Pratt & srud

Dear Student,

We are excited you decided to take a course in a field we have dedicated our life to teaching. We understand this is likely your first in-depth exposure to the study of taxation and do not necessarily share our passion for taxes. Indeed, if you're like most, taxation is probably a subject that you have been dreading. So, in every edition we have been very careful to match our enthusiasm and experience with the expectations of the first-time student. What you will discover is a unique and proven pedagogy. At first glance, the tax law appears to be an endless maze of boring rules and regulations. However, we try to make sense of the complexity. Throughout the text, we explain the rationale underlying the rule. We have found that students who understand the reason for the rule also have an easier time in learning how the rule applies. It's a simple but effective approach. This technique has helped thousands of students we have taught not only to learn more about taxes but have fun doing it.

Since staying current on the latest tax laws and regulations is important, we continue, as we have with every edition, to highlight the changes. We wait to the last possible moment to go to press so as not to miss any key changes. In addition, at our website **www.prattkulsrud.com** you will see we continue to supplement the book with updates for new legislation and other current developments that affect the taxation of individuals, corporations, partnerships, estates, and trusts.

Finally, if you find yourself in need of additional learning tools, you will find at our website an online study guide. With its chapter review, study guide questions and true-false/multiple-choice questions, the study guide is an excellent companion to the text.

We wish you the very best in your course and your career.

Cordially,

Jim Pratt & Bill Kulsrud

Corporate, Partnership, Estate and Gift
Taxation
2017 Edition

James W. Pratt
William N. Kulsrud

Contributing Authors

Christine C. Cheng, Ph.D.
Louisiana State University

Marguerite R. Hutton, Ph.D., C.P.A.
Western Washington University

Robert W. Jamison, Ph.D., C.P.A.
Indiana University

William N. Kulsrud, Ph.D., C.P.A.
Indiana University

Nathan Oestreich, Ph.D., C.P.A.
San Diego State University

James W. Pratt, D.B.A., C.P.A.
University of Houston

Roby B. Sawyers, Ph.D., C.P.A.
North Carolina State University

Edward J. Schnee, Ph.D., C.P.A.
University of Alabama

Steven C. Thompson, Ph.D., C.P.A.
Texas State University

Pratt & Kulsrud

VAN-GRINER

Corporate, Partnership, Estate and Gift Taxation

2017 Edition

James W. Pratt
William N. Kulsrud

Printed in the United States of America
10 9 8 7 6 5 4 3 2 1
ISBN: 978-1-61740-364-4

Van-Griner Publishing
Cincinnati, Ohio
www.van-griner.com

CEO: Mike Griner
President: Dreis Van Landuyt
Project Manager: Maria Walterbusch
Customer Care Lead: Julie Reichert

Pratt 364-4 W16
171007
Copyright © 2017

Preface

Welcome to the 2017
Pratt & Kulsrud Taxation Series

Proven Approach

Our focus has always been one that blends Code and context. We try to decipher the law and explain it in a way students can appreciate and understand. Then, we incorporate thousands of examples to provide students with the right amount of context. Because students are more likely to remember the rules when they're set in a historical perspective, we try to provide the underlying rationale whenver it makes sense. Students not only learn the "what" of the tax law, but they better understand the "how" and the "why" as well. As tax professionals and authors, we have been explaining the fundamentals of the statutory law clearly and efficiently for over 30 years, helping to better prepare our students for what awaits them in their careers. Interestingly, even the IRS has used our book for their training programs!

Our approach to teaching the taxation of business entities is tried and true—we take a life-cycle approach. We normally start by examining the tax consequences of formation of the business followed by a discussion of operations, distributions, liquidations and sales. Throughout the discussions, we reference the applicable sections of the Code and other relevant authority.

Thorough and Flexible

The sheer number of rules and regulations makes it nearly impossible to cover all the material in the course time allotted. Do you want to cover controlled groups, redemptions by related corporations, Section 338 elections, mergers and acquisitions, disproportionate distributions by a partnerships, QSSTs, ESBTs, and more? Maybe yes—and maybe no. While other books may channel you into covering a specific set of topics, we cover all topics and let you decide which topics best meet the needs of your students. Regardless of your approach, the content you need is in our books, so you can tailor your syllabus to meet your requirements. It's all in there, so cover (and cut) what you want. We also offer custom options and can create a unique book that suits your particular course, department, or curriculum. Ask us about our custom options.

Tax Return Problems and the Software to do Them

Most students like to do tax returns, and we provide an assortment of problems that helps students develop basic skills in preparing tax returns for all of the entities, as well as a fiduciary income tax return. We have a straightforward Form 1120 in Chapter 1 and another one that is a bit more challenging in Chapter 2. For instructors who want to demonstrate the differences between C corporations, S corporations and partnerships, it's easily done. The same basic fact pattern for the Chapter 2 1120 is repeated in Chapters 9 and 11 so that the partnership and S corporation rules can be applied. In this way, students can observe the different results that may be obtained, depending on the owner's choice of entity.

To enhance the real-world simulation, each new book includes H&R Block software. Students can build problem solutions, adjust for new and additional facts, and test the way different data affects outcomes.

As We Go to Press

This textbook has been revised to reflect tax law changes and significant judicial and administrative developments during the past year. As we go to press, Congress is considering various proposals that may lead to significant and immediate changes in the tax law. Should any of these proposals be enacted, we will continue our long-standing policy of posting these changes to the Pratt & Kulsrud instructor website, **www.prattkulsrud.com.**

For the Student

A *Study Guide to Accompany Corporate, Partnership, Estate and Gift Taxation 2017* is available online at **www.prattkulsrud.com.** Written by one of the contributing authors, Steve Thompson, the Study Guide provides in-depth chapter reviews, study exercises, and true-false/multiple-choice questions. These materials may be used in students' initial study of the chapter content, and also in their review. The Study Guide is only available online.

Enhanced and Updated Support for Instructors

Instructor Website. The 2017 edition continues with its one-stop instructor resource website. At **www.prattkulsrud.com** you will find access to all of these items. To register for access, visit the site and complete the registration form.

- **Solutions Manual.** Solutions to end-of-chapter discussion questions and computational problems are included in this manual. Specific pages and examples from the text are referenced, as are supporting statutory and administrative authorities, when appropriate.

- **Instructor's Resource Guide and Test Bank.** This guide contains answers to the tax research questions found in the text as well as solutions to the tax return problems, complete with filled-out forms. In addition, the Instructor's Guide includes a test bank of more than 750 objective questions (true-false and multiple choice), whose answers reference specific pages and examples in the text.

- **PowerPoint® Slides.** Designed for classroom use, there are slides for each chapter's principal topics. In addition, there are slides containing solutions for many problems. These solution slides typically are animated so that parts of the solution can be revealed however the instructor desires.

- **Lecture Outlines.** These outlines provide additional background on various subjects contained in the chapters as well as useful tips on how to teach the topics.

- **Legislative Updates.** Page-specific updates, tax law changes, and inflation adjustments are posted on a regular basis to the Pratt & Kulsrud website: **www.prattkulsrud.com.**

Instructor Resources

Instructor ancillaries—including the Solutions Manual, Instructor's Resource Guide and Test Bank, PowerPoint Slides, and Lecture Outlines—are provided online at our website. Moreover, if you have any questions, any problems, any comments, you can contact Professor Kulsrud directly at wkulsrud@iupui.edu. How many other textbooks encourage you to contact the authors! These resources give instructors the ultimate tool for preparing and customizing lectures, presentations, and exams. The test bank files are provided in Microsoft® Word so they can be modified easily for your use.

Additional Offerings from the Pratt & Kulsrud Taxation Series

The series includes new editions of:

Federal Taxation
2017 Edition
ISBN 978-1-61740-365-1

To offer maximum flexibility in your course, the text not only focuses on the Federal income taxation of individuals, but also covers additional topics, such as the income taxation of regular corporations and shareholders; the taxation of partnerships and S corporations; Federal estate and gift taxation; the income taxation of estates, trusts, and beneficiaries; and the major aspects of family tax planning. Includes H&R Block™ desktop software.

Individual Taxation
2017 Edition
ISBN 978-1-61740-366-8

Numerous examples and computational illustrations explain the more complex rules concerning the Federal income taxation of individuals, making this text ideal for a first course in Federal taxation for undergraduate or graduate accounting, business or law students. Includes H&R Block™ desktop software.

Acknowledgments

The editor and author team would like to thank particularly Jan Meade of the University of Houston, Randle Pollard and James Motter of Indiana University, Leonard Goodman of Rutgers University, Brigitte Muehlmann of Babson University, Ramon Fernandez of St. Thomas University, and Teresa Stephenson of the University of South Dakota for their comments and suggestions. In addition, the editors and authors would like to acknowledge Van-Griner's Project Manager, Maria Walterbusch, who has gone beyond the call of duty in helping us compile this year's book. Her work on this edition has led to a strong revision that will benefit both students and instructors.

Brief Contents

Contents

Part 4   Multijurisdictional Taxation

Appendices

Corporate Taxation

PART 1

Income Taxation of Corporations

Learning Objectives

Upon completion of this chapter you will be able to:

LO.1 Identify the alternative forms of doing business.

LO.2 Define a corporation for Federal income tax purposes.

LO.3 Compare and contrast corporate and individual taxation.

LO.4 Compute the corporate income tax, including the tax for personal service corporations and controlled corporations.

LO.5 Identify important features of the corporate alternative minimum tax (AMT).

LO.6 Describe the corporate tax forms and filing requirements.

Chapter Outline

Introduction

Every business organized and operated within the United States is classified for Federal income tax purposes as *one* of the following five business forms:

1. Sole proprietorship
2. Partnership
3. Regular corporation
4. S corporation
5. Limited liability company

Usually a taxpayer has a choice of which of these tax forms his or her business will take. The choice may be based on *tax* or *nontax* factors, or some combination of both. For example, the dominant tax reason for not operating a business in the regular corporate form is the avoidance of *double taxation* of the same source of income. If the business is operated as a regular corporation, its income is taxed once at the corporate level *and* again (as dividends) when the income is distributed to the shareholder(s). Conversely, the most significant nontax reason for selecting the corporate form is the *limited liability* that this form offers to its owner or owners. Unfortunately, this nontax benefit may be of little value to small business owners who must personally guarantee repayment of corporate debt, or to professional corporations of physicians, CPAs, and attorneys who cannot avoid personal liability for their professional services under state law. For these corporations, insurance provides the greatest protection against liability just as it does for the unincorporated business.

Although there are many other tax and nontax factors that should be considered in selecting a particular business form, the purpose of this chapter is to examine the Federal income taxation of regular corporations. One logical way to do this is to compare and contrast corporate taxation with the taxation of income earned by the other business forms. Thus, a brief overview of these business forms is presented below.

Overview of Business Forms

LO.1

Identify the alternative forms of doing business.

As stated above, a business can be operated as a *sole proprietorship,* a *partnership,* or a *corporation.* If the corporate form is selected, and certain requirements are met, the owner or owners may *elect* to be treated as an S corporation for Federal income tax purposes. In addition to these traditional entities, a business can be operated as a limited liability company that combines nontax features of corporations with tax features of partnerships. Each of these business forms is discussed below.

SOLE PROPRIETORSHIPS

More businesses are operated as proprietorships than any other form. This is partially a reflection of our entrepreneurial society. It is also the simplest form available—personally, legally, and for tax purposes. A proprietorship's net income or net loss is computed much the same as for any other business. The major difference is that in taxation the proprietorship is *not* separated from its owner. As a result, the owner cannot enter into taxable transactions with the proprietorship as a creditor, an employee, a customer, or in any other role.

For information purposes, proprietorship *ordinary income* and *deductions* are reported on *Schedule C* (or Schedule F if a farming operation) which is a supporting document for the owner's Form 1040.[1] Proprietorship net ordinary income also is the basis for calculating any *self-employment* tax liability.[2] All items subject to special tax treatment, such as capital gains and losses, charitable contributions, and dividend income, are reported on the appropriate tax return schedules as though incurred by the owner rather than the proprietorship.

---

[1] Code §§ 61(a) and 162. Please note that this and all future references to the Code are to the Internal Revenue Code of 1986. The section symbol (§) will be used throughout the text to indicate the particular section of the Code referred to. See Chapter 18 for a discussion of tax citations.

[2] See § 6017.

In essence, the sole proprietorship serves as a *conduit*—that is, all items of income, gain, loss, deduction, or credit it possesses flow through to the individual.

Example 1

T is employed as an accounting professor at State University where he earns a salary of $94,000. T also operates a consulting practice as a sole proprietorship which earned $35,000 during the year. In connection with his consulting practice, T generated a $400 general business tax credit. The sole proprietorship does not file a separate return and pay a tax (net of the general business credit) on its income. Instead, T reports the sole proprietorship income on Schedule C and includes this income along with his salary on his personal tax return (Form 1040). In addition to the regular income tax imposed on T, he must add his self-employment tax (computed on Schedule SE, Form 1040) and subtract the $400 general business credit (computed on Form 3800).

PARTNERSHIPS

Like the sole proprietorship, the partnership is a conduit for Federal income tax purposes. This means that the partnership itself is never subject to the Federal income tax and that all items of partnership income, expense, gain, or loss *pass through* to the partners and are given their tax effect at the partner level.[3] The partnership is required to file a return, however. This return (Form 1065) is merely an information return reporting the results of the partnership's transactions and how those results are divided among the partners. Using this information, the partners each report their respective share of the various items on their own tax return.[4] Because the partner pays taxes on his or her share of the partnership income, distributions made by the partnership to the partner generally are not taxable to the partner.[5]

Example 2

For calendar year 2016, AB Partnership had net income subject to tax of $98,000. During the year, each of its two equal partners received distributions of $45,000. The partnership is not subject to tax, and each partner must include $49,000 in her annual income tax return despite the fact that each partner actually received less than this amount. The partnership must file an annual income tax return reporting its transactions and the ways in which those transactions affect each partner.

In some respects, the partnership is treated as a separate entity for tax purposes. For example, many tax elections are made by the partnership,[6] and a partnership interest generally is treated as a single asset when sold.[7] In transactions between the partners and the partnership, the parties generally are treated like unrelated parties.[8] These and other controlling provisions related to the Federal income tax treatment of partnerships are discussed in Chapter 9 and Chapter 10.

S CORPORATIONS

The Internal Revenue Code provides the possibility for certain closely held corporations to elect to be treated as conduits (like partnerships) for Federal income tax purposes. This election is made pursuant to the rules contained in Subchapter S of the Code.[9] For this reason, such corporations are referred to as S corporations. If the corporation elects S status, it is taxed in virtually the same fashion as a partnership. Like a partnership, the S corporation's items of income, expense, gain, or loss pass through to the shareholders to be taxed at

---

[3] § 701.

[4] § 702(a).

[5] § 731(a).

[6] § 703(b).

[7] § 741 states that the sale or exchange of an interest in a partnership shall generally be treated as the sale of a capital asset.

[8] § 707(a).

[9] §§ 1361 through 1379.

the shareholder level. The S corporation files an information return (Form 1120S), similar to that for a partnership, reporting the results of the corporation's transactions and how those results are allocated among the shareholders. The individual shareholders report their respective shares of the various items on their own tax returns. Unlike a partnership, however, an S corporation may, in certain limited circumstances, be subject to taxation at the entity level. Chapters 11 and 12 contain a discussion of the taxation of S corporations and their shareholders.

CORPORATE TAXPAYERS

Section 11 of the Code imposes a tax on all corporations. The tax applies to all of the income, whether from a U.S. or foreign source, of any domestic corporations, as well as any U.S.-source income (and/or foreign-source income effectively connected with a U.S. trade or business) of any foreign corporation.[10] Although § 11 requires all corporations to pay tax, other provisions in the law specifically exempt certain types of corporations from taxation. For example, a corporation organized not for profit but for religious, charitable, scientific, literary, educational, or certain other purposes is generally not taxable.[11] However, if a non-profit organization conducts a business which is not related to the purpose for which its exemption was granted, any resulting taxable income would be subject to tax.[12] In addition to the special provisions governing taxation of nonprofit corporations, the rules applying to S corporations vary from those applying to "regular" corporations as mentioned above.

While the overall taxation of corporations is similar to the taxation of individuals, several important differences exist. For example, the basic formula for computing the corporate tax varies from that used for individuals. Also, the treatment of dividend income received by a corporation is not the same as that imposed on dividends received by an individual.[13] These and other differences are discussed later in this chapter.

LIMITED LIABILITY COMPANIES

Every state has enacted or introduced legislation that approves the formation of limited liability companies (LLCs). As with a corporation, an LLC generally offers limited liability to its members. At the same time, however, the LLC avoids the Federal tax disadvantages of regular corporations by providing the flow-through characteristics of a partnership.

Limited liability companies are created under state law by filing articles of organization. The owners of an LLC are called *members*. Although some states allow single-member LLCs, the entity generally must be formed by two or more members (these members can be individuals, partnerships, regular corporations, S corporations, trusts, or other LLCs). Like a corporation, an LLC can act on its own behalf and can sue and be sued. Also like a corporation, members generally possess limited liability except that they may be liable for their own acts of malpractice in those states that allow professionals to form LLCs.

In contrast to the treatment of corporations, LLCs may be treated as partnerships for Federal income tax purposes. Under a "check-the-box" system made effective on January 1, 1997, an LLC that has at least two members will, without an election to the contrary, be classified as a partnership and an LLC with only a single member will be treated as a sole proprietorship. This system of selecting a form of doing business is described in more detail in the next section.

Although it resembles an S corporation, an LLC is not burdened by the eligibility requirements and certain tax disadvantages of an S corporation. As a result, an LLC may be the preferred form of doing business for many taxpayers.

What Is a Corporation?

LO.2

Define a corporation for Federal income tax purposes.

A corporation is an artificial "person" created by state law. The state may impose restrictions on the issuance of shares and the type of business conducted. The state also specifies the requirements for incorporation, such as the filing of articles of incorporation, the issuance of a corporate charter, and the payment of various fees (e.g., franchise taxes).

---

[10] § 882(a). See Chapter 13 for more details.

[11] § 501(a).

[12] § 501(b).

[13] See §§ 243 through 246.

Federal tax law provides that a tax will be imposed upon the taxable income of every corporation. For this purpose, a *corporation* is a business entity organized under a Federal or state statute, if the statute refers to the entity as incorporated or as a corporation, body corporate, or body politic.[14] This definition includes entities such as insurance companies, state-statute authorized joint-stock companies or associations, banks with any FDIC-insured deposits, businesses wholly owned by state or political subdivisions, and business entities, such as publicly traded partnerships, that are treated as corporations. The regulations also classify a list of specified foreign entities as corporations.

ASSOCIATIONS

Historically, an association that was not treated as a corporation under state or Federal law (e.g., a partnership) could be classified as a corporation for Federal income tax purposes and thus be inadvertently exposed to the disadvantages of the regular (C) corporate form of doing business. The aspects that were addressed in determining whether an association should be classified and taxed as a corporation included:[15]

1. Continuity of life,
2. Centralized management,
3. Limited liability, and
4. Free transferability.

If three of these four characteristics were satisfied, an entity would be taxed as a corporation, even if the entity was treated differently under state law. For example, a limited liability partnership (LLP) or a limited liability company (LLC) could be treated as a corporation for tax purposes if it had, along with limited liability, two of the other three characteristics (e.g., centralized management and no restrictions on the transfer of interests).

It is important to note what could happen to any anticipated tax benefits if an organization was unexpectedly classified as an association. For example, if the owners of a real estate business expected excess losses in the early years of operations, the corporate tax entity would not be the best choice of business form unless the organization qualified for and elected S corporation status. If the business was treated as a partnership or an S corporation, the excess losses flowed through to the owners and could be deductible on their personal tax returns, subject to the passive activity loss rules. However, if the entity was classified as an association and was thereby taxable as a regular corporation, the excess losses simply accumulated at the corporate level in the form of net operating loss carryovers, the tax benefit of which expired at the end of 20 years.[16] Obviously, if the organization's owners did not think that the business was a corporation, they certainly would not file the required election to be treated as an S corporation for Federal income tax purposes. Thus, unless the organization qualified as a partnership for tax purposes, any anticipated tax benefits would *either* be lost or, at best, unduly delayed.

Naturally, the above classification rules led to a great number of conflicts between the IRS and taxpayers. To simplify this process, the IRS issued regulations effective January 1, 1997 that replaced the old rules for classifying entities with a "check-the-box" system.[17] Under these rules, an entity organized as a corporation under state law, or an entity classified under the Code as a corporation, will be treated as a corporation and will not be allowed to make an election. However, any other business entity (e.g., an LLC) that has at least two members may elect to be treated as a corporation or a partnership for tax purposes (an entity with only one member will be treated as a corporation or a sole proprietorship). In general, existing entities will continue to operate as they are as long as there is a reasonable basis for the current classification. These rules greatly simplify the process of selecting the form of business in which the owners wish to operate.

An important exception to the classification rules, however, is the so-called *publicly traded partnership* (PTP). A partnership meeting the definition of a PTP will be treated *and* taxed as a regular corporation. Basically, a partnership is a PTP if it (1) is a limited partnership, (2) was organized after December 17, 1987, and (3) has interests that are traded

---

[14] § 7701(a)(3).

[15] Reg. § 301.7701-2 (in effect prior to January 1, 1997).

[16] See § 172(b)(1)(B).

[17] Reg. § 301.7701-3.

on an established securities market or are readily tradeable on a secondary market. Certain exceptions exist for PTPs in existence on December 17, 1987 and for those with income consisting primarily of interest, dividends, rental income from real property and gains from the sale of such property; gains from the sale of capital or § 1231 assets; and income and gains from development, mining or production, refining, transportation, or marketing of any mineral or natural resource. These rules are discussed in Chapter 9.

LIMITED LIABILITY COMPANIES

The "check-the-box" rules eliminate the need for LLCs to create artificial features (e.g., limits on centralized management, restrictions on transferability, limits on life of the entity) to receive the desired entity classification. Under a default system, a newly formed LLC will automatically be classified as a partnership if it has at least two members unless it affirmatively elects to be taxed as a corporation. Thus, LLCs can easily and effectively provide limited liability to their members while still being treated as a partnership for Federal tax purposes.

SHAM CORPORATIONS

In some instances the IRS will ignore the fact that an entity is considered a corporation as defined by its state law. This may happen when a corporation's only purpose is to reduce taxes of its owners or to hold title to property. If the corporation has no real business or economic function, or if it conducts no activities, it may be a "sham," or "dummy," corporation.[18] Generally, as long as there is a business activity carried on, a corporation will be considered a separate taxable entity.[19]

Example 3

M owns a piece of real estate. To protect it from his creditors, M forms X Corporation and transfers the land to it in exchange for all of X Corporation's stock. The only purpose of X Corporation is to hold title to the real estate, and X Corporation conducts no other business activities. It is properly incorporated under state law. The IRS is likely to designate X Corporation as a sham corporation and to disregard its corporate status. Any income and expenses of X Corporation will be considered as belonging to M.

If X Corporation had conducted some business activities (such as leasing the property and collecting rents), it is likely that it will not be considered a sham corporation.

Generally the IRS, but not the taxpayer, is allowed to disregard the status of a corporation. The courts have frequently agreed that if a taxpayer has created a corporation, he or she should not be allowed to ignore its status (i.e., in order to reduce taxes). However, the Supreme Court has ruled that a taxpayer could use a corporate entity as the taxpayer's agent in securing financing.[20] Thus, under certain conditions, taxpayers may use a corporation for a business purpose and not have it treated as a corporation for Federal tax purposes.

Comparison of Corporate and Individual Income Taxation

LO.3

Compare and contrast corporate and individual taxation.

A corporation's taxable income is computed by subtracting various deductions from its gross income.[21] Although this appears to be the same basic computation as for individual taxpayers, there are numerous important differences. In order to highlight these differences, Exhibit 1-1 and Exhibit 1-2 contain the tax formulas for corporate and individual taxpayers.

---

[18] See *Higgins V. Smith*, 40-1 USTC ¶9160, 23 AFTR 800, 308 U.S. 473 (USSC, 1940).

[19] *Moline Properties, Inc.*, 43-1 USTC ¶9464, 30 AFTR 1291, 319 U.S. 436 (USSC, 1943).

[20] *Jesse C. Bollinger*, 88-1 USTC ¶9233, 61 AFTR2d 88-793, 108 S.CT. 1173 (USSC, 1988).

[21] § 63(a).

EXHIBIT 1-1	Tax Formula for Corporate Taxpayers

Income (from whatever source)	**$xxx,xxx**
Less: Exclusions from gross income	– xx,xxx
Gross income	**$xxx,xxx**
Less: Deductions	– xx,xxx
Taxable income	**$ xx,xxx**
Applicable tax rates	xx%
Gross tax	**$ xx,xxx**
Less: Tax credits and prepayments	– x,xxx
Tax due (or refund)	**$ xx,xxx**

EXHIBIT 1-2	Tax Formula for Individual Taxpayers

Total income (from whatever source)		**$xxx,xxx**
Less: Exclusions from gross income		– xx,xxx
Gross income		**$xxx,xxx**
Less: Deductions for adjusted gross income		– xx,xxx
Adjusted gross income		**$xxx,xxx**
Less:		
1. The larger of		
a. Standard deduction	$x,xxx	
or	*or*	– x,xxx
b. Total itemized deductions	$x,xxx	
2. Number of personal and dependency exemptions × exemption amount		– x,xxx
Taxable income		**$xxx,xxx**
Applicable tax rates (From Tables or Schedules X, Y, or Z)		xx%
Gross tax		**$ xx,xxx**
Less: Tax credits and prepayments		– x,xxx
Tax due (or refund)		**$ xx,xxx**

GROSS INCOME

The definition of gross income is the same for both corporations and individuals.[22] However, there are some differences in the exclusions from gross income. For example, capital contributions to a corporation (e.g., purchase of corporate stock by shareholders) are excluded from gross income.[23]

DEDUCTIONS

Corporations have no "Adjusted Gross Income." Thus for corporations, there are no "deductions for AGI" or "deductions from AGI." All corporate expenditures are either deductible or not deductible. All allowable deductions are subtracted from gross income in arriving at taxable income.

---

[22] § 61(a).   [23] See §§ 118(a) and 1032.

Corporations are considered to be "persons" only in a legal sense, and are *not* entitled to the following "personal" deductions that are available for individuals:

1. Personal and dependency exemptions
2. Standard deduction
3. Itemized deductions

All activities of a corporation are considered to be business activities. Therefore, corporations usually deduct all their losses since such losses are considered business losses.[24]

In addition, corporations do not have to reduce their casualty losses by either the $100 statutory floor or by 10% of adjusted gross income.

Corporations do not have "nonbusiness" bad debts, since all activities are considered business activities. All bad debts of a corporation are business bad debts.[25]

There are several deductions that are available only for corporations.[26] These are deductible in addition to the other business deductions and include the dividends-received deduction and the amortization of organizational expenditures.

DIVIDENDS-RECEIVED DEDUCTION

As mentioned earlier, double taxation occurs when corporate profits are distributed in the form of dividends to the shareholders. The corporation is not allowed a deduction for the dividends paid, and an individual shareholder is not entitled to an exclusion (although the shareholder will be subject to a 20% maximum rate of tax on qualified dividends). Therefore, when one corporation is a shareholder in another corporation, *triple* taxation might occur. To prevent this, Congress provided corporations with a deduction for dividends received.[27]

General Rule

The dividends-received deduction (DRD) generally is 70% of the dividends received from taxable domestic (U.S.) corporations.[28] However, a corporation that owns at least 20 percent—but less than 80 percent—of the dividend-paying corporation's stock is allowed to deduct 80% of the dividends received.[29] In addition, members of an *affiliated group* are allowed to deduct 100% of the dividends that are received from another member of the same group. A group of corporations is considered affiliated when at least 80% of the stock of each corporation (except the common parent) is owned by other members of the group.[30]

Taxable Income Limitation

The 70% dividends-received deduction may not exceed 70% of the corporation's taxable income computed without the deduction for dividends-received, net operating loss carryovers or carrybacks, and capital loss carrybacks.[31] However, if the dividends-received deduction adds to *or* creates a net operating loss for the current year, the 70% of taxable income limitation *does not* apply.

Like the dividends-received deduction percentage, the taxable income limitation percentage becomes *80%* rather than 70% if the dividend-paying corporation is at least 20% owned by the recipient corporation. In the unlikely event a corporation receives dividends subject to *both* the 70% and 80% rules, a special procedure must be followed. First, the 80% limitation is applied by treating the "70% dividends" as other income. The 70% limitation is then applied by treating the "80% dividends" as if they had not been received.[32]

Exhibit 1-3 contains a format for the computation of the 70% dividends-received deduction, and *Examples 4, 5,* and *6* illustrate this computational procedure.[33]

---

[24] § 165(a). Like individuals, certain corporations are subject to the passive-loss rules discussed in Chapter 9.

[25] § 166.

[26] § 241.

[27] §§ 243 through 246.

[28] § 243(a)(1).

[29] § 243(c).

[30] §§ 243(a)(3), 243(b)(5), and 1504.

[31] § 246(b).

[32] § 246(b)(3).

[33] To apply the 80% rules, simply substitute 80% for 70% in the exhibit and accompanying examples.

EXHIBIT 1-3	**Computation of Corporate Dividends-Received Deduction**

Step 1:   Multiply the dividends-received from taxable domestic (U.S.) corporations by 70 percent. This is the tentative dividends-received deduction (DRD).

Step 2:   Compute the tentative taxable income for the current year, using the tentative DRD (from Step 1):

   Total revenues (including dividend income)
   Less: Total expenses
   Equals: Taxable income (before DRD)
   Less: Tentative DRD (Step 1)
   Equals: Tentative taxable income (loss)

   If the tentative taxable income is *positive*, the taxable income limitation may apply. Go to Step 3.

   If the tentative taxable income is *negative*, there is no taxable income limitation. The dividends-received deduction is the amount computed in Step 1.

Step 3:   Compute the taxable income limitation:

   Taxable income (before DRD) (Step 2)
   Add: Any net operating loss carryovers or carrybacks from other years that are reflected in the taxable income
   Add: Any capital loss carrybacks from later years that are reflected in taxable income
   Equals: Taxable income (before DRD), as adjusted
   Times: 70%
   Equals: Taxable income limitation

Step 4:   Compare the tentative DRD (Step 1) to the taxable income limitation (Step 3). Choose the smaller amount. This is the corporate dividends-received deduction.

Example 4

R Corporation has the following items of revenue and expense for the year:

Dividends received from domestic corporations	$40,000
Revenue from sales.	60,000
Cost of goods sold and operating expenses	54,000

The dividends-received deduction is computed as follows:

Step 1: $40,000 dividends received
× 70%

$28,000 *tentative* dividends-received deduction (DRD)

Step 2:

Dividend income	$ 40,000
Revenue from sales	+ 60,000
Total revenues	$100,000
Less: Total expenses	– 54,000
Taxable income (before DRD)	$ 46,000
Less: Tentative DRD	– 28,000
Tentative taxable income	$ 18,000

Since the tentative taxable income is *positive*, the taxable income limitation may apply. Go to Step 3.

Step 3:   Compute the taxable income limitation:

Taxable income (before DRD)	$ 46,000
Times 70%	× 70%
Taxable income limitation	$ 32,200

Step 4:   Compare the tentative DRD ($28,000) to the taxable income limitation ($32,200). Choose the *smaller* amount ($28,000). In this case, R Corporation's dividends-received deduction is $28,000 (not subject to limitation).

Example 5

Assume the same facts as in *Example 4* except that the revenue from sales is $50,000. The dividends-received deduction is computed as follows:

Step 1: $40,000 dividends received
× 70%

$28,000 *tentative* DRD

Step 2:

Dividend income	$40,000
Revenue from sales	+50,000
Total revenues	$90,000
Less: Total expenses	–54,000
Taxable income (before DRD)	$36,000
Less: Tentative DRD	–28,000
Tentative taxable income	$ 8,000

Since the tentative taxable income is *positive*, the taxable income limitation may apply. Go to Step 3.

Step 3:   Compute the taxable income limitation:

Taxable income (before DRD)	$36,000
Times 70%	× 70%
Taxable income limitation	$25,200

Step 4:   Compare the tentative DRD ($28,000) to the taxable income limitation ($25,200). Choose the *smaller* amount ($25,200). In this case, R Corporation's dividends-received deduction is $25,200 (limited to 70% of taxable income).

Example 6

Assume the same facts as in *Example 4* except that the revenue from sales is $41,000. The dividends-received deduction is computed as follows:

Step 1: $40,000 dividends received
          × 70%
          _____

          $28,000 *tentative DRD*

Step 2:

Dividend income	$40,000
Revenue from sales	+41,000
Total revenues	$81,000
Less: Total expenses	−54,000
Taxable income (before DRD)	$27,000
Less: Tentative DRD	−28,000
Tentative taxable income (loss)	$ (1,000)

Because the tentative taxable income (loss) is *negative,* there is no taxable income limitation. The dividends-received deduction is $28,000.

The taxable income limitation discussed above *does not* apply to dividends received from affiliated corporations that are entitled to the 100% dividends-received deduction.[34]

Other Restrictions on Dividends-Received Deduction

There are three additional limitations or restrictions that may be imposed on the dividends-received deduction. First, unless a corporation has held the stock for more than 45 days during a 90-day period (beginning 45 days before the ex-dividend date) before its sale or other disposition, any dividends-received on such stock will not be eligible for the dividends-received deduction.[35] This restriction was created to stop the perceived abuse of corporate taxpayers purchasing dividend-paying stock shortly before dividends were declared and selling such stock immediately after the right to receive the dividends became fixed (i.e., the date of record or ex-dividend date).

Example 7

The treasurer of R Inc. temporarily invested $1,000 of R's working capital by purchasing stock in D Corporation. Shortly thereafter, R received a dividend of $100 from D, causing the value of the D stock owned by R to drop to $900. R then sold the stock and realized a short-term capital loss of $100 ($900 − $1,000). Economically, R is no better off than before the dividend because it spent $1,000 and received $1,000 ($900 + $100). From a tax view, however, the corporation effectively reports a loss from the transaction of $70 ($30 dividend income − $100 capital loss), assuming the capital loss can be used[36] and the dividends-received deduction is allowed. The 45-day rule attempts to prevent such schemes by requiring the taxpayer to accept the risk of holding the stock for a period of time.

---

[34] § 246(b)(1).

[35] § 246(c)(1).

[36] The tax treatment of a corporation's capital gains and losses is discussed later in this chapter.

Note that the plan revealed in *Example 7* succeeds if the taxpayer is willing to accept the risk of holding the stock for more than 45 days. Another rule aimed at such plans attacks so-called *extraordinary dividends*.[37] If a corporation receives an extraordinary dividend within the first two years that the stock is owned, the basis of the stock must be reduced by the nontaxable portion of the dividend (but not below zero). When the nontaxable portion exceeds the stock's basis, the excess is included in income in the year the dividend is received. An extraordinary dividend generally is any dividend that equals or exceeds 10% of the taxpayer's basis of common stock, or 5% of the basis of preferred stock. If the taxpayer can prove the value of the stock, the taxpayer can use such value instead of basis to determine if the dividend is extraordinary.

Example 8

Assume the same facts as in *Example 7,* except that the stock was sold three months after it was purchased. In this case, the dividends-received deduction is allowed. However, the dividend is an extraordinary dividend because the amount is at least 10% of the cost of the stock ($100 = [10% × $1,000]). Thus, R must reduce the basis of the stock by the nontaxable portion of the dividend, $70. Therefore, on the sale of the stock R recognizes a loss of only $30 ($900 − $930). Observe that the required reduction in basis produces the right economic result; that is, R is now unaffected from a tax view ($30 dividend income − $30 capital loss = $0).

A third restriction on a corporation's dividends-received deduction prohibits corporations from taking advantage of this deduction by borrowing funds and using them to purchase dividend-paying stock.

Example 9

This year, X Corporation borrowed money and purchased dividend-paying stock. During the year, X received $1,000 of dividend income but paid $1,000 of interest expense. Although the income and expense wash from an economic view, without a special rule, X would be taxed on only $300 of income because of the dividends-received deduction.

To prohibit arbitrage transactions such as that described in *Example 9* above, the Code denies corporations the dividends-received deduction to the extent the purchase price of the stock was financed with borrowed funds.

The restriction on the dividends-received deduction applies to so-called *debt-financed portfolio stock*. Generally, the term applies to any stock that was either acquired by debt financing or refinanced by the taxpayer, *and* where all or a portion of the indebtedness remained unpaid prior to the receipt of dividends on the stock. In such cases, the deduction for these dividends is limited to the product of

1. 70 percent,[38] and
2. 100% minus the *average indebtedness percentage.*

For this purpose, the average indebtedness percentage is calculated by dividing the average unpaid indebtedness for the period by the stock's adjusted basis.[39]

---

[37] § 1059(a).

[38] § 246A(a)(1); 80% in the case of any dividend from a 20% or more owned corporation.

[39] See §§ 246A(a)(2) and 246A(d).

> ### Example 10
>
> On September 1, 2016, T Corporation received dividends of $10,000 from General Electric Corporation. T had purchased the General Electric stock with $200,000 of borrowed funds in 2015. Assuming the average unpaid balance of the debt between dividend dates was $80,000, T Corporation's average indebtedness percentage is 40 percent, and the dividends-received deduction for this stock is limited to $4,200.
>
> | | |
> |---|---:|
> | Dividends received on debt-financed portfolio stock | $10,000 |
> | Times: 70% × (100% − 40%) | × 42% |
> | Dividends-received deduction | $ 4,200 |

ORGANIZATIONAL EXPENDITURES

When a corporation is formed, various expenses directly related to the organization process are incurred, such as attorneys' fees, accountants' fees, and state filing charges. Although some of the attorneys' and accountants' fees may be ordinary and necessary business expenses that do not benefit future periods (and are therefore deductible), most of these expenditures will benefit future periods and are therefore capitalized as *organizational expenditures*. These organizational expenditures are intangible assets that have value for the life of the corporation.

Generally, assets with indefinite lives may not be amortized for Federal income tax purposes. However, Congress has given corporations a special option for organization expenses. Under § 248 corporations, both C and S, normally are permitted to deduct up to $5,000 of organization expenses in the tax year in which the business begins. As a practical matter, this provision permits most corporations to expense all of their qualified organization costs immediately since the costs of incorporating normally are less than $5,000. If organization expenses should exceed $5,000, the excess must be amortized over the 180-month period (15 years) beginning with the month in which the business begins.[40] If organization expenses exceed $50,000, the $5,000 allowance is reduced one dollar for each dollar in excess of $50,000.

The Regulations give the following examples of organizational expenditures:[41]

1. Legal services incident to the organization of the corporation, such as drafting the corporate charter, by-laws, minutes of organizational meetings, and terms of original stock certificates.
2. Necessary accounting services.
3. Expenses of temporary directors and of organizational meetings of directors or stock holders.
4. Fees paid to the state of incorporation.

The Regulations also give several examples of items that are *not* considered organizational expenditures, such as costs of issuing stock.[42] The costs of issuing stock are considered selling expenses, and therefore are a reduction in the proceeds from selling the stock. They reduce stockholders' equity and do not create any tax deduction.

It is important to note that only those organizational expenditures *incurred* before the end of the corporation's first taxable year will qualify for deduction.[43] Neither the taxable year of actual payment nor the corporation's method of accounting (i.e., cash or accrual) affect this requirement. However, any subsequent expenditures, such as for corporate charter or by-laws revisions, are not eligible for amortization.

[40] § 248.
[41] Reg. § 1.248-1(b)(2).
[42] Reg. § 1.248-1(b)(3).
[43] Reg. § 1.248-1(a).

Example 11

N Corporation was formed on July 1, 2016 and incurred and paid qualifying organizational expenditures of $3,000. N Corporation can elect to deduct all $3,000 of the organization expenses in 2016.

Example 12

Same facts as above except N incurred $23,000 of organization expenses. In this case, it could deduct $5,000 immediately and amortize the remaining balance of $18,000 over 15 years (180 months) beginning in July. This would result in amortization of $100/month for 180 months. The deduction for organization expenses for 2016 would be $5,600 computed as follows:

First year allowance	$5,000
Amortization ($18,000/180 = $100/month × 6 months)	600
Total organization expense deduction in first year	$5,600

In 2017, N's would continue to amortize the remaining organization expenses, resulting in a deduction of $1,200 ($100/month × 12).

Example 13

In March, 2016 TRX, a multinational, publicly traded corporation formed a subsidiary, SUB Inc., to operate in Germany. SUB incurred organization expenses of $52,000. SUB's immediate expensing allowance of $5,000 must be reduced one dollar for each dollar of organization expense exceeding $50,000. In this case, the allowance is reduced by $2,000 ($52,000 − $50,000) to $3,000. Thus SUB may deduct $3,000 plus amortization of the remaining $49,000, resulting in a deduction of $5,720 computed below.

First year allowance ($5,000 − [$52,000 − $50,000 = $2,000])		$ 3,000
Amortization:		
Total expense	$52,000	
First year allowance	(3000)	
Amortizable balance	$49,000	
Amortization:		
($49,000/180 = $272/month × 10 months)		2,720
Total organization expense deduction in first year		$ 5,720

Note that if SUB had incurred $55,000 or more of organization expenses, the $5,000 immediate write-off would be reduced to zero and all $55,000 of the expenses would be amortized over 180 months.

For many years, a corporation had to file a statement with its first tax return electing to amortize its organization expenses. Under current law, however, the corporation is deemed to make such an election unless it elects to opt out.[44] If the election is not made, the organizational expenditures may not be amortized.

A similar election is available for the organizational costs of partnerships.[45] This is discussed in Chapter 9.

---

[44] Reg. § 1.248-1(c).   [45] § 709.

NET OPERATING LOSS

Corporations, like individuals, are entitled to deduct net operating loss carryovers in arriving at taxable income. Numerous modifications are required in computing an individual's net operating loss.[46] However, only two modifications are considered in computing a corporation's net operating loss. These two modifications are the net operating loss deductions[47] and the dividends-received deduction.[48] Net operating loss deductions for each year are considered separately. Therefore, the net operating loss deductions for other years are omitted from the computation of the current year's net operating loss. The modification relating to the dividends-received deduction is that the 70% (or 80%) taxable income limitation is ignored (i.e., the dividends-received deduction is allowed in full).

  A corporate net operating loss may be carried back two years and carried forward 20 years.[49] The loss is first carried back to the earliest year. Any unabsorbed loss is carried to the first prior year (the first year before the loss was created), and then forward until the loss is completely used or the 20-year period expires. Net operating losses generated in subsequent tax years are used in a first-in, first-out (FIFO) order (i.e., losses are carried to the earliest of the taxable years to which they may be carried).

  A corporation may elect not to carry the loss back.[50] If a corporation makes this election, the loss would be carried forward for 20 years. No loss would be carried back. This election is irrevocable.

Example 14

T Corporation had the following items of revenue and expense for 2016:

Revenue from operations.	$42,000
Dividends from less than 20% owned corporation.	40,000
Expenses of operations	63,000

T Corporation's net operating loss for 2016 is computed as follows:

Revenue from operations.	$42,000
Dividend income	40,000
Total revenue.	$82,000
Less: Total expenses.	−63,000
Less: Dividends-received deduction (ignore the taxable income limitation)	−28,000
Net operating loss (negative taxable income).	$ (9,000)

The 2016 net operating loss is carried back two years to 2014. If T Corporation's taxable income for 2014 is $3,000, the 2016 net operating loss is treated as follows:

2014 taxable income.	$ 3,000
Less: NOL carryback	− 9,000
NOL carryover to 2015	$ (6,000)

  A corporate net operating loss is carried back by filing either Form 1120X (Amended U.S. Corporation Income Tax Return) or Form 1139 (Corporation Application for Tentative Refund). T Corporation should receive a refund of its 2014 income tax paid.

---

[46] § 172(d).

[47] § 172(d)(1).

[48] § 172(d)(5).

[49] § 172(b)(1).

[50] § 172(b)(3)(C).

PASSIVE LOSS RULES

The passive loss rules of § 469 generally do not apply to C corporations. Presumably, their immunity is based on the theory that individuals normally cannot benefit from losses locked inside the corporate form. Congress, however, did not want taxpayers to be able to circumvent the passive loss rules merely by incorporating. Absent a special rule, a taxpayer could utilize corporate immunity to shelter income derived from personal services. Taxpayers would simply incorporate as a personal service corporation and acquire tax shelter investments at the corporate level. The losses produced by the tax shelters would offset not only the service income but also income from any investments made at the corporate level. Consequently, the passive loss rules apply to *personal service corporations* (PSCs). Passive losses of a PSC can be deducted only to the extent of passive income. For this purpose, a PSC is a corporation whose principal activity is the performance of any type of personal services and such services are primarily performed by employee-owners who own the stock of the corporation either directly or indirectly (e.g., through family members).[51]

Without additional restrictions, any taxpayer—not just one who derives income from services—could incorporate his or her portfolio and offset the investment income with losses from tax shelters. To prohibit this possibility, the passive loss rules also apply in a limited fashion to all closely held C corporations (i.e., a regular C corporation where five or fewer individuals own more than 50% of the stock either directly or indirectly). A closely held corporation may not use passive losses to offset its portfolio income. However, such corporations may offset losses from passive activities against the income of any active business carried on by the corporation.

CHARITABLE CONTRIBUTIONS

A corporation's charitable contribution deduction is much more limited than the charitable contribution deductions of individuals. As with individuals, the charitable contributions must be made to qualified organizations.[52] The amount that can be deducted in any year is the amount actually donated during the year and, *if the corporation is on the accrual basis,* any amounts that are authorized during the year by the board of directors may be added as well, provided the amounts are actually paid to the charity by the 15th day of the third month following the close of the tax year.[53]

Example 15

C Corporation donated $3,000 cash to United Charities (a qualified charitable organization) on June 3, 2016. On December 20, 2016 the board of directors of C Corporation authorized a $2,500 cash donation to United Charities. This $2,500 was actually paid to United Charities on March 12, 2017. C Corporation uses the calendar year as its accounting period.

If C Corporation is a *cash basis* corporation,

> only the $3,000 contribution to United Charities made in 2016 may be deducted in 2016. The additional $2,500 authorized contribution may not be deducted until 2017.

If C Corporation is an *accrual basis* corporation,

> then $5,500 ($3,000 + $2,500) may be deducted in 2016.

Note: If the $2,500 donation authorized on December 20, 2016 had been paid after March 15, 2017, the $2,500 contribution deduction would not be allowed until 2017.

---

[51] § 469(j)(2) defining personal service corporation by reference to § 269A(b)(2) with certain modifications.

[52] § 170(c).

[53] §§ 170(a)(1) and (2).

Contributions of Ordinary Income Property

When property is contributed, the fair market value of the property at the time it is donated may generally be deducted. There are, however, several exceptions to this general rule. One exception involves donations of *ordinary income property*.[54] The Regulations define ordinary income property as property that would produce a gain *other than* long-term capital gain if sold by the contributing corporation for its fair market value. The charitable contribution deduction for ordinary income property generally may not exceed the corporation's basis in the property.

Example 16

G Corporation donates some of its inventory to a church. The inventory donated is worth $5,000 and has an adjusted basis to G Corporation of $2,000. G Corporation's deduction for this contribution is $2,000, its adjusted basis in the inventory.

Three exceptions permit corporate taxpayers to claim contribution deductions in excess of the basis of the ordinary income property. A corporation is allowed to deduct its basis *plus* one-half of the unrealized appreciation in value (the deduction cannot exceed twice the basis) of (1) any inventory item donated to a qualifying charity and used solely for the care of the ill, the needy, or infants,[55] (2) a gift to a college or university of a corporation's newly manufactured scientific equipment if the recipient is the original user of the property and at least 80% of its use will be for research or experimentation,[56] and (3) a contribution of computer technology and equipment to U.S. primary and secondary schools.[57] Under any of these exceptions, the corporation is required to obtain a written statement from the charity indicating that the use requirement has been met.

Contributions of Capital Gain Property

In three situations a corporation also is limited in the amount of deduction it may take when appreciated long-term capital gain property is contributed.[58] The *first* situation occurs when tangible personal property donated to a charity is put to a use that is not related to the charity's exempt purpose. The *second* situation in which a limitation will apply is the donation of appreciated property to certain private foundations. The limitation applied in these cases is that the fair market value of the property must be reduced by the unrealized appreciation (i.e., the deduction is limited to the property's adjusted basis).

Example 17

L Corporation donated a painting to a university. The painting was worth $10,000 and had an adjusted basis to L Corporation of $9,000. If the painting is placed in the university for display and study by art students, this is considered a use related to the university's exempt purpose.[59] The limitation mentioned above would not apply, and L Corporation's charitable contribution deduction would be $10,000, the fair market value of the painting.

If, however, the painting is immediately sold by the university, this is considered to be a use that is not related to the university's exempt purpose. L Corporation's contribution deduction would be limited to $9,000, its basis of the painting ($10,000 fair market value – $1,000 unrealized appreciation).

---

[54] Reg. § 1.170A-4(b)(1).

[55] § 170(e)(3).

[56] § 170(e)(4).

[57] § 170(e)(6).

[58] § 170(e)(1).

[59] Reg. § 1.170A-4(b)(3).

Reduction for unrealized appreciation is also required in a *third* situation. In practice, it is common for businesses to contribute patents and similar property to research universities and other not-for-profit organizations, providing opportunities for further development. According to the IRS, the values of such property—and therefore the deductions—were being significantly overstated. To eliminate this abuse, the reduction for appreciation is required for contributions of patents, trademarks, trade names, trade secrets, certain copyrights, know-how, software or similar property.[60] However, in a special twist, the corporation is entitled to additional deductions in future years for a portion of the income attributable to such items.

Annual Deduction Limitations

In addition to the limitations based on the type of property contributed, there is a maximum annual limitation. The limitation is 10% of the corporation's taxable income before certain deductions.[61] The 10% limitation is based on taxable income without reduction for charitable contributions, the dividends-received deduction, net operating loss carrybacks, or capital loss carrybacks. However, taxable income *must* be reduced by *both* net operating loss and capital loss carryovers from prior years. Amounts contributed in excess of this limitation may be carried forward and deducted in any of the five succeeding years.[62] In no year may the total charitable contribution deduction exceed the 10% limitation. In years in which there is *both* a current contribution and a carryover, the current contribution is deductible first. At the end of the five-year period, any carryover not deducted expires.

Example 18

M Corporation has the following for tax year 2016:

Net income from operations	$100,000
Dividends received (subject to 70% rules)	10,000
Charitable contributions made in 2016	8,000
Charitable contribution carryforward from 2015	5,000

M Corporation's contribution deduction for 2016 is limited to $11,000, computed as follows:

Net income from operations	$100,000
Dividends received	+ 10,000
Taxable income without the charitable contribution deduction and the dividends-received deduction	$110,000
Multiply by 10% limitation	× 10%
Maximum contribution deduction for 2016	$ 11,000

Taxable income for the year will be $92,000, computed as follows:

Net income from operations		$100,000
Dividends received		+ 10,000
		$110,000
Less: Special corporate deductions:		
Charitable contributions $11,000	$11,000	
Dividends received (70% of $10,000)	+ 7,000	
Total special deductions		− 18,000
M Corporation's 2016 taxable income		$ 92,000

---

[60] § 170(e)(1)(B)(iii).

[61] § 170(b)(2).

[62] § 170(d)(2).

Example 19

Based on the facts in *Example 18,* M Corporation has a $2,000 charitable contribution carryover remaining from 2015. The first $8,000 of the $11,000 allowed deduction for 2016 is considered to be from the current year's contributions, and the $3,000 balance is from the 2015 carryover. Thus, the remaining (unused) $2,000 of the 2015 contributions must be carried over to 2017.

CAPITAL GAINS AND LOSSES

The definition of a capital asset, the determination of holding period, and the capital gain and loss *netting process* are essentially the same for corporations as they are for individuals. Under the first step of the netting process, each taxpayer combines short-term capital gains and losses, and the result is either a *net* short-term capital gain or a *net* short-term capital loss. Likewise, the taxpayer combines long-term capital gains and losses with a result of either a *net* long-term capital gain or a *net* long-term capital loss. If the taxpayer has *both* a net short-term capital gain and a net long-term capital gain—or a net short-term capital loss and a net long-term capital loss—*no* further netting is allowed. If the taxpayer has *either* a net short-term capital gain and a net long-term capital loss, or a net short-term capital loss and a net long-term capital gain, these results are combined in the second stage of the netting process. The *three* possible results of the netting process are:[63]

1. *Capital gain net income*—either a net short-term capital gain with no further netting allowed, or the *excess* of a net short-term capital gain over a net long-term capital loss.

2. *Net capital gain*—either a net long-term capital gain with no further netting allowed, or the *excess* of a net long-term capital gain over a net short-term capital loss.

3. *Net capital loss*—either a net short-term capital loss or a net long-term capital loss with no further netting allowed, the *sum* of both net short-term and net long-term capital losses, the *excess* of a net short-term capital loss over a net long-term capital gain, or the *excess* of a net long-term capital loss over a net short-term capital gain.

Capital Gains

Historically, the tax law treated short-term capital gains (i.e., capital gain net income) of both individuals and corporations as ordinary income while providing favorable treatment for long-term capital gains (i.e., net capital gains). In 1986, this tradition ended when the special treatment of long-term capital gains for corporations was eliminated. Corporations include both net long-term capital gains and net short-term capital gains along with other income and compute the tax liability at the prevailing rates.[64] Thus, a corporation's long-term and short-term capital gains are effectively treated as ordinary income.

Capital Losses

Individuals and corporations treat capital losses quite differently. As a general rule, individuals are allowed to offset capital losses against capital gains and up to $3,000 of ordinary income annually. If both a net short-term capital loss and a net long-term capital loss exist, the taxpayer first offsets the net short-term capital loss against ordinary income. Any short-term or long-term capital loss not absorbed is carried forward until it is exhausted. Capital losses retain their character as either short-term or long-term when they are carried forward.

Capital losses of a corporation offset only capital gains.[65] A corporation is never permitted to reduce ordinary income by a capital loss. As a result, corporations cannot deduct their excess capital losses for the year. Instead, a corporation must carry the excess capital losses back for three years and forward for five years,[66] to use them to offset capital gains in those years. The losses are first carried back three years. They will reduce the amount of capital

---

[63] See §§ 1222(9), (10), and (11).

[64] § 1201(a).

[65] § 1211(a).

[66] § 1212(a).

gains reported in the earliest year. Any amount not used to offset gain in the third previous year can offset gain in the second previous year and then the first previous year. If the sum of the capital gains reported in the three previous years is less than the capital loss, the excess is carried forward. Losses carried forward may be used to offset capital gains recognized in the succeeding five tax years. Capital losses created in subsequent tax years are used in FIFO order (i.e., they are carried back to the earliest of the taxable years to which they may be carried). Losses unused at the end of the five-year carryforward period expire.

Example 20

B Corporation has income, gains, and losses as follows:

	2013	2014	2015	2016
Ordinary income	$100,000	$100,000	$100,000	$100,000
Net capital gain or (loss)	4,000	3,000	2,000	(10,000)
Total income	$104,000	$103,000	$102,000	$ 90,000

B reported taxable income in years 2013, 2014, and 2015 of $104,000, $103,000, and $102,000, respectively, since net capital gains are added into taxable income. In 2016, B must report $100,000 taxable income because capital losses are nondeductible. However, B Corporation is entitled to carry the net capital loss back to years 2013, 2014, and 2015 and file a claim for refund for the taxes paid on the capital gains for each year. Because the 2016 capital loss carryback ($10,000) exceeds the sum of the capital gains in the prior three years ($9,000), B has a $1,000 capital loss carryforward. This loss carryforward can be used to offset the first $1,000 of net capital gains recognized in years 2017 through 2021.

Corporations treat all capital loss carrybacks and carryovers as short-term losses. At the present, this has no effect on the tax due and it is often immaterial whether the carryover is considered long-term or short-term. However, if Congress ever reinstates special treatment for corporate long-term capital gains, keeping short-term and long-term carryovers separate will once again have meaning.

SALES OF DEPRECIABLE PROPERTY

Corporations generally compute the amount of § 1245 and § 1250 ordinary income recapture on the sales of depreciable assets in the same manner as do individuals. However, Congress added Code § 291 to the tax law in 1982 with the intent of reducing the tax benefits of the accelerated cost recovery of depreciable § 1250 property (e.g., buildings) available to corporate taxpayers. As a result, corporations must treat as ordinary income 20% of any § 1231 gain *that would have been* ordinary income if Code § 1245 rather than § 1250 had applied to the transaction.[67] Similar rules apply to amortization of intangible drilling costs incurred by corporate taxpayers. The amount that is treated as ordinary income under § 291 is computed in the following manner:

Amount that would be treated as ordinary income under Code § 1245		$xx,xxx
Less:	Amount treated as ordinary income under § 1250	(x,xxx)
Equals:	Difference between recapture amounts	$xx,xxx
Times:	Rate specified in § 291	× 20%
Equals:	Amount that is treated as ordinary income	$xx,xxx

---

[67] See Appendix H for the current ACRS depreciation tables, including the straight-line recovery percentages.

The § 1250 recapture amount—generally the excess of accelerated depreciation over straight-line—for most § 1250 properties will be zero.[68] Nevertheless, as the following example demonstrates, § 291 still applies regardless of the method of depreciation.

Example 21

D Corporation sells residential rental property for $500,000 in 2016. The property was purchased for $400,000 in 2004. Assume that the corporation claimed straight-line depreciation of $232,000. D Corporation's depreciation recapture and § 1231 gain are computed as follows:

Step 1: Compute realized gain:

Sales price		$500,000
Less: Adjusted basis		
Cost	$400,000	
MACRS depreciation	−232,000	−168,000
Realized gain		$332,000

Step 2: Compute excess depreciation:

Actual depreciation	$232,000
Straight-line depreciation	−232,000
Excess depreciation	$ 0

Step 3: Compute § 1250 depreciation recapture:

Lesser of realized gain of	$332,000
or	
Excess depreciation of $0	
Section 1250 depreciation recapture	$ 0

Step 4: Compute depreciation recapture if § 1245 applied:

Lesser of realized gain of $332,000	
or	
Actual depreciation of $232,000	
Depreciation recapture if § 1245 applied	$232,000

Step 5: Compute § 291 ordinary income:

Depreciation recapture if § 1245 applied	$232,000
Section 1250 depreciation recapture	− 0
Excess recapture potential	$232,000
Times: § 291 rate	× 20%
Section 291 ordinary income	$ 46,400

Step 6:

Realized gain	$332,000
Less: Ordinary income	− 46,400
Section 1231 gain	$285,600

---

[68] Before 1987, residential rental and commercial buildings could be depreciated using accelerated methods. For commercial buildings, all accelerated depreciation is recaptured (§ 1245). For residential property, only the excess of accelerated over straight-line is recaptured (§ 1250). Residential buildings acquired during 1981–1986 were normally depreciated using at most a 19-year life. These buildings were fully depreciated by the end of 2005 and there will be no § 1250 recapture.

Chapter 1 *Income Taxation of Corporations*

TRANSACTIONS BETWEEN CORPORATIONS AND THEIR SHAREHOLDERS

Like noncorporate taxpayers, corporations are not allowed to deduct a loss incurred in a transaction between related parties.[69] For example, a loss on the sale of the property from a corporation to a shareholder who owns more than 50% of the corporation is not deductible. In such case, the unrecognized loss must be suspended and may be used by the shareholder to offset gain when the property is sold. A corporation also may be denied deductions for *accrued* but *unpaid* expenses incurred in transactions between related parties. For example, an accrual basis corporation may not deduct accrued expenses payable to related parties on a cash basis *until* the amount actually is paid.[70] For this purpose, a related party is any person owning directly or constructively more than 50% of the corporation's outstanding stock. In calculating constructive ownership, stock owned by family members and other entities owned by the taxpayer are included.[71] With respect to the matching of income and deduction provision only, tax law expands the definition of a related party in the case of a *personal service corporation* to include any employee-owner who owns any of the corporation's stock. For this purpose, a personal service corporation is one where the principal activity of the corporation is the performance of personal services *and* where such services are substantially performed by employee-owners. This rule applies to firms engaged in the performance of services in the fields of health, law, engineering, architecture, accounting, actuarial science, performing arts, or consulting.

The sale of property at a *gain* between a corporation and its controlling shareholders is not affected by the disallowance rules. Instead, the gain is *reclassified* as ordinary income rather than capital or § 1231 gain if the property is *depreciable* by the purchaser.[72] For purposes of this rule, a controlling shareholder is defined the same as under the disallowed loss rule (i.e., more than 50% ownership).[73] In calculating ownership, stock owned by other entities and the taxpayer's spouse must be included with the taxpayer's direct ownership.[74] In addition, sales of depreciable property between a corporation and a more than 50% shareholder are ineligible for the installment method.[75]

Computation of Corporate Income Tax

LO.4

Compute the corporate income tax, including the tax for personal service corporations and controlled corporations.

The basic corporate income tax rates in effect for 2016 are as follows:[76]

Taxable Income	Tax Rate
$ 0 – $ 50,000	15%
50,001 – 75,000	25
75,001 – 10,000,000	34
Over $10,000,000	35

Example 22

Z Corporation has taxable income of $100,000 for its calendar year 2016. Its tax liability is computed as follows:

15% ×	$ 50,000	=	$ 7,500
25% ×	25,000	=	6,250
34% ×	25,000	=	8,500
Taxable income	$100,000		$22,250 Tax

Z Corporation's tax liability before credits is $22,250.

---

[69] § 267(a)(1).

[70] § 267(a)(2).

[71] §§ 267(b) and (c).

[72] § 1239(a).

[73] § 1239(c)(1).

[74] § 1239(c)(2).

[75] § 453(g).

[76] § 11(b).

There are two exceptions to the basic tax rates shown above. First, in an effort to restrict the tax benefit of the lower graduated rates to small corporate businesses with taxable incomes of $100,000 or less, a 5% *surtax* is imposed on corporate taxable income in excess of $100,000, up to a maximum surtax of $11,750—the net "savings" of having the first $100,000 of corporate income taxed at the lower rates rather than at 34 percent.[77]

Example 23

L Corporation has taxable income of $120,000 for its 2016 calendar year. Its tax liability is computed as follows:

15% × $50,000	=	$ 7,500
25% × 25,000	=	6,250
34% × 45,000	=	15,300
Tax liability before surtax		$29,050
Plus: 5% surtax on $20,000		+ 1,000
Total tax liability for 2016		$30,050

Example 24

P Corporation has taxable income of $335,000 for its 2016 tax year. Its tax liability is computed as follows:

15% × $ 50,000	=	$ 7,500
25% × 25,000	=	6,250
34% × 260,000	=	88,400
Tax liability before surtax		$102,150
Plus: 5% surtax on $235,000		+ 11,750
Total tax liability for 2016		$113,900

Note that the 5% surtax on the $235,000 income in excess of $100,000 completely offsets the benefit of the lower graduated tax rates of 15% and 25%. Thus, corporations with taxable income of $335,000 or more will have a flat tax rate of 34% ($335,000 × 34% = $113,900).

Second, in the case of a corporation that has taxable income in excess of $15 million, the amount of tax is increased by the lesser of 3% of the excess taxable income over $15 million or $100,000. This surtax is designed to recapture the tax savings from using the 34% rate on the first $10 million of taxable income.

Taking the 5% and 3% surtaxes into account, Exhibit 1-4 presents a corporate tax rate schedule applicable to *most* corporations. The rate structure contained in Exhibit 1-4 is not available to so-called personal service corporations or to certain related corporations. The specific rules applicable to these corporations are discussed below.

---

[77] *Ibid.*

EXHIBIT 1-4	Corporate Tax Rate Schedule

If Taxable Income Is

Over	But Not Over	The Tax Is	+	% on Excess	Of the Amount Over
$ 0	$ 50,000	------------	+	15%	$ 0
50,001	75,000	$ 7,500	+	25%	50,000
75,001	100,000	13,750	+	34%	75,000
100,001	335,000	22,250	+	39%	100,000
335,001	10,000,000	113,900	+	34%	335,000
10,000,001	15,000,000	3,400,000	+	35%	10,000,000
15,000,001	18,333,333	5,150,000	+	38%	15,000,000
18,333,334	------------	6,416,666	+	35%	18,333,333

PERSONAL SERVICE CORPORATIONS

As described earlier, a personal service corporation (PSC) is a corporation whose principal activity is the performance of services in the fields of health, law, engineering, architecture, accounting, actuarial science, the performing arts, or consulting, *and* substantially all of the stock is owned by employees, retired employees, or their estates.[78] Apparently concerned that PSCs were being used to shield income from the employee-owners' higher individual tax rates, Congress denied the benefits of the lower tax rates to such corporations for taxable years after 1987. As a result, the taxable income of a PSC is subject to a flat rate of 35 percent.[79]

CONTROLLED CORPORATIONS

Certain related corporations must share the tax benefits of the lower graduated tax rates. That is, corporations that are members of a *controlled group* are allowed only one layer of income to qualify for *each* of the tax rates below the top marginal rate. Without such a rule, the owner(s) of a corporation that earns more than $75,000 in 2016 could obtain substantial tax savings simply by creating another corporation to which sales or services and the resulting income could be diverted. Such income would then be taxed at marginal rates lower than the top marginal rate plus the surtax imposed on the original corporation.

Example 25

Quik-Fix Inc. operates a very successful auto repair business at a single location in Los Angeles. Projected income and the resulting tax liability for 2016 are $150,000 and $41,750 ($22,250 + $19,500 [$150,000 − $100,000 = $50,000 × 39%]), respectively. Absent a related corporation rule, the shareholder(s) of Quik-Fix Inc. could create another separately owned corporation, or have Quik-Fix Inc. create a subsidiary corporation to which enough repair work could be directed, in order to split the anticipated $150,000 taxable income. By splitting the income between two corporations, a $14,250 ($41,750 − $27,500 [$13,750 tax per corporation × 2]) tax savings could be achieved.

---

[78] § 448(d)(2). See Rev. Rul. 91-30, 1991-1 C.B. 61, in which the IRS has ruled that a veterinary corporation may be a PSC.

[79] § 11(b)(2). Note that a PSC is not subject to the 5% or 3% surtax since it does not benefit from the lower corporate tax rates.

The members of the controlled group are permitted to allocate the use of the lower tax rates in any manner they so *elect,* provided every corporate member of the group agrees to the allocation. If the members of the group do not elect a particular apportionment, however, they will be required to share each lower tax rate bracket *equally.*[80] This requirement could result in a loss of some of the tax benefit of the lower corporate tax rates.

Example 26

In 2016, M Corporation reported taxable income of $75,000 while N Corporation suffered a loss of $25,000. If M and N are members of a controlled group, they are allowed only one benefit of the lower tax rate schedule. If they do not elect to apportion this benefit, their respective tax liabilities will be $19,625 and zero. M Corporation's tax is computed as follows:

15% × $25,000	=	$ 3,750
25% × 12,500	=	3,125
34% × 37,500	=	12,750

Taxable income:	$75,000
Tax liability:	$19,625

Note that the failure to elect a particular apportionment of the lower tax rate schedule results in an equal division of the $50,000 and $25,000 income (i.e., $25,000 and $12,500 each) subject to the 15 and 25% rates, even though none of N Corporation's income is subject to these rates. If an election is made to apportion the full amount of the rate brackets to M Corporation, the tax liability of M is reduced to $13,750 ([15% × $50,000 = $7,500] + [25% × $25,000 = $6,250]), the same tax liability due if M were unrelated to N.

In addition to the rate bracket limitation described above, a controlled group of corporations is also subject to one accumulated earnings credit, and one $40,000 exemption amount for purposes of the corporate alternative minimum tax. Therefore, it is important to properly determine whether a group of corporations is a "controlled group" for these purposes. If it is, additional information must be recorded on the corporate tax return (see Schedule J, Line 1 on the Form 1120 located at the end of this chapter).

Code § 1563(a) defines controlled groups to include:

1. Parent corporations and their 80% owned subsidiaries (referred to as a *parent subsidiary* controlled group).

2. Two or more corporations where five or fewer noncorporate shareholders who collectively own more than 50% of the stock of each corporation (referred to as a *brother-sister* controlled group).

3. Three or more corporations, each of which is a member of either a parent-subsidiary controlled group *or* a brother-sister controlled group, *and* at least one of which is both the common parent corporation of a parent-subsidiary controlled group and a member of a brother-sister controlled group (referred to as a *combined* controlled group).

Parent-Subsidiary Controlled Group

A parent-subsidiary controlled group consists of one or more chains of corporations connected through stock ownership with a common parent corporation.[81] Such a group exists if one corporation—the parent—*directly* owns 80% or more of the total combined voting power of all classes of stock entitled to vote or 80% of the total value of all classes of stock of another corporation—a subsidiary.[82] Additional corporations are included in the group if at least 80% of their voting stock or 80% of the value of their stock is directly owned by a parent and/or subsidiary corporation.

---

[80] § 1561(a).

[81] § 1563(a)(1).

[82] A parent-subsidiary controlled group is essentially the same type of group that is eligible to file a consolidated tax return. See Chapter 8 for a discussion of consolidated tax returns.

Example 27

P Corporation is the sole shareholder of Q Corporation. Because of this stock ownership, P and Q Corporations are members of a parent-subsidiary controlled group. If P Corporation acquires all of the stock of T Corporation, the parent-subsidiary controlled group expands to include P, Q, and T Corporations. Assuming Q Corporation and T Corporation each own 45% of the outstanding stock of U Corporation, the parent-subsidiary controlled group is expanded to include U Corporation. Note that P Corporation (the common parent) need not own any of U Corporation's stock for U to be included as a member of the controlled group. It is sufficient that other members of the group (Q and T) own at least 80% (in value or voting power) of another corporation for such corporation to be included in the group. (See Exhibit 1-5 for an illustration of this parent-subsidiary controlled group.)

EXHIBIT 1-5	Illustration of a Parent-Subsidiary Controlled Group

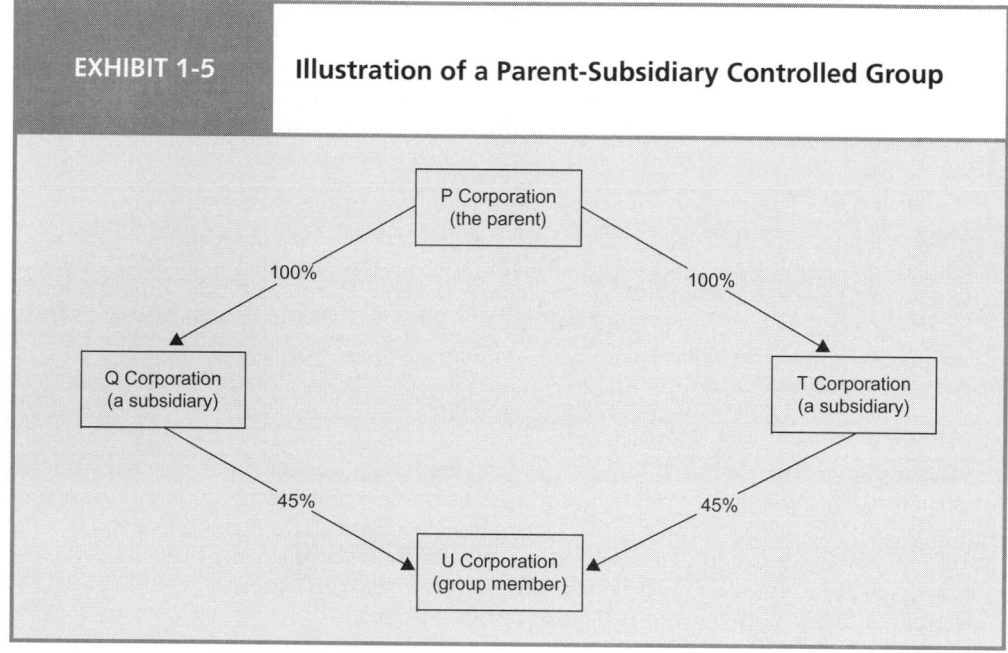

Brother-Sister Controlled Group

A brother-sister controlled group consists of two or more corporations connected through the stock ownership of certain noncorporate shareholders. Such a group exists if five or fewer individuals, estates, or trusts own more than 50% of the total combined voting power of all classes of stock entitled to vote or more than 50% of the total value of shares of all classes of stock of each corporation, taking into account only the *lowest* stock ownership percentage of each shareholder that is identical with respect to each corporation.[83]

Example 28

The stock of Corporations X, Y, and Z is owned by the following unrelated shareholders:

Individuals	Corporations			Lowest Identical Ownership
	X	Y	Z	
A	40%	20%	30%	20%
B	30	40	20	20
C	30	40	50	30
Total				70%

---

[83] § 1563(a)(2).

Corporations X, Y, and Z are members of a brother-sister controlled group because the sum of the identical ownership percentages of each of the members of this same shareholder group (A, B, and C) is 70 percent, thereby exceeding the 50% threshold. (See Exhibit 1-6 for an illustration of a brother-sister controlled group.)

EXHIBIT 1-6	**Illustration of a Brother-Sister Controlled Group**

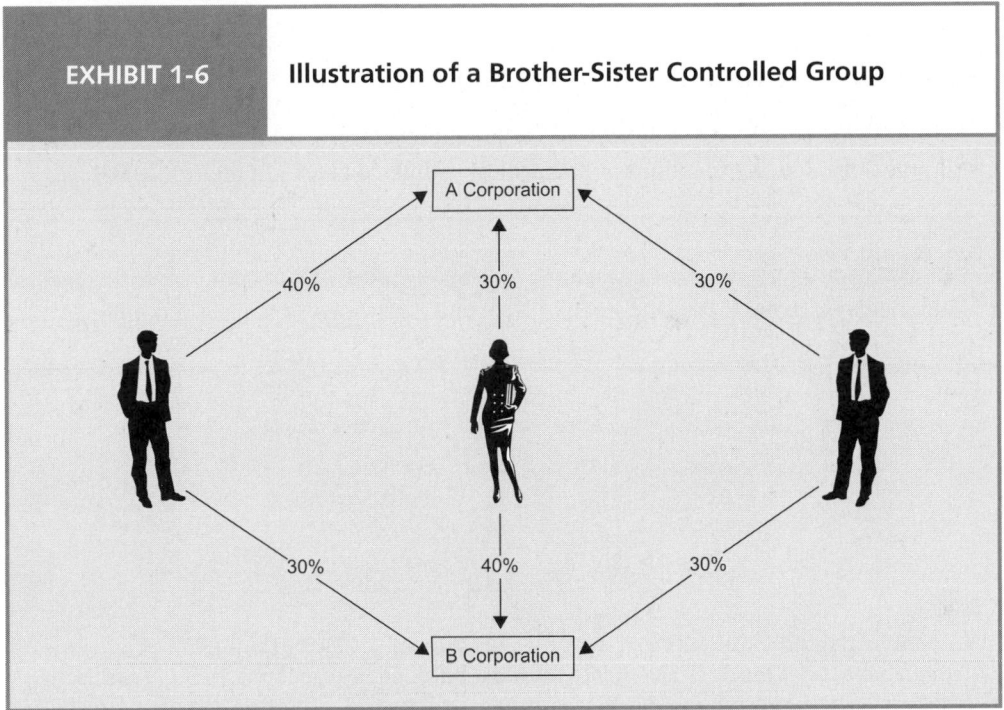

Example 29

Changing the facts in *Example 28,* the stock ownership of X, Y, and Z Corporations appears as follows:

	Corporations			Lowest Identical Ownership
Individuals	X	Y	Z	
A	70%	10%	20%	10%
B	20	70	10	10
C	10	20	70	10
Total				30%

In this situation, the lowest identical stock ownership does not exceed 50%. Thus X, Y, and Z are not members of a brother-sister controlled group.

Example 30

J owns 100% of the stock of L Inc., and 100% of the stock M Inc. J's common identical ownership is 100 percent, so L and M are a controlled group. This is perhaps the simplest example of a controlled group but also the most common—one individual owns two or more corporations.

Additional 80% Test. For tax years beginning *before* October 22, 2004, corporations were not a brother-sister controlled group unless the five or fewer shareholder group also owned 80% of the stock of each corporation.[84] While the 80% test no longer applies in determining whether allocation is required for the tax brackets, AMT exemption, and accumulated earnings credit, it is still used by a number of provisions in the law that rely on the definition of a controlled group in § 1563. These provisions involve the following:

- Limited expensing allowance [§ 179(d)(7)].

- Percentage of completion method [§ 460(e)(3)].

- Transactions between related parties [§ 267(b)(3)].

- Research expenditures [§ 41(f)(1)(A)(i)].

- Large corporation exception for payment of estimated taxes [§ 6655(g)(2)(B)].

Example 31

Individuals A, B and C own the stock of X, Y, and Z as follows (same as *Example 28*).

Shareholder	Corporations X	Y	Z	Common Ownership
A	40%	20%	30%	20%
B	30	40	20	20
C	30	40	50	30
Total	100%	100%	100%	70%

In applying the controlled group test for purposes of § 179 and the other provisions listed above, both the 50% and 80% tests must be taken into account. In this case, both tests are met—corporations X, Y, and Z are members of a brother-sister controlled group because (1) at least 80% of the stock of each corporation is owned by a group of five or fewer persons who own stock in each corporation (thereby meeting the 80% ownership test) and (2) the sum of the identical ownership percentages of each of the members of this same shareholder group (A, B, and C) is 70 percent, thereby exceeding the 50% threshold.

For purposes of the 80% test, a shareholder's stock ownership is counted only if stock in each of the potential group members is owned.[85]

Example 32

Individuals R and S own the stock of X and Y Corporations as follows:

Individuals	Corporations X	Y	Lowest Identical Ownership
R	100%	60%	60%
S	0	40	0
Total	100%	100%	60%

Although it would initially appear that both the 80% and 50% tests are met, they are not. S's ownership in Y is not counted toward the 80% test because S does not own any of the stock in X. If S's 40% is eliminated, only 60% of X and Y is owned.

---

[84] Technically, the shareholders must own 80% of the total combined voting power of all classes of stock entitled to vote or 80% of the total value of all classes of stock of each corporation.

[85] See *U.S. v. Vogel Fertilizer Co.,* 82-1, USTC ¶9134, 49 AFTR2d 82-491, 455 U.S. 16 (USSC, 1982).

Exhibit 1-7 contains an illustration of a combined controlled group.

EXHIBIT 1-7 — **Illustration of Combined Controlled Group**

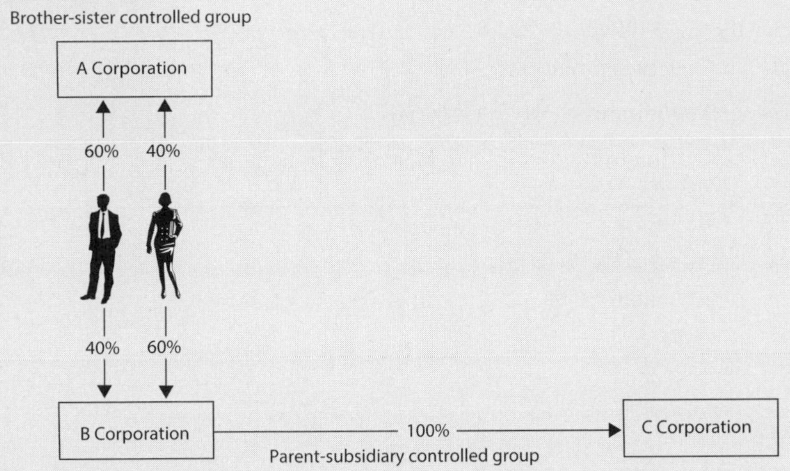

ALTERNATIVE MINIMUM TAX

Like individuals, corporations are subject to the alternative minimum tax (AMT). However, unlike individuals, certain small corporations are exempt from the AMT as discussed below. The tax is computed at a 20% rate on alternative minimum taxable income (AMTI) in excess of $40,000.[86] The $40,000 exemption is reduced by 25% of the amount of AMTI in excess of $150,000.[87] Consequently, the exemption is completely eliminated for AMTI in excess of $310,000 ([$310,000 − $150,000 = $160,000] × 25% = $40,000).

The computation of a corporation's AMT is shown in Exhibit 1-8. Note that a corporation will have an AMT liability *only if* its tentative AMT (reduced by allowable credits) *exceeds* its regular tax liability for the year.

LO.5
Identify important features of the corporate alternative minimum tax (AMT).

AMT Adjustments

AMT adjustments reflect timing differences. Relative to the regular tax treatment, the AMT provisions normally postpone deductions and accelerate income. Several of these adjustments are identified in Exhibit 1-9. For the items shown in Exhibit 1-9, the adjustments are positive initially (i.e., added back to regular taxable income in computing AMTI) but are reversed in later years (i.e., subtracted from taxable income to arrive at AMTI). Perhaps the best example of this phenomenon is depreciation. Regular tax depreciation for personal property (MACRS) generally is computed using a 200% declining-balance method, a specified cost recovery, and the appropriate convention. Under current law, regular tax depreciation for real property is computed using the straight-line method, the mid-month convention, and a life of 39 years for nonresidential realty and 27.5 years for residential realty. In contrast, depreciation for AMTI is generally computed using the appropriate conventions and the straight-line method for realty and the 150% declining-balance method for personalty.[88] AMT depreciation uses the same class life that is used for regular tax purposes (prior to 2002, the AMT class life for personalty may have been longer than that used for the regular tax and the AMT class life for realty was 40 years). Therefore, there is no depreciation adjustment for real property placed in service in 2002 and later. However, because AMT depreciation for personalty is determined under a different method than the method used for regular tax, positive or negative adjustments are required in computing AMTI.[89]

[86] See §§ 56(a) and (b).
[87] § 55(d)(3)(A).
[88] § 56(a)(1)(A)(ii).
[89] The taxpayer may elect to use AMT depreciation for regular tax purposes to avoid separate depreciation schedules.

EXHIBIT 1-8	**Calculation of the Corporate Alternative Minimum Tax**

Start with:	Regular taxable income		$xxx,xxx
Plus/Minus:	AMT adjustments, Exhibit 1-9	±	xx,xxx
Equals:	AMT adjusted taxable income		$xxx,xxx
Plus:	Sum of tax preference items, Exhibit 1-11	+	xx,xxx
Equals:	Alternative minimum taxable income (AMTI)		$xxx,xxx
Less:	Exemption ($40,000 – 25% of [AMTI – $150,000])	–	xx,xxx
Equals:	AMTI base		$xxx,xxx
Times:	AMT rate	×	xx%
Equals:	Gross alternative minimum tax		$xxx,xxx
Less:	AMT foreign tax credit	–	xx,xxx
Equals:	Tentative AMT		$xxx,xxx
Less:	Regular tax liability	–	xx,xxx
Equals:	Alternative minimum tax		$ xx,xxx

EXHIBIT 1-9	**Selected AMT Adjustments**

1. Regular tax cost recovery deductions on property placed in service after 1986 in excess of amount allowed for AMT purposes*
2. Regular tax deductions for pollution control facilities and mining, exploration, and development costs in excess of required AMT depreciation*
3. Excess of AMT gain reported from long-term contracts on the percentage completion method over amount reported as regular tax gain under the completed contract method*
4. Regular tax NOLs in excess of AMT NOL deduction*
5. Seventy-five percent (75%) of the adjusted current earnings (ACE) in excess of AMTI (computed before this adjustment item)*

* Each of these items represents a timing difference. As such they are *positive adjustments (i.e., additions to regular taxable income in arriving at AMTI) in the early years; when reversed, they become negative adjustments.*

Example 33

T Corporation placed an asset costing $100,000 in service on February 15, 2016. Assuming the asset is "three-year property," the effect on alternative minimum taxable income (AMTI) is computed as follows:

	2016	2017	2018	2019
Regular tax deduction (200%)	$33,330	$44,450	$ 14,810	$ 7,410
AMT deduction (150%)	(25,000)	(37,500)	(25,000)	(12,500)
Effect of adjustment on AMTI	$ 8,330	$ 6,950	$(10,190)	$ (5,090)
	Increase	Increase	Decrease	Decrease

Note that the above example illustrates the need to maintain one set of depreciation records for each tax system in order to compute the basis of assets for gain or loss determination. It is also important to note that this depreciation adjustment applies *only* to assets placed in service after 1986. The excess depreciation on assets placed in service before 1987 will give rise to a tax preference item *rather* than an AMT adjustment.

The most significant aspect of the corporate AMT is the adjustment for "adjusted current earnings" (ACE). Congress was concerned that certain corporations were reporting income for financial accounting purposes yet reporting little or no taxable income. To address this problem, Congress created the ACE adjustment to ensure that all corporations would pay some minimum tax on book income. In theory, the ACE adjustment simply requires taxpayers to compare book income to taxable income to determine the amount of financial accounting income that somehow escaped tax. The computation of AMTI requires that a portion of this amount be added to taxable income. Technically, the ACE adjustment is equal to 75% of the difference between *adjusted current earnings* and AMTI.[90] In this calculation, adjusted current earnings serves as a proxy for book income.

Example 34

Z Corporation has adjusted current earnings (ACE) of $80,000 and alternative minimum taxable income (without regard to the ACE adjustment) of $50,000. Because ACE exceeds AMTI by $30,000, 75% of this amount must be added to Z Corporation's AMTI. As a result, the corporation's AMTI for the year is $72,500 ($50,000 + $22,500 [$30,000 × 75%]).

The computation of adjusted current earnings begins with alternative minimum taxable income (AMTI) calculated before the adjustments for ACE or the AMT NOL. To determine the ACE amount, positive or negative adjustments are made to AMTI for special items that have not already been included in the calculation of AMTI. The formula for computing the ACE adjustment is shown in Exhibit 1-10.

One final observation should be made about the ACE adjustment. The ACE adjustment can be positive or negative. However, any negative adjustment cannot exceed prior net positive adjustments. For this reason, the corporation may want to keep track of its ACE adjustments each year even if it is not subject to the AMT.

Example 35

In 2015, X Corporation had an AMTI of $100,000 and an ACE amount of $300,000. The positive ACE adjustment that is added to AMTI is $150,000 (75% × [$300,000 − $100,000]). In 2016, X had an AMTI of $400,000 and an ACE amount of $100,000. In this case, the negative ACE amount is $225,000 (75% × [$100,000 − $400,000]). The negative adjustment to AMTI is limited to $150,000, the positive adjustment in prior years.

[90] § 56(g).

	EXHIBIT 1-10	Calculation of the ACE Adjustment

	AMTI	
	Plus:	Income excluded from AMTI but included for ACE:
		State and municipal bond interest income
		Life insurance proceeds > cash surrender value (e.g., key person life insurance)
		Income element included in cash surrender value of life insurance
		Entire gain on installment sale (except when interest is charged)
		Certain other adjustments
		Deductions not allowed for ACE:
		70% dividends-received deduction (80% and 100% generally are allowed for ACE)
		Amortization of organization expenses
		Excess of FIFO over LIFO
	Less:	Expenses attributable to income excluded above:
		Life insurance expenses
		Interest incurred on debt to acquire tax-exempt bonds
Equals:	Adjusted current earnings (ACE)	
	Less:	AMTI
Equals:	Base	
	Times:	75%
Equals:	ACE adjustment (positive or negative)	

Tax Preference Items

Corporations are required to use many of the tax preferences that individuals use in arriving at AMTI. These items are presented in Exhibit 1-11.[91]

	EXHIBIT 1-11	Tax Preference Items for Corporations

1. Depletion in excess of basis with respect to natural resources

2. Excess intangible drilling and development costs

3. Tax-exempt interest income (net of expenses related to its production) from private activity bonds

4. Excess accelerated depreciation (over straight-line amount) on nonrecovery real property placed in service before 1981

5. Excess accelerated cost recovery deductions (over straight-line alternative) on 19- and 18-year real property placed in service before 1987

Minimum Tax Credit

To alleviate the possibility of double taxation under the two tax systems, Congress enacted an alternative minimum tax credit. Basically, the alternative minimum tax paid in one year may be used as a credit against the taxpayer's future regular tax liability—but only to the

---

[91] § 57 sets forth all the tax preference items and the specifics of each calculation.

extent of the excess of the regular tax liability over the tentative minimum tax for the carryover year. The credit may be carried forward indefinitely until used—however, the credit cannot be carried back *nor* can it be used to offset any future minimum tax liability.[92]

Example 36

K Corporation's total AMT liability for 2016 is $85,000. This amount is carried forward to 2017 to reduce the regular tax (but not the minimum tax) in that year. If the 2017 regular tax is $130,000 (the minimum tax liability would be $70,000), the $85,000 credit carryover may be used to offset only $60,000 of the regular tax ($130,000 regular tax − $70,000 minimum tax). The remaining $25,000 credit may be carried over to 2018.

Exemption from AMT for Small C Corporations

Small C corporations are not subject to the AMT. A small corporation is one that has less than $5 million in average annual gross receipts for all prior taxable years. Once a C corporation qualifies as a small C corporation, it will not lose its status until its average annual gross receipts exceed $7.5 million.[93]

TAX CREDITS

Most of the same tax credits available to individuals also are available to corporations. However, corporations are not entitled to credits that apply only to individuals (e.g., the earned income credit).

ACCOUNTING PERIODS AND METHODS

Accounting Periods

A corporation generally is allowed to choose either a calendar year or fiscal year for its reporting period.[94] However, a personal service corporation (PSC) is subject to special rules. For this purpose, a PSC is defined by reference to § 269 and includes any service business. PSCs must use a calendar year for tax purposes unless it can satisfy IRS requirements that there is a business purpose for a fiscal year or a special election is made.[95] If a PSC elects to use a fiscal year, it is subject to special rules governing the deductions for payments to employee-owners during the year.[96] Like PSCs, S corporations generally must use a calendar year for tax purposes.[97] Exceptions to this rule are discussed in Chapter 11.

Accounting Methods

Unlike individuals, most corporations are denied the use of the cash method of accounting for tax purposes. There are three basic exceptions, however. The cash method may be used by the following:

1. Corporations with average annual gross receipts of $5 million or less in all prior taxable years.
2. S corporations.
3. Personal service corporations (as defined in § 448 referring to those C corporations that provide services in one of eight specified fields).[98]

---

[92] § 53(a).

[93] § 55(e).

[94] § 441.

[95] §§ 441(i) and 444.

[96] § 280H.

[97] § 1378(b). But see § 444 for an exception and Chapter 9 for further discussion.

[98] § 448.

Corporate Tax Forms and Filing Requirements

LO.6

Describe the corporate tax forms and filing requirements.

Corporations are required to report their income and tax liability on Form 1120. Page 1 of this form contains the summary of taxable income and tax due the Federal government or the refund due the corporation. There are separate schedules for the computation of cost of goods sold, compensation of officers, dividends-received deduction, and tax computation.

In addition to the computational schedules, Form 1120 also has several schedules that contain additional information, such as financial balance sheets for the beginning and end of the year. Form 1120 also contains *three* schedules of reconciliation, Schedules M-1, M-2, and M-3. Corporations with less than $250,000 of gross receipts and less than $250,000 in assets are not required to complete Schedule L, Schedule M-1, or Schedule M-2. The M-3 must be completed only by corporations (or a group of corporations filing a consolidated return) that file Form 1120 and have assets of $10 million or more.

Schedule M-1

Schedule M-1 is a reconciliation of income per books and income per tax returns. Both permanent and timing differences will appear in this schedule.

Example 37

Z Corporation reports the following data for 2016:

Net income per books	$44,500
Federal income tax liability (accrued)	7,500
Officer's life insurance premiums	5,000
Excess accelerated cost recovery	6,000
Excess charitable contributions	1,000
Municipal bond interest	2,000

A completed Schedule M-1 is shown below.

Schedule M-1	**Reconciliation of Income (Loss) per Books With Income per Return** **Note.** The corporation may be required to file Schedule M-3 (see instructions).					
1	Net income (loss) per books	44,500.00	7	Income recorded on books this year not included on this return (itemize):		
2	Federal income tax per books	7,500.00				
3	Excess of capital losses over capital gains		a	Tax-exempt interest $ 2,000.00		
4	Income subject to tax not recorded on books this year (itemize):		b	Other (itemize):		
						2,000.00
			8	Deductions on this return not charged against book income this year (itemize):		
5	Expenses recorded on books this year not deducted on this return (itemize):		a	Depreciation . . $ 6,000.00		
a	Depreciation . . . . $		b	Charitable contributions $		
b	Charitable contributions $ 1,000.00		c	Other (itemize):		
c	Travel and entertainment $					
d	Other (itemize):					6,000.00
	Key Employee Ins. = 5,000.00	6,000.00	9	Add lines 7 and 8		8,000.00
6	Add lines 1 through 5	58,000.00	10	Income—line 6 less line 9		50,000.00

The starting point in completing the M-1 is the net income per books of $44,500. Added to this amount are items that are deducted in computing net income per books but are not allowed in computing taxable income. Among such items are the federal income tax, charitable contributions in excess of the ten percent taxable income limitation, and premiums on "key employee" life insurance. Next, the net income per books is decreased by income included in book income but not included in taxable income (i.e., municipal bond interest). Finally, there is an adjustment for accelerated cost recovery in excess of straight-line depreciation allowed for income tax purposes but not allowed for book income determination.

A problem sometimes arises with respect to the Federal income tax (FIT) adjustment on the Schedule M-1. If the actual FIT amount is entered in Line 2, this amount may differ from the FIT expense accrued by the corporation. In this case, an over or under accrual amount must be determined so that the net effect is to adjust the book income by the accrued expense. Thus, in *Example 37,* if the actual FIT were entered on Line 2 in the amount of $7,500 but the corporation accrued FIT expense of $9,000, there would be an over accrual amount of $1,500 that must be shown on the Schedule M-1. This adjustment may be made on Line 5. An under-accrual amount may also be shown on Line 5 as a negative entry.

For the IRS, the M-1 is usually considered *the* most important part of Form 1120. This schedule, by revealing how a corporation's book reporting differs from its tax reporting, helps the IRS spot possible tax issues, potential tax avoidance and perhaps fraudulent accounting. When there are wide disparities between book and tax amounts (e.g., more income is being reported to shareholders than to Uncle Sam), or other inconsistencies, such differences could be a sign of tax shelter activity. In a sense, the M-1 provides the government a roadmap that it can use to identify high risk areas and aggressive transactions that may warrant greater government scrutiny.

Recently, the IRS has expressed its need for additional disclosure and the shortcomings of the M-1. According to the IRS, the financial shenanigans unveiled in the corporate scandals involving Enron, WorldCom and others underscore the need for greater openness in both tax and financial reporting. Enron's situation is instructive. Through its creative tax shelters, Enron was able to completely avoid paying taxes on the $2.3 billion of profit it reported for financial accounting purposes for the years 1996–1999. In the government's view, the book-tax differences reported on the M-1—which was created in 1964—were insufficient to expose potential problems in these cases. As most of the tax profession admits, differences between book and tax reporting as shown on the M-1 are often obscured and uninformative because (1) the starting point, book income, is not necessarily the same for every corporation (i.e., no uniform definition of "book income"); (2) corporations freely net amounts, reducing the amount of differences; (3) the reporting categories are too broad; and (4) corporations had too much flexibility in how they reported the various differences.

In order to make corporate reporting "more transparent," the IRS created a new model in 2004: the Schedule M-3. One of the primary goals of the M-3 is to help the IRS see more clearly how creative tax reporting may impact a corporation's book income and cash flow. The IRS believes that the increased reporting required by the M-3 will improve audit efficiency by improving its ability to identify returns and items that need extended examination. No doubt it is also hoped that the new M-3 will alert the government to inappropriate tax shelter activity.

Schedule M-3

In lieu of filing Schedule M-1, larger corporations must file Schedule M-3. The M-3 must be completed by any corporation that files Form 1120 and has assets of $10 million or more at the end of the year. If a group of corporations file a consolidated tax return, the $10 million is measured on a consolidated basis (i.e., the assets of the group are aggregated). In measuring whether its assets meet the $10 million threshold, a corporation must use the same basis as it prepares its financial statements. Thus, a cash-method taxpayer which prepares accrual based financial statements must use the accrual method to determine whether the M-3 is required. If a corporation is required to file an M-3 but its assets subsequently fall below $10 million, it can choose between the M-3 and the M-1. However, if total assets again exceed $10 million, the corporation must resume filing the M-3.

Schedule M-3, like its sibling, Schedule M-1, requires a reconciliation of book income with taxable income. However, the M-3 is much more detailed—much much more. The M-3 fills three pages and is divided into three parts. The M-1 takes up less than one-fourth of a page and there are no separate parts. The M-1 asks for no details about the company, its financial statements, or the net income per books that is reported on line 1 of the M-1. The M-3 requests information regarding all of these items and fills the entire first page.

Part I of the Schedule M-3 addresses the first defect of Schedule M-1 noted above: the lack of a uniform definition of "book income." It requires the taxpayer to identify its source of "book income" that is used in the reconciliation of book income to taxable income that occurs in Parts II and III. The book income that must be used in the reconciliation process depends on the type of financial statements that the corporation prepares. The following hierarchy is used:

1. SEC Form 10-K
2. Certified income statement
3. Other financial statements
4. No financial statement issued (report net income as determined from the company's books and records)

If the corporation files a SEC Form 10-K, has an audited financial statement, or prepares an income statement for the year, it must complete Part I. If none of these conditions apply, the net income per the corporation's books and records is entered on line 11, and the remainder of Part I is left blank.

The primary function of Part I is to isolate U.S. book income of the corporations that are included in the tax return. The starting point is normally the corporation's worldwide book income including all entities computed using U.S. generally accepted accounting principles. From here, income from nonincludible entities, both foreign and domestic, is removed. Thus Part I requires the corporation to identify and report any income or loss from foreign entities whose income and loss is not subject to U.S. taxation.

Example 38

P, a multinational corporation, is the parent company of a world-wide organization of over 50 entities that files a consolidated tax return. It has more than $1 billion in gross receipts and is required to file Schedule M-3. The first item to be eliminated from P's worldwide consolidated financial statement income as reported on Schedule M-3 is the income (loss) of its foreign subsidiaries (since foreign entities are normally not includible in a consolidated return). P must also make adjustments for the income or loss of any entity in which P owns between 50 and 80% since such entities must be consolidated for financial statement purposes, but not for tax purposes. Other items to be eliminated might be the income or loss of other subsidiaries that are not includible in a consolidated return such as life insurance companies or real estate investment trusts. After making these adjustments, the end result is the book income of only those entities that are included in P's consolidated return. It is this amount that must be reconciled to the taxable income reported on the tax return. For example, if the corporation files a Form 10-K with the SEC and also has a certified income statement, it must use the net income from Form 10-K.

After completing Part I and determining the "net income per books" to be used in reconciling book and taxable income, the actual reconciliation is done in Parts II and III. Part II deals with income items while Part III handles expense items. Both parts attempt to remedy the remaining problems identified above: netting, overly broad categories and flexibility.

Parts II and III require corporate taxpayers to complete a detailed reconciliation. It requires the corporation to separately report more than 70 items of income and expense in preparing the reconciliation. The long list of categories with specific labels clearly identifies what is to be reported. This reduces the opportunity for netting positive differences with negative differences, resulting in little or no difference. It also prevents taxpayers from using arcane or euphemistic terminology to conceal significant book-tax differences. The overall objective is to provide a trail that the government can easily follow so it can understand how the corporation's taxable income is derived from the company's books. The increased number of categories also limits the flexibility corporations had. The M-3 instructions indicate that all differences "must be *separately* stated and adequately disclosed." Apparently there is no materiality threshold. Moreover, the book income to be used must match the income in Part I and the taxable income must be that shown on the return.

Parts II and III not only require corporations to identify the differences between book and taxable income, but they must also report the portion of the difference that is permanent or temporary (timing differences). The IRS' principal focus is the permanent differences. Permanent differences often reflect aggressive transactions that once reported disappear from the corporation's books never to be seen again. For example, stating that an income item reported on the financial statements should never be included in taxable income is a permanent difference that will never be shown again on the tax return. Most of the aggressive tax shelters involve transactions that create permanent differences. For this reason, it is no surprise that the IRS is pleased to have these revealed.

Both Parts II and III contain four columns. Column A of Part II asks for the amount of the *income* item per the *books* while Column D asks for the amount of the income item per the *return*. Columns A and D of Part III ask for the same information for *expenses*. In between columns A and D are Columns B and C which are used to reconcile the differences between A and D. Taxpayers are required to report any difference that is temporary in Column B and any difference that is permanent in Column C. In the first year a Schedule M-3 is required, the corporation may omit the disclosures of book and tax amounts for each item (Columns A and D) on Schedules II and III and report only the differences for each item.

The M-3 also serves another purpose. Pursuant to additional reporting rules, certain taxpayers that participate in a *reportable transaction* are required to disclose the transaction on Form 8886, *Reportable Transaction Disclosure Statement*. One of the six categories of reportable transactions is a transaction with a significant book-tax difference, generally a difference of more than $10 million.[99] This particular rule generally applies only to taxpayers that are publicly traded or have book assets of $250 million or more. The IRS has indicated that filing the M-3 will satisfy the reporting requirement.[100] This alternative eliminates some of the overlap between the Form 8886 and the M-3.

The new M-3 has received mixed reactions. While most feel that its goals are worthy, there is concern that the costs to achieve them may be too high. Practitioners are concerned about the increased amount of reporting. Businesses are concerned that they may be required to make costly revisions in their accounting and information gathering systems just to capture each of the specified items on the form. The M-3 has also changed the way firms will approach reporting. In the past, the critical issue was whether a corporation should disclose a particular item. This usually involved a legal analysis of the issues. Now the concern has shifted to determining how the corporation can find everything that should be disclosed, more of a controls issue. Regardless of the profession's view, the IRS believes the M-3 can increase its audit coverage in areas with high compliance risk without using too much of its resources. Some see the M-3 as simply an intrusive government fishing expedition. Unfortunately, the M-3 cannot be ignored since failure to properly disclose results in substantial penalties. Moreover, there is little doubt that it is here to stay. In fact, the IRS has also developed Schedule M-3 forms for partnerships and S corporations.

Schedule M-2

Reconciles opening and closing retained earnings. This schedule uses *accounting* rather than tax data. Corporations without any special transactions will show an increase in retained earnings for net income and a decrease for distributions (i.e., dividends) as the major items in Schedule M-2.

Example 39

This is a continuation of *Example 37*. Additional information with respect to Z Corporation includes:

Retained earnings balance at beginning of year	$150,000
Cash dividends paid	10,000

A completed Schedule M-2 is shown below.

Schedule M-2	Analysis of Unappropriated Retained Earnings per Books				
1	Balance at beginning of year	150,000.00	5	Distributions: **a** Cash	10,000.00
2	Net income (loss) per books	44,500.00		**b** Stock	
3	Other increases (itemize):			**c** Property	
			6	Other decreases (itemize):	
			7	Add lines 5 and 6	10,000.00
4	Add lines 1, 2, and 3	194,500.00	8	Balance at end of year (line 4 less line 7)	184,500.00

The use of these schedules is further illustrated in an example of a corporate tax return presented later in this chapter.

---

[99] Reg. § 1.6011-4(b).

[100] Rev. Proc. 2004-45, 2004-31 I.R.B. 140.

SCHEDULE M-3 (Form 1120) Department of the Treasury Internal Revenue Service	**Net Income (Loss) Reconciliation for Corporations** **With Total Assets of $10 Million or More** ► Attach to Form 1120 or 1120-C. ► Information about Schedule M-3 (Form 1120) and its separate instructions is available at *www.irs.gov/form1120*.	OMB No. 1545-0123 2015

Name of corporation (common parent, if consolidated return)	Employer identification number

Check applicable box(es):   (1) ☐ Non-consolidated return   (2) ☐ Consolidated return (Form 1120 only)

(3) ☐ Mixed 1120/L/PC group   (4) ☐ Dormant subsidiaries schedule attached

Part I   Financial Information and Net Income (Loss) Reconciliation (see instructions)

1a Did the corporation file SEC Form 10-K for its income statement period ending with or within this tax year?
  ☐ **Yes.** Skip lines 1b and 1c and complete lines 2a through 11 with respect to that SEC Form 10-K.
  ☐ **No.** Go to line 1b. See instructions if multiple non-tax-basis income statements are prepared.

b Did the corporation prepare a certified audited non-tax-basis income statement for that period?
  ☐ **Yes.** Skip line 1c and complete lines 2a through 11 with respect to that income statement.
  ☐ **No.** Go to line 1c.

c Did the corporation prepare a non-tax-basis income statement for that period?
  ☐ **Yes.** Complete lines 2a through 11 with respect to that income statement.
  ☐ **No.** Skip lines 2a through 3c and enter the corporation's net income (loss) per its books and records on line 4a.

2a Enter the income statement period: Beginning MM/DD/YYYY Ending MM/DD/YYYY

b Has the corporation's income statement been restated for the income statement period on line 2a?
  ☐ **Yes.** (If "Yes," attach an explanation and the amount of each item restated.)
  ☐ **No.**

c Has the corporation's income statement been restated for any of the five income statement periods immediately preceding the period on line 2a?
  ☐ **Yes.** (If "Yes," attach an explanation and the amount of each item restated.)
  ☐ **No.**

3a Is any of the corporation's voting common stock publicly traded?
  ☐ **Yes.**
  ☐ **No.** If "No," go to line 4a.

b Enter the symbol of the corporation's primary U.S. publicly traded voting common stock . . . . ☐☐☐☐☐

c Enter the nine-digit CUSIP number of the corporation's primary publicly traded voting common stock . . . . ☐☐☐☐☐☐☐☐☐

4a Worldwide consolidated net income (loss) from income statement source identified in Part I, line 1 .	**4a**	
b Indicate accounting standard used for line 4a (see instructions): (1) ☐ GAAP (2) ☐ IFRS (3) ☐ Statutory (4) ☐ Tax-basis (5) ☐ Other (specify) _____		
5a Net income from nonincludible foreign entities (attach statement)	**5a**	( )
b Net loss from nonincludible foreign entities (attach statement and enter as a positive amount) . . .	**5b**	
6a Net income from nonincludible U.S. entities (attach statement)	**6a**	( )
b Net loss from nonincludible U.S. entities (attach statement and enter as a positive amount)	**6b**	
7a Net income (loss) of other includible foreign disregarded entities (attach statement)	**7a**	
b Net income (loss) of other includible U.S. disregarded entities (attach statement)	**7b**	
c Net income (loss) of other includible entities (attach statement)	**7c**	
8 Adjustment to eliminations of transactions between includible entities and nonincludible entities (attach statement)	**8**	
9 Adjustment to reconcile income statement period to tax year (attach statement)	**9**	
10a Intercompany dividend adjustments to reconcile to line 11 (attach statement)	**10a**	
b Other statutory accounting adjustments to reconcile to line 11 (attach statement)	**10b**	
c Other adjustments to reconcile to amount on line 11 (attach statement)	**10c**	
11 **Net income (loss) per income statement of includible corporations.** Combine lines 4 through 10 .	**11**	

Note: Part I, line 11, must equal Part II, line 30, column (a) or Schedule M-1, line 1 (see instructions).

12 Enter the total amount (not just the corporation's share) of the assets and liabilities of all entities included or removed on the following lines.

	Total Assets	Total Liabilities
a Included on Part I, line 4 . . . . ►		
b Removed on Part I, line 5 . . . . ►		
c Removed on Part I, line 6 . . . . ►		
d Included on Part I, line 7 . . . . ►		

For Paperwork Reduction Act Notice, see the Instructions for Form 1120.   Cat. No. 37961C   Schedule M-3 (Form 1120) 2015

Schedule M-3 (Form 1120) 2015 | Page **2**

Name of corporation (common parent, if consolidated return)	Employer identification number

Check applicable box(es): **(1)** ☐ Consolidated group **(2)** ☐ Parent corp **(3)** ☐ Consolidated eliminations **(4)** ☐ Subsidiary corp **(5)** ☐ Mixed 1120/L/PC group

Check if a sub-consolidated: **(6)** ☐ 1120 group **(7)** ☐ 1120 eliminations

Name of subsidiary (if consolidated return)	Employer identification number

Part II Reconciliation of Net Income (Loss) per Income Statement of Includible Corporations With Taxable Income per Return (see instructions)

Income (Loss) Items (Attach statements for lines 1 through 12)	(a) Income (Loss) per Income Statement	(b) Temporary Difference	(c) Permanent Difference	(d) Income (Loss) per Tax Return
1 Income (loss) from equity method foreign corporations				
2 Gross foreign dividends not previously taxed				
3 Subpart F, QEF, and similar income inclusions				
4 Section 78 gross-up				
5 Gross foreign distributions previously taxed				
6 Income (loss) from equity method U.S. corporations				
7 U.S. dividends not eliminated in tax consolidation				
8 Minority interest for includible corporations				
9 Income (loss) from U.S. partnerships				
10 Income (loss) from foreign partnerships				
11 Income (loss) from other pass-through entities				
12 Items relating to reportable transactions				
13 Interest income (see instructions)				
14 Total accrual to cash adjustment				
15 Hedging transactions				
16 Mark-to-market income (loss)				
17 Cost of goods sold (see instructions)	( )			( )
18 Sale versus lease (for sellers and/or lessors)				
19 Section 481(a) adjustments				
20 Unearned/deferred revenue				
21 Income recognition from long-term contracts				
22 Original issue discount and other imputed interest				
23a Income statement gain/loss on sale, exchange, abandonment, worthlessness, or other disposition of assets other than inventory and pass-through entities				
b Gross capital gains from Schedule D, excluding amounts from pass-through entities				
c Gross capital losses from Schedule D, excluding amounts from pass-through entities, abandonment losses, and worthless stock losses				
d Net gain/loss reported on Form 4797, line 17, excluding amounts from pass-through entities, abandonment losses, and worthless stock losses				
e Abandonment losses				
f Worthless stock losses (attach statement)				
g Other gain/loss on disposition of assets other than inventory				
24 Capital loss limitation and carryforward used				
25 Other income (loss) items with differences (attach statement)				
26 **Total income (loss) items.** Combine lines 1 through 25				
27 **Total expense/deduction items** (from Part III, line 38)				
28 Other items with no differences				
29a Mixed groups, see instructions. All others, combine lines 26 through 28				
b PC insurance subgroup reconciliation totals				
c Life insurance subgroup reconciliation totals				
30 **Reconciliation totals.** Combine lines 29a through 29c				

Note: Line 30, column (a), must equal Part I, line 11, and column (d) must equal Form 1120, page 1, line 28.

Schedule M-3 (Form 1120) 2015

Schedule M-3 (Form 1120) 2015   Page **3**

Name of corporation (common parent, if consolidated return)	Employer identification number

Check applicable box(es): **(1)** ☐ Consolidated group   **(2)** ☐ Parent corp   **(3)** ☐ Consolidated eliminations   **(4)** ☐ Subsidiary corp   **(5)** ☐ Mixed 1120/L/PC group

Check if a sub-consolidated: **(6)** ☐ 1120 group   **(7)** ☐ 1120 eliminations

Name of subsidiary (if consolidated return)	Employer identification number

Part III   Reconciliation of Net Income (Loss) per Income Statement of Includible Corporations With Taxable Income per Return—Expense/Deduction Items (see instructions)

Expense/Deduction Items	(a) Expense per Income Statement	(b) Temporary Difference	(c) Permanent Difference	(d) Deduction per Tax Return
1 U.S. current income tax expense				
2 U.S. deferred income tax expense				
3 State and local current income tax expense				
4 State and local deferred income tax expense				
5 Foreign current income tax expense (other than foreign withholding taxes)				
6 Foreign deferred income tax expense				
7 Foreign withholding taxes				
8 Interest expense (see instructions)				
9 Stock option expense				
10 Other equity-based compensation				
11 Meals and entertainment				
12 Fines and penalties				
13 Judgments, damages, awards, and similar costs				
14 Parachute payments				
15 Compensation with section 162(m) limitation				
16 Pension and profit-sharing				
17 Other post-retirement benefits				
18 Deferred compensation				
19 Charitable contribution of cash and tangible property				
20 Charitable contribution of intangible property				
21 Charitable contribution limitation/carryforward				
22 Domestic production activities deduction				
23 Current year acquisition or reorganization investment banking fees				
24 Current year acquisition or reorganization legal and accounting fees				
25 Current year acquisition/reorganization other costs				
26 Amortization/impairment of goodwill				
27 Amortization of acquisition, reorganization, and start-up costs				
28 Other amortization or impairment write-offs				
29 Reserved				
30 Depletion				
31 Depreciation				
32 Bad debt expense				
33 Corporate owned life insurance premiums				
34 Purchase versus lease (for purchasers and/or lessees)				
35 Research and development costs				
36 Section 118 exclusion (attach statement)				
37 Other expense/deduction items with differences (attach statement)				
38 **Total expense/deduction items.** Combine lines 1 through 37. Enter here and on Part II, line 27, reporting positive amounts as negative and negative amounts as positive				

Schedule M-3 (Form 1120) 2015

FILING REQUIREMENTS

Form 1120 must be filed by the 15th day of the third month following the close of the corporation's tax year.[101] As mentioned previously, a regular corporation is permitted to elect either a calendar or a fiscal year. The decision generally is unaffected by the tax years of its shareholders.[102] The selection is made by filing the first return by the appropriate due date; for calendar year corporations, the due date is March 15. The return must be signed by an officer or other authorized person.[103]

Corporations may obtain an automatic six-month extension of time to file the tax return.[104] The extension only covers the return—not the tax due. The request for extension (Form 7004) must be accompanied by the full amount of estimated tax due. The extension can be terminated by the government on ten days' notice.

ESTIMATED TAX PAYMENTS

Corporations are required to file and pay estimated tax (including any estimated AMT liability).[105] The estimates are due the 15th day of the 4th, 6th, 9th, and 12th months of the tax year. For a calendar year corporation, the payment dates for estimated taxes are as follows:

- April 15
- June 15
- September 15
- December 15

One-fourth of the estimated tax due is to be paid on each payment date.

To avoid a penalty for underpayment of the estimated tax, at least 100% of the corporation's tax due for the year must be paid as estimated taxes.[106] Specifically, the corporation must pay *one-fourth* of this amount—25% (100% ÷ 4) of the tax shown on its return—by the due date of each installment.[107] However, the underpayment penalty is not normally imposed where the installment for any period is:

1. At least 25% of the tax shown on the prior year's return (if such a return was for 12 months and showed a tax liability); or
2. Equal to or in excess of 100% of the tax due for each quarter based on annualized taxable income.[108]

Example 40

B Corporation, a calendar year corporation, made timely 2016 estimated tax payments of $20,000 each quarter. The actual tax liability for 2016 is $120,000; the 2015 tax liability was $98,000. Income was earned evenly throughout the year.

B could have avoided the underpayment penalty by paying installments of $24,500, the lesser of $30,000 or $24,500, as computed below.

$$\text{100\% of current year's tax: } \frac{100\% \times \$120,000}{4} = \$30,000$$

$$\text{100\% of last year's tax: } \frac{100\% \times \$98,000}{4} = \$24,500$$

---

[101] § 6072(b).

[102] Although a regular corporation's selection of a calendar or fiscal year is not affected by the tax years of its shareholders, a corporation electing to be treated as a conduit (flow-through) entity under Subchapter S of the Code generally is required to adopt the same tax year as its shareholders. Chapter 11 for greater detail.

[103] § 6062.

[104] § 6081(b).

[105] § 6655.

[106] § 6655(b).

[107] *Ibid.*

[108] See §§ 6655(d) and (e) for these exceptions, and Chapter 19 for a discussion of underpayment penalties.

> Because the estimated payments were insufficient, B must pay a penalty based on the underpayment that occurred with each installment, $4,500 ($24,500 − $20,000). Note that the annualized income exception is not available because income is earned ratably throughout the year.

A so-called *large* corporation—one with taxable income of $1 million or more in any of its immediately three preceding taxable years—is not allowed to use exception 1 above *except* for its first estimated tax payment of the year.[109] If a large corporation uses the first-quarter exception, any deficiency between the normal required amount (i.e., 100% of the current year's tax) and the amount paid under the first-quarter exception (100% of last year's tax) must be made up with the second installment.

Example 41

Assume the same facts as in *Example 40,* except that the corporation's taxable income for the last three years was as follows:

Year	Taxable Income
2013	$ 900,000
2014	1,200,000
2015	800,000

Because the corporation has taxable income in one of its last three taxable years that is $1 million or more (i.e., 2014), it is considered a large corporation. Consequently, unlike other corporations, it is allowed to base its installment payments on last year's tax *only* for the first payment. Therefore, its first installment would be $24,500. Its second installment payment amount would be $35,500, computed as follows:

Normal installment for large corporation	$30,000	$30,000
Installment based on last year's tax	(24,500)	
Deficiency	$ 5,500	5,500
Second installment		$35,500

Note that the third and fourth installments would drop to the normal 100% amount of $30,000.

Finally, a corporation whose tax liability for the year is less than $500 is not subject to the underpayment penalty.[110] If a corporation does not qualify for any of the exceptions, its underpayment penalty is computed on Form 2220.

---

[109] § 6655(d)(2).   [110] § 6655(f).

EXAMPLE OF CORPORATE TAX RETURN

The next few pages contain an illustration of a corporation's annual Federal income tax return (Form 1120). This return is based on the following information:

R Corporation is a calendar year, cash method taxpayer that operates a men's clothing store. John Beyond owns 100% of R Corporation's stock and is employed as the company's only officer. The corporation had the following items of income and expense for the current year:

Gross sales	$3,900,000
Sales returns	20,000
Inventory at beginning of year	120,000
Purchases	1,100,000
Inventory at end of year	140,000
Salaries and wages	
Officers	400,000
Other	150,000
Rent expenses	120,000
Interest expense	50,000
Interest income	
Municipal bonds	7,000
Other	10,000
Charitable contributions	79,000
Depreciation	110,000
Dividend income	30,000
Advertising expenses	50,000
Professional fees paid	20,000
Taxes paid (state income and payroll taxes)	40,000
Premiums paid on key employee life insurance policy	45,500

R Corporation timely paid $600,000 in estimated income tax payments based on its prior year's tax liability of $595,200. All dividends received by the corporation qualify for the 70% dividends received deduction. The corporation declared and paid dividends of $65,000 to its sole shareholder. Additional information is provided in the balance sheets in Schedule L. R Corporation's 2016 tax liability is $612,000 ($1,800,000 × 34%).

Note: The sample corporate tax return is on 2015 tax forms because the 2016 forms were not available at the publication date of this text.

Form **1120**	**U.S. Corporation Income Tax Return**	OMB No. 1545-0123
Department of the Treasury Internal Revenue Service	For calendar year 2015 or tax year beginning _____, 2015, ending _____, 20 ____ ▶ Information about Form 1120 and its separate instructions is at *www.irs.gov/form1120.*	20**15**

A Check if:
1a Consolidated return (attach Form 851) ☐
 b Life/nonlife consolidated return ☐
2 Personal holding co. (attach Sch. PH) ☐
3 Personal service corp. (see instructions) ☐
4 Schedule M-3 attached ☐

TYPE OR PRINT

Name: R. Corporation
Number, street, and room or suite no. If a P.O. box, see instructions.
123 Jones Avenue
City or town, state, or province, country, and ZIP or foreign postal code
Anywhere, U.S.A. 98765

B Employer identification number
74 – 0987650
C Date incorporated
1 – 1 – 2013
D Total assets (see instructions)
$ 2,184,925 00

E Check if: **(1)** ☐ Initial return **(2)** ☐ Final return **(3)** ☐ Name change **(4)** ☐ Address change

Income

1a	Gross receipts or sales	1a	3,900,000	00
b	Returns and allowances	1b	20,000	00
c	Balance. Subtract line 1b from line 1a	1c	3,880,000	00
2	Cost of goods sold (attach Form 1125-A)	2	1,080,000	00
3	Gross profit. Subtract line 2 from line 1c	3	2,800,000	00
4	Dividends (Schedule C, line 19)	4	30,000	00
5	Interest	5	10,000	00
6	Gross rents	6		
7	Gross royalties	7		
8	Capital gain net income (attach Schedule D (Form 1120))	8		
9	Net gain or (loss) from Form 4797, Part II, line 17 (attach Form 4797)	9		
10	Other income (see instructions—attach statement)	10		
11	**Total income.** Add lines 3 through 10 ▶	11	2,840,000	00

Deductions (See instructions for limitations on deductions.)

12	Compensation of officers (see instructions—attach Form 1125-E) ▶	12	400,000	00
13	Salaries and wages (less employment credits)	13	150,000	00
14	Repairs and maintenance	14		
15	Bad debts	15		
16	Rents	16	120,000	00
17	Taxes and licenses	17	40,000	00
18	Interest	18	50,000	00
19	Charitable contributions	19	79,000	00
20	Depreciation from Form 4562 not claimed on Form 1125-A or elsewhere on return (attach Form 4562)	20	110,000	00
21	Depletion	21		
22	Advertising	22	50,000	00
23	Pension, profit-sharing, etc., plans	23		
24	Employee benefit programs	24		
25	Domestic production activities deduction (attach Form 8903)	25		
26	Other deductions (attach statement) Professional Fees	26	20,000	00
27	**Total deductions.** Add lines 12 through 26 ▶	27	1,019,000	00
28	Taxable income before net operating loss deduction and special deductions. Subtract line 27 from line 11.	28	1,821,000	00
29a	Net operating loss deduction (see instructions)	29a		
b	Special deductions (Schedule C, line 20)	29b	21,000	00
c	Add lines 29a and 29b	29c	21,000	00

Tax, Refundable Credits, and Payments

30	**Taxable income.** Subtract line 29c from line 28 (see instructions)	30	1,800,000	00
31	Total tax (Schedule J, Part I, line 11)	31	612,000	00
32	Total payments and refundable credits (Schedule J, Part II, line 21)	32	600,000	00
33	Estimated tax penalty (see instructions). Check if Form 2220 is attached ▶ ☐	33		
34	**Amount owed.** If line 32 is smaller than the total of lines 31 and 33, enter amount owed	34		
35	**Overpayment.** If line 32 is larger than the total of lines 31 and 33, enter amount overpaid	35	12,000	00
36	Enter amount from line 35 you want: **Credited to 2016 estimated tax** ▶ 12,000 00 **Refunded** ▶	36		

Sign Here

Under penalties of perjury, I declare that I have examined this return, including accompanying schedules and statements, and to the best of my knowledge and belief, it is true, correct, and complete. Declaration of preparer (other than taxpayer) is based on all information of which preparer has any knowledge.

▶ *John Beyond*   3–14–17   ▶ President
Signature of officer   Date   Title

May the IRS discuss this return with the preparer shown below (see instructions)? ☐ Yes ☐ No

Paid Preparer Use Only

Print/Type preparer's name	Preparer's signature	Date		PTIN
	Sherry L. Hartman	3–12–17	Check ☐ if self-employed	454-24-9464
Firm's name ▶ Roy W. Hartman & Daughters			Firm's EIN ▶ 74 – 2735841	
Firm's address ▶ 11318 Kingsland Blvd., Sealy, TX			Phone no. (281) 489 – 6443	

For Paperwork Reduction Act Notice, see separate instructions.   Cat. No. 11450Q   Form **1120** (2015)

Form 1120 (2015) Page **2**

Schedule C	Dividends and Special Deductions (see instructions)	(a) Dividends received	(b) %	(c) Special deductions (a) × (b)
1	Dividends from less-than-20%-owned domestic corporations (other than debt-financed stock)	30,000	70	21,000
2	Dividends from 20%-or-more-owned domestic corporations (other than debt-financed stock)		80	
3	Dividends on debt-financed stock of domestic and foreign corporations		*see instructions*	
4	Dividends on certain preferred stock of less-than-20%-owned public utilities . . .		42	
5	Dividends on certain preferred stock of 20%-or-more-owned public utilities		48	
6	Dividends from less-than-20%-owned foreign corporations and certain FSCs . . .		70	
7	Dividends from 20%-or-more-owned foreign corporations and certain FSCs . . .		80	
8	Dividends from wholly owned foreign subsidiaries		100	
9	**Total.** Add lines 1 through 8. See instructions for limitation			21,000
10	Dividends from domestic corporations received by a small business investment company operating under the Small Business Investment Act of 1958		100	
11	Dividends from affiliated group members		100	
12	Dividends from certain FSCs		100	
13	Dividends from foreign corporations not included on lines 3, 6, 7, 8, 11, or 12 . . .			
14	Income from controlled foreign corporations under subpart F (attach Form(s) 5471) .			
15	Foreign dividend gross-up			
16	IC-DISC and former DISC dividends not included on lines 1, 2, or 3			
17	Other dividends			
18	Deduction for dividends paid on certain preferred stock of public utilities			
19	**Total dividends.** Add lines 1 through 17. Enter here and on page 1, line 4 . . . ▶	30,000		
20	**Total special deductions.** Add lines 9, 10, 11, 12, and 18. Enter here and on page 1, line 29b . . . . ▶			21,000

Form **1120** (2015)

Form 1120 (2015)			Page **3**

Schedule J | **Tax Computation and Payment** (see instructions)

Part I–Tax Computation

1	Check if the corporation is a member of a controlled group (attach Schedule O (Form 1120)) . . . . . ▶ ☐			
2	Income tax. Check if a qualified personal service corporation (see instructions) . . . . . ▶ ☐		**2**	612,000 00
3	Alternative minimum tax (attach Form 4626)		**3**	
4	Add lines 2 and 3		**4**	612,000 00
5a	Foreign tax credit (attach Form 1118)	**5a**		
b	Credit from Form 8834 (see instructions)	**5b**		
c	General business credit (attach Form 3800)	**5c**		
d	Credit for prior year minimum tax (attach Form 8827)	**5d**		
e	Bond credits from Form 8912	**5e**		
6	**Total credits.** Add lines 5a through 5e		**6**	
7	Subtract line 6 from line 4		**7**	612,000 00
8	Personal holding company tax (attach Schedule PH (Form 1120))		**8**	
9a	Recapture of investment credit (attach Form 4255)	**9a**		
b	Recapture of low-income housing credit (attach Form 8611)	**9b**		
c	Interest due under the look-back method—completed long-term contracts (attach Form 8697)	**9c**		
d	Interest due under the look-back method—income forecast method (attach Form 8866)	**9d**		
e	Alternative tax on qualifying shipping activities (attach Form 8902)	**9e**		
f	Other (see instructions—attach statement)	**9f**		
10	**Total.** Add lines 9a through 9f		**10**	
11	**Total tax.** Add lines 7, 8, and 10. Enter here and on page 1, line 31		**11**	612,000 00

Part II–Payments and Refundable Credits

12	2014 overpayment credited to 2015		**12**	
13	2015 estimated tax payments		**13**	600,000 00
14	2015 refund applied for on Form 4466		**14**	( )
15	Combine lines 12, 13, and 14		**15**	600,000 00
16	Tax deposited with Form 7004		**16**	
17	Withholding (see instructions)		**17**	
18	**Total payments.** Add lines 15, 16, and 17		**18**	600,000 00
19	Refundable credits from:			
a	Form 2439	**19a**		
b	Form 4136	**19b**		
c	Form 8827, line 8c	**19c**		
d	Other (attach statement—see instructions).	**19d**		
20	**Total credits.** Add lines 19a through 19d		**20**	
21	**Total payments and credits.** Add lines 18 and 20. Enter here and on page 1, line 32		**21**	600,000 00

Schedule K | **Other Information** (see instructions)

		Yes	No
1	Check accounting method: **a** ☐ Cash **b** ☐ Accrual **c** ☒ Other (specify) ▶ Hybrid _____		
2	See the instructions and enter the:		
a	Business activity code no. ▶ 448110		
b	Business activity ▶ Men's Clothing Store		
c	Product or service ▶ Clothing		
3	Is the corporation a subsidiary in an affiliated group or a parent-subsidiary controlled group?		X
	If "Yes," enter name and EIN of the parent corporation ▶		
4	At the end of the tax year:		
a	Did any foreign or domestic corporation, partnership (including any entity treated as a partnership), trust, or tax-exempt organization own directly 20% or more, or own, directly or indirectly, 50% or more of the total voting power of all classes of the corporation's stock entitled to vote? If "Yes," complete Part I of Schedule G (Form 1120) (attach Schedule G)		X
b	Did any individual or estate own directly 20% or more, or own, directly or indirectly, 50% or more of the total voting power of all classes of the corporation's stock entitled to vote? If "Yes," complete Part II of Schedule G (Form 1120) (attach Schedule G) .	X	

Form **1120** (2015)

Form 1120 (2015)   Page **4**

Schedule K	**Other Information** *continued* (see instructions)			Yes	No

5 At the end of the tax year, did the corporation:

a Own directly 20% or more, or own, directly or indirectly, 50% or more of the total voting power of all classes of stock entitled to vote of any foreign or domestic corporation not included on **Form 851,** Affiliations Schedule? For rules of constructive ownership, see instructions. If "Yes," complete (i) through (iv) below.   **No: X**

(i) Name of Corporation	**(ii)** Employer Identification Number (if any)	**(iii)** Country of Incorporation	**(iv)** Percentage Owned in Voting Stock

b Own directly an interest of 20% or more, or own, directly or indirectly, an interest of 50% or more in any foreign or domestic partnership (including an entity treated as a partnership) or in the beneficial interest of a trust? For rules of constructive ownership, see instructions. If "Yes," complete (i) through (iv) below.   **No: X**

(i) Name of Entity	**(ii)** Employer Identification Number (if any)	**(iii)** Country of Organization	**(iv)** Maximum Percentage Owned in Profit, Loss, or Capital

6 During this tax year, did the corporation pay dividends (other than stock dividends and distributions in exchange for stock) in excess of the corporation's current and accumulated earnings and profits? (See sections 301 and 316.) . . . .   **No: X**

If "Yes," file **Form 5452,** Corporate Report of Nondividend Distributions.

If this is a consolidated return, answer here for the parent corporation and on Form 851 for each subsidiary.

7 At any time during the tax year, did one foreign person own, directly or indirectly, at least 25% of **(a)** the total voting power of all classes of the corporation's stock entitled to vote or **(b)** the total value of all classes of the corporation's stock? . . . .   **No: X**

For rules of attribution, see section 318. If "Yes," enter:

(i) Percentage owned ▶ _____ and **(ii)** Owner's country ▶ _____

(c) The corporation may have to file **Form 5472,** Information Return of a 25% Foreign-Owned U.S. Corporation or a Foreign Corporation Engaged in a U.S. Trade or Business. Enter the number of Forms 5472 attached ▶ _____

8 Check this box if the corporation issued publicly offered debt instruments with original issue discount . . . . ▶ ☐

If checked, the corporation may have to file **Form 8281,** Information Return for Publicly Offered Original Issue Discount Instruments.

9 Enter the amount of tax-exempt interest received or accrued during the tax year ▶ $ 7,000

10 Enter the number of shareholders at the end of the tax year (if 100 or fewer) ▶ 1

11 If the corporation has an NOL for the tax year and is electing to forego the carryback period, check here . . . . . ▶ ☐

If the corporation is filing a consolidated return, the statement required by Regulations section 1.1502-21(b)(3) must be attached or the election will not be valid.

12 Enter the available NOL carryover from prior tax years (do not reduce it by any deduction on line 29a.) ▶ $ _____

13 Are the corporation's total receipts (page 1, line 1a, plus lines 4 through 10) for the tax year **and** its total assets at the end of the tax year less than $250,000? . . . .   **No: X**

If "Yes," the corporation is not required to complete Schedules L, M-1, and M-2. Instead, enter the total amount of cash distributions and the book value of property distributions (other than cash) made during the tax year ▶ $ _____

14 Is the corporation required to file Schedule UTP (Form 1120), Uncertain Tax Position Statement (see instructions)? . . . . .

If "Yes," complete and attach Schedule UTP.

15a Did the corporation make any payments in 2015 that would require it to file Form(s) 1099? . . . .

b If "Yes," did or will the corporation file required Forms 1099? . . . .

16 During this tax year, did the corporation have an 80% or more change in ownership, including a change due to redemption of its own stock? . . . .

17 During or subsequent to this tax year, but before the filing of this return, did the corporation dispose of more than 65% (by value) of its assets in a taxable, non-taxable, or tax deferred transaction? . . . .

18 Did the corporation receive assets in a section 351 transfer in which any of the transferred assets had a fair market basis or fair market value of more than $1 million? . . . .

Form **1120** (2015)

Form 1120 (2015)   Page **5**

Schedule L | **Balance Sheets per Books** | Beginning of tax year | | End of tax year | |

	Assets	(a)	(b)	(c)	(d)
1	Cash		30,000		320,000
2a	Trade notes and accounts receivable . . .	180,000		210,000	
b	Less allowance for bad debts	( )	180,000	( )	210,000
3	Inventories		120,000		140,000
4	U.S. government obligations				100,000
5	Tax-exempt securities (see instructions) . .				104,425
6	Other current assets (attach statement) . .				
7	Loans to shareholders				
8	Mortgage and real estate loans		200,000		
9	Other investments (attach statement) . . .				970,500
10a	Buildings and other depreciable assets . .	420,000		420,000	
b	Less accumulated depreciation	(50,000)	370,000	(80,000)	340,000
11a	Depletable assets				
b	Less accumulated depletion	( )		( )	
12	Land (net of any amortization)				
13a	Intangible assets (amortizable only) . . .				
b	Less accumulated amortization	( )		( )	
14	Other assets (attach statement)				
15	Total assets		900,000		2,184,925
	Liabilities and Shareholders' Equity				
16	Accounts payable		150,000		110,000
17	Mortgages, notes, bonds payable in less than 1 year				
18	Other current liabilities (attach statement) . .				
19	Loans from shareholders				
20	Mortgages, notes, bonds payable in 1 year or more				
21	Other liabilities (attach statement)				
22	Capital stock: a Preferred stock				
	b Common stock	10,000	10,000	10,000	10,000
23	Additional paid-in capital		90,000		90,000
24	Retained earnings—Appropriated (attach statement)				
25	Retained earnings—Unappropriated . . .		650,000		1,974,925
26	Adjustments to shareholders' equity (attach statement)				
27	Less cost of treasury stock		( )		( )
28	Total liabilities and shareholders' equity . .		900,000		2,184,925

Schedule M-1 | **Reconciliation of Income (Loss) per Books With Income per Return**

Note: The corporation may be required to file Schedule M-3 (see instructions).

1	Net income (loss) per books	1,389,925	7	Income recorded on books this year not included on this return (itemize):	
2	Federal income tax per books	472,575			
3	Excess of capital losses over capital gains .			Tax-exempt interest $ 7,000	
4	Income subject to tax not recorded on books this year (itemize):_____			Municipal Bond Interest	
					7,000
			8	Deductions on this return not charged against book income this year (itemize):	
5	Expenses recorded on books this year not deducted on this return (itemize):			a Depreciation . . $ 80,000	
a	Depreciation . . . . $_____			b Charitable contributions $_____	
b	Charitable contributions . $_____				
c	Travel and entertainment . $_____				
	Key Employee Ins. Premiums	45,500			80,000
			9	Add lines 7 and 8	87,000
6	Add lines 1 through 5	1,908,000	10	Income (page 1, line 28)—line 6 less line 9	1,821,000

Schedule M-2 | **Analysis of Unappropriated Retained Earnings per Books (Line 25, Schedule L)**

1	Balance at beginning of year	650,000	5	Distributions: a Cash	65,000
2	Net income (loss) per books	1,389,925		b Stock	
3	Other increases (itemize):_____			c Property . . .	
			6	Other decreases (itemize):_____	
	_____		7	Add lines 5 and 6	65,000
4	Add lines 1, 2, and 3	2,039,925	8	Balance at end of year (line 4 less line 7)	1,974,925

Form **1120** (2015)

DISCUSSION QUESTIONS

1-1 *What Is a Corporation?* Although an entity may be a corporation under state law, what characteristics must the entity possess to be treated as a corporation for Federal tax purposes? What difference will it make on the Federal tax classification if the entity possesses all or only a few of these characteristics?

1-2 *Disregard of Corporate Form.* Why might the IRS try to disregard an entity that meets the state law requirements of a corporation? Under what circumstances might shareholders try to use the corporate form but attempt to disregard it for Federal tax purposes?

1-3 *Corporate versus Individual Taxation.* What are the differences in income tax treatment of corporations and individuals for the items below?
   a. Dividends received
   b. Classification of deductions
   c. Casualty losses
   d. Charitable contribution limitations
   e. Net capital gain treatment
   f. Capital loss deduction
   g. Capital loss carryovers and carrybacks
   h. Gain on sale of depreciable realty

1-4 *Dividends-Received Deduction.* Why is a corporation allowed a dividends-received deduction? Under what circumstances is the recipient corporation allowed an 80% rather than the usual 70% dividends-received deduction?

1-5 *Limitations on Dividends-Received Deduction.* What arc thc limitations imposcd on a corporation's dividends-received deduction? Under what circumstances can one of these limitations be disregarded?

1-6 *Charitable Contribution Carryovers.* Under what circumstances must a corporation carry over to subsequent years its qualifying contributions? If contributions are made in the current year and the corporation has a contribution carryover from a prior year, which contributions are deducted first? Why do you suppose Congress imposes this ordering of contribution deductions?

1-7 *Controlled Corporate Groups.* What types of related corporations are subject to the limitation of one graduated tax rate structure? Describe each group of related corporations subject to this restriction.

1-8 *Five Percent Surtax.* Which corporations are subject to the five percent surtax? What is the marginal tax rate on the last dollar of taxable income of a corporation with 2016 taxable income of $170,000? What is the flat tax rate imposed on a corporation with 2016 taxable income of $335,000?

1-9 *Alternative Minimum Tax.* Some taxpayers believe that the alternative minimum tax is an amount of tax paid in lieu of the regular income tax. Are these taxpayers correct? Explain.

1-10 *Adjusted Current Earnings Adjustment.* The tax law contains an adjustment to the corporate alternative minimum tax calculation for adjusted current earnings (ACE). Notice that alternative minimum taxable income must be adjusted upward by nontaxable income (e.g., tax-exempt interest, key-person life insurance proceeds), and the dividends-received deduction. What was Congress trying to accomplish with this ACE adjustment?

PROBLEMS

1-11 *Comparison of Corporate versus Individual Taxation.* In each of the situations below, explain the tax consequences if taxpayer T were either a corporation or a single individual.
   a. For the current year, T has gross income of $60,000, including $10,000 dividends from Ford Motor Company. Without regard to taxable income, how much of the dividend income will be subject to tax?

b. During the current year, T sustains a total loss of an asset. The asset was valued at $2,000 shortly before the loss and had an adjusted basis of $2,700. If the casualty loss was incurred by T as an individual, it would be a personal rather than a business loss. Without regard to any taxable income limitation, what is the measure of the casualty loss deduction?

c. For the calendar year 2016, T has long-term capital gains of $10,000 and short-term capital losses of $4,000. What is the maximum amount of Federal income tax T will be required to pay as a result of these capital asset transactions?

d. During 2016, T had $8,000 of long-term capital gains and $3,000 of short-term capital gains. During 2015, the only prior year with capital asset transactions, T had a short-term capital loss of $6,000. How much of T's 2016 gross income will consist of capital gains?

e. T's taxable income for 2016, before any deduction for charitable contributions, is $50,000. If T were an individual, adjusted gross income would be $60,000. If T made cash contributions of $40,000 during the year, what is the maximum amount that could be claimed as a deduction for 2016?

f. T sells residential rental property for $250,000 in 2016. The property was purchased for $200,000 in 2006. Assume that T claimed straight-line depreciation of $80,000. Calculate T's depreciation recapture and § 1231 gain on the sale.

1-12 *Capital Gains and Losses.* Y Corporation incurred the following items of capital gain and loss in 2016:

STCG	$ 20,000
STCL	(10,000)
LTCG	5,000
LTCL	(28,000)

A review of Y's past tax returns shows that Y Corporation reported the following net capital gain/(loss) in prior years: 2012—$6,000; 2013—$8,000; 2014—($3,000); and 2015—$1,000.

a. Calculate Y's net capital gain (loss) for 2016. How is this reported on the 2016 Form 1120?

b. Calculate the amount of capital loss carryback to 2012, 2013, 2014, and 2015.

c. Calculate the amount of capital loss carryforward to 2017. How will this loss be treated in 2017 (i.e., as a short-term or long-term capital loss)?

1-13 *Dividends-Received Deduction.* K Corporation has the following items of revenue and expense for the current year:

Sales revenue, net of returns	$100,000
Cost of sales	30,000
Operating expenses	40,000
Dividends (from less than 20% owned corporation)	20,000

a. What is K Corporation's dividends-received deduction for the current year?

b. Assuming that K Corporation's operating expenses were $72,000 instead of $40,000, compute its dividends-received deduction for the current year.

1-14 *Dividends-Received Deduction.* During 2016, R Corporation (a cash method, calendar year taxpayer) has the following income and expenses:

Revenues from operations	$170,000
Operating expenses	178,000
Dividends (from less than 20% owned corporation)	40,000

a. What is R Corporation's 2016 dividends-received deduction?

b. Assuming R Corporation's 2016 tax year has not yet closed, compute the effect on its dividends-received deduction if R accelerated $5,000 of operating expenses to 2016 that were planned for 2017.

1-15 *Organizational Expenditures.* G Corporation, an accrual basis taxpayer, incurred and paid $41,000 of qualifying organizational expenditures in 2016. Assuming G Corporation makes an election under § 248 to maximize its deductions, compute the maximum amount that may be deducted for each of the following years if G Corporation adopts a calendar tax year.
   a. For 2016, if G Corporation began business on September 1?
   b. Calendar year 2017?
   c. Calendar year 2021?
   d. How would your answer to (a) change if the $41,000 had been paid in February 2017?
   e. How would your answer to (a) change if G Corporation were a cash basis taxpayer and the $41,000 had been paid in February 2017?
   f. How would your answer to (a) change if G Corporation had incurred $12,000 of the $41,000 qualified expenditures in January 2017?

1-16 *Organizational Expenditures.* Which of the following expenditures qualify under § 248 for deduction or amortization?
   a. Expenses of a market survey to determine the feasibility of starting a new business.
   b. Expenses of temporary directors.
   c. Legal services incident to the organization of the corporation.
   d. Fees paid to the state of incorporation.
   e. Expenses incident to the issuance of stock.
   f. Accounting services incident to the organization of the corporation.

1-17 *Charitable Contribution Deductions.* T Corporation has the following for tax year 2016:

Net income from operations	$600,000
Dividends (from less than 20% owned corporation)	100,000

   a. What is T Corporation's maximum charitable contribution deduction for 2016?
   b. Assuming T Corporation made charitable contributions of $68,000 during 2016 and had a $10,000 charitable contribution carryover from 2015, compute how much of its 2015 carryover will be carried over to 2017.

1-18 *Charitable Contribution Pledges.* All of the board members of Z Corporation were invited to a gala New Year's Eve party hosted by the American Theatrical Society (a qualified charitable organization). About an hour before midnight on December 31, 2016, representatives of the charity asked the invited guests to make generous charitable contributions. Z's board members held an impromptu meeting and decided to pledge $10,000 (well within the statutory limits for corporate charitable contributions). Z is a calendar year, accrual basis corporation. Assuming Z Corporation made actual payment of the pledged amount on February 28, 2017, will Z be entitled to a charitable contribution deduction for 2016? Would your answer change if the payment were made on March 29, 2017?

1-19 *Sale of Depreciable Realty.* Z Corporation purchased a mini-warehouse unit in December 2011 for $400,000. Z Corporation deducted depreciation of $87,000 prior to the sale. The unit was sold in January 2016 for $410,000. What are the amount and character of Z Corporation's gain?

1-20 *Computation of Corporate Tax Liability.* L Corporation had taxable income of $150,000 for 2016. What is L Corporation's 2016 income tax liability before credits or prepayments?

1-21 *Five Percent Surtax Computation.* F Corporation had taxable income of $250,000 for 2016. What is F Corporation's 2016 income tax liability before credits or prepayments? If F Corporation is a personal service corporation, what is its 2016 income tax liability before credits or prepayments?

1-22 *Members of Controlled Groups.* R, U, S, and T Corporations each have only one class of outstanding stock. Given the stock ownership of these corporations by the four un-related individuals indicated below, indicate which of the corporations are members of controlled groups.

	Corporations			
Individuals	R	U	S	T
A	30%	5%	40%	50%
B	10	10	10	20
C	40	5	10	10
D	20	80	0	20

1-23 *Alternative Minimum Tax Computation.* V Corporation has regular taxable income of $100,000 for 2016. The following items were taken into consideration in arriving at this number:

1. A building acquired in 1986 was depreciated using ACRS. The depreciation claimed was $90,000; straight-line depreciation over a 40-year life is $60,000.
2. Key-person life insurance proceeds of $80,000 were received but were not included in taxable income.

In light of these facts, perform the following computations.
a. Compute V Corporation's alternative minimum taxable income (AMTI).
b. Assuming V has no tax credits for 2016, compute the corporation's alternative minimum tax liability for 2016.

1-24 *Corporate Tax Computation.* T Corporation had the following items of income for its 2016 calendar year:

Net income from operations	$150,000
Dividends received (from less than 20% owned corporations)	10,000
Charitable contributions	30,000
Net operating loss carryover from 2015	30,000
Long-term capital gains	8,000
Long-term capital losses	6,000
Short-term capital gains	3,000
Capital loss carryover from 2015	9,000

a. Compute T Corporation's 2016 income tax liability before credits or prepayments.
b. What are the nature and amount of any carryovers to 2017?

1-25 *Schedules M-1, M-2.* P Corporation reports the following information for 2016:

Net income per books	$125,730
Federal income taxes (accrued)	10,500
Net capital loss	3,600
Travel and entertainment (50% portion disallowed for FIT)	300
Proceeds of life insurance on president	75,000
Insurance premiums on life of president	1,250
Tax-exempt interest	3,500
ACRS deductions in excess of straight-line depreciation used for book purposes	1,400
Excess charitable contributions	520
Unappropriated retained earnings (beginning of 2016)	200,000
Dividends paid during the year	23,500

Complete Schedules M-1 and M-2 below.

Schedule M-1	**Reconciliation of Income (Loss) per Books With Income per Return**				
	Note. The corporation may be required to file Schedule M-3 (see instructions).				
1	Net income (loss) per books		7	Income recorded on books this year not included on this return (itemize):	
2	Federal income tax per books				
3	Excess of capital losses over capital gains		a	Tax-exempt interest $_____	
4	Income subject to tax not recorded on books this year (itemize): _____		b	Other (itemize): _____	
	_____			_____	
	_____		8	Deductions on this return not charged against book income this year (itemize):	
5	Expenses recorded on books this year not deducted on this return (itemize):		a	Depreciation . . $_____	
a	Depreciation . . . . $_____		b	Charitable contributions $_____	
b	Charitable contributions $_____		c	Other (itemize): _____	
c	Travel and entertainment $_____			_____	
d	Other (itemize): _____			_____	
	_____		9	Add lines 7 and 8	
6	Add lines 1 through 5		10	Income—line 6 less line 9	

Schedule M-2	**Analysis of Unappropriated Retained Earnings per Books**					
1	Balance at beginning of year		5	Distributions:	a Cash	
2	Net income (loss) per books				b Stock	
3	Other increases (itemize): _____				c Property . . .	
	_____		6	Other decreases (itemize): _____		
	_____					
	_____		7	Add lines 5 and 6		
4	Add lines 1, 2, and 3		8	Balance at end of year (line 4 less line 7) .		

For Paperwork Reduction Act Notice, see the Instructions for Form 1120-F.   Cat. No. 49678K   Schedules M-1 and M-2 (Form 1120-F) 2015

1-26 *Reconciliation of Book and Taxable Income.* D Corporation, a calendar year, accrual basis corporation, reported net income per books of $300,000 for the tax year ended December 31, 2016. Included in the calculation of net book income were the following items:

Accrued federal income tax	$ 90,000
Life insurance proceeds on officer who died in 2016	120,000
Insurance premiums on key employee life insurance	6,000
Net loss on sale of securities held for investment	4,000
Depreciation	50,000

Depreciation claimed on the tax return was $86,000. The actual tax calculated on the tax return was $80,000 (i.e., D Corporation had an overaccrual of federal income tax of $10,000). What is D Corporation's taxable income for 2016?

1-27 *Schedule M-3.* Indicate whether the following statements regarding the Schedule M-3 are true or false and if false, explain why.

a. A corporation can file Schedule M-3 or alternatively use Schedule M-2.

b. Only publicly traded companies are required to file Schedule M-3.

c. One of the alleged defects of the M-1 concerns the source of the "book income" number used in the reconciliation.

d. Corporations that are required to use the M-3 must complete SEC Form 10-K and use the financial statement income reported on such form in completing the reconciliation between book income and taxable income.

e. Reporting the actual book-tax differences on the M-3 is identical to that for the M-1 except the M-3 identifies about 70 specific items that must be reported while the M-1 reports about 10.

f. In the first year that a corporation files the M-3, it need not report the book and tax numbers but only the differences and whether they are permanent or temporary.

g. Filing of the M-3 satisfies the reportable transaction requirement.

1-28 *Schedule M-3.* Upon reviewing the staff member's preparation of the M-3, the senior manager notices that the depreciation difference is classified as a permanent difference. He wonders whether this is correctly classified or whether an error has been made. If such a difference is incorrectly classified as a permanent difference, what might the IRS conclude and what might occur?

1-29 *Corporate Estimated Tax.* F Corporation, a calendar year corporation, reported the following information with respect to its tax liabilities for 2015 and 2016:

Actual 2016 tax liability (regular tax)	$120,000
Actual 2016 alternative minimum tax	15,000
Actual 2015 tax liability (regular tax)	100,000

F made timely quarterly estimated tax payments of $26,000 each quarter during 2016. F Corporation is not a "large" corporation (i.e., it did not have taxable income of $1 million or more in any of the three preceding taxable years). The 2015 tax liability was for a full 12-month period.

Compute the amount of quarterly underpayment for F Corporation, if any.

1-30 *Corporate Estimated Tax.* Refer to *Problem 1-29.* Assume that F Corporation is a "large" corporation.

Compute the amount of quarterly underpayment for F Corporation, if any.

1-31 *Transaction between Corporation and Its Shareholder.* In 2015, G, a shareholder in ABC Corporation, sold to her 90% controlled corporation 20 shares of IBM stock for $2,000. The stock was acquired in 2013 for $4,000. In 2016, ABC sold the stock to an unrelated party for $5,000.

a. What amount of gain or loss will G report on her 2015 tax return?

b. What amount of gain or loss will ABC report on its 2016 tax return?

1-32 *Transaction between Corporation and Its Shareholder.* H owns a residential rental property (an apartment unit) that he purchased in 1986 for $100,000 ($80,000 allocated to the building and $20,000 to the land). Now that the building is fully depreciated and is no longer generating tax benefits, H has decided to sell the building and land to XYZ, H's solely owned C corporation, for $200,000 ($160,000 allocated to the building and $40,000 to the land). XYZ will continue to operate the property as an apartment unit. H is in the 34% marginal income tax bracket; XYZ is in the 34% marginal tax bracket.

a. What is H's motive behind this sale?

b. How does the tax law treat the sale from H to XYZ?

1-33 Sam Smith (446-46-4646) and Jane Jones (312-12-1212) own and operate The Bike Shop, Inc. The corporation was formed on May 1, 1998. Sam is the president and owns 70% of the stock while Jane is the secretary-treasurer and owns the remaining 30 percent. Both are full-time employees. Sam received a salary of $150,000 and Jane received a salary of $60,000. Other pertinent information is given below.

- The corporation is an accrual-method, calendar-year taxpayer.
- Inventories are determined using the lower of cost or market method.
- The corporate headquarters are located at 1234 Wheeling Road, Cincinnati, OH 45202.
- The employer identification number is 75-4476243.

A tentative income statement and balance sheet for the corporation are given below.

Assets	January 1, 2015	December 31, 2015
Cash	$ 110,000	$ 691,000
Accounts receivable	14,000	31,000
Allowance for doubtful accounts	(2,000)	(6,000)
U.S. Treasury bonds	20,000	20,000
Stocks	50,000	70,000
Inventory	375,000	375,000
Equipment	295,000	405,000
Land	164,000	164,000
Building	500,000	500,000
Accumulated depreciation	(211,000)	(251,000)
	$1,315,000	$1,999,000

Liabilities and Equity	January 1, 2015	December 31, 2015
Accounts payable	65,000	350,000
Notes payable (due within 1 year).........	500,000	400,000
Capital stock (all common)	150,000	150,000
Retained earnings (unappropriated)........	600,000	1,099,000
	$1,315,000	$1,999,000

	Debit	Credit
Sales		$2,100,000
Purchases	$700,000	
Dividends		5,000
Interest income on U.S. Treasury bonds.....		10,000
Salaries-officers	210,000	
Salaries-sales and clerical	265,000	
Repairs and maintenance..............	20,000	
Bad debt expense	5,000	
Interest expense	14,000	
Charitable contributions...............	60,000	
Depreciation (per books)	40,000	
Advertising	14,000	
Meals and entertainment..............	16,000	
Taxes (state, local and payroll)...........	50,000	
Life insurance premiums	10,000	
Long term capital gain................		7,000
Long term capital loss	9,000	
Federal income taxes paid	150,000	

The company provided the following additional information:

- The corporation distributed a cash dividend of $60,000 during the year.
- Tax depreciation for the year was $50,000.
- Meals and entertainment includes the corporation's expense for a suite at Paul Brown Stadium, home of professional football's Cincinnati Bengals. The cost of the suite was $10,000, which includes event tickets of $4,000.
- The corporation's estimated bad debt expense for the year was $5,000. Actual bad debts were $1,000.
- Life insurance premiums were paid on term policies covering the lives of the two owners. The corporation is the beneficiary.
- Dividends received were from stock investment in less than 20% owned U.S. corporations.
- The company took a physical count of its inventory on the last day of the year. On that date, it was determined that ending inventory was $360,000. This is not reflected in the financial statements above.
- Each of the four $37,500 timely made estimated tax payments were recorded as Federal income taxes paid.

Prepare Form 1120 for the corporation.

TAX RETURN PROBLEM

1-34 Paul Schroeder is the owner of ABC Manufacturing Corporation in Denver, Colorado. Paul is in the process of preparing the 2015 income tax return for ABC and needs guidance on how to depreciate recently acquired assets (personalty) for regular tax purposes. His problem is that, because of a substantial amount of alternative minimum tax (AMT) adjustments, ABC is exposed to the AMT for 2015. Of course, he wants to choose a depreciation method that will minimize ABC's negative tax consequences from application of the AMT. Paul has heard that he can avoid creating an AMT adjustment by electing to depreciate ABC's assets acquired in 2015 by using the 150% declining-balance method. Paul thinks it might be a good idea to elect this AMT method so that exposure to the AMT in 2015 is not made worse. The facts of this case are:

1. Paul estimates that ABC Corporation will have net income of $300,000 without regard to depreciation of the assets acquired in 2015.
2. ABC Corporation has other AMT adjustments of $200,000.
3. If Paul uses MACRS (modified ACRS) to depreciate the personalty acquired, the depreciation amount will be $50,000. If he elects to use the 150% declining-balance method to avoid creation of an AMT adjustment, the first-year depreciation will amount to $37,500.

Prepare Form 4626 assuming that Paul elects to use MACRS to depreciate ABC's personalty acquired in 2015. Prepare a second Form 4626 assuming that Paul elects to use the 150% declining balance method under ADS. Which depreciation method should Paul use for ABC Corporation?

TAX RESEARCH PROBLEM

1-35 Linda Smith is a single investor living in Phoenix, Arizona who wants to buy an apartment building for $240,000 in Houston, Texas. Because real estate prices are currently attractive, Linda plans to acquire the property at a good price and hold it until the real estate market improves (hopefully, within the next five years).

By agreeing to make a $40,000 down payment on the apartment building, Linda has obtained a loan commitment from National Mortgage Company for $200,000 on a nonrecourse note with a 14% interest rate (the interest rate is high because of the speculative nature of the investment). However, because Texas usury law limits the interest rate to 12% when a loan is made to a noncorporate entity, the lender requires that the loan be made to a corporate entity.

Linda is concerned about the negative tax implications of holding the investment in the corporate form. She wants to receive the tax benefits from the investment (e.g., loss pass-throughs) for use on her personal return (she will qualify for the $25,000 actively managed rental realty exception to the passive activity loss rules). Linda knows that losses generated by a regular corporation will not pass through to her and may be used only to offset future corporate income.

Linda has also considered forming a corporation under state law and making the S corporation election for Federal income tax purposes. Although this looks like a good alternative, she is concerned that her pass-through losses will soon exceed her $40,000 direct investment in the corporation and the remaining losses will be suspended just as they would be with a regular corporation.

Linda has also considered forming a regular corporation under state law and having the corporation treated as her agent (i.e., a nontaxable entity). This would be a great alternative if it works, because she could obtain her loan and still have the investment losses pass through for use on her personal return. Can this be done? What specific steps must she take to ensure that the IRS will not treat the corporation as a taxable entity?

Research aid:

Jesse C. Bollinger, 88-1 USTC ¶ 9233, 61 AFTR2d 88-793, 108 S.Ct. 1173 (USSC, 1988).

2

Corporate Formation and Capital Structure

Learning Objectives

Upon completion of this chapter you will be able to:

LO.1 Explain the basic tax consequences of forming a new corporation, including how to:

- Determine the gain or loss recognized by the shareholders and the corporation.
- Determine the basis of the shareholder's stock in the corporation and the corporation's basis in the property received.

LO.2 Describe the requirements for qualifying a transfer to a corporation for tax-free treatment.

LO.3 Recognize the tax consequences of transferring property to an existing corporation.

LO.4 Understand the effects of transferring liabilities to a corporation.

LO.5 Describe special problems involved in computing depreciation of assets transferred to the corporation.

LO.6 Explain the effect of contributions to capital by shareholders and nonshareholders.

LO.7 Identify the tax considerations in determining whether the corporation's capital structure should consist of stock or debt.

Chapter Outline

Introduction

The previous chapter examined the fundamental rules of corporate income taxation. Beginning with this chapter and extending through Chapter 7, attention is directed to a variety of special tax problems that often arise in organizing and operating a corporation. For example, this chapter focuses on the tax consequences of forming a corporation. In addition, this chapter considers how the tax law affects a corporation's decision to use debt or stock to raise capital. Subsequent chapters look at the tax problems associated with distributions by the corporation to its shareholders (e.g., dividends, redemptions, and liquidations) and tax aspects of corporate mergers, acquisitions, divisions, and other types of reorganizations that a corporation may undergo.

The technical discussion contained in this and the next several chapters concerning corporations and their shareholders ultimately seeks to answer two basic questions:

1. What is the tax effect of the transaction on the corporation?
2. What is the tax effect of the transaction on the shareholder?

The pages that follow all concern the rules and the rationale necessary for answering these two seemingly straightforward inquiries.

Incorporation in General

Prior to examining the tax aspects of forming and transferring property to a corporation, a few comments reviewing the incorporation process may be helpful. Forming a corporation is generally a very simple procedure. In most states, the law requires an application, entitled the "Articles of Incorporation," to be filed with the appropriate state agency for the privilege of operating as a corporation. The information typically required in the articles of incorporation includes (1) the name and address of the corporation, (2) the period for which it will exist, (3) the purpose for which the corporation is organized, (4) the number and type of shares of stock that the corporation will have authority to issue, (5) the provisions relating to the regulation of the internal affairs of the business, and (6) the number and names of the initial board of directors of the corporation. Once drafted, the articles of incorporation are submitted along with any funds necessary for payment of fees charged by the state. The representative of the state subsequently reviews the articles, and approval is routinely given. Upon approval, the state grants the corporation the right to operate within its boundaries pursuant to state law.

Once the decision to incorporate has been made, an important question concerns the selection of the state of incorporation. Two factors are generally considered: (1) the various advantages and disadvantages of a state's laws governing the operations of corporations within its jurisdictions (e.g., are the laws of Delaware more favorable than those of Nevada?), and (2) the costs of incorporating in the state where the corporation will be operating versus the costs of qualifying as a foreign corporation authorized to do business in that state. With respect to this latter factor, state and local taxes are often extremely important.

The final step in the incorporation process requires the transfer of assets by the investors to the corporation. In the simple case, investors merely contribute cash and other assets to the corporation in exchange for stock. As a practical matter, however, even simple transfers require numerous considerations.

Example 1

Several years ago, R and S started manufacturing plastic spikes for golf shoes in R's basement and selling the final product to local retailers. Business grew at such a rate that they were forced to acquire additional equipment and to move their operation from R's home to a small building that S owned. They were so successful that in their third year of operations they were unable to fill all of their orders on a timely basis. To attract the capital necessary to expand and meet demand, they decided to incorporate their business. The two contacted numerous people who indicated they would be interested in investing in the corporation. Accordingly, they met with their attorney and accountant, who provided the services related to incorporation.

Examination of the situation in the example above suggests numerous concerns that should be addressed. For instance, R and S must initially determine which assets and liabilities of their existing business they should transfer to the corporation. In addition, they must determine the method of transfer: should the property be contributed in exchange for stock and/or debt, or perhaps leased or sold to the corporation? With respect to the other investors, some may wish to contribute cash for stock while others may desire debt in exchange for their investment. Another consideration relates to the method of compensating the attorney and the accountant. When a cash shortage exists, it is not unusual for these individuals to receive stock—an equity interest in the corporation—as payment for their services. As analysis of this example indicates, there are many decisions confronting those forming a corporation. Interestingly, tax factors play an important role in determining how these decisions should be resolved.

IDENTIFYING THE TAX CONSEQUENCES

The tax consequences related to incorporating a new business *or* making transfers to an existing corporation are a direct result of the form of the transaction. In the typical situation, the taxpayer transfers property to the corporation in exchange for stock. It is the exchange feature of this transaction that has tax implications. Under the general rule of Code § 1001, an exchange is treated as a taxable disposition, and the taxpayer must recognize gain or loss to the extent that the value of the property received exceeds or is less than the adjusted basis of the property transferred.

Example 2

G currently operates a restaurant as a sole proprietorship but he is contemplating the incorporation of the business. Under the arrangement proposed by his accountant, G would transfer the following assets to the corporation.

Asset	Adjusted Basis	Fair Market Value
Equipment.	$12,000	$10,000
Building.	30,000	50,000
Total	$42,000	$60,000

In exchange for the assets, G would receive stock worth $60,000. As a result, G would realize a gain of $18,000, representing the difference between his amount realized, stock valued at $60,000, and the adjusted basis in his assets of $42,000. Note that under the general rule of § 1001, G would be required to recognize the gain and pay tax—a cost that may cause him to change his mind about the virtues of incorporating.

Also note that if the transaction were taxable, G's basis in his stock would be its value of $60,000 and the corporation's basis in the equipment and the building also would be their values of $10,000 and $50,000 respectively.

The problems of applying the general rule requiring recognition of gain or loss on transfers to a corporation are twofold. First, when gain is recognized, the tax cost incurred may prohibit the taxpayer from using the corporate form where otherwise it is entirely appropriate. Second, since losses are also recognized, taxpayers could arbitrarily create artificial losses even though they continue to own the asset, albeit indirectly through the corporation.

Example 3

Consider the facts in *Example 2* above. Without any special provision, G could transfer the equipment to the corporation and recognize a $2,000 loss ($10,000 − $12,000) even though he still maintained control of the asset through ownership of the corporation.

LO.1

Explain the basic tax consequences of forming a new corporation, including how to:

- Determine the gain or loss recognized by the shareholders and the corporation.

- Determine the basis of the shareholder's stock in the corporation and the corporation's basis in the property received.

In 1921, Congress recognized these difficulties and enacted a special exception. Under this provision, no gain or loss is recognized on most transfers to controlled corporations. This treatment was based on the so-called *continuity of interest* principle. According to this principle, when the transferor exchanges property for stock in a corporation controlled by that transferor, there is merely a change of ownership and nothing more. In essence, the transferor's economic position is unaffected since investment in the asset is continued through investment in the corporation.[1] Congress believed that as long as this "continuity of interest" was maintained, it was inappropriate to treat the exchange as a taxable event. This is not to say, however, that any gain or loss realized goes permanently unrecognized. Rather, similar to the treatment of a like-kind exchange, any gain or loss realized on the transaction is postponed until that time when the transferor liquidates the investment or "cashes in"— usually when the stock is sold.[2]

A rather intricate set of statutory provisions exists to ensure that the policy objectives underlying nonrecognition are achieved, yet not abused. Due to these provisions, several questions must be addressed whenever a transfer is made to a corporation.

1. Has the transferor or the corporation realized any gain, loss, income, or deduction on the transfer that must be recognized? If so, what is its character?

2. What is the basis and holding period of any property received by the transferor and the corporation?

Although the answers to these questions can be elusive at times, the general rules—which are mandatory if the requirements are satisfied—may be summarized as follows:

1. No gain or loss is recognized by the transferor or the corporation on the exchange.[3]

2. The transferor substitutes the basis of the property transferred to the corporation as the basis of the stock received (substituted basis).[4]

3. The corporation uses the transferor's basis as its basis for the property received (carryover basis).[5]

Example 4

During the year, T decided to incorporate her copying business. She transferred her only asset, a copying machine (value $25,000, adjusted basis $15,000), to the corporation in exchange for stock worth $25,000. Although T realized a $10,000 gain on the exchange ($25,000 − $15,000), no gain is recognized. T's basis for her stock is the same as her basis for the asset she transferred, $15,000. In other words, she substituted the basis of the old property for the new. The basis assigned to the machine by the

---

[1] Reg. § 1.1002-1(c).

[2] *Portland Oil Co. v. Comm.*, 40-1 USTC ¶9234, 24 AFTR 225, 109 F.2d 479 (CA-1, 1940).

[3] §§ 351(a) and 1032.

[4] § 358.

[5] § 362.

corporation is the same as that used by T, $15,000—in effect, the shareholder's basis carries over to the corporation. Note that these basis rules preserve future recognition of the gain originally realized. For example, if T immediately sells her stock for its $25,000 value, she would recognize the $10,000 gain that was postponed on the transfer to the corporation. Similarly, if the corporation were to sell the copying machine for $25,000, it would recognize the $10,000 gain previously deferred.

Unfortunately, these rules can serve only as guidelines. The specific provisions of the Code that contain various exceptions are discussed below.

Section 351: Transfers to Controlled Corporations

Section 351 provides the general rule governing transfers to controlled corporations. This provision applies to transfers to regular C corporations as well as transfers to S corporations.[6] In addition, the rule governs not only transfers to newly organized corporations but to existing corporations as well. For example, after a corporation has been formed and operated for a time, an infusion of capital to the business might be necessary, requiring either a new or an old shareholder, or both, to make a transfer to the corporation. If the transfer falls within the scope of § 351, that provision's rules apply. Section 351(a) reads as follows:

> **General Rule.** *No gain or loss shall be recognized if property is transferred to a corporation by one or more persons solely in exchange for stock in such corporation and immediately after the exchange such person or persons are in control of the corporation.*

A close examination of this rule reveals three basic requirements that must be satisfied before the deferral privilege is granted:

1. Only transferors of *property* are eligible.
2. Transferors of property qualify only if they *control* the corporation after the exchange.
3. Transferors of property who are in control receive nonrecognition only to the extent that they receive *solely stock.*

These three aspects of § 351 are analyzed below.

LO.2
Describe the requirements for qualifying a transfer to a corporation for tax-free treatment.

THE PROPERTY CONDITION

Only those persons who transfer *property* to the corporation are eligible for nonrecognition. Although the Code does not define property, the term has been broadly construed to encompass virtually all of those items that one would normally believe to constitute property. For example, the term property includes money, all real property such as land and buildings, and all personal property such as inventory and equipment. In addition, such items as accounts receivable (including the unrealized receivables of a cash basis taxpayer), notes receivable, installment receivables, patents, and other intangibles are considered property.

Property versus Services

Although the Code does not define property, § 351 does provide that property does not include services.[7] Apparently, Congress believed that an exchange of *services for stock* was not the economic equivalent of an exchange of *property for stock*. When property is exchanged, the form of ownership merely changes from direct to indirect. When services are

---

[6] Section 351 does not apply to transfers of property to corporations considered investment companies under § 351(e). Section 351 may not apply to transfers to controlled corporations outside the U.S. (see § 367).

[7] § 351(d).

exchanged, however, the transaction is more akin to a cash payment for the services, followed by a purchase of stock by the party performing the services. Section 351 adopts this view and, therefore, does not treat services as property. Instead, stock received for services is considered compensation for such services, and the shareholder must recognize ordinary income equal to the value of the stock received for the services rendered.[8] Consistent with the recognition of income, the service shareholder assigns a basis to the stock received equal to the amount of income recognized—in effect, the cost of the stock. The corporation is allowed to treat the issuance of stock for the services just as if it had paid cash.[9] Accordingly, the corporation may deduct or capitalize the costs, depending on the nature of the services.

Example 5

This year, B decided to incorporate his construction business. B's attorney drafted the articles of incorporation and handled all other legal aspects of forming the corporation. Upon approval by the state, B transferred the assets to the corporation in exchange for 90 shares of stock. In addition, his attorney received 10 shares valued at $10,000 as compensation for his legal services. The attorney is not entitled to defer recognition of the compensation since he transferred services to the corporation and not property. Therefore, he recognizes $10,000 of ordinary income, and his basis in the stock is $10,000, reflecting the fact that he was required to report income on the exchange. The corporation treats the issuance of stock as payment for an organization expense.

THE CONTROL CONDITION

As indicated above, the purpose of § 351 is to grant deferral to those exchanges where there has been no substantive change in the transferor's economic position. This policy is reflected in the statute by the presence of a requirement concerning *control*. According to § 351, deferral is permitted only if those who transferred property (rather than services) control the corporation. Control is defined as ownership of (1) at least 80% of the total combined voting power of all classes of stock entitled to vote *and* (2) 80% of the total number of shares of each class of nonvoting stock of the corporation immediately after the exchange.[10] Note that when a corporation issues only voting common stock (as is usually the case with most newly formed corporations), the second part of the control test is irrelevant. To simplify the subsequent discussion, it is assumed that the corporation issues a single class of stock, voting common. Note also that, in the application of the control test, stock does not include stock rights or stock warrants[11] and certain debt-like preferred stock referred to as nonqualified preferred stock.[12]

Example 6

This year, H, I, and J formed a new corporation. H exchanged equipment for 50% of the stock, I exchanged land for 40% of the stock, and J exchanged cash for the remaining 10% of the stock. Section 351 applies to all of the exchanges because the transferors of property—H, I, and J, *as a group*—own at least 80% of the stock immediately after the exchange.

It is not necessary that the transferors of property acquire control on the exchange. It is sufficient if the transferors own 80% of the stock after the exchange, taking into account the stock received on the exchange as well as any stock already owned by the transferors.

---

[8] Reg. § 1.351-1(a)(2) Ex. 3, but see § 83.

[9] Rev. Rul. 217, 1962-2 C.B. 59.

[10] § 368(c); Rev. Rul. 59-259, 1959-2 C.B. 115.

[11] Reg. § 1.351-1(a)(1)(ii).

[12] § 351(g).

Example 7

For the last several years, X Corporation has had 100 shares of stock outstanding: 60 shares owned by J and 40 shares owned by K. This year, J transferred property to X in exchange for an additional 100 shares. Although J received stock representing only 50% of the shares outstanding ($100 \div 200$), the control test is satisfied because both the stock received and the stock owned by the transferor prior to the exchange are counted towards control. Since after the exchange J owns 160 of the 200 shares outstanding, the 80% control test is satisfied, and § 351 applies to his exchange.

Example 8

Assume the same facts as above, except that K, who originally owned 40 shares made the transfer and received the 100 shares. In this case, K owns only 140 shares of the 200 shares outstanding, or 70%. Thus, the 80% test is not satisfied and K's transfer is taxable.

Stock Received for Services

In determining whether the control test is satisfied, only the stock of those who transfer *property* is counted. Since property, by definition, does not include services, stock received in exchange for services normally is not counted towards control.

Example 9

During the year, B and C formed T Corporation with the help of A, an attorney, who agreed to be compensated in stock. The three individuals contributed the following in exchange for stock:

Transferor	Transfer	Shares Received
A	Services	20
B	Machine	20
C	Land	60
		100

Since the transferors of property, B and C, own 80% of T's outstanding stock after the transfers, their exchanges are nontaxable under § 351. Because A's only contribution to T was services, his ownership is not included in determining whether control exists, and his exchange is not governed by § 351. Instead, A is treated as simply receiving compensation in the form of property, and must report income equal to the value of the stock. In addition, A's basis in the stock will be equal to the value reported as income.

Example 10

Assume the same facts as above, except that A received 40 shares of stock for his services. In this case, § 351 does not apply to any of the exchanges since the transferors of property, B and C, own only 67% ($80 \div 120$) of the stock after the exchange. Thus, the exchanges of property by B and C, as well as A's contribution of services, are taxable. Note that if those who exchange *only* services receive *more than* 20% of the stock, application of § 351 is denied for all transferors.

Transfers of Both Property and Services

In situations where some persons transfer property to the corporation while others provide services, it is clear that the stock ownership of the service shareholder is disregarded for purposes of the control test. A question arises, however, as to the treatment of the transferor who contributes both property and services in exchange for stock. The Regulations address this problem by generally providing that *all* of the stock received by a transferor of both property and services is considered in determining whether control is achieved.[13]

Example 11

E, F, and G have decided to form a corporation. According to their plan, E will transfer equipment worth $40,000 (basis $25,000) to the corporation for 40 shares of stock while F will transfer land worth $10,000 (basis $2,000) for 10 shares. G is still contemplating what his contribution to the corporation will be. If G contributes solely services worth $50,000 to the corporation for 50 shares of stock, neither E nor F will qualify for nonrecognition since the transferors of property, E and F, would own only 50% of the stock outstanding ([40 + 10] ÷ [40 + 10 + 50]).

Example 12

Assume the same facts as above, except that G contributes property worth $20,000 and services worth $30,000 for 50 shares of stock. In this case, all of the stock received—not just that portion received for the property—is considered in applying the control test. Therefore, G is treated as a transferor of property, and all of his ownership is counted toward meeting the 80% standard. Thus, the transferors of property own 100% of the stock ([40 + 10 + 50] ÷ [40 + 10 + 50]). Although § 351 grants nonrecognition to this transaction, G still recognizes income equal to the value of the services rendered, $30,000. In all cases, an individual who is compensated for services must recognize income.

Nominal Property Transfers

Certain situations exist when a small contribution of property by a transferor could produce very favorable results. For instance, consider a transaction that does not qualify for § 351 treatment because the service shareholder receives more than 20% of the stock. Given the general rule of the Regulations, the service shareholder could enable his or her stock to be counted toward control by simply transferring $1 of cash or other property along with the services. To discourage this practice, the Regulations indicate that nominal transfers of property for the purpose of qualifying the service shareholder's stock are ignored.[14] The IRS has elaborated further on this rule, specifying that for advance ruling purposes, the value of the property transferred must not be less than 10% of the value of the services rendered (value of property ÷ value of service ≥ 10%).[15] For example, if T exchanges services worth $10,000 for stock, she would also have to give property of $1,000 if her stock were to count for the control test.

---

[13] *Supra*, Footnote 8.

[14] Reg. § 1.351-1(a)(1)(ii).

[15] Rev. Proc. 77-37, 1977-2 C.B. 568, Sec. 3.07.

Example 13

As part of an incorporation transaction, B provides services worth $30,000 and transfers property worth $20,000 (basis $8,000) for 50% of the stock. C transfers equipment for the other 50% of the stock. In this case, all of B's stock (not just those shares received for property) is counted in determining control because the property transferred is not relatively small in value compared to the value of the services provided. In fact, the property's value exceeds the 10% threshold prescribed by the IRS for advance ruling purposes ($20,000 ÷ $30,000, or 67 percent, exceeds 10%). Since B's ownership is considered toward control, the transferors of property own 100% of the stock, and thus the exchanges of property qualify for nonrecognition. As noted above, however, even though the property transfers qualify under § 351, B's transfer of services does not, and therefore he would recognize income of $30,000 on the exchange.

A second situation when the nominal transfer issue arises involves the admission of a new shareholder to the corporation. A prospective shareholder may be unwilling to be the sole transferor of property because receipt of less than an 80% interest causes any gain or loss realized to be recognized. In such case, existing shareholders may transfer property along with the new shareholder so that the existing shareholders' stock could also be counted toward control. By counting both the old and the new shareholders' ownership, the 80% test would be satisfied and the new shareholder would not recognize any gain or loss on the transaction. To prevent abuses (e.g., the transfer of $1 of property by the existing shareholders) the Regulations provide that nominal transfers of property are ignored. In this regard, the IRS has indicated that for advance ruling purposes, a property transfer is counted toward control if the value of the property transferred is equal to 10% or more of the value of the stock already owned by the transferor (value of property ÷ value of preexisting ownership ≥ 10%).[16]

Example 14

T owns all 80 shares of X Corporation, which has a value of $200,000. She wishes to admit N as a new shareholder. N would contribute property worth $50,000 (basis $5,000) for 20 shares of stock. As structured, N would recognize a gain on the exchange since he would own only 20% of the stock after the exchange. However, if T also contributes at least $20,000 (the IRS benchmark: 10% of her $200,000 share value), her stock ownership would be counted along with that of N in determining control. In such case, the transferors would own 100% of the stock after the exchange, and thus N's gain would be deferred.

Control "Immediately after the Exchange"

The statute provides that the point in time when control is measured is immediately after the exchange. Read literally, this condition suggests that all transfers must be made precisely at the same time if nonrecognition is to be obtained. However, according to the Regulations, simultaneous transfers are unnecessary. It is sufficient if all of the transfers are made pursuant to a prearranged plan that is carried out expeditiously.[17] Thus, if the transfers satisfying the 80% test are made in a timely manner, nonrecognition is permitted.

---

[16] *Supra,* Footnote 15.   [17] Reg. § 1.351-1(a)(1).

> ## Example 15
>
> Four individuals, A, B, C, and D, decided to form a corporation with each owning 25% of the stock. A, B, and C make their transfers in January while D makes her transfer in March. If control is measured after A, B, and C have contributed their property, their transfers would be tax free under § 351 since they own 100% of the shares outstanding immediately after the exchange. In contrast, D's contribution may be considered an isolated transfer. Therefore, her transfer would be taxable since she was the only transferor and she owned only 25% of the stock after the exchange. If D desires nonrecognition, her transfer must be considered part of a prearranged plan that calls for her contribution.

In certain circumstances, a transferor may find nonrecognition undesirable. For example, if the transferor would realize a loss on the transfer, recognition may be the preferred treatment. In such case, a transferor may deliberately attempt to separate his or her transfer from other qualifying transfers. It should be emphasized, however, that the transfer may be treated as part of the plan unless it is sufficiently delayed so as to be completely disassociated from the other transfers.

Another problem associated with the "control-immediately-after-the-exchange" requirement involves so-called momentary control. The issue is whether the 80% test is satisfied when the transferors have control for a brief moment after the exchange only to lose it because they dispose of sufficient shares to reduce their ownership below the necessary 80 percent. Note that the same difficulty could arise if the corporation subsequently issues additional shares.

> ## Example 16
>
> W has decided to incorporate his business. He anticipates transferring all of the assets to the corporation for 100% of its stock. Immediately after the exchange, W plans to give 15% of the stock to his son and sell another 20% to an interested investor. If control is measured prior to W's gift and sale of shares, § 351 applies since the 80% test is met. However, if control is measured after the gift and sale, W would own only 65% and § 351 would not allow nonrecognition.

As a general rule, "momentary control" normally is sufficient if the transferor does indeed have control. Control is evidenced by the fact that the transferor has—upon the receipt of the stock—the freedom to retain or dispose of the stock as desired.[18] As long as the subsequent transfers are not a part of a prearranged plan that inevitably leads to the transferors' loss of control, the statute should be satisfied. In any event, transfers immediately after the exchange should be considered carefully so that the dramatic effect of loss of control can be avoided.

SOLELY FOR STOCK AND THE "BOOT" EXCEPTION

The general rule of § 351 indicates that a transfer qualifies only if the transferor receives *solely* stock in exchange for the property transferred. The solely-for-stock requirement ensures that nonrecognition is granted when the transferor has not used the exchange to effectively liquidate or "cash in" on the investment in the property transferred. However, receipt of property other than stock (e.g., cash) does not completely disqualify an exchange. Instead, § 351(b) requires that the transferor recognize gain to the extent that other property—so-called "boot"—is received.

Several aspects of the "boot" exception require clarification.[19] First, the amount of the gain recognized—as determined by the amount of the boot received—can never exceed the gain actually realized on the exchange.[20] Second, receipt of boot never triggers recognition

---

[18] See, for example, *Intermountain Lumber Co.*, 65 T.C. 1025 (1976).

[19] § 351(b)(1).

[20] If more than one asset is transferred, Rev. Rul. 68-55, 1968-1 C.B. 140 adopts a separate property approach for computing

gain or loss. The gain or loss realized and recognized is separately computed for each property transferred, assuming that a proportionate share of the stock, securities, and boot is received for each property (e.g., an asset representing 10% of the value of all properties transferred is allocated 10% of the stock and boot).

of losses, even if a loss is realized.[21] This latter rule can be traced to one of the original purposes of § 351: a transferor should not be able to obtain losses when control of the asset is maintained. The final aspect of the boot rule warranting emphasis concerns liabilities and is discussed later in this section. Suffice it to say here that the transfer of liabilities by the transferor is generally not considered boot for purposes of determining recognized gain or loss.[22]

Example 17

AAA Corporation has been in business several years. This year the original shareholders, Q and R, decided to contribute additional assets. Q transferred land worth $10,000 (basis $8,000) that was subject to a mortgage of $1,000 in exchange for stock worth $6,000 and cash of $3,000. R transferred equipment valued at $15,000 (basis $20,000) for stock worth $9,000 and cash of $6,000. Since Q and R own 100% of the stock after the exchange, nonrecognition under § 351 is permitted but only to the extent that stock is received. The tax consequences of the exchange are determined as follows:

	Q	R
Amount realized:		
Stock	$ 6,000	$ 9,000
Cash	3,000	6,000
Liability relief	1,000	0
Total amount realized	$10,000	$15,000
Adjusted basis of property transferred	(8,000)	(20,000)
Gain (loss) realized	$ 2,000	$(5,000)
Gain recognized:		
Lesser of		
Boot received	$ 3,000	$ 6,000
Gain realized	$ 2,000	0
Gain recognized	$ 2,000	
Loss recognized		$ 0

Q recognizes a gain of $2,000. Note that Q's gain recognized is limited to the gain realized even though the boot exceeded the realized gain. Also observe that the liability transferred (and from which Q was relieved) was not treated as boot. In contrast, R recognizes none of his realized loss even though he receives boot.

Securities as Boot

For many years, an exchange qualified for nonrecognition under § 351 if the transferor received stock *or securities* (e.g., long-term notes). Apparently, the original drafters of § 351 believed that the long-term creditor interest that a transferor obtained with the receipt of securities was sufficiently equivalent to the equity interest obtained with stock to warrant tax-free treatment. In effect, the authors of § 351 felt that the use of long-term debt satisfied the continuity of interest principle. In 1989, however, this approach was rejected, and § 351 was

---

[21] § 351(b)(2). If solely nonqualified preferred stock is received and no other stock is received, loss can be recognized.   [22] § 357(a).

altered to allow nonrecognition only where stock is received.[23] In revising § 351, Congress presumably felt that an exchange for securities was more similar to a sale than a continuation of the transferor's investment. As a result, securities or debt of any type received as part of the exchange is now treated as boot. Thus, any gain realized on the exchange must be recognized to the extent of any securities received. However, Proposed Regulations provide that such gain may be recognized as the debt is repaid (i.e., using the installment method).[24] Loss is not recognized. The impact of this treatment of securities on the corporation's capital structure is discussed later in this chapter.

Character of Gain

Once it is known that gain must be recognized on the exchange, the character of that gain must be determined. The character of the gain depends on the nature of the asset in the hands of the transferor. If the asset is a capital asset, the gain is either short- or long-term capital gain depending on the transferor's holding period. If the asset is § 1231 property—generally real or depreciable property used in a trade or business held for more than one year—the gain is a § 1231 gain except to the extent that the recapture provisions such as §§ 1245 and 1250 require gain to be treated as ordinary income due to depreciation allowed on the property. Similarly, the gain could be considered ordinary income under § 1239 (relating to sales or exchanges of property between related parties if the property is depreciable in the hands of the corporation).

LIABILITIES ASSUMED BY THE CORPORATION

LO.4

Understand the effects of transferring liabilities to a corporation.

Many incorporation transactions involve the transfer of property encumbered by debt or the assumption of the transferor's liabilities by the corporation. For example, when a sole proprietor incorporates his or her business, it would not be unusual to find a transfer of mortgaged real estate as well as the transfer of routine accounts payable to the corporation. Normally, when a taxpayer is relieved of a liability, it is treated as if the taxpayer received cash and then paid off the liability. If such treatment were extended to § 351 transfers, the transferor would be deemed to have received boot for any liabilities transferred and, therefore, required to recognize any gain realized.[25] However, Congress recognized that the practical effect of treating liabilities as boot was to make many incorporation transactions taxable. This in turn interfered with the taxpayer's choice of business form, a result that is inconsistent with the underlying policy of § 351. As a result, Congress enacted a special provision governing the treatment of liabilities.

Currently, § 357(a) provides that when a corporation assumes the liabilities of a transferor as part of a § 351 transaction, the liability is not treated as boot for purposes of computing gain or loss recognized.[26]

Example 18

This year, T transferred land worth $20,000 (basis $15,000) to his wholly owned corporation. The land was subject to a mortgage of $10,000. Normally, T would be treated as having received a cash payment equal to the liability from which he was relieved, $10,000. Under § 357(a), however, relief of a liability is not treated as boot and thus no gain is recognized.

Although immunizing the transferor from gain when liabilities are transferred was warranted, it created an additional problem: the potential for tax avoidance. Sections 357(b) and (c) address these difficulties.

---

[23] § 351(a) as revised by the Revenue Reconciliation Act of 1989.

[24] Prop. Reg. § 1.453-1(f)(3). Note that the shareholder's stock basis increases immediately even though the gain is deferred. In contrast, the corporation increases its basis in the assets received as the shareholder recognizes the gain.

[25] 38-1 USTC ¶9215, 20 AFTR 1041, 303 U.S. 564 (USSC 1938).

[26] Section 357(d) defines whether the corporation is treated as having assumed a liability.

Section 357(b): Curbing Tax Avoidance

To understand the abuse that could occur without any special provisions, consider the following examples:

Example 19

B, a taxpayer in the 15% bracket, owns land worth $100,000 (basis $25,000), which he plans to contribute to his wholly owned corporation. He also is in need of cash of $20,000. B could contribute the land to the corporation for 80 shares of stock worth $80,000 and cash of $20,000. In such case, he would be required to recognize $20,000 of his realized gain because of the boot received. Consequently, B would pay tax of $3,000 ($20,000 × 15%) on the gain. After the transaction, B would have 80 additional shares of stock and cash of $17,000.

Example 20

Assume the same facts as above, except that immediately before the exchange, B mortgages the land and receives $20,000 in cash. Subsequently, B transfers the land now subject to the $20,000 mortgage to the corporation for 80 shares of stock worth $80,000. Since the liabilities transferred by B are not treated as boot, B recognizes no gain. After the transaction, B has 80 additional shares of stock and cash of $20,000.

A comparison of the result in *Example 19* to that in *Example 20* quickly reveals that by capitalizing on the general rule of § 357(a), B is able to cash in on the appreciation of his investment without paying any tax. Because liabilities are not treated as boot, B was able to avoid $3,000 in tax. Moreover, he has been completely relieved of his obligation to pay the debt. Although B would be required to reduce the basis of the stock received for the liability, the reduction might be a small price to pay for the deferral of the gain. Congress recognized that the purpose of § 351 could be undermined in this fashion and addressed the problem in § 357(b).

Section 357(b) requires that the principal purpose of the liability transfer be scrutinized. If, after taking all of the circumstances into consideration, it appears that the principal purpose of the liability transfer is to avoid tax or alternatively there is no bona fide business reason for the transfer, all liabilities are treated as boot.[27] Observe that *all* liabilities are treated as boot and not just those that had an improper purpose.[28] It should be noted that the IRS requires that the corporate purpose for any liability assumption must be stated on the tax return for the year the assumption occurs.[29]

As suggested above, whether liabilities must be treated as boot can be determined only in light of the surrounding circumstances. Since most liabilities arise from routine business operations, the bona fide business purpose test normally insulates the taxpayer from application of § 357(b). Perhaps the liabilities on which the transferor is most vulnerable are those incurred shortly before they are transferred. Nevertheless even these should withstand attack if the transferor can support them with a good business purpose. However, any personal obligations of the transferor that might be assumed by the corporation are unlikely candidates for satisfying the business purpose test and most probably would be treated as boot. In this regard it should be remembered that if one tainted liability is transferred (e.g., a personal obligation) it could be disastrous since *all* liabilities would be treated as boot—even those incurred for business reasons.

[27] For an illustration, see *R.A. Bryan v. Comm.*, 60-2 USTC ¶9603, 6 AFTR2d 5191, 281 F.2d 233 (CA-4. 1960).

[28] Reg. § 1.357-1(c).

[29] Rev. Proc. 83-59, 1983-2 C.B. 575.

Section 357(c): Liabilities in Excess of Basis

Section 357(c) was enacted to eliminate a technical flaw in the law that arises when liabilities on property transferred exceed the property's basis. The following example illustrates the problem.

Example 21

Z transferred an office building subject to a mortgage to her wholly owned corporation. The office building is worth $100,000 and has a low basis of $45,000 due to depreciation deductions. The mortgage has a balance of $70,000. Upon the transfer, Z received stock valued at $30,000 (the difference between the property's value and the mortgage) and thus realized a gain of $55,000 ($30,000 + $70,000 − $45,000). Under the general rule of § 357(a), Z recognizes no gain on the transfer since the liabilities are not treated as boot. Given that the purpose of § 351 is to defer the gain, Z's basis should be set equal to an amount that would result in a $55,000 gain if she were to sell her stock for its $30,000 value. In order to do this, the basis of the stock must be a negative $25,000. Alternatively, the basis could be reduced only to zero, in which case Z would effectively escape tax on $25,000—a subsequent sale for $30,000 would yield a $30,000 gain ($30,000 − $0) when the theoretically correct gain should be $55,000. Note that the $25,000 that would escape tax is the amount by which the liability exceeds the property's basis.

As the above example reveals, the problem faced by the courts was which method of dealing with the problem was more acceptable: (1) allow a negative basis—a concept that would be unprecedented in the Code but would ensure that the proper gain would be preserved; (2) allow a zero basis and enable a portion of the gain to escape tax; or (3) require the taxpayer to recognize gain to the extent the liability exceeded basis—an approach consistent with the view that the transferor is, in fact, better off to that extent (i.e., the transferor has in effect received a cash payment that exceeds the transferor's investment in the property as reflected by its basis). After the courts struggled with the issue, Congress provided a solution in 1954 with the enactment of § 357(c).[30] This provision requires that the taxpayer recognize gain to the extent that the total liabilities transferred on the exchange exceed the total basis of all property transferred.[31] Note that this is an *aggregate* rather than an asset-by-asset test.

Example 22

Assume the same facts as in *Example 21*. Under Code § 357(c), Z must recognize gain to the extent that the $70,000 mortgage on the property exceeds its $45,000 basis. Thus, Z recognizes $25,000 ($70,000 − $45,000) of the total $55,000 gain realized on the exchange. As discussed below, Z's basis will become zero, and a later sale of the stock for $30,000 would cause her to recognize the remaining portion of the $55,000 gain realized, $30,000.

According to Regulation § 1.357-2(b), the character of the gain is determined by allocating the total recognized gain among all assets except cash based on their relative fair market values. The type of asset and its holding period are used to determine the character of the gain allocated to it.

Note that if both § 357(b) (liability bailouts) and § 357(c) (liabilities in excess of basis) apply, § 357(b) controls, causing *all* liabilities to be treated as boot.[32]

---

[30] See, for example, *Woodsam Associates, Inc. v. Comm.*, 52-2 USTC ¶9396, 42 AFTR 505, 198 F.2d 357 (CA-2, 1952).

[31] § 357(c)(1).

[32] § 357(c)(2)(A). In *Peracchi v. Comm.*, 98-1 USTC ¶50,374 81, AFTR2d 98-1754, 143 F. 3d 487 (CA-9, 1998) *rev'g* T.C. Memo. 1996-191, a taxpayer's own note had basis and, consequently, a contribution of the note eliminated the excess of liabilities over basis [but see § 357(d) as revised for transfers after October 18, 1998].

Liabilities of the Cash Basis Taxpayer

Prior to 1978, requiring a transferor to recognize gain when liabilities exceeded basis posed difficulties when the transferor used the cash method of accounting. The following example demonstrates the dilemma.

Example 23

D, an accountant, uses the cash method of accounting. This year he decided to incorporate his practice, transferring the following assets and liabilities to the corporation:

	Fair Market Value	Adjusted Basis
Cash	$ 3,000	$3,000
Accounts receivable	40,000	0
Furniture and equipment	5,000	5,000
	$48,000	
Accounts payable	$35,000	0
Notes payable	7,000	7,000
Net worth	6,000	0
	$48,000	

When determining whether gain should be recognized, liabilities transferred must be compared to the basis of the assets transferred. The difficulty confronting the cash basis taxpayer stems from the fact that some of the assets transferred have a zero basis—in this case, the accounts receivable have no basis. Thus, if the term *liability* is construed literally, the taxpayer has transferred liabilities of $42,000, which exceed the $8,000 ($5,000 + $3,000) basis of his assets by $34,000. Under a strict interpretation of the rule, D would be required to recognize gain of $34,000. Note that if D were an accrual basis taxpayer, the receivables would have a basis, thus preventing recognition of gain.

As shown in the example, the problem confronting the courts was the definition of liabilities. Some courts believed that accounts payable of a cash basis taxpayer should be ignored while others did not.[33] After much conflict, § 357 was amended to clarify what liabilities were to be considered. As now defined, liabilities do not include those that would give rise to a deduction by a cash basis taxpayer when paid.[34] However, a liability incurred for an expense that must be capitalized is considered a liability.[35]

Example 24

Assume the same facts as in *Example 23,* except that one of the accounts payable represents a bill of $500 for architectural drawings of D's planned office building. The remaining accounts payable are for routine deductible expenses. Upon the transfer of assets and liabilities to the corporation, D is considered as having transferred liabilities of $7,500. The $7,500 is the sum of the $7,000 notes payable, which when paid

---

[33] See *John P. Bongiovanni v. Comm.*, 73-1 USTC ¶9133, 31 AFTR2d 73-409, 470 F.2d 921 (CA-2, 1972); *Peter Raich*, 46 T.C. 604 (1966); and *Donald D. Focht*, 68 T.C. 223 (1977).

[34] § 357(c)(3). As discussed within, these liabilities are also ignored for basis purposes [see § 358(d)(2)].

[35] § 357(c)(3)(B).

would not be deductible, and the $500 account payable for the drawings, which when paid must be capitalized. The remaining accounts payable are not treated as liabilities because the corporation may deduct their payment when made. Because the $7,500 of liabilities does not exceed the $8,000 basis of the assets transferred ($3,000 + $5,000), D recognizes no gain on the exchange under § 357(c).

BASIS OF TRANSFEROR'S STOCK

The rules for computing the transferor's basis for any stock received reflects Congressional desire to defer rather than eliminate recognition on the exchange. As indicated above, the purpose of § 351 is to allow nonrecognition only as long as the transferor maintains an interest in the property transferred. Thus, any gains and losses not recognized on the original exchange should be recognized when the transferor or the corporation effectively severs its interest in the property. This policy is achieved in the provisions governing the basis assigned to the transferor's stock and the basis computed for the property transferred to the corporation.

Example 25

T transfers property with a value of $100 and a basis of $40 to a corporation in exchange for stock worth $100. Under § 351, none of the $60 gain realized is recognized. This gain does not escape tax, but is preserved by assigning a basis to the stock equal to the basis of the property transferred, $40. If the stock is later sold for its $100 value, the taxpayer would recognize the $60 gain initially postponed.

The transferor's basis for the stock received is often referred to as a *substituted* basis since the basis of the property transferred is generally substituted as the basis for the stock received.

If a shareholder recognizes gain due to the receipt of boot, only the portion of the gain that is not recognized needs to be built into the basis of the stock. This approach is reflected in the formula for the computation of the transferor's basis in Exhibit 2-1.[36] As seen in the formula, the transferor's basis is initially the same as the property transferred, but is increased for the gain recognized on the exchange so that this amount will not be taxed twice. The combination of these two amounts represents the transferor's basis for the stock and boot received. A portion of this total is then allocated to the boot by subtracting the *value* of the boot. In effect, the basis assigned to the boot is its value, while the remaining basis is assigned to the stock. This arithmetic ensures that the deferred gain is built into the transferor's basis for the stock.

EXHIBIT 2-1	Transferor's Basis of Stock Received

	Adjusted basis of property transferred	$xx,xxx
+	Gain recognized	x,xxx
−	Boot received	(xxx)
−	Liabilities transferred	(xxx)
=	Basis of stock received	$xx,xxx

---
[36] § 358.

Example 26

T transfers property with a value of $120 and a basis of $40 to C Corporation in exchange for stock worth $90 and $30 cash. T realizes an $80 ($90 + $30 – $40) gain, $30 of which is recognized due to the boot received. As determined below, T's basis in the stock is $40, while his basis in the cash is its value of $30.

	Basis of property transferred	$40
+	Gain recognized.	30
–	Boot received.	(30)
=	Basis of stock.	$40

Note how a subsequent sale of the stock for its $90 value would cause T to recognize the previously postponed gain of $50 ($90 – $40).

Effect of Liabilities

Although liabilities transferred by the transferor are not considered boot for purposes of computing gain or loss recognized on the exchange, they normally are treated as boot in determining the transferor's basis.[37] This treatment ensures eventual recognition of the gain or loss deferred on the exchange.

Example 27

K, a cash basis taxpayer, transferred land to her corporation. The land was valued at $80,000 (basis $35,000) and was subject to a $30,000 mortgage. In exchange for the land, K received stock worth $50,000. Although K realizes a $45,000 gain ($30,000 + $50,000 – $35,000), none of the gain is recognized because the corporation's acquisition of the property subject to the debt is not considered boot for purposes of gain or loss recognition. In contrast, K's basis for the stock received is computed treating the liability as boot as follows:

	Adjusted basis of property transferred	$35,000
+	Gain recognized.	0
–	Boot received (including liabilities transferred)	(30,000)
=	Basis of stock.	$ 5,000

K's basis in the stock is $5,000. Should K subsequently sell the stock for its $50,000 value, the $45,000 gain postponed on the exchange would be recognized. Note that the effect of this approach is the equivalent of treating the shareholder as receiving a cash payment, which is considered a nontaxable return of capital.

It should be noted that not all liabilities are treated as boot for purposes of determining basis. As explained earlier, Code § 357(c)(3) provides that those liabilities relating to routine deductible expenditures are not considered liabilities in determining whether liabilities exceed basis. Similarly, when computing the shareholder's basis, such liabilities are also ignored.[38]

---

[37] § 358(d).   [38] § 358(d)(2).

Example 28

Assume the same facts as in *Example 27* above, except that the corporation also assumed $20,000 of K's routine accounts payable that would be deductible when paid and the value of the stock received is $30,000. K still recognizes no gain on the transaction since the payables are ignored because the corporation could deduct the payments when made. Similarly, these liabilities are ignored in computing basis. Thus, K's basis also remains the same.

Holding Period

The transferor's holding period may affect the tax treatment if the property received in the exchange is disposed of in the future. In determining the transferor's holding period of the stock and boot received, the rules of § 1223 apply. This provision allows a transferor to add the time that the property transferred was held to the actual holding period of the property received if both of the following conditions are satisfied:[39]

1. The property transferred was a capital asset or § 1231 property (generally real or depreciable business property) in the hands of the transferor.

2. The basis of the property received was determined in reference to the basis of the property transferred to the corporation.

Since the basis of the transferor's stock is determined by using the basis of the property transferred as a starting point, the transferor's holding period for the stock includes the holding period of the transferred property, but only if the property transferred is a capital asset or § 1231 property. The holding period of any boot received begins on the date of the exchange since its basis is not determined in reference to the property transferred but is its value.

CORPORATION'S GAIN OR LOSS

The treatment of the corporation on the exchange is very straightforward relative to that of the transferor shareholder. The corporation recognizes no gain or loss when it receives money, property, or services in exchange for its stock.[40] This rule applies whether the stock exchanged is previously unissued stock or treasury stock.[41] As stated earlier, however, the corporation treats the issuance of stock for services just as if a cash payment had been made. In such case, the corporation may capitalize or deduct the amount depending on the type of services rendered.[42]

CORPORATION'S BASIS FOR PROPERTY RECEIVED

Like the basis rules for the transferor, those for the corporation ensure that any gain or loss deferred on the exchange is properly recognized if the corporation subsequently disposes of the property. The basis assigned to the property received by the corporation is sometimes referred to as a *carryover* basis. This term is used because the transferor's basis is "carried over" and generally serves as the corporation's basis as well. However, if the transferor recognizes any gain on the exchange, the amount of gain is added to the corporation's basis to prevent the gain from being recognized twice. The formula for computing the corporation's basis is shown in Exhibit 2-2.[43]

---

[39] § 1223(1).

[40] § 1032.

[41] *Supra*, Footnote 40.

[42] *Supra*, Footnote 9.

[43] § 362. Under § 362(d)(1), basis may not be increased above the property's fair market value on account of gain recognized by the transferor as a result of a liability assumed by the corporation. For this purpose, fair market value is determined without regard to § 7701(g) (which provides that the value is not less than the amount of nonrecourse debt to which it is subject).

EXHIBIT 2-2	Basis of Assets Received by the Corporation

	Adjusted basis of property to the transferor.	$x,xxx
+	Gain recognized on the exchange	xxx
=	Aggregate basis of property received.	$x,xxx

Example 29

During the current year, Y transferred land worth $50,000 (basis $10,000) to her wholly owned corporation for 40 shares of stock worth $47,000 and cash of $3,000. Y realizes a $40,000 gain ($47,000 + $3,000 − $10,000). She recognizes $3,000 of the gain since she received boot of $3,000. The corporation's basis in the land is $13,000 (transferor's $10,000 basis + transferor's $3,000 gain recognized).

The basis calculation for the corporation is not troublesome when the transferor recognizes no gain on the exchange. In such case, the corporation merely "steps into the shoes" of the transferor and its basis for each asset received is identical to the transferor's basis. However, if the transferor contributes more than one asset and recognizes gain, it is unclear how the aggregate basis should be allocated among the various assets. Since it is generally assumed that each asset transferred should have a basis at least equal to that of the transferor, the crucial question concerns the allocation of the gain recognized. Perhaps the most logical method would be to allocate the gain to the asset(s) responsible for it. Unfortunately, several other methods have been suggested and the acceptable one has yet to be identified.

Duplication of Losses

Over the years, the government has raised concerns about tax avoidance schemes that are structured to take a single economic loss and magically convert it into two tax losses. Such manipulations were among the tax abuses discovered in the investigation of Enron by the Joint Committee of Taxation.[44]

Example 30

This year P formed a subsidiary, S, by transferring property worth $1 million (basis $5 million) to S in exchange for all of S's stock. The transaction is nontaxable under § 351. P's basis in the stock of S is a substituted basis of $5 million and S's basis in its assets is a carryover basis of $5 million. If P sells the S stock for its value of $1 million, it recognizes a $4 million loss ($1,000,000 − $5,000,000). Similarly, if S sells the assets, it recognizes a $4 million loss. Note how P has duplicated the loss by transferring the loss assets to a C corporation and taking advantage of the basis rules. It should also be emphasized that a single gain is similarly duplicated when assets with a built-in gain are contributed to a C corporation.

To prevent the duplication of losses, § 362(e)(2) was enacted in 2004. This special rule applies for exchanges subject to § 351 as well as contributions to capital.[45] Under this provision, if the aggregate basis of the property transferred exceeds the value of such assets—that is, there is a net built-in loss—the basis of the loss assets is limited to their fair

---

[44] See *Report of Investigation of Enron Corporation and Related Entities Regarding Federal Tax and Compensation Issues, and Policy Recommendations* (JCS-3-03), February, 2003.

[45] § 362(e)(1) operates in a similar manner where losses are imported to the U.S.

market value. In such case, the basis of each loss asset is reduced by the loss asset's proportionate share of the total net built-in loss.[46] In lieu of reducing the basis of the assets, if both the shareholder-transferor and corporate-transferee both elect, the transferor can reduce the basis of the stock received. By making this election, the basis of the stock is equal to the fair market value of the assets.

Example 31

L transfers three parcels of land to his wholly-owned corporation in a transaction qualifying as a § 351 exchange. The value and basis of the assets are shown below. In this case, the aggregate basis of the assets immediately after the transfer of $170,000 exceeds the aggregate value of $160,000. Consequently, a net built-in loss of $10,000 exists, and a basis reduction is required. As shown below, the total basis of the assets of $170,000 is reduced by the net built-in loss of $10,000 to $160,000. The $10,000 basis reduction is allocated between the loss assets (Badacre and Pooracre) in proportion to their respective built-in losses before the transaction.

	Badacre	Pooracre	Subtotal	Goodacre	Total
Fair market value.........	$ 10,000	$ 30,000	$ 40,000	$120,000	$160,000
Adjusted basis	(50,000)	(90,000)	(140,000)	(30,000)	(170,000)
Built-in gain (loss)	$(40,000)	$(60,000)	$(100,000)	$ 90,000	$ (10,000)
Basis reduction..........	$ 4,000*	$ 6,000**	$ 10,000	$ 0	$ 10,000
Revised adjusted basis	$ 46,000	$ 84,000	$ 130,000	$ 30,000	$160,000

* $40,000/$100,000 × $10,000
** $60,000/$100,000 × $10,000

Alternatively, if L and the corporation both elect, L may reduce the basis of his stock by the net built-in loss from $170,000 to $160,000 instead of the corporation reducing the basis of its assets.

The basis reduction rule applies only if the *aggregate* basis of the assets transferred exceeds the aggregate value. For this purpose and for purposes of computing the net built-in loss of the corporation, the aggregate basis immediately after the transaction includes any basis increase attributable to gain recognized by the transferor.

In many cases, there are multiple transferors that contribute property. In this case, the loss duplication rule is applied separately to each transferor. In other words, a transfer of assets with an aggregate net built-in loss by one transferor does not cause the rule to apply to other transferors involved in the transaction.

Holding Period

The rule governing the corporation's holding period for property received is consistent with the notion that the corporation essentially "steps into the shoes" of the transferor in a § 351 exchange. Accordingly, the corporation's holding period for all assets received includes that of the transferor.[47]

SPECIAL CONSIDERATIONS

Several additional concerns arise when a corporation is formed or property is transferred to a controlled corporation. For example, the corporation must identify the taxable year it wants to use. Another issue that must be considered is the application of the depreciation recapture rules. Still another issue concerns the method of applying the Modified Accelerated Cost Recovery System (MACRS) to determine the proper amount of depreciation for the year. These and other problems are addressed below.

---

[46] See Prop. Reg. § 1.362-4.   [47] § 1223(2).

Selection of Tax Year and Short Taxable Years

When a corporation is formed, it must select its taxable year. As noted in Chapter 1, C corporations may elect to report using either the calendar year or a fiscal year. Note that there are no restrictions on the year that C corporations may select as there are with other entities (e.g., S corporations, partnerships, and trusts normally must use the calendar year).

As a practical matter, when a corporation is formed, the taxable year selected usually results in a short taxable year (i.e., a year with less than 12 months). For example, a corporation may be formed on August 5 and elect to use a calendar year, resulting in a short taxable year running from August 5 through December 31. In calculating the tax liability for a short taxable year, the law usually requires taxpayers to annualize their income. However, the annualization requirement only applies when a *change* in the tax year creates a short year. There is no need to annualize income in the case of a newly formed entity.[48]

Recapture of Depreciation

The depreciation recapture provisions of §§ 1245 and 1250 sometime require the taxpayer to recognize gain on what otherwise would be a nontaxable transaction. This treatment makes certain that the potential recapture is not avoided. When property is transferred to a controlled corporation, recapture is not triggered.[49] However, any gain that the shareholder must recognize on the transfer is treated as ordinary income to the extent of any recapture potential. Any remaining recapture potential carries over to the corporation. Therefore, if the corporation subsequently disposes of the property at a gain, it must recapture not only amounts related to the depreciation it has claimed, but also the appropriate amount of any depreciation claimed by the transferor.

Example 32

In a transaction qualifying for § 351 treatment, T transferred equipment worth $12,000 (original cost of $8,000 less $3,000 depreciation claimed and deducted = $5,000 adjusted basis) to C Corporation in exchange for stock worth $11,000 and $1,000 cash. Although T realized a gain of $7,000 ($12,000 − $5,000), only $1,000 must be recognized because the boot received was $1,000. All $1,000 of the gain is recaptured under § 1245 and is therefore treated as ordinary income. The balance of the depreciation that has not been recaptured, $2,000 ($3,000 − $1,000), carries over to the corporation for possible recapture upon a subsequent disposition.

Depreciation Computations

Often depreciable property is placed in service prior to its transfer to a corporation. When such property (e.g., property currently being used in business) is transferred, certain rules must be adhered to in computing the depreciation deduction and in allocating it between the transferor and the corporation. When the property transferred qualifies for depreciation using MACRS, depreciation for the year of the transfer and subsequent years generally is computed using the transferor's period and method.[50] For the year of transfer, the depreciation must be allocated between the transferor and the corporation according to the number of months held by each.[51] In determining the number of months that each holds the property, the corporation is assumed to hold the property for the entire month in which the property is transferred.

LO.5

Describe special problems involved in computing depreciation of assets transferred to the corporation.

---

[48] § 443(b)(1).

[49] §§ 1245(b)(3) and 1250(d)(3).

[50] § 168(i)(7) and Prop. Reg. § 1.168-5(b)(2)(B). Special rules apply for depreciating any gain element in the corporation's basis. See Prop. Reg. § 1.168-5(b)(7).

[51] Prop. Reg. § 1.168-5(b)(4)(i).

Example 33

In 2011, S retired from the military and started his own copying business. After being in business for several years, he decided to incorporate. On September 23, 2016, he transferred assets of the business to a corporation in exchange for all of its stock. Among the assets transferred was an automobile purchased for $10,000 in June 2015. In 2015, S's depreciation deduction using the optional MACRS tables (contained in Appendix H) for five-year property was $2,000 (20% × $10,000). For the year of the transfer, 2016, depreciation of the automobile is computed using the same method used by the transferor S. Thus, depreciation for the year of the transfer is $3,200 (32% of $10,000). The $3,200 depreciation deduction must be allocated between S and the corporation based on the number of months held by each. S is treated as having held the property for eight months (January–August) while the corporation is given credit for holding the asset for the remaining four months of the year (the month of the transfer, September, through December). S may deduct $2,134 ($3,200 × 8 ÷ 12) and the corporation may deduct the remaining depreciation ($3,200 × 4 ÷ 12).

It should be emphasized that any computations made with respect to S, such as computing his basis in the stock received or his gain or loss on the transfer, must reflect the depreciation allocated to him. Therefore, the basis of the property transferred (which generally is substituted for the basis of the stock received) is $5,866 ($10,000 – $2,000 – $2,134). Note that the corporation's basis is also $5,866 on the day of the transfer, but it uses the *full $10,000* cost to compute its future depreciation deductions just as S would have, had he retained the property.

Example 34

Assume the same facts as above. In 2017 the corporation continues to compute depreciation on the automobile using S's period and method. Therefore, the corporation's depreciation for 2017 is $1,920 ($10,000 × 19.2%).

The MACRS operating rules also require a modification in the normal depreciation calculation for property *other than real property* when a corporation has a short taxable year and the contributed property has not been previously used in business. In determining whether the corporation has a short taxable year, for purpose of the depreciation rules, the taxable year does not include any month prior to the month in which the business begins. For example, if two individuals form a calendar year corporation that starts business on September 14, it is treated as having a short taxable year beginning in September and ending on December 31. When property is placed in service during a short taxable year, standard depreciation conventions (i.e., half-year, mid-month, and mid-quarter) must be followed in computing the depreciation deduction. For example, personal property placed in service during a short taxable year of four months is treated as having been in service for half the number of months in that year (i.e., two months).[52] As a result, the corporation would be entitled to 2/12 of the *annual* depreciation amount. If depreciation is calculated using the optional tables, however, the deduction would be 4/12 of the amount normally computed using the table. This fraction, 4/12, is used instead of 2/12 since the rate prescribed in the table for the first year already reflects the half-year convention. Consequently, if the tables are used for calculating the deduction, depreciation is computed by multiplying the amount determined in the normal manner by the fraction of the year—expressed in months—during which the corporation was in business.[53]

---

[52] Conference Agreement, Conference Report H.R. 3838 (9/18/86), U.S. Government Printing Office: 1986, 99th Congress, 2d Session, Report 99-841, p. 11-46.

[53] Prop. Reg. § 1.168-2(f)(1).

Example 35

After many years of wanting to have her own company, B finally decided in 2016 to test her fortunes in the limousine business. On May 17, 2016, she transferred $50,000 in cash to a corporation in exchange for all of its stock. On the same day, the corporation purchased a limousine (five-year property) for $30,000. The corporation adopted the calendar year for reporting. Since the corporation was not in business prior to May, it has a short taxable year of eight months. Consequently, the depreciation deduction is $4,000, computed as follows:

Cost of equipment.	$30,000
Rate per depreciation tables (Appendix)	× 20%
Short taxable year fraction.	× 8/12
Depreciation	$ 4,000

Observe that if B had contributed a limousine that she was currently using in her business (and therefore depreciating), depreciation for the vehicle would be computed in the normal manner—without adjustments for the short year—and simply allocated between B and the corporation.

There are no special modifications needed in computing the depreciation for real property acquired in a short taxable year. This follows from the fact that depreciation for real property is computed using a mid-month convention. For example, consider a calendar year corporation formed on August 1 that purchases a warehouse in November. In this case, the corporation should receive 1½ months of depreciation (½ month for November and 1 month for December). This result (and the proper depreciation percentage) can be obtained from the table by assuming there was no short taxable year and using that rate given for property placed in service in the eleventh month of the year (i.e., the company's normal taxable year). For the year of formation, this process would yield a percentage of 0.321 (see Appendix H).

Contributions to Capital

The previous section examined transfers to controlled corporations when the transferor received stock and other property in exchange. From time to time, transfers may be made to a corporation when the transferor receives nothing in exchange. Such transfers are termed *contributions to capital* and are subject to special tax treatment. As discussed below, the tax treatment of capital contributions generally depends on the source of the contribution: shareholders or nonshareholders.

> **LO.6**
> Explain the effect of contributions to capital by shareholders and nonshareholders.

SHAREHOLDER CONTRIBUTIONS

The tax treatment of a *cash* contribution to capital made by a shareholder normally presents little difficulty. A corporation may exclude the contribution from its gross income as long as it is truly a contribution and not merely disguised compensation for something the corporation has provided or will provide to the shareholder.[54] If the facts suggest the latter, the corporation recognizes income on the transfer. Assuming the transfer is a contribution and not compensation, the shareholder treats the contribution as an additional cost of the stock previously owned and increases the basis in the stock.[55]

If a contribution of *property* is made by a shareholder, the treatment varies only with respect to the basis computations. Assuming the contribution is voluntary, the shareholder's basis in his or her stock is increased by the basis of the property transferred plus any gain recognized—which usually does not arise. The corporation's basis for the property is the same as the transferor's, increased by any gain recognized.

---

[54] § 118.   [55] Reg. § 1.118-1.

A question that arises frequently in this area concerns the treatment of a loan, or some other debt made by the shareholder to the corporation, which the shareholder subsequently forgives. It is not uncommon, particularly in small closely held corporations, for shareholders to make advances to their corporations which as a practical matter are never repaid and ultimately are forgiven by the shareholder. As a general rule, when a debt is cancelled, the debtor must recognize income. When the debtor-creditor relationship is between a corporation and its shareholders, however, the courts have normally characterized the transaction as a nontaxable contribution to capital as long as the facts suggested that the shareholder intended to make a contribution.[56]

NONSHAREHOLDER CONTRIBUTIONS

Capital contributions are not limited to those made by shareholders. Nonshareholders also make contributions to businesses notwithstanding their lack of a proprietary interest. These contributions are usually prompted by the hope of deriving some indirect benefit. For example, in their drive to create jobs, governmental units and other types of nonshareholders often provide attractive financial packages to lure corporations to locate in their area. When the economic incentives include capital contributions, special tax considerations arise.

A nonshareholder contribution may be excluded by the corporation from gross income if the transfer is an inducement rather than payment for corporate goods or services.[57] If the corporation receives a contribution of property, the basis of the property is considered zero so that normal tax benefits associated with basis (e.g., depreciation) cannot be obtained.[58] Note that a corporation could circumvent this result by requesting a cash contribution and using it to acquire property, which would then have a basis equal to its cost. To preclude such action, the corporation must reduce the basis of any property acquired with the money during the next 12-month period.[59] If all or a part of the money has not been used at the end of this period to acquire property, the basis of other property must be reduced by the amount not spent. The basis of property subject to depreciation, depletion, or amortization is reduced first.[60] Any further reductions required are applied to other property.

Example 36

To attract a professional football team to locate in its area, the city government contributed a practice facility worth $4 million to the corporation owning the team. The corporation recognizes no income from the contribution, and the basis of the facility is zero. Had the city contributed $4 million in cash to the corporation, which subsequently acquired an office building for $3 million, the corporation would have a basis in the office building of zero. In addition, if the remaining $1 million had not been spent at the end of the 12-month period, the basis of other corporate property must be reduced by $1 million.

The Corporation's Capital Structure

In financing corporate operations, management primarily relies on the issuance of stock or debt or some combination thereof to secure necessary capital. The ultimate configuration of stock and debt used—normally referred to as the corporation's *capital structure*—is shaped by many factors, including the tax law. Various tax provisions have significant implications for whether a corporation's capital should be acquired by issuing stock or by creating debt. The principal tax considerations in deciding between stock or debt are discussed in the following sections.

---

[56] Reg. § 1.61-12(a); See, for example, *Hartland Assocs.*, 54 T.C. 1580 (1970).

[57] § 118.

[58] § 362(c)(1).

[59] § 362(c)(2).

[60] Reg. § 1.362-2(b).

STOCK VERSUS DEBT: A COMPARISON

Appreciated Property

Prior to the revisions of § 351 in 1989, a corporation could issue stock *or debt* in exchange for property without tax consequences. Consequently, a corporation had the flexibility to issue stock or debt as otherwise suited its needs. Normally, this meant a heavy dosage of debt was used in the capital structure because of its many advantages, discussed below. However, the Revenue Reconciliation Act of 1989 altered the traditional playing field. As explained earlier, Congress revised § 351 so that the receipt of securities is treated as boot. Therefore, if debt is issued in exchange for property that has appreciated, the transferor must recognize gain. This may serve as an important limitation on the use of debt. However, the Proposed Regulations do allow any gain attributable to receipt of the debt to be reported as the debt is collected using the installment sales method; this may reduce the impact of the change.[61]

> **LO.7**
>
> Identify the tax considerations in determining whether the corporation's capital structure should consist of stock or debt.

It should be observed that the treatment of securities as boot has no effect if the transferor does not realize any gain on the exchange. For example, contributions of cash or loss property in exchange for securities can be made without tax consequences. Thus, the 1989 Act did not kill the corporation's use of securities to raise capital but only imposed an important limitation that must be considered when planning the formation of the corporation and subsequent exchanges.

Interest versus Dividends

No doubt the most obvious distinction between stock and debt concerns the tax treatment of interest and dividends. Quite simply, the corporation can deduct interest payments eliminating double taxation, but cannot do so with dividend payments. Since interest payments reduce taxable income while dividend payments do not, the corporation's cost of using debt to raise capital may be less than the cost for stock. Assuming a corporation paid Federal and state taxes at about a 40% rate, that corporation would be required to earn $100 to pay a $60 dividend while only $60 of income is needed to pay the same amount in interest. Historically this difference looms as such a powerful incentive that commentators have criticized this apparent advantage for leading to excessive debt financing.[62] In addition, debt has traditionally served as an excellent vehicle for shareholders of a closely held corporation to bail out the earnings and profits of a corporation at the cost of a single tax.

Example 37

J and B each received $500,000 from their father to start their own businesses. J transferred his $500,000 to his corporation for shares of stock worth $200,000 and a note bearing 10% interest, payable in annual installments of $20,000 for 15 years. B invested his $500,000 in exchange solely for stock. Both corporations are equally successful. Ignoring salary payments, J and B both desire $30,000 from their corporations. By designing his capital structure to include debt, J's corporation distributes the $30,000 to J in the form of a deductible interest payment, thus avoiding the double tax penalty. In contrast, the distribution from B's corporation represents a nondeductible dividend. Consequently, B's $30,000 has been taxed twice—once when the corporation earns the income and again when the income is distributed as dividends to B.

---

[61] *Supra,* Footnote 24.

[62] See, for example, U.S. Department of the Treasury, *Blueprints for Basic Tax Reform,* p. 69.

While *Example 37* above clearly illustrates the benefits of debt, the new preferential tax rates applying to dividends (i.e., 15% or 5%) dilute—at least somewhat—this historical preference for debt. For example, consider an investor in the 35% tax bracket. To provide the investor with a $100 of after-tax income from an investment, a corporation would be required to pay either a dividend of about $118 [$118 − (15% × $118 = 18) = $100] or interest of $153 [$153 − (35% × $153 = $53) = $100]. Consequently, the corporation, assuming it pays taxes at a 40% rate, must earn $153 to pay the deductible interest or $197 [$197 − (40% × $197 = 79) = $118] to pay the nondeductible dividend. In contrast, if the corporation pays taxes at a 15% rate, it needs to earn only $139 [$139 − (15% × $139 = $21) = $118] to produce the desired return to the investor. As this example illustrates, depending on the facts, the new rates for dividends may alter the traditional playing field.

Debt Repayment versus Stock Redemption

Another distinction between stock and debt concerns the tax consequences resulting from repayment of debt as compared to redemption of stock. When the investor in a publicly held corporation needs funds, a sale of a portion of the investment (stock or debt) enables a tax-free recovery of the investment's cost and a capital gains tax on any excess. For an investor in a closely held corporation, however, the situation changes dramatically. In this case, there probably is little market for the investment, and even if there were, a transfer to an outsider is probably not acceptable. For the investor whose investment is in stock, the alternative is a sale of the stock to the corporation (i.e., a redemption). Notwithstanding the fact that a "sale" may occur in form, the Code generally provides that such sales are treated as dividends.[63] On the other hand, if the investor's investment takes the form of debt, repayments of the debt generally are treated as a tax-free return of the debt's principal. Although the end result of a redemption (i.e., capital gain or dividend treatment) is taxed at a favorable rate, this outcome still falls short of the nontaxable treatment available with debt. Like the interest-dividend distinction, the difference between repayments of debt and redemptions of stock affords shareholders of a closely held corporation an excellent opportunity to bail out corporate earnings.

Example 38

Assume the same facts as in *Example 37* above. In addition to receiving an annual interest payment of $30,000, J also receives an annual principal payment of $20,000 that is tax free. If B desires to receive a similar payment of $20,000, he could sell stock to his corporation worth $20,000 (note that a sale to an outside third party is normally an unacceptable alternative when the corporation is closely held). Although the transaction may be structured as a sale, the redemption provisions of the Code require that this amount be treated as a dividend since the distribution has all the characteristics of a dividend (i.e., B's interest has not been reduced, the distribution is pro rata). Consequently, B acquires the $20,000 at the cost of two taxes.

As the above examples suggest, shareholders of closely held corporations have long preferred debt to stock when exchanging their assets with the corporation. Consequently, the closely held corporation's capital structure has usually been heavily tipped in favor of debt. When this condition exists—the capital structure consists primarily of debt and little stock—the corporation is said to be *thinly capitalized*. If a corporation is too thinly capitalized, all or a portion of its debt may be treated as stock. Of course, if debt is reclassified as stock, all of the advantages of debt are lost. While the significance of this distinction may have diminished with dividends now being taxed at a lower rate, it still looms as a serious concern. The possible characterization of debt as stock is considered in more detail below.

Accumulated Earnings Tax Considerations

Another difference between stock and debt involves application of the accumulated earnings tax provisions. These provisions impose a penalty tax in addition to the regular corporate tax

---

[63] § 302. The redemption provisions are discussed in Chapter 4.

to dissuade taxpayers from shifting income to the corporation, where it may be taxed at lower corporate rates. For example, income could be shifted to the corporation and taxes saved if the actual corporate rate paid (e.g., 15% on the first $50,000) was less than the rate paid by the individual (e.g., 10 percent, 15 percent, 25 percent, 28 percent, 33 percent, 35 percent, or 39.6 percent). To foil attempts by individuals who wish to take advantage of shifting income, the accumulated earnings tax levies a penalty when corporations accumulate earnings beyond the reasonable needs of the business. Herein lies the importance of debt. The repayment of debt is considered a reasonable need.[64] Thus, the corporation is allowed to accumulate the funds necessary to discharge the debt. In contrast, the redemption of stock is not considered a reasonable need and hence accumulations for such purpose are not permitted. As a result, the presence of debt in the capital structure serves as a justification for accumulations, whereas the presence of stock does not.

Worthless Debt versus Worthless Stock

Since not all businesses prosper, an investor must consider the tax result if his or her investment in the corporation goes sour. The tax consequences attributable to worthless stock and debt can vary widely depending on the circumstances. For this reason, the subject of worthless investments is considered in detail later in this chapter. Basically, however, if stock or debt becomes worthless, a capital loss is usually recognized. Thus, deductions for worthlessness are normally restricted to the extent of capital gains *plus* $3,000. The major exception to this rule is contained in § 1244, which generally provides special treatment for the first million dollars of stock issued. Investors who own § 1244 stock are entitled to ordinary loss treatment if the stock is disposed of at a loss or if it becomes worthless. Since many businesses do not succeed, this distinction must be carefully weighed before using a substantial amount of debt in the capital structure.

DEBT TREATED AS STOCK

In view of the favorable tax treatment given to debt, corporations, particularly those that are closely held, have often tried to exploit its advantages by using a high proportion of debt in their capital structures. The lack of taxpayer restraint in this area was well illustrated in one case where the shareholders had advances outstanding to the corporation exceeding 100 times the value of the stock.[65] In these circumstances, the government is apt to ignore the fact that the instrument is debt on its face (i.e., it contains all the formal characteristics of debt), and focus instead on its substance. If it is determined that the alleged debt instrument is simply a disguised equity interest, it may be reclassified and treated as stock.

A recharacterization of debt as stock can be disastrous. For example, all interest payments previously made are treated as dividends, and are therefore not deductible, resulting in double taxation. Similarly, repayments of debt principal are treated as payments in redemption of stock and are likely to be treated as dividends. In short, the favorable tax treatment is lost and unfavorable treatment is imposed.

Whether a purported debt instrument is debt or stock has been a subject of scores of cases. In fact, the problem so plagues the government that in 1969 Congress enacted the now infamous § 385. The primary thrust of § 385 is to authorize the Treasury to draft Regulations clarifying the circumstances that would warrant a recharacterization of debt as stock. To this date, however, Treasury has been unable to write Regulations that are both acceptable to the financial community and at the same time not easily circumvented or abused. Consequently, over 42 years after the enactment of § 385, Regulations still do not exist.

Section 385 does identify certain factors that should be considered in determining whether a true debtor-creditor relationship has been established. The factors to be considered are:

1. Whether there is a written unconditional promise to pay on demand or on a specified date a sum certain in money in return for an adequate consideration in money or money's worth, and to pay a fixed rate of interest.

---

[64] Reg. § 1.537-2(b)(3). The accumulated earnings tax is discussed in Chapter 6.

[65] In *Glenmore Distilleries Co.*, 47 B.T.A. 213 (1942, capital stock was $1,000 while shareholder advances were $131,458).

2. Whether there is subordination to or preference over any indebtedness of the corporation.

3. The ratio of debt to equity of the corporation.

4. Whether there is convertibility into the stock of the corporation.

5. The relationship between holdings of stock in the corporation and holdings of the interest in question.

Unfortunately, this list is simply a distillation of factors already identified by the courts.[66] Consequently, in absence of Regulations, the courts continue their struggle to distinguish debt from equity. Whether an instrument is stock or debt seems to be a question of risk. An early court case captured the definitional problem well, stating:

> [the] vital difference between the shareholder and the creditor [is that the] shareholder is an adventurer in the corporate business; he takes the risk, and profits from success. The creditor, in compensation for not sharing the profits, is to be paid independently of the risk of success, and gets a right to dip into capital when the payment date arrives.[67]

Unfortunately, the threshold of risk at which an investor transcends creditor status and becomes a shareholder has not been clearly identified. The various cases suggest that the issue must ultimately be resolved in light of the taxpayer's intent: did the investor intend to provide risk capital susceptible to the fortunes of the business or to establish a debtor-creditor relationship? Consequently, most of the court cases involve an examination of various factors that may be indicative of the investor's true intention.

The reclassification controversy takes place on two fronts. The first involves instruments that have all the formal characteristics of debt. These instruments, normally considered *straight debt*, contain an unqualified promise to pay a sum certain at a maturity date along with a fixed percentage in interest. Straight debt normally has a maturity date that is reasonably close in time, and interest that is payable regardless of the corporation's income. In addition, the debt is not subordinated to those of general creditors but has similar rights, and the debt also gives the holder the right to enforce payment upon maturity or default. The second type of debt involves *hybrid* securities, so-called because they are really neither stock nor debt but a blend. A hybrid security is often convertible to stock or contains some feature normally associated with stock. For example, the security may entitle the holder to vote on corporate affairs much like a shareholder, or the security's interest payments may be contingent on earnings much like dividends.

A review of the various court decisions indicates that hybrid securities usually have more difficulty in qualifying as debt than does straight debt. Courts apparently are somewhat reluctant to grant debt status to instruments that are obviously not debt on their face (e.g., instruments structured with conversion or participation features). On the other hand, straight debt is not above suspicion. An instrument that meets the classical definition of debt may still be characterized as stock depending on the surrounding circumstances. For example, straight debt is particularly vulnerable where there is an excessive debt-to-equity ratio or the debt is held in the same proportion as stock.

As suggested earlier, the clearest signal that debt is not what it is purported to be is a high debt-to-equity ratio. Although no particular ratio is conclusive, a ratio exceeding 4:1 suggests that things are not what they might seem.[68] Where the ratio of debt to equity is high—such as in an extreme case when all of the capital is in the form of debt—all or

---

[66] For a recent illustration of the problem, see *Indmar Products Co, Inc. v. Comm.*, 2006-1 USTC 50,270, 97 AFTR 2d 2006-1956, 444 F3d 771 (CA-6, 2006) rev'g TC Memo 2005-32 where the appellate court analyzed 11 nonexclusive factors.

[67] *Commissioner v. O.P.P. Holding Corp.*, 35-1 USTC ¶9179, 15 AFTR 379, 76 F.2d 11, 12 (CA-2, 1935).

[68] Prior to the Supreme Court's decision in *John Kelley Co. v. Comm.*, 46-1 USTC ¶9133, 34 AFTR 314, 326 U.S. 521 (USSC, 1946), the Tax Court bestowed debt status notwithstanding ratios that were far greater than 4:1. In Kelley's companion case, *Talbot Mills*, the Court, in stating that a 4:1 ratio was not "obviously excessive," provided a benchmark of sorts for about a decade. Later decisions, however, indicated that there was no "magic" ratio and consequently no discernible pattern developed. The Regulations that were proposed contained certain safe harbor ratios. For example, straight debt was classified as debt where the ratio is less than 3:1.

virtually all of the risk is borne by creditors. In such situations, repayment of the debt is so linked with the fortunes of the business—since there are no other sources for payment—that it must be said that it represents risk capital and warrants recharacterization as stock.

The fact that shareholders hold debt in the same proportion as they hold stock (e.g., a 60% shareholder holds 60% of the debt) normally raises a strong inference that the shareholders never intended to act like creditors. Accordingly, the courts have been willing to reclassify the instrument. This inference stems from the theory that a shareholder-creditor who holds debt in a greater proportion than stock (e.g., 70% debt, 30% stock) is more likely to act like a creditor and exercise his or her legal right to recover the excess should circumstances warrant.

Example 39

When J and K incorporated their business, J contributed 60% of the funds while K contributed the other 40%. For his contribution J received 30 shares of stock worth $30,000 and a $24,000 demand note while K received 20 shares of stock worth $20,000 and a $16,000 demand note. Thus, J received 60% of the stock (30 ÷ 50) and 60% of the debt ($24,000 [$24,000 + $16,000]) while K received 40% of the stock (20 ÷ 50) and 40% of the debt ($16,000 ÷ [$24,000 + $16,000]). After several years of operations, it became evident that the business could fail. At that time, the corporation had $20,000 in cash and some equipment that had no value if the business ceased. Its only liabilities included the two notes to J and K. In this situation, neither J nor K has an incentive to act like a creditor since their holdings in stock are identical to those in debt. J and K would share the remaining assets in the same 60–40 split regardless of whether they exercised their legal rights as creditors. On the other hand, if their holdings were disproportionate (e.g., J owned 80% of the debt and 20% of the stock while K owned 20% of the debt and 80% of the stock), it is unlikely that J would abandon his creditor rights since to do so would severely reduce his recovery.

The conclusion to be drawn from the previous example is merely this: disproportionate holdings support a debtor-creditor relationship while proportionate holdings do not.[69] The converse is not necessarily true, however. Proportionate holdings are not conclusive evidence that the debt is equity since considering them as such would deny the principle that an investor can be both a shareholder and a creditor. For example, if debt were always treated as stock when proportional holdings existed, a one-person corporation could never make a "loan" to his or her corporation since shareholder debt and equity would always be held in the same proportion. Therefore, proportional holdings normally must be coupled with some other factor such as an unreasonably high interest rate before the instrument is reclassified.[70] The high interest rate would simply add further credence to the need for reclassification since it suggests the shareholder was using the debt to bail earnings out of the corporation.

LOSSES ON STOCK AND DEBT INVESTMENTS

As most individuals who form corporations know, not all businesses succeed. When a corporation is unprofitable, the failure ultimately must be borne by those who provided the capital (i.e., the holders of the corporation's debt or stock). For this reason, an investor must understand the tax consequences resulting from losses on stock or debt and use this knowledge in choosing between them.

An investor's losses may be classified into four categories: (1) worthless securities (i.e., stock and certain types of debt), (2) business and nonbusiness bad debts, (3) losses on sale of stock and debt, and (4) losses on § 1244 stock. Each of these are discussed below.

---

[69] See, for example, *Wachovia Bank & Trust Co. v. U.S.*, 61-1 USTC ¶9362, 7 AFTR2d 1071, 288 F.2d 750 (CA-4, 1961).

[70] *Piedmont Corp. v. Comm.*, 68-1 USTC ¶9189, 21 AFTR2d 534, 388 F.2d 886 (CA-4. 1968).

Worthless Securities

When a security becomes worthless, special rules govern the loss.[71] These rules apply only to those items satisfying the definition of security. The term security means stock, stock rights, bonds, debentures, or any other evidence of indebtedness issued by a corporation or the government with interest coupons or in registered form.[72] In addition, the security must be considered a capital asset before the special rules apply. If a qualifying security becomes worthless at any time during the year, the resulting loss is treated as arising from the sale or exchange of a capital asset on the last day of the taxable year. Therefore, losses from worthlessness are treated as either short- or long-term capital losses.

Example 40

M incorporated her business on November 1, 2016, receiving 100 shares of stock. The stock had a basis of $25,000. On July 1, 2017, seven months after M acquired her stock, the corporation declared bankruptcy. Since the stock is worthless, M has a capital loss of $25,000. In addition, the loss is considered long-term since the holding period exceeds one year—November 1, 2016 to December 31, 2017, the day on which the hypothetical sale is deemed to occur. Due to the limitations on deductions of capital losses, M may deduct a maximum of $3,000 (assuming she has no capital gains) and the unused loss of $22,000 could be carried over until it is exhausted.

As noted within, however, if stock qualifies as § 1244 stock the loss on worthlessness may be ordinary. Another variation in the general treatment permits ordinary loss treatment for a corporation where the securities are in certain affiliated corporations—generally an 80% owned subsidiary that has less than 10% of its receipts from passive sources.

Bad Debts

If a debt does not meet the definition of a security (e.g., securities such as bonds), a loss due to worthlessness is governed by the rules for bad debts.[73] The tax treatment depends on whether it is a business or a nonbusiness bad debt. Business bad debts that are totally or partially worthless may be deducted as ordinary losses. In contrast, a nonbusiness bad debt can only be deducted when it is totally worthless and is always treated as a short-term capital loss.

Given the significantly different treatments accorded business and nonbusiness bad debts, the distinction between the two is very important. According to the Code, a debt is considered a business bad debt only if it is incurred by a corporation or is created or acquired in connection with the taxpayer's trade or business.[74] The imprecision of this definition has led to a great deal of litigation.

The most perplexing problem in this area concerns shareholder advances. It is very common in a closely held corporation where business is suffering for shareholders to periodically lend the corporation funds on open account. If the loans subsequently become worthless, the shareholder attempts to characterize the loans as arising from a trade or business so that an ordinary loss can be claimed. To the dismay of many shareholders, the Supreme Court has held that a shareholder who is merely an investor is not considered as being in a trade or business.[75] Thus, the loan is considered a nonbusiness bad debt and treated as a short-term capital loss.

Although the Supreme Court's ruling settled the turmoil when the shareholder is only an investor, controversy still exists when a shareholder is also an employee or has some other type of business relationship with the corporation. For example, numerous cases have held that when the motive for the loan by the shareholder-employee is to protect his or her employment with the corporation and thus maintain a salary, the debt is considered as arising from the taxpayer's trade or business.[76]

---

[71] § 165(g).

[72] § 165(g)(2). Observe that a simple note payable is not a security.

[73] § 166.

[74] § 166(d)(2).

[75] *A.J. Whipple v. Comm.*, 63-1 USTC ¶9466, 11 AFTR2d 1454, 373 U.S. 193 (USSC 1963).

[76] See, for example, *John M. Trent v. Comm.* 61-2 USTC ¶9506, AFTR2d 1599, 291 F.2d 669 (CA-2, 1961). See *U.S. v. Edna Generes*, 72-1 USTC ¶9259, 29 AFTR2d 72-609, 405 U.S. 93 (USSC, 1972) where the Supreme Court held that job protection must be the dominant motivation for the loan.

SECTION 1244 STOCK

Absent special rules, the $3,000 limitation on deductions for capital losses would discourage investment in new corporations. For example, if an individual invested $30,000 in a new corporation's stock and the stock became worthless, it could take as long as ten years to deduct the loss. In contrast, a sole proprietor or partner is able to directly recover the worthless investment without limitation. In 1958 Congress addressed these problems by enacting § 1244. Under § 1244, losses on "Section 1244 stock" generally are treated as ordinary rather than capital losses.

Eligible Shareholders

Ordinary loss treatment is available only to *individuals* who are the *original* holders of the stock, including individuals who were partners in a partnership when the partnership originally purchased the stock.[77] If these persons transfer the stock (e.g., sell, give, devise, or in the case of a partnership, distribute the stock to its partners), the § 1244 advantage does not transfer to the subsequent holder.

Ordinary Loss Limitation

If § 1244 stock is sold at a loss or the stock becomes worthless, the taxpayer may deduct up to $50,000 annually as an ordinary loss.[78] Taxpayers who file a joint return may deduct up to $100,000 regardless of whether the stock is owned jointly or separately. When the loss in any one year exceeds the $50,000 or $100,000 limitation, the excess is considered a capital loss subject to normal restrictions. Note that gains on the sale of § 1244 stock are treated in the normal fashion.

Example 41

K, married, is one of the original purchasers of WNK Corporation's stock, which qualifies for special treatment under § 1244. She separately purchased the stock two years ago for $150,000. During the year, she sold all of the stock for $30,000 resulting in a $120,000 loss. On her joint return for the current year, she may deduct $100,000 as an ordinary loss. The portion of the loss exceeding the limitation, $20,000 ($120,000 − $100,000), is treated as a long-term capital loss. Assuming K has no capital gains, she may deduct $3,000 of the remaining loss and carryover $17,000 ($20,000 − $3,000) as a long-term capital loss to the following year.

Without some special provision, § 1244 would enable a taxpayer to convert a capital loss into an ordinary loss. For example, assume a taxpayer owns a capital asset that has a basis of $30,000 and a value of $20,000. If the individual shareholder sold the asset, he or she would recognize a $10,000 capital loss. Assume instead that the shareholder transferred the property to a corporation in exchange for § 1244 stock. The basis of the stock would be $30,000. If the taxpayer subsequently sold the stock for $5,000, an ordinary loss of $25,000 would be recognized under § 1244, and the taxpayer would have successfully converted the $10,000 capital loss into an ordinary loss. To prohibit this scheme, the taxpayer is required to reduce the basis of the § 1244 stock to the value of the property at the time of the transfer.[79] If this principle had been applied in the illustration above, the taxpayer would have a § 1244 loss of $15,000 ($5,000 − $20,000), and the remaining $10,000 loss would be a capital loss. Note that the capital loss has been preserved.

---

[77] Reg. § 1.1244(a)-1(b).

[78] § 1244(b)(1).

[79] § 1244(d)(1).

Section 1244 Stock Defined

Stock issued by a corporation qualifies as § 1244 stock only if certain requirements are satisfied. As a practical matter, these conditions are easily met and § 1244 treatment is automatic for a limited amount of stock issued. As a general rule, § 1244 treatment applies when a domestic corporation issues stock for money or property and the corporation is (1) a "small business corporation" when the stock is issued, and (2) an "operating company" when the shareholder's loss is sustained.[80]

Stock for Money and Property

Section 1244 treatment is available only for stock that is issued for money and property other than stock or securities. For this purpose, stock includes common stock and preferred stock (if such preferred stock was issued after July 18, 1984). It should be emphasized that this rule precludes favorable treatment for stock issued for services or convertible securities. In addition, further contributions to capital that increase a shareholder's stock are not treated as allocable to the § 1244 stock.

Small Business Corporation

The corporation must qualify as a small business corporation (SBC) at the time the stock was issued for § 1244 to apply.[81] A corporation is an SBC if its total capitalization (amounts received for stock issued, contributions to capital, and paid-in surplus) does not exceed $1 million. In determining the corporation's capitalization, the amount of stock issued for property is determined by using the property's adjusted basis reduced by any liability to which the property is subject or which is assumed by the corporation. This requirement effectively limits § 1244 treatment to those individuals who originally invest the first $1 million in money and property in the corporation.

Example 42

In 2016, R and S provided the initial capitalization for CBT Corporation. R purchased 600 shares at a cost of $1,000 a share for a total cost of $600,000. S transferred property worth $200,000 (basis of $125,000) that was subject to a mortgage of $50,000 in exchange for 150 shares of stock worth $150,000. In 2017, R and S convinced their good friend T to purchase 500 shares of stock at a cost of $1,000 per share or a total of $500,000. All of the shares of both R and S qualify since the amount received for stock by the corporation, $675,000 ($600,000 cash + property with an adjusted basis of $125,000 – the liability of $50,000), did not exceed $1 million. Only 325 of T's shares qualify for § 1244 treatment, however, since 175 of the 500 purchased were issued when the corporation's total capitalization exceeded $1 million.

It should be emphasized that the corporation need not be an SBC at the time the shareholder incurs the loss. SBC status is required only when the shareholder receives the stock.

Operating Company

Another condition that must be satisfied before § 1244 applies concerns the nature of the corporation's activities. The corporation must be considered an *operating company* at the time the shareholder incurs the loss.[82] A corporation is treated as an operating company if at least 50% of its gross receipts for the five most recent taxable years (or the years it has been in existence if less) ending before the date of the loss are derived from sources *other than* royalties, rents, dividends, interest, annuities, and gains from sales or exchanges of stocks or securities. Without this rule, a taxpayer could convert a loss, which normally would be a capital loss if suffered in an individual capacity, into an ordinary loss. This requirement is ignored when a corporation's deductions for the test period—other than the dividends-received deduction and the deduction for net operating losses—exceed its gross income.[83]

---

[80] § 1244(c). Special rules apply for stock issued before November 7, 1978.

[81] § 1244(c)(3).

[82] § 1244(c)(1)(C).

[83] § 1244(c)(2)(C).

QUALIFIED SMALL BUSINESS STOCK

A discussion of the capital structure of a corporation would not be complete without addressing a special tax incentive created to stimulate investment in small businesses. In 1994, Congress enacted § 1202, which normally allows noncorporate investors (i.e., individuals, partnerships, estates, and trusts) to exclude 50% of the gain on the sale of *qualified small business stock* (QSB stock or § 1202 stock) held for more than five years. Stock is considered QSB stock if it was issued after August 10, 1993 and meets a long list of requirements.

1. At the time the stock is issued, the corporation issuing the stock must be a *qualified small business*. A corporation is a qualified small business if:
    *   The corporation is a domestic C corporation. Stock in an S corporation does not qualify.
    *   The corporation's gross assets do not exceed $50 million (i.e., cash plus the fair market value of contributed property measured at the time of contribution plus the adjusted basis of other assets). For this purpose, a parent-subsidiary controlled group (using a 50% test rather than an 80% test) is treated as one corporation.

2. The seller is the original owner of the stock.

3. The stock is issued for money, property other than stock, or as compensation for services (other than underwriting).

4. During substantially all of the seller's holding period of the stock, the corporation was engaged in an active trade or business other than the following:
    *   A business involving the performance of providing services in the fields of health, law, engineering, architecture, accounting, actuarial science, performing arts, consulting, athletics, financial services, brokerage services, or any other business where the principal asset is the reputation or skill of one or more of its employees.
    *   Banking, insurance, financing, leasing, or investing.
    *   Farming.
    *   Businesses involving the production or extraction of products eligible for depletion.
    *   Business of operating a hotel, motel, or restaurant.

5. The corporation generally cannot own:
    *   Real property with a value that exceeds 10% of its total assets unless such property is used in the active conduct of a trade or business (e.g., rental real estate is not an active trade or business).
    *   Portfolio stock or securities with a value that exceeds 10% of the corporation's total assets in excess of its liabilities.

Note that the active trade or business requirement and the prohibition on real estate holdings severely limits the exclusion. These conditions effectively grant the exclusion to corporations engaged in manufacturing, retailing, or wholesaling businesses.

The new provision also imposes a restriction, albeit a liberal one, on the amount of gain eligible to be excluded on the sale of a particular corporation's stock. The maximum amount of gain that may be excluded on the sale of one corporation's stock is the *larger* of:

1. $10 million reduced by previously excluded gain on the sale of such corporation's stock; or

2. 10 times the adjusted basis of all qualified stock of the corporation that the taxpayer sold during the tax year.

In determining the taxpayers' net capital gain and capital losses, any gain excluded on the sale of § 1202 stock is not taken into account. For example, assume a taxpayer sells § 1202 stock for a gain of $60,000 and regular stock for a long-term capital loss of $40,000. The excluded gain of $30,000 is removed from the calculation prior to netting, and the taxpayer reports a long-term capital loss of $10,000 ($30,000 − $40,000). Also note that one-half of the *excluded* gain (one-fourth of the entire gain) is a tax preference item for purposes of the alternative minimum tax. In addition, the excluded gain is generally not considered investment income for purposes of determining the investment interest limitation.

Treatment of Gain

Normally taxpayers may exclude 50% of the gain on § 1202 stock. However, the exclusion is increased to 75% for QSB stock acquired after February 17, 2009 and before September 28, 2010 and to 100% for QSB stock acquired after September 27, 2010 and before January 1, 2014. Also note that the lower rates for long-term capital gains (0, 15, or 20 percent) are not available for § 1202 stock. Instead half of the gain is taxed at a rate of 28% (or the taxpayer's ordinary rate if lower). In some situations, taxpayers might pay less tax if the full gain was taxed at the lower rates rather that half of the gain at 28 percent. But, application of § 1202 is not elective. However, as a practical matter, taxpayers could secure the lower rate by intentionally failing the five year holding period.

Rollover Provision

Perhaps the most important aspect of § 1202 stock is the ability for the taxpayer to postpone gain realized on the sale of stock. Under § 1045, if an individual realizes a gain on the sale of such stock held for six months, he or she can defer recognition of the gain if the sales proceeds are used to purchase other QSB stock. In such case, the taxpayer's basis in the newly acquired QSB stock is its cost reduced by the deferred gain.

Basis of Qualified Small Business Stock

The addition of § 1202 creates a new wrinkle in the basis calculation for stock received in a § 351 exchange when the stock received is qualified small business stock. When qualified stock is received for property other than money or stock, the basis of the stock received *for purposes of determining the amount eligible for exclusion* is no less than the fair market value of the stock at the time of acquisition [§ 1202(i)]. This rule prohibits taxpayers from transferring appreciated property to a corporation, selling the stock, and effectively obtaining the exclusion for appreciation that accrued prior to contribution of the property and formation of the corporation.

Example 43

This year R formed a new corporation, transferring property worth $100,000 (basis $20,000) in exchange for all of the stock of the corporation. After holding the stock for the required holding period of more than five years, R sold the stock for $150,000. Under the general rule, R's basis in the stock is a substituted basis of $20,000 and, consequently, he would recognize a long-term capital gain on the sale of $130,000 ($150,000 − $20,000). In this case, however, the stock is considered qualified small business stock since R was the original owner of the stock and the company's gross assets at the time the stock was issued did not exceed $50 million. Therefore, a portion of the gain is eligible for the 50% exclusion. For purposes of determining the amount of gain that may be excluded, the basis is no less than the fair market value of the stock at the time it was acquired or $100,000. As a result, the amount eligible for the 50% exclusion is $50,000 ($150,000 − $100,000) and R may exclude $25,000 (50% × $50,000). Thus, R reports a long-term capital gain of $105,000 ($130,000 − $25,000). Note that the $105,000 consists of the $80,000 of appreciation that had accrued on the contributed property prior to its contribution to the corporation and one-half of the appreciation, $25,000 (50% × $50,000), accruing after the stock was received. Also note that the gain that had accrued on the property prior to its contribution to the corporation, $80,000 ($100,000 − $20,000), was not eligible for exclusion. Only the gain that accrued after incorporation, $50,000, qualified for the special exclusion.

TAXABLE VERSUS NONTAXABLE TRANSFERS TO CONTROLLED CORPORATIONS

At the beginning of this chapter, it was noted that there were various ways to transfer property to a corporation. This chapter went to great lengths exploring § 351, which generally enables a taxpayer to transfer property without consequences. In certain situations, however, the taxpayer may find that greater benefits can be obtained by avoiding § 351 and making the transfer a taxable transaction. For example, a taxpayer may desire to recognize a loss on property that is to be transferred to a corporation.

Example 44

J has decided to transfer assets to a new corporation. Among the assets he plans to transfer is equipment, which has a basis of $10,000 but is only worth $3,000. If J transfers the equipment in a wholly nontaxable transaction under § 351, the potential loss on the equipment will not be recognized currently but will be depreciated over the next few years. On the other hand, if the transaction were taxable, J could recognize the loss immediately.

Another situation where the taxpayer historically has reaped rewards by avoiding § 351 involves appreciated property. In the typical scenario, the taxpayer traded recognition of gain—minimized through use of the capital gain and installment sales provisions—for a step-up in the basis of property. Moreover, assuming the taxpayer received debt on the exchange, all of the advantages of debt were also secured.

Example 45

About 15 years ago, R purchased land for $10,000. Over the years, the land has continued to appreciate and R now estimates that the land, with some development (roads, sewers, etc.), could be subdivided and sold for a total of $510,000. Although the land currently constitutes a capital asset in R's hands, if he were to subdivide it and sell the lots, any income would most probably be ordinary income. R might convert the ordinary income into favorable capital gain by establishing a corporation that would purchase and develop the land. R, along with other investors, could organize a corporation to which he would then sell the property for $510,000. In payment, the corporation would give R a note payable for the entire sales price. The note would be payable in installments over four years. The corporation would develop, subdivide, and sell the land. By following these steps, R achieves substantial tax savings. Although he sold the land to the corporation and must recognize gain, the entire gain is capital gain taxed at 15% instead of 39.6 percent. In addition, assuming the installment sales method is used, the gain will be reported ratably over the four years that he receives the note payments. If the corporation sells the land for what it is worth, $510,000, it recognizes no gain since its basis in the land is its cost, $510,000. Lastly, by selling the land for debt R has created a vehicle for obtaining cash out of his corporation via deductible interest payments and tax-free payments of principal. These interest payments essentially replace dividends that otherwise might have been necessary to obtain the cash from the corporation.

Example 46

Assume the same facts as above, except that the property transferred is an apartment complex which currently generates substantial taxable income. In this case, R increased his basis of depreciable property at the cost of a capital gains tax which—like that in the situation above—is reduced by deferring it over the installment period. By so doing, R may benefit through increased depreciation deductions which reduce the taxable income produced by the property. R has also maintained his ownership of the property so that he can further benefit if it continues to appreciate.

As the above examples illustrate, a taxable transfer may pay handsomely. Taxpayers usually avert nonrecognition in one of three ways: (1) selling the property to the corporation—usually for debt, (2) exchanging the property in a § 351 transaction in which boot received (e.g., securities) causes recognition, and (3) exchanging the property with the corporation when § 351 does not apply [e.g., the transferor(s) do not have the requisite 80% control]. These plans are far from fail safe, however. Before examining the tax risks of each of the three taxable transfers, two preliminary considerations must be addressed.

Transfers to Related Parties

When the taxpayer attempts to recognize gain or loss on the transfer of property to a corporation, the initial hurdles are §§ 1239 and 267—the former applying where appreciated property is sold to the corporation and the latter where the property has declined in value. As previously discussed, § 1239 causes the gain on the sale of depreciable property (including patents) between a taxpayer and his or her more than 50% owned corporation to be treated as ordinary income.[84] In addition, § 453(g) provides that the installment sales method cannot be used when the sale is between "related parties" as defined in § 1239 (i.e., a taxpayer and his or her more than 50% owned corporation). But notice that §§ 1239 and 453(g) are ineffective as long as the taxpayer is not treated as owning more than 50% of the stock.

Example 47

Assume the same facts as in *Example 46,* above. R could collaborate with another unrelated individual, say S, to develop the land. S might contribute sufficient cash or other property to the newly formed corporation for 50% or more of the stock. If he does, R receives 50% or less of the stock and § 1239 does not apply to his sale—thus, capital gain and an installment sale are assured.

Further, the installment sales method can be used when it can be established that none of the principal purposes of the sale was tax avoidance. Thus, if the taxpayer can show a good business reason for the sale, the installment sales technique is still available.

When the taxpayer sells property hoping to recognize a loss, § 267 may cause difficulty. It might be remembered that this provision in part prohibits the taxpayer from deducting any losses on sales between the taxpayer and his or her more than 50% owned corporation. Like § 1239, however, this provision is defeated when the taxpayer does not own, actually or constructively, more than 50% of the corporation.

The Code provides yet another pitfall that clearly reduces the advantage of an installment sale in this and other situations. Section 453(i) requires that gain must be recognized on the installment sale in the year of the sale to the extent of any recapture income under §§ 1245, 1250, and 291. Such treatment applies *regardless* of the amount that is received during the year of sale. This rule effectively accelerates to the sale year the recognition of gain that otherwise would be deferred. As a result, the cost of obtaining a step-up in basis may be substantially increased in the case of an installment sale of depreciable property.

---

[84] Note that § 1239 does not apply to sales of land. In contrast, compare § 1239 to § 707(b) for partnerships that normally causes gains on the sales of all property to be treated as ordinary.

Sales to a Controlled Corporation

Since a sale is normally structured so that the transferor-seller receives debt on the exchange—enabling installment recognition of gain—the transaction risks being treated as tax-free under § 351. This can occur if the debt is considered stock. Such treatment spells disaster for the taxpayer. Under § 351, the basis of the property carries over to the corporation and, without the step-up in basis, potential capital gain benefits and higher depreciation deductions are lost.

Notwithstanding the fact that the transaction is structured as a sale, § 351 may apply because in effect the seller is exchanging property for what may be considered stock of the corporation. Recall that § 351 requires nonrecognition when stock is received by the transferor. Whether § 351 is ultimately applied, however, normally depends on whether the debt received by the seller can be considered stock.

Example 48

In *Aqualane Shores*, three individuals transferred $600 to a corporation in exchange for all of its stock.[85] Immediately thereafter, the three sold appreciated land to the corporation for notes of about $192,000 which were to be paid by the corporation in five equal installments. The corporation developed, subdivided, and sold the land as residential property. Upon audit of the corporation, the IRS challenged the amount of income reported, asserting that the basis of the land should have been the lower basis of the individuals since the "purported sale" was truly a nontaxable exchange under § 351. The court agreed with the IRS, suggesting that the debt of the corporation was truly stock. In so doing, it emphasized that the corporation was undercapitalized and had failed to pay the installments on the notes when due.

Transfers for Boot

The above technique relied on sale treatment to make the transaction taxable. In using that method, the taxpayer attempts to avoid § 351. Another technique, however, generally achieves the same result within the confines of § 351. According to this plan, the transferor simply exchanges his or her property under § 351 for boot—usually short-term notes.[86] Short-term notes are used because there is less likelihood that they might be considered stock. This method does not achieve the desired result when loss property is transferred to the corporation since losses are not recognized under § 351.

Transfers Not Qualifying under § 351

Still another technique involves not satisfying the requirements of § 351. For example, if property is transferred and those who made the transfer do not own 80% of the stock of the corporation immediately after the exchange, the transaction is taxable since § 351's control test is not met.[87] In this situation, the transfer is taxable just as if the taxpayer had sold the property to the corporation.

APPRECIATED PROPERTY: TRANSFER VERSUS LEASE

The previous section and much of this chapter has often concerned itself with or made reference to the transfer or sale of *appreciated* property to a corporation. Despite this attention, such transfers to a C corporation may be extremely unwise. In fact, a contribution of property that has appreciated or is expected to appreciate in the future may lead to disastrous tax consequences. The problem arises when the corporation later sells the property and distributes the after-tax proceeds to the shareholders. In such case, the gain on the sale

[85] 59-2 USTC ¶9632, 4 AFTR2d 5346; 269 F.2d 116 (CA-5, 1959); also see *Burr Oaks Corp. v. Comm.*, 66-2 USTC ¶9506, 18 AFTR2d 5018, 365 F.2d 24 (CA-4, 1966); for cases where the taxpayer was victorious in this area see *Sun Properties, Inc.*, 55-1 USTC ¶9261, 47 AFTR 273, 220 F.2d 171 (CA-5, 1955).

[86] The taxpayer was successful in using this approach in *Jolana S. Bradshaw v. U.S.*, 82-2 USTC ¶9454, 50 AFTR2d, 82-5238, 683 F.2d 365 (Ct. Cls., 1982).

[87] See *Granite Trust Co. v. U.S.*, 57-1 USTC ¶9201, 50 AFTR 763, 238 F.2d 670 (CA-1, 1957).

of the property is taxed twice: once at the corporate level and again when the proceeds are distributed to the shareholder as a dividend or in liquidation (see Chapters 3 and 5). For this reason, current wisdom suggests that shareholders personally own property, particularly real estate, and lease the property to the corporation. Leasing property to the corporation rather than transferring it not only avoids the problem of double taxation but provides other benefits as well.

- Leasing provides one of the same benefits as debt: it gives the taxpayer a technique for withdrawing capital from the corporation. Rental payments on the lease may be deducted by the corporation; hence, double taxation is avoided.

- A leasing arrangement can be structured to produce passive income or loss. In the early years of a lease, rental income normally is adequate to pay operating expenses and satisfy debt payments, resulting in before-tax break-even cash flow. However, depreciation of the property will provide passive deductions that can be used to the extent of the $25,000 allowance or to offset passive income. If the property appreciates and the corporate business is profitable, the rental income can be increased, producing passive income that can absorb passive losses from other sources.

- New businesses that lose money during the first years of operations often cannot use the additional deductions that owning the property may produce. Shareholders-lessors may secure immediate benefits from the deductions if they own and lease the property.

At the point when the leased property no longer produces benefits to the shareholder-lessor (e.g., the asset is fully depreciated), the property becomes a perfect vehicle to shift income to lower-bracket family members. The property may be given to the family member or a trust for the benefit of the family member and subsequently leased to the corporation. By so doing, the shareholder-lessor shifts rental income to the family member (or trust), where it is taxed at a lower rate.

SECTION 351 ECONOMICS AND PRECONTRIBUTION ALLOCATIONS

Taxpayers must also give attention to any difference between the basis of the property that they transfer to the corporation and its fair market value. Most individuals who contribute properties that have a value equivalent to properties from their fellow contributors are satisfied if they receive an equivalent value of stock. For example, if K transfers $10,000 cash to a corporation while L transfers property worth $10,000 (basis $3,000), it would not be unlikely for both to receive 50% of the corporation's stock. However, this would be an inequitable allocation of the stock. In effect, K has purchased a 50% interest in the property transferred to the corporation by L and consequently should enjoy the tax benefits from that property (e.g., depreciation) *as if* it had a basis of $10,000 (or $5,000 with respect to him [50% of $10,000]). Since the tax basis of the property carries over to the corporation, K effectively benefits from a basis of $1,500 rather than $5,000. Consequently, some adjustment should be made to take into account the inequity which results from the difference between the transferor's basis in the property and its fair market value.

Problem Materials

DISCUSSION QUESTIONS

2-1 *Considerations When Incorporating.* During the year, J decided to incorporate her boutique, which she has operated as a sole proprietorship for several years. The business has various assets including a building, office equipment, accounts receivable, and inventory. Prepare a list of tax-related issues that should be discussed with J concerning the incorporation of her business.

2-2 *Rationale for § 351.* Discuss briefly the theory underlying the nonrecognition treatment provided for transfers to controlled corporations.

2-3 *Section 351: Requirements.* Identify the general conditions that must be satisfied before nonrecognition is permitted on an exchange of assets for stock of a corporation.

2-4 *Service Shareholders.* During the year, R and S formed C Corporation. For each of the following independent situations, indicate whether § 351 applies to the exchange.
  a. R contributed property worth $70,000 (basis $50,000) in exchange for 70 shares of stock and S contributed services worth $30,000 in exchange for 30 shares of stock.
  b. R contributed property worth $70,000 (basis $50,000) in exchange for 70 shares of stock and S contributed services worth $25,000 for 25 shares of stock in addition to property worth $5,000 for 5 shares of stock.
  c. R contributed property worth $70,000 (basis $50,000) in exchange for 70 shares of stock and S contributed services worth $29,000 for 29 shares in addition to cash of $1,000 for 1 share.

2-5 *Contributions of Services in Exchange for Stock.* P and Q formed a new corporation this year. P contributed property and Q contributed services.
  a. What is the maximum percentage of the outstanding stock that Q may receive if P's exchange of property is to qualify for nonrecognition under § 351?
  b. Under what circumstances could Q receive a greater percentage of stock for services than specified above?

2-6 *Control Test: General Rules.* Indicate whether § 351 applies to the following exchanges.
  a. This year, M, N, and O formed R Corporation. Each contributed property in exchange for 60, 30, and 10 shares of R stock, respectively.
  b. Two years after the formation of R Corporation, M transferred additional property in exchange for 100 more shares of stock.

2-7 *Section 351 versus Section 721.* Below is the Code section governing the transfers of property to a partnership, § 721. It is the counterpart of § 351 in the partnership area.

Section 721. Nonrecognition of gain or loss on contribution

(a) General rule. No gain or loss shall be recognized to a partnership or to any of its partners in the case of a contribution of property to the partnership in exchange for an interest in the partnership.

Assume you were starting a small business and expected to admit new investors from time to time. Based on your reading of § 721 above and your knowledge of § 351, which entity, a C corporation, an S corporation, or a partnership, would make more sense (i.e., provide more flexibility)? Explain.

2-8 *Solely Stock.* S transferred appreciated property to a newly created corporation for 60% of its stock while T transferred appreciated property for 40% of the stock and the corporation's 20-year note, payable in equal installments with 10% interest.
  a. Does § 351 apply to either of these exchanges?
  b. How may T report any gain to be recognized from this exchange?

2-9 *Immediately after the Exchange.* R, S, and T all transferred property to JOB Corp. In exchange, each individual received 50 shares of stock. R and S contributed their assets in early January of the current year, and T transferred her assets near the end of March.
  a. Does § 351 apply to any of these exchanges?
  b. Why might T have waited to make her transfer?

2-10 *Property Requirement.* T is considering transferring the following to a new corporation in exchange for stock. Which of these items do not qualify as property under § 351?
  a. Building
  b. Machinery
  c. Inventory
  d. Services
  e. Patent
  f. Note receivable from X

2-11 *Exchange for Stock.* Below is a list of items that a corporation may transfer to a prospective shareholder. Indicate which items would cause gain recognition to the transferor, assuming the exchange otherwise qualifies under § 351?
   a. Preferred stock of the transferee corporation.
   b. Rights to purchase stock of the transferee corporation.
   c. Twenty-year note of the transferee corporation, payable in equal installments with 10% interest.
   d. Convertible bonds of the transferee corporation.
   e. Money.

2-12 *Avoiding § 351.* Under what circumstances might a transferor deliberately violate the provisions of § 351?

2-13 *Transfer of Liabilities.* Indicate whether the following statements are true or false, assuming a transferor contributes liabilities to a corporation as part of a § 351 exchange. If the statement is false, explain why.
   a. The transfer of liabilities normally is not treated as boot received for purposes of computing gain recognized on the transfer.
   b. The transfer of liabilities normally is not treated as boot received for purposes of computing basis of property received.
   c. The transfer of liabilities causes any gain realized to be recognized to the extent total liabilities exceed the total basis of the assets transferred.
   d. The transfer of any liabilities incurred without business purpose or for the purpose of avoiding taxes causes all liabilities to be treated as boot for purposes of gain recognition.
   e. If the liabilities transferred exceeded the aggregate basis of the assets transferred and were incurred for the purpose of avoiding taxes, the liabilities are treated as boot.
   f. Liabilities of a cash basis taxpayer do not include accounts payable which when paid would give rise to a deduction.

2-14 *Accommodation Exchange.* S's father, F, has agreed to admit him as a shareholder of the business for his contribution of appreciated property. S would receive 9% of the stock. However, S is unwilling to contribute the property if gain must be recognized. What steps might be taken to ensure that S does not recognize gain?

2-15 *Post-Transfer Dispositions.* G has decided to incorporate her sole proprietorship. She plans to give 25% of the stock to her daughter and sell 30% of the stock to an interested investor immediately after the business is incorporated. What tax risks might G encounter under this arrangement?

2-16 *Depreciation Recapture.* D incorporated his accounting practice this year receiving only stock on the exchange. As part of the incorporation transaction, he transferred a computer worth $5,000. Depreciation claimed by him prior to the transfer was $1,000. Two months after the transfer the corporation sold the computer, realizing a $2,500 gain. Briefly explain how the depreciation recapture provisions operate in this situation.

2-17 *Section 351 and Corporate Gain or Loss.* Indicate the effect, if any, on the corporation's taxable income as a result of the following:
   a. Corporation issues its own previously unissued stock to A in exchange for property in a transaction qualifying under § 351.
   b. Corporation issues its own previously unissued stock to A in exchange for property in a transaction not qualifying under § 351.
   c. Corporation issues its treasury stock to A in exchange for property in a transaction qualifying under § 351.
   d. Corporation issues its own previously unissued stock to A in exchange for legal services that A provided in conjunction with the incorporation transaction.

2-18 *Corporation's and Transferor's Bases and Holding Periods.* Briefly indicate how a transferor and a corporation determine bases and holding periods for property received in the following exchanges qualifying under § 351.

    a. Machine purchased December 3, 2013 is transferred to a corporation in exchange for stock on March 7, 2016.

    b. Legal services are provided to a corporation on May 5, 2016 in connection with the articles of incorporation. The transferor receives stock for the services on May 30, 2016.

    c. Inventory purchased June 6, 2016 is transferred to a corporation on December 20, 2016 in exchange for stock and a note payable in one year with 10% interest.

2-19 *Sale to an S Corporation.* J owns and operates a small delicatessen in downtown Chicago. The business is located in a 12-story building that J inherited in 2000. The building is located two blocks from a major convention center currently under construction. J's basis in the land and building is $25,000 but the property is currently worth $500,000. D is a real estate developer interested in renovating the building and converting it to a 600-room hotel. Recently he approached J about a joint venture where J would contribute the land and building and D would contribute the funds required for development. D expects operating losses in the first two years of business but profits thereafter. J and D have asked your advice on whether J should sell the property to a newly formed S corporation or exchange the property for the corporation's stock. Briefly discuss these two alternatives.

2-20 *Contributions to Capital.* JEL Inc., one of the new "high-tech" firms, relocated their headquarters to Metropolis this year because the city contributed $250,000 of seed money to the corporation for research. In addition, the city gave the corporation an office building.

    a. Discuss the tax consequences of the contributions to JEL.

    b. How would your answer in (a) above change if a group of JEL shareholders currently living in Metropolis had made the contributions?

2-21 *Comparison of Stock and Debt.* Prepare a list containing the advantages and disadvantages of using stock and debt in the capital structure of a corporation.

2-22 *Debt Recharacterization.* Answer the following questions:

    a. Outline the circumstances when debt is highly suspect and likely to be reclassified as stock.

    b. Explain what is meant when a corporation is said to be "thinly capitalized."

    c. Briefly discuss the tax consequences if the corporation's debt is reclassified as stock.

2-23 *Losses: Stock versus Debt.* Q and R incorporated their partnership two years ago, each receiving 50 shares of stock and a 10-year note which is payable in equal installments with 13% interest. To the dismay of Q and R, the economy slowed and the business crumbled. Both the stock and debt became worthless this year. Q and R are not only shareholders but also employees of the business.

    a. Discuss the tax consequences resulting from the losses on the debt and stock.

    b. Assume that Q advanced the corporation money on open account during the last six months of operations. His aim was to keep the business afloat. How should Q treat the worthless advances?

2-24 *Section 1244 Stock.*

    a. Explain the significance of owning "§ 1244" stock.

    b. G owns 100 shares of DSA Corp. stock that she received from sources described below. In each case indicate whether the shares received constitute § 1244 stock, assuming the stock qualified as § 1244 stock in the hands of the person from whom she received it.

        1. 20 shares inherited from her uncle.

        2. 35 shares given to her by her father.

        3. 15 shares purchased from C.

        4. 20 shares issued to G for a contribution of cash when the corporation's total capital was $300,000.

        5. 10 shares issued to G for a contribution of services to the corporation when the corporation's total capital was $300,000.

2-25 *Qualified Small Business Stock.* In each of the following situations indicate whether the stock is qualified small business stock in the hands of the purchaser.

    a. T purchased 100 shares of B&N Corporation stock when it was initially offered to the public. B&N's total assets at the time were $30 million.

    b. Dr. Payne incorporated his medical practice this year, transferring $100,000 of cash in exchange for all of the corporation's stock. The corporation immediately elected to be treated as an S corporation.

    c. When Symon Corporation went public, V purchased 100 shares. This year he sold them for a gain of $20,000. At the time V purchased the shares, the corporation was a major player in the appliance retail business. Over time, however, the slow economy forced the corporation to close many of its outlets (freestanding stores), which it subsequently leased to other businesses.

PROBLEMS

2-26 *Control Test Individuals.* M, N, and O quit their jobs this year and started a business selling and servicing lawn mowers and garden equipment.

    a. M contributed machinery worth $10,000 (basis $12,000) for 10 shares of stock and N contributed equipment worth $20,000 (basis $15,000) for 20 shares of stock. O agreed to be in charge of the service department and received 20 shares for services to be performed during the first year of business. Does the exchange qualify for special tax treatment provided by § 351?

    b. Same as (a), except that O received five shares.

2-27 *Corporate Formation—Services.* This year, F and G decided to organize FG, Inc. They received stock in exchange for the following asset contributions to the corporation:

Transferor	Contributed	Market Value	Transferor's Basis	Shares Received
F	Equipment	$50,000	$33,000	50
G	Cash	20,000	20,000	20

In addition, services were performed in exchange for 30 shares of stock worth $30,000. Compute (1) each transferor's recognized gain or income, (2) each transferor's basis in the stock, and (3) FG's basis in the assets for each of the following situations.

    a. Y performed the services involved in the incorporation of FG.

    b. Y performed the services two years after F and G made their contributions.

    c. F performed the services involved in the incorporation of FG.

    d. G performed the services involved in the incorporation of FG.

2-28 *Transfers to Controlled Corporations: Fundamentals.* During the year, A and B formed a new corporation. Each received 100 shares of stock for contributing the following assets:

Transferor	Property Transferred	Transferor's Basis	Fair Market Value
A	Cash	$100,000	$100,000
B	Land and building	20,000	70,000
	Equipment	40,000	30,000

    a. Compute the gain or loss realized and recognized by A and B.

    b. Compute the basis of the stock received by A and B.

    c. Compute the gain or loss recognized by the corporation.

    d. Compute the bases of the assets received by the corporation.

2-29 *Control—Additional Contributions.* Q owns 550 shares and Z owns 150 shares of QZ, Inc. Six years after QZ's formation, X contributes land ($60,000 market value and $20,000 basis) for 200 shares of QZ. At the same time, Q contributes $30,000 cash for an additional 100 shares of QZ. Determine the likely tax effects of these additional contributions.

2-30 *Corporate Formation.* F and V, retired carpenters, decided to organize the SWS Corporation which would build wooden swing sets for children. The items transferred and received were as follows:

Transferor	Asset Transferred	Market Value	Transferor's Basis	Shares Received
F	Equipment	$20,000	$18,000	50
V	Warehouse	25,000	10,000	50
	Mortgage on warehouse	5,000		

   a. Compute the gain or loss recognized by F and V.
   b. Compute the gain or loss recognized by SWS Inc.
   c. Compute the bases of the stock received by F and V.
   d. Compute the bases of the assets received by SWS Inc.

2-31 *Section 351 and Boot.* X Corporation was formed several years ago by Q and R to operate a custom T-shirt shop in Dayton. Each received 50 shares of stock. This year, Q and R decided to expand and bring in S, T, and U, who operated a similar shop in Toledo. To this end, the following investments were made by the new and existing shareholders.

Transferor	Property Transferred		Transferor's Basis	Fair Market Value	Received
S	Shirt inventory		$ 60,000	$110,000	100 shares, $10,000 cash
T	Land and building		74,000	80,000	70 shares, $10,000 cash
U	Embroidery equipment				30 shares, $10,000 cash
	Cost	$75,000			
	Depreciation	$ 9,000	66,000	40,000	
R	Cash		100,000	100,000	100 shares

   a. Does the transaction qualify for § 351 treatment?

   For the remaining questions, assume the transaction is eligible for § 351 treatment.
   b. Compute the gain or loss recognized by S, T, and U.
   c. Compute the bases of the stock received by S, T, and U.
   d. Compute the bases of the assets received by the corporation.

2-32 *Corporate Formation—Boot.* This year, E, H, and K decided to organize EHK, Inc. They received stock in exchange for the following asset contributions to the corporation:

Transferor	Property Contributed	Market Value	Transferor's Basis	Shares Received
E	Land	$70,000	$68,000	35
H	Patent	70,000	15,000	35
K	Equipment	60,000	80,000	30

   Compute (1) each transferor's recognized gain or loss, (2) each transferor's basis in the stock, and (3) EHK's basis in the assets for each for the following situations.
   a. All three exchanges were made simultaneously.
   b. All three exchanges were made simultaneously and each shareholder received a four-year note from EHK for $10,000 in lieu of five shares of stock. Equal note payments are to be made plus 10% interest each December 31.
   c. K's exchange occurred by an agreement made two years after the exchanges by E and H.

2-33 *Comprehensive Corporate Formation.* M's Diner Inc. (MDI) was formed by M, A, F, and V on April 1, 2016 to operate a restaurant. M transferred restaurant equipment worth $13,000 purchased by him on October 3, 2011 for $12,000. He had deducted $4,000 of depreciation. For her interest, A contributed a building (and the land on which it sat) in which the restaurant would be housed. The building was worth $25,000 (basis $13,000) and was subject to a $15,000 mortgage which was assumed by the corporation. No depreciation had been claimed on the building. F contributed tables and chairs that she had used in another venture. The furniture was worth $11,000 (basis $16,000). V provided legal services incident to the incorporation worth $10,000. Each individual received 100 shares of MDI stock worth $100 per share. In addition, M and F received notes payable in one year with 10% interest in the amount of $3,000 and $1,000, respectively.

   a. Does the transaction qualify as a nontaxable exchange? Explain.

   For the remaining questions, assume that the transfer qualifies for treatment under § 351 and all parties use the calendar year for tax purposes.

   b. Compute the gain or loss realized and recognized by each of the shareholders.
   c. Compute the basis of the stock and other property received by each of the shareholders.
   d. What effect does the exchange have on MDI's taxable income?
   e. Compute the basis of the property received by MDI.
   f. On what date does M's holding period begin for the stock he received?
   g. On what date does MDI's holding period begin for the restaurant equipment?
   h. Comment on the application of the depreciation recapture provisions to this transaction.

2-34 *Sections 357(b) and (c) Calculations.* M owns all of the stock of RCC Inc., a land development company. Two years ago M contributed land worth $150,000 (basis of $90,000 and subject to a $100,000 mortgage) to the corporation in exchange for stock worth $50,000. Upon audit this year, the IRS determined that M had mortgaged the property shortly before transferring it to the corporation. For this reason, the IRS asserted that the liability was incurred to avoid taxes and has proposed an adjustment to M's tax liability for the year of the transfer. Assuming M is in the 50% bracket, how much additional tax would be imposed if the IRS adjustment is ultimately upheld?

2-35 *Liabilities of Cash Basis.* Taxpayer Dr. Q has operated his medical practice as a sole proprietorship for the last two years. Like most individuals he uses the cash method of accounting. This year, he decided to incorporate his practice to take advantage of certain employee fringe benefits. He transferred the following assets and liabilities in exchange for all of the stock.

	Value
Cash	$1,000
Unrealized accounts receivable	8,000
Equipment	6,800
Accounts payable	4,000
Note payable on equipment	1,500

The equipment had a basis of $2,000. In addition, the accounts payable are all for routine deductible expenditures except a $200 bill from his attorney for services relating to the incorporation of his business.

   a. Is Dr. Q required to recognize any gain on the transfer?
   b. Compute Dr. Q's basis for his stock.

2-36 *Section 357(c) Liabilities.* During the year, D transferred the following assets and liabilities to his wholly owned corporation in exchange for stock worth $50,000.

Asset	Adjusted Basis	Fair Market Value
Land and warehouse.................	$90,000	$150,000
Mortgage on warehouse..............	0	(100,000)
Total	$90,000	$ 50,000

   a. Compute D's gain or loss realized.
   b. Compute D's gain or loss recognized.
   c. Compute the basis of the stock received by D.
   d. Compute the bases of the assets to the corporation.
   e. After being apprised of the tax consequences of the transfer described above, D is having second thoughts. How might any gain recognition above be avoided, assuming D still wants to contribute the land to the corporation?

2-37 *Section 357: Treatment of Liabilities.* Each of the transfers below qualifies as a § 351 transaction. In addition, the transferor is a cash basis taxpayer and the corporation assumes the liabilities involved in the transfer. For each transfer, compute the following:

   1. Transferor's recognized gain.
   2. Transferor's basis in the stock received.
   3. Corporation's basis in each asset received.

      a. R transfers land worth $120,000 (basis of $60,000) and subject to a mortgage of $20,000 in exchange for stock worth $100,000.
      b. S transfers a crane worth $120,000 (basis of $40,000) and a $50,000 note payable secured by the crane in exchange for stock worth $70,000.
      c. Same facts as (b) above, except that the note was created two weeks before the transfer and S used the proceeds to take his wife on a vacation to the Virgin Islands.
      d. T transfers accounts receivable worth $12,000, dental equipment with a basis of $15,000, a $10,000 note payable secured by the equipment, and routine accounts payable for lab bills of $7,000 for stock worth $50,000.

2-38 *Section 351 and Depreciation Recapture.* Several years ago, B transferred all of the assets of his sole proprietorship to a newly formed corporation in exchange for all of its stock. Among the assets contributed was equipment that B had purchased for $10,000 and for which he had claimed $2,000 of depreciation. Since the transfer, the corporation has claimed $1,500 of depreciation. This year, the corporation sold the asset for $14,000. Compute the corporation's gain recognized on the sale and its character.

2-39 *Contributions to Capital: Calculations.* MND Corp. recently announced its plan to close a fabrication plant in Terraville and build a new facility in another city. The plant closing would eliminate over 1,000 jobs. Since the economy of Terraville was closely tied to the plant's operations, the city government voted to give land worth $30,000 to MND that could be used as a site for a new structure. In addition, the Chamber of Commerce agreed to raise $200,000 which it would contribute to the corporation to apply to the construction cost of a new plant. Due to these actions by the city and the Chamber, MND decided to remain in Terraville. Assuming MND received the land and cash and constructed a plant for $900,000, what are the tax consequences?

2-40 *Depreciation of Contributed Property.* On October 1, 2016, K incorporated his rug cleaning business which he has operated for several years. As part of the incorporation, he transferred a truck which he had purchased for $5,000 in 2015 and for which he had claimed depreciation using MACRS percentages for five-year property of $1,000. On October 15, 2016 the corporation purchased a new van for $10,000. Both K and his corporation use the calendar year for tax purposes. (Ignore § 179 limited expensing.)

    a. Using the tables in Appendix H-3, compute the corporation's depreciation on the truck and the van for 2016.

    b. Assume that prior to October 2016 K had never been in business and the corporation acquired the truck for $5,000 and the van for $10,000 on October 15, 2016. Compute the depreciation on the two items for 2016.

    c. Same facts as (b) above, except the corporation purchased a building for $100,000 on October 15, 2016.

2-41 *Section 1244 Stock: Calculations.* Several years ago, S, single, contributed $210,000 cash to HJI, Inc. for 80 shares of § 1244 stock. This year, S sold the stock for $40,000. S's taxable income is $70,000, including a short-term capital gain of $1,000 but excluding the sale of HJI stock. What is S's taxable income after accounting for the HJI stock sale?

2-42 *Section 1244: Basis Problems.* M, who is single, transferred property worth $120,000 and a basis of $300,000 to Z Corporation in exchange for § 1244 stock. Two years later, M sold all of his stock for $90,000. Assuming M has no other property transactions during the year, compute the effect on M's AGI.

2-43 *Worthless Stock, Debt, and Advances.* Twenty years ago, P formed WRE Corp. receiving stock and a 25-year note on the exchange. This year the stock (basis $50,000) and debt (basis $10,000) became worthless when the corporation declared bankruptcy. During the demise of WRE, P advanced the business $20,000 on open account and now these loans are also uncollectible. Assuming the purpose of P's advances were to protect her employment and $75,000 a year salary, how will the losses affect her taxable income?

2-44 *Stock versus Debt.* Compare the tax implications of situations A and B.

	Situation A	Situation B
Stock issued...................	$120,000	$80,000
Debt owed to shareholders	0	40,000

The debt was issued as a 10-year note with 10% annual interest. Each year's interest and one-fifth of the note are payable each December 31. Shareholders will receive $30,000 from the corporation each year, which is considered first as payment of any debt obligations, and second as dividends. Assume marginal tax rates are 34% for the corporation and 28% for the shareholders. Compute the tax savings and costs for (1) the corporation and (2) the shareholders for Situations A and B in the first year when $30,000 is distributed. (Assume interest for the year is $4,000.)

2-45 *Worthless Stock versus Debt.* Refer to *Problem 2-44.* At the end of year 2, before distributions to shareholders, the corporation declares bankruptcy, and shareholders will receive nothing from the corporation for their stock or debt. Assume a 28% marginal tax rate for two individuals, X and Y, each filing as head of household and on the cash basis. X and Y own the stock and debt as follows:

	Situation A	Situation B
Stock issued to X	$84,000	$56,000
Y	36,000	24,000
Debt owed to X		10,000
Y		20,000
Interest owed to X		1,000
Y		2,000

Compute the tax savings for X and Y as a result of reporting the losses for Situations A and B in the current year.

2-46 *Capital Structure: Qualified Small Business Stock.* On September 1, 2014, B started her own rare book store. To get started, she contributed $100,000 to a newly formed corporation in exchange for all of its stock. After a slow start, the corporation became quite successful. In 2020, B decided to capitalize on her success and sold all of the stock in the company to a publicly held company that had super book stores all over the country.

   a. Assuming B sold all of the stock for $5,000,000, what is her taxable gain?
   b. Assuming B sold all of the stock for $15,000,000, what is her taxable gain?
   c. Same as (a), above, except in lieu of cash B contributed rare books that were worth $100,000 (basis $20,000).
   d. Same as (a). Must B recognize the gain realized on the sale? Does she have any options?

2-47 *Section 351 Planning.* Once bitter rivals, H. R. and S. W. decided to join forces this year and form a corporation that would manufacture doodads. H. R. will finance the deal by contributing $100,000. S. W. will contribute various assets used in his sole proprietorship worth $100,000 (basis $30,000). As currently planned, each would receive 40 shares of the corporation's voting common stock worth a total of $180,000. To incorporate the business, the two men have engaged the services of D. Q., an attorney, who will provide her services for 20 shares of preferred stock worth $40,000.

   a. If you were advising S. W., would you tell him to consummate the transaction as currently structured? If you believe that it would be in S. W.'s best interests to go ahead with the deal, explain why. If not, explain why not and how you might restructure the deal so that it would be an equitable arrangement.
   b. Same as (a), except you are the accountant for H. R.

TAX RETURN PROBLEMS

2-48 During 2015, Lisa Cutter and Jeff McMullen decided they would like to start their own gourmet hamburger business. Lisa and Jeff believed that the public would love the recipes used by Lisa's mom, Tina Woodbrook. They also thought that they had the necessary experience to enter this business, as Jeff currently owned a fast-food franchise business while Lisa had experience operating a small bakery. After doing their own market research, they established Slattery's Inc., which was incorporated on February 1, 2016. The company's address is 5432 Partridge Pl., Tulsa, Oklahoma 74105 and its employer identification number is 88-7654321.

The company started modestly. After refurbishing an old gas station that it had purchased, the company opened for business on February 25, 2016. Shortly after business began, however, business boomed. By the close of 2016, the company had established two other locations. Slattery's has three shareholders who own stock as follows:

Shareholder	Shares
Lisa Cutter.	500
Jeff McMullen	200
Tina Woodbrook (Lisa's mother)	300
Total outstanding	1,000

Slattery's was formed on February 1, 2016. On that date, shareholders made contributions as follows:

   • Lisa Cutter contributed $30,000 in cash and 200 shares of MND stock, a publicly held company, which had a fair market value of $20,000. Lisa had purchased the MND stock on October 3, 2011 for $8,000.
   • Jeff McMullen contributed equipment worth $20,000 which he had used in his own business until he contributed it. The equipment's basis was $48,000 (original cost in February 2014, $100,000; depreciation using MACRS accelerated percentages for five-year property, $52,000).
   • Tina Woodbrook contributed $30,000 in cash.

The company is on the accrual basis and has chosen to use the calendar year for tax purposes. The corporation's adjusted trial balance for financial accounting purposes reveals the following information:

	Debit	Credit
Cash	$229,200	
Ending inventory	0	
Equipment	35,000	
Land	10,000	
Building	15,000	
Improvements to building	55,000	
Accumulated depreciation		$ 9,000
Notes payable		93,000
Accounts payable		45,000
Taxes payable		8,000
Salaries payable		20,000
Capital stock		100,000
Sales		600,000
Gain on sale of MND stock		18,000
Dividend from MND Corporation		2,000
Legal expenses	5,500	
Accounting expenses	3,000	
Miscellaneous expenses	2,100	
Premium on key employee life insurance policy	800	
Advertising	8,600	
Purchases	300,000	
State income taxes	8,000	
Federal income taxes	48,000	
Payroll taxes	12,500	
Salary expenses	120,000	
Insurance	9,000	
Repairs	6,500	
Charitable contributions	17,600	
Depreciation per books	9,000	
Interest expense	200	

The company has provided additional information below.

- The company took a physical count of inventory on December 31, 2016. On that date, it was determined that ending inventory was $16,000. This ending inventory must be recorded on the company's books and will result in a reduction in cost of goods sold.
- On February 9, 2016, the corporation purchased an old gas station for $25,000 to house the restaurant. Of the $25,000 purchase price, $10,000 was allocated to the land while $15,000 was allocated to the building. Prior to opening, the old gas station was renovated. Improvements to the structure were made during February at a cost of $55,000. Assume the building and improvements are 39-year property.
- The legal costs were for work done by Slattery's attorney in February for drafting the articles of incorporation and by-laws. Accounting fees that were paid in May were for setting up the books and the accounting system. Miscellaneous expenses included a $100 fee paid in February to the State of Oklahoma to incorporate.
- The MND stock was sold for $38,000 on April 3, 2016. Shortly before the sale, MND had declared and paid a dividend. Slattery's received $2,000 on April 1, 2016. MND was incorporated in Delaware.
- The corporation purchased refrigeration equipment (7-year property) on February 15, 2016 for $15,000. (Ignore bonus depreciation.)
- Slattery's has elected not to use the limited expensing provisions of Code § 179. In addition, it claimed the maximum depreciation with respect to all other assets. Any other elections required to minimize the corporation's tax liability were made.

- Lisa Cutter (Social Security no. 444-33-2222) is president of the corporation and spends 90% of her working time in the business. Salary expense includes her salary of $60,000 and an accrued bonus to her as of December 31 of $15,000. No other officers received compensation. The key employee life insurance policy covers Lisa's life and the corporation is the beneficiary.
- The company paid estimated income taxes during the year of $48,000 ($12,000 on each installment due date). For simplicity's sake, in completing the tax return do not adjust the books to reflect the actual tax due.

Required: Prepare Form 1120 and other appropriate forms, schedules, and elections for Slattery's. On separate schedule(s), show all calculations used to determine all reported amounts except those for which the source is obvious or which are shown on a formal schedule to be filed with the return.

TAX RESEARCH PROBLEMS

2-49 JKL, Inc. is a rapidly growing development and construction company operating in Denver. Several years ago it decided to expand its business to the mountains so it could take advantage of the lucrative condominium market. To this end, the corporation persuaded M, N, and O, all of whom had built several projects in mountain communities to become a part of JKL. M, N, O, and JKL contributed assets to a new corporation, X, in a transaction qualifying under § 351. M contributed the following assets for 25% of the stock, worth $450,000, and $50,000 cash: land worth $300,000 (basis $25,000); office building worth $70,000 (basis $90,000); and a crane worth $130,000 (basis $100,000). This year the corporation subdivided the land and began selling the unimproved property. What basis should X corporation assign to the land for purposes of computing gain and loss on the lot sales?

2-50 Q and R, both single, formed SLI Inc. in 2012 and opened a small amusement park. The park's main attraction was a water slide, five stories high. Pursuant to the incorporation agreement, Q and R both contributed cash of $400,000. In exchange they each received 100 shares of the stock worth $100,000 and a six-year note for $300,000 payable in equal installments with 10% interest annually. During 2016, business became sluggish.

   a. Q and R believe the business is going to fail. Can Q and R obtain ordinary loss treatment for their investment should it become worthless? Answer this question independent of the facts in (b).

   b. After much deliberation, Q and R decided that the business could still succeed. The pair decided they needed something to spur profits, such as a stand-up roller coaster. On March 7, 2016, Q and R both contributed an additional $500,000 for 500 shares of stock. In August it was determined that the corporation required additional capital and S was admitted as a shareholder. S received 500 shares for a $500,000 contribution on August 15, 2016. In June, 2017 SLI was adjudged bankrupt and the stock of SLI became worthless. How will Q, R, and S treat their stock losses? How will Q and R treat their loss on the unpaid note?

2-51 T, an individual taxpayer, plans to incorporate his farming and ranching activities, currently operated as a sole proprietorship. His primary purpose of incorporating is to transfer a portion of his ownership in land to his son and daughter. T believes that gifts of stock rather than land will keep his business intact. Included in the property he plans to transfer is machinery purchased two years earlier. T's current thought is to incorporate and immediately transfer 40% of the corporate stock to his two children. What potential tax problems might result if T pursues his current plans? Would it make any difference if T received all voting stock and had the new corporation transfer nonvoting stock to the children?

Partial list of research aids:

   Rev. Rul. 59-259, 1959-2 C.B. 115.

   Reg. § 1.47-3(f)(5).

   W.F. Blevins, 61 T.C. 547 (1974).

2-52 RST Corporation is currently owned by three individuals: R, S, and T. The corporation has a net worth of $300,000 and has 500 shares (1,000 shares authorized) of common stock outstanding. R owns 200 shares (40%), and S and T each own 150 shares (30%). Individual E owns land worth $90,000, which the corporation could use as a new plant site. However, E is not interested in selling the land now because it would result in a large capital gain tax. E is willing to transfer the land to the corporation in exchange for 60 shares of its common stock or securities of equivalent value, but only if the transfer will be nontaxable. How would you advise the parties to structure the transaction?

Research aids:

> Rev. Rul. 73-472, 1973-2 C.B. 115.
>
> Rev. Proc. 76-22, 1976-1 C.B. 562.
>
> Reg. § 1.351-1(a)(1)(ii).

2-53 This year, the Brock brothers, Buster and H. R., decided to open a video store. Buster had the capital, and H. R. had the location. After closely studying the economics of the entire deal, the two negotiated an agreement that called for the following:

- Buster would contribute $50,000.
- H. R. would transfer a building having an appraised value of $75,000 (basis $12,000) and subject to a $25,000 mortgage.
- Buster and H. R. have agreed that both would get 50% of the stock of the new corporation.

Upon review of the proposed agreement, the brothers' attorney, Mr. Barry Stare, indicated that H. R. would be required to recognize gain on the transfer. Mr. Stare has suggested that H. R. could eliminate the problem if both he and Buster were to give a personal note to the corporation for $13,000 in exchange for additional stock. The brothers have now come to you, their accountant, to review the proposed agreement and Mr. Stare's advice.

a. Would you advise Buster to consummate the deal as planned? Would you advise H. R. to complete the deal as proposed? Evaluate the plan from the perspectives of both Buster and H. R. and discuss the tax problems and risks inherent in the proposal.

b. After you have reviewed the proposal with the brothers, H. R. and Buster indicate that a new twist to the deal has developed. Because they have had little experience in retail sales, they will be bringing in a friend of Buster's, X, to help manage the business. However, X has demanded an equity interest before she becomes a member of the team. Consequently, as part of the incorporation agreement, the three parties have agreed that each of the brothers will receive 58 shares of voting common stock worth $58,000 in exchange for their contributions while X will receive 10 shares of nonvoting common stock worth $10,000 for her future services. Discuss how this new proposal would affect your answer to (a) above and give any suggestions that you might have for the parties.

2-54 In 1995, Michael Malone, a professor of computer science and a specialist in digital technology, realized that it was only a short time before the computer would change the way people lived. Although he was 59 and quite happy with his $70,000 annual salary, he decided that this was an opportunity he just could not pass up. In 1998, he formed a new corporation, investing virtually all of his accumulated wealth, $200,000, in exchange for 51% of its stock. Three other individuals contributed additional cash for the remaining 49% of the stock. In the first few years of operation, the corporation was immensely successful. In 2005 Mike retired from the university and turned all of his attention to the business. All went well. In fact, things went so well that, by 2008, Mike turned over the supervision of everyday operations to several trusted employees; he began spending more time at the golf course and less time at the office. He was completely content working 20 hours a week and drawing an annual salary of $70,000. That income combined with his pension from the university of $20,000 a year was more than enough to keep him happy. During 2009, however, the competition in the computer business became fierce and the corporation had cash flow problems. As a result, Michael loaned the corporation $150,000 to keep it afloat. Unfortunately, the corporation was not able to survive and declared bankruptcy in 2016. How should Michael treat the worthless loan?

2-55 This year MHS Associates, LLC signed a contract with the city of Nashville to build a downtown mall. The mall was to have three upscale department stores. These stores would serve as anchor tenants that would attract additional businesses to locate in the mall. Among the possible anchor tenants that MHS sought was Sack's Third Avenue, a department store out of Los Angeles known all over the world. To secure Sack's, MHS offered the company $5,000,000 if it would agree to operate a store in the mall for the next 20 years. Assuming you are providing tax advice to Sack's on the proposed transaction, how would Sack's treat the amount received?

3

Corporate Distributions: Cash, Property, and Stock Dividends

Learning Objectives

Upon completion of this chapter you will be able to:

LO.1 Define a dividend for tax purposes.

LO.2 Compare the concept of retained earnings with the concept of earnings and profits.

LO.3 Explain how earnings and profits are calculated, and the function of earnings and profits in measuring dividend income.

LO.4 Identify the special problems related to distributions of property (other than cash), including how to:

- Determine the amount of the dividend to the shareholder.

- Determine the shareholder's basis of the property distributed.

- Determine the amount of gain or loss recognized by the distributing corporation.

- Determine the effect of a distribution of property on the corporation's earnings and profits.

LO.5 Identify a constructive distribution.

LO.6 Explain the tax consequences of a stock dividend.

Chapter Outline

Introduction

After shareholders have formed a corporation and operations are underway, one of their primary concerns is getting money out of the corporation. Unfortunately, this area, *corporate distributions,* can be somewhat complex. The difficulty stems from the vastly differing treatments applying to distributions whose forms differ ever so slightly. For example, if a corporate distribution is considered a dividend, it is not deductible by the corporation, so double taxation results. However, the maximum tax rate on dividends is generally limited to 15% (although it could be as high as 23.8% for high income taxpayers). In contrast, if the distribution to the shareholder is considered a type of payment that is deductible by the corporation, double taxation does not occur but the applicable tax rate may be as high as 39.6 percent. For example, if a corporation pays a shareholder a salary for services performed, the corporation may deduct the payment and while the distribution avoids double taxation, it is taxed at a higher rate and is subject to employment taxes as well. In most cases, shareholders, particularly those in closely held corporations, normally go to great lengths to avoid distributing "dividends." As might be expected, they prefer to characterize distributions as salary or rent or interest or anything other than a dividend. Consequently, one of the first problems in solving the distribution puzzle is trying to determine whether a distribution is in reality a payment with respect to the shareholder's stock—a potential dividend—or some other type of payment.

Even if one assumes that the distribution to a shareholder is *with respect to the shareholder's stock,* a determination must be made as to whether the distribution represents a return *on* the shareholder's investment (i.e., a distribution of corporate earnings—a dividend) or a return *of* the shareholder's capital. Prior to 2003, this distinction was critical since dividends were taxed as ordinary income while distributions of capital were tax free to the extent of the shareholder's investment (i.e., stock basis) and taxable as favorable capital gain to the extent they exceed the stock's basis. The distinction has diminished somewhat in that dividends (other than those to corporate shareholders) and capital gains are now taxed at the same rate. Of course, if the distribution is a return on capital, a capital gain still results only if the amount exceeds the stock basis, continuing to make the distinction important.

The rules governing corporate distributions are further complicated because they may take a variety of forms. A corporation may distribute cash or property including its own stock and obligations. Upon receipt of a corporate distribution, a shareholder may or may not surrender stock. After the distribution, the corporation may continue in the same or some modified form, or may completely terminate its operations. To determine whether a distribution under these various circumstances is a return on capital or a return of capital, the Code provides an intricate—almost mazelike—system of rules. These rules are the subject of this and the following chapter.

Corporate distributions generally fall into one of the following categories:

1. Section 301 distributions: distributions of property including cash where the shareholder normally does not surrender stock and which may be treated as a dividend or a return of capital, depending on whether the distributions are made from earnings and profits of the corporation.

2. Distributions of stock and stock rights of the distributing corporation.

3. Redemptions: distributions to a shareholder in exchange for stock and the corporation continues to operate.

4. Redemptions in partial liquidation: distributions to a shareholder in exchange for stock and the corporation terminates a portion of its business.

5. Redemptions in complete liquidation: distributions to a shareholder in exchange for stock and the corporation ceases to conduct business.

6. Spin-offs, split-offs, and split-ups: distributions of stock of one or more subsidiaries as part of a corporate division.

This chapter focuses on the first two categories of distributions, or what are commonly known as cash, property, and stock dividends. The other types of corporate distributions are considered in subsequent chapters.

As a practical matter, virtually all distributions consist of cash and constitute ordinary dividend income to the shareholders. However, the Code contains a somewhat elaborate system to accommodate distributions of property and to ensure that returns of capital are nontaxable. Section 301 contains the general rule governing the tax treatment of distributions of property to a shareholder. For this purpose, property is defined broadly to include money, securities, and other property except stock (or rights to purchase stock) of the distributing corporation.[1] The following material considers the basic rules governing distributions. This discussion is followed by an examination of the special problems arising when a corporation distributes property other than money. The treatment of stock distributions is considered later in this chapter.

TAXATION OF DISTRIBUTIONS TO SHAREHOLDERS: STATUTORY SCHEME

When a corporation distributes property, § 301 requires the shareholder to include the amount of the distribution in gross income to the extent that it constitutes a *dividend*.[2] The treatment of the dividend depends on the type of shareholder that receives it. Dividends received by individuals are treated as ordinary income and potentially taxable at the individual's highest marginal tax rate, currently 39.6 percent. However, *qualified dividends* received by individuals are taxed at a maximum rate of 15% (5% if the individual is in the 15 or 10 percent tax bracket or 20% for taxpayers in the 39.6% bracket). Qualified dividends generally include all dividends distributed by domestic C corporations. It makes no difference whether the dividend is distributed by a publicly traded corporation or a corporation with a single shareholder. In contrast, dividends received from a foreign corporation normally are qualified only if the corporation's stock is readily tradable on an established U.S. securities market. Note also that dividends may be subject to the 3.8% tax on net investment income for those with modified adjusted gross incomes exceeding $200,000 ($250,000 for joint filers).

If the recipient of the dividend is a C corporation, the corporation normally is entitled to a dividends received deduction. As explained in Chapter 1, subject to a special limitation based on taxable income, the deduction is normally 70% of the dividend but is increased to 80% if the corporation owns 20% or more of the stock of the distributing corporation.

The term *dividend,* a precisely defined word as explained below, generally means any distribution of property that is out of the corporation's earnings and profits.[3] The critical presumption contained within the distribution provisions is that any distribution made by the corporation with respect to its stock is deemed first to be a distribution out of earnings and profits to the extent thereof. Therefore, as long as the corporation has sufficient earnings and profits, distributions are treated as taxable dividends. Amounts that are not considered dividends because of inadequate earnings and profits are treated as nontaxable returns of capital to the extent of the shareholder's basis for the stock.[4] In effect, the nondividend portion of the distribution is applied to and reduces the basis of the stock. Should the return of capital distribution exceed the shareholder's basis, the excess is treated as gain from the sale of the stock, normally capital gain if the stock is a capital asset.[5]

> **LO.1**
> Define a dividend for tax purposes.

Example 1

On December 1, JKL Inc. distributed $10,000 to its sole shareholder, T. At the close of the year, the corporation had earnings and profits of $6,000 before taking into account the distribution. Assuming T's basis in her stock is $3,000, the $10,000 distribution is treated as follows: a taxable dividend to the extent of the corporation's earnings and profits, $6,000; a tax-free return of capital to the extent of her basis in the stock, $3,000; and a capital gain to the extent the return of capital distribution exceeds her basis, $1,000 ($4,000 − $3,000). Note that in this case, the return of capital distribution reduces T's basis in her stock to zero.

As this example suggests, the treatment of property distributions is closely tied to the notion of earnings and profits.

---

[1] § 317(a).

[2] § 301(c).

[3] § 316(a).

[4] § 301(c)(2).

[5] § 301(c)(3).

EARNINGS AND PROFITS

LO.2

Compare the concept of retained earnings with the concept of earnings and profits.

Under the statutory scheme, a dividend can be distributed only if the corporation has earnings and profits—or as it is usually called, E&P.[6] Interestingly, the Code, which normally goes to great lengths to define its words, fails to define the term *earnings and profits*. Although the statute offers some guidance concerning how certain transactions affect E&P, the meaning of E&P is conspicuously absent.[7] As a result, the Treasury and the courts have had to fashion a definition of E&P in light of its purpose. The primary function of E&P is to provide a measure of the amount a corporation can distribute without "dipping" into its capital. In so doing, it provides a standard for determining whether a distribution represents a taxable dividend or a potentially tax-free return of capital.

Given the definition of E&P—an amount that can be distributed without impairing the corporation's capital—E&P generally represents the corporation's economic income that can be distributed. In this regard, E&P actually consists of two parts: *current E&P*, which represents current economic income computed on an annual basis; and *accumulated E&P*, which is simply the sum of each year's current E&P reduced by distributions. Generally, current taxable income, as adjusted for certain items, serves as a proxy for the corporation's current economic income (i.e., current E&P).

Example 2

X and Y Corporation were both formed this year. For the year, X Corporation reported a loss while Y reported $20,000 of income after taxes. If X makes a distribution, the distribution is a return of the shareholders' capital since X has no current or accumulated E&P. In contrast, any distribution made by Y—up to $20,000—is treated as having been paid out of its current earnings (i.e., current E&P) and is, therefore, a taxable dividend.

E&P is somewhat similar to the legal concept of "earned surplus" and the accounting concept of "retained earnings," neither of which include paid-in-capital or subsequent contributions to capital. This is not to say, however, that E&P is equivalent to either retained earnings or earned surplus. Indeed, in many cases E&P may bear little resemblance to either. For example, when a corporation issues a stock dividend, generally accepted accounting principles require the capitalization of part of the retained earnings balance (i.e., the transfer of an amount equal to the market value of the stock from the retained earnings account to the capital stock account). If this were allowed for tax purposes, corporations could avoid paying dividends simply by declaring nontaxable stock dividends that would eliminate their E&P at no cost to the shareholders. For tax purposes, however, a nontaxable stock dividend has no effect on the corporation's ability to pay dividends, and consequently the E&P balance is unaffected.

Current E&P is not the same as current taxable income. Nor is accumulated E&P simply the sum of each year's taxable income. Taxable income, fraught with special provisions designed to achieve some objective or furnish some relief, is not necessarily representative of the corporation's economic income. For the most part, taxable income provides only a blurred picture of the corporation's capacity to pay dividends. Nevertheless, taxable income has traditionally been used as the starting point in the computation of E&P.

Since E&P represents the corporation's economic income, numerous adjustments to taxable income must be made to arrive at the corporation's E&P. For example, tax-exempt interest must be added to taxable income because it represents economic income that the corporation could distribute without violating its capital account. A general formula for computing E&P is presented in Exhibit 3-1. Each of these adjustments to taxable income is considered in detail below.

---

[6] § 316(a).   [7] § 312 describes the effect of certain transactions *on* E&P.

EXHIBIT 3-1	Calculations of Current Earnings and Profits

Current taxable income (or net operating loss)

\+ Exempt and nondeferrable income

\- Items not deductible in computing taxable income

\+ Deductions not permitted in computing E&P

\= Current earnings and profits (or deficit)

The calculation of E&P is normally made using the same accounting methods used to compute taxable income.[8] For example, a corporation that adopts the cash receipts and disbursements method of accounting uses the same method for determining E&P. Over the years, however, Congress has often required corporate taxpayers to adopt accounting methods for computing E&P that vary from those they use for computing taxable income. The objective of many of these modifications is to conform E&P more closely to the economic concept of income. For example, when calculating E&P, taxpayers are not allowed to use the Modified Accelerated Cost Recovery System (MACRS) to compute depreciation. Instead, they must use the slower-paced Alternative Depreciation System (ADS) with its straight-line method and longer class lives. A partial list of the special adjustments that must be made in computing E&P appears in Exhibit 3-2.

Modifications for E&P: Excluded and Deferred Income

Under the Regulations, all income normally *excluded* in computing taxable income must be included in determining E&P. Accordingly, E&P must be increased for items such as tax exempt interest on state and local bonds[9] and life insurance proceeds. Several items that are technically excluded from income by the Code are not added back to taxable income to determine E&P since they do not represent income. For example, contributions to capital, gifts, and bequests would be ignored in making the computation.

Income items are generally included in E&P in the year in which they are *recognized*. Consistent with this principle, gain postponed under the like-kind exchange provisions or the rules permitting nonrecognition on certain involuntary conversions is not reflected in E&P in the year realized but in the year recognized.[10] In contrast, the installment sales method may not be used for computing E&P. As a result, the entire amount of any gain realized on an installment sale must be included in E&P in the year of the sale.[11] Similarly, income and deductions of a corporation using the completed-contract method of accounting must be accounted for using the percentage of completion method.[12]

As explained below, distributions of appreciated property cause the distributing corporation to recognize gain. These gains must be included in the computation of E&P prior to any reduction to E&P caused by the distribution.[13]

Items Nondeductible for E&P

The Code provides a lengthy list of items which, although deductible in computing taxable income, cannot be deducted currently in calculating E&P. In this category of required adjustments is one affecting all corporations that account for inventory using the LIFO method. These corporations must generally use the FIFO method in computing cost of goods sold for determining E&P.[14]

---

[8] Reg. § 1.312-6(a).

[9] Reg. § 1.312-6(b).

[10] § 312(f)(1).

[11] § 312(n)(5).

[12] § 312(n)(6).

[13] § 312(b). As explained within, E&P is increased for any gain recognized on the distribution. The increase by itself may create sufficient E&P to cause taxation of the distribution to the shareholder. Following the distribution, E&P is reduced by the property's value.

[14] § 312(n)(5), effective for taxable years beginning after September 30, 1984.

EXHIBIT 3-2	**Partial List of Adjustments Used in Computing Current Earnings and Profits**

Taxable Income:

Plus:

Tax-exempt interest income

Deferred gain on installment sales

Dividends-received deduction

Excess of accelerated depreciation over straight-line depreciation

Excess of ACRS depreciation over ADS straight-line depreciation [§ 312(k)(3)]

Excess of LIFO cost of goods sold over FIFO cost of goods sold

Four-fifths (4/5) of deduction for immediate expensing of assets under § 179 taken during the current year [§ 312(k)(3)(B)]

Excess of deductions for construction period interest and taxes over the amortization of such costs

Excess of depletion taken over cost depletion

Increases in cash surrender value of life insurance when the corporation is the beneficiary (directly or indirectly)

Proceeds of life insurance when the corporation is the beneficiary (directly or indirectly)

Amortization of organization and circulation expenditures

Net operating loss deductions carried over from other years

Federal income tax refunds

Recoveries of bad debts and other deductions, but only if they are *not* included in taxable income under the tax benefit doctrine

Income based on the percentage-of-completion method rather than the completed-contract method

In the year they are reflected in taxable income: charitable contribution carryovers, capital loss carryovers, and other timing differences (since they reduced E&P in the year they originated)

Minus:

Federal income taxes

Nondeductible expenses:

Penalties and fines

Payments to public officials not reflected in taxable income

Expenses between related parties not deductible under § 267

Interest expense related to the production of tax-exempt income

Life insurance premiums when the corporation is the beneficiary (directly or indirectly)

Travel, entertainment, and gift expenses that do not meet the substantiation requirements of § 274(d)

Fifty percent of meals and entertainment disallowed as a deduction under § 274(n)

Other expenses that are disallowed to the corporation as the result of an IRS audit

Nondeductible losses between related parties under § 267

Charitable contributions in excess of the 10% limitation

Excess capital losses for the year that are not deductible

Gains on sales of depreciable property to the extent that accelerated depreciation or MACRS (or ACRS) exceeds the straight-line depreciation method used for computing increases in E&P

Gains on sales of depletable property to the extent that depletion taken exceeds cost depletion

One-fifth (1/5) of any immediate expensing deduction under § 179 taken during the previous four years [§ 312(k)(3)(B)]

Foreign taxes paid that have been treated as credits on the corporation's tax return

Equals: **Current Earnings and Profits**

Note: The above exhibit does not include the effect of corporate distributions and dividends on E&P —this is discussed later in the chapter.

Several other modifications in this group involve the methods used to account for capital expenditures. No doubt the most important of these concerns depreciation. As mentioned above, depreciation deductions for E&P generally must be calculated using a straight- line method.[15] For property subject to MACRS depreciation, the Alternative Depreciation System (ADS) straight-line method must be used. The recovery periods for ADS are summarized in Exhibit 3-3, while the ADS depreciation percentages are shown in Exhibits 3-4 and 3-5. Assets expensed under the limited expensing provision of § 179 must be depreciated using the straight-line method over a five-year period.

EXHIBIT 3-3	Alternative Depreciation System Recovery Periods

General Rule: Recovery period is the property's class life unless:
1. There is no class life (see below), or
2. A special class life has been designated (see below).

Type of Property	Recovery Period	
Personal property with no class life	12	years
Nonresidential real property with no class life	40	years
Residential real property with no class life	40	years
Cars, light general purpose trucks, certain technological equipment, and semiconductor manufacturing equipment	5	years
Computer-based telephone central office switching equipment	9.5	years
Railroad track	10	years
Single-purpose agricultural or horticultural structures	15	years
Municipal waste water treatment plants, telephone distribution plants	24	years
Low-income housing financed by tax-exempt bonds	27.5	years
Municipal sewers	50	years

Example 3

In January of this year, T Corporation purchased an apartment building for $110,000, $10,000 of which was allocable to the land. Under MACRS, T claims a depreciation deduction of $3,485 ($100,000 × 3.485% per Appendix H) in computing taxable income. Under ADS, which must be used in computing E&P, depreciation is $2,396 ($100,000 × 2.396% per Exhibit 3-5). Consequently, in computing E&P, taxable income must be increased by $1,089 ($3,485 − $2,396), the excess of MACRS depreciation over ADS depreciation. The difference is attributable to the different recovery periods: 40 years for ADS and 27.5 years for MACRS.

---

[15] § 312(k)(1) is applicable only for taxable years beginning after June 30, 1972.

EXHIBIT 3-4	ADS Straight-Line Depreciation Percentages Using the Half-Year Convention for Property with Certain Recovery Periods

	Recovery Period (Class Life)	
Recovery Year	5 Years	12 Years
1	10.00%	4.17%
2	20.00	8.33
3	20.00	8.33
4	20.00	8.33
5	20.00	8.33
6	10.00	8.33
7		8.34
8		8.33
9		8.34
10		8.33
11		8.34
12		8.33
13		4.17

Source: Rev. Proc. 87-57, 1987-2 C.B. 687, Table 8.

EXHIBIT 3-5	ADS Straight-Line Depreciation Percentages for Real Property Using the Mid-Month Convention

Residential Property and Nonresidential Real Property

	Recovery Year		
Month Placed in Service	1	2–40	41
1	2.396%	2.500%	0.104%
2	2.188	2.500	0.312
3	1.979	2.500	0.521
4	1.771	2.500	0.729
5	1.563	2.500	0.937
6	1.354	2.500	1.146
7	1.146	2.500	1.354
8	0.938	2.500	1.562
9	0.729	2.500	1.771
10	0.521	2.500	1.979
11	0.313	2.500	2.187
12	0.104	2.500	2.396

Source: Rev. Proc. 87-57, 1987-2 C.B. 687, Table 13.

Similar to the modifications for depreciation, adjustments must be made for the following:

1. *Depletion.* Only cost depletion may be used in computing E&P.[16]
2. *Intangible drilling costs.* These costs must be capitalized and amortized over 60 months.[17]

---

[16] Reg. § 1.312-6(c)(1).

[17] § 312(n)(2)(A).

3. *Mineral exploration and development costs.* These costs must be capitalized and amortized over 120 months.[18]

4. *Construction period interest, taxes, and other carrying charges.* These costs must be capitalized and amortized over the life of the related property.[19]

5. *Organization and circulation expenditures.* Deduction or amortization of these costs is not permitted in computing E&P. These costs must be capitalized.[20]

Another adjustment required in computing E&P involves the dividends-received deduction. Since this deduction does not affect the corporation's ability to pay dividends, it must be added back to taxable income when computing E&P.

Example 4

During the year, C Corporation received dividends of $100,000. Because of the dividends-received deduction, only $30,000 of the $100,000 is included in the corporation's taxable income ($100,000 − [70% × $100,000]). In computing E&P, the corporation must include the full $100,000. Consequently, a positive adjustment of $70,000 must be made to the corporation's taxable income to arrive at the proper balance of E&P.

The net operating loss deduction must also be added back, since this deduction simply represents a carryover or carryback of a loss incurred in another year. Losses reduce E&P in the year they are incurred.

Items Nondeductible for Taxable Income

Items that cannot be deducted in computing taxable income are deducted in computing E&P since they reduce the amount that could be paid out to shareholders. Several of the more important expenses and losses that are subtracted include the following:

1. *Federal income taxes.* An accrual basis taxpayer reduces current E&P for the taxes imposed on current taxable income, while a cash basis taxpayer reduces current E&P only for those taxes paid. A special adjustment is required for Federal income taxes since they are not deductible in computing taxable income. Note, however, that no special adjustment is required for state income taxes since they are deductible in computing taxable income.

2. *Charitable contributions.* Those in excess of the 10% limitation are also deductible in computing E&P (i.e., contributions are deductible in full in the year paid).

3. *Expenses related to tax-exempt income.*

4. *Premiums paid on key-person life insurance policies.* These amounts may be deducted to the extent they exceed any increase in the policy's cash surrender value.

5. *Excess of capital losses over capital gains.* Since net capital losses are not deductible in computing current year taxable income, they must be deducted in computing E&P.

6. *Related party losses and expenses.* Losses and expenses disallowed under the related party rules of § 267 are subtracted in computing current E&P (e.g., accrued bonus to a more-than-50% shareholder).

Although the above list identifies numerous nondeductible items that must be considered in computing E&P, it is by no means exhaustive. Any outlay that reduces the amount available to distribute, yet is not a capital expenditure, may represent a potential adjustment for E&P (e.g., nondeductible political contributions, lobbying expenses, and penalties).

---

[18] § 312(n)(2)(B).   [20] § 312(n)(3).

[19] § 312(n)(1).

Example 5

This year, D Corporation sold securities yielding a short-term capital loss of $25,000. The corporation had no capital gains during the year. As a result, none of the loss is deductible in computing current taxable income. Nevertheless, E&P must be reduced by $25,000 since the loss reduces the corporation's ability to pay dividends.

Example 6

E Corporation maintains a life insurance policy of $500,000 on its president, T. During the year, the corporation paid the annual premium of $5,000. In addition, the cash surrender value of the policy increased by $2,000. Although the annual premium payments are not deductible, they do reduce E&P. Similarly, increases in the cash surrender value of the policy that are nontaxable are included in E&P. Consequently, E&P would be reduced by the $5,000 premium and increased by the $2,000 increase in the cash surrender value.

Several years later, T died when the cash surrender value was $60,000. The corporation received the face amount of the policy, $500,000. Although the $500,000 is nontaxable, E&P must be adjusted. Since the corporation has adjusted E&P previously for increases in the cash surrender value and because part of the $500,000 represents a return of that value, only $440,000 ($500,000 − $60,000) is added to E&P.[21]

CURRENT VERSUS ACCUMULATED E&P

As noted above, E&P consists of two basic parts: current E&P and accumulated E&P. The distinction between current and accumulated E&P is very important for, as explained below, the two are often viewed as two separate pools of earnings from which distributions can be made. As a result, under the current approach a corporation can make taxable dividend distributions if it has current E&P, notwithstanding the fact that it may have a deficit in accumulated E&P.

DIVIDEND DISTRIBUTIONS

LO.3

Explain how earnings and profits are calculated, and the function of earnings and profits in measuring dividend income.

Under the statutory approach described above, only that portion of a distribution which is a dividend is included in the shareholder's gross income.[22] A *dividend* is defined as a distribution paid *out of either current or accumulated E&P*.[23] In this regard, any distribution made during the year is deemed to come first from any current E&P that may exist.[24] If the distribution exceeds current E&P, then the distribution is considered as having been paid from any *accumulated E&P* of prior years.[25] The presumption that every distribution is first out of current E&P and then from accumulated E&P produces the following rules that must be applied in determining the source of the distribution:[26]

1. Current E&P is allocated among *all* distributions made during the year on a pro rata basis, as follows:

$$\frac{\text{Amount of distribution}}{\text{Total current distributions}} \times \text{Current E\&P} = \text{Distribution's share of current E\&P}$$

---

[21] Rev. Rul. 54-230, 1954-1 C.B. 114.

[22] §§ 301(c)(1) and 316.

[23] § 316(a).

[24] § 316(a)(2).

[25] § 316(a)(1).

[26] Reg. § 1.316-2.

2. For this purpose, current E&P is computed on the last day of the taxable year *without* reduction for any distributions made during the year.

3. Accumulated E&P is allocated among distributions made during the year in *chronological* order. If there is a deficit in current E&P (e.g., a current operating loss), it is prorated on a daily basis against any accumulated E&P existing on the date of the distribution. For example, if there is a distribution on February 1, the amount of the deficit that occurs through January 31 is determined and netted against accumulated E&P. If the actual deficit suffered prior to the date of distribution can be determined, that amount is used rather than the amount determined under the proration method.

4. If a deficit in accumulated E&P exists, it is ignored and all distributions are dividends to the extent of their share of current E&P.

5. If there is a deficit *in both* accumulated and current E&P, any distribution is not a dividend but rather a return of capital.

These operating rules are summarized in Exhibit 3-6 and illustrated in the following examples.

EXHIBIT 3-6	Determining Available E&P and Its Allocation to Distributions

	AE&P	CE&P	AVAILABLE E&P
1.	+	+	Allocation • CE&P pro rata • AE&P chronologically
2.	–	+	Do not net • Dividend to extent of CE&P • Allocate CE&P pro rata

3.	+	–	Net
			• Compute E&P at date of distribution
			• Prorate deficit on daily basis (or actual)
			  • Net against AE&P at distribution date
			  • Dividend to extent of net AE&P – prior distributions

4.	–	–	No E&P, no dividend

Example 7

At the beginning of the taxable year, K Inc. had accumulated E&P of $40,000. Current E&P for the year was $27,000. During the year, K made cash distributions to its sole shareholder, J, of $30,000 on April 1 and $60,000 on October 1. The treatment of these distributions is shown below.

Distribution				Accumulated		
Date	Amount	Current E&P $27,000*	Remaining Distribution	E&P $40,000	Return of Capital	Sale
4/1	$30,000	$ 9,000	$21,000	$21,000	0	0
10/1	60,000	18,000	42,000	19,000	$15,000	$8,000

$$* \frac{\$30,000}{\$30,000 + \$60,000} \times \$27,000 = \$9,000$$

$$* \frac{\$60,000}{\$30,000 + \$60,000} \times \$27,000 = \$18,000$$

As shown above, both distributions are deemed to consist of their allocable share of current E&P. The April 1 distribution represents a $9,000 distribution from current E&P while the October 1 distribution represents $18,000 of current E&P. Accumulated E&P is allocated on a chronological basis; thus, $21,000 of the $40,000 balance is allocated to the remaining portion of the April 1 distribution (i.e., the distribution not out of current E&P, $30,000 − $9,000) and the remaining accumulated E&P of $19,000 is allocated to the October 1 distribution. As a result, the entire $30,000 distribution on April 1 is treated as a dividend while only $37,000 ($18,000 + $19,000) of the October 1 distribution of $60,000 is a dividend. The remaining $23,000 balance ($60,000 − $37,000) of the October 1 distribution is considered a return of the shareholder's basis. Assuming J has a $15,000 basis in his stock, the $23,000 is applied to and reduces J's basis to zero, while the $8,000 ($23,000 − $15,000) excess over his basis is considered capital gain from the sale of his stock.

Note that in the example above the allocation process had no effect on the amount of dividend income that J reports (i.e., J's dividend after the allocation is $67,000, the same as the sum of current and accumulated E&P) because he was the corporation's only shareholder. However, if there are changes in ownership during the year, the allocation process can affect the amount of dividend income that the shareholder must include in income.

Example 8

On June 30, 2016, M sold 100% of the stock of L Inc. to B for $12,000. L had accumulated E&P at the beginning of the year of $20,000, while current E&P for the year was $40,000. The corporation made distributions of $40,000 on April 1 and $40,000 on October 1. As computed below, all of the $40,000 distribution to M on April 1 is a dividend while only $20,000 of the $40,000 distribution to B is a dividend. Although both M and B owned 100% of the corporation for six months of the year and both received equal distributions, M must report twice as much dividend income because accumulated E&P is allocated chronologically.

Distribution		Current E&P $40,000*	Remaining Distribution	Accumulated E&P $20,000	Return of Capital	Sale
Date	Amount					
4/1	$40,000	$20,000	$20,000	$20,000	0	0
10/1	40,000	20,000	20,000	0	$12,000	$8,000

$$* \quad \frac{\$40,000}{\$40,000 + \$40,000} \times \$40,000 = \$20,000$$

Example 9

At the beginning of the year, K Corporation had accumulated E&P of $60,000. Unprofitable operations for the year resulted in a $36,500 deficit in K Corporation's current E&P. During the year, the corporation made cash distributions of $30,000 on April 1 and $60,000 on October 1. The deficit is prorated on a daily basis (excluding the date of distribution) and reduces any accumulated E&P otherwise available on the date of distribution. Accordingly, in determining accumulated E&P as of the date of the first distribution, April 1, the beginning balance of accumulated E&P is reduced by $9,000 of the current deficit ($36,500 ÷ 365 × 90), leaving $51,000 ($60,000 − $9,000) available for distribution. Since accumulated E&P exceeds the April 1 distribution, all $30,000 of the distribution is a dividend. Accumulated E&P available for the October distribution is $2,700 [$60,000 − deficit to October 1 of $27,300 (273 ÷ 365 × $36,500) − previous distribution of $30,000], reflecting both the deficit through September 30 and the previous distribution of $30,000.

Example 10

At the beginning of the year, D Corporation had a deficit in accumulated E&P of $100,000 resulting from unprofitable operations in prior years. This year, the corporation had an excellent year, with current E&P of $60,000. On November 30 of this year, the corporation distributed $70,000 to its sole shareholder, M, who had a basis in her stock of $16,000. M must report a dividend of $60,000, representing a distribution of current E&P—notwithstanding the fact that the corporation had a deficit in accumulated E&P. Note that a deficit in accumulated E&P is *not* netted with current E&P. The remaining distribution of $10,000 reduces M's basis in her stock to $6,000 ($16,000 − $10,000).

Distributions of Property

In the previous section, it was assumed that all distributions made by a corporation to its shareholders were cash distributions. Although the vast majority of corporations distribute only cash, in certain cases the corporation may distribute land, inventory, or other property in lieu of or in addition to cash. As a general rule, property distributions are treated in the same manner as cash distributions. Indeed, when the basis of the distributed property is equal to its fair market value, the treatment is essentially identical with that accorded cash distributions. In theory, the *result* is the same as if the corporation had sold the property and distributed the cash proceeds from the sale. In such case, there would be no concern with gain or loss at the corporate level and any resulting adjustment to E&P, since the property's value and basis are equivalent. Unfortunately, the basis and value of the property are rarely equal, leading one to ask how far the "as if sold" approach is taken. In short, the distribution of property raises several additional questions that are not present with cash distributions:

1. Does the corporation *recognize gain or loss* on the distribution?
2. What is the effect of the distribution on the corporation's *E&P*?
3. What is the *amount* of the distribution to the shareholder?
4. What is the *basis* of the distributed property in the hands of the shareholder?

These and other considerations related to property distributions are addressed below. Before proceeding, it should be mentioned that the following rules apply to distributions of virtually all types of property, including the corporation's own securities (e.g., bonds and notes).[27] However, distributions of the corporation's own stock (e.g., stock dividends), as well as rights to acquire such stock, are subject to a special set of provisions discussed later in this chapter.

LO.4

Identify the special problems related to distributions of property (other than cash), including how to:

- Determine the amount of the dividend to the shareholder.
- Determine the shareholder's basis of the property distributed.
- Determine the amount of gain or loss recognized by the distributing corporation.
- Determine the effect of a distribution of property on the corporation's earnings and profits.

EFFECT OF PROPERTY DISTRIBUTION ON THE SHAREHOLDER: AMOUNT AND BASIS OF PROPERTY DISTRIBUTION

The effect of a distribution of property on a shareholder is determined using the same basic rules that apply to cash distributions. Like cash distributions, property distributions generally are treated as dividends to the extent they are out of E&P and otherwise are treated as nontaxable returns of capital to the extent of the shareholder's basis. The only pitfall presented by property distributions in this regard concerns the unique problems of appreciated property. As the discussion below warns, a distribution of appreciated property could increase E&P, which in turn could affect the amount of the dividend to the shareholder.

When a distribution of property is made, two issues uncommon to cash distributions arise: (1) what is the *amount* of the distribution; and (2) what is the shareholder's *basis* of the property distributed? When cash distributions are made, the amount of the distribution is simply the value of the cash received, and of course the basis of the cash is also its value. When a property distribution is made, however, the Code sets forth special rules for determining its amount and basis to the shareholder.

---

[27] §§ 301 and 317(a).

Amount

The "amount" of any property distribution is the property's fair market value as of the date of distribution. This amount properly reflects the value of the benefit received by the shareholder.[28] If, in connection with the distribution, the shareholder assumes a liability of the distributing corporation or takes the distributed property subject to a liability, the amount of the distribution must be reduced by the liability (but not below zero).[29] This modification is necessary because the shareholder's wealth has increased only by the net amount of the distribution (fair market value less the liability). In short, the shareholder's income includes as a dividend the fair market value of any property received (adjusted for liabilities) to the extent the distribution is out of E&P.

Basis

The shareholder's basis for the property received is the property's fair market value.[30] This basis reflects the fact that the shareholder has been taxed on such value and any future gain or loss is properly measured from this point. In contrast to the computation of the amount of the distribution, the shareholder's basis in the property is *not* affected—neither decreased nor increased—by any liabilities assumed in connection with the distribution. Note that this approach is in essence the same as that used for any other basis computations. For example, if property is purchased for $10,000, the taxpayer's basis for the property is its cost, regardless of whether $10,000 in cash is paid or a $10,000 note is given. In effect, the liability assumed is included in the basis because it represents part of the taxpayer's cost of the property.

Example 11

During the year, G Inc. distributed land worth $150,000 to its sole shareholder, B. The corporation acquired the land for $60,000. B took the property subject to a mortgage of $20,000. The amount of the distribution is $130,000 ($150,000 − $20,000) and is treated as a dividend, assuming the corporation has that much E&P. B's basis in the land is its fair market value of $150,000. Note that if B immediately sold the land for $150,000 and paid the $20,000 liability, no gain or loss would be recognized and B would be better off by $130,000, the amount of the distribution included in income.

CORPORATE GAIN OR LOSS ON PROPERTY DISTRIBUTIONS

General Rule

Section 311 provides that a corporation must recognize gain—*but not loss*—upon the distribution of property other than its own obligations.[31] The gain to be recognized is computed as if the corporation had sold the property to the distributee shareholder for the property's fair market value.

Example 12

P Corporation distributed land worth $100,000 (basis $20,000) and equipment worth $30,000 (basis $45,000) to its sole shareholder, O. P must recognize the $80,000 ($100,000 − $20,000) gain realized on the distribution of the land. Although P also realizes a loss on the distribution of the equipment, the loss is not recognized. Note that gain and loss are computed on an asset-by-asset basis.

---

[28] § 301(b)(1)(A).

[29] § 301(b)(2).

[30] § 301(d)(1).

[31] §§ 311(a) and (b).

Observe that the gain recognition rule of § 311 ensures that the appreciation on distributed property does not escape tax. This would otherwise occur because the shareholder's basis in the property is its fair market value. For instance, in *Example 12* above, the shareholder's basis in the land would be $100,000. Therefore, a subsequent sale of the land for $100,000 would result in no gain at the shareholder level. For this reason, the corporation is required to recognize the gain just as if it had sold the property. This treatment ensures that—at least in the case of appreciated property—there is no distinction between sales of property followed by a distribution and distributions of property. In both cases, two taxes occur: one at the corporate level upon the sale or distribution, and one at the shareholder level upon receipt of the sales proceeds or property.

Losses

The restriction against loss recognition was enacted to prohibit taxpayers from circumventing the basic rule requiring gain recognition. For example, assume a wholly owned corporation holds appreciated land worth $1,000, which its sole shareholder wishes to extract for his own use. Assume for the sake of simplicity that the land has a basis of zero. Also assume the owner of the corporation holds equipment that has a fair market value of zero but a basis of $1,000. Absent a prohibition against losses, the owner could take the following steps to avoid the tax on the gain recognized by the corporation when the property is distributed. First, the owner would contribute the equipment (with the built-in loss) to the corporation, for which the corporation would take a $1,000 carryover basis. Second, the corporation would distribute *both* the property and the equipment. If the $1,000 loss on the equipment (value $0, basis $1,000) were allowed, it would offset the $1,000 gain on the land that must be recognized (value $1,000, basis $0). Moreover, the taxpayer would not pay any tax on the distribution of the equipment since it has a value of zero, and the taxpayer would still hold the equipment after the series of transactions is complete.[32] The rule against loss recognition prevents such possibilities.

The no-loss rule also bars taxpayers from creating artificial losses when the property is still under the taxpayer's control. For example, consider a wholly owned corporation that desires losses to reduce its income. Absent the loss prohibition rule, it could distribute loss property to its sole shareholder and recognize the loss even though the property was still controlled by the shareholder. Section 311 foils this scheme by disallowing the loss.

Property Subject to a Liability

When property subject to a liability is distributed, the corporation is relieved of an obligation. In such case, the effect to the corporation is the same as if it had sold the property for cash equal to the liability and paid off the debt. Consistent with this approach, § 311 provides that the fair market value of the property is deemed to be *no less* than the amount of the liability.[33] Thus, when the liability exceeds both the fair market value and the basis of the property, the corporation must recognize gain equal to the excess of the liability over the basis. If the liability does not exceed the property's fair market value, it is ignored for gain recognition purposes and the fair market value is used.

Example 13

T corporation owns land with a basis of $10,000 and that is subject to a liability of $40,000. Due to recent rezoning, the property has declined in value to $25,000. During the year, T distributed the land as a dividend to its sole shareholder, R. Since the liability exceeds the value of the property, the corporation has essentially received cash equal to the liability. Thus, the corporation must recognize a gain of $30,000 ($40,000 liability − $10,000 basis). Had the liability been $3,000, T Corporation would have recognized a gain of $15,000 ($25,000 value − $10,000 basis) because the liability is ignored in this instance.

---

[32] Note that the shareholder would have a zero basis in the equipment, so no further loss would result.

[33] § 311(b)(2).

EFFECT OF PROPERTY DISTRIBUTIONS ON THE CORPORATION'S E&P

Like distributions of cash, distributions of property require the corporation to make appropriate adjustments to its E&P. The general rule of Code § 312 demands that the corporation reduce E&P by the *adjusted basis* of the distributed property—in effect, the unrecovered amount of E&P tied up in the asset.[34]

Example 14

K Corporation purchased equipment several years ago for $10,000. After claiming $2,000 of depreciation on the asset, the corporation distributed it to its shareholder when it had a value of $5,000. The corporation must reduce E&P by the adjusted basis of the equipment, $8,000 ($10,000 − $2,000).

Although the general rule applies in most cases, special adjustments must be considered in three instances: (1) distributions of appreciated property; (2) distributions of property subject to a liability; and (3) distributions of the corporation's own obligations (e.g., bonds).

Distributions of Appreciated Property

When a corporation calculates its E&P, special care must be taken in determining the effect of distributions of appreciated property. These distributions present unique problems because the corporation is required to recognize gain.

Due to the gain recognition requirement, the impact of appreciated property distributions on E&P is twofold.[35] First, E&P must be increased by the gain recognized on the distribution. Second, E&P must be decreased by the fair market value of the property.[36] The effect of these adjustments is equivalent to what would have occurred had the corporation sold the property (thereby increasing E&P by the gain on the sale) and distributed the cash proceeds from the sale. Generally, the *net* effect is to reduce E&P by the original basis of the distributed property. However, E&P would decrease for any taxes resulting from the gain recognized.

Example 15

During the year, D Inc. distributed land worth $50,000 (basis $10,000). Since the distributed property is appreciated, the corporation must recognize a gain of $40,000 ($50,000 − $10,000). The gain increases D's current E&P by $40,000. D's E&P is then reduced by the fair market value of the property, $50,000. Thus, the net effect of the distribution on the corporation's E&P—ignoring any taxes paid on the gain—is to decrease E&P by $10,000, as follows:

Increase E&P by gain recognized	$ 40,000
Decrease E&P by value of property	(50,000)
Net decrease in E&P	$(10,000)

As suggested above, the effect of the distribution is the same as if the corporation had sold the property for $50,000 (thereby increasing E&P by the $40,000 gain) and distributed the $50,000 proceeds (thereby decreasing E&P by $50,000). Note also that the net decrease in E&P is equal to the original basis of the distributed property, $10,000.

---

[34] § 312(a).

[35] § 312(b).

[36] It may be useful to think of the basis to the distributing corporation as being increased by the gain recognized. By so doing, the general rule would still apply.

Corporations sometimes overlook the nuances in property distributions only to be surprised that what they originally thought would be a nontaxable return of capital distribution is in fact a dividend.

Example 16

Near year-end, T, the accountant for Z Inc., examined the corporation's financial position to determine the possible consequences of a property distribution. Upon inspection, he determined that the corporation had neither accumulated E&P nor current taxable income. Based on this assessment, T believed that the time was right for distributing land worth $100,000 (basis $20,000) since the distribution apparently would be a nontaxable distribution to the shareholder. On the distribution, however, the corporation is required to recognize a gain of $80,000 ($100,000 − $20,000). The gain in turn increases E&P, causing the distribution to be treated as a dividend to the extent of any E&P created on the distribution itself.

Property Subject to a Liability

When property subject to a liability is distributed, or when the shareholder assumes liabilities in connection with the distribution, the corporation benefits from the relief of the liability. To reflect this benefit, the normal charge to E&P must be reduced by the amount of the liability.[37] Note that this decrease itself is reduced by the liability so the effect is to increase E&P by the amount of the liability distributed.

Example 17

During the year, C Corporation, which has substantial E&P, distributed land worth $60,000 (basis $80,000) to its sole shareholder. The land is subject to a $30,000 mortgage. Under the general rule, C reduces E&P by the basis of the property, $80,000. This charge must be reduced, however, by the amount of the mortgage, $30,000. Thus, C's E&P is reduced by $50,000 ($80,000 − $30,000).

Example 18

D Corporation distributed a building worth $100,000 (basis $70,000) to its sole shareholder. The building is subject to a mortgage of $40,000. In contrast to the previous example, the property has appreciated, thus requiring an additional adjustment to E&P. The net effect of the distribution is to reduce E&P by $30,000, determined as follows:

Increase E&P by the gain recognized	$ 30,000
Decrease E&P by the value of property	(100,000)
Normal charge to E&P	$(70,000)
Reduction for liability	40,000
Net decrease in E&P	$(30,000)

---

[37] § 312(c).

Example 19

E Corporation distributed a warehouse worth $50,000 (basis $40,000) to its sole shareholder. The warehouse is subject to a mortgage of $75,000. The net effect of the distribution is to *increase* E&P by $35,000, determined as follows:

Increase E&P by gain recognized ($75,000 – $40,000)	$ 35,000
Decrease E&P by value (not less than the liability)	(75,000)
Normal charge to E&P	$(40,000)
Reduction for liability	75,000
Net increase in E&P	$ 35,000

Note that reducing the normal charge to E&P by the liability effectively increases E&P by $75,000. This properly reflects the fact that the corporation is better off without the liability.

Obligations of the Distributing Corporation

When a corporation distributes its own obligation (e.g., a bond), E&P is normally reduced by the principal amount of the obligation.[38] Without some modification, corporations could use this general rule essentially to eliminate E&P at little or no cost to the shareholder.

Example 20

K Corporation has $500,000 of E&P, which it would like to eliminate to make return of capital distributions. To this end, it issued bonds with a principal amount of $500,000 to its shareholders. Since the bonds bear interest at a rate of only 2 percent, they are worth only $100,000. As a result, the noncorporate shareholders report dividend income of only $100,000, but the corporation, in the absence of a special rule, could reduce its E&P account by the principal amount of the bonds, $500,000. In effect, the corporation could wipe out $500,000 of E&P at the cost of a tax on $100,000.

To end the discrepancy between the amount of the dividend reported and the amount of the E&P reduction, Congress modified the general rule. Where the corporation distributes its own obligations that have original issue discount, E&P is reduced by the "issue price" of the obligation.[39] The issue price is normally the same as the obligation's value.

Example 21

Same facts as in *Example 20*. The reduction to E&P is limited to the issue price of the securities, which normally approximates the securities' fair market value. Accordingly, K would reduce E&P by $100,000, leaving it with a balance of $400,000.

The rules governing the treatment of property distributions are summarized in Exhibit 3-7.

---

[38] § 312(a)(2). Note that there is a distinction between distributions of property subject to liabilities to third parties and distributions of the corporation's own obligations.

[39] *Ibid.*

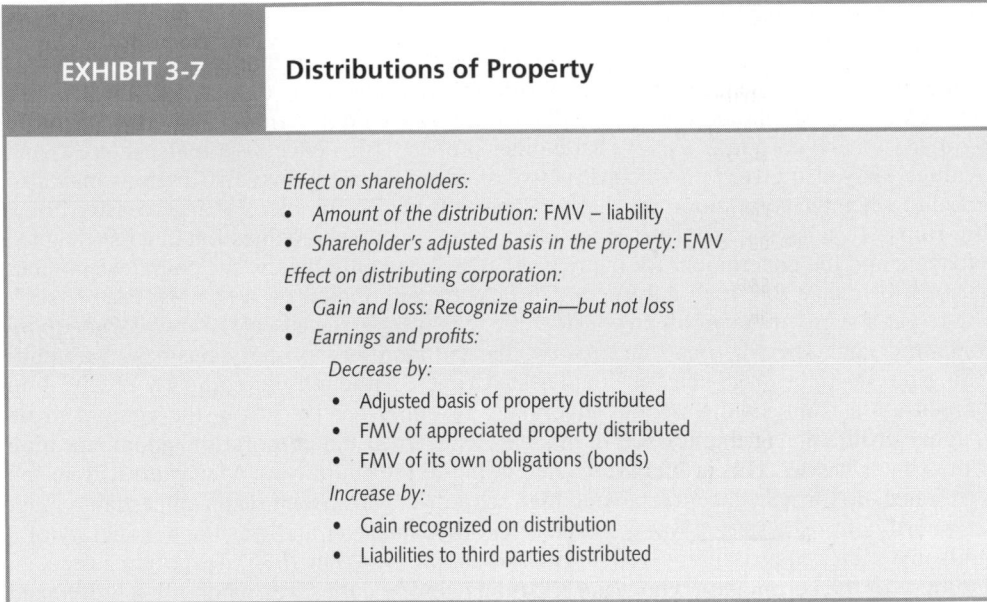

EXHIBIT 3-7   **Distributions of Property**

Effect on shareholders:

- *Amount of the distribution:* FMV – liability
- *Shareholder's adjusted basis in the property:* FMV

Effect on distributing corporation:

- *Gain and loss: Recognize gain—but not loss*
- *Earnings and profits:*

  Decrease by:
  - Adjusted basis of property distributed
  - FMV of appreciated property distributed
  - FMV of its own obligations (bonds)

  Increase by:
  - Gain recognized on distribution
  - Liabilities to third parties distributed

Constructive Distributions

LO.5

Identify a constructive distribution.

The rules governing corporate distributions apply solely to distributions paid with respect to the shareholder's stock and only if paid to the shareholder while in a shareholder capacity.[40] Consequently, when a shareholder receives payments as an employee for services rendered or as a creditor in satisfaction of a debt, the distribution rules are inapplicable. Similarly, the distribution rules do not apply when the corporation's payments are for property (e.g., a purchase) or for the use of property (e.g., rent), since the shareholder is not receiving these payments as a shareholder.

This is not to say, however, that the distribution rules are reserved solely for those distributions that have been formally authorized by the corporation's board of directors. For tax purposes, the failure to officially "declare a dividend" in the manner required by state law does not absolve the distribution from dividend treatment. If a corporation informally provides a benefit to a shareholder, it may be construed as a *constructive* or *disguised* distribution. The finding of a constructive distribution can be disastrous because the shareholder must report the distribution as a dividend and the corporation is not permitted to deduct the payment. Consequently, double taxation occurs.

The likelihood of discovering constructive distributions is greatest when the corporation is closely held. Constructive dividends are normally found in this setting because the dealings between the corporation and the shareholders are usually unstructured and informal. The fact that the corporation is an entity distinct from its owners is frequently overlooked because the corporation often is merely the alter ego of the shareholder. In effect, the shareholder who is also the chief executive officer and chairman of the board is likely to treat the corporate checkbook as his or her own. As a result, transactions often occur that are not made at arm's length. Some of these transactions may represent a deliberate attempt on the part of the shareholders to secure the use of corporate earnings without suffering the double tax penalty that arises upon a formal dividend distribution. For example, the corporation may try to disguise a nondeductible dividend simply by classifying the payment as a deductible bonus. Other transactions, however, may be recast as dividend distributions even though their effect was unintentional. Suffice it to say here that dealings between closely held corporations and their shareholders are quite vulnerable to dividend treatment.

Constructive dividends can take many forms. In all cases, however, a dividend is not imputed unless the transaction is deemed to be for the personal benefit of the shareholder rather than the corporation—often a difficult determination. The transactions most commonly recast as a dividend are summarized below.

---

[40] § 301(a).

EXCESSIVE COMPENSATION

When a corporation pays a shareholder-employee compensation that is deemed excessive for the services provided, that portion considered unreasonable is treated as a constructive dividend to the shareholder and is not deductible by the corporation. Similarly, excessive payments for the corporate use of shareholder property (i.e., excessive rents, interest, and royalties) may also give rise to a constructive dividend. Constructive distributions may also be found when the corporation purchases property from a shareholder at an excessive price. Unfortunately, what is considered excessive in these situations is a question that has plagued taxpayers and the government for many years. One need only review the countless number of cases to realize that reasonableness can only be determined on a case-by-case basis.[41]

To get a sense of the problem, consider the taxpayers in the cases of *Summit Publishing Company*[42] and *Menard, Inc.*[43] In *Summit,* the corporation's primary business was publishing the in-flight magazine for Southwest Airlines. Although the company received no compensation from Southwest, the advertising revenues received from the venture made it highly profitable. The sole issue in this case concerned the corporation's compensation of the owner's wife, Marcia Magavaro. According to the court, Mrs. Magavaro had no job experience, no formal education beyond high school, and no special skills other than typing. Yet, shortly after she started work, she became office manager and was the beneficiary of a handsome salary, approaching $72,000 in 1984 and $184,000 in 1985. At the same time, an employee of the corporation who was performing similar duties was paid only $40,000 and $50,000. Although it might seem that her salary is obviously out of line, this is only half right. The Tax Court, after closely reviewing the facts, found that the amount in the first year was justified by on-the-job-training, significant responsibilities, and the corporation's policy of generous compensation. Although the taxpayer escaped the first year, the court had a change of heart in the second year, holding that the tremendous increase was unreasonable.

In *Menard, Inc.* the nation's third-largest home improvement chain gave its founder, controlling shareholder, and CEO John Menard a compensation package exceeding $20.6 million (base salary of $157,500, profit sharing of $3 million, and a bonus of nearly $17.5 million). The IRS determined that the Mr. Menard's compensation was unreasonable. The IRS also challenged the arrangements relating to Team Menard Inc., a race-car operation, owned and operated by John Menard. Team Menard was used by the corporation in various promotional capacities. The corporation paid certain of Team Menard's expenses without any formal written agreement regarding the payments or reimbursement of the race car expenses. The IRS argued that Menard Inc.'s payment of Team Menard's expenses was a constructive dividend to John Menard.

In its analysis, the Tax Court found that the rate of return on investment generated by the Menard Inc. for the year at issue would be acceptable to an "independent investor" notwithstanding the compensation to John Menard. According to the Court, satisfaction of this so-called *independent investor test* established a presumption of reasonableness for the compensation. However, the Court still believed that the compensation was not reasonable when compared with that paid by competitors. The Court emphasized that under Regulation § 1.162-(b)(3) reasonable and true compensation "is only such amount as would ordinarily be paid for like services by like enterprises under like circumstances."

Relying on the government's comparison of CEO compensation for comparable companies (Home Depot, Kohl's, Lowe's, Staples, and Target), and a Black-Scholes stock option valuation model, the Court believed that the evidence demonstrated that comparable publicly traded companies paid substantially less compensation to their CEOs. Moreover, the evidence was sufficient to rebut the presumption of reasonableness. The Court ultimately found that about $7 million of the compensation was reasonable, thus denying a deduction for about $13 million. The court also believed that the arrangement with Team Menard resulted in a constructive dividend to Mr. Menard. Despite the Tax Court's interesting analysis, its decision was reversed on appeal.

---

[41] For examples, see *Mayson Manufacturing Co. v. Comm.*, 49-2 USTC ¶9467, 38 AFTR 1028, 178 F.2d 115 (CA- 6, 1949) concerning excessive compensation; and *Fairmount Park Raceway Inc. v. Comm.*, 64-1 USTC ¶9183, 13 AFTR2d 416-B, 327 F.2d 780 (CA-7, 1964) concerning excessive rents.

[42] 59 TCM 833, T.C. Memo 1990-288.

[43] 2009-1 USTC ¶50270, 103 AFTR2d 2009-1280 (CA-7, 2009), *rev'g* 66 TCM 833, T.C. Memo 2004-207.

The moral of these and other cases in this area is that the outcome is highly dependent on the facts in each situation. Nevertheless, taxpayers who have achieved success have generally relied on some or all of the following factors: (1) a written compensation policy approved by the board of directors that documents the rationale for the compensation; (2) a bonus system that is tied not to net earnings but to some other measure of business performance, such as sales or cost control; (3) a consistent, even if nominal, dividend history to develop a historical return on equity; and (4) compensation of shareholder-employees that is not in the same ratio as stock ownership.

One final note on reasonable compensation is warranted. Historically, most corporations have taken a very simple approach to the problem. They deduct all distributions to shareholder-employees as compensation and hope that the IRS never comes knocking on their door. And, even if these corporations lose the audit lottery, they presumably can rest easy knowing that the IRS will allow at least a "reasonable" amount to be deducted. However, a recent decision reveals that this approach can be quite dangerous.

In *O.S.C. & Associates, Inc.*, the IRS disallowed $3.1 million but not all of the corporation's $4.4 million deduction for compensation to its two shareholder-employees during 1990–1992.[44] The taxpayers contended that at least some portion of the disallowed amount represented reasonable compensation. Moreover, at trial the IRS conceded that a substantially larger amount should be deductible. However, the Courts disagreed. Both the Tax and Appellate Courts observed that the taxpayer neither met the reasonableness criteria nor proved that the distributions were intended to represent compensation. As a result, the Courts sustained the Commissioner's original position and rejected the dissenting opinion's call for greater apportionment to compensation. In addition, the Courts upheld the negligence penalty of $217,741 for failing to exercise due care. Based on this holding, taxpayers whose strategy has been to deduct all distributions as compensation and then wait for the IRS to determine how much is reasonable clearly risk losing the deduction for even the reasonable portion!

LOANS

One method of avoiding any type of taxable distribution to the shareholder (e.g., salary, dividend, or rent) is to loan the shareholder funds as may be required. Because taxation can be completely avoided, corporate advances to shareholders are highly vulnerable for recharacterization as dividends. To avoid recharacterization, the advance must represent a *bona fide loan*. A bona fide debtor-creditor relationship is generally suggested by the following: the advance is recorded on the books of the corporation and is evidenced by a note; the shareholder has made payments on the note according to a fixed schedule; the note bears a reasonable charge for interest; the note is secured by collateral; the due dates for payments have been enforced. Advances on open account, demand loans, loans that do not bear adequate interest, and loans that have no fixed maturity date are likely to be treated as disguised dividends.

In 1984, Congress ended the controversy concerning low-interest or no-interest loans to shareholders and employees. Section 7872 imputes a daily interest payment, at the applicable Federal rate, compounded semiannually, from the borrower (e.g., the shareholder or employee) to the corporation, which the corporation is deemed to have paid back to the borrower. The borrower generally is permitted to deduct the hypothetical interest payment made to the corporation. In addition, the borrower treats the transfer from the corporation as a dividend or compensation, depending on the borrower's status. On the other hand, the corporation may deduct the payment if it is considered compensation. The corporation is denied a deduction if the payment is treated as a dividend. Recently proposed regulations provide guidelines to be used in determining whether the hypothetical payment to a shareholder-employee is compensation or a dividend.[45] When the corporation is publicly held, the payment is treated as a dividend if the shareholder-employee owns more than 0.05% of the stock. In contrast, if the corporation is not publicly held, the payment is treated as a dividend if the shareholder-employee owns more than five percent of the stock. These guidelines are to be followed unless there exists convincing evidence to the contrary.

---

[44] 99-2 U.S.T.C. ¶ 50,765, 84 AFTR2d 99-5735, (CA-9, 1999) *aff'g* 73 TCM 3231 and T.C. Memo 1997-300.

[45] Prop. Reg. § 1.7872-9.

Although these rules can be quite onerous, § 7872 provides limited relief. The provision does not apply for any day that the loan between the corporation and the shareholder and/or employee does not exceed $10,000. For this purpose, loans to a husband and wife are aggregated and treated as a single loan.

Example 22

On January 1, 2016, Z Corp. loaned R, a 40% shareholder, $100,000, payable on demand without interest. At the end of the year, the loan was still outstanding. Assuming the applicable Federal rate of interest is 10% for the entire year, R is treated as having made an interest payment of $10,250 (10% compounded semiannually = 10.25% × $100,000) to the corporation. In addition, he is deemed to have received a dividend of $10,250. Whether this deemed transaction is merely a wash for R (i.e., the imputed income is offset by a deduction for the imputed payment) depends on whether R may deduct the interest. On the other hand, the corporation is not entitled to a deduction for the $10,250 payment because it is considered a dividend.

PAYMENTS FOR THE SHAREHOLDER'S BENEFIT

If the corporation pays the personal obligation of a shareholder, the payment may be treated as a constructive distribution. Whether the payment is ultimately treated as a distribution depends on the purpose of the expenditure. When it can be shown that the expenditure is incurred primarily for the benefit of the corporation, distribution treatment is avoided. Conversely, a constructive distribution ordinarily results when the expenditure is primarily for the benefit of the shareholder. As one might expect, it is usually difficult to ascertain the primary purpose for the outlay. Constructive distributions arising from a payment for the shareholder's benefit have been found to exist when the corporation paid the following: the shareholder's debt; charitable contributions where shareholders or their relatives receive benefits from the charity; the shareholder's expenses for financial and accounting services; and the payment of the shareholder's travel and entertainment expenses.

SHAREHOLDER USE OF CORPORATE PROPERTY

Constructive distributions can also occur when a shareholder uses corporate property for personal purposes at no cost. The most common distribution in this category is use of the company car. Of course, use of other company-owned property such as boats, airplanes, and entertainment facilities, including hunting lodges, also risks distribution treatment. Distributions of this type are typically avoided by having the shareholder reimburse the corporation for any personal use of the property or by including the value of such benefits in the shareholder's income as compensation.

BARGAIN PURCHASES

Corporations often allow shareholders to purchase corporate property at a price less than the property's fair market value. These so-called bargain purchases (to be distinguished from qualified employee discounts) are treated as constructive distributions to the extent the fair market value of the property exceeds the amount paid for the property by the shareholder.

Distributions of Stock and Stock Rights

As previously mentioned, corporate distributions of its own stock—commonly referred to as stock dividends—are not governed by the property distribution rules discussed above. Due to the unique characteristics of stock dividends, Congress has created a special set of rules prescribing their treatment. These provisions, currently found in § 305, are the product of many controversies over stock dividends that began early in tax history.

STOCK DIVIDENDS: A HISTORICAL PERSPECTIVE

The Revenue Act of 1913, the first tax statute, provided no information on whether stock dividends were taxable. As a result, the government attempted to tax stock dividends under the all-inclusive definition of income. Although they succeeded in the lower courts, the Supreme Court ruled in *Towns v. Eisner* that a stock dividend was not income under the 1913 Act.[46] Congress attempted to address the problem in the Revenue Act of 1916 by requiring the taxation of all dividends. Shortly thereafter, however, the Supreme Court, in the landmark case of *Eisner v. Macomber,* ruled that the provisions of the 1916 Act were unconstitutional where a corporation made a distribution of common on common.[47] Congress responded to this decision by providing in the Revenue Act of 1921 that stock dividends were nontaxable. This general rule still exists today in § 305.

> **LO.6**
> Explain the tax consequences of a stock dividend.

The general rule, as originally authored by the Supreme Court, was based on the theory that "a stock dividend really take[s] nothing from the property of the corporation and add[s] nothing to that of the shareholder."[48] This rationale still represents the guiding principle for determining the taxability of a stock dividend. When a corporation distributes its own stock, it is not distributing an asset of the business; indeed, the corporation's assets remain completely intact. On the shareholder side, assuming all shareholders receive their proportionate share of the stock distributed, they have essentially received nothing because their interest in corporate assets remains unchanged. Since the net effect is to leave both the corporation and the shareholder in the same economic position as they held prior to the distribution, the stock dividend—a misnomer in this case—is nontaxable. Note, however, that when the distribution is not pro rata (i.e., not all shareholders received their proportionate share of the distribution), the shareholders' interests have been altered, thus suggesting an alternative tax treatment.

Over the years, the general rule excluding all stock dividends from tax has been modified to prohibit sophisticated schemes designed by management to satisfy the desires of their shareholders. For example, absent a special rule, the corporation could distribute cash to some shareholders and stock to others and the stock distribution would escape tax even though the interests of the shareholders have changed dramatically. In this case, the shareholders who received stock have exchanged immediate returns of ordinary income for possible capital gain. To prohibit this and other possibilities, Congress has provided that certain types of stock dividends are taxable. The specific provisions applying to stock dividends are discussed below.

NONTAXABLE DISTRIBUTIONS OF STOCK AND RIGHTS

Subject to five exceptions considered below, § 305 provides that gross income does not include distributions of stock of the distributing corporation. Similarly, when a corporation distributes rights to acquire its own shares, the distribution is nontaxable. The sole effect of a nontaxable distribution of stock or rights concerns the shareholder's basis.

Basis of Distributed Stock: Nontaxable Distribution

If the distribution of stock is nontaxable, only the shareholder's basis *per share* is altered. Specifically, the shareholder must allocate a portion of the basis of the original stock to the distributed stock. Technically, the basis is allocated between the "old" and "new" stock in proportion to the relative fair market values of the old and new stock on the date of distribution, as illustrated in Exhibit 3-8.[49] When the old shares are identical to the new shares, however, the basis for each share is simply determined by dividing the basis of the old stock by the total number of shares held by the shareholder after the distribution. Since the cost basis of the old shares effectively carries over to the new shares, the holding period of the old shares also carries over to the new shares.[50] Thus, the shareholder is treated as holding the new stock for the same period as the old stock.

---

[46] *Henry R. Towns v. Eisner*; 1 USTC ¶14, 3 AFTR 2959, 245 U.S. 418 (USSC, 1918).

[47] 1 USTC ¶32, 3 AFTR 3020, 252 U.S. 189 (USSC, 1920).

[48] *Ibid.*

[49] § 307.

[50] § 1223(b).

Example 23

B owned 30 shares of XYZ Corporation common stock, which she acquired on July 8, 2009 for $900. On May 1, 2016, the corporation declared a 3 for 2 stock split for common shareholders. [Note that this split is the equivalent of a 50% stock dividend ($[3 - 2] \div 2$).] As a result, B received 15 additional shares of common stock. The common shares had a value of $40 on the date of distribution. Each of the 45 shares held after the distribution has a basis of $20 per share, determined as follows:

$$\frac{\text{Basis in old stock}}{\text{Number of shares after distribution}} \times \frac{\$900}{45} = \$20 \text{ per share}$$

The holding period for both the old and new shares begins on July 8, 2009, the acquisition date of the original stock.

If the nontaxable stock distribution consists of shares that are not identical to the original shares, the basis allocation using relative values as shown in Exhibit 3-8 must be used.

Example 24

Assume the same facts as in *Example 23*, except that the 15 shares received were preferred stock worth $160 per share. A distribution of preferred on common is nontaxable since the proportionate interest of the common shareholders does not change. The basis allocation is computed as follows:

Step 1:   Determine total fair market value (FMV) of old and new stock.

FMV of old stock (30 shares × $40)	$1,200
+ FMV of new stock received (15 shares × $160)	2,400
Total FMV of stock	$3,600

Step 2:   Allocate original basis of old stock between old and new stock according to relative FMVs.

$$\frac{\text{FMV of old stock}}{\text{Total FMV of stock}} \times \text{Original basis of old stock} = \text{New basis of old stock}$$

$$\frac{\$1,200}{\$3,600} \times \$900 = \$300$$

$$\frac{\text{FMV of new stock}}{\text{Total FMV of stock}} \times \text{Original basis of old stock} = \text{Basis of new stock received}$$

$$\frac{\$2,400}{\$3,600} \times \$900 = \$600$$

The revised basis of the common stock is $300. The basis of the preferred stock is $600. The holding periods of both the common and preferred stock begin on July 8, 2009.

EXHIBIT 3-8	Basis of Stock and Rights Received in Nontaxable Distribution

Basis of Stock:

Step 1: Determine total fair market value (FMV) of old and new stock.

FMV of old stock	$xx,xxx
+ FMV of new stock received	xx,xxx
Total FMV of stock	$xx,xxx

Step 2: Allocate original basis of old stock between old and new stock according to relative FMVs.

$$\frac{\text{FMV of old stock}}{\text{Total FMV of stock}} \times \text{Original basis of old stock} = \text{New basis of old stock}$$

$$\frac{\text{FMV of new stock}}{\text{Total FMV of stock}} \times \text{Original basis of old stock} = \text{Basis of new stock received}$$

Basis of Rights:

Step 1: Determine total fair market value (FMV) of old stock and the rights received.

FMV of old stock	$xx,xxx
+ FMV of rights received	xx,xxx
Total FMV of stock	$xx,xxx

Step 2: If FMV of rights ≥ (15% of value of stock), allocation of basis between old stock and rights required; otherwise elective.

Step 3: Allocate original basis of old stock between old and new rights received according to relative FMVs.

$$\frac{\text{FMV of old stock}}{\text{Total FMV of stock}} \times \text{Original basis of old stock} = \text{New basis of old stock}$$

$$\frac{\text{FMV of old rights}}{\text{FMV of stock and rights}} \times \text{Original basis of old stock} = \text{Basis of new stock received}$$

Stock Rights

The treatment of nontaxable distributions of rights follows the pattern designed for nontaxable distributions of stock. As a general rule, the shareholder must allocate the basis of the original stock between the stock and the rights in proportion to their relative fair market values. The formula for allocating the basis of the original stock is shown in Exhibit 3-8. As indicated there (Step 2), however, if the fair market value of the rights is less than 15% of the fair market value of the stock as of the date of distribution, the basis of the rights is zero *unless* the shareholder elects to make the normal allocation.[51] The election must be filed with the shareholder's return for the year in which the rights are received.[52] Failure to properly make the election results in a zero basis for the rights. If the basis allocation is made, the holding period of the original stock carries over to the rights. If the rights are subsequently exercised to purchase stock, the holding period of the acquired stock begins on the date of acquisition.

A shareholder who receives stock rights has three alternatives with respect to their use: (1) the rights may be sold, in which case the gain or loss is measured using the basis that was assigned to the rights; (2) the rights may be exercised, in which case any basis assigned to the rights is added to the basis of the stock acquired with the rights; or (3) the rights may lapse, in which case any basis that may have been assigned to the rights reverts back to the original stock—in other words, a loss cannot be created by allocating basis to the rights and then allowing them to lapse.[53]

Example 25

T Corporation distributed nontaxable stock rights to its shareholders on January 3. C received 100 rights on the 100 shares of common stock he purchased three years ago for $1,000. On the date of distribution, T Corporation's common stock had a value of $15 per share and the rights had a value of $5 each. On March 1, C sold the rights for $7 each. The stock had a value of $17 per share on March 1. C is required to allocate his stock basis between the stock and the rights because the value of the rights is at least 15% of the value of the stock ($500 ÷ $1,500 = 33%). The allocation is based on the relative fair market values of the stock and the rights as of January 3, the date of the distribution. The March 1 value of the stock is irrelevant. The basis allocation is computed as follows:

Step 1:	FMV of C's common stock (100 × $15).....................................	$1,500
	FMV of C's stock rights (100 × $5)	500
	Total FMV of stock and stock rights	$2,000

(a)

$$\frac{\text{FMV of C's common stock}}{\text{Total FMV of stock and stock rights}} \times \text{Old basis}$$

$$\frac{\$1,500}{\$2,000} \times \$1,000 = \underline{\$750} \ (\$7.50 \ per \ share)$$

(b)

$$\frac{\text{FMV of C's stock rights}}{\text{Total FMV of stock and stock rights}} \times \text{Old basis}$$

$$\frac{\$500}{\$2,000} \times \$1,000 = \underline{\$250} \ (\$250 \ per \ share)$$

C's gain on the sale of his stock rights is computed as follows:

Selling price of stock rights (100 × $7)..	$700
Less: Basis in stock rights..	(250)
Gain on sale of stock rights	$450

---

[51] § 307(b)(1).

[52] Reg. § 1.307-2.

[53] Reg. § 1.307-1(a).

Example 26

Assume the same facts as in *Example 25*, except that C does not sell the stock rights, but allows them to lapse on June 1. Since the stock rights lapsed, rather than being exercised or sold, there is no basis allocated to them. C has no recognized loss (since the rights have no basis) and the basis of the old shares remains $1,000.

Example 27

Assume the same facts as in *Example 25*, except that the fair market values of the stock and rights on January 3 were $19 and $1, respectively. Since the total value of the rights ($100) is less than 15% of the value of the stock (15% of $1,900 = $285), no allocation is required. C would have a $700 gain on the sale of the stock rights since their basis was zero. The gain would be long-term because the holding period of the rights includes the holding period of the stock.

Example 28

Assume the facts from *Example 27*, except that C elected to allocate basis between the stock and the stock rights. The basis of the rights is computed as follows:

$$\frac{\text{FMV of stock rights}}{\text{FMV of stock and stock rights}} \times \text{Old basis}$$

$$\frac{\$100 \text{ rights} \times \$1}{(100 \text{ rights} \times \$1) + (100 \text{ shares} \times \$19)} \times \$1,000 \text{ old basis}$$

$$\frac{\$100}{(\$2,000)} \times \$1,000 = \underline{\$50} \text{ basis in stock rights}$$

Here, the sale of the rights for $700 would result in a $650 gain ($700 − $50).

Effect on Distributing Corporation

Nontaxable stock or right distributions have no effect on the distributing corporation. The corporation recognizes no gain or loss.[54] In addition, in contrast to the capitalization of earnings required for financial accounting purposes, E&P of the distributing corporation is unchanged.[55]

TAXABLE STOCK DIVIDENDS

As noted above, five exceptions contained in § 305 require the taxation of certain stock dividends. When these exceptions apply, the stock or right distributions become subject to the special rules governing property distributions discussed above.[56] With respect to the

---

[54] § 311(a)(1).

[55] § 312(d).

[56] § 305(b).

shareholder's treatment of the distribution, the *amount* of the distribution is the fair market value, regardless of whether the shareholder is a corporation or an individual.[57] Of course, the amount of the distribution is treated as a dividend to the extent it is considered out of E&P. The shareholder's basis of the stock is its fair market value and the holding period begins on the date of distribution. With respect to the effect of the taxable distribution on the corporation, the corporation recognizes no gain or loss.[58] However, the corporation does reduce E&P by the fair market value of the taxable stock or rights distributed at the time of distribution.

The distributions selected for taxation reflect the basic principle first announced in *Eisner v. Macomber:* distributions that do not alter the proportionate interests of the shareholders are tax-free, while those that do are taxable. The taxable stock and right distributions are:[59]

1. *Distributions in Lieu of Money:* Distributions in which the shareholder may elect to receive the corporation's stock or other corporate property.

2. *Disproportionate Distributions:* Distributions in which some shareholders receive property and the other shareholders receive an increase in their proportionate share of corporate assets or E&P.

3. *Distributions of Common and Preferred Stock:* Distributions in which some common shareholders receive common stock while other common shareholders receive preferred stock.

4. *Distributions on Preferred Stock:* Any distribution on preferred stock, other than an increase in the conversion ratio of convertible preferred stock made solely to take into account a stock dividend or stock split with respect to the stock to which the convertible may be converted. Note that a distribution of preferred on common is nontaxable since the equity interests of the common shareholders are not affected.

5. *Distributions of Convertible Preferred Stock:* Distributions of convertible preferred stock unless it is established that they are not substantially disproportionate.

In addition to these taxable distributions, dividend income may arise from a variety of other events (e.g., a change in the redemption or conversion price) affecting the corporation's outstanding stock.[60] A complete discussion of these rules is beyond the scope of this book.

Tax Planning

As may be apparent from previous reading, the corporate entity offers many tax advantages. For example, corporate tax rates historically have been substantially lower than individual tax rates. Indeed, the difference between corporate and individual tax rates has ranged as high as 65 percentage points in the short history of our income tax Exhibit 3-9. This disparity alone has caused many taxpayers to operate their businesses in the corporate form to avoid high individual tax rates. Although this trend was reversed in 1987, the new relationship did not endure long. Currently, the top individual rate is 39.6% (2016), and the maximum corporate rate is 35% (34% for corporations with less than $10 million of taxable income). In any event, the corporation, as a separate taxable entity, provides a means to split income. By splitting income between the taxpayer and one or more corporations, the taxpayer can minimize the tax rate that applies to such income.

---

[57] Reg. § 1.305-1(b).

[58] § 311(a).

[59] § 305(b)(1) through (5).

[60] § 305(c).

Example 29

J is married and files a joint return. This year, J's sole proprietorship had net income of $100,000 before taxes. Ignoring the availability of any deductions or exemptions, J's personal tax liability based on a joint return for 2016 is $16,543. If J incorporates the business and draws a salary of $50,000, he will pay an individual tax of only $6,573. The balance of the income, $50,000 ($100,000 – $50,000) is taxed to the corporation. The 2016 corporate tax on such income is $7,500. As a result, the total tax paid on the $100,000 income is $14,073 ($7,500 + $6,573). As summarized below, by splitting the income between the corporation and himself, J has saved taxes of $2,470 ($16,543 – $14,073). Note that the result would be the same if J opted to operate his business as an S corporation or a partnership instead of a sole proprietorship.

		C Corporation Tax	Married S Corporation Partnership Tax
2016 corporate tax on $100,000		$22,250	
2016 individual tax on $100,000			$16,543
Tax if $100,000 is split equally: $50,000 to each			
Corporation	$ 7,500		
Individual	6,573		
Total	$14,073	(14,073)	(14,073)
Tax savings		$ 8,177	$ 2,470

The results are even more dramatic when an income stream of $200,000 is split equally.

		C Corporation Tax	Married S Corporation Partnership Tax
2016 corporate tax on $200,000		$61,250	
2016 individual tax on $200,000			$42,986
Tax if $200,000 is split equally: $100,000 to each			
Corporation	$22,250		
Individual	16,543		
Total	$38,793	(38,793)	(38,793)
Tax savings		$22,457	$ 4,193

In addition to the potential for income splitting, other advantages are obtained by incorporation. For instance, the dividends-received deduction and certain nontaxable fringe benefits (including health and life insurance) are available only through use of the corporate form. Whenever the corporate form is used, however, the potential for double taxation exists. Thus, much of the planning related to corporate taxation involves capitalizing on the attractions of the corporate entity while at the same time avoiding or at least reducing the double-tax penalty. In short, the obvious aim of most planning concerned with distributions has been to devise ways of extracting earnings from the corporation without suffering the double-tax penalty resulting from dividend treatment. It should be emphasized, however, that when the *shareholder* is a corporation, dividend treatment is generally preferable because of the dividends-received deduction.

	Individual and Corporate Tax Rates:
EXHIBIT 3-9	**A Comparison of the Top Marginal Rates**

Year(s)	Individual Rate (%)	Corporate Rate (%)	Difference
1913–15	7	1	6
1916	15	2	13
1917	67	6	61
1918	77	12	65
1919–21	73	10	63
1922–23	58	12.5	45.5
1924	46	12.5	33.5
1925	25	13	12
1926–27	25	13.5	11.5
1928	25	12	13
1929	25	11	14
1930–31	25	12	13
1932–35	63	13.75	49.25
1936–37	79	15	64
1938–39	79	19	60
1940	79	24	55
1941	81	31	50
1942–43	88	40	48
1944–45	94	40	54
1946–49	91	38	53
1950	91	42	49
1951	91	51	40
1952–53	92	52	40
1954–63	91	52	39
1964	77	50	27
1965–67	70	48	22
1968–69	70	52.8	17.2
1970	70	49.2	20.8
1971–78	70	48	22
1979–81	70	46	24
1982–86	50	46	4
1987	38.5	40	–1.5
1988–90	28	34	–6
1991–92	31	34	–3
1993–2000	39.6	35	4.6
2001	39.1	35	4.1
2002	38.6	35	3.6
2003–12	35	35	0
2013–16	39.6	35	4.6

Sources: Corporate tax rates from Tax Policy Center http://www.taxpolicycenter.org/taxfacts/Content/PDF/corporate_historical_bracket.pdf; Individual tax rates from Tax Foundation: U.S. Federal Individual Income Tax Rates History, 1913–2011 (Nominal and Inflation-Adjusted Brackets) http://www.taxfoundation.org/files/federalindividualratehistory-20080107.pdf

AVOIDING DISTRIBUTIONS OUT OF EARNINGS AND PROFITS

Since a distribution is taxable as a dividend only to the extent it is made out of earnings and profits, dividend treatment can be avoided simply by making the distribution when the corporation does not have E&P.

Example 30

Z Corporation has a deficit in both accumulated and current E&P for the current year. Despite recent losses, it expects operations to become profitable next year. Assuming the corporation plans to make a distribution, timing is critical. Given its projections, a distribution in the current year would be a return of capital, while a distribution in the following year would be taxable as a dividend to the extent of the corporation's current E&P for that year. As the above example illustrates, dividend treatment was avoided by making the distribution when the corporation did not have E&P. Similar results can be obtained if the corporation eliminates E&P prior to the distribution. One way E&P can be eliminated at little or no cost is by distributing property that has a high basis but a low market value.

Example 31

T corporation has no current E&P but has accumulated E&P of $40,000. If T distributes property with a market value of $1,000 and a basis of $40,000, the E&P would be totally eliminated at the cost of a tax on a dividend of only $1,000. This advantage is secured because E&P is reduced by the basis of any property distributed, while the amount of the dividend is the property's market value. Note that a subsequent cash distribution would not be a dividend because the property distribution wiped out E&P. Although this technique eliminates E&P, its cost may be prohibitive because the $39,000 loss realized on the property distribution is not recognized and would forever be lost.

NONDIVIDEND DISTRIBUTIONS

Double taxation also can be avoided to the extent the corporation makes deductible payments either directly or indirectly to its shareholders. The best examples of such payments—which in effect are distributions—are those that are nontaxable to the shareholder-employee but are immediately deductible by the corporation. For example, the corporation can establish a medical reimbursement plan that pays the medical expenses of its shareholders. In the context of a one-person corporation, this is an extremely valuable benefit because the payment is nontaxable to the shareholder-employee. In addition, the benefit is not subject to FICA or FUTA taxes. Moreover, the corporation is entitled to deduct all of the payment, which, if made by the shareholder-employee, could be deducted only to the extent it exceeded 7.5% of adjusted gross income. Similar advantages can be obtained for group term life insurance, meals and lodging, and certain other employee fringe benefits.

In addition, the corporation could pay expenses that benefit the shareholder personally. For example, travel and entertainment may be primarily for the benefit of the corporation but also indirectly benefit the shareholder-employee. In effect, the ability to deduct the costs of country club memberships, tickets for sporting events and the theater, sumptuous dining, travel, and other perquisites for the shareholder-employee provides a means to extract earnings from the corporation at no tax cost. Clearly, combining business with pleasure has its rewards. In making such payments, however, the parties must be concerned with the possibility that the IRS may prescribe dividend treatment for the transaction. In the case of nonstatutory fringe benefits that the shareholder-employee *indirectly* receives, dividend treatment is usually avoided if it can be shown that the expenditure was undertaken primarily for the benefit of the corporation rather than for the shareholder.

Charitable contributions by closely held corporations illustrate the dilemma the IRS faces in determining whether the payments primarily benefit the corporation or the shareholders. It seems that charitable contributions made by a closely held corporation, which is effectively the alter ego of its shareholders, clearly benefit the shareholder rather than the corporation. Nevertheless, in a private letter ruling, the IRS has held that no benefit inures to the shareholder—and thus no dividend—unless the contribution by the corporation satisfies the shareholder's charitable pledge.[61] Given this interpretation, for the charitably minded owner, earnings are easily obtained from the corporation without penalty as long as the taxpayer has no obligation to make a charitable contribution.

The second category of corporate payments that avoid dividend treatment are those that are deductible but tax deferred. This next best alternative consists primarily of payments to qualified pension and profit-sharing plans. Contributions to these plans on behalf of the shareholder-employee are immediately deductible by the corporation but not taxable until the shareholder-employee receives the benefits. More important, the earnings on the contributions are not taxed until distributed. Contributions to qualified plans essentially provide another means to secure the earnings of the corporation without double taxation, since the contributions are working for the shareholder-employee's benefit. Moreover, subject to limitations, the shareholder-employee can borrow from these plans. In so doing, the shareholder is paying interest to himself or herself, thus compounding interest tax-free for later distribution.

The third technique for avoiding dividend treatment is making deductible payments that are taxable to the shareholder-employee. For example, the corporation may make salary payments to compensate the shareholder for services to the corporation, interest payments on loans made by the shareholders to the corporation, or payments of rent for property leased from the shareholder. In this regard, however, the parties must take care that the distributions not be considered as excessive and hence as dividends.

In the previous paragraphs, methods for obtaining corporate earnings by completely avoiding double taxation have been considered. An alternative approach is to accept double taxation but attempt to reduce the cost of the second tax. For example, if the shareholder was in the 35% tax bracket, a sale of the stock would produce a maximum tax on the resulting capital gain of 15 percent, or if the stock is § 1202 qualified small business stock, a rate of 14 percent.

Problem Materials

DISCUSSION QUESTIONS

3-1 *Distributions in General.* The Code contains an intricate scheme governing the tax consequences of a distribution by a corporation to its shareholders. This system is attributable, at least in part, to the fact that corporate distributions can assume a variety of forms.

    a. Briefly outline the various forms or types of distributions, indicating the characteristic (or characteristics) distinguishing one from the other.

    b. What are the principal objectives underlying the rules prescribing the treatment of corporate distributions?

3-2 *Earnings and Profits Concept.* The concept of earnings and profits serves an important role in the taxation of corporate distributions. Address each of the following:

    a. What does E&P represent (i.e., conceptually) and what is its function?

    b. Explain the relationship between E&P, "retained earnings," and "earned surplus."

3-3 *Sections 301 and 316: Statutory Framework.* Assuming a shareholder receives a cash distribution from a corporation, briefly explain the general rules governing the tax consequences to the shareholder.

3-4 *Reporting Corporate Distributions.* Schedule B of Form 1040 is used by individual taxpayers to report dividend and interest income. Two lines in that form require the reporting of "capital gain distributions" and " nontaxable distributions," respectively. To what does each of these lines refer?

---

[61] See Letter Rul. 8152094 and *Henry J. Knott*, 67 T.C. 681 (1977).

3-5 *E&P Computation in General.* Briefly explain the following:
   a. How is current E&P computed (i.e., the general formula)?
   b. How is accumulated E&P computed?
   c. Why is there a need to distinguish between current and accumulated E&P?

3-6 *Distributions: Operating Rules.* Indicate whether the following statements are true or false. If the statement is false, explain why.
   a. Since most corporations make distributions only when they are profitable and then only to the extent of their current earnings, there generally is no need to compute accumulated E&P.
   b. A distribution made during a year when the corporation has neither accumulated E&P nor current E&P cannot be a dividend.
   c. Assuming R Corporation has $50,000 of accumulated E&P at the beginning of its second year of operations, a distribution of $10,000 will have the same effect to the shareholder whether it is made in the first year or second year of operations.
   d. A corporation with a deficit in accumulated E&P that substantially exceeds current E&P cannot make a dividend distribution.
   e. If a corporation makes four equal distributions, each of which exceeds current E&P of $10,000 and accumulated E&P of $0, the amount of the first distribution that constitutes a dividend will exceed the amount of the last distribution that constitutes a dividend. Assume all distributions are made during one taxable year.
   f. If a corporation makes four equal distributions, each of which exceeds current E&P of $10,000 and accumulated E&P of $5,000, the amount of the first distribution that constitutes a dividend will exceed the amount of the last distribution that constitutes a dividend. Assume all distributions are made during one taxable year.

3-7 *Property Distribution: "Amount."* When a corporation makes a distribution of property, the "amount" of the distribution must be determined to ascertain the distribution's effect on the shareholder. Briefly explain the rules for determining the "amount" of a property distribution.

3-8 *Property Distributions: Effect on Corporate Taxable Income.* Code § 311 contains the general rule governing the tax consequences to corporations on distributions of property. According to this rule, does a corporation usually recognize gain or loss on distributions of property? Explain.

3-9 *Property Distributions and Liabilities.* Corporations sometimes distribute property encumbered by a liability. Indicate whether the following are true or false, and if false, explain why.
   a. The liability has no effect on the amount of the dividend to be reported by the shareholder.
   b. The liability has no effect on the shareholder's basis for the property.
   c. Distributing the liability increases the corporation's E&P.

3-10 *Property Distributions: Effect on E&P.* When a corporation makes a distribution of property, a series of adjustments may be required.
   a. Is E&P ever increased as a result of a property distribution? If so, explain why.
   b. As a general rule, by what amount is E&P reduced when property is distributed?
   c. As a practical matter, when can this general rule be relied upon? Explain.

3-11 *Constructive Distributions.* The rules governing corporate distributions apply only to distributions paid *with respect to the shareholder's stock.* Can the distribution rules cause dividend treatment in the absence of a formal corporate resolution declaring a dividend? Explain.

3-12 *Stock Dividends.* As a general rule, stock dividends are nontaxable. However, like so many general rules in the Code, this one is also subject to exceptions.
   a. Why are stock dividends usually nontaxable?
   b. Under what circumstances will stock dividends be taxable? Include in your answer the reason why taxation results.
   c. Are distributions of rights to purchase stock of the distributing corporation treated in the same manner as stock dividends?

PROBLEMS

3-13 *E&P Computation.* For its current taxable year, K Corporation, a manufacturer of nuts and bolts, reported the following information using the accrual method of accounting:

Income:

Sales	$575,000
Cost of goods sold (LIFO)	(175,000)
Gross profit from operations	$400,000
Interest income:	
Municipal bonds	9,000
Corporate bonds	20,000
Dividends received	10,000
Ordinary income on installment sale	14,000
Life insurance proceeds	50,000

Expense:

Selling and administrative expenses	90,000
Amortization of organization expense	500
Fines for overweight trucks	1,000
Depreciation	50,000
Long-term capital loss	3,000
Net operating loss from prior year	60,000

In addition to the information above, the company's records reveal:

1. Cost of goods sold using FIFO would have been $150,000.
2. The dividends were received from a 30% owned domestic corporation.
3. The installment sale income arose from the sale of land for $100,000 (basis $30,000); $20,000 cash was received this year. The income was ordinary due to previous reporting of net § 1231 losses.
4. Life insurance proceeds arose from the death of the company's chief executive officer; K Corporation had paid the premiums on a term insurance policy covering the officer.
5. Organization expense represented amortization of total organization expense of $2,500.
6. Depreciation was computed using accelerated methods; straight-line depreciation using the appropriate recovery periods would have been $37,000.
7. Cash distributions to shareholders during the year were $12,000.

Required:
   a. Compute K Corporation's taxable income.
   b. Compute K's current E&P.

3-14 *E&P Computation.* USC Corp. reported $600,000 of taxable income during the year. A review of the corporation's financial records revealed this additional information:
   1. Taxable income included $50,000 of accelerated depreciation in excess of straight-line depreciation.
   2. A short-term capital loss of $30,000 was incurred this year, and USC had no current or prior year capital gains.
   3. Gross income of the corporation included $100,000 dividends received from a 50% owned domestic corporation.
   4. Interest income of $13,000 from bonds issued by the city of Chicago was included in the company's income reported for financial accounting purposes.
   5. The corporation made contributions of $9,000 in excess of the amount currently deductible.
   6. Cash distributions to shareholders during the year were $20,000. Compute the corporation's current E&P.

3-15 *Single Cash Distributions—Deficit E&P.* The books of P Inc. and Q Inc. reveal the following information at year-end before each corporation makes a $25,000 cash distribution on the last day of the taxable year:

	P Inc.	Q Inc.
Capital stock	$150,000	$200,000
Current E&P (deficit)	30,000	(30,000)
Accumulated E&P (deficit).	(40,000)	40,000

Compute the tax effects of each distribution for P Inc., P's shareholders, Q Inc., and Q's shareholders.

3-16 *Operating Rules: Single Cash Distribution.* F Inc. made a $50,000 distribution on February 1 of this year to its sole shareholder, H. H has a basis in her stock of $12,000. Determine the tax consequences of the distribution to H for each of the following situations:

	Accumulated E&P	Current E&P
a.	$ 6,000	$ 30,000
b.	(20,000)	15,000
c.	60,000	(25,550)
d.	(8,000)	(4,550)

3-17 *Operating Rules: Multiple Cash Distributions.* W Corporation was owned by C prior to a sale of all of his stock (basis at the beginning of the year, $5,000) to D in June for $10,000. During the year, W Corporation distributed $60,000 on May 1 and $40,000 on September 1. Indicate how the distributions would be treated by individual shareholders C and D in the following situations:

	Accumulated E&P	Current E&P
a.	$ 10,000	$ 50,000
b.	(70,000)	50,000
c.	95,000	(18,250)

3-18 *Multiple Cash Distributions—Positive E&P.* Z Corporation's books reveal the following information at year-end before cash distributions are considered:

Capital stock	$100,000
Current E&P	22,000
Accumulated E&P	32,000

M is a 10% shareholder whose basis for 1,000 shares is $8 per share, or $8,000 total. Compute the tax consequences to Z and M if corporate cash distributions during the year were:
a. $30,000 on December 31.
b. $12,000 for each of the first two quarters and $18,000 for each of the last two quarters.

3-19 *Distribution of Appreciated Property: General Concepts.* During the year, XYZ Sand and Gravel Corporation distributed a parcel of land to its sole shareholder, A. The land (value $20,000, cost $3,000) had been used in the corporation's quarry operations.
a. What is the effect of the distribution on the shareholder's taxable income?
b. What is A's basis in the land?
c. What is the effect of the distribution on XYZ's taxable income?
d. What is the effect of the distribution on XYZ's E&P?
e. How would your answers to (a), (b), (c), and (d) change if A were a corporation?

3-20 *Distribution of Property Subject to a Liability.* Answer *Problem 3-19,* assuming the property was subject to a mortgage of $7,000.

3-21 *Property Distributions: Comprehensive Problem.* M, an individual, owns all of the stock of MDI Corporation. MDI has $100,000 of E&P. During the year, MDI made the distributions described below.

   a. For each distribution indicate the following:

      1. The effect of the distribution on the shareholder's taxable income;

      2. The shareholder's basis for the property received;

      3. The effect of the distribution on MDI's taxable income; and

      4. The effect of the distribution on MDI's E&P.

         a. Land used by the corporation in its business since its purchase, value $5,000 (cost $1,000).

         b. Same as (a), except the land was subject to a mortgage of $3,500.

         c. Business equipment worth $3,000 (cost, $8,000; depreciation claimed, $1,000).

         d. MDI 10-year, 4 percent, $10,000 bond (value $8,500).

   b. Would the answers above change if M were a corporation rather than an individual?

3-22 *Property Distributions: Effect on Noncorporate Shareholder.* During the year, WRK Corp. distributed the items listed below to its sole shareholder, F, an individual. WRK has substantial E&P. For each of the distributed items, answer the following:

   1. What is the effect of the distribution on the shareholder's taxable income?

   2. What is the shareholder's basis of the property received?

      a. A small acreage of land used in the corporation's farming business was distributed, having a value of $70,000 (basis $20,000).

      b. Same as (a), except the acreage was subject to a mortgage of $30,000, which F assumed.

      c. A warehouse worth $60,000 (adjusted basis $90,000). Straight-line depreciation of $10,000 had been deducted since the property's acquisition.

3-23 *Effect of Distributions: Corporate Shareholder.* Answer *Problem 3-22,* assuming that F is a corporate shareholder.

3-24 *Effect of Distributions on Corporate Taxable Income.* Indicate the effect of the distributions identified in *Problem 3-22* on the corporation's taxable income, assuming that shareholder F is an individual.

3-25 *Effect of Distributions on Corporate E&P.* Indicate the effect of the distributions identified in *Problem 3-22* on the corporation's E&P, assuming that shareholder F is an individual.

3-26 *Property Distributions.* L Corporation has the following information at year-end before year-end property distributions are made.

Capital stock	$440,000
Current E&P	90,000
Accumulated E&P	110,000

Assume L's marginal tax rate is 34% and its shareholders' marginal tax rate is 28 percent. The property distributed is:

   a. T Inc. preferred stock held as an investment by L with a $40,000 market value and a $50,000 basis;

   b. Depreciable equipment with a $30,000 market value, a $45,000 cost, $20,000 accumulated depreciation, and a $25,000 basis; and

   c. Land with a $32,000 market value, $28,000 basis; and a mortgage of $34,000.

Compute L's gain or loss and E&P after the distributions.

3-27 *Disguised Distributions.* SDF Corporation, a home developer, is owned equally by F and S, father and son. Briefly discuss the tax consequences arising from the following situations:

    a. A review of the corporation's books reveals an account entitled "F Suspense." Closer examination discloses that the corporation debits this account for checks made payable to F. Most of these checks are cash advances to F made during the current year. The average balance of this account during the current year exceeded $20,000.

    b. One of the checks charged to a suspense account maintained for S was for $6,000. The payment was for a garage that was added on to S's home to house the company car that he drives.

    c. S drives a car that was purchased by the corporation and is titled in the corporation's name. S uses a credit card issued to the corporation (also in the corporation's name) by a major oil producer to purchase all of his gas and pay for miscellaneous repairs on the company car. The corporation routinely pays the credit card bill, which for this year was $3,000.

    d. During the year, the corporation paid S's daughter, D, $12,000 to empty the trash and vacuum the corporate offices (about 2,000 square feet of office space) once a week.

    e. The corporation added a screened-in porch to F's home at a cost of $3,500. The corporation normally charges cost plus 30% on projects of this type but charged F only $3,500.

    f. F sold land to the corporation for $100,000. The corporation plans to develop a subdivision on the property. Similar land was available for $75,000.

3-28 *Stock Dividends: Computations.* R owns 50 shares of A Corporation common stock, which he purchased in 2012 for $100 per share. On January 1 of the current year, A Corporation declared a dividend of one share of new preferred stock for each share of common. The shares were distributed on March 1. On that date, the common stock was selling for $150 per share and the preferred stock for $50 per share.

    a. How much income must R recognize on the receipt of the preferred stock?

    b. What is R's basis in the preferred stock?

    c. On June 1, R sells 25 shares of common stock for $175 per share and 25 shares of preferred stock for $75 per share. What is R's recognized gain or loss? Is it long-term or short-term?

3-29 *Stock Dividends: Computations.* E, an individual, has the following stock dividend information:

	Purchase Date	Stock Purchase Price	Stock Dividend	Market Price per Share at Distribution Common	Preferred
a.	5/13/2007	1,000 shares common in S Inc., $5,000	100 shares common	$ 6	
b.	10/3/2010	100 shares common in T Inc., $1,000	50 shares preferred	$15	$10
c.	11/2/2011	20 shares preferred in U Inc., $1,200	2 shares preferred		$75

All stock dividends were distributed in the current year, and all shareholders were required to receive the shares. Compute the tax effects to E for each of the three stock dividends.

3-30 *Stock Rights: Computations.* Y Corporation's profits had taken a deep dive in recent years. To encourage purchase of its stock, the corporation issued one stock right for each share of outstanding common stock. The rights allow the holder to purchase a share of stock for $1. The common stock was selling for $1.50 when the rights were issued (June 1). The value of the stock rights on June 1 was $0.50 each. A owns 1,000 shares of common stock for which he paid $20 per share 10 years ago, and therefore received 1,000 stock rights. A sold 100 rights on July 1 for $175. He exercised 100 rights on August 1 when the stock was selling for $1.80 per share. The remaining rights lapsed on December 30.

   a. How much dividend income must A recognize on June 1?
   b. How much gain or loss must A recognize on the July 1 sale of the stock rights? Is it long-term or short-term?
   c. What is A's recognized loss when the remaining rights lapse?
   d. What is the basis of the original 1,000 shares on December 31?

3-31 *Stock Rights: Computations.* K, an individual, received 100 stock rights with a $300 (100 × $3) market value on 1,000 shares of common stock with a value of $25,000 (1,000 × $25) and a basis of $18,000. Compute the tax effects for the following situations.

   a. K makes no special elections. He sells 25 rights for $3.50 each ($3.50 × 25 = $87.50), exercises 50 rights when the per-share price is $25 plus one right (50 × $25 = $1,250 paid), and forgot to exercise or sell the remaining 25 rights.
   b. Same as (a) except K makes the election to allocate basis to the rights.

3-32 *Transactions Affecting E&P.* For each of the following transactions, indicate whether a special adjustment must be made in computing R Corporation's current E&P. Answer assuming that E&P has already been adjusted for current taxable income.

   a. During the year, the corporation paid estimated Federal income taxes of $25,000 and estimated state income taxes of $10,000.
   b. The corporation received $5,000 of interest income from its investment in tax-exempt bonds.
   c. The corporation received a $10,000 dividend from General Motors Corporation.
   d. The corporation purchased machinery for $9,000 and expensed the entire amount in accordance with Code § 179.
   e. The corporation reported a § 1245 gain of $20,000.
   f. The corporation had a capital loss carryover of $7,000 from the previous year. This year the corporation had capital gains before consideration of the loss of $10,000.

3-33 *Transactions Affecting E&P.* For each of the following transactions, indicate whether a special adjustment must be made in computing K Corporation's current E&P. Answer assuming that E&P has already been adjusted for current taxable income.

   a. Negligence penalty of $5,000 for failure to issue Form 1099 to independent contractors.
   b. Realized gain of $10,000 on like-kind exchange, $4,000 of which was recognized.
   c. Distribution of formally declared dividend of $10,000 to shareholders.
   d. Income from long-term contract completed this year as reported on completed contract basis was $70,000. Twenty percent of the work was done this year.
   e. Charitable contribution of $12,000 in cash, of which $10,000 was deducted.

3-34 *Depreciation and E&P.* During 2016, D Corporation purchased a new light duty truck for $10,000. D computed depreciation using MACRS and deducted $2,000 of depreciation. What adjustment, if any, must be made in computing D's E&P for 2016?

3-35 *Gain for E&P.* Using the same facts as in *Problem 3-34* above, assume D Corporation sold the truck for $9,000 on June 30, 2017. Depreciation for 2017, using MACRS, was $1,600 ($10,000 × 32% × ½). What adjustment, if any, must be made in computing D's E&P for 2017? Assume E&P has been properly adjusted for all previous years.

TAX RESEARCH PROBLEM

3-36 P Inc. owns all of the stock of T Corporation, which operates a chain of ice cream shops throughout the Southwest. B Corp., a food conglomerate, wishes to expand into the ice cream business and is planning to acquire T. T currently has substantial cash balances. B's controller has suggested the following proposal for consummating the acquisition. Under the proposal, T distributes all of its cash to P, followed by a sale of the stock of T to B. The price of the T stock would reflect the shrinkage in T's value due to the cash distribution to R. Evaluate the proposal from the perspectives of both P and B.

Research aids:

Rev. Rul. 75-493, 1975-2, C.B. 108.

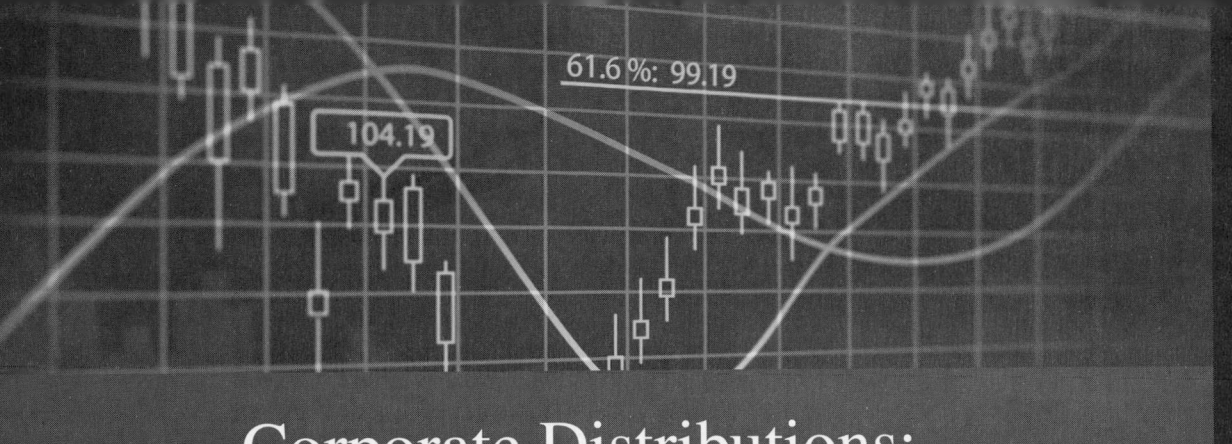

4

Corporate Distributions: Stock Redemptions and Partial Liquidations

Learning Objectives

Upon completion of this chapter you will be able to:

LO.1 Define a redemption and distinguish it from other types of nonliquidating distributions.

LO.2 Recognize when a redemption is treated as a sale rather than a dividend.

LO.3 Apply the constructive stock ownership rules to determine the effect of a redemption.

LO.4 Identify the tax consequences of a redemption to shareholders, including how to:
- Calculate the effect on shareholder taxable income.
- Calculate the shareholder's basis in any property received.
- Determine the effect on the basis of any stock held by the shareholder that was not redeemed.

LO.5 Define a partial liquidation and explain its tax treatment.

LO.6 Describe when redemptions related to paying death taxes are given sale treatment.

LO.7 Identify the tax consequences of a redemption to the distributing corporation, including how to:
- Calculate the effect on the corporation's taxable income.
- Calculate the effect on the corporation's earnings and profits.

LO.8 Identify when sales of stock to a related corporation are treated as a redemption by such corporation of its own stock.

LO.9 Explain a preferred stock bailout and the tax consequences relating to a sale or redemption of § 306 stock.

Chapter Outline

Introduction

In this chapter, the emphasis switches from distributions with respect to the shareholder's stock—dividend distributions—to distributions in *redemption* of the shareholder's stock. A redemption is defined as the acquisition by a corporation of its own stock from a shareholder in exchange for property. From the shareholder's point of view, the transaction appears to be identical to a sale to a third party, warranting favorable capital gain treatment.[1] However, appearances may be deceiving. Under certain circumstances, what in form may look like a sale may in effect be no different than a dividend. Historically, the significantly different tax treatment of sales and dividends (capital gain versus ordinary income) caused shareholders to structure distributions from their corporations as redemptions. As one might expect, the Code does not sit idly by letting shareholders select dividend or capital gain treatment as they please. As will be seen in this chapter, redemptions that are *essentially equivalent* to a dividend are treated as such. This chapter examines the problems inherent in determining how redemption distributions are taxed.

Stock Redemptions

LO.1

Define a redemption and distinguish it from other types of nonliquidating distributions.

Before examining the tax problems associated with redemption transactions, it may be helpful to consider why shareholders redeem rather than sell their stock to a third party. Redemptions often occur for the same reasons that other sales occur. For example, the shareholder may simply desire to withdraw from the business. This situation might arise when a shareholder wishes to make an investment elsewhere or wants to retire from the business. In contrast, sale of the shareholder's interest might be prompted by his or her death. In such case, the corporation may be obligated under some type of buy-sell agreement with the shareholders to purchase the decedent's interest from the estate.

Regardless of the circumstances, for some shareholders who wish to sell their stock, the only prospective buyer may be the corporation itself. Such a limited market typically exists when the corporation is closely held. In this setting, the other shareholders often do not have the resources to purchase the stock, yet all parties concerned do not want the stock to be sold to an outsider. When this situation arises, the corporation may have funds available to purchase all or a portion of the shareholder's stock. Similarly, if a shareholder wants to sell to a third party, the prospective buyer may have insufficient cash or other assets to make the purchase. In this case, the corporation may in effect finance the transaction in a "bootstrap acquisition," so called because the buyer's lack of funds is supplemented by those from the corporation. In an acquisition of this type, the corporation purchases some of the shareholder's stock and the remaining shares are purchased by the outsider.

Redemption of the corporation's own stock may also be appropriate from a corporate viewpoint. Indeed, a search of the Internet for so-called stock "buybacks" or "share-repurchase" reveals that they have become quite popular recently. Management likes them in part because they can signal the market that the stock is undervalued and may cause the stock price to increase. Financial ratios like earnings per share and return on equity may also improve. They can also be used to eliminate a hostile shareholder (e.g., a corporate raider). Shareholders like them because they are more tax efficient. Unlike a dividend, shareholders can choose the time when they will pay their taxes by simply electing not to sell their shares. Moreover, as discussed below, the shareholders' tax on a $1,000 buyback (redemption) is normally less than that on a $1,000 dividend because the shareholders can recover their basis in the shares they sold. They can also create capital gains to absorb capital losses.

Still another use of redemptions occurs when corporate management decides to take a publicly held company private. In this case, the corporation redeems all of the stock that is publicly traded, leaving the corporation's ownership in the hands of a few key individuals.

---

[1] § 317(b).

Another common use of redemptions, at least historically, has been to extract E&P out of the corporation at a cost significantly lower than that incurred with dividends. The cost is lower because the redemption transaction is treated as a sale. Over the years, sale treatment usually has produced substantial savings since any gain would be considered favorable capital gain. In effect, the shareholder paid a cheap second tax and avoided the harsh double tax penalty normally associated with dividends. It is this possibility—that is, the potential for bailing out E&P at the cost of a capital gains tax—that has necessitated a set of complex rules to distinguish whether the redemption was a true sale or merely a disguised dividend. However, the 2003 changes making the tax rate on dividends equivalent to those on capital gains has diminished this concern. Nonetheless, sale treatment can still be more favorable. Sale treatment enables a shareholder to recover any basis in the stock before having to report income. In addition, capital gain treatment is beneficial for those taxpayers with capital losses in excess of $3,000. Finally, sale treatment enables the taxpayer to use the installment sales method to lengthen the period over which any gain is reported.

In contending with the redemption provisions, it is important to remember the traditional role of dividends and capital gains in the tax arena. Tax practitioners generally equate dividends with the most undesirable tax result—*double* taxation of the same income! On the other hand, capital gain treatment has long been the taxpayer's proverbial pot of gold at the end of the tax rainbow, worthy of whatever steps are necessary to obtain it. For this reason, the area of redemptions has always been quite fertile for controversy: is the distribution a dividend or is it capital gain? In digesting the redemption rules, understand that these rules were designed when the stakes were high, and the government wanted to ensure that only deserving taxpayers were rewarded.

TREATMENT OF STOCK REDEMPTIONS: GENERAL CONSIDERATIONS

A quick look at a redemption reveals that it has the same characteristics as an ordinary sale: the stock of the shareholder is *exchanged* for property of the corporation. In such case, the transaction normally would receive capital gain treatment. Upon closer scrutiny, however, the transaction may have an effect that more closely resembles a dividend than a sale. That this may be true is easily seen in the classic example in which a corporation redeems a portion of its *sole* shareholder's stock. Although the shareholder surrenders stock as part of the exchange, like a dividend distribution, the interest of the shareholder in corporate assets as well as the shareholder's control over corporate affairs is completely unaffected.

LO.2
Recognize when a redemption is treated as a sale rather than a dividend.

Example 1

K Corporation has 100 shares of outstanding stock, all of which are owned by B. If K Corporation redeems 30 of B's shares, B still owns 100% of the stock outstanding. Since the redemption has not substantially affected B's interest in the corporation, the redemption distribution does not qualify for exchange treatment. Rather, it is treated as a dividend to the extent of K's E&P.

In the case of the one-owner corporation as illustrated above, it is somewhat obvious that the transaction more closely resembles a dividend than a sale. Dividend treatment is not limited to this situation alone, however. The effect is similar whenever the redemption is pro rata among all shareholders (e.g., a redemption of 10% of the stock held by each shareholder) since each shareholder's interest after the transaction is the same as before.

Standing in contrast to pro rata redemptions are those that are non-pro rata, or disproportionate. For example, a corporation might redeem 10% of one shareholder's stock and 20% of another's. For disproportionate redemptions such as this, the shareholder's interest (e.g., the rights to vote and to receive dividends and assets upon liquidation) is normally diluted just as if the shareholder had sold stock to a third party. Because such redemptions more closely resemble a sale to a third party, they are usually entitled to sale treatment. However, disproportionate redemptions may still warrant dividend treatment when the relationships between shareholders are considered.

> ### Example 2
>
> H and W each own 50% of the stock of KIN Corporation. If, in a non-pro rata redemption, the corporation redeems all of H's shares and none of W's shares, it is clear that H's interest has been significantly altered and that sale treatment would be appropriate. However, if H and W were husband and wife, it is easy to conclude that the redemption has had no effect on the *family's* interest in or control over the corporation.

As early as 1921, Congress recognized that the effect of a redemption may be indistinguishable from that of a dividend; consequently, Congress took action. From that time until 1954, sale treatment was granted only to redemptions that were *not essentially equivalent to a dividend*. If dividend equivalency was found, the amount paid by the corporation for the stock was taxed as a dividend to the extent that the corporation had E&P. To the dismay of all concerned, however, Congress provided no clues as to when a redemption was equivalent to a dividend. Lacking guidance, the courts generally found dividend equivalency only when the redemption was pro rata; yet in some cases, pro rata redemptions received sale treatment when a valid business purpose for the transaction was found. As a result, the courts were barraged by redeeming shareholders hoping to establish a satisfactory purpose or to find another road to capital gain treatment.

With the enactment of the 1954 Code, Congress attempted to clarify those situations in which redemptions would qualify for sale treatment. Current law, contained in § 302, provides sale treatment for the following redemptions:

1. The redemption is not essentially equivalent to a dividend.[2]
2. The redemption is substantially disproportionate.[3]
3. The redemption is in complete termination of the shareholder's interest.[4]
4. The redemption is in partial liquidation of the distributing corporation.[5]
5. The redemption is made in order to pay death taxes.[6]

In addition, special rules exist to police so-called redemptions through related corporations:[7] sales of stock of one corporation that the shareholder controls to another corporation that the shareholder also controls. In designing all of these rules, Congress took into account the problems presented where shareholders of the corporation are related (see *Example 2* above) by enacting § 318. This provision contains "constructive ownership" rules, which must be considered in determining how the shareholder's interest has been affected by the redemption.

Before proceeding with a discussion of the constructive ownership rules and each of the redemption provisions, it should be emphasized that the critical question in all cases is whether the distribution is treated as a payment in exchange for the shareholder's stock (i.e., as a sale) or a distribution of property to which § 301 applies (i.e., as a possible dividend).[8] This question is critical since other tax consequences flow from this initial determination. For example, if the redemption is treated as a distribution of property rather than as a sale, all of the rules discussed in Chapter 3 concerning property distributions under § 301 come into play.

---

[2] § 302(b)(1).

[3] § 302(b)(2).

[4] § 302(b)(3).

[5] § 302(b)(4).

[6] § 303.

[7] § 304.

[8] §§ 302(a) and (d). In the following discussion, the term *sale* is used for "distribution as payment in exchange for stock," and it is normally assumed that the sale results in capital gain rather than ordinary income treatment. Similarly, the term *dividend* is generally used to imply a distribution of property subject to § 301 even though the distribution is only a dividend to the extent it is out of E&P.

Whether the redemption is treated as a sale or a dividend, consideration must be given to the following questions in each case:

1. Is the redemption treated as a sale or as a distribution of property?
2. If the redemption qualifies as a sale, what is the shareholder's gain or loss realized and recognized, and what is its character? If the redemption is treated as a distribution of property, what amount is considered dividend income and/or return of capital?
3. How is the basis of the shareholder's stock affected?
4. What is the shareholder's basis in any property received?
5. Does the corporation recognize any gain or loss on the redemption?
6. What is the effect of redemption on the corporation's E&P?

TREATMENT OF THE SHAREHOLDER: SALE VERSUS DIVIDEND

The following sections examine the rules that must be applied to determine whether the redemption is treated as a sale or a dividend distribution. But first, it is crucial to understand the possible outcomes of this determination.

Sale or Exchange Treatment

If the redemption qualifies as a sale, the transaction is treated like any other sale of stock. The shareholder's gain or loss realized is the difference between the amount realized as paid by the corporation and the adjusted basis of the stock. The realized gain or loss normally is recognized and treated as a capital gain or loss. However, § 267 prohibits recognition of the loss if the shareholder owns more than 50% of the stock. If the corporation redeems the stock with property, the shareholder's basis in the property is its fair market value.

Dividend Treatment

If the redemption does not qualify for sale or exchange treatment, the *entire* amount received by the shareholder for the stock (*not* just the amount in excess of the stock's basis) is considered a property distribution and thus a dividend to the extent that it is out of E&P. In addition, all other rules related to property distributions discussed previously apply.

Another issue arising when the redemption is treated as a dividend concerns the basis of the stock that the shareholder has surrendered. The Regulations permit the shareholder to add the basis of the surrendered stock to the basis of the remaining shares owned by the shareholder.[9]

Example 3

R owns all 100 shares of the outstanding stock of Z Corporation. R's basis for the shares is $50,000 or $500 per share. This year, the corporation redeemed 20 shares of R's stock for a $25,000 note, payable in equal installments with interest over the next 10 years. If this transaction is treated as a sale, R would report a long-term capital gain of $15,000 ($25,000 – $10,000), deferred over the next 10 years using the installment method. However, since the effect of this distribution is the same as a dividend, R must report the entire amount of the note, $25,000, as dividend income this year, assuming that Z Corporation has adequate E&P. Observe that R not only lost any benefit to be derived from capital gain treatment but also the right to offset his basis against the distribution ($25,000 dividend instead of a $15,000 capital gain). Thus, R's total basis for his remaining 80 shares is $50,000. Because the distribution is treated as a dividend, R's basis in his remaining shares has increased from $500 per share to $625 per share. Note also that without sale treatment, R cannot defer the gain over the next 10 years. Instead, he must report the entire $25,000 of dividend income this year because the distribution of the note is a distribution of property subject to all the normal distribution rules. This treatment could produce a significant hardship for R because he has not received any cash from the transaction that could be used to pay the tax.

---

[9] When the shareholder owns no other shares in the corporation (e.g., when the interest is completely terminated), the basis is added to the shares owned by related parties whose ownership is attributed to the shareholder. See Reg. § 1.302-2(c).

Corporate Shareholders

Although sale treatment normally is favored by noncorporate shareholders, corporate shareholders usually prefer dividend treatment due to the dividends-received deduction available only to corporate taxpayers. For many years, ingenious corporations were able to parlay this deduction and the basis rules for redemptions to their advantage.

Example 4

LAR Inc. recently learned that BIG Inc., a publicly held corporation, would be redeeming 200,000 of its 1 million shares outstanding for $100 per share, if tendered to BIG within the next 60 days. LAR immediately bought 10,000 shares of BIG for $100 a share or $1 million. LAR then tendered 2,000 of the shares to BIG for exactly what it paid, receiving $200,000. Assuming the sale to BIG was treated as a *dividend*, LAR reports $60,000 ($200,000 – dividends-received deduction of $140,000 [70% × $200,000]) as income and its basis in the remaining 8,000 shares remains at $1 million. The value of the stock immediately after the redemption was still worth $100 per share since both the assets and the number of shares outstanding declined proportionately. LAR later sold its remaining 8,000 shares for $100 per share or $800,000 and reported a capital loss of $200,000 ($800,000 – $1 million). As a result of these transactions, LAR reported $60,000 of income and a capital loss of $200,000—in effect a $140,000 loss (assuming the short-term capital loss can be used against short-term capital gains). Note that this loss and the resulting tax savings were obtained without any real economic loss. LAR's cash outlay was $1 million—but it was totally recovered through the redemption and the sale ($200,000 + $800,000).

In 1986 Congress moved to ensure that corporations could not obtain the advantages illustrated above. For corporate taxpayers, any amount received in a redemption that is non-pro rata—yet is treated as a dividend—is treated as an *extraordinary dividend*. Similarly, any distribution a corporation receives that is in partial liquidation and is considered a dividend, is treated as an extraordinary dividend. Both rules operate without regard to the amount of the dividend or the period for which the stock was held.[10] As a result, the corporation must reduce its basis in its remaining stock by the untaxed portion of the dividend. To the extent that the untaxed portion of the dividend exceeds the basis of the stock, the corporate shareholder must recognize gain as if it had sold the stock. These rules are intended to prohibit corporations from engaging in arbitrage transactions similar to those discussed in Chapter 1.

Example 5

Assume the same facts as in *Example 4*. The redemption distribution received by LAR would be treated as an extraordinary dividend since it is treated as a dividend and is non-pro rata (i.e., the same proportion of stock, say 10 percent, was not redeemed from all shareholders). Consequently, LAR must reduce the basis of its remaining stock by the untaxed portion of the dividend, $140,000. Due to this adjustment, on the subsequent sale by LAR of the stock for $800,000, the corporation's loss is reduced from $200,000 to $60,000 determined as follows:

Amount realized		$ 800,000
Adjusted basis:		
Original basis	$1,000,000	
– Untaxed portion of the dividend	(140,000)	
= Revised basis		(860,000)
Loss recognized on sale		$ (60,000)

Note that the $60,000 loss exactly offsets the $60,000 gain reported earlier on receipt of the dividend. This treatment ensures that the tax rules reflect the economic reality that no gain or loss was actually incurred on the series of transactions.

---

[10] § 1059(e).

CONSTRUCTIVE OWNERSHIP RULES

The tests for dividend equivalency contained in the redemption provisions focus on the shareholder's ownership interest in the corporation before and after the redemption to determine how that interest has been affected. Generally, if after the redemption the shareholder does not have control of the corporation and has had a substantial reduction in ownership, the redemption qualifies for sale treatment. As shown above, the relationships existing among the shareholders of the corporation must be considered in determining whether a shareholder's interest truly has been altered. Section 318 provides that in determining whether the shareholder's ownership interest has changed, the shareholder is treated as not only owning the shares that are actually or directly owned but also those shares of certain related parties. In other words, stock owned by one party is attributed to another party. As noted below, however, the constructive ownership rules do not apply to redemptions made in order to pay death taxes. In addition, the *family* attribution rules may be waived under certain circumstances. The attribution rules are summarized below.[11]

LO.3
Apply the constructive stock ownership rules to determine the effect of a redemption.

Attribution to Family Members

An individual is considered as owning the stock owned by his or her spouse and other family members, including children, grandchildren, and parents.[12] Note that an individual does not own the stock owned by his or her brothers, sisters, or grandparents. Also observe that stock that is attributed to one family member cannot be reattributed from that family member to another family member.[13] To do so would otherwise expand the statutory definition of family.

Example 6

H and W are married and have one son, S. These individuals, S, H, W, and W's father, F, each own 25% of D Corporation's outstanding stock as shown below.

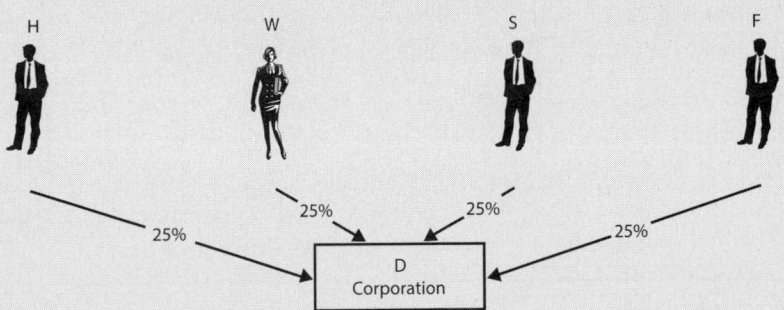

Under the attribution rules, H is considered as owning 75% of the stock [25% directly, 25% indirectly through his wife, and 25% indirectly through his son—note that H does not own the stock of his father-in-law, F, since stock attributed to one family member (W) is not reattributed to another family member]. W owns 100% of the stock (25% directly, and the other 75% indirectly through her husband, son, and father). S is considered as owning 75% of the stock (25% directly, 25% indirectly through his mother, and 25% indirectly through his father—note that S does not own the stock of his grandfather, F). F is considered as owning 75% of the stock (25% directly, 25% indirectly through his daughter W, and 25% indirectly through his grandson, S).

---

[11] § 1059(e).

[12] § 318(a)(1).

[13] § 318(a)(5)(B).

Entity-to-Owner Attribution

Stock owned either directly or indirectly (i.e., stock owned constructively) by an entity is generally considered as owned proportionately by those having an interest in the entity.[14]

1. *Partnerships.* Stock owned by a partnership is considered as owned proportionately by its partners (e.g., if a partner owns a 30% interest in the partnership, the partner owns 30% of whatever stock the partnership owns).[15]

2. *Estates and Trusts.* Stock owned by an estate is considered as owned proportionately by the beneficiaries of the estate.[16] A similar rule applies to trusts.[17]

3. *Corporations.* Stock owned by a corporation is considered as owned proportionately only by shareholders owning either directly or indirectly *at least* 50% of the corporation's stock.[18]

Example 7

R owns 60% of the stock of X Corporation and 30% of the stock of Y Corporation. The remaining 70% of Y's stock is owned by X. This ownership pattern is diagrammed below.

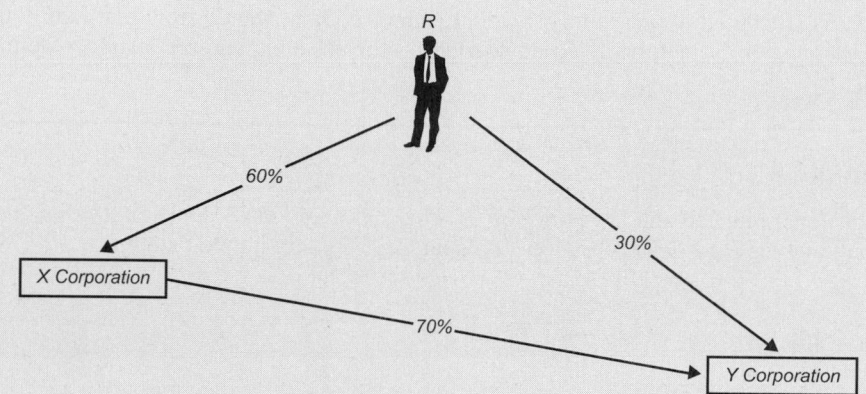

R is considered as owning 72% of Y (30% directly and 42% [60% × 70%] indirectly through X). If R's ownership in X had been less than 50 percent, none of X's ownership in Y would be attributed to R, and thus R would own only 30% of Y.

---

[14] § 318(a)(2).

[15] § 318(a)(2)(A). Whether stock indirectly owned by the partnership is reattributed to the partners is clarified in § 318(a)(5).

[16] *Ibid.*

[17] § 318(a)(2)(B).

[18] § 318(a)(2)(C).

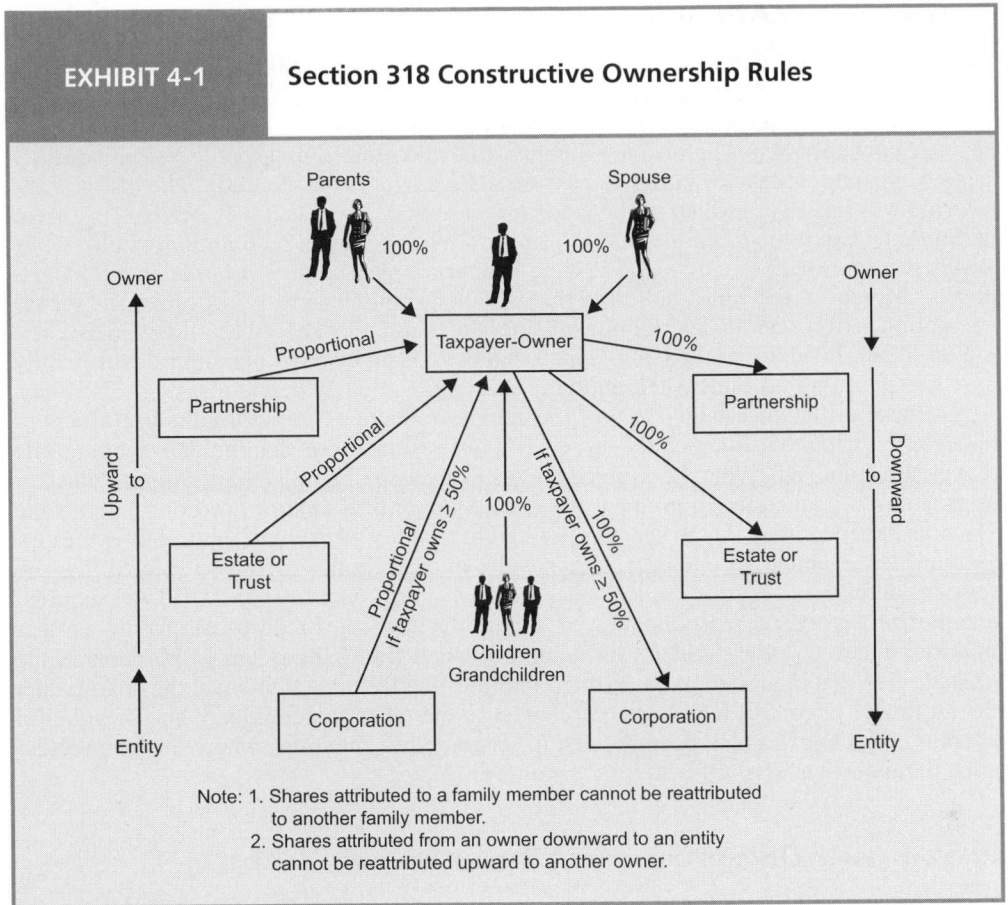

EXHIBIT 4-1   **Section 318 Constructive Ownership Rules**

Note: 1. Shares attributed to a family member cannot be reattributed
to another family member.
2. Shares attributed from an owner downward to an entity
cannot be reattributed upward to another owner.

Owner-to-Entity Attribution

Stock owned by those having an interest in an entity is generally attributed in *full* to the entity.[19] Thus, stock owned by a partner is considered as owned by the partnership, while stock owned by the beneficiaries of an estate is considered as owned by the estate. Stock owned by a shareholder is attributed to the corporation only if the shareholder owns either directly or indirectly at least 50% of the corporation. Similar rules apply to trusts.

Example 8

Same as *Example 7* above. X Corporation is considered as owning 100% of the stock of Y (70% directly and 30% indirectly through R). If R had owned less than 50% of the stock of X, X would be treated as owning only 70% of Y.

Section 318 contains several other rules clarifying problems concerning reattribution and options that must be considered when applying the constructive ownership rules in practice.[20] The constructive ownership rules are summarized in the diagram in Exhibit 4-1.

[19] § 318(a)(3).   [20] §§ 318(a)(4) and (5).

REDEMPTIONS NOT EQUIVALENT TO A DIVIDEND: § 302(b)(1)

Although the 1954 Code made substantial changes in the redemption provisions, as in prior law, a subjective dividend equivalency test was maintained. Section 302(b)(1) currently grants sale treatment if the redemption is "not essentially equivalent to a dividend." Although the language contained in this provision is identical to that contained in its predecessor, it quickly became apparent that the two provisions were to be interpreted differently. The thrust of the new rule was initially clarified in the landmark case of *U.S. v. Maclin P. Davis.*[21] In *Davis*, the Supreme Court modified the rule of prior law, holding that a redemption would not be considered equivalent to a dividend if there is a *meaningful reduction in the shareholder's interest.* Moreover, the Court indicated that whether a valid business purpose exists for the redemption is irrelevant in determining whether the transaction should be classified as a sale or a dividend. In addition, the Court stated that the constructive ownership rules generally must be taken into account when applying the dividend equivalency test of § 302(b)(1).

Because of the uncertainty of the "meaningful reduction" principle, the usefulness of § 302(b)(1) is limited. It generally serves as a last resort where shareholders seeking sale treatment cannot satisfy the other objective tests discussed below. In determining whether the meaningful reduction requirement is satisfied, the critical factor to be considered is the effect of the redemption on the shareholder's right to vote and exercise control over the corporation. For example, in one case, a taxpayer's interest dropped from 85% to 61.7% and was considered meaningfully reduced because a two-thirds majority (66 2/3%) was required to authorize a merger or consolidation or to alter the articles of incorporation.[22] In another situation, where the shareholder's ownership dropped from 57 percent to 50 percent, the Service ruled that the redemption resulted in a meaningful reduction since the shareholder was no longer in control but was merely equal to the other shareholder.[23] The meaningful reduction principle has also been applied in several other situations where the shareholder failed the objective tests of §§ 302(b)(2) and (3).

SUBSTANTIALLY DISPROPORTIONATE REDEMPTIONS: § 302(b)(2)

Dissatisfaction with the subjective dividend equivalency test of Code § 302(b)(1) caused Congress to establish several situations where sale treatment is assured if certain requirements are satisfied. The first safe harbor is contained in § 302(b)(2) concerning substantially disproportionate redemptions. Under this provision, a redemption is considered substantially disproportionate and qualifies for sale treatment if each of the following conditions are met:

1. Immediately after the redemption, the shareholder owns *less than 50%* of the total combined voting power of all classes of stock entitled to vote.

2. Immediately after the redemption, the shareholder's *percentage* ownership of *voting* stock is *less than 80%* of the shareholder's *percentage* ownership immediately before the redemption.

3. Immediately after the redemption the shareholder's percentage ownership of *common* stock is *less than 80%* of the shareholder's percentage ownership immediately before the redemption.

Note that if the corporation has only one class of *voting common* stock outstanding, conditions 2 and 3 above effectively merge to become a single requirement since satisfaction of 2 also satisfies 3 and vice versa. To simplify subsequent discussion, it is assumed that the corporation's only stock outstanding is voting common.

The thrust of the substantially disproportionate test is twofold: if the shareholder is no longer in control after the redemption (50% test) and has what amounts to a 20% loss in ownership (80% test), the redemption has significantly altered the shareholder's interest and the transaction should receive sale treatment. Two operational aspects of this test should be emphasized. First, when applying the 80% test, note that it is the shareholder's *percentage* ownership that must drop below 80% of what it was prior to the redemption and not the shareholder's number of shares. Second, when applying both the 50 and 80 percent tests, the constructive ownership rules must be used.

---

[21] 70-1 USTC ¶9289, 25 AFTR2d 70-287, 397 U.S. 301 (USSC, 1970).

[22] *William F. Wright v. U.S.*, 73-2 USTC ¶9583, 32 AFTR2d 73-5490, 482 F.2d 600 (CA-8, 1973).

[23] Rev. Rul. 75-502, 1975-2 C.B. 111.

Example 9

TNT Corp. has 100 shares of outstanding stock which are owned by three unrelated individuals as follows: A owns 60 shares, B 30 shares, and C 10 shares. During the year, TNT redeemed 15 of A's shares for $20,000. A's basis for all 60 shares was $12,000 or $200 per share. Examination of A's ownership before and after the redemption reveals the following:

	Shares Owned by A in TNT	
	Pre-Redemption	Post-Redemption
Directly	60	45
Indirectly	0	0
Total owned	60	45
Percentage owned	60% (60 ÷ 100)	53% (45 ÷ 85)

In order for the redemption to be substantially disproportionate, A's percentage ownership after the redemption must be (1) less than 50 percent, and (2) less than 80% of his percentage ownership before the redemption or 48% (60% × 80%). Since his post-redemption ownership of 53% exceeds the 50% threshold, the redemption does not qualify for sale treatment. Even if A's post-redemption percentage had fallen to 49 percent, the redemption would not be substantially disproportionate because the post-redemption percentage must drop below 48 percent. In this regard, note that A's stock ownership after the redemption, 45 shares, is less than 80% of the *number of shares* that he owned before the redemption, 48 shares (60 × 80%). This is irrelevant, however; it is his *percentage ownership* in TNT that must be considered.

Since the redemption does not qualify for sale treatment, the entire $20,000 distribution is treated as a dividend assuming TNT had adequate E&P. The basis of the 15 shares redeemed is added to the basis of the 45 shares A continues to hold. Thus, his total basis remains as $12,000 but his per-share basis has increased from $200 per share to $267 per share ($12,000 ÷ 45).

Example 10

Assume the same facts as in *Example 9* above, except that TNT redeems 30 shares. A's post-redemption percentage ownership is now 43% (30 ÷ [100 − 30]). Since the post-redemption percentage is less than 50% and less than 80% of what he owned before (48%), the redemption qualifies for sale treatment. Thus, A recognizes a capital gain of $14,000 ($20,000 amount realized − $6,000 basis in the 30 shares redeemed). The basis in the remaining 30 shares is still $200 per share or $6,000 in total.

Example 11

Assume the same facts as in *Example 10* above, except that shareholder C is A's 70% owned corporation. A's ownership must be recomputed to give effect to the constructive ownership rule as follows:

	Shares Owned by A in TNT	
	Pre-Redemption	Post-Redemption
Directly	60	30
Indirectly through C.	7 (70% × 10)	7 (70% × 10)
Total owned.	67	37
Percentage owned.	67% (67 ÷ 100)	53% (37 ÷ 70)

Since A's post-redemption ownership has not fallen below 50 percent, the redemption does not qualify for sale treatment. Thus, the result is the same as in *Example 9* above. Had A owned only 40% of the stock in C Corporation, none of C's ownership would have been attributed to A. In such case, the redemption would qualify for sale treatment and the result would be identical to that in *Example 10* above.

REDEMPTIONS IN COMPLETE TERMINATION OF THE SHAREHOLDER'S INTEREST: § 302(b)(3)

Section 302(b)(3) provides sale treatment for redemptions that are "in complete termination of a shareholder's interest." At first glance, it appears that this provision is unnecessary since any redemption that terminates the shareholder's interest would qualify for sale treatment as a substantially disproportionate redemption. The important distinction between the two provisions concerns application of the family attribution rules. If the shareholder's *direct* interest is completely terminated, the *family* attribution rules may be waived.[24] Thus, the termination of interest rule permits sale treatment even though the shareholder's family continues ownership of the corporation.

Example 12

M and her daughter, D, started a corporation 15 years ago. M and D each own 50 shares of the 100 shares of stock outstanding. M now wants to retire. D wants to continue to operate the corporation by herself but has insufficient funds to purchase her mother's stock. To meet M's desires, the corporation redeems all 50 shares of M's stock. This redemption does not qualify as a substantially disproportionate distribution since M is deemed to own 100% of the stock both before and after the redemption. However, because the redemption completely terminates M's direct interest, she may elect to waive the family attribution rules. If the election is made, none of D's stock is attributed to M and the redemption qualifies for sale treatment.

The family attribution rules may generally be waived only if the redeeming shareholder agrees to totally sever his or her interest in the corporation. In order to waive the attribution rules the following conditions must be satisfied:[25]

1. The shareholder must not retain any interest in the corporation except as a creditor. The statute expressly prohibits the shareholder from continuing as an officer, director, or employee.

2. The shareholder cannot acquire any interest in the corporation for at least 10 years from the date of the redemption. The sole exception to this prohibition is stock that is acquired by bequest or inheritance.

---

[24] § 302(c)(2).   [25] Ibid.

3. The shareholder must file an agreement with the IRS that indicates that the shareholder will notify the Service if a prohibited interest is acquired within the 10-year period. The agreement must be attached to the return for the year in which the redemption occurs.

Whether the redeeming shareholder is considered to have acquired a so-called prohibited interest may be unclear in some instances. The IRS generally considers the performance of any type of service to be an acquisition of an interest even if the shareholder is not compensated.[26] As a result, a former shareholder may be at risk whenever he or she is asked for counsel.

Entities are also permitted to waive the family attribution rules that might otherwise prohibit a complete termination of their interest in the corporation. Waiver is authorized if *both* the entity and the individuals whose ownership is attributed to the entity do not have a prohibited interest.

Example 13

H, his wife, W, and their son S, each own 25 of the 100 shares of outstanding stock of KIN Corp. The remaining 25 shares are owned by a trust established for the benefit of S. Prior to the redemption of any of the trust's shares, the trust is considered as owning all 100 shares (25 directly and 75 through S, the beneficiary of the trust; note that the stock of H and W attributed to S may be reattributed to the trust). Any redemption of the trust's shares would not affect the ownership of the trust, because it would still be treated as owning all of the remaining shares outstanding through S. In order to waive family attribution and thus avoid attribution of the shares of H and W to S, and reattribution to the trust, all of the shares of both S and the trust must be redeemed since neither the trust nor the beneficiary may retain an interest.

REDEMPTIONS QUALIFYING AS PARTIAL LIQUIDATIONS

LO.5
Define a partial liquidation and explain its tax treatment.

The Code also extends sale treatment to certain redemptions that occur due to a termination or a contraction of a portion of the corporation's business—a so-called partial liquidation. Sale treatment is apparently justified in this case on the theory that the redemption proceeds represent a portion *of* the shareholder's capital which was formerly employed in the business rather than a return *on* capital. Technically, § 302(b)(4) grants sale treatment only when the redemption distribution is to a *noncorporate shareholder* and is in *partial liquidation* of the distributing corporation. A distribution is considered in partial liquidation only if:[27]

1. The distribution is not essentially equivalent to a dividend; or
2. The distribution is attributable to the termination of one of two or more "qualified" businesses.

In addition to satisfying either of the above requirements, the distribution must be made pursuant to a plan and must be made within the taxable year that the plan is adopted or in the following taxable year.

Dividend Equivalency Test for Partial Liquidations

As noted above, a distribution qualifies for partial liquidation treatment if it is *not essentially equivalent to a dividend*. Although identical language appears in § 302(b)(1), as discussed previously, the Code makes it clear that the phrase is to be interpreted differently in the partial liquidation area. In determining dividend equivalency for a distribution in partial liquidation, the focus is on the distribution's effect on the distributing corporation. This is in contrast to the dividend equivalency test of § 302(b)(1) where the concern was the effect of the redemption on the shareholder.

A distribution in partial liquidation is not considered equivalent to a dividend if it is attributable to a genuine contraction of the corporation's business. The "corporate contraction theory" is illustrated in the Regulations, which use an example based on the Tax Court's decision in *Joseph W. Imler* in 1948.[28] In this case, a fire destroyed the upper two stories of

---

[26] Rev. Rul. 70-104, 1970-1 C.B. 66.

[27] § 302(e).

[28] 11 T.C. 836 (1948); Reg. § 1.346-1(a)(2).

a seven-story building that the corporation owned. The upper two stories had been rented in part to another company. Upon receipt of the insurance proceeds, the corporation decided it was too costly to rebuild and distributed the cash to its shareholders, one of whom was Mr. Imler. Although the government argued that the distribution to Mr. Imler should be treated as an ordinary dividend, the Tax Court held that there had been a "bona fide contraction in the business" and granted partial liquidation treatment. Unfortunately, in other situations it is often difficult to determine whether a contraction has occurred. The Service has allowed partial liquidation treatment where a full line department store was converted to a discount apparel store and there was a reduction in inventory, employees, and related items.[29] On the other hand, the Regulations indicate that the distribution of funds attributable to a reserve for an expansion program that has been abandoned does not qualify as a partial liquidation.[30]

Termination of Business

In 1954, Congress recognized the uncertainty inherent in the dividend equivalency test and created a safe harbor where the taxpayer can be assured of sale treatment. To qualify as a partial liquidation under the safe harbor rules, a distribution must satisfy the following:

1. The distribution must be attributable to either the corporation's ceasing to conduct a "qualified business" or must consist of the assets of a "qualified business."

2. Immediately after the distribution, the corporation must be actively engaged in a qualified business.

Note that these two rules require the corporation to have at least two qualified businesses, one that is retained and another that is sold or distributed. For these purposes, a *qualified business* is a business that satisfies the following conditions:

1. The activities in which the corporation engages constitute a business (rather than an investment).

2. The business was conducted throughout the five-year period ending on the date of the distribution.

3. The business was not acquired in a taxable transaction in the five-year period ending on the date of distribution.

These requirements were designed to prevent the bailout of the corporation's E&P as capital gain. It should be remembered, however, that in light of the 2003 rate reductions on dividends the treatment of long-term capital gains and dividends may not be substantially different.

Example 14

C Inc. is owned and operated by J. Over the past several years, the corporation has accumulated cash which J would now like to obtain without suffering the double tax penalty associated with dividends. He plans to use the cash to acquire a small apartment complex which is currently under construction by T Corp. A normal redemption is unavailable since none of the standards of §§ 302(b)(1), (2), or (3) (meaningful reduction, substantially disproportionate, termination of interest) could be satisfied. As an alternative, J has suggested that he could cause the corporation to purchase the apartment building, operate it for a short time, then distribute the building in partial liquidation of some of his shares. This transaction, however, would not meet the safe harbor tests for partial liquidations for several reasons: the apartment project would be acquired in a taxable transaction within five years of the distribution; the project may not be considered a business but rather investment property; and the project activities will have been conducted for less than five years prior to the distribution.

As the above example illustrates, the safe harbor tests prevent the corporation from *purchasing* assets desired by the shareholder and subsequently distributing them with the hope that such distributions would be considered in partial liquidation and thus qualify for capital gain treatment. The rules do enable legitimate contractions to qualify for capital gain treatment, however.

[29] Rev. Rul. 74-296, 1974-1 C.B. 80.   [30] Reg. § 1.346-1(a)(2).

Example 15

C Corporation was organized in 2007 to manufacture video games. The corporation was immediately successful and diversified by purchasing from Q Corporation a small computer business in 2009. By 2016, the profitability in the video game market had become nominal, and C sold the entire business to a competitor who continued to market games under C's name. C distributed the proceeds from the sale to its shareholders in redemption of 5% of their stock. The distributions qualify for partial liquidation treatment since all of the conditions are satisfied; that is, the distribution was attributable to the termination of an active business (video business) that had not been acquired in a taxable transaction in the five years prior to the distribution and that had been conducted for at least five years. In addition, the corporation retained an active computer business which had not been acquired in a taxable transaction in the five years prior to the distribution and which had been conducted for at least five years.

Example 16

Same facts as in *Example 15* above, except assume that C had acquired the computer company from Q in 2013 in an exchange qualifying for nonrecognition under § 351 concerning transfers to controlled corporations. In addition, assume Q had operated the computer business since 2004. The distribution still satisfies all of the conditions for partial liquidation treatment. The acquisition of the computer company within five years of the distribution is permissible since it was acquired in a nontaxable transaction. Note that the distributed business must qualify and that the corporation must have at least one retained business that qualifies. Also note that the distributing corporation need not operate the business for five years. It is sufficient if it was conducted by anyone for five years.

The tests for determining whether a group of activities constitutes a qualified trade or business are virtually identical to those pertaining to the active business requirement, contained in § 355, relating to corporate divisions discussed in Chapter 7. Additional aspects of these tests are considered in that discussion.

Effect of Partial Liquidation on Shareholders

As noted above, if the distribution qualifies as a partial liquidation, a noncorporate shareholder is entitled to sale treatment. Corporate shareholders, however, are not eligible for partial liquidation treatment. Thus, such a redemption distribution to a corporate shareholder is subject to the other redemption tests of § 302(b). Similarly, if the distribution does not qualify as a partial liquidation for a noncorporate shareholder, the distribution is also governed by the other redemption provisions of §§ 302(b) or 303. Note that in the case of a corporate shareholder, if the distribution is treated as a dividend, it is treated as an extraordinary dividend.[31]

---

[31] § 1059(e).

Example 17

S, an individual, and LJK Inc. each own 50 of the 100 outstanding shares of PLQ Corporation stock. Both S and LJK have a basis of $5,000 ($100 per share) for their stock, which they have held for 15 years. PLQ has manufactured shirts and ties for 25 years. This year it sold the tie portion of the business. In a transaction qualifying as a partial liquidation, PLQ redeemed 20 shares of stock from both S and LJK for $20,000. PLQ has substantial E&P. Since the redemption qualifies as a partial liquidation, S, the noncorporate shareholder, is treated as having sold her stock. Thus, she reports capital gain of $18,000 ($20,000 − [$100 × 20]). On the other hand, LJK does not receive sale treatment since it is not a noncorporate shareholder. Thus, the treatment of LJK's distribution must be determined under the other tests of § 302. Since LJK's ownership after the distribution is not less than 50% (30 ÷ 60), the redemption is not substantially disproportionate and thus it is treated as a dividend. Consequently, LJK reports a dividend of $20,000 which is eligible for the 80% dividends-received deduction. However, the dividend is also treated as an extraordinary dividend. As such, LJK is required to reduce its basis in the stock by the untaxed portion of the dividend, $16,000 (80% × $20,000). Since the basis reduction of $16,000 exceeds LJK's original basis of $5,000, LJK is required to report—in addition to the dividend income—gain from the sale of stock of $11,000 ($16,000 − $5,000).

REDEMPTIONS TO PAY DEATH TAXES: § 303

LO.6

Describe when redemptions related to paying death taxes are given sale treatment.

In § 303, Congress carves out yet another situation where sale treatment is guaranteed. Under § 303, a redemption of stock that has been included in the decedent's gross estate generally qualifies for sale treatment if the stock's value represents a substantial portion of the value of the estate. Sale treatment is granted under § 303 notwithstanding the fact that the redemption may not meet the basic tests established in § 302 discussed above.

The special rules of § 303 evolved from Congressional concern that the financial burden of paying death taxes may force the sale of family businesses. When the estate is comprised primarily of stock of a corporation, the only source of funds for payment of the estate tax may be from the corporation itself since the market for the corporation's shares may be limited. Absent a special rule, a redemption of the shares of the estate or beneficiary may be treated as a dividend and consequently represents a costly method to finance the estate tax. The only reasonable alternative that may exist is sale to an outside party. To reduce the need for such sales, § 303 was designed to lower the cost of a redemption by granting it sale treatment. The benefits of sale treatment in this context are particularly favorable since the basis of the shares is normally equivalent to their fair market value due to the step-up permitted for inherited property. As a result, the family not only avoids a dividend tax, but usually escapes tax entirely! That said, the importance of § 303 has diminished recently since the number of estates subject to estate taxes has decreased. In 2016, only estates exceeding $5,450,000 are subject to estate taxes.

To secure sale treatment under § 303, the following conditions must be satisfied.

1. *Thirty-Five Percent Test.* The value of the redeeming corporation's stock must be more than 35% of the *adjusted gross estate.*[32] The adjusted gross estate is the total gross estate—generally the fair market value of all of the property owned by the decedent at date of death—reduced by deductions permitted by §§ 2053 and 2054 for funeral and administrative expenses, claims against the estate, debts, and casualty losses. In determining whether the 35% test is met, stock in two or more corporations may be combined if at least 20% of the total value of each outstanding stock is included in the gross estate.[33]

2. *Qualifying Amount.* The maximum amount of the redemption distribution that can qualify for sale treatment is limited to the sum of all taxes imposed on account of the shareholder's death (both Federal and state taxes such as estate and inheritance taxes) and the deductions allowed on the estate tax return for funeral and administrative expenses.[34]

---

§ 303(b)(2)(A).

§ 303(b)(2)(B).

§ 303(a)(1).

3. *Shareholder Restrictions.* Section 303 applies to a redemption distribution only to the extent that the recipient shareholder's interest in the decedent's estate is directly reduced because of the payment of those items noted above: death taxes and funeral and administrative expenses.[35]

4. *Time Limits.* Section 303 generally applies only to distributions made within 90 days after the statute of limitations for assessment of the estate tax expires. Since the limitations period expires three years after the due date for filing of the estate tax return—which is nine months after the date of death—the distribution normally must be made within approximately four years after the date of death (3 years + 9 months + 90 days = 4 years). This period may be extended under certain conditions.[36]

Example 18

R died owning $11,200,000 of property, including a 15% interest in X Corporation valued at $4,000,000 (100,000 shares at $40 per share) and a 30% interest in Y Corporation worth $1,650,000. R's funeral and administrative expenses were $300,000, while claims against the estate totaled $900,000. R's adjusted gross estate is $10 million ($11,200,000 − $900,000 − $300,000). Since the $4,000,000 value of the X stock exceeds 35% of the adjusted gross estate of $3,500,000 (35% of $10 million), a redemption of the X stock qualifies for sale treatment subject to the other limitations of § 303. The Y stock cannot be redeemed pursuant to § 303, because its $1,650,000 value does not exceed the 35% benchmark of $3,500,000 nor can it take advantage of the aggregation rule. Although Y stock is eligible to be combined with other stocks for this test—since at least 20% of its value is included in the estate—it can only be combined with other 20% stocks. Because only 15% of the value of the X stock is included in the gross estate, no other stock can be combined with it. Had at least 20% of X been included in the gross estate, the stock of both X and Y could have been combined, thus enabling Y to qualify.

Example 19

Same facts as in *Example 18* above but assume the following additional facts. Assume the Federal estate tax and state inheritance tax imposed on account of R's death totaled $1,700,000. According to R's will, his estate, after payment of expenses and claims, would be shared equally by his son, S, and daughter, D. The total amount qualifying for § 303 treatment is limited to $2,000,000, the sum of the death taxes of $1,700,000 and the funeral and administrative expenses of $300,000. In addition, since S's share of the estate bears one-half of the burden of all of these expenses, a subsequent redemption of his shares qualifies for § 303 treatment but not to exceed $1,000,000. A similar conclusion is reached for D.

Example 20

Same facts as in *Example 18* above. Two years after the death of R, all of the estate's assets are distributed to S and D. At that time, S's basis in his 50,000 shares of X stock is $2,000,000 (50,000 × $40 per share, the stock's fair market value at R's death) and the stock is now worth $5,000,000 or $100 per share. During the year, X distributed $3,000,000 in redemption of 30,000 shares of S's X stock. Of the $3,000,000 distributed, $1,000,000 qualifies as payment in *exchange* for S's stock under § 303. S reports long-term capital gain on this deemed sale of $600,000 ($1,000,000 sales price − $400,000 basis of the shares that could be purchased for $1,000,000 [$1,000,000 ÷ $100 × $40 basis per share]). The remaining distribution of $2,000,000 would qualify for sale treatment only if it satisfies the requirements of § 302.

---

[35] § 303(b)(3).

[36] §§ 303(b)(1)(A), (B), and (C).

TREATMENT OF THE REDEEMING CORPORATION

LO.7

Identify the tax consequences of a redemption to the distributing corporation, including how to:

■ Calculate the effect on the corporation's taxable income.

■ Calculate the effect on the corporation's earnings and profits.

An analysis of basic redemption rules would be incomplete without considering the effect of the redemption distribution on the redeeming corporation. Two questions must be considered:

1. Does the corporation recognize gain or loss on the distribution of property?
2. What is the effect of the distribution on the redeeming corporation's E&P?

Gain or Loss

Code § 311—which was discussed in conjunction with property distributions in Chapter 3—provides the rule applying to all nonliquidating distributions. Recall that under § 311, the distributing corporation must recognize gain—*but not loss*—upon the distribution of property other than its own obligations. Thus, when the corporation distributes property in redemption of stock, it must recognize any gain inherent in the property while any loss goes unrecognized.

When property subject to a liability is distributed, the fair market value of the property is deemed to be *no less* than the amount of the liability.[37] Thus, when the liability exceeds the property's fair market value and the basis of the property, the corporation must recognize gain equal to the excess of the liability over the basis. If the liability does not exceed the property's fair market value, it is ignored for gain recognition purposes and the fair market value is used.

Example 21

T contributed land to a corporation many years ago, which the corporation uses as a parking lot. This year T has decided to retire from the business and is willing to take the land in payment for his 20% interest in the business. The basis of his interest is $15,000. The land is worth $50,000 and has a basis of $10,000. If the corporation accepts T's proposal and redeems the stock by distributing the land, the corporation must recognize gain of $40,000 ($50,000 − $10,000). Gain must be recognized regardless of whether the distribution receives sale or dividend treatment. Note that if the property's value had been only $3,000, the corporation would not have recognized any loss. Moreover, such loss would be permanently lost since the basis of the property to the distributee would have been its value of $3,000!

Example 22

V Corporation operates a hat and glove business. This year V liquidated the hat business and—as part of a transaction qualifying as a partial liquidation—distributed the following assets to its sole shareholder, M: cash of $5,000; furniture worth $10,000 (cost, $18,000 and depreciation, $5,000); and a small warehouse worth $30,000 which had a basis of $20,000 and which was subject to a mortgage of $45,000. Although the corporation realizes a $3,000 loss ($10,000 − [$18,000 − $5,000]) on the distribution of the furniture, none of the loss is recognized. In contrast, the corporation must recognize a gain on the distribution of the warehouse of $25,000 ($45,000 liability − $20,000 basis).

Earnings and Profits

The E&P of a corporation must be adjusted to reflect any redemption distributions. First, if the corporation must recognize gain on the distribution under § 311, E&P must be increased for the gain.[38]

The amount of the reduction of E&P on account of the distribution depends on whether the distribution qualifies for sale treatment. If the distribution does not qualify for sale treatment, E&P is reduced according to the rules applying to property distributions.

If the redemption qualifies for sale treatment under §§ 302 or 303, only a portion of the distribution is charged against E&P. E&P is reduced by the redeemed stock's proportionate share of E&P but not more than the amount of the redemption distribution.[39]

---

[37] § 311(b)(2).

[38] § 312(b)(1).

[39] § 312(n)(7).

Example 23

K Corporation has 100 shares outstanding, 40 of which are owned by B. K has $100,000 of E&P. During the year, K redeemed all of B's shares for $50,000. If the redemption qualifies as a sale, E&P must be reduced by the amount of E&P attributable to the stock. Since 40% of the stock was redeemed (40 ÷ 100), 40% of E&P or $40,000 is eliminated, leaving a $60,000 balance. Had K redeemed the 40 shares for $25,000, the reduction in E&P would have been limited to $25,000, the lesser of 40% of E&P or the amount of the redemption distribution.

The various rules applying to redemptions are summarized in Exhibit 4-2.

EXHIBIT 4-2	Section 302 Redemptions: Summary	

Type	Sections 302(b)(1), (2), and (3)	Section 302(b)(4) Partial Liquidation
Comments	**Sale If**	**Noncorporate S/H Only Sale If**
	1. Not essentially equivalent to a dividend (shareholder level)	1. Not essentially equivalent to a dividend (corporate contraction)
	2. Substantially disproportionate: post-redemption percentage ownership less than	2. Attributable to termination of qualified business
	a. 50% overall; and	a. Business, not investment
	b. 80% of preredemption ownership	b. Conducted five years pre-redemption
	3. Complete termination of interest: family attribution waived if prohibited interest not acquired for 10 years	c. Not acquired in taxable transaction in five years preredemption
	Otherwise:	**Otherwise:**
	Section 301 Distribution	Section 301 Distribution unless § 302(b)(1), (2), or (3) applicable.
Effect on Shareholder	**Sale:**	**Sale:**
	Gain/loss realized = FMV − AB	Gain/loss realized = FMV − AB
	Section 301:	**Section 301:**
	Dividend to extent of E&P	Dividend to the extent of E&P
Shareholder's Adjusted Basis	**In Remaining Stock:**	**In Remaining Stock:**
	Sale: Unchanged	*Sale:* Unchanged
	Section 301:	*Section 301:*
	Increase by AB of stock surrendered	Increase by AB of stock surrendered
	In Property Received:	**In Property Received:**
	Sale: FMV	*Sale:* FMV
	Section 301: FMV	*Section 301:* FMV
Effect on Distributing Corporation's Taxable Income	**Gain:** Recognized	**Gain:** Recognized
	Loss: Not Recognized	**Loss:** Not Recognized
Effect on Distributing Corporation's E&P	**Reduction**	**Reduction**
	Sale:	*Sale:*
	By redeemed stock's share of E&P not > amount distributed	By redeemed stock's share of E&P not > amount distributed
	Section 301:	*Section 301:*
	By money, AB of property	By money, AB of property

Stock Redemption by Related Corporations

LO.8

Identify when sales of stock to a related corporation are treated as a redemption by such corporation of its own stock.

As seen in the previous sections, Congress has devised an intricate scheme to prohibit shareholders from bailing out E&P from their corporations by using carefully planned redemptions. Absent special provisions, however, the rules discussed thus far could be easily defeated when a shareholder controls two or more corporations through a brother-sister or parent-subsidiary arrangement (see Exhibit 4-3).[40]

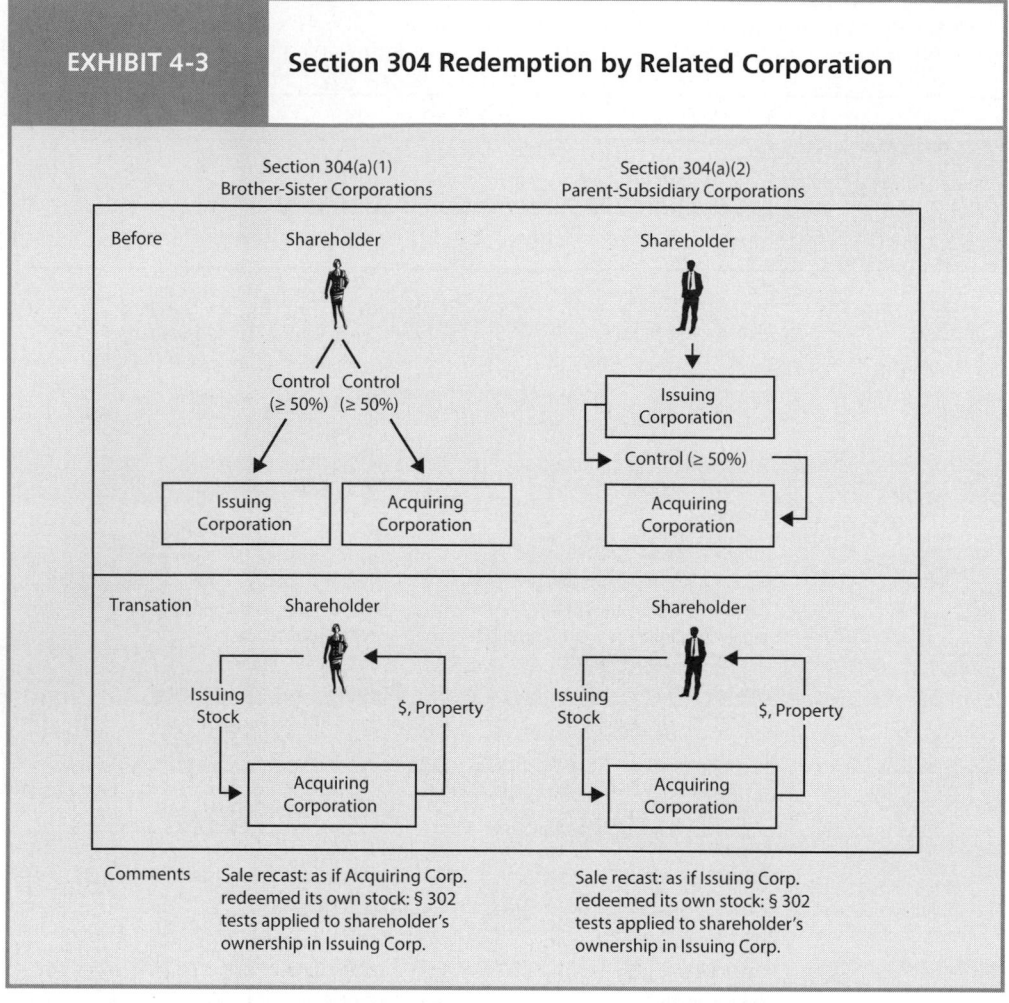

EXHIBIT 4-3	Section 304 Redemption by Related Corporation

Section 304(a)(1)
Brother-Sister Corporations

Section 304(a)(2)
Parent-Subsidiary Corporations

Before

Shareholder → Control (≥ 50%) / Control (≥ 50%) → Issuing Corporation / Acquiring Corporation

Shareholder → Issuing Corporation → Control (≥ 50%) → Acquiring Corporation

Transaction

Shareholder — Issuing Stock / $, Property — Acquiring Corporation

Shareholder — Issuing Stock / $, Property — Acquiring Corporation

Comments

Sale recast: as if Acquiring Corp. redeemed its own stock: § 302 tests applied to shareholder's ownership in Issuing Corp.

Sale recast: as if Issuing Corp. redeemed its own stock: § 302 tests applied to shareholder's ownership in Issuing Corp.

---

[40] See for example, *John Wanamaker, Trustee,* 49-2 USTC
¶9486, 38 AFTR 1014, 178 F.2d 10 (CA-3, 1949).

Example 24

A owns 100% of the stock of both X and Y. (**Note:** When a shareholder(s) controls two or more corporations in this manner, the corporations are referred to as brother-sister corporations.) If X redeems some of its stock from A, dividend treatment results under § 302 since A's interest is not changed by the redemption. A similar result would occur if Y were to redeem some of its shares from A. Alternatively, A might sell some of his X stock to Y for $10,000. In effect, A has received a dividend distribution of $10,000 since he still controls both corporations after the sale. However, the normal redemption provisions of § 302 would not apply to the sale since neither corporation acquired its own stock. Thus, without additional rules, a shareholder could obtain cash at will from his or her controlled corporations at the cost of a capital gains tax.

Example 25

Assume the same facts as in *Example 24* above, except that X owns 100% of Y. (Note here that the relationship between the corporations is parent-subsidiary.) A sale of A's X stock to Y for $10,000 has the same effect as described above: a dividend distribution of $10,000 since A's interest in X is unaffected by the transaction because X controls Y.

To prevent shareholders from effectively redeeming stock through sales to related corporations, Congress enacted § 304. This provision recasts the "sale" to the related corporation as a redemption and applies the tests of § 302 to determine the tax treatment. The rules apply only when control is present (see Exhibit 4-3).[41] For this purpose, control generally means ownership of at least 50% of each corporation's stock. In determining whether control exists, the constructive ownership rules of § 318 are applied with a slight modification. Attribution of stock to and from a corporation occurs as long as the shareholder constructively owns at least 5% of the corporation.[42] If control is found, a special set of rules applies, depending on whether the brother-sister or parent-subsidiary relationship exists between the corporations.

BROTHER-SISTER REDEMPTIONS

As noted above and illustrated in Exhibit 4-3, a brother-sister relationship exists where one or more shareholders are in control in each of two corporations and neither corporation controls the other (as is the case with a parent-subsidiary relationship). In this situation, if the controlling shareholder (or shareholders) sells stock of one corporation (referred to as the issuing corporation) to the other corporation (referred to as the acquiring corporation), the brother-sister redemption rules apply. According to these rules, the sale by the shareholder to the acquiring corporation is recast as a redemption by the acquiring corporation of its own stock. The stock of the issuing corporation that is actually obtained by the acquiring corporation is treated as a contribution to the acquiring corporation's capital in exchange for some of the acquiring corporation's stock.

Section 304(a)(1) creates a hypothetical (and clearly bewildering) two-step transaction. First, the stock of the issuing corporation actually obtained by the acquiring corporation is deemed to have been contributed to the acquiring corporation's capital in exchange for some of the acquiring corporation's stock. The acquiring corporation is then treated as having redeemed its own stock that it just issued, for the price it actually paid. The basis assigned to the acquiring corporation's stock that is considered redeemed is the same as the stock of the issuing corporation that was actually sold (or deemed contributed to the acquiring corporation's capital). The critical ownership tests of § 302 are applied to the shareholder's interest in the issuing corporation.[43]

---

[41] Note that § 303 might also be applied.

[42] § 304(c)(3)(B). Note also that downward attribution from a shareholder to a corporation is proportional if less than 50% is owned [Code § 304(c)(3)(B)(ii)(11)].

[43] For this purpose, attribution from a corporation to its shareholder or from a shareholder to a corporation occurs without regard to the 50% threshold normally required [§ 304(b)(1)].

If the distribution does not qualify for sale treatment, the distribution is treated as having been made by the acquiring corporation to the extent of its E&P and then by the issuing corporation to the extent of its E&P.[44] In addition, since the distribution is treated as a dividend, the basis of the issuing corporation's stock that was actually sold is added to the shareholder's basis for the acquiring corporation's stock. The basis of the issuing corporation's stock in the hands of the acquiring corporation is the shareholder's basis.[45]

Example 26

S owns all of the 100 shares of outstanding stock of I Corp. and 70 of the 100 shares of outstanding stock of A Corp. He purchased the I shares for $500 per share (total $50,000) and the A shares for $300 per share (total $21,000) several years ago. A has $10,000 of E&P while I has $70,000 of E&P. As shown below, S sold 40 shares of I (basis $20,000) to A (acquiring corporation) for $60,000.

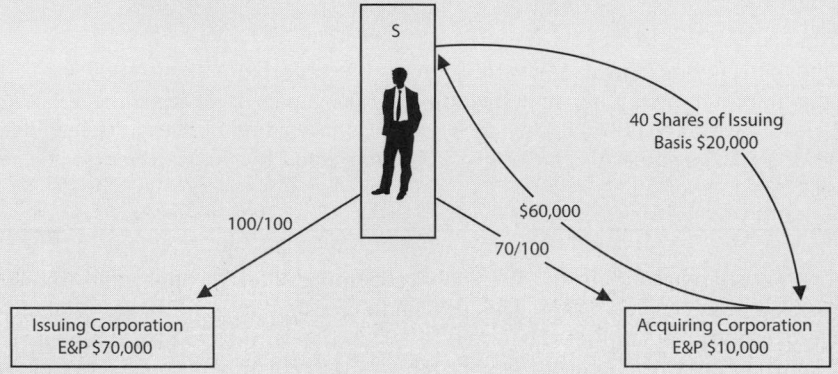

Since S controls (owns at least 50%) both I and A, the brother-sister redemption rules apply to the sale. S is treated as having contributed the I (issuing corporation) stock to the capital of A in exchange for A shares. S assigns a basis of $20,000 to these A shares, the same as the basis of the I stock contributed to A's capital. A is then treated as having redeemed the A shares just issued for the amount which was actually paid, $60,000. The hypothetical redemption is tested by examining S's ownership in the issuing corporation, I, before and after the hypothetical redemption.

	Shares Owned in Issuing Corporation	
	Pre-Redemption	*Post-Redemption*
Directly	100	60
Indirectly	0	28 (70% × 40)
Total	100	88
Percentage owned	100%	88%

Since the redemption is not substantially disproportionate (S owns neither less than 50% after the redemption nor less than 80% of what he owned before), is not a complete termination of his interest, or is not made to pay death taxes, it is treated as a $10,000 dividend out of A's E&P and as a $50,000 dividend out of I's E&P. S increases his basis in his A stock by the basis of the I stock redeemed, $20,000. Thus, his total basis in A stock is $41,000 ($20,000 + $21,000). A's basis in the I stock, hypothetically acquired by a contribution to capital, is $20,000, which is the basis of the I stock in the hands of S.

---

[44] § 304(b)(2).

[45] Although the basis as determined under § 362 is technically the shareholder's basis increased by any gain recognized, any dividend income recognized on the transaction is not considered gain. See Reg. § 1.304-2(c) Ex. (1).

Example 27

Assume the same facts as *Example 26* above, except that A had a deficit in E&P of $9,000 attributable to several years of losses. The amount of the dividend in this case is still $60,000 attributable to the E&P of I Corp.

If the redemption is treated as a sale, it is considered a sale of the acquiring corporation's stock that was deemed issued in exchange for the issuing corporation's stock. For purposes of computing gain or loss on the sale, as noted above, the basis assigned to the acquiring corporation's shares is that of the issuing corporation's stock that was actually sold. The sale has no effect on the shareholder's basis in the remaining stock of either the issuing corporation or the acquiring corporation. In other words, the basis of the shares that the shareholder has not transferred remains the same.[46] The acquiring corporation's basis in the issuing corporation's stock that it purchased is the cost of that stock.[47]

Example 28

Assume the same facts as in *Example 26* above, except that before the redemption S owned 50 shares of I Corp.

	Shares Owned in Issuing Corporation	
	Pre-Redemption	*Post-Redemption*
Directly	50	10
Indirectly	0	28 (70% × 40)
Total	50	38
Percentage owned	50%	38%

Since S's percentage ownership after the redemption is less than 50% and less than 80% of his ownership prior to the redemption (38% is less than 40% [80% of 50%]), the redemption qualifies for sale treatment under the substantially disproportionate rules of § 302(b)(2). Thus, S is treated as having sold A shares with a basis of $20,000 (the same as his basis in the I shares actually sold) for $60,000 resulting in a long-term capital gain of $40,000. S's basis in the remaining 10 shares of I is unaffected by the sale and remains as $5,000 ($500 × 10). S's basis in his A Corp. stock is also unaffected by the sale and remains as $21,000. A's basis in the stock it has purchased from S is the cost of that stock, $60,000.

PARENT-SUBSIDIARY REDEMPTIONS

Section 304(a)(2) is designed to address the problems arising when a shareholder sells stock of a parent corporation to the parent's subsidiary (see Exhibit 4-3). For this purpose, the required parent subsidiary relationship exists when the parent owns 50% of the stock of the subsidiary. Note that the shareholder need not control either corporation as is required in the brother-sister context. Rather, the question is whether one corporation controls the other.

In the parent-subsidiary situation, if a shareholder sells stock of the parent (issuing corporation) to the subsidiary (acquiring corporation), the exchange is recast as a redemption by the issuing parent of its own stock. This approach differs from that for brother-sister redemptions where the acquiring corporation is considered as having redeemed its own stock.

---

[46] Reg. § 1.304-2(a).

[47] See the Tax Reform Act of 1986, Act § 1875(c), and the House Committee Report.

As in the brother-sister redemption rules, however, the § 302 tests pertaining to ownership are applied to the shareholder's interest in the issuing parent corporation. Also, as in the brother-sister redemption rules, if the redemption does not qualify for sale treatment, the distribution is treated as having been made by the acquiring subsidiary corporation to the extent of its E&P and then by the issuing parent corporation to the extent of its E&P.[48] In addition, the shareholder's basis in any remaining stock held in the issuing parent corporation is increased by the basis of the stock surrendered to the acquiring subsidiary.[49] Note that the basis adjustment is made to the issuing parent corporation's stock in this case while it was made to the acquiring corporation's stock in the brother-sister situation. The basis of the stock acquired by the subsidiary is its cost.[50]

Example 29

K owns 60 of the 100 shares of outstanding stock of P Corp. She acquired the shares several years ago for $60,000. In addition, P owns 80% of the outstanding stock of its subsidiary, S Corp. P Corp. has $100,000 of E&P while S has $30,000 of E&P. During the year, K sold 10 shares of her P stock to S for $70,000 (basis $10,000).

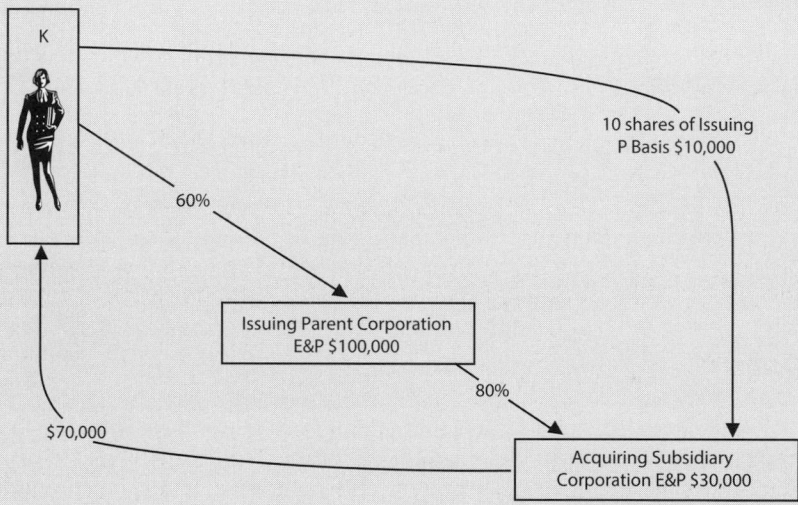

The ownership tests of § 302 are applied to the shareholder's interest in the issuing parent corporation P. As shown below, before the redemption, K owned 60% of P and after the redemption she owned 54% (50 shares directly and four shares indirectly through P [her new ownership in P, 50% × P's ownership in S, 80% × S's ownership of P, 10%]).

	Shares Owned in Issuing Corporation	
	Pre-Redemption	Post-Redemption
Directly...	60	50
Indirectly...	0	4 (50% × 80% × 10)
Total..	60	54
Percentage owned.................................	60%	54%

---

[48] § 304(b)(2).

[49] Reg. § 1.304-3(a).

[50] With respect to the basis of the stock in the hands of the acquiring subsidiary, in absence of any provisions contained in the Code or Regulations, the basis of the stock should be its cost under § 1012.

Since K's ownership in P Corp. after the redemption is not less than 50 percent, the redemption does not qualify as a substantially disproportionate redemption under § 302(b)(2) and thus does not qualify for sale treatment. Accordingly, the distribution is treated as a $70,000 dividend, $30,000 out of the E&P of S Corp. and $40,000 out of the E&P of P Corp. K's basis in her remaining stock of the issuing parent corporation P is increased by $10,000, the basis of the P shares sold. Thus, her total basis in the P Corp. stock is still $60,000; however, this is the basis for 50 shares of stock rather than 60 shares, as was the case before the redemption. The basis of the P stock acquired by S Corp. is $70,000, its cost.

If the parent-subsidiary redemption qualifies for sale treatment, the shareholder computes gain or loss in the normal fashion using the basis of the issuing parent's stock in the calculation. In this case, the shareholder's bases in the remaining stock of both the issuing parent and acquiring subsidiary corporations are unaffected and thus remain the same.

Example 30

Assume the same facts as *Example 29* above, except that the sale qualifies as a redemption made in order to pay death taxes under § 303. In this case, the shareholder has a $60,000 long-term capital gain ($70,000 − $10,000). The basis in her remaining 50 shares of P Corp. stock is $50,000 while the basis in her S Corp. stock is not affected.

Preferred Stock Bailouts: § 306

LO.9

Explain a preferred stock bailout and the tax consequences relating to a sale or redemption of § 306 stock.

As may be apparent from the previous discussion, shareholders have devised various schemes over the years to extract E&P out of the corporation without suffering the double tax penalty incurred with dividend distributions. A popular technique that achieved this objective prior to 1954 was the so-called *preferred stock bailout*. According to this plan, the corporation declared a dividend of nonvoting preferred stock to be distributed to holders of the corporation's common stock. Notwithstanding efforts by the government to treat this as a taxable stock dividend, the distribution of preferred stock on common is considered nontaxable since it has no effect on the interest of the common stock shareholders. Upon receipt of the nontaxable stock dividend, a portion of the shareholder's basis in the common stock was allocated to the preferred stock. The next step in the plan was a prearranged sale of the preferred stock by the shareholder to a friendly third party. The sale normally resulted in favorable long-term capital gain to the shareholder. The corporation subsequently redeemed the third party's stock with the cash that would have been distributed as a dividend to the shareholder. The third party was willing to participate in the scheme since the corporation redeemed the stock at a price which exceeded its cost to the third party as a reward for facilitating the bailout. By following these steps, the shareholder was able to obtain cash out of the corporation—albeit indirectly through an accommodating third party—at the cost of a capital gains tax. The courts approved this scheme, as illustrated below.[51]

Example 31

T owns all 100 shares of the outstanding common stock of P Corporation. T had acquired these shares for $20,000 several years ago. During the year, T caused the corporation to distribute a nontaxable preferred stock dividend of 10 shares. At the time of the dividend, the common stock was worth $40,000 and the preferred stock was worth $10,000. T assigned a basis of $4,000 to the shares [$10,000 ÷ ($10,000 + $40,000) × $20,000] and sold them to his friend F for $10,000, realizing a long-term

---

[51] *C.P. Chamberlain v. Comm.*, 53-2 USTC ¶9576, 44 AFTR 494, 207 F.2d 462 (CA-6, 1953).

> capital gain of $6,000 ($10,000 – $4,000). P Corporation subsequently redeemed the 10 shares from F for $10,500. After the transactions have been completed, T reports a long-term capital gain of $6,000 that should have been characterized as a dividend of $10,000 assuming the corporation had adequate E&P at the time the preferred stock was distributed.

In 1954, Congress enacted § 306 to prohibit taxpayers from using the preferred stock bailout to avoid taxes. The thrust of this provision is to assign the § 306 "taint" to the preferred stock received as a nontaxable stock dividend and cause a subsequent sale or redemption of such "tainted" stock to result in ordinary or dividend income. However, as explained below, since 2003 both the ordinary income and the dividend income for individual taxpayers are taxed at favorable rates for long-term capital gains. Consequently, the effect of § 306 is not quite as harsh as it once was for individual taxpayers.

SECTION 306 STOCK DEFINED

As suggested above, if "§ 306 stock" is sold or redeemed, the provisions of § 306 generally operate to deny the benefits of sale treatment. Section 306 stock is defined as follows:[52]

1. *Stock Received as a Dividend.* Stock (other than common stock distributed with respect to common) that is received as a nontaxable dividend.

Example 32

Same facts as in *Example 31* above. The nontaxable distribution of preferred stock is § 306 stock.

2. *Stock Received in a Corporate Reorganization or Division.* Stock (other than common stock) that is received tax-free in a corporate reorganization or division where the effect of the transaction was substantially the same as the receipt of a stock dividend, or where the stock was received in exchange for § 306 stock.

Example 33

T owns all of the outstanding common stock of X Corporation. Y Corporation and X agree to a merger where Y will absorb X. Pursuant to the merger transaction, T receives common and preferred stock in Y, and T's stock in X is cancelled. The preferred stock is § 306 stock since this is a nontaxable reorganization and the receipt of the preferred stock by T has the same effect as a nontaxable stock dividend.

3. *Stock with a Substituted or Carryover Basis.* Stock that has a basis determined in reference to the basis of § 306 stock.

Example 34

B gave 100 shares of § 306 stock worth $50,000 (basis $10,000) to her son Z. Since the basis of the stock in Z's hands is the donor's basis of $10,000, the stock is § 306 stock.

Note that stock inherited from a decedent loses the § 306 taint since the basis of the stock is its fair market value (i.e., it is not determined by reference to the basis of the decedent).

---

[52] § 306(c)(1).

4. *Stock Received in § 351 Exchange.* Stock, other than common stock, acquired in a § 351 exchange if the receipt of money (in lieu of the stock) would have been treated as a dividend to any extent.[53]

Even though stock may satisfy one of the definitions above, it is not considered § 306 stock if the corporation had no current or accumulated E&P at the time the stock was distributed.[54] Stock escapes the § 306 taint in this case because a distribution at such time would not have been taxable as a dividend.

Example 35

Same facts as *Example 31* above. If the corporation had no E&P at the time that the preferred stock was distributed, the stock would not be § 306 stock.

DISPOSITIONS OF § 306 STOCK

The provisions of § 306 apply whenever there is a disposition of § 306 stock. However, the effect of § 306 differs somewhat depending on whether the stock is sold to a third party or redeemed by the distributing corporation.

Sales of § 306 Stock

If a shareholder sells or disposes of § 306 stock other than by redemption, potential bailout is prohibited by effectively dividing the amount realized into two components: an ordinary income component and a return of capital component. The amount realized is treated as ordinary income to the extent that the shareholder would have had a dividend if *at the time of distribution* cash had been distributed (in lieu of stock) in an amount equal to the fair market value of the stock.[55] Thus, the ordinary income component is measured by E&P at the date the § 306 stock is distributed. Although § 306 characterizes this amount as ordinary income, § 306(a)(1)(D) provides that such amount is to be considered dividend income for purposes of the special tax rates applicable to qualified dividends under § 1(h)(11). The favorable treatment takes much of the bite out of § 306. Since the transaction is treated as a sale (rather than a distribution), note also that the corporation makes no adjustment to its E&P account. The remainder of the amount realized is treated as a return of the shareholder's basis. To the extent that the return of capital component exceeds the shareholder's basis, the shareholder recognizes gain from the sale of stock, usually capital gain. If the shareholder's basis is not fully recovered, no loss is recognized for the unrecovered basis. Rather, the shareholder adds the unrecovered basis of the preferred stock to the basis of the common stock with respect to which the preferred stock was distributed.

---

[53] In making this determination, rules similar to those contained in Code § 304(b)(2) must be considered.

[54] § 306(c)(2).

[55] § 306(a)(1).

Example 36

T owns all 100 shares of the outstanding common stock of PSB Corp. T had acquired these shares for $20,000 several years ago. On May 1, 2013, when the corporation had E&P of $7,000, it distributed to T a nontaxable preferred stock dividend of 10 shares worth $15,000. T assigned a basis of $4,000 to the preferred shares. On June 7, 2016 T sold the preferred shares to his friend F for $12,000. At the time of the sale, the corporation had E&P of $30,000. Absent § 306, T would report a long-term capital gain of $8,000 ($12,000 − $4,000). Pursuant to § 306, however, T reports ordinary income of $7,000 and long-term capital gain of $1,000 determined as follows:

Amount realized	$12,000
Ordinary income:	
Amount that would have been a dividend had cash been distributed in lieu of stock	(7,000)
Return of capital	$ 5,000
Adjusted basis	(4,000)
Gain on sale	$ 1,000

Although T reports ordinary income of $7,000, it is eligible for the special tax rates extended to long-term capital gain. Note that the amount of the $15,000 distribution that would have been a dividend had cash been distributed in lieu of stock is measured by the corporation's E&P at the time of distribution, $7,000.

Example 37

Assume the same facts as above, except that E&P at the time of the distribution, May 1, 2013 was $11,000. In this case, $11,000 is ordinary income and taxed at favorable rates. However, no loss is recognized for the unrecovered basis of $3,000; rather, the basis of the common stock on which the stock was distributed is increased by $3,000 to $19,000 ($16,000 + $3,000). These results are summarized below.

Amount realized	$12,000
Ordinary income:	
Amount that would have been a dividend had cash been distributed in lieu of stock	(11,000)
Return of capital	$ 1,000
Adjusted basis	(4,000)
Loss not recognized	$ 3,000

Redemptions of § 306 Stock

If a shareholder redeems § 306 stock, the amount realized is considered a distribution of property subject to the normal rules of § 301. As a result, the amount realized in this case is treated as a *dividend* to the extent of the corporation's E&P *at the time of the redemption.* To the extent the distribution exceeds E&P, it is treated as a return of the shareholder's basis with any excess considered gain from the sale of stock. Any basis which is not recovered is added to the basis of the common shares with respect to which the § 306 stock was distributed. Since the distribution is treated as a normal property distribution, the corporation must make an adjustment to its E&P. Recall also that dividends are taxed at a favorable rate.

> ### Example 38
>
> Assume the same facts as in *Example 36* above, except that instead of selling the stock to F, the corporation redeemed the shares. Here, the entire amount realized of $12,000 is treated as a dividend since E&P at the date of the redemption is $30,000. The $4,000 basis of the shares is added to the shareholder's basis for the common stock, resulting in a total basis for the common stock of $20,000 ($4,000 + $16,000). Note that this result is very harsh since only $7,000 of ordinary income would have been recognized had a cash distribution been made in lieu of stock at the date of distribution.

EXCEPTIONS TO § 306

The special rules governing redemptions and other dispositions of § 306 stock are disregarded for certain dispositions where the shareholder's interest is terminated or where the § 306 taint is retained by the transferor, transferee, or both. The exception granted for transactions that completely terminate the shareholder's interest is justified on the theory that the series of transactions no longer resembles an ordinary dividend distribution since the shareholder's interest has substantially changed. The other exception is not truly an exception because the § 306 taint remains. Section 306 provides several other exceptions as well.[56]

Tax Planning

EXTRACTING CORPORATE EARNINGS AT CAPITAL GAINS RATES

Notwithstanding the gauntlet of requirements that redemptions must run, they provide opportunities for withdrawing corporate earnings at a cost lower than that incurred with a dividend distribution. For this reason, the taxpayer should always consider the possibility of structuring a distribution as a redemption rather than as a dividend. In planning, however, two factors should be remembered: (1) dividends are currently taxed at the same rates as long-term capital gains and (2) a *corporate* shareholder cannot obtain a benefit from structuring the redemption as a dividend due to the extraordinary dividend rules.

REDEMPTIONS OF GIFTED STOCK

When planning for the owner of an interest in a closely held business, gifts of stock are often made to shift income to family members in a lower bracket (e.g., children). This technique is particularly useful when the corporation has elected to be taxed as an S corporation since the income of the entity flows through to the lower-bracket family member. Whether the corporation is an S corporation or a regular corporation, the stock given to the children can later be redeemed by the corporation to provide funds as their own needs arise. For example, corporate stock could be transferred in trust to a child who is seven years old, and the stock could be redeemed during his or her college age years to provide funds for tuition and other expenses. In order to secure sale treatment, however, the redemption must be postponed for more than 10 years from the date the stock was gifted. The conclusion derives from several special rules regarding the family attribution waiver under Code § 302(b)(3). According to this provision, the family attribution rules cannot be waived if any of the redeemed stock was acquired from a related person within 10 years of the redemption.[57] This rule prohibits a father from giving his son or another related party some of his stock, immediately followed by a redemption of the son's stock with favorable sale treatment. Thus, in order for this technique to be successful, stock must be gifted more than 10 years before the anticipated redemption. Alternatively, the child could acquire the stock directly from the corporation for a contribution (e.g., when the value of the stock was low when the corporation was formed) and the restriction would be avoided.

---

[56] See § 306(b).   [57] § 302(c)(2)(B)(i).

BOOTSTRAP ACQUISITIONS

As suggested earlier in this chapter, redemptions are often used as a means to finance the sale of a shareholder's stock. Oftentimes, a prospective buyer has insufficient cash to make the purchase. However, if the corporation has cash, or perhaps desirable property, the buyer can purchase some of the shareholder's stock while the corporation redeems the remaining shares. This technique is referred to as a "bootstrap acquisition."

Example 39

R owns all 100 shares of X Corporation's outstanding stock worth $100,000. S wishes to buy the corporation from R but can secure only $20,000 for the purchase. Assuming X has sufficient assets, S could purchase 20 of the shares from R while X redeemed the other 80 shares. In this case, the redemption would qualify as a complete termination of R's interest, and sale treatment would be secured.

The IRS initially disputed the results achieved in bootstrap acquisitions, arguing the distribution would have been treated as a dividend to the seller if the redemption had occurred prior to the sale. Currently, however, favorable results can be achieved if the redemption is carefully planned.[58]

REDEMPTIONS TO PAY DEATH TAXES

The provisions pertaining to redemptions to pay death taxes provide an excellent vehicle for extracting earnings from the corporation at favorable rates. As explained earlier, because the basis of the redeemed stock is stepped up to its value at the decedent's death, there may be little if any tax to pay on the redemption. Because of these favorable aspects, owners of a closely held corporation should consider arranging for a redemption after death to provide their estate with assets to pay the death taxes. This may entail gifts of property prior to the death of the shareholder to ensure that the stock ultimately represents more than 35% of the decedent's adjusted gross estate. In this regard, it should be mentioned that for this purpose gifts within three years of the decedent's death are included in the adjusted gross estate. Thus, any gifting to qualify the stock under § 303 should be planned far in advance.

In planning a § 303 redemption, the timing of the redemption is very important. The Regulations indicate that the limitation of § 303 treatment to the amount of death taxes and funeral and administrative expenses is allocated on a chronological basis.[59] This rule must be followed even if one of the redemptions would qualify for sale treatment under the general rules of § 302.

Example 40

When R died, total funeral and administrative expenses were $25,000, while death taxes were $275,000. As a result, § 303 treatment is limited to $300,000 ($275,000 + $25,000). In the year following R's death, T—one of R's heirs—redeemed all of her inherited stock, receiving $250,000. During the second year, the estate redeemed $100,000. Only $50,000 of the estate's redemption qualifies under § 303 since the first $250,000 allowable was allocated to T's redemption. This would be true even if T's redemption qualified for capital gain treatment under § 302.

As the above example illustrates, steps should be taken to ensure that § 303 treatment is not wasted on a redemption that otherwise would qualify for capital gains under § 302.

Another attractive feature of the § 303 redemption is that accumulations to redeem stock once the shareholder has died are exempt from the accumulated earnings tax. Thus, if the redemption is to take place over a period of years, accumulations by the corporation would be justified.

---

[58] *Fern R. Zenz v. Quinlivan*, 54-2 USTC ¶9445, 45 AFTR 1672, 213 F.2d 914 (CA-6, 1954).

[59] Reg. § 1.303-2(g)(2).

REDEMPTIONS AND CHARITABLE CONTRIBUTIONS

For owners of a closely held corporation, redemptions can serve as an attractive means to obtain charitable contributions. As discussed in Chapter 3, the corporation may make the contribution for the owner directly as a means to avoid double taxation. Another technique for charitable giving involves redemptions. This method enables the shareholder to obtain a charitable deduction without having to part with the cash immediately.

Example 41

K is the sole shareholder of X Corporation. During the year, she decided to contribute $100,000 to her alma mater, Indiana University. Initially she planned to give a small amount each year. On the advice of her accountant, she transferred all of her nonvoting preferred stock (not § 306 stock), worth $100,000, to the school. Subsequently, the corporation redeems the stock, giving the school a note for $100,000 payable over 20 years. In this situation, K is entitled to a charitable contribution deduction of $100,000 in the year she transfers the stock. Note that this is true even though the cash is actually paid to the charity in installments. Moreover, K has no dividend income and has not lost any control over X. In addition, the corporation is entitled to reduce its E&P account for the E&P attributable to the shares redeemed.

The favorable treatment obtained in this example is secure as long as the charity is not required to surrender the shares for redemption.

Problem Materials

DISCUSSION QUESTIONS

4-1 *Redemptions in General.* When a shareholder sells stock in a corporation, the transaction normally results in capital gain or loss. The Code may alter this result, however, when the sale of the stock is made to the corporation that issued the stock.

   a. What term is used to describe a corporation's acquisition of its own stock?

   b. Why might a corporation acquire its own stock? Answer from the point of view of both the shareholder and the corporation.

   c. Indicate the alternative treatment accorded such exchanges and explain why a different treatment might be necessary.

4-2 *Redemptions: Tax Consequences to Shareholders.* R Corporation, which has substantial E&P, redeems 50 of T's 70 shares (basis of $100 per share) for $60,000.

   a. What effect does the redemption have on T's taxable income and the basis for his stock, assuming the transaction qualifies as a sale?

   b. What effect does the redemption have on T's taxable income and the basis for his stock, assuming the distribution does not qualify for sale treatment?

4-3 *Redemptions: Dividend Equivalency.* A redemption is treated as payment in exchange for the shareholder's stock when it is not essentially equivalent to a dividend. When is a redemption distribution not equivalent to a dividend? Include in your answer comments concerning all tests used to determine dividend equivalency, as well as comments on how the following factors affect the dividend equivalency determination: valid business purpose, pro rata distributions, and relationships among the shareholders.

4-4 *Attribution Rules.* Answer the following:
  a. What is the purpose of the constructive ownership rules of § 318?
  b. Give an example of (1) family attribution, (2) entity-to-owner attribution, and (3) owner-to-entity attribution.
  c. Are the constructive ownership rules applicable to all situations where stock ownership must be considered? If not, indicate those situations where they are not applicable.

4-5 *Redemptions to Pay Death Taxes.* In § 303, Congress has provided special treatment for redemptions of stock included in the gross estate of the decedent. In light of this general rule, address the following questions.
  a. What is the significant difference between § 303 and § 302, the general provision governing redemptions? Why is the treatment of § 303 particularly favorable?
  b. In general, when are the benefits of § 303 available?
  c. As a practical matter, the benefits of § 303 have become quite limited over the years. What prompts such a conclusion?

4-6 *Partial Liquidations in General.* Under § 302(b)(4), sale treatment is granted to a redemption distribution qualifying as a partial liquidation if it is "not essentially equivalent to a dividend." This same language appears in the general redemption rule of § 302(b)(1).
  a. Is this phrase interpreted in the same fashion for both provisions? Explain.
  b. The partial liquidation provisions contain a safe harbor test, which a shareholder can utilize to secure sale treatment without concern for the vague dividend equivalency test mentioned above. Outline the requirements of this test and explain their purpose.

4-7 *Redemptions: Effect on Corporate Taxable Income.* Do the rules governing the tax consequences to the corporation on the distribution of property in a redemption differ from those applying to § 301 distributions of property? Explain.

4-8 *Redemptions: Effect on Corporate E&P.* Z Corporation, which had $100,000 of E&P at the end of the year, redeemed 60 shares of its 100 shares outstanding for $70,000. Briefly explain the series of adjustments to Z's E&P that must be made if:
  a. The redemption is treated as a dividend.
  b. The redemption is treated as a sale or exchange.

4-9 *Redemptions by Related Corporations.* By definition, a corporation cannot "redeem" the stock of another corporation, yet the title of § 304 clearly suggests otherwise.
  a. Explain the purpose of § 304 (concerning sales of stock by a shareholder to a related corporation). Include in your answer an explanation of why this provision not only looms as a trap for the unwary but also serves as a device to police possible abuse of the corporate redemption provisions.
  b. How are the ownership tests of § 302 applied to a brother-sister redemption? A parent subsidiary redemption?
  c. If one of the related corporations in a brother-sister or parent-subsidiary redemption has a deficit of $10,000 in E&P, while the other has positive E&P of $10,000, sale treatment effectively results regardless of how the transaction is characterized. Is this statement true or false? Explain.

4-10 *Preferred Stock Bailouts.* Section 306 provides special treatment on the sales of certain stock.
  a. Explain the abuse that § 306 is designed to curb.
  b. How does § 306 eliminate the loophole described above?
  c. The treatment under § 306 varies depending on whether stock is sold or redeemed. What is the critical difference?

PROBLEMS

4-11 *Redemptions: § 302(b)(2).* Z Corporation has 1,000 shares of stock outstanding owned as follows:

Shareholder	Shares Owned	Adjusted Basis
A...	100	$10,000
B...	100	10,000
C...	200	20,000
D...	600	60,000
	1,000	

All shareholders paid $100 per share for their stock. Z has substantial earnings and profits.
  a. During the year, the corporation redeemed 400 shares of D's stock for $400,000. What is the effect of the redemption on D?
  b. Same as (a) except the corporation redeemed 200 shares of D's stock for $200,000.

4-12 *Redemptions: § 302(b)(3).* X Corporation has 1,000 shares of stock outstanding owned as follows:

Shareholder	Shares Owned
E	100
F	100
H..	200
W	600
	1,000

H and W are husband and wife. For each of the following *independent* situations, indicate whether the redemption would qualify for sale treatment. Assume the transaction qualifies unless otherwise implied.
  a. X redeemed all of H's stock. H received cash of $50,000 and a $100,000 note payable in annual installments with interest over the next five years.
  b. X redeemed all of E's stock. E will continue his employment with X as vice president.
  c. Several years ago, X redeemed all of the stock of F's father, G. At that time, G filed the appropriate agreement with his tax return, indicating he would notify the IRS if he acquired any stock in X within 10 years of the redemption. This year F died, leaving all of his stock to his father.

4-13 *Redemptions: Basics.* B owns 60 shares of X Corporation while his wife and son own 30 and 10 shares, respectively. Each of the shareholders has a basis in his or her stock of $1,000 per share. X has substantial E&P. What are the consequences to B if the corporation redeems 30 shares of his stock for $150,000?

4-14 *Family Attribution.* Ms. B owns 30% of the stock of F Corporation. The remaining 70% of the stock is owned by the members of her family. Indicate whether Ms. B would be treated as constructively owning the stock owned by the following individuals under the family attribution rules of § 318.
  a. Her father
  b. Her daughter
  c. Her sister
  d. Her grandfather
  e. Her grandson
  f. Her father-in-law
  g. Her son-in-law
  h. Her uncle

4-15 *Entity to Owner Attribution.* C Corporation has 100 shares outstanding, owned as shown below.

Shareholder	Shares
L	20
Partnership A (L is a 10% partner)	20
Partnership B (L is a 60% partner)	20
Corporation X (L is a 10% shareholder)	20
Corporation Y (L is a 60% shareholder)	20
	100

Under the constructive ownership rules of § 318, how many shares of stock is L deemed to own?

4-16 *Entity to Owner Attribution.* C Corporation has 100 shares outstanding, 90% of which are owned by the A&B Partnership. Mr. A owns a 70% interest in the partnership and Mr. B owns a 30% interest in the partnership. Answer the following questions in light of the constructive ownership rules of § 318.
  a. How many shares do A and B each own in C?
  b. Same as (a) except A&B is a corporation.

4-17 *Owner to Entity/Attribution.* D Corporation has 100 shares outstanding, owned as shown below. For each situation, determine how many shares the named entity owns in D Corporation under the constructive ownership rules of § 318.
  a. How many shares does Partnership X own in D?

Shareholder	Shares in D
Mr. J	60
Partnership X (J is a 20% partner)	40
	100

  b. How many shares does Corporation X own in D?

Shareholder	Shares in D
Mr. J	60
Corporation X (J is a 20% shareholder)	40
	100

  c. Same as (b) except J owns 80% of X.

4-18 *Constructive Ownership Rules.* M, Inc.'s 1,000 shares of stock are owned as follows:

Shareholder	Shares in D
B	300
D, B's wife	190
F, B's brother	80
H, D's mother	70
J, Inc.	110
L, a partnership	120
N, a trust	130
Total	1,000

Both J, Inc. and L are owned 60% by B and 40% by F. N was established by H for the benefit of B's and D's children, ages 7 and 10. Determine the direct and indirect ownership interest in M, Inc. attributable to each of M's shareholders.

4-19 *Redemptions and Constructive Ownership Rules.* Z Corporation has 200 shares of common stock outstanding, 100 owned by A and 100 owned by B. Z plans to redeem all 100 shares owned by A. If A is related to B in each of the following ways, will the redemption qualify for sale treatment? (Indicate the number of shares owned by A after the redemption in each of the following cases.)

   a. B is A's wife.

   b. B is A's estranged wife. They continue to be married only for political reasons.

   c. B is a corporation. A owns 50% of B's stock.

   d. B is a corporation. A owns 40% of B's stock.

   e. A is a corporation. B owns 50% of A's stock.

   f. B is the wife of A's son, R.

   g. A is a trust whose sole beneficiary is B's son.

4-20 *Multiple Shareholder Redemption.* T Corporation has 100 shares of stock outstanding owned, as indicated below. Buck Smith is married to Tina Smith, while John Brown is the father of Lucy Brown. The Smiths and the Browns are not related. During the year, the corporation redeemed 33 shares from the shareholders as shown below, paying $2,000 for each share redeemed. Each shareholder had a $200 basis in each share of stock owned prior to the redemption.

Name	Shares Before	Shares Redeemed
Buck Smith	40	23
Tina Smith	10	2
John Brown	45	4
Lucy Brown	5	4
	100	33

   a. What are the tax consequences of the redemption to Buck Smith? Indicate the income, its character, and the basis of his remaining stock.

   b. What are the tax consequences of the redemption to John Brown? Indicate the income, its character, and the basis of his remaining stock.

4-21 *Section 311 and Redemption Distributions.* This year, C Corporation redeemed all of the stock of two of its shareholders, A and B. The corporation distributed land worth $75,000 (basis $10,000) to A and equipment worth $30,000 (basis $40,000) to B. What are the effects of the distributions, if any, on C's taxable income?

4-22 *Earnings and Profits.* A distribution is made when D, Inc. has assets valued at $500,000 (basis of $300,000), E&P of $80,000, and 10,000 shares of stock outstanding. T receives assets valued at $100,000 (basis of $60,000) for all his D stock (2,000 shares with a basis of $25,000). Compute the corporation's E&P balance after the exchange if it is treated as (a) a dividend, or as (b) a sale.

4-23 *Section 302 Redemptions.* H and D (unrelated), F and S (father and son), and PAC Corporation own the outstanding shares of stock of CEL Corporation, as follows:

Shareholder	Adjusted Basis for Stock	Pre-Redemption Ownership
H............................	$ 5,000	40
D............................	10,000	10
F............................	15,000	25
S............................	1,000	5
PAC.........................	25,000	20
Total		100

In addition, H owns 80% of PAC, while F owns the remaining 20 percent. CEL Corporation has $100,000 of E&P. Each individual is an employee of CEL.

    a. What are the tax consequences to H and CEL if CEL redeems 20 shares of H's stock for $15,000? Include in your answer the effect on (1) H's taxable income, (2) H's basis of his stock in CEL, (3) CEL's taxable income, and (4) CEL's E&P.

    b. Same as (a) except H owns 45% of PAC.

    c. S wishes to redeem his shares only if he can obtain sale treatment. Can S's desires be accommodated? Explain.

    d. What amount of gain or loss, if any, must CEL recognize if it distributes a crane worth $50,000 (cost $40,000, depreciation $10,000) to PAC for five of its shares?

    e. Same as (d) except the property's basis to CEL was $75,000.

4-24 *Partial Liquidations: Qualification.* HPI Corp. has 500 shares outstanding, 400 owned by B and 100 owned by R. HPI operates the following:

    1. A tavern which it purchased for $100,000 cash from its prior owners in 2002.

    2. A sporting goods store it obtained in March 2013 from B in exchange for 300 shares of HPI stock. B had operated the store as a sole proprietor since 1993. Prior to this acquisition, HPI had 200 shares outstanding, 100 owned by both B and R.

    3. An apartment building which it purchased three years ago. The building was new when it was acquired.

Each of the activities described above are equivalent in value. HPI desires to distribute one of these to B in exchange for 167 shares of stock on December 1, 2016. Of those listed, which may B receive and be assured of sale treatment? Explain your answer.

4-25 *Partial Liquidation: Shareholder Treatment.* C, an individual, owns all 100 of the outstanding shares of Y Corporation. She had acquired the stock for $100 per share several years ago. In a transaction qualifying as a partial liquidation, Y redeemed 20 shares of C for $30,000.

    a. What are the tax consequences to C?

    b. Same as (a) except assume that C is a corporation.

4-26 *Partial Liquidation: Computations.* DSA Corp., which is in the printing business, is owned equally by the following parties: individuals Q, R, S, and corporation TUV. Each shareholder has a $10,000 basis in the 25 shares of stock owned, which they acquired 10 years ago when they formed the corporation. During the year, DSA redeemed 10 shares from Q for $15,000. Assuming the redemption qualifies as a partial liquidation, answer the following:

    a. What is the effect of the redemption on the taxable income of Q?

    b. Assume DSA obtained Q's shares in exchange for photocopying equipment worth $15,000 (cost $8,000 in 2010, depreciation $6,000). What amount of gain or loss, if any, must DSA recognize on the transfer?

    c. Same as (a) except DSA redeemed 10 shares from TUV for $15,000.

4-27 *Partial Liquidation: Computations.* CRS Corp. is owned and operated by individuals J, K, and L, and UGH, Inc. J owns 40 shares (basis $20,000), which he acquired when the corporation was organized in 2006. K owns 15 shares (basis $7,500), which she also acquired upon organization. L owns 20 shares, which he acquired from K in 2014 for $12,000. UGH owns the remaining 25 shares (basis $9,000). CRS has E&P of $200,000. As part of a transaction qualifying as a partial liquidation, CRS redeemed the following in 2016: 20 shares from J for $20,000; 10 shares from K in exchange for a warehouse used in CRS's business worth $10,000 (cost in 2009 was $7,000, depreciation claimed using the straight-line method was $3,000); 15 shares from L in exchange for land used in the business worth $15,000 (basis $25,000).

 For each of the shareholders identified in (a–d) below, indicate (1) the effect of the redemption on taxable income; and (2) the basis of any property received.
  a. J
  b. K
  c. L
  d. What is the effect of the redemption on the taxable income of CRS?

4-28 *Death Tax Redemptions: Qualification/Computations.* On January 1, 2016 K died. His gross estate of $8 million included a 10% interest (10,000 shares) in XYZ Corporation worth $3,200,000 and a 25% interest in ABC Inc. worth $400,000. Funeral and administrative expenses deductible under §§ 2053 and 2054 were $240,000. Deductible debts were $960,000. Federal estate taxes in 2016 were $540,000. The entire estate after payment of claims and taxes was payable to K's sole heir Z.
  a. Would a redemption of either XYZ or ABC stock qualify for sale treatment under § 303?
  b. On August 1, 2016 XYZ redeemed 1,000 shares of its stock for $320,000 from the estate. What are the tax consequences to the estate?
  c. Refer to (b). Would additional redemptions of XYZ stock qualify for § 303 treatment? If so, in what amount?

4-29 *Brother-Sister Redemptions.* T owns 50 of the 100 outstanding shares of ISC Corp. stock and 80 of the 100 outstanding shares of ACC Corp. stock. The remaining shares of each corporation are held by a party unrelated to T. T has a basis in the ISC stock of $5,000 ($100 per share) and a basis in the ACC Corp. stock of $4,000 ($50 per share). The E&P of ISC and ACC are $10,000 and $15,000, respectively. During the year, T sold 30 shares of ISC to ACC for $20,000.
  a. Compute T's gain or loss on the sale and state its character.
  b. What is T's basis in her remaining shares of ISC?
  c. What is T's basis in her shares of ACC?
  d. What is ACC's basis in the ISC shares purchased?
  e. Answer (a–d) assuming T owns 60 of ACC's shares.

4-30 *Parent-Subsidiary Redemptions.* T owns 120 of the 200 outstanding shares of P Corporation stock. His basis in the shares is $6,000 ($50 per share). P owns 90 of the 100 outstanding shares of S Corporation stock. The E&P of P and S are $25,000 and $30,000, respectively. During the year, T sold 80 shares of P stock to S for $40,000.
  a. Compute T's gain or loss on the sale and state its character.
  b. What is T's basis in his remaining shares of P?
  c. What is S's basis in the P shares purchased?
  d. Answer (a–c) assuming T sells 20 shares.

4-31 *Preferred Stock Bailouts: Computations.* T owns 100 shares of the outstanding common stock of WIC Corp. On June 3, 2012 the corporation distributed 20 shares of preferred stock as a nontaxable dividend to T. The preferred stock was worth $50,000. Accumulated E&P on June 3, 2012 was $40,000. The basis allocated to the preferred stock was $8,000.
  a. Assume T sells the preferred stock to a third party for $42,000 on July 15, 2016, when WIC's E&P is $65,000. What are the tax consequences to T and WIC?
  b. Same as (a) except WIC redeems the preferred stock.

4-32 *Application of § 306.* For each of the following situations, indicate whether § 306 applies, and if so, how?

   a. T received a nontaxable distribution of preferred stock with respect to her common stock on May 2, 2016, when the corporation had a deficit in E&P of $50,000.

   b. R received a nontaxable distribution of common stock (value $40,000) with respect to his common stock on June 1, 2016, when the corporation had E&P of $70,000.

   c. X Corporation decided to reshuffle its capital structure. Consequently, it issued one share of common stock and one share of preferred stock to each common shareholder in exchange for all of the outstanding shares of common stock. The transaction qualified as a tax-free recapitalization under the reorganization provisions.

   d. G inherited 50 shares of § 306 stock from his uncle.

   e. H gave 30 shares of § 306 stock to her nephew.

   f. E sold 50 shares of TYX common and 30 shares of TYX preferred that was § 306 stock to her father. This completely terminated her direct interest in TYX.

TAX RESEARCH PROBLEMS

4-33 D Corporation has 100 shares outstanding owned as shown below.

Shareholder	Shares
Mr. J	60
Partnership X (J is a 20% partner)	20
Partnership Y (J is a 70% partner)	20
	100

Under the constructive ownership rules of § 318, determine the number of shares owned by each of D's shareholders.

Research source:

   § 318 (a)(5).

4-34 C Corporation has 100 shares outstanding, owned as shown below.

Shareholder	Shares
Mr. R	60
Corporation X (R is a 20% shareholder)	20
Corporation Y (R is a 70% shareholder)	20
	100

Under the constructive ownership rules of § 318, determine the number of shares owned by each of C's shareholders.

Research source:

   § 318 (a)(5)

4-35 Bennie and his son, Ted, formerly owned Aluminum Tennis Frames Incorporated (ATF) equally. The corporation has manufactured and sold aluminum tennis frames to the leading sellers of tennis racquets in the United States for the past 10 years. In 2008 Bennie decided to turn his entire business over to his son and retire to the good life. To this end, ATF redeemed all of Bennie's shares to completely terminate his interest. ATF redeemed the shares by giving Bennie a note payable with 10% interest in 10 annual installments. Bennie filed the appropriate agreement necessary to waive the family attribution rules and hence, reported the gain on the redemption as a capital gain as each installment payment was received.

In 2016 Bennie, yearning for the excitement of business, decided he wanted to go back into business. During his absence from ATF, the business had grown and prospered. Consequently, ATF had more orders than it could handle properly. Knowing this, Bennie approached his son about supplying ATF with racquet frames. Bennie and his son are considering signing an agreement whereby Bennie's company will provide racquet frames to ATF. It is anticipated that in 2016 all of Bennie's business will consist of sales to ATF. During 2017 and 2018, the percentage of Bennie's business attributable to the agreement with ATF is expected to drop slightly as the company plans to produce racquets for other companies, as well as a unique "elephant size" racquet (the Dumbo), which it will sell directly to tennis retailers and via mail order.

Bennie and his son have come to you to ask whether there are any tax ramifications related to the planned agreement.

4-36 In 2002 Perry and his wife, Della, incorporated his construction business. The business was quite successful, allowing the couple to enjoy the finer things in life. Over the years, however, Perry and Della became disenchanted with each other and decided to go their separate ways. Nevertheless, Della would not divorce Perry, fearing that it would have a negative impact on her political career.

Recently, Della decided to run for the state legislature. Needing money for her campaign, she is considering selling some of her stock back to the corporation. Can she obtain sale treatment if the corporation redeems a portion of her shares?

4-37 Julie Caesar owns all of the stock of Checkers Corporation, which operates a chain of pizza shops. Several years ago, Julie thought she should expand into the hamburger business, so she formed JC Enterprises, which operates a chain of gourmet hamburger restaurants. Checkers owns 75% of the stock of JC Enterprises, and Julie and her daughter, Lily, own 15 and 10 percent, respectively. This year Julie was suddenly murdered, leaving a large estate entirely to Lily. Her estate tax return revealed the following information:

Gross estate:

Checkers stock	$ 9,000,000
JC Enterprises stock	1,000,000
Other assets	15,000,000
Funeral and administrative expenses	500,000
Claims against the estate	4,500,000
State inheritance and estate taxes	8,000,000

The executor of Julie's estate now wants to arrange a redemption of JC Enterprises stock in order to pay some of the expenses of the estate. Will a redemption of JC Enterprises qualify for § 303 treatment?

COMPREHENSIVE PROBLEM

4-38 Walter Bedd and Lester Lazyboy started Couch Potato Furniture 35 years ago. Since that time Walter has brought his daughter, Emmie, and son-in-law, Chester, into the corporation, giving them stock 20 years ago. On January 1, the 100 shares of outstanding stock of the corporation were owned as follows:

Name	Shares Owned
Walter Bedd	30
Chester Dror	3
Emmie Dror	12
Lilly Dror	5
Lester Lazyboy	30
L&Z Partnership	10
LLL Corporation	10

Walter is Emmie's father. Chester and Emmie are happily married with one child, Lilly, who is 17 years old. The couple gave Lilly her stock 6 years ago. Lester owns a 40% interest in the L&Z partnership and 40% of the stock of LLL Corporation. All of the shareholders have a basis in each share of stock of $1,000 per share. All of the individual shareholders currently work for the corporation, including Lilly who works part-time. Couch Potato has $200,000 of E&P. Answer the following questions:

a. On August 1 of this year, Walter decided to curb his involvement in the corporation. What is the minimum number of shares that Walter must surrender in order to qualify for sale treatment? For purposes of the redemption test, how many shares of the corporation does Walter own before and after the redemption?

b. Assume the corporation distributed land (an outlot at a shopping mall held for future expansion) worth $50,000 (basis $15,000) and a car worth $10,000 (basis $13,000) to Walter in redemption of his stock that qualified for sale treatment. What amount of gain or loss, if any, must the corporation recognize?

c. Assume Walter redeems 20 shares of stock for $60,000 cash and the redemption qualifies for sale treatment. What is the effect of the redemption distribution on the corporation's E&P?

d. Lilly is 17 and preparing to enter college next year. Her parents' financial adviser has suggested that the corporation redeem her stock and Lilly could use the proceeds to help pay her tuition. He suggests this in lieu of a sale by the parents who would then use their proceeds to pay for her tuition. Comment on the advantages and disadvantages of this plan. Your comments should include all the information that you would want to convey to Lilly and her parents at an upcoming meeting.

e. Due to various poor investments Lester is short of cash and is considering selling some of his stock back to the corporation. How many shares is he currently treated as owning in Couch Potato?

f. Lester has thought about solving his cash flow problems by selling some of his Couch Potato stock to LLL Corporation. What issues, if any, must be addressed before giving Lester advice on this transaction?

Complete Liquidations

5

Learning Objectives

Upon completion of this chapter you will be able to:

LO.1 Explain some of the reasons for liquidating a corporation.

LO.2 Determine the tax consequences of a liquidation to a shareholder.

LO.3 Determine the tax consequences of a liquidation to the liquidating corporation.

LO.4 Discuss the special rules that apply when a parent corporation liquidates a subsidiary.

LO.5 Explain the special election available to an acquiring corporation allowing it to treat the purchase of a target corporation's stock as a purchase of its assets.

Chapter Outline

Introduction

LO.1

Explain some of the reasons for liquidating a corporation.

Chapter 3 and Chapter 4 considered several types of corporate distributions: distributions of property and stock as well as those relating to redemptions and partial liquidations. In all of these situations, the corporation continues to operate all or part of its business. At some time during the corporation's life, however, it may be appropriate to terminate the corporation's existence. In such case, the corporation must wind up its business affairs and proceed with a *complete liquidation*.

A liquidation may be desirable for a number of reasons. Many liquidations occur because the business's profitability, or lack thereof, no longer justifies continuing the corporation. Liquidation also may be desirable where shareholders simply seek the corporation's cash and other assets to meet other needs.

A liquidation often occurs in conjunction with a sale of the corporation's business. For example, a party interested in acquiring a target corporation's business might purchase the target's assets—rather than its stock. In such case, the corporation may sell the assets and subsequently distribute the sale proceeds to its shareholders in complete liquidation. Alternatively, the corporation may distribute its assets to its shareholders in complete liquidation whereupon the shareholders sell the assets to the interested buyer. On the other hand, the buyer may purchase the target's stock and subsequently liquidate its new subsidiary to obtain the subsidiary's assets. Regardless of how the sale is consummated, knowledge of the tax provisions governing liquidations is mandatory.

Still other tax factors may provide the motive for liquidation. Shareholders and management may wish to discard the corporate form to avoid such tax problems as double taxation or the risk of incurring the accumulated earnings tax or the personal holding company tax—special penalty taxes imposed on corporations that have improperly accumulated their earnings. If the corporation is suffering losses, another form of business such as a partnership would enable deduction of the losses by the owners.

Regardless of the reason for the corporate liquidation, the transaction should not be planned without a full awareness of the tax consequences. This chapter examines various tax aspects of complete liquidations as well as the related problems of so-called *collapsible corporations*.

Complete Liquidations in General

The various liquidation rules do not operate unless the distribution is considered a distribution in complete liquidation. According to the Code, a distribution is treated "as in complete liquidation of a corporation if the distribution is one of a series of distributions in redemption of all of the stock of the corporation pursuant to a plan."[1] The Regulations elaborate, providing that liquidation treatment applies only if the corporation is in a "status of liquidation."[2] This status exists when a corporation ceases to be a going concern and is engaged in activities whose sole function is the winding up of its business affairs. Interestingly, a formal written plan indicating the intention to liquidate is not required; factors merely suggesting the intention to liquidate may be sufficient to warrant liquidation treatment. In addition, it is not necessary for the corporation to dissolve for the liquidation to be complete.[3] In fact, the corporation may retain a nominal amount of assets provided the reason for the retention is to preserve the corporation's legal existence.[4] Because of the imprecision in the definition of a corporate liquidation, it is sometimes difficult to determine whether the corporation is in a status of liquidation and thus whether the liquidation provisions apply.

Since a complete liquidation results in the termination of the corporation, its treatment differs somewhat from that accorded stock redemptions and other corporate distributions. Nevertheless, the basic tax question that must be addressed in both situations is the same: what is the effect of the liquidation on the liquidating corporation and its shareholders?

The tax treatment of the shareholders of the liquidating corporation is normally governed by Code § 331. This rule provides that a shareholder treats the property received in liquidation of a corporation as proceeds obtained from the *sale* of stock. Therefore, the shareholder must recognize gain or loss. The gain or loss is typically capital gain or loss since the

---

[1] § 346(a).

[2] Reg. § 1.332-2(c).

[3] *Ibid.*

[4] *Ibid.*

shareholder's stock is usually a capital asset. The basis of any property received by the shareholder is its fair market value.[5]

The tax treatment of the liquidating corporation is normally governed by Code § 336. Section 336 generally provides that the corporation must recognize gain and loss on the distribution of property to its shareholders as part of a complete liquidation. As part of the liquidation, the corporation's earnings and profits are usually eliminated as is the corporation's basis in any property it distributes.

Example 1

Corporation X owns one asset, land, with a basis of $1,000 and a fair market value of $10,000. According to a plan of complete liquidation of X, the corporation distributes the asset to its sole shareholder, Y, who purchased his stock for $500. Section 331 requires Y to recognize a gain of $9,500 ($10,000 − $500) as if he had sold the stock. Y's basis in the property is its fair market value of $10,000. Pursuant to § 336, the corporation must recognize a gain on the distribution of the land of $9,000 ($10,000 − $1,000).

In addition to these general provisions governing complete liquidations, special rules exist that apply when a parent corporation causes a subsidiary to liquidate. These rules are contained primarily in §§ 332 and 337. A special set of rules contained in Code § 338 may come into play as part of an acquisition when a parent corporation purchases the stock of another corporation and continues to operate it as a subsidiary.

The remainder of this chapter discusses the detailed tax treatment of corporate liquidations. It is normally assumed that the corporation is in the process of liquidating and fulfills the requirements evidencing a "status of liquidation" as discussed previously. If a "status of liquidation" does not exist, the following rules do not apply. Instead, the corporation and the shareholders are considered as having made and received a dividend distribution or distribution in redemption of part of the corporation's stock and are treated accordingly.

Complete Liquidations: Effect on Shareholders

When a shareholder receives a distribution in complete liquidation of a corporation, two questions must be addressed:

LO.2
Determine the tax consequences of a liquidation to a shareholder.

1. What is the amount of gain or loss recognized and what is its character?
2. What is the basis of any property received?

The answers to these questions depend on whether the rules generally covering all liquidations apply—those contained in § 331—or the special rules of § 332 concerning liquidations of a subsidiary. In this section, the general rules governing all liquidations other than those of an 80-percent-owned subsidiary are considered.

THE GENERAL RULE: § 331

Gain or Loss

Under the general liquidation rules prescribed by § 331, amounts received by shareholders in complete liquidation of a corporation are considered as payment in full for their stock. Each shareholder recognizes gain or loss equal to the difference between the *net* fair market value of the property received (fair market value of the assets received less any liabilities assumed) and the basis of the stock surrendered.[6] If the stock was purchased at different times and for different amounts, the gain or loss is computed on each separate lot.[7] The liquidating distribution is allocated according to the number of shares in each lot.

---

[5] § 334(a).

[6] § 1001.

[7] Reg. § 1.331-1(e).

Example 2

C purchased 200 shares of ABC Corporation stock for $8,000 on January 1, 2011. On June 1, 2016, C purchased an additional 100 shares for $15,000. On October 7, 2016, C received $30,000 in complete liquidation of ABC. The allocation of the $30,000 between the two lots of stock and C's gain and loss on the deemed sale is computed below.

	2011 Lot	2016 Lot
Number of shares	200	100
Fraction of total	200/300	100/300
× Total received	× $30,000	× $30,000
Amount realized	$ 20,000	$ 10,000
Adjusted basis	(8,000)	(15,000)
Gain (loss) recognized	$ 12,000	$ (5,000)

Generally, corporate stock is a capital asset. Therefore, the gains and losses recognized under § 331 are capital gains and losses. Since each stock acquisition is treated separately, it is possible for a shareholder to have a long-term gain or loss on one block of stock and a short-term gain or loss on another block.

Example 3

Same facts as *Example 2*. The gain on the stock acquired in 2011 is long-term, while the loss on the stock acquired in 2016 is short-term.

Time of Recognition

Shareholders could receive liquidating distributions all in one year or in a series over several years. When the shareholder receives all of the distributions in one taxable year, the exact amount of the gain or loss is reported in the year of receipt. If the payments are received in two or more taxable years, the shareholder must use the *cost recovery method* for recognition of gain or loss.[8] Under this method, each payment received is first applied against the basis of the stock.[9] After reducing the stock's basis to zero, all subsequent receipts are recognized as gain when received. In no case is loss recognized until all distributions are received.

Example 4

J owns 100 shares of M Corporation with a basis of $10,000. From 2016 to 2019, J received the following series of liquidating distributions from M Corporation.

Date of Distribution	Amount of Distribution
December 31, 2016	$7,000
January 7, 2017	2,000
January 12, 2018	3,000
January 21, 2019	4,000

---

[8] Rev. Rul. 68-348, 68-2 C.B. 141.

[9] When a shareholder receives a distribution of property of indeterminable value, income may be reported under the open transaction doctrine causing a different result in some instances. See, for example, *Stephen H. Dorsey*, 49 T.C. 606 (1968).

Since she is receiving installments over several years, she uses the cost recovery method to report her gain. As shown below, the first $7,000 is nontaxable and reduces her basis from $10,000 to $3,000. The 2017 distribution of $2,000 is also nontaxable but further reduces her basis to $1,000. The first $1,000 received in 2018 is nontaxable. The remaining amounts are taxable when received. Therefore, J has a $2,000 gain in 2018 and a $4,000 gain in 2019.

	2016	2017	2018	2019
Remaining basis.	$10,000	$3,000	$1,000	$ 0
Distribution	(7,000)	(2,000)	(3,000)	(4,000)
Remaining basis.	$ 3,000	$1,000	$ 0	$ 0
Gain recognized.	$ 0	$ 0	$2,000	$4,000

Example 5

Assume the same facts as in *Example 4*, except that J receives only the 2016 and 2017 distributions. Again J uses the cost recovery method. She recognizes a $1,000 loss in 2017 following the final distribution—10,000 (basis) − ($7,000 + $2,000 [2016 and 2017 distributions]).

Installment Notes

Absent special rules, the distribution of an installment note by a liquidating corporation to its shareholders would create a hardship for the shareholder. Under the general liquidation rules, shareholders must compute their gain on the "sale" of the stock using the full fair market value of the note. For example, consider a corporation that distributes a note to its sole shareholder worth $100,000 that is payable over the next five years in annual installments of $20,000. Under § 331, gain on the distribution must be computed as if the shareholder had received the entire $100,000 when the note was received—even though cash is actually collected over the next five years! Such treatment obviously could create a cash flow problem since the tax would be due currently but note payments would not be received until later. To eliminate this problem, a special exception has been created.

If a shareholder receives an installment note attributable to a sale of property by the liquidating corporation, the cash collections on the note (rather than the receipt of the note itself) may be treated as payment for the *stock*.[10] This special treatment is available only if the sale by the liquidating corporation that produces the installment note occurs within the 12-month period beginning on the date the plan of liquidation is adopted, and the liquidation is completed by the close of this 12-month period. If the liquidation takes more than 12 months (i.e., more than 12 months have elapsed from the time the plan is adopted to the time the final distribution to shareholders is made), the rule does not apply. Similarly, the rule does not apply to installment notes arising from sales *prior* to the adoption of the plan of liquidation. In addition, the special rule does not apply to installment obligations arising from the sales of inventory unless all the inventory of a trade or business is sold to one person in one transaction—a so-called *bulk sale*.[11] If the corporation is engaged in two or more businesses, a sale of the inventory of each business can qualify as a bulk sale. The effect of these rules is to reserve this special treatment for installment obligations attributable to sales of property—other than routine sales of inventory—occurring during the 12-month liquidation period.

---

[10] § 453(h)(1)(A). Note that the corporation must recognize gain on the distribution of the installment note under § 336.

[11] § 453(h)(1)(B).

Example 6

Z Corporation opened its first discount fur coat store in 2007 and was immediately successful. Over the next seven years, it expanded rapidly, establishing over 50 stores in 20 states. To obtain additional cash for expansion, it sold a warehouse on June 1, 2015, receiving $100,000 cash and a note for $500,000 payable in 10 annual installments. In 2016 the corporation was no longer able to compete and adopted a plan of liquidation on May 1, 2016. It had "going out of business" sales during the month of June at all of its locations. All of the inventory not sold at the end of June was sold on July 12, 2016 to its biggest competitor, E Corporation, for a $900,000 note payable over the next five years. Z distributed all of its assets, including the two notes, to its sole shareholder, D, on December 15, 2016. The sequence of events and their treatment are shown below.

In reporting her gain on the liquidation, D is entitled to special treatment on the note received from E Corporation since it arose from a sale occurring after the plan of liquidation was adopted, and the liquidation was completed within 12 months. Although the property sold to E was inventory, special treatment is still allowed since the sale qualifies as a bulk sale (i.e., substantially all of its inventory was sold to one person in one transaction). The note arising from the sale of the warehouse does not qualify for special treatment since it arose prior to the time the plan of liquidation was adopted.

When a shareholder receives an installment note that satisfies each of the requirements, a special calculation is made. The shareholder is effectively treated as having sold part of the stock for the note and the remaining part for any other property received. To determine the gain on each of the sales, the shareholder's basis in the stock is allocated between the note and the other property received based on their relative values. The gain or loss on the sale of the stock for the other property received is reported currently while the gain on the note is reported as payments are received.

Example 7

At the time N Corporation adopts a plan of liquidation, it owns the following assets:

	Basis	Fair Market Value
Cash	$10,000	$10,000
Land	10,000	25,000

Following adoption of the plan, N sells the land for $25,000 and receives the purchaser's installment note. N distributes the cash and installment note to its stockholder, B, whose basis in the stock is $3,500. B allocates his basis as follows:

$$\frac{\text{Cash}}{\text{Total receipts}} = \frac{\$10,000}{\$35,000} \times \$3,500 = \$1,000 \text{ basis allocated to cash}$$

$$\frac{\text{Note}}{\text{Total receipts}} = \frac{\$25,000}{\$35,000} \times \$3,500 = \$2,500 \text{ basis allocated to cash}$$

B recognizes $9,000 gain on the cash received ($10,000 received − $1,000 basis). B's basis in the installment note becomes $2,500. Therefore, B will recognize gain equal to 90% of each dollar received on the note ([$25,000 face amount − $2,500 basis = $22,500 gain] ÷ $25,000 face amount).

BASIS TO SHAREHOLDER

When a shareholder uses the general rule of § 331 to determine gain or loss on the liquidation, the shareholder's basis in the property received in the liquidation is its fair market value on the date of distribution.[12] In effect, the shareholders are treated as if they had purchased the assets using stock as the consideration.

Example 8

K owned 100 shares of stock in L Corporation. K's adjusted basis in the stock was $400. L Corporation completely liquidated and distributed to K $200 cash and office equipment worth $700 in exchange for his stock. K's recognized gain is computed as follows:

Cash received by K	$200
Fair market value of property distributed to K	700
Amount realized	$900
Less: K's adjusted basis in his stock	(400)
Realized gain	$500

K's entire realized gain of $500 is recognized. K's basis in the cash received is $200. K's basis in the office equipment received is $700, its fair market value on the date of distribution.

Complete Liquidation: Effect on the Corporation

The previous discussion examined the effect of a complete liquidation on the shareholder. In this section, the effects of the liquidation on the liquidating corporation are considered. The primary concern is whether the corporation recognizes gain or loss on the distribution.

LO.3
Determine the tax consequences of a liquidation to the liquidating corporation.

GAIN OR LOSS TO THE LIQUIDATING CORPORATION

Section 336 provides that a corporation generally must recognize gain *and* loss on the distribution of property as part of a complete liquidation. The gain and loss are computed as if such property were sold to the shareholder at its fair market value.

Example 9

Sleep Inc., a waterbed retailer, fell on hard times and decided to dissolve the business. This year, the corporation adopted a plan of liquidation and completely liquidated. The furniture that the corporation was unable to move in their going-out-of-business sale was distributed to its sole shareholder. This inventory was worth $5,000 (basis $1,000). In addition, the corporation distributed land held for investment worth $8,000 (basis $10,000). The corporation must recognize $4,000 of ordinary income ($5,000 − $1,000) on the distribution of inventory, and a $2,000 capital loss ($8,000 − $10,000) on the distribution of the land.

---

[12] § 334(a).

Note that the gain and loss recognition rule of § 336 ensures that the appreciation on distributed property does not escape tax. This avoidance would otherwise occur because the shareholder's basis in the property is its fair market value. For instance, in *Example 9* above, the shareholder's basis in the inventory would be $5,000. Therefore, a subsequent sale for $5,000 would result in no gain at the shareholder level. For this reason, the corporation is required to recognize the gain just as if it had sold the property.[13]

Liabilities

If the shareholder assumes a corporate liability, the fair market value of the property is treated as being no less than the liability.[14] Therefore, where the liability exceeds the value of the property, gain must be recognized to the extent the liability exceeds the basis of the property.

Example 10

T Corporation's only asset is a building with a basis of $100,000 that is subject to a liability of $400,000. The low basis is attributable to accelerated depreciation. The property is currently worth $250,000. Pursuant to a liquidation, T distributed the building to its sole shareholder, R. T Corporation must recognize a gain of $300,000 ($400,000 liability – $100,000 basis). Had the liability been $200,000, T would have ignored the liability and recognized a gain of $150,000 ($250,000 value – $100,000 basis).

Loss Recognition

The treatment of distributions in liquidation differs from that in nonliquidating distributions in that the corporation is normally allowed to recognize loss on a liquidating distribution.[15] This is not true for all liquidating distributions, however. As with nonliquidating distributions, Congress was concerned that taxpayers may utilize the loss recognition privilege to circumvent the gain recognition rule. To prohibit possible abuse, § 336(d) provides two exceptions concerning the treatment of losses.

Distributions to Related Parties

Section 336(d)(1) prohibits the liquidating corporation from recognizing losses on distributions to *related parties* if the distribution is either:

1. Non-pro rata (i.e., each shareholder did not receive his or her pro rata share of each type of property); or

2. The distributed property was acquired by the corporation during the five-year period prior to the distribution in either a nontaxable transfer under § 351 (relating to transfers to controlled corporations) or a contribution to capital.

For this purpose, a related party is the same as that defined in Code § 267 (e.g., an individual who owns either directly or constructively more than 50% of the distributing corporation's stock).

---

[13] Prior to 1987, corporations recognized gain only under limited circumstances and never recognized loss on the distribution or sale of property in connection with a liquidation.

[14] § 336(b).

[15] Note that § 267 concerning sales between related parties does not apply to a corporate distribution in complete liquidation. See § 267(a)(1).

Example 11

J is the sole shareholder of Z Corporation. In anticipation of the corporation's liquidation, J contributed a dilapidated warehouse to the corporation with a built-in loss of $100,000 (value $200,000, basis $300,000). J elected to reduce her stock basis instead of the corporation reducing the asset's basis. Shortly thereafter, Z distributed the warehouse along with land worth $90,000 (basis $20,000). Absent a special rule, the corporation would recognize a loss of $100,000 which would offset the gain on the land that it must recognize of $70,000 ($90,000 − $20,000). Under the loss prohibition exception, however, no loss is recognized since the distribution is to a related party, J, and the property was acquired as a contribution to capital within five years of the liquidation.

Example 12

B and C own 70 and 30% of the stock of X Corporation, respectively. Pursuant to a plan of liquidation, X disposed of most of its assets, having only cash and two parcels of undeveloped land remaining:

Assets	Adjusted Basis	Fair Market Value
Cash	$400,000	$ 400,000
Goodland	100,000	300,000
Badland	450,000	300,000
		$1,000,000

During the year, X distributed 70% of the assets to B and 30% of the assets to C. B received Badland and the cash while C received Goodland. X must recognize a $200,000 ($300,000 − $100,000) gain on the distribution of Goodland. However, none of the $150,000 loss on the distribution of Badland is recognized since the distribution of the loss property was to a related party (i.e., B owned more than 50% of the stock) and the distribution was disproportionate (i.e., B did not receive his 70% share of the property but rather 100%).

Example 13

Same facts as above except B received Goodland while C received Badland. In this case, X recognizes both the gain and loss. The loss is recognized since the loss property was not distributed to a related party but rather a minority shareholder. Even if the loss property had been contributed four years ago, the loss would be recognized since it is not distributed to a related party (but see discussion below concerning tax-motivated contributions of loss property).

Tax Avoidance Exception. The loss limitation rule of § 336(d)(1) applies only when loss property is distributed to a related party. Absent an additional rule, the loss prohibition could be avoided by distributing recently contributed loss property to a minority shareholder. To prevent this possibility, a second limitation on losses is imposed. Under § 336(d)(2), the amount of loss recognized by a liquidating corporation on the sale, exchange, or distribution of any property acquired in a § 351 transaction or as a contribution of capital is reduced. However, this rule applies only if the principal purpose for the acquisition was the recognition of a loss by the corporation in connection with the liquidation.

It is generally presumed that any property acquired in the above manner after the date that is two years before the date on which a plan of liquidation is adopted was acquired for the purpose of recognizing a loss. When the tax-avoidance motive is found, the rule effectively limits the loss deduction to the decline in value that occurs while the property is in the hands of the corporation. In other words, any built-in loss existing at the time of contribution is not deductible.

To ensure that any built-in loss is not deducted, the Code provides a special computation. For purposes of determining the *loss* on the disposition of the tainted property, the basis of such property is reduced (but not below zero) by the amount of the built-in loss (i.e., the excess of the property's basis over its value at the time the corporation acquired it). By reducing the basis, any subsequent loss recognized is reduced.

Example 14

R, S, T, and U own the stock of Q Corporation. Knowing that the corporation planned to liquidate, R contributed land to the corporation with a built-in loss of $100,000 (value $200,000, basis $300,000) in exchange for shares of Q stock, which qualified for nonrecognition under Code § 351. R elected to reduce her stock basis by the built-in loss. During the course of liquidation, the corporation sold the property for $160,000. Under the general rule, the corporation would recognize a loss of $140,000 ($160,000 amount realized − $300,000 carryover basis). However, since the property was acquired in a § 351 exchange and the principal purpose of the transaction was to recognize loss on the property in liquidation, the special rule applies. The loss recognized is limited to that which occurred in the hands of the corporation, $40,000 ($200,000 value at contribution − $160,000 amount realized). In other words, the loss computed in the normal manner, $140,000, must be reduced by the built-in loss of $100,000. Technically, Q Corporation would compute the loss by reducing its basis in the property by the amount of built-in loss as follows:

Amount realized			$160,000
Adjusted basis:			
Carryover basis		$300,000	
− Basis reduction:			
Carryover basis	$300,000		
− Value at contribution	(200,000)		
Built-in loss		(100,000)	
Adjusted basis			(200,000)
Loss recognized			$ (40,000)

As noted above, loss property transferred more than two years before the plan of liquidation is adopted is generally exempt from the loss prohibition rule. In many cases, however, this rule may provide little relief for those situations where abuse clearly was not intended. For this reason, Congress instructed the IRS to write regulations creating at least two additional exceptions. First, the basis reduction rule generally does not apply to property acquired during the first two years of a corporation's existence. Thus, persons who form a new corporation by transferring assets to it are not penalized if they are later forced to liquidate the venture. Second, the basis reduction rule applies only if there is no "clear and substantial relationship" between the contributed property and the corporation's current or anticipated business. For example, if the shareholders contribute raw land in New Mexico to a corporation that conducts all of its business in the Northeast and that does not expect to expand, there is not a clear and substantial relationship between the property and the corporation's business; thus, the basis reduction rule would apply.

BASIS AND EFFECT ON EARNINGS AND PROFITS

When a corporation liquidates, it normally distributes all its assets and dissolves. As a result, the corporation has no property remaining for which to compute basis. Similarly, the liquidating distributions effectively eliminate all the corporation's earnings and profits.

Liquidation of a Subsidiary

EFFECT ON THE PARENT: CODE § 332

General Rule

Although a shareholder generally recognizes gain or loss on the receipt of a liquidating distribution, Code § 332 provides an important exception when the shareholder is a parent corporation and it causes its subsidiary to liquidate. Under § 332, a parent corporation generally recognizes no gain or loss on property it receives from the liquidation of a subsidiary corporation. This provision was originally designed to permit corporations to simplify complex corporate structures tax-free. In such case, any gain or loss not recognized is deferred through the basis provisions. The bases of the assets generally carry over from the subsidiary to the parent, ensuring that any unrecognized gain is recognized on a subsequent sale of the assets.

LO.4
Discuss the special rules that apply when a parent corporation liquidates a subsidiary.

Example 15

S Corporation is a wholly owned subsidiary of P Corporation. S Corporation's only asset is land, which is leased to P. The land has a basis to S of $100,000 and a fair market value of $500,000. P's basis in the S stock is $150,000. P liquidates S and receives the land. Under the normal liquidation rules, P would recognize a gain of $350,000. However, under the parent-subsidiary liquidation rules of § 332, P does not recognize any gain. P's basis for land is $100,000, the same as S's basis. Note that P's basis in its S Corporation stock is ignored in determining P's basis in the land.

Section 332 applies only if *three* requirements are satisfied:

1. *Ownership.* The parent corporation must own at least 80% of the voting power and at least 80% of the total value of the stock (except nonvoting, nonparticipating preferred stock) on the date of adoption of a plan of liquidation and at all times thereafter until the liquidation is completed.[16] Section 332 and the related provisions apply only to the parent. Minority shareholders—those owning less than 80% of the stock—are subject to the general liquidation rules of § 331 discussed earlier in this chapter.

2. *Cancellation of stock.* All of the subsidiary's property must be distributed in complete cancellation or redemption of the subsidiary's stock pursuant to a plan. The timing of the distributions depends on the nature of the corporation's plan of liquidation.

3. *Plan and time limits.* The liquidating distributions must be made pursuant to a plan of liquidation and within certain time limits. If all distributions occur within one taxable year of the subsidiary, no *formal* plan is necessary.[17] In such case, a shareholder's resolution authorizing the liquidating distributions constitutes a plan. Where the distributions do not take place within one taxable year, a formal plan must exist and the distributions must be made within three years of the close of the year in which the first distribution is made.[18] For example, assuming the subsidiary is a calendar year taxpayer and the first distribution is made during 2016, the final distribution can occur no later than December 31, 2019. In effect, the liquidation can occur over a four-year period.

---

[16] § 332(b)(1).

[17] § 332(b)(2).

[18] § 332(b)(3).

If any of the above requirements are not satisfied (e.g., distributions are not made in a timely manner), the special liquidation-of-a-subsidiary rules of § 332 do not apply to any of the distributions. Instead, the general rule of § 331 applies. On the other hand, it is important to note that § 332 is *not elective*. If the above conditions are met, § 332 and the related provisions must be followed.

Insolvent Subsidiary

Section 332 does not apply if the subsidiary is insolvent since the parent corporation would not receive any assets in exchange for its *stock,* which is a requirement of a liquidation. Instead, § 165(g), concerning worthless securities (e.g., the subsidiary's stock), applies. This provision states that the corporation has a capital loss on a deemed exchange on the last day of the year. The loss is ordinary if the subsidiary is an affiliated corporation under § 165(g)(3). The subsidiary is considered an affiliated corporation if two conditions are satisfied. First, the parent corporation must own at least 80% of the voting power and at least 80% of each class of nonvoting stock (except nonvoting, nonparticipating preferred stock). Second, the subsidiary must have more than 90% of its gross receipts for all taxable years from sources other than rents, royalties, dividends, interest, and gains from sales or exchanges of stock and securities.

Example 16

As part of a plan of expansion into the fast-food business, P Corporation purchased all of the stock of T Corporation for $100,000. This year, T became insolvent, having liabilities of $400,000 and assets of $250,000. As a result, P liquidated T, receiving all of its assets and assuming all of its liabilities. The liquidation rules do not apply since T is insolvent. P Corporation may deduct $100,000 as an ordinary loss since T is an affiliated corporation *and* it is an operating company (i.e., more than 90% of its gross receipts are not from passive sources).

EFFECT ON SUBSIDIARY: CODE § 337

Under the general rules governing liquidations, a liquidating corporation normally must recognize gain or loss on the distribution of property in complete liquidation. However, gain or loss recognition is not theoretically necessary when the gain or loss inherent in the distributed property is preserved for later recognition by the distributee. Preservation normally is accomplished by requiring the distributee shareholder to assume the liquidating corporation's basis. Under the normal liquidation rules of § 331, however, the shareholder recognizes gain or loss and takes a basis in the distributed property equal to its fair market value. In such case, recognition by the liquidating corporation is consistent since the gain or loss is not preserved.

Pursuant to the parent-subsidiary liquidation rules of § 332, the parent corporation does not recognize gain on the receipt of property from its subsidiary since the property is still held in the corporate form. In addition, under § 334(b) discussed below, the subsidiary's basis of the property carries over to the parent. As a result, any gain or loss attributable to the subsidiary is preserved for later recognition when the property is disposed of by the parent. Since the gain or loss is preserved, it is inappropriate to require a subsidiary to recognize gain or loss on a distribution of property when § 332 applies. Consequently, a special exception exists, exempting liquidating subsidiaries from gain or loss recognition. (See Exhibit 5-1 for a comparison of the general liquidation rules to the parent-subsidiary rules.)

Section 337

Under § 337, a subsidiary does not recognize gain or loss on the distribution of property to its *parent* corporation. The nonrecognition provision applies only to distributions of property *actually* transferred to the parent. Property distributed to any minority shareholder is generally governed by § 336, which requires gain or loss recognition. But as explained below, loss on distributions of property to minority shareholders is not recognized.

	EXHIBIT 5-1	**Summary of Corporate Liquidation Provisions**

Type	§ 331: General Liquidation	§ 332: Subsidiary Liquidation
Comments	Shareholders surrender all stock in exchange for property and liquidating corporation ceases to exist	Parent recognizes no gain or loss and can elect purchase or carryover basis if 1. 80% control 2. Plan of liquidation 3. Distribution within one taxable year or three years after close of year plan adopted
Effect on Shareholder	**Sale Treatment** Gain or loss realized = FMV − AB; Exception: Gain reported on installment obligation as payments received	**Sale Treatment** Gain or loss: Parent recognizes no gain or loss
Shareholder's Adjusted Basis	**In Assets Received** FMV [§ 334(a)]	**In Assets Received** Carryover Basis
Effect on Distributing Corporation's Taxable Income	**Sale Treatment** Gains and losses recognized	**Gain or Loss** Carryover Basis No gain or loss on liquidation
Effect on Distributing Corporation's E&P and Tax Attributes	E&P eliminated; other tax attributes disappear	**Carryover Basis** Parent inherits subsidiary's attributes

Example 17

P Corporation owns 90% of the outstanding stock of S Corporation while the remaining 10% is owned by unrelated parties. In a liquidation pursuant to § 332, S distributed property to P with a fair market value of $90,000 (basis $40,000). In addition, S distributed property to the minority shareholders worth $10,000 (basis $8,000). S recognizes no gain on the distribution to P since § 337 exempts a subsidiary from gain or loss recognition on distributions of property to its parent. However, S must recognize a gain of $2,000 ($10,000 − $8,000) on the distribution to the minority shareholders.

Gain and loss recognition is based on how the property is actually distributed, rather than on some hypothetical pro rata distribution to all shareholders.

Example 18

P Corporation owns 80% of the stock of S Corporation while the remaining 20% is owned by a minority shareholder, M. S Corporation owns assets valued at $200,000, consisting of land worth $160,000 (basis $60,000) and $40,000 cash. During the year, S liquidated under § 332, distributing the land to P and the cash to M.

> S recognizes no gain on the distribution of the property since it was distributed in its entirety to the parent corporation. Absent the rule discussed above, it may have been argued that S would be required to recognize 20% of the gain on the land as if 20% of the land had been distributed to M.

Absent any limitation, the above rule would allow the subsidiary to distribute gain assets to the parent to avoid gain recognition and loss assets to the minority shareholders to obtain loss recognition. To prohibit this scheme, § 336(d)(3) provides that no loss is recognized on distributions to minority shareholders under § 332.

Indebtedness of Subsidiary to Parent

Ordinarily when one taxpayer is indebted to another and the debt is satisfied using property, the indebted taxpayer realizes gain or loss as if it had sold the property and used the proceeds to pay the debt. Section 337(b) contains an exception to this general rule. The exception states that when a subsidiary corporation is indebted to its parent corporation and the subsidiary liquidates under § 332, no gain or loss is recognized by the subsidiary when it transfers property to the parent to satisfy the debt.

Example 19

S Corporation is a wholly owned subsidiary of P Corporation. S owes P $100,000 on account. As part of a complete liquidation, S transfers appreciated property worth $100,000 (basis $25,000) to P in settlement of the debt. Since S is being liquidated under § 332, it does not recognize any of the $75,000 gain realized on the transfer of property in payment of the debt. Note that P's basis in the property would be the same as S's, $25,000.

SECTION 334: BASIS OF ASSETS

Section 334(b)(1): The General Rule

When a subsidiary is liquidated by its parent corporation, the basis of the assets transferred from the subsidiary to the parent must be determined. Generally, the basis of each of the assets transferred is the same for the parent corporation as it had been for the subsidiary—a so-called *carryover basis*.[19] This rule applies not only to property transferred in cancellation of the subsidiary's stock, but also to property transferred in order to satisfy the subsidiary's debt to the parent. The amount of the parent's investment in the subsidiary's stock is ignored. The parent's basis is determined solely by the subsidiary's basis.

Example 20

S Corporation had assets with a basis of $1 million and no liabilities. P Corporation bought all of the stock of S Corporation for $1.2 million. Several years after the purchase, when S Corporation's assets have a basis of $800,000, P Corporation liquidates S Corporation in a tax-free liquidation under § 332. P Corporation's basis in the assets received from S Corporation is $800,000, the same basis as S Corporation had in the assets. The $400,000 difference between the basis of the assets and P Corporation's basis in the stock of S Corporation is lost.

---

[19] § 334(b)(1). If the liquidated subsidiary is a foreign subsidiary the parent may have to use fair market value instead of carryover basis. See § 334(b)(1)(B).

Example 21

Assume the same facts as in *Example 20*, except that P Corporation had paid $700,000 (instead of $1.2 million) for S Corporation's stock. P Corporation's basis in the assets received from S Corporation is still $800,000, the same as S Corporation's basis in the assets. In this example, rather than losing a $400,000 investment, P Corporation received a $100,000 tax-free increase in its basis in S Corporation and its assets ($800,000 basis in S Corporation's assets – $700,000 basis that P Corporation had in S Corporation's stock).

As demonstrated above, this carryover of the basis of assets from a subsidiary to its parent can be either beneficial (*Example 21*) or detrimental (*Example 20*) to the parent corporation. For this reason, a parent corporation that plans to sell the business of its subsidiary must carefully evaluate whether a sale of stock or a sale of assets is preferable.

When the parent corporation in a § 332 liquidation uses the carryover basis of the subsidiary as its basis in the assets received [§ 334(b)(1)], the subsidiary recognizes no gain or loss on the distribution. This approach—nonrecognition with a carryover basis—ensures that any gain or loss inherent in the subsidiary's assets is preserved for later recognition. Note, also, that when the carryover basis rules of § 334(b)(1) are used, the depreciation recapture rules are not triggered.[20] Any recapture potential shifts to the parent corporation. In addition, the holding periods of the assets received by the parent corporation in the liquidation include their holding period while the assets were owned by the subsidiary.[21]

When § 332 and the carryover basis provisions of § 334(b)(1) apply, the parent corporation inherits the tax attributes of the subsidiary under § 381. The E&P of the subsidiary is added to the E&P of the parent. (However, a deficit in the subsidiary's E&P cannot reduce a positive balance in the parent's E&P.) If the subsidiary has any net operating loss carryovers, § 381 generally entitles the parent to use such losses.[22] This rule in effect provides corporations with the opportunity to shop for other corporations that have net operating losses that they are unable to use for immediate benefit. To prevent so-called *trafficking in NOLs*, Congress enacted § 269, which authorizes the government to disallow the deduction where the principal purpose of the acquisition was to evade or avoid tax. The ability to use "purchased" NOLs is also limited by § 382. The limitations applying to use of NOLs obtained through acquisitions are discussed in greater detail in Chapter 7.

The *Kimbell-Diamond* Problem

The general requirement calling for the subsidiary's basis to be carried over to the parent was the subject of dispute in *Kimbell-Diamond Milling Co. v. Comm.*[23] In this case, Kimbell-Diamond's plant was destroyed by fire and the corporation wished to purchase replacement property to avoid recognizing gain on the involuntary conversion. The only desirable plant was owned by another corporation that would not sell. To acquire the asset, Kimbell-Diamond purchased the corporation's stock and then liquidated the corporation. Kimbell-Diamond then used the basis of the assets of the liquidated corporation as its basis for the assets pursuant to §§ 332 and 334(b)(1). The amount that Kimbell-Diamond had paid for the stock of the corporation was much less than the liquidated corporation's basis in the assets. Thus, by using the carryover basis, Kimbell-Diamond received much larger depreciation deductions (and therefore had much smaller taxable income) than if it had actually purchased the plant. Upon audit, the IRS reclassified the transaction as a *purchase of assets* rather than a purchase of stock followed by a separate liquidation. As a result, the basis of the plant and other assets of the acquired corporation was their cost (i.e., their value) rather than a higher carryover basis. Upon further review, the Tax Court as well as the Fifth Circuit Court of Appeals agreed with the IRS that the two transactions should be treated as a "single transaction," thus creating the now infamous *Kimbell-Diamond* exception.

---

[20] §§ 1245(b)(3) and 1250(d)(3).

[21] § 1223(2).

[22] The amount of NOL usable in any year may be limited if there has been an ownership change. See Chapter 7 for a discussion of this rule.

[23] 14 T.C. 74 (1950), aff'd, 51-1 USTC ¶9201, 40 AFTR 328, 187 F.2d 718 (CA-5, 1951).

Under the *Kimbell-Diamond* rule, if the original purpose of the stock acquisition was to acquire assets, the acquiring corporation was required to use as its basis for the subsidiary's assets the cost of the subsidiary's stock rather than a carryover basis. Unfortunately, application of this principle was extremely troublesome since the basis of the liquidated subsidiary's assets ultimately depended on ascertaining the intent of the acquiring corporation—a subjective determination that all too often led to litigation. To make matters worse, the IRS found that corporate taxpayers could use the *Kimbell-Diamond* exception to their advantage. For example, consider a target corporation that has assets with a low basis but a high value. In this situation, the acquiring corporation would attempt to avoid the carryover basis rules and obtain a cost basis in the subsidiary's assets by relying on the *Kimbell-Diamond* decision. Of course, in this case, the IRS found itself on the other side of the fence, arguing that the *Kimbell-Diamond* rule did not apply.

Example 22

S Corporation had a single asset worth $800,000 and a basis of $500,000. During the year, P Corporation purchased all of the stock of S for $800,000 and promptly liquidated it. Under the normal parent-subsidiary liquidation rules, P's basis would be $500,000. However, if P could successfully argue that the *Kimbell-Diamond* approach applied, its basis would be a cost basis of $800,000, that is, the price that P paid for S's stock.

The effect of the *Kimbell-Diamond* decision was to create a great deal of controversy. In some cases, a parent corporation would argue that the *Kimbell-Diamond* exception applied, and, therefore, its basis in the liquidated subsidiary's assets would be essentially the fair market value (i.e., the purchase price of the subsidiary's stock). In other cases, a parent would argue that the normal carryover basis rules applied. As a practical matter, a parent was often unsure what its basis ultimately would be.

Beginning in 1954, Congress tried several times to eliminate the problems with corrective legislation. However, a truly palatable solution was not found until the enactment of Code § 338 in 1982. Section 338 provides a rather unique solution in that it allows the parent corporation to select the basis that it would prefer (i.e., a carryover basis or a basis equal to the asset's fair market value). As explained below, however, this choice does not come without a price.

SECTION 338: STOCK PURCHASES TREATED AS ASSET PURCHASES

LO.5

Explain the special election available to an acquiring corporation allowing it to treat the purchase of a target corporation's stock as a purchase of its assets.

Under § 338, if the parent corporation purchases the stock of a subsidiary, it may *elect* to treat the *stock* purchase as a purchase of assets. This election essentially enables the parent to obtain the same basis that it would have obtained had it purchased the assets directly (i.e., a basis equal to fair market value rather than a carryover basis). If the election is made, the Code creates an interesting fiction to reach this result: the subsidiary is treated as having sold all of its assets to itself for the assets' fair market value. As a result, gain or loss is generally recognized and the subsidiary's basis for its assets is equal to the price paid by the parent corporation for the subsidiary's stock. In short, § 338 enables the corporation to choose between a carryover or purchase basis for the subsidiary's assets.

Although § 338 treats the stock acquisition as if it were an acquisition of the assets, there is no requirement in the statute that the subsidiary be acquired with the intent to obtain its assets. If the formal requirements of § 338 are met, the rules apply. Therefore, the acquisition of stock need not be for any particular purpose. In addition, there is no requirement that the subsidiary *actually* be liquidated.

Qualified Stock Purchase

To qualify under § 338, the parent corporation must make a *qualified stock purchase:* a *purchase* of stock of the target corporation possessing at least 80% of the voting power and representing at least 80% of the value of all the stock (except nonvoting, nonparticipating, preferred stock).[24] To qualify as a *purchase*, the stock may not be acquired from a related party, in a transaction that qualifies under Code § 351 (relating to nontaxable corporate formations), or in any transaction that results in the purchaser using a carryover basis (e.g., gift or tax-free reorganizations).[25] As suggested above, the acquisition of control may occur in a series of transactions; however, the parent must obtain at least 80% control within any 12-month period.[26]

Example 23

S Corporation has 100 shares of stock outstanding. P Corporation purchases stock from unrelated parties as follows:

January 2, 2016	5 shares
May 5, 2016	50 shares
November 6, 2016	20 shares
February 12, 2017	15 shares

P Corporation acquires control of S on February 12, 2017, the first date that P owns at least 80% of S. Although the purchases extended more than 12 months, since 80% of the stock was obtained in a 12-month period (May 5, 2016 through February 12, 2017), the acquisitions constitute a qualified stock purchase. The fact that P purchased five shares of S stock on January 2, 2016 is immaterial.

If the parent corporation meets the purchase requirement, it must elect to treat the acquisition as an asset purchase by the fifteenth day of the ninth month following the month of acquisition.[27] After the election, the subsidiary generally increases or decreases the basis of its assets to the price paid for the stock. The election, once made, is irrevocable. Failure to make the election results in the parent being treated as purchasing stock and thus prohibits the subsidiary from adjusting the basis of its assets.

Technical Effect of § 338

As mentioned above, § 338 does not require a liquidation. As a result, both the parent and the subsidiary may continue to exist. To accomplish its objective, § 338 effectively treats the target subsidiary as two distinctly different corporations: *old target* and *new target*. Under § 338, old target is treated as having sold all of its assets to new target for their fair market value as of the close of the acquisition date. The results of this fantasy are twofold. First, the subsidiary (i.e., old target) must recognize gain and loss on the hypothetical sale—a fully taxable transaction. Any gain or loss recognized on the hypothetical sale is reported on the *final* return of the old target for the period ending on the acquisition date. Second, the basis of the assets to the subsidiary (i.e., new target) is their cost, generally the price paid by the acquiring corporation for the subsidiary's stock as adjusted for certain items discussed below.

Example 24

P Corp. purchased 100% of the outstanding stock of S Corp. for $1 million. S had only one asset, land with a basis of $600,000 and a fair market value of $1 million. Assuming a § 338 election is made, S must recognize a $400,000 gain on the deemed sale of the land. Its basis in the land then becomes $1 million.

---

[24] § 338(d)(3).

[25] § 338(h)(3). Stock acquired from a related corporation (including that where the basis of the stock carries over) may be treated as *purchased* if at least 50% of the stock of the related corporation was purchased. § 338(h)(3)(C).

[26] §§ 338(d) and (h).

[27] § 338(g).

For purposes of determining the subsidiary's new basis in its assets, the deemed purchase price is generally equal to the price that the parent corporation paid for the subsidiary's stock. This price must be adjusted for ownership of less than 100% (i.e., the portion not owned by the parent) as well as liabilities of the subsidiary and other relevant items.[28] Note that in increasing the purchase price of the stock for liabilities of the subsidiary, such liabilities include the tax liability attributable to income arising from the deemed sale.

Example 25

During the year, P Corporation purchased all of the stock of S Corporation for $1 million. S's only asset is land with a basis of $200,000. It has no liabilities. Assuming P makes the appropriate election under § 338, S is deemed to have sold its assets, in this case the land, for its fair market value, $1 million. Thus, S must recognize a gain of $800,000 ($1,000,000 − $200,000). The tax liability arising from the deemed sale is $272,000 ($800,000 × 34%). After the hypothetical sale and repurchase, P's basis in the land is $1,272,000, its purchase price of the stock, $1 million, increased by the liability arising on the deemed sale of $272,000. Note that P, as the new owner of S, bears the economic burden of the tax liability. Consequently, assuming the value of the land is truly $1 million, P would no doubt desire to reduce the purchase price of the stock by the liability that arises with a § 338 election; that is, it probably would try to buy the stock for $728,000 ($1,000,000 − $272,000). If P did buy the stock for $728,000, the gain on the deemed sale would still be $800,000 since the land is considered sold for its value of $1 million. In such case, the tax liability would still be $272,000 and the basis of the land under § 338 would be $1 million ($728,000 purchase price of the stock + $272,000 tax liability). Note that the effect of these rules is to reduce the value of the target subsidiary by an amount equal to the tax liability that would arise if § 338 were elected.

If the parent corporation owns less than 100% of the subsidiary, the deemed price must be "grossed up" to take into account the minority interest. The adjustment for a minority interest results in a deemed purchase price called the *grossed-up basis*. This grossed-up basis is obtained by multiplying the actual purchase price of the stock by a ratio, the numerator being 100% and the denominator equal to the percentage of the subsidiary stock owned by the parent.[29] This computation can be expressed as follows:

$$\text{Grossed-up basis} = \frac{\text{Parent corporation's basis in the}}{\text{subsidiary's stock on the acquisition date}} \times \frac{100\%}{\substack{\text{Percentage of subsidiary's stock held} \\ \text{by parent on the acquisition date}}}$$

Example 26

P Corporation purchased 90% of the outstanding stock of S Corporation for $900,000. S Corporation had only one asset, land with a basis of $200,000. Assume that there are no liabilities or other relevant items that affect the deemed purchase price. Since P owns less than 100% of S, a grossed-up basis must be calculated. The result is $1 million ($900,000 purchase price × [100 ÷ 90, the percentage of S owned by P]). If P elects § 338, S's basis for the land is $1 million. Note that the grossed-up purchase price will be increased by the liabilities of S Corporation.

---

[28] § 338(a). Section 338(b) provides that the basis is the sum of the grossed-up basis of stock purchased during the 12-month acquisition and the basis of stock not purchased during that period, adjusted as necessary.

[29] § 338(b)(4). Note that this approach must be modified when the parent holds stock not acquired during the 12-month period.

Allocation of Deemed Purchase Price

The temporary regulations under Code § 338 provide that the deemed purchase price of the stock is to be allocated to the subsidiary's assets using the *residual value* approach.[30] Under this technique, assets must be grouped into seven classes for purposes of making the allocation:

1. *Class I:*   Cash, demand deposits, and other cash equivalents;
2. *Class II:*   Certificates of deposit, U.S. government securities, readily marketable securities, and other similar items;
3. *Class III:* Accounts receivable;
4. *Class IV:*   Inventory;
5. *Class V:*   All assets other than those in Classes I, II, III, IV, VI, or VII;
6. *Class VI:*   Section 197 intangibles other than goodwill or going concern value; and
7. *Class VII:* Intangible assets in the nature of goodwill and going concern value.

According to the system, the purchase price is first allocated to Class I assets in proportion to their relative fair market values as determined on the date following the acquisition. Because Class I assets are either cash or cash equivalents, the basis assigned to them is their face value. Once this allocation is made, any excess of the purchase price over the amount allocated to Class I assets is allocated to Class II assets, again based on relative fair market values. Any excess purchase price remaining after making the allocation to Class II assets is allocated to Class III assets based on relative fair market values. Any excess of purchase price over amounts allocated to Classes I, II, and III is allocated to Class IV assets based on relative fair market values. In allocating such excess to Class II through Class IV assets, the amount allocated *cannot exceed the fair market value* of the asset. Thus, any purchase price that remains after the allocation to the Class I, II, III, and IV assets is assigned to Class V assets—hence, the reason for calling this method the *residual* value approach. By limiting the allocation to Class I, II, III, and IV assets to the assets' fair market values, the rules generally seek to ensure that corporate taxpayers allocate the proper amount to goodwill.

For purpose of these allocation rules, the temporary regulations provide that the fair market value of the asset is its gross value computed without regard to any mortgages, liens, or other liabilities related to the property. These rules are illustrated below.

Example 27

P Corporation purchases from an unrelated person 100% of the stock of S Corporation on June 1, 2016. Assume the purchase price adjusted for all relevant items is $100,000. S's assets at acquisition date are:

	Basis	Fair Market Value
Cash	$10,000	$10,000
Accounts receivable	20,000	20,000
Inventory	25,000	55,000
Total	$55,000	$85,000

The purchase price is first allocated to cash in the amount of $10,000. This leaves $90,000 to be allocated. Since there are no Class II assets, the allocation is to Class III next. Thus $20,000 is allocated to the accounts receivable. If the residual approach were not required, the taxpayer might allocate all of the remaining $70,000 to the inventory despite the fact that its value is only $55,000. If this were allowed, a subsequent sale of the inventory would result in a loss. However, since the remaining purchase price ($70,000) exceeds the fair market value of the Class IV assets, the basis of the assets in this class is their fair market value, $55,000 for the inventory. This leaves $15,000 of the purchase price that has not been allocated. It is all assigned to goodwill since there are no Class V or VI assets.

---

[30] Reg. § 1.338-6.

Other Consequences of § 338 Election

Section 338 not only entitles the subsidiary to a stepped-up basis for its assets, it also treats the subsidiary as a new corporation in every respect. As a result, the subsidiary may adopt any tax year it chooses, unless it files a consolidated return with the parent corporation, in which case it must adopt the parent's tax year. It may adopt new accounting methods if it desires. MACRS depreciation may be used for all of the hypothetically purchased property—the antichurning rules being inapplicable since the old and new subsidiary are considered unrelated. The new subsidiary acquires none of the other attributes of the old subsidiary. The earnings and profits of the old subsidiary are eliminated and any net operating loss carryovers of the old subsidiary are unavailable to the new subsidiary.

Consistency Provisions

In most situations, the target subsidiary has some assets that have appreciated in value (i.e., fair market value exceeds the asset's basis) and other assets whose value is less than the basis. In such case, the acquiring corporation, desiring the highest basis possible for the assets, might first purchase the appreciated property, then purchase the subsidiary's stock, and then liquidate the subsidiary under § 332. By so doing, the acquiring corporation would obtain the best of both worlds: a basis for the appreciated property equal to its fair market value and a carryover basis for the other assets. In the latter case, the basis is higher than it would have been had the assets themselves been purchased or had the stock been purchased followed by an election under § 338. To prohibit the acquiring corporation from effectively selecting the basis that is most desirable for each separate asset, the Code contains the so-called *consistency* provisions. Under the regulations implementing the consistency rules, a violation of the consistency provision due to the purchase of an asset from the target will not result in a deemed or required § 338 election. Instead, the acquiring corporation will be forced to use a carryover basis for the asset instead of a cost basis.[31] There are also consistency rules for the acquisition of two or more subsidiaries from one affiliated group. These rules apply only to the extent necessary to prevent avoidance of the asset consistency rules.

Section 338(h)(10) Election

In most situations, corporations are reluctant to make the § 338 election because the tax cost of the election exceeds the tax benefit. To be more precise, the tax on the gain from the deemed sale of the target's assets normally exceeds the present value of the future tax savings attributable to the increase in the basis of the target's assets resulting from the § 338 election. However, § 338 contains another provision that can be very beneficial—the § 338(h)(10) election.

The rationale for the creation of the "(h)(10)" election is best understood from an example. Consider a parent corporation that owns 100% of the stock of a subsidiary that it would like to sell. If the parent sells all of the stock of the subsidiary (the target), the parent would pay a tax on the sale and the acquiring corporation could obtain a cost basis in its assets by making the § 338 election that would result in a second tax. However, by restructuring the transaction, the same result could be obtained by paying only *a single tax*. To illustrate, if the target sold its assets to the acquiring corporation then distributed the sales proceeds to its parent in a nontaxable § 332 liquidation, the acquiring corporation would obtain a cost basis in the target's assets and the parent would end up with the sales proceeds with only a single tax (i.e., the tax on the sale by the target). A single tax could also result if the target distributed its assets to its parent in a nontaxable § 332 liquidation and the parent sold the target's assets to the acquiring corporation. The authors of § 338 recognized that corporations could easily avoid double taxation in this situation so they created a special rule—the § 338(h)(10) election—that produces the desired result with a sale of the target's stock rather than a sale of the target's assets.

---

[31] Reg. § 1.338-4(a)(1).

Liquidation of a Subsidiary   **5-21**

     If a parent corporation sells at least 80% of the target corporation's stock and an election is made under § 338(h)(10), the parent does not recognize any gain or loss on the sale of the stock. Instead, the target recognizes gain or loss as if it sold its assets and the basis of its assets to the acquiring corporation is generally the purchase price of the stock. Specifically, if the (h)(10) election is made, a regular § 338 election is deemed made for the target and the old target is treated as selling all of its assets to the new target for their fair market value. Old target recognizes all gain and loss realized on the deemed sale. However, the parent reports the gain or loss from the target's deemed sale of its assets on its return. If the parent and the target file consolidated returns, the gain or loss is included on the consolidated return and therefore may be offset by any net operating losses of the group. In addition, the selling parent inherits the targets attributes, including any net operating losses which the parent could use in the consolidated return of the selling group. The acquiring corporation's aggregate basis of the assets is generally equal to the price it paid for the target's stock adjusted for liabilities. The aggregate basis is allocated among the target's assets as explained above. The selling group and the buying group have joint and several liability for the tax on the deemed sale. For this reason, both the selling and the acquiring corporations must make the election. Observe that the buying group may not want to make the election if it has concerns about the parent's payment of the tax.

Example 28

Parent Corporation owns all of the stock of Target Corporation (value $1,000,000, basis $400,000). Target's assets have a value of $1,000,000 and a basis of $400,000. This year Acquiring Corporation purchased all of Target's stock from Parent. If Acquiring Corporation simply made a § 338 election, Target would recognize a $600,000 gain on the deemed sale of the assets and Parent would recognize another $600,000 gain on the sale of the stock. As a result, Acquiring would obtain a cost basis of $1,000,000 and two taxes would be paid.

Example 29

Assume the same facts as in *Example 28* above. If Acquiring and Parent agree to make the § 338(h)(10) election, the Target still reports a $600,000 gain on the deemed sale of its assets and pays the appropriate tax. If Parent and Target file a consolidated return, this gain is reported on the consolidated return of Parent and Target and any other members of the consolidated group. However, Parent's gain of $600,000 on the sale of stock is not recognized. Thus, Acquiring is able to get a basis for the assets of Target of $1,000,000 at the cost of a single tax. Observe that if the Parent-Target consolidated group have any net operating losses, such losses can be used to absorb the gain on the deemed sale of Target's assets and the transaction can take place with little tax cost. Also note that the Acquiring Corporation may be unwilling to make the election because it is liable (along with the Parent group) for the tax on the deemed sale of assets by Target.

     Observe that the gain reported by the parent corporation with the (h)(10) election is not necessarily the same as it would be without the election. This occurs when the parent's basis of the target's stock differs from the target's basis in its assets.

> **Example 30**
>
> Parent Corporation owns all of the stock of Target Corporation. Target has assets valued at $10 million (basis $2 million). Parent's basis in its Target stock is $3 million. If Parent sells all of the Target stock to Acquiring Corporation for $10 million, Parent recognizes gain of $7 million from the stock sale. If Parent and Acquiring make an (h)(10) election, Target recognizes a gain of $8 million from the deemed asset sale, but no gain from the stock sale will be reported. Parent recognizes an additional gain of $1 million if the (h)(10) election is made or $1,000,000 more than what would be reported from the actual stock sale. This occurs because Parent's basis in its Target stock of $3 million was higher than the inside basis of Target's assets.

SECTION 336(e): STOCK DISPOSITION TREATED AS ASSET DISPOSITION

As previously discussed, only a corporate acquisition of control of another corporation permits a § 338 election. To qualify to make a § 338(h)(10) election, a parent corporation must sell the stock of a subsidiary to another corporation. However, if the stock is sold to anyone other than a corporation, § 338 will not apply. As a result, if a corporation sells the stock of a subsidiary to a private equity fund or to the public in an IPO, the parent corporation will recognize gain or loss on the sale of the stock and the acquired corporation will have carryover basis on its assets.

To permit additional dispositions of a subsidiary with a step-up basis, Congress enacted § 336(e). This section applies to a parent corporation's disposition of its subsidiary's stock. The stock can be acquired by individuals, partnerships as well as corporations. Upon enactment, Congress required Treasury to issue regulations to detail the requirements and taxation of these transactions. Recently, the required regulations were issued. In general, the regulations permit a parent corporation that disposes of a subsidiary to make a § 336(e) election that treats the stock dispositions in a manner similar to a stock sale under § 338(h)(10).

To make the election, the stock must be stock of a domestic subsidiary owned by a domestic corporation. The parent corporation must dispose of control (at least 80% of the voting power and at least 80% of the fair market value) within a 12 month period. The disposition may be a sale, exchange or distribution of the stock. The disposition may not qualify as a tax free § 351 transaction, a tax-free reorganization or a tax free corporate division. The § 336(e) election can be made if the disposing corporation and the acquirers enter into a binding agreement to make the election by the due date of the tax return of the disposing corporation that includes the disposition.

If the disposing corporation makes a § 336(e) election, it does not report gain or loss on the stock disposition. Instead, the subsidiary is treated as selling its assets for the price paid for the stock if sold, or fair market value, if the stock is distributed to the shareholders of the parent corporation. If the stock is sold, the subsidiary recognizes gain or loss for the deemed asset sales. If the stock is distributed, the subsidiary will recognize gain but not loss from the deemed asset sales. If the parent's basis in the subsidiary's stock is equal to the subsidiary's basis in its assets, the gain on the deemed asset sale will equal the realized gain on the stock disposition. If the stock basis is greater than the asset basis, a larger gain will be reported; and if the stock basis is less than the asset basis, then a smaller gain will be reported.

The parent corporation will want to make the election if the gain it is required to report from the deemed asset sales is equal to or less than the realized gain on the stock sale. It will not want to make the election if it will report a larger gain. Taxpayer that acquires the stock will want a § 336(e) election to be made if the value of the assets exceeds its basis. It will not want an election made if the value is less than basis. If the acquirer wants a § 336(e) election but the seller does not, it is possible that the price paid for the stock can be adjusted to make a § 336(e) election beneficial to both parties.

BUYING AND SELLING BUSINESSES

Although the term *liquidation* usually carries negative connotations, such is not always the case. Liquidations often arise in conjunction with a sale of a business. For this reason, knowledge of the tax rules governing liquidation is imperative whenever a business is being sold or purchased.

There are numerous methods that can be used for buying and selling the business of a corporation. Interestingly, the liquidation provisions play an important role in determining how the transaction is structured. Assuming the disposition of the business is to be taxable, the transfer normally takes one of two forms: a sale of assets, or a sale of stock. In most transactions, the parties must first determine whether the buyer will purchase stock or assets. Once this initial decision is made, most stock and assets sales follow a similar pattern.

When the buyer and seller agree upon a sale of assets, the transfer can be consummated in one of two ways. The target corporation may sell the assets desired by the buyer and distribute the sale proceeds and any unwanted assets to the shareholders in complete liquidation. Alternatively, the shareholders could sell the assets of the target. This could be accomplished by causing the target to distribute the assets to the shareholders in complete liquidation, followed by a sale of the assets by the shareholders.

A stock acquisition is far more straightforward. The selling shareholder simply sells the stock to the buyer. The buyer may decide to operate the corporation or, alternatively, liquidate the business.

Nontax Considerations

Several nontax factors may dictate the form of the transaction (i.e., a sale of stock or assets). For example, stock sales are far easier to carry out than asset sales. When assets are sold, titles must be changed—perhaps for hundreds of assets—and creditors must be notified in conformance with the applicable bulk sales laws. Stock sales are much simpler in this regard since the seller merely sells the stock to the buyer.

Another important factor that may control the form of the sale, if present, is the existence of some nonassignable right such as a license, lease, trademark, or other favorable contractual arrangement. If such contracts cannot be assigned, only a sale of stock can preserve such rights.

Perhaps the most important factor to consider is the possibility of unknown or contingent liabilities. In a risky business, the seller wants to absolve himself from all liability—both known and unknown. Consequently, a sale of stock is desirable since the purchaser obtains not only all of the assets but all of the liabilities. Of course, the purchaser in this case wants to limit any exposure and may be unwilling to accept responsibility for the unknown (e.g., product liability or adjustments in prior taxes). When a stock sale is otherwise desirable, this problem may be alleviated by having the seller indemnify the buyer for any undisclosed liabilities.

Still other considerations may determine the form of the transaction. A sale of assets may be desirable where minority shareholders may be unwilling to sell their stock and the buyer does not want to share the business with outsiders. Similarly, the corporation may have undesirable assets that the buyer does not want to pay for. In such case, an asset sale would be favored.

Tax Considerations

Tax factors must also be considered when buying or selling a business. In this regard, a thorough understanding of the rules governing liquidations is indispensable.

From the seller's perspective, a sale of stock is often desirable. This derives from the fact that the sale of stock results in only a *single tax* at what historically have been favorable capital gains rates. On the other hand, a sale of assets normally results in two taxes: one at the corporate level on the sale or distribution of the business's assets, and one at the shareholder level upon liquidation. Obviously, the seller normally would prefer to sell stock to avoid the additional tax. Unfortunately, buyers may be willing to purchase the stock only at a substantial discount in light of the unfavorable consequences of *buying* stock.

On the buyer's side, the most important consideration is the basis in the assets acquired. In a purchase of stock, the basis of the acquired assets remains unchanged and does not reflect the purchase price of the stock. The buyer can obtain a basis equal to the asset's value only if the corporation is liquidated, or in the case of a corporate purchaser, an election is made pursuant to § 338. In such case, the buyer would bear the burden of the second tax. On the other hand, if the buyer purchases assets, the basis of such assets is their cost and the burden of the corporate-level tax is shifted to the seller. For this reason, the buyer is unwilling to purchase the stock at a price equal to the value of the corporation's assets.

Example 31

Target Corporation is 100% owned by Seller who has a basis in his stock of $10,000. Target's sole asset is a steel mill worth $100,000 (basis $30,000). If Buyer purchases the stock of Target for $100,000, the results are twofold. Seller would pay a single tax on a gain of $90,000 ($100,000 − $10,000) while Buyer would own a corporation that holds a steel mill with a basis in the mill of $30,000. In effect, Buyer's basis in the assets acquired is far less than cost. Buyer could obtain a step-up in basis, however, but only at the cost of a second tax. If Buyer is a corporation, the § 338 election could be made, resulting in a deemed sale of the mill and a tax on a gain of $70,000 ($100,000 − $30,000). If Buyer is a noncorporate purchaser, a liquidation under the general rules would have the same result: the corporation would recognize a gain of $70,000 on the distribution of the property in liquidation. (Note that in such case, Buyer would have no gain on the liquidation since the basis in the stock, $100,000, is equivalent to the value of the assets received.) In each case, Buyer would incur a tax in order to obtain a cost basis in the assets. For this reason, a tax-wise Buyer would only be willing to purchase the stock at a price reflecting the tax inherent in the appreciated assets. From Seller's view, the value of his business is diminished by the corporate level tax which must be paid either directly in a sale of assets or indirectly in the form of a reduced sales price for the stock.

It should be emphasized that the above discussion deals with the typical situation where the assets have a value exceeding their basis. Other facts may suggest a different approach to disposing of the business.

Example 32

Just last year, P Corporation purchased all of the stock of S Corporation for $1 million. S has a basis in its assets of $1.5 million. This year, Buyer Corporation has indicated that it would like to purchase the business of S for $1.2 million. In this case, P should liquidate S Corporation under § 332 and then sell the assets received from S. In so doing, it would recognize a loss of $300,000 ($1.2 million sales proceeds − $1.5 million carryover basis in S Corporation's assets), whereas a sale of stock would have produced a gain of $200,000 ($1.2 million − $1 million basis in S Corporation stock). Of course, the Buyer would prefer to buy stock in this instance so that it could enjoy a $1.5 million basis which exceeds its $1.2 million cost.

Section 338: Election

When a corporate purchaser acquires another corporation, perhaps the most important tax consideration to be addressed is whether the § 338 election should be made. The § 338 election normally results in a step-up in the target corporation's assets equal to the assets' fair market value, with any additional basis assigned to goodwill. *(See Example 27.)* This step-up, however, can only be obtained at a tax cost arising on the deemed sale that results when the § 338 election is made. Therefore, the propriety of making the § 338 election can only be determined by evaluating whether the tax benefits to be obtained from the step-up in basis are worth the immediate tax cost.

Normally, the tax benefits to be secured from the step-up in basis enabled by a § 338 election (e.g., increased depreciation) are deferred. In some instances, such as where part of the basis is assigned to land, no benefit is obtained from the basis step-up until the acquired business is sold. In addition, basis assigned to Class VI and Class VII assets will be recovered over 15 years provided the assets meet the definition of § 197 amortizable intangibles. Consequently, a proper assessment of whether a § 338 election is worthwhile would involve discounting the future tax savings to determine their present value and comparing such benefits to their cost.

SHAREHOLDER CONSIDERATIONS

When the general liquidation provisions of § 331 apply, consideration should be given to the possibility of spreading the gain to be recognized by the shareholder over more than one year. By arranging for a series of liquidating distributions that spans several years, the gain is recognized in smaller increments thus reducing the marginal tax rate which otherwise would apply if the shareholder received the distribution in lump sum or all in one year.

Taxes might also be saved by making gifts of the stock prior to the liquidation to family members who are in low tax brackets. Gifts in trusts where the donor retains a reversionary interest in the trust, must be avoided, however, since a sale of the stock or property is normally attributed to the donor.

LIQUIDATING A SUBSIDIARY

Any time a corporation purchases control of another corporation, consideration should be given to a § 338 election. The analysis should compare the future tax benefit of the basis step-up (e.g., increased depreciation and cost of goods sold) with the current tax liability resulting from the deemed sale.

Occasionally, a subsidiary is formed to enter a new business or to expand to a new geographical location. These new businesses often are unprofitable to the extent of bordering on insolvency. In these cases (especially if the subsidiary is insolvent), the parent should compare the tax treatment afforded by § 165(g) concerning worthless securities to that resulting from liquidating the subsidiary. Section 165(g) provides for an ordinary loss on the worthlessness of a subsidiary's stock. This treatment is more favorable than the nonrecognition, carryover basis rules of subsidiary liquidations contained in § 332. To receive the favored treatment, the stock must be worthless. Therefore, all the assets must be transferred to creditors. If any asset is distributed to the parent in exchange for the stock, the security is obviously not worthless and a liquidation is deemed to occur. Therefore, it may be more beneficial to allow the creditors to take all of the subsidiary's assets rather than receiving a nominal amount that will preclude a loss deduction.

Problem Materials

DISCUSSION QUESTIONS

5-1 *Complete Liquidations in General.* ABC Inc., a furniture store, is owned and operated by two brothers, F and G. While at dinner one evening they decided that they should no longer continue the business. As a result, they advertised a going-out-of-business sale to begin on June 1. Prior to that date the corporation began distributing cash and other assets of the business. As the assets of the business were sold, other distributions were made and creditors were paid off. At the close of the year, all of the assets had been distributed and the corporation was a mere shell. No stock was ever actually surrendered and cancelled. Will the distributions be treated as being made in complete liquidation? Explain and include the reasons why the determination is important.

5-2 *Section 331: Effect on Shareholder.* K Corporation was no longer profitable. As a result, J, an individual and the sole shareholder of the corporation, decided to completely liquidate under the general liquidation provisions of § 331. The corporation distributed assets worth $100,000 to J in exchange for his stock, which he had acquired several years earlier for $20,000. How will J treat the liquidating distribution?

5-3 *Section 334(a): Shareholder Basis.* JCT Corp., a publishing firm, was owned by M. The corporation had published only one successful book in its 10-year history and consequently M decided to terminate its existence. JCT distributed cash of $15,000, equipment worth $40,000 (basis $8,000), and land worth $60,000 (basis $12,000) to M for all of her stock which had a basis of $3,000. What is the basis of the assets to M assuming the general rules applying to liquidations are followed?

5-4 *Section 336: Treatment of the Distributing Corporation.* P Corp. adopted a plan of complete liquidation on June 1 of this year and subsequently distributed its only two assets, a patent worth $20,000 (basis $25,000) and land worth $50,000 (basis $10,000). What are the tax consequences to the corporation assuming the general rules applying to liquidations are followed?

5-5 *General Rules: §§ 331, 334(a), 336.* The balance sheet for M Corporation immediately prior to its liquidation appears below:

Cash	$10,000	Accounts payable	$ 6,000
Machinery	30,000	Earnings and profits	54,000
Land	25,000	Common stock	5,000
Total	$65,000	Total	$65,000

The fair market values of all the assets were equivalent to their bases except for the land, which was worth $40,000. M Corporation distributed all of its assets to its sole shareholder, Q, for all of her stock which she had acquired two years earlier for $30,000. Assuming the general rules applying to liquidations are followed, answer the questions below:

   a. What amount of gain or loss must M Corporation recognize, and what amount of tax, if any, will it be required to pay?

   b. What amount of gain or loss must Q recognize?

   c. What is the basis of the assets received by Q?

5-6 *Liquidation of a Subsidiary: §§ 332 and 334(b)(1).* E Corp., a manufacturer of components for computers, has decided that a logical expansion of its operations would be in the robotics industry. T Inc. is presently building robots to be used in the automotive industry but is not profitable. E believes that with their expertise they can make T a profitable firm in three years. T's principal asset is worth $100,000 but has a basis of $150,000. E desires to acquire T and liquidate it to take advantage of T's losses and the high basis in its asset. What steps must E take to achieve their objective?

5-7 *Kimbell-Diamond Exception.* Consider the facts in *Problem 5-6* above and answer the following questions:

   a. How might the *Kimbell-Diamond* exception frustrate the objective of E?

   b. Is the *Kimbell-Diamond* exception still applicable under the current statutory scheme?

5-8 *Section 338: Stock versus Asset Purchases.* L Inc. is contemplating expansion by acquiring M Corporation. The principal asset of M is a manufacturing plant that is worth $500,000 and has a basis of $200,000, net of depreciation of $100,000. Assuming that L desires to buy the stock of M for $500,000, answer the following:

   a. What steps can be taken, if any, by L to obtain a stepped-up basis for the plant?

   b. Can L obtain the step-up in basis in a nontaxable transaction?

5-9 *Consistency Provisions.* J Corporation has decided to expand by acquiring M Inc. M Inc. owns land worth $100,000 (basis $25,000) and equipment worth $200,000 (basis $500,000). In order to obtain the highest basis for M's assets, J's advisor has suggested that it should initially purchase the land for $100,000. Subsequent to the land acquisition, the corporation was advised to purchase all of the stock of M for $200,000 and liquidate the company under § 332 and utilize the carryover basis provisions of § 334(b)(1). Comment on the validity of the advisor's plan.

5-10 *Section 338(h)(10) Election.* Explain why a Parent Corporation planning to sell one of its subsidiaries at a substantial gain would prefer the "(h)(10)" election rather than simply having the acquiring corporation make the regular § 338 election.

PROBLEMS

5-11 *Liquidations—General Rules (§§ 331 and 336).* G an individual owns all the stock of T Corporation. G purchased the stock 15 years ago for $450,000. G decided to completely liquidate T Corporation. The balance sheet of T Corporation immediately prior to the liquidation is as follows:

		Basis	Fair Market Value
Cash		$ 30,000	$ 30,000
Marketable securities.		100,000	90,000
Equipment.	$400,000		
Less: Accumulated depreciation	(170,000)	230,000	280,000
Land		760,000	810,000
Total assets		$1,120,000	$1,210,000
Retained earnings		$ 670,000	$ 0
Common stock		450,000	1,210,000
Total equity		$1,120,000	$1,210,000

Assume that G is in the 35% tax bracket and that T corporation is in the 34% tax bracket before the liquidation. Also assume that earnings and profits prior to liquidation were equivalent to retained earnings.

  a. How much gain or loss, if any, will T corporation recognize as a result of the liquidation?

  b. What is G's recognized gain or loss?

  c. What is G's basis in the assets received?

5-12 *Liquidation—General Rules (§§ 331 and 336).* Assume the same facts as *Problem 5-11* except G purchased the stock 15 years ago for $1,400,000.

  a. How much gain or loss, if any, will T Corporation recognize as result of the liquidation?

  b. What is G's recognized gain or loss?

  c. What is G's basis in the assets received?

5-13 *Loss Considerations.* Assume the same facts as in *Problem 5-11* except that the marketable securities were contributed in anticipation of the liquidation. How much gain or loss will T Corporation recognize on the liquidation?

5-14 *Liquidations (§ 332).* Assume the same facts as in *Problem 5-11* except that the stock is owned by G, Inc. and the liquidation is pursuant to § 332.

  a. How much gain or loss, if any, must T Corporation recognize as a result of the liquidation?

  b. How much gain or loss, if any, must G, Inc. recognize?

  c. What is the basis of the assets received by G, Inc.?

  d. Assume T Corporation has a deficit in earnings and profits and an NOL carryover. Will these facts affect G, Inc.?

5-15 *Limitation on Losses (§ 336).* X Corporation is owned 90% by T and 10% by A, two unrelated individuals. In anticipation of liquidation, T contributes land with a basis of $200,000 and a fair market value of $140,000 to X.

  a. What is the effect on X Corporation if the land is distributed to T as part of the liquidation at a time when its value is $120,000?

  b. What is the effect on X Corporation if the land is distributed to A as part of the liquidation at a time when its value is $120,000?

  c. What is the effect on X Corporation if the land is sold for $120,000 and the proceeds are distributed to T and A as part of the liquidation of X?

5-16 *Liquidation—General Rules (§§ 331 and 336).* I, an individual, owns all of the stock of T Corporation. I formed the business seven years ago in a tax-free § 351 transaction by contributing $100,000 cash and assets with a basis of $300,000 and a fair market value of $700,000. I decided to completely liquidate T Corporation and all the assets of T are distributed to I. The balance sheet for T immediately prior to the liquidation is as follows:

		Basis	Fair Market Value
Cash		$ 10,000	$ 10,000
Accounts receivable		100,000	70,000
Equipment	$400,000		
Less: Accumulated depreciation	(250,000)	150,000	120,000
Total assets		$ 260,000	$ 200,000
Retained earnings (deficit)		$(140,000)	$ 0
Common stock		400,000	200,000
Total equity		$ 260,000	$ 200,000

    a. How much gain or loss, if any, will T Corporation recognize as a result of the liquidation?

    b. What is I's recognized gain or loss?

    c. What is I's basis in the assets received?

5-17 *Liquidation—General Rules (§§ 331 and 336).* Assume the same facts as in *Problem 5-16*, except that the basis of the assets other than money that I contributed was $90,000 instead of $300,000.

    a. What is I's recognized gain or loss?

    b. What is I's basis in the assets received?

    c. How much gain or loss, if any, will T Corporation recognize as a result of the liquidation?

5-18 *Section 331: Gain on Series of Distributions.* MAV Corporation decided to liquidate in 2016. In December 2016 the corporation distributed $30,000 to its sole shareholder, Y. The corporation also made liquidating distributions of $50,000 and $60,000 in 2017 and 2018, respectively. Y purchased all of her stock in 2011 for $35,000.

    a. Compute the amount of the gain or loss that must be recognized by Y on each of the distributions.

    b. Same as (a) except Y's basis in her stock is $200,000.

5-19 *Section 331: Gain on a Series of Distributions.* Assume the same facts as in *Problem 5-18*, except that Y purchased one-half the stock in 2008 for $20,000 and the remaining stock in 2011 for $90,000. Compute the gain or loss that must be recognized by Y on each distribution.

5-20 *Distribution of Installment Obligations.* As of June, 2016 X Corporation has the following assets when a plan of liquidation is adopted:

	Basis	Fair Market Value
Cash	$18,000	$ 18,000
Marketable securities	15,000	25,000
Undeveloped real estate	40,000	100,000

On July 5, 2016 X sells the land for $100,000 in exchange for the purchaser's installment note. X Corporation immediately distributed the securities and note to its sole shareholder, J. J's basis in X stock is $20,000. X Corporation retains the $18,000 cash to pay its final income tax liability.

a. What is J's recognized gain in 2016?

b. Assume that in 2017 J receives the first installment on the note of $25,000. How much gain must J recognize?

c. What is J's basis in the assets received?

d. Does X Corporation recognize any gain? If so, how much?

5-21 *Section 336: Gain or Loss on Distributions.* MOD Inc. operated a restaurant in downtown Phoenix. The business prospered for eight months, until several customers became stricken with food poisoning. Fearing the impact of this event on business, the company liquidated, distributing the items noted below to its sole shareholder. Indicate the effect on the distributing corporation for each of the following distributions, assuming the liquidation is a general liquidation under § 331.

a. Land adjacent to the restaurant used as a parking lot worth $100,000 (basis $40,000).

b. Land and building in which the restaurant was housed worth $200,000 (basis $90,000). Straight-line depreciation of $30,000 had been claimed and deducted.

c. Restaurant supplies such as paper napkins, towels, etc., for which the corporation had claimed a deduction of $5,000.

d. Oven equipment worth $10,000 (basis $15,000). Accelerated depreciation of $5,000 had been claimed. Straight-line depreciation would have been $3,000.

e. One hundred cases of XXX wine, the house wine worth $12,000 (basis $7,000). The wine was accounted for using the LIFO method. Basis using the FIFO method would have been $9,000.

f. A note receivable arising from the sale of land which occurred prior to the adoption of the plan of liquidation. The note had a face and fair market value of $100,000 (basis $35,000).

g. Same as (f) except the sale occurred after the plan of liquidation was adopted.

5-22 *Section 336: Liabilities.* L Corporation purchased land with a building for $1.5 million, paying $600,000 cash and an $900,000 note payable at the end of five years. To date the corporation has claimed depreciation of $700,000. As a result of a zoning change to adjacent land, the property has a fair market value of $825,000. L decides to liquidate and distribute the land and building to its sole shareholder V. How much gain or loss must L recognize?

5-23 *Section 336: Liabilities—Effect on Shareholders.* Assume the same facts as in *Problem 5-22.* Further, assume that V purchased the stock five years ago for $300,000. The land, building and note are the only items V received as a result of the liquidation. How much gain or loss must V recognize?

5-24 *Code § 336 Limitations on Losses.* Unrelated shareholders R, S, and T own 60, 30, and 10 percent of the stock of Dynamic Developer Inc., respectively. Pursuant to a plan of liquidation, Dynamic sold all of its assets except for the following:

Assets	Adjusted Basis	Fair Market Value
Cash	$300,000	$300,000
Land	10,000	80,000
Warehouse	220,000	120,000
	$530,000	$500,000

Indicate the amount of gain or loss that Dynamic must recognize in the following situations.

a. The corporation distributed the warehouse and $180,000 of cash to R, land and $70,000 of cash to S, and $50,000 of cash to T.

b. The corporation distributed the land and $220,000 of cash to R, the warehouse and $30,000 of cash to S, and $50,000 to T.

c. The corporation distributed the cash to the shareholders in their respective shares and distributed the land and warehouse, having each retitled such that each shareholder would own his or her respective shares.

d. Same as (c) except the warehouse had been contributed by R to the corporation four years ago in a nontaxable transaction at which time the property was worth $300,000 (basis $250,000).

e. Same as (b) except the warehouse had been contributed by R to the corporation one year ago in a nontaxable transaction at which time the property was worth $200,000 (basis $250,000).

5-25 *Section 338: Election.* T Corporation purchased 100% of X Corporation stock on January 15, 2016 for $600,000. At that time X Corporation has two assets: appreciated land and equipment. The land was worth $500,000 (basis $30,000) and was subject to a $150,000 mortgage. The equipment was worth $250,000 (basis $90,000 net of $50,000 of depreciation.) Assuming T makes an election under § 338 concerning the basis of the assets, indicate whether the following statements are true or false. If false, indicate why.

a. The basis allocated to the assets of X will exceed $600,000.

b. Assuming the basis allocated to the land and equipment is $777,000 ($600,000 cost + liability + tax) the basis of the land will be $518,000 and the equipment will be $259,000.

c. X Corporation recognizes gain of $50,000 as a result of the election.

d. Assuming T purchased only 80% of X's stock for $520,000, the basis of the assets would not differ from that which would result had T purchased 100% of X's stock.

e. X Corporation may use MACRS in depreciating the equipment even if it was not doing so prior to the acquisition.

f. X Corporation's E&P will not be affected by the election.

5-26 *Section 338: Basis Calculation.* On January 1, 2016 P Corporation purchases from an unrelated person all the outstanding stock of S Corporation for $90,000. S's balance sheet on the purchase date is as follows:

Assets	Basis	Fair Market Value
Cash	$ 5,000	$ 5,000
Accounts receivable.	20,000	20,000
Inventory (LIFO)	20,000	40,000
Equipment (accumulated depreciation of $10,000)	30,000	45,000
Total assets	$75,000	$110,000
Liabilities		
Accounts payable	$20,000	$ 20,000
Equity	55,000	90,000
Total liabilities and equity.	$75,000	$110,000

P properly elects § 338. S's tax rate is 34 percent.
   a. What is the aggregate basis of S's assets after this transaction?
   b. What is the basis for each individual asset?

5-27 *Liquidation (§ 332).* X Corporation purchased 90% of the stock of S Corporation 10 years ago for $900,000. The remaining 10% is owned by Q, an unrelated individual who purchased her S stock five years ago for $70,000. X has decided to liquidate S Corporation. X will receive assets with a fair market value of $1,425,000 and a basis to S Corporation of $850,000. S will distribute undeveloped land to Q with a fair market value of $140,000 and a basis of $126,000 as part of the liquidation.
   a. How much gain or loss must X recognize?
   b. What is the basis of the assets received by X?
   c. How much gain or loss must S recognize?
   d. How much gain or loss must Q recognize?
   e. What is the basis of the land received by Q?
   f. How would your answer to (a), (b), (c), (d), and (e) change if the basis of the land immediately prior to distribution was $171,000?

5-28 *Liquidation of Insolvent Subsidiary.* R Corporation formed V Corporation eight years ago. R Corporation contributed cash of $100,000 and assets with a fair market value of $900,000 and a basis of $600,000. R Corporation has loaned V Corporation $200,000 on open account. V Corporation has never made a profit. At the current time, V has liabilities of $1,400,000 and assets with a basis and fair market value of $725,000. R is considering liquidating V Corporation. How much gain or loss will R Corporation recognize if V Corporation is liquidated?

5-29 *Selling a Business: § 332 versus § 338.* On June 1 of this year Public Corporation acquired all of the stock of Private Corporation from Seller for $1.5 million. Seller's basis for his stock was $200,000. Private's balance sheet on June 1 revealed the following information:

Assets	Adjusted Basis	Fair Market Value
Cash	$ 50,000	$ 50,000
Accounts receivable.	475,000	475,000
Inventory.	400,000	525,000
Equipment (net of depreciation)	170,000	350,000
Land	105,000	400,000
	$1,200,000	$1,800,000

Liabilities and Equity		
Accounts payable	$ 300,000	$ 300,000
Retained earnings	700,000	
Common stock	200,000	1,500,000
	$1,200,000	$1,800,000

In addition to the information above, an inspection of Private's prior tax returns indicated that the equipment was originally purchased in 2012 at a cost of $300,000. Private also has accumulated earnings and profits of $1,100,000 and a capital loss carryover of $90,000. Private is in the 35% marginal tax bracket.

a. What are the tax consequences to Seller on the sale of the stock to Public?

b. What are the tax consequences to Public and Private if Public liquidates Private shortly after the purchase and the § 338 election is not made? Indicate the gains and losses realized and recognized for each corporation, the basis of Private's assets to Public and the treatment of Private's earnings and profits and capital loss carryover.

c. What are the tax consequences to Public and Private if Public liquidates Private shortly after the purchase and the § 338 election is properly made? Indicate the gain or loss realized and recognized for each corporation, the basis of Private's assets to Public and the treatment of Private's earnings and profits and capital loss carryover.

d. Should the § 338 election be made? Explain why or why not.

5-30 *Sale of Subsidiary's Business.* On May 1 of this year, P Corporation, a bank, acquired all of the stock of S Corporation, an insurance company, for $4 million. Shortly thereafter, state law was altered such that banks could no longer hold the stock of insurance companies. Consequently, P liquidated S under § 332 and sold all of S's assets for their fair market value of $4 million.

a. Compute P's gain or loss assuming S's basis for its assets is $3 million.

b. Compute P's gain or loss assuming S's basis for its assets is $5 million.

c. Compute P's gain or loss assuming it sold the stock of S.

d. Based on the results obtained above, what advice can you give P?

5-31 *Comprehensive Corporate Liquidation Problem.* Sun Corporation is owned 80% by Sky Corporation and 20% by A. Blue, a valued former employee. A recent balance sheet of Sun is as follows:

	Basis	Fair Market Value
Cash	$ 300,000	$ 300,000
Inventory	200,000	400,000
Equipment (net of $250,000 depreciation)	600,000	400,000
Land	300,000	950,000
Total assets	$1,400,000	$2,050,000
Accounts payable	$ 200,000	$ 200,000
Notes payable	400,000	400,000
Common stock	200,000	200,000
Retained earnings	600,000	1,250,000
Total liabilities and equity	$1,400,000	$2,050,000

Sky Corporation has a basis of $700,000 in its Sun stock and Blue has a basis of $125,000 in his Sun stock. Both Sky and Blue have held their Sun stock for several years.

Required:

a. Determine the tax consequences to each of the three parties if a pro-rata liquidation of Sun (i.e., each shareholder would receive its ratable share of Sun's assets and would assume its ratable share of Sun's liabilities).

b. Is there any alternate way of structuring the liquidation of Sun to achieve a more desirable tax result than that from a pro-rata liquidation?

c. Assume that Sky's basis in Sun is $1,400,000 instead of $700,000. Would a liquidation of Sun under § 332 continue to be a desirable alternative from a tax standpoint? Explain.

TAX RESEARCH PROBLEMS

5-32 S, an individual, manufactures and sells high-speed, high-quality portable printers to be used with personal computers. A major computer manufacturer agrees to buy all of S's output and to sell the printer with its computer, provided S will guarantee to double production by the end of the year. The only way S can fulfill the contract is to acquire additional machines to manufacture laser printers. After unsuccessfully trying to buy the machines, S buys all the outstanding stock of M Corporation which owns the machines that S needs. S paid $600,000 for the stock. The basis of the machines (M's only assets) is $200,000. S immediately liquidates M and uses the machines in her business. What is the basis of the machines to S?

Research aids:

> *Kimbell-Diamond Milling Co.*, 14 T.C. 74 (1950) *aff'd*, 51-1 USTC ¶9201, 40 AFTR 328, 187 F.2d. 715 (CA-5), 1955.
>
> *H.B. Snivley*, 19 T.C. 850, *aff'd*, 55-1 USTC ¶9221, 46 AFTR 1703, 219 F.2d. 266 (CA-5, 1955).
>
> *Chrome Plate, Inc.*, 78-1 USTC ¶9104, 40 AFTR2d 77-6122, *aff'd*, 80-1 USTC ¶9332, 45 AFTR2d 80-1241.

5-33 Data Corporation is interested in acquiring Sales Corporation. Since Data will pay a premium over book value for the stock, it will only make the purchase if it can make a valid § 338 election. Data has insufficient cash to buy all the stock whereas Sales has an excess of working capital. Therefore, Data plans the following:
1. Purchase 40% of Sales stock on the open market in September 2016.
2. At the next shareholders meeting, convince the remaining shareholders of Sales Corporation to sell 30% of their stock to Data and have the corporation redeem the remaining 30 percent. The purchases will occur between March and August 2017. The redemptions will occur in November and December 2017.

If the transactions occur as planned, will Data be able to make a § 338 election?

5-34 Average Corporation is wholly owned by J, an individual. Although Average has not been very profitable, its assets have appreciated in value. J wants to liquidate Average. However, he does not want to pay the tax on the appreciation at the corporate level. Therefore, he plans to contribute depreciated property to the corporation, which will sell it to an unrelated third party. J then plans to wait two years and one month and adopt a plan of liquidation. The corporation will distribute the appreciated property to J. J expects to use the capital loss carryover from the property he contributed to offset the gain on the distribution. Will J's plan succeed?

5-35 Consulting, Inc. is a professional service corporation owned by John Smith. The corporation uses the cash method of accounting. The corporation has just received notice that its largest client has filed under Chapter 11, voluntary bankruptcy. The client owes Consulting, Inc. $3 million for prior services. John Smith realizes that the Consulting, Inc. will be unable to pay its bills and, therefore, must liquidate. What is the tax effect on Consulting, Inc. and John Smith if it completely liquidates by transferring all of its assets, including the $3 million claim to John?

Penalty Taxes on Corporate Accumulations

Learning Objectives

Upon completion of this chapter you will be able to:

LO.1 Understand the rationale for the two corporate penalty taxes: the accumulated earnings tax and the personal holding company tax.

LO.2 Identify the circumstances that must exist before the accumulated earnings tax will apply.

LO.3 Recognize when earnings have accumulated beyond the reasonable needs of the business.

LO.4 Explain how the accumulated earnings tax is computed.

LO.5 Indicate when the personal holding company tax applies.

LO.6 Apply the stock ownership and income tests to determine if a corporation is a personal holding company.

LO.7 Explain how the personal holding company tax is computed and how it might be avoided.

Chapter Outline

Introduction

LO.1

Understand the rationale for the two corporate penalty taxes: the accumulated earnings tax and the personal holding company tax.

In addition to the regular tax, a corporation may be subject to two penalty taxes—the *accumulated earnings tax* and the *personal holding company tax*. As the label "penalty" suggests, the primary goal of these taxes is not to raise revenues but rather to prohibit certain activities. The objective of the accumulated earnings tax and the personal holding company tax is to discourage individual taxpayers from using the corporate entity solely for tax avoidance. These taxes contend with potential abuse by imposing limitations on the amount of earnings a corporation may retain without penalty. The rationale for these taxes is readily apparent when some of the opportunities for tax avoidance using the corporate structure are considered.

Perhaps the best illustration of how the corporate entity could be used to avoid taxes involves the 70% dividends-received deduction. As discussed in Chapter 1, this deduction is available only to corporate taxpayers. Nevertheless, individuals could take advantage of the deduction by establishing a corporation and transferring their dividend-paying stocks to it. By so doing, all dividend income would be taxable to the corporation instead of the individual. Using this arrangement, the corporation would pay tax on dividends at an effective rate of 10.5% or lower (35% × [100% − 70%]) in 2016. Most individual taxpayers with taxable dividend income would reap substantial tax savings from this arrangement since all individual marginal rates are 10% or higher. This is but one of the alluring features of the corporate entity.

Another corporate advantage that individuals previously used to avoid taxes concerned the difference between individual and corporate tax rates. Until the current year, because the highest individual tax rate exceeded the top corporate tax rate, individuals operating a business in the corporate form could benefit by leaving earnings in the corporation and reinvesting at this lower tax rate. The savings obtained by utilizing this disparity, the dividends-received deduction, and other advantages of the corporate entity, illustrate that individuals could achieve wholesale tax avoidance if not for some provision denying or discouraging such plans.

The two penalty taxes were developed to battle avoidance schemes such as those above by attacking their critical component: the accumulation. This can be seen by examining the two previous examples. The fate of both tax savings schemes rests on whether the shareholder can reduce or totally escape the second tax normally incurred when the income is ultimately received. In other words, the success of these arrangements depends on the extent to which double taxation is avoided. Herein lies the role of corporate accumulations. As long as the earnings are retained in the corporation, the second tax is avoided and the taxpayer is well on the way to obtaining tax savings. To foil such schemes, Congress enacted the accumulated earnings tax and the personal holding company tax. Both taxes are imposed on unwarranted accumulations of income—income that normally would have been taxable to the individual at individual tax rates if it had been distributed. By imposing these taxes on unreasonable accumulations, Congress hoped to compel distributions from the corporation and thus prevent taxpayers from using the corporate entity for tax avoidance.

Although these penalty taxes are rarely incurred, each serves as a strong deterrent against possible taxpayer abuse. However, with the reduction in the tax rate on dividends to 20 percent, imposition of these penalties or change in corporate behavior is even less likely. This chapter examines the operation of both the accumulated earnings tax and the personal holding company tax.

Mitigation of the double tax penalty and any resulting tax savings are not achieved solely through corporate accumulations. The effect of double taxation can be reduced or avoided in other ways. The most common method used to avoid double taxation is by making distributions that are deductible. Typical deductible payments include compensation for services rendered to the corporation, rent for property leased to the corporation by the shareholder, and interest on funds loaned to the corporation. All of these payments are normally deductible by the corporation (thus effectively eliminating the corporate tax) and taxable to the shareholder. Avoidance of the double tax penalty does not ensure tax savings, however. All of these payments are taxable to the shareholder; thus, savings through use of the corporate entity may or may not result. For example, savings could occur if the payments are made to shareholders after they have dropped to a tax bracket lower than the one in which they were when the earnings were initially realized by the corporation. In addition, even if the shareholder's tax bracket remains unchanged, deferral of the tax could be beneficial.

Example 1

L operates a home improvement company, specializing in kitchen renovations. He is in the 35% bracket in 2016. Assume that he incorporates his business in 2016 and it earns $100,000, of which $50,000 is paid to him as a salary and $50,000 is accumulated. In 2016 L saves $10,000 ([35% − 15%] × $50,000) in taxes on the $50,000 not distributed. However, if the $50,000 accumulated is distributed to L as a salary in 2021 when he is still in the 35% bracket, the $10,000 of taxes originally saved is lost. Although no taxes have been saved, L continues to benefit because he has been able to postpone the $10,000 in tax for five years. Assuming his after-tax rate of return is 10 percent, the present value of the $10,000 tax is reduced to $6,209—a savings of $3,791, or almost 38%. Note that the savings would have increased if the distribution had been made to L when his tax bracket dropped below 35%.

Accumulated Earnings Tax

The accumulated earnings tax, unlike most taxes previously discussed, is not computed by a corporation when filing its annual income tax return. There is no form to file to determine the tax. Normally, the issue arises during an audit of the corporation. Consequently, the actual tax computation is made only after it has been determined that the penalty must be imposed.

AN OVERVIEW

The accumulated earnings tax applies whenever a corporation is "formed or availed of" for what is generally referred to as the *forbidden purpose*, that is, "for the purpose of avoiding the income tax with respect to its shareholders … by permitting earnings and profits to accumulate instead of being … distributed."[1] Whether a corporation is in fact being used for the forbidden purpose and thus subject to penalty is an elusive question requiring a determination of the taxpayer's *intent*. Without guidance from the law, ascertaining the taxpayer's intent might prove impossible. However, the Code states that the required intent is deemed present whenever a corporation accumulates earnings beyond its reasonable needs unless the corporation can prove to the contrary by a preponderance of evidence.[2] The problems concerning intent are considered in detail below.

Not all corporations risk the accumulated earnings tax. The Code specifically exempts tax-exempt corporations, personal holding companies, and passive foreign investment companies.[3] In addition, the tax normally does not apply to an S corporation since it does not shield shareholders from tax. An S corporation's earnings are taxed to its shareholders annually.

If it applies, the accumulated earnings tax is imposed on the annual increment to the corporation's total accumulated earnings, not on the total accumulated earnings balance. This annual addition is referred to as *accumulated taxable income*. The tax is 20% of the corporation's accumulated taxable income.[4] This tax does not replace any other taxes (e.g., the corporate income tax or the alternative minimum tax) but is imposed in addition to these taxes.

LO.2
Identify the circumstances that must exist before the accumulated earnings tax will apply.

Example 2

In an audit of P Corporation, it was determined that the company had accumulated earnings beyond the reasonable needs of its business. In addition, the corporation's accumulated taxable income was $150,000. Since evidence of the forbidden purpose is present and the corporation has accumulated taxable income, the accumulated earnings tax must be paid. P Corporation's accumulated earnings tax is $30,000 ($150,000 × 20%).

[1] § 532(a).
[2] § 533(a).
[3] § 532.
[4] § 531.

In short, the corporation actually pays the accumulated earnings tax only if the forbidden purpose is found and it has accumulated taxable income. The following sections examine the determination of the taxpayer's intent and the computation of accumulated taxable income.

INTENT

The accumulated earnings tax is imposed only if the corporation is formed or used for the purpose of avoiding income tax on its shareholders by accumulating earnings.[5] Unfortunately, the Code provides no objective, mechanical test for determining whether a corporation is in fact being used for the forbidden purpose. As a result, application of the accumulated earnings tax rests on a subjective assessment of the shareholders' intent. The Code and regulations offer certain guidelines for making this assessment. Section 533 provides that a corporation is deemed to have been formed or used for the purpose of avoiding tax on its shareholders in two situations:

1. If the corporation has accumulated earnings beyond the reasonable needs of the business; or

2. If the corporation is a mere holding or investment company.

The first situation is the most common cause of an accumulated earnings tax penalty. Consequently, avoidance of the accumulated earnings tax normally rests on whether the corporation can prove that its balance (i.e., the amount in excess of the $250,000 or $150,000 threshold) in accumulated earnings and profits is required by the reasonable needs of the business. Before discussing what constitutes a "reasonable need" of the business, it should be noted that other circumstances may indicate that the forbidden purpose does or does not exist.

According to the Regulations, the following factors are to be considered in determining whether the corporation has been used to avoid tax:[6]

1. Loans to shareholders or expenditures that benefit shareholders personally;

2. Investments in assets having no reasonable connection with the corporation's business; and

3. Poor dividend history.

Although these factors are not conclusive evidence, their presence no doubt suggests improper accumulations.

In determining whether the requisite intent exists, the courts have considered not only the criteria mentioned above but also whether the corporation's stock is widely held. As a general rule, the accumulated earnings tax does not apply to publicly held corporations. Publicly held corporations normally are protected since the number and variety of their shareholders usually preclude the formation of a dividend policy to minimize shareholder taxes. Nevertheless, the tax has been applied to publicly held corporations in which management was dominated by a small group of shareholders who were able to control dividend policy for their benefit.[7] Moreover, in 1984, Congress eliminated any doubts as to whether publicly held corporations are automatically exempt from the penalty tax. Section 532(c) currently provides that the tax be applied without regard to the number of shareholders of the corporation. Thus, the tax may be imposed on a publicly held corporation if the situation warrants.

While publicly held corporations usually are immune from the penalty tax, closely held corporations are particularly vulnerable since dividend policy is easily manipulated to meet shareholders' desires. Indeed, it may be a formidable task to prove that the corporation was not used for tax avoidance in light of the *Donruss* decision.[8] In that case, the Supreme Court held that the tax avoidance motive need not be the primary or dominant motive for the accumulation of earnings before the penalty tax is imposed. Rather, if tax avoidance is but one of the motives, the tax may apply.

---

[5] § 532(a).

[6] Reg. § 1.533-1(a)(2).

[7] See *Trico Products*, 42-2 USTC ¶9540, 31 AFTR 394, 137 F.2d 424 (CA-2, 1943). In *Golconda Mining Corp.*, 58 T.C. 139 (1972), the Tax Court held that the tax applied where management controlled 17% of the outstanding stock of a publicly held corporation but the Ninth Circuit reversed, suggesting the tax should be applied solely to closely held

corporations, 74-2 USTC ¶9845. 35 AFTR2d 75-336, 507 F.2d 594 (CA-9, 1974). Tax applied to publicly held corporation in *Alphatype Corporation v. U.S.* 76-2 USTC ¶9730, 38 AFTR2d 76-6019 (Ct. Cls., 1976). In Rev. Rul. 73-305, *1975-2 C.B. 228* the IRS confirmed its position that it will apply the tax to publicly held corporations.

[8] *U.S. v. Donruss*, 69-1 USTC ¶9167, 23 AFTR2d 69-418, 393 U.S. 297 (USSC, 1969).

As a practical matter, it is difficult, if not impossible, to determine the actual intent of the corporation and its shareholders. For this reason, the presumption created by § 533(a) looms large in virtually all accumulated earnings tax cases. Under this provision, a tax avoidance purpose is deemed to exist if earnings were accumulated beyond the reasonable needs of the business.[9] As might be expected, most of the litigation in this area has concerned what constitutes a reasonable need of the business. In fact, many cases do not even mention intent, implying that the accumulated earnings tax will be applied in all cases in which the accumulation exceeds business needs. Except in the unusual case in which a corporation's intent can be demonstrated, a corporation should be prepared to justify the accumulations based on the needs of the business.

REASONABLE NEEDS OF THE BUSINESS

The Code does not define the term "reasonable needs of the business." Instead it states that the reasonable needs of the business include the *reasonably anticipated needs* of the business.[10] The Regulations clarify the term reasonably anticipated needs.[11] First, the corporation must have specific, definite, and feasible plans for the use of the accumulation. The funds do not have to be expended in a short period of time after the close of the year. In fact, the plans need only require that the accumulations be expended within a *reasonable* time in the future. However, if the plans are postponed indefinitely, the needs will not be considered reasonable. As a general rule, the plans must not be vague and uncertain. If the plans are based on specific studies containing dollar estimates and are approved by the board of directors, the corporation is in a better position to prove that the plans qualify as reasonable business needs.

In addition to reasonably anticipated needs, the Code and Regulations identify certain specific reasons for accumulations that are considered to be reasonable needs of the business.[12] Several of these reasons are discussed below.

Stock Redemptions from an Estate

A corporation is allowed to temporarily accumulate earnings in order to redeem the stock of a deceased shareholder in conjunction with Code § 303 (discussed in Chapter 4).[13] The accumulations may commence *only after* the death of a shareholder. The fact that a shareholder dies after accumulations have been made and the corporation redeems his or her stock under § 303 is ignored in evaluating pre-death accumulations.[14] If the shareholder owned stock in two or more corporations, each corporation is entitled to accumulate only a portion of the total redeemable amount unless the estate's executor or administrator has indicated that more shares of one of the corporations will be offered for redemption than will those of another corporation.[15] The requirements of § 303 (relating to redemption of stock to pay death taxes) must be met in order for this provision to apply.

Product Liability Loss Reserves

The Code also allows accumulations to cover product liability losses.[16] Product liability is defined as damages for physical or emotional harm as well as damages and loss to property as a result of the use of a product sold, leased, or manufactured by the taxpayer.[17] The amount accumulated can cover both actual and reasonably anticipated losses.

Business Expansion or Plant Replacement

Perhaps the most common reason for accumulating earnings that the Regulations specifically authorize is for *bona fide* expansion of business or replacement of plant.[18] This provision includes the purchase or construction of a building.[19] It also includes the modernization,

[9] § 533(a).
[10] § 537(a)(1).
[11] Reg. § 1.537-1(b).
[12] See § 537(a) and (b), and Reg. § 1.537-2.
[13] § 537(b)(1).
[14] § 537(b)(5).
[15] Reg. § 1.537-1(c)(3).
[16] § 537(b)(4).
[17] § 172(f).
[18] Reg. § 1.537-2(b)(1).
[19] *Sorgel v. U.S.*, 72-1 USTC ¶9427, 29 AFTR2d 72-1035, 341 F. Supp. 1 (D. Ct. Wisc., 1972).

rehabilitation, or replacement of assets.[20] However, this provision does not shield a corporation which has not adequately specified and documented its expansion needs.[21]

Acquisition of a Business Enterprise

A second reason offered in the Regulations for accumulating earnings is for the acquisition of a business enterprise through the purchase of stock or assets.[22] This provision appears to encourage business expansion, since the Regulations state that the business for which earnings can be accumulated includes any line of business the corporation wishes to undertake, and not just the line of business previously carried on.[23] However, this provision for accumulation is limited by the statement in the Regulations that investments in properties or securities that are *unrelated* to the activities of the business of the corporation are unacceptable reasons for accumulations.[24] The statements in the Regulations raise a question as to the validity of accumulations for diversification. On one hand the corporation can acquire an enterprise or expand its business into any field. On the other hand the acquisition should be related to the corporation's activities. This apparent conflict in the Regulations is reflected in court decisions. A corporation that manufactured automobile clutches was permitted to accumulate income to acquire a business that would make use of the corporation's metalworking expertise, whereas a corporation in the printing business was not permitted to accumulate income to acquire real estate.[25] The extent to which a corporation can diversify is uncertain. It appears that diversification into passive investments is unacceptable whereas diversification into an operating business, no matter how far removed from the original line of business, is acceptable.

Retirement of Indebtedness

The Regulations also provide for the accumulation of earnings to retire business indebtedness.[26] The debt can be to either a third party or a shareholder as long as it is a bona fide business debt.

Investments or Loans to Suppliers or Customers

The Regulations state that earnings may be accumulated to provide for investments or loans to suppliers or customers.[27] However, loans to shareholders, friends and relatives of shareholders, and corporations controlled by shareholders of the corporation making the loan indicate that earnings are possibly being accumulated beyond reasonable business needs.[28]

Contingencies

Although the Regulations do not specifically allow accumulations for contingencies, they do imply approval of such accumulations as long as the contingencies are not unrealistic.[29] Unfortunately, the distinction between realistic and unrealistic contingencies is difficult to define. However, the more specific the need, the more detailed the cash estimate, and the more likely the occurrence, the easier it will be to prove the accumulation is reasonable.

Redemption of Stock

As noted above, accumulations to redeem stock from a decedent's estate under § 303 constitute a reasonable need of the business. This provision does not cover any other stock redemption. Several cases have held that a redemption may be a reasonable need provided the redemption is for the benefit of the corporation and not the shareholder.[30] For example, the redemption of a dissenting minority shareholder's stock can be for the corporation's benefit

---

[20] *Knoxville Iron*, 18 TCM 251, T.C. Memo 1959-54.

[21] *I.A. Dress Co.*, 60-1 USTC ¶9204, 5 AFTR2d 429, 273 F.2d 543 (CA-2, 1960), aff&g. 32 T.C. 93; *Herzog Miniature Lamp Works, Inc.*, 73-2 USTC ¶9593, 32 AFTR2d 73-5282, 273 F.2d 543, (CA-2, 1973).

[22] Reg. § 1.537-2(b)(2).

[23] Reg. § 1.537-3(a).

[24] Reg. § 1.537-2(c)(4).

[25] *Alma Piston Co.*, 22 TCM 948, T.C. Memo 1963-195; *Union Offset*, 79-2 USTC ¶9550, 44 AFTR2d 79-5652. 603 F.2d 90 (CA-9, 1979).

[26] Reg. § 1.537-2(b)(3).

[27] Reg. § 1.537-2(b)(5).

[28] Reg. §§ 1.537-2(c)(1), (2), and (3).

[29] Reg. § 1.537-2(c)(5).

[30] See *John B. Lambert & Assoc. v. U.S.*, 38 AFTR2d 6207 (Ct. Cls., 1976); *C.E. Hooper, Inc. v. U.S.*, 38 AFTR2d 5417, 539 F.2d 1276 (Ct. Cls.,1976); *Mountain State Steel Foundries, Inc. v. Comm.*, 6 AFTR2d 5910, 284 F.2d 737 (CA-4, 1960); and *Koma, Inc. v. Comm.*, 40 AFTR 712, 189 F.2d 390 (CA-10, 1951).

whereas the redemption of a majority shareholder's stock would be for the shareholder's benefit. It might also be possible to prove that the redemption was necessary to reduce or eliminate disputes over management or conduct of the business.

Working Capital

Another reason mentioned in the Regulations for a reasonable accumulation of earnings and profits is the need for working capital.[31] This is one of the primary justifications corporations use for the accumulation of earnings. A corporation is permitted to retain earnings to provide necessary working capital. Initially, the courts tried to measure working capital sufficiency by using rules of thumb. A current ratio of 2.5 to 1 generally meant that the corporation had not accumulated income unreasonably.[32] The courts considered a current ratio more than 2.5 to 1 an indication of unreasonable accumulation.

In the 1965 case of *Bardahl Mfg. Corp.*, the Tax Court utilized a formula to compute the working capital needs of a corporation.[33] Under this approach (called the *Bardahl* formula), the working capital needed for one operating cycle is computed. This amount in essence represents the cash *needed* to meet expenses incurred during the operating cycle—the period required for a business to convert cash into inventory, sell the merchandise, convert the customer's accounts receivable into cash, and pay its accounts payable. This necessary working capital is then compared to actual working capital. If necessary working capital is greater than actual working capital, an accumulation of earnings to meet the necessary working capital requirements is justified. If actual working capital is greater than the working capital needed, the corporation must show other reasons for the accumulation of earnings in order to avoid the accumulated earnings tax.

The initial step of the *Bardahl* formula is to calculate the inventory, accounts receivable, and accounts payable cycle ratios. These ratios are computed as follows:

$$1. \quad \text{Inventory cycle ratio} = \frac{\text{Average inventory}}{\text{Cost of goods sold}}$$

$$2. \quad \text{Accounts receivable cycle ratio} = \frac{\text{Average accounts receivable}}{\text{Net sales}}$$

$$3. \quad \text{Accounts payable cycle ratio} = \frac{\text{Average accounts payable}}{\text{Purchases}}$$

The ratios resulting from these calculations represent the cycle expressed as a percentage of the year. In other words, if the accounts receivable cycle ratio is 10 percent, then it normally takes about 36 days (10% × 365) to collect a receivable once it has been generated by a sale.

Instead of using the *average* inventory and the average receivables, a corporation can use *peak values* if it is in a seasonal business. If the corporation uses peak values for the other ratios, it may be required to use peak payables.

Once computed, the three ratios are combined. The result represents the number of days—expressed as a fraction of the year—during which the corporation needs working capital to meet its operating expenses. The operating cycle ratio is computed as follows:

> Inventory cycle ratio
> + Accounts receivable cycle ratio
> − Accounts payable cycle ratio
> = Operating cycle ratio

The operating cycle ratio is multiplied by the *annual operating expenses* to compute the necessary working capital. Operating expenses are defined as the cost of goods sold plus other annual expenses (i.e., general, administrative, and selling expenses). The operating expense category does not include depreciation since depreciation does not require the use of cash.

---

[31] Reg. § 1.537-2(b)(4).

[32] *J. Scripps Newspaper*, 44 T.C. 453 (1965).

[33] *Bardahl Mfg. Corp.*, 24 TCM 1030, T.C. Memo 1965-200.

However, the category can include income taxes if the corporation pays estimated taxes and will make a tax payment during the next operating cycle.[34] Other expenses should be included if they will require the expenditure of cash during the next operating cycle.

The required working capital computed by the *Bardahl* formula is compared to actual working capital to determine if there have been excess accumulations. Since the computed working capital is based on accounting data, it is normally compared to actual working capital (current assets – current liabilities) computed from the corporation's financial statements. There are exceptions to this rule. Financial statements are not used if they do not clearly reflect the company's working capital. The Supreme Court authorized the use of fair market value instead of historical cost to value a firm's current assets in *Ivan Allen Co.*[35] The assets in question were marketable securities that had appreciated. The decision is broad enough to permit the Internal Revenue Service to determine actual working capital based on current value any time there is a significant difference between cost and market.

Any corporation whose actual working capital does not exceed required working capital (per the *Bardahl* formula) should be exempt from the accumulated earnings tax. If the actual working capital exceeds required working capital, the excess is considered an indication of unreasonable accumulations. This excess is compared to the reasonable needs of the business (other than working capital) to determine if the accumulations are unreasonable. To the extent that the corporation has needs, it may accumulate funds. If all of the excess working capital is not needed, the tax is imposed. The tax is based on the accumulated taxable income and not the excess working capital.

Example 3

K owns and operates K's Apparel, Inc. (KAI). After hearing that a friend's corporation was recently slapped with an accumulated earnings tax penalty, she asked her accountant to determine the vulnerability of her own business. The following is a balance sheet and income statement for 2015 and 2016 for KAI.

Balance Sheet

	2015	2016
Current assets:		
Cash	$ 55,000	$ 67,000
Marketable securities	10,000	8,000
Accounts receivable (net)	45,000	55,000
Inventory	30,000	20,000
Total current assets	$140,000	$150,000
Property, plant, and equipment (net)	300,000	425,000
Total assets	$440,000	$575,000
Current liabilities:		
Notes payable	$ 5,000	$ 4,000
Accounts payable	50,000	30,000
Accrued expenses	8,000	16,000
Total current liabilities	$ 63,000	$ 50,000
Long-term debt	37,000	40,000
Total liabilities	$100,000	$ 90,000
Stockholders' equity:		
Common stock	10,000	10,000
Earnings and profits	330,000	475,000
Total liabilities and stockholders' equity	$440,000	$575,000

---

[34] *Empire Steel*, 33 TCM 155, T.C. Memo 1974-34.

[35] *Ivan Allen Co. v. U.S.*, 75-2 USTC ¶9557, 36 AFTR2d 75-5200, 422 U.S. 617 (USSC, 1975).

Income Statement

Sales	$400,000	$500,000
Cost of goods sold:		
Beginning inventory	$ 40,000	$ 30,000
Purchases	300,000	320,000
Ending inventory	(30,000)	(20,000)
Total	$310,000	$330,000
Gross profit	$ 90,000	$170,000
Other expenses:		
Depreciation	$ 40,000	$ 55,000
Selling expenses	10,000	15,000
Administrative	20,000	50,000
Total	$ 70,000	$120,000
Net income before taxes	$ 20,000	$ 50,000
Income tax expense	(2,000)	(5,000)
Net income	$ 18,000	$ 45,000

In addition to this information, K indicated that at the end of 2016 the securities were worth $15,000 more than their book value, or $23,000. K also estimates that her reasonable needs for the current year 2016 amount to $20,000.

Under the *Bardahl* formula, her working capital needs are determined as follows:

Step 1: Operating cycle expressed as a fraction of the year (in thousands):

$$\text{Inventory cycle} = \frac{\text{Average inventory}}{\text{Cost of goods sold}} = ([30 + 20]/2)/330 = 0.0758$$

$$+\ \text{Receivable cycle} = \frac{\text{Average accounts receivable}}{\text{Net sales}} = ([45 + 55]/2)/500 = 0.1000$$

$$-\ \text{Payable cycle} = \frac{\text{Average accounts payable}}{\text{Purchases}} = ([50 + 30]/2)/320 = (0.1250)$$

Step 2: Computation of operating expenses:

Operating expenses:	
Cost of goods sold	$330,000
Selling expenses	15,000
Administrative expenses	50,000
Taxes	5,000
Total operating expenses	$400,000

Step 3: Working capital needs:

Operating expenses (Step 2)	$400,000
× Operating cycle (Step 1)	× 0.0508
= Working capital needs	$ 20,320

K's working capital needs, $20,320, must be compared to actual working capital using the assets' fair market value. Any excess of actual working capital over required working capital must be compared to the current year's needs to determine if unwarranted accumulations exist. Assuming the marketable securities are actually worth $23,000, the comparison is made as follows:

Actual working capital:	
Current assets ($150,000 + $15,000)	$165,000
– Current liabilities	(50,000)
= Actual working capital	$115,000
– Required working capital (Step 3)	(20,320)
= Excess working capital	$ 94,680
– Reasonable needs	(20,000)
= Accumulations beyond current needs	$ 74,680

The accumulated earnings tax focuses on whether the corporation has accumulated liquid assets beyond its reasonable needs that could be distributed to shareholders. In this case, actual working capital exceeds required working capital and other needs of the business by $74,680, implying that the accumulated earnings tax applies. If so, the actual penalty tax is computed using accumulated taxable income, as explained below.

COMPUTATION OF THE ACCUMULATED EARNINGS TAX

LO.4

Explain how the accumulated earnings tax is computed.

The purpose of the accumulated earnings tax is to penalize taxpayers with unwarranted accumulations. To accomplish this, a 20% tax is imposed on what the Code refers to as accumulated taxable income. Accumulated taxable income is designed to represent the amount that the corporation could have distributed after funding its reasonable needs. In essence, the computation attempts to determine the corporation's dividend-paying capacity. Exhibit 6-1 shows the formula for computing accumulated taxable income.[36]

EXHIBIT 6-1	Accumulated Taxable Income[37]

Taxable income:

Plus:
1. The dividends-received deduction
2. Any net operating loss deduction that is reflected in taxable income
3. Any capital-loss carryovers from other years that are reflected in taxable income

Minus:
1. Federal income taxes for the year, but not the accumulated earnings tax or the personal holding company tax
2. The charitable contributions for the year in excess of the 10% limitation
3. Any net capital loss incurred during the year reduced by net capital gain deductions of prior years that have not previously reduced any net capital loss deduction
4. Any net capital gain (net long-term capital gain – the net short-term capital loss) for the year minus the taxes attributable to the gain and any net capital losses of prior years that have not reduced a net capital gain deduction in determining the accumulated earnings tax

Equals: *Adjusted taxable income*

Minus:
1. Accumulated earnings credit (see Exhibit 6-2)
2. Dividends–paid deduction (see Exhibit 6-3)

Equals: *Accumulated taxable income*

[36] § 535.

[37] § 535. Several additional adjustments are required for computing accumulated taxable income of a holding or investment company.

The computation of accumulated taxable income begins with an imperfect measure of the corporation's ability to pay dividends-taxable income. To obtain a more representative measure of the corporation's dividend-paying capacity, taxable income is modified to arrive at what is often referred to as *adjusted taxable income*.[38] For example, the deduction allowed for dividends received is added back to taxable income since it has no effect on the corporation's ability to pay dividends. The same rationale can be given for the net operating loss deduction. In contrast, charitable contributions in excess of the 10% limitation may be deducted in determining adjusted taxable income since the corporation does not have the nondeductible amount available to pay dividends. For the same reason, Federal income taxes may be deducted in computing adjusted taxable income.

The deduction for capital gains stems from the assumption that these earnings are used to fund the corporation's needs and consequently may be accumulated with impunity. Capital losses are deductible since these amounts are unavailable for payment of dividends and are not reflected in taxable income. As shown in Exhibit 6-1, however, the deductions for capital gains as well as capital losses must be modified.

Prior to 1984, corporations were entitled to reduce taxable income not only by the amount of their net capital gains (reduced by related taxes) but also by the full amount of their net capital losses, depending on whether a net capital gain or loss occurred. Consequently, there was an advantage in recognizing capital gains in one year and capital losses in another year in order to avoid netting and thus permit both gains and losses to be deductible in full. For example, if the corporation had a capital loss of $1,000 this year and a capital gain of $5,000 next year (ignoring taxes), both could be deducted in full each year in computing adjusted taxable income. However, if they occurred in the same year, the deduction would be limited to $4,000. To eliminate this planning opportunity, corporations are now required to reduce their net capital losses by any net capital gain deductions that have been used to arrive at adjusted taxable income in prior years. Under these rules, it is immaterial in what order or in what year gains and losses are recognized. In effect, taxable income is reduced only by the overall net gain or loss that the corporation has recognized to date.

Example 4

T Corporation has the following income and deductions for 2016:

Income from operations.	$ 150,000
Dividend income (from less than 20% owned corporations)	40,000
Charitable contributions.	25,000

T Corporation computes its taxable income as follows:

Income from operations.		$ 150,000
Dividend income		40,000
Income before special deductions		$ 190,000
Special deductions:		
Charitable contribution (limited).	$19,000	
Dividend-received deduction	28,000	
Total special deductions		(47,000)
Taxable income		$ 143,000

---

[38] This term is not found in the Code; it is used here solely for purposes of exposition.

T Corporation's Federal income taxes for 2016 are $39,020. T Corporation's adjusted taxable income is computed as follows:

Taxable income		$143,000
Plus: Dividend-received deduction		28,000
		$171,000
Minus the sum of		
Federal income taxes	$39,020	
Actual charitable contributions for the year minus the charitable contribution deduction reflected in taxable income ($25,000 − $19,000)	6,000	(45,020)
Equals: Adjusted taxable income		$125,980

Two additional deductions are permitted in computing accumulated taxable income: the accumulated earnings credit and the dividends-paid deduction. The deduction allowed for dividends is consistent with the theory that the tax should be imposed only on income that has not been distributed. The accumulated earnings credit allows the taxpayer to accumulate without penalty $250,000 or an amount equal to the reasonable needs of the business, whichever is greater.

ACCUMULATED EARNINGS CREDIT

In creating the accumulated earnings tax, Congress realized that a corporation should not be penalized for keeping enough of its earnings to meet legitimate business needs. For this reason, in computing accumulated taxable income, a corporation is allowed—in effect— a reduction for the amount out of current year's earnings necessary to meet such needs. This reduction is the *accumulated earnings credit*.[39] Note that despite its name, the credit actually operates as a deduction. As a practical matter, it is this credit that insulates most corporations from the accumulated earnings tax.

Specifically, the credit is the greater of two amounts as described in Exhibit 6-2 and discussed further below. Generally, however, the credit for the current year may be determined as follows:

Reasonable business needs (or $250,000 if larger)	$xxx,xxx
Less: Beginning accumulated E&P	(xx,xxx)
Accumulated earnings credit	$xxx,xxx

EXHIBIT 6-2	Accumulated Earnings Credit[40]

The accumulated earnings credit is the greater of
1. *General Rule:* Earnings and profits for the taxable year that are retained to meet the reasonable needs of the business, minus the net capital gain for the year (reduced by the taxes attributable to the gain), or
2. *Minimum Credit:* $250,000 ($150,000 for personal service corporations) minus the accumulated earnings and profits of the corporation at the close of the *preceding* taxable year, adjusted for dividends paid in the current year *deemed* paid in the prior year.

Part 1 of Exhibit 6-2 contains the general rule authorizing accumulations. It permits corporations to accumulate earnings to the extent of their reasonable needs without penalty.[41] In determining the amount of the earnings and profits for the taxable year that have been retained to meet the reasonable needs of the business, it is necessary to consider to what extent the accumulated earnings and profits are available to cover these needs.[42] In effect,

[39] § 535(c).
[40] § 535(c)(1).
[41] *Ibid.*
[42] Reg. § 1.535-3(b)(1)(ii).

prior accumulations reduce the amount that can be retained in the current year. If the corporation's accumulated earnings and profits are sufficient to meet the reasonable needs of the business, *none* of the current earnings and profits will be considered to be retained to meet the reasonable needs of the business.

Part 2 of Exhibit 6-2 is the so-called *minimum credit*.[43] For most corporations the amount of the minimum credit is $250,000. For personal service corporations, the minimum credit is $150,000. Personal service corporations are corporations that provide services in the area of health, law, engineering, architecture, accounting, actuarial science, performing arts, or consulting. The lower credit for personal service corporations reflects the fact that their capital needs are relatively small when compared to retail or manufacturing businesses.

To determine the amount of the minimum credit available for the current year, the base amount, $250,000 ($150,000), must be reduced by the accumulated earnings and profits at the close of the preceding tax year. For purposes of this computation, the accumulated earnings and profits at the close of the preceding year are reduced by the dividends that were paid by the corporation within 2½ months after the close of the preceding year.[44]

Example 5

X Corporation, a calendar year retail department store, had current earnings and profits for 2016 of $75,000. Its accumulated earnings and profits at the close of 2015 were $200,000. X Corporation has paid no dividends for five years. X Corporation's taxable income for 2016 included a net capital gain of $20,000. [The taxes related to this net capital gain were $6,800 (34% × $20,000).] The reasonable needs of X Corporation are estimated to be $240,000. The amount of X Corporation's current earnings and profits that are retained to meet reasonable business needs is computed as follows:

Estimated reasonable needs of X Corporation	$240,000
Less: Accumulated earnings and profits as of 12/31/2015	(200,000)
Extent to which current earnings and profits are needed to cover the reasonable needs of the business	$ 40,000

Even though the current earnings and profits are $75,000, only $40,000 of the current earnings and profits are needed to meet the reasonable needs of the business.

The accumulated earnings credit is the greater of

1. Current earnings and profits to meet the reasonable needs of the business		$ 40,000
Minus: Net capital gain	$20,000	
Reduced by the taxes attributable to the gain	(6,800)	(13,200)
General rule credit		$ 26,800
or		
2. $250,000		$250,000
Minus: Accumulated earnings and profits as of 12/31/2015		(200,000)
Minimum credit		$ 50,000

X Corporation's accumulated earnings credit is $50,000, the greater of the general rule credit ($26,800) or the minimum credit ($50,000).

---

[43] § 535(c)(2). [44] § 535(c)(4).

Example 6

Assume the same facts as in *Example 5*, except that X Corporation is an engineering firm (i.e., a personal service corporation). The general rule credit would still be $26,800, but the minimum credit would be computed as follows:

$150,000.	$150,000
Minus: Accumulated earnings and profits as of 12/31/2015	(200,000)
Minimum credit (the minimum credit cannot be a negative number).	$ 0

In this situation the accumulated earnings credit is $26,800, the greater of the general rule credit ($26,800) or the minimum credit ($0).

Two aspects of the accumulated earnings credit deserve special mention. First, the minimum credit has a very limited role. Since the $250,000 (or $150,000 for service corporations) is reduced by the prior accumulations, the minimum credit will always be zero for firms that have greater than $250,000 of accumulated earnings. In other words, accumulations in excess of $250,000 must be justified by business needs.

The second aspect involves capital gains. As discussed previously, capital gains (net of related taxes) are subtracted from taxable income in arriving at adjusted taxable income. Therefore, a corporation can accumulate all of its capital gains without the imposition of the accumulated earnings tax. At the same time, however, capital gains are subtracted from business needs in arriving at the general credit (see Exhibit 6-2). As a result, a capital gain may cause accumulations of ordinary income to be subject to the special tax even though the capital gain itself escapes penalty. In effect, the computations are based on the assumption that business needs are funded first from capital gains and then from income from operations.

DIVIDENDS-PAID DEDUCTION

Exhibit 6-1 indicated that both the accumulated earnings credit and the dividends-paid deduction are adjustments in computing accumulated taxable income. Exhibit 6-3 lists the types of dividends that constitute the dividends-paid deduction.

EXHIBIT 6-3	Dividends-Paid Deduction[45]

1. Dividends paid during the taxable year,[46]
2. Dividends paid within 2½ months after the close of the taxable year,[47]
3. Consent dividends, plus[48]
4. Liquidating distributions,[49]

   Equals: **Dividends-Paid Deduction**

To qualify for the dividend deduction, the distribution must constitute a "dividend" as defined in § 316.[50] As previously discussed, § 316 limits dividends to distributions out of current earnings and profits and accumulated earnings and profits since 1913. Property distributions qualify only to the extent of their adjusted basis.[51]

---

[45] §§ 561 through 565.

[46] § 561(a)(1).

[47] § 563(a).

[48] § 565.

[49] § 562(b)(1).

[50] § 562(a).

[51] Reg. § 1.562-1(a).

Throwback Dividends

The dividends-paid deduction includes not only dividends paid during the year, but also so-called *throwback dividends*, dividends paid during the 2½ months following the close of the tax year.[52] Amounts paid during the 2½-month period *must* be treated as if paid in the previous year.[53] This treatment is mandatory and not elective by the shareholders or the corporation.

Consent Dividends

In addition to actual dividends paid, the corporation is entitled to a deduction for consent dividends.[54] Sometimes a corporation may have a large amount of accumulated earnings, but insufficient cash or property to make a dividend distribution. In order to avoid the accumulated earnings tax, the corporation may obtain a dividends-paid deduction by using consent dividends—so called because the shareholders consent to treat a certain amount as a taxable dividend on their tax returns even though there is no distribution of cash or property. Not only are the shareholders deemed to receive the amount to which they consent, but they also are treated as having reinvested the amount received as a contribution to the corporation's capital.

To qualify a dividend as a consent dividend, the shareholders must file a consent form (Form 972) with the corporate income tax return. The consents must be filed by the due date (including extensions) of the corporate tax return for the year in which the dividend deduction is requested. Only shareholders who own stock on the last day of the tax year need file consent forms. On the forms, each shareholder must specify the amount of the consent dividend and then include this amount as a cash distribution by the corporation on his or her individual income tax return. Consent dividends are limited to the amount that would have qualified as a dividend under Code § 316 had the dividend been distributed in cash.[55] Only shareholders of common and participating preferred stock may consent to dividends.[56]

Liquidating Distributions

If the distribution is in liquidation, partial liquidation, or redemption of stock, the portion of the distribution chargeable to earnings and profits is included in the dividend deduction.[57] For partial liquidations and redemptions, this is the redeemed stock's proportionate share of accumulated E&P. For complete liquidations, any amount distributed within the two years following the adoption of a plan of liquidation and that is pursuant to the plan is included in the dividends-paid deduction, but not to exceed the corporation's current earnings and profits for the year of distribution.[58]

Personal Holding Company Tax

As mentioned earlier in this chapter, the accumulated earnings tax is not the only penalty tax applicable to corporations. Congress has also enacted the personal holding company tax. This tax evolved in 1934 from the need to stop the growing number of individuals who were misusing the corporate entity despite the existence of the accumulated earnings tax. The personal holding company tax was designed to thwart three particular schemes prevalent during that period.

The first two schemes specifically aimed to take advantage of the disparity between individual and corporate tax rates. At that time, the maximum individual tax rates were approximately 45 percentage points higher than the maximum corporate rates. A typical plan used to take advantage of this differential involved the formation of a corporation to hold an individual's investment portfolio. This plan allowed an individual's interest and dividends to

---

[52] § 563.

[53] Reg. § 1.563-1.

[54] § 565.

[55] Reg. § 1.565-2(a).

[56] § 565(f).

[57] § 562(b)(1).

[58] § 562(b)(1)(B).

become taxable to the corporation rather than to the individual and consequently to be taxed at the lower corporate rates. Another, somewhat more sophisticated, technique enabled the transfer of an individual's service income to a corporation. The blueprint for this plan required the formation of a corporation by an individual (e.g., movie star) who subsequently became an employee of the corporation. With the corporation in place, parties seeking the individual's services were forced to contract with the corporation rather than with the individual. The individual would then perform the services, but the corporation would receive the revenue. Finally, the corporation would pay the individual a salary that was less than the revenue earned. Through this plan, the individual succeeded in transferring at least some of the revenue to the corporation, where it would be taxed at the lower corporate rates.

The final scheme was not specifically designed to take advantage of the lower corporate rates. Instead, its attraction grew from the practical presumption that all corporate activities are business activities. Given this presumption, an individual would transfer his or her personal assets (e.g., a yacht, race car, or vacation home) along with other investments to the corporation. Under the veil of the corporation, the expenses relating to the personal assets, such as maintenance of a yacht, would be magically transformed from nondeductible personal expenses to deductible business expenses which could offset the income produced by the investments. In short, by using the corporate form, individuals were able to disguise their personal expenses as business expenses and deduct them.

Although the Internal Revenue Service tried to curb these abuses using the accumulated earnings tax, such attempts often failed. These failures normally could be attributed to the problem of proving that the individuals actually intended to avoid taxes. Aware of this problem, Congress formulated the personal holding company tax, which could be applied without having to prove that the forbidden purpose existed. In contrast to the accumulated earnings tax, which is imposed only after a subjective assessment of the individual's intentions, the personal holding company tax automatically applies whenever the corporation satisfies two objective tests.

Not all corporations that meet the applicable tests are subject to the penalty tax, however. The Code specifically exempts certain corporations. These include S corporations, tax-exempt corporations, banks, life insurance companies, surety companies, foreign corporations, lending and finance companies, and several other types of corporations.[59]

If the personal holding company tax applies, the tax is 20% of undistributed personal holding company income.[60] Like the accumulated earnings tax, the personal holding company tax is levied in addition to the regular tax.[61] The personal holding company tax differs from the accumulated earnings tax however, in that the corporation is required to compute and remit any personal holding tax due at the time it files its annual return. Form 1120-PH is used to compute the tax and must be filed with the corporation's annual Form 1120. In those cases where both the accumulated earnings tax and the personal holding company tax are applicable, only the personal holding company tax is imposed.[62]

PERSONAL HOLDING COMPANY DEFINED

LO.5

Indicate when the personal holding company tax applies.

The personal holding company tax applies only if the corporation is considered a personal holding company (PHC). As might be expected in light of the schemes prevalent at the time the tax was enacted, a corporation generally qualifies as a personal holding company if it is closely held and a substantial portion of its income is derived from passive sources or services. Specifically, the Code provides that a corporation is deemed to be a personal holding company if it satisfies both of the following tests.[63]

1. *Ownership*—At any time during the last half of the taxable year, more than 50% of the value of the corporation's outstanding stock is owned by five or fewer individuals.[64]

2. *Passive income*—At least 60% of the corporation's adjusted ordinary gross income consists of personal holding company income (PHCI).[65]

---

[59] § 542(c).

[60] § 541.

[61] *Ibid.*

[62] § 532(b)(1).

[63] § 542.

[64] § 542(a)(2).

[65] § 542(a)(1).

Before each of these tests is examined in detail, the distinction between the personal holding company tax and the accumulated earnings tax should be emphasized. The accumulated earnings tax applies only when it is proven that it was the shareholder's intention to use the corporation to shield income from individual tax rates. In contrast, application of the personal holding company tax requires only that two mechanical tests be satisfied. As a result, a corporation may fall victim to the personal holding company tax where there was no intention to avoid tax by misusing the corporation. For example, consider a closely held corporation in the process of liquidating. During liquidation, the corporation may have income from operations and passive income from temporary investments (investments made pending final distributions). If the passive income is substantial—60% or more of the corporation's total income—the corporation will be treated as a personal holding company subject to the penalty tax even though there was no intention by the shareholders to shelter the passive income. As this example illustrates, the mechanical nature of the personal holding company tax, unlike the subjective nature of the accumulated earnings tax, presents a trap for those with the noblest of intentions.

PHC OWNERSHIP TEST

As indicated above, the first part of the two-part test for personal holding company status concerns ownership. Apparently it was Congressional belief that the tax-saving schemes described above succeeded primarily in those cases where there was a concentration of ownership. For this reason, the ownership test is satisfied only if five or fewer individuals own more than 50% of the value of the corporation's outstanding shares of stock at any time during the last half of the taxable year.[66] As a quick study of this test reveals, a corporation having less than ten shareholders always meets the ownership test since there will always be a combination of five or fewer shareholders owning more than 50% of the stock (e.g., 100% ÷ 9 = 11%; 11% × 5 > 50%). Thus, it becomes apparent that closely held corporations are extremely vulnerable to the tax.

In performing the stock ownership test, the shareholder's *direct and indirect* ownership must be taken into account.[67] Indirect ownership is determined using a set of constructive ownership rules designed specifically for the personal holding company area.[68] According to these rules, a taxpayer is considered owning indirectly the following:

1. Stock owned directly or indirectly by his or her family, including his or her brothers, sisters, spouse, ancestors, and lineal descendents;[69]
2. His or her proportionate share of any stock owned by a corporation, partnership, estate, or trust in which he or she has ownership (or of which he or she is a beneficiary in the case of an estate or trust);[70] and
3. Stock owned indirectly or directly by his or her partner in a partnership.[71]

In using these rules, the following guidelines must be observed: (1) stock attributed from one family member to another cannot be reattributed to yet another member of the family,[72] (2) stock attributed from a partner to the taxpayer cannot be reattributed to a member of his or her family or to yet another partner,[73] (3) stock on which the taxpayer has an option is treated as being actually owned,[74] and (4) convertible securities are treated as outstanding stock.[75] In addition, Code § 544 contains other rules that may affect an individual's stock ownership.

INCOME TEST

Although the stock ownership test may be satisfied, a corporation is not considered a personal holding company unless it also passes an income test. In general terms, this test is straightforward: At least 60% of the corporation's income must be derived from either passive sources or certain types of services. Unfortunately, the technical translation of this requirement is somewhat more complicated. According to the Code, at least 60% of the

---

[66] § 542(a)(2).
[67] *Ibid.*
[68] § 544.
[69] § 544(a)(2).
[70] § 544(a)(1).
[71] § 544(a)(2).
[72] § 544(a)(5).
[73] *Ibid.*
[74] § 544(a)(3).
[75] § 544(b).

corporation's adjusted ordinary gross income must be *personal holding company income*.[76] This relationship may be expressed numerically as follows:

$$\frac{\text{Personal holding company income}}{\text{Adjusted ordinary gross income}} \geq 60\%$$

As will be seen below, the definition of each of these terms can be baffling. However, the general theme of each term and the thrust of the test should not be lost in the complexity. Personal holding company income is generally passive income, while adjusted ordinary gross income is just that, ordinary gross income with a few modifications. Performing the income test is, in essence, a matter of determining whether too much of the corporation's income (adjusted ordinary gross income) is passive income (personal holding company income).

Example 7

K, a high-bracket taxpayer, wished to reduce her taxes. Upon the advice of an old friend, she transferred all of her stocks and bonds to a newly formed corporation of which she is the sole owner. During the year, the corporation had dividend income of $40,000 and interest income of $35,000. In this case, the corporation is treated as a personal holding company because both the stock ownership test and the income test are satisfied. The stock ownership test is met since K owned 100% of the stock in the last half of the year. The income test is also met since all of the corporation's income is passive income—or more specifically, its personal holding company income, $75,000 ($40,000 dividends + $35,000 interest) exceeds 60% of its adjusted ordinary gross income, $45,000 (60% of $75,000).

The technical definitions of adjusted ordinary gross income and personal holding company income are explored below.

ADJUSTED ORDINARY GROSS INCOME

The first quantity that must be determined is adjusted ordinary gross income (AOGI).[77] As suggested above, the label given to this quantity is very appropriate since the amount which must be computed is just what the phrase implies; that is, it includes only the ordinary gross income of the corporation with certain adjustments. In determining AOGI, the following amounts must be computed: (1) gross income, (2) ordinary gross income, and (3) the adjustments to ordinary gross income to arrive at AOGI. Therefore, the starting point for the calculation of AOGI is gross income.

Gross Income

The definition of gross income for purposes of the personal holding company provisions varies little from the definition found in § 61. Accordingly, gross income includes all income from whatever source except those items specifically excluded. In addition, gross income is computed taking into consideration cost of goods sold. The only departure from the normal definition of gross income concerns property transactions. Only the net gains from the sale or exchange of stocks, securities, and commodities are included in gross income.[78] Net losses involving these assets do not reduce gross income. Similarly, any loss arising from the sale or exchange of § 1231 property is ignored and does not offset any § 1231 gains.

Ordinary Gross Income

In applying the income test, capital-gain type items are ignored and consequently have no effect on whether the corporation is treated as a personal holding company. Therefore, since the quantity desired is adjusted "ordinary" gross income, the second step of the calculation requires the removal of capital-gain type items from gross income. As seen in Exhibit 6-4, all capital

---

[76] § 542(a)(1).

[77] § 543(b)(2).

[78] Prop. Reg. § 1.543-12(a). Also see Reg. §§ 1.542-2 and 1.543-2.

gains and § 1231 gains are subtracted from gross income to arrive at ordinary gross income.[79] It should be noted that this amount, "ordinary gross income," is not simply a subtotal in arriving at AOGI. As discussed below, ordinary gross income (OGI) is an important figure in determining whether certain types of income are treated as personal holding company income.[80]

EXHIBIT 6-4	Ordinary Gross Income[80]

Gross income
Minus: a.   Capital gains
            b.   (b) Section 1231 gains
Equals: **Ordinary gross income (OGI)**

Adjustments to OGI

For many years, OGI generally served as the denominator in the income-test fraction shown above. In 1964, however, modifications were necessary to discourage the use of certain methods taxpayers and their advisors had forged to undermine the income test. The popular schemes capitalized on the fact that $1 of gross rental income could shelter 60 cents of passive personal holding company income. This particular advantage could be obtained even though the rental activity itself was merely a break-even operation. Consequently, a taxpayer could easily thwart the income test and reap the benefits of the corporate entity by investing in activities that produced substantial gross rents or royalties, notwithstanding the fact that these activities were not economically sound investments.

Example 8

Refer to the facts in *Example 7*. Absent special rules, K could circumvent the income test by purchasing a coin-operated laundry which generated gross rents of more than $50,000 (e.g., $51,000) and transferring it to the corporation. In such case, assuming the rents would not be treated as personal holding income, the personal holding company income would still be $75,000 (dividends of $40,000 + interest of $35,000). However, when the laundry rents are combined with the personal holding company income to form the new AOGI, personal holding company income would be less than 60% of this new AOGI [$75,000 < 60% × ($40,000 + $35,000 + $51,000) = $75,600]. Although the laundry business might not show a profit, this would be irrelevant to K since she would have gained the advantage of the dividends-received deduction and avoided personal holding company status.

To deter the type of scheme illustrated above, the calculation now requires rental and royalty income to be reduced by the bulk of the expenses typically related to this type of income: depreciation, interest, and taxes. This requirement reduces the ability of the activities to shelter income. For instance, in *Example 8* above, K would be required to reduce the gross rental income by depreciation, interest, and taxes—which would severely curtail the utility of purchasing the laundry business.[81] The specific modifications that reduce ordinary gross income to arrive at adjusted ordinary gross income are shown in Exhibit 6-5.[82] Exhibit 6-6 and Exhibit 6-7 illustrate the adjustments required to be made to gross income from rents and mineral, oil, and gas royalties for purposes of computing adjusted ordinary gross income.

---

[79] § 543(b)(1).

[80] *Ibid.*

[81] Under current law, it is also likely that the rents would be treated as PHCI, thus further spoiling the plan.

[82] § 543(b)(2).

EXHIBIT 6-5	**Adjusted Ordinary Gross Income**[83]

Ordinary gross income (OGI)

Minus:
    a. Depreciation, property taxes, interest expense, and rents paid related to gross rental income. These deductions may not exceed gross rental income. (Gross rental income is income for the use of corporate property and interest received on the sales price of real property held as inventory.)

    b. Depreciation and depletion, property and severance taxes, interest expense, and rents paid related to gross income from mineral, oil, and gas royalties. These deductions may not exceed the gross income from the royalties.

    c. Interest on tax refunds, on judgments, on condemnation awards, and on U.S. obligations (only for a dealer in the obligations).

Equals: **Adjusted ordinary gross income (AOGI)**

EXHIBIT 6-6	**Adjusted Income from Rents**[84]

Gross rental income

Minus:
    a. Depreciation
    b. Property taxes
    c. Interest expense
    d. Rents paid

Equals: **Adjusted income from rents**

EXHIBIT 6-7	**Adjusted Income from Mineral, Oil, and Gas Royalties**[85]

Gross income from mineral, oil, and gas royalties (including production payments and overriding royalties)

Minus:
    a. Depreciation
    b. Property and severance taxes
    c. Interest expense
    d. Rents paid

Equals: **Adjusted income from mineral, oil, and gas royalties**[86]

PERSONAL HOLDING COMPANY INCOME (PHCI)

Following the computation of AOGI, the corporation's personal holding company income must be measured to determine whether it meets the 60% threshold. Although personal holding company income can be generally characterized as passive income and certain income from

[83] § 543(a)(1).
[84] § 543(a)(1).
[85] *Ibid.*
[86] § 543(b)(4).

services, the Code identifies eight specific types of income which carry the personal holding company taint.[87] These are listed in Exhibit 6-8. Selected items of PHCI are discussed below.

EXHIBIT 6-8	**Personal Holding Company Income (PHCI)**

Dividends, interest, royalties (except mineral, oil, or gas royalties, copyright royalties, and certain software royalties), and annuities.

Plus:

a. Adjusted income from rents, *but* the adjusted income from rents is not added to PHCI *if*

 1. The adjusted income from rents is 50% or more of AOGI, and
 2. The dividends paid, the dividends considered paid, and the consent dividends equal or exceed

  i. PHCI computed without the adjusted income from rents
  ii. Minus 10% of OGI.

b. Adjusted income from mineral, oil, and gas royalties, *but* the adjusted income from these royalties is not added to PHCI *if*

 1. The adjusted income from the royalties is 50% or more of AOGI,
 2. PHCI computed without the adjusted income from these royalties does not exceed 10% of OGI, and
 3. The § 162 trade or business deductions equal or exceed 15% of AOGI.

c. Copyright royalties, *but* the copyright royalties are not added to PHCI *if*

 1. The copyright royalties are 50% or more of OGI,
 2. PHCI computed without the copyright royalties does not exceed 10% of OGI, and
 3. The § 162 trade or business deductions related to the copyright royalties equal or exceed 25% of

  i. The OGI minus the royalties paid, plus
  ii. The depreciation related to the copyright royalties.

d. Software royalties, *but* these are not added to PHCI *if*

 1. The royalties are received in connection with the licensing of computer software by a corporation which is actively engaged in the business of developing, manufacturing, or production of such software,
 2. The software royalties are 50% or more of OGI,
 3. Research and experimental expenditures, § 162 business expenses, and § 195 start-up expenditures allocable to the software business are generally 25% or more of OGI computed with certain adjustments, and
 4. Dividends paid, considered paid, and the consent dividends equal or exceed

  i. PHCI computed without the software royalties and certain interest income
  ii. Minus 10% of OGI.

e. Produced film rents, but the produced film rents are not added to PHCI if the produced film rents equal or exceed 50% of OGI.

f. Rent (for the use of tangible property) received by the corporation from a shareholder owning 25% or more of the value of the corporation's stock. This rent is only included in PHCI if PHCI computed without this rent and without the adjusted income from rents exceeds 10% of OGI.

g. Income from personal service contracts *but only if*

 1. Someone other than the corporation has the right to designate who is to perform the services or if the person who is to perform the services is named in the contract, and
 2. At some time during the taxable year, 25% or more of the value of the corporation's outstanding stock is owned by the person performing the services.

h. Income of estates and trusts taxable to the corporation.

Equals: **Personal holding company income (PHCI)**

---

[87] § 543.

Dividends, Interest, Royalties, and Annuities

The most obvious forms of PHCI are those usually considered passive in nature: dividends, interest, royalties, and annuities.[88] Generally, identification and classification of these items present little problem. The most noteworthy exception concerns royalties. Mineral, oil, gas, copyright, and computer software royalties generally are included in this category of PHCI. However, as seen in Exhibit 6-8, items (b), (c), and (d), these royalties are not treated as PHCI if certain additional tests are satisfied.

Example 9

B Corporation has three stockholders. Its income consisted of

Gross income from a grocery	$52,000
Interest income	38,000
Capital gain	6,000

B Corporation's OGI (See Exhibit 6-4) is $90,000, computed as follows:

Gross income ($52,000 + $38,000 + $6,000)	$96,000
Minus: Capital gains	(6,000)
OGI	$90,000

In this example, AOGI is the same as OGI since the amounts which are subtracted from OGI to arrive at AOGI are zero (see Exhibit 6-5).

B Corporation's PHCI is $38,000, the amount of the interest income (see Exhibit 6-8). Since the corporation's PHCI ($38,000) is not 60% or more of its $90,000 AOGI ($90,000 × 60% = $54,000), it does not meet the income requirement.

Although B Corporation meets the stock ownership requirement since it has only three shareholders, it does not meet *both* the ownership requirement and the income requirement. As a result, it is not a personal holding company and is not subject to the personal holding company tax.

Example 10

Assume the same facts as in *Example 9* except that B Corporation had received $88,000 of interest income.

B Corporation's OGI and AOGI would be computed as follows:

Gross income ($52,000 + $88,000 + $6,000)	$146,000
Minus: Capital gains	(6,000)
OGI (also AOGI)	$140,000

B Corporation's PHCI is now $88,000, the amount of the interest income. Since the corporation's $88,000 of PHCI is more than 60% of the $140,000 AOGI ($140,000 × 60% = $84,000), it meets the income requirement.

Since B Corporation meets both the ownership requirement and the income requirement, *it is* a personal holding company.

Adjusted Income from Rents

Rental income presents a special problem for the personal holding company provisions. Normally, rents—generally defined as compensation for the use of property—represent a passive type of income. However, for many corporations, most notably those involved in renting real estate and equipment, rental operations are not merely a passive investment but represent a true

---

[88] § 543(a)(1).

business activity. If all rental income were considered personal holding income, closely held corporations involved in the rental business could not escape PHI status. To provide these corporations with some relief, rental income is not treated as PHCI under certain circumstances.

The amount of rental income potentially qualifying as PHCI is referred to as the *adjusted income from rents*.[89] As seen in Exhibit 6-6, adjusted income from rents consists of the corporation's gross rental income reduced by the adjustments required for determining AOGI—depreciation, property taxes, interest expense, and rental payments related to such income (e.g., ground lease payments). The corporation's adjusted income from rents is treated as PHCI unless it can utilize the relief measure suggested above. Specifically, adjusted income from rents is PHCI unless: (1) it is 50% or more of the corporation's AOGI, and (2) the corporation's dividends during the taxable year as well as dividends paid within the first 2½ months of the following year *and* consent dividends are not less than the amount by which nonrental PHCI (e.g., dividends and interest) exceeds 10% of OGI.[90]

These relationships may be expressed as follows:

1. Adjusted income from rents $\geq$ (50% $\times$ AOGI); *and*

2. Dividends $\geq$ (nonrental PHCI – [10% $\times$ OGI]).

As the latter expression indicates, when rents represent a substantial portion of OGI relative to nonrental PHCI (as typically would be the case where a corporation is truly in the rental "business"), no dividends are required. In other words, as long as nonrental income is not a major portion of the corporation's total income—does not exceed 10% of the corporation's OGI—dividends are unnecessary. Otherwise, a corporation in the rental business is forced to make dividend distributions to avoid penalty.

Example 11

D Corporation had four shareholders in 2016 and therefore met the stock ownership requirement. The following information is available for D Corporation for 2016:

Interest income	$10,000
Gross rental income	25,000
Depreciation, property taxes, and interest expense related to rental income	24,000
Maintenance and utilities related to rental income	3,000
Dividends paid during 2016	8,000

OGI (Exhibit 6-4) is $35,000 ($10,000 + $25,000). AOGI (see Exhibit 6-5) is computed as follows:

OGI	$35,000
Minus: Depreciation, property taxes, and interest expense related to rental income	(24,000)
AOGI	$11,000

D Corporation's adjusted income from rents is computed as follows (see Exhibit 6-6):

Gross rental income	$25,000
Minus: Depreciation, property taxes, and interest expense related to rental income	(24,000)
Adjusted income from rents	$ 1,000

Note that in determining AOGI and adjusted income from rents, the maintenance and utility expenses are ignored. Such expenses are also not taken into account in determining gross income or OGI. The next step is to determine if the adjusted income from rents is to be added to PHCI. It is *not* added to PHCI if *both* of the following tests are met.

---

[89] § 543(b)(3).   [90] *Ibid.*

Test 1. (50% test): Is the adjusted income from rents (AIR) 50% or more of AOGI? This test also can be expressed as:

- AIR ≥ (50% × AOGI).
- AIR = $1,000.
- (50% × AOGI) = (50% × $11,000 = $6,500).
- Since AIR of $1,000 is not at least $6,500 (50% of AOGI) Test 1 is not met.
- The adjusted income from rents is excluded from PHCI only if both Test 1 and Test 2 are met. Since Test 1 is not met, the adjusted income from rents is included in PHCI, and there is no need to go on to Test 2. However, Test 2 is done here for illustrative purposes.

Test 2. (10% test): Does the total of the dividends paid, the dividends considered paid, and the consent dividends equal or exceed PHCI (computed without the adjusted income from rents) reduced by 10% of OGI? This test also can be expressed as:

- Dividends ≥ (Nonrental PHCI − [10% × OGI]).
- Nonrental PHCI = $10,000 (interest income).
- 10% × OGI = (10% × $35,000) = $3,500.
- Dividends ≥ ($10,000 − $3,500 = $6,500).
- Since the total dividends, $8,000, exceeds $6,500, Test 2 is met.
- As noted above, however, both Test 1 and Test 2 must be met if the adjusted income from rents is to be excluded from PHCI. Since both tests are not met, adjusted income from rents is considered PHCI. Note that when nonrental PHCI is zero no dividend payment is necessary.

D Corporation's PHCI is computed as follows (see Exhibit 6-8):

Interest income	$10,000
Adjusted income from rents	1,000
PHCI	$11,000

D Corporation's $11,000 PHCI is more than 60% of the $11,000 AOGI. In this example, in fact, PHCI is 100% of AOGI since all of the income is personal holding company income. D Corporation, therefore, meets *both* the ownership requirement and the income requirement, and thus is a personal holding company.

The rules relating to mineral, oil, gas, copyright, and software royalties are very similar to those discussed above for rents. See Exhibit 6-7 and Exhibit 6-8, items (b), (c), and (d).

Income from Personal Service Contracts

The shifting of service income to a corporation by highly compensated individuals, such as actors and athletes, is sharply curtailed by the personal holding company provision. The PHC provisions attack the problem by treating service income as PHCI under certain conditions. Generally, amounts received by a corporation for services provided are treated as PHCI if the party desiring the services can designate the person who will perform the services and that person owns 25% or more of the corporation's stock[91] (see Exhibit 6-8, item (g)).

Example 12

T Corp., a producer of motion pictures, wanted RK to act in a new movie it was producing. Assume that RK's services could be obtained only by contracting with his wholly owned corporation, RK Inc. Accordingly, a contract is drafted providing that RK Inc. will provide the services of RK to T Corp. for $500,000. All of the income is PHCI to RK Inc. since RK owns at least 25% of the corporation *and* he is actually designated in the contract to perform the services.

---

[91] § 543(a)(7).

Given the general rule, it would appear that virtually all service corporations are likely candidates for the PHC tax. This problem was considered in Revenue Ruling 75-67.[92] According to the facts of the ruling, a corporation's primary source of income was attributable to the services of its only employee, a doctor, who also owned 80% of the corporation's stock. In this case, all the facts suggested that the income would be PHCI. The only question was whether the doctor's patients formally designated him as the one to perform the services. Although a formal designation was lacking, it was implicit since the doctor was the only employee of the corporation and the patients never expected someone other than the doctor to perform the services. Despite evidence to the contrary, the IRS ruled that the income was not PHCI on the theory that there was no indication that the corporation was obligated to provide the services of the doctor in question. In addition, the ruling emphasized that the services to be performed were not so unique as to prohibit the corporation from substituting someone else to perform them. The Service also relied on the uniqueness rationale in situations involving a CPA who had incorporated his or her practice and a musical composer who had incorporated his or her song-writing activities.[93] Apparently, as long as the services are not so unique as to preclude substitution and there is no formal designation of the individual who will perform the services, a service business can escape PHC status.

COMPUTATION OF THE PHC TAX

The personal holding company penalty tax is 20% of the *undistributed personal holding company income*. Undistributed personal holding company income is defined as adjusted taxable income minus the dividends-paid deduction.[94] The computation of adjusted taxable income and undistributed PHCI is shown in Exhibit 6-9.

LO.7

Explain how the personal holding company tax is computed and how it might be avoided.

EXHIBIT 6-9	Undistributed Personal Holding Company Income[95]

Taxable income

Plus:
- a. Dividends-received deduction.
- b. Net operating loss deduction (but not a net operating loss of the preceding year computed without the dividends-received deduction).
- c. The amount by which the § 162 (trade or business) deductions and the § 167 (depreciation) deductions related to rental property exceed the income produced by the rental property, unless it can be shown that the rent received was the highest possible and that the rental activity was carried on as a bona fide business activity.

Minus:
- a. Federal income taxes (but not the accumulated earnings tax or the personal holding company tax).
- b. The amount by which actual charitable contributions exceeds the charitable contributions deduction reflected in net income.
- c. Net capital gain reduced by the taxes attributable to the net capital gain.

Equals: Adjusted taxable income
Minus: Dividends-Paid Deduction
Equals: Undistributed Personal Holding Company Income

Like the computation of accumulated taxable income, the calculation attempts to determine the corporation's dividend-paying capacity. As a practical matter, the tax is rarely paid because of a deduction allowed for "deficiency dividends," which can be made once it has been determined the PHC tax applies.

---

[92] Rev. Rul. 75-67, 1975-1 C.B. 169.

[93] Rev. Rul. 75-290, 1975-1 C.B. 172; Rev. Rul. 75-249, 1975-1 C.B. 171; and Rev. Rul. 75-250, 1975-1 C.B. 179.

[94] § 545(a). The term "adjusted taxable income" is not found in the Code.

[95] § 545.

Dividends-Paid Deduction

The dividends-paid deduction for personal holding companies is similar to the one for the accumulated earnings tax. It includes the following types of distributions:

1. Dividends paid during the taxable year;

2. Throwback dividends: dividends paid within 2½ months after the close of the taxable year (but subject to limitation as discussed below);

3. Consent dividends;

4. Liquidating distributions; and

5. Deficiency dividends.

Note that this list of qualifying distributions is identical to that provided in Exhibit 6-3 for the accumulated earnings tax, except for the special deficiency dividend. In addition, personal holding companies are entitled to a dividend carryover, which is not available for accumulated earnings tax purposes.[96]

Throwback Dividends. As in the accumulated earnings tax computation, a personal holding company is allowed a deduction for throwback dividends (i.e., dividends paid within 2½ months after the close of the taxable year).[97] However, the PHC throwback dividend differs from that for the accumulated earnings tax in two ways. First, it is included in the dividends-paid deduction only if the corporation makes an election at the time the corporate tax return is filed to treat the dividends as applying to the previous year.[98] Second, the amount treated as a throwback dividend is limited to the smaller of the following:[99]

1. Twenty percent of the dividends actually paid during the taxable year in question; or

2. Undistributed PHCI (computed without the dividends paid during the 2½-month period).

Consent Dividends. The rules for consent dividends are the same for personal holding companies as for the accumulated earnings tax.[100] As mentioned previously, a consent dividend is an amount that a shareholder agrees to consider as having been received as a dividend even though never actually distributed by the corporation. Consent dividends are limited to shareholders who own stock on the last day of the tax year. Their shares must be either common stock or participating preferred stock. Consent dividends do not include preferential dividends. A shareholder who consents to a dividend is treated as having received the amount as a cash dividend and contributing the same amount to the corporation's capital on the last day of the year.

Dividend Carryover. A personal holding company is also entitled to a dividend carryover as part of its dividends-paid deduction.[101] If the dividends paid in the two prior years exceed the adjusted taxable incomes (See Exhibit 6-9) for those years, the excess may be used as a dividend carryover (and therefore as part of the dividends-paid deduction) for the year in question.

Deficiency Dividends. Once a determination has been made that a corporation is subject to the personal holding company tax, the tax can still be abated by the use of a *deficiency dividend*.[102] Following the determination of the personal holding company tax, the corporation is given 90 days to pay a deficiency dividend. A deficiency dividend must be an *actual cash dividend* which the corporation elects to treat as a distribution of the personal holding company income for the year at issue, and it is taxable to the shareholders. It does not reduce the personal holding company income of any year other than the year at issue. A deficiency dividend effectively reduces the amount of the penalty tax. However, interest and penalties are still imposed as if the deduction were not allowed. Thus, the corporation may

---

[96] § 561(a)(3).

[97] § 563.

[98] § 563(b).

[99] *Ibid.*

[100] § 565.

[101] § 564.

[102] § 547.

be able to escape the tax itself—but not any interest or penalties related to such tax. It should also be noted that the deficiency dividend is available *only* to reduce the personal holding company tax. This escape is not available to those corporations subject to the accumulated earnings tax.

Example 13

C Corporation determined that it was a personal holding company and had to file Form 1120-PH. Its records for 2015 reveal the following:

Gross profit from operations	$150,000
Dividend income	400,000
Interest income	350,000
Long-term capital gain	30,000
Gross income	$930,000
Compensation	(30,000)
Selling and administrative	(100,000)
	$800,000
Dividends-received deduction	(280,000)
Charitable contributions	(80,000)
Taxable income	$440,000
Federal income tax at 34%	$149,600

Charitable contributions actually made during the year were $90,000, but are limited to $80,000 (10% × $800,000 taxable income before the deductions for contributions and dividends received). C paid dividends of $20,000 in 2015 and $10,000 during the first 2½ months of 2016, which it *elects* to throw back to 2015 in computing the dividends-paid deduction. The personal holding company tax is computed as follows:

	Taxable income	$440,000
+	Dividends-received deduction	280,000
–	Excess charitable contributions	(10,000)
–	Federal income taxes	(149,600)
–	Long-term capital gain net of tax ($30,000 – [34% × $30,000])	(19,800)
	Adjustable taxable income	$540,600
–	Dividends paid deduction:	
	2015	(20,000)
	2016 throwback (Limited to 20% of 2015 dividends)	(4,000)
	UPHCI	$516,600
	Times: PHC tax rate	× 20%
	PHC tax	$103,320

C Corporation's tax liability for 2015 is $252,920 ($149,600 regular tax + $103,320 PHC tax). The PHC tax could be avoided by paying a deficiency dividend equal to UPHCI ($516,600). However, the payment of the dividend would not eliminate any penalties or interest that might be assessed on the $103,320 PHC tax due if Form 1120-PH is not filed in a timely manner.

ACCUMULATED EARNINGS TAX

For taxpayers wanting to use the corporate form to shield their income from individual taxes, the accumulated earnings tax represents a formidable obstacle. Although there is an obvious cost if the tax is incurred, that cost may be far more than expected. This result often occurs because the imposition of the tax for one year triggers an audit for all open years. In addition, the IRS usually takes the position that the negligence penalty of Code § 6653 should be imposed whenever the accumulated earnings tax is applicable. Moreover, in contrast to the personal holding company tax which can normally be averted using the deficiency dividend procedure, the accumulated earnings tax, once levied, cannot be avoided. At the time of the audit, it is too late for dividend payments or consent dividends!

Despite the potential cost of the tax, the rewards from avoidance—or at least the deferral—of double taxation are often so great that the shareholders are willing to assume the risk of penalty. Moreover, many practitioners believe that with proper planning the risk of incurring the accumulated earnings tax is minimal, particularly since the tax is not self-assessed but dependent on the audit lottery. In addition, it is possible to shift the burden of proof to the IRS. The discussion below examines some of the means for reducing the taxpayer's exposure to the accumulated earnings tax.

Liquid Assets and Working Capital

Normally, the accumulated earnings tax is not raised as an issue unless the corporation's balance sheet shows cash, marketable securities, or other liquid assets that could be distributed easily to shareholders. The absence of liquid assets indicates that any earnings that have been retained have been reinvested in the business rather than accumulated for the forbidden purpose. It is a rare occasion, however, when such assets do not exist. Consequently, most IRS agents routinely assess whether the level of the corporation's working capital is appropriate by applying the *Bardahl* formula.

The courts have made it clear that the *Bardahl* formula serves merely as a guideline for determining the proper amount of working capital. In *Delaware Trucking Co., Inc.*, the court held that the amount needed using the *Bardahl* formula could be increased by 75% due to the possibility of increased labor and other operating costs due to inflation.[103] Nevertheless, in those instances where working capital appears excessive, the Internal Revenue Manual directs agents to require justification of such excess. Therefore, the corporation should closely control its working capital to ensure that it does not exceed the corporation's reasonable needs.

One way to reduce working capital is to increase shareholder salaries, bonuses, and other compensation. Since these payments are deductible, double taxation is avoided. This technique also has the benefit of reducing taxable income, which in turn reduces the accumulated earnings tax should it apply. However, this method of reducing working capital may not be feasible if the compensation paid exceeds a reasonable amount. To the extent that the compensation is unreasonable, the payments are treated as dividends and double taxation results. In addition, if the unreasonable compensation is not pro rata among all shareholders, the dividend will be considered preferential and no deduction will be allowed for the dividend in computing adjusted taxable income.

Another method for reducing working capital is for the corporation to invest in additional assets. However, the taxpayer must be careful to avoid investments that are of a passive nature or that could be considered unrelated to the corporation's existing or projected business. With respect to the latter, the courts have ruled that the business of a controlled subsidiary is the business of the parent while the business of a sister corporation normally is not the business of its brother.[104]

Reasonable Needs

The courts have accepted a variety of reasons as sufficient justification for the accumulation of earnings. On the one hand, the needs deemed reasonable have been both certain and

---

[103] 32 TCM 104, T.C. Memo 1973-29.

[104] For example, see *Latchis Theatres of Keene, Inc. v. Comm.*, 54-2 USTC ¶9544, 45 AFTR 1836, 214 F.2d 834 (CA-1, 1954).

well-defined, such as the repayment of corporate debt. On the other hand, the courts have approved needs as contingent and unknown as those arising from possible damage from future floods.

One contingency that seemingly could be asserted by all corporations as a basis for accumulating funds is the possibility of a business reversal, depression, or loss of major customer. Interestingly, the courts have often respected this justification for accumulations, notwithstanding the fact that it is a risk assumed by virtually all business entities. Acceptance of this need, however, appears to be dependent on the taxpayer's ability to establish that there is at least some chance that a business reversal could occur that would affect the taxpayer. For example, in *Ted Bates & Co.*, the corporation was in the advertising business and received 70% of its fees from only five clients.[105] In ruling for the taxpayer, the court held that the corporation was allowed to accumulate amounts necessary to cover its fixed costs for a period following the loss of a major client. Much of the court's opinion was based on its view that the advertising business was extremely competitive and the possibility of losing a client was not unrealistic. A similar decision was reached where a manufacturer sold all its products to one customer and had to compete with others for that customer's business. The court believed that accumulations were necessary to enable the corporation to develop new markets if it lost its only customer. Relying on a possible downturn in business as a basis for accumulations has not always sufficed. In *Goodall*, the company accumulated earnings in light of the prospect that military orders would be lost.[106] The court upheld the penalty tax, indicating that even if the loss occurred, it would not have a significant effect because the corporation's business was expanding.

Although the courts have sustained various reasons for accumulations, a review of the cases indicates that the taxpayer must demonstrate that the need is realistic. This was made clear in *Colonial Amusement Corp.*[107] In this case, the corporation's accumulations were not justified when it wanted to construct a building on adjacent land and building restrictions existed that prohibited construction.

In establishing that a need is realistic, a taxpayer's self-serving statement normally is not convincing. Proper documentation of the need is critical. This is true even when the need is obvious and acceptable. In *Union Offset,* the corporation stated at trial that its accumulations were necessary to retire outstanding corporate debt, a legitimate business need.[108] To the taxpayer's dismay, however, the Tax Court still imposed the tax because the corporation had failed to document in any type of written record its plan to use the accumulations in the alleged manner. In this case, a simple statement in the Board of Directors' minutes concerning the proposed use of the funds would no doubt have saved the taxpayer from penalty.

S Corporation Election

In those cases where it is difficult to justify accumulations, the shareholders may wish to elect to be treated as an S corporation. Since the earnings of an S corporation are taxed to the individual shareholders rather than the corporation, S corporations cannot be used to shelter income and thus are immune to the accumulated earnings tax. However, the election insulates the corporation only prospectively (i.e., only for that period for which it is, an S corporation). Prior years open to audit are still vulnerable. In addition, the S election may raise other problems. The shareholders will be required to report and pay taxes on the income of the corporation even though it may not be distributed to them. As a result, cash flow problems may occur. Further, because the corporation has accumulated earnings and profits, the excess passive income tax specifically designed for C corporations that have elected S status may apply. In addition, the corporation may be subject to the built-in gains tax.[109] For these reasons, an S election should be carefully considered.

PERSONAL HOLDING COMPANY TAX

The personal holding company tax, like the accumulated earnings tax, is clearly a tax to be avoided. Unfortunately, the personal holding company tax differs from the accumulated earnings tax in that it is not reserved solely for those whose intent is to avoid taxes. Rather, it is applied on a mechanical basis, regardless of motive, to all corporations that fall within

---

[105] 24 TCM 1346, T.C. Memo 1965-251.

[106] *Robert A. Goodall Estate v. Comm.*, 68-1 USTC ¶9245, 21 AFTR2d 813, 391 F.2d 775, (CA-8.1968).

[107] 7 TCM 546.

[108] 79-2 USTC ¶9550, 603 F.2d 90 (CA-9, 1979).

[109] See Chapter 12 for a discussion of these special taxes that may be imposed on S corporations.

its purview. For this reason, it is important to closely monitor the corporation's activities to ensure that it does not inadvertently become a PHC.

One important responsibility of a practitioner is to recognize potential personal holding company problems so that steps can be taken to avoid the tax or the need to distribute dividends. This responsibility not only concerns routine operations but extends to advice concerning planned transactions that could cause the corporation to be converted from an operating company to an investment company. For example, a corporation may plan to sell one or all of its businesses and invest the proceeds in passive type assets. Similarly, a planned reorganization (discussed in Chapter 7) may leave the corporation holding stock of the acquiring corporation. Failure to identify the possible personal holding company difficulty which these and other transactions may cause can lead to serious embarrassment.

Although the thrust of most tax planning for personal holding companies concerns how to avoid the tax, there are certain instances when a planned PHC can provide benefits. Both varieties of personal holding companies, the planned and the unplanned, are discussed below.

PHC Candidates

All corporations could fall victim to the PHC tax. However, some corporations are more likely candidates than others. For this reason, their activities and anticipated transactions should be scrutinized more carefully than others.

Potential difficulties often concern corporations that are involved in rental activities and those that have some passive income. In this regard, it should be noted that the term "rent" is defined as payments received for the use of property. As a result, "rental companies" include not only those that lease such items as apartments, offices, warehouses, stadiums, equipment, vending machines, automobiles, trucks, and the like, but also those that operate bowling alleys, roller and ice skating rinks, billiards parlors, golf courses, and any other activity for which a payment is received for use of the corporation's property. All of these corporations are at risk since each has rental income which could be considered passive personal holding company income unless it satisfies the special two-prong test for rental companies.

There are several other types of corporations that must be concerned with PHC problems. Investment companies—corporations formed primarily to acquire income producing assets such as stock, bonds, rental properties, partnership interests, and similar investments—clearly have difficulties. Corporations that derive most of their income from the services of one or more of their shareholders also are vulnerable. In recent years, however, the Service has taken a liberal view toward the professional corporations of doctors, accountants, and several others. Another group of corporations that are probable targets of the PHC tax includes those that collect royalty income. The royalty income might arise from the corporation's development and licensing of a product (e.g., patent on a food processor or franchises to operate a restaurant). Other logical candidates for the PHC tax are banks, savings and loans, and finance companies since the majority of their income is interest income from making loans and purchasing or discounting accounts receivable and installment obligations. Banks and savings and loans need not worry, however, since they are specifically excluded from PHC status. Finance companies are also exempt from the penalty tax, but only if certain tests—not discussed here—are met. Consequently, those involved with finance companies should review their situation closely to ensure such tests are satisfied.

Avoiding PHC Status

In general, if a corporation is closely held and 60% of its income is derived from passive sources or specified personal services, the PHC tax applies. Thus, to avoid the PHC tax *either* the stock ownership test or the income test must be failed.

Stock Ownership Test

The stock ownership test is satisfied if five or fewer persons own more than 50% of the stock. This test is the most difficult to fail since it requires dilution of the current shareholders' ownership. Moreover, dilution is very difficult to implement in practice due to the constructive ownership rules. The rules make it virtually impossible to maintain ownership in the family since stock owned by one family member or an entity in which the family member has an interest is considered owned by other family members. Therefore, to fail the ownership test, sufficient stock must be owned by unrelated parties to reduce the ownership of the five largest shareholders to 50% or less. Unfortunately, it is often impossible to design an arrangement that meets these conditions yet is still desirable from an economic viewpoint.

Passive Income Test

The corporation is deemed to satisfy the passive income test if 60% of its adjusted ordinary gross income (AOGI) is personal holding company income (PHCI)—income from dividends, interest, annuities, rents, royalties, or specified shareholder services. The potential for failing this test is perhaps more easily seen when this test is expressed mathematically:

$$\frac{PHCI}{AOGI} \geq 60\%$$

The steps that can be taken to fail this test fall into three categories: (1) increasing operating income or AOGI, (2) reducing PHCI, and (3) satisfying the exceptions to remove the PHC taint from the income.

Increasing Operating Income

One way to fail the 60% test is to increase the denominator in the income test fraction, AOGI, without increasing the numerator. This requires the corporation to increase its operating income without any corresponding increase in its passive income. Obtaining such an increase is not easy since it is essentially asking that the corporation generate more gross income. This does not necessarily mean that sales must increase, however. The corporation might consider increasing its profit margin. Although this could reduce sales, the resulting increase in gross income could be sufficient to fail the test. Alternatively, the corporation might consider expanding the operating portion of the business. Expansion not only increases AOGI but also may have the effect of reducing PHCI if the investments generating the PHCI are sold to invest in the expansion.

Reducing Personal Holding Income

Failing the income test normally is accomplished by reducing personal holding company income. It is sometimes asserted that merely reducing PHCI is not sufficient since both the numerator and the denominator in the test fraction are reduced by the same amounts. (This occurs because AOGI includes PHCI.) A mathematical check of this statement shows that it is incorrect and that a simple elimination of PHCI aids the taxpayer.

Example 14

Z Corporation has $100,000 of AOGI, including $70,000 of interest income that is PHCI. Substituting these values into the test fraction reveals that the corporation has excessive passive income.

$$\frac{PHCI}{AOGI} = \frac{\$70,000}{\$100,000} = 70\%$$

If Z Corporation simply reduces its interest income by $30,000, the corporation would fail the income test despite the fact that both the numerator and the denominator are reduced by the same amounts.

$$\frac{PHCI}{AOGI} = \frac{\$40,000}{\$70,000} = 57.1\%$$

One way a corporation could eliminate part of its PHCI is by paying out as shareholder compensation the amounts that otherwise would be invested to generate PHCI. Alternatively, the corporation could eliminate PHCI by switching its investments into growth stocks where the return is generated from capital appreciation rather than dividends. Of course, the taxpayer would not necessarily want to switch completely out of dividend-paying stocks since the advantage of the dividends-received deduction would be lost.

The corporation could also reduce its PHCI by replacing it with tax-exempt income, capital gains, or § 1231 gains. This would have the same effect as simply eliminating the PHCI altogether.

Example 15

Same as *Example 14* above except the corporation invests in tax-exempt bonds which generate $20,000 of tax-exempt, rather than taxable, interest. In addition, the corporation realizes a $10,000 capital gain instead of taxable interest. The effect of replacing the taxable interest of $30,000 with capital gains of $10,000 and tax-exempt income of $20,000 would produce results identical to those above. This derives from the fact that the tax-exempt interest and capital gains are excluded from both the numerator, PHCI, and the denominator, AOGI, creating fractions identical to those shown above.

Removing the PHC Taint

In some situations, income which is normally considered PHCI (e.g., rental income) is not considered tainted if certain tests are met. For example, the Code provides escape hatches for rental income; mineral, oil, and gas royalties; copyright royalties; and rents from the distribution and exhibition of produced films. Although additional tests must be met to obtain exclusion for these types of income, there is one requirement common to each. *Generally,* if a corporation's income consists predominantly (50% or more) of only one of these income types, exclusion is available. More importantly, this condition can normally be obtained without great difficulty. To satisfy the 50% test, the taxpayer should take steps to ensure that a particular corporation receives only a single type of income. This may require forming an additional corporation that receives only one type of income, but by so doing the 50% test is met and the PHC tax may be avoided.

With proper control of their income, these corporations will have no difficulty in satisfying the income test since at least 50% of their AOGI is from one source. For corporations with rental income, however, dividends equal to the amount that their nonrental PHC income exceeds 10% of their OGI still must be paid. Note, however, that if a corporation has little or no nonrental PHC income, no dividends are necessary to meet the test. Also note that each additional dollar of gross rents, unreduced by expenses, decreases the amount of dividend that must be paid.

Example 16

G Corporation has $60,000 of OGI, including $53,000 of rental income and $7,000 of dividend income. In this case, dividends of only $1,000 are necessary since nonrental PHCI exceeds the 10% threshold by only $1,000 ($7,000 − [10% of OGI of $60,000]). If the taxpayer wants to avoid distributing dividends, consideration should be given to increasing gross rents. Note how an increase of $10,000 in gross rents to $63,000 would increase OGI and concomitantly eliminate the need for a dividend. This increase in gross rents would be effective even if the typical adjustments for depreciation, interest, and taxes reduce the taxpayer's net profit to zero or a loss. This is true because such adjustments are not included in determining OGI, but only AOGI. Thus, an incentive exists for the corporation to invest in breakeven or unprofitable activities as a means to eliminate the dividend.

Reducing the PHC Tax with Dividends

If the tests for PHC status cannot be avoided, the penalty can be eliminated or minimized by the payment of dividends. Although a similar opportunity exists for the accumulated earnings tax, the treatment of dividends differs in several important respects.

On the one hand, the PHC tax requires quicker action than the accumulated earnings tax. For accumulated earnings tax purposes, all dividends paid within the 2½-month period after the close of the taxable year are counted as paid for the previous year. However, for purposes of the PHC tax, the after-year-end dividends are limited to 20% of the amount actually paid during the year. Thus, if no dividends are paid during the year, then none can be paid during the 2½-month period. On the other hand, the PHC tax can almost always be avoided through payment of a deficiency dividend, which is not available for the accumulated earnings tax. The deficiency dividend may come at a high price, however. As previously mentioned, any interest and penalties that would have been imposed had the penalty tax applied must be computed and paid as if the PHC tax were still due.

Planned Personal Holding Companies

Treatment of a corporation as a personal holding company is normally considered a dire consequence. Yet, in certain cases, PHC status may not be detrimental and at times can be beneficial. Two of these situations are outlined below.

Certain taxpayers seeking the benefits of the corporate form are unable to avoid characterization as a personal holding company. For example, an athlete or movie celebrity may seek the benefits reserved solely for employees, such as group-term life insurance, health and accident insurance, medical reimbursement plans, and better pension and profit-sharing plans. In these situations, if the individual incorporates his or her talents, the corporation will be considered a PHC since all of the income for services will be PHCI. This does not mean that the PHC tax must be paid, however. The PHC tax is levied only upon undistributed PHCI. In most cases, all of the undistributed PHCI can be eliminated through the payments of deductible compensation directly to the individual or deductible contributions to his or her pension plan. As a result, the individual can obtain the benefits of incorporation without concern for the PHC tax. This technique was extremely popular prior to 1982, when the benefits of corporate pension plans were significantly better than those available to the self-employed (i.e., Keogh plans).

Over the years, personal holding companies have been used quite successfully in estate planning in reducing the value of the taxpayer's estate and obtaining other estate tax benefits. Under a typical plan, a taxpayer with a portfolio of securities would transfer them to a PHC in exchange for preferred stock equal to their current value and common stock of no value. The exchange would be tax free under Code § 351. The taxpayer would then proceed to give the common stock to his or her children at no gift tax cost since its value at the time is zero. The taxpayer would also begin a gift program, transferring $10,000 of preferred stock annually to heirs, which would also escape gift tax due to the annual gift tax exclusion. There were several benefits arising from this arrangement.

First and probably foremost, any appreciation in the value of the taxpayer's portfolio would accrue to the owners of the common stock and thus be successfully removed from the taxpayer's estate, avoiding both gift and estate taxes. Second, the corporation's declaration of dividends on the common stock would shift the income to the lower-bracket family members. Dividends on the preferred stock would also be shifted to the extent that the taxpayer has transferred the preferred stock. The dividends paid would in part aid in eliminating any PHC tax. Third, the taxpayer's preferred stock in the PHC would probably be valued at less than the value of the underlying assets for estate and gift tax purposes. Although the IRS takes the position that the value of the stock in the PHC is the same as the value of the corporation's assets, the courts have consistently held otherwise. The courts have normally allowed a substantial *discount* for estate and gift tax valuation, holding that an investment in a closely held business is less desirable than in the underlying shares since the underlying securities can easily be traded in the market while the PHC shares cannot.[110]

---

[110] For example, see *Estate of Maurice Gustane Heckscher*, 63 T.C. 485 (1974). Also, See Chapter 15 for possible limitations on this estate planning technique.

Problem Materials

DISCUSSION QUESTIONS

6-1 *Double Taxation.* List four approaches that corporations use to avoid the effects of double taxation.

6-2 *Accumulated Earnings Tax.* What is the purpose of the accumulated earnings tax?

6-3 *Accumulated Earnings Tax.* What is the accumulated earnings tax rate? Why do you suppose Congress chose this particular tax rate?

6-4 *Accumulated Taxable Income.* What is the difference between accumulated taxable income and taxable income?

6-5 *Accumulated Earnings Credit.* What is the accumulated earnings credit? How does it affect the accumulated earnings tax?

6-6 *Dividends-Paid Deduction.* What constitutes the dividends-paid deduction for purposes of the accumulated earnings tax?

6-7 *Throwback Dividend.* What is a throwback dividend?

6-8 *Consent Dividends.* What is a consent dividend? What is its purpose?

6-9 *Intent of Accumulations.* What situations are considered to indicate the intent of a corporation to unreasonably accumulate earnings?

6-10 *Reasonable Needs.* List six possible reasons for accumulating earnings that might be considered reasonable needs of the business.

6-11 *Reasonable Needs—The Bardahl Formula.* What is the *Bardahl* formula? How is it used?

6-12 *Personal Holding Company Tax.* What is the purpose of the personal holding company tax?

6-13 *Personal Holding Company.* What requirements must be met by a corporation in order for it to be a personal holding company?

6-14 *Ownership Requirement.* What is the ownership requirement for personal holding companies? What constructive ownership rules apply?

6-15 *Income Requirement.* What is the income requirement for personal holding companies? What terms must be defined in order to determine if a corporation meets the income requirement?

6-16 *Income Requirement.* What tests must be met in order to determine whether the adjusted income from rents is included in personal holding company income?

6-17 *Computing the Personal Holding Company Tax.* How is the personal holding company penalty tax computed?

6-18 *Adjusted Taxable Income.* How does adjusted taxable income differ from taxable income?

6-19 *Dividends-Paid Deduction.* How does the dividends-paid deduction for personal holding company tax purposes differ from the dividends-paid deduction for accumulated earnings tax purposes?

6-20 *Deficiency Dividends.* What is a deficiency dividend? What is its purpose? What effect does it have on the personal holding company tax?

PROBLEMS

6-21 *Computing the Accumulated Earnings Tax.* X Corporation had accumulated taxable income of $220,000 for the current year. Calculate X Corporation's accumulated earnings tax liability.

6-22 *Computing Adjusted Taxable Income.* R Corporation has the following income and deductions for the current year:

Income from operations.	$200,000
Dividend income (from less than 20% owned corporations)	60,000
Charitable contributions.	40,000

Compute R Corporation's adjusted taxable income.

6-23 *Minimum Accumulated Earnings Tax Credit.* D Corporation, a calendar year manufacturing company, had accumulated earnings and profits at the beginning of the current year of $70,000. If the corporation's earnings and profits for the current year are $290,000, what is D Corporation's minimum earnings tax credit?

6-24 *Accumulated Earnings Tax Credit.* Assume the same facts as *Problem 6-23* above except that D corporation has estimated reasonable business needs of $190,000 at the end of the current year.
  a. Compute D Corporation's accumulated earnings tax credit for the current year.
  b. Would your answer differ if D Corporation was an incorporated law practice owned and operated by one person? If so, by how much?

6-25 *Computing the Accumulated Earnings Tax.* U Corporation had accumulated earnings and profits at the beginning of 2016 of $340,000. It has never paid dividends to its shareholders and does not intend to do so in the near future. The following facts relate to U Corporation's 2016 tax year:

Taxable income	$210,000
Federal income tax	64,750
Dividends received (from less than 20% owned corporations)	50,000
Reasonable business needs as of 12/31/2016	364,950

  a. What is U Corporation's accumulated earnings tax?
  b. If U Corporation's sole shareholder wanted to avoid the accumulated earnings tax, what amount of consent dividends would be required?

6-26 *Dividends-Paid Deduction.* J Corporation, a small oil tool manufacturer, projects adjusted taxable income for the current year of $200,000. Its estimated reasonable business needs are $500,000; and the corporation has $380,000 of prior years' accumulated earnings and profits as of the beginning of the current year. Using this information, answer the following:
  a. Assuming no dividends-paid deduction, what is J Corporation's accumulated earnings tax for the current year?
  b. If J Corporation paid $50,000 of dividends during the year, what is J Corporation's accumulated earnings tax liability?
  c. If J Corporation's shareholders are willing to report more dividends than the $50,000 actually received during the year, what amount of consent dividends is necessary to avoid the accumulated earnings tax?
  d. If the corporation's shareholders are not interested in paying taxes on hypothetical dividends, what other possibility is available to increase the dividends-paid deduction?

6-27 *Working Capital Needs—The Bardahl Formula.* Y Corporation wishes to use the *Bardahl* formula to determine the amount of working capital it can justify if the IRS agent currently auditing the company's records raises the accumulated earnings tax issue. For the year under audit, Y Corporation had the following:

Annual operating expenses	$315,000
Inventory cycle ratio	0.43
Accounts receivable cycle ratio	0.59
Accounts payable cycle ratio	0.84

  a. How much working capital can Y Corporation justify based on the above facts?
  b. If Y Corporation's turnover ratios are based on annual averages, what additional information would you request before computing working capital needs based on the *Bardahl* formula?

6-28 *Working Capital Needs—Bardahl Formula.* B owns and operates BKA Inc., which is a retail toy store. One Wednesday morning in January 2017, she noticed in the *Wall Street Journal's* tax column an anecdote about a small corporation that was required to pay the accumulated earnings tax. Concerned, B presented the following information to her tax advisor to evaluate her exposure as of the end of 2016.

Balance Sheet

	2015	2016
Current assets:		
Cash	$ 15,000	$ 30,000
Marketable securities (cost)	10,000	23,000
Accounts receivable (net)	55,000	45,000
Inventory	30,000	50,000
Property, plant, and equipment (net)	500,000	552,000
Total assets	$610,000	$700,000
Current liabilities:		
Accounts payable	$ 13,000	$ 31,000
Long-term debt	147,000	119,000
Common stock	50,000	50,000
Earnings and profits	400,000	500,000
Total liabilities and equity	$610,000	$700,000

Income Statement

Sales		$400,000
Cost of goods sold:		
Beginning inventory	$ 30,000	
Purchases	220,000	
Ending inventory	(50,000)	
Total		(200,000)
Gross profit		$200,000
Other expenses:		
Depreciation	$ 70,000	
Selling expenses and administrative	25,000	
Interest	5,000	
Total		(100,000)
Net income before taxes		$100,000
Income taxes		(25,750)
Net income		$ 74,250

B noted that the market value of the securities was $40,000 as of December 31, 2016. In addition, B estimates the future expansion of the business (excluding working capital) will require $25,000. Determine whether the accumulated earnings tax will apply to B.

6-29 *Personal Holding Company—Income Requirement.* L Corporation is equally owned and operated by three brothers. L Corporation's gross income for the current year is $95,000, which consists of $15,000 of dividend income, interest income of $50,000 and a long-term capital gain of $30,000.

    a. Calculate ordinary gross income.

    b. Calculate adjusted ordinary gross income.

    c. Is L Corporation a personal holding company?

6-30 *Personal Holding Company—Rent Exclusion.* T Corporation has gross income of $116,000, which consists of gross rental income of $86,000, interest income of $20,000, and dividends of $10,000. Depreciation, property taxes, and interest expense related to the rental property totaled $16,000. Assuming T Corporation has seven shareholders and has no dividends-paid deduction, answer the following:

    a. What is T Corporation's ordinary gross income?

    b. Adjusted ordinary gross income?

    c. Does the rental income constitute personal holding company income?

    d. Is T Corporation a personal holding company?

6-31 *Personal Holding Company—Income.* T Corporation is equally owned by two shareholders. The corporation reports the following income and deductions for the current year:

Dividend income	$35,000
Interest income	12,000
Long-term capital gain	11,000
Rental income (gross)	90,000
Rental expenses:	
Depreciation	12,000
Interest on mortgage	10,000
Property taxes	4,000
Real estate management fees	9,000

    a. Calculate ordinary gross income.

    b. Calculate adjusted ordinary gross income.

    c. Calculate adjusted income from rentals.

    d. Calculate personal holding company income.

    e. Is T Corporation a personal holding company?

    f. If T Corporation paid $5,000 of dividends to each of its two shareholders during the current year, how would this affect your answers to (d) and (e) above?

6-32 *Items of PHC Income.* Indicate whether the following would be considered personal holding company income.

    a. Income from the sales of inventory.

    b. Interest income from AT&T bond.

    c. Interest income from State of Texas bond.

    d. Dividend income from IBM stock.

    e. Long-term capital gain.

    f. Short-term capital gain.

    g. Rental income from lease of office building (100% of the corporation's income is from rents).

    h. Fees paid to the corporation for the services of Jose Greatfoot, internationally known soccer player.

6-33 *PHC Income Tax Test.* All of the stock of X Corporation is owned by A. Next year, the corporation expects the following results from operations:

Sales	$550,000
Costs of goods sold	225,000
Other operating expenses	50,000
Interest income	20,000

What is the maximum amount of dividend income that the corporation can have without being classified as a personal holding company?

6-34 *Computing the Personal Holding Company Tax.* P Corporation is owned by five individuals. For the current year P had the following:

Taxable income	$200,000
Federal income tax	60,750
Dividends received (from less than 20% owned corporations).	40,000
Long-term capital gain.	10,000

Compute P Corporation's personal holding company tax assuming that P meets the income test, P did not pay dividends, and the long-term capital gain was taxed at 34 percent.

6-35 *Personal Holding Company—Dividend Deduction.* Y, a personal holding company, anticipates having undistributed personal holding company income of $150,000 before any dividend deduction for 2016. The company wishes to distribute all of its income to avoid the penalty. Because of cash flow problems, it wishes to pay as much of this dividend as it can in the 2½ months after the close of the tax year.
   a. What is the maximum that Y can distribute during 2017 to accomplish its task if dividends of $60,000 were paid in 2016?
   b. What is the minimum amount that Y can distribute during 2016 and still be able to defer until 2017 the payment of any additional dividends?

6-36 *Personal Holding Company—Service Income.* J, an orthopedic surgeon, is the sole owner of J Inc. The corporation employs surgical nurses and physical therapists in addition to J. The nurses assist Dr. J on all operations, and the therapists provide all follow-up treatment. J Inc. bills all clients for all services rendered and pays the employees a stated salary. Will any of J Inc.'s fee be personal holding company income?

6-37 *PHC Dividends—Paid Deduction.* Indicate whether the following distributions would qualify for the personal holding company dividends-paid deduction for 2016. Assume that the corporation is a calendar year taxpayer.
   a. Cash dividends paid on common stock in 2016.
   b. Dividend distribution of land (value $30,000 basis $10,000) paid on common stock in 2016.
   c. Cash dividends paid on common stock March 3, 2017.
   d. Cash dividends paid on common stock in 2015.
   e. Consent dividends, the 2016 corporate tax return was filed on March 3, 2017, the consent was filed on May 15, 2017.
   f. Cash dividend paid on 2019 shortly after it was determined that the corporation was a personal holding company.
   g. The corporation adopted a plan of liquidation in 2014 and the final liquidating distribution was made during 2016.

6-38 *Accumulated Earnings Tax Dividends—Paid Dividends.* Indicate whether the distributions identified in *Problem 6-37* would qualify for the accumulated earnings tax dividends paid deduction for 2016.

6-39 *Understanding the PHC Tax.* Indicate whether the following statements regarding the personal holding company tax are true or false.
   a. The PHC tax is self-assessed and, if applicable, must be paid in addition to the regular income tax.
   b. An S corporation or partnership may be subject to the PHC tax.
   c. A corporation that can prove that its shareholders did not intend to use it as a tax shelter is not subject to the PHC tax.
   d. A publicly traded corporation normally would not be subject to the PHC tax.
   e. A corporation that derives virtually all of its income from leasing operations does not risk the PHC tax, even though such income is normally considered passive.
   f. Federal income taxes reduce the base on which the PHC tax is assessed.

   g. Long-term capital gains are not subject to the PHC tax.

   h. A corporation that consistently pays dividends normally would not be subject to the PHC tax.

   i. Throwback dividends are available to reduce the corporation's potential liability without limitation.

   j. Corporations without cash or property that they can distribute cannot benefit from the dividends-paid deduction.

   k. The PHC tax is not truly a risk because of the deficiency dividend procedure.

   l. A corporation may be required to pay both the accumulated earnings tax and the personal holding company tax in the same year.

6-40 *Understanding the Accumulated Earnings Tax.* Indicate whether the statements in *Problem 6-39* are true or false regarding the accumulated earnings tax.

TAX RESEARCH PROBLEMS

6-41 H Corporation is owned and operated by William and Wilma Holt. The corporation's principal source of income for the past few years has been net rentals from five adjacent rent houses located in an area that the city has condemned in order to expand its freeway system. The Holts anticipate a condemnation award of approximately $400,000, and a resulting gain of $325,000. Although convinced that they will have the corporation reinvest the proceeds in other rental units, the Holts would like to invest the corporation's condemnation proceeds in a high-yield certificate of deposit for at least three years. They have come to you for advice.

   a. What advice would you give concerning the reinvestment requirements of Code § 1033?

   b. If H Corporation will have substantial interest income in the next few years, could the § 541 tax be a possibility?

   c. If the Holts have considered liquidating the corporation and reinvesting the proceeds in rental units, what additional information would you need in order to advise them?

6-42 Stacey Caniff is the controlling shareholder of Cotton, Inc., a textile manufacturer. She inherited the business from her father. In recent years earnings have fluctuated between $0.50 and $3.00 per share. Dividends have remained at $0.10 per share for the past ten years with a resulting increase in cash. On audit, the IRS agent has raised the accumulated earnings tax issue. In your discussion with Stacey, she has indicated that the dividends are so low because she is afraid of losing the business (as almost happened to her father during the Depression), of decreased profitability from foreign competition, and of the need to modernize if OSHA were to enforce the rules concerning cotton dust. Evaluate the possibility of overcoming an accumulated earnings tax assessment.

Advanced Corporate Tax Topics

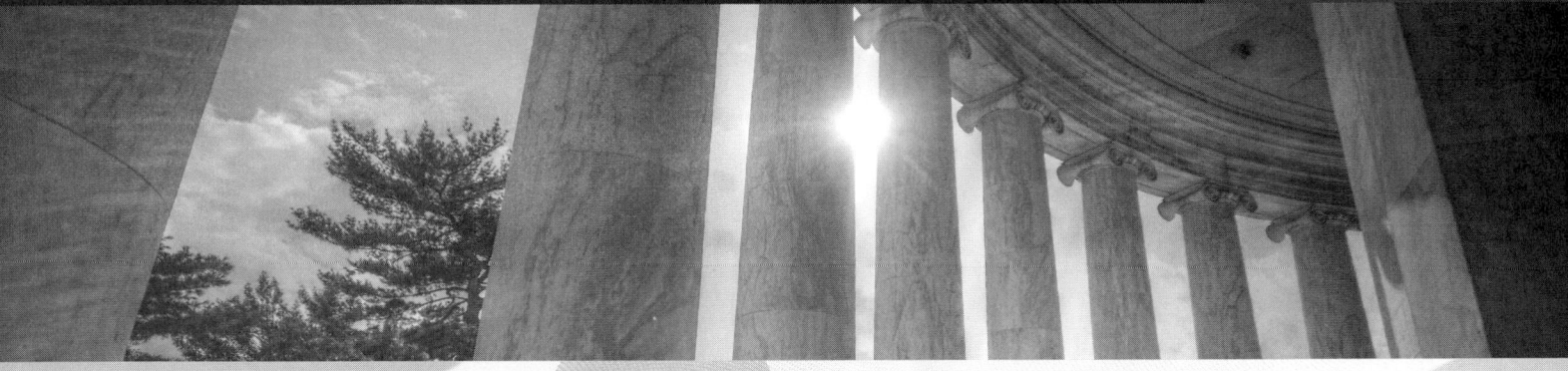

Corporate Reorganizations

7

Learning Objectives

Upon completion of this chapter you will be able to:

LO.1 Understand the basic tax consequences arising from corporate reorganizations, including corporate mergers, acquisitions, and divisions.

LO.2 Describe the seven different types of reorganizations and what requirements must be met for nontaxable treatment.

LO.3 Discuss the tax treatment of the acquiring corporation, the target corporation, and the target's shareholders.

LO.4 Explain the rules governing the carryover of the tax attributes from one corporation to another.

Chapter Outline

Introduction

During its life, circumstances may arise that cause a corporation to alter the form in which it conducts its business. For instance, a corporation may want to combine its business operations with another corporation, or conversely, split its operations into several parts. Over the past 25 years, corporations have often found that restructuring is necessary for economic survival and growth. As a result, business combinations—mergers and acquisitions—and divisions have been rampant. Perhaps the most striking example of a corporate restructuring was the breakup of American Telephone and Telegraph Corporation in 1983 into eight separate companies. This divestiture can be contrasted with the merger of General Electric and RCA. Since these corporate divisions and combinations usually involve exchanges of stock and property, they normally would be taxable transactions without special treatment. To ensure that the tax laws would not impede corporate realignments, Congress enacted certain provisions that allow for nonrecognition of gain or loss in various types of corporate reorganizations.

The reorganization provisions contained in the tax law are not confined to situations involving corporate giants such as AT&T. Rather, they exist to enable corporations of any size to restructure to meet business needs without the interference of taxes. The following example illustrates a typical situation in which the reorganization rules apply.

Example 1

A highly successful cable television company, CTV, desires to expand by acquiring FM, a corporation, owning a radio station in Chicago. CTV's management is convinced that their expertise can be used to make FM a very profitable operation. The acquisition of the radio station could be made in several ways. CTV could purchase the stock of FM from its shareholders and operate the newly acquired corporation as a subsidiary. This method would result in tax to the FM shareholders—perhaps an undesirable result—and may require CTV to use its cash, which it may be unwilling to do. Alternatively, CTV and FM could agree to a merger in which CTV would acquire FM using its own stock rather than using cash or other considerations. If a merger occurred, CTV would issue CTV stock to the FM shareholders in *exchange* for their stock. As a result, FM would be absorbed into CTV and the FM shareholders would become CTV shareholders. Since a merger generally qualifies as a reorganization, the exchange of FM stock for CTV stock by FM's shareholders is nontaxable.

If CTV desired not to absorb FM in a merger transaction—perhaps because the license granted to FM to operate the radio station cannot be assigned to CTV under government regulations—it could simply issue CTV stock to the FM shareholders in *exchange* for their FM stock and operate FM as a subsidiary. As above, the FM shareholders would become CTV shareholders instead of FM shareholders, and everyone would enjoy tax-free treatment since a stock-for-stock exchange normally qualifies as a reorganization.

Note that in both situations described above, CTV is able to restructure its operations generally unaffected by tax considerations. However, any gain or loss realized on the transactions does not go permanently unrecognized. The basis rules applying to reorganizations ensure that recognition occurs if and when there is a subsequent disposition of the stock or property.

Reorganizations are normally nontaxable because the shareholders have not liquidated their investment but merely have continued it in a modified form. In other words, they remain shareholders, albeit in a reorganized corporation. Since the shareholders have not converted their equity interests into cash, they have not realized (in an accounting sense) any of the appreciation in their investment, nor have they received the equivalent of a corporate distribution. Moreover, the shareholders lack the ability to pay any tax since they have not "cashed in" but rather still own property. In light of these circumstances, Congress has permitted properly structured reorganizations to be carried out without the imposition of tax.

The reorganization provisions are very similar to the like-kind exchange rules, which enable taxpayers to exchange properties held for productive use or investment tax-free.

As with like-kind exchanges, however, if the shareholders involved in a reorganization receive boot or terminate their interest in the property, there may be tax consequences. In addition, the unrecognized gains and losses are preserved through the basis assigned to the various properties.

This chapter discusses the various types of reorganizations and the requirements that must be satisfied if a reorganization is to be considered a nontaxable transaction.

Tax-Free Reorganizations: General Requirements

In order for a transaction to be given nonrecognition treatment under the reorganization provisions, it must meet several general requirements.

> **LO.1**
> Understand the basic tax consequences arising from corporate reorganizations, including corporate mergers, acquisitions, and divisions.

1. The reorganization must meet certain tests in the Regulations regarding "continuity of interest" and "continuity of business enterprise."

2. The reorganization must be conducted according to one of several acceptable patterns—there are seven qualifying forms or types of reorganizations eligible for nonrecognition.

3. The reorganization must meet the judicially imposed condition requiring a "business purpose" for the transaction.

4. A plan of reorganization must exist and such plan must be adopted by each corporation involved in the transaction.

Before examining these requirements, the general context in which they are applied as well as some terminology must be understood. The important characteristics of a reorganization can be readily seen in a merger transaction that qualifies as a so-called "A" reorganization. In a merger, one corporation, E, referred to as the *transferee,* acquires the assets of another corporation, T, called the *transferor,* in exchange for E stock, securities, and other considerations. The shareholders of the transferor, T, exchange their stock of the transferor for the package of consideration provided by the transferee and the T stock is cancelled. This somewhat confusing set of transactions is illustrated in Exhibit 7-2 and is examined in detail later in this chapter. In considering the tax treatment of these exchange transactions, the somewhat more descriptive term, *acquiring corporation,* is normally used in lieu of *transferee corporation.* Similarly, the transferor corporation is typically referred to the *target,* or *acquired corporation.* References to prior or former shareholders are to the shareholders of the target (transferor) corporation since they are no longer shareholders in the target but rather shareholders in the acquiring corporation.

CONTINUITY OF INTEREST

As previously suggested, nonrecognition of gains on exchanges related to a reorganization is premised on the theory that the shareholders have a *continuity of interest;* that is, they retain a substantial proprietary interest in the continuing business. This concept was first developed by the court in *Cortland Specialty Co.*[1] and is now contained in the Regulations. The Regulations state:

> The purpose of the continuity of interest requirement is to prevent transactions that resemble sales from qualifying for nonrecognition of gain or loss available to corporate reorganizations. Continuity of interest requires that in substance a substantial part of the value of the proprietary interests in the target corporation be preserved in the reorganization.[2]

Much of our understanding of the meaning and limits of the continuity of interest requirement was developed through cases. The results were sometimes contradictory and often difficult to apply to new fact patterns. As a result Treasury rewrote the regulations to provide greater certainty and simplicity.

---

[1] *Cortland Specialty Co. v. Comm.,* 3 USTC ¶980, 11 AFTR 857, 60 F.2d 937 (CA-2, 1932).

[2] Reg. § 1.368-1(e)(1)(i).

As quoted above, to meet the continuity of interest requirement, a substantial part of the proprietary interests in the target company must be preserved. An interest is preserved if it is exchanged for a proprietary interest in the acquiring corporation.[3] An interest is not preserved if it is acquired for property other than stock or the stock that is issued is redeemed by the acquiring corporation.[4]

The thrust of the continuity-of-interest doctrine is to limit the types of consideration items that an acquiring corporation can offer to the target's shareholders. If the exchange is to qualify for favorable treatment, it is clear that the consideration package must contain stock of the acquiring corporation in order that the target's shareholders have an equity interest in the acquiring corporation. The percentage of consideration that is stock has never been precisely specified by the Regulations or the Courts. The IRS has indicated its position, however. For ruling purposes, the Service requires at least 50% of the consideration to be stock of the acquiring corporation.[5] However, based on an example in recently revised regulations, it appears that taxpayer will meet the continuity of interest requirement if taxpayer receives stock worth at least 40% of the total amount received.[6] This is not to say that at least 40% of what each shareholder receives must be stock. Instead, the test is applied to the target's shareholders as a group—not individually. As a result, an acquiring corporation has great flexibility in designing the package of consideration that the target's owners will receive.

Example 2

B Corporation wishes to merge with Target Corporation. Most of Target's shareholders are in favor of the merger; however, a minority of Target's shareholders have threatened a lawsuit if the merger is consummated. If B Corporation restructures the transaction so that the shareholders of Target who oppose the merger receive cash and the majority of Target's shareholders receive stock, the transaction should meet the continuity of interest requirement.

Another aspect of the continuity-of-interest requirement concerns subsequent transactions involving the proprietary interests received. As a general rule, the former shareholders of target are permitted to dispose of the stock received in the reorganization without violating the requirement. However, if the stock is redeemed by the acquiring corporation, the regulations treat the target shareholder as having received cash and not stock.[7] As a result, the target shareholders may not have maintained sufficient continuing interest for the transaction to be a tax-free reorganization.

CONTINUITY OF BUSINESS ENTERPRISE

A reorganization is classified as a nontaxable transaction because it results in a continuation of the *business* in modified form. To ensure that the business is continued, the Regulations contain a *continuity of business enterprise* requirement.[8] To meet this requirement, the acquiring corporation must either continue the target corporation's historic business or use a significant portion of the target corporation's assets in a business.[9]

Example 3

Target Corporation, which contains substantially appreciated assets, has been only marginally profitable the last few years. Its shareholders would like to liquidate the corporation and invest in another business. C Corporation has a large capital loss carryforward and needs additional cash for expansion. Target is merged into C with

---

[3] See Rev. Rul. 77-415, 1977-2 C.B. 311 and Rev. Rul. 77-479, 1977 C.B. 119.

[4] For example, see *LeTulle v. Scofield*, 40-1 USTC ¶9150, 23 AFTR 789, 308 U.S. 415 (USSC, 1940).

[5] Rev. Proc. 77-37, 1977-2 C.*B. 568.* The regulations contain an example in which 40% stock was sufficient. See Reg. § 1.368-1T(e)(2)(v) Ex. 1.

[6] Reg. § 1.368-1(e)(2)(v) Ex. 6.

[7] Reg. § 1.368-1(e)(i) and (ii).

[8] Reg. § 1.368-1(d).

[9] Reg. § 1.368-1(d)(2).

> Target's shareholders receiving C stock. C immediately sells Target's assets and invests the cash in its existing business. This transaction does not meet the continuity of business enterprise requirement. Note that Target's shareholders do not end up owning stock in a corporation that will continue Target's old business but rather have sold the old corporation and invested in C.

Continuing the target corporation's historic business generally requires continuing the target's most recently conducted line of business.[10] It does not require continuing all of the acquired corporation's lines of business nor does it require continuing the business in the exact same manner. If the target corporation has more than one line of business, the test is satisfied where the most significant line is continued. In addition, reasonable changes can be made in the management of the business, and duplicative or unnecessary assets can be sold. The extent of the changes will be viewed in context of all the facts and circumstances.

Using a significant portion of the acquired corporation's assets means using a significant portion of the assets used by the target (or acquired) corporation in its historic business.[11] It does not mean using all the assets nor does it mean using the assets in the same manner.

Example 4

P Corporation manufactures computers and Target Corporation manufactures components for computers. Target sells all of its output to P. On January 1, 2016 P decides to buy imported components only. On March 1, 2016 Target merges into P. P retains Target's assets as a backup source of supply. P is considered to be using a significant part of Target's assets even though they are kept as a backup.[12]

CONTROL

In addition to imposing the continuity requirement, the reorganization provisions frequently require that the acquiring corporation obtain control of the target corporation or that the shareholders of the acquiring corporation be in control of the corporation immediately after the transaction. For these purposes, control is defined as at least 80% of the total voting power and at least 80% of all other classes of stock.[13] To meet the latter test, the shareholders must own at least 80% of the total number of shares of each class of nonvoting stock.[14] This is the same definition of control that is applied for purposes of corporate formations under § 351.

Acceptable Patterns of Reorganization: Types A–G

There are seven qualifying patterns of reorganization. The descriptions, which are contained in 368(a)(1)(A) through (G), are as follows:

Type A— a statutory merger or consolidation;

Type B— the acquisition by one corporation, in exchange solely for all or a part of its voting stock (or in exchange solely for all or a part of the voting stock of a corporation which is in control of the acquiring corporation), of stock of another corporation if, immediately after the acquisition, the acquiring corporation has control of such other corporation (whether or not such acquiring corporation had control immediately before the acquisition);

LO.2

Describe the seven different types of reorganizations and what requirements must be met for nontaxable treatment.

---

[10] Reg. § 1.368-1(d)(3)(iii).

[11] Reg. § 1.368-1(d)(4).

[12] Reg. § 1.368-1(d)(5) Ex. 2.

[13] § 368(c).

[14] Rev. Rul. 59-259, 59-2 C.B. 115.

Type C— the acquisition by one corporation, in exchange solely for all or a part of its voting stock (or in exchange solely for all or a part of the voting stock of a corporation which is in control of the acquiring corporation), of substantially all of the properties of another corporation, but in determining whether the exchange is solely for stock the assumption by the acquiring corporation of a liability of the other, or the fact that property acquired is subject to a liability, shall be disregarded;

Type D— a transfer by a corporation of all or a part of its assets to another corporation if immediately after the transfer the transferor, or one or more of its shareholders (including persons who were shareholders immediately before the transfer), or any combination thereof, is in control of the corporation to which the assets are transferred; but only if, in pursuance of the plan, stock or securities of the corporation to which the assets are transferred are distributed in a transaction which qualifies under §§ 354, 355, or 356;

Type E— a recapitalization;

Type F— a mere change in identity, form, or place of organization of one corporation, however effected; or

Type G— a transfer by a corporation of all or part of its assets to another corporation in a Title 11 or similar case, but only if, in pursuance of the plan, stock or securities of the corporation to which the assets are transferred are distributed in a transaction which qualifies under Code §§ 354, 355, or 356.

In referring to the different types of reorganizations, tax practitioners generally shorten the reference and simply call each by the subparagraph in which it is described. Therefore, the seven transactions are usually referred to as "A," "B," "C," "D," "E," "F," or "G" reorganizations.

The seven acceptable patterns of reorganization may be classified into two categories: divisive and nondivisive. As the name suggests, a *divisive reorganization* is one in which a single corporation is divided into two or more corporations. After the division, the original corporation may or may not survive. The "D" reorganization is the sole divisive reorganization. All other reorganizations are *nondivisive*.

The nondivisive reorganizations can be further subdivided into two groups: those that are acquisitive reorganizations and those that are not. In the *acquisitive reorganizations*— the "A," "B," "C," and acquisitive "D" reorganizations—one corporation acquires another corporation's stock, assets, or some combination thereof. Note while studying these reorganizations that one of the distinctions between them is what is acquired (e.g., stock or assets). Another distinction is the type of consideration that may be used by the acquiring corporation. Although the rules concerning consideration that may be used reflect the continuity-of-interest requirement (i.e., stock of the acquiring corporation must be exchanged), variations in the consideration packages exist.

The other nondivisive reorganizations are the "E," "F," and "G" reorganizations. In the "E" reorganization, a single corporation reconfigures its capital structure (e.g., issues stock to its shareholders in exchange for their bonds). The "F" reorganization rules govern the tax consequences when the corporation merely changes its name or place of incorporation, or makes some other alteration in its form. The "G" reorganization concerns bankrupt corporations.

As this brief overview indicates, reorganizations come in various shapes and sizes. They vary in the number of corporations involved, the type of consideration that may be used, the properties transferred, and other subtle ways. Exhibit 7-1 summarizes the general characteristics of the various reorganizations. Each of the reorganizations is explored in detail below.

"A" REORGANIZATION

The "A" reorganization is defined as a statutory merger or consolidation.[15] "Statutory" means that the reorganization qualifies as a merger or consolidation under the appropriate state law or similar statute.[16] In a merger, one corporation (the acquiring corporation)

---

[15] § 368(a)(1)(A).   [16] Reg. § 1.368-2(b)(1).

absorbs another corporation (target corporation). There are basically two steps in a merger. First, the target corporation transfers all of its assets and liabilities to the acquiring corporation in return for stock and securities (and possibly other property) of the acquiring corporation. Then the target corporation, which now contains solely the stock and securities (and other property) of the acquiring corporation, dissolves by exchanging the acquiring corporation's stock for its own stock. As a result, the former shareholders of the target corporation become shareholders in the acquiring corporation; and the acquiring corporation is the sole corporation that survives. This is illustrated in Exhibit 7-2.

Example 5

J owns all the stock of Target Corporation. B owns all the stock of Acquiring Corporation. J and B agree to merge Target and Acquiring in an "A" reorganization. Target Corporation transfers its assets and liabilities to Acquiring Corporation in return for Acquiring Corporation stock. Target Corporation then dissolves by transferring the Acquiring stock to J in exchange for its (Target's) stock. Acquiring is the sole surviving corporation. J and B are the shareholders of Acquiring Corporation.

A consolidation is a statutory combination of two or more corporations in a new corporation. It involves the same two steps as a merger. First, the target corporations transfer their assets to the new consolidated corporation in return for stock and securities of the new corporation. Then the target corporations dissolve by distributing the new corporation's stock to their shareholders in return for their own stock. This is illustrated in Exhibit 7-3.

Example 6

J owns all the stock of T1 Corporation, whose assets have a fair market value of $500,000. B owns all the stock of T2 Corporation, whose assets have a fair market value of $300,000. C owns all the stock of T3 Corporation, whose assets have a fair market value of $200,000. J, B, and C agree to consolidate their corporations in an "A" reorganization. T1, T2, and T3 transfer their assets to A Corporation, a new entity, in return for shares of stock. Assuming A Corporation issues 1,000 shares of stock, T1 receives 500 shares, T2 receives 300 shares, and T3 receives 200 shares. T1, T2, and T3 then dissolve by transferring the A stock to its shareholder in return for its outstanding stock. J, B, and C become the shareholders of A Corporation.

The "A" reorganization requires that the merger or consolidation qualify as such under an applicable statute. Therefore, both domestic and foreign corporations can merge under the rules of an "A" reorganization. Although laws differ, they generally require that the merger be approved by the board of directors and the shareholders of each corporation involved in the reorganization. This can be a time-consuming and expensive requirement. It is usually considered one of the major disadvantages of the "A" reorganization. The other major disadvantage of the "A" reorganization is that the acquiring corporation will be responsible for all the liabilities of the target corporation, including contingent liabilities.

EXHIBIT 7-1		**Reorganization Characteristics**			

		Acquiring Corporation		Target Corporation	
Reorg.	Shortened Title	Transfers	Receives	Transfers	Receives
A	Merger	Stock, securities, and/or other property	Target's assets and liabilities	All property and liabilities	Goes out of existence
	Consolidation	Stock, securities, and/or other property	Target's assets and liabilities	All property and liabilities	Goes out of existence
B	Stock acquisition	Solely voting stock	Controlling stock of target	—	—
C	Asset acquisition	Solely voting stock and possibly other property	Substantially all the assets of target	Substantially all its assets	Voting stock of acquiring corporation
	Acquisitive	Substantially all its assets	Goes out of existence	Controlling stock	Assets of acquiring corporation
D	Divisive	Some of its assets	Controlling stock and securities of target (distributes to shareholders)	Controlling stock and securities	Assets of acquiring corporation
E	Recapitalization	New stock and securities	Its old stock and securities	—	—
F	Change in identity	New stock and securities	Its old stock and securities	—	—
G	Bankruptcy	Some or all of its assets	Stock and securities of target (distributes to shareholders)	Stock and securities	Assets from acquiring corporation

The "A" reorganization, unlike the "B" and "C" reorganizations, does not contain any statutory limitations on the consideration that the acquiring corporation can issue to the target corporation in return for its assets. As long as applicable law permits, the acquiring corporation can issue its common stock (voting and nonvoting), preferred stock (voting, nonvoting, participating, and nonparticipating), and securities. The exact percentages of each are dictated by the business considerations and the desires of the shareholders of the target corporation. This ability to issue a variety of considerations makes the "A" reorganization very flexible. Yet, this flexibility is not unlimited. The transaction must meet the continuity-of-interest requirement. The shareholders of the target corporation must receive enough stock of the acquiring corporation so that they have a continuing financial interest in the reorganized firm. There is no minimum percent of the total consideration paid that must be in the stock of the acquiring corporation. As indicated previously, however, it is the government's position for issuing advanced rulings that at least 50% of the consideration used must be stock of the acquiring corporation.[17] The computation is made in the aggregate for all the shareholders of the target corporation, not on an individual shareholder basis.

---

[17] Rev. Proc. 77-37, 1977-2 C.B. 568.

EXHIBIT 7-1	Continued

	Acquiring Corporation's Shareholders			Target Corporation's Shareholders	
Transfers	Receives	Realized Gain Recognized	Transfers	Receives	Realized Gain Recognized
—	—	—	Exchange stock and securities	Stock and securities of new corp.	To extent boot is received
Exchange stock and securities	Stock and securities of new corp.	To extent boot is received	Exchange stock and securities	Stock and securities of new corp.	To extent boot is received
—	—	—	Controlling stock	Voting stock of acquiring corporation	None
—	—	—	Stock and securities of target	Stock and securities of target plus boot	To extent boot is received
Stock and securities	Controlling stock and securities of target	To extent boot is received	—	—	—
May transfer stock and securities	Controlling stock and securities of target	To extent boot is received	—	—	—
Old stock and securities	New stock and securities	To extent boot is received	—	—	—
Old stock and securities	New stock and securities	To extent boot is received	—	—	—
May transfer stock and securities	Controlling stock and securities of target	To extent boot is received	—	—	—

Example 7

Individuals J and B each own 50% of Target Corporation. The fair market value of all the outstanding shares of Target Corporation is $10,000. On March 1, Target is merged into Acquiring Corporation. Acquiring Corporation transfers to Target Corporation shares of its common stock with a fair market value of $6,000 and bonds worth $4,000. On the dissolution of Target Corporation, J receives common stock of Acquiring Corporation worth $5,000, and B receives stock of $1,000 and bonds of $4,000. This transaction meets the continuity-of-interest requirement because the stock of Acquiring Corporation received by J and B had a fair market value of $6,000, which exceeds 50% of the value of the out standing stock of Target Corporation prior to the merger. The fact that B received all the bonds and that the Acquiring Corporation's stock she received is less than 50% of the value of the Target stock she surrendered is immaterial for qualification as an "A" reorganization.

Transfers to a Subsidiary (Drop-Downs)

The end result of an "A" reorganization, whether merger or consolidation, is one surviving corporation. This may not be the most useful form.

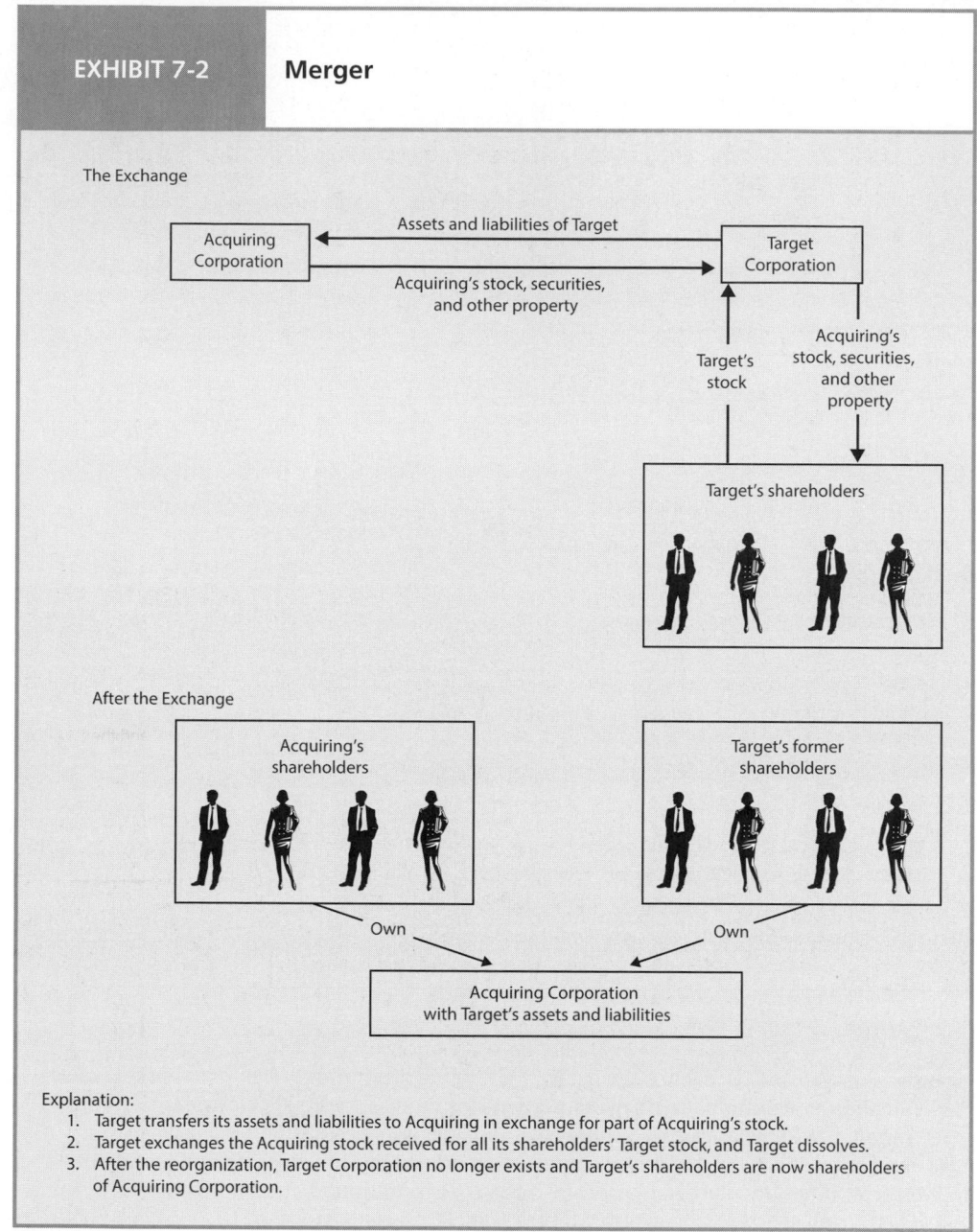

EXHIBIT 7-2	Merger

Explanation:
1. Target transfers its assets and liabilities to Acquiring in exchange for part of Acquiring's stock.
2. Target exchanges the Acquiring stock received for all its shareholders' Target stock, and Target dissolves.
3. After the reorganization, Target Corporation no longer exists and Target's shareholders are now shareholders of Acquiring Corporation.

EXHIBIT 7-3	Consolidation

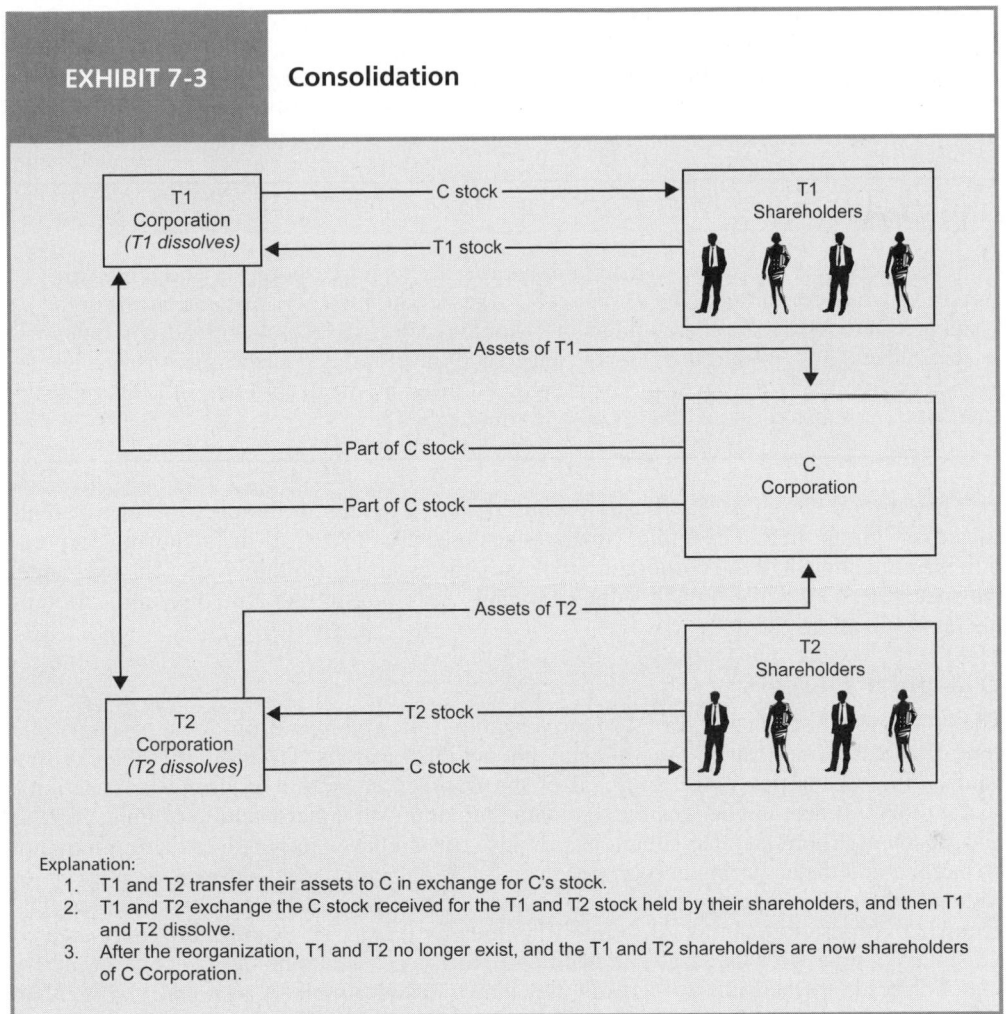

Explanation:
1. T1 and T2 transfer their assets to C in exchange for C's stock.
2. T1 and T2 exchange the C stock received for the T1 and T2 stock held by their shareholders, and then T1 and T2 dissolve.
3. After the reorganization, T1 and T2 no longer exist, and the T1 and T2 shareholders are now shareholders of C Corporation.

Example 8

The ABC Insurance Company wishes to expand into the brokerage business and mutual funds. It has located T Corporation, which it desires to acquire. The shareholders of T are interested in a nontaxable merger. However, combining the two corporations could cause ABC problems. First, it might violate state insurance rules against diversification. Second, it might change the asset reserves that the state requires ABC to maintain since the total assets that ABC owns will have increased. Finally, the management of T receives bonuses based on profitability that would be difficult to maintain if the corporations are merged.

As the above example illustrates, a merger may be undesirable where management of the acquiring corporation does not want to combine the assets of its corporation with those of the target. A possible solution to the one-corporation problem of the "A" reorganization would be for the acquiring corporation to create a new subsidiary following the reorganization. The acquiring corporation would transfer the assets of the target company to the newly formed (or existing) subsidiary in a nontaxable § 351 exchange. The two steps would solve the problem. Normally when a transaction consists of two related steps, the government applies the step transaction doctrine and denies independent tax treatment to the "independent" steps. If the step transaction doctrine were applied to the suggested solution, the transaction could not be an "A" reorganization because the acquiring corporation does not end up with the assets of the target. Since 1954, however, the Code has permitted the transfer of all or part of the assets received from the target corporation to a subsidiary of the acquiring corporation without disqualifying the "A" reorganization.[18]

Example 9

Same facts as *Example 8*. ABC could acquire the target corporation and still maintain separate corporations in a nontaxable transaction. First, T Corporation would be merged into ABC. The shareholders of T would receive ABC stock and thereby satisfy their needs. ABC would then create Newco and transfer the assets acquired from T to Newco in a § 351 transaction. The merger followed by the drop-down of the target's assets to a subsidiary qualifies as an "A" reorganization.

The drop-down of assets illustrated in *Example 9* results in the creation of a parent-subsidiary group. In that example, Newco is a subsidiary of ABC. If the acquiring corporation is not in control of the corporation receiving the assets immediately after the exchange, the special rule allowing transfers does not apply, resulting in probable disqualification of the reorganization.

Triangular Mergers

The "A" reorganization and the "A" reorganization followed by a drop-down of assets to a controlled subsidiary can be used in many but not all situations. The stumbling block often confronting the parties is the approval of the transaction by the acquiring corporation's shareholders. It may not be feasible to obtain their approval either because of time, cost, or disagreement. There are also situations, because of state laws, in which the target may not be merged into the acquiring corporation even if it is only temporary before a drop-down. In addition, the acquiring corporation may be unwilling to assume the target's liabilities. The acquiring corporation can avoid these difficulties by having an existing or newly created subsidiary merge with the target. In such case, the target's shareholders become minority shareholders in the subsidiary—a result they may find undesirable. A *triangular merger* can overcome this problem.[19] In a *forward* triangular merger, the target corporation is merged directly into an existing or newly created subsidiary. Instead of using its own stock as consideration, however, the subsidiary transfers stock of its parent corporation to the target in exchange for the assets. The target dissolves by distributing the stock of the parent to its shareholders in return for its own stock. A forward triangular merger starts with a parent and subsidiary corporation and ends up with a parent and an enlarged subsidiary. The shareholders of the parent corporation are the former owners of the parent plus the former owners of the target. The transaction is illustrated in Exhibit 7-4.

There are three requirements for a forward triangular merger.[20] First, a controlled subsidiary (at least 80% owned by the parent) must receive substantially all the assets of the target corporation in the merger. It is the government's position that *substantially all* means at least 90% of the fair market value of the net assets *and* at least 70% of the fair market value of the gross assets.[21] Second, the transaction must have satisfied the requirements of an "A" reorganization if the target had been merged into the parent corporation instead of the subsidiary. Third, no stock of the controlled subsidiary can be used.

[18] § 368(a)(2)(C).

[19] § 368(a)(2)(D).

[20] *Ibid.*

[21] Rev. Proc. 77-37. 1977-2 C.B. 568.

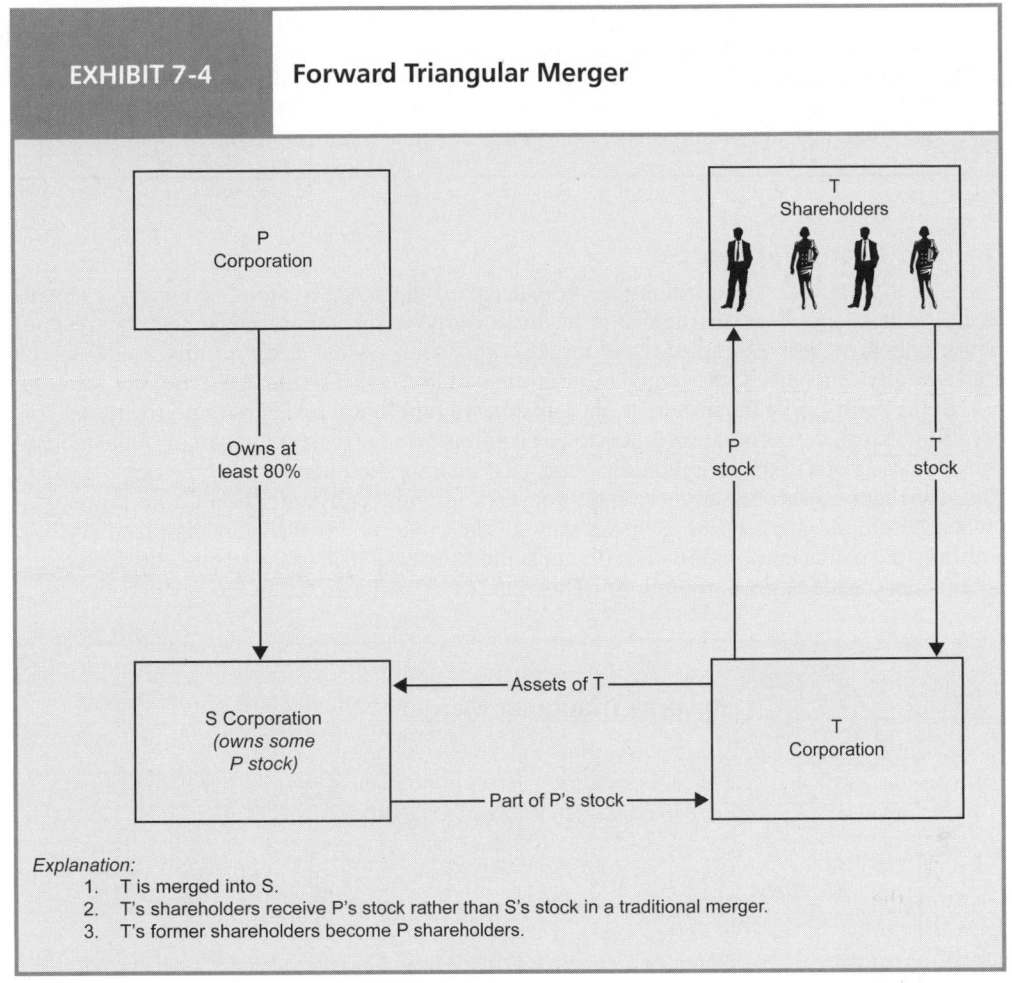

EXHIBIT 7-4   **Forward Triangular Merger**

Explanation:
1. T is merged into S.
2. T's shareholders receive P's stock rather than S's stock in a traditional merger.
3. T's former shareholders become P shareholders.

Example 10

Bank Company owns all the stock of Savings Corp. Bank Company desires to acquire First Federal Inc. as part of its subsidiary Savings Corp. To this end, First Federal is merged into Savings Corp. First Federal transferred all of its assets, except land acquired for expansion, to Savings in return for 1,000 shares of Bank Company stock. The assets transferred to Savings have a fair market value of $10 million. First Federal dissolves by transferring the stock of Bank Company, with a fair market value of $10 million, and the land, with a fair market value of $1 million, to its shareholders in return for its stock. The transaction is a valid forward triangular merger since all three requirements are satisfied. Savings received more than 90% of First Federal's assets; therefore it received substantially all the assets of the target corporation. In addition, if First Federal had been merged directly into Bank Company, it would have been a valid "A" reorganization. Finally, the only stock transferred to First Savings was stock of the parent company (i.e., Bank Company).

Example 11

Same facts as *Example 10* except First Federal transferred all of its assets to Savings and received Bank Company stock with a fair market value of $1 million and long-term bonds with a fair market value of $10 million. This would probably not be a valid triangular merger. Although Savings received substantially all the assets and the only stock transferred was stock of Bank Company, less than 10% of the total consideration given to First Federal shareholders was stock. Such a small percentage of stock would probably not pass the continuity-of-interest requirement.

Reverse Triangular Merger

There is a variation of the triangular merger called the *reverse triangular merger*.[22] This variation is used whenever there is a business purpose for maintaining the target corporation's identity. For example, if the target corporation owned licenses that could not be conveniently transferred, the target corporation would have to be the surviving corporation.

In the reverse triangular merger, the subsidiary corporation is merged into the target corporation; that is, the corporation that is to be acquired. Voting stock of the parent of the merged subsidiary is given to the shareholders of the target corporation in return for the target's stock. The law requires that the target corporation end up with "substantially all" the property it owned before the merger and "substantially all the property" of the merged subsidiary.[23] In addition, the parent corporation must obtain control (at least 80% of the voting and 80% of the other stock) of the target corporation.[24] This transaction is illustrated in Exhibit 7-5.

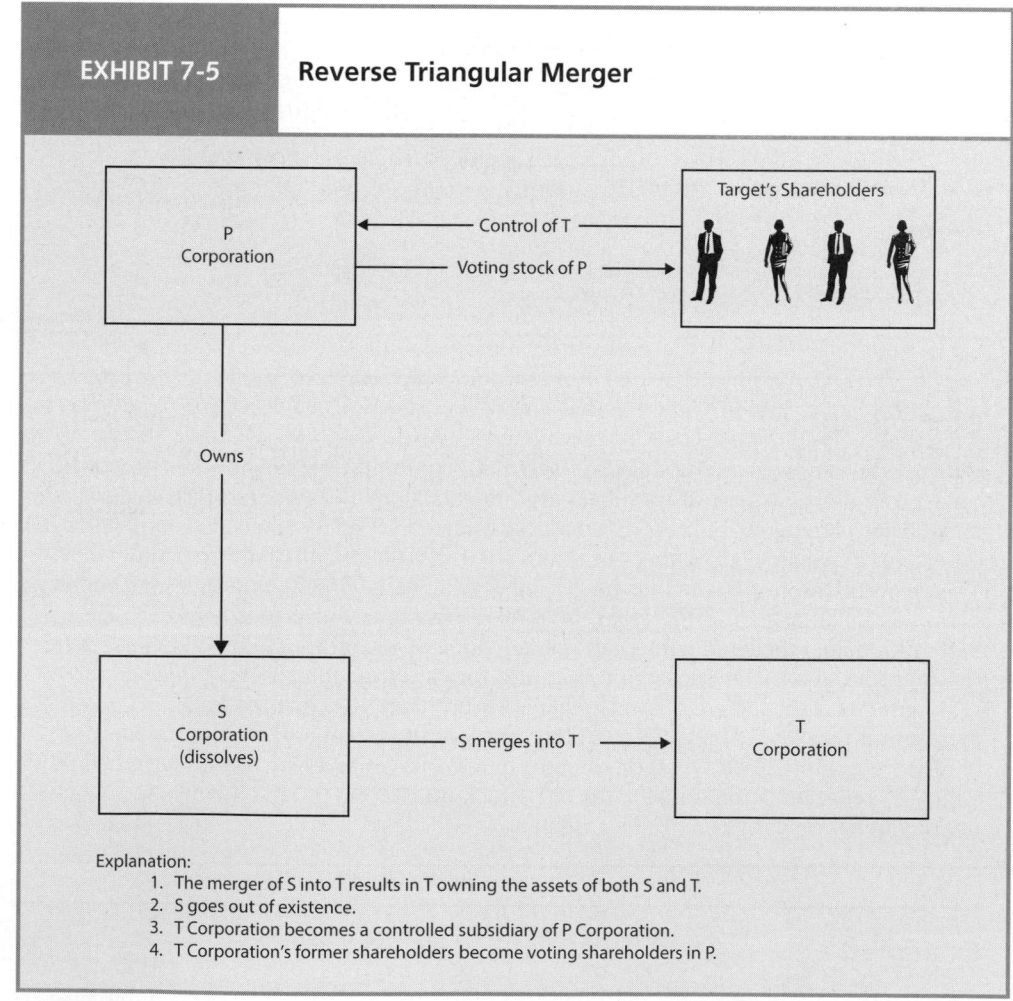

| EXHIBIT 7-5 | **Reverse Triangular Merger** |

P Corporation

Target's Shareholders

← Control of T —

— Voting stock of P →

Owns

S Corporation (dissolves)

— S merges into T →

T Corporation

Explanation:
1. The merger of S into T results in T owning the assets of both S and T.
2. S goes out of existence.
3. T Corporation becomes a controlled subsidiary of P Corporation.
4. T Corporation's former shareholders become voting shareholders in P.

---

[22] § 368(a)(2)(E).

[23] § 368(a)(2)(E)(i).

[24] § 368(a)(2)(E)(ii).

Example 12

CTV is a highly successful cable television company. It desires to expand into the radio broadcasting business by acquiring FM. However, FM's FCC license cannot be transferred to another corporation. CTV creates a wholly owned subsidiary R. R is merged into FM. FM's shareholders receive voting stock of CTV in return for all their shares of FM. This is a valid reverse triangular merger. R, CTV's initial subsidiary, goes out of existence. FM becomes a wholly owned subsidiary of CTV and FM's original shareholders become shareholders in CTV.

"B" REORGANIZATION

In contrast to the "A" reorganization in which one corporation acquires the assets of another, the "B" reorganization is defined as the acquisition of *stock* of one corporation by another.[25] Thus, the target corporation becomes a subsidiary of the acquiring corporation. There are two requirements of a "B" reorganization:

1. The target's stock must be acquired using solely voting stock.
2. Immediately after the exchange, the acquiring corporation must be in control of the target corporation.

The "B" reorganization is illustrated in Exhibit 7-6.

The consideration that the acquiring corporation can use is restricted to *solely voting stock*. The transfer of nonvoting stock, securities, or cash as part of the consideration for the target's stock violates this solely-for-voting-stock requirement and invalidates the "B" reorganization. The voting stock can be either the stock of the acquiring corporation or of the corporation that controls the acquiring corporation (i.e., its parent). Stock of both the acquiring corporation and its parent may not be used.

Example 13

Acquiring Corporation desires to acquire Target Corporation. Target Corporation's shareholders insist that the transaction be nontaxable. Acquiring offers Target Corporation shareholders one share of Acquiring Corporation voting stock for every five shares of Target Corporation stock they own as part of a plan of reorganization. All of Target Corporation's shareholders accept the offer. The exchange of Acquiring stock for Target stock qualifies as a "B" reorganization since Acquiring obtained control of Target for solely voting stock.

Example 14

Same facts as *Example 13* except the offer permits the shareholders of Target to receive one share of Acquiring stock or cash of $100. The cash was included to buy out a dissident minority of Target's shareholders. Ninety-five percent of Target's shareholders accept the stock, and the remainder accept the cash. The transaction does not qualify as a "B" reorganization since it does not meet the solely-for-voting-stock requirement.

---

[25] § 368(a)(1)(B).

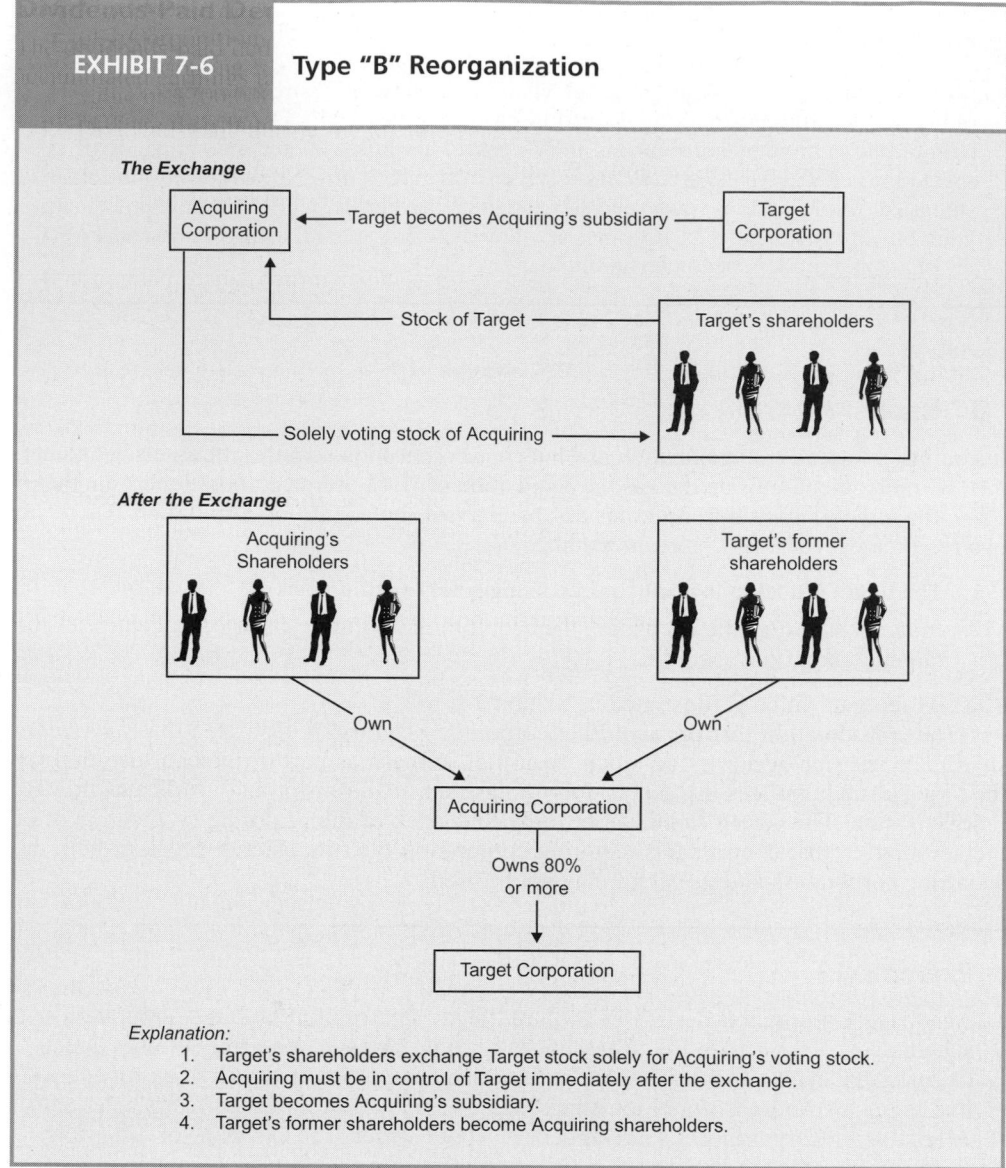

EXHIBIT 7-6   **Type "B" Reorganization**

The Exchange

Acquiring Corporation ← Target becomes Acquiring's subsidiary — Target Corporation

— Stock of Target —

Target's shareholders

— Solely voting stock of Acquiring →

After the Exchange

Acquiring's Shareholders — Own →

Target's former shareholders — Own →

Acquiring Corporation

Owns 80% or more

Target Corporation

Explanation:
1. Target's shareholders exchange Target stock solely for Acquiring's voting stock.
2. Acquiring must be in control of Target immediately after the exchange.
3. Target becomes Acquiring's subsidiary.
4. Target's former shareholders become Acquiring shareholders.

As indicated above, the second condition of the "B" reorganization requires the acquiring corporation to be in control of the target corporation immediately after the acquisition. It is not necessary that control be acquired in the transaction. It is sufficient if control exists after the exchange.

Example 15

Acquiring Corporation owns 90% of Target Corporation (and thus already has the requisite control). Acquiring can acquire the remaining 10% of Target's stock in a nontaxable "B" reorganization provided it only uses voting stock in the transaction.

The Regulations sanction what is referred to as a *creeping* "B" reorganization—so called because the requisite control is acquired through a series of acquisitions using solely voting stock. For each separate acquisition to qualify, several requirements must be satisfied:[26]

1. The acquisition must be one of a series of acquisitions that are part of an overall plan to acquire the requisite control.
2. The plan of acquisition must be carried out in a relatively short period of time, such as 12 months.
3. The acquisition must be made solely for voting stock.

Prior cash purchases of the target's stock are permissible within this scheme, provided the purchase is a separate transaction and not part of the overall plan.

Example 16

Acquiring purchased 30% of Target's stock in 2008. Acquiring can acquire the remaining 70% of Target's stock in 2016 in a "B" reorganization as long as only voting stock is used. The prior cash purchase is ignored since it clearly is not part of an expeditious plan to acquire Target's stock.

Example 17

Same facts as in *Example 16* except Acquiring purchased the 30% of Target's stock during the last half of 2015. The cash acquisition was made through a tender offer by which Acquiring had hoped to obtain control of Target. Having failed to acquire the necessary 80 percent, Acquiring then offered its own voting stock for the remaining 70% under a plan of reorganization. Acquiring obtained the remaining stock during the first half of 2016. The stock-for-stock exchanges qualify as a "B" reorganization. As in the previous example, the prior cash purchase is ignored. Note also that control need not be acquired in the stock exchanges for those exchanges to qualify as a "B" reorganization. Although only 70% of the stock was acquired solely for voting stock, the exchanges still qualify since the acquiring corporation had control after the plan of acquisition was complete. (See *Example 15* above where the same result would occur had the 90% been purchased in a previous transaction.)

Regardless of whether the corporation acquires control in the transaction or already has control, the "B" reorganization has as its end product a parent/subsidiary relationship between the acquiring and target corporation. For instance, in both *Example 16* and *Example 17,* Target is a subsidiary of Acquiring after the reorganization.

"C" REORGANIZATION

The "C" reorganization is defined as the acquisition of substantially all the assets of a corporation solely for voting stock of the acquiring corporation or its parent.[27] In this reorganization, the target corporation transfers assets to the acquiring corporation in exchange for the acquiring corporation's voting stock and in some circumstances a limited amount of other consideration. The target corporation must liquidate as part of the plan of reorganization unless the IRS waives this requirement.[28] As a result, the shareholders of the target corporation become shareholders in the acquiring corporation. In determining the tax consequences to the liquidating target, the reorganization provisions govern—*not* the liquidation rules of §§ 336 and 337.[29] The "C" reorganization is illustrated in Exhibit 7-7.

---

[26] Reg. § 1.368-2(c).

[27] § 368(a)(1)(C).

[28] § 368(a)(2)(G).

[29] § 361(b)(1)(A).

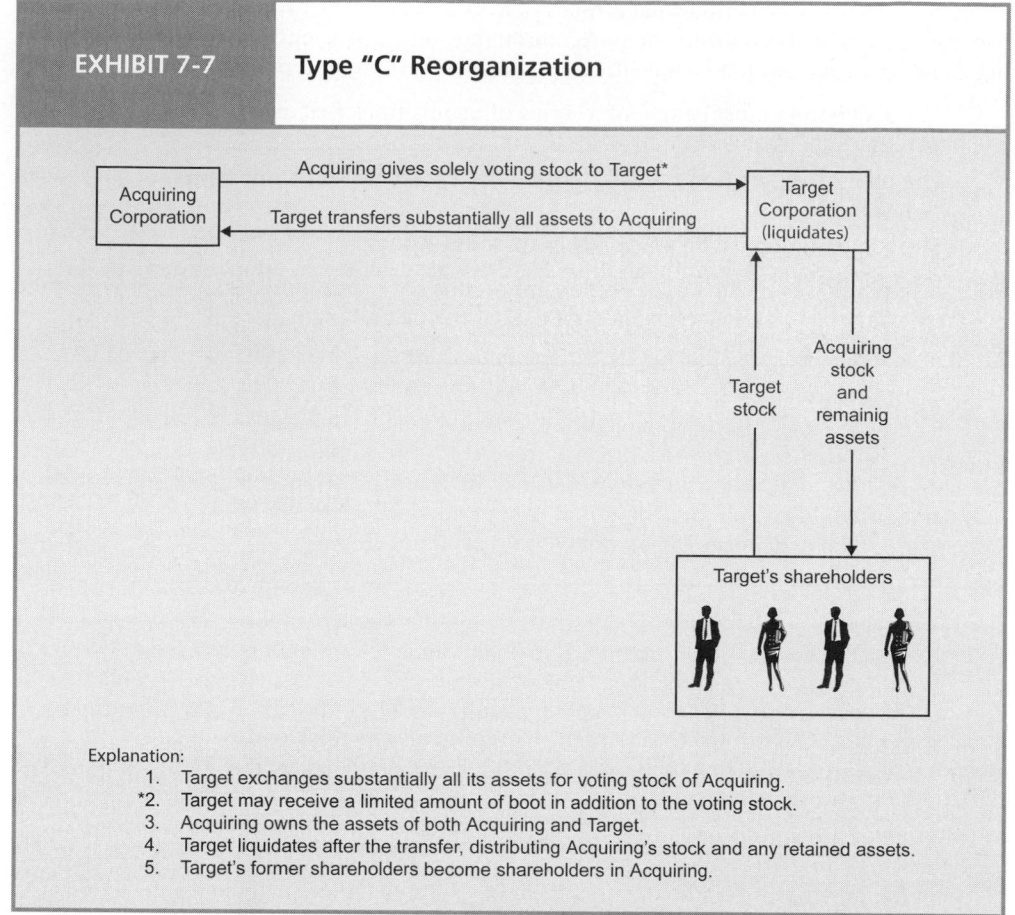

| EXHIBIT 7-7 | Type "C" Reorganization |

Explanation:
1. Target exchanges substantially all its assets for voting stock of Acquiring.
*2. Target may receive a limited amount of boot in addition to the voting stock.
3. Acquiring owns the assets of both Acquiring and Target.
4. Target liquidates after the transfer, distributing Acquiring's stock and any retained assets.
5. Target's former shareholders become shareholders in Acquiring.

Example 18

Retail Corp. desires to obtain the operations of one of its suppliers, Manufacturing Corp. Under a plan of reorganization, Retail Corp. issues voting stock, equal to 30% of its total outstanding stock, in exchange for all the assets of Manufacturing Corp. Immediately after the exchange, Manufacturing Corp. liquidates, distributing the stock of Retail Corp. to its shareholders. The exchange qualifies as a "C" reorganization.

The "C" reorganization is easily distinguished from a "B" reorganization but is sometimes similar to an "A" merger. The "C" reorganization differs from the "B" reorganization in two major aspects. First, the acquiring corporation obtains assets in the "C" reorganization whereas it obtains stock in a "B" reorganization. Second, the target corporation becomes a subsidiary in the "B" reorganization while in a "C" reorganization the target corporation goes out of existence.

On the other hand, a "C" reorganization closely resembles an "A" merger. The target corporation must liquidate after the exchange, distributing the acquiring corporation's stock and any remaining assets to its shareholders.[30] Therefore, the end result is the same as a merger: the acquiring corporation holds the assets of the target and the target's shareholders become shareholders in the acquiring corporation. Thus, the "C" reorganization is sometimes called the "practical merger." The "C" reorganization permits a business combination where mergers are not practical or allowed under state law. In a "C" reorganization, the acquiring corporation's shareholders need not formally approve of the acquisition. The target's shareholders, however, normally must approve the sale of the assets and the liquidation.

---

[30] § 368(a)(2)(G).

As indicated above, the acquiring corporation must obtain substantially all of the target's assets. The phrase "substantially all the assets" is not defined in the Code. For advanced ruling purposes, however, the Service requires that the acquiring corporation obtain at least 70% of the gross assets *and* 90% of the net assets.[31]

Example 19

Target Corporation owns assets with a fair market value of $1 million and a basis of $400,000. Target's liabilities equal $200,000. Acquiring Corporation receives assets with a fair market value of $800,000 and a basis of $250,000 in exchange for its voting stock as part of a plan of reorganization. Since Acquiring Corporation has obtained 80% of the gross assets ($800,000 ÷ $1 million) *and* 100% of the net assets ($800,000 ÷ [$1 million − $200,000]), it satisfies the *substantially all* test.

The type of assets retained by the target corporation is just as important as the amount of assets. The courts generally require that those assets critical to the continuation of the target's business must be transferred. Failure to do so may cause the transaction to fall outside the scope of a "C" reorganization.

The definition of a "C" reorganization also contains a solely-for-voting-stock requirement. In determining whether this requirement is satisfied, liabilities receive special treatment. The assumption of the target corporation's liabilities—which is normally considered the giving of boot—is disregarded. The amount of the liabilities is immaterial except in the situation described below. Without this rule, the "C" reorganization would rarely be used. Few creditors would allow the transfer of property without the transfer of the related debt for fear that the original debtor will be unable to repay the liability.

Example 20

Same facts as *Example 19* except that Acquiring Corporation assumes the $200,000 of liabilities. The assumption of the liabilities is ignored and Acquiring Corporation is considered to have obtained substantially all of Target's assets for solely voting stock.

In addition to assuming liabilities, the acquiring corporation may transfer a limited amount of boot along with voting stock.[32] The amount of boot is limited to not more than 20% of the total consideration. In other words, 80% or more of the fair market value of *gross assets* (i.e., ignoring liabilities) received by the acquiring corporation must be in exchange for voting stock. For purposes of this test, boot includes the liabilities assumed by the acquiring corporation. In effect, the amount of boot is limited to 20% of the fair market value of the assets transferred reduced by any liabilities assumed. If the liabilities exceed 20% of the value of the assets, only voting stock can be used since these liabilities are ignored if no boot is transferred.

Example 21

X Corporation transfers all of its assets, with a fair market value of $100,000, to Y Corporation for Y Corporation's voting stock. Y Corporation assumes $30,000 of X Corporation's liabilities. This can qualify as a "C" reorganization since the liabilities are disregarded as long as no boot is transferred.

---

[31] Rev. Proc. 77-37, 1977-2 C.B. 568. The same test is applied to triangular mergers.

[32] § 368(a)(2)(B).

Example 22

Same facts as *Example 21* except Y Corporation also transfers $1,000 to X Corporation. The total boot is $31,000 ($30,000 liabilities + $1,000 cash). Since the boot exceeds 20% of the fair market value of the assets ($31,000 > 20% × $100,000), this will not qualify as a "C" reorganization.

Example 23

W Corporation desires to acquire the assets of Z Corporation in a "C" reorganization. The assets of Z have a fair market value of $200,000. W will be assuming liabilities of $23,000. The maximum amount of boot that can be transferred in addition to the voting stock is $17,000 ([20% of $200,000 assets] − the $23,000 liabilities assumed).

The "C" reorganization permits the acquiring corporation to restructure the target's operation. Some or all of the assets received can be transferred to a corporation controlled by the acquiring corporation without affecting the "C" reorganization.[33]

Example 24

Retail Corporation acquires all the assets of Manufacturing Corporation in a "C" reorganization. Following the reorganization, Retail transfers the assets received to a newly formed subsidiary, Supply Corp., in a § 351 transaction. The transfer of the assets to Supply Corp. does not affect the "C" reorganization.

Example 25

Same facts as *Example 24* except Manufacturing Corporation also owned some retail outlets in addition to the manufacturing operations. Retail transfers only the manufacturing assets to Supply. The acquisition of Manufacturing still qualifies as a "C" reorganization. Retail was able to restructure Manufacturing so that it is solely a manufacturing company and Retail contains all of the marketing operations.

In lieu of dropping down the assets to a controlled subsidiary, a controlled subsidiary could be used as the acquiring corporation. In such case, the subsidiary may use the voting stock of the corporation that is in control of it (i.e., its parent corporation) in lieu of its own voting stock.[34] The acquiring corporation may not use both its own and its parent's voting stock. This rule is identical to the one for a type "B" reorganization.

"D" REORGANIZATION

There are two types of "D" reorganizations.[35] The first is referred to as an *acquisitive "D" reorganization* since it results in the acquisition of target's assets by the acquiring corporation. In this transaction, the acquiring corporation transfers substantially all of its assets to the

---

[33] § 368(a)(2)(C).

[34] § 368(a)(1)(C).

[35] § 368(a)(1)(D).

target corporation in exchange for control of the target corporation.[36] The acquiring corporation then distributes any remaining assets and the target corporation's stock to its shareholders.[37] Although the acquiring corporation does not have to legally liquidate, the distribution of all its assets is a *de facto* liquidation. The shareholders of the acquiring corporation that has been liquidated (either in fact or in effect) become the controlling shareholders of the target corporation. The transaction is illustrated in Exhibit 7-8.

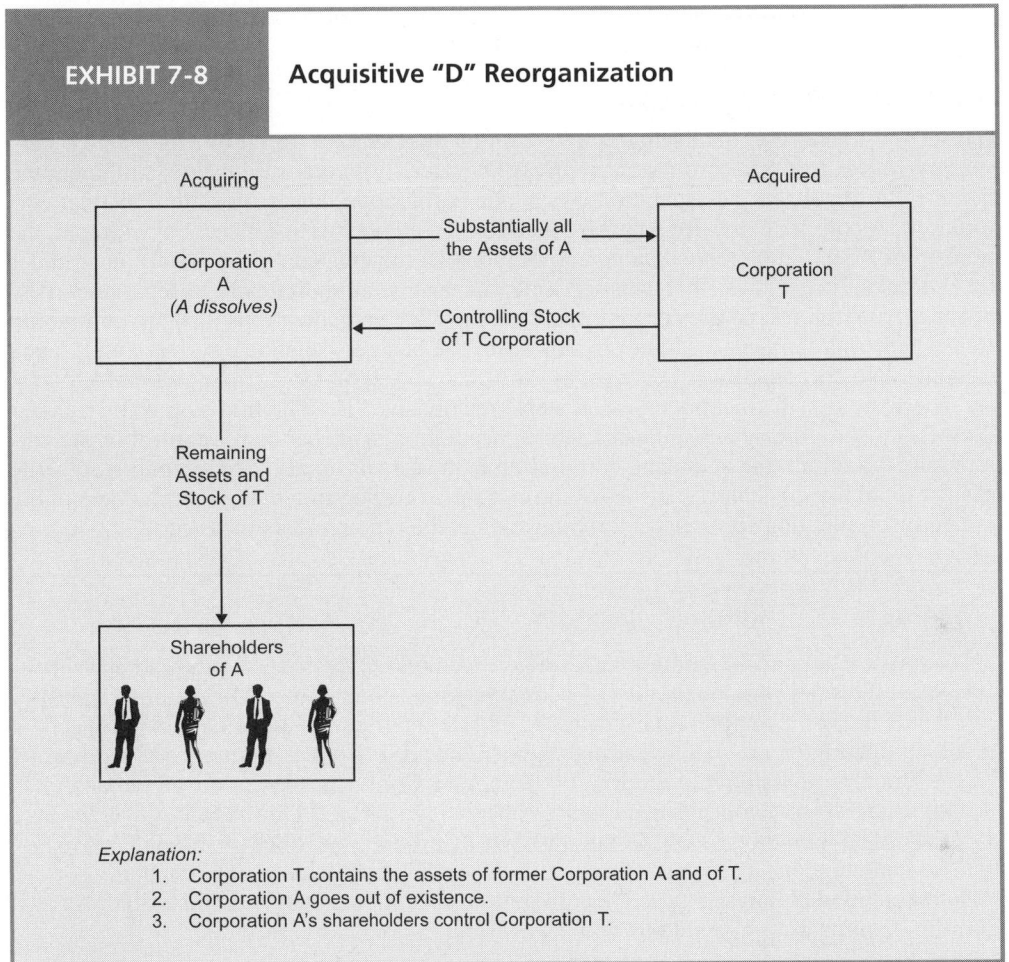

EXHIBIT 7-8	Acquisitive "D" Reorganization

Explanation:
1. Corporation T contains the assets of former Corporation A and of T.
2. Corporation A goes out of existence.
3. Corporation A's shareholders control Corporation T.

Example 26

Coal Corporation desires to acquire Power Co., its major customer. However, Power Co. must be the surviving corporation because of certain nontransferable licenses. Coal Corp. transfers all its assets to Power Co. in return for 1,000 shares of Power Co., which is 90% of the total issued and outstanding stock of Power Co. Coal Corporation then dissolves by transferring Power Co. stock to its shareholders in return for its own stock. The transaction qualifies as an acquisitive "D" reorganization. Power Co. owns all of the assets it previously owned plus all the assets of Coal Corporation, and Coal Corporation's shareholders receive stock of Power Co. sufficient for control.

---

[36] §§ 354(b)(1)(A) and 368(a)(1)(D).   [37] § 354(b)(1)(B).

It is possible for a transaction to meet the requirements of *both* the "C" reorganization *and* the acquisitive "D" reorganization. In these cases, the transaction is treated as a "D" reorganization.[38]

The result of an acquisitive "D" reorganization is that the shareholders of the acquiring corporation (the transferor of assets) end up in control of the target corporation. For purpose of this reorganization, control is defined as ownership of stock possessing at least 50% of the voting power or at least 50% of the total value of all classes of stock.[39] This special definition of control was enacted to prevent certain tax avoidance schemes that were popular prior to the repeal of the General Utilities doctrine.

Divisive "D" Reorganization

The second transaction qualifying as a "D" reorganization is referred to as a *divisive "D" reorganization*. In contrast to the acquisitive "D" where two corporations are combined, the divisive "D" results in the separation of a single corporation into two or more distinct corporations. A corporate division may be called for in a number of instances. For example, the breakup of AT&T into eight separate corporations was mandated by the government under the Federal antitrust laws. On a smaller scale, management might desire to separate a risky business from the rest of the corporation. Divisive "D" reorganizations also are commonly used where shareholders disagree. In this case, the business is split up, thus giving each group its own corporation.

There are two distinct but essential steps in a divisive "D." The first step is the transfer of assets constituting an active business to a corporation in exchange for control of the corporation.[40] In effect, the acquiring corporation creates a subsidiary. The second step is the transfer of all the stock and securities of the controlled corporation to the shareholders of the transferor corporation. This distribution must meet the requirements of § 355.[41]

Example 27

Computer Corp. manufactures and sells computers. Over time, Computer has increased the sales of its manufactured components to competitors. On the other hand, sales of its own computers have dropped and its retail outlets have had to stock and sell competing brands. This year management decided to separate the manufacturing and retailing operations. Accordingly, Computer Corp. transferred all of the assets used in the manufacturing operation to a new corporation, Manufacturing, in return for all of its common stock. Computer then distributed the stock of Manufacturing to its shareholders. The transaction is a divisive "D" reorganization. Computer Corp. has been divided into two separate corporations—Computer and Manufacturing. As a result, Computer's shareholders now own shares of both corporations.

The final ownership of the two resulting corporations in a divisive "D" depends on (1) the manner in which the controlled corporation's stock is distributed—pro rata or non-pro rata,[42] and (2) whether the receiving shareholders are required to exchange shares of the original corporation's stock for the shares of the new corporation's stock they receive.[43] The method of distribution and/or exchange produces one of three different types of divisions. These are referred to as the spin-off, the split-off, and the split-up.

Spin-Off

In a *spin-off,* the original corporation transfers some of its assets to a newly formed subsidiary in exchange for all of the subsidiary's stock, which it then distributes to its shareholders (see Exhibit 7-9). The shareholders of the original corporation do not surrender any of their ownership in the original corporation for the subsidiary's stock. Consequently, the

---

[38] § 368(a)(2)(A).

[39] § 368(a)(2)(H).

[40] §§ 368(a)(1)(D) and 355(a)(1)(C).

[41] § 355(a)(1)(D)(i). The transferor corporation may keep some stock provided it distributes control to its shareholders

and can prove that the retention was not motivated by tax avoidance § 355(a)(1)(D)(ii).

[42] § 355(a)(2)(A).

[43] § 355(a)(2)(B).

shareholders of the original corporation are still shareholders of the original corporation as well as shareholders of the newly formed subsidiary. Note that the entire transaction is virtually identical to a normal dividend distribution. Yet, if all the reorganization requirements are satisfied, the distribution is tax-free to the shareholders.

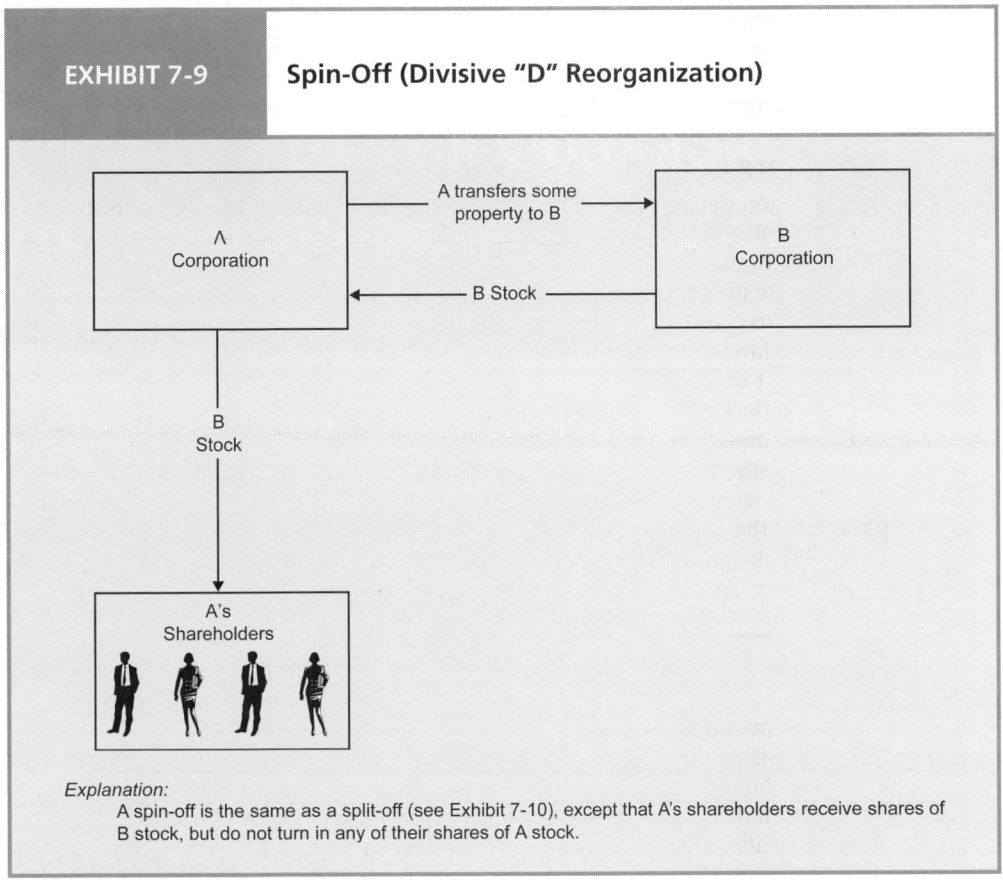

EXHIBIT 7-9	Spin-Off (Divisive "D" Reorganization)

Explanation:
A spin-off is the same as a split-off (see Exhibit 7-10), except that A's shareholders receive shares of B stock, but do not turn in any of their shares of A stock.

The spin-off transaction is often used when management decides that corporate operations should be divided but the shareholders want to continue an investment in both the original and new corporation.

Example 28

P Corporation, a water company, owns 100% of S Corporation. P established S many years ago to hold a reservoir and the surrounding land for future development. This year P's management determined that it would be in the best interest of P to withdraw from the real estate development business and concentrate on its utility business. Accordingly, P distributed all of its shares in S to its shareholders. The distribution is referred to as a spin-off. Although it is virtually indistinguishable from a dividend distribution, it is a tax-free distribution if the requirements of § 355 are satisfied.

Split-Off

When shareholders prefer different investments in the future operations of the corporation, a *split-off* is used. In a split-off, the original corporation transfers some of its assets to a newly formed subsidiary in exchange for all of the subsidiary's stock, which it then distributes to some or all of its shareholders in exchange for some portion of their original stock. As a result, the two corporations are held by the original shareholders but in a proportion that differs from that which they held in the original corporation. The split-off is presented in Exhibit 7-10.

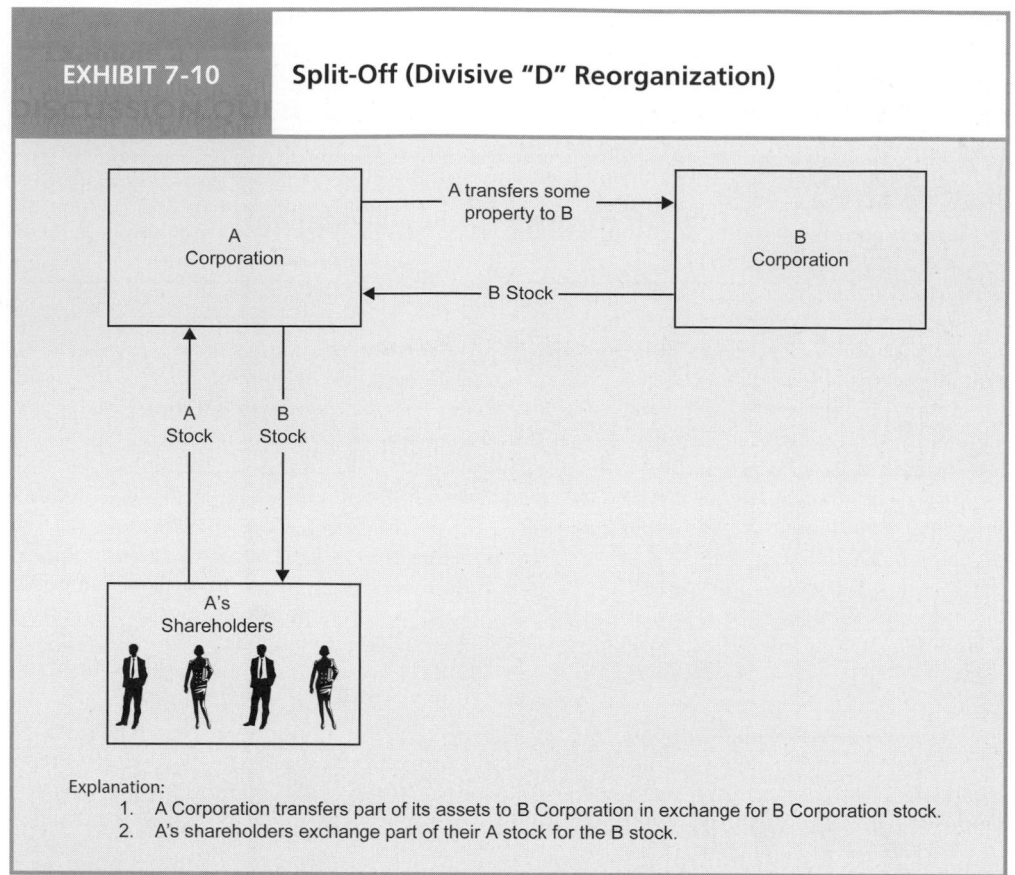

EXHIBIT 7-10   **Split-Off (Divisive "D" Reorganization)**

Explanation:
1. A Corporation transfers part of its assets to B Corporation in exchange for B Corporation stock.
2. A's shareholders exchange part of their A stock for the B stock.

Example 29

S Corp. is owned equally by B and his three sons: C, D, and E. The corporation has been in the electronics business for a long time and recently has become involved in computers. B died this year and willed equal interests in S Corp. to each of his three sons. Apparently, B had been the glue that held the family business together, for shortly after his death the brothers disagreed. D and E decided that the company should invest more in computers and less in electronics. On the other hand, C is somewhat reluctant about becoming too heavily involved in computers and feels that the corporation's efforts should remain primarily in its traditional business of electronics. As a compromise, the three decide to separate the corporation into two corporations. S Corp. transfers the assets of the computer business to a new corporation, T, in exchange for all of its stock. It subsequently transfers all of the T stock to D and E in exchange for all of their interest in S. As a result, D and E own T Corp. while C owns S Corp. The transaction qualifies as a divisive "D" reorganization.

The sole difference between the spin-off and split-off concerns the shareholder exchange. In a spin-off, shareholders do not surrender any stock in the original corporation for the stock they receive, while in a split-off they do. Consequently, the transaction is similar to a redemption. However, like a spin-off, the transaction is nontaxable if all the rules related to reorganizations are followed.

Split-Up

A *split-up* varies little from a split-off. In a split-up, the original corporation transfers some of its assets to one newly created subsidiary and the remainder of the assets to another newly created subsidiary. The original corporation then liquidates, distributing the stock of both subsidiaries in exchange for its own stock. The effect of the split-up is to create two new corporations. The dissolution of the original corporation distinguishes this transaction from a split-off and also causes it to be similar to a liquidation. The split-up is illustrated in Exhibit 7-11.

EXHIBIT 7-11	Split-Up (Divisive "D" Reorganization)

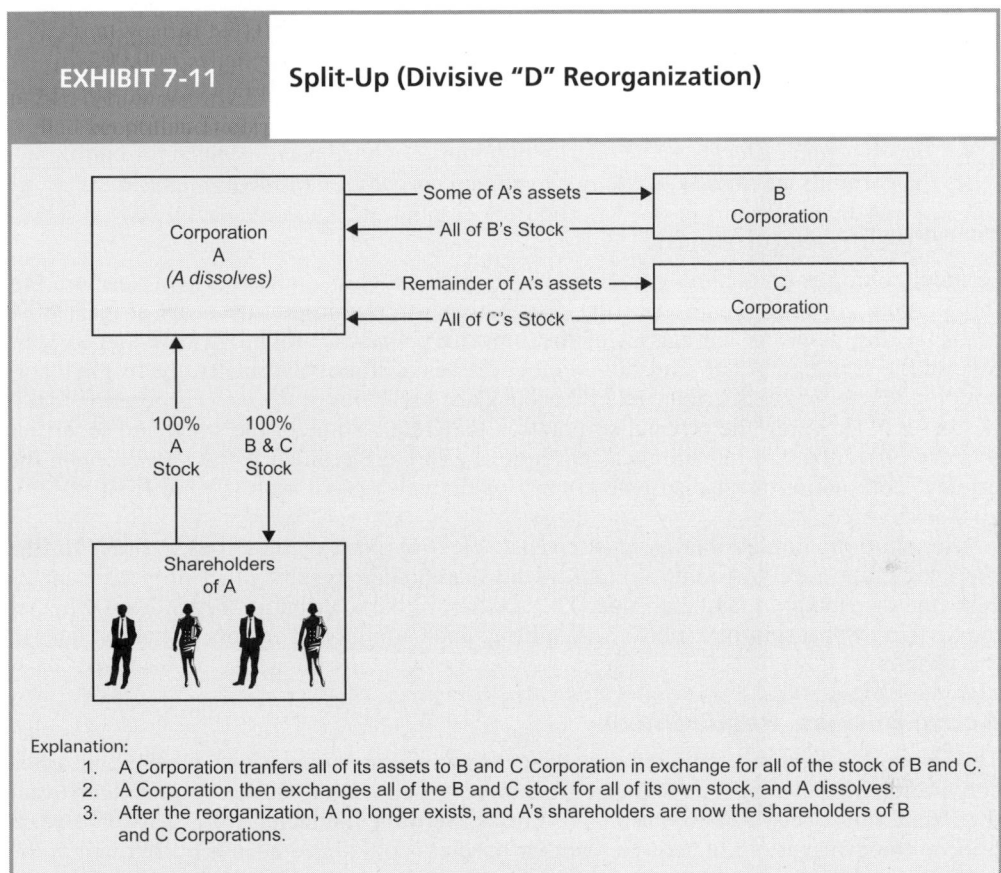

Explanation:
1. A Corporation tranfers all of its assets to B and C Corporation in exchange for all of the stock of B and C.
2. A Corporation then exchanges all of the B and C stock for all of its own stock, and A dissolves.
3. After the reorganization, A no longer exists, and A's shareholders are now the shareholders of B and C Corporations.

Example 30

Same facts as in *Example 29*. Instead of continuing S Corp. in its present form, C, D, and E decide to set up two new corporations: X Inc. and Y Inc. The assets of the computer business are transferred to X in exchange for all of the X stock while the assets of the electronic business are transferred to Y in exchange for all of the Y stock. In liquidation of S Corp., the X stock is distributed to D and E in exchange for all of their S stock and the Y stock is distributed to C in exchange for all of his S stock. D and E are now shareholders in X while C is the sole shareholder of Y.

Existing Subsidiary

In a divisive "D" reorganization, a corporation transfers assets to one or more newly created subsidiaries and subsequently distributes the stock. In some cases, a corporation simply distributes the stock of an *existing* subsidiary that it may have acquired or formed at another time. In such case, the reorganization provisions of § 368 do not apply. Nevertheless, the distribution is still subject to § 355 and will therefore be nontaxable, assuming the requirements discussed below are met.

Requirements for Divisive "D" Reorganization

As noted above, spin-offs, split-offs, and split-ups must satisfy the requirements imposed by § 355 in order to qualify for favorable treatment as "D" reorganizations. These requirements are as follows:

1. *Distribution of Control*—The original corporation must distribute to its shareholders stock of the newly created subsidiary that constitutes control.

2. *Character of Distribution*—The property distributed by the original corporation must consist solely of stock or securities of the newly created subsidiary. Distribution of other property (including certain preferred stock and securities in certain circumstances) constitutes boot, and gain must be recognized.

3. *Active Business*—Immediately after the distribution, both the original corporation and the controlled subsidiary must be engaged in the active conduct of a trade or business.

4. *Tax-Avoidance Device*—The distribution must not have been a device for bailing out the earnings and profits of either the original corporation or the new subsidiary.

Distribution Requirement

Nonrecognition is granted only to distributions of stock of a "controlled" corporation. For this purpose, control is present if the distributing parent corporation owns at least 80% of the voting power of all classes of the subsidiary's stock entitled to vote and at least 80% of the total number of shares of all other classes of stock.[44] Normally, the original corporation is required to distribute all of the stock and securities of the new corporation that it possesses.[45] However, the original corporation may retain some of the stock and securities if it can prove that the retention was not motivated by tax avoidance.[46] As a *minimum*, the original corporation must distribute control of the new corporation (i.e., at least 80% of all stock).

In addition, the distribution must consist solely of stock or securities in order for the shareholders to receive nonrecognition. If the shareholders receive other property such as cash, the distribution may be taxable. The taxation of the distribution depends on whether the division was a spin-off, split-off, or split-up and certain other factors discussed later in this chapter.

Active Business Requirement

The *active business test* requires that both the transferor corporation and the controlled corporation must be engaged in the active conduct of a trade or business immediately after the transfer of assets.[47] These businesses must have been conducted for at least five years prior to the distribution. In addition, neither business could have been acquired within the five-year period in a taxable transaction.[48] These conditions are designed to prevent a corporation from using the "D" reorganization to bail out accumulated cash and other assets in the original corporation at capital gains rates instead of ordinary income rates. Without this rule, the bailout could be accomplished by a "D" reorganization followed by a liquidation or sale of the distributed stock.

Example 31

F Corporation has excess accumulated cash. If it paid a dividend, its shareholders would be required to report ordinary dividend income. Instead, F transfers the cash to Newco, a newly created subsidiary, and distributes Newco stock to its shareholders in what it hopes is a nontaxable "D" reorganization. The shareholders then liquidate Newco and report capital gains on the liquidation. Under the active business test, the original transaction does not qualify as a "D" reorganization because Newco fails to engage in any business after the distribution. Consequently, the shareholders are required to report dividend income on the receipt of Newco stock.

---

[44] § 355(a)(1)(A).

[45] § 355(a)(1)(D)(i).

[46] § 355(a)(1)(D)(ii).

[47] § 355(b)(1)(A).

[48] § 355(b)(2).

> ### Example 32
>
> Same facts as *Example 31* except F uses the cash to buy an existing business. It transfers the business to Newco and distributes the Newco stock to its shareholders. The shareholders sell the Newco stock and report capital gains. Since the business transferred to Newco was acquired in a taxable transaction (i.e., a purchase), the transaction does not satisfy the active business test and thus is not a valid "D" reorganization. The shareholders must report dividend income on the receipt of Newco stock.

The determination of whether or not a corporation is engaged in an active business is made based on all the facts and circumstances. The minimum requirement for an active business is that the corporate activities include every step in the process of earning income.[49] Ordinarily, this would include collection of income and payment of expenses. In addition, the Regulations indicate that the active conduct of a trade or business does not include either (1) the holding of stock, securities, or other property for investment purposes or (2) the ownership or operation (including leasing) of real or personal property used in a trade or business unless the owner performs significant services with respect to the operation and management of the property.[50]

> ### Example 33
>
> L Corporation desires to transfer the land it owns to a new corporation, N, in a "D" reorganization. Some of the land will be held for future appreciation. The remainder would be leased back to L as a parking lot. The assets transferred to N probably would not be considered a trade or business. The investment land lacks the requisite collection of income and payment of expense activities. The leasing activities probably do not contain sufficient services to be considered a business.

As noted above, the active business must have been conducted for at least five years prior to the distribution. It need not be conducted by the original corporation for all of the required five years. In this regard, additions of new products and other similar changes are disregarded provided they do not constitute the acquisition of a new business.[51]

> ### Example 34
>
> Manufacturing Corporation has been in the business of manufacturing and selling television and stereo equipment for the past 15 years. During the last five years, it discontinued production of black-and-white TVs and started producing miniature portable sets following the construction of a new plant. The changes during the past five years should not prevent Manufacturing from being considered to have been in the business of manufacturing and selling televisions for more than five years.

The nebulous features of the active business requirement have led to a significant amount of litigation. Taxpayers have been successful in separating two businesses, dividing one business into two complete businesses,[52] and dividing a single business along functional lines.[53] Whether a particular division qualifies, however, must be determined in light of all the facts and circumstances.

---

[49] Reg. § 1.355-3(b)(2)(ii).

[50] Reg. § 1.355-3(b)(2)(iv)(B).

[51] Reg. § 1.355-3(b)(3)(ii).

[52] *Coady*, 33 T.C. 771 (1960).

[53] *Wilson*, 42 T.C. 914 (1964); *Leslie, Jr.*, 40 T.C. 947 (1963).

Device Limitation

For a valid "D" reorganization, taxpayers must be able to prove that the transaction was not principally a device for distributing the earnings of the distributing or controlled corporation.[54] Although the device question must be answered based on all the facts and circumstances, there are several factors that indicate that the transaction was used to avoid taxes. For example, subsequent sales of stock by the shareholders, transfer or retention of liquid assets in excess of business needs, and operation of the controlled corporation in a manner similar to that of the pretransfer operation all suggest an improper motive.[55]

Example 35

Bank Corporation has been in existence for 20 years. Six years ago it started performing bookkeeping and accounting work for the public. D, an individual, desires to purchase the bookkeeping and accounting business. Rather than sell the business, Bank distributes the assets to a new corporation, Book, and distributes Book's stock to its shareholders. The shareholders sell half of Book's stock to D. The transaction would probably be considered a device for the distribution of earnings.[56]

Example 36

Same facts as *Example 35* except that Bank transfers cash in excess of Book's needs to Book along with the other assets. The shareholders sell half the stock to E, an individual who expressed interest in Book following the transaction. The fact that excess cash was transferred to Book and the shareholders sold some of the stock, even though not part of the original plan, will probably result in the transaction being considered a device for the distribution of earnings.[57]

The transaction is not considered a device if the distribution to the shareholder would otherwise qualify as a sale under the stock redemption provisions of § 302.[58]

Example 37

X Corporation transfers an active business to Z Corporation in exchange for all of Z's stock. The Z stock is then distributed to individual J in exchange for all of her X stock. The exchange of Z stock for all of J's stock, standing alone, would be considered a redemption of J's entire interest qualifying for sale treatment under § 302. Therefore, the transaction will not be considered a device for distributing earnings. This *safe harbor* rule favors the split-up over the spin-off and possibly the split-off, which could not meet the conditions of § 302.

"E" REORGANIZATION

The "E" reorganization is defined as a *recapitalization*.[59] Although not defined in the Code, the term *recapitalization* refers to exchanges of stock and securities by the corporation's shareholders and security holders for new stock and/or securities. In essence,

---

[54] § 355(a)(1)(B).

[55] Reg. § 1.355-2(d)(2) and (3).

[56] See Reg. § 1.355-2(c)(4) Ex. 1.

[57] See Reg. § 1.355-2(d)(4) Ex. 3.

[58] Reg. § 1.355-2(c)(5).

[59] § 368(a)(1)(E).

the "E" reorganization permits a corporation to alter the configuration of its capital structure. As such, the "E" reorganization involves only one corporation. Also, the regulations exempt the "E" reorganization from both the continuity of interest and the continuity of business enterprise doctrines.

Four exchanges are included under the general heading of recapitalization. They are:

1. Stock for Stock
2. Bonds for Stock
3. Bonds for Bonds
4. Stock for Bonds

As a general rule, only the first three exchanges qualify as "E" reorganizations.

Stock for Stock

The exchange of stock in a corporation for other stock in the same corporation qualifies as an "E" reorganization. It is immaterial whether the transaction involves common for common, common for preferred, preferred for common, or preferred for preferred.[60] Also, differences in the voting rights, dividend rates, and preferences on liquidation are ignored.

Example 38

ABC Corporation is equally owned by S and her son. S desires to retire from active involvement in the corporation. She exchanges all of her common stock for nonvoting, nonparticipating, preferred stock. The exchange can qualify as an "E" reorganization.

Example 39

XYZ Corporation has been unable to pay a dividend on its noncumulative, nonvoting, preferred stock. To forestall a fight at the shareholders' meeting, XYZ agrees to exchange one share of participating, cumulative, preferred stock for each share of preferred stock currently outstanding. The exchange can qualify as an "E" reorganization.[61]

Example 40

W Corporation is owned equally by C and his sister K. C and K cannot agree on the future direction of W Corporation. K agrees to exchange all of her W stock for the stock of S, a wholly owned subsidiary of W. This cannot be an "E" reorganization because K is not receiving stock in the same corporation.

Although the "E" reorganization includes exchanges of preferred stock, it does not cover preferred stock with dividends in arrears. The stock received for the dividends will be taxable under the rules of § 305, which makes stock dividends paid on preferred stock taxable.[62]

---

[60] Reg. § 1.368-2(e)(2) and (3).

[61] The transaction would also receive nonrecognition treatment under § 1036.

[62] Reg. § 1.368-2(e)(5).

Bonds for Stock

The exchange of bonds for stock by a security holder qualifies as an "E" reorganization. This provision effectively permits the corporation to pay off its debts with stock.[63] Creditors may be willing to make such an exchange where equity participation appears more profitable. The stock can be either common or preferred. The "E" reorganization does not cover the issuance of stock for accrued interest. The fair market value of the stock distributed must equal the face amount of the debt surrendered to avoid forgiveness of indebtedness income.[64]

Bonds for Bonds

The exchange of bonds for other bonds of the corporation by a security holder qualifies as an "E" reorganization.[65] However, if the principal amount of the bonds received exceeds the principal amount of the bonds surrendered, gain must be recognized by the bondholder.[66]

Example 41

As part of an "E" reorganization, T exchanges 100 shares of common stock and bonds with a face amount of $1,000 for 50 shares of preferred stock and bonds with a face amount of $1,200. T has received $200 ($1,200 − $1,000) of excess principal on the bonds. He is required to recognize gain on the exchange.

Stock for Bonds

As a general rule, an exchange of stock for bonds by a shareholder does not qualify as an "E" reorganization since the shareholder has upgraded his or her investment position.[67] Even if it did qualify as a reorganization, the bonds received would be treated as "boot." Therefore, the shareholder must recognize income. The income is treated as dividends or capital gains depending on whether the receipt of the bonds was the equivalent of a dividend (e.g., a pro rata distribution).

"F" REORGANIZATION

An "F" reorganization is defined as "a mere change in identity, form, or place of organization of one corporation, however effected."[68] Like the "E" reorganization, it is also exempt from the continuity of interest and continuity of business enterprise doctrines. The "F" reorganization rules normally apply when the corporation changes its name, state of operation, or makes other changes in its corporate charter. In such case, there is a deemed transfer from the old corporation to the new corporation.

Example 42

The change in name from American Building Corporation to "American Corporation" in the corporate charter is an "F" reorganization. There is a deemed transfer from the old corporation (American Building Corporation) to a new corporation (American Corporation).

"G" REORGANIZATION

A "G" reorganization applies to a reorganization as part of bankruptcy.[69] It permits the transfer of some or all of the assets of a failing corporation to a new controlled corporation provided the stock and securities of the controlled corporation are distributed to the old corporation's shareholders under the rules for distributions in a "D" reorganization.

[63] Reg. § 1.368-2(e)(1).

[64] § 108(e)(8).

[65] *Trust of Neustadt v. Comm.*, 42-2 USTC ¶9751, 30 AFTR 320, 131 F.2d 528 (CA-2, 1942).

[66] § 354(a)(2)(A).

[67] *Bazley*, 47-1 USTC ¶9288, 35 AFTR 1190, 311 U.S. 737 (USSC 1947).

[68] § 368(a)(1)(F).

[69] § 368(a)(1)(G).

Judicial Limitations

The courts have not felt constrained to grant nonrecognition treatment to a transaction simply because it falls within the definition of a reorganization and can pass the continuity requirements. From almost the beginning, the courts have required corporations and their shareholders to show a business purpose for the reorganization. The earliest and best known case imposing this requirement was *Gregory v. Helvering*.[70] In order to avoid the receipt of dividend income, Gregory had a corporation that she owned undergo what today would meet the definition of a divisive "D" reorganization. According to her instructions, her wholly owned corporation transferred assets to a new corporation in exchange for its stock. The corporation then distributed the shares of stock to Gregory. Shortly after receiving the shares of the new corporation she liquidated it, thereby acquiring its assets at capital-gains rates rather than dividend rates. The Supreme Court acknowledged that the transaction met the literal requirements of a reorganization. However, they refused to grant it nonrecognition treatment on the grounds that it lacked a business purpose other than tax avoidance. Although this case arose prior to the 1954 Code, the courts continue to require a business purpose before a transaction is considered a reorganization.

There is no specific definition of business purpose. The Regulations provide little guidance, indicating only that a transaction that "puts on the form of a reorganization as a disguise for concealing its real character, and the object and accomplishment of which is the consummation of a preconceived plan having no business or corporate purpose, is not a plan of reorganization." Similarly, in § 355, the Regulations provide that "a corporate business purpose is a real and substantial non-Federal tax purpose germane to the business."[71] Unfortunately, these statements provide little insight as to what may or may not constitute a business purpose.

Plan of Reorganization

The final requirement for a valid reorganization is the existence of a plan of reorganization. This requirement is not contained in § 368, the definitional section, but appears in § 361, the operational section that provides for nonrecognition treatment. The plan must be adopted by each corporation involved in the transaction.[72] However, the fact that the corporations adopt a plan will not result in transactions being classified as reorganizations unless they meet the specific requirements discussed above.[73]

Tax Consequences of Reorganization

The benefits afforded a reorganization are generally limited to "parties to the reorganization." The parties to the reorganization are the acquiring corporation, the target corporation, and any corporation formed during the reorganization.[74] If stock of a corporation that controls the acquiring corporation is used in the exchange, the controlling corporation is also a party to the reorganization. Finally, if the assets acquired from the target are transferred to a subsidiary, the subsidiary is a party to the reorganization.

LO.3
Discuss the tax treatment of the acquiring corporation, the target corporation, and the target's shareholders.

The shareholders of a party to the reorganization are not parties to the reorganization themselves. Their tax treatment is determined by the property exchanged. Generally, if they exchange stock and/or securities of a party to the reorganization for stock and securities of another party to the reorganization (the same corporation or a different one), the exchange is nontaxable.[75]

The tax treatment of the various participants is discussed below.

---

[70] 35-1 USTC ¶9043, 14 AFTR 1191, 293 U.S. 465 (USSC, 1935).

[71] Reg. § 1.355-2(b).

[72] Reg. § 1.368-3(a).

[73] Reg. § 1.368-2(g).

[74] § 368(b).

[75] § 354(a).

Acquiring Corporation

Gain or Loss

In a reorganization, the acquiring corporation transfers its stock, securities, and perhaps boot to the target corporation in exchange for its property or stock. Since the acquiring corporation is treated as having issued stock for a contribution of property, it recognizes neither gain nor loss under the general rule allowing nonrecognition of gain on the contribution of property to a corporation.[76] Similarly, the issuance of securities in a reorganization has historically been granted nonrecognition. In contrast, if the acquiring corporation transfers other property or boot, it must recognize gain or loss on the transfer of such boot measured by the difference between its fair market value and adjusted basis at the time of transfer.[77]

Example 43

In a "C" reorganization, Acquiring Corporation transfers its stock worth $800,000 and land worth $200,000 (basis $50,000) to Target Corporation in exchange for all of its assets and liabilities. Acquiring Corporation must recognize a $150,000 gain on the transfer of the land just as if it had sold the land for cash and transferred such cash to Target Corporation. No gain or loss is recognized on the transfer of the stock.

Distribution of Stock and Securities of a Controlled Corporation

As a general rule, a parent corporation that distributes stock or securities of a subsidiary in a spin-off, split-off, or split-up transaction or any other distribution to which § 355 applies does not recognize gain or loss. However, §§ 355(d) and (e) prescribe special rules to prevent corporate taxpayers from using this provision to convert what is in reality a sale to a nontaxable distribution.

Example 44

P Corporation owns all of the stock of a subsidiary, S. P purchased the stock of S several years ago for $10,000, and it is now worth $100,000. P now wishes to sell S but does not want to recognize any gain. During the year, Buyer purchased 40% of P's stock on the open market for $100,000. Shortly thereafter, as part of a qualifying split-off, P distributed all of its stock in S (worth $100,000) to Buyer in exchange for all of Buyer's P stock (worth $100,000). In effect, P has sold all of the S stock for $100,000. Yet under the general rule, P would not recognize any gain on the transaction.

To ensure that taxpayers cannot disguise sales as nontaxable distributions, Congress adopted two special rules. Section 355(d) generally requires a corporation to recognize gain—but not loss—on the distribution of a subsidiary's stock if, immediately after the distribution, a shareholder holds at least a 50% interest in either the subsidiary or the parent that is attributable to stock that was purchased within the five-year period prior to the distribution. Note that the shareholder is not affected by this provision.

Example 45

Same facts as *Example 44* above. P must recognize a gain of $90,000 ($100,000 − $10,000) on the distribution of S stock because Buyer received at least a 50% interest in S (it actually received a 100% interest) as a result of its purchase of P stock during the preceding five years.

---

[76] § 1032.

[77] § 361(a) does not apply to the transfer of boot.

Under § 355(e), the distributing corporation must recognize gain on the distribution of stock of a controlled corporation if the distribution is part of a plan where one or more persons acquire 50% or more of the controlled or distributing corporation. A plan is presumed if one or more persons acquire at least 50% of stock during the four year period starting two years before the date of distribution. The presumption is rebuttable. The section also provides that the acquisition of the assets of either controlled or distributing in a nontaxable reorganization will be treated as the acquisition of stock of the corporation from which the assets were acquired.

Example 46

P Corporation runs two separate businesses. A Corporation wishes to acquire one of these businesses. P Corporation transfers the unwanted business to a new corporation S, and distributes the stock of S to its shareholders. Following the distribution, A Corporation acquires all the stock of P Corporation in exchange for its stock. P Corporation will be required to recognize gain of the distribution of S stock as if it sold the stock for its fair market value.

Both §§ 355(d) and (e) prevent disguised sales by requiring the distributing corporation to recognize gain. Section 355(d) is triggered by the purchase of stock whereas § 355(e) is triggered by any acquisition of 50% or more of the stock of either controlled or distributing corporations within the four-year period.

Basis of Acquired Property or Stock

When the acquiring corporation obtains the assets of the target corporation, the basis of such assets must be determined. The acquiring corporation's basis in such property is the same as that of the target corporation increased by any gain recognized by the target (normally none, as discussed below).[78] In other words, the basis of the target corporation's assets generally carries over completely intact to the acquiring corporation. These rules apply even if the acquiring corporation receives stock or securities of the target corporation. This calculation is shown in Exhibit 7-12.

EXHIBIT 7-12	Acquiring Corporation's Basis for Property Received

Transferor's basis in property transferred		$xxx,xxx
Plus:	Gain recognized by the transferor on the transfer	xx,xxx
Equals:	Basis of property to acquiring corporation	$xxx,xxx

Example 47

In a statutory merger (an "A" reorganization), Target Corporation transfers assets worth $500,000 (basis $400,000) in exchange for Acquiring Corporation stock worth $500,000. Acquiring Corporation's basis in the assets received is the same as Target Corporation's basis, $400,000.

---

[78] § 362(b).

> ### Example 48
>
> In a "B" reorganization, Acquiring Corporation transferred stock worth $1 million to T, the sole shareholder of Target Corporation, in exchange for all of his stock. T's basis in his stock was $50,000. Acquiring Corporation's basis in Target Corporation's stock is the same as T's, $50,000.

As shown in Exhibit 7-12, the basis of the property acquired by the acquiring corporation is the same as the target's basis increased by any gain recognized by the target. The target corporation will not recognize gain on the transfer of assets to the acquiring corporation except in the case of a transfer of liabilities. Consequently, in computing the basis of the assets to the acquiring corporation there generally will be no gain to consider. In addition, any gain that might be recognized by the target corporation on the transfer to its shareholders, as well as any gain recognized by the shareholders on the receipt of a distribution by the target corporation, does not affect the acquiring corporation's basis in the assets received.

> ### Example 49
>
> In a "C" reorganization, Acquiring Corporation transfers its own stock worth $800,000 and cash of $200,000 to Target Corporation in exchange for all of Target's assets with a basis of $500,000. Target subsequently liquidates as required, distributing the cash and stock to its shareholders. Although Target Corporation's shareholders must recognize gain, the basis of the assets to Acquiring Corporation is limited to $500,000, the basis of the assets in the hands of the Target Corporation. The gain recognized by the shareholders of Target is not added to the basis of the assets.

ACQUIRED (TARGET) CORPORATION

Gain or Loss

In acquisitive reorganizations, the target corporation transfers its assets to the acquiring corporation in exchange for stock, securities, and boot. In such case, the target corporation recognizes no gain or loss on the *receipt* of the stock and securities. In addition, no gain will be recognized on the receipt of boot provided it is distributed to target's shareholders.[79]

> ### Example 50
>
> As part of a "C" reorganization, Target Corporation transfers all of its assets with a basis of $600,000 and a fair market value of $800,000 for stock of the Acquiring Corporation worth $700,000 and cash of $100,000. Target recognizes no gain or loss on the receipt of the stock or cash.

The assumption of the target corporation's liabilities is not considered the receipt of boot.[80] However, if the principal purpose for the transfer of the liabilities is tax avoidance, the total amount of the liabilities is considered boot.[81] Unlike a corporate formation under § 351, the transfer of liabilities in excess of basis does not produce gain except in the case of a divisive "D" reorganization.[82]

---

[79] § 361(b).

[80] § 357(a).

[81] § 357(b).

[82] § 357(c).

Example 51

As part of a "C" reorganization, Target Corporation transfers assets with a basis of $800,000 and a fair market value of $1 million. The acquiring corporation gave Target its stock with a fair market value of $900,000 and assumes $100,000 of Target's liabilities. Although Target realizes a $200,000 gain, it does not recognize any gain since liabilities surrendered are not treated as boot. Had the assumption of the liabilities been motivated by tax avoidance, Target would have been treated as having received $100,000 of boot.

Example 52

Target transfers assets with a basis of $800,000 and a fair market value of $1 million plus a liability of $950,000 to Acquiring Corporation for stock worth $50,000 in a "C" reorganization. Although Target realizes a $200,000 gain ($950,000 + $50,000 − $800,000), none is recognized since liabilities exceeding basis are ignored *except* in a "D" reorganization. Had the transfer been to a controlled corporation in a "D" reorganization, Target would recognize gain of $150,000, the excess of liabilities over basis ($950,000 − $800,000).

Basis

In most cases, the target corporation has little concern for determining basis since it normally receives stock, securities, or cash, which it distributes to its shareholders in liquidation. As explained below, the shareholders who receive such property determine their bases in the property under special rules.

One special situation regarding the target's basis that must be addressed concerns receipts by the target corporation of property *other than* stock, securities, or cash. This particular case requires attention because of the ramifications to the target corporation on a later distribution of such property. When the target receives boot other than cash, the basis of the boot is the same as it would be in the hands of the acquiring corporation, increased by any gain and decreased by any loss recognized by the acquiring corporation on the transfer.[83] As discussed above, the acquiring corporation must recognize gain or loss on the transfer of boot. Consequently, the basis of any boot received by the target is its fair market value.

Example 53

As part of a "C" reorganization, Acquiring Corporation transferred its own stock worth $900,000 and two parcels of land, one worth $60,000 (basis $10,000) and another worth $40,000 (basis $70,000), to Target Corporation for all of its assets. Acquiring must recognize a $50,000 gain on the transfer of one parcel and a $30,000 loss on the transfer of the other parcel. As a result, Target's basis in the two parcels of land is $60,000 ($10,000 basis + gain of $50,000) and $40,000 ($70,000 basis − loss of $30,000), respectively.

Liquidation of the Target (Transferor) Corporation

In a "C" or acquisitive "D" reorganization, the transferor corporation is *required* to liquidate. Accordingly, the transferor must distribute the stock, securities, and any boot received from

---

[83] Target is treated *as if* it purchased the boot property.

the acquiring (i.e., transferee) corporation, as well as any remaining assets to its shareholders. Although the transferor corporation liquidates, the liquidation rules do not cover this transaction. Instead, Code § 361 prescribes the treatment for the transferor on the distribution. Under this provision, the transferor corporation does not recognize any gain or loss on the distribution of the acquiring corporation's stock or securities.[84] However, the Code requires the transferor to recognize gain (but not loss) on the distribution of any appreciated property.[85] As a practical matter the transferor recognizes gain only on appreciated property that was not transferred to the acquiring corporation, since the basis of any property received from the acquiring corporation is its fair market value.

Example 54

In a "C" reorganization, Target Corporation transferred all of its assets except land to Acquiring Corporation. The land was worth $300,000 (basis $260,000). The assets transferred were worth $10 million and had a basis of $8 million. In exchange for the assets, Target received stock of the Acquiring Corporation worth $9.7 million, cash of $100,000, and an office building worth $200,000 (basis to Acquiring of $70,000). Acquiring Corporation must recognize gain on the transfer of $130,000. Target's basis in the office building is $200,000 (Acquiring's basis of $70,000 + the gain recognized by Acquiring of $130,000). Target recognizes no gain on the receipt of the stock and other assets. However, it must recognize gain of $40,000 ($300,000 − $260,000) on the distribution of the land that was not transferred to Acquiring. Target recognizes no gain on the distribution of the office building since its basis in the building, $200,000, is the same as its value. Note that the effect of the rule requiring the target corporation to recognize gain on the distribution of property operates to cause only the gain on retained property to be recognized. This is appropriate since the acquiring corporation previously recognized gain on the transfer of the boot.

SHAREHOLDERS

Gain or Loss

The Code specifically provides nonrecognition for shareholders and security holders if they exchange stock and securities of a party to a reorganization *solely* for stock and securities of another party to the reorganization.[86] The exchange must be pursuant to the plan of reorganization. Subsequent distributions or exchanges that are not part of the plan are not exempt from taxation even if they consist solely of stock and securities of a party to the reorganization.

The receipt of "nonqualified preferred stock" will be treated as the receipt of boot in both acquisitive and divisive reorganizations (except if received in exchange for nonqualified preferred stock or "E" reorganization of family corporations). "Nonqualified preferred stock" is redeemable preferred stock and preferred stock whose dividends vary based on changes in interest rates or commodity prices. The definition of "unqualified preferred stock" is the same for reorganizations as it is in corporate formation under § 351.

The amount of securities that can be received tax-free is limited to the principal amount of securities surrendered.[87] The fair market value of securities received in excess of the amount surrendered is considered boot.

Example 55

As part of a plan of reorganization, B, an individual, exchanges 100 shares of stock and a security in the principal amount of $1,000 for 300 shares and a security in the principal amount of $1,500. The security received had a fair market value of $1,800 on the date of receipt. B is considered to have received boot of $600 as determined below.

---

[84] § 361(c)(1).
[85] § 361(c)(2).
[86] § 354(a)(1).
[87] § 354(a)(2)(A).

Principal amount of securities received. $1,500

− Principal amount of securities . . . . (1,000)

Excess principal amount received. . . . . $ 500

$$\frac{\text{Excess principal amount}}{\text{Total current distributions}} \times \text{FMV of security received} = \begin{array}{c}\text{FMV of excess principal}\\\text{amount (i.e., boot)}\end{array}$$

$$\frac{\$500}{\$1,500} \times \$1,800 = \$600$$

The solely for stock and securities requirement has been modified to permit a limited amount of boot.[88] The receipt of boot causes the recognition of gain up to the amount of money plus the fair market value of property received. The receipt of boot does not permit the recognition of loss on the transaction, however.[89]

Example 56

As part of a plan of reorganization, A, an individual, received the following in exchange for a share of stock having an adjusted basis to her of $85:

One share of stock worth $100

Cash 25

Other property worth 50

Total $175

A's realized gain is $90 ($175 − $85). Total boot received is $75 ($25 + $50). A recognizes income of $75, the lesser of the amount of boot received or the gain realized.

The type of gain recognized is determined by the type of exchange. If the shareholder receives the distribution without having to surrender stock and securities (e.g., a spin-off), then the boot is treated as a dividend.[90] If the shareholder exchanges stock in the transaction and the boot has the effect of a dividend distribution (e.g., a pro rata distribution to all shareholders), the shareholder recognizes dividend income to the extent of his or her ratable share of accumulated earnings and profits.[91] Boot not having the effect of a dividend, or in excess of the shareholder's ratable share of accumulated earnings, is treated as an amount received on the sale of property.

In *Donald E. Clark,* the Supreme Court ruled that the determination of dividend equivalency is to be made by applying the redemption rules contained in § 302.[92] Using the approach employed by the Court, the target shareholder is deemed to have transferred his or her stock solely for stock of the *acquiring* corporation. Consequently, if the target shareholder actually receives boot, he or she is treated as having received acquiring corporation stock equal to the value of the boot. The stock hypothetically received for the boot is then treated as redeemed by the acquiring corporation. The redemption tests of § 302 are applied to the target shareholder's interest to determine the character of the gain. If the distribution has the effect of a dividend as determined under § 302, the amount of *gain* treated as a dividend is limited to the shareholder's ratable share of the earnings and profits of the acquiring corporation. Note, however, that the current equality in the tax rate applied to both dividends and capital gains reduces the significance of this distinction.

---

[88] § 356.

[89] § 356(c).

[90] § 356(b).

[91] § 356(a)(2).

[92] *Comm. v. Clark,* 89-1 USTC ¶9230, 63 AFTR 2d 89-860, 109 S. Ct.1455 (USSC, 1989).

Example 57

Target Corporation's stock is owned as follows:

Shareholder	Shares	Basis	Fair Market Value
B	100	$ 10,000	$200,000
W	100	10,000	200,000
Total	200		$400,000

This year, Acquiring Corporation acquired all of the assets of Target in a statutory merger. Prior to the merger, Acquiring had 100,000 shares outstanding worth $40 per share. B and W surrendered their stock in Target for the items noted below and computed their realized and recognized gain as follows:

	B	W	Total
Amount realized:			
Stock in Acquiring Corp.			
5,000 shares at $40/share	$200,000	—	$200,000
1,000 shares at $40/share	—	$ 40,000	40,000
Total stock	$200,000	$ 40,000	$240,000
Cash	—	160,000	160,000
Amount realized	$200,000	$200,000	$400,000
Adjusted basis	(10,000)	(10,000)	
Gain realized	$190,000	$190,000	
Gain recognized to extent of boot	none	$160,000	

The character of W's gain is determined by applying § 302, treating W as having received additional shares of stock in lieu of the cash actually received. Since the stock is worth $40 per share, she is deemed to have received an additional 4,000 shares ($160,000/$40). As a result, the transaction is recast such that W receives 5,000 shares of stock worth $200,000 rather than 1,000 shares worth $40,000 and cash of $160,000. W is then treated as having redeemed the 4,000 shares for the $160,000 cash she received. For purposes of § 302, the corporation is treated as having 110,000 shares outstanding prior to the redemption, the 100,000 prior to the merger plus the 6,000 actually issued and the 4,000 hypothetically issued to W. Prior to the hypothetical redemption, W is treated as owning 4.55% (5,000/110,000). After the redemption of the 4,000 shares, she is treated as owning 0.94% (1,000/106,000). Because her stock has dropped below 80% of what she owned before, 3.64% (80% × 4.55%), the gain of $160,000 is treated as capital gain.

When the target shareholder receives securities, the *Clark* rule is applied in a similar manner. For this purpose, the amount of the boot would be the fair market value of the excess principal amount received.

Basis

In those cases in which the shareholder exchanges stock and securities, the shareholder must calculate the basis of the stock and securities received. The stock and securities have a substituted basis;[93] that is, the basis equals the basis of the stock and securities given up. The basis is increased for gain recognized by the shareholder and decreased for boot received. The basis calculation is shown in Exhibit 7-13.

EXHIBIT 7-13	Target Shareholders' Basis of Stock and Securities Received	
Basis of stock and securities transferred		$ x,xxx
Plus:	Gain recognized	xxx
	Dividend income	xxx
Minus:	Money received	(xxx)
	FMV of property received	(xxx)
Equals:	Basis of stock and securities received	$ x,xxx

The basis of the boot received is its fair market value.[94] If the taxpayer surrenders both stock and securities for stock and securities, the basis is calculated separately for each exchange.[95]

> ## Example 58
>
> Same facts as *Example 56*. The basis of the stock received is $85 ($85 [basis of stock transferred] + $30 [dividend income] + $45 [gain on exchange] − $25 [cash received] − $50 [other boot received]). The basis of the boot property is $50.

Carryover of Tax Attributes

LO.4

Explain the rules governing the carryover of the tax attributes from one corporation to another.

From the moment of formation, a corporation begins to accumulate certain tax characteristics. For example, the corporation must select its tax year and method of accounting. Over the years, other characteristics develop. These characteristics include such items as the corporation's accumulated earnings and profits, capital loss carryovers, and net operating loss carryovers. These characteristics are referred to as the corporation's *tax attributes*. In most cases, these tax attributes are carried forward to be used by the corporation. This treatment is much like that given to individual taxpayers. For example, an individual is permitted to carry forward (and carry back) losses to use against other income to mitigate the effects of the annual accounting period requirement. Applying similar logic to corporate taxpayers, it would appear that as long as the *legal identity* of the corporation is maintained, the corporation should be permitted to use the accumulated tax attributes. However, such an approach ignores the fact that a corporation's ownership may change. If the ownership of the corporation should change, the question arises as to whether the tax attributes should be carried over to be used by the corporation under the new ownership, or die with the old ownership. Similarly, if the corporation changes its business, should the attributes arising from the old business be carried over to be used by the new business? The significance of this question becomes apparent when the attribute in question is a *loss carryover*.

---

[93] § 358(a).

[94] § 358(a)(2).

[95] Reg. § 1.358-2(b)(4).

Example 59

L Corporation has a large net operating loss carryover, deriving from several years of unprofitable operations. P Corporation is a very profitable corporation that manufactures semiconductors. P currently has plans to manufacture its own line of computers. To this end, P might purchase all of the stock of L, and with the infusion of new assets and the creation of a new computer manufacturing business, convert L to a profitable corporation. In this case, P would like to see the attributes of L survive the change in ownership so that L's loss carryover can offset current and future profits. Alternatively, P might absorb L in a merger. As in the first situation, P would want L's losses to survive the transfer to offset P's profits. In addition, P would want to inherit L's deficit in E&P (if any) in order to reduce its own E&P and perhaps eliminate any subsequent dividends.

Prior to 1954, there was great controversy over how and when a corporation's tax attributes carried over. This issue was particularly difficult when there was a reorganization such as a merger where the acquiring corporation simply absorbs the target corporation. To eliminate the confusion, Congress established specific rules regarding attribute carryovers in 1954.

CODE § 381: CARRYOVERS IN CERTAIN CORPORATION ACQUISITIONS

The general rules governing the carryover of tax attributes are contained in § 381. This section provides that where a corporation acquires the assets of another corporation in certain tax-free reorganizations and liquidations, selected attributes of the target corporation are carried over to the acquiring corporation. The reorganization transactions in which the tax attributes of the target survive are the "A," "C," acquisitive "D," "F," and "G" reorganizations. In each of these reorganizations, the acquiring corporation obtains the assets of the target corporation and the basis of such assets carries over. Consistent with this approach, the attributes of the target corporation also carry over. An acquiring corporation also inherits the target's attributes when it liquidates the target under the parent-subsidiary liquidation rules of § 332. As may be recalled from Chapter 5, in a § 332 liquidation, no gain or loss is recognized by the parent or subsidiary and the basis of the subsidiary's assets carries over to the parent—thus justifying the carryover of the tax attributes.

The nonqualifying reorganizations in which the attributes are not subject to the carry over rules are the "B," divisive "D," and "E." The "B" and "E" reorganizations were omitted since in both cases the corporation continues exactly as before only with changed ownership. There is no need for specific rules for carryovers, since the carryover occurs automatically. The divisive "D" was omitted since the transferor stays in existence and continues an active business. The transferor maintains all carryovers and the controlled corporation is considered a new entity.[96]

Following one of the specified reorganizations, § 381 provides for the termination of the tax year of the transferor corporation.[97] The termination occurs on the date the corporation transfers or distributes its assets.[98] Unless the transfer occurs on the last day of the corporation's tax year, this provision results in the corporation having to file a short period tax return.

In addition to providing for the close of the transferor's tax year, § 381 contains a long list of items that carry over or must be considered by the acquiring corporation (see Exhibit 7-14). As can be seen in this exhibit, § 381 allows the carryover of net operating loss and earnings and profits. Without further limitation, these rules would allow a profitable corporation to acquire and use for its benefit the NOLs of a loss corporation as well as any deficit the loss corporation has in E&P (see *Example 59* above). As might be expected, however, Congress took additional steps to prevent possible abuse concerning these particular attributes.

---

[96] Earnings and profits must be allocated between the transferor and controlled corporation under § 312(h).

[97] § 381(b)(1). There is an exception for the "E" reorganization. The corporation's tax year does not close.

[98] § 381(b)(2).

EXHIBIT 7-14	Tax Attributes

1. Net operating loss carryovers
2. Earnings and profits
3. Capital loss carryovers
4. Method of accounting
5. Inventories
6. Method of computing depreciation allowance
7. Installment method
8. Amortization of bond premium or discount
9. Treatment of certain mining development and exploration expenses
10. Contributions to pension and other benefit plans
11. Recovery of bad debts, prior taxes, or delinquency amounts
12. Involuntary conversions under § 1033
13. Dividend carryover of personal holding company
14. Indebtedness of certain personal holding companies
15. Certain obligations of the transferor corporation
16. Deficiency dividend of personal holding company
17. Percentage depletion on extraction of ores or mining from the waste or residue of prior mining
18. Charitable contribution carryovers
19. Successor insurance companies
20. General business credit
21. Deficiency dividend of regulated investment company
22. Method of computing recovery allowance
23. Minimum tax credit

EARNINGS AND PROFITS

Section 381(c)(2) is designed to prohibit a profitable corporation from eliminating its own positive balance in E&P by acquiring a loss corporation with a deficit in E&P. In general, the E&P of the target corporation simply carries over and is combined with that of the acquiring corporation. However, a loss corporation's deficit cannot be used to offset any E&P of the profitable corporation existing at the date of the transfer. Rather, such deficit can be used only to offset the E&P arising from the combined corporation's operations after the transfer. Moreover, since dividends are deemed to come first from current E&P, and current E&P is unaffected by any deficit in accumulated E&P, the deficit may provide little or no benefit to the profitable corporation as long as the combined corporations produce current E&P.

Example 60

Effective December 31, 2015 Profit Corporation with E&P of $100,000 merged with Loss Corporation that had a deficit of $1.2 million. The $1.2 million deficit of Loss Corporation carries over to Profit Corporation but cannot be used to eliminate Profit's $100,000 of E&P as of December 31.

> During 2016, the combined operation generated a profit of $400,000. If the corporation made distributions during 2016, such distributions would be treated as dividends to the extent of current E&P of $400,000. Note that the inherited deficit of Loss Corporation has no effect on the status of the distributions since they are deemed to be dividends to the extent of any current E&P—unaffected by any deficit in accumulated E&P.

Example 61

Assume the same facts as above except that in 2016, the corporation made no distributions. In 2017, the corporation had no current E&P but distributed $400,000. In this case, only $100,000 of the distribution would be treated as a dividend since the deficit of the Loss Corporation eliminates the $400,000 of postacquisition E&P. The $100,000 represents the E&P of Profit Corporation accumulated before the acquisition that is unaffected by the deficit of Loss Corporation.

CARRYOVER OF NET OPERATING LOSS

Although all tax attributes are important and should be considered in planning a reorganization, the net operating loss (NOL) undoubtedly draws the most attention. To the extent that the NOL of the target corporation can be used to offset income of the acquiring corporation (e.g., in a merger), it provides needed cash for the business and reduces the actual cost of acquiring the target corporation. This advantage has led to substantial abuse. Indeed frequent advertisements formerly appeared in *The Wall Street Journal* for corporations indicating that their NOLs made them desirable candidates for acquisition. To limit such abuses Congress has enacted certain restrictions.

The law provides that the target corporation's NOL can be carried forward and deducted by the acquiring corporation on the return for the first taxable year ending after the date of transfer.[99] However, the actual amount deductible on that first return is limited to:

$$\frac{\text{Income of acquiring corporation} \times \text{Number of days in year after transfer}[100]}{\text{Number of days in a year}}$$

Example 62

Target Corporation is merged into Acquiring Corporation in an "A" reorganization on October 31, 2016. Target has an October 31 year-end and an NOL carryover of $365,000. Acquiring Corporation has taxable income before any NOL deduction of $730,000 and a fiscal year ending November 30. On the tax return of Acquiring Corporation for the year ended November 30, 2016, Acquiring can deduct $60,000 of Target's NOL ($730,000 × 30 days in November following merger ÷ 365 days). The remaining $305,000 NOL is carried over to 2017.

Unless the restrictions of § 382 apply (discussed below), there are no special limitations on the NOL carryover for years other than the first year. However, the law does prevent the *carryback* of an NOL generated *after* the reorganization to a tax year of the *transferor* corporation.[101] This prevents a corporation that is suffering losses from acquiring a profitable corporation and using its current loss as an offset against past profits of the target corporation to obtain a refund of prior taxes paid by the target corporation.

---

[99] § 381(c)(1)(A).

[100] § 381(c)(1)(B).

[101] § 381(b)(3).

> **Example 63**
>
> Loss Corporation manufactured steel and had been unprofitable for the past several years. During the current year, Loss acquired Profit Corporation, which had taxable income of $10 million for each of the past three years. During the first year of combined operations, the corporation generated a loss of $5 million due to the poor performance of the steel business. None of the $5 million loss can be carried back to a prior year of Profit Corporation to recover taxes paid by Profit Corporation on its taxable income.

Limitation on NOL Carryovers

The availability of the NOL as a carryover led to many corporate acquisitions motivated by the tax avoidance potential of the carryforward. To prevent the trafficking in losses, Congress enacted § 382, which applies to all acquisitions of corporations with NOLs. The thrust of this provision is that any NOL is in effect the property of the shareholders of the corporation when it incurred the losses. From the view of the architects of § 382, "income generated under different corporate owners which is attributable to capital over and above the capital used in the loss business, is related to a pre-acquisition loss only in the formal sense that it is housed in the same corporate entity."[102] As this statement suggests, the drafters of § 382 were obviously concerned about the possibility that new owners could infuse new capital into the business or divert income-producing opportunities to the corporation and obtain greater utilization of the loss corporation's NOLs than the former owners. Consequently, limitations on the use of a loss carryover are imposed whenever there is a *change of ownership* in the loss corporation such that those shareholders who suffered the economic burden of the corporation's NOLs are no longer in control. Before identifying what changes in ownership trigger the loss limitation, the limitation itself is considered.

Calculation of the Limitation

Following a significant change of ownership in the loss corporation, the maximum amount of NOL carryover that can be used in any year is limited. The limitation is based on the theory that the loss should be used only to offset income attributable to the loss corporation's assets, and not the income derived from the profitable corporation's business. Section 382 takes an objective approach instead of determining the amount of income that the loss corporation's assets actually generate, thus avoiding the inherent difficulties in making such a determination. The provision assumes that the equity of the loss corporation immediately before the change in ownership is invested in tax-exempt securities that pay interest at a rate prescribed by statute. Thus, the amount of any NOL carryover that can be used when the limitation applies is the product of the fair market value of the corporation's stock before the change and the "long-term tax-exempt rate."[103] Under this approach, the new owners of the corporation obtain the same result as would occur had they invested the amount paid for the loss corporation in tax-exempt securities instead of buying the loss corporation. In making the computation, the value of the loss corporation's stock is normally the price at which the stock changed hands. The long-term tax-exempt rate is generally the highest interest rate on U.S. obligations (e.g., Treasury bonds) with remaining terms exceeding nine years, reduced to reflect the difference in rates on taxable and tax-exempt obligations. This rate is to be published monthly by the IRS.

---

[102] Tax Reform Bill of 1986, Senate Finance Committee Report on H.R. 3838, Report 99-313, 99th Congress, 2d Sess., p. 231.

[103] § 382(b).

> ### Example 64
>
> B, an individual, purchased all of the stock of Loss Corporation for $1 million. Loss Corporation had an NOL carryover of $700,000. Since there was a complete change of ownership, the limitation on the NOL carryover applies. In computing the limitation, the value of the loss corporation is assumed to be equal to the amount paid by B, $1 million. Assuming that at the time of the purchase the long-term tax-exempt rate was 6 percent, the maximum amount of NOL carryover that can be used in any year is $60,000 ($1 million × 6%). Thus, assuming the corporation becomes profitable under the new ownership and generates $100,000 of taxable income, only $40,000 would be taxable since $60,000 of the corporation's NOL can be used. In effect, the new corporation earned $60,000 of taxable income that was not subject to tax, the same as if B had invested $1 million in tax-exempt securities yielding 6%.

Change in Ownership

As noted above, the limitation of § 382 operates only in the taxable year after there has been a substantial change in ownership—a so-called ownership change. This condition ensures that the new owners cannot benefit from losses that were in fact the economic burden of the previous owners. Generally, the requisite ownership change is deemed to occur whenever there has been more than a 50 percentage point *increase* in ownership by one or more shareholders who own 5% of the corporation.[104]

> ### Example 65
>
> Loss Corporation is owned by individual R. During the year, Profit Corporation purchased all of the stock of Loss Corporation from R. The § 382 limitation applies since the ownership of the 5% shareholders has increased by more than 50 percentage points immediately after the change. The same result would occur if three unrelated individuals each purchased 20% of the stock.

The Code indicates that the test to determine whether an ownership change has occurred must be made whenever there is an "owner shift involving a 5% shareholder" or an "equity structure shift."[105] An "owner shift involving a 5% shareholder" (an *owner shift*) is defined as *any change* in the stock ownership of the corporation that affects the percentage of stock in the corporation owned by any person who is a 5% shareholder before or after the change.[106] For example, an owner shift occurs and the test for an ownership change must be made whenever a 5% shareholder either sells or buys stock. Similarly, an owner shift occurs if a purchaser not owning 5% acquires sufficient stock to meet the 5% threshold. Note also that an owner shift could occur even though the shareholder did not buy or sell stock. For example, if an event occurs such as the issuance of stock or a stock redemption that changes a 5% shareholder's interest or causes a shareholder to become a 5% shareholder, an owner shift has occurred. In effect, § 382 tracks the holdings of 5% shareholders to determine whether an ownership change has occurred.

The second event that triggers a test for an ownership change is an *equity structure shift*. An equity structure shift is simply defined as a reorganization other than an "F," divisive "D," or divisive "G" reorganization.[107] Thus, as a practical matter, whenever a reorganization occurs the test for an ownership change must be made.

If either an owner shift or equity structure shift has occurred, the test for an ownership change must be made. The first step in applying this test is identification of the 5% shareholders. A 5% shareholder is any shareholder holding 5% or more of the corporation's

---

[104] § 382(g).

[105] *Ibid.*

[106] § 382(g)(2).

[107] § 382(g)(3).

stock at any time during the testing period.[108] The testing period is the three-year period ending on the day of the owner shift or equity structure shift. Once all 5% shareholders have been identified, their percentage *increase* in ownership for each year during the testing period must be determined. The percentage increase is determined by comparing the shareholder's percentage interest immediately after the owner shift or equity structure shift with the shareholder's lowest percentage interest in the loss corporation during the testing period. The percentage increases of all 5% shareholders are then summed to determine if the total increase exceeds 50 percentage points. If the total increase exceeds 50 percent, the § 382 limitation applies.

The following examples illustrate the rules used to determine whether a sufficient change in ownership has occurred.

Example 66

M owns 10% of Loss Corporation. During the year, M purchased additional stock of Loss Corporation, increasing her ownership to 15%. The purchase constitutes an owner shift since the holdings of a 5% shareholder have changed. Consequently, the test for an ownership change is required. There has been a 50% increase in M's ownership. However, there has been only a 5 *percentage point* increase. Consequently, an ownership change has not occurred.

Example 67

K owns 15% of Loss Corporation. On February 1, 2016 K purchased additional shares of Loss Corporation's stock to increase her ownership to 45%. The purchase constitutes an owner shift since the holdings of a 5% shareholder have changed. As a result, the test for an ownership change is required. Assuming there have been no other stock transactions since February 2, 2013 (the beginning of the testing period), this is not an ownership change since the 30 percentage point increase did not exceed 50 percentage points.

On June 3, 2017 J, an unrelated party, purchased 25% of Loss Corporation from persons other than K. The purchase constitutes an owner shift since the holdings of J, a 5% shareholder, have changed. The 5% shareholders during the testing period (6/4/2014 to 6/3/2017) are J and K. J has a 25 percentage point increase in his holdings and K's holdings have increased 30 percentage points, for a total of 55 percentage points. Since the percentage point increase of 55 points exceeds 50, Loss Corporation's ability to use its NOL carryforwards is limited.

Example 68

R has owned all 1,000 shares of stock of Loss Corporation since its formation several years ago. On May 7, 2016 R sold 400 of his shares to S. On June 3, 2017 the Loss Corporation issued 200 shares each to T and U.

The sale on May 7, 2016 is an owner shift involving two 5% shareholders, R and S. There is no ownership change, however, since the increase of the only 5% shareholder whose ownership increased during the testing period (5/6/2013 to 5/7/2016), S, was only 40 percentage points. R's ownership decrease is ignored.

The issuance of 200 shares to both T and U on June 3, 2017 is an owner shift involving 5% shareholders, T and U (200 ÷ 1,400 = 14.29% each). In addition, the issuance of the shares reduces the interest of R and S to 42.86% (600 ÷ 1,400) and 28.57% (400 ÷ 1,400), respectively. The issuance of these shares causes an ownership change

---

[108] § 382(k)(7).

as determined below. Note that the decrease in R's percentage ownership is ignored and does not offset the increases occurring in the other shareholder's interest.

5% Shareholders	Ownership Percentage After	Lowest Percentage Before	Increase
R	42.86%	60%	0.00%
S	28.57	0	28.57
T	14.29	0	14.29
U	14.29	0	14.29
			57.15%

In determining whether there is an owner shift involving a 5% shareholder, all of the shares not owned by 5% shareholders are aggregated and treated as if they were held by a single hypothetical shareholder. In the case of an equity structure shift (i.e., a qualifying reorganization), each group of less than 5% shareholders of each corporation is treated as a separate 5% shareholder.

Example 69

Loss Corporation has been a publicly held company since 2007. During the three-year period ending on December 31, 2016, the stock has been actively traded such that there has been a complete change of ownership. However, at no time during this period did any one shareholder own 5% of the stock. Despite the complete turnover in ownership, there has not been an "ownership change" since under the aggregation rule 100% of the stock is deemed to be owned at all times by a single shareholder. Accordingly, this hypothetical shareholder's interest has not changed during the testing period.

Example 70

Loss Corporation has been owned equally by X and Y since its inception in 2002. On July 7 of this year, the corporation issued stock to the public representing 70% of its outstanding stock. No person acquires 5% or more of the stock. Neither X nor Y acquires additional stock, so together they own the remaining 30%. This is an owner shift since the interests of 5% shareholders have been affected (i.e., X, Y and the hypothetical shareholder). Since all of the shares owned by the less than 5% shareholders are aggregated and treated as owned by a single hypothetical shareholder, this shareholder's ownership has increased by 70 percentage points. Thus, an ownership change has occurred.

Example 71

On June 1, 2016 Loss Corporation was merged into Profit Corporation pursuant to state law. Both corporations were publicly traded corporations and neither had a shareholder owning 5% or more of its stock. As part of the merger, the shareholders of Loss Corporation received 40% of Profit's stock. The merger of Loss Corporation is an equity structure shift since the transaction qualified as a type "A" reorganization. Moreover, an ownership change has occurred since Profit Corporation's shareholders (who are treated as a single 5% shareholder) have *effectively* increased their percentage ownership in the Loss Corporation (although it does not survive) by more than 50 percentage points [from 0 before the reorganization to 60% (100% − 40%) after the reorganization].

Continuity of Business Requirement

In addition to limiting the use of NOL carryovers where there is a change of ownership in the loss corporation, § 382 may disallow their use entirely. If the loss corporation does not continue its business enterprise for at least two years after there has been an ownership change, none of the NOL carryover can be used.[109] For this purpose, the definition of *business enterprise* is given the same meaning that it has under the continuity of business enterprise doctrine discussed earlier in this chapter. Under this doctrine, the target corporation's historic business must be continued, or alternatively, a significant portion of the target's assets must be used in a business.

Although the above discussion describes the essence of § 382, it should be emphasized that various other complexities of this provision were not considered. As a practical matter a careful study of § 382 is required if the acquisition of a loss corporation is contemplated.

BUILT-IN GAINS

Section 382 limits the ability of a profitable corporation to acquire a net operating loss by purchase or reorganization. It does not affect acquisitions by loss corporations, however. As a result, it has been possible for a corporation with an NOL carryover to acquire a corporation with a *built-in gain* (fair market value of assets exceeding basis) and use its NOL to offset the gain on the sale of the acquired corporation's assets. Today, however, this potential is limited by Code § 384.

Two conditions must exist before § 384 will apply. First, there must be a "qualified acquisition." A qualified acquisition is defined as either a stock acquisition or an asset acquisition. In a qualified stock acquisition, the acquiring corporation purchases (or obtains by reorganization) stock of the target sufficient for the acquiring corporation and the target to form an affiliated group (one eligible to file a consolidated return).[110] A qualified asset acquisition is the acquisition of assets in the liquidation of a subsidiary under § 332, or as the result of an "A," "C," or "acquisitive D" reorganization. The second condition that must he present is that either the target or the acquiring corporation must be a "gain corporation." A *gain corporation* is defined as any corporation with a built-in gain. A corporation will meet this condition if the excess of the fair market value of its assets over their adjusted basis exceeds the lesser of $10 million *or* 15% of the value of the assets.

Following a qualified acquisition, § 384 provides that the NOL carryover cannot offset any recognized built-in gain during the five-year period following the qualified acquisition. As a result, the corporation will pay tax on any recognized gains even though it has unused loss carryovers. It is possible for both §§ 382 and 384 to apply to a reorganization.

SECTION 269

Sections 381 and 382 limit the carryover of certain tax attributes based on objective rules. The IRS can also apply § 269 to prevent tax avoidance. This section provides that if an individual or corporation acquires control of a corporation with the principal purpose of avoiding tax by obtaining a deduction or credit, the Service can disallow the deduction or credit. For purposes of § 269, control is defined as 50% or more of the voting power, or 50% or more of the fair market value of all the stock. This section is not applied unless the *principal purpose* of the acquisition was the avoidance of tax. "Principal purpose" means that the avoidance of tax exceeds any other purpose.[111] Section 269 is very broad in scope and permits the IRS to selectively disallow items. Since it requires a forbidden purpose, the exact extent of its reach is unknown.

---

[109] § 382(c).

[110] Affiliated groups are discussed in Chapter 8.

[111] Reg. § 1.269-3(a).

Example 72

G purchases all the stock of Drug Corporation that has an NOL carryover of $300,000. Immediately after purchase, G contributes a profitable hardware business to Drug Corporation. Drug continues to operate both businesses—drugs at a break-even point and hardware profitably. The purchase and transfer will be considered an acquisition for tax avoidance, and the NOL carryover is denied under § 269.[112]

Problem Materials

DISCUSSION QUESTIONS

7-1 *Reorganizations in General.* For many, the term *reorganization* brings to mind thoughts of failing businesses and their financial overhaul. For tax purposes, however, the term has a far different meaning.
  a. Discuss the term *reorganization* and its implications for tax purposes.
  b. What is the significance of qualifying a transaction as a reorganization?

7-2 *Principles of Reorganizations.* Explain the justification underlying the nonrecognition treatment accorded qualifying reorganizations and how, as a practical matter, it has been implemented.

7-3 *Reorganization Situations.* T Corporation has 100 shares of outstanding stock owned by two friends, B and C. The corporation was started by B and C several years ago to publish a computer magazine and has had great success.
  a. Identify two sets of circumstances where an acquisitive reorganization may be appropriate.
  b. Identify two sets of circumstances where a divisive reorganization may be appropriate.

7-4 *Control.* Define the term *control* as used in reorganization.

7-5 *"A" Reorganizations.* Define an "A" reorganization.

7-6 *Triangular Mergers.* Describe a triangular merger and explain the circumstances where its use is appropriate.

7-7 *Reverse Triangular Mergers.* Describe a reverse triangular merger and explain the circumstances where its use is appropriate.

7-8 *"B" Reorganizations.* Define a "B" reorganization. What is meant by the term *creeping* "B" reorganization?

7-9 *"C" Reorganizations.* Define a "C" reorganization.

7-10 *Substantially All Test.* What is the definition of *substantially all the assets* as it applies to "C" reorganization?

7-11 *Transfer of Liabilities.* What is the effect of the transfer of liabilities in addition to assets in a "C" reorganization?

7-12 *Acquisitive "D" Reorganizations.* Define an acquisitive "D" reorganization.

7-13 *Divisive "D" Reorganizations.* Define a divisive "D" reorganization.

---

[112] Adapted from example in Reg. § 1.269-3(b)(1).

7-14 *Corporate Divisions in General.* Address the following concerning corporate divisions:
- **a.** A corporate division may be necessary for a number of reasons. List several factors that might prompt a corporate division.
- **b.** A division can be accomplished through various means: by dividend, redemption, partial liquidation, or under the corporate division rules of § 355. What distinguishes corporate divisions pursuant to § 355 from the other methods?
- **c.** Once it is determined that a division will take place, the division can assume three different forms. Identify the three types of corporate divisions, what they resemble, and how they differ.

7-15 *Corporate Divisions: Requirements of § 355.* List the requirements that must be satisfied under § 355 to secure favorable treatment. Include in your list a brief statement of the purpose of each requirement.

7-16 *Corporate Divisions: Effect on Shareholders.* Address the following concerning corporate divisions:
- **a.** If all of the conditions of § 355 are satisfied, how is the distribution of stock of the controlled corporation treated by the shareholder?
- **b.** Explain the concept of boot and the tax consequences to the shareholder if boot is received as part of the corporate division.
- **c.** How is the character of any recognized gain determined?
- **d.** How are the shareholder's bases determined in the stock, securities, and boot received?

7-17 *Corporate Divisions: Effect on Distributing Corporation.* Address the following questions concerning corporate divisions:
- **a.** Assuming a corporation distributes solely stock or securities of the controlled corporation, how is the distributing corporation's taxable income affected?
- **b.** Under what circumstances, if any, does the distributing corporation recognize gain or loss?

7-18 *"E" Reorganizations.* Describe an "E" reorganization.

7-19 *"F" Reorganizations.* Describe an "F" reorganization.

7-20 *"G" Reorganizations.* Describe a "G" reorganization.

7-21 *Acquisitive Reorganizations: Tax Consequences.* Briefly describe the tax consequences resulting from an acquisitive reorganization for the following:
- **a.** Acquiring corporation.
- **b.** Target corporation.
- **c.** Target corporation's shareholders.

7-22 *Carryover of Tax Attributes.* Some reorganizations are prompted by the ability to carry over certain tax attributes. Explain.

PROBLEMS

7-23 *Continuity of Interest: Consideration.* Bob, Bill, and Brad each own 100% of the stock of three separate corporations. They combine their separate corporations into a new corporation called Tri-B. Under state law the transaction is a consolidation. Bob receives all the common stock of Tri-B valued at $500,000. Bill receives all of the non-voting preferred stock of Tri-B valued at $300,000 and Brad receives all of the 20-year bonds (valued at $200,000) issued by Tri-B. Does the transaction qualify as a reorganization?

7-24 *Continuity of Interest: Consideration.* Retail Corporation is the wholly owned subsidiary of Holding Corporation. On January 2 of this year, Supply Corporation is merged into Retail under state law. Supply's shareholders receive 10% of Holding Corporation's common stock (worth $90,000) and $100,000 of Retail's 20-year debenture bonds (worth $100,000) in exchange for all of Supply's common stock. Is this transaction a qualified reorganization?

7-25 *Statutory Merger.* P Corporation, a widely held conglomerate, has 200,000 shares of a single class of common stock outstanding. Each share is worth $90. P has E&P of $900,000. P plans on merging with S Corporation, which manufactures furniture. S's 2,000 shares are owned equally by I, J, K, L, and M. I and J each paid $50 per share while the other three shareholders paid $120 for their shares. S's stock is now worth $100 per share. S has $250,000 of E&P. I and K are also creditors of S. Each paid $75,000 for S's 10-year bonds. The bonds have a $75,000 face value, pay 8% interest and are currently worth $90,000 each. Under the terms of the merger agreement, each S shareholder receives 500 shares of P Corporation. Each of S's creditors receives 1,200 shares of S stock.

   a. What gain or loss is realized and recognized by the shareholders and creditors of S?

   b. What is each shareholders basis for the stock received?

   c. What are the tax consequences to P and S?

   d. Answer questions (a) through (c) above, assuming each S shareholder receives 400 shares of B stock and $5,000 cash and each creditor received 1,250 shares of P stock for its bonds.

7-26 *"A" Reorganization: Consideration.* Movie King, Inc., the giant of video rental, plans to acquire the stock of Video World, a video store that has 25 stores in Illinois and Indiana. Movie King is currently in the process of negotiating with Video's shareholders, R and S who own 60% and 40% of the stock, respectively. R and S have agreed to take $1 million in consideration for their interests. The attorneys handling the deal have suggested several alternative arrangements for consummating the acquisition. Assuming the proposed transactions below will qualify as mergers under state law, indicate how each would be treated for tax purposes. For *each case,* assume the shareholders split the consideration according to their respective interests unless otherwise noted.

   a. King would give the shareholders cash of $1 million in exchange for all of their stock (a cash merger).

   b. King would give the shareholders 100,000 shares of King nonvoting preferred stock worth $1 million in exchange for all of their stock.

   c. King would give cash of $100,000, bonds worth $500,000, and 40,000 shares of King common stock worth $400,000.

   d. S has some misgivings about the deal. Consequently, he has demanded and will receive cash of $400,000. On the other hand, R will get 60,000 shares of King's common stock worth $600,000.

   e. King would give 100,000 shares of voting common stock to R and S. After the transaction R and S would own about two percent of King's outstanding stock.

   f. King would give 100,000 shares of common stock to R and S. Shortly after the transaction is consummated, R sells all of his stock for cash and goes to the Bahamas.

   g. Before completing the deal, King decided that there were several locations that it was not interested in obtaining. Consequently, Video sold those stores. The merger was consummated shortly thereafter. Any problems?

7-27 *"B" Reorganization.* In 2009, Sales Corporation acquired 85% of the common stock of Supply Corporation in a qualified "B" reorganization. In 2016, Sales obtains the remaining 15% pursuant to a plan of reorganization. Is this a qualified "B" reorganization?

7-28 *"B" Reorganization: Prior Cash Purchase.* Computer Corporation desires to acquire Component Corporation in a nontaxable "B" reorganization. However, 5% of Component's shareholders oppose the transaction. On December 15, 2016 Component redeems the shares of the 5% opposing the reorganization for cash. On June 30, 2017, pursuant to a plan of reorganization, Component's shareholders exchange Component common stock for Computer's common stock. Is this a qualified "B" reorganization?

7-29 *"B" Reorganization.* As a plan of expansion and diversification, Acquiring Corporation desired to acquire Target Corporation in a friendly takeover. Target was started by I. J. whose ingenuity built Target into a prosperous and growing firm. I. J. now owns 65% of the stock while the remaining 35% is owned by unrelated investors. Target's stock is currently worth $2 million. Indicate whether the following transactions qualify as a "B" reorganization.

  a. Acquiring transfers newly issued Acquiring voting preferred stock to I. J. and the other shareholders in exchange for all of their Target stock.

  b. Acquiring transfers newly issued Acquiring stock to I. J. and the other shareholders for all of their S stock. In addition, several shareholders receive cash in lieu of fractional shares.

  c. While I. J. is excited about the deal, the other shareholders do not share his enthusiasm and prefer to receive cash rather than stock. Acquiring plans to capitulate to their demand and give them cash.

  d. Assume the same facts as in (c), except that Target will redeem the shares of the minority with notes payable due in one year.

  e. Prior to the acquisition, Acquiring's representatives advise I. J. and his board that state law imposes a fiduciary duty on them to ensure that the transaction is fair to their shareholders. To fulfill this obligation, Target's board hired the investment banking firm Alls Well to evaluate the offer, render a fairness opinion and stand ready to advise the board in the event of any hostile takeover activity, in order to consummate the deal. Acquiring paid Target's expenses for Alls Well's services as well as those for Target's own legal counsel.

7-30 *"B" Reorganization: Acquiring Control.* In each of the following situations, which of the transactions qualify for treatment as a type "B" reorganization?

  a. Big purchased for cash 40% of the Little stock from Little's shareholders last year. This year it acquired the remaining 60% for Big voting stock.

  b. Assume the same facts as in (a), except that Big acquired the remaining 60% in two transactions, 30% in March and 30% in November.

  c. At the beginning of this year, Big purchased 10% of the Little stock for $100,000. Now Big wants to acquire the remaining 90% (fair market value = $900,000) by issuing Big voting preferred stock. Will this qualify as a "B" reorganization? What advice might you give to Big?

  d. To consummate the deal, Big transferred Big shares to a newly formed subsidiary, Sub, which then transferred all of the Big shares to the Little shareholders in exchange for their stock.

7-31 *"C" Reorganization: Substantially All Test.* Small Corporation owns assets with a fair market value of $3 million and a basis of $2.1 million. Small's liabilities equal $250,000. Small transfers assets with a fair market value of $2.75 million and a basis of $1.2 million to Parent Corporation as part of a reorganization. Small keeps the other assets to pay off its liabilities. Has Parent Corporation received substantially all of the assets of Small?

7-32 *"C" Reorganization.* Target Corporation owns assets with a fair market value of $2 million and a basis of $1.6 million. Target's liabilities equal $500,000. Target transfers all its assets plus liabilities to Acquirer in exchange for 30% of Acquirer's voting stock. Target liquidates, distributing the acquiring stock to its shareholders. Is this a valid "C" reorganization? Explain.

7-33 *"C" Reorganization.* Assume the same facts as in *Problem 7-32*, except that the basis of Target's assets is $400,000. Is this a valid "C" reorganization? Explain.

7-34 *"C" Reorganization.* Assume the same facts as in *Problem 7-32*, except that Acquirer transfers cash of $50,000 in addition to its stock. Is this a valid "C" reorganization? Explain.

7-35 *Reorganization Definition.* Assume the same facts as in *Problem 7-33*, except that Acquirer transfers 55% of its voting stock. Is this a valid reorganization? What is the tax effect on Target Corporation?

7-36 *Triangular Reorganizations.* H. C. Corporation is a insurance holding company. It would like to acquire C, an operating insurance company using a statutory merger. State law prohibits C Corporation from merging with H. C. Therefore H. C. creates Sub Corporation under § 351, transferring H. C. Corporation voting stock. C Corporation merges with Sub Corporation. Is this a valid reorganization? Explain.

7-37 *Triangular Reorganizations.* Assume the same facts as *Problem 7-36* except that before the merger, C Corporation redeems 18% of its stock in exchange for land it has purchased to be used for future expansion. Is this a valid reorganization? Explain.

7-38 *Triangular Reorganizations.* Assume the same facts as *Problem 7-36* except that H. C. Corporation created Sub Corporation using its stock and cash. The cash was 35% of the total value of the initial contribution. As part of the transaction, C Corporation distributes the cash and stock to its shareholders. Is this a valid reorganization? Explain.

7-39 *Triangular Reorganizations.* Assume the same facts as in *Problem 7-36,* except that Sub Corporation is merged into C Corporation with C Corporation being the survivor. Is this a valid reorganization? Explain.

7-40 *"C" Reorganization: Computation of Gain/Loss and Basis.* Target Corporation has assets of $2 million (basis $1.6 million) and liabilities of $150,000. Target transfers all of its assets and liabilities to Acquiring Corporation. Target receives common stock worth $1.5 million and property worth $350,000 with a basis of $100,000 in the exchange. Target subsequently liquidates.
   a. How much gain or loss, if any, must Target recognize?
   b. How much gain or loss, if any, must Acquiring Corporation recognize?
   c. Compute Acquiring Corporation's basis for Target's assets

7-41 *"B" Reorganization: Computation of Gain/Loss and Basis.* L owns 2,000 shares of X Corporation's common stock. She purchased the stock five years ago for $80 per share. L also owns $90,000 of X's bonds which she purchased for $90,000. As part of a "B" reorganization L exchanges her stock and bonds for 700 shares of A Corporation's common stock with a fair market value of $250 per share plus $100,000 of A Corporation's bonds with a fair market value of $95,000.
   a. Compute L's realized and recognized gain or loss.
   b. Compute L's basis in the A Corporation's stock and bonds.
   c. Same facts as above except L's share of X's accumulated earnings and profits is $15,000. Would this change your answer to (a) or (b) above?

7-42 *Effect on Shareholder.* A, an individual, owns 25% of the stock of Target Corporation. Her basis in the stock is $100,000. Target Corporation's accumulated earnings and profits are $60,000. As part of a valid reorganization, A is given the choice between 10% of Acquirer's common stock or 6% of Acquirer's common stock plus $25,000. Assume that A accepts the 10% common stock option.
   a. How much gain or loss, if any, must she recognize?
   b. What is the basis of the Acquirer's stock she received?

7-43 *Effect on Shareholder.* Assume the same facts as in *Problem 7-42*, except that A accepted the stock plus cash.
   a. How much gain or loss, if any, must she recognize?
   b. What type of income is it?
   c. What is the basis of the Acquirer's stock she received?

7-44 *Exchange of Securities.* In an otherwise qualified type "A" reorganization, Jane exchanges bonds of T Corporation with a face amount and basis of $75,000 for bonds of A Corporation with a face amount of $90,000 and a fair market value of $75,000. What is the tax effect of this exchange for Jane?

7-45 *Type "A" Reorganization: Effects.* Acquiring Corporation operates a rapidly expanding hotel business. At the beginning of the year, it had 3,000 shares of stock outstanding owned equally by X, Y, and Z. This year, Acquiring convinced Mr. Seller to join its ranks. Seller owned all of the stock of Target Corporation, which owned a string of motels on the Emerald Coast of Florida. Target Corporation had assets worth $600,000 (basis $175,000). Seller, who was nearing retirement, wanted cash for his company, but Acquiring convinced him to take stock and some cash as part of a merger of Seller's corporation with Acquiring. As part of the deal, Acquiring gave Seller 2,000 shares of Acquiring common stock worth $500,000 and cash of $100,000 in a transaction qualifying as a statutory merger. Seller had a basis in his stock of $10,000.

    a. Will the transaction qualify as a type "A" reorganization?

    b. Assuming that the transaction qualifies as an "A" reorganization, why might Seller want to merge his corporation with Acquiring rather than sell it? Explain.

    c. What is Seller's gain or loss recognized and what is its character?

    d. What is Seller's basis in the stock of Acquiring Corporation?

    e. What is the effect on Acquiring Corporation?

7-46 *Selecting the Reorganization.* Foods Galore owns and operates several chains of fine restaurants, including Burrito Greato, Boogie's Burgers, and Captain Hook Fish and Chips. It now wishes to get into the chicken business. To this end, it is negotiating with Uncle Jimmy's Southern-Fried Chicken. Uncle Jimmy's has units primarily in the Rockies, including Colorado, Idaho, Wyoming, and Montana. It began negotiating with Uncle Jimmy's several weeks ago. How would each of the following factors affect the form of reorganization that may be used? Discuss briefly whether an "A," triangular "A" (forward or reverse), "B," or "C" reorganization will work given each factor. Assume each is an independent case.

    a. Uncle Jimmy's has been under audit by the FDA for possible violation of health codes. In addition, the corporation's prior-year tax returns are currently under audit.

    b. While the principal shareholder, James Robert Smith, wants to push forward on the deal, two minority shareholders, Bubba Jones and Sissy Brown, want out. They will not take Foods stock but only cash.

    c. Several vocal shareholders who own significant interests in Foods do not want to pursue the deal.

    d. The state of Montana will not allow foreign corporations (i.e., out of state) to merge with Montana corporations.

    e. Uncle Jimmy's has a few units in Atlanta, where the company got its start. A few of these units do have favorable locations but are not making money since there are plenty of places in the South that offer Jimmy's brand of Southern-fried chicken. Consequently, Foods is not interested in acquiring them.

    f. Uncle Jimmy's has leased the ground on which most of its units sit, and all but a few of these leases are for a long term and have favorable terms.

    g. Foods already owns a 30% stake in Jimmy's, having acquired the stock last year for cash.

7-47 *Corporate Divisions.* Do the following corporate divisions meet the § 355 requirements relating to the active conduct of a trade or business? If yes, do they qualify as a spin-off, a split-off, or a split-up? Assume all other requirements for a corporate division are met.

   a. R, Inc. has produced T-shirts for the U.S. and European markets for the past eight years. The officers of R decide to move all European production activities to the East Coast of the United States. In addition, the assets necessary for its European production process will be transferred to E, Inc., a corporation being organized for this purpose. Stock in E, Inc. will be distributed to R, Inc. shareholders. Shareholders will not surrender any of their shares.

   b. Although M, Inc. has been an active manufacturer for eight years, it is subject to the alternative minimum tax, primarily because of its substantial investment in equipment. The officers of M propose to transfer all equipment acquired since 2008 to P, Inc., a corporation to be organized for the purpose of owning all equipment to be used by M. After the transfer, M will lease the equipment from P. M will hold 60% of P stock and distribute 40% to M shareholders. Shareholders will not surrender any of their M shares.

   c. Twelve years ago, V and W corporations were formed as wholly owned subsidiaries of U, Inc. U has no other assets. Y and Z are equal owners of U, Inc. Y and Z are in complete disagreement about the future of the three corporations. Unable to reconcile these differences, Y and Z agree to have U distribute all its stock in V to Z and all its stock in W to Y. In exchange, Y and Z will surrender all their shares in U, and U will be terminated.

7-48 *Spin-Off: Effect on Shareholder.* In 2005, XYZ Corporation was formed by I, J, K, and L. Each contributed $50,000 for 100 shares of the corporation's stock. The corporation was established to capitalize on the public's need for exercise activities. XYZ's first transaction in 2005 was the purchase of a yoga studio. Based on the exercise craze in the late nineties, the corporation purchased all the stock of B Corporation in 2008. B Corporation sells and repairs bicycles. In 2013, XYZ purchased all the stock of F Corporation, which had manufactured a line of health food since 1986.

   a. XYZ's management currently believes that it has grown too fast and consequently should divest itself of B or F. Will a spin-off of either subsidiary be non-taxable?

   On December 1, 2016 XYZ distributed all of its B stock pro-rata in a transaction that satisfies the requirements of § 355. Immediately after the distribution, the XYZ stock and B stock were valued at $250,000 and $60,00 respectively. In addition, XYZ distributed 13 securities pro-rata worth $25,000 (face value $30,000). I received B stock valued at $15,000 and securities worth $7,500. XYZ has $100,000 of E&P. B's net worth is $70,000.

   b. State the amount of realized gain or loss, if either is recognized by I and its character.

   c. What is I's basis in her XYZ stock and her stock and securities of B?

7-49 *Split-Off: Effect on Shareholder.* Same facts as *Problem 7-48* except I surrenders all her stock of XYZ for all of the B stock and securities.

   a. State the amount of gain or loss, if either is recognized by I and its character.

   b. What is I's basis in her stock and securities of B?

7-50 *Carryover of NOL: Section 382 Limitations.* Loss Corporation's common stock is owned as follows:

R	45 shares
S	45 shares
T	10 shares

On December 15, 2016 E purchased the stock owned by S and T. He purchased the stock because Loss has a very large NOL carryover.

   a. Will the NOL carryover be limited by § 382?

   b. Same facts as above except Loss is merged into Profit Corporation. R, S, and T each receive 1,200 shares of Profit out of the total of 8,000 shares issued and outstanding. Can Profit carry over Loss's NOL without limitation under § 382?

7-51 *Carryover of NOL: Computation.* Loss Corporation merged into Profit Corporation on December 1, 2016. Loss' NOL is $600,000. Profit Corporation has taxable income before considering Loss's NOL of $204,500 for the year ended December 31, 2016. Compute Profit's taxable income for 2016. (Assume the § 382 limit is greater than the deductible loss.)

7-52 *Section 384 Limitation.* On December 31, 2016 Profitable Corporation merged into Loss Corporation. Profitable Corporation's only asset is land with a fair market value of $1 million and a basis of $500,000. Loss Corporation has a $5 million NOL carryover from 2015. In 2017, Loss Corporation breaks even on its operations. In addition, Loss Corporation sold the land acquired from Profitable for $1 million. Compute Loss Corporation's taxable income for 2017.

TAX RESEARCH PROBLEMS

7-53 Stable Corporation is an old, established corporation in a mature industry. It has more cash than is needed for its operations. Stable decides to invest its spare cash in corporate stock. After much investigation, Stable purchased 5% of Glamour Corporation in February 2015. The purchase was so successful that Stable Corporation acquires an additional 10% of Glamour during 2016. In 2016, the IRS audits Stable's 2014 tax return. The agent raises, but does not pursue, an excess accumulated earnings penalty issue. To avoid future problems, Stable decides to diversify. To implement this plan, the corporation tenders its voting stock for the outstanding voting stock of Glamour in a "B" reorganization. The shareholders of Glamour accept the offer and exchange Glamour voting stock for Stable voting stock on January 2, 2017. Will the prior cash purchases of Glamour stock invalidate the "B" reorganization?

7-54 Jim and Jane each own 50% of T Corporation. They disagree on the future direction of the business. To settle the dispute, it is agreed that T Corporation will transfer its retail operations to Newco in exchange for all of its stock. The stock is worth $360,000. T Corporation will exchange the stock of Newco for all the stock of T Corporation owned by Jim. To even up values, T Corporation will also distribute $40,000 cash to Jim. Assuming the transaction qualifies as a "divisive D" reorganization, determine the tax treatment of $40,000 cash distributed to Jim.

8

Consolidated Tax Returns

Learning Objectives

Upon completion of this chapter you will be able to:

LO.1 Discuss the advantages and disadvantages of filing a consolidated return.

LO.2 Identify who is eligible to file a consolidated return.

LO.3 Compute consolidated taxable income and tax liability.

LO.4 Determine the treatment of an intercompany transaction.

LO.5 Explain the rules limiting the use of one member's losses and credits against the income and tax of other consolidated group members.

LO.6 Explain how a corporation accounts for its investment in a subsidiary.

Chapter Outline

Introduction

Although most corporations are required to file their own separate tax returns, certain related corporations (e.g., a parent corporation and its 80% owned subsidiary) are entitled to file a *consolidated tax return*. The consolidated tax return is essentially a method by which to determine the tax liability of a group of affiliated corporations. The tax computation is based on the view that the businesses of the related corporations represent a single enterprise. Accordingly, it is appropriate to tax the aggregate income of the group rather than the separate income of each corporation. This is not to say, however, that a consolidated return simply reports the sum of each member corporation's taxable income as if the group were one enlarged single corporation. The applicable Treasury Regulations[1] modify the aggregate results by providing special rules requiring the statement of certain items on a consolidated basis (e.g., capital gains) and adjustments for intercompany transactions. The intricacies of these consolidated return rules are the subject of this chapter.

The History of the Consolidated Return

The origin of the consolidated tax return can be found in the early regulations concerning the tax imposed on excess profits during World War I. These regulations authorized the Commissioner of the Internal Revenue Service to prescribe rules necessary to prevent corporations from avoiding the tax by eliminating their "excess profit" by arbitrarily shifting income to another corporation where it would not be considered excessive. As early as 1917, the Commissioner used this power to require the filing of consolidated tax returns by affiliated corporations to limit the benefits of multiple corporations. By 1918, Congress had made the filing of consolidated returns mandatory for affiliated groups for purposes of not only the excess profits tax but also the income tax. In addition, the Commissioner's authority to issue Regulations governing consolidated returns was codified.

The end of the war produced several changes affecting consolidated returns. The war's end eliminated the need for the excess profits tax and consequently it was repealed. At the same time, the forerunner of § 482 was enacted. This provision permitted the IRS to apportion income, expenses, or credits between two or more organizations that are under common control in order to prevent tax avoidance and clearly reflect income. The repeal of the excess profits tax and the extension of the Commissioner's authority to reallocate income reduced the opportunity for distorting income and thus the need for mandatory consolidated returns for affiliated groups. As a result, in 1921, Congress made the filing of a consolidated return optional.

For the next 14 years, consolidated returns remained optional, although an additional 1% tax was imposed on the privilege of filing a consolidated return in 1932. In 1934, influenced by the effects of the Great Depression and the ability of a loss corporation to offset the income of a profitable one, Congress abolished the use of the consolidated tax return.[2] The consolidated tax return soon reappeared with the beginning of World War II as Congress extended corporations the privilege of filing a consolidated return in 1942. This time, however, the cost for filing a consolidated return was increased. Congress imposed a 2% penalty on consolidated taxable income—a penalty that was to remain until its repeal in 1964. Since 1942, the filing of a consolidated return has been optional.

---

[1] See generally Reg. §§ 1.1502-11, 12, and 13.

[2] This election still remained available for certain railroad corporations.

Although certain benefits could be gained through filing consolidated returns, for many years affiliated groups often opted to file separate returns to obtain the benefits accorded multiple corporations.

Example 1

P, S, and T are an affiliated group of corporations. Each corporation had taxable income of $50,000 for the year. The group's major competitor, Z Inc., a separate corporation, had taxable income of $150,000. If P, S, and T file their own separate returns reporting $50,000 of taxable income on each return, their combined tax liability will be $22,500 ($7,500 × 3). In contrast, Z's tax liability for its $150,000 of taxable income is $41,750, which is $19,250 greater than the combined liability of P, S, and T. Note that the taxes saved are attributable to the fact that the group's taxable incomes are never taxed at the higher rate (i.e., 34%) or subject to the additional 5% surtax.

In 1969, the benefits of multiple corporations illustrated above were severely curtailed. Under the Tax Reform Act of 1969,[3] affiliated corporations were effectively treated as a single corporation (e.g., in the example above, P, S, and T would be treated like Z) notwithstanding the fact that each corporation filed a separate return.[4] With the elimination of these benefits, there has been increasing interest in the filing of consolidated returns.

The Consolidated Return Regulations

As previously mentioned, Congress granted the Commissioner (IRS) the authority to promulgate regulations for filing a consolidated tax return. Specifically, Code § 1502 states in part:

> The Secretary shall prescribe such regulations as he may deem necessary in order that the tax liability of any affiliated group of corporations making a consolidated return and of each corporation in the group, both during and after the period of affiliation, may be returned, determined, computed, assessed, collected and adjusted, in such a manner as clearly to reflect the income tax liability and the various factors necessary for the determination of such liability, and in order to prevent avoidance of such tax liability.[5]

It takes little imagination to see that Congress has granted the IRS broad authority to write regulations governing the filing of a consolidated tax return. These regulations, referred to as legislative regulations,[6] grant a nearly absolute power to the Secretary of the Treasury to prescribe the rules for consolidated tax returns. Although not statutory in form, these regulations have the *force* and *effect* of law and remain effective unless overturned by the courts or restricted by Congress.

As early as 1928[7] and then again in 1954,[8] Congress contemplated codifying the consolidated return regulations. In 1954, the House Ways and Means Committee wanted the regulations written into the statutes on the grounds that the regulations had become generally accepted and should be formalized. The Senate Finance Committee, however, rejected this notion.[9] The Senate felt that the detailed consolidated return rules should remain in regulation format. By leaving the regulations in that form, any rule or tax law change could be readily addressed by the IRS without requiring further action by Congress.[10]

---

[3] §§ 1561 and 1563.

[4] See discussion on controlled groups in Chapter 1.

[5] § 1502.

[6] Legislative regulations should be contrasted with interpretive regulations (see Chapter 17 for a discussion).

[7] S. Rept. No. 960, 70th Cong., 1st Session.

[8] H. Rept. No. 1337, 83rd Cong., 2nd Session.

[9] S. Rept. No. 1622, 83rd Cong., 2nd Session.

[10] Whether this logic still applies today with nearly annual tax law changes may be a subject for debate. It often takes years to get Regulations proposed and finalized.

In 1966, the IRS completely overhauled the system governing consolidated returns by replacing the old regulations with a lengthy and intricate set of new regulations. The 1966 regulations rejected the accounting principles that had long served as the basis of the old regulations and replaced them with an entirely different approach. These 1966 regulations remained in effect until 1990 when new regulations began to appear. These new regulations reflected the repeal of the *General Utilities* doctrine by the Tax Reform Act of 1986. As a result, new rules have been adopted for basis determination, loss disallowance, intercompany transactions and the manner in which the separate company net operating losses are carried into the consolidated return. The thrust of the new rules is to treat the affiliated group of corporations as a single entity rather than an aggregate of separate companies.

Advantages and Disadvantages of the Consolidated Tax Return

LO.1

Discuss the advantages and disadvantages of filing a consolidated return.

Although filing a consolidated tax return has advantages, numerous disadvantages exist as well. A review of the various advantages and disadvantages that must be considered before filing a consolidated return is presented below.

ADVANTAGES OF CONSOLIDATED RETURNS

A partial list of the advantages of filing a consolidated income tax return includes the following:

1. Unused losses (both ordinary and capital) and credits of an affiliate may be used to offset the income and tax liability of other affiliated group members in the current year. By utilizing these losses and credits in the current year, the group receives immediate tax benefits and thereby avoids the need for carryovers to recover the benefits. In addition, any excess losses or credits can also be carried back or carried over to subsequent consolidated return years.

2. Intercompany profits on the sale of property and services may be deferred until later years. This deferral has the added benefits of postponing depreciation recapture as well as investment tax credit recapture.

3. Intercompany dividends between group members are eliminated from income and are not subject to tax.

4. Deductions and credits that are subject to percentage limitations can be determined on a consolidated rather than on a separate company basis. This permits a single corporation subject to such limitations to effectively avoid them.

5. The basis in the stock of a subsidiary is increased by taxable and tax-exempt income accumulated during consolidated return years. Thus, when a parent corporation disposes of a subsidiary any resulting gains are reduced or losses increased.

DISADVANTAGES OF CONSOLIDATED RETURNS

Some of the more important disadvantages of filing a consolidated return include the following:

1. Electing to file consolidated returns requires compliance with the consolidated return regulations. This could create additional costs and administrative burdens.

2. The consolidated return election is binding for future years. This election can only be terminated by disbanding the affiliated group or by obtaining permission from the IRS to file separate returns.

3. Separate return credits and capital losses can be limited by operating losses and capital losses from other members of the group. Thus, the credit and loss carryovers may expire unused due to heavy losses by an affiliated member.

4. A subsidiary member is required to change its tax year to the same year as that of the common parent corporation. This can create a short tax year that is considered a complete tax year for purposes of carrybacks or carryovers in the case of unused losses and credits.

5. Losses of a subsidiary that reduce the tax liability of the group also decrease the parent's tax basis in the subsidiary. This serves to increase a gain or decrease a loss by the parent corporation on the sale of its subsidiary.

6. Under controversial *loss disallowance rules,* losses on the sale of a subsidiary's stock can possibly be disallowed for tax purposes.

7. The rights of minority shareholders must be respected both legally and ethically. As a result, the presence of minority shareholders may create situations that may have adverse effects for the affiliated group.

Eligibility for Filing the Consolidated Return

Code § 1501 grants an affiliated group the privilege of filing a consolidated tax return on the condition that all eligible members *elect* to do so. If a corporation is a member for a fractional part of a year, the consolidated return must include the income for the short period that the affiliate is a member of the group. As may be expected, these rules are precise and complex.

LO.2
Identify who is eligible to file a consolidated return.

AFFILIATED GROUPS

The term *affiliated group* refers to one or more chains of includible corporations connected through stock ownership with a common parent corporation.[11] This definition contains two requirements that must be satisfied before the related corporations are treated as an affiliated group. First, the corporation must be an *includible corporation,* and second, the group must pass a *stock ownership test.* If a corporation fails either test, it is not eligible to file a consolidated return with the remaining qualifying corporations.

Includible Corporations

The term includible corporation is defined by exception.[12] In other words, an includible corporation is any corporation other than one of the following entities:

1. A corporation exempt from taxation under § 501 (e.g., a nonprofit organization).
2. A corporation electing a U.S. Possession tax credit under § 936.
3. Certain life or mutual insurance companies not covered by a separate election.[13]
4. A foreign corporation.[14]
5. A regulated investment company or real estate investment trust.
6. A Domestic International Sales Corporation (DISC).

Stock Ownership Test

The stock ownership requirements are satisfied when the following tests are met:

1. An includible parent corporation owns directly at least 80% of the total voting power *and* 80% of the fair market value of the stock of at least one of the other includible corporations.

2. An includible corporation (other than the parent) has at least 80% of its voting stock *and* 80% of the fair market value of its nonvoting stock owned directly by one or more of the other corporations in the group.

---

[11] § 1504.

[12] § 1504(b).

[13] Two or more domestic insurance companies can be treated as includible corporations for purposes of filing a consolidated return for the insurance companies alone. See § 1504(c)(1) and Rev. Rul. 77-210, 1977-1 C.B. 267.

For years beginning in 1981, insurance companies taxed under §§ 802 or 821 may elect to file consolidated returns with non-life insurance companies, subject to limitations under § 1504(c)(2).

[14] A limited exception exists for wholly owned Canadian or Mexican corporations.

The stock ownership test requires that a group must have a common parent [defined in (1) above] *and* at least one includible subsidiary [defined in (2) above]. If either test is not met the group is ineligible for filing a consolidated return. When applying the stock ownership tests, nonvoting preferred stock that is not convertible into another class of stock or stock that does not significantly participate in corporate growth is generally ignored.

Example 2

Individual A owns 100% of both J and K Corporations. J Corporation owns 60% of T Corporation, the remaining 40% of which is owned by K (see Exhibit 8-1). Neither J nor K qualifies as a parent corporation and consequently the group cannot file a consolidated tax return.[15] It should be noted that neither corporation is owned 80% or more by other corporations, so the second test is failed as well. Had J owned 80% of T, then both tests would have been met for the affiliated group composed of J and T.

EXHIBIT 8-1	Diagram of Ownership in Example 2

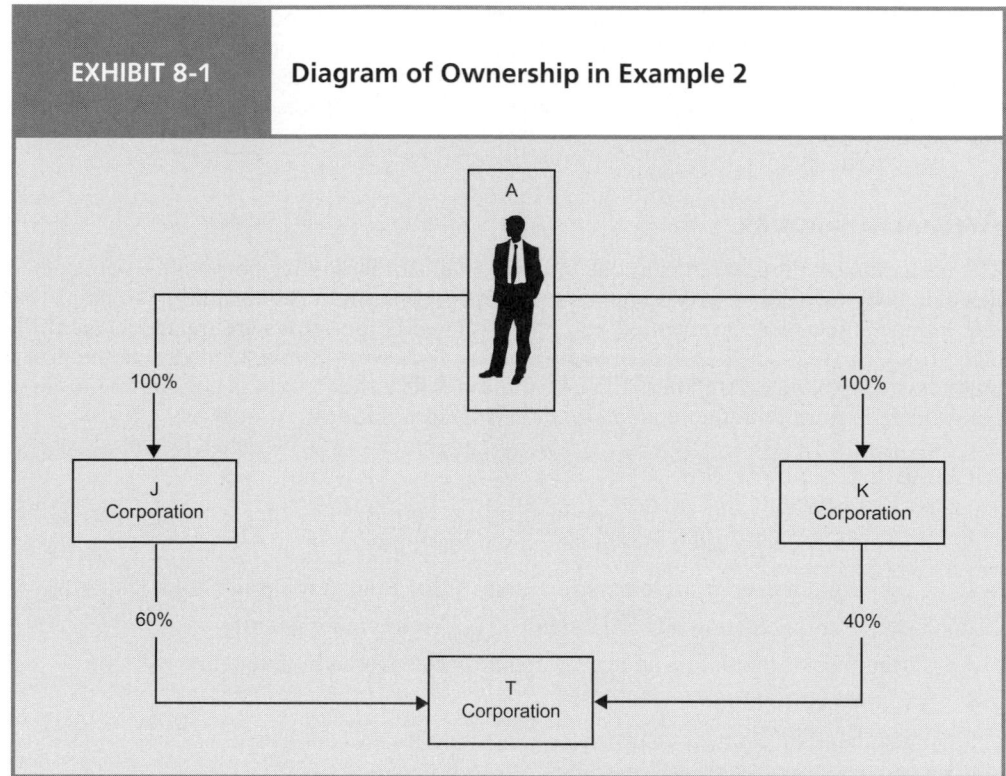

Example 3

P corporation owns 100% of the stock of both E and F corporations. E and F each owns 50% of the stock of G Corporation (see Exhibit 8-2). If all corporations are includible corporations, then P, E, F, and G are considered affiliated corporations with P as the parent. G is included in the affiliated group because it is more than 80% owned by other members of the group (E and F). The affiliated group composed of P, E, F, and G is eligible for filing a consolidated tax return.

---

[15] These corporations would fall within the controlled group provisions of §§ 1561 through 1564.

EXHIBIT 8-2	Diagram of Ownership in Example 3

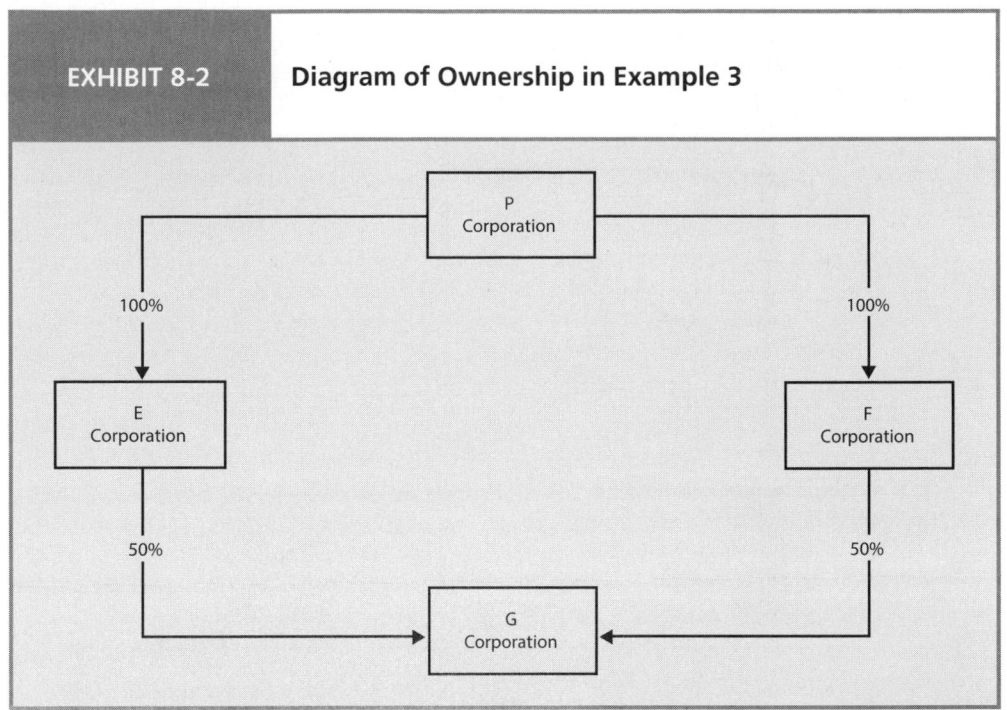

Example 4

P Corporation owns 80% of both L and Q Corporations. L owns 100% of M Corporation and Q owns 80% of both R and S Corporations. R and S own 80% and 20% of T Corporation, respectively (see Exhibit 8-3). If L is a newly formed life insurance company, M a second life insurance company, and S a regulated investment company, two affiliated groups exist. L and M make up an affiliated insurance group with L as the parent. P, Q, R, and T make up a second affiliated group with P as the parent. L and M are not includible corporations within the exception of § 1504(c)(2) and S is not includible by definition. Although T is owned 20% by S (not an includible corporation), T is owned 80% by R, an includible corporation, so it is included within the affiliated group. Under a special rule, L and M are eligible to file their own consolidated tax return.

Affiliated Group versus Controlled Group

An *affiliated group* is treated as a single taxable entity and is eligible to file a consolidated tax return. On the other hand, a *controlled group* is also treated as a single taxable entity, but may not satisfy the definition of affiliated group and thus be denied the privilege of filing a consolidated tax return. The rules defining an affiliated group are quite similar to those defining a parent-subsidiary relationship in a controlled group.[16]

---

[16] See Chapter 1 for a discussion of parent-subsidiary controlled groups.

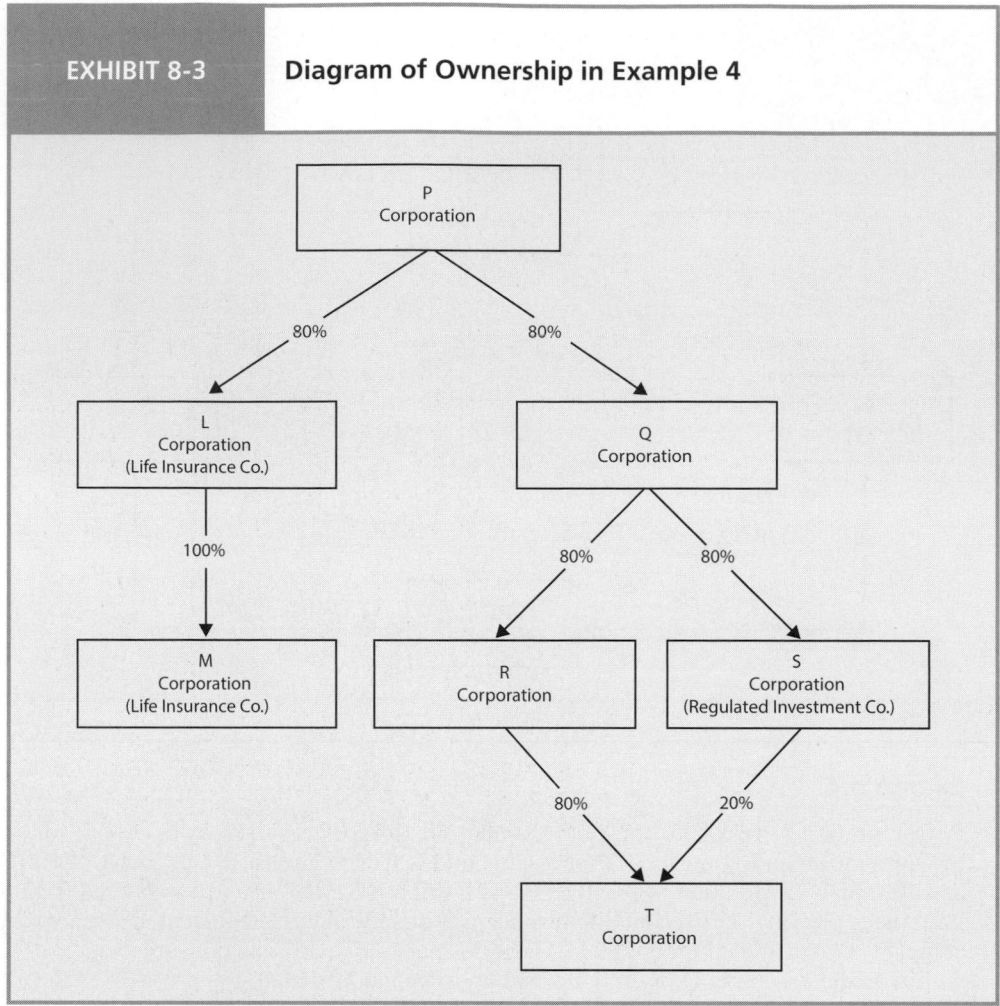

EXHIBIT 8-3   Diagram of Ownership in Example 4

Indeed, at first glance these provisions appear to be identical. The fundamental difference, however, rests in the stipulation of "direct" ownership. An affiliated group requires direct ownership, while a parent-subsidiary controlled group does not. An example might best illustrate the differences.

Example 5

X Corporation owns 70% of both Y and Z Corporations. The remaining 30% of Z is owned by Y and the remaining 30% of Y is owned by Z (see Exhibit 8-4). Under the provisions defining a controlled group, identical ownership is ignored so that X *indirectly* owns 100% of both Y and Z.[17] For purposes of an affiliated group, the 80% *direct* ownership test is not met and thus X, Y, and Z cannot file a consolidated tax return.

THE ELECTION

If an affiliated group wishes to file a consolidated tax return, all eligible subsidiaries must consent and all must join in the filing of a consolidated return. Each subsidiary must indicate their consent by filing Form 1122 Authorization and Consent of Subsidiary Corporation to be included in a Consolidated Income Tax Return (see Exhibit 8-5). These consent forms must

---

[17] See Reg. § 1.1563-1(a)(2), Ex. 4 for a more detailed explanation.

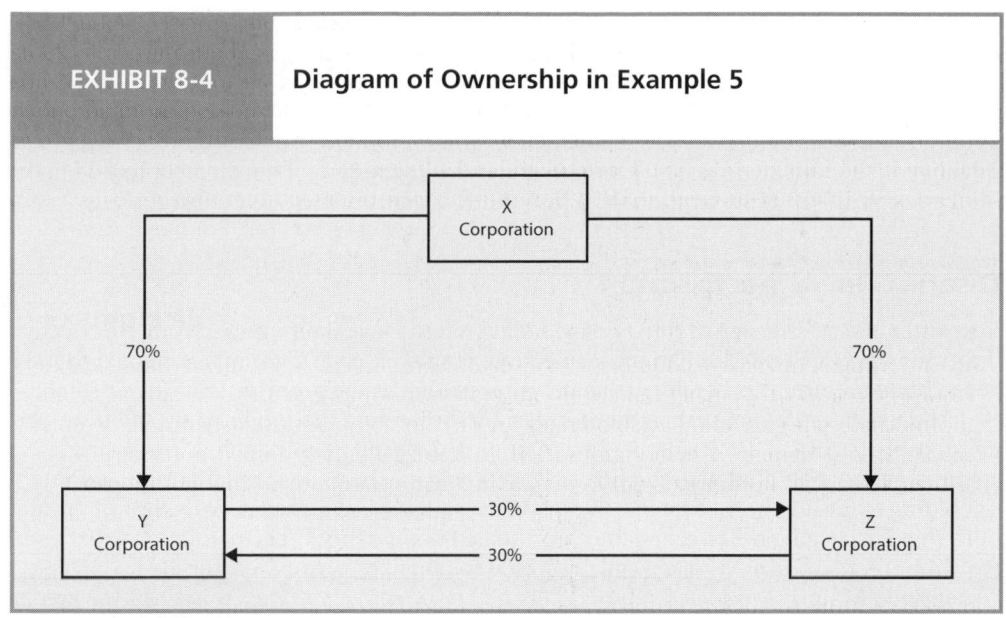

EXHIBIT 8-4   **Diagram of Ownership in Example 5**

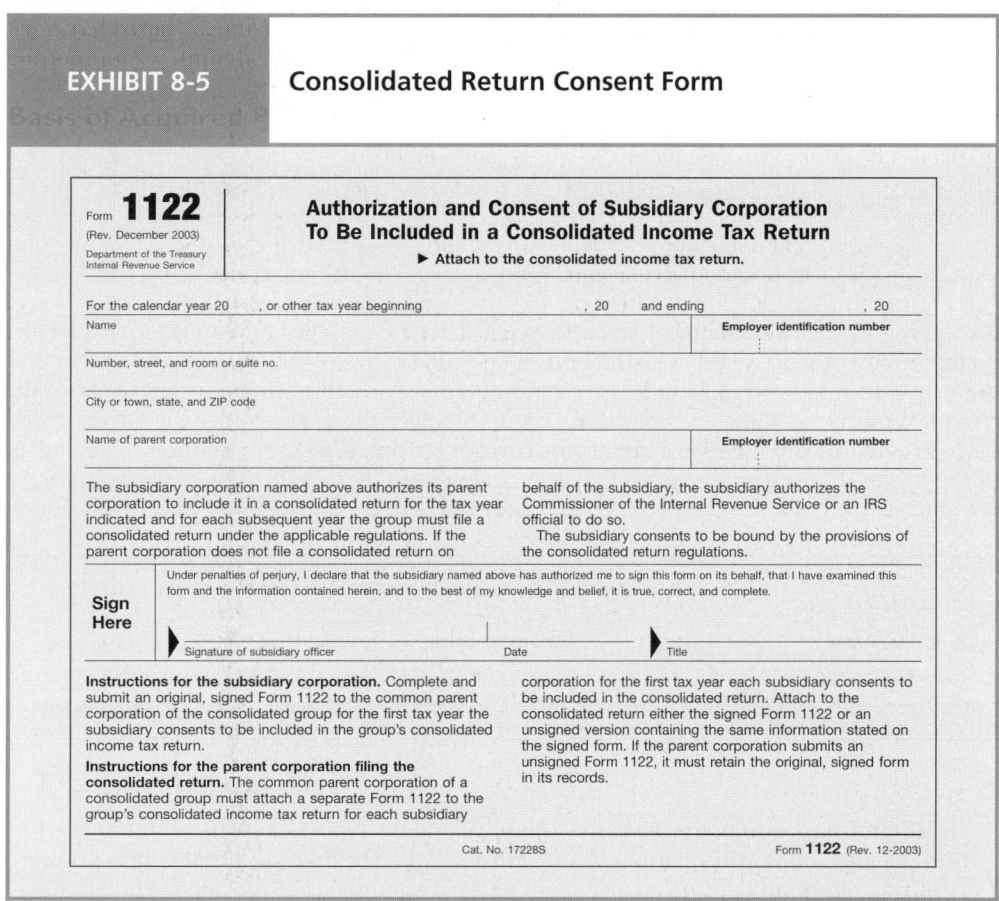

EXHIBIT 8-5   **Consolidated Return Consent Form**

be attached to the initial consolidated tax return, Form 1120. In addition, the first consolidated tax return must contain Form 851 Affiliations Schedule that indicates the ownership of the members of the affiliated group. The election must be filed on or before the common parent's due date (including extensions) for filing its tax return. The group can, at any time prior to the extended due date, change its decision and revoke its election to file a consolidated return. Once the extended due date passes, however, the election cannot be withdrawn,[18] and consolidated returns must be filed until the group terminates.

If any member of the group fails to file a consent form or does not join in the filing of a consolidated return, a consolidated tax return cannot be filed. In such case, the tax liability of each member is determined as if separate returns were filed.[19] If the common parent can establish to the satisfaction of the Commissioner that the failure of the member to join in the filing was an inadvertent error, the election to file a consolidated tax return remains valid.

DISCONTINUING THE ELECTION

Very often the advantages of filing consolidated returns lose their utility. When this occurs, the group may desire to discontinue its election. However, once a group has elected to file a consolidated return, it is bound by that decision as long as the group remains in existence.[20]

The election may be discontinued either by disbanding the group or by securing permission of the IRS. Permission is granted only if the group can establish *good cause*. An application must be filed with the IRS at least 90 days before the due date of the tax return (including extensions). An example of a good cause would be a change in the law or regulations that has an adverse effect on the consolidated tax liability.[21] The regulations also grant the Commissioner discretionary authority to issue blanket permission for all taxpayers to discontinue filing consolidated returns. This authority is generally exercised only when an amendment to the Code or regulations has an adverse effect on a group or class of corporate taxpayers.[22]

If a corporation is included in a consolidated return and then ceases to be a member of the affiliated group, that corporation (or its successor) cannot return to be reincluded as a member of the affiliated group for a specified period. That period generally ends on the 61st month beginning after the corporation's first taxable year in which it ceased being a member of the group. The Commissioner, however, is authorized to waive application of this rule under conditions it deems appropriate.

DETERMINING THE YEAR INCOME IS REPORTED

According to the regulations, a consolidated tax return must be filed on the basis of the common parent's tax year.[23] This requires a subsidiary that is not on the same tax year as the parent to make a change in its accounting period to conform to the taxable year of the parent. As a result, the consolidated tax return includes the parent's income for the entire tax year, and the subsidiary's income only for that portion of the year that it was a member of the group.[24] This usually means that a separate return must be filed by the subsidiary for the short period before it joins the group or for the period after it ceases to be a member.[25]

Example 6

P, S, and T file a consolidated tax return for 2015 on a calendar year basis. If P sells the stock of T to an individual on March 1, 2016, the consolidated tax return for 2016 includes the income of T from January 1 to March 1, 2016. T files a short-period tax return for the remaining 10 months (March through December). If on July 21, 2016 P purchases all the stock of X, a calendar year corporation, the consolidated tax return for 2016 must also include the income or loss for X from July 21 through December 31, 2016. X also must file a short period tax return for the period January 1 through July 20, 2016.

---

[18] Reg. § 1.1502-75(a)(1).

[19] Reg. § 1.1502-75(b)(3).

[20] Although a group normally terminates when a parent corporation ceases to exist, certain exceptions apply relating to reverse acquisitions, F reorganizations, and downstream mergers.

[21] Reg. § 1.1502-75(c)(1).

[22] Reg. § 1.1502-75(a)(2). Also see Rev. Proc. 95-11, 1995-1 C.B. 505, issued as a result of new investment adjustment rules in 1994.

[23] Reg. § 1.1502-76(a)(1).

[24] Reg. § 1.1502-76(b)(1).

[25] Reg. § 1.1502-76(b)(2).

In 1994, the Treasury revised Regulation § 1.1502-75(d)(1) to include the following sentence. "A group remains in existence for a tax year if the common parent remains as the common parent and at least one subsidiary that was affiliated with it at the *end* of the prior year remains affiliated with it at the *beginning* of the year, whether or not one or more corporations have ceased to be subsidiaries at any time after the group was formed." The thrust of the revision suggests that a parent corporation that begins a tax year filing a consolidated return with a subsidiary will continue to file a consolidated return with all subsidiaries if on the last day of the taxable year at least one subsidiary exists—even though the subsidiaries at the beginning and end of the year may be different.

Example 7

P, a calendar year corporation, owns 100% of the stock of S Corporation. For the year 2015, P and S file a consolidated tax return. On March 15, 2016 P sells all of the stock of S. On August 15, 2016 P acquires all of the stock of T, also a calendar year corporation. Because P ended 2015 and began 2016 with S as its subsidiary, P will file a consolidated return for 2016 that will include all subsidiaries owned by P during 2016. It makes no difference that a period existed during the year when P owned no subsidiary. Thus, T will include all of its income from August 16, 2016 through December 31, 2016 on P's consolidated tax return. T must file a separate tax return from January 1, through August 15, 2016. S's income from January 1, through March 15, 2016 will also be included in the consolidated return of P.

Example 8

Assume the same facts as *Example 7* except that P acquires all the stock of T on January 1, 2017. Although P is required to file a consolidated return for 2016, P does not begin 2017 with a subsidiary that was included in the prior year's consolidated return. Thus, if P desires to file a consolidated return with T, a new election must be made.

Filing a Separate Return

In filing the separate return, the subsidiary's income and deductions must be allocated between the consolidated and separate return years. The due date for these separate returns is generally the earlier of the subsidiary's due date (on a 12-month basis) or the due date of the consolidated tax return. The regulations require that an allocation for purposes of determining separate taxable income be made according to the permanent records of the company.[26] In most cases, this requires an *actual* closing of the subsidiary's books. To ameliorate the administrative burdens of closing the books, regulations allow certain subsidiaries the opportunity to elect to prorate taxable income to the short period. The rule allows subsidiaries that are *not* required to change their taxable year upon joining or leaving the group to elect to have their nonextraordinary items of income, gain, or deductions for the year allocated between the group's year and the separate return year of the subsidiary. Extraordinary items are not subject to the ratable allocation election and must be included in income at the time that they occur. Among other things, extraordinary items include capital gains and losses, § 1231 gains and losses, and income from passthrough entities, such as partnerships.[27]

It should be noted that when a subsidiary files a separate return, the short period is treated as a separate taxable year.[28] This separate year is counted in determining the number of years that a loss or credit carryover can be applied.

---

[26] Reg. § 1.1502-76(b).

[27] Reg. § 1.1502-76(b)(2)(ii)(C).

[28] Reg. § 1.1502-76(d).

Computation of the Consolidated Tax Liability: An Overview

LO.3

Compute consolidated taxable income and tax liability.

The consolidated tax return evolved from the premise that the tax liability of a group of related corporations should be based on the results of transactions with parties that are not affiliated with the group. Accordingly, *consolidated taxable income* is generally thought of as simply the combination of the taxable incomes of each individual corporation with transactions between members of the group eliminated. Unfortunately, the actual tax computation is somewhat more complicated. The regulations specifically provide that consolidated taxable income is the aggregate of (1) the separate taxable incomes of each member of the affiliated group, and (2) those items of income and deduction that must be excluded from the computation of separate taxable income and computed on a consolidated basis. The computation of consolidated taxable income normally involves three steps:

1. The taxable income of each member corporation is determined as if it filed a separate return.

2. Certain modifications are made to the taxable incomes computed in step 1 to eliminate (a) transactions between members of the group (e.g., a sale of property from one member to another), and (b) certain items that must be accounted for on a consolidated basis (e.g., capital gains). The result is called *separate taxable income*.

3. The separate taxable incomes of each member corporation, including the necessary modifications, are combined with those items that must be stated on a consolidated basis to arrive at consolidated taxable income.

Example 9

P Corp. owns 100% of S Inc. P's taxable income during the year was $110,000, including a long-term capital gain of $4,000 and $6,000 of income attributable to a sale of land to S which S treated as a capital expenditure. S had taxable income of $50,000, including a $3,000 short-term capital loss. Consolidated taxable income is the aggregate of the separate taxable income of each corporation and those items which must be reported on a consolidated basis—in this case, the capital gains and losses. The separate taxable income of P is $100,000 ($110,000 total taxable income − $6,000 profit from sales to a member of the group − $4,000 capital gain that must be eliminated and restated on a consolidated basis), and the separate taxable income of S is $53,000 ($50,000 + $3,000 capital loss, which must be eliminated and restated on a consolidated basis). The consolidation of each member's capital gains and losses of the group results in a long-term capital gain of $1,000 ($4,000 long-term capital gain of P − $3,000 short-term capital loss of S). Consolidated taxable income is $154,000 ($100,000 + $53,000 + $1,000).

A detailed discussion of the computation of consolidated taxable income follows.

Separate Taxable Income

The first step in computing consolidated taxable income is to determine the *separate taxable income* of each member of the affiliated group. Separate taxable income is defined as the corporation's taxable income calculated as if it were filing separately except for two modifications. Notwithstanding the two modifications, the calculation of separate taxable income is made applying all of the principles normally encountered when a corporation determines its taxable income. As indicated above, the two modifications required to arrive at separate taxable income concern transactions between members of the affiliated group—so-called separate company transactions—and certain items that must be computed on a consolidated basis.

Separate Company Transactions

The regulations identify seven types of *separate company transactions* that must be accounted for in a particular manner. These are listed below and discussed later in this chapter.

1. Intercompany transactions.[29]
2. Intercompany distributions with respect to a member's stock and redemptions of stock, bonds, or other obligations of members of the group.[30]
3. Built-in deductions.[31]
4. Mine exploration expenditures that are limited by Code § 617(h).[32]
5. Income or loss from changes in accounting methods.[33]
6. Initial inventory adjustments.[34]
7. Recapture of excess loss accounts.[35]

Single-Entity Modifications

The second modification to separate taxable income concerns certain items that must be recomputed on a consolidated basis (e.g., as if one corporation made all of the charitable contributions). Each of the following items is eliminated in computing separate taxable income.

1. Net operating losses.
2. Net capital gains and losses.
3. Section 1231 gains and losses.
4. Charitable contribution deductions.
5. Dividends-received and dividends-paid deductions.

CONSOLIDATED ITEMS

Once the separate taxable income of each member corporation is determined, calculations must be made concerning those items that must be treated on a consolidated basis. These items are the same as those that were eliminated from each group member's separate taxable income as noted above (e.g., the member's capital gains and losses and charitable contributions). The various items are combined as if the group were a single corporation. For example, the capital loss of one member offsets the capital gain of another member. In effect, the limitations that normally apply separately to each member are applied to the group as a whole. This can be very advantageous where one member has a net operating loss deduction since the deduction can be used to offset the income of another member, thus producing immediate benefits (i.e., the loss does not have to be carried over to a year when the loss corporation has income, which may never occur).

The combination of these various items results in the following:

1. The consolidated net operating loss deduction.
2. The consolidated capital gain net income.
3. The consolidated § 1231 loss.
4. The consolidated casualty and theft loss.
5. The consolidated charitable contributions deduction.
6. The consolidated dividends-received and dividends-paid deduction.

---

[29] Reg. § 1.1502-13.

[30] Reg. § 1.1502-14.

[31] Reg. § 1.1502-15.

[32] Reg. § 1.1502-16.

[33] Reg. § 1.1502-17.

[34] Reg. § 1.1502-18.

[35] Reg. § 1.1502-19.

COMPUTATION OF THE CONSOLIDATED TAX LIABILITY

After the separate taxable income of each member has been determined and the calculations concerning consolidated items have been completed, *consolidated taxable income* may be computed. Consolidated taxable income is determined by combining the separate taxable income of each member with the consolidated items above. This amount is then multiplied by the tax rates normally applying to corporations to determine the group's gross tax. From this amount, the group may deduct any consolidated credits and prepayments to arrive at the net tax liability. The process for computing the consolidated tax liability is presented in Exhibit 8-6 and applied in Exhibits 8-7 and 8-8.

DUAL RESIDENT CORPORATIONS

Code § 1503(d) disallows a loss in consolidation for certain "dual resident" corporations. This subsection provides that if a U.S. corporation is subject to a foreign country's tax on worldwide income, any taxable loss it incurs cannot again reduce the taxable income of any other member of a U.S. affiliated group. This provision is effective for taxable years beginning after 1986. Carryforward losses of dual resident corporations incurred prior to 1987 are still available to offset income of other members of U.S. affiliated groups.

EXHIBIT 8-6	The Consolidated Tax Formula

Combine separate taxable incomes to arrive at combined taxable income.

Eliminate:
- Intercompany dividends
- Disallowed built-in deductions
- Net operating loss deductions
- Capital gains and losses
- Section 1231 gains and losses
- Charitable contribution deductions
- Dividends-received deductions

Adjust for:
- Deferred intercompany gains and losses
- Gains and losses on nondividend intercompany distributions
- Intercompany profits in inventory
- Excess losses of affiliates

Deduct:
- Consolidated net operating losses
- Consolidated § 1231 losses
- Consolidated charitable contributions
- Consolidated dividends-received deduction
- Consolidated dividends-paid deduction

Add:
- Consolidated net capital gains

Equals:
- Consolidated taxable income

EXHIBIT 8-7	Example of Computing Consolidated Tax Liability

Descriptions	P	S	T	Combined	Consolidating Adjustment *(see below) No.	Consolidating Adjustment *(see below) Amount	Consolidated
Gross income:							
Gross receipts..............	$330,000	$ 80,000	$20,000	$430,000			$430,000
Cost of goods sold...........	100,000	25,000	5,000	130,000			130,000
Gross profit	$230,000	$ 55,000	$15,000	$300,000			$300,000
Dividends.................	50,000	10,000	5,000	65,000	1.	$(50,000)	15,000
Other interest	70,000	6,000	2,000	78,000			78,000
Net capital gains	12,000			12,000	2.	(9,000)	3,000
Total income..............	$362,000	$ 71,000	$22,000	$455,000		$(59,000)	$396,000
Deductions:							
Compensation of officers......	$ 50,000	$ 25,000	$ 9,600	$ 84,600			$ 84,600
Salaries and wages...........	120,000	30,000	3,300	153,300			153,300
Repairs....................	6,000	4,200	1,000	11,200			11,200
Bad debts..................	3,000	2,000	700	5,700			5,700
Rents	7,200	6,000	3,000	16,200			16,200
Taxes	1,500	1,000	900	3,400			3,400
Interest	1,000	2,200	200	4,400			4,400
Contributions...............	4,000		200	4,200	3.	$ (4,200)	0
Depreciation	56,000	104,000	800	161,600			161,600
Advertising.................	1,400	2,100	100	3,600			3,600
Other deductions............	900	1,000		1,900			1,900
Total deductions...........	$251,000	$ 178,300	$20,800	$450,100		$ (4,200)	$445,900
Taxable income (loss) before NOL and special deductions..........	$111,000	$(107,300)	$ 1,200	$ 4,900		$(54,800)	$ (49,900)
NOL deduction		(20,000)		(20,000)	4.	20,000	0
Special deductions............	(50,000)	(8,000)	(4,000)	(62,000)	1.	50,000	(12,000)
Taxable income (loss)..........	$ 61,000	$(135,300)	$ (2,800)	$ (77,100)		$ 15,200	$ (61,900)

*Explanation
1. To eliminate intercompany dividends from T to P.
2. To record a separate company capital loss carryforward not deductible by S but which may be used to offset P's capital gain.
3. To eliminate the contribution deductions since consolidated taxable income is a loss.
4. To eliminate SRLY NOL by S (explained within).

EXHIBIT 8-8	U.S. Corporation Income Tax

Form 1120
Department of the Treasury
Internal Revenue Service

U.S. Corporation Income Tax Return
For calendar year 2015 or tax year beginning _____, 2015, ending _____, 20 ____
► Information about Form 1120 and its separate instructions is at *www.irs.gov/form1120.*

OMB No. 1545-0123

2015

A Check if:
1a Consolidated return (attach Form 851) [X]
b Life/nonlife consolidated return . . [ ]
2 Personal holding co. (attach Sch. PH) . [ ]
3 Personal service corp. (see instructions) . [ ]
4 Schedule M-3 attached [ ]

TYPE OR PRINT

Name
P INC and Includible Subsidiaries

Number, street, and room or suite no. If a P.O. box, see instructions.
5757 Westheimer

City or town, state, or province, country, and ZIP or foreign postal code
Houston, TX 77027

B Employer identification number
76 – 5432104

C Date incorporated
1 – 1 – 2004

D Total assets (see instructions)
$ 592,874 00

E Check if: (1) [ ] Initial return　(2) [ ] Final return　(3) [ ] Name change　(4) [ ] Address change

Income	1a	Gross receipts or sales	1a	430,000	00
	b	Returns and allowances	1b		
	c	Balance. Subtract line 1b from line 1a	1c	430,000	00
	2	Cost of goods sold (attach Form 1125-A)	2	130,000	00
	3	Gross profit. Subtract line 2 from line 1c	3	300,000	00
	4	Dividends (Schedule C, line 19)	4	15,000	00
	5	Interest	5	78,000	00
	6	Gross rents	6		
	7	Gross royalties	7	3,000	00
	8	Capital gain net income (attach Schedule D (Form 1120))	8		
	9	Net gain or (loss) from Form 4797, Part II, line 17 (attach Form 4797)	9		
	10	Other income (see instructions—attach statement)	10		
	11	**Total income.** Add lines 3 through 10 ►	11	396,000	00
Deductions (See instructions for limitations on deductions.)	12	Compensation of officers (see instructions—attach Form 1125-E) ►	12	84,600	00
	13	Salaries and wages (less employment credits)	13	153,300	00
	14	Repairs and maintenance	14	11,200	00
	15	Bad debts	15	5,700	00
	16	Rents	16	16,200	00
	17	Taxes and licenses	17	3,400	00
	18	Interest	18	4,400	00
	19	Charitable contributions	19		
	20	Depreciation from Form 4562 not claimed on Form 1125-A or elsewhere on return (attach Form 4562)	20	161,600	00
	21	Depletion	21		
	22	Advertising	22		
	23	Pension, profit-sharing, etc., plans	23	3,600	00
	24	Employee benefit programs	24		
	25	Domestic production activities deduction (attach Form 8903)	25		
	26	Other deductions (attach statement)	26	1,900	00
	27	**Total deductions.** Add lines 12 through 26 ►	27	445,900	00
	28	Taxable income before net operating loss deduction and special deductions. Subtract line 27 from line 11.	28	– 49,900	00
	29a	Net operating loss deduction (see instructions)	29a		
	b	Special deductions (Schedule C, line 20)	29b	12,000	00
	c	Add lines 29a and 29b	29c	12,000	00
Tax, Refundable Credits, and Payments	30	**Taxable income.** Subtract line 29c from line 28 (see instructions)	30	– 61,900	00
	31	Total tax (Schedule J, Part I, line 11)	31		
	32	Total payments and refundable credits (Schedule J, Part II, line 21)	32	2,000	00
	33	Estimated tax penalty (see instructions). Check if Form 2220 is attached ► [ ]	33	0	00
	34	**Amount owed.** If line 32 is smaller than the total of lines 31 and 33, enter amount owed	34		
	35	**Overpayment.** If line 32 is larger than the total of lines 31 and 33, enter amount overpaid	35	2,000	00
	36	Enter amount from line 35 you want: **Credited to 2016 estimated tax** ►　Refunded ►	36	2,000	00

Sign Here
Under penalties of perjury, I declare that I have examined this return, including accompanying schedules and statements, and to the best of my knowledge and belief, it is true, correct, and complete. Declaration of preparer (other than taxpayer) is based on all information of which preparer has any knowledge.

► *John Beyond*　　2–5–16　► President
Signature of officer　　Date　　Title

May the IRS discuss this return with the preparer shown below (see instructions)? [ ] Yes [ ] No

Paid Preparer Use Only

Print/Type preparer's name	Preparer's signature	Date	Check [ ] if self-employed	PTIN
S. Nykol Pratt	*S. Nykol Pratt*	2–1–16		468–18–7240

Firm's name ► TaxCo P.C.
Firm's address ► 321 Main Blvd., Houston, TX 77066
Firm's EIN ► 74 – 1897652
Phone no. (713) 743 – 4835

For Paperwork Reduction Act Notice, see separate instructions.　　Cat. No. 11450Q　　Form **1120** (2015)

An intercompany transaction is any transaction between corporations that are members of the same consolidated group immediately after the transaction.[36] For example, a subsidiary might sell or rent property to another subsidiary or borrow money from its parent. Similarly, a parent might provide services to a subsidiary or license technology from it. Intercompany transactions such as these create several troublesome accounting problems for corporations filing consolidated returns. To illustrate, consider IBM and its wholly owned subsidiary, Lotus. Assume Lotus sells software for $100 (basis $80) to its parent, IBM, that includes the software as a component in its personal computers. There are three major issues that must be addressed in this transaction: (1) when is the gain realized on the intercompany transaction recognized; (2) how much gain will be recognized by each member of the group; and (3) what is its character. To ensure that the taxable income of the affiliated group is clearly reflected and to prevent transactions that could create, accelerate, avoid, or defer consolidated taxable income, the regulations provide special rules governing intercompany transactions.

> **LO.4**
> Determine the treatment of an intercompany transaction.

Before proceeding to the technical complexities of these rules, an understanding of their basic thrust may be useful. Under the current rules (much like those in the old regulations), intercompany transactions are usually treated as if they occurred between two divisions of a single corporation. Consequently, gains and losses on intercompany sales are normally postponed until the property is sold outside the group. For example, in the case above, assume that IBM has two divisions, Lotus and its personal computer division, PC. If Lotus were a division of IBM (rather than a subsidiary), it would *not* recognize the income of $20 ($100 − $80) upon the sale to its parent. Similarly, under this division approach, the PC division of IBM would still have a basis in the software of $80. If the PC division later sells the computer and $130 of the computer's sales price is attributable to the Lotus software, IBM would have a gain of $50 ($130 − $80), $20 reported by its subsidiary, Lotus, and $30 reported by IBM itself. Note that the total income of $50 in this transaction is recognized and reported on the consolidated return as if the separate corporations were simply divisions of a single entity (the single-entity approach). However, the actual reporting of the income or the location of the income is determined as if the corporations were separate entities (the separate-company approach, Lotus reporting $20 and IBM reporting $30).

As explained below, the regulations also contain a *matching rule* and an *acceleration rule* that attempt to secure a result that is consistent with the single-entity approach. For example, in the case of intercompany rentals or licensing, say IBM licenses technology from Lotus, IBM's taxable income (i.e., consolidated taxable income) would not be effected since there has been merely a shift in assets within a single taxable entity (i.e., Lotus' rental income is matched against IBM's rental expense).

Much of the difficulty in applying the intercompany transaction rules arises from trying to decipher whether the single-entity or separate-companies approach is used. As demonstrated above, the location of intercompany gain, loss, deduction, and income is usually done on a separate company basis while the timing is done on a single-entity basis. As will be seen, the trick is determining when each approach applies. Fortunately, the regulations provide numerous examples.

DEFINITIONAL APPROACH

The current regulations operationalize the treatment of intercompany transactions described above using what can be confusing terminology. The regulations start simply, explaining that in an intercompany transaction, S will be deemed to be the selling member while B will be the buying member. S's items of income, gain, deduction and loss that arise in an intercompany transaction are referred to as its *intercompany items*.[37] On the other side of the transaction, B's tax items arising from the same intercompany transaction are referred to as *corresponding items*.[38] For example, consider the example above concerning IBM and Lotus. In this transaction, Lotus is S, the seller, while IBM is B, the buyer. Upon S's sale of software (basis $80) to B for $100, S has an *intercompany item,* a gain on the sale of $20 ($100 − $80), and B has a *corresponding item* related to the sale in an amount yet to be determined. Similarly, if B rented property from S, B's rental expense would be the intercompany item

---

[36] Reg. § 1.1502-13(b)(1).

[37] Reg. § 1.1502-13(b)(2)(i)(A).

[38] Reg. § 1.1502-13(b)(2)(ii)(A).

while S's rental income would be the corresponding item. The next quantity is the most cumbersome: the *recomputed corresponding item*. A recomputed corresponding item is the corresponding item (e.g., the gain) that B would take into account if S and B were divisions in a single corporation and the intercompany transaction was between those divisions. For example, again assume that the software purchased by B from S is sold as a component of a personal computer with $130 of the sales price attributable to the software. In this case, B has a corresponding item, a recognized gain of $30 ($130 − $100) that it reports as part of its separate taxable income. B's recomputed corresponding item is a $50 gain, the gain that B would have had if the transaction had occurred between two divisions of a single corporation ($130 − $80). Since B's corresponding item, $30, is taken into account by B as part of its separate taxable income, S reports its deferred item of gain, $20, as part of its separate taxable income for the year. Technically, however, the regulations arrive at the same answer a bit differently. The regulations provide that the amount of the *intercompany item* that S is to report is the difference between B's *recomputed corresponding item*, the $50 gain that B would have had if the transaction had occurred between two divisions of a single corporation ($130 − $80 = $50), and B's *corresponding item* of $30, or $20 ($50 − $30). This approach is diagrammed in Exhibit 8-9. Note that the consolidated group would report gain of $50 ($30 from B + $20 from S). Observe also that this $50 is the same gain that would have been reported had S and B been two divisions of a single corporation.

EXHIBIT 8-9   Computation of Intercompany Items

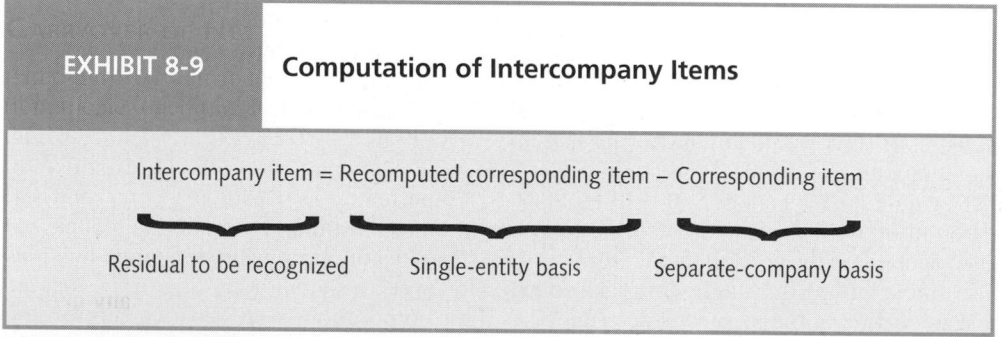

Intercompany item = Recomputed corresponding item − Corresponding item

Residual to be recognized   Single-entity basis   Separate-company basis

---

Example 10

Parent B and its wholly owned subsidiary S file a consolidated return. This year S sold equipment with a basis of $70 to B for $100. S's realized gain and intercompany item is its $30 gain ($100 − $70). Although S has realized a gain on a separate company basis, S does not report the realized gain until B recognizes its corresponding item (e.g., when the equipment is sold outside the group). Shortly thereafter, B sold the equipment outside the group for $90. B's corresponding item is the loss on the resale of $10 ($90 − $100). Upon the resale, the matching rule is triggered and B reports the loss of $10 while S reports its deferred gain of $30. Using the definitional approach, the $30 gain reported by S would be computed as follows:

B's recomputed corresponding item as if between two divisions of a single entity ($90 − $70)	$ 20
Less B's corresponding item computed on a separate company basis ($90 − $100)	(10)
S's income to be reported	$ 30

In computing consolidated taxable income, S's separate taxable income would contain a $30 gain while B's separate taxable income would contain a $10 loss, resulting in a consolidated gain of $20. Note that the computation of the recomputed corresponding item is a fictitious computation. Neither S nor B actually takes the recomputed corresponding item into account. Such amount is simply a necessary element in the computation of S's intercompany item that is recognized. Also observe that if B had not resold the equipment shortly after its purchase but recovered its cost through depreciation, its depreciation deductions would be corresponding items, triggering gain to be recognized by S.

MATCHING RULE

To ensure that a group's intercompany transactions are reported as if the enterprise were a single entity, the regulations also contain a matching rule. Like the other rules discussed thus far, the matching rule is designed to produce the same effect that would occur if the group members were divisions of a single corporation (rather than separate corporations). In this regard, the matching rule deals with two primary issues: (1) the character of the gain or loss recognized (i.e., character issues), and (2) the period in which an item is to be recognized (i.e., timing issues).

Character

In determining the character of a particular item, the activities of both S and B are taken into account.[39] For example, if S holds property for sale to unrelated customers in the ordinary course of its trade or business and sells the property to B, S's intercompany items as well as B's corresponding items may be ordinary items solely by reason of S's activities. There is no bright line test that can be used in this regard. The result can be determined only after an assessment of all of the surrounding facts and circumstances.

Example 11

Big Corporation is a real estate development company, concentrating on residential housing. Typically, Big causes its subsidiary, S, to purchase land that S holds for investment until Big believes the time is right for development. S usually sells land to its parent, Big, but may sell the land to an outsider. When Big buys a parcel of land from S, it usually does all of the development work then subdivides the property and sells the lots to builders. Big and S file a consolidated return. In 20X1, S purchased 100 acres of land on the north side of town for $300,000. Five years later in 20X6, S sold the land to Big for $800,000, realizing a gain of $500,000 ($800,000 − $300,000). Big prepared the ground for selling, putting in sewers and roads at a cost of $600,000. In 20X9, Big sold all of the lots for $2,100,000. S's intercompany gain of $500,000 is not recognized until Big reports its corresponding item, its gain of $700,000 ($2,100,000 − [$800,000 + $600,000]). Big and S are treated as divisions of a single entity for purposes of determining the character of the gain. Since the combined activities of both Big and S suggest that the land was held primarily for resale the gains of both Big and S would be considered ordinary. This is true even though the land in S's hands was held for investment and may have given rise to capital gain had it been sold to a nonmember.

Holding Periods

Because the character and other attributes of an intercompany transaction are determined by treating S and B as divisions, the matching rule normally aggregates the holding periods of S and B with respect to property transferred in an intercompany transaction. However, certain exceptions apply.[40]

Timing

Under the matching rule, S, the seller, generally takes into account its intercompany items in the year that B's corresponding items are taken into account.[41]

---

[39] Reg. § 1.1502-13(c)(1)(i).

[40] Reg. § 1.1502-13(c)(1)(ii).

[41] Reg. § 1.1502-13(c)(2)(ii).

Example 12

In Year 1, subsidiary S sells land with a basis of $80 to its parent B for $100, realizing a gain of $20. Two years later, in Year 3, B sells the land outside the group for $130. Under the matching rule, S does not report its $20 intercompany gain until B takes into account its corresponding item under its method of accounting. Since B does not recognize its $20 corresponding item until Year 3, S does not recognize any of its gain in Year 1 or 2. Instead, S defers recognition until Year 3, reporting its $20 gain at the same time that B reports its $30 gain. Thus consolidated taxable income would increase in year 3 by $50 ($20 + $30).

The sale of depreciable property between members follows the single-entity approach. B's corresponding item of depreciation is depreciation computed on a separate entity approach (i.e., its cost). B's recomputed corresponding item is depreciation as if B and S were divisions within a single entity (i.e., depreciation using S's basis). In other words, B computes its depreciation as if it were S to the extent of S's basis in the property (i.e., its recomputed corresponding item) and, to the extent that B's basis exceeds S's basis, B treats the excess as newly purchased property for purposes of depreciation. S's gain is generally the same as any additional depreciation that B would report due to any higher basis.

Example 13

On January 15, 2016, subsidiary S purchased an office building for $1,100,000 ($100,000 is attributable to the land). It sold the building to its parent B on July 20, 2020 for $1,400,000. Depreciation for S using the nonresidential realty tables found in would be computed as follows:

Year	S's Depreciation
2016 (2.461% × $1,000,000)	$ 24,610
2017 (2.564% × $1,000,000)	25,640
2018 (2.564% × $1,000,000)	25,640
2019 (2.564% × $1,000,000)	25,640
2020 (2.564% × $1,000,000 × 6.5/12)	13,888
Accumulated depreciation	$115,418

At the time of sale, S's basis in the depreciable property is $884,582 ($1,000,000 − $115,418). In computing its gain, it allocated $100,000 of the sales price to the land, resulting in no gain on the sale of the land. The gain on the sale of the building was $415,418 ([$1,400,000 − $100,000 = $1,300,000] − $884,582). In computing B's depreciation, B is treated as S to the extent its basis does not exceed S's basis. Thus in the year of sale, B claims the balance of the year's depreciation that S would have claimed, $11,752 in 2019 ($25,640 − $13,888). With respect to the excess basis of $415,418 ($1,300,000 − $884,582), which is the same as S's intercompany gain, it computes depreciation as if the property were newly placed in service. Using the factor for nonresidential realty that is placed in service in the seventh month of the year, depreciation would be $4,889 ($415,418 × 1.177%). The portion of S's $415,418 gain that is taken into account reflects the difference between B's depreciation and the depreciation that would have been claimed had B and S been separate divisions within the same single-entity (i.e., the recomputed depreciation). For 2020, B takes into account depreciation of $16,641 ($11,752 + $4,889). The recomputed depreciation would have been the $11,752, i.e., the amount that would have been reported if they were divisions with a single entity. Therefore, S reports a gain of $4,889 ($16,641 − $11,752). This can be summarized as follows:

S's separate depreciation	$11,752
S's portion of intercompany gain recognized	(4,889)
B's depreciation if it had been S	$13,888
B's depreciation of excess basis	4,889
Depreciation effect on consolidated taxable income	$25,640

In the following year, B's depreciation as if it had been S would be $25,640. The depreciation on the excess basis would be $10,651 ($415,418 × 2.564%). B's total reported depreciation would be $36,291 ($25,640 + $10,651). B's recomputed depreciation would have been $25,640 (as if B and S were divisions of a single entity). Therefore, S would recognize gain of $10,651 ($36,291 − $25,640). The net effect on consolidated taxable income (assuming the character is the same) is a reduction of $25,640.

B's depreciation if it had been S	$25,640
B's depreciation of excess basis	10,651
S's portion of intercompany gain recognized	(10,651)
Depreciation effect on consolidated taxable income	$25,640

Under the matching rule, reporting is not technically triggered by particular events but rather when B's corresponding items are taken into account.

Example 14

Subsidiary S sells a parcel of land, Whiteacre, to parent B, realizing an intercompany gain of $1,000. B subsequently transfers Whiteacre to N, a nonmember, in exchange for another parcel of land, Blackacre. Under the like-kind exchange provisions of § 1031, B recognizes no gain on the exchange of Whiteacre for Blackacre. As a result, B's *corresponding item,* its recognized gain, is zero. In addition, B's recomputed corresponding item (i.e., the gain that B would have had if the transaction had taken place between two divisions of a single-entity) is also zero. Consequently, no gain is taken into account by S under the matching rule even though the property is transferred outside the group. Instead, S's gain remains deferred and is taken into account based on B's corresponding items with respect to the replacement property, Blackacre. Under the old regulations, S's gain would have been recognized due to the transfer of the property outside of the group.

ACCELERATION RULE

The purpose of the acceleration rule is to take items into account to the extent that they cannot be taken into account under the matching rule. The acceleration rule generally applies in two situations: first, where the matching rule will not fully account for the items from an intercompany transaction in consolidated taxable income,[42] and second, where the intercompany transaction is reflected by a nonmember.[43]

---

[42] Reg. § 1.1502-13(d)(1)(i)(A).   [43] Reg. § 1.1502-13(d)(1)(i)(B).

The first situation in which the acceleration rule can apply is where either S or B becomes a nonmember of the affiliated group, and any remaining intercompany items and corresponding items can no longer be matched. In such a case, the intercompany items are taken into account immediately before S or B becomes a nonmember.

Example 15

P, the parent corporation, owns 100% of both S and B. S owns land with a basis of $70 and a value of $100. On January 1, 2016 S sells the land to B for $100. On July 1, 2018 P sells 60% of S's stock to unrelated X for $60 and, as a result, S becomes a nonmember. Under the matching rule, none of S's $30 gain is taken into account in years 1 through 3 (2016, 2017, and 2018) because there is no difference between B's corresponding gain ($0) and B's recomputed gain (also $0). Under the acceleration rule, S's gain must be taken into account because the matching rule will never produce the proper effect once S becomes a nonmember. Thus, S takes its $30 gain into account in 2018 immediately before becoming a nonmember. In addition, S's gain is reflected in P's basis in the S stock immediately before P's sale of the stock. Notwithstanding the acceleration of S's gain, B continues to take its corresponding items into account under its accounting method. Thus, B's corresponding items (i.e., its gain or loss on the sale of the land) are taken into account based on subsequent events on a separate-company basis.

Example 16

Assume the same facts as in *Example 15* except that P sells the B stock (rather than S stock) to X for $60 and, as a result, B becomes a nonmember of the affiliated group. Once again, because the effect of treating S and B as divisions of a single corporation cannot be produced once B becomes a nonmember, S takes its $30 gain into account under the acceleration rule immediately (the day before) before B becomes a nonmember.

The second situation in which the acceleration rule can apply occurs when B purchases property from S and transfers it tax-free to an entity (e.g., to a partnership under § 721 or to a nonmember corporation under § 351). Because the transferee entity now succeeds to B's corresponding item cost basis in the property, the acceleration rule requires S to take its intercompany items into account immediately before the event, rendering single-entity treatment impossible.[44]

Under special circumstances, the acceleration rule might also apply outside the scope of the two common situations. One such event might occur if S's gain or loss from the sale of property to B exceeds the effect of the intercompany transaction on the basis of the property.

Example 17

B owns a building with a basis of $2,000,000 and a value of $5,000,000. The building is destroyed by fire, and B uses insurance proceeds to buy a replacement building from S. S's gain or loss will not conform to B's basis in the building because B takes a substituted basis under the involuntary conversion rules of § 1033. If the amount of S's gain or loss exceeds the effect of the intercompany sale on the building's basis, S's gain or loss will not be fully taken into account under the matching rule because there will not be a sufficient difference between the corresponding items B takes into account and its recomputed items. Consequently, the acceleration rule applies at the time of the intercompany sale to take the excess amount into account. Unfortunately, S's gain or loss is accelerated because it is not possible to treat S and B as divisions of a single corporation, and acceleration is the only justifiable alternative.

---

[44] The primary difference between this rule and the situation of *Example 14* is that if B were to dispose of the property in an exchange with a nonmember under § 1031, the intercompany items would not be taken into account under the acceleration rule because the nonmember would not succeed to B's cost basis.

SIMPLIFICATION OF INVENTORY RULES

In 1995, the IRS incorporated simplification rules that treat inventory transactions like other intercompany transactions. However, the Service determined that a special rule is warranted for certain intercompany inventory transactions where applying the matching and acceleration rules would be extremely burdensome, such as dollar-value LIFO methods. Thus, if either S or B uses dollar-value LIFO inventory method, the regulations provide several inventory counting options to take into account their items from intercompany inventory transactions.

ANTI-AVOIDANCE RULES

The Service realized that the regulations could not address every situation where adjustments may be required to achieve neutrality in the overall determination of consolidated taxable income. Accordingly, the new regulations contain anti-avoidance rules that allow the IRS the flexibility to make adjustments where a transaction is structured with the principal purpose of avoiding treatment under the new intercompany transactions regulations.[45] The scope of this rule is illustrated with several examples in the regulations.[46]

Election to Report Currently

With the consent of the IRS, a group may elect not to defer gain or loss on *all* deferred intercompany transactions. In such a case, the gain or loss is recognized at the time of the transaction. Once approved, the election is binding to all future consolidated return years unless permission to revoke is given.[47] Such an election may be useful to eliminate laborious bookkeeping chores, especially for multiple intercompany transactions or transfers of long-lived assets.

Other Provisions Affecting Intercompany Transactions

Special rules exist that may further defer a loss on the sale of those assets beyond the rules found in the consolidated return regulations. If a member of an *affiliated* group ceases to be a member of that group but continues to be a member of a *controlled* group immediately after deconsolidation, regulations under § 267(f), in many instances, override the restoration rules previously discussed for deferred intercompany transactions.[48]

Example 18

P and its wholly owned subsidiary S join in the filing of a consolidated tax return for taxable year 2016, in which P sells property to S for a loss. Due to the deferral requirements, the loss is eliminated in consolidation. On January 1, 2017 all of the stock of S is transferred to P's sole shareholder. Although P and S are no longer affiliated corporations and must file separate tax returns, they remain members of a controlled group and restoration of the loss will not take place.

Intercompany Distributions

Whether income is recognized on an intercompany distribution depends on the type of distribution that is made. As a general rule, a distribution paid out of earnings and profits (i.e., a dividend) is eliminated from gross income in the consolidated tax return.[49] Because the dividends are eliminated, no dividends-received deduction is available with respect to these dividends.[50] To the extent that a distribution is not a dividend [i.e., a return of capital under §§ 301(c)(2) and (3)], the distributee reduces its basis in the stock of the subsidiary. Contrary to the case under the separate return rules, if the distribution exceeds basis, gain is not recognized. Instead, it is deferred in an account known as an *excess loss account* until the occurrence of some subsequent event such as the sale of a subsidiary's stock. The excess loss account is discussed in detail later in this chapter.

---

[45] Reg. § 1.1502-13(h)(1).

[46] Reg. § 1.1502-13(h)(2).

[47] Reg. § 1.1502-13(e)(3).

[48] See Reg. § 1.267(f)-1(c).

[49] Reg. § 1.1502-13(f).

[50] Reg. § 1.1502-26(b).

Example 19

P and its newly created subsidiary S file a consolidated tax return for the current year. During the year, S distributes $12,000 cash to P. P's basis in its S stock is $7,000 and S has current earnings and profits for its first year of $4,000 and no other gains are recognized. The first $4,000 is treated as a dividend and eliminated in consolidation. The next $7,000 reduces P's basis under § 301(c)(2) to zero. The remaining $1,000 is not taxed as a capital gain but simply increases the excess loss account.

If, as a result of a property distribution, the *distributing* corporation is required to recognize gain or loss, the amount of the gain or loss is to be treated under the intercompany transaction rules. The basis of the property to the distributee is the basis of the property in the hands of the distributing subsidiary increased by any gain recognized on the distribution.

Consolidated Items

As indicated above, certain items must be eliminated from separate taxable income and accounted for on a consolidated basis. Each of these items is examined below.

THE CONSOLIDATED NET OPERATING LOSS

LO.5

Explain the rules limiting the use of one member's losses and credits against the income and tax of other consolidated group members.

Perhaps the most important advantage of a consolidated return is that the net operating losses of one group member can be used currently to offset the taxable income of another member. This benefit is often the major reason for electing to file a consolidated return.

To arrive at the consolidated NOL, the first step is to determine each member's separate taxable income or loss. This calculation is made without regard to any NOL *carryovers* or *carrybacks* to the current taxable year. The separate taxable incomes and NOLs are then combined. If the separate NOLs exceed the separate taxable incomes, a consolidated NOL results. Only the consolidated NOL may be carried back or over. In computing the consolidated NOL that is carried over or back, certain items eliminated in computing separate taxable income are taken into account. The items generally restored are the dividends-received deduction, the charitable contribution deduction, the net capital gains or losses, and the § 1231 loss.[51] The consolidated net operating loss can be carried back or carried over subject to certain limitations discussed later in this chapter.

CONSOLIDATED CAPITAL GAINS AND LOSSES

The regulations require that capital gains and losses must be computed and reported on a consolidated basis. The first step in the computation is to separate capital gains and losses for each member of the group. The consolidated capital gain net income is then determined by taking into account the following:[52]

1. The aggregate of capital gains and losses from the affiliated members.
2. The consolidated § 1231 gains.
3. The consolidated net capital loss carryovers.

---

[51] Reg. § 1.1502-21(f).   [52] Reg. § 1.1502-22(a)(1).

Example 20

Corporations P, S, and T file consolidated tax returns for 2016 and 2017. In 2017, the members had the following capital asset transactions:

1. P sold to T a § 1231 asset for $12,000 (basis of $8,000).
2. S sold an asset to an unrelated individual for $1,000. S had purchased the asset from P in 2014 for $3,000. P had deferred a capital gain of $800 on the sale to S.
3. T sold an asset to an unrelated individual for $15,000 (basis of $7,000).
4. The group had a consolidated capital loss carryover of $5,000.

The consolidated net capital gain for the group is determined as follows:

P's net capital gain restored into income due to S's disposal	$ 800
T's net capital gain ($15,000 – $7,000)	8,000
S's net capital loss ($1,000 – $3,000)	(2,000)
Capital loss carryover	(5,000)
The $4,000 gain ($12,000 – $8,000) on P's intercompany transaction is not taken into account for this year	0
Consolidated net capital gain	$1,800

Consolidated net capital losses cannot be used to offset consolidated taxable income. An analysis of capital losses and possible limitations is continued in the discussion on loss carryovers later in this chapter.

THE CONSOLIDATED DIVIDENDS-RECEIVED DEDUCTION

The rules for determining the consolidated dividends-received deduction for nonmember dividends (intercompany dividends are eliminated) are essentially the same as the computations performed on a separate company basis.[53] The only difference is that the (70 or 80) percent limitation is based on consolidated taxable income excluding the consolidated NOL deduction, the consolidated net capital loss carryback, and the consolidated dividends-paid deduction for certain dividends under § 247.

Example 21

Corporations P, S, T, and U file a consolidated tax return for the year showing consolidated taxable income of $90,000. The companies received dividends during the year from less than 20% owned nonmember domestic corporations as follows:

Corporation	Nonmember Dividends	Separate Taxable Income
P	$ 10,000	$20,000
S	20,000	30,000
T	70,000	40,000
U	0	(10,000)
	$100,000	$80,000

The dividends-received deduction is limited to the lesser of 70% of $100,000 (the domestic dividends) or 70% of $80,000 (consolidated taxable income), unless a net operating loss is generated for the year. Since an NOL is not created, the dividends-received deduction is limited to $56,000 (70% × $80,000). Notice that on a separate company basis, the aggregate of the dividends-received deductions would produce a $70,000 deduction determined as follows:

Corporation	Deduction	
P	$ 7,000	($10,000 × 70%)
S	14,000	($20,000 × 70%)
T	49,000*	($70,000 × 70%)
	$70,000	

* This amount is not limited to 70% of $40,000 because the deduction would create a net operating loss.

THE CONSOLIDATED CHARITABLE CONTRIBUTION DEDUCTION

The amount that can be deducted as a consolidated charitable contribution is the *lesser* of the following computations.

1. The combined charitable contributions of the individual group members (before limitations) plus any consolidated charitable contribution carryovers to the current year.
2. 10% of adjusted consolidated taxable income.[54]

Adjusted taxable income is consolidated taxable income computed without regard to the dividends-received or the dividends-paid deductions, consolidated loss carryovers, and the consolidated charitable contribution deduction itself.[55]

To the extent that the consolidated charitable contribution exceeds the limitation, the excess amount plus any remaining contributions from separate return years can be carried over to the next year. The five-year carryforward of § 170(d) also applies to the consolidated charitable contribution deduction. If an affiliated corporation ceases to be a member of the group, part of the contribution carryover attributable to the member must be allocated to it. The regulations prescribe the manner for making this allocation.[56]

THE CONSOLIDATED TAX LIABILITY

For corporations other than insurance companies, the consolidated tax liability consists of one or more of the following taxes:

1. The § 11 corporate income tax on consolidated taxable income.
2. The § 541 tax on consolidated undistributed personal holding company income.
3. The § 531 tax on consolidated accumulated taxable income.
4. The § 56 alternative minimum tax liability on consolidated minimum taxable income.

In computing its § 11 corporate income tax on consolidated taxable income, the group is only entitled to a single graduated tax bracket amount under the controlled group limitations of § 1561(a). For purposes of applying the additional 5% surtax on corporations having taxable income in excess of $100,000, the members of the affiliated group are treated as a single corporation. The same holds true for taxable income in excess of $10,000,000.

---

[54] The regulations still state five percent, but the IRS has conformed to the 10% amount under Code § 170. Reg. § 1.1502-24(a)(1) and (2).

[55] Reg. § 1.1502-24(c).

[56] Reg. § 1.1502-79(e)(2).

THE CONSOLIDATED TAX CREDIT

The consolidated tax liability of the group is reduced by any available tax credits also computed on a consolidated basis. Although the regulations specifically recognize only two credits—the investment tax credit and foreign tax credit—only the investment tax credit is discussed here. An analysis of credit carryovers is reserved for a later portion of this chapter dealing with carryover limitations.

Investment Tax Credit

The investment tax credit became part of the general business credit contained in § 38 in 1984.[57] However, the investment tax credit was generally repealed as part of the Tax Reform Act of 1986 for property placed in service after 1985. Nevertheless, it remains intact for certain transition property, energy property, and qualified rehabilitation expenditures.[58] In addition to the investment tax credit, § 38 also includes the targeted jobs credit, the alcohol fuels credit, the research credit, and the low-income housing credit.

The amount of the general business credit should generally be the sum of the consolidated business credits earned in that year, and the consolidated business credit carryovers and carrybacks. The consolidated business credit carryovers and carrybacks should also include any unused credits of members of the group arising in separate return years that can be carried over or back to the taxable year under consideration.[59]

Credit Recapture

Investment credit must be recaptured whenever property is disposed of outside of the group or ceases to be qualifying property. Any recapture must be added to the consolidated tax liability of the group. If a group member disposes of qualifying property during a separate return year, the member is totally liable for any resulting investment tax credit recapture—regardless of whether the property was placed in service in a consolidated return year.[60] It should be noted that a sale or exchange between group members is not treated as a disposition for credit recapture purposes. The *purchasing member* must assume liability for the recapture tax in the event separate returns are filed.[61]

Limitations and Adjustments Due to Consolidation

One of the attractions of filing a consolidated tax return is the ability of a profitable entity to use the losses and credits of an unprofitable entity. One can only imagine the abuses that would result if some form of limitation were not imposed. As a result, the consolidated return regulations impose certain restrictions. These involve the following:

1. Separate return limitation years.
2. Built-in deductions.
3. Reverse acquisitions.
4. Carryovers and carrybacks to separate return years.

In addition to these limitations, the regulations provide for several other adjustments. These serve to maintain the integrity of a single-entity concept while preventing certain abuses (e.g., the double counting of subsidiary losses) and mitigating the hardships of double taxation when a subsidiary's stock is sold. These include the following:

1. Adjustments for investment in subsidiaries.
2. The excess loss account.
3. Adjustments for earnings and profits.

---

[57] See Reg. § 1.1502-3 for the application of the investment tax credit to an affiliated group filing consolidated returns before 1984.

[58] § 46(a)(2) and (3); § 49(b)(1) and (e).

[59] See Reg. § 1.1502-3(a) and (b)(1).

[60] Reg. § 1.1502-3(f)(1).

[61] Reg. § 1.1502-3(f)(2).

SEPARATE RETURN LIMITATION YEARS

When a corporation incurs a net operating loss in a separate return year and subsequently carries that loss to a consolidated return year, the Regulations limit the deductible amount of the loss carryover.[62] The limitation is imposed only if the loss year is considered a *separate return limitation year* (SRLY). Generally, this means any loss year for which a separate return was filed, except where the corporation was a member of the group for the entire year or the corporation is the parent in the year to which the loss is being carried. The amount of loss incurred in a SRLY that may be deducted in a consolidated year before 1997 is limited to the excess of consolidated taxable income (computed without regard to the net operating loss deduction) over consolidated taxable income as reduced by the loss member's income and deductions.[63] In essence, the group's deduction for any member's SRLY losses cannot exceed the member's contribution to consolidated taxable income.[64]

Example 22

P and S are members of an affiliated group for 2015 and file a consolidated tax return. T Corporation, owned by an individual, incurs a $15,000 net operating loss for 2015. On January 1, 2016, P acquires all the stock of T. In 2015, P, S, and T file a consolidated tax return showing consolidated taxable income of $40,000, of which $6,000 is attributable to the efforts of T. Because of the SRLY rules, only $6,000 of the $15,000 loss can be carried over to 2016. The carryover is limited to $6,000, which is T's contribution to consolidated taxable income. The remaining $9,000 ($15,000 − $6,000) may be carried over to 2017 and is subject to the SRLY rules and NOL carryover limitations, as discussed under the modified SRLY rules later in this chapter.

Exceptions to SRLY Rules

According to the definition of a SRLY noted above, the corporation designated as the common parent for an affiliated group is generally not subject to the SRLY rules since its years are not considered SRLY years. Under this so-called *lonely parent rule*, the parent's losses from a "pre" or "post" affiliation year may be used to offset the earnings of other members in a consolidated return year.[65] This exception does not apply if there has been a reverse acquisition[66] or similar merger of a parent into a subsidiary.

Example 23

In Year 1, P, a first-year corporation, files a separate return with an operating loss of $12,000. On January 1, Year 2, P acquires all the stock of S Corporation. For Year 2, P and S file a consolidated tax return reflecting P's taxable income of $5,000 and S's taxable income of $24,000. In this case, the SRLY rules are not applicable since P is the common parent. Consequently, all $12,000 of the loss carryover is utilized in Year 2.

Example 24

Assume the same facts as in *Example 23,* except that P sells all the S stock on January 1, Year 3. If P incurs a $14,000 loss for Year 3, the SRLY rules do not restrict P from carrying back the loss from this post-affiliation year to a consolidated return year since P was the parent in the year to which the loss is carried. Therefore, the full amount of the loss can be carried back to Year 2 to offset consolidated taxable income without limitation. (Note that the SRLY rules apply to carrybacks as well as carryovers.)

---

[62] Reg. § 1.1502-21.

[63] Prop. Reg. § 1.1502-21(c)(2).

[64] If there are carryovers from more than one year, they are absorbed in chronological order.

[65] *F.C. Donovan, Inc. v. U.S.*, 261 F.2d 470 (CA-1, 1958).

[66] Defined later in this chapter.

The SRLY rules are also inapplicable for a corporation's separate return year (SRY) if that corporation was a member of the group for each day of such year.[67] This would occur when the corporation was a member of a group that elected *not* to file on a consolidated basis.[68]

Related Provisions

The SRLY rules are not just restricted to net operating losses. The rules also apply to net capital losses, the investment tax credit, and foreign tax credits. Note, however, that charitable contribution carryovers do not fall within these restrictions.

MODIFIED SRLY RULES

On January 28, 1991, the Internal Revenue Service issued proposed regulations amending the separate return limitation year rules of Reg. §§ 1.1502-21 and 1.1502-22 regarding net operating loss and capital loss carrybacks and carryovers. These proposed regulations were replaced with temporary regulations in 1997.[69] The modifications to the SRLY rules diverge from the former regulations in three significant aspects. First, the manner in which the member's contribution to consolidated taxable income is determined has been changed. Second, the manner in which a subsidiary uses its SRLY losses is based upon a *cumulative* contribution to taxable income. Third, the manner in which a SRLY loss is used is computed on a *subgroup,* rather than a member-by-member basis. Each of these is discussed below.

A Member's Contribution to Taxable Income

Under the former regulations, a member's contribution to the taxable income of the group was determined on a "with and without" basis. Under the current regulations (since 1997), a member's contribution to consolidated taxable income is based upon the member's items of income, gain, deduction, and loss.[70] Thus, the amount of SRLY that may be absorbed in any given consolidated return year is established solely by reference to that member's contribution to consolidated taxable income. Under this method, a member's contribution to taxable income cannot be diminished by another member's net operating loss or capital loss unless it is a member of a subgroup (discussed below).

Cumulative Contribution to Consolidated Taxable Income

Under the modified regulations, the ability to use a SRLY loss is based upon the member's cumulative contribution to taxable income since it became a member of the group.[71] As a result, if a subsidiary with SRLY losses becomes a member of an affiliated group and continues to generate losses after affiliation, the new member must first contribute income toward consolidated taxable income in the amount of its post-affiliation losses before it has the opportunity to utilize its SRLY losses.

Example 25

P and S, both calendar year corporations, become affiliated on January 1, 2016, when S had a NOL carryover of $40,000. During 2016 P and S have consolidated taxable income of $100,000, of which $16,000 is attributable to S. In 2017, P and S experience a consolidated loss of $85,000, of which $50,000 is attributable to S. In 2018, P and S have $120,000 of consolidated taxable income, of which $31,000 is attributable to S. Under the new SRLY rules, in 2016, S can utilize up to $16,000 of its NOL carryforward and the remaining $24,000 ($40,000 − $16,000) will continue to carry

[67] Reg. § 1.1502-1(f). See *Braswell Motor Freight Line, Inc. v. U.S.*, 477 F.2d 594 (CA-5, 1973), where a corporation was formed in 1955 and became a member of the group in July of 1957. Although the corporation had no assets or taxable income prior to July 1957, the loss generated in the latter half of the year was subject to the SRLY rules because the corporation was not a member for each day of the year (1957).

[68] Reg. § 1.1502-1(f). The same rule applies to a predecessor of any group member that was a member of the group on each day of the year. A predecessor is a transferor or distributor of assets to the member in a transaction to which § 381(a) applies.

[69] Temp. Reg. § 1.1502-21(c).

[70] Temp. Reg. § 1.1502-21(c)(1).

[71] *Ibid.*

forward. In 2017, because S has made no contribution to taxable income, none of the NOL carryforward can be utilized. In 2018, even when S contributes taxable income of $31,000, none of the NOL carryforward can be used because S has made a negative contribution to consolidated taxable income on a cumulative basis since affiliation ($16,000 − $50,000 + $31,000 = −$3,000). Until S can recover to a cumulative positive contribution to the consolidated taxable income, none of the SRLY loss can be utilized. Under the prior rules, S could have utilized the remaining $24,000 of its NOL in 2018 because it made a positive contribution to taxable income for that year.

Alternatively, because of the cumulative approach, SRLY losses can now be absorbed in a year in which the member has *no* taxable income, provided the member has contributed to consolidated taxable income in excess of its losses in earlier affiliated years.

SRLY Subgroups

To be consistent with new regulations promulgated under Code § 382 for consolidated groups, the extent to which a group can absorb a SRLY loss must be determined on a subgroup basis.[72] In other words, all corporations within that subgroup are treated as a single entity for purposes of determining a cumulative contribution to consolidated income. A SRLY subgroup is a group composed of all members that have been continuously affiliated with the member since the loss arose. A separate SRLY subgroup is formed for each SRLY loss. Once a SRLY subgroup is established, no other corporations can become a member of that subgroup unless they become classified as "successor" corporations.

Example 26

On December 31, 2016, P and S, affiliated calendar year corporations, have a NOL carryforward of $40,000, which is not a SRLY loss. On January 1, 2017, M purchases all the stock of P and S. P and S now become a "subgroup," and their $40,000 NOL becomes a SRLY loss with respect to the income that the subgroup can contribute to the M-P-S affiliated group.

Because more than one SRLY loss may be carried forward, a corporation may be considered a member of more than one SRLY subgroup. When this is the case, the regulations provide "anti-duplication" rules to ensure that items of income and deductions are not taken more than once in determining the SRLY absorption.[73] In addition, losses utilized by the consolidated group are absorbed on a FIFO basis using the principles of § 172.

Example 27

Assume the same facts as *Example 26*, and for 2017 the M-P-S affiliated group experiences a consolidated taxable loss of $55,000. Accordingly, none of the $40,000 SRLY subgroup loss can be utilized. If on January 1, 2018, L corporation buys all the stock of M corporation, two SRLY subgroups are formed: P-S, with a SRLY loss of $40,000, and M-P-S, with a SRLY loss of $55,000. Because P and S are in both subgroups, special "anti-duplication" rules will prevent any positive taxable income generated by these corporations in the future from being used more than once in absorbing SRLY carryovers to the L-M-P-S affiliated group.

---

[72] Temp. Reg. § 1.1502-21(c)(2).
[73] Temp. Reg. § 1.1502-21(c)(2)(iv).

Final SRLY Regulations

Final SRLY regulations, issued on June 25, 1999, generally adopted the rules of the temporary regulations, with minor modifications and one major change. The change, referred to as the "overlap rule," arose from the belief by Treasury that a § 382 limitation reasonably approximates a corresponding SRLY limitation. Thus, the simultaneous imposition of both rules was not necessary and only served to complicate the limitation of net operating loss carryovers. Accordingly, the final regulations generally eliminate the SRLY limitation in circumstances in which its application *overlaps* with that of § 382.[74] These regulations are effective for consolidated return due dates that arise after June 25, 1999.

The Overlap Rule

Generally, to qualify for the net operating loss overlap rule (and elimination of the SRLY calculation), a corporation must become a member of a consolidated group (a SRLY event) within six months of the change date of an ownership change that gives rise to a § 382(a) limitation (a § 382 event). If the § 382 event occurs on the same date as the SRLY event or precedes that SRLY event, the overlap rule is applicable to the tax year that includes the SRLY event. If the SRLY event precedes the § 382 event, the elimination of SRLY is delayed until the first tax year that begins after the § 382 event. The delay is necessary to ensure that an adequate limitation is always in effect for a net operating loss carryover.

Example 28

On April 1, P Corporation purchases 60% of S corporation (a § 382 event) and on September 1 of the same year, P acquired an additional 20% of S (a SRLY event). Because a SRLY event occurred within six months after the § 382 event, only a § 382 limitation will be applied. In absence of the overlap rule, those losses would also be subject to a SRLY limitation.

Example 29

Assume a SRLY event occurs December 1 for a calendar year consolidated group in Year 1, and a § 382 event occurs on April 1, Year 2. Even though an overlap situation results, because the SRLY event occurred first, it is necessary to maintain the application of the SRLY rules until the end of Year 2. Beginning in Year 3, only the § 382 limit will apply.

Subgroups

The final regulations also provide special overlap rules for subgroups. In general, the overlap rule applies to the subgroup and not separately to the members of the subgroup. However, the overlap rule does not apply unless the SRLY subgroup is coextensive with the § 382 loss subgroup.[75]

Example 30

Assume that the S consolidated group (composed entirely of S and T) has a $200 consolidated net operating loss, of which $100 is attributable to S and $100 is attributable to T. If the M group acquires the S group, S and T compose both a SRLY subgroup and a § 382 loss subgroup. Because the subgroups are coextensive, the overlap rule applies to eliminate the application of SRLY in the M group for the $200 consolidated net operating loss. If the subgroups had not been composed of the same corporations (even though both limitations occurred at the same time), the overlap rule would not apply to eliminate a SRLY computation.

---

[74] Reg. § 1.1502-21(g)(1).　　　　[75] Reg. § 1.1502-21(g)(4).

BUILT-IN LOSSES

The regulations also impose restrictions on the use of *built-in losses*.[76] A built-in loss is a deduction or loss that economically accrues in a separate return year but is recognized in a consolidated return year for tax purposes.

Example 31

S Corporation purchased an investment in 2012 for $22,000. On January 1, 2016, P Corporation purchased all of the stock of S. At that time, S's investment was worth $13,000. If P and S sell the investment in 2016 and file a consolidated tax return for the year, $9,000 ($22,000 − $13,000) is considered a built-in loss because it economically accrued in years before 2016.

Under the regulations,[77] a built-in loss can be deducted in determining consolidated taxable income only to the extent of the acquired member's contribution toward consolidated taxable income. The effect of this limitation is the same as if the loss had occurred in pre-affiliation years subject to the SRLY rules for net operating losses. Deductions and losses not currently used are carried forward indefinitely to succeeding years.[78]

New regulations for built-in losses become effective for corporations that become members of a consolidated group for years beginning after 1996.[79] The new regulations apply the rules of § 382(h) in determining the presence of built-in losses. The presence of a built-in loss must be determined on a subgroup basis at the time of affiliation. A built-in loss subgroup is composed of the member recognizing the loss and all members of the consolidated group that have been continuously affiliated with that member for 60 consecutive months prior to subgroup status.

Exceptions

There are two exceptions to the built-in loss rule. First, the limitation does not apply to the assets that a group acquires either directly or by acquiring a new member if the acquisition occurred more than five years before the first day of the taxable year in which the sale occurs.[80] Second, the limitation does not apply if immediately before the acquisition of the assets, the aggregate adjusted basis of all assets acquired (excluding cash and marketable securities) did not exceed the fair market value of such assets by more than 15% or $10 million (whichever is smaller).[81] Cash and marketable securities are excluded from the computation in order to prevent avoidance of this rule by making additional cash and security contributions immediately before acquisition.

Example 32

On May 24, 2016, P acquires all the stock of S Corporation. At the time of the acquisition, S's only assets are land (fair market value of $12,000; basis of $7,000) and machinery (fair market value of $8,000; basis of $15,000). If in a subsequent year the group sells the machinery for $8,000, the built-in loss rules will not apply since at the time of the original acquisition the aggregate basis of S's assets ($7,000 + $15,000 = $22,000) did not exceed their fair market value ($12,000 + $8,000 = $20,000) by more than 15% ($20,000 × 115% = $23,000).

---

[76] Temp. Reg. § 1.1502-15.

[77] Temp. Reg. § 1.1502-15(a).

[78] *Ibid.*

[79] Temp. Reg. § 1.1502-15(f).

[80] Temp. Reg. § 1.1502-15(a)(4)(i)(a).

[81] Temp. Reg. § 1.1502-15(a)(4)(i)(b).

Example 33

Assume the same facts as in *Example 32,* except that the only asset of S was the machinery. In this case the basis exceeds the fair market value by 87.5% ([$15,000 − $8,000] ÷ $8,000) and the built-in loss limitation would apply. However, if the group had waited until January 1, 2022 to sell the machinery, the limitation would not apply because the acquisition took place more than five years before the year of the sale.

REVERSE ACQUISITIONS

In 1966, the regulations[82] first addressed the problems caused by reverse acquisitions. The problem arose whenever a taxpayer merged a smaller corporation into a larger group and then selected the smaller corporation to be the common parent because of the favorable tax attributes that would survive the merger.[83]

Example 34

Profitable P Corporation plans a merger with loss corporation S. If S merges into P, S's attributes (i.e., NOLs) are limited under the SRLY rules. However, should P merge into S, P's attributes disappear and S's attributes would appear to survive.

If the transaction qualifies as a reverse acquisition—whether intended or not—the results can have adverse tax consequences to the surviving members. A reverse acquisition occurs when:

1. A common parent ("first corporation"), or subsidiary of the first corporation, acquires (in exchange for stock of the first corporation) either another corporation (second corporation) or group of corporations (second group); and

2. The second corporation's (second group's) shareholders own more than 50% the fair market value of the outstanding stock of the first corporation.

Example 35

R Corporation and its two wholly owned subsidiaries S and T have filed a consolidated tax return for the past five years, showing large consolidated profits each year. R Corporation is owned equally by individuals A, B, and C. N Corporation and its two wholly owned subsidiaries O and P are owned 100% by individual D. The N group has been experiencing consolidated losses each year since its formation three years ago. The ownership of these groups is shown in Exhibit 8-10.

On January 1 of the current year, the R group merges into the N group with the R shareholders receiving 90% of the fair market value of the outstanding stock of N. The results of this merger are shown in Exhibit 8-11. Because N ("first corporation") has acquired, in exchange for its stock, R ("second corporation") and the R shareholders (second corporation's shareholders) own more than 50% of the outstanding stock of N, a reverse acquisition has taken place. In other words, although N survives, R's former shareholders control N.

---

[82] Reg. § 1.1502-75(a)(3).

[83] The relative size of the two groups is determined by stock ownership in the surviving common parent.

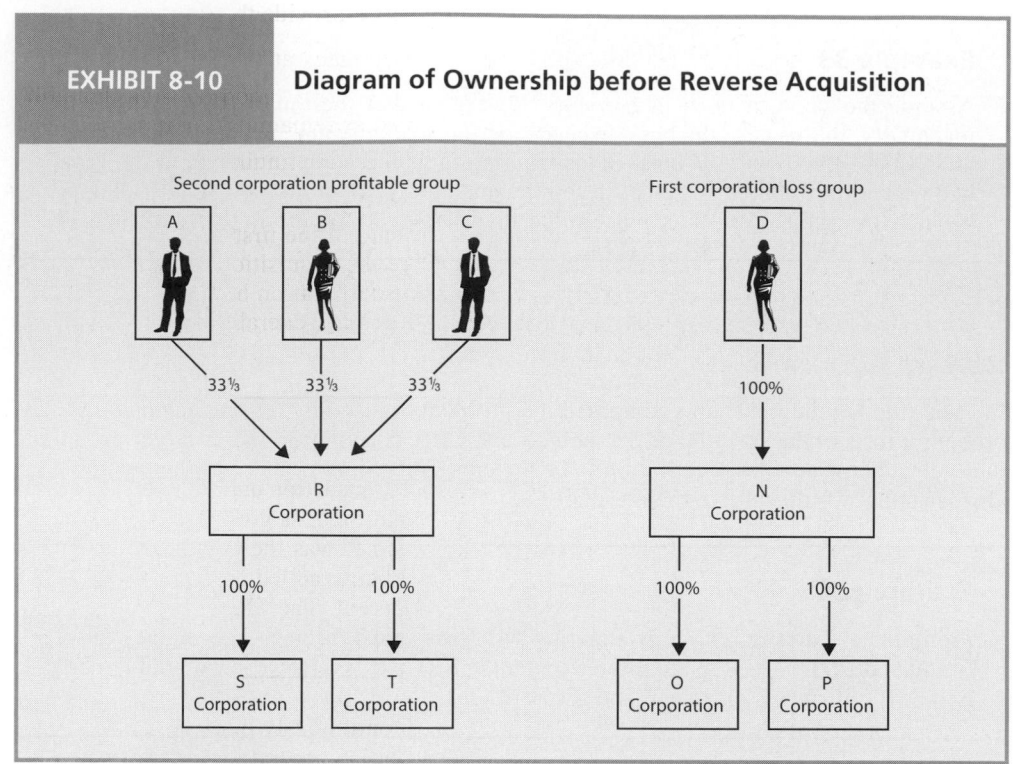

EXHIBIT 8-10   Diagram of Ownership before Reverse Acquisition

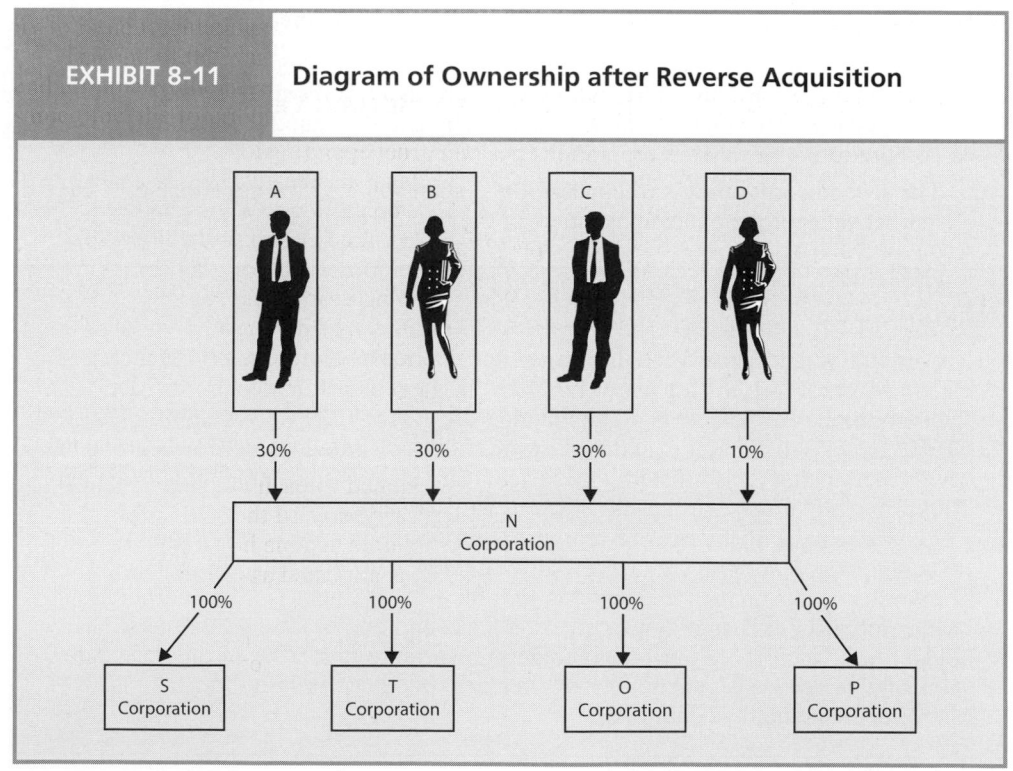

EXHIBIT 8-11   Diagram of Ownership after Reverse Acquisition

If the rules for a reverse acquisition are met, the regulations provide the following:[84]

1. The first corporation's group (the loss group) terminates at the date of acquisition (N above).

2. The second corporation's group (R above) is treated as remaining in existence.

3. The first corporation (N) still becomes the parent of the continuing group even though its group does not survive.

When a reverse acquisition has occurred, the taxable years of the first corporation's group (e.g., the loss corporation, N above) ending on or before the acquisition date are subject to the SRLY limitations regardless of the fact that the first corporation becomes the common parent. The taxable years of the second corporation's group generally are not subject to SRLY rules.[85]

Example 36

Assume the same facts as in *Example 35*. Because the transaction qualifies as a reverse acquisition, corporations N, O, and P ("first group and the loss group") terminate on the date of the merger. The group (S and T) of which R was the common parent is treated as continuing in existence with N, O, and P being added as members of the group and N taking the place of R as the common parent. The SRLY rules apply to corporations N, O, and P and not to corporations S and T.[86]

A special elective rule exists for groups that have continuously owned at least 25% of the fair market value of the stock of the acquired ("second") corporation for five years. The election essentially gives the electing corporation the flexibility of choosing which group survives the acquisition.

CARRYBACKS AND CARRYOVERS TO SEPARATE RETURN YEARS

The previous discussion has addressed the carryover of net operating losses from separate return years to consolidated return years. Consideration must also be given to situations where the loss occurs in a consolidated return year and must be carried to a separate return year.

Once a consolidated net operating loss is computed, the rules that apply are similar to those for a single corporation. The consolidated net operating loss is carried back two years and any unused portion is carried over to the 20 succeeding years. Customarily, these NOLs are computed and carried back or forward on a consolidated basis. In some cases, however, the carryback year is a year in which the corporation filed a separate return. When this is the case, special rules must be followed.

Loss Carrybacks

A consolidated net operating loss must first be apportioned to each member of the group. Once apportioned, the NOL—absence an election to carryforward the NOL—must be carried back to the second prior year and applied to the separate taxable income of the member. The regulations[87] prescribe that the consolidated NOL is allocated as follows:

$$\frac{\text{Member's separate NOL}}{\text{Sum of separate NOLs of all losss members}} \times \text{Consolidated NOL} = \frac{\text{Member's portion}}{\text{of consolidated NOL}}$$

---

[84] Reg. § 1.1502-75(d)(3)(i)(b).

[85] Reg. § 1.1502-1(f)(3).

[86] The SRLY rules do not have any effect on profitable corporations.

[87] Reg. §§ 1.1502-79A(a) and 1.1502-21(b).

Example 37

T, a first-year unaffiliated corporation, had taxable income for 2015 of $350,000. On January 1, 2016 the affiliated group of P and S purchases all the stock of T and files a consolidated return for 2016 showing a consolidated loss of $800,000 computed as follows:

	Consolidated Taxable Income
P	$(300,000)
S	400,000
T	(900,000)
Total	$(800,000)

T's share of the apportioned consolidated NOL is $600,000 ($800,000 × [$900,000 ÷ ($300,000 + $900,000)]) of which $350,000 is carried back to its first year. The remaining $250,000 is carried over to 2016 and may be combined with any of the remaining $200,000 loss attributable to P.

Under § 172(b)(3)(C), a parent can elect to forgo the two-year carryback period. If such an election is made, the loss is carried forward as a consolidated NOL and any refund generated from such loss is paid to the parent. If the election to forgo the carryback is not made, the refund is paid to the affiliated member.[88]

Example 38

Assume the same facts as in *Example 37,* except that P made an election to forgo the carryback. The entire $800,000 loss is carried over to 2017 and is applied toward any 2017 consolidated taxable income. If P had not made this election, any refund generated from the carryback to T's 2015 return would have been paid directly to T.

When a portion of a consolidated net operating loss is attributable to a member that cannot use the loss in a carryback year because the member was not in existence, the other members of the group may be able to utilize the loss if certain conditions are met.[89] The carryback may be used by other members of the group in an equivalent consolidated return year if the corporation unable to use the loss became a member of the group immediately after its organization. This is known as the "offspring" rule.

Example 39

Assume the same facts as in *Example 37*. In addition, assume that P and S had the following consolidated taxable income for earlier years of:

2014	$975,000
2015	100,000

Since T was not a member of the group immediately after its organization, P and S can only carry back its share of the loss, $200,000, to 2014. T may carry back $350,000 of its $600,000 share of the loss to 2015. T's remaining loss of $250,000 carries over to 2016 as a consolidated NOL.

If T had been formed on January 1, 2016 and had become a member of the P and S group immediately after its organization, no carryback period would exist for T. Thus, under the offspring rule, T's share of the loss could be used by the other members. Because T would be considered a member of the group for the entire period, its $600,000 share of the loss could be used to offset the consolidated taxable income of 2014.

---

[88] Reg. § 1.1502-78(b)(1).   [89] Reg. § 1.1502-79(a)(2).

Loss Carryovers

Under the regulations,[90] if a corporation ceases to be a member of a group during a consolidated return year, any consolidated net operating loss carryover from a prior taxable year must first be carried to the current consolidated return year. This requirement is observed notwithstanding the fact that all or a portion of the consolidated net operating loss is attributable to the terminating member. Only the portion of the terminating member's loss not absorbed in consolidation can be carried over to the first separate return year.

> ### Example 40
>
> Assume the same facts as in *Example 37*. Assume further that on June 15, 2016 P sells all the T stock to an outsider. For 2016, P and S file a consolidated return (which includes the income of T for the period January 1 to June 15) while T files a separate return. The 2015 unabsorbed loss carryover attributable to T of $250,000 must be applied first to the 2016 consolidated taxable income. Any unused loss is then applied toward T's 2016 income and any balance is carried forward by T.

CONSOLIDATED RETURN CHANGE OF OWNERSHIP

The rules for a *consolidated return change of ownership* (CRCO) were derived from the early (pre-1986) rules of Code § 382 concerning the carryover of NOLs. In 1986, Congress modified the rules of § 382, but never addressed the impact of the provision on consolidated tax returns. Thus, the only bridge between § 382 and taxpayer abuses were the CRCO regulations. Effective for years beginning after 1997, new regulations require that § 382 be applied to consolidated groups on a single-entity basis. As a result, the CRCO rules are no longer necessary and have been repealed.[91]

RELATIONSHIP TO § 382

The rules under § 382, which were discussed in conjunction with liquidations and reorganizations,[92] may also restrict the use of net operating losses by an affiliated group. The limitations imposed by § 382, however, are far more harsh than those imposed by the consolidated return regulations. If the taxpayer comes within the purview of § 382, the NOL carryovers can be disallowed in full or limited to a fraction of their total.[93]

> ### Example 41
>
> P, S, and T file a consolidated tax return for calendar year 2015 reflecting a consolidated net operating loss attributable in part to each member. P owns 80% of S's stock, and S owns 80% of T's stock. On January 1, 2016 A purchases 60% of P's stock. During 2016, T's business is discontinued. Because there has been a more than 50 percentage point increase in the ownership of P, the common parent of the group, and since T has not continued in the same trade or business after the increase, under § 382, the portion of the 2015 consolidated NOL attributable to T cannot be included for 2016 or any subsequent years, whether consolidated or separate.[94]

---

[90] Temp. Reg. § 1.1502-21(b)(2)(ii)(A).

[91] Reg. § 1.1502-21A.

[92] See Chapter 5 and Chapter 7.

[93] *Ibid.*

[94] Reg. § 1.1502-21(e)(1)(iii). Note that § 382 disallows any use of the NOL because T's business is discontinued. Had T's business been continued, § 382 would limit the amount of the NOL carryover deduction. See Chapter 7.

The Internal Revenue Service issued a detailed set of regulations containing provisions governing the applicability of § 382 to consolidated groups. Generally, the § 382 regulations adopt a single-entity approach in the application of its provisions to consolidated groups. Thus, the determination of whether an ownership change is made for consolidated basis is done in the same manner as it is done for a stand-alone corporation.[95] Like the new SRLY rules, § 382 is applied on a subgroup basis rather than a member-by-member basis when members leave or join a consolidated group. Consequently, all members of a group filing a consolidated tax return will be treated as a single entity and referred to as a *Loss Group*. Single entity tests are applied to the Loss Group to determine whether an ownership change occurs.[96] The § 382 *limitations* with respect to the Loss Group losses apply to any testing date commencing on or after January 1, 1998.

Example 42

Assume the same facts as in *Example 41* except that T's business continues after the purchase of P's stock. Under the consolidated § 382 regulations, P, S, and T become a Loss Group. The value of the Loss Group is determined and multiplied by the Federal long-term tax-exempt rate to compute the § 382 limitation. This limitation is used to determine the portion of the consolidated NOL that can be used in each of the subsequent consolidated tax years of the Loss Group.

The consolidated § 382 rules can also apply to a new corporation joining the affiliated group that brings with it a SRLY loss. This newly acquired member, known as a *New Loss Member,* must separately track its losses until either (1) a new ownership change occurs, or (2) the New Loss Member has been a member of the affiliated group for five consecutive years. This rule also applies to a new subgroup that joins the affiliated group known as the *New Loss Subgroup*.[97]

Investment in Subsidiaries

BASIS ADJUSTMENTS

LO.6

Explain how a corporation accounts for its investment in a subsidiary.

At the end of each consolidated return year, the parent's basis in the stock of a subsidiary must be adjusted to reflect the economic results of operations. Generally, this requires increasing the parent's basis by any undistributed gains of the subsidiaries and reducing the basis by any losses sustained by the subsidiaries. The purpose of these adjustments is to prevent duplication of gain or loss on a later disposition of the subsidiaries' stock. In theory, following the basis rules is no more difficult than keeping a running checkbook balance. In practice, however, these rules involve a series of intricate net positive and net negative adjustments.

BASIS RULES FOR YEARS BEGINNING ON OR AFTER JANUARY 1, 1995

Effective for years beginning on or after January 1, 1995, the regulations amended the consolidated return investment adjustment system.[98] The amendments delink the adjustments to stock basis from the adjustments to earnings and profits (E&P). Under the new system, stock basis adjustments are determined by reference to a modified computation of a subsidiary's taxable income rather than to the subsidiary's E&P. A subsidiary's E&P, however, continue to tier up to a parent corporation, but under a separate E&P adjustment system. Separating the stock basis and E&P adjustments prevents policies specific to one system from distorting the other.

---

[95] Reg. § 1.382-2.

[96] Reg. §§ 1.1502-91 through 1.1502-93.

[97] Reg. § 1.1502-96(a).

[98] Reg. § 1.1502-32.

Under the 1995 regulations, a parent's stock basis is adjusted under rules similar to the rules for adjusting the basis of a partnership interest or stock in an S corporation. Investment adjustments under the new Regulations are generally based on items calculated annually and reflected in a subsidiary's tax return or permanent records. The annual computation (as illustrated in Exhibit 8-12) is the net of the following positive and negative adjustments:

- Increase or decrease for taxable income or loss;

- Increase for tax-exempt income;

- Decrease for noncapital or nondeductible expenses; and

- Decrease for distributions with respect to the subsidiary.

EXHIBIT 8-12	Computation of Investment in Subsidiaries

Beginning basis in the stock of a subsidiary
Plus:
Positive adjustments:
   Taxable income
   Tax-exempt income (including):
- Intercompany dividends
- Dividends-received deduction
- Federal tax refunds

Less:
Negative adjustments:
   Taxable losses
   Noncapital, nondeductible expenses (including):
- Federal income taxes
- Disallowed losses under § 311(a)
- Expiring NOLs
   Distributions under § 301

Equals:
Ending basis in the stock of a subsidiary

Taxable Income or Loss

A subsidiary's taxable income or loss is determined as if the subsidiary were the only member of the consolidated group. The subsidiary's deductions and losses are taken into account to the extent that they are absorbed by the subsidiary or any other member of the affiliated group. This includes loss carrybacks and carryforwards. To the extent that loss carrybacks or carryforwards cannot be absorbed, they will not produce a negative adjustment.[99]

Tax-Exempt Income

A subsidiary's tax-exempt income is its income and gain that is taken into account for financial purposes but excluded from gross income. To the extent that a subsidiary's taxable income is offset by a deduction of loss that does not reduce the basis of the subsidiary's assets, this amount will be treated as tax-exempt income. For example, if a subsidiary receives a $100 dividend subject to a $70 dividends-received deduction, the $70 will be treated as tax-exempt income.[100]

---

[99] Reg. § 1.1502-32(b)(3)(i).   [100] Reg. § 1.1502-32(b)(3)(ii).

Noncapital, Nondeductible Expenses

A subsidiary's noncapital, nondeductible expenses are its expenses that are taken into account for financial purposes but permanently eliminated in determining taxable income (e.g., a subsidiary's share of federal income tax). Similarly, if a net operating loss carryover expires unused, it becomes a noncapital, nondeductible expense. Any decrease in the basis of a subsidiary's assets may be a noncapital, nondeductible expense to the extent that it is permanently excluded from reducing the subsidiary's taxable income.[101]

Distributions

Distributions will be treated as negative adjustments to the extent that the distribution is taxed under § 301. This includes any other distributions treated as dividends; under other provisions of the code.[102]

Example 43

During the current year, the calendar year P-S group has consolidated taxable income of $500. Taking into account only the income and expenses of S, the P-S group would have a taxable loss of $100. In addition, S has tax-exempt interest income of $60 and related expenses of $35 for the year that would not be deductible under § 265. Under the basis adjustment rules, P will make a net negative adjustment of $75 in its basis in S stock. This adjustment includes a negative adjustment of $100 for S's loss, a positive adjustment for S's tax-exempt income of $60, and a negative adjustment for the $35 of nondeductible expenses related to the tax-exempt income ([$100] + $60 − $35 = [$75]).

Adjustments to basis are made as of the close of each consolidated return year or at any other time if a determination is necessary to determine the tax liability of a person (e.g., a parent's sale of a subsidiary's stock). If a negative adjustment exceeds a parent's basis in the subsidiary, the excess will be treated as an excess loss account (discussed later).[103] When one subsidiary owns stock in another subsidiary, the adjustment in the higher-tier subsidiary cannot be made until the adjustment is made for the lower-tier subsidiary. For years beginning on or after January 1, 1995, the basis of a subsidiary's stock must be determined or redetermined as if the *new* rules were in effect for all consolidated return years of the group.

Expiring Net Operating Losses

One of several controversial areas addressed by the net final Regulations is the rule requiring a negative stock basis adjustment for an expiring net operating loss (NOL). Whereas most taxpayers agreed that losses arising while a subsidiary is a member of the affiliated group should be treated as noncapital nondeductible items in the year that they expire, many disagreed with this treatment for losses that arose before the subsidiary became a group member. As a result of this disagreement, the final Regulations provide a special rule that allows a consolidated group to avoid a negative adjustment when a subsidiary carries over an NOL from a separate return year.

Under Regulation § 1.1502-32(b)(4), the group may make an irrevocable election to treat all or any portion of a loss carryover as expiring immediately before a subsidiary becomes a member of a consolidated group. Thus, a negative basis adjustment in the stock of a subsidiary will not be required for any portion of the loss carryover that is waived. To waive a carryover, the Regulations require the amount to be waived to be identified in a statement filed with the group's consolidated return for the first year that the subsidiary with the loss becomes a member of the group.

---

[101] Reg. § 1.1502-32(b)(3)(iii).

[102] Reg. § 1.1502-32(b)(3)(v).

[103] Reg. § 1.1502-32(a)(3)(ii).

Example 44

P, a calendar year corporation and the parent of the P-S affiliated group, purchases all of the stock of T corporation on November 6 of the current year. T has a $100,000 NOL that will expire in three years. If the P-S-T group makes the irrevocable election, the $100,000 loss arising in a separate return year will be treated as if it never existed (for purposes of the new group only). If the election is not made, to the extent that any of the $100,000 loss still remains when it expires in three years, a negative adjustment will be made to P's basis in the T stock. Obviously, this election is beneficial where the SRLY rules or § 382 severely restricts the use of the NOL.

EXCESS LOSS ACCOUNT

When a group files a consolidated tax return, the losses of a subsidiary can exceed the group's investment in that corporation. Instead of denying a deduction for a portion of the losses that exceed basis under the notion that a negative basis is generally not recognized, the regulations provide for an extension of the basis adjustment rules known as an *excess loss account*.[104] This account maintains a record of these excess deductions until they are recovered.

Example 45

On January 1, 2015, P created a wholly owned subsidiary S. On the same date, S organized a wholly owned subsidiary, T. P invested $5,000 in S while S invested $3,000 in the stock of T. Consolidated tax returns are filed for the years 2015 through 2017 showing the following separate incomes and losses:

	T	S	P
2015	$(2,000)	$ 1,200	$25,000
2016	(1,800)	300	33,000
2017	600	(6,400)	42,000

No distributions were made by S or T for any of the years. As of December 31, 2017 the adjusted bases for the stock of S and T are computed as follows:

	S in T	P in S
2015		
Original basis	$ 3,000	$ 5,000
Loss of T	(2,000)	(2,000)
Undistributed earnings of S	0	1,200
Basis	$ 1,000	$ 4,200
2016		
Loss of T	$(1,800)	$(1,800)
Undistributed earnings of S	0	300
Basis	0	$ 2,700
Excess loss amount	($800)	0
2017		
Undistributed earnings of T	$ 600	$ 600
Loss of S	0	(6,400)
Basis	0	0
Excess loss amount	$ (200)	$(3,100)

---

[104] Reg. § 1.1502-19.

> Note that if it had not been for the requirement that P's basis in S must reflect T's operations, P would not have an "excess loss account" with respect to S.

Recovery of Excess Loss Account

The excess loss account generally must be recaptured and included in the investor's income when there is a disposition of the stock outside of the group.[105] On a disposition, gain is always recognized to the extent of the excess loss account.[106]

Dispositions can include a sale, a redemption, or worthlessness of a subsidiary's stock, as well as the termination of a consolidated return.[107] Upon a disposition, the gain to be recognized is generally treated as a capital gain.[108] In the case of an insolvent subsidiary, the excess loss is treated as ordinary income.[109]

Example 46

Same facts as in *Example 45,* except that on January 1, 2018, S sells all of its stock in T to an unrelated individual. Because at the end of 2017 S has an excess loss account in the T stock of $200, all $200 must be recognized by S as capital gain. This recognition is in addition to any other gain or loss that may be taxable on the sale stock.

Loss Disallowance Rule

Beginning in 1990, the Internal Revenue Service adopted controversial *loss disallowance rules* in regulations effective for transactions occurring on or after March 9, 1990.[110] These rules, applicable to any disposition or deconsolidation, serve to deny a deduction for any loss recognized by a member corporation with respect to the stock of a subsidiary. A *disposition* is defined as any event in which gain or loss is recognized in whole or in part. A *deconsolidation* refers to any event that causes a share of stock of a subsidiary to be no longer owned by a member of a consolidated group in which the subsidiary is a member. In order to maintain the integrity of this rule, the regulations also provide for "anti-stuffing" rules that prevent members of the affiliated group from transferring appreciated assets to absorb any losses that would be disallowed in the event of a disposition or deconsolidation.[111]

Example 47

P buys all the stock of T for $100, thus making T a member of the P-T affiliated group. T owns an asset with a basis of $20 and a fair market value of $120. If T sells the asset for its value, $120, P increases its basis to $200 under the investment adjustment system. Five years later if P sells its T stock for $125, the regulations disallow the $75 loss to P on its disposition of T.

---

[105] Reg. § 1.1502-32(e)(2). When an excess loss amount has been triggered, any subsequent net positive adjustments must first be applied to reduce the excess loss before any increase can be made to the basis of stock.

[106] Reg. § 1.1502-19(a)(1).

[107] Although a number of exceptions for carryover basis exist (i.e., reorganizations, liquidations, etc.), a discussion of these techniques is beyond the scope of this chapter.

[108] Reg. § 1.1502-19(a)(2).

[109] Reg. § 1.1502-19(a)(1).

[110] Reg. § 1.1502-20(a)(1).

[111] Reg. § 1.1502-20(d)(1).

> ### Example 48
>
> P buys all 100 shares of S stock for $100, thus making S a member of the P-S affiliated group. The value of the S stock declines to $50, and P sells 60 shares to an unrelated party for $30. The sale causes a deconsolidation of the remaining 40 shares of S stock. Accordingly, P must reduce the basis of the remaining S stock from $40 to $20 (its current value). In addition, the loss of $30 on the disposition of the 60 shares of S stock is also disallowed to P. If P had attempted to circumvent the loss disallowance rule by transferring appreciated assets to S immediately prior to the sale, the regulations would have triggered the "anti-stuffing rules," requiring a *gain* to be recognized to the extent of the loss disallowance.

On March 7, 2002, the Treasury Department added yet another chapter to the painful history of the loss disallowance rules. In the wake of the government's loss in *Rite Aid Corporation v. United States*,[112] in which the Federal Circuit found the "loss duplication" factor of Treas. Reg. § 1.1502-20(c) to be an invalid exercise of regulatory authority, proposed and temporary "interim" consolidated return loss disallowance regulations were created.[113] These interim regulations effectively replace the loss disallowance rules of Treas. Reg. § 1.1502-20 with a loss disallowance regime that allows a loss on the disposition of a subsidiary's stock to the extent the taxpayer can demonstrate that the loss is not attributable to the subsidiary's recognition of built-in gain. In other words, the regulations create a "tracing" regime that was last-effective for years before 1991.

Recently added regulations under Reg. § 1.1502-36, finalized in September of 2008, attempt to patch the network of regulations written under Regs. § 1.337(d) and § 1.1502-35 in an effort to resolve the post-*Rite-Aid* saga dealing with loss duplication limitations. The new regulations adopt a three-pronged approach to the anti-loss duplication and *General Utilities* repeal protections. These rules contain the following characteristics:

- First, to deal with non-economic losses created by distortive allocations of income and loss items under the investment adjustment rules;

- Second, to deal with non-economic "son-of-mirror" type transactions that generate a tax loss without the occurrence of an economic loss); and

- Third, to create an attribute reduction rule that prevents the creation of two tax losses where one economic loss exists.

EARNINGS AND PROFITS

In order to determine the tax treatment on distributions made by the affiliated group, each member must compute and maintain its own separate E&P account. The computation is similar to the standard rules governing the determination of E&P; however, the following transactions must be taken into account:

1. Gains or losses on intercompany transactions (i.e., the selling member must adjust for intercompany gains and losses for E&P purposes even though the transaction is deferred for taxable income purposes).

2. The initial and recovery inventory adjustment (i.e., these adjustments must be made to the selling member's computation of E&P).

---

[112] 255 F.3d 1357, 2001-2 USTC ¶50,516, 88 AFTR2d 5058 (Fed. Cir. 2001), *petition for rehearing denied* (October 3, 2001) and *rev'g* Fed. Cl., 46 Fed Cl. 500, 2001-1 USTC ¶50,429, 85 AFTR2d 1439 (2000).

[113] Treas. Reg. §§ 1.337(d)-2, 1.1502-20(i), and 1.1502-32(b)(4)(v), T.D. 8984, 67 Fed. Reg. 11,034 (March 12, 2002).

3. Dividend distributions between members (i.e., the distributing corporation must reduce E&P while the distributee increases its E&P).

4. Dispositions of a subsidiary's stock or obligations.

5. An allocable share of the consolidated tax liability (i.e., the member's share of the tax liability decreases its E&P).

Earnings and profits are never calculated on a consolidated basis. For years after 1975, each member must reflect its subsidiary's E&P in the computation of its own E&P at the end of each taxable year. The computations are made in a fashion similar to those discussed for basis adjustments in a subsidiary. The higher-tiered corporation makes a series of net negative and net positive adjustments for the lower-tiered subsidiary.[114]

Because the earnings and profits of a subsidiary are directly reflected in a parent's E&P, special computations are not necessary on a later disposition of a subsidiary's stock. Essentially, these adjustments create a situation that is very similar to consolidated E&P without formally requiring an E&P computation on a consolidated basis.

Example 49

P forms S Corporation on January 1, 2016, with a contribution to capital of $1,000. P and S file consolidated returns for 2016 and 2017 with S earning $100 and $300, respectively. In 2016, S distributes $150 in dividends to P. On December 31, 2017, P sells its stock in S for $1,200. As a result of these transactions, P's earnings and profits are increased by $100 and $300 for the 2016 and 2017 earnings. The $150 distribution decreases P's E&P. The disposition of S stock decreases E&P by $50 ($1,200 sales price − [$1,000 contribution + $100 and $300 in earnings − $150 distribution]).

The adjustment to E&P to reflect the earnings or loss of subsidiaries is mandatory for years after 1975. For years ending before 1976, adjustments can be made for these earnings only if an election to apply the adjustment rules is made. Once an election is made by the group, it cannot be revoked and remains in effect for all subsequent taxable years.[115]

Allocating Tax Liability

One of the primary adjustments in the computation of earnings and profits concerns the consolidated group's Federal income tax liability. Because taxes paid or accrued decrease the E&P of a member, § 1552 provides methods for allocating the consolidated tax liability to member corporations. The Code and regulations provide four options for making the allocation. In the event the group fails to elect a specific allocation method, § 1552(b) provides that the tax liability is to be apportioned in the ratio that each member's taxable income bears to consolidated taxable income.

Example 50

P Corporation is the common parent, owning all the stock of corporations S and T. The group files a consolidated tax return for the current year. For the year, the corporations had the following taxable incomes:

P	$ 0
S	12,000
T	(2,000)
Total	$10,000

---

[114] Reg. § 1.1502-33(c)(4)(ii).   [115] Reg. § 1.1502-33(c)(4)(iii).

The group has not made an election to allocate the tax liability, so the allocation is made under Code § 1552(b). Assume the consolidated tax liability for the year is $1,500 ($10,000 × 15%), all of which is allocable to S (the only profitable company). As a result, S reduces its E&P by $1,500 regardless of which corporation in the group pays the tax liability. If S pays the liability, no further accounting is required. If, however, P pays the tax liability (and this payment is not treated as a loan), P is treated as having made a contribution to S's capital account in the amount of $1,500. On the other hand, if T pays the liability, T is treated as having made a distribution to P, and P, in turn, is treated as having made a contribution to S's capital account. If P is treated as having made a contribution to capital, it increases the basis in its stock.

Operating Rules

The regulations contain a series of detailed administrative procedures that become operative whenever a group of entities join together to file a consolidated return. Included in these provisions are the following requirements:

1. All group members conform to the same accounting period.
2. The estimated tax payments are to be determined in the aggregate.
3. Each member of the group is liable for the entire tax liability of the group.
4. The parent corporation has the power to act as the agent for the group.

COMMON ACCOUNTING PERIODS

A consolidated tax return must be filed on the basis of the common parent's taxable year. Accordingly, each subsidiary must adopt the parent's annual accounting period for the initial consolidated tax return.[116] The regulations do not require that a subsidiary obtain advance permission from the Commissioner to change its tax year to conform to the accounting period of the parent.[117] The IRS, however, has ruled that it will allow a parent corporation to change its taxable year to that of its subsidiaries.[118] In such case, a consolidated tax return is permitted for the short taxable year.

ESTIMATED TAX PAYMENTS

If a group files a consolidated tax return for two consecutive years, estimated tax payments must be made on a consolidated basis for each subsequent taxable year until separate returns are filed.[119] If estimated tax payments are made on a consolidated basis but the group files separate returns, the common parent may apportion the estimated payments in any method satisfactory to the Commissioner.[120]

For the first two years that a group files a consolidated return, it may make estimated payments on either a consolidated or separate return basis.[121] If payments are made on a separate company basis, the amounts of any estimated tax payments are aggregated and credited against the consolidated tax liability for the year. As with rules governing the estimated tax payments, any penalties computed under § 6655 (underpayment of estimated taxes) may be determined on a separate or consolidated basis for the first two consolidated return years. This computation is made without regard to whether the estimated taxes were paid on a separate or consolidated basis.

---

[116] Reg. § 1.1502-76(a)(1).

[117] Reg. § 1.442-1(d) states that a Form 1128 need not be filed by a subsidiary.

[118] Rev. Rul. 55-80, 1955-1 C.B. 387.

[119] Reg. § 1.1502-5(a)(1).

[120] Reg. § 1.1502-5(b)(4).

[121] Reg. § 1.1502-5(a)(2).

TAX LIABILITY OF THE GROUP

Each member of a consolidated tax return is liable for the entire consolidated tax liability of the group.[122] This liability includes not only taxes but any deficiencies assessed against the group for its consolidated return years. If a subsidiary ceases to be a member of a group before a deficiency is assessed, the IRS may assess the former subsidiary only its allocable share of the deficiency. This allocation is only available, however, if the subsidiary's cessation came from a bona fide sale or exchange of its stock.[123] A tax-sharing agreement entered among the affiliated members is not sufficient to protect any member from imposition of the entire consolidated tax liability.[124] Nevertheless, this agreement may be useful to allow the subsidiary to recover the taxes from the other members.

COMMON PARENT AS AGENT

The common parent corporation is considered to be the sole agent for each subsidiary in the group. Except for minor situations—other than the initial election to be taxed on a consolidated basis—the common parent has full authority to make elections and act for the group. In fact, the Regulations specifically prohibit the subsidiary from exercising these powers.[125] Thus, the IRS must deal only with a single corporation, unless, after giving notice to the common parent, it chooses to deal with a specific subsidiary. If the parent corporation contemplates dissolution, it is required to notify the IRS and designate another affiliated member to act as agent in its place. Failure to designate another group member as agent before dissolution allows the remaining members to choose a replacement agent.[126]

Problem Materials

DISCUSSION QUESTIONS

8-1 *Consolidated Regulations.* Describe why regulations for consolidated tax returns are more authoritative than the Regulations for controlled groups.

8-2 *Choosing to File a Consolidated Return.* Before filing a consolidated return, consideration should be given to both the advantages and disadvantages of such returns. Describe the following:
   a. Four advantages of filing such returns.
   b. Four disadvantages of filing a consolidated return.

8-3 *Eligibility to File.* The privilege of filing a consolidated tax return is available only to an affiliated group. Briefly describe the two tests that are necessary to satisfy the requirements of an affiliated group.

8-4 *Includible Corporations.* In each of the following situations, determine whether the corporation is an "includible" corporation.
   a. John Smith, P.C., an S corporation.
   b. Southwest Pipe, NA., a foreign corporation.
   c. Jet Tool and Die, Inc., an Alaskan corporation.
   d. AVCO, Inc., a wholly owned finance subsidiary.
   e. Malbert, Inc., a captive insurance company.
   f. A trust taxable as an association.

---

[122] Reg. § 1.1502-6(a).

[123] Reg. § 1.1502-6(b).

[124] Reg. § 1.1502-6(c).

[125] Reg. § 1.1502-77(a).

[126] Reg. § 1.1502-77(d).

8-5 *Controlled Groups.* Explain how related corporations can be considered a parent-subsidiary controlled group yet not satisfy the requirements to file a consolidated tax return.

8-6 *Election to File Consolidated Returns.* Answer the following questions regarding a corporation's election to file consolidated tax returns.
   a. At what date must the election be made?
   b. Can the election be revoked?
   c. On what form is the election made?
   d. Describe two situations in which the election can be discontinued.

8-7 *Stock Ownership Test.* Briefly describe the two requirements that must be met in order to satisfy the stock ownership rules.

8-8 *Consolidated Tax Concepts.* Briefly describe the steps necessary to compute consolidated taxable income.

8-9 *Intercompany Transactions.* Distinguish between intercompany transactions and deferred intercompany transactions.

8-10 *Intercompany Item Recognition.* Describe the two events that trigger recognition of deferred intercompany transactions.

8-11 *Intercompany Transactions.* Briefly define the following terms:
   a. Intercompany item
   b. Corresponding item
   c. Recomputed corresponding item

8-12 *Investment in Subsidiaries.* Consider the following:
   a. Briefly describe why adjustments are made to the basis of the stock of subsidiaries that are held by members of the affiliated group filing a consolidated tax return.
   b. Identify the positive adjustments.
   c. Identify the negative adjustments.

8-13 *Excess Loss Account.* Answer the following:
   a. Define an "Excess Loss Account" and explain why such an account exists.
   b. Must an "Excess Loss Account" always be used in accounting for an investor's investment? Explain.

8-14 *Separate Return Limitation Year.* Answer the following:
   a. Define a SRLY and describe situations in which it arises.
   b. Are there any exceptions to the SRLY limitations?
   c. What is the "lonely parent rule"?

8-15 *Built-In Deductions.* Address the following questions:
   a. When do the restrictions concerning built-in deductions apply?
   b. Explain when the limited deductions can be utilized.
   c. Are there any exceptions to the built-in deduction rules? Explain.

8-16 *Reverse Acquisitions.* Explain a reverse acquisition and its implications for filing consolidated returns.

8-17 *Operating Rules.* Answer the following:
   a. Assuming the parent is on a July 31 year-end and the subsidiary is on a calendar year-end, can a consolidated return be filed?
   b. In the first consolidated return year, how are estimated tax payments to be made?
   c. In the third consolidated return year, how are estimated tax payments to be made?
   d. Who is generally liable for the tax liability of the affiliated group?
   e. Will a tax-sharing agreement among the members be of any use?
   f. Under what circumstances may a subsidiary deal with the IRS?

8-18 *Year Income Is Reported.* On January 18, 2016, P, a calendar year corporation, acquires all the stock of calendar year S corporation.
a. How may S file for 2016?
b. Same as above except that P is on an October 31 year-end.
c. Same as above but S is on an October 31 year-end.
d. Same as above but S was purchased on December 7, 2016.

PROBLEMS

8-19 *Intercompany Transactions.* P Corporation, a manufacturer of plumbing equipment, has two subsidiaries: S, a plumbing sales corporation, and T, a plumbing maintenance corporation. P, S, and T file a consolidated return. During 2016, T performs the following for its affiliated members in addition to its services for its customers: (1) July 1, 2016, a $28,750 charge for installation of a water cooling system for P; and (2) October 15, 2016, $125 charge to repair a cracked water line for S.
a. How are the services to P reported by T?
b. How are the services to S reported by T?
c. If P places the $28,750 charge on account to be paid at a later date, does it matter that P is an accrual basis taxpayer and T is a cash basis taxpayer?

8-20 *Intercompany Items Recognized.* Assume the same facts as in *Problem 8-19* above. In addition, assume the water cooling system is being depreciated over a ten-year period using the straight-line method. How much income must T report in 2016? In 2017?

8-21 *Consolidated Capital Gains.* P, S, and T file a consolidated tax return for 2015 and 2016. During 2016 the group had the following capital transactions:
1. S sold to T land for $35,000 (basis of $12,000).
2. P sold equipment to its president, Individual X, who owns 40% of P's stock, for $11,000 (basis of $20,000). The remainder of P's stock is owned by X's brother.
3. T sold depreciable equipment for $22,000 which it purchased from P in 2014 for $20,000. The equipment was being depreciated over a five-year period using MACRS.
4. There is a capital loss carryover from 2015 of $13,000.

Determine the consolidated net capital gain or loss for the year.

8-22 *Separate Return Limitation Years (SRLY).* On January 1, 2016, affiliated group P, S, and T buys loss corporation X with a net operating loss carryover of $120,000. During 2016, the group has consolidated taxable income as follows:

P	$40,000
S	60,000
T	(20,000)
X	15,000
Consolidated taxable income	$95,000

a. How much of X's NOL can be utilized in 2016?
b. How much of the loss can be carried over to 2017?
c. Suppose that the shareholders of X, instead of selling their stock, purchased all of the stock of S Corporation from the affiliated group. Assuming the same income figures for 2016, what is the amount of X's NOL that can be utilized in 2016?

8-23 *Built-In Deductions.* P Corporation acquires all the stock of S on January 1, 2016, which has the following assets:

	Fair Market Value	Basis
Cash	$10,000	$10,000
Machinery...	8,000	20,000
Land	16,000	14,000
Totals..	$34,000	$44,000

a. If S sells the machinery for $6,000 on May 24, 2016, how much can be deducted in a consolidated tax return if consolidated taxable income is as follows:

P..	$17,000
S..	4,000
Consolidated taxable income.....................................	$21,000

b. Would your answer to (a) above change if the land was worth $25,000?
c. Same as (a) above, but S shareholders contribute $30,000 prior to their sale of S stock to P.

8-24 *Reverse Acquisition.* On January 1, 2016, individual A purchases the stock of P Corporation and merges P Corporation into L, receiving 80% of the outstanding stock of L Corporation. L has a $40,000 NOL carryover to 2016. L and P file a consolidated return for 2016 showing the following:

L..	$10,000
P..	20,000
Consolidated taxable income.....................................	$30,000

a. How much of the NOL can be used to offset the consolidated taxable income of $30,000?
b. How much of the NOL is carried forward to 2017?
c. Can any of the unused loss be applied to P's prior profitable years?

8-25 *Net Operating Loss Carryovers and Carrybacks.* Corporations P, S, and T file a consolidated tax return for 2016 reflecting separate taxable income in each corporation as follows:

P..	$ (4,000)
S..	(8,000)
T..	3,000
Consolidated taxable income (loss)	$ (9,000)

a. How much of the loss is apportioned to P?
b. How much of the loss is apportioned to S?
c. How much of the loss is apportioned to T?
d. Assuming that S was an unaffiliated corporation for 2014 and 2015, determine the amount of its carryback assuming the taxable incomes in each of the following separate return years.

2014..	$ 3,500
2015..	4,000

e. If P, the parent, makes an election to carry forward the NOL, how much can S carry back to its separate return years?
f. If the election in (e) above is in effect for 2017 and S is sold on July 1, 2017, what effect will this have on the carryover?

8-26 *Investment in Subsidiaries.* P, a calendar year corporation, acquires all the stock of S corporation for $15,000 on January 1, 2016. At the time of the purchase, S has accumulated E&P of $3,000. For 2016 S had earnings of $4,000 and made distributions of $2,500 on April 1 and October 1, 2016.

   a. What is P's basis in S as of December 31, 2016?

   b. Assume the same facts above but that S acquires T Corporation on July 1, 2017, for $8,000. T has no prior E&P but earns $3,000 for the entire year of 2017. What is S's basis in T if half the earnings are attributable to the consolidated return period?

   c. Assume the same facts as (b). What is P's basis in S as of December 31, 2017, if S earns $2,300 and makes no distributions during the year?

8-27 *Excess Loss Account.* On January 1, 2015, P acquires subsidiary S, which in turn acquires subsidiary T. P invests $12,000 in S, and S invests $4,000 in T. Consolidated tax returns filed for 2015 through 2017 reflecting the separate taxable income of each as follows:

	P	S	T
2015	$10,000	$ (3,000)	$(3,500)
2016	15,000	1,600	(2,700)
2017	20,000	(10,400)	500

   a. What is P's basis in S for 2015?

   b. What is S's basis in T for 2015?

   c. What is P's basis in S for 2017?

   d. What is S's basis in T for 2017?

   e. How much gain or loss must S report if it sells all of its stock in T for $6,000 on December 31, 2017? What is the character?

8-28 *Earnings and Profits.* P Corporation acquires all the stock of corporations S and T on January 1, 2016. P, S, and T file a consolidated tax return for 2016 and 2017. During this two-year period, the corporations had the following earnings (E&P) and made the following distributions:

	Earnings			Distributions		
	P	S	T	P	S	T
2016	$10,000	$50,000	$30,000	$30,000	$12,000	$ 0
2017	12,000	80,000	35,000	40,000	20,000	5,000

Assume P made distributions to its shareholders of $30,000 and $40,000, respectively, for 2016 and 2017. Determine the taxability of each distribution and the effects it will have on E&P for each year. (Assume no balance in E&P prior to 2016.)

8-29 *Allocating Tax Liability.* For 2016, the affiliated group of P, S, and T files a consolidated tax return reflecting the following taxable incomes and yielding a consolidated tax liability of $3,200:

P	$ 6,000
S	18,000
T	(8,000)
Consolidated taxable income	$16,000

   a. What is P's share of the liability?

   b. What is S's share of the liability?

   c. What is T's share of the liability?

   d. If P pays the entire tax liability, what effect does it have on S and T?

TAX RESEARCH PROBLEMS

8-30 On January 15, 2016, R Corporation purchased all the stock of S and T Corporations. R, S, and T are all calendar year corporations. It was mutually determined and documented in the corporation minutes that an election to file on a consolidated basis would be made for tax year 2016. On February 1, 2017, R inadvertently filed with the Internal Revenue Service a separate tax return for 2016. Realizing the mistake on February 15, 2017, all three corporations joined in the filing of a consolidated automatic application for extension of time, Form 7004. The extension was granted through September 15, 2017. On September 21, 2017, R, S, and T submitted their 2016 consolidated tax return to the Internal Revenue Service.

Based upon these facts and circumstances, will R Corporation be able to file a consolidated tax return with its subsidiaries S and T? Does the inadvertent filing of a separate tax return by R have any effect on your answer?

Research aids:

Reg. § 1.1502-75(a)(1)

Rev. Rul. 56-67, 1956-l C.B. 437

Rev. Rul. 76-393, 1976-2 C.B. 255

Millette and Associates, Inc. v. Comm., T.C. Memo 1978-180

8-31 P and its wholly owned subsidiaries S, T, and U constitute an affiliated group that has filed consolidated returns for the past five years. Each corporation has been both a "selling member" and a "purchasing member" in a variety of deferred intercompany transactions for which deferred gains currently exist. Because of the prevailing economic climate, P is contemplating the sale of its subsidiaries. If no suitable buyer is found, P may consider liquidating S, T, and U into P. In view of these considerations, what are the "restoration" consequences with respect to the deferred gains that exist among the members? If neither of these alternatives is acceptable, what are the "restoration" consequences if all the members receive permission to discontinue filing a consolidated tax return?

Research aids:

Reg. § 1.1502-13(f)(1)

Reg. § 1.1502-75(d)(1)

Reg. § 1.1502-13(c)(6)

Flow-Through Entities

9

Taxation of Partnerships and Partners

Learning Objectives

Upon completion of this chapter you will be able to:

LO.1 Define the terms *partner* and *partnership* for federal income tax purposes.

LO.2 Distinguish between the entity theory and the aggregate theory of partnerships.

LO.3 Explain the role of the partnership agreement.

LO.4 Analyze the tax consequences of forming a new partnership, including:

- The recognition of gain or loss by a partner upon the contribution of cash, property, or services to a partnership.

- The recognition of gain or loss by a partnership upon the exchange of a partnership interest for cash, property, or services contributed by a partner.

- The computation of the partners' bases in their new partnership interests.

- The computation of the partnership's basis in its new assets.

LO.5 Determine the effect of partnership liabilities on the partners' bases in their partnership interests.

LO.6 Compute partnership taxable income or loss and identify any separately computed items of partnership income, gain, loss, deduction, or credit.

LO.7 Explain how the tax consequences of partnership operations are reported on the tax returns of the partners and how the partners' bases in their partnership interests are adjusted to reflect these tax consequences.

LO.8 Define the term *substantial economic effect* and describe other limitations on allocations of partnership items to partners.

LO.9 Compute the three potential limitations on the current deductibility of a partner's distributive share of partnership loss.

LO.10 Determine the tax consequences of various transactions between a partner and a partnership.

Chapter Outline

Introduction

When two or more parties agree to go into business together, they must first decide which form of business to use. Should the business be incorporated or should it operate as a partnership? Although the corporate form predominates for large companies, it is certainly not appropriate for all businesses. Consequently, partnerships are widely used throughout the business world.

Partnerships come in a wide assortment of shapes and sizes. For example, two accountants may form a professional partnership through which to conduct their business, or a family may organize a partnership to manage real estate or operate a corner delicatessen. In contrast, two international corporations may form a partnership to develop a new product or to conduct research. Partnerships may also be used as investment vehicles. For instance, hundreds or thousands of people may invest in partnerships that drill for oil, construct office buildings, or make movies. For whatever reason, when two or more parties decide to pool their resources in order to carry on a profit-making activity, they often choose to do so as partners in a partnership.

Definitions

The federal tax consequences of business activities that meet the statutory definition of a partnership are governed by the provisions of Subchapter K of the Internal Revenue Code (§§ 701 through 777). This chapter begins with an analysis of this definition and a brief introduction to several other important concepts that underlie Subchapter K. The chapter also includes discussions of the formation and operation of a partnership, the mechanics by which partnership income or loss is allocated to and taken into account by each partner, and the tax consequences of common transactions between partners and partnerships. The more advanced topics of current and liquidating partnership distributions and dispositions of partnership interests are included in Chapter 10.

WHAT IS A PARTNERSHIP?

LO.1

Define the terms *partner* and *partnership* for federal income tax purposes.

The Uniform Partnership Act defines a partnership quite simply as "an association of two or more persons to carry on as co-owners a business for profit."[1] This basic definition is expanded in the Code to include a syndicate, group, pool, joint venture, or any other unincorporated organization.[2] For an organization to constitute a partnership, it must have at least two partners. Note that there are no restrictions on either the maximum number of partners or on the type of entity that may be a partner. Individuals, corporations, trusts, estates, and even other partnerships may join together as partners to carry on a profit-making activity.

---

[1] Uniform Partnership Act, § 6(1).   [2] § 761(a).

As a practical matter, determining whether an organization qualifies as a partnership is rarely a problem. For example, any organization formed under the Uniform Partnership Act or the Uniform Limited Partnership Act should expect to be treated as a partnership. However, as explained in Chapter 1, certain unincorporated organizations may or may not be treated as partnerships for tax purposes. Under the "check the box" regulations, all business entities incorporated under a state law providing for a separate corporation, a joint stock company, an insurance company, a bank, or certain foreign entities will be classified as corporations for federal tax purposes.[3] All other business entities, known as associations, which are not automatically defined as a corporation can *elect* to be taxed as a corporation. Any association, including any limited liability company[4] having two or more owners and that does not make the election, will be treated as a partnership.[5]

A foreign entity in which all owners have limited liability will be treated as a corporation. A foreign entity in which one or more owners have unlimited liability will be treated as a partnership unless it makes the election to be taxed as a corporation.[6]

Other treasury regulations clarify that certain arrangements are not treated as partnerships for federal tax purposes. A joint undertaking is not a partnership if the only joint activity is the sharing of expenses. For example, if two adjacent property owners share the cost of a dam constructed to prevent flooding, no partnership exists. Similarly, joint ownership of property is not a partnership if the co-owners merely rent or lease the property and provide minimal services to the lessees. In such case, the co-owners are not actively conducting a trade or business. If, however, these co-owners provide substantial tenant services, they may elevate their passive co-ownership to active partnership status.[7]

ELECTING OUT OF SUBCHAPTER K

Section 761(a) allows certain unincorporated organizations that potentially constitute partnerships for federal tax purposes to be excluded from the application of the statutory rules of Subchapter K. An organization may elect out of the statutory rules governing the taxation of partners and partnerships if it is formed for (1) investment purposes only and not for the active conduct of a business, or (2) the joint production, extraction, or use of property. The members of such an organization must be able to compute their separate incomes without the necessity of computing partnership taxable income (i.e., income for the organization as a whole). The election is made by attaching a statement to a properly filed Form 1065 (U.S. Partnership Return of Income) for the first taxable year for which the organization desires exclusion from Subchapter K. The statement must identify all members of the organization and indicate their consent to the election.[8]

GENERAL AND LIMITED PARTNERSHIPS

There are two types of partnerships: *general* partnerships and *limited* partnerships. The two differ primarily in the nature of the rights and obligations of the partners; the major differences can be summarized as follows:

1. General partnerships are owned solely by general partners, whereas limited partnerships must have at least one general partner and one or more limited partners.

2. General partners have *unlimited liability* for partnership debt, whereas limited partners are usually liable only to the extent of their capital contributions to the partnership.

---

[3] Reg. §§ 301.7701-1(b) and 301.7701-2(b).

[4] All 50 states and the District of Columbia authorize limited liability companies.

[5] A limited liability company with only one owner cannot be considered a partnership for tax purposes. Instead, such

an entity will be treated as either a corporation or sole proprietorship.

[6] See Reg. §§ 301.7701-1(b) and 301.7701-4.

[7] Reg. § 1.761-1(a).

[8] Reg. § 1.761-2(b)(2).

3. General partners participate in the management and control of the partnership business, whereas limited partners are not allowed to make management decisions.[9]

4. General partners are subject to self-employment taxes on partnership business earnings even if they do not perform services for the partnership, whereas limited partners are not.

Two other types of entities that are usually taxed as partnerships are limited liability companies (LLC) and limited liability partnerships (LLP). In an LLC, all members (i.e., owners) have limited liability. Generally, the partners in an LLP have better liability protection than general partners, but more liability exposure than limited partners. LLP partners usually have unlimited liability, except any particular partner is not personally liable for claims arising from a tort that was committed by a different partner. Nevertheless, the partner committing the tort is personally liable for the claims resulting from his or her actions.

All references throughout the text are to general partners and general partnerships unless otherwise stated.

ENTITY AND AGGREGATE THEORIES

LO.2

Distinguish between the entity theory and the aggregate theory of partnerships.

Most rules governing the taxation of partnerships are based on either the entity or aggregate theory of partnerships.[10] According to the *entity theory*, partnerships should be regarded as entities distinct and separate from their owners. As such, partnerships may enter into taxable transactions with partners, may hold title to property in their own names, are not legally liable for debts of partners, are required to file annual returns (Form 1065) that report the results of operations, and can make tax elections concerning partnership activities that apply to all partners.

In contrast, the *aggregate theory* views a partnership as a collection of specific partners, each of which indirectly owns an undivided interest in partnership assets. Under this theory, the partnership itself has no identity distinct from that of its partners. The fact that a partnership is a pass-through rather than a taxable entity, functioning only as a conduit of income to the partners, is a clear reflection of the aggregate theory. The aggregate theory also prevents the recognition of gain or loss on several types of transactions between partners and their partnerships.

The inconsistent application of the entity and aggregate theories throughout Subchapter K certainly complicates the taxation of partners and their partnerships. In extreme cases, a single Code section may contain elements of both theories. In spite of this confusion, taxpayers and their advisers who can determine which theory underlies a particular rule of partnership tax law will gain valuable insight into the proper application of that rule to a specific fact situation.

Forming a Partnership

LO.3

Explain the role of the partnership agreement.

The first step in the formation of any partnership is the drafting of a partnership agreement by the prospective partners. A *partnership agreement* is a legal contract stipulating the rights and obligations of the co-owners of the business. Ideally a partnership agreement should be drafted by a competent attorney, should be in writing, and should be signed by each partner. However, even oral partnership agreements between business associates have been respected as binding contracts by the courts.[11]

A partner's *interest in a partnership* is an intangible asset—an equity interest in the partnership business, the exact nature of which is defined in the partnership agreement. Under the typical agreement, each partner has a specified interest in partnership cash and property. The dollar amount of such interest at any time is reflected by the balance in each partner's *capital account* in the equity section of the partnership balance sheet. In addition to his or her

---

[9] A limited partner who takes part in the control of the partnership business may become liable to the creditors of the partnership by doing so. Revised Uniform Limited Partnership Act (1976), § 303(a).

[10] For an interesting historical discussion of the development of these conflicting theories, see Arthur B. Willis, John S.

Pennell, and Philip F. Postlewaite, *Partnership Taxation* (Colorado Springs, Co.: Shepard's/McGraw-Hill, Inc.), Chapter 4.

[11] See, for example, *Elrod*, 87 T.C. 1046 (1986).

capital interest, each partner has an interest in any income or loss generated by the partnership's activities. This interest is usually expressed as a *profit-and-loss sharing ratio* among the partners. If the partners consent, the terms of their agreement may be modified with respect to a particular taxable year at any time before the unextended due date by which the partnership return for such year must be filed.[12]

Partners may certainly agree to share profits and losses in different ratios. They may also agree that these ratios will be independent of the relative amounts of capital to which the partners are entitled.

Example 1

Lawyers J and K decide to form a general partnership to carry on a law practice. Both individuals contribute $50,000 of cash to the partnership so that both have an initial capital account balance of $50,000. The partnership will use the cash to purchase equipment and supplies and to lease office space. J has been in local practice for several years and has an established reputation, while K recently graduated from law school. Consequently, the partnership agreement provides that J will be allocated 65% of profits and losses, while K will be allocated 35%. The agreement stipulates that J and K will renegotiate this profit-and-loss sharing ratio after three years.

CONTRIBUTIONS OF PROPERTY

Partners may make initial contributions to partnership capital in the form of cash, property, or a combination of both. When a partner transfers property to a partnership in exchange for an ownership interest, § 721 provides that neither the partner nor the partnership recognizes any gain or loss on the exchange.[13] The partner's tax basis in the transferred property carries over to become the partnership's basis in the property (i.e., a *carryover* basis).[14] The tax basis in the transferring partner's newly acquired partnership interest equals the basis of the transferred property plus any amount of cash contributed to the partnership (i.e., a *substituted* basis).[15] Tax professionals who specialize in the partnership area have coined the term *inside basis* to refer to the tax basis of assets owned by a partnership. In contrast, the term *outside basis* refers to the tax basis of a partner's interest in a partnership. Although neither term is used in the Code or Regulations, they provide a descriptive and easy way to differentiate between these two basis concepts.

The partnership's holding period for contributed assets includes the holding period of the assets in the hands of the contributing partner.[16] If the assets were either capital assets or § 1231 assets to the contributing partner, the partner's holding period for these assets becomes the holding period for his new partnership interest.[17] If the contributed assets were not capital or § 1231 assets, the partner's holding period for his interest begins on the date the interest is acquired.

LO.4
Analyze the tax consequences of forming a new partnership, including:

- The recognition of gain or loss by a partner upon the contribution of cash, property, or services to a partnership.
- The recognition of gain or loss by a partnership upon the exchange of a partnership interest for cash, property, or services contributed by a partner.
- The computation of the partners' bases in their new partnership interests.
- The computation of the partnership's basis in its new assets.

Example 2

A contributes § 1231 assets with a fair market value of $25,000 and an adjusted basis of $15,500, and B contributes $25,000 cash to the AB Partnership. The capital accounts on the partnership books are credited to reflect the equal $25,000 contributions of each partner. A does not recognize any gain on the exchange of the appreciated business assets for his interest in the AB Partnership. However, A's initial outside basis in his

---

[12] § 761(c).

[13] This nonrecognition rule does not apply to gain realized on the transfer of appreciated stocks and securities to an investment partnership. § 721(b). Also, special rules—beyond the scope of this text—apply to transfers to partnerships with foreign persons and transfers of intangibles to foreign partnerships. See §§ 721(c) and 721(d).

[14] § 723. If contributed property is depreciable, the partnership will continue to use the cost recovery method and life used by the contributing partner. § 168(i)(7).

[15] § 722.

[16] § 1223(2).

[17] § 1223(1).

> partnership interest is only $15,500. A's holding period for this interest includes the period of time for which A owned the contributed § 1231 assets. Even though the partnership recorded the contributed assets on its books at their $25,000 fair market value, the partnership's inside basis in these assets is only $15,500. B's initial tax basis in her partnership interest is $25,000, and her holding period for this interest begins on the date of contribution.

The above example illustrates two important points. First, a partner's outside basis is not necessarily equal to the balance in his or her capital account on the partnership's financial books and records. The partnership *book* capital accounts reflect the economic value of contributions to the partnership, while the partners' outside bases in their partnership interests reflect the tax basis of their respective contributions. Second, the tax rules governing contributions to partnerships result in an initial equilibrium between the partners' aggregate outside bases and the total inside basis of partnership assets. In *Example 2,* A and B have aggregate outside bases of $40,500. The AB Partnership has total inside basis in its assets of $40,500 ($25,000 cash + $15,500 carryover basis of its § 1231 assets). This equilibrium reflects the aggregate theory of partnerships under which A and B are considered to own indirect interests in AB's assets. However, it is possible that during the partnership's existence the aggregate outside basis will differ at times from the total inside basis.

A partner may have a divided holding period in his or her partnership interest in two circumstances. If a divided holding period occurs, the portion of a partnership interest to which a holding period relates is based on the relative fair market values of the properties contributed.[18] This will occur if the partner acquired portions of the partnership interest at different times.[19]

Example 3

R purchased a 10% interest in Z Partnership for $10,000 on January 1, 2016. She purchased another 5% interest in Z for $5,000 on November 1, 2016. As of January 1, 2017, R has a one-year holding period in two-thirds of her partnership interest ($10,000/$15,000), and a two-month holding period for one-third ($5,000/$15,000) of her interest.

A partner will also have a divided holding period in his or her partnership interest if the partner contributed more than one property for the partnership interest, and these properties had different holding periods in the hands of the partner.[20]

Example 4

E contributes cash of $2,000 and a capital asset (basis = $1,000; value = $2,000) held for five years for a 25% interest in Partnership Y. The portion of E's interest attributable to the cash, 50% ($2,000/[$2,000 + $2,000]), will have a holding period beginning the day after the contribution. The portion of his interest attributable to the capital asset (50%) has a five-year holding period.

Effect of Partnership Liabilities on Basis

LO.5

Determine the effect of partnership liabilities on the partners' bases in their partnership interests.

When a partnership borrows money, the general partners typically have unlimited liability for repayment of the debt to the partnership's creditors. If the partnership itself is unable to repay its debts, each partner must contribute personal funds to satisfy the unpaid balance.

---

[18] Reg. § 1.1223-3(b)(1).

[20] Reg. § 1.1223-3(a)(2).

[19] Reg. § 1.1223-2(a); for transfers of partnerships interests after September 20, 2000.

As a result, a partner's economic investment in a partnership consists not only of the contribution of cash or property reflected in his or her capital account, but also the share of partnership debt for which the partner might ultimately be held responsible.

Section 752(a) acknowledges this responsibility by providing that any increase in a partner's share of the liabilities of a partnership or any assumption of a partnership debt by a partner is treated as a contribution of money to the partnership. This constructive cash contribution increases the partner's outside basis in his or her partnership interest. Conversely, § 752(b) provides that any decrease in a partner's share of the liabilities of a partnership or any assumption of a partner's debt by a partnership is treated as a distribution of money from the partnership to the partner. This constructive cash distribution reduces the partner's outside basis.[21]

Example 5

M and N are equal partners in the M&N Partnership. On January 1 of the current year, both M and N had a $25,000 outside basis in their partnership interests, and the partnership had no debt on its balance sheet. On January 31, the partnership borrowed $15,000 from a local bank and used the funds to buy business assets. Because this transaction increased M and N's respective shares of the partnership's liabilities by $7,500, each was considered to have contributed this amount of cash to the partnership. As a result, their outside bases as of January 31 increased to $32,500.

On June 1, the partnership repaid $6,000 of the outstanding debt. Because this payment decreased M and N's respective shares of partnership debt, each was considered to have received a $3,000 cash distribution from the partnership. As a result, their outside bases as of June 1 decreased to $29,500.

	M	N
January 1 outside basis	$25,000	$25,000
Plus: Increase in share of partnership debt on 1/31	7,500	7,500
Less: Decrease in share of partnership debt on 6/1	(3,000)	(3,000)
June 1 outside basis	$29,500	$29,500

Note that in the above example, the inclusion of partnership debt in the partners' outside bases maintained the equilibrium between inside and outside basis. Between January 1 and June 1, M and N's aggregate outside bases increased by a net amount of $9,000. During this same period, the basis of partnership assets also increased by $9,000 ($15,000 debt proceeds − $6,000 cash distribution).

Partner's Share of Partnership Liabilities

The combined result of § 752(a) and (b) is that on any particular date, a partner's outside basis includes a share of the various debts reflected on the partnership balance sheet as of that date. The Treasury regulations under § 752 provide a lengthy and complex set of rules for determining a partner's share of partnership liabilities. Under these regulations, each partner's share of any specific debt depends on the classification of the debt itself and whether the partner is a general or limited partner. All partnership debts are classified as either recourse or nonrecourse. A debt is *recourse* if the creditor can look to the personal assets of any general partner to satisfy the unpaid portion of the debt in the event the partnership does not have sufficient assets for repayment. A debt is *nonrecourse* if the creditor cannot look beyond the assets of the partnership for repayment.

[21] § 733.

A partner's share of recourse debt equals the portion of such debt for which that partner bears the *economic risk of loss*.[22] Because limited partners generally bear no responsibility for the repayment of partnership liabilities, they have no risk of loss with respect to partnership recourse debt. Consequently, no amount of such debt is apportioned to any limited partner.

The extent to which general partners are deemed to bear the economic risk of loss for partnership recourse debt is generally determined by using the results from a hypothetical *constructive liquidation scenario*.[23] The basic idea behind these rules is to consider which partners would have to actually satisfy these liabilities if the absolute worst scenario imaginable (i.e., all liabilities are due but all partnership assets are worthless) happened to the partnership. The following transactions are assumed to occur, simultaneously, at the end of the partnership's taxable year:

1. All liabilities must be paid immediately in full.
2. All partnership assets, including cash, are assumed to have a fair market value of zero.
3. All partnership assets are sold for no consideration, which results in a recognized loss for each asset equal to the asset's adjusted basis.
4. These losses are allocated to the partners according to the loss sharing ratios in the partnership agreement.
5. The partners reduce their respective capital accounts by the amount of the losses.
6. The partnership liquidates. Consequently, any partner having a negative capital account after step five is deemed to make a cash contribution to the partnership, equal to this negative amount, so that his or her ending capital account will be zero.
7. The partnership is deemed to use this cash to pay off the recourse liabilities of the partnership.
8. Any remaining cash is deemed to be distributed to partners that have positive capital account balances.

The amount of cash that is deemed to be contributed to the partnership under step six is the partner's share of the recourse liabilities.

Example 6

Individuals W and X are general partners and individuals Y and Z are limited partners in the WXYZ Partnership. Partnership losses are allocated 20% to W, 30% to X, and 25% respectively to Y and Z. As of December 31 of the current year, the partnership has $100,000 of recourse debt. The partnership's balance sheet as of December 31 is as follows:

	Basis	Fair Market Value
Cash	$ 50,000	$ 50,000
Inventory	75,000	200,000
Machinery and equipment	75,000	150,000
	$200,000	$400,000
Recourse liabilities	$100,000	$100,000
W, capital	20,000	60,000
X, capital	30,000	90,000
Y, capital	25,000	75,000
Z, capital	25,000	75,000
	$200,000	$400,000

---

[22] Reg. § 1.752-2(a).

[23] Reg. § 1.752-2(b). In so-called straight-up partnerships in which the partners' profit-and-loss sharing ratios correspond to the ratios of their respective capital account balances, the application of this analysis has the same result as an apportionment based on loss-sharing ratios.

If the assets were worthless and sold for no consideration, a $200,000 loss would be recognized. In allocating this loss to the partners, the limited partners cannot have a negative capital account since they have limited liability. Therefore, whereas Y and Z would otherwise each be allocated $50,000 of loss ($200,000 × 25%), each is limited to a loss allocation of $25,000. The remaining $150,000 of loss is allocated to W and X based on their relative loss sharing ratios, as follows:

W: $150,000 × 20%/(20% + 30%) = $60,000
X: $150,000 × 30%/(20% + 30%) = $90,000

After allocation of these losses, the capital accounts are as follows:

	W	X	Y	Z
Capital, 12/31	$ 20,000	$ 30,000	$25,000	$25,000
Loss allocation	(60,000)	(90,000)	(25,000)	(25,000)
	$(40,000)	$(60,000)	0	0

The WXYZ Partnership is now assumed to liquidate. W and X must contribute $40,000 and $60,000 to the partnership, respectively, to restore their capital accounts to zero. This $100,000 is then used to pay the $100,000 recourse liability. Therefore, W and X are allocated $40,000 and $60,000 of the recourse liability, respectively, while Y and Z are not allocated any of the liability.

If a partnership defaults on the repayment of a nonrecourse debt and partnership assets are insufficient to satisfy the debt, the creditor cannot look to the personal assets of any partner for satisfaction. Therefore, no partner—general or limited—bears any economic risk of loss with regard to partnership nonrecourse debt. As a result, separate rules are provided for the allocation of nonrecourse debt. In general, the Regulations provide that nonrecourse debt is apportioned to all partners based on their profit-sharing ratios. However, an exception is provided to this rule if a partner has contributed property to the partnership encumbered with nonrecourse debt that has a built-in gain. In this case, the contributing partner is first allocated nonrecourse debt to the extent of the lower of (1) the built-in gain on the contributed property, or (2) the excess of the non-recourse debt over the adjusted basis of the contributed property. Any remaining debt is then allocated to all the partners based on their profit-sharing ratios.[24] This apportionment rule reflects the fact that such debt will be repaid from partnership profits and that both general and limited partners alike will pay tax on their allocated shares of such profits.

Example 7

Individuals G and H are general partners and individuals I and J are limited partners in the GHIJ Partnership. Partnership profits are allocated 10% to G, 20% to H, and 35% respectively to I and J. As of December 31 of the current year, the partnership has $100,000 of nonrecourse debt. This $100,000 debt is attached to property that was contributed by G. At the time of contribution, the property had an adjusted basis to G of $80,000 and a fair market value of $120,000. The first $20,000 of the $100,000 debt is allocated to G as follows:

Lower of
1. the built-in gain on the property, $40,000 ($120,000 – $80,000),
   or
2. the excess of the non-recourse debt over the adjusted basis of the contributed property, $20,000 ($100,000 – $80,000)

The remaining $80,000 of nonrecourse debt is allocated based on the profit sharing ratios.

[24] Reg. § 1.752-3(a); these regulations also include the concept of minimum gain for allocations of nonrecourse debt, but that discussion is beyond the scope of this book.

In summary, the $100,000 nonrecourse debt is allocated as follows:

	G	H	I	J
Built-in gain	$20,000	$ 0	$ 0	$ 0
Profit ratio	8,000	16,000	28,000	28,000
	$28,000	$16,000	$28,000	$28,000

Consequently, G, H, I, and J may include $28,000, $16,000, $28,000, and $28,000 of the debt respectively in the outside bases of their partnership interests.

Liabilities Transferred to the Partnership

A partner who contributes property to a partnership in exchange for an ownership interest may negotiate for the partnership to assume a recourse liability of the partner as part of the exchange transaction. Similarly, the property contributed to the partnership may be subject to a nonrecourse liability. In both cases, the rules of § 752 have an impact on the computation of the contributing partner's outside basis.

Any debt for which the contributing partner is relieved of personal liability reduces that partner's basis in his or her new partnership interest. However, this outside basis is also increased by any amount of such debt apportioned to the contributor in his or her capacity as partner. Because this decrease and increase occur simultaneously as the result of a single transaction, only the net increase or decrease is taken into account in computing the contributing partner's basis.[25] The net increase or decrease for the contributing partner's basis can be computed as: amount of liability transferred × (100% − partner's percentage share of debt).

Example 8

Individual T contributes business assets with an adjusted basis of $50,000 to a partnership in exchange for a 25% general interest in partnership capital, profits, and losses. As part of the contribution, the partnership assumes $12,000 of T's business recourse debt, relieving T of personal liability. The partnership has no other debts. Although T is relieved of the $12,000 debt in her individual capacity, she continues to bear the economic risk of loss for 25% of the debt in her capacity as general partner. Accordingly, T's outside basis in her partnership interest immediately subsequent to her contribution is $41,000 ($50,000 basis of contributed property − $9,000 net relief of debt).

Basis of contributed property		$50,000
Less:	Relief of personal liability	(12,000)
Plus:	Liability for debt as general partner (25% × $12,000)	3,000
T's outside basis in partnership interest		$41,000

Example 9

Individual O contributes a tract of investment land with an adjusted basis of $340,000 to a partnership; the land is subject to a $125,000 nonrecourse mortgage. In exchange for the encumbered land, O receives a 10% limited interest in partnership capital, profits, and losses. The partnership has no other debts. Although O is relieved of the $125,000 mortgage in his individual capacity, he is allocated 10% of the debt in his capacity as limited partner.[26] Accordingly, O's outside basis in his partnership interest

---

[25] Reg. § 1.752-1(f).

[26] Because the mortgage is nonrecourse, O was not personally liable for its repayment prior to contribution of the encumbered land to the partnership. However, § 752(c)

and Reg. § 1.752-1(e) clarify that nonrecourse debt (to the extent of the fair market value of the property) is treated as a personal liability of the owner.

immediately subsequent to his contribution is $227,500 ($340,000 basis of contributed property − $112,500 net relief of debt).

Basis of contributed property		$340,000
Less:	Relief of liability	(125,000)
Plus:	Liability for debt as limited partner (10% × $ 125,000)	12,500
O's outside basis in partnership interest		$227,500

A partnership's assumption of a contributing partner's debt has tax consequences not only to the contributor but to the other partners as well. The outside bases of the non-contributing partners will increase by the amount of newly assumed debt apportioned to them and decrease by the amount of existing partnership debt apportioned to the newly admitted partner.

Example 10

Individual L contributes business assets with a fair market value of $23,600 and adjusted basis of $10,000 to a partnership in exchange for a one-third general interest in partnership capital, profits, and losses. As part of the contribution, the partnership assumes $3,600 of L's business recourse debt, relieving L of personal liability. Consequently, L's contribution has a net value of $20,000 ($23,600 − $3,600) and a net basis of $6,400 ($10,000 − $3,600). The partnership has $6,000 of existing debt as of the date of contribution. Immediately after the contribution, the partnership has the following balance sheet:

		Inside Basis	Fair Market Value
Contributed assets		$10,000	$23,600
Existing assets		30,000	46,000
		$40,000	$69,600
Assumed debt		$ 3,600	$ 3,600
Existing debt		6,000	6,000
Capital:	Partner L (33.3%)	6,400	20,000
	Partner M (33.3%)	12,000	20,000
	Partner N (33.3%)	12,000	20,000
		$40,000	$69,600

L's outside basis in his new partnership interest is $9,600 [$10,000 basis of contributed property − $2,400 ($3,600 × 66.7%) net relief of the assumed debt + $2,000 ($6,000 × 33.3%) assumption of one-third of existing partnership debt].

Prior to L's admission to the partnership, partners M and N each had $15,000 of outside basis in his partnership interest. This basis number represented a one-half interest in the $24,000 net inside basis of existing partnership assets plus one-half of the $6,000 of existing partnership debt. Upon L's admission, M and N are each apportioned $1,200 of the assumed debt. However, they are each relieved of $1,000 of existing debt. Subsequent to L's admission, their outside bases have each increased to $15,200 ($15,000 + $200 net increase in share of partnership liabilities).

Note that in *Example 10,* the inclusion of $9,600 of total partnership debt in the partners's outside bases maintains the equilibrium between the $40,000 total aggregate outside bases (L's $9,600 basis + M's $15,200 basis + N's $15,200 basis) and the $40,000 total inside basis of the partnership assets.

Relief of Debt in Excess of Basis

Section 733 provides a general rule that a cash distribution from a partnership to a partner represents a nontaxable reduction in the partner's outside basis. This same section prohibits a negative basis (a basis of less than zero) in a partnership interest. Section 731(a)(1) resolves the potential conflict between these rules by providing that a partner who receives a cash distribution in excess of outside basis must recognize the excess as gain from a sale of the partnership interest.

If a contributing partner receives a constructive cash distribution in the form of net relief of liability, and the amount of such relief exceeds the total basis of the property contributed to the partnership, the contributor must recognize a taxable gain to the extent of the excess.

Example 11

Individual B contributes business assets with a fair market value of $75,000 and an adjusted basis of $30,000 to a partnership in exchange for a 15% general interest in partnership capital, profits, and losses. As part of the transaction, the partnership assumes $45,000 of B's business recourse debt, relieving B of personal liability. The partnership has no other debts. Because B's $38,250 net relief of debt (85% of $45,000) exceeds the $30,000 basis of the contributed assets, B will have a zero basis in her partnership interest and must recognize an $8,250 gain on the constructive distribution of cash in excess of her outside basis.

If B seeks competent tax advice before she completes the transaction described in the above example and is informed of the consequences of the excess relief of debt, she can easily avoid gain recognition by retaining personal liability for the necessary portion of her business debts. If, however, the $45,000 debt represents a nonrecourse lien on the business assets B wishes to contribute to the partnership, the tax planning solution is not as obvious. Because B had no personal liability for such debt before contribution, she cannot retain personal liability without significantly altering the legal nature of the debt.

Fortunately, the § 752 regulations provide a special apportionment rule to protect a contributing partner from immediate gain recognition in this situation. If property contributed to a partnership is subject to a nonrecourse debt, any amount of the debt in excess of the property's basis is apportioned to the contributing partner. The balance of the debt is then apportioned to all partners based on their profit sharing ratios.[27]

Example 12

Refer to the facts in *Example 11*. If the $45,000 debt is a nonrecourse mortgage on the assets B contributes to the partnership, $15,000 of such debt (the excess of the debt over the $30,000 basis of the assets) is apportioned to B for inclusion in her outside basis. The $30,000 balance of the debt is apportioned to all the partners based on their profit-sharing ratios. Accordingly, B is apportioned an additional $4,500 (15% of $30,000) of the debt. Because B's net relief of debt is only $25,500 ($45,000 original debt – $19,500 debt apportioned to B as a partner), her outside basis in her partnership interest is $4,500 ($30,000 basis of contributed assets – $25,500 net relief).

Basis of contributed property		$30,000
Less:	Relief of liability	(45,000)
Plus:	Excess of nonrecourse debt over contributed basis	15,000
	Liability for remaining debt as limited partner (15% × $30,000)	4,500
B's outside basis in partnership interest		$ 4,500

---

[27] Reg. § 1.752-3(a)(3).

CONTRIBUTION OF SERVICES

The nonrecognition rule of § 721 does not apply when an incoming partner contributes personal services to a partnership in exchange for an ownership interest. The tax consequences of such an exchange to both parties depend on whether the service partner receives an interest in partnership *capital* or merely an interest in the *future profits* of the partnership business.

Receipt of a Capital Interest

If a service partner receives an interest in the existing capital of a partnership, the partner must recognize ordinary compensation income to the extent of the value of such interest.[28] The amount of income recognized becomes the partner's initial outside basis in the interest received.[29]

Example 13

C agrees to perform services for the AB Partnership in exchange for a 20% interest in partnership capital, profits, and losses. On the date that C is admitted to the partnership, the net value of the partnership assets is $250,000. The value of C's newly acquired interest is $50,000 (20% of $250,000), which equates to the value of the assets that C would receive if the partnership were to immediately liquidate and distribute its assets to each partner based on their relative capital account balances. C must recognize $50,000 of compensation income on the exchange and will have a $50,000 outside basis in her partnership interest.

If the service partner's legal rights in his capital interest are not subject to any restriction, the partner will recognize compensation income in the year the interest is received. However, if the interest is subject to a *substantial risk of forfeiture* so that the partner's rights in the interest are nonvested, § 83(a) defers the recognition of income until the risk of forfeiture lapses.

Example 14

Refer to the facts in *Example 13*. Assume that the partnership agreement between service partner C and existing partners A and B stipulates that C must surrender her capital interest back to A and B if she fails to perform services exclusively for the partnership business at any time during the next three years. Because her capital interest is subject to a substantial risk of forfeiture, C will not recognize ordinary income until the year in which the restriction lapses. The amount of income she will recognize will depend upon the value of the capital interest in that future year.

Partners who perform services in exchange for a restricted ownership interest may elect to include the current value of the interest in gross income for the year of receipt.[30] This election is attractive if the partner believes that the current value of the restricted interest is significantly less than the projected future value of the interest in the year the restriction will lapse. The election, though, is not without risk. A partner who eventually forfeits the interest back to the partnership may not claim a deduction for any unrecovered basis in the interest.[31]

---

[28] Reg. § 1.721-1(b)(1).

[29] Reg. § 1.722-1.

[30] § 83(b). The election must be made within 30 days after the interest is received by the service partner.

[31] § 83(b)(1).

> ### Example 15
>
> Refer to the facts in *Example 14*. In the year that C receives her restricted 20% interest in the capital, profits, and losses of the AB Partnership, the interest has a value of $50,000. Because C projects that this interest will be worth at least $100,000 in the year the restriction lapses, she elects to include $50,000 in her current-year gross income. Accordingly, her basis in the interest is $50,000. Unfortunately, C cannot get along with A and B and leaves the partnership the next year. Even though C must forfeit her interest back to A and B, she cannot deduct her $50,000 basis in the interest.

Impact on Partnership and Other Partners. The performance of services in exchange for a capital interest in a partnership has tax consequences for the partnership (and therefore the other partners) as well as for the service partner. By transferring a capital interest, the partnership has incurred a business expense to acquire the services. The partnership should either deduct this expense currently or capitalize it, depending on the nature of the services.[32] However, the expense is not in the form of a cash payment but of an undivided interest in partnership assets. For tax purposes, the transfer of an asset in payment for services is treated as if the transferor sold the asset for cash (recognizing gain or loss accordingly) and then used the cash to make payment. In other words, the transfer represents a fully taxable exchange of the asset for fair market value.

More specifically, a partnership's transfer of a capital interest for services is treated as if the partnership constructively exchanges an undivided interest in each of its assets and recognizes gain or loss equal to the difference between the fair market value of the interest and a corresponding share of each asset's tax basis.[33] The incoming partner who receives the undivided interest in exchange for the performance of services recognizes ordinary income equal to the interest's fair market value.[34] The partner is treated as immediately contributing the undivided interest back to the partnership to establish an initial capital account balance. The partnership's basis in the contributed interest equals its fair market value.

The partnership tax consequences described in the preceding paragraphs should affect only the original partners. In other words, any current deduction for the payment to the service partner (or any future amortization of the capitalized cost of the services) should be allocated to only the other partners. Similarly, any gain or loss recognized on the constructive exchange of partnership assets for services should be allocated entirely to the original partners. The requirements for such special allocations are discussed later in this chapter.

> ### Example 16
>
> In return for services rendered to it by Z, the XY Partnership transfers a one-third capital interest to Z when it has the following assets and no liabilities:
>
> | | Inside Basis | Fair Market Value |
> |---|---|---|
> | Land | $15,000 | $ 30,000 |
> | Building | 60,000 | 90,000 |
> | Total | $75,000 | $120,000 |
>
> The partnership is treated as exchanging a one-third interest in both the land and the building for an amount realized of $40,000 ($120,000 total fair market value of both assets ÷ 3). The partnership's aggregate basis in the one-third interest is $25,000 ($75,000 total basis of both assets ÷ 3). As a result, the partnership must recognize a $15,000 gain ($40,000 − $25,000), the character of which depends on the character and holding period of each asset. If the payment for Z's services is a current expense, the partnership may claim a $40,000 deduction.

---

[32] For example, if the services consisted of the architectural design of a new building, the partnership would capitalize the payment for the services to the cost of the building. See *Jackson E. Cagle*, 63 T.C. 86 (1974), aff'd in 76-2 USTC ¶9672, 38 AFTR2d 76-5834, 539 F.2d 409 (CA-5, 1976).

[33] See *United States v. General Shoe Corp.*, 60-1 USTC ¶9927, 22 AFTR2d 44512, 282 F.2d 9 (CA-6, 1960) and Reg. § 1.83-6(b).

[34] This is a guaranteed payment, as discussed later in this chapter. Reg. § 1.721-1(b)(2).

Incoming partner Z must recognize $40,000 of compensation income upon receipt of the one-third interest in the partnership land and building. He is treated as contributing this interest back to the partnership, thereby establishing his initial capital account of $40,000. Z's outside basis in his new partnership interest is $40,000, and the partnership's inside bases in its assets are increased as follows:

	2/3 Old Basis	+	Z's 1/3 Interest	=	New Basis
Land	$10,000		$10,000		$20,000
Building	40,000		30,000		70,000
	$50,000		$40,000		$90,000

Note that the partnership's basis in each of its assets has been increased to reflect the gain recognized as a result of the deemed asset exchange. Also note that this gain and the $40,000 deduction arising from the payment for services should be allocated only to the original partners and not to new partner Z.

Receipt of a Profits Interest

The partners in an established partnership may be reluctant to give up any part of their equity in existing partnership assets (i.e., a capital interest) as compensation to a newly admitted service partner. These partners might be more willing to give the service partner an interest in the future profits of the business—profits partially attributable to the new partner's efforts on behalf of the partnership.

Example 17

J agrees to perform services for the GHI partnership in exchange for a 25% interest in future partnership profits and losses. On the date that J is admitted to the partnership, the net value of the partnership's assets is $800,000. However, J is not given an initial capital account and has no legal interest in these assets. If the partnership were to immediately liquidate and distribute its assets to the partners based on their relative capital account balances, J would receive nothing. If the partnership generates income subsequent to J's admission, J will be entitled to 25% of such income.

The tax consequences to a service partner who receives nothing more than an interest in future partnership profits have been the subject of heated debate among tax experts for many years. The courts have also struggled with this issue with confusing and inconclusive results.[35] Currently, the uneasy consensus of opinion is that a service partner does not recognize current income upon the receipt of a profits interest because the interest has no immediate liquidation value.[36] Consequently, the service partner's initial basis in the interest is zero. The partner will, of course, recognize income to the extent of his or her share of future partnership profits.

Proposed Regulations Change Rules for Services

Proposed regulations issued in 2005 provide that an employer that transfers a capital partnership interest to a service provider would not have to recognize gain or loss on the transaction.[37] In *Example 16,* the partnership would not recognize the $15,000 gain if these regulations take effect. Under the proposed regulations, service providers would still recognize income on the receipt of a capital interest (but not a profits interest) and the employer

---

[35] See *Sol Diamond*, 56 T.C. 530 (1971), aff'd 74-1 USTC ¶9306, 33 AFTR2d 74-852, 492 F.2d 286 (CA-7, 1974) and *William G. Campbell*, 59 TCM 236, T.C. Memo 1990-162, rev'd 1991-2 USTC ¶50,420 (CA-8, 1991).

[36] See Rev. Proc. 93-27, 1993-2 C.B. 343 and Rev. Proc. 2001-43 for further guidance on this issue.

[37] Prop. Reg. §§ 1.721-1(b) and 1.83-3(e).

would receive a compensation deduction for the value of the interest (unless the payment is an organization expense). However, this conclusion is reached in a slightly different fashion than existing law. The proposed regulations provide that the value of the partnership interest is its current liquidation value immediately after the transaction. Profits interest would have no liquidation value, so service providers receiving a profits interest would have no income.

Operating the Partnership

Section 701, the first section in Subchapter K, states that "A partnership as such shall not be subject to the income tax imposed by this chapter. Persons carrying on business as partners shall be liable for income tax only in their separate or individual capacities." Even though partnerships are not taxable entities, they are required to file an annual information return, Form 1065 (U.S. Partnership Return of Income). Basically, this return shows the computation of partnership taxable income and how such income is allocated to each partner. Form 1065 is due by the 15th day of the third month following the close of the partnership taxable year.[38] For calendar year partnerships, this would be March 15. An automatic extension of six months is available (to September 15 for calendar year partnerships).

The correct tax treatment of all partnership items of income, gain, deduction, and loss is determined at the partnership level through *unified audit proceedings*.[39] Each partnership must designate a *tax matters partner* to represent the partnership in any dispute with the IRS or any subsequent litigation. After the correct treatment of a partnership item has been finally resolved, the IRS may assess each partner for any additional tax liability with respect to such item without initiating an audit of the partner's return.[40]

In order to compute its annual taxable income, a newly formed partnership must make a number of initial elections, including the adoption of both an accounting method (or methods) by which to compute income and the partnership taxable year. The fact that these important elections are made by the partnership itself rather than by each partner is a very practical application of the entity theory of partnerships.[41] As a general rule, partnerships are free to elect the cash receipts and disbursements method, the accrual method, or a hybrid method of accounting for tax purposes.[42] As explained in the next section of the chapter, they have much less flexibility in the choice of a taxable year.

THE PARTNERSHIP'S TAXABLE YEAR

Income generated by a partnership is included in the taxable income of a partner for the partner's year in which the partnership's taxable year ends.[43] If partnerships had no restrictions as to their choice of taxable year, this simple timing rule could be used to achieve a significant deferral of income recognition.

Example 18

R and S, calendar year individuals, decide to operate a business as equal partners. The RS Partnership begins business on February 1, 2016. During its first year of operations the partnership generates $3,000 of taxable income each month. If the partnership could adopt a fiscal year ending January 31, its $36,000 of first year income ($33,000 of which was earned in 2016) would be included in the partners' 2017 tax returns because 2017 is the partners' taxable year in which the partnership's fiscal year ends. For each subsequent year that the RS Partnership remains in existence, eleven months of income earned in one calendar year would not be taxed at the partner level until the following calendar year.

---

[38] § 6031; § 6072(a). For tax years before 2016 the due date was the 15th day of the fourth month following the close of the partnership's tax year end.

[39] § 6221. The unified audit proceedings do not apply to certain small partnerships with 10 or fewer partners. See § 6231(a)(1)(B).

[40] § 6231(a)(6).

[41] § 703(b).

[41] § 703(b).

[42] § 446(c). Section 448(a) limits the use of the cash method for a partnership that (1) is a tax shelter, or (2) has a C corporation as a partner. However, § 448(b) provides several important exceptions to this restrictive limitation.

[43] § 706(a).

Subchapter K contains a set of complex rules designed to minimize the potential for income deferral through use of a partnership. A partnership must adopt the taxable year used by one or more partners who own more than a 50% aggregate interest in partnership capital and profits. If no such *majority interest taxable year* exists, the partnership must adopt the taxable year used by its principal partners (those partners owning at least a 5% interest in partnership capital or profits).[44] If the principal partners use different taxable years, the partnership must adopt a taxable year resulting in the least aggregate deferral of income to the partners. The taxable year resulting from the application of these rules is known as the "required taxable year."

Under the *least aggregate deferral method*,[45] all year-ends that any of the partners have must be tested, and the one that produces the least amount of deferral for the partners as a group is the required tax year. The deferral for each partner is computed as the time from the year-end being tested until the next year-end of the partner. The months of deferral are then weighted by each partner's profits interest. The least aggregate deferral method is illustrated by the following example:

Example 19

M and N are equal corporate partners in the MN Partnership. M has a year-end of March 31 and N has a year-end of November 30. Since M and N each own 50% of the partnership, no partner, or group of partners, that have the same year-end own a more than 50% interest in the partnership. MN Partnership has two principal partners, but the principal partners do not have the same year end. Therefore, the least aggregate deferral method must be used. The two months that must be tested are March and November.

Test of March 31 Year-End

Partner	Year-End	Profit Interest	×	Months of Deferral	Weighted Deferral
M	3/31	50%	×	0	0.0
N	11/30	50%	×	8	4.0
				Aggregate Deferral	4.0

Test of November 30 Year-End

Partner	Year-End	Profit Interest	×	Months of Deferral	Weighted Deferral
M	3/31	50%	×	4	2.0
N	11/30	50%	×	0	0.0
				Aggregate Deferral	2.0

Therefore, the required year end is November 30 since it produces the least amount of deferral for the partners as a group.

If the partners wish to use a year different from the "required tax year," the Code offers relief from these mechanistic rules by allowing a partnership to adopt any taxable year (without reference to the taxable years of its partners) if it can convince the IRS that there is a valid *business purpose* for such year.[46] The IRS will generally agree that a partnership has a business purpose for adopting a taxable year that conforms to its *natural business year*. For example, a partnership operating a ski resort might have a natural business year that ends on April 30. The IRS should allow this partnership to adopt this fiscal year for tax purposes, regardless of the taxable years used by the various partners. A partnership can also use a different year-end from its required year-end if it meets the 25% test. This test holds that a

---

[44] § 706(b)(1)(B)(i) and (ii).

[45] Reg. § 1.706-1(b)(3).

[46] § 706(b)(1)(C).

partnership may change its tax year if at least 25% of the taxpayer's annual gross receipts are recognized in the last two months of the tax year to which the partnership wishes to change, and this 25% test is met for three consecutive years.[47]

Section 444 adds further complexity to the web of rules governing the adoption of a partnership taxable year. Under this section, partnerships may elect to use a taxable year other than the "required tax year" if the deferral period inherent in such year is no more than three months. Therefore, a partnership with a required taxable year-end of December 31 could elect to have a year-end of September 30, October 31, or November 30. Partnerships electing under § 444 must make a cash deposit with the federal government. This non-interest-bearing deposit, the amount of which must be adjusted annually, approximates the amount of tax on partnership income that is deferred annually because of the election.[48]

ORGANIZATION COSTS AND SYNDICATION FEES

Any costs incurred to organize a partnership, such as legal fees for drafting the partnership agreement and filing fees charged by the state in which the partnership is formed, must be capitalized and are not deductible as ordinary and necessary business expenses. The partnership must expense the first $5,000 of these *organization costs* and amortize the remainder over a period of 180 months, beginning with the month in which the partnership begins business (unless the partnership elects to not do so).[49] The $5,000 amount to be expensed must be reduced, but not below zero, by the amount of organizational expenses in excess of $50,000. Any *syndication fees* connected with the issuance and marketing of partnership interests must also be capitalized. These fees may not be amortized and will remain as an intangible asset on the partnership books until the partnership is liquidated.[50]

COMPUTATION OF PARTNERSHIP TAXABLE INCOME

LO.6

Compute partnership taxable income or loss and identify any separately computed items of partnership income, gain, loss, deduction, or credit.

Partnership taxable income is computed in the same manner as the taxable income of an individual.[51] However, for reporting purposes, the partnership must classify the various components of its income into two groups: (1) the separately stated items and (2) the non-separately stated items. The partnership must separately state any item of income, gain, deduction, loss, or credit potentially subject to special treatment at the partner level.[52] Separately stated items include capital gains and losses, § 1231 gains and losses, investment income and expenses, net rental income or loss, and charitable contributions. Nonseparately stated items are all taxable items of income, gain, loss or deduction that do not have to be separately stated. These items are combined into a single total referred to on the partnership's tax return as *ordinary business income or loss*. Ordinary income is reported on page 1, line 22 of Form 1065. Ordinary income includes such items as gross profit on sales, operating expenses such as employee salaries, guaranteed payments to partners (discussed below) and other administrative expenses. Ordinary income also includes income characterized as ordinary income under the depreciation recapture rules of §§ 1245 and 1250 since this income receives no special treatment (see Form 1065, p. 1, line 6, net gain from Form 4797). In contrast, all separately stated items are listed as such on page 3, Schedule K of Form 1065. Note that the partnership's taxable income is the sum of the partnership's ordinary income or loss and the separately stated items. (See Exhibit 9-1 for an illustration of a partially completed Form 1065 and the accompanying Schedules K and K-1. See Exhibit 9-2 for a summary of Separately and Nonseparately Stated Items.)

---

[47] Rev. Proc. 2002-39, 2002-22 I.R.B. 1046, provides the guidelines for changing from the required tax year because of the business purpose test and the 25% gross receipts test. Also see Rev. Rul. 87-57, 1987-2 C.B. 117 for other examples of circumstances that may or may not be considered valid business purposes.

[48] This deposit is described in § 7519.

[49] § 709(b).

[50] § 709(a).

[51] § 703(a).

[52] § 702(a). Reg. § 1.702-1(a)(8)(ii) explains that each partner must be able to take into account separately his or her distributive share of any partnership item that results in an income tax liability different from that which would result if the item were not accounted for separately.

EXHIBIT 9-1	Partnership Tax Return Form 1065

Form 1065

Department of the Treasury
Internal Revenue Service

U.S. Return of Partnership Income

For calendar year 2015, or tax year beginning _____ , 2015, ending _____ , 20 _____ .

▶ Information about Form 1065 and its separate instructions is at *www.irs.gov/form1065.*

OMB No. 1545-0123

2015

A Principal business activity Retail	
B Principal product or service Clothing	
C Business code number 448110	

Type or Print	Name of partnership T Company
	Number, street, and room or suite no. If a P.O. box, see the instructions. 8122 South 8th Street
	City or town, state or province, country, and ZIP or foreign postal code Norfolk, VA 23508

D Employer identification number
88 – 9138761

E Date business started
1 – 1 – 15

F Total assets (see the instructions)
$ 322,000 00

G Check applicable boxes: **(1)** [X] Initial return **(2)** [ ] Final return **(3)** [ ] Name change **(4)** [ ] Address change **(5)** [ ] Amended return
(6) [ ] Technical termination - also check (1) or (2)

H Check accounting method: **(1)** [ ] Cash **(2)** [X] Accrual **(3)** [ ] Other (specify) ▶ _____

I Number of Schedules K-1. Attach one for each person who was a partner at any time during the tax year ▶ 2

J Check if Schedules C and M-3 are attached . . . . [ ]

Caution. *Include **only** trade or business income and expenses on lines 1a through 22 below. See the instructions for more information.*

Income

1a	Gross receipts or sales	**1a**	470,000 00	
b	Returns and allowances	**1b**	0 00	
c	Balance. Subtract line 1b from line 1a	**1c**	470,000 00
2	Cost of goods sold (attach Form 1125-A)	**2**	300,000 00
3	Gross profit. Subtract line 2 from line 1c	**3**	170,000 00
4	Ordinary income (loss) from other partnerships, estates, and trusts (attach statement) . .	**4**	
5	Net farm profit (loss) (attach Schedule F (Form 1040))	**5**	
6	Net gain (loss) from Form 4797, Part II, line 17 (attach Form 4797)	**6**	
7	Other income (loss) (attach statement)	**7**	
8	**Total income (loss).** Combine lines 3 through 7	**8**	170,000 00

Deductions (see the instructions for limitations)

9	Salaries and wages (other than to partners) (less employment credits)	**9**	48,000 00
10	Guaranteed payments to partners . . $24,000 + $700 Employee Benefit . .	**10**	24,700 00
11	Repairs and maintenance	**11**	12,000 00
12	Bad debts	**12**	
13	Rent	**13**	
14	Taxes and licenses . $3,000 Property Taxes + $4,000 Payroll Taxes . .	**14**	7,000 00
15	Interest	**15**	3,300 00
16a	Depreciation (if required, attach Form 4562)	**16a**	15,000 00	
b	Less depreciation reported on Form 1125-A and elsewhere on return	**16b**	0 00	**16c**	
17	Depletion **(Do not deduct oil and gas depletion.)**	**17**	
18	Retirement plans, etc. . . . . . . Life Insurance Coverage, Utilities,	**18**	
19	Employee benefit programs . . . . & Tele = $2,500 + Office Supp =	**19**	1,400 00
20	Other deductions (attach statement) . $1,100 + Insurance = $3,100 . .	**20**	6,700 00
21	**Total deductions.** Add the amounts shown in the far right column for lines 9 through 20 .	**21**	118,100 00
22	**Ordinary business income (loss).** Subtract line 21 from line 8	**22**	51,900 00

Sign Here

Under penalties of perjury, I declare that I have examined this return, including accompanying schedules and statements, and to the best of my knowledge and belief, it is true, correct, and complete. Declaration of preparer (other than general partner or limited liability company member manager) is based on all information of which preparer has any knowledge.

▶ *adolph Z.T.*

Signature of general partner or limited liability company member manager

▶ 3 – 31 – 16

Date

May the IRS discuss this return with the preparer shown below (see instructions)? [ ] **Yes** [ ] **No**

Paid Preparer Use Only

Print/Type preparer's name	Preparer's signature	Date	Check [ ] if self-employed	PTIN
Firm's name ▶			Firm's EIN ▶	
Firm's address ▶			Phone no.	

For Paperwork Reduction Act Notice, see separate instructions.   Cat. No. 11390Z   Form **1065** (2015)

EXHIBIT 9-1   **Continued**

Form 1065 (2015)   Page **2**

Schedule B **Other Information**		**Yes**	**No**

1 What type of entity is filing this return? Check the applicable box:

a ☒ Domestic general partnership	**b** ☐ Domestic limited partnership		
c ☐ Domestic limited liability company	**d** ☐ Domestic limited liability partnership		
e ☐ Foreign partnership	**f** ☐ Other ▶		

2 At any time during the tax year, was any partner in the partnership a disregarded entity, a partnership (including an entity treated as a partnership), a trust, an S corporation, an estate (other than an estate of a deceased partner), or a nominee or similar person? . . . . **No: X**

3 At the end of the tax year:

a Did any foreign or domestic corporation, partnership (including any entity treated as a partnership), trust, or tax-exempt organization, or any foreign government own, directly or indirectly, an interest of 50% or more in the profit, loss, or capital of the partnership? For rules of constructive ownership, see instructions. If "Yes," attach Schedule B-1, Information on Partners Owning 50% or More of the Partnership . . . . **No: X**

b Did any individual or estate own, directly or indirectly, an interest of 50% or more in the profit, loss, or capital of the partnership? For rules of constructive ownership, see instructions. If "Yes," attach Schedule B-1, Information on Partners Owning 50% or More of the Partnership . . . . **No: X**

4 At the end of the tax year, did the partnership:

a Own directly 20% or more, or own, directly or indirectly, 50% or more of the total voting power of all classes of stock entitled to vote of any foreign or domestic corporation? For rules of constructive ownership, see instructions. If "Yes," complete (i) through (iv) below . . . .

(i) Name of Corporation	**(ii)** Employer Identification Number (if any)	**(iii)** Country of Incorporation	**(iv)** Percentage Owned in Voting Stock

b Own directly an interest of 20% or more, or own, directly or indirectly, an interest of 50% or more in the profit, loss, or capital in any foreign or domestic partnership (including an entity treated as a partnership) or in the beneficial interest of a trust? For rules of constructive ownership, see instructions. If "Yes," complete (i) through (v) below . . **No: X**

(i) Name of Entity	**(ii)** Employer Identification Number (if any)	**(iii)** Type of Entity	**(iv)** Country of Organization	**(v)** Maximum Percentage Owned in Profit, Loss, or Capital

		Yes	**No**

5 Did the partnership file Form 8893, Election of Partnership Level Tax Treatment, or an election statement under section 6231(a)(1)(B)(ii) for partnership-level tax treatment, that is in effect for this tax year? See Form 8893 for more details . . . . **No: X**

6 Does the partnership satisfy **all four** of the following conditions?

a The partnership's total receipts for the tax year were less than $250,000.

b The partnership's total assets at the end of the tax year were less than $1 million.

c Schedules K-1 are filed with the return and furnished to the partners on or before the due date (including extensions) for the partnership return.

d The partnership is not filing and is not required to file Schedule M-3 . . . . **No: X**

If "Yes," the partnership is not required to complete Schedules L, M-1, and M-2; Item F on page 1 of Form 1065; or Item L on Schedule K-1.

7 Is this partnership a publicly traded partnership as defined in section 469(k)(2)? . . . . **No: X**

8 During the tax year, did the partnership have any debt that was cancelled, was forgiven, or had the terms modified so as to reduce the principal amount of the debt? . . . . **No: X**

9 Has this partnership filed, or is it required to file, Form 8918, Material Advisor Disclosure Statement, to provide information on any reportable transaction? . . . . **No: X**

10 At any time during calendar year 2015, did the partnership have an interest in or a signature or other authority over a financial account in a foreign country (such as a bank account, securities account, or other financial account)? See the instructions for exceptions and filing requirements for FinCEN Form 114, Report of Foreign Bank and Financial Accounts (FBAR). If "Yes," enter the name of the foreign country. ▶ **No: X**

Form **1065** (2015)

EXHIBIT 9-1	Continued

Form 1065 (2015)   Page **3**

Schedule B   **Other Information** *(continued)*

		Yes	No
11	At any time during the tax year, did the partnership receive a distribution from, or was it the grantor of, or transferor to, a foreign trust? If "Yes," the partnership may have to file Form 3520, Annual Return To Report Transactions With Foreign Trusts and Receipt of Certain Foreign Gifts. See instructions	X	
12a	Is the partnership making, or had it previously made (and not revoked), a section 754 election? . . . . . . See instructions for details regarding a section 754 election.		X
b	Did the partnership make for this tax year an optional basis adjustment under section 743(b) or 734(b)? If "Yes," attach a statement showing the computation and allocation of the basis adjustment. See instructions		X
c	Is the partnership required to adjust the basis of partnership assets under section 743(b) or 734(b) because of a substantial built-in loss (as defined under section 743(d)) or substantial basis reduction (as defined under section 734(d))? If "Yes," attach a statement showing the computation and allocation of the basis adjustment. See instructions		X
13	Check this box if, during the current or prior tax year, the partnership distributed any property received in a like-kind exchange or contributed such property to another entity (other than disregarded entities wholly owned by the partnership throughout the tax year) . . . . ▶ ☐		X
14	At any time during the tax year, did the partnership distribute to any partner a tenancy-in-common or other undivided interest in partnership property?		X
15	If the partnership is required to file Form 8858, Information Return of U.S. Persons With Respect To Foreign Disregarded Entities, enter the number of Forms 8858 attached. See instructions ▶		X
16	Does the partnership have any foreign partners? If "Yes," enter the number of Forms 8805, Foreign Partner's Information Statement of Section 1446 Withholding Tax, filed for this partnership. ▶		X
17	Enter the number of Forms 8865, Return of U.S. Persons With Respect to Certain Foreign Partnerships, attached to this return. ▶		
18a	Did you make any payments in 2015 that would require you to file Form(s) 1099? See instructions		X
b	If "Yes," did you or will you file required Form(s) 1099?		
19	Enter the number of Form(s) 5471, Information Return of U.S. Persons With Respect To Certain Foreign Corporations, attached to this return. ▶		
20	Enter the number of partners that are foreign governments under section 892. ▶		

Designation of Tax Matters Partner (see instructions)

Enter below the general partner or member-manager designated as the tax matters partner (TMP) for the tax year of this return:

Name of designated TMP ▶		Identifying number of TMP ▶	
If the TMP is an entity, name of TMP representative ▶		Phone number of TMP ▶	
Address of designated TMP ▶			

Form **1065** (2015)

EXHIBIT 9-1   Continued

Form 1065 (2015)   Page **4**

Schedule K		Partners' Distributive Share Items				Total amount
Income (Loss)	1	Ordinary business income (loss) (page 1, line 22)			1	51,900 00
	2	Net rental real estate income (loss) (attach Form 8825)			2	
	3a	Other gross rental income (loss)	3a		3c	
	b	Expenses from other rental activities (attach statement)	3b			
	c	Other net rental income (loss). Subtract line 3b from line 3a			3c	
	4	Guaranteed payments . . Includes $700 Life Ins. Premiums			4	24,700 00
	5	Interest income			5	
	6	Dividends: a Ordinary dividends			6a	2,000 00
		b Qualified dividends	6b	2,000 00		
	7	Royalties			7	
	8	Net short-term capital gain (loss) (attach Schedule D (Form 1065))			8	1,000 00
	9a	Net long-term capital gain (loss) (attach Schedule D (Form 1065))			9a	
	b	Collectibles (28%) gain (loss)	9b			
	c	Unrecaptured section 1250 gain (attach statement) . .	9c			
	10	Net section 1231 gain (loss) (attach Form 4797)			10	
	11	Other income (loss) (see instructions) Type ▶			11	
Deductions	12	Section 179 deduction (attach Form 4562)			12	
	13a	Contributions			13a	7,000 00
	b	Investment interest expense			13b	
	c	Section 59(e)(2) expenditures: (1) Type ▶ _____ (2) Amount ▶			13c(2)	
	d	Other deductions (see instructions) Type ▶			13d	
Self-Employ-ment	14a	Net earnings (loss) from self-employment . $51,900 + $24,700 G Pmt. . .			14a	76,600 00
	b	Gross farming or fishing income			14b	
	c	Gross nonfarm income			14c	
Credits	15a	Low-income housing credit (section 42(j)(5))			15a	
	b	Low-income housing credit (other)			15b	
	c	Qualified rehabilitation expenditures (rental real estate) (attach Form 3468, if applicable)			15c	
	d	Other rental real estate credits (see instructions) Type ▶ _____			15d	
	e	Other rental credits (see instructions) Type ▶ _____			15e	
	f	Other credits (see instructions) Type ▶ Rehabilitation Credit			15f	2,000 00
Foreign Transactions	16a	Name of country or U.S. possession ▶ _____				
	b	Gross income from all sources			16b	
	c	Gross income sourced at partner level			16c	
		Foreign gross income sourced at partnership level				
	d	Passive category ▶ _____ e General category ▶ _____ f Other ▶			16f	
		Deductions allocated and apportioned at partner level				
	g	Interest expense ▶ _____ h Other . . . . ▶			16h	
		Deductions allocated and apportioned at partnership level to foreign source income				
	i	Passive category ▶ _____ j General category ▶ _____ k Other ▶			16k	
	l	Total foreign taxes (check one): ▶ Paid ☐ Accrued ☐			16l	
	m	Reduction in taxes available for credit (attach statement)			16m	
	n	Other foreign tax information (attach statement)				
Alternative Minimum Tax (AMT) Items	17a	Post-1986 depreciation adjustment			17a	
	b	Adjusted gain or loss			17b	
	c	Depletion (other than oil and gas)			17c	
	d	Oil, gas, and geothermal properties—gross income			17d	
	e	Oil, gas, and geothermal properties—deductions			17e	
	f	Other AMT items (attach statement)			17f	
Other Information	18a	Tax-exempt interest income			18a	
	b	Other tax-exempt income			18b	
	c	Nondeductible expenses			18c	
	19a	Distributions of cash and marketable securities			19a	12,000 00
	b	Distributions of other property			19b	7,000 00
	20a	Investment income . . . . Dividends . .			20a	2,000 00
	b	Investment expenses			20b	
	c	Other items and amounts (attach statement)				

Form **1065** (2015)

EXHIBIT 9-1   **Continued**

Form 1065 (2015)   Page **5**

Analysis of Net Income (Loss)

1   Net income (loss). Combine Schedule K, lines 1 through 11. From the result, subtract the sum of Schedule K, lines 12 through 13d, and 16l . $51,900 + $2,000 + $1,000 + $24,700 − $7,000 =   **1**   **72,600 | 00**

2   Analysis by partner type:

	(i) Corporate	(ii) Individual (active)	(iii) Individual (passive)	(iv) Partnership	(v) Exempt Organization	(vi) Nominee/Other
a General partners		72,600.00				
b Limited partners						

Schedule L   Balance Sheets per Books

	Assets	Beginning of tax year (a)	(b)	End of tax year (c)	(d)
1	Cash				
2a	Trade notes and accounts receivable				
b	Less allowance for bad debts				
3	Inventories				
4	U.S. government obligations				
5	Tax-exempt securities				
6	Other current assets (attach statement)				
7a	Loans to partners (or persons related to partners)		First		
b	Mortgage and real estate loans		Year		
8	Other investments (attach statement)		Partnership		
9a	Buildings and other depreciable assets				
b	Less accumulated depreciation				
10a	Depletable assets				
b	Less accumulated depletion				
11	Land (net of any amortization)				
12a	Intangible assets (amortizable only)				
b	Less accumulated amortization				
13	Other assets (attach statement)				
14	Total assets				322,000.00
	Liabilities and Capital				
15	Accounts payable				
16	Mortgages, notes, bonds payable in less than 1 year				
17	Other current liabilities (attach statement)				
18	All nonrecourse loans				
19a	Loans from partners (or persons related to partners)				
b	Mortgages, notes, bonds payable in 1 year or more				
20	Other liabilities (attach statement)				
21	Partners' capital accounts				
22	Total liabilities and capital				322,000.00

Schedule M-1   Reconciliation of Income (Loss) per Books With Income (Loss) per Return

Note. The partnership may be required to file Schedule M-3 (see instructions).

1	Net income (loss) per books	47,900.00*	**6**	Income recorded on books this year not included on Schedule K, lines 1 through 11 (itemize):	
2	Income included on Schedule K, lines 1, 2, 3c, 5, 6a, 7, 8, 9a, 10, and 11, not recorded on books this year (itemize):		**a**	Tax-exempt interest $	
3	Guaranteed payments (other than health insurance)	24,700.00	**7**	Deductions included on Schedule K, lines 1 through 13d, and 16l, not charged against book income this year (itemize):	
4	Expenses recorded on books this year not included on Schedule K, lines 1 through 13d, and 16l (itemize):		**a**	Depreciation $	
a	Depreciation $		**8**	Add lines 6 and 7	
b	Travel and entertainment $		**9**	Income (loss) (Analysis of Net Income (Loss), line 1). Subtract line 8 from line 5	72,600.00
5	Add lines 1 through 4	72,600.00			

Schedule M-2   Analysis of Partners' Capital Accounts

1	Balance at beginning of year		**6**	Distributions: **a** Cash	12,000.00
2	Capital contributed: **a** Cash			**b** Property	7,000.00
	b Property		**7**	Other decreases (itemize):	
3	Net income (loss) per books	47,900.00			
4	Other increases (itemize):		**8**	Add lines 6 and 7	19,000.00
5	Add lines 1 through 4	47,900.00	**9**	Balance at end of year. Subtract line 8 from line 5	28,900.00

Form **1065** (2015)

*Book income = $51,900 + $2,000 dividends + $1,000 capital gain − $7,000 contribution

EXHIBIT 9-1	Continued

651113

OMB No. 1545-0123

☐ Final K-1 ☐ Amended K-1

Schedule K-1
(Form 1065)

20**15**

Department of the Treasury
Internal Revenue Service

For calendar year 2015, or tax

year beginning _____ , 2015

ending _____ , 20 _____

Partner's Share of Income, Deductions, Credits, etc. ► See back of form and separate instructions.

Part III	Partner's Share of Current Year Income, Deductions, Credits, and Other Items

1	Ordinary business income (loss) 51,900	15	Credits U 2,000
2	Net rental real estate income (loss)		
3	Other net rental income (loss)	16	Foreign transactions
4	Guaranteed payments 24,700		
5	Interest income		
6a	Ordinary dividends 2,000		
6b	Qualified dividends 2,000		
7	Royalties		
8	Net short-term capital gain (loss)		
9a	Net long-term capital gain (loss) 1,000	17	Alternative minimum tax (AMT) items
9b	Collectibles (28%) gain (loss)		
9c	Unrecaptured section 1250 gain		
10	Net section 1231 gain (loss)	18	Tax-exempt income and nondeductible expenses
11	Other income (loss)		
12	Section 179 deduction	19	Distributions 19,000
13	Other deductions 7,000 Charitable Contribution	20	Other information
14	Self-employment earnings (loss) 76,600		

Part I **Information About the Partnership**

A Partnership's employer identification number
88 – 9138761

B Partnership's name, address, city, state, and ZIP code

T Company
1822 South 8th Street
Norfolk, VA 23508

C IRS Center where partnership filed return
Memphis, TN

D ☐ Check if this is a publicly traded partnership (PTP)

Part II **Information About the Partner**

E Partner's identifying number
467 – 63 – 5052

F Partner's name, address, city, state, and ZIP code
Adolph Z.T.
1291 Maple Street
Norfolk, VA 23508

G ☒ General partner or LLC member-manager   ☐ Limited partner or other LLC member

H ☒ Domestic partner   ☐ Foreign partner

I1 What type of entity is this partner? Individual

I2 If this partner is a retirement plan (IRA/SEP/Keogh/etc.), check here . . . . ☐

J Partner's share of profit, loss, and capital (see instructions):

	Beginning	Ending
Profit	100 %	100 %
Loss	80 %	80 %
Capital	80 %	80 %

K Partner's share of liabilities at year end:
Nonrecourse . . . . $ _____
Qualified nonrecourse financing . $ _____
Recourse . . . . $ 40,000

L Partner's capital account analysis:
Beginning capital account . . . $ _____ *
Capital contributed during the year $ _____
Current year increase (decrease) . $ 47,900 *
Withdrawals & distributions . . $ (19,000)
Ending capital account . . . . $ _____ *

☒ Tax basis ☐ GAAP ☐ Section 704(b) book
☐ Other (explain)

M Did the partner contribute property with a built-in gain or loss?
☐ Yes ☐ No
If "Yes," attach statement (see instructions)

*See attached statement for additional information.

For IRS Use Only

For Paperwork Reduction Act Notice, see Instructions for Form 1065.   IRS.gov/form1065   Cat. No. 11394R   **Schedule K-1 (Form 1065) 2015**

* Note this is not taxable income but book income ($51,900 ordinary income +
$2,000 dividends + $1,000 capital gain – $7,000 contribution)

	EXHIBIT 9-2	**Separately and Nonseparately Stated Items**

For each of the following items of income, deduction, loss, and credit an "×" in the appropriate column indicates whether the item is includible in a partnership's ordinary income or loss (reported on Form 1065, page 1, Schedule K, line 1; and Schedule K-1, line 1) or whether the item must be separately stated (reported on Schedules K and K-1, lines 2 and following).

		Ordinary Income or (Loss) (Form 1065, p. 1)	Separately Stated Item (Schedule K)	Reason
a.	Sales	×		No special partner treatment
b.	Income or loss from rental activities		×	Passive income or loss for § 469 purpose
c.	Dividends		×	Investment (portfolio) income
d.	Taxable interest		×	Investment (portfolio) income
e.	Tax-exempt interest		×	May affect partner deduction under § 265
f.	Cost of sales	×		No special partner treatment
g.	State and local taxes	×		No special partner treatment
h.	Net long-term capital gain or loss		×	Requires netting at partner level
i.	Net short-term capital gain or loss		×	Requires netting at partner level
j.	Net gain from sales of collectibles		×	Requires netting at partner level
k.	Net unrecaptured § 1250 gain		×	Requires netting at partner level
l.	Gain from sales of qualified small business stock		×	Requires netting at partner level
m.	Charitable contribution		×	Subject to limitation at partner level
n.	Foreign income		×	Required for foreign tax credit computation
o.	Foreign taxes		×	Subject to limitation at partner level
p.	Medical expenses		×	Subject to AGI limitation of partner, not deductible by partnership
q.	Investment interest		×	Subject to investment interest limitation
r.	MACRS or ACRS on plant and equipment	×	×	Subject to AMT tax liability at partner level*
s.	Recovery of a bad debt		×	Subject to § 111 determination at partner level*
t.	Advertising	×		No special partner treatment
u.	Repairs and maintenance	×		No special partner treatment
v.	Expenses for production of income (§ 212)		×	Miscellaneous itemized deduction at partner level
w.	All credits		×	Subject to tax liability at partner level

* Any preference or adjustment resulting from the use of accelerated depreciation must be separately reported, along with any § 179 expense.

The character of any item of partnership income, gain, deduction, or loss is determined with reference to the activities of the partnership rather than the activities of the individual partners.[53] For example, gain on the sale of land held by a partnership as an investment for two years is long-term capital gain. This characterization holds even if some of the partners to whom the gain will be taxed are real estate developers in whose hands the land would have been inventory. Similarly, the gain is long-term even if some of the partners have owned their partnership interests for less than one year.[54]

Section 724 contains three exceptions to the general rule that tax characteristics are determined at the partnership level.

---

[53] § 702(b).   [54] Rev. Rul. 67-188, 1967-1 C.B. 216.

1. In the case of unrealized receivables contributed to the partnership by a partner, any gain or loss recognized when the partnership disposes of the receivables must be treated as ordinary gain or loss.

2. In the case of inventory contributed to the partnership by a partner, any gain or loss recognized on disposition within the five-year period subsequent to contribution must be treated as ordinary gain or loss.

3. In the case of a capital asset contributed to the partnership by a partner, any loss recognized on disposition within the five-year period subsequent to contribution must be treated as capital loss to the extent the basis of the asset exceeded its fair market value at date of contribution.

Example 20

Three years ago, D exchanged land that he held as an investment ($50,000 fair market value and $65,000 basis) and an inventory asset from his sole proprietorship ($20,000 fair market value and $18,000 basis) for an interest in the DEF Partnership. Both assets had a carryover basis to the partnership under § 723. Both contributed assets were used in the partnership business, and therefore were characterized as § 1231 assets at the partnership level. During the current year, the partnership sold both assets, realizing a $22,000 loss on the sale of the land and a $3,500 gain on the sale of the former inventory asset.

Because the sales took place within the five-year period subsequent to contribution, the partnership must recognize $15,000 of the loss on the land sale (excess of $65,000 contributed basis over $50,000 contributed value) as capital loss and the $7,000 remainder as § 1231 loss. The partnership must recognize the entire gain on the sale of the former inventory as ordinary income. If the sales had taken place after the expiration of the five-year period, both the recognized loss and gain would have been § 1231 in nature.[55]

REPORTING OF PARTNERSHIP ITEMS BY PARTNERS

LO.7

Explain how the tax consequences of partnership operations are reported on the tax returns of the partners and how the partners' bases in their partnership interests are adjusted to reflect these tax consequences.

Partners must take into account their distributive shares of partnership ordinary income and any separately stated partnership items in computing their taxable incomes.[56] This pass-through of partnership items to the partners is deemed to occur on the last day of the partnership's taxable year. Consequently, the pass-through items are included in each partner's return for the partner's taxable year within which the partnership year ends.[57]

Each partner's distributive share of every partnership item is reported on a Schedule K-1 for that partner (see Exhibit 9-1). Partnerships must include a copy of each Schedule K-1 with the annual partnership return filed with the IRS. A second copy is transmitted to each partner. Rev. Proc. 2012–17 provides that if the partner consents, the K-1 can be transmitted electronically. Upon receipt, partners must incorporate the information reported on the Schedule K-1 into their tax. However, the Schedule K-1 is not included in the partner's tax return.

---

[55] § 704(c) also requires a special allocation of both loss and gain among the partners. This allocation rule is discussed in a later section of the chapter.

[56] § 702(a). Section 772(a) provides a simplified reporting system for certain electing large partnerships. Large

nonservice partnerships with 100 or more members can elect to reduce the number of items that must be separately reported to their numerous partners. See §§ 771 through 777.

[57] § 706(a).

Example 21

Mr. A and B Inc. are calendar year taxpayers and equal partners in the AB Partnership, which uses a September 30 fiscal year-end for tax purposes. In December 2016, each partner received a Schedule K-1 showing the following results of partnership operations from October 1, 2015 through September 30, 2016:

Ordinary income from business activities (partnership taxable income)	$42,300
Dividend income	2,300
Net long-term capital loss	(4,000)
Investment interest expense	(5,500)
Charitable contributions	(1,900)

Individual A will include his $42,300 share of ordinary business income on Schedule E, his $2,300 share of dividend income on Schedule B, and his $4,000 share of the long-term capital loss on Schedule D of his 2016 Form 1040. Per § 163(d), A's $5,500 share of investment interest expense is deductible only to the extent of his net investment income for 2016. Furthermore, the deductible portion of the interest expense and A's $1,900 share of the charitable contribution must be reported as itemized deductions on Schedule A, Form 1040.

Corporation B will include both its $42,300 share of ordinary business income and its $5,500 share of investment interest expense on page 1, and its $4,000 share of long-term capital loss on Schedule D of its 2016 Form 1120. [Corporations are not subject to the § 163(d) limitation.] B will include its $2,300 share of dividend income on Schedule C (Dividends and Special Deductions) and will compute an appropriate dividends-received deduction. B's $1,900 share of the charitable contribution may be deducted on page 1 of Form 1120 to the extent that the corporation's total charitable contributions for 2016 do not exceed 10% of taxable income.

SELF-EMPLOYMENT INCOME AND ESTIMATED TAX PAYMENTS

Individuals who are general partners in business partnerships must report their distributive shares of partnership ordinary income plus any guaranteed payments received for services performed for the partnership as self-employment income subject to the federal self-employment tax.[58] For this purpose, self-employment income does not include any depreciation recapture income. In contrast, individuals who are limited partners have self-employment income only if they receive a guaranteed payment as compensation for services performed for the partnership.[59]

Individual partners are required to make quarterly estimate payments of both the income tax and self-employment tax attributable to their distributive share of partnership income for the year.[60] In computing the required amount of each quarterly payment, a partner must take into account his or her estimated share of partnership income attributable to those months in the partnership year that precede the month in which the installment date falls.[61]

Example 22

T is a general partner in the TUV Partnership. Both T and the partnership use a calendar year for tax purposes. During the current year, T's only source of income is his distributive share of TUV's taxable income. T must base his first quarterly payment for the year (due on April 15) on his estimate of TUV's income for the first three months of the year.

---

[58] § 1402(a). Guaranteed payments are discussed later in the chapter.

[59] However, note that in 2011 the Tax Court ruled that partners in limited liability companies who are active in the business are subject to self-employment taxes [*Renkemeyer, Campbell & Weaver, LLC v. Comm.*, 136 T.C. No. 7 (Feb. 9, 2011)].

[60] § 6654.

[61] Reg. § 1.6654-2(d)(2).

ADJUSTMENTS TO PARTNER'S BASIS

A partner's distributive share of annual partnership income is determined without reference to actual cash distributions made by the partnership to its partners. If a partner's share of annual partnership income exceeds any cash received from the partnership during the year, the undistributed income will be recorded as an increase in that partner's capital account balance (his or her equity in the partnership) at year-end. On the other hand, in a year in which a partnership operates at a loss, a partner's share of such loss will be recorded as a capital account decrease.

The fluctuating nature of a partnership investment is also reflected in the basis of the partner's interest in the partnership. Outside basis is *increased* by a partner's distributive share of both taxable and nontaxable partnership income.[62] Outside basis is *decreased* by distributions made by the partnership to the partner and by the partner's distributive share of partnership losses and nondeductible current expenditures.[63] These basis adjustments are made in the above order at the end of the partnership taxable year.[64] Even if cash distributions representing advances or draws against a partner's share of current income are made at various dates throughout the year, the effect of these distributions on basis is determined as of the last day of the year.[65]

Example 23

M owns a 40% interest in the capital, profits, and losses of the KLMN Partnership. Both M and KLMN use a calendar year for tax purposes. At the beginning of the current year, M's outside basis in her partnership interest was $35,000. During the year, M received four cash distributions of $5,000 each as advances against her share of current-year income. At the end of the year, the partnership has $20,000 of nonrecourse debt. M's Schedule K-1 for the current year showed the following distributive shares:

Ordinary income	$33,000
Tax-exempt interest income	4,000
Net long-term capital gain	8,100
Nondeductible penalty	(1,700)
Nondeductible 50% business meals and entertainment	(600)

As of the last day of the current year, M's outside basis is increased by $8,000 ($20,000 × 40%) for her share of the debt and by $45,100 (her share of partnership taxable and tax-exempt income), decreased by the $20,000 of cash distributions made during the year, and decreased by $2,300 (her share of the partnership nondeductible current expenses). Consequently, M's outside basis as of the first day of the next taxable year is $65,800.

Partners' Distributive Shares

The income or loss generated by a business conducted in partnership form is measured and characterized at the partnership level, then allocated to the various partners for inclusion on their income tax returns. Each partner's *distributive share* of any item of partnership income, gain, loss, deduction, or credit is determined by reference to the partnership agreement.[66] Consequently, the partners themselves can decide exactly how the profits or losses from their business are to be shared. The sharing arrangement as specified in the partnership agreement can be an equal allocation of profits and losses to each partner or a more elaborate arrangement under which different items of gain or loss are shared in different ratios among different categories of partners.

Although partners certainly have a great deal of flexibility in determining the allocation of partnership income and loss, § 704(b) warns that such allocations must have *substantial economic effect* if they are to be respected by the Internal Revenue Service. If the IRS concludes that the allocation of any partnership item lacks substantial economic effect,

---

[62] § 705(a)(1).

[63] § 705(a)(2).

[64] Reg. § 1.705-1(a).

[65] Reg. § 1.731-1(a)(1)(ii).

[66] § 704(a).

it may reallocate the item among the partners. Such reallocation will be based upon the partners' true economic interests in the partnership, as determined by the IRS upon examination of all relevant facts and circumstances.

SUBSTANTIAL ECONOMIC EFFECT

Treasury regulations provide an intricate set of rules for determining whether partnership allocations meet the substantial economic effect test of § 704(b). The basic objective of the regulations is to "ensure that any allocation is consistent with the underlying economic arrangement of the partners. This means that in the event there is an economic benefit or economic burden that corresponds to an allocation, the partner to whom the allocation is made must receive such economic benefit or bear such economic burden."[67] The economic benefit or burden of an allocation equates to the impact of the allocation on a partner's interest in partnership capital. In other words, an allocation of income or loss for tax purposes must correspond to an allocation of dollars to or from a partner's capital account on the partnership books.

> **LO.8**
> Define the term *substantial economic effect* and describe other limitations on allocations of partnership items to partners.

The regulations attempt to ensure this correspondence through a three-pronged test for economic effect.[68] Any allocation for tax purposes will have economic effect only if the following three conditions are met:

1. The allocation is reflected in the partners' capital accounts for book purposes.
2. Upon liquidation of the partnership, liquidating distributions of cash and property are made to the partners based on the balances in their capital accounts.
3. Partners with deficit balances in their capital accounts upon liquidation are unconditionally required to restore such deficit balance to the partnership. (This obligation may be expressly stated in the partnership agreement or imposed by state law.)[69]

Example 24

The RST Partnership agreement provides that taxable income or loss will be allocated 50% to R and 25% respectively to S and T. The agreement provides that this allocation will be reflected in the partnership capital accounts, that liquidating distributions will be based on capital account balances, and that any partner with a deficit capital account balance must restore the deficit immediately prior to liquidation.

For the current year, the RST Partnership generated $48,000 taxable income, $24,000 of which was reported as R's distributive share on his Schedule K-1 and $12,000 of which was reported as S and T's respective distributive shares on their Schedules K-1. Each partner's capital account was increased by the amount of income reported as his distributive share for tax purposes. Because the allocation meets the three-pronged test, it has economic effect and should be respected by the IRS.

Note that in the above example, the taxable income allocated to each partner matched the increase in each partner's capital account balance for the year. Moreover, upon liquidation of the partnership, the partners will receive an amount of dollars (or property) equal to the balances in their capital accounts. Contrast this result with that in the following example.

Example 25

The XYZ partnership agreement provides that taxable income or loss will be allocated 50% to X and 25% respectively to Y and Z. The agreement states that for book purposes income will be allocated equally to each partner. For the current year, the XYZ Partnership generated $48,000 of taxable income, $24,000 of which was reported as X's distributive share on his Schedule K-1 and $12,000 of which was reported as Y and Z's respective distributive shares on their Schedules K-1. However, each partner's capital account on the partnership books was increased by $16,000.

---

[67] Reg. § 1.704-1(b)(2)(ii)(a).

[68] The additional requirement that economic effect be *substantial* is discussed in Reg. § 1.704-1(b)(2)(iii).

Any discussion of this difficult regulation is beyond the scope of this text.

[69] Reg. § 1.704-1(b)(2)(ii)(c).

In this example, the allocation of taxable income fails to reflect the allocation of dollars to the partners. Because this tax allocation obviously lacks economic effect, the IRS can reallocate the taxable income to the partners based upon its determination of how the partners actually intend to share the economic benefit of the income. The facts of this simple example indicate that X, Y, and Z intend to share the dollars generated by their partnership business equally. Consequently, the IRS will allocate $16,000 of current year taxable income to each partner.

Example 26

The ABC Partnership agreement provides that taxable income or loss will be allocated equally to partners A, B, and C. The agreement also states that this allocation will be reflected in the partnership capital accounts. The agreement provides that when the partnership liquidates, 40% of all liquidating distributions will be made to A, while 30% of such distributions will be made to B and C, respectively.

The tax allocation in *Example 26* lacks economic effect because it violates the second requirement of the three-pronged test. Although the current-year tax allocation is reflected by an increase in each partner's capital account balance, such balances will not control when the final distribution of partnership dollars is made. Regardless of capital account balances, A will receive 40% of any liquidating distribution, and B and C will each receive 30% of such distribution. Because the facts indicate that the economic sharing arrangement among A, B, and C does not correspond to their equal allocation of taxable income, the IRS may reallocate such income in the ratio (40 percent, 30 percent, 30 percent) in which the partners will ultimately divide up the partnership assets.

Example 27

The RS Partnership agreement provides that taxable income or loss will be allocated equally between partners R and S. The agreement also states that this allocation will be reflected in the partnership capital accounts, that liquidating distributions will be based on capital account balances, and that any partner with a deficit capital account balance must restore the deficit immediately prior to liquidation. At the beginning of the current year, the partnership balance sheet showed the following:

Assets	$70,000			
		Capital:	R	$50,000
			S	20,000
				$70,000

For the current year, the RS Partnership generated a $60,000 net operating loss, $30,000 of which was reported as R and S's respective distributive shares on their Schedules K-1. Each partner's capital account was reduced by the amount of loss reported as his distributive share for tax purposes. As of the close of the year, the partnership balance sheet showed the following:

Assets	$10,000			
		Capital:	R	$20,000
			S	(10,000)
				$10,000

If the partnership were to liquidate as of the close of the current year, S would be obligated to restore his $10,000 deficit account balance by contributing $10,000 to the partnership. The $20,000 of partnership assets could then be distributed to R in accordance with his capital account balance. Because of S's deficit restoration obligation, his $30,000 allocated tax loss for the year matches his potential $30,000 economic loss. Consequently, the tax allocation has economic effect.

If the RS Partnership agreement or state law failed to obligate S to restore his $10,000 deficit balance, only $20,000 of the $30,000 current-year tax loss allocated to S would have economic effect. S would not be required to contribute $10,000 to the partnership upon liquidation, and his economic loss would be limited to the $20,000 reduction in his capital account for the current year. Because of the insufficiency of partnership assets, the liquidating distribution to R would be $10,000 less than the balance in his capital account. Consequently, R's economic loss would exceed his allocated tax loss by $10,000. In such case, the IRS could restore equilibrium between the tax allocation and the dollar impact of the current-year loss by reallocating $10,000 of the loss for tax purposes from S to R.

ALLOCATIONS WITH RESPECT TO CONTRIBUTED PROPERTY

When a partner contributes property to a partnership and the value of such property is more or less than the contributing partner's tax basis in the property, subsequent allocations of taxable income, gain, loss, and deduction with respect to the contributed property will lack substantial economic effect within the meaning of § 704(b).

Example 28

M contributed an asset (fair market value $20,000, adjusted basis $14,000) and N contributed $20,000 cash to M&N Partnership in exchange for a one-half interest in partnership capital, profits, and losses. The asset contributed by M was recorded on the partnership books at $20,000 but had a carryover tax basis to the partnership of $14,000. The capital accounts for both M and N were credited with the $20,000 values of their respective contributions. Three months after its formation, the partnership sold the contributed asset for $20,000. For tax purposes, the partnership recognized a $6,000 gain on sale. For book purposes, the partnership realized no gain and made no entry to either partner's capital account.

Because of the initial difference between the contributed *value* and the contributed *basis* of the asset in the above example, the taxable gain on the sale did not equal the gain realized for book purposes. Consequently, any allocation of the taxable gain to the partners did not have substantial economic effect because the allocation would not be reflected in book capital accounts.

Section 704(c) solves this problem by mandating a special allocation rule for items of income, gain, loss, and deduction attributable to contributed assets.[70] Essentially, any difference between the amount of the item for tax purposes and for book purposes at the time of contribution must be allocated to the contributing partner when the partnership disposes of the asset. The remainder of the item is allocated for both tax and book purposes according to the sharing ratios specified in the partnership agreement. The application of this special rule to the $6,000 taxable gain recognized in *Example 28* results in an allocation of the entire $6,000 gain to contributing partner M. Note that this amount of gain equals the deferred gain that M was not required to recognize upon the contribution of the appreciated asset to the partnership.

---

[70] The following discussion reflects the *traditional method* of making § 704(c) allocations as prescribed in Reg. § 1.704-3(b). Any discussion of the alternate methods allowed in the regulation is beyond the scope of this text.

Example 29

O contributed an asset (FMV $20,000, adjusted basis $26,000) and P contributed $20,000 cash to O&P Partnership in exchange for a one-half interest in partnership capital, profits, and losses. The asset contributed by O was recorded on the partnership books at $20,000 but had a carryover tax basis to the partnership of $26,000. The capital accounts for both O and P were credited with the $20,000 values of their respective contributions. Seven months after its formation, the partnership sold the contributed asset for $17,000. For tax purposes, the partnership recognized a $9,000 loss on sale, while for book purposes it realized only a $3,000 loss (the decline in the value of the asset subsequent to its contribution to the partnership). The first $6,000 of the tax loss must be allocated to contributing Partner O. The remaining $3,000 loss is allocated equally between O and P.

The effect of the contributions and the subsequent allocation of the tax loss on the partners' outside bases in their partnership interests and their capital accounts are shown in the following table.

	Partner O		Partner P	
	Outside Basis in PS Interest	*Capital Account*	*Outside Basis in PS Interest*	*Capital Account*
Initial contribution	$26,000	$20,000	$20,000	$20,000
Allocation of tax loss on sale	(7,500)		(1,500)	
Allocation of book loss on sale.	0	(1,500)	0	(1,500)
Total	$18,500	$18,500	$18,500	$18,500

This table emphasizes two important points concerning the mandatory allocation rule of § 704(c). First, the allocation eliminates the difference between contributing partner O's initial outside basis and his initial capital account. Second, the allocation gives the two equal partners an equal outside basis in their partnership interests.

Section 704(c) affects the allocation of depreciation deductions attributable to contributed property as well as allocations of gains and losses recognized by the partnership upon disposition of the property. These tax depreciation deductions are first allocated to the noncontributing partners in an amount equal to their allocable share of book depreciation (depreciation computed on the contributed value of the property). Any remaining tax depreciation is allocated to the partner who contributed the property.

Example 30

D contributed a depreciable asset (fair market value $60,000, adjusted basis $48,000) and E contributed $120,000 cash to DEF Partnership in exchange for a one-third and a two-thirds interest respectively in partnership capital, profits, and losses. The partnership will depreciate the asset over five years on a straight-line basis. In each year, tax depreciation on the contributed asset is $9,600 (20% of the $48,000 contributed basis), while book depreciation is $12,000 (20% of the $60,000 contributed value). Two-thirds and one-third of the book depreciation is allocated to E and D, respectively. Each year noncontributing partner E is allocated the first $8,000 of tax depreciation (her two-thirds share of the $12,000 book depreciation). The remaining $1,600 of the annual tax depreciation is allocated to contributing partner D.

The effects of the contributions and the subsequent special allocation of the tax depreciation on the partners' outside basis in their partnership interests and their capital accounts are shown in the following table.

	Partner D		Partner E	
	Outside Basis in PS Interest	Capital Account	Outside Basis in PS Interest	Capital Account
Initial contribution	$48,000	$60,000	$120,000	$120,000
Allocation of tax depreciation for five years	(8,000)		(40,000)	
Allocation of book depreciation for five years	0	(20,000)	0	(40,000)
Total	$40,000	$40,000	$ 80,000	$ 80,000

Note that at the end of the five-year period over which both the asset's tax basis and book basis are depreciated to zero, the special § 704(c) allocation of tax depreciation has resulted in an equalization of D's outside basis in his partnership interest and his capital account as well as a restoration of the one-third/two-thirds ratio between D and E's outside bases in their partnership interests. Unfortunately, the special allocation rule may not always work to produce this desired result. The Treasury Regulations under Section 704(c) contain a *ceiling rule* limiting the special allocation of taxable gain, loss, and depreciation attributable to contributed property to the total amount of such gain, loss, or depreciation recognized by the partnership for the year.[71]

Example 31

Refer to the facts in *Example 30*. If the contributed basis of D's asset had been $36,000 rather than $48,000, annual tax depreciation would be only $7,200. This total amount is less than noncontributing partner E's $8,000 share of book depreciation. Nonetheless, only $7,200 of tax depreciation can be allocated to E because of the ceiling rule.

As another example of the ceiling rule, if in *Example 28* the partnership had sold the asset for $18,000, the gain of $4,000 ($18,000 − $14,000) would be allocated to M. Even though the precontribution gain was $6,000 for the asset, the ceiling rule limits the allocation of gain to M to $4,000 since that was all the gain recognized from the sale.

RETROACTIVE ALLOCATIONS

In addition to the substantial economic effect requirement of § 704(b) and the special allocation rule of § 704(c), the determination of each partner's annual distributive share of partnership income, gain, loss, deduction, or credit must take into account any change in the partner's equity interest in the partnership during the year.[72] This *varying interest rule* was enacted to prevent retroactive allocations of partnership items to new partners who were admitted to the partnership after the items were recognized or incurred.

---

[71] Reg. § 1.704-3(b)(1).   [72] § 706(d)(1).

Example 32

K and L have been equal partners in the calendar year cash basis K&L Partnership since 2011. On November 1 of the current year, M contributed $100,000 cash in exchange for a one-third interest in partnership capital. The partnership generated a $108,000 operating loss for the current taxable year. The maximum amount of this loss that can be allocated to M under the revised partnership agreement among K, L, and M is $18,049, the portion of the loss attributable to the last 61 days of the year during which M owned an interest in the partnership. Note that this allocation represents a 100% loss-sharing allocation for M, even though M owns only a one-third capital interest.

In *Example 32,* the amount of the annual operating loss attributable to the last two months of the year was determined by a daily proration of the loss. As an alternative, K&L could perform an interim closing of its books on October 31 in order to determine the precise amount of the loss incurred before and after the admittance of partner M.[73] Under this alternative, K&L might be tempted to inflate the amount of loss attributable to the period of time subsequent to M's admission by delaying payment of deductible expenses until year-end. The statute forestalls this planning technique by requiring cash basis partnerships to use the accrual method to account for certain items during a year in which a new partner is admitted. Such items include payments for interest, taxes, services, the use of property, and any other item specified in Treasury regulations.[74]

Example 33

Partner T was admitted to the calendar year cash basis RST Partnership on December 1 of the current year. On December 15, RST paid $36,000 of rent attributable to the last 4 months of the current year and $15,600 of property taxes attributable to the 12-month period beginning on January 1 of the current year. In computing the results of operations subsequent to the admission of partner T, the partnership may deduct only $9,000 (one month) of the rent payment and $1,300 (one month) of the tax payment.

BASIS LIMITATION ON LOSS DEDUCTIBILITY

LO.9

Compute the three potential limitations on the current deductibility of a partner's distributive share of partnership loss.

Under § 704(d), a partner's distributive share of partnership loss is deductible only to the extent of the partner's outside basis in his or her partnership interest as of the end of the partnership year in which the loss was incurred. Any nondeductible portion of a current-year loss is carried forward indefinitely into future years and can be deducted if and when sufficient outside basis is restored. This loss limitation rule is applied only after a partner's basis has been increased by any distributive share of current year partnership income and decreased by any distributions made to the partner for the year.[75]

---

[73] Reg. § 1.706-1(c)(2)(ii).

[74] § 706(d)(2).

[75] Reg. § 1.704-1(d)(2).

Example 34

F is a partner in the calendar year DEFG Partnership. At the beginning of the current year, F's outside basis in her partnership interest was $14,500. During the year, F received a $3,000 cash distribution from DEFG. At the close of the year, Schedule K-1 showed that her distributive share of the partnership's current year operating loss was $20,000, while her shares of current year dividends and long-term capital gains were $3,400 and $1,300 respectively. F will increase her outside basis by $4,700 (her share of partnership income) and decrease it by the $3,000 cash distribution. Under § 704(d), F may deduct her allocated partnership loss only to the extent of her $16,200 remaining outside basis, thereby reducing her year-end basis to zero. The $3,800 nondeductible portion of F's loss will carry forward into subsequent taxable years.

F's January 1 outside basis	$14,500
Plus: Allocated share of income	4,700
Less: Distributions	(3,000)
Deductible share of allocated loss	(16,200)
F's December 31 outside basis	$ 0
F's loss carryforward	$ 3,800

If a partner is allocated a distributive share of more than one type of loss and the partner's outside basis is insufficient to absorb the aggregate amount of losses, the § 704(d) limitation is applied proportionately to each type of loss.[76]

Example 35

Refer to the facts in *Example 34*, but assume that F is allocated a $6,000 § 1231 loss in addition to the $20,000 operating loss. F's currently deductible amounts of each type of loss are computed as follows:

Operating loss:	($20,000 ÷ $26,000) × $16,200 =	$12,462
§ 1231 loss:	($ 6,000 ÷ $26,000) × $16,200 =	$ 3,738

The nondeductible $7,538 operating loss and $2,262 § 1231 loss are carried forward into the subsequent year.

ADDITIONAL LOSS LIMITATIONS

Even when a partner has sufficient year-end basis in his or her partnership interest to avoid the § 704 limitation, the sequential application of two additional statutory limitations may result in nondeductibility for some portion, or even all, of the current year partnership loss. These additional limitations are not located in Subchapter K, and apply to all types of business losses—not just to those generated by partnerships. Moreover, these limitations only apply to individual taxpayers and certain closely held corporations. Consequently, they have no impact on partnership losses allocated to many corporate partners.

---

[76] Reg. § 1.704-1(d)(2).

At-Risk Limitation

Under § 465(a), individuals and certain closely held corporations engaged in any business or income-producing activity may deduct their share of losses from the activity only to the extent of their *at-risk amount* in such activity. For activities conducted in the partnership form, a partner's at-risk amount corresponds very closely to the outside basis in the partnership interest. The major difference between the two is any nonrecourse debt included in the partner's basis under § 752(a). Any debt for which a partner is not personally liable is generally excluded from his or her at-risk amount.[77] The major exception to the rule is *qualified nonrecourse financing*, defined as nonrecourse debt incurred in a real estate activity and borrowed from a commercial lender, such as a bank or savings and loan association.[78]

Example 36

Limited partner L and general partner G own equal interests in the L&G Partnership, which purchases, develops, and manages commercial real estate. At the end of the current year, the partnership has $15,000 of recourse debt, all of which is allocated to G for inclusion in the basis of her partnership interest, and $100,000 of nonrecourse debt, $50,000 of which is allocated to both L and G for inclusion in their bases. Only $40,000 of the nonrecourse debt is qualified nonrecourse financing.

Of the $65,000 total debt included in G's basis, only $35,000 ($15,000 recourse debt for which G is personally liable + $20,000 qualified nonrecourse financing) is included in her at-risk amount. Of the $50,000 of debt included in L's partnership basis, only the $20,000 of qualified nonrecourse financing is included in his at-risk amount.

A partner's at-risk amount with respect to a partnership is reduced by any partnership losses currently allowed as a deduction under § 465(a).[79] To the extent that a partner's distributive share of current-year partnership losses exceeds his or her at-risk amount, such nondeductible excess may be carried forward into future years and deducted if and when the partner increases his or her at-risk amount above zero.[80]

Example 37

Partner J, an individual taxpayer, was allocated a $36,000 loss for the current year from the JKLM Partnership. Before consideration of this loss, J's basis in his partnership interest was $25,000, while his at-risk amount in the partnership was only $18,000. Under § 704(d), J may deduct only $25,000 of his allocated loss. Consequently, the outside basis in his partnership interest is reduced to zero and he has an $11,000 loss carryforward for § 704(d) purposes. Unfortunately, the at-risk rules further limit the current deductibility of the $25,000 loss to only $18,000. J's at-risk amount is also reduced to zero and he has a second loss carryforward of $7,000 for § 465 purposes.

Passive-Activity Limitation

Partnership losses that escape limitation under § 704(d) and § 465 face a third and final obstacle in the form of the § 469 limitation on *passive-activity losses*. If a partnership interest represents a passive activity, the partner's distributive share of partnership losses can be deducted only against current income from other passive activities; the losses cannot

---

[77] § 465(b)(2)(A).

[78] § 465(b)(6)(B).

[79] § 465(b)(5).

[80] § 465(a)(2).

be deducted against the partner's earned income, income from nonpassive business activities, or portfolio income (i.e., investment income such as interest and dividends).[81] Any nondeductible passive-activity loss with respect to the partnership is suspended and carried forward into future taxable years. Such loss can be deducted against future passive-activity income or against any type of income in the year in which the partner disposes of the partnership interest in a fully taxable transaction.[82]

Example 38

Refer to the facts in *Example 37*. If J's partnership interest is not a passive activity within the meaning of § 469, J may deduct $18,000 of his $36,000 distributive share of partnership loss against any type of current year income. If, however, the interest is a passive activity, the $18,000 loss is only deductible to the extent of J's current year income from other passive activities. If J has no passive-activity income for the current year, the entire $18,000 loss is suspended and carried forward for § 469 purposes.

A partnership interest is considered a passive activity if (1) the partnership conducts an active trade or business in which the partner does not *materially participate,* or (2) the partnership conducts a rental activity. A partner is treated as materially participating in a partnership business only if the partner is involved in the day-to-day operation of the business on a regular, continuous, and substantial basis.[83] The statute specifies that limited partners, by definition, cannot materially participate in a partnership business.[84] Note that the classification of an interest in an active business partnership depends upon each partner's relationship to the business.

Example 39

Corporation A (which is neither closely held nor a personal service corporation) and individuals B, C, and D are equal partners in the ABCD Partnership. A and B are limited partners. C and D are general partners; however, only C materially participates in the partnership business. For the current year, each partner's distributive share of partnership loss is $20,000. The losses are not limited under either § 704(d) or § 465.

Section 469 is not applicable to corporate partner A so that A's share of the loss is fully deductible on A's current year Form 1120. Because individual B is a limited partner, her share of the loss is a passive-activity loss. Because C materially participates in the partnership business, his share of the loss is a fully deductible business loss not subject to the § 469 limitation. Because D does not materially participate, her share of the loss is a passive-activity loss.

Rental Real Estate Exception

If a partnership operates a rental activity, such activity is passive regardless of the level of participation by any of the partners.[85] Section 469(i) contains an important exception to the passive activity loss limitation for the first $25,000 of losses attributable to rental real estate activities in which a partner actively participates during the year. This *active participation*

---

[81] Per § 469(a)(2), individuals, fiduciaries, closely held C corporations, and personal service corporations are subject to the passive-activity loss limitation. However, closely held corporations that are not personal service corporations may offset passive-activity losses against net active business income. § 469(e)(2).

[82] See § 469(g)(1).

[83] § 469(h)(1). Temp. Reg. § 1.469-5T provides extensive guidance on the material participation standard.

[84] § 469(h)(2).

[85] The Revenue Reconciliation Act of 1993 amended § 469 to provide that *real estate professionals* engaged in a *real property trade or business* are conducting a business, rather than a rental activity. Consequently, if the real estate professional meets the material participation requirement, losses from the activity are not subject to the § 469 limitation.

requirement is less stringent than the material participation standard for nonrental business activities. A partner actively participates in a partnership real estate rental activity if (1) the partner owns at least a 10% interest in the activity, and (2) the partner is involved in significant management decisions concerning the rental property. Again, the statute specifies that limited partners are deemed not to meet this active participation standard.[86]

The rental real estate exception is phased out for individuals whose adjusted gross incomes exceed $100,000. The $25,000 maximum exception is reduced by one dollar for every two dollars of adjusted gross income in excess of the $100,000 threshold. Thus, the exception is completely eliminated for taxpayers with adjusted gross incomes greater than $150,000.

Example 40

Individuals M and N each own a 25% general interest in the MNOP partnership, which manages rental real estate. Both partners are involved in making management decisions concerning the partnership's various rental properties. For the current year, both M and N are allocated $40,000 of partnership loss. These losses are not limited under either § 704(d) or § 465. Neither partner has any passive-activity income for the year.

Before consideration of such loss, M's adjusted gross income is $95,000. Consequently, M may deduct $25,000 of his allocated loss against any source of current year income. The $15,000 remainder of the loss is a passive-activity loss.

Before consideration of such a loss, N's adjusted gross income is $112,000. N may deduct only $19,000 of her allocated loss ($25,000 − [$12,000 excess AGI ÷ 2]) against any other source of current-year income. The $21,000 remainder of the loss is a passive-activity loss.

Transactions between Partners and Partnerships

LO.10

Determine the tax consequences of various transactions between a partner and a partnership.

Under the entity theory, a partner and a partnership are separate and distinct entities that can transact with each other at arm's length. This perspective is adopted in § 707(a), which states that "if a partner engages in a transaction with a partnership other than in his capacity as a member of such partnership, the transaction shall, except as otherwise provided in this section, be considered as occurring between the partnership and one who is not a partner." Because of this general rule, a partner can assume the role of unrelated third party when dealing with the partnership. For example, a partner can lend money to or borrow money from a partnership, rent property to or from a partnership, buy property from or sell property to a partnership, or provide consulting services to a partnership as an independent contractor. The tax consequences of all the above transactions will be determined as if the partnership were dealing with a nonpartner.[87]

The major exception to the general rule of § 707(a) concerns partners who work in the partnership business on a regular and ongoing basis. The point was made earlier in the chapter that general partners are considered self-employed individuals, rather than employees of their partnership. Consequently, partners cannot be paid a salary or wage by the partnership, even if they perform exactly the same duties as nonpartner employees. However, partners who work in a partnership business certainly expect to be compensated for their time and effort. The tax consequences of compensatory payments made by partnerships to partners in their capacities as such are governed by § 707(c). The annual amounts of such payments are typically determined with reference to the extent and nature of the services performed, without regard to the income of the partnership for that year. Such *guaranteed payments* must be recognized as ordinary income by the recipient partner. The partnership will either deduct the guaranteed payment as a § 162 business expense or capitalize it to an appropriate asset account as required by § 263.[88]

---

[86] § 469(i)(6)(C).

[87] Under § 267(a)(2), a payment made by an accrual basis taxpayer to a cash basis related party may not be deducted by the payor until the taxable year in which the payee includes the payment in gross income. Under § 267(e), a partnership and any partner are related parties for purposes of this matching rule. The rule does not apply to § 707(c) guaranteed payments.

[88] Guaranteed payments can also be made with respect to a partner's capital account. Such payments are functionally equivalent to interest, always represent ordinary income to the recipient partner, and will be either deducted or capitalized by the partnership.

Example 41

P has a one-third interest in the calendar year OPQ Partnership. Unlike partners O and Q, P works in the partnership business on a full-time basis. The partnership agreement provides that for the current year P will receive a monthly guaranteed payment of $4,000 from the partnership. The partnership business generates $175,000 of annual income before consideration of P's guaranteed payment.

Based on the nature of the work performed by P, the partnership may claim a current deduction for the guaranteed payment; accordingly its net income for the year is $127,000 ($175,000 − $48,000 total guaranteed payments), and each partner's one-third distributive share is $42,333. P will report total partnership income for the year of $90,333 ($48,000 guaranteed payment + $42,333 distributive share), while O and Q will each report only their $42,333 distributive shares of income.

Example 42

Assume the same facts as in *Example 41*, except that the OPQ Partnership generates only $30,000 of annual income before consideration of P's guaranteed payment. In this case, the deduction of the payment results in an $18,000 net *loss* of which each partner's distributive share is $6,000. P will report total partnership income for the year of $42,000 ($48,000 guaranteed payment − $6,000 loss), while O and Q will each report only their $6,000 distributive shares of loss.

From an economic perspective, a guaranteed payment received by a partner is functionally equivalent to a salary received by an employee. Nonetheless, for tax purposes several important differences distinguish the two. An employer is required by law to withhold federal, state, and local income taxes and employee payroll taxes from an employee's salary. Guaranteed payments are not subject to any similar withholding requirement. At the end of each calendar year, employees receive a Form W-2 on which gross annual compensation and various withheld amounts are summarized. Guaranteed payments are reported only as a line item on the recipient partner's Schedule K-1 issued by the partnership. Finally, while cash basis employees must recognize salary payments as gross income in the year the payments are received, guaranteed payments are deemed to be paid to partners on the last day of the tax year, regardless of when they are actually paid during the year.[89]

Example 43

Refer to the facts in *Example 42*, but assume the OPQ Partnership is on a fiscal year ending September 30. As a result, P actually received three $4,000 guaranteed payments in October, November, and December of the prior calendar year and only nine $4,000 payments during the current calendar year. Notwithstanding, P will report the entire $48,000 of guaranteed payments in the current year because all twelve months of guaranteed payments are deemed to be paid on September 30. Note that this result holds regardless of the amount of any renegotiated guaranteed payment that P may receive during the last three months of the current year.

---

[89] Reg. § 1.707-1(c).

In addition to their taxable salaries, employees may receive a variety of nontaxable fringe benefits, such as group-term life insurance and health insurance coverage, or employer-provided meals or lodging.[90] Many of these nontaxable forms of compensation are not available to partners. For example, if a partnership pays for insurance coverage for its partners, the payments are considered § 707(c) guaranteed payments, which are fully includible in the partners' gross incomes and deductible by the partnership.[91] Partners may claim any health insurance premium payments as a deduction for adjusted gross income. Partners are not eligible to participate in qualified retirement plans sponsored by the partnership for its employees. However, each partner may establish a Keogh plan, which can provide tax-sheltered retirement benefits for the partner comparable to the benefits available under employee retirement plans.[92]

SALES BETWEEN PARTNERS AND CONTROLLED PARTNERSHIPS

Section 707(b) defines two situations in which the general rule of § 707(a) is overridden and the tax consequences of transactions between partners and partnerships are not determined as if the transaction were negotiated at arm's length between independent parties. The situations involve a sale of property between (1) a partnership and any person owning more than a 50% interest in either partnership capital or profits, or (2) two partnerships in which the same persons own more than a 50% interest in either capital or profits.[93]

If such a sale results in a recognized loss to the seller, such loss is disallowed. If the purchaser of the property subsequently disposes of the property at a gain, the originally disallowed loss may be used to offset such gain.[94]

Example 44

T owns a 60% interest in the TV Partnership. During the current year, T sells investment land to TV for $100,000; T's basis in the land is $145,000. T may not recognize his $45,000 loss realized on the sale, and TV will take a $100,000 cost basis in the land. If the partnership subsequently sells the land for more than $100,000, T's $45,000 disallowed loss may be used to offset the amount of taxable gain the partnership must recognize. If the partnership sells the land for less than $100,000, T's disallowed loss will have no effect on the amount of the taxable loss the partnership will recognize.

If a sale of property between a partner and a related partnership results in a recognized gain, and the property is *not* a capital asset in the hands of the purchaser, the gain must be characterized as ordinary income.[95]

Example 45

Refer to the facts in *Example 44,* but assume that T's basis in the investment land was $70,000. If the TV Partnership uses the land in its trade or business, rather than holding it as a capital asset, T's $30,000 recognized gain on the sale must be characterized as ordinary income.

---

[90] See §§ 79, 106, and 119.

[91] Rev. Rul. 91-26, 1991-1 C.B. 184.

[92] See § 401(d).

[93] Percentage ownership is determined with reference to the constructive ownership rules of § 267(c) other than paragraph (3) of such section. § 707(b)(3).

[94] § 707(b)(1). Note the similarity to the more general loss disallowance rule of § 267(a)(1).

[95] § 707(b)(2). An almost identical (and therefore redundant) gain characterization rule can be found in § 1239(a).

Before entrepreneurs can decide whether to organize a new business venture as a corporation, a partnership, or a limited liability company, they must carefully consider the contrasting legal characteristics of these alternatives. The check-the-box regulations have made it possible for unincorporated entities (i.e., LLCs) to be taxed as partnerships, even if they have all four primary corporate characteristics (limited liability, continuity of life, free transferability of interests, and centralized management). Therefore, many new business entities may organize as limited liability companies so they can have limited liability for all of their owners, yet still be taxed as a partnership.

There are distinct federal tax advantages to the use of the partnership form. Because they are nontaxable conduit entities, partnerships allow entrepreneurs to avoid an entity level tax on business income. The income earned by a partnership is taxed only once at the partner level, regardless of the amount of cash distributed to the partners during the year. In contrast, income earned by a corporation and distributed as dividends to the shareholders is taxed both at the entity level and at the shareholder level. Operating losses generated by a partnership may yield an immediate tax benefit to the extent they are currently deductible at the partner level. Corporate losses are trapped at the entity level and yield a tax benefit only in the form of a net operating loss carryback or carryforward deduction against corporate taxable income.

The partnership form provides maximum flexibility in the manner in which items of income, gain, deduction, loss, or credit generated by a business or investment activity may be shared among the co-owners. Varying allocation ratios for different items may be specified in the partnership agreement; such *special allocations* that pass the substantial economic effect test of § 704(b) will control for tax purposes. Special tax allocations of pass-through items cannot be accomplished through the use of an S corporation. Although S corporations are conduit entities, they may have only a single class of outstanding stock. Consequently, each share of S corporation stock must confer an identical right to every item of corporate income, gain, deduction, loss, or credit.[96]

The Treasury has expressed its increasing concern that taxpayers can abuse the partnership form by structuring certain transactions to achieve tax results inconsistent with the underlying economic arrangement. Regulation § 1.701-2 applies to any partnership undertaking a transaction with a principal purpose of substantially reducing the present value of the partner's aggregate federal tax liability in a manner that is inconsistent with the intent of Subchapter K. If a partnership transaction runs afoul of this *anti-abuse* regulation, the IRS may disregard the partnership arrangement "in whole or in part" in determining the proper tax consequences. Because of the broad scope of this new regulation, taxpayers and their advisers will have to exercise an added measure of caution in tax planning with partnerships.

Once a group of entrepreneurs has decided to form a partnership, their rights and responsibilities as partners should be carefully documented in a professionally drafted partnership agreement. The new partners must decide upon the nature and amount of their capital contributions and consider the potential tax consequences thereof. Partners can plan to exchange cash or appreciated property for an equity interest without recognizing any current gain. On the other hand, partners who own property the value of which is less than its adjusted basis may want to deliberately avoid the nonrecognition rule of § 721 by selling or leasing the property to the partnership. Partners who intend to perform services in exchange for an equity interest should determine to what extent the value of the interest received will represent current-year compensation income. Finally, the tax effect of a partnership assumption of the debt of a contributing partner should be carefully analyzed to determine if the assumption might trigger immediate gain recognition at the partner level.

Exhibit 9-3 contains a summary of the tax effects of partnership formations. Exhibit 9-4 summarizes the effects of operating a partnership, and Exhibit 9-5 summarizes the tax effects of partner/partnership transactions.

---

[96] Reg. § 1.1361-1(i)(1).

EXHIBIT 9-3	Summary of Tax Effects for Partnership Formations

	Transaction	Effect on Partnership	Effect on Partner
1.	Contribution of cash or property for a capital interest	Nontaxable; partner's basis becomes partnership's basis in contributed assets (i.e., carryover basis)	Nontaxable; partner's basis in contributed assets becomes partner's outside basis in partnership interest (i.e., substituted basis)
2.	Partner's share of partnership liabilities increases	No effect	Increases partner's outside basis based on P & L ratio
3.	Partner's share of partnership liabilities decreases	No effect	Decreases partner's outside basis, based on P & L ratio; includible income to the extent this "cash distribution" exceeds the partner's outside basis
4.	Contribution of appreciated or depreciated property	Special allocations of gain or loss, depreciation and depletion attributable to contributed assets	Special allocations of gain or loss, depreciation and depletion attributable to contributed assets
5.	Taint on contributed property:		
a.	Accrued losses on capital assets	Capital losses when recognized (for five years)	Precontribution capital losses flow through to the contributing partner
b.	Inventory	Ordinary gains or losses when recognized (for five years)	Precontribution ordinary gains or losses flow through to the contributing partner
c.	Unrealized receivables	Ordinary gains or losses when recognized	Precontribution ordinary gains or losses flow through to the contributing partner
6.	Contributions of services:		
a.	Unrestricted capital interest received	FMV is either a deductible expense or capitalized, depending on the type of service; treated as a sale of undivided interest in assets	FMV is includible ordinary income and the outside basis in the partnership interest
b.	Restricted capital interest	Same as above when restrictions removed	a. FMV at date restrictions are removed is includible income on that date or b. May elect that current FMV is includible income currently Amount recognized is the outside basis in the partnership interest
c.	Interest in profits only	Distribution of profits	Includible ordinary income (probably as profits are received)

EXHIBIT 9-4　Summary of Tax Effects for Operating the Partnerships

Transaction	Effect on Partnership	Effect on Partner
1. Net ordinary income	Reported on Form 1065	Distributive share flows through and increases outside basis; includible ordinary income
2. Net ordinary loss	Same as above	Distributive share flows through to the extent of outside basis and decreases the basis (but not below zero); deductible ordinary loss to the extent of the flow-through; losses in excess of basis are carried forward until outside basis is positive
3. Other income, expenses, gains, losses, and credits	Reported on Schedules K (if more than 10 partners) and K-1	Same as above, character flows through with all items
4. Self-employment income:		
a. General partner	Same as above	Distributive share of ordinary net income (adjusted) plus guaranteed payments
b. Limited partner	Same as above	Guaranteed payment for services performed
5. Partnership elections	All but three must be made by the partnership	Section 703 lists elections to be made individually by each partner

EXHIBIT 9-5　Summary of Tax Effects for Partner/Partnership Relations

Transaction	Effect on Partnership	Effect on Partner
1. Partner as an employee	Not applicable—a partner cannot be an employee of a partnership	Not applicable
2. Partner compensation treated as a guaranteed payment	Deductible or capitalized, depending on the type of service performed	Includible ordinary income as of partnership's year-end
3. Partner compensation based on partnership profits	Distribution of profits	Nontaxable to extent of basis; any excess is capital gain
4. Other payments to a partner in a nonpartner status (e.g., interest on debt, rent, and royalty payments)	Deductible when the payment is includible by the partner	Includible as though received from an unrelated party
5. Losses on sales to partnership (partner owns more than 50% of partnership with constructive ownership rules)	FMV is basis; future gain is not recognized to the extent of the partner's disallowed losses	No deduction
6. Gain on sales to partnership (partner owns more than 50% of partnership with constructive ownership rules)	Treated as a purchase from a nonpartner	All gain is ordinary income if asset is not a capital asset in the hands of the purchaser

Problem Materials

DISCUSSION QUESTIONS

9-1 *Partnership versus Corporation.* List both tax and nontax advantages or disadvantages of operating a business as a partnership rather than as a corporation.

9-2 *Entity Classification.* How are limited liability companies classified for federal income tax purposes?

9-3 *General versus Limited Partners.* Distinguish between the legal rights and responsibilities of a general partner and a limited partner.

9-4 *Aggregate versus Entity Theory.* How does the aggregate theory of partnerships differ from the entity theory of partnerships? Give a specific example of a Subchapter K rule that reflects each theory.

9-5 *Partnership Agreement.* How often may a partnership agreement be amended and will such amendments be effective for federal tax purposes?

9-6 *Contributions of Property.* Is the statement that neither a partner nor a partnership ever recognizes gain or loss on the contribution of property in exchange for a partnership interest true or false? Explain your conclusion.

9-7 *Outside Basis versus Capital Account.* In what circumstances would the amount of a partner's outside basis in her partnership interest differ from her capital account balance on the partnership books?

9-8 *Partnership Liabilities as Basis.* What is the economic rationale for including a portion of partnership recourse debt in the partners' bases of their partnership interests? What is the rationale for the inclusion of nonrecourse debt?

9-9 *Contributions of Services.* Distinguish between the tax consequences to a partner who contributes services in exchange for a capital interest in a partnership and one who contributes services in exchange for an interest in future profits.

9-10 *Contributions of Services.* Explain how a contribution of services in exchange for a capital interest in an existing partnership might trigger gain or loss recognition to the noncontributing partners.

9-11 *Organization Costs versus Syndication Fees.* Compare the tax treatment of partnership organization costs to that of syndication fees.

9-12 *Partnership Taxable Year.* What choices are available to a business partnership when selecting a taxable year?

9-13 *Partnership Elections.* Are tax elections concerning the computation of partnership income generally made at the partnership level or by each partner? Does your answer to this question reflect the aggregate or the entity theory of partnerships?

9-14 *Timing of Income Recognition.* At what point in time does a cash basis partner recognize income for the following:
    a. Distributive share of partnership taxable income?
    b. Guaranteed payments for personal services?
    c. Interest income on a loan to the partnership?

9-15 *Loss Limitations.* Identify the three potential limitations on the deductibility of partnership losses by individual partners. In what order are these limitations applied?

9-16 *Basis Adjustments.* Indicate whether each of the following occurrences increases, decreases, or has no effect on a general partner's basis in his partnership interest. Assume all liabilities are recourse liabilities.
    a. The partnership borrows cash that will be repaid in two years.
    b. The partnership earns tax-exempt interest on municipal bonds.
    c. The partnership generates an operating loss for the year.
    d. The partnership distributes cash to its partners.
    e. The partnership incurs a nondeductible penalty.
    f. The partnership makes a principal payment on a mortgage secured by partnership property.
    g. The partnership recognizes a long-term capital gain on the sale of marketable securities.

9-17 *Partners' Transactions with Partnerships.* Give three examples of a transaction be-tween a partnership and a partner that will be treated as a transaction between the part-nership and a nonpartner for tax purposes. Does such arm's length treatment reflect the aggregate or the entity theory of partnerships?

9-18 *Partners as Employees.* May a general partner be an employee of the partnership for federal tax purposes? Explain your conclusion.

PROBLEMS

9-19 *Formation—No Liabilities.* J and G form the JG Partnership and contribute the fol-lowing business assets:

Asset	Fair Market Value	Basis	Contributed By
Land	$60,000	$30,000	J
Inventory.	50,000	28,000	G
Auto	10,000	14,000	G

J and G will share profits and losses equally.
   a. Calculate each partner's realized and recognized gain or loss.
   b. Calculate each partner's basis in his or her partnership interest.
   c. Calculate the partnership's basis in each asset.

9-20 *Formation—No Liabilities.* The A-E Partnership is being formed by five individuals who each contribute assets in exchange for a 20% capital and profit/loss interest. Calculate the following for each partner: (1) recognized gain or loss, (2) each part-ner's basis in his or her partnership interest, (3) the partnership's basis for each asset, and (4) the holding period of the partnership interest for the partner and the asset for the partnership. Assume all contributed assets will be used in the partnership's trade or business.
   a. A contributes business furniture with a market value of $10,000. The furniture cost $16,000 when purchased four years ago and A's adjusted basis in the furni-ture is $5,000.
   b. B contributes business equipment with a market value of $10,000. The equipment cost $20,000 when purchased two years ago and B's adjusted basis in the equip-ment is $12,000.
   c. C contributes business inventory with a market value of $10,000. The inventory cost $9,000 when purchased 16 months ago.
   d. D and E contribute $10,000 cash each.

9-21 *Formation—Liabilities.* Refer to *Problem 9-20,* but assume that D and E made the following contributions instead of cash. How do these new facts change your answers for each partner?
   a. D contributes land with a market value of $16,000. The land was acquired 10 months ago for $9,000 cash and a $6,000 note payable (recourse debt). The $6,000 note payable is also transferred to the partnership.
   b. E contributes land with a market value of $18,000. E received the land three years ago as a gift from a relative and has a basis of $5,000. In addition, E transfers an $8,000 mortgage (nonrecourse debt) on the land to the partnership.

9-22 *Partner's Holding Period.* Individuals X and Y contributed $50,000 each to the equal Z Partnership on January 1, 2016. On July 1, 2016, X contributed land with an adjusted basis of $10,000 and fair market value of $25,000 to Z for an increased in-terest in the partnership. X had owned the property as an investment for six months. On October 1, 2016, Y contributed land with an adjusted basis of $30,000 and fair market value of $15,000 to Z for an increased interest in the partnership. Y, a dealer in real property, had owned the land for three years. As of December 31, 2016, what are the partners' holding period in their partnership interests?

9-23 *Allocation of Partnership Liabilities—General Partnership.* In the current year, individuals M, N, and O form a general partnership, making no initial capital contributions. The three partners share partnership profits and losses in the following manner: 10% to M, 45% to N, and 45% to O. The partnership borrows $50,000 cash on a recourse basis. The partnership also borrows $180,000 on a nonrecourse basis. The nonrecourse debt is secured by investment land purchased by the partnership at a total cost of $200,000 ($20,000 cash plus the $180,000 proceeds of the nonrecourse debt).

   a. Calculate the effect of the two partnership liabilities on each partner's basis in the partnership.
   b. How does the calculation change if M, N, and O have respective 10 percent, 45 percent, and 45% interests in partnership profits but share losses equally (i.e., each partner has a 33.3% interest in partnership losses)?

9-24 *Allocation of Partnership Liabilities—Limited Partnership.* Refer to the facts in *Problem 9-23*, but assume that individual M is a general partner and individuals N and O are limited partners. How does this change in facts affect the calculation of each partner's basis in the partnership?

9-25 *Allocation of Recourse Debt.* Individuals A and B are general partners and individual L is a limited partner in the ABL Partnership. Partnership losses are allocated 40% to A, 35% to B, and 25% to L. As of December 31 of the current year, the partnership has $50,000 of recourse debt. The partnership's balance sheet as of December 31 is as follows:

	Basis	Fair Market Value
Cash	$ 25,000	$ 25,000
Receivables	50,000	75,000
Land	25,000	40,000
	$100,000	$140,000
Recourse liabilities	$ 50,000	$ 50,000
A, capital	20,000	36,000
B, capital	20,000	36,000
L, capital	10,000	18,000
	$100,000	$140,000

How would the $50,000 of recourse debt be allocated to A, B, and L?

9-26 *Relief of Debt in Excess of Basis.* Corporation C contributed land used in its business to the Beta Partnership in exchange for a 40% general interest in partnership capital, profits, and loss. The land had a $320,000 basis to the corporation and an appraised fair market value of $850,000, and was subject to a $635,000 recourse mortgage. Beta assumed the mortgage in the exchange transaction; as of the date of the exchange, Beta had no other liabilities.

   a. What are the tax consequences to Corporation C of its contribution of the land to Beta? What initial basis does Corporation C have in its partnership interest?
   b. How would your answers to (a) change if the $635,000 mortgage were nonrecourse rather than recourse?
   c. How would your answers to (a) change if Beta had $200,000 of other recourse liabilities on its books as of the date of Corporation C's contribution of the land?

9-27 *Receipt of Partnership Interest for Services.* In return for services rendered to the AX Partnership, T receives a 20% unrestricted interest in partnership capital. On the day T receives her interest, the partnership owned the following assets:

	Basis	Fair Market Value
Inventory	$ 5,000	$10,000
Equipment	10,000	14,000
Land	15,000	21,000
Building	40,000	50,000
Totals	$70,000	$95,000

Assuming the partnership has no liabilities and that before T's admission it is owned 60% by partner A and 40% by partner X, answer the following questions.
a. How much compensation income must be reported by T?
b. What is T's basis in the partnership interest received?
c. What are the tax consequences of this transfer to the AX Partnership? To partners A and X?
d. What is the partnership's basis in each of its assets following the transfer?

9-28 *Contribution of Services.* The G-H equal partnership was formed several years ago. Because the business has grown so rapidly, the partnership was expanded to include E and F. E and F each obtained a 20% profit and capital interest in the partnership in exchange for their services. E's services—the investigation and acquisition of property—have been completed. and he received an unrestricted capital interest at the beginning of the year. F has agreed to serve as a manager of the new operation. Her ownership interest is subject to her continuing as the manager for five consecutive years. At the beginning of the year, the partnership's net assets had a basis of $100,000 and a market value of $300,000. Thus, a 20% interest is valued at $60,000. The partners anticipate the business having a value of approximately $500,000 at the end of the five years when the restriction is removed from F's interest. Determine the tax effect on the partnership and each of the four partners for:
a. E's service contribution.
b. F's service contribution.

9-29 *Required Taxable Year.* F, G, and H are partners in the FGH Partnership. F, G, and H have profit-sharing ratios of 30 percent, 50 percent, and 20 percent, respectively. F has a year-end of December 31, G of February 28, and H of September 30. What is the required year-end for FGH Partnership?

9-30 *Partnership Taxable Year.* R, S, and T each owned a retail store as sole proprietors. R and S have a December 31 year-end, and T has a January 31 year-end. In order to take advantage of certain economies of scale, they combined their operations by forming a partnership on December 1, 2015. Each partner has a one-third interest in partnership profits. The partnership's net income was as follows:

December 1–December 31, 2015	$30,000
January 1–January 31, 2016	10,000
February 1–November 30, 2016	50,000
December 1–December 31, 2016	25,000

a. What tax year(s) may the partnership adopt? Discuss all options.
b. Assuming the partnership adopts a December 31 year-end, how much income from the partnership will T report on its tax return for the year ending January 31, 2016?
c. Assuming the partnership could adopt a January 31 year-end, how much income from the partnership will R report on his December 31, 2015 tax return? On his December 31, 2016 return?

9-31 *Computation of Partnership Taxable Income.* N is a 10% general partner in the KLMN Partnership. The partnership's records for the current year show the following:

Gross receipts from sales	$670,000
Cost of sales	(500,000)
Operating expenses.	(96,000)
Net income from rental real estate.	48,000
Dividend income	10,000
Business meals and entertainment	(6,700)
Section 1231 loss.	(13,500)

N's outside basis in his partnership interest was $125,000 at the beginning of the year. During the year, partnership recourse liabilities increased by $55,000; the partnership has no nonrecourse liabilities. KLMN made no distributions during the year to its partners.

  a. Calculate the partnership's taxable income (Form 1065, page 1) for the current year.

  b. Calculate N's basis in the partnership at the end of the year.

9-32 *Organization and Syndication Costs.* The Sigma Limited Partnership was organized during May and June of the current year. During these two months, the partnership paid $40,000 to a law firm to draft the partnership agreement and $10,000 to a CPA to set up an accounting system for the partnership business. The partnership also paid a $2,500 filing fee to the state of Illinois and $18,000 to advertise and market the sale of limited interests to potential investors. Sigma began business in August of the current year and properly adopted a fiscal year ending September 30 for tax purposes. Based on these facts, what portion of the above expenses may be expensed and amortized on Sigma's first Form 1065?

9-33 *Outside Basis and Taxation of Partners.* The TVX Partnership, formed in 2012, owns several office rental buildings. Selected year-end information for its first five years reveals the following:

	2012	2013	2014	2015	2016
Recourse liabilities	$100,000	$120,000	$130,000	$150,000	$160,000
Nonrecourse liabilities	500,000	400,000	300,000	250,000	200,000
Net income (or loss).	(300,000)	(200,000)	(110,000)	(40,000)	70,000
Cash distributed to partners. . . .	50,000	100,000	150,000	100,000	0

All liabilities were incurred by the partnership.

  Partner A contributed property with a basis of $50,000 and a market value of $75,000 in exchange for her partnership interest. Nine other partners contributed $75,000 cash each. A is a general partner and the other nine partners are limited partners. They share profits and losses equally, 10% each. Prepare a schedule showing (a) the distributive share of profits and losses, and (b) the outside basis of the partnership interest at the end of each year for the general partner and for one of the limited partners.

9-34 *Substantial Economic Effect.* The EFG Partnership agreement provides that taxable income, gain, deduction, and loss will be allocated equally among the partners. The agreement states that tax allocations will be reflected in the partners' capital accounts per books, and that liquidating distributions will be made in accordance with capital account balances. It also specifies that no limited partner is under any legal obligation to the general partner to restore any deficit capital account balance upon the liquidation of EFG. Under state law, general partners must restore any deficit capital account balance upon partnership liquidation. At the beginning of the current year, the partnership balance sheet reveals the following:

Assets	$300,000	
Debt		$200,000
Capital General partner E		15,000
Limited partner F		60,000
Limited partner G		25,000
		$300,000

For the current year, the partnership generates a $90,000 operating loss. How must this loss be allocated for tax purposes in order to meet the substantial economic effect requirement of § 704(b)?

9-35 *Contributed Property—Allocations.* The H and I Equal Partnership was formed at the beginning of the year. H contributed cash of $40,000 and I contributed equipment with a market value of $40,000 and an adjusted basis of $25,000. For the sake of simplicity, assume the partnership's depreciation rate for the current year on this equipment is 20 percent. The partnership's net ordinary income, excluding depreciation deductions on the equipment, is $60,000.

  a. Calculate H's distributive share of partnership net ordinary income (after depreciation is deducted).

  b. H asks you what the tax consequences would have been if the partnership had sold the equipment for $39,000 only five months after I transferred it to the partnership. (Assume no depreciation on the equipment was deducted by the partnership.)

9-36 *Contributed Property—Allocations.* At the beginning of the current year, S contributed depreciable business property (market value $90,000 and basis $67,200) and T contributed investment land (market value $180,000 and basis $145,000) to form the ST Partnership. S has a one-third interest and T has a two-thirds interest in partnership capital, profits, and loss.

  a. The ST Partnership will depreciate the property contributed by S on a straight-line basis over six years. Compute the amount of first-year tax depreciation on the property and allocate the depreciation between partners S and T.

  b. How would your answer to (a) change if the contributed basis of the business property had been $55,500 rather than $67,200?

  c. Refer to the original facts in the problem. Assume the partnership sells the property contributed by S on the first day of the partnership's third taxable year. The amount realized on sale is $65,000. Compute the taxable gain or loss recognized on the sale and allocate the gain or loss between partners S and T.

  d. How would your answer to (c) change if the amount realized on sale had been $54,000 rather than $65,000?

  e. During its fourth taxable year, the ST Partnership sells the land contributed by T for $200,000. Compute the taxable gain recognized on sale and allocate the gain between partners S and T.

9-37 *Sale of Contributed Property—Allocations.* Two years ago, X contributed property, which was part of his proprietorship inventory, to the D Partnership in exchange for a one-third partnership interest. At the date of contribution, the property had a basis of $120,000 and a value of $145,000. The property was used in the partnership's business as a nondepreciable § 1231 asset. The partnership sold the property for $160,000 in the current year.

    a. Calculate the amount and character of the taxable gain recognized on the sale allocable to X.

    b. How would the answer for (a) change if the sale occurred six years rather than two years after contribution?

    c. How would the answer for (a) change if the property had been sold for $100.000 rather than $160,000?

9-38 *Retroactive Allocations.* On September 1 of the current year, Corporation M contributed $125,000 cash in exchange for an interest in Topper Partnership, a calendar year, accrual basis partnership. For the current year, Topper recognized a $180,000 net operating loss; $82,000 of this loss had accrued as of August 31. In June of the same year, Topper sold marketable securities, recognizing a $63,000 capital gain.

    a. If Topper does not make an interim closing of its books on August 31, what is the maximum amount of current-year net operating loss and capital gain that can be allocated to Corporation M? Explain your conclusion. (In answering the question, you may assume that any allocation will have substantial economic effect.)

    b. If Topper does make an interim closing of its books on August 31, what is the maximum amount of current-year net operating loss and capital gain that can be allocated to Corporation M? Explain your conclusion. (In answering the question, you may assume that any allocation will have substantial economic effect.)

9-39 *Retroactive Allocations.* On November 16 of the current year, Corporation Q contributed $250,000 cash in exchange for an interest in Mega Ltd., a calendar year cash basis partnership. Mega's financial books and records indicate that Mega's operations through November 15 generated a $320,000 operating loss, while operations from November 16 through December 31 generated an additional $205,000 of loss. In December, Mega expensed the following payments:

Legal fee (for services rendered to the partnership in June and July of the current year)	$50,000
Interest expense (for annual interest accrued from January 1 through December 31 of the current year).	72,000

Based on these facts, what is the maximum amount of the $205,000 post-admission loss that the partnership can allocate to newly admitted partner Corporation Q? (In answering the question, you may assume that any allocation will have substantial economic effect.)

9-40 *Losses—Section 704(d).* Z has a 60% interest in the capital, profits, and losses of the Zeta Partnership. Both Z and Zeta are calendar year taxpayers. At the beginning of the current year, Z's basis in her partnership interest was $100,000. For the current year, Zeta incurred a $200,000 ordinary loss from its business operation, earned $14,600 of dividend and interest income on its investments, and recognized a $62,000 capital gain on the sale of a partnership capital asset. On March 12 of the current year, Z received a $15,000 cash distribution from Zeta. Assume that there was no change in the amount of Zeta's liabilities during the current year.

    a. How much of the $200,000 operating loss may Z deduct on her current-year tax return? In answering this question, ignore any impact of the at-risk or passive-activity loss limitations.

    b. Calculate Z's basis in her partnership interest at the end of the year.

9-41 *Losses—Section 704(d).* Corporation Q owns a 50% interest in the capital, profits, and loss of the QRST Partnership. Both Q and QRST are calendar year taxpayers. At the beginning of the current year, Q's outside basis in its partnership interest was $30,000. For the current year, the partnership earned $14,000 of tax-exempt interest on its investment in municipal bonds, incurred a $106,000 ordinary loss from its business operation, and recognized a $42,000 capital loss on the sale of a partnership capital asset. QRST made no distributions to partners during the year, and it did not change the amount of partnership debt on its books. Based on these facts, how much of the partnership's operating loss and capital loss may Corporation Q deduct in the current year? (In answering this question, assume that Q has sufficient current-year capital gains against which to deduct any amount of partnership capital loss.)

9-42 *Sections 704(d) and 465.* A cattle ranch, operated as a partnership, has the following year end information for a four-year period:

	Year 1	Year 2	Year 3	Year 4
Net income (loss)	$(90,000)	$(40,000)	$(20,000)	$(40,000)
Cash to partners	0	45,000	30,000	20,000
Recourse debt	45,000	42,000	39,000	36,000
Nonrecourse debt	80,000	70,000	60,000	50,000

G acquired a 10% general interest at the beginning of year 1 for $20,000. He has received his 10% share of the cash distributed during the four years. Calculate his § 704(d) basis and his § 465 at-risk amount at the beginning of years 2 through 5.

9-43 *Sections 704(d) and 465.* Refer to *Problem 9-42,* but assume the partnership activity is a real estate leasing business and that the nonrecourse debt is qualified nonrecourse financing. Calculate G's 704(d) basis and his § 465 at-risk amount at the beginning of years 2 through 5.

9-44 *Passive Activity Loss Limitation.* Corporation M (not a closely held or personal service corporation) is a 25% general partner in the MNOP Partnership, which operates a manufacturing business. Individuals N and O are 25% general partners, while individual P is a 25% limited partner. Partner N works full time in the partnership business, while the other general partners only participate in making occasional management decisions concerning broad aspects of MNOP's operations. At the beginning of the current year, each partner had an outside basis and at-risk amount in the partnership of $100,000. For the current year, MNOP generated a $480,000 operating loss. Assuming that none of the partners has any passive-activity income, determine how much of MNOP's loss each partner may deduct in the current year.

9-45 *Transactions between Partners and Partnerships.* A calendar year, accrual basis partnership rents property from a calendar year, cash basis partner, paying an arm's-length rent of $4,000 per month. The December rent payment for the current year was not received by the partner until January 5 of the subsequent year. The partnership pays this same partner a guaranteed payment for services rendered to the partnership of $10,000 per month. The December guaranteed payment was not received by the partner until January 10 of the subsequent year.
   a. In what year should the partnership deduct the December rent payment, and in what year should the partner include this payment in gross income?
   b. In what year should the partnership deduct the December guaranteed payment, and in what year should the partner include this payment in gross income?

9-46 *Payments for Partner Services.* LLB, a cash basis partnership, has a September 30 taxable year-end. Partner B, a calendar year, cash basis individual, received a guaranteed payment for services rendered to the partnership of $4,500 a month for the partnership's year ending September 30, 2016. The partnership agreed to increase the payment to $6,000 a month for the next fiscal year. On October 12, 2016, B also received a $12,000 payment from the partnership for professional services. B performs these professional services for a variety of clients in his sole proprietorship business. How much income attributable to these payments should B report in 2016?

9-47 *Guaranteed Payments.* B and G are partners in the DR Partnership. B oversees the daily operations of the business and therefore receives compensation of $50,000, regardless of the amount of the partnership's net income. In addition, his distributive share of profits and losses is 50 percent.
   a. If the partnership had $75,000 ordinary income before any payments to partners, determine the amount and character of B's total income.
   b. Same as (a), but assume the partnership had $30,000 ordinary income before payments to partners.
   c. Same as (a), except assume the partnership had $25,000 ordinary income and $50,000 long-term capital gain before payments to partners.

9-48 *Guaranteed Payments.* At the end of the current year, the three partners in the ABC Partnership had the following preclosing balances in their capital accounts.

Partner A.	$ 70,000
Partner B	89,000
Partner C.	105,000

The ABC Partnership agreement provides that (1) each partner will receive an annual guaranteed payment for the use of capital equal to 6% of the pre-year-end closing balance in his or her capital account and (2) any remaining income or loss for the year will be allocated equally among the partners. Before accounting for any guaranteed payments to the partners, ABC had $54,000 of taxable income for the current year. How much taxable income is allocated to each partner?

9-49 *Computation of Partner's Taxable Income.* T is a 30% partner who works in the partnership business. Both T and the partnership use the calendar year for tax purposes. The partnership's records for the current year show:

Gross profit	$240,000
Guaranteed payments to T	(20,000)
Life insurance premium for T.	(500)
Operating expenses.	(60,000)
Charitable contributions.	(5,000)
Net long-term capital gain.	10,000

T is single, has no other income, and no itemized deductions for the year. T received the $20,000 guaranteed payments and withdrew an additional $10,000 during the year. T's basis in the partnership was $40,000 at the beginning of the year.
   a. Calculate the partnership's ordinary income (Form 1065, page 1) for the year.
   b. Calculate T's taxable income for the year.
   c. Calculate T's basis in the partnership at the end of the year.

9-50 *Sale to Related Partnership—Loss.* V, a 60% partner, sells land to the partnership for $8,000. V's basis in the land is $ 9,000.
   a. Determine (1) V's recognized loss and (2) the partnership's basis in the land after the transaction.
   b. What are the tax consequences to the partnership if it sells the land six months later for (1) $7,500, (2) $8,600, or (3) $9,300?
   c. How would your answers to (a) and (b) differ if V were a 40% partner?

9-51 *Sale to a Related Partnership—Loss.* The RS Partnership is owned 40% by R and 60% by S. R and S are unrelated. The partnership, expanding its very successful efforts, contracts to purchase two plots of land at market value, one owned by R and one by S. The relevant information is as follows:

Asset	Purchase Price	Partner's Basis	Seller
Plot 1.	$20,000	$23,000	R
Plot 2.	24,000	28,000	S

   a. Calculate the realized and recognized loss for each seller.
   b. Calculate RS's basis in each of the two plots.
   c. Calculate the realized and recognized gain or loss for the partnership and each partner if, two years later, the partnership sells Plot 1 for $22,000 and Plot 2 for $29,000.

9-52 *Sale to a Related Partnership—Gain.* During the current year, Corporation J sold investment land with a $400,000 basis to the Kappa Partnership for a selling price of $525,000. Determine the amount and character of Corporation J's recognized gain on the sale under each of the following sets of assumptions:
   a. Corporation J owns a 75% interest in the capital, profits, and loss of Kappa, and Kappa also holds the land as an investment asset.
   b. Corporation J owns a 35% interest in the capital, profits, and loss of Kappa, and Kappa uses the land in its business operation.
   c. Corporation J owns a 75% interest in the capital, profits, and loss of Kappa, and Kappa uses the land in its business operation.

9-53 *Contribution of Inventory with Built-In Gain.* V is a 40% partner in the TUV Partnership. V is a dealer in computer equipment, and V contributes computers to TUV that the partnership will use in its business operations. The computers have a basis to V of $10,000 and a fair market value of $16,000. What are the tax consequences to V and to TUV under the following circumstances?
   a. TUV sells the computers six months later for $15,000. Assume the basis is the same.
   b. TUV sells the computers six years later for $3,000. Assume the basis is zero at that time.
   c. What would your answer be if the facts are the same as in part a, except that TUV also is a dealer in computer equipment?

9-54 *Contribution of Capital Asset with Built-In Loss.* W is a 20% partner in the WXY Partnership. W has owned a parcel of land as an investment for three years. W contributes this land to WXY. WXY is a dealer in land. The land has a basis to W of $120,000 and a fair market value of $100,000. What are the tax consequences to W and to WXY under the following circumstances?
   a. WXY sells the land six months later for $100,000.
   b. WXY sells the land six months later for $90,000.
   c. WXY sells the land six years later for $90,000.
   d. WXY sells the land six years later for $150,000.

9-55 *Self-Employment Taxes.* T is a general partner and owns a one-third interest in the RST Partnership. All partners are actively involved in the partnership's operations. For the current calendar year, RST reports ordinary income of $100,000, before guaranteed payments, and a long-term capital gain of $12,000. Additionally, T receives the only guaranteed payment of $10,000.
   a. What is the impact of these transactions on T's self-employment income for the current year?
   b. Same as part (a), except T is a limited partner, is not involved in partnership operations, but receives the guaranteed payment for use of his capital.

TAX RETURN PROBLEM

9-56 *Tax Return Problem.* Phil Smith and Kate Jones formed the P&K General Partnership on March 1, 2012 to provide computer consulting services. Partnership profits and losses are allocated 60% to Phil and 40% to Kate. The business code and employer identification numbers are 7370 and 24-3897625, respectively. The business office is located at 3010 East Apple Street, Atlanta, Georgia 30304. Phil and Kate live nearby at 1521 South Elm Street and 3315 East Apple Street, respectively. Their Social Security numbers are 403-16-5110 for Phil and 518-72-9147 for Kate.

The calendar year, cash basis partnership's December 31, 2015 balance sheet and December 31, 2016 trial balance (both prepared for tax purposes) contain the following information:

	Balance Sheet 12/31/2015		Trial Balance 12/31/2016	
	Debit	Credit	Debit	Credit
Cash	$ 12,000		$ 22,000	
Investments (1)	14,000		14,000	
Equipment (2, 3)	150,000		190,000	
Accumulated depreciation		$ 38,000		$ 63,500
Recourse notes payable (4)		58,000		87,200
Nonrecourse notes payable		36,000		30,000
Phil, capital		28,000		28,000
Phil, drawing (5)			25,440	
Kate, capital		16,000		16,000
Kate, drawing (5)			16,960	
Revenues				235,000
Dividend income (1)				1,000
Interest income (1)				400
Section 1245 gain (depreciation recapture) (2)				3,500
Compensation (6)			110,000	
Rent expense			12,000	
Interest expense			16,600	
Tax expense (property and payroll)			13,800	
Repair expense			5,800	
MACRS depreciation			29,200	
Health insurance expense (7)			1,600	
Property insurance expense			1,500	
Office supplies expense			3,000	
Utility expense			2,200	
Charitable contribution			500	
Total	$176,000	$176,000	$464,600	$464,600

1. The investment account consists of marketable securities of U.S. corporations and U.S. Treasury Bonds. All of the dividends are considered qualified dividends.
2. Equipment was sold May 12, 2016 for $9,800. It was purchased new on May 1 of the prior year for $10,000 and its basis when sold was $6,300.
3. New equipment was purchased March 1, 2016 with $5,000 cash and a $35,000 three-year recourse note payable. The first note payment is March 1, 2017. (**Note:** The correct amount of tax depreciation is included in the depreciation expense account in the trial balance.)
4. Notes payable are long-term except for $20,000 of the recourse notes to be paid next year. All liabilities were created by the partnership.
5. The partners' drawing accounts record cash distributions made to the partners throughout the year.
6. Compensation is composed of guaranteed payments of $30,000 each to Phil and to Kate and $50,000 to unrelated employees.
7. Health insurance premiums paid were for the unrelated employees.

Prepare a 2016 (or 2015 if the 2016 tax forms are not yet available) Form 1065, Schedule K, Schedules L and M (even though not required by the IRS instructions to Form 1065), and Schedule K-1 for Phil. Complete all pages, including responses to all questions. If any necessary information is missing in the problem, assume a logical answer and record it. Do not prepare Schedule K-l or other required supplemental forms for Kate at this time. Use the Worksheet for Figuring Net Earnings (Loss) from Self-Employment included in the Form 1065 instructions to calculate the partners' self-employment income. Note that if you are preparing a 2015 Form 1065 you will need to adjust all indicated years in this problem to fit the 2015 tax year.

9-57 *Tax Return Problem.* Early in the current year, Lisa Cutter and Jeff McMullen decided they should start their own gourmet hamburger business. Lisa and Jeff believed that the public would love the recipes used by Lisa's mom, Tina Woodbrook. They also were confident that they had the necessary experience to enter this business, because Jeff currently owns a fast-food franchise and Lisa formerly managed a small bakery. After conducting their own market research, Lisa, Jeff, and Tina agreed to form Slattery's General Partnership. They signed a partnership agreement on February 1 and opened their first restaurant for business on February 25. The restaurant was housed in a renovated gas station that the partnership purchased with funds borrowed from a local bank. The partnership's business address is 5432 Partridge Place, Tulsa, Oklahoma, 74105, and its employer identification number is 88-7654321.

Lisa Cutter contributed $30,000 cash and 200 shares of MND stock to partnership capital. Lisa had purchased the stock on October 3, 2012 for $8,000; at date of contribution, the stock was worth $20,000. Jeff McMullen contributed business equipment with a fair market value of $35,000 and an adjusted basis of $28,000, and Tina Woodbrook contributed $30,000 cash and her box of recipes. Lisa, Jeff, and Tina agreed to share partnership profits and losses 40 percent, 30 percent and 30 percent, respectively.

The partnership elected to use the accrual method of accounting and a calendar year for tax purposes. Its adjusted trial balance for the current year (the first year of operations) reveals the following information:

	Debit	Credit
Cash	$144,800	
Ending inventory	16,000	
Equipment	35,000	
Land	10,000	
Building	15,000	
Improvements to building	55,000	
Accumulated depreciation		$ 11,500
Note payable to bank		93,000
Accounts payable		40,000
Taxes payable		8,000
Accrued salaries payable		20,000
Capital accounts		115,000
Sales		400,000
Gain on sale of MND stock		18,000
Dividend from MND Corporation		2,000
Cost of goods sold	84,000	
Legal expenses	6,000	
Accounting expenses	4,000	
Miscellaneous expenses	2,150	
Premium on life insurance policy	800	
Advertising	3,600	
Utilities	5,200	
Payroll taxes	5,600	
Salaries and wages	71,350	

	Debit	Credit
Guaranteed payment to Lisa Cutter.	$ 60,000	
Insurance.	7,700	
Repairs	6,100	
Charitable contributions.	17,600	
Depreciation expense	11,500	
Interest expense	5,200	
Distribution to partners	150,000	

The partnership records provide certain additional information:

1. The partnership took a physical count of its inventory of foodstuffs and supplies on December 31 and determined that ending inventory was $16,000.
2. Ten percent of the principal balance of the note payable is due each year for the next ten years.
3. The legal expense was paid to the partnership's attorney in February for drafting the partnership agreement. The accounting expense was paid to a CPA firm in May for establishing an accounting system for the business. Miscellaneous expenses include a $100 state registration fee for new business partnerships.
4. The partnership sold the MND stock on April 3 for $38,000.
5. Slattery's CPA correctly computed current-year tax depreciation as $11,500. The partnership simply used this number as its depreciation expense per books.
6. Lisa Cutter (Social Security No. 447-52-7943) is the managing partner for Slattery's. During the current year, she devoted over 1,800 hours to the business and received a $60,000 guaranteed payment for her services. Neither Jeff nor Lisa worked in the partnership business. The partnership purchased a $100,000 insurance policy on Lisa's life. Slattery's is both the owner and beneficiary of this policy.
7. Because the partnership's business was so profitable, the three partners each took a cash distribution of $50,000 on December 15.

Prepare a current-year Form 1065, Schedule K, Schedules L and M (even though not required by the IRS instructions to Form 1065), and Schedule K-1 for Lisa. Complete all pages, including responses to all questions. If any necessary information is missing in the problem, assume a logical answer and record it. Do not prepare Schedule K-l or other required supplemental forms for other partners at this time. Use the Worksheet for Figuring Net Earnings (Loss) from Self-Employment included in the Form 1065 instructions to calculate the partners' self-employment income.

10

Partnership Distributions, Dispositions of Partnership Interests, and Partnership Terminations

Learning Objectives

Upon completion of this chapter you will be able to:

LO.1 Determine the tax consequences of both current and liquidating distributions, including:

- The recognition of gain or loss by the recipient partner.
- The basis of distributed property in the hands of the recipient partner.
- The character of gain or loss recognized on a subsequent disposition of distributed property.
- The postdistribution basis of the recipient partner's interest in the partnership.

LO.2 Explain the function of § 736 as it applies to liquidating distributions and compute the amount of any § 736(a) payment included in a distribution.

LO.3 Identify the circumstances in which a partnership must make an adjustment to the inside bases of its assets because of a distribution to a partner.

LO.4 Recognize a disproportionate distribution and calculate the tax consequences to both the distributing partnership and recipient partner.

LO.5 Analyze the tax consequences of a sale of a partnership interest to both the seller and purchaser.

LO.6 Apply the family partnership rules to partnership interests created by gift.

LO.7 Recognize a termination of a partnership and summarize the tax consequences of the termination to the partners.

Chapter Outline

Introduction

The tax consequences of partnership formations and the operation of a business in partnership form were the major topics covered in Chapter 9. In this chapter, the more advanced topics of partnership distributions, dispositions of partnership interests, and partnership terminations are discussed. The statutory rules governing the tax consequences of these various transactions are among the most complex in the Internal Revenue Code. Understanding a particular rule often becomes easier if the rule can be identified as a logical extension of either the entity or the aggregate theory of partnerships. Under the *entity theory,* partners own equity interests in the partnership as a whole. A partnership interest is analogous to stock in a corporation, and should be viewed as a capital asset in its own right. Under the *aggregate theory,* partners indirectly own a proportionate interest in partnership assets, and the tax consequences of any transaction involving a partnership interest can be determined only by reference to those assets.

The aggregate theory predominates in the sections of Subchapter K (§§ 731 through 737) devoted to partnership distributions. Under this theory, a partner who receives a distribution of cash or property is merely converting his or her indirect interest in partnership assets to direct ownership of the distributed assets. This change in ownership form should not be a taxable event and should have no effect on the tax basis of the distributed assets. This theoretical foundation is clearly discernible in the set of rules explained in the following section.

Partnership Distributions

LO.1

Determine the tax consequences of both current and liquidating distributions, including:

- The recognition of gain or loss by the recipient partner.

- The basis of distributed property in the hands of the recipient partner.

- The character of gain or loss recognized on a subsequent disposition of distributed property.

- The postdistribution basis of the recipient partner's interest in the partnership.

This first section of Chapter 10 is an analysis of the broad set of rules applicable to partnership distributions to which the specialized provision of § 751(b) does not apply. (This difficult provision and its impact on the tax consequences of disproportionate distributions of certain types of partnership assets are examined in a subsequent section.) All partnership distributions can be classified as either current or liquidating. A *current distribution* reduces a partner's interest in partnership capital but does not extinguish the interest. In other words, subsequent to the receipt of a current distribution, a partner is still a partner. In contrast, a *liquidating distribution* extinguishes the recipient partner's entire equity interest in the partnership. An ongoing partnership may make liquidating distributions to any of its partners who terminates an interest. When a partnership itself terminates, it will make a final liquidating distribution to all its partners.

CURRENT DISTRIBUTIONS

Cash Distributions

Partners may withdraw cash from their partnerships at various times throughout the partnership's taxable year in order to meet their personal short-term liquidity needs or as advance payments of their anticipated distributive shares of current-year partnership income. Partners may also receive periodic cash distributions as guaranteed payments for ongoing services rendered to the partnership. Finally, partners may receive constructive cash distributions in the form of reductions in their respective shares of partnership liabilities.[1]

---

[1] § 752(b).

Regardless of the nature of a current cash distribution, § 731(a) provides that the recipient partner does not recognize gain upon its receipt. The cash distribution is instead treated as a nontaxable return of capital that reduces the recipient's outside basis in his or her partnership interest.[2] However, the basis of a partnership interest can never be reduced below zero. Consequently, a partner who receives a cash distribution in excess of outside basis must recognize the excess as gain derived from sale of the partnership interest.[3]

Guaranteed payments and other cash distributions representing advances against the recipient's share of current-year partnership income are taken into account as of the last day of the partnership year.[4] This timing rule minimizes the possibility that distributions will trigger gain recognition at the partner level.

Example 1

Partnership WXYZ and 25% partner Z both use a calendar year for tax purposes. At the beginning of the current year, Z's outside basis was $50,000, and partnership debt totaled $60,000 ($15,000 of which was properly included in Z's outside basis). On July 7, the partnership made a $75,000 cash distribution to Z. As of the last day of the year, partnership debt totaled $80,000. Partnership income for the current year consisted of $109,000 ordinary income and a $5,600 capital loss. Z's outside basis at the end of the year is computed as follows:

Basis on January 1		$50,000
Increased by:	25% share of ordinary income	27,250
	25% share of $20,000 increase in partnership debt	5,000
Decreased by:	July 7 cash distribution	(75,000)
	25% share of capital loss	(1,400)
Basis on December 31		$ 5,850

The effect of the July 7 distribution is determined as if the distribution had occurred on the last day of the partnership year. Because Z's outside basis is first increased by his distributive share of partnership income and his share of WXYZ's increased debt load, the distribution is treated as a nontaxable return of capital.

If the $75,000 distribution had not been a guaranteed payment or advance against income, its tax effect would have been determined on July 7. Assuming that the partnership debt on this date was still $60,000, Z must recognize a $25,000 capital gain equal to the excess of the distribution over his $50,000 basis. Subsequent to the distribution, Z's outside basis would have been reduced to zero.

Property Distributions

As a general rule, a current distribution of partnership property to a partner does not cause gain or loss recognition at either the partnership or the partner level.[5] The recipient partner simply takes a *carryover* basis in the distributed property and reduces the outside basis in her partnership interest by a corresponding amount.[6]

---

[2] § 733.

[3] § 731(a)(1). This gain is capital gain per § 741.

[4] Reg. § 1.731-1(a)(1)(ii).

[5] § 731(a) and (b). Section 731(c) provides that certain marketable securities are treated as money rather than property for purposes of § 731(a). Consequently, the distribution of such securities by a partnership may trigger gain recognition to the recipient partner. Discussion of this special rule is beyond the scope of this text.

[6] §§ 732(a)(1) and 733.

Example 2

S receives a current distribution of property from the STUV Partnership. At date of distribution, the property has a fair market value of $14,000 and an inside basis to the partnership of $7,500. Immediately prior to the distribution, S's outside basis in her partnership interest was $12,000. Neither the partnership nor S recognizes a gain on the distribution. S's basis in the property becomes $7,500 and her outside basis is reduced to $4,500 ($12,000 − $7,500).

Note that in the above example the $7,500 inside basis of the distributed property (i.e., the carryover basis) was preserved by shifting $7,500 of S's outside basis to the property. If the recipient partner's outside basis is less than the inside basis of the distributed property, the distribution is referred to as a *substituted* basis transaction. In such a situation, the basis of the distributed property in the hands of the partner is limited to his or her outside basis amount.[7]

Example 3

Refer to the facts in *Example 2*. If S's predistribution outside basis had been only $6,000, S's basis in the distributed property would be $6,000 and her postdistribution outside basis would be zero ($6,000 − $6,000). Note that S simply substitutes her outside basis as the basis in the distributed asset.

If a partnership distribution consists of multiple assets and the recipient partner's outside basis is less than the aggregate inside bases of the assets, the outside basis must *first* be reduced by any amount of cash included in the distribution. The remaining basis is allocated between two categories of noncash assets in the following order of priority:

1. To any unrealized receivables and inventory (Category 1) in an amount not to exceed the basis of these assets in the hands of the partnership.[8]
2. To any other distributed properties (Category 2).

Basis is allocated to multiple assets within either of these two categories under a *basis decrease formula*. The basis decrease is first allocated to property with unrealized depreciation (i.e., inside basis greater than fair market value) to the extent of the unrealized depreciation in each property.[9]

Example 4

J receives a current distribution from the JKL Partnership consisting of the following:

	JKL Basis	FMV
Cash	$4,000	$4,000
Accounts receivable	0	3,000
Inventory	2,000	2,900
Capital asset 1	1,000	1,500
Capital asset 2	3,000	1,000

---

[7] § 732(a)(2).

[8] An unrealized receivable is any right to payment for goods or services provided to customers in the ordinary course of business that has not been recognized by the partnership as ordinary income. Reg. § 1.732-1(c)(1) and § 751(c).

[9] § 732(c)(3)(A).

Immediately prior to the distribution, J's outside basis in his partnership interest was $8,000. This basis is first reduced by the $4,000 cash distribution. The $4,000 remaining basis is allocated to the Category 1 assets in an amount not to exceed JKL's inside basis:

	Partner J's Basis
Unrealized receivables	$ 0
Inventory.	2,000

Because J's $2,000 remaining outside basis is less than the aggregate inside bases of the Category 2 assets distributed, the basis decrease formula must be used to allocate this amount to the two capital assets received. First, the amount of the basis decrease is computed to be $2,000 by subtracting J's remaining outside basis amount ($2,000) from the aggregate inside bases ($1,000 + $3,000 = $4,000) of these assets. The $2,000 basis decrease is then allocated to any of these assets with unrealized depreciation; in this case only capital asset 2. Thus, J's basis in capital asset 2 is $1,000 ($3,000 − $2,000). J's resulting basis in each of these assets is reflected below:

	Inside Basis	FMV	Unrealized Depreciation	Partner J's Basis
Capital asset 1	$1,000	$1,500	$ 0	$1,000
Capital asset 2	3,000	1,000	2,000	1,000

After the distribution, J's outside basis in his partnership interest is reduced to zero.

If more than one of the distributed assets from the same category has depreciated in value, the basis decrease is allocated based on relative depreciation.

Example 5

Assume the same facts in *Example 4* above, except that the fair market value of Capital asset 1 is $500 instead of $1,500. In this case, the basis decrease is allocated between the two capital assets based on relative depreciation. J's basis in each of these assets is determined as follows:

	Inside Basis	FMV	Unrealized Depreciation
Capital asset 1	$1,000	$ 500	$ 500
Capital asset 2	3,000	1,000	2,000

	J's Basis
Capital asset 1:	
$1,000 carryover basis − $400 ([$500/$2,500] × $2,000 basis decrease) = ...	$ 600
Capital asset 2:	
$3,000 carryover basis − $1,600 ([$2,000/$2,500] × $2,000 basis decrease) = ...	1,400

Finally, if the required basis decrease exceeds the unrealized depreciation of the assets, any further decrease is allocated in proportion to the assets relative bases (as previously adjusted).[10]

---

[10] § 732 (c)(3)(B).

Example 6

Assume the same facts as in *Example 5* above, except that the total amount of the required basis decrease is $2,800 instead of $2,000. In this case, the bases of capital assets 1 and 2 would first be reduced by the existing depreciated amount to $500 and $2,000, respectively. The $300 remaining basis decrease would be allocated between these assets in proportion to these reduced bases. J's basis in each of the capital assets would be computed as follows:

	JKL Basis	Unrealized Depreciation	Reduced Basis	$300 Basis Decrease		J's Basis
Capital asset 1	$1,000	$ 500	$ 500	$100	([$500/$1,500] × $300)	$400
Capital asset 2	3,000	2,000	1,000	200	([$1,000/$1,500] × $300)	800

There is one exception to the rule that the partnership does not recognize gain or loss on partnership distributions. The IRS has recently ruled that gain may be recognized if appreciated property is given to a partner to satisfy a guaranteed payment obligation.[11] For example, if a partner has an $80,000 guaranteed payment and the partnership uses property with a basis of $60,000 and fair market value of $80,000 to satisfy this obligation, the partnership must recognize gain of $20,000.

Distributions of Contributed Property

A partner who contributes property to a partnership in exchange for a partnership interest does not recognize gain or loss on the exchange. The contributed property takes a carryover basis in the hands of the partnership so that if the partnership subsequently disposes of the property in a taxable transaction, the precontribution gain or loss inherent in the property will be recognized. Moreover, under the rule of § 704(c)(1)(A), such gain or loss must be specially allocated to the contributing partner.

Example 7

Three years ago, Y contributed investment land ($50,000 fair market value and $32,000 basis) in exchange for a 50% interest in the YZ Partnership. Y was not required to recognize the $18,000 appreciation in the value of the land as income at the date of contribution. The partnership's tax basis in the land is $32,000. If the partnership sells the land during the current year, the first $18,000 of gain recognized (the precontribution gain) must be specially allocated to Partner Y.

In the above example, recognition of the $18,000 gain realized by Y on the exchange of appreciated land for a partnership interest is deferred only until the partnership sells the land. Congress wanted to ensure the same result if the partnership eventually disposes of the land through a distribution to another partner. Consequently, § 704(c)(1)(B) provides an exception to the general rule that a distribution of property by a partnership is a nontaxable event. If (1) distributed property had been contributed to the partnership within the seven-year period prior to date of distribution, and (2) the property is distributed to a *noncontributing* partner, the contributing partner must recognize gain or loss to the extent that partner would have been specially allocated gain or loss under § 704(c)(1)(A) if the property had been sold.[12] The character of the gain or loss is determined by the character of the gain or loss that would have resulted had the contributed property actually been sold. Both the contributing partner's outside basis and the inside basis of the distributed property are increased (decreased) by the amount of gain (loss) recognized.[13]

---

[11] Rev. Rul. 2007-40, 2007-25 IRB 1426.

[12] See §§ 721 and 723.

[13] § 704(c)(1)(B)(iii).

Example 8

Refer to the facts in *Example 7*. During the current year, the partnership distributed the land contributed by Y to partner Z. At date of distribution, the fair market value of the land was $61,000 and Z's outside basis in his partnership interest was $112,000.

Because the land was distributed to noncontributing partner Z within seven years of its contribution to the partnership, contributing partner Y must recognize an $18,000 gain in the current year. (If the partnership had sold the land for $61,000, $18,000 of the $29,000 taxable gain recognized would have been specially allocated to Y.) Y increases his outside basis by $18,000 and the partnership increases its $32,000 predistribution inside basis in the land to $50,000.

Upon receipt of the land, Z will decrease his outside basis in his partnership interest by $50,000 and take a $50,000 carryover basis in the land.

Distributions to Contributing Partners

Section 737 describes a second situation in which the distribution of property triggers gain recognition at the partner level. If a partner receives a distribution of property the fair market value of which is in excess of the outside basis in his or her partnership interest immediately prior to distribution, the partner must recognize gain equal to the lesser of (1) the excess value over basis, or (2) the net precontribution gain allocated to the partner.[14] *Net precontribution gain* is the net gain (if any) that would be triggered if all property contributed by the partner to the partnership within the seven-year period prior to distribution had been distributed to a noncontributing partner.[15] The recipient partner's outside basis is increased by the amount of § 737 gain; this increase is deemed to occur immediately prior to distribution. The inside basis of the partner's contributed property is also increased by the amount of gain recognized on the distribution.[16]

Example 9

Refer to the facts in *Example 7*. Assume that the land contributed by Y to the partnership three years ago is still owned by the partnership. During the current year, Y received a distribution of equipment with a fair market value of $40,000 and an inside basis to the partnership of $25,000. Y's predistribution outside basis in his partnership interest was $13,000. Because the distribution of the equipment occurred within seven years of Y's contribution of the land, Y must recognize an $18,000 gain (the lesser of the $27,000 excess FMV of the equipment over Y's outside basis or his $18,000 net precontribution gain).

The partnership increases its $32,000 inside basis in Y's contributed land by $18,000. Y increases his outside basis by the $18,000 gain recognized and decreases it by his $25,000 carryover basis in the equipment.

Y's predistribution basis	$13,000
Increased by: § 737 gain	18,000
Decreased by: Carryover basis in equipment	(25,000)
Y's postdistribution basis	$ 6,000

The gain recognition rule of § 737 was designed to prevent Y from accomplishing a tax-free exchange of land for equipment by making a nontaxable contribution of the land to a partnership and receiving a nontaxable distribution of the equipment. Accordingly, this gain

---

[14] § 737(a). The character of the gain is determined by reference to the character of the precontribution gain.

[15] § 737(b).

[16] § 737(c).

recognition rule does not apply to a distribution of property that the recipient partner had originally contributed to the partnership.[17]

Example 10

Refer to the facts in *Example 9*. If the land that Y originally contributed to the partnership was distributed back to Y, the general rule that a distribution of property by a partnership is a nontaxable event would hold. Y would reduce his outside basis in his partnership interest to zero and take a $13,000 basis in the distributed land.

LIQUIDATING DISTRIBUTIONS

Cash Distributions

When a partner's entire interest in a partnership is extinguished upon receipt of a liquidating cash distribution, the partner will recognize capital gain to the extent of any amount of cash in excess of the outside basis in his partnership interest. Conversely, if the cash distribution is less than the outside basis, the partner may recognize the amount of unrecovered basis as capital loss.

Example 11

C receives a liquidating distribution of $20,000 cash from the ABC Partnership. (This distribution equals the $20,000 value of C's capital account as of the date of distribution.) Because she is no longer a partner, C is relieved of $13,000 of partnership debt. C's total cash distribution is $33,000 ($20,000 actual cash + $13,000 constructive cash in the form of debt relief).

If C's outside basis immediately prior to distribution is $24,500, she must recognize an $8,500 capital gain equal to the excess of the $33,000 cash distribution over this basis.

If C's outside basis immediately prior to distribution is $35,000, she may recognize a $2,000 capital loss equal to the excess of this basis over the $33,000 cash distribution.

Property Distributions

Liquidating distributions of property generally do not result in gain or loss recognition to either partnership or partner.[18] When a partnership distributes property as a liquidating distribution, the recipient partner's outside basis (reduced by any amount of cash included in the distribution) is allocated to the distributed property.[19] In most cases, this substituted basis rule defers the recognition of any economic gain or loss realized by the partner upon liquidation.

---

[17] § 737(d)(1).

[18] *Supra*, Footnote 5.

[19] § 732(b).

Example 12

M receives a liquidating distribution of $6,000 cash and a partnership § 1231 asset with a fair market value of $25,000 and a $14,600 inside basis to the partnership.

Assume M's predistribution outside basis is $40,000. This basis is reduced by the $6,000 cash distribution, and the remaining $34,000 basis is substituted as the basis of the distributed asset to M. Neither M nor the partnership recognizes gain or loss because of the distribution.

Assume M's predistribution outside basis is $9,000. This basis is reduced by the $6,000 cash distribution, and the remaining $3,000 basis is substituted as the basis of the distributed asset to M. Neither M nor the partnership recognizes gain or loss because of the distribution.

Assume M's predistribution outside basis is only $4,000. M must recognize the $2,000 cash distribution in excess of basis as capital gain. The distributed asset will have a zero basis to M.

If a liquidating distribution includes multiple assets, the recipient partner's outside basis (reduced by any cash distributed) is allocated between two categories of noncash assets in the following order of priority:

1. To any unrealized receivables and inventory (Category 1) in an amount not to exceed the basis of these assets in the hands of the partnership.

2. To any other distributed properties (Category 2).

Unlike the current (nonliquidating) distribution rules that limit the distributee partner's bases in *any* assets to the distributing partnership's inside basis (i.e., a carryover basis), only the bases of unrealized receivables or inventory (Category 1 assets) are subject to this rule in a liquidating distribution. If the distributee partner's outside basis exceeds the partnership's inside basis of any unrealized receivables or inventory distributed, the remaining outside basis must be assigned to any asset received from Category 2.[20] If the partner does not receive any Category 2 assets, then the excess of the outside basis over the inside basis of the Category 1 assets is recognized as a loss by the partner.[21] However, if Category 2 assets are received, the partner can never recognize a loss.

Example 13

R receives a liquidating distribution from the RST Partnership that consists of the following:

	RST Basis	FMV
Cash	$2,500	$2,500
Accounts receivable	0	2,000
Inventory	3,000	4,000
Capital asset	5,000	9,000

R's predistribution outside basis in his partnership interest was $12,000. This basis must first be reduced by the $2,500 cash distribution. The $9,500 remaining basis is allocated to the Category 1 assets in an amount not to exceed RST's inside basis:

	Partner R's Basis
Unrealized receivables	$ 0
Inventory	3,000

The $6,500 remaining basis is allocated to the capital asset (Category 2 asset), even though this substituted basis exceeds the RST Partnership's $5,000 inside basis. In addition, neither R nor the RST Partnership recognizes gain or loss because of the distribution.

[20] § 732(c).   [21] § 731(a)(2).

Example 14

N receives a liquidating distribution from the MNOP Partnership that consists of the following:

	MNOP Basis	FMV
Cash	$ 700	$ 700
Accounts receivable	0	800
Inventory asset 1	1,000	1,300
Inventory asset 2	2,100	2,500

Immediately prior to the distribution, N's outside basis is $4,000. This basis must first be reduced by the $700 cash distribution. Only $3,100 of the $3,300 remaining basis is allocable to the Category 1 assets.

	Partner N's Basis
Unrealized receivables	$ 0
Inventory asset 1	1,000
Inventory asset 2	2,100

N may recognize her $200 unrecovered outside basis as a capital loss.

Example 15

Refer to the facts in *Example 14*. If N's predistribution outside basis had been $3,000, N would recognize no loss. N's basis would be reduced by the $700 cash distribution, and the entire $2,300 remaining basis would be allocated to the Category 1 assets in proportion to their inside bases to MNOP.

	Partner N's Basis
Unrealized receivables	$ 0
Inventory asset 1	
($1,000 ÷ $3,100) × $2,300	742
Inventory asset 2	
($2,100 ÷ $3,100) × $2,300	1,558

Note that in *Example 14* and *Example 15* partner N received a liquidating distribution with a total fair market value of $5,300, so in both examples N realized an economic gain upon termination of her partnership interest. The Subchapter K rules governing the tax consequences of partnership property distributions ensure that a partner's economic gain or loss with respect to the distribution is deferred until subsequent disposition of the property.

Example 16

Refer to the facts in *Example 14*. Although N recognized a $200 tax loss upon receipt of the liquidating distribution, she realized a $1,300 economic gain ($5,300 value of assets received in excess of $4,000 basis in N's liquidated partnership interest). However, N's basis in the distributed assets is only $3,100. If N were to sell the unrealized receivables and inventory for their aggregate value of $4,600, she would recognize a $1,500 taxable gain.

The result in *Example 16* is consistent with the aggregate theory of partnerships, under which N has not severed her interest in the MNOP Partnership until she no longer owns any interest in partnership *assets*. When N finally sells the distributed MNOP assets, her $1,500 recognized gain on sale netted against her $200 recognized loss upon distribution equates to her $1,300 economic gain attributable to the termination of her partnership interest.

Finally, when partners receives more than one Category 2 asset in a liquidating distribution, their remaining outside basis must be allocated between the assets using one of the following:

1. *Basis decrease formula*—where the sum of the bases of the distributed Category 2 assets *exceeds* the distributee partner's outside basis remaining after reduction for any cash received and basis allocated to any unrealized receivables or inventory (Category 1 assets).

2. *Basis increase formula*—where the sum of the bases of the distributed Category 2 assets is *less* than the distributee partner's outside basis remaining after reduction for any cash received and basis allocated to any unrealized receivables or inventory (Category 1 assets).

Example 17

After reduction for a distribution of cash and the required allocation of basis to unrealized receivables and inventory received in a liquidating distribution from the RST Partnership, partner T's remaining outside basis of $25,000 must be allocated to the following capital assets:

	RST's Basis	FMV
Capital asset 1	$10,000	$20,000
Capital asset 2	30,000	10,000

Because T's $25,000 remaining outside basis is less than the aggregate bases of the Category 2 assets, the basis decrease formula must be used. First, the amount of the basis decrease is computed to be $15,000 by subtracting T's outside basis amount ($25,000) from the aggregate inside bases ($40,000) of these assets. The $15,000 basis decrease is then allocated to any of the assets with unrealized depreciation; in this case only Capital asset 2. T's basis in each of these assets is reflected below:

	Inside Basis	FMV	Unrealized Depreciation	Partner T's Basis
Capital asset 1	$10,000	$20,000	$ 0	$10,000
Capital asset 2	30,000	10,000	20,000	15,000

Note that even though the depreciation in value of Capital asset 2 is $20,000, the total basis decrease is only $15,000. Thus, the $30,000 inside basis in that asset is reduced to $15,000 in T's hands.

If more than one of the distributed assets from the same category has depreciated in value, the basis decrease is allocated based on relative depreciation.

Example 18

Assume the same facts in *Example 17* above, except that the fair market value of Capital asset 1 is $5,000 instead of $20,000. In this case, the $15,000 total basis decrease is allocated between the two capital assets based on relative depreciation as follows:

	T's Basis
Capital asset 1:	
$10,000 carryover basis − $3,000 ([$5,000/$25,000] × $15,000 basis decrease) = ...	$ 7,000
Capital asset 2:	
$30,000 carryover basis − $12,000 ([$20,000/$25,000] × $15,000 basis decrease) = ...	18,000

Example 19

After reduction for a distribution of cash and the required allocation of basis to unrealized receivables and inventory received in a liquidating distribution from the RST Partnership, partner T's remaining outside basis of $25,000 must be allocated to the following capital assets:

	RST's Basis	FMV
Capital asset 1	$10,000	$20,000
Capital asset 2	5,000	25,000

Because the aggregate bases of the Category 2 assets is *less* than T's remaining outside basis, the basis *increase* formula must be used. First, the amount of the basis increase is computed to be $10,000 by subtracting the aggregate inside bases ($15,000) of these assets from T's outside basis amount ($25,000). The $10,000 basis increase is then allocated to the assets based on relative unrealized appreciation. T's basis in each of these assets is reflected below:

	Inside Basis	FMV	Unrealized Appreciation	Basis Increase
Capital asset 1	$10,000	$20,000	$10,000	$3,333
Capital asset 2	5,000	25,000	20,000	6,667

T's basis in Capital asset 1 will be $13,333 ($10,000 carryover basis + $3,333 basis increase) and his basis in Capital asset 2 will be $11,667 ($5,000 carryover basis + $6,667 basis increase). Note that the total of T's bases in these assets ($13,333 + $11,667 = $25,000) equals his $25,000 remaining predistribution outside basis.

If only one of the assets in *Example 19* above had unrealized appreciation, it would have been allocated all of the basis increase up to its total fair market value. In the event that the basis increase exceeded the unrealized appreciation, any remaining basis increase amount would be allocated between the assets based on relative fair market values.

Closing of Partnership Year

When a partner's entire interest in a partnership is liquidated, the partnership taxable year closes with respect to that partner.[22] As a result, the partner may have to include a proportionate share of more or less than 12 months of partnership income in his or her taxable year in which the liquidation occurs.

---

[22] § 706(c)(2)(A)(ii).

Example 20

The BCD Partnership and partner B both use a calendar year for tax purposes. On September 30, 2016 B received a liquidating distribution from BCD that terminated her interest in the partnership. BCD's taxable year closed with respect to B on September 30. As a result, B will include her proportionate share of BCD's income from January 1 through September 30 (9 months) in her 2016 tax return. BCD's taxable year does not close with respect to the remaining partners, who will include their proportionate shares of BCD's income for the full calendar year on their respective returns.

Example 21

Refer to the facts in *Example 20*. If BCD uses a fiscal year ending May 31 for tax purposes, two partnership years (June 1, 2015 through May 31, 2016 and the short year June 1, 2016 through September 30, 2016) ended within partner B's 2016 taxable year. As a result, B will include her proportionate share of BCD's income from June 1, 2015 through May 31, 2016 (12 months) and from June 1, 2016 through September 30, 2016 (4 months) in her 2016 tax return.

In *Examples 20* and *21*, B's outside basis in her partnership interest immediately prior to the receipt of her liquidating distribution should reflect her distributive share of BCD's income or loss through September 30, 2016.[23] Therefore, B cannot determine the tax consequences of the distribution itself until she receives her final Schedule K-1 from the BCD Partnership.

Section 736 Payments

The amount of a liquidating distribution paid to a partner who is terminating an interest in an ongoing partnership should theoretically equal the partner's proportionate interest in the value of the partnership assets. In reality, partners may negotiate for and partnerships may agree to pay liquidating distributions in excess of such amount. In such case, § 736 provides that only the portion of the total distribution attributable to the partner's interest in partnership assets is subject to the statutory rules dealing with partnership distributions. The remainder of the distribution (labeled a *§ 736(a) payment*) is not subject to the normal distribution rules. Instead, § 736(a) payments that are determined without regard to the income of the partnership are classified as *guaranteed payments*. Section 736(a) payments determined with reference to partnership income are classified as *distributive shares* of such income.

LO.2

Explain the function of § 736 as it applies to liquidating distributions and compute the amount of any § 736(a) payment included in a distribution.

Example 22

R, a 20% general partner in the RSTU Partnership, retired from the partnership business during the current year. As of the date of R's retirement, the partnership had the following balance sheet:

	Inside Basis	FMV
Cash	$ 50,000	$ 50,000
Business assets	65,000	90,000
	$115,000	$140,000

[23] § 705(a). If a partner who terminates his or her entire interest in a partnership has suspended losses under § 704(d), these losses expire on termination. *Sennett*, 80 T.C. 825 (1983).

	Inside Basis	FMV
Debt	$ 5,000	$ 5,000
Capital: R.	22,000	27,000
Other partners	88,000	108,000
	$115,000	$140,000

Even though R's capital account balance was only $27,000, the other partners agreed to pay R $40,000 cash in complete liquidation of his equity interest. The additional $13,000 payment was in grateful recognition of R's long years of faithful service to the business.

The total liquidating payment to R consisted of $41,000 ($40,000 actual cash + $1,000 relief of 20% of the partnership debt). R's 20% interest in the value of partnership assets was $28,000 (as evidenced by the $27,000 value of his capital account and 20% share of the partnership debt). Therefore, only $28,000 of the liquidating payment is treated as a distribution. If R's outside basis in his partnership interest was $23,000, R must recognize a $5,000 capital gain equal to the excess of the cash distribution over this basis.

The $13,000 § 736(a) payment to R was determined without regard to partnership income. Consequently, it is classified as a guaranteed payment, which R must recognize as ordinary income and the partnership may deduct as a current expense.

Example 23

Refer to the facts in *Example 22*. Assume that R's partners agreed to pay R $27,000 cash plus 40% (rather than the normal 20%) of current-year partnership income in complete liquidation of his equity interest in the partnership. Partnership taxable income for the year totaled $90,000 ($60,000 ordinary income and $30,000 long-term capital gain). As a result, R received a total liquidating payment of $64,000 ($27,000 cash payment + $1,000 relief of 20% of the partnership debt + 40% of partnership income). Only $28,000 of the liquidating payment is treated as a distribution. If R's outside basis in his partnership interest was $23,000, R must recognize a $5,000 capital gain equal to the excess of the cash distribution over this basis.

The $36,000 § 736(a) payment is determined with reference to partnership income and is therefore treated as R's distributive share of that income. R must recognize $24,000 (40% of $60,000) as ordinary income and $12,000 (40% of $30,000) as long-term capital gain.

Payments for Unrealized Receivables and Unspecified Goodwill

Section 736 contains a special rule concerning liquidating payments made with respect to a partner's interest in certain partnership assets. Payments made with respect to unrealized receivables must be considered § 736(a) payments rather than distributions.[24] Payments made with respect to goodwill are similarly classified unless the partnership agreement specifies that a withdrawing partner will be paid for his or her share of goodwill. Prior to the enactment of the Revenue Reconciliation Act of 1993, this special rule applied to liquidating payments made to any partner by any partnership. The 1993 Act limited its application to payments made to *general* partners by partnerships *in which capital is not a material income-producing factor.*[25]

---

[24] § 751(c) provides that, for § 736 purposes, the term *unrealized receivables* includes only zero basis accounts receivable and not § 1245, § 1250, or other types of ordinary income recapture.

[25] § 736(b)(3). Capital is not a material income-producing factor if substantially all of the partnership's income consists of fees, commissions, or other compensation for personal or professional services performed by individuals.

Example 24

E is a 10% general partner in the Beta Partnership, a professional service partnership in which capital is not a material income-producing factor. During the current year, E had a serious disagreement with the other partners and decided to withdraw from the partnership. As of the date of E's withdrawal, the partnership had the following balance sheet:

	Inside Basis	FMV
Cash	$ 35,000	$ 35,000
Accounts receivable	0	24,000
Business assets	100,000	145,000
	$135,000	$204,000
Debt	$ 15,000	$ 15,000
Capital: E	12,000	18,900
Other partners	108,000	170,100
	$135,000	$204,000

After considerable negotiation, the other partners agreed to pay E $20,000 cash in complete liquidation of her equity interest. The partners determined that this was a fair price for E's 10% capital interest because the partnership business has considerable goodwill and going concern value that is not recorded as an asset on its balance sheet. The Beta Partnership agreement does not provide for specific payments with respect to partnership goodwill.

The total liquidating payment to E consisted of $21,500 ($20,000 actual cash + $1,500 relief of 10% of the partnership debt). E's 10% interest in the value of the recorded partnership assets was $20,400 (as evidenced by the value of her $18,900 capital account and 10% share of the partnership debt). However, the $2,400 payment made with respect to E's 10% interest in Beta's unrealized receivables must be classified as a § 736(a) payment. Consequently, only $18,000 of the liquidating payment ($20,400 − $2,400) is treated as a distribution. If E's outside basis in her partnership interest was $13,500, E must recognize a $4,500 capital gain equal to the excess of the cash distribution over this basis.

The $3,500 § 736(a) payment to E represents the value of her 10% interest in Beta's accounts receivable and unspecified goodwill. Because the payment was determined without regard to partnership income, it is classified as a guaranteed payment, which E must recognize as ordinary income and Beta may deduct as a current expense.

Installment Payments

If a partnership has insufficient cash on hand to fund a liquidating distribution to a withdrawing partner, it may negotiate to make a series of payments over a fixed number of years. In such cases, the partnership agreement may specify to what extent each annual payment consists of a liquidating distribution and a § 736(a) payment.[26] If the agreement is silent on this point, Treasury Regulations state that each year's payment shall consist of a proportionate amount of liquidating distribution and § 736(a) payment.[27] In either case, all debt relief is taken into account in Year 1.

---

[26] Reg. § 1.736-1(b)(5)(iii).   [27] Reg. § 1.736-1(b)(5)(i).

Example 25

Refer to the facts in *Example 24*. Assume that Beta agreed to pay the $20,000 cash to partner E over a four-year period, but the partnership agreement failed to specify the character of each annual payment for tax purposes. The total liquidating payment of $21,500 consists of a liquidating distribution of $18,000 (83.7% of the total) and a § 736(a) payment of $3,500 (16.3% of the total). Accordingly, 83.7% of each annual payment will represent a liquidating distribution, while 16.3% of each payment will be a § 736(a) payment. The following table breaks down each payment into its two components and shows the tax consequences of each component.

	Liquidating Distribution	Basis Reduction	Capital Gain	Section 736(a) Payment	Ordinary Income	Total
Year 1*	$ 5,442	$ 5,442	$ 0	$1,058	$1,058	$ 6,500
Year 2	4,186	4,186	0	814	814	5,000
Year 3	4,186	3,872	314	814	814	5,000
Year 4	4,186	0	4,186	814	814	5,000
	$18,000	$13,500	$4,500	$3,500	$3,500	$21,500

* The Year 1 payment consists of $5,000 cash + $1,500 debt relief.

In *Example 25,* partner E does not recognize any capital gain attributable to the liquidating distribution until Year 3, when the cumulative amount of the distribution finally exceeds E's outside basis in her partnership interest. In contrast, E must recognize each annual § 736(a) payment as ordinary income.

DISPOSITIONS OF DISTRIBUTED PROPERTY

If a partner who received either a current or liquidating distribution of partnership unrealized receivables subsequently collects the receivables or disposes of them in a taxable transaction, that partner must recognize the excess of the amount realized over the zero basis in the receivables as ordinary income.[28] Similarly, if a partner sells inventory distributed from a partnership within five years of the date of distribution, any gain or loss recognized must be characterized as ordinary gain or loss.[29]

Example 26

Two years ago, G received a current distribution of land from the EFG Partnership, which operates a real estate development business. The land was an inventory asset to EFG and took a carryover basis of $140,000 in G's hands. G held the land as an investment and sold it in the current year for $200,000. Because she sold the land within five years of the date of its distribution by EFG, G must recognize her gain as ordinary income, even though the land was a capital asset in her hands.

A partner who receives a distribution of a partnership asset may include the partnership's holding period for the asset in his or her holding period.[30]

---

[28] § 735(a)(1). This paragraph provides that either gain or loss realized on a partner's disposition of partnership unrealized receivables is characterized as ordinary gain or loss. Except in unusual circumstances, such receivables will have a zero basis in the hands of a distributee partner; consequently, their disposition can only trigger gain recognition.

[29] § 735(a)(2).

[30] § 735(b).

Example 27

Partnership JKL purchased land in June 2015 and held it as an investment. In April 2016 the land was distributed to K, who took a carryover basis of $35,000. K also held the land as an investment and sold it in October 2016 for $46,000. Because K's holding period for the land extended back to June 2015, he recognized an $11,000 long-term capital gain on the sale.

Basis Adjustments to Partnership Property

Under the general rules governing the tax consequences of partnership distributions, no gain or loss is recognized at either the partnership or the partner level and distributed assets simply take a carryover basis in the hands of the recipient partner. However, in certain circumstances, a partner may be required to recognize either capital gain or loss because of a distribution. In other cases, the inside basis of a distributed partnership asset does not carry over to the recipient partner.

These exceptions to the general rules can be viewed as anomalies that violate the aggregate theory of partnerships. Subchapter K provides a mechanism to correct these anomalies in the form of an adjustment to the inside basis of undistributed partnership property. Specifically, if a partnership has a *§ 754 election* in effect, it is allowed to increase the basis of partnership property by (1) any amount of gain recognized by a partner as the result of a distribution, and (2) any reduction of the inside basis of a distributed partnership asset in the hands of the recipient partner.[31]

LO.3

Identify the circumstances in which a partnership must make an adjustment to the inside bases of its assets because of a distribution to a partner.

Example 28

Partner L received a current distribution from the LMNO Partnership that consisted of $5,000 cash and partnership inventory with an inside basis of $1,500. Because L's predistribution outside basis was only $3,600, L recognized a $1,400 capital gain and took a zero basis in the distributed inventory. If LMNO has a § 754 election in effect, it may increase the inside basis in its remaining assets by $2,900 ($1,400 gain recognized by L + $1,500 reduction in the basis of the distributed inventory).

In *Example 28,* $1,400 of the positive basis adjustment counterbalances the current gain recognized at the partner level by decreasing the amount of future gain the partnership will recognize on a sale of assets (a $1,400 basis increase is equivalent to a $1,400 decrease in gain potential). The remaining $1,500 positive basis adjustment to LMNO's assets compensates for the $1,500 lost basis in the distributed inventory.

A partnership with a § 754 election in effect is required to *decrease* the basis of partnership property by (1) any amount of loss recognized by a partner as the result of a distribution, and (2) any increase in the basis of a distributed partnership asset in the hands of the recipient partner.[32]

Example 29

Partner E received a liquidating distribution of $5,000 cash from the EFGH Partnership. Because E's predistribution outside basis was $7,000, E recognized a $2,000 capital loss. Partner F received a liquidating distribution from EFGH consisting of a capital asset with an inside basis of $10,000. Because F's predistribution outside basis was $14,500, F took a $14,500 substituted basis in the distributed asset.

---

[31] § 734(b)(1).   [32] § 734(b)(2).

> If EFGH has a § 754 election in effect, it must decrease the basis in its remaining assets by $6,500 ($2,000 loss recognized by E + $4,500 increase in the basis of the distributed capital asset).

In *Example 29*, $2,000 of the negative basis adjustment counterbalances the current loss recognized at the partner level by decreasing the amount of future loss the partnership will recognize on a sale of assets (a $2,000 basis decrease is equivalent to a $2,000 decrease in loss potential). The remaining $4,500 negative basis adjustment to EFGH's assets compensates for the $4,500 additional basis in the distributed capital asset.

The optional basis adjustment is allocated to the same asset class in which the distributed property falls. For purposes of this adjustment, the partnership's assets are divided into two property classes:

1. Capital assets and § 1231 property (i.e., capital gain property), and
2. All other assets (i.e., ordinary income property).

However, any loss resulting from the distribution of cash, unrealized receivables, and inventory, must be allocated to the partnership's capital gain property. Further, any gain recognized from the distribution of cash must also be allocated to the capital gain property.

For allocations of increases in basis within a class, the increase must be allocated first to any properties in that class with unrealized appreciation. If more than one property has unrealized appreciation, the increase is allocated in proportion to each asset's unrealized appreciation. However, in no case can the allocated increase for an asset exceed that asset's unrealized appreciation. If any increase remains after this allocation, it is allocated to properties within that class in proportion to their fair market values.

The rules are similar for a decrease in basis. The decrease must be allocated first to any properties in that class with unrealized depreciation. If more than one property has unrealized depreciation, the decrease is allocated in proportion to each asset's unrealized depreciation. However, in no case can the allocated decrease for an asset exceed that asset's unrealized depreciation. If any decrease remains after this allocation, it is allocated to properties within that class in proportion to their adjusted bases. The adjusted bases used for this allocation include any adjustments already made as part of the overall allocation process.[33] In no case can the adjusted basis for an asset be reduced below zero. If the bases of all assets within a class have been reduced to zero, any remaining decreases are suspended until the partnership acquires property in that class.[34]

It is important to note that the rules for increases and decreases are similar, except that any remaining adjustment after the initial allocations are based on relative *fair market values* for increases, but on relative *adjusted bases* for decreases.

Example 30

Refer to the facts in *Example 28*. The § 754 adjustment was $2,900: $1,400 for the gain from the cash distribution and $1,500 due to the reduction in basis for the distributed inventory. The $1,400 for the gain must be allocated to capital gain property. Since inventory is an ordinary asset, the $1,500 for the inventory basis must be allocated to the ordinary income class.

Assume that LMNO Partnership owns the following two capital assets:

	Adjusted Basis	FMV	Unrealized Appreciation
Capital asset A...	$1,000	$3,000	$2,000
Capital asset B...	1,000	1,000	0

Since the only capital asset with unrealized appreciation is asset A, its basis is increased by $1,400 to $2,400.

---

[33] Reg. § 1.755-1(c)(2).   [34] Reg. § 1.755-1(c)(4).

Alternatively, assume that LMNO Partnership owns the following two capital assets:

	Adjusted Basis	FMV	Unrealized Appreciation
Capital asset A....................................	$1,000	$2,200	$1,200
Capital asset B....................................	1,000	1,800	800

The $1,400 basis increase is allocated to the assets based on the relative unrealized appreciation. Therefore, asset A receives a basis increase of $840 ($1,200/$2,000 × $1,400). Asset B receives a basis increase of $560 ($800/$2,000 × $1,400). Note that these basis increases are allowed because neither exceeds the unrealized appreciation for the respective asset. Asset A's basis is increased from $1,000 to $1,840, and asset B's basis is increased from $1,000 to $1,560.

Example 31

Refer to the facts in *Example 29*. The § 754 adjustment was $6,500: $2,000 for the loss recognized and $4,500 for the increase in basis of the capital asset. This results in a $6,500 decrease in the basis of capital assets, because all losses due to distributions are allocated to capital assets, as are adjustments due to the distribution of capital assets. Assume that LMNO Partnership owns the following two capital assets:

	Adjusted Basis	FMV	Unrealized Appreciation
Capital asset A....................................	$12,000	$ 4,000	$8,000
Capital asset B....................................	10,000	12,000	0

Since the only capital asset with unrealized depreciation is asset A, its basis is decreased by $6,500 to $5,500.

The § 754 Election

A partnership will adjust the inside basis of its assets as the result of a distribution to a partner only if it has a § 754 election in effect for the year of the distribution. A partnership makes a § 754 election simply by attaching a statement to that effect to its Form 1065 for the first taxable year for which the election is to be effective. Once made, the election applies for all subsequent years unless the Internal Revenue Service agrees to its revocation.[35]

Substantial Basis Reduction

Even if a § 754 election is not in effect, the rules discussed above will apply if there is a substantial basis reduction to partnership property as the result of a distribution. A substantial basis reduction occurs if the sum of (1) the partner's loss on the distribution, and (2) the basis increase to the distributed properties is more than $250,000.[36]

Example 32

Partner B has a basis of $4,000,000 in her partnership interest in Partnership AB. Partnership AB does not have a § 754 election in effect. She receives a liquidating distribution of land from the partnership having a fair market value of $3,500,000 and

---

[35] Reg. § 1.754-1.

[36] See § 734(d)(1). These rules apply for distributions made after October 22, 2004. Different rules apply for electing investment partnerships. A discussion of these rules is beyond the scope of this text.

a basis of $1,800,000. She will recognize no gain or loss on the distribution. Her basis in the land will be $4,000,000 and the basis in her partnership interest will be reduced to zero. Since the basis of the land has increased by more than $250,000 (by $2,200,000, from $1,800,000 to $4,000,000) a substantial basis reduction has occurred. Therefore, Partnership AB will have to reduce the basis of its other properties by $2,200,00 according to the rules of § 754.

Disproportionate Distributions

LO.4

Recognize a disproportionate distribution and calculate the tax consequences to both the distributing partnership and recipient partner.

The various rules governing the tax consequences of both current and liquidating partnership distributions are only applicable to the extent that § 751(b) does not apply to the distribution in question. Section 751(b) governs the tax consequences of *disproportionate distributions* in which the recipient partner receives either more or less than a proportionate share of any partnership unrealized receivables or substantially appreciated inventory. Consequently, the first step toward mastering the intricacies of § 751(b) is to define these two categories of partnership assets, which for convenience's sake tax practitioners have simply labeled *hot assets*.

PARTNERSHIP HOT ASSETS

Unrealized Receivables

The term unrealized receivables as used in § 751 includes zero basis trade accounts receivables generated by a cash basis partnership. The term also includes the § 1245 and § 1250 ordinary income recapture potential inherent in depreciable partnership assets.[37] All partnership unrealized receivables are deemed to have a zero tax basis.[38]

Example 33

The cash basis ABC Partnership owns the following assets:

		Tax Basis	FMV
Cash		$ 15,000	$ 15,000
Accounts receivable		0	33,000
Furniture and fixtures—cost	$ 45,000		
Accumulated depreciation	(27,000)	18,000	15,000
Equipment—cost	$100,000		
Accumulated depreciation	(30,000)	70,000	80,000
Buildings—cost	$600,000		
Accumulated depreciation (straight-line)	(165,000)	435,000	630,000
Land		200,000	210,000
		$738,000	$983,000

If the partnership were to sell its furniture and fixtures for their $15,000 current value, it would recognize a $3,000 § 1231 loss; therefore, the furniture and fixtures have no § 1245 ordinary income recapture potential. However, if the partnership were to

---

[37] § 751(c). The term unrealized receivables also includes many esoteric types of ordinary income recapture potential, such as § 1254 recapture of intangible drilling

and development costs of oil and gas wells and mining development and exploration expenditures.

[38] Reg. § 1.751-1(c)(5).

> sell its equipment for market value, it would recognize a $10,000 gain, all of which would be recaptured as § 1245 ordinary income. The sale of the building would not result in any § 1250 recapture because the partnership has been using the straight-line method to calculate depreciation.
>
>   Based on this list of assets, ABC Partnership has § 751 unrealized receivables of $43,000 ($33,000 zero basis accounts receivable + $10,000 § 1245 recapture potential).

Substantially Appreciated Inventory

Section 751(d) provides a very expansive definition of the term inventory for purposes of Subchapter K. Partnership inventory includes not only stock in trade and property held primarily for sale to customers in the ordinary course of business but also any other property that is not a capital asset or a § 1231 asset to the partnership.[39] Partnership inventory is considered substantially appreciated if its aggregate fair market value exceeds 120% of its aggregate basis.[40] For § 751 purposes, the fair market value of inventory refers to the replacement value of the inventory, not to the price at which the inventory is offered for sale to customers.[41] If a partnership deliberately purchases inventory property in order to decrease the amount of aggregate appreciation in its inventory so as to fail the 120% test, such property will be disregarded in applying the test.[42]

Example 34

The accrual basis MNO Partnership owns the following assets:

	Tax Basis	FMV
Cash	$ 7,000	$ 7,000
Accounts receivable	29,000	27,000
Stock in trade	330,000	410,000
Capital and § 1231 assets	250,000	390,000
	$616,000	$834,000

Both MNO's accounts receivable and stock in trade are inventory within the meaning of § 751 because accounts receivable are not a capital or § 1231 asset to the partnership.[43] Furthermore, the inventory is substantially appreciated because its aggregate FMV of $437,000 exceeds 120% of its aggregate basis (120% of $359,000 = $430,800).

THE AGGREGATE THEORY AND PARTNERSHIP DISTRIBUTIONS

Hot assets are essentially those properties that generate ordinary income upon their collection, sale, or exchange. Under the aggregate theory of partnerships, each partner owns a proportionate interest in partnership hot assets and has a corresponding obligation to recognize a proportionate share of the unrealized ordinary income accrued in the assets during the period of time the partner has been an owner.

---

[39] § 751 inventory also includes any partnership property that would be inventory if held by a selling or distributee partner. § 751(d)(3).

[40] § 751(b)(3)(A).

[41] Regs. § 1.751-1(d)(1) and § 1.471-4(a).

[42] § 751(b)(3)(B).

[43] Accounts receivable of a cash basis partnership are both an unrealized receivable and an inventory item for purposes of § 751.

Example 35

The CDE Partnership has the following simplified balance sheet:

	Tax Basis	FMV
Inventory	$320,000	$ 400,000
Capital and § 1231 assets (no recapture)	600,000	800,000
	$920,000	$1,200,000
Capital: Partner C	$230,000	$ 300,000
Other partners	690,000	900,000
	$920,000	$1,200,000

CDE has a hot asset in the form of substantially appreciated inventory (FMV of partnership inventory exceeds 120% of basis). Partner C owns a 25% interest in partnership capital, profits, and loss. Under the aggregate theory, C is deemed to own a 25% interest in CDE's inventory. Upon sale of the inventory for its current value, $20,000 of the $80,000 ordinary income realized by CDE will be allocated to C.

A strict application of the aggregate theory suggests that if C reduces her percentage ownership interest in CDE (by means of a current distribution) or terminates her interest (by means of a liquidating distribution), she is indirectly disposing of either a portion of or her entire interest in partnership inventory. As a result, she should be obligated to recognize an appropriate amount of the ordinary income accrued in the inventory rather than shifting such income to CDE's remaining partners.

Example 36

Refer to the facts in *Example 35*. Assume that CDE agrees to distribute partnership assets worth $300,000 to C in complete liquidation of her partnership interest. The distribution will be proportionate (i.e., will consist of a 25% interest in each of the partnership's assets):

	Distributed Tax Basis	Distributed FMV
Inventory	$ 80,000	$100,000
Capital and § 1231 assets	150,000	200,000
	$230,000	$300,000

Under the general rules of § 731, neither C nor the partnership will recognize any gain or loss on the distribution. If C's outside basis in her partnership interest is $230,000, this basis will be allocated to the distributed partnership assets. Under the rules of § 732, her 25% interest in the inventory will have an $80,000 basis and her 25% interest in the capital and § 1231 assets will have a $150,000 basis.

In the case of a proportionate distribution of hot assets, the general rules governing the tax consequences of distributions are compatible with the aggregate theory because they ensure that the recipient partner's interest in unrealized ordinary income of the partnership is preserved. Note that in *Example 36,* if ex-partner C sells her distributed share of the inventory and the capital and § 1231 assets for their current value, she will recognize $20,000 of ordinary income and $50,000 of capital/§ 1231 gain.[44]

For obvious practical reasons, few distributions consist of the recipient partner's proportionate interest in each asset owned by the partnership. The typical distribution consists of cash or nonoperating partnership assets. In such case, application of the general rules could result in a serious violation of the aggregate theory as it applies to hot assets. In *Example 36,* if rather than making a proportionate distribution, CDE distributes capital assets worth $300,000 (partnership basis $225,000) to C in complete liquidation of her interest, then under the general distribution rules, neither C nor the partnership will recognize any gain or loss on the distribution. C's $230,000 outside basis will become C's basis in the distributed capital assets. Note that C will now recognize $70,000 of capital gain if she sells the distributed capital assets for their current value. Because C did not receive her proportionate share of CDE's inventory, her 25% share of CDE's potential ordinary income has been effectively converted into capital gain. The remaining partners in CDE will eventually recognize 100% (rather than their 75% proportionate share) of the ordinary income accrued in CDE's inventory through the date on which C's interest terminated.

Mechanics of § 751(b)

Congress enacted § 751(b) to prevent a partnership distribution from resulting in an unwarranted shift of ordinary income among partners. This subsection overrides the general distribution rules, the application of which in *Example 36* would result in a shift of $20,000 of ordinary income from C to her former partners. Section 751(b) applies only to *disproportionate distributions* that include either more or less than the recipient partner's proportionate share of partnership hot assets. To the extent that the recipient partner receives excess hot assets, he or she is deemed to have received the excess *in exchange for* his or her interest in other partnership assets of equal value. Conversely, to the extent the recipient partner receives less than his or her share of partnership hot assets, he or she is deemed to have surrendered the shortage *in exchange for* an interest in other partnership assets of equal value. In either case, the constructive exchange between partner and partnership is a fully taxable event to both parties.

Example 37

Refer to the facts in *Example 36.* The distribution of capital assets worth $300,000 to C is disproportionate because it includes none of C's $100,000 share of CDE's substantially appreciated inventory. Therefore, § 751(b) overrides the general rules governing partnership distributions. The tax consequences of this override are explained in the following paragraphs.

Tax Consequences to the Recipient Partner

Application of the constructive exchange rule of § 751(b) at the partner level involves a three-step process.[45]

Step 1. C is deemed to have received a proportionate distribution of 25% of CDE's inventory. The value of the constructive distribution is $100,000.

Step 2. C takes an $80,000 carryover basis in her 25% interest in the inventory. Her $230,000 outside basis in her partnership interest is reduced by this carryover basis amount to $150,000.

Step 3. C immediately exchanges her interest in the inventory for capital assets of equal value ($100,000). This constructive exchange triggers $20,000 of ordinary income recognition ($100,000 amount realized − $80,000 basis surrendered) to C.

---

[44] This conclusion is based on the assumptions that (1) C either sells the inventory within five years or the inventory retains its character as such in C's hands [§ 735(a)(2)] and (2) the capital and § 1231 assets retain their character as such in C's hands.

[45] Reg. § 1.751-1(b)(2).

The following exchange table summarizes the information presented in the above three steps:

	FMV of Actual Distribution Received by C	FMV of Constructive Proportionate Distribution of Assets	Excess/(Shortage) of Assets
Hot assets:............................	$ 0	$100,000	$ (100,000)
Other assets:.........................	300,000	200,000	100,000
	$300,000	$300,000	$ 0

The third column represents C's constructive exchange of her proportionate interest in CDE's inventory for an excess amount of CDE's capital assets. Because C is deemed to have acquired $100,000 of capital assets in a fully taxable exchange, she has a $100,000 cost basis in this portion of her capital assets.

The $200,000 remainder of the capital assets C received (her proportionate share of CDE's other assets) represents a liquidating distribution to which the general tax rules apply. C's remaining $150,000 of outside basis (refer to *Step 2* above) becomes the substituted basis in this remainder, so that C's aggregate basis in her $300,000 worth of capital assets totals $250,000 ($100,000 cost basis + $150,000 substituted basis).

Tax Consequences to the Distributing Partnership

Application of the constructive exchange rule of § 751(b) at the partnership level involves just two steps.

Step 1.   CDE is deemed to have made a proportionate distribution of 25% of its inventory to C. The distributed inventory is worth $100,000 and has an inside basis of $80,000.

Step 2.   CDE immediately reacquires this inventory in exchange for $100,000 worth of its capital assets with an inside basis of $75,000. This constructive exchange triggers $25,000 of capital gain recognition ($100,000 amount realized − $75,000 basis surrendered) to CDE.

Because CDE is deemed to have acquired $100,000 of inventory in a fully taxable exchange, it has a $100,000 cost basis in this portion of its inventory. The following analysis of the partnership's inventory account shows the net effect of the above two steps.

	Tax Basis	FMV
Inventory before § 751(b) exchange	$320,000	$400,000
§ 751(b) exchange: *Step 1* constructive distribution	(80,000)	(100,000)
Step 2 constructive reacquisition	100,000	100,000
Inventory after § 751(b) exchange	$340,000	$400,000

Summary of Tax Consequences

A summary of the tax consequences of the disproportionate distribution by CDE to C reveals that § 751(b) does, in fact, prevent a shift of ordinary income from C to the ongoing partnership. Because of the distribution, C must recognize $20,000 of ordinary income, her proportionate share of the income accrued in the partnership inventory immediately prior to the distribution. Although CDE still owns all of the inventory, its basis has been increased by a net amount of $20,000. Consequently, when the partnership sells the inventory, it will recognize only $60,000 of ordinary income, the remaining partners' proportionate share of the income accrued immediately prior to the distribution.

The application of § 751(b) to even the simplest partnership distribution is a forbidding computational task. An apparently straightforward nontaxable distribution can be contorted into a constructive exchange of assets triggering unanticipated gain recognition to both the distributing partnership and the recipient partner. Fortunately, § 751(b) applies only to disproportionate distributions by partnerships with hot assets. If a partnership has no unrealized receivables or substantially appreciated inventory, it is immune to the subsection.

The most common way for a partner to dispose of a partnership interest is through a liquidating distribution from the partnership itself. There are, however, a number of other types of dispositions, each of which has a unique set of tax consequences to both partner and partnership.

SALES OF PARTNERSHIP INTERESTS

Partnership agreements typically place restrictions on the partners' right to sell their equity interests in the partnership to third parties. For example, an agreement might provide that a partner must offer his or her interest to the partnership itself or to the existing partners before offering it to a third-party purchaser. The agreement may also provide that a prospective purchaser must be approved by the general partners or by a majority of all partners. Because of such limits on transferability, partnership interests are considered illiquid assets.

LO.5

Analyze the tax consequences of a sale of a partnership interest to both the seller and purchaser.

When a partner sells his or her entire interest in a partnership, the partnership's taxable year closes with respect to that partner.[46] The selling partner's outside basis in the partnership interest immediately prior to sale includes his or her distributive share of partnership income or loss through date of sale.[47] The tax consequences of the sales transaction itself to both seller and purchaser are governed by specific rules in Subchapter K.

Tax Consequences to Seller

Upon sale of a partnership interest, the seller recognizes gain or loss to the extent the amount realized exceeds or is less than the outside basis of the interest. Section 741 contains a general rule that such gain or loss is capital in nature. This rule reflects the entity theory, under which a partnership interest represents the partner's equity in the partnership as a whole rather than a proportionate interest in each specific asset owned by the partnership.

Literally in mid-sentence, § 741 shifts to the aggregate theory by cautioning that the general rule is inapplicable to the extent the partnership owns unrealized receivables or inventory (whether or not substantially appreciated).[48] In such case, the amount of gain or loss for the hot assets (unrealized receivables and inventory) is determined by assuming that these assets are sold by the partnership in a fully taxable transaction for cash in an amount equal to the fair market value of the properties. The partner selling his partnership asset is allocated the portion of the ordinary income that would have been allocated to him if these assets had actually been sold by the partnership.[49]

Example 38

K sold her 10% interest in the KLM Partnership to P for $45,000 cash. KLM used the cash method of accounting and had the following balance sheet as of the date K sold her interest. K's outside basis in her interest was $35,500.

	Inside Basis	FMV
Cash	$ 40,000	$ 40,000
Accounts receivable	0	30,000
Stock in trade	90,000	100,000
Section 1231 assets (no recapture)	225,000	300,000
	$355,000	$470,000

---

[46] § 706(c)(2)(A)(i). Refer to the discussion of the closing of a partnership year with respect to a partner at, *supra*.

[47] *Supra*, Footnote 23.

[48] § 751(a). Note that for sales or exchanges, inventory is considered a § 751 hot asset whether or not it is substantially appreciated.

[49] Reg. § 1.751-1(a)(2).

	Inside Basis	FMV
Debt	$ 20,000	$ 20,000
Capital: K.	33,500	45,000
Other partners	301,500	405,000
	$355,000	$470,000

At date of sale, the partnership had both unrealized receivables of $30,000 (zero basis accounts receivable) and $100,000 of inventory.

If the hot assets were sold by the partnership at fair market value the partnership would recognize $40,000 of ordinary income ($130,000 fair market value − $90,000 basis). Ten percent of this income, or $4,000, would be allocated to K. Therefore, on the sale of her partnership interest K must recognize $4,000 of ordinary income under § 751(a).

Subsequent to the application of § 751(a), the amount realized on the sale of K's partnership interest has been reduced to $34,000 ($47,000 total amount realized—$13,000 attributable to hot assets). K's outside basis in her partnership interest has been reduced to $26,500 ($35,500 predistribution basis—$9,000 basis allocated to hot assets). Under the general rule of § 741, K recognizes a $7,500 capital gain on the sale of her partnership interest.

These computations can be summarized as follows:

	Total	Hot Assets [§ 751(a)]	Other (§ 741)
Amount realized	$47,000	$13,000	$34,000
Adjusted basis	(35,500)	(9,000)	(26,500)
Recognized gain/loss.	$11,500	$ 4,000	$ 7,500
		Ordinary income	Capital gain

The application of § 751(a) in *Example 38* converted $4,000 of potential capital gain into ordinary income. However, application of the subsection may actually trigger the recognition of ordinary income in a situation in which a partner realizes a loss on the sale of a partnership interest.

Example 39

U sold his 20% interest in the accrual basis TUV Partnership to P for $22,000 cash. As of the date of sale, U's outside basis in his interest was $40,000 and the partnership had the following balance sheet:

		Inside Basis	FMV
Cash		$ 5,000	$ 5,000
Accounts receivable.		7,000	7,000
Stock in trade		45,000	80,000
Equipment cost	$30,000		
Accumulated depreciation	(9,000)	21,000	28,000
Other § 1231 assets (no recapture)		122,000	50,000
		$200,000	$170,000
Debt		$ 60,000	$ 60,000
Capital: U		28,000	22,000
Other partners		112,000	88,000
		$200,000	$170,000

At date of sale, TUV had unrealized receivables of $7,000 (§ 1245 recapture potential in equipment), accounts receivable of $7,000 and $80,000 of inventory.

If the hot assets were sold by the partnership at fair market value the partnership would have an amount realized of $94,000 ($80,000 for the inventory, $7,000 for the accounts receivable, and $7,000 for the depreciation recapture). The partnership's basis in these assets is $52,000 (note that the basis in the recapture is zero). Therefore, the partnership would have ordinary income of $42,000. Twenty percent of this income, or $8,400, would be allocated to U. Therefore, on the sale of his partnership interest U must recognize $8,400 of ordinary income under § 751(a).

Subsequent to the application of § 751(a), the amount realized on sale of U's partnership interest has been reduced to $15,200 ($34,000 total amount realized—$18,800 attributable to hot assets). U's outside basis in his partnership interest has been reduced to $29,600 ($40,000 predistribution basis—$10,400 basis allocated to hot assets). Under the general rule of § 741, U recognizes a $14,400 capital loss on the sale of his partnership interest.

	Total	Hot Assets [§ 751(a)]	Other (§ 741)
Amount realized	$34,000	$18,800	$ 15,200
Adjusted basis	(40,000)	(10,400)	(29,600)
Recognized gain/loss	$ (6,000)	$ 8,400	$(14,400)
		Ordinary income	Capital loss

In addition to the recognition of ordinary income if the partnership has hot assets, the seller of a partnership interest may also have special tax treatment in three other situations: collectibles gain, § 1250 capital gain, and residual long-term capital gain or loss.

First, if at the time of the sale of a partnership interest (which has been held for more than one year) the partnership holds collectibles with unrealized appreciation, the gain attributable to this appreciation is taxed at 28 percent.[50] A collectible includes any work of art, rug, antique, metal, gem, stamp, coin, or alcoholic beverage.[51]

Example 40

H and G are individuals that have been equal partners in HG for the last three years. The partnership owns gems that qualify as collectibles that have an adjusted basis of $500 and a fair market value of $1,100. H sells her interest in HG to I. As a result, $300 of H's gain from the sale will be characterized as collectibles gain (50% of the $600 gain that HG would have realized if it sold its collectibles in a fully taxable transaction).

Second, unrecaptured § 1250 gain is taxed at a 25% maximum rate. Unrecaptured § 1250 gain is the capital gain that would be treated as ordinary income if § 1250(b)(1) required all depreciation to be recaptured as ordinary income. If a partner sells an interest in a partnership, and the partnership has unrecaptured § 1250 gain, then the partner must take into account his or her portion of that gain in computing the tax results.[52]

Example 41

Assume in *Example 40* above that HG also owns residential rental property. At the time of H's sale, the property had a fair market value of $110,000 and adjusted basis of $60,000. The property's original cost basis was $100,000. Straight-line depreciation of

---

[50] § 1(h)(6)(B).

[51] § 408(m)(3).

[52] Reg. § 1.1(h)-1(b)(3)(ii).

$40,000 had been claimed on the property. At the time of H's sale, one must compute what H's share of unrecaptured § 1250 gain would be if the property was sold. Since the property is realty and straight-line depreciation was used there would be no § 1250 recapture. Consequently, the entire gain ($50,000) would be a § 1231 gain. However, the § 1231 gain would be treated as a 25% gain to the extent of any straight-line depreciation claimed ($40,000). H's share of the 25% gain is $20,000. Consequently, of the total gain recognized by H on the sale of his partnership interest, $20,000 will be 25% gain due to the § 1250 unrecaptured gain.

The collectibles gain and § 1250 unrecaptured gain that are allocable to a partner that has sold his or her partnership interest are together known as the look-through capital gain.[53] The residual long-term capital gain or loss is computed as follows:

Residual long-term capital gain/loss =
§ 741 long-term capital gain or loss (after application of § 751),
Minus,
Look-through capital gain or loss.

Example 42

G and H are individuals that have been equal partners in Partnership B for the last two years. B owns collectibles with a basis and fair market value of $3,000 and $5,000, respectively. G sells his interest in partnership B to R and has a total recognized gain of $500. After the application of the § 751 hot assets rules, assume that G recognizes ordinary income of $2,000 and § 741 long-term capital loss of $1,500 (i.e., the pre-look through long-term capital loss). G's share of the collectibles gain (i.e., the look-through capital gain) is $1,000 ([$5,000 − $3,000] × 50%).

Total gain	$ 500
§ 751 hot asset ordinary income	(2,000)
Pre-look through long-term capital loss	(1,500)
Gain from collectibles	1,000
Residual long-term capital loss	$(2,500)

To summarize, G has $2,000 of ordinary income, $1,000 collectibles gain taxed at 28 percent, and a $2,500 capital loss.

Tax Consequences to Purchaser

Section 742 states that the basis of a partnership interest acquired other than by contribution shall be determined under the normal basis rules provided in § 1011 and following. Thus, the purchaser of a partnership interest takes a *cost basis* in the interest. The cost basis includes the amount of cash and the value of any noncash property paid to the seller plus the amount of any partnership liabilities assumed by the purchaser in his or her role as a new partner.

The fact that a purchaser is given a cost basis in the partnership interest rather than in a proportionate share of partnership assets reflects the entity theory of partnerships. Section 743(a) reinforces this perspective by specifying that the basis of partnership property shall not be adjusted as the result of a transfer of an interest in a partnership by sale or exchange. This general rule typically results in an imbalance between a purchasing partner's outside basis and the inside basis of his or her proportionate share of partnership assets.

---

[53] § 1(h)(1)(D); Reg. § 1.1(h)-1(b)(1).

Example 43

P purchased a 10% interest in the accrual basis KLM Partnership from K for $45,000 cash. As of the date of sale, the partnership had the following balance sheet:

	Inside Basis	FMV
Cash	$ 40,000	$ 40,000
Accounts receivable	30,000	30,000
Stock in trade	90,000	100,000
Depreciable assets	225,000	300,000
	$385,000	$470,000
Debt	$ 20,000	$ 20,000
Capital: K (replaced by P)	36,500	45,000
Other partners	328,500	405,000
	$385,000	$470,000

P's cost basis in his new partnership interest is $47,000 ($45,000 cash + 10% of KLM's debt). The transaction between P and K had no effect on the basis of the partnership assets, so that P's aggregate inside basis in 10% of KLM's assets is only $38,500.

The imbalance between P's outside and inside bases in *Example 43* has several negative implications for P. If the partnership sells its entire stock in trade for $ 100,000, P will be allocated $1,000 of ordinary income (the excess of the $10,000 value of 10% of the stock in trade over its $9,000 basis), even though P indirectly paid $10,000 to acquire his share of this asset. Similarly, P will be allocated tax depreciation computed on the $22,500 inside basis of 10% of KLM's depreciable assets, even though P indirectly paid $30,000 to acquire his share of these assets.

Special Basis Adjustment for Purchaser

Strict adherence to the entity theory is relaxed if a purchaser acquires an interest in a partnership with a § 754 election in effect.[54] In this case, § 743(b) provides that any excess of the purchaser's outside basis over the inside basis of his or her proportionate share of partnership assets becomes a *positive* adjustment to that partner's inside basis.[55] Conversely, any excess of a purchaser's inside basis in his or her proportionate share of partnership assets over outside basis becomes a *negative* adjustment to that partner's inside basis.

Any positive or negative adjustment to the inside basis of the partnership property must be allocated to specific assets in such a manner as to reduce the difference between the fair market value and the tax basis of the asset. For purposes of this adjustment, the partnership's assets are divided into two property classes:[56]

1. Capital assets and § 1231 property (i.e., capital gain property), and
2. All other assets (i.e., ordinary income property).

The allocation of the optional basis adjustment between these two classes is based on the gain or loss that would be allocated to the transferee partner based on a hypothetical sale of all the partnership's assets. Therefore, it is possible that a positive adjustment could be made to the capital assets and a negative adjustment to the other assets, or vice versa.

[54] The § 754 election is discussed at, *supra*.
[55] § 743(b)(1).
[56] § 755.

The adjustment to the ordinary income class is the amount of income, gain, or loss allocated to the transferee partner from the hypothetical sale of all ordinary income property at fair market value for cash. The adjustment to the capital asset class is then the difference in the total adjustment less the adjustment to the ordinary income class. However, any decrease in basis adjustment for the capital asset class cannot reduce the basis of the capital assets below zero. Once the basis of the capital assets is reduced to zero, any remaining negative adjustment must be used to reduce the basis of ordinary income property.[57]

The adjustment to each class must then be allocated to assets within that class. Generally, the adjustment to each item of ordinary income property equals the amount of income, gain, or loss allocated to the transferee partner in a hypothetical sale of the item. The adjustment for each item in the ordinary income class is determined as shown below.

Example 44

G sells his 25% interest in the JJG Partnership to D on March 15, 2016. JJG Partnership previously made a § 754 election. D paid $50,000 to G and assumed G's share of partnership liabilities. JJG's balance sheet at the date of sale is as follows:

	Inside Basis	FMV
Cash	$ 40,000	$ 40,000
Accounts receivable	20,000	15,000
Inventory	42,000	50,000
Building	70,000	85,000
Land	20,000	40,000
	$192,000	$230,000
Debt	$ 30,000	$ 30,000
Capital: G (replaced by D)	40,500	50,000
Other partners	121,500	150,000
	$192,000	$230,000

Since the JJG Partnership has a § 754 election in effect, D is entitled to a $9,500 basis adjustment (the excess of his $57,500 outside basis over the $48,000 inside basis of his 25% share of JJG's assets [$192,000 × 25%]). Note that his outside basis is computed as the $50,000 cash payment plus 25% of the partnership's debt. The $9,500 is labeled as a § 743(b) adjustment.

The § 743(b) adjustment is allocated between classes and among properties based on the allocations of income, gain, or loss that the transferee partner would receive from a hypothetical sale of all partnership assets.

Allocation between Classes:

	D's Allocable Share (25%)		
Ordinary Income Property	Adjusted Basis	FMV	Gain/(Loss)
Accounts receivable	$ 5,000	$ 3,750	$(1,250)
Inventory	10,500	12,500	2,000
Total	$15,500	$16,250	$ 750
Capital Gain Property			
Building	$17,500	$21,250	$ 3,750
Land	5,000	10,000	5,000
Total	$22,500	$31,250	$ 8,750

Therefore, the § 743(b) adjustment is allocated $750 to the ordinary income property and $8,750 to the capital gain property.

---

[57] Reg. § 1.755-1(b).

Allocation within Classes:

If a hypothetical sale occurred, D would be allocated a loss of $1,250 from the sale of the receivables and a gain of $2,000 from the sale of the inventory. D would also be allocated a gain of $3,750 for the building and a gain of $5,000 for the land. Therefore, these amounts are D's basis adjustment for each of these assets.

To summarize, D's allocation of the inside basis of JJG's assets is as follows:

	Inside Basis	25% of Basis	Section 743(b) Adjustment	Adjusted Inside Basis
Cash	$40,000	$10,000	$ 0	$10,000
Accounts receivable	20,000	5,000	(1,250)	3,750
Inventory	42,000	10,500	2,000	12,500
Building	70,000	17,500	3,750	21,250
Land	20,000	5,000	5,000	10,000
				$57,500

Note that D's total outside basis of $57,500 is now equal to his allocation of the inside basis of the partnership's assets.

Effect of the Adjustment

A § 743(b) special basis adjustment belongs only to the purchasing partner and has no effect on the other partners. Although any benefit of a § 743(b) basis adjustment accrues only to the purchasing partner, the burden of record keeping for the adjustment falls upon the partnership. This disparity is one reason partnerships may be reluctant to make the § 754 election necessary to activate § 743(b). If a partner has a special basis adjustment with respect to an asset disposed of by the partnership in a taxable transaction, the adjustment will be taken into account in calculating that partner's distributive share of gain or loss.

Example 45

If the JJG Partnership in the previous example sells its inventory for $50,000 and recognizes $8,000 of ordinary income, D's 25% share of that is $2,000. However, D's $2,000 special basis adjustment in the inventory reduces his distributive share of the partnership ordinary income to zero.

If a partner has a special basis adjustment with respect to a depreciable or amortizable asset, the adjustment will generate an additional cost recovery deduction for that partner.[58] Therefore, D can depreciate the $3,750 step-up in basis for the building in *Example 44*.

Substantial Built-In Loss

Even if a § 754 election is not in effect, the rules discussed above will apply if there is a substantial built-in loss to the partnership immediately after the transfer of the partnership interest. A substantial built-in loss occurs if the partnership's basis in its assets exceeds the fair market value of those assets by more than $250,000.[59]

---

[58] A § 743(b) basis adjustment to depreciable property is considered a newly purchased asset placed in service in the year in which the adjustment arises. Prop. Reg. § 1.168-2(n).

[59] See § 743(d)(1). These rules apply for distributions made after October 22, 2004. Different rules apply to electing investment partnerships. A discussion of these rules is beyond the scope of this text.

> ### Example 46
>
> Partner M sells his 20% partnership for $500,000 at a time when the MN Partnership has a basis and fair market value in assets of $3,000,000 and $2,500,000, respectively. Since the basis of the partnership's assets exceeds the fair market value by more than $250,000 (by $500,000 [$3,000,000 − $2,500,000]), a substantial built-in loss exists. Therefore, even if Partnership MN does not have a § 754 election in effect, the partnership must reduce the acquiring partner's share of the basis in its assets by $100,000, the proportional amount of the $500,000 built-in loss according to the rules of § 755.

Special Rule for Built-In-Losses

If the seller of a partnership interest had previously contributed built-in-loss property to the partnership, special rules apply. As was explained in Chapter 9, if a partner contributes property with built-in losses, § 704(c) requires that when the property is sold, any recognized loss must be allocated to the contributing partner to the extent of the built-in loss, with any remaining loss allocated per the partnership agreement. However, § 704(c)(1)(C) requires that in determining the amount of items allocated to other (non-contributing) partners, the basis of the property is assumed to be its fair market value at the time of contribution.[60]

> ### Example 47
>
> Partner L contributes land to equal partnership LO with a basis of $100 and a fair market value of $80. Therefore, the land has a built-in loss of $20. If the partnership sold the land for $80, the $20 loss would be allocated to L.
>
> Assume that L sells his partnership interest to M for $80. L would recognize a loss of $20 from the sale of his partnership interest. Under previous law, M would "step into the shoes" of L and the first $20 loss from the future sale of the land would be allocated to M. § 704(c)(1)(C) now requires that the basis of the land be treated as $80 (its fair market value on the date of contribution) for purposes of allocating any tax items to partners M and O. Thus, if the land was later sold by the partnership for $70, the basis of the land would be $80 (not $100). The sale would create a $10 loss ($70 amount realized less $80 basis), none of which is a built-in loss. The $10 loss would be allocated equally to partners M and O.

The purpose of this rule is to prevent the partners from benefiting from a double loss. If L recognizes a loss of $20 on the sale of the partnership interest and M could recognize another loss of $20 when the land was sold, a double benefit would be created.

OTHER DISPOSITIONS OF PARTNERSHIP INTERESTS

Exchanges

As a general rule, an exchange of a partnership interest for another asset is a fully taxable event. The tax consequences to the original partner who surrenders the interest and the new partner who acquires the interest are identical to the consequences to a seller and purchaser of a partnership interest. Even if the asset received in exchange for an interest in one partnership is an interest in another partnership, the exchange is taxable; § 1031(a), which permits the nontaxable exchange of like-kind business or investment properties, is inapplicable to exchanges of partnership interests.[61] Nevertheless, the IRS has ruled that an exchange of interests *in the same partnership* (for example, an exchange of a general interest for a limited interest)

---

[60] This provision does not apply to contributions of property made before October 23, 2004.

[61] § 1031(a)(2)(D).

is a nontaxable event.[62] A contribution of a partnership interest to a corporation in exchange for corporate stock is nontaxable if the exchange meets the strict requirements of § 351(a).[63]

Abandonments

If a taxpayer voluntarily surrenders legal interest in a business or investment asset, he or she is entitled to deduct any amount of unrecovered basis in the asset as an *abandonment loss*.[64] A partner may abandon an interest in a partnership by manifesting his or her decision by "some overt act or statement reasonably calculated to give a third party notice of the abandonment."[65] For example, a partner who unequivocally announced his withdrawal from a partnership at a partners' meeting and refused to participate in any further partnership activities was deemed to have abandoned his interest, even though applicable state law provided no explicit procedure for doing so.[66]

As a general rule, the abandonment of property results in an ordinary loss. Because the taxpayer receives no payment of any kind for the abandoned asset, the disposition cannot be considered a sale or exchange and therefore cannot result in a capital loss.[67] However, if a partner who withdraws from a partnership by abandoning his or her interest is thereby relieved of any amount of partnership debt, such relief is considered a distribution of cash to the partner. This distribution, in turn, is considered an amount realized on the sale of the partnership interest.[68] As a result, the partner must recognize a capital rather than an ordinary loss upon abandonment.[69]

Example 48

R and S each owned a 20% interest in the Summa Partnership. R, a limited partner, had a $4,000 outside basis in her interest while S, a general partner, had a $10,000 outside basis. Both R and S withdrew from Summa by abandoning their partnership interests. Immediately prior to the partners' withdrawal, Summa owed $30,000 of recourse debt. Under § 752(a), none of this debt was included in limited partner R's outside basis but $7,500 of the debt was included in general partner S's outside basis.

Under § 752(b), the decrease in S's portion of Summa's debt upon his withdrawal from the partnership is considered a $7,500 cash distribution in liquidation of his interest. Consequently, S recognizes a $2,500 capital loss upon the abandonment of his interest. Because none of Summa's debt was included in R's outside basis in her interest, R received no constructive distribution of cash upon her withdrawal and can recognize a $4,000 ordinary loss on the abandonment.[70]

Gifts of Partnership Interests and Family Partnerships

Dispositions of partnership interests by gift generally have no income tax consequences to either donor or donee, although the donor may be liable for a gift tax on the transfer.[71] The donee will take a basis in the partnership interest as determined under § 1015. The transfer of a partnership interest by gift does not close the partnership taxable year with respect to the donor. However, the partnership income for the year during which the gift occurs must be allocated between the donor and donee based on the number of days that each owned the interest.[72]

LO.6
Apply the family partnership rules to partnership interests created by gift.

[62] Rev. Rul. 84-52, 1984-1 C.B. 157 and Rev. Rul. 95-37, 1995 IRB 130.

[63] Rev. Rul. 84-111, 1984-2 C.B. 88 provides a complete analysis of the tax consequences of the incorporation of a partnership business.

[64] § 165(a).

[65] *Echols v. Comm.*, 91-2 USTC ¶50,360, 68 AFTR2d 5157, 935 F.2d 703 (CA-5, 1991), *rev'g* 93 T.C. 553 (1989).

[66] *Ibid.*

[67] Section 1222 defines a capital loss as a loss from the sale or exchange of a capital asset.

[68] § 731(a).

[69] *Citron*, 97 T.C. 200 (1991).

[70] Rev. Rul. 93-80, 1993-2 C.B. 239.

[71] If the donor's relief of partnership liabilities attributable to the gift of the partnership interest exceeds the donor's outside basis in the interest, the excess relief over basis must be recognized as a gain on sale of the interest. Reg. § 1.1001-1(e).

[72] Reg. § 1.706-1(c)(5).

Transfers of partnership interests by gift usually involve donors and donees who are members of the same family, and therefore often result in the creation of family partnerships. Such partnerships can be an effective way to divide the income from a family business among various family members. To the extent the income can be allocated and taxed to individuals in the lower marginal tax brackets, family partnerships can also achieve a significant tax savings.

Not surprisingly, the tax laws restrict the use of family partnerships as income-shifting devices. If the income earned by a partnership is primarily attributable to the individual efforts and talents of its partners, any allocation of that income to nonproductive partners would be an unwarranted assignment of earned income. Accordingly, a family member cannot be a partner in a personal or professional service business unless he or she is capable of performing the type of services offered to the partnership's clientele.[73]

A family member can be a partner in a business in which capital is a material income-producing factor.[74] In contrast to a service partnership, the mere ownership of an equity interest in a capital intensive partnership entitles a partner to a share of partnership income. Under the general rules of § 704, a partner's allocable share of income does not have to be in proportion to his or her interest in partnership capital as long as the allocation has substantial economic effect. However, § 704(e)(2) provides that in the case of any partnership capital interest *created by gift*, the income allocable to such interest cannot be proportionally greater than the income allocated to the donor's capital.

Example 49

M creates a partnership with his son S and daughter D by giving each child an equity interest in his business. M is in the highest marginal tax bracket, while his children are in the 15% marginal tax bracket. The initial MSD Partnership balance sheet appears as follows:

Contributed business assets	$300,000		
		Capital: M	$200,000
		S	50,000
		D	50,000
			$300,000

If S and D's interests had not been created by gift, the partnership agreement could allocate any amount of partnership income to S and D as long as the allocation had substantial economic effect. Because the interests were created by gift, the maximum percentage of income allocable to S and D respectively is 16.7% ($50,000 donee's capital ÷ $300,000 total capital of both donor and donees).

Section 704(e)(2) also requires that any allocation of income with respect to donor and donee partners take into account the value of services rendered to the partnership by the donor. This statutory requirement prevents a donor partner from forgoing reasonable compensation from the partnership in order to maximize the amount of income shifted to the donee partners.

---

[73] See *Comm. v. Culbertson*, 337 U.S. 733 (USSC, 1949).

[74] § 704(e)(1). Capital is a material income producing factor if the operation of the partnership business requires substantial inventories or a substantial investment in plant, machinery, or equipment. Reg. § 1.704-1(e)(1)(iv).

Example 50

Refer to the facts in *Example 49*. If M performs services for MSD during its first taxable year that are reasonably worth $25,000, he must be compensated for the services before any amount of partnership income may be allocated to S and D. If the partnership earns $145,000 of operating income during its first year, the maximum amount of such income allocable to S and D respectively is $20,000 (16.7% of [$145,000 operating income − $25,000 compensation to M]).

Note that the restrictions illustrated in *Examples 48* and *49* technically apply to any partnership interest created by gift, regardless of any familial relationship between donor and donee. Realistically, these restrictions most frequently apply to family partnerships. In order to prevent families from circumventing these restrictions, the statute states that a partnership interest purchased from a family member is considered to have been acquired by gift.[75]

Death of a Partner

When an individual partner dies, his or her partnership interest passes to a *successor in interest* in the partnership.[76] Because the death of a partner causes a closing of the partnership's tax year with respect to that partner, items of income, gain, loss, deduction, or credit attributable to the deceased partner's interest up to date of death will be included on the final tax return of the decedent. Any amounts for the remainder of the partnership's tax year must be reported by the deceased partner's successor in interest.[77]

Example 51

Individual Z, who owned a 40% interest in the capital, profits, and loss of the calendar year XYZ Partnership, died on November 3 of the current year. Under the terms of Z's will, all his assets (including his interest in XYZ) passed to his estate. Because the partnership's tax year closes with respect to Z on the date of his death, XYZ's income or loss attributable to this interest from January 1 to November 3 will be included in Z's final tax return. Income or loss attributable to this 40% interest for the remainder of the year must be included in the first fiduciary income tax return filed on behalf of Z's estate.

Deceased partners obviously can no longer participate in or contribute to the success of partnership activities. Consequently, many partnerships do not allow a deceased partner's successor in interest to continue to share in the profits and losses of the partnership business. The agreements governing such partnerships specify that a successor in interest cannot become a partner and must accept a liquidating distribution from the partnership or sell the interest to the surviving partners. Typically, such forced dispositions are effective as of the date of the partner's death. In such case, the partnership taxable year closes with respect to the deceased partner as well as any successor in interest.[78]

Example 52

Refer to the facts in *Example 51*. Assume that the XYZ Partnership agreement stipulates that upon the death of any partner, the successor in interest is obligated to sell

---

[75] § 704(e)(3). For purposes of this rule, a partner's family members include a spouse, ancestors, and lineal descendants.

[76] The successor in interest is named under the decedent partner's will or determined by reference to state intestacy laws if the decedent died without a will.

[77] § 706(c)(2)(A)(ii).

[78] Reg. § 1.706-1(c)(3)(iv).

the interest back to XYZ for its fair market value as of date of death. In this case, XYZ's current taxable year closes with respect to Z on November 3. Z's final tax return will include his 40% distributive share of partnership income or loss from January 1–November 3 of the current year. Because Z's estate does not become a partner, no amount of XYZ's current-year income or loss will be included in the first fiduciary income tax return.

A deceased partner's gross estate for federal estate tax purposes includes the fair market value of the partnership interest at date of death. As a general rule, the decedent's successor in interest takes an outside basis in the interest equal to such fair market value plus the successor's share of partnership liabilities.[79] This general rule does not apply to the extent of any item of income in respect of a decedent inherent in the interest.[80] *Income in respect of a decedent* (IRD) includes any item of gross income to which a decedent was entitled at death but was not includible in the decedent's final tax return because of the decedent's method of accounting.[81] Under this definition, partnership income earned prior to the death of a partner but reported on the tax return of the partner's successor in interest is IRD.[82]

Example 53

Refer to the facts in *Example 51*. On November 3 of the current year, cash basis Partnership XYZ had the following balance sheet:

	Inside Basis	FMV
Accounts receivable	$ 0	$ 45,000
Business assets	197,500	265,000
	$197,500	$310,000
Debt	$ 10,000	$ 10,000
Capital: Z (replaced by estate of Z)	75,000	120,000
Other partners	112,500	180,000
	$197,500	$310,000

As of the date of Z's death, his interest in the XYZ Partnership was valued at $120,000. This total value equaled $102,000 (the value of 40% of XYZ's net business assets) plus $18,000 (the value of 40% of XYZ's current-year income earned through November 3). The Estate of Z's 40% share of XYZ's income for the remainder of the year was $2,000 for the period November 4–December 31. The estate must recognize the full $20,000 distributive share, including $18,000 of IRD, as gross income on its first income tax return.[83] The estate's outside basis in its partnership interest is $106,000 (the $102,000 date-of-death value of the partnership interest exclusive of IRD plus the estate's $4,000 share of XYZ's debts).

The fact that the outside basis in a partnership interest transferred at death is stepped up (or down) to fair market value can result in an imbalance between outside basis and inside basis. Such imbalance may have negative implications for a successor in interest who continues as a partner in the partnership.

---

[79] Reg. § 1.742-1.

[80] § 1014(c).

[81] Reg. § 1.691(a)-1(b).

[82] Reg. § 1.706-1(c)(3)(v). Any § 736(a) payments received by a deceased partner's successor in interest also represent IRD. § 753.

[83] § 691(a). The estate may be entitled to a § 691(c) deduction for federal estate tax with respect to the IRD.

> ## Example 54
>
> Refer to the facts in *Example 53*. The estate of Z's outside basis in its 40% interest in XYZ is $106,000 (the $120,000 date-of-death value of the partnership interest − $18,000 value of IRD + $4,000 share of partnership debt). However, the estate's proportionate share of the inside basis of the partnership business assets is only $79,000 ($40% of $197,500). The estate's future share of any gain recognized on the sale of these assets or cost recovery deductions attributable to the assets will reflect the lower inside basis rather than the stepped-up outside basis.

An imbalance between a successor in interest's outside and inside bases is remedied if the partnership has a § 754 election in effect. In such case, § 743(b) permits a special adjustment with respect to the inside basis of the partnership assets.[84] If the XYZ Partnership in *Example 54* has made the § 754 election, the estate of Z will have a $27,000 positive basis adjustment (the excess of its $106,000 outside basis over the $79,000 inside basis in 40% of XYZ's assets) to be allocated to the partnership's appreciated business assets.

Partnership Termination

LO.7
Recognize a termination of a partnership and summarize the tax consequences of the termination to the partners.

One of the important legal characteristics of the partnership form of business is *limited life*. Under state law, a partnership is dissolved whenever any partner ceases to be associated in the carrying on of the partnership business.[85] From a legal perspective, a partnership's identity, and therefore its existence, is dependent upon the continued association of a particular group of partners. This perspective is consistent with the aggregate theory of partnerships. Nevertheless, it would be totally impractical to require a partnership to close its taxable year and make a final accounting of its business activities every time an existing partner left or a new partner joined the partnership.

Section 708(a) adopts the entity theory by providing that a partnership does not terminate for tax purposes simply because it may be dissolved under state law. In other words, a partnership shall continue in existence as an entity for purposes of Subchapter K even if the association of partners changes. Section 708(b) provides that a partnership shall terminate for tax purposes *only if*:

1. No part of any business, financial operation, or venture is being conducted by the partnership (*natural termination*), or

2. Within a 12-month period there is a sale or exchange of 50% or more of the total interest in partnership capital and profits (*technical termination*).

TECHNICAL TERMINATIONS

When a partnership ceases to conduct any type of economic activity, its termination for federal tax purposes marks the natural end of its life as a business entity. In contrast, a partnership that is terminated because of a sale or exchange of a 50% or greater interest may be conducting a vital, ongoing business. Moreover, the partners who were not involved in the sale or exchange may be unaware that the terminating transaction even occurred!

Only sales or exchanges of partnership interests can trigger a technical termination. Other types of dispositions, such as gifts or transfers at death, are ignored. Similarly, changes in the relative ownership interests of partners because of contributions to or distributions from a partnership cannot result in termination. Sales or exchanges will not cause termination unless a 50% or greater cumulative interest in both capital and profits changes hands within a 12-month period.

---

[84] This is the same statutory remedy available to a purchaser of a partnership interest.

[85] Uniform Partnership Act, § 29.

Example 55

Partners A, B, and C have owned equal interests in the capital and profits of the ABC Partnership since 2002.

- On January 12, 2016 A sold her one-third interest to new partner D.

- On July 8, 2016 B sold 10 percentage points of his interest to new partner E.

- On November 22, 2016 C gave his one-third to new partner F.

- On January 9, 2017 F exchanged this interest for stock in a new corporation; the exchange was nontaxable under § 351.

The January 12 sale did not terminate the ABC Partnership because only a 33.3% interest in capital and profits was sold. The July 8 sale did not terminate the partnership because at that point in time only a 43.3% cumulative interest in capital and profits had been sold within a 12-month period. The November 22 gift did not enter into the termination calculation. The January 9 exchange did result in a termination of the ABC Partnership; within the 12-month period beginning on January 12, 2016, a cumulative 76.6% interest in the partnership was sold or exchanged. If F had delayed his exchange until after January 11, 2017, the transaction would not have triggered a termination.

In determining whether a cumulative 50% interest has been sold or exchanged within the crucial 12-month time period, multiple transfers of the *same interest* are counted only once.[86] In *Example 55*, if D (rather than F) had exchanged his one-third interest for corporate stock on January 9, 2017, the exchange would not have resulted in a technical termination.

EFFECT OF TERMINATION

Upon termination, a partnership's taxable year closes with respect to all its partners. If the partnership and any partner use different taxable years, a bunching of more than 12 months of income may occur.

Example 56

The QRS Partnership uses a calendar year for tax purposes, while corporate partner Q uses a fiscal year ending June 30. The partnership terminated on March 31, 2017 and closed its taxable year on that date. Because two partnership years (calendar year 2016 and the short taxable year from January 1–March 31, 2017) ended within its fiscal year ending June 30, 2017, Q must include its distributive share of 15 months of partnership income in its taxable income for the year.

Pursuant to a natural termination, a partnership typically will wind up its affairs and distribute all remaining cash and assets to the partners in complete liquidation of their interests.[87] In a technical termination, the partnership contributes all of its assets and liabilities to a new partnership in exchange for an interest in the new partnership. The terminated partnership then distributes interests in the new partnership to the purchasing partner and all other remaining partners.[88] The result of the application of these rules is that the technical termination does not automatically result in adjustments to the bases of the partnership assets because no assets are treated as being distributed.[89]

---

[86] Reg. § 1.708-1(b)(2).

[87] Reg. § 1.708-1(b)(1).

[88] Reg. § 1.708-1(b)(4).

[89] A complete analysis of the potential tax consequences of technical terminations is beyond the scope of an introductory text.

PARTNERSHIP MERGERS AND DIVISIONS

If the partners in two or more partnerships decide to combine operations by merging their partnerships, the new partnership will be considered a *continuation* of a merged partnership if the former partners of that partnership own more than 50% of the capital and profits of the new partnership. Any merged partnership that is not continued is terminated as of the date of merger.[90]

Example 57

A and B own equal interests in the AB Partnership, which has a net worth of $80,000. Y and Z own equal interests in the YZ Partnership, which has a net worth of $160,000. The four individuals decide to merge the two partnerships into the new ABYZ Partnership. A and B will each receive a 16.7% interest in partnership capital, profits, and loss. Y and Z will each receive a 33.3% interest in partnership capital, profits, and loss. Because Y and Z own a 66.7% aggregate interest in ABYZ, this partnership is a continuation of the original YZ Partnership. The AB Partnership terminates (and its taxable year closes) as of the date of merger.

If an existing partnership divides into two or more partnerships, any resulting partnership will be considered a continuation of the original partnership if its partners owned more than a 50% interest in the capital and profits of the original partnership.[91]

Example 58

The HIJKL Partnership (net worth $500,000) had five equal partners. The partnership divided into the HIJ Partnership (three equal partners and net worth $300,000) and the KL Partnership (two equal partners and net worth $200,000). Because the partners in HIJ owned a 60% interest in HIJKL, HIJ is a continuation of the original HIJKL Partnership. Consequently, only partners K and L terminated their interests in the continuing partnership. These two partners are deemed to have (1) received liquidating distributions of property from HIJKL, and (2) contributed such property in exchange for an interest in the new KL Partnership.

Problem Materials

DISCUSSION QUESTIONS

10-1 *Current versus Liquidating Distributions.* Explain the difference between a current distribution and a liquidating distribution from a partnership.

10-2 *Aggregate Theory.* How do the general rules applicable to partnership distributions reflect the aggregate theory of partnerships?

10-3 *Current Distributions.* Is the statement that a partner never recognizes a loss upon the receipt of a current distribution true or false? Explain your conclusion.

10-4 *Liquidating Distributions.* Under what circumstances will a partner recognize a capital loss upon the receipt of a liquidating distribution?

10-5 *Closing of Partnership Year.* Partner Z received a liquidating distribution from a calendar year partnership on April 3 of the current year. Explain why Z could not determine the tax consequences of the distribution until the end of the year.

---

[90] Reg. § 1.708-1(c).   [91] Reg. § 1.708-1(d)(1).

10-6 *Section 736(a) Payments.* Why would a partner who is terminating his or her interest in a partnership prefer a liquidating distribution to a § 736(a) payment of the same dollar amount?

10-7 *Partnership Goodwill.* Explain the difference in tax consequences to both partner and partnership of liquidating payments with respect to (1) specified and (2) unspecified partnership goodwill.

10-8 *Distributed Inventory.* During the current year, N received a partnership distribution consisting of four tracts of undeveloped land that the partnership held as inventory. N's accountant has advised her to hold the land for a minimum of five years before she attempts to sell it. What favorable tax consequences will this strategy achieve for N?

10-9 *Optional Basis Adjustments.* Under what circumstances would a partnership that has made a distribution to a partner decide not to make a § 754 election resulting in adjustments to the inside bases of its assets?

10-10 *Partnership Hot Assets.* Define the two types of hot assets that a partnership might own.

10-11 *Sale of a Partnership Interest.* Is the statement that the sale of an interest in a partnership owning hot assets can result in either ordinary gain or loss recognition true or false? Explain your conclusion.

10-12 *Sale of a Partnership Interest.* Does the fact that a partner recognizes capital gain or loss on the sale of an interest in a partnership with no hot assets reflect the entity or aggregate theory of partnerships?

10-13 *Tax Consequences to Purchaser.* Explain why the outside basis in a purchased interest in a partnership without a § 754 election in effect is usually different than the purchaser's proportionate share of the inside basis of partnership assets. Does this result reflect the entity or aggregate theory of partnerships?

10-14 *Section 754 Election.* Discuss the various reasons why a partnership might refuse to make a § 754 election when a new partner purchases an interest in the partnership.

10-15 *Abandonment of a Partnership Interest.* A partner who abandons a partnership interest may recognize either capital loss or ordinary loss. Explain.

10-16 *Family Partnerships.* In what ways does the tax law restrict the use of a family partnership as a device to shift income to individuals in the lower marginal tax brackets?

10-17 *Inherited Partnership Interests.* How is the basis of a partnership interest inherited from a decedent partner calculated?

10-18 *Death of a Partner.* How is any partnership income, gain, loss, deduction, or credit attributable to a deceased partner's interest allocated between that partner's final tax return and that of the successor in interest? Assume for purposes of your answer that death occurred on August 15th and that both the partnership and the deceased were calendar year taxpayers.

10-19 *Partnership Terminations.* Distinguish between the dissolution of a partnership under state law and the termination of a partnership for federal tax purposes.

10-20 *Partnership Mergers.* Under what circumstances could the merger of three partnerships into a single resulting partnership cause the termination of only two of the original partnerships?

PROBLEMS

10-21 *Current Distributions—Proportionate.* X is a 50% partner in XY, a calendar year partnership. X had a basis in her partnership interest of $10,000 at the beginning of the year. On October 1, she and the other partner withdrew $15,000 cash each as an advance against their anticipated share of partnership income for the year. The partnership's ordinary taxable income for the year was $60,000.

    a. How much gain or loss must X recognize on October 1?

    b. What is X's distributive share of partnership taxable income for the year, and what is the basis in her partnership interest at the end of the year?

    c. How would the answers to (a) and (b) change if partnership taxable income had been $6,000 instead of $60,000?

10-22 *Current Distribution—Proportionate.* The JK Partnership proposes making a proportionate current distribution to 50% partner K of *either* (a) $50,000 cash or (b) partnership inventory ($50,000 market value and $28,000 basis). Prior to any distribution, K's basis in his partnership interest is $40,000. Based on these facts, what are the tax consequences of the alternative distributions, and what factors should K consider in deciding which alternative to accept?

10-23 *Current Distribution—Proportionate.* During the current year, partner J received a proportionate distribution from HIJK Partnership, consisting of $13,000 cash and land (an investment asset to the partnership). The land had a basis to the partnership of $20,000 and FMV of $33,000. Prior to the distribution, J's basis in his partnership interest was $40,000. The distribution had no effect on J's profit and loss sharing ratio.

    a. How much gain or loss must J recognize because of this distribution? What basis will J have in the land? What basis will J have in his partnership interest after the distribution?

    b. Does the partnership recognize any gain on the distribution of the appreciated land to J?

    c. How would the answer to (a) change if J's basis in his interest prior to distribution had been $25,000 rather than $40,000?

10-24 *Current Distribution of Inventory.* C received a current proportionate distribution consisting of partnership inventory with an inside basis of $25,000 and a FMV of $31,000. C's predistribution outside basis in his partnership interest was $22,500.

    a. How much gain or loss must C recognize because of this distribution?

    b. What basis will C take in the distributed inventory and what will be C's postdistribution outside basis?

    c. How would your answers to (a) and (b) change if C's predistribution outside basis had been $29,000 rather than $22,500?

10-25 *Dispositions of Distributed Inventory.* Refer to the facts in *Problem 10-24*.

    a. What will be the tax consequences to C if he sells the distributed inventory for $30,000 in the first year following the distribution?

    b. How does your answer to (a) change if C waits for six years and then sells the distributed inventory for $40,000?

10-26 *Optional Adjustment to Basis—Current Proportionate Distribution.* Refer to *Problem 10-24(b)* and *(c)*. The partnership has a § 754 election in effect. Determine the § 734 basis adjustment for the partnership assets.

10-27 *Current Distribution—Proportionate.* A partnership is curtailing some of its operations and decides to make a proportionate distribution of excess assets to its two equal partners. P's share of each of the distributed assets is as follows:

	Inside Basis	Fair Market Value
Cash	$4,000	$4,000
Inventory	5,000	7,000
Investment stocks	2,000	3,000
Equipment	6,000	2,000

Calculate P's recognized gain or loss, basis in each asset, and basis in his partnership interest after distribution if P's basis in the partnership before distribution is:
a. $20,000,
b. $14,000,
c. $8,000.

10-28 *Optional Adjustment to Basis—Current Proportionate Distribution.* Refer to *Problem 10-27*. The partnership has a § 754 election in effect. Determine the § 734 basis adjustment for the partnership assets.

10-29 *Basis of Distributed Property—Current Distribution.* R receives a current distribution from the RST Partnership consisting of the following:

	Inside Basis	Fair Market Value
Cash	$10,000	$10,000
Accounts receivable	0	7,500
Inventory	4,000	5,000
Capital asset 1	5,000	4,000
Capital asset 2	8,000	6,000

Immediately prior to the distribution, R's outside basis in her partnership interest was $22,000. What are R's bases in the distributed assets, and what is her basis in the partnership interest after the distribution?

10-30 *Distribution of Contributed Property.* Four years ago, partner L contributed a nondepreciable investment asset to the LMNO Partnership in exchange for a 15% interest in partnership profits and capital. At date of contribution, the asset had a fair market value of $95,000 and a basis to L of $70,000.
a. During the current year, the partnership distributed the investment asset to partner O. Immediately prior to distribution, the investment asset had a fair market value of $132,000, and O's outside basis in her partnership interest was $400,000. What are the tax consequences of the distribution to partners L and O?
b. How would your answer to (a) change if L's contribution of the asset occurred eight (rather than four) years ago?
c. How would your answer to (a) change if the current-year distribution of the investment asset had been to L (rather than O), and L's predistribution outside basis in his partnership interest was $92,000?

10-31 *Distributions to Contributing Partners.* Two years ago, corporate partner S contributed Greenacre (a 425-acre tract of investment land) to the RST Partnership in exchange for a 45% interest in partnership profits and capital. At date of contribution, Greenacre had a fair market value of $200,000 and a basis to S of $60,000. The partnership does not have a § 754 election in effect.
a. During the current year, the partnership distributed a tract of commercial real estate to partner S. Immediately prior to distribution, the real estate had a fair market value of $232,000 and an inside basis of $205,000, and S's outside basis in its partnership interest was $83,000. The RST Partnership still owns Greenacre, which has a current fair market value of $225,000. What are the tax consequences of the distribution to S and the RST Partnership?
b. How would your answer to (a) change if S's contribution of the asset occurred nine (rather than two) years ago?

10-32 *Liquidating Distribution—Proportionate.* Immediately prior to its termination, the FN Partnership owned the following assets:

	Inside Basis	Fair Market Value
Cash	$ 40,000	$40,000
Equipment.	100,000	70,000
Accumulated depreciation	(60,000)	
Capital asset	10,000	30,000

F, a 50% partner, receives a one-half interest in each of the assets in complete liquidation of her partnership interest. F's outside basis in this interest is $45,000.
a. Calculate F's basis for each asset received in the distribution.
b. How would your answer to (a) change if F's outside basis in her partnership interest is $60,000?

10-33 *Liquidating Distribution—Proportionate.* The three partners in the ABC Real Estate Partnership decided to liquidate their business by distributing equal, undivided interests in partnership assets to each partner. Immediately prior to liquidation, ABC owned $63,000 cash and two tracts of land, Whiteacre and Blackacre, both of which were held for sale to customers in the ordinary course of the partnership business. Whiteacre had a fair market value of $185,000 and an inside basis of $120,000, and Blackacre had a fair market value of $318,000 and an inside basis of $270,000. The partnership owned no other assets and had no outstanding debt.
a. Partner A's preliquidation basis in his partnership interest was $200,000. How much gain or loss must A recognize on receipt of his one-third share of ABC's assets, and what basis will A take in his undivided interests in Whiteacre and Blackacre?
b. Partner C's preliquidation basis in her partnership interest was $125,000. How much gain or loss must C recognize on receipt of her one-third share of ABC's assets, and what basis will C take in her undivided interests in Whiteacre and Blackacre?

10-34 *Basis of Distributed Property—Liquidating Distribution.* After reduction for a distribution of cash and the required allocation of basis to unrealized receivables and inventory received in a liquidating distribution from the HIJ Partnership, Partner J has an outside basis of $100,000. J also receives the following capital assets as part of the liquidating distribution:

	Inside Basis	Fair Market Value
Capital asset 1	$25,000	$60,000
Capital asset 2	50,000	20,000

What basis does J take in each of the capital assets following this distribution?

10-35 *Section 734 Basis Adjustment.* Partner F received a liquidating distribution of $9,000 cash from the EFG Partnership. F's predistribution outside basis was $12,000. Assume that EFG has a § 754 election in effect. Partnership EFG owns the following assets after the distribution to F:

	Inside Basis	Fair Market Value
Cash	$20,000	$20,000
Inventory.	12,000	15,000
Capital asset M	14,000	10,000
Capital asset N.	10,000	8,000

a. What is F's gain or loss from the distribution?
b. What are the § 734 basis adjustments for the partnership's remaining assets?

10-36 *Substantially Appreciated Inventory.* A partnership has the following assets:

	Inside Basis	Fair Market Value
Cash	$10,000	$10,000
Accounts receivable	15,000	15,000
Inventory	30,000	38,000
Capital assets	40,000	46,000

a. Is the inventory substantially appreciated within the meaning of § 751(b)?
b. Would the answer to (a) change if the accounts receivable had a basis of zero instead of $15,000?
c. Would the answer to (a) change if the accounts receivable had a basis of zero and a fair market value of $5,000, and the fair market value of the inventory was only $30,000?

10-37 *Disproportionate Distribution.* RHS is a cash basis, calendar year partnership. At the beginning of the year, it had the following assets:

	Inside Basis	Fair Market Value
Cash	$10,000	$10,000
Inventory	8,000	15,000

Partner R, who was having cash flow problems, wanted to terminate his one-fourth interest in the partnership. On January 1, he received $6,250 cash as a liquidating distribution. R's outside basis in his interest immediately before the distribution was $4,500. How much gain or loss must R and RHS recognize as a result of the transaction?

10-38 *Disproportionate Distribution.* Q is a one-third partner in the QRS Partnership. The partnership makes a liquidating distribution to Q consisting of $54,000 worth of partnership inventory with an inside basis of $43,200. QRS does not have a § 754 election in effect. Immediately prior to the distribution, QRS had the following balance sheet:

	Inside Basis	Fair Market Value
Inventory	$ 48,000	$ 60,000
§ 1231 and capital assets	72,000	102,000
	$120,000	$162,000
Partners' capital	$120,000	$162,000

Q's predistribution basis in his partnership interest was $40,000.
a. How much gain or loss must Q recognize on the receipt of the distribution, and what basis will Q have in the inventory?
b. How much gain or loss must the QRS Partnership recognize because of the distribution, and how will the distribution affect the basis of the partnership's remaining assets?
c. How would your answers to (a) and (b) change if the predistribution basis in the partnership inventory had been $55,000 (rather than $48,000) and the inside basis in the $54,000 worth of inventory distributed to Q had been $49,500 (rather than $43,200)?

10-39 *Payments to a Retiring Partner.* The balance sheet of EFG Partnership shows the following:

	Inside Basis	Fair Market Value
Cash	$20,000	$20,000
Unrealized receivables	0	12,000
§ 1231 assets.	60,000	80,000
Goodwill	0	16,000

E, a 30% general partner, is retiring from the business. The partnership has agreed to pay $38,400 to E as a liquidating distribution. E's predistribution basis in her partnership interest is $24,000. Capital is not a material income-producing factor to the EFG Partnership.

a. Determine the tax consequences of the distribution to E and the partnership if the partnership agreement does not mention goodwill.

b. Determine the tax consequences of the distribution to E and the partnership if the partnership agreement states that retiring partners will be paid for their interest in partnership goodwill.

c. Determine the tax consequences of the distribution to E and the partnership if the partnership agreement does not mention goodwill and the $38,400 will be paid in five equal amounts over five years. E receives $7,680 in the first year.

10-40 *Payments to a Retiring Partner.* The balance sheet of RST Partnership shows the following:

	Inside Basis	Fair Market Value
Cash	$ 30,000	$ 30,000
Accounts receivable.	20,000	20,000
Inventory.	105,000	112,000
§ 1231 assets.	94,000	147,000
	$249,000	$309,000
Liabilities	$ 9,000	$ 9,000
R, Capital.	80,000	100,000
S, Capital.	80,000	100,000
T, Capital.	80,000	100,000
	$249,000	$309,000

During the current year, partners S and T agree to liquidate R's interest in the partnership for $115,000, to be paid in annual installments of $23,000 each over a five-year period. R's basis in his interest (including his one-third share of partnership liabilities) is $83,000. Capital is a material income-producing factor to the RST Partnership and the partnership has no unrecorded goodwill.

a. What are the tax consequences to R of the series of cash distributions from the partnership?

b. What are the consequences to the partnership of the liquidating distributions?

10-41 *Section 754 Election and Partnership Distributions.* Refer to the facts in *Problem 10-40*. What are the tax consequences to the continuing partnership if a § 754 election is in effect for the year in which R's interest is liquidated?

10-42 *Sale of a Partnership Interest.* Refer to the facts in *Problem 10-40*. Assume that U, an unrelated party, will purchase R's interest in RST Partnership for a lump sum payment of $115,000.

a. What are the tax consequences of the sale to R?

b. Compute U's basis in his newly purchased partnership interest.

c. What is the effect of U's purchase of R's partnership interest on the inside basis of partnership assets if RST Partnership does not have a § 754 election in effect?

10-43 *Consequences of a § 754 Election to a Purchasing Partner.* Refer to the facts in *Problem 10-42*. What are the tax consequences to new partner U and to RST Partnership if a § 754 election is in effect for the year in which U purchases R's partnership interest?

10-44 *Sale of a Partnership Interest.* Records of a CPA partnership show the following:

	Inside Basis	Fair Market Value
Cash	$ 8,000	$ 8,000
Accounts receivable	0	40,000
§ 1231 assets	130,000	100,000
Accumulated depreciation	(50,000)	0
	$ 88,000	$148,000
Liabilities	$ 28,000	$ 28,000
Partners' capital	60,000	120,000
	$ 88,000	$148,000

The § 1231 assets have potential § 1245 and § 1250 recapture of $4,000. M, a 25% partner, has an outside basis in his partnership interest of $22,000 (including 25% of partnership liabilities). M sells the 25% interest to J for $30,000 cash.

a. What is the amount and character of M's recognized gain on sale?

b. How would your answers differ if M's outside basis in his partnership interest had been $28,000?

10-45 *Consequences of a § 754 Election to a Purchasing Partner.* Refer to the facts in *Problem 10-44*. During the first month after J purchased his 25% interest from M, the CPA partnership collected half of its $40,000 accounts receivable.

a. Calculate J's and the other partners' distributive shares of this $20,000 of ordinary income, and determine the tax consequences to J if the partnership does not have a § 754 election in effect for the year.

b. Calculate J's and the other partners' distributive shares for this $20,000 of ordinary income, and determine the tax consequences to J if the partnership does have a § 754 election in effect for the year.

10-46 *Sale of Partnership Interest with Hot Assets.* T, a general partner in the accrual basis TUV Partnership, sells her one-third partnership interest to D at the end of the current year for $50,000 cash. The partnership's balance sheet at the end of the year is as follows:

	Basis	FMV		Basis	FMV
Cash	$61,000	$ 61,000	T, capital	$30,000	$ 50,000
Inventory	21,000	39,000	U, capital	$30,000	$ 50,000
Land	8,000	50,000	V, capital	$30,000	$ 50,000
	$90,000	$150,000		$90,000	$150,000

a. What is T's gain or loss from this sale?

b. What basis does D have in her partnership interest?

c. If the partnership sells the land for $50,000 immediately after D purchases her interest, what is the tax effect to D?

d. What should D request that the partnership do to prevent the result in part (c) from occurring?

e. Instead of inventory, assume that the partnership owns collectibles with a basis of $21,000 and fair market value of $39,000. Also, assume that instead of land, the partnership owns a building with a basis of $8,000, fair market value of $50,000, depreciation claimed of $30,000 (of which $20,000 would have been straight-line depreciation). What is T's gain or loss on the sale?

10-47 *Section 754 Election.* Based on the facts from *Problem 10-46*, what would the tax result be to D upon the sale of the land if the partnership had a § 754 election in effect?

10-48 *Dispositions of Partnership Interests.* K owns a limited interest in the Kappa Investment Partnership. The interest has a FMV of $50,000 and a basis to K of $37,000. No amount of partnership debt is included in this basis number. What are the tax consequences to K in each of the following situations?
   a. K exchanges the interest for a general interest in Kappa that is worth $50,000.
   b. K exchanges the interest for investment land worth $50,000.
   c. K dies and bequeaths the interest to her nephew.
   d. K exchanges the interest for newly issued stock in Gamma Inc. Immediately after the exchange, K owns 12% of Gamma's outstanding stock.
   e. K determines that the value of the interest is not $50,000 but is zero. Consequently, she abandons the interest.

10-49 *Dispositions of Partnership Interests Holding Built-In Loss Property.* C and D create the equal CD Partnership in 2015. C contributes cash of $1,000 and D contributes land (holding period is 5 years) having a basis of $1,400 and a fair market value of $1,000. What are the tax consequences to the partners in the following *independent* situations? Assume that the partnership has not made a § 754 election.
   a. The partnership sales the land for $800 on January 15, 2016.
   b. D sells his partnership interest to E for $900 on March 15, 2016.
   c. After D sells the partnership interest to E, the partnership sells the land for $800.

10-50 *Family Partnerships.* Individuals K, L, and M are general partners in the KLM Partnership, in which capital is a material income-producing factor. Under the terms of the partnership agreement, the partners have equal interests in partnership profit and loss. However, K's capital account is $100,000, whereas L's and M's capital accounts are only $20,000. KLM Partnership generated $370,000 of ordinary taxable income during the current year. Based on these facts, how much current-year income is allocable to the three partners under each of the following sets of facts?
   a. K, L, and M are unrelated individuals who formed the partnership through cash contributions four years ago.
   b. K, L, and M are brothers; L and M purchased their interests in the partnership from K four years ago, paying fair market value for their interests.
   c. L and M are K's sons; L and M purchased their interests in the partnership from K four years ago, paying fair market value for their interests.
   d. K, L, and M are unrelated, but have been close friends for years. L and M received their partnership interests as gifts from K four years ago.
   e. Same facts as in (a). During the year, K performed occasional services for the partnership but received no compensation for her work. The services were worth approximately $8,000. L and M performed no services during the year.
   f. Same facts as in (d). During the year, K performed occasional services for the partnership but received no compensation for her work. The services were worth approximately $8,000. L and M performed no services during the year.

10-51 *Partnership Termination.* At the beginning of 2016 Beta Partnership was owned by four equal partners. On June 8, 2016 Partner A sold her one-fourth interest to B, one of the other three partners. On November 19, 2016 new partner G contributed cash and property in exchange for a 55% interest in partnership capital and profits. On March 31, 2017 G sold a 30% interest to a new partner P. Beta and all its partners use the calendar year for tax purposes.
   a. Do any of the capital transactions described above terminate the Beta Partnership?
   b. What is the effect of any termination on Beta's taxable year?

10-52 *Partnership Merger.* The respective partners of Mega and Zeta Partnerships decide to merge their businesses into the M-Z Partnership. Mega used a calendar year for tax purposes, while Zeta used a fiscal year ending September 30. The merger occurred on June 1, 2016. The former partners of Mega own 62% of the capital and profits of the M-Z Partnership, while the former partners of Zeta own the remaining 38 percent.
   a. Is M-Z a continuation of either Mega or Zeta?
   b. What is the effect of the merger on the taxable years of the two merged partnerships?

10-53 *Partnership Division.* The capital and profits of WHB Partnership are owned by three partners: W (55%), H (15%), and B (30%). The three partners no longer agree on how to manage the partnership's business and have decided to divide the business assets between two newly formed partnerships. W and H will own 75 percent and 25 percent, respectively, of new partnership WH. B and H will own 80 percent and 20 percent, respectively, of new partnership BH. Based on these facts, does the WHB Partnership terminate upon the division of its assets into two new partnerships? Explain.

TAX RESEARCH PROBLEMS

10-54 *Family Partnership.* B operates a proprietorship that manufactures and sells utility tables. Net ordinary income has been increasing approximately 20% each year. Last year, net ordinary income was $60,000 on net assets of $225,000. B needs $75,000 to expand the business. Although B's daughter is only 18 years old, she plans to join her father in the business at some point in the future. B is considering forming a partnership with his daughter. His ownership interest would be 75% and hers would be 25 percent. If the daughter's interest is held in trust until she reaches 21, can B serve as the trustee without disqualifying the partnership arrangement?

Research aids:

§ 704 and accompanying Regulations

Stern, 15 T.C. 521 (1950)

Bateman v. U.S., 74-1 USTC ¶9176, 33 AFTR2d 74-483, 490 F.2d 549 (CA-9, 1973)

Ginsberg v. Comm., 74-2 USTC ¶9660, 34 AFTR2d 74-5760, 502 F.2d 965 (CA-6, 1974)

10-55 *Distribution of a Partner's Debt by a Partnership.* Two years ago, Corporation Z, a 10% partner in XYZ Partnership, borrowed $150,000 from the partnership in an arm's-length transaction. Corporation Z gave the partnership a properly executed note stipulating that it would repay the loan at the end of three years and that it would pay the partnership 9% interest each year on the outstanding principal balance. During the current year, Corporation Z decided to withdraw from the partnership. Both Z and the other partners agreed that the fair market value of Z's capital account was $150,000 and that the partnership would liquidate this interest by distributing Z's own note back to the corporation. On the date of the liquidating distribution, Z's outside basis in its 10% interest in XYZ was $116,000. What are the consequences of this transaction to Corporation Z and the XYZ Partnership?

Research aids:

Rev. Rul. 93-7, 1993-1 C.B. 125.

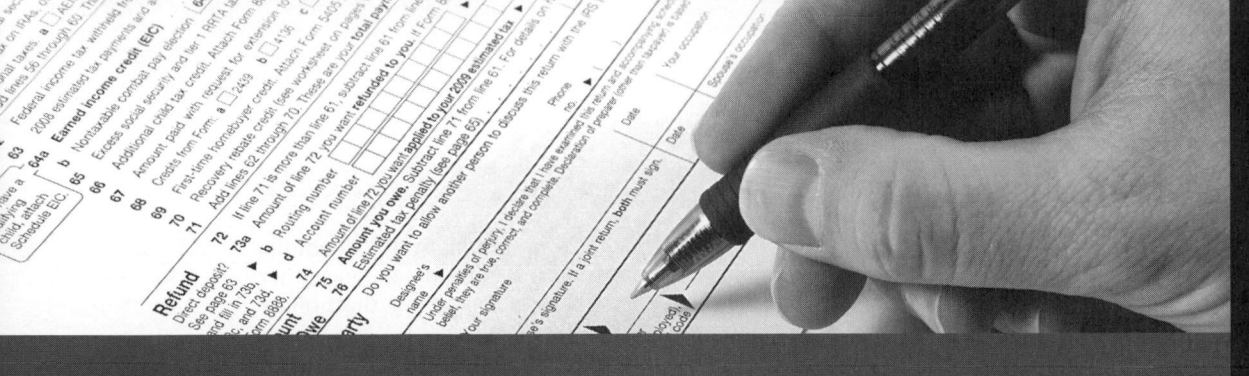

11

S Corporations:
General Rules Applicable
to All S Corporations

Learning Objectives

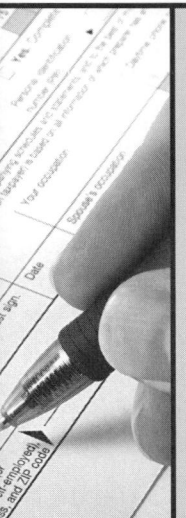

Upon completion of this chapter you will be able to:

LO.1 Identify the requirements necessary to attain S corporation status.

LO.2 Recognize the actions that terminate S status.

LO.3 Compute the taxable income or loss for an S corporation and the impact of S corporate operations on shareholders' taxable income.

LO.4 Determine the shareholders' basis in the S corporation stock and debt, and understand the significance for loss deductions and distributions.

LO.5 Recognize transactions between shareholders and their S corporations that are subject to special treatment.

LO.6 Determine the appropriate taxable year for an S corporation.

LO.7 Explain the unique concepts relevant to family members concerning ownership attribution, compensation, benefits and income allocation.

LO.8 Calculate gain or loss for the S corporation and its shareholders when cash distributions are made and the S corporation has no Accumulated Earnings and Profits (AE&P).

Chapter Outline

Introduction

Congress added Subchapter S to the Internal Revenue Code in 1958, giving birth to a unique tax entity: the S corporation. The S corporation passes taxable income, losses, and other items to its owners, similar to a partnership. However, this entity has all of the nontax (and some tax) characteristics of a corporation. In providing this distinctive treatment, Congressional intent was to allow small businesses to have "the advantages of the corporate form of organization without being made subject to the possible tax disadvantages of the corporation."[1] As this statement suggests, Congress recognized that many taxpayers who normally would incorporate their businesses to secure limited liability were reluctant to do so because of the possibility of double taxation. Accordingly, one of the major objectives of the Subchapter S legislation was to minimize taxes as a factor in the selection of the form of business organization. To accomplish this objective, a complete set of special rules were designed, most of which are contained in Subchapter S.

Although the treatment of S corporations resembles that of partnerships, this goal was not achieved under the 1958 legislation. As originally written, the rules governing S corporations (or Subchapter S corporations as they were initially called) bore little resemblance to partnership rules. Many of these differences were eliminated, however, with the substantial modifications introduced by the Subchapter S Revision Act of 1982. Under the revised rules, Federal income tax treatment of S corporations and their shareholders is similar to that of partnerships and their partners, although there are some significant differences between the two tax entities. The S corporation generally is not subject to the corporate *Federal income tax*. Rather, like a partnership, the S corporation is merely a conduit. The income, deductions, gains, losses, and credits of the S corporation flow through to its shareholders. An S corporation, however, may be subject to a special tax, such as the tax on excessive passive income or on built-in gains.

Even though the Federal income tax treatment of an S corporation resembles that of a partnership, this entity is subject to many rules that apply to regular corporations. For example, since an S corporation is formed in the same manner as a regular corporation (defined as "C" corporations), the basic rules governing organization (i.e., the nonrecognition rules contained in § 351 concerning transfers to a controlled corporation discussed in Chapter 2) of all corporations also apply to S corporations. Similarly, redemptions of an S corporation's stock, as well as liquidation and reorganization of an S corporation, generally are subject to the rules applying to regular corporations. As a practical matter, however, each provision must be closely examined to determine whether special treatment is provided for S corporations.

Perhaps one of the most significant differences between an S corporation and a partnership deals with the conversion of the entity to or from C corporation status. If a C corporation becomes a partnership, the transaction is a corporate liquidation and formation of a partnership. Although the formation of the partnership is usually a tax free transaction, the same is not true for the liquidation of the C corporation. This liquidation is a taxable event, both to the corporation and to its shareholders. Thus it is rarely advantageous to convert a corporation to partnership status for tax purposes. See Chapter 5 for a discussion of corporate liquidations.

In contrast, most conversions of C corporations to S corporation status are tax free events, at least at the time of conversion. There is one exception, which applies if the corporation uses the LIFO inventory method. In this case the corporation recognizes a deemed sale of its inventory at the lower of FIFO cost or market on its final day as a C corporation. This fictional transaction is termed LIFO recapture.

There are also complications in the distribution rules for former C corporations. In addition, they may be subject to taxes at the corporate level on Investment Credit recapture, built-in gains and excess passive investment income. These topics, as well as the LIFO recapture rules, are included in Chapter 12. This chapter is concerned with the principal rules applicable to all S corporations.

---

[1] S. Rept. No. 1622, 83rd Cong., 2d Sess., 119 (1954).

S Corporation Eligibility Requirements

The special tax treatment provided for S corporations is available only if the corporation is a *small business corporation* and its shareholders *consent* to the corporation's election to be taxed under Subchapter S. A small business corporation must:[2]

LO.1
Identify the requirements necessary to attain S corporation status.

1. Be an *eligible domestic* corporation;
2. Not have more than 100 shareholders, all of whom must be eligible persons or entities; and
3. Have only *one class of stock* outstanding.

The corporation must meet all of these requirements when it files its S corporation election and at all times thereafter. Failure at any time to qualify as a small business corporation terminates the election, and as of the date of termination, the corporation is taxed as a regular corporation (hereafter referred to as a C corporation).[3]

The phrase *small business corporation* may be a misnomer. As the requirements for this status indicate, the sole restriction on the size of the corporation is the limitation imposed on the *number* of shareholders. Corporations are not denied use of Subchapter S due to the amount of their assets, income, net worth, or any other measure of size. In addition, the S corporation is not required to conduct an active business. Merely holding assets does not bar the corporation from Subchapter S.

ELIGIBLE CORPORATIONS

Subchapter S status is reserved for *eligible domestic corporations*.[4] Thus, foreign corporations do not qualify. In addition, certain types of domestic corporations are considered ineligible. These ineligible corporations include insurance companies, banks that use the reserve method of accounting for bad debts, corporations electing the special possessions tax credit under Code § 936 and domestic international sales corporations (DISCs).[5]

Only corporations or entities that are considered corporations may take advantage of Subchapter S. A limited liability company (LLC) or other unincorporated entity can qualify as an S corporation if it elects to be treated as a corporation under the check-the-box regulations (see Chapter 1).[6] Under these rules, the entity could only be considered an S corporation if it opts to be taxed as a corporation *and* subsequently or concurrently makes a valid S election. In other words, an LLC or partnership that elects to be treated as a corporation is treated as a C corporation until the corporation files an S election. An association that wants to be treated as an S corporation must satisfy the S corporation rules for eligible owners, number of owners, and a single class of ownership interest.

Although there once was a restriction about ownership of subsidiaries, S corporations may own stock in *C corporations* without limitation. Thus, S corporations have the freedom to structure their ownership in C corporations to meet the needs of their organization. For example, an S corporation may establish a wholly owned C corporation as a subsidiary to hold a risky business, thereby protecting the assets of the parent. However, S and C corporations cannot file a consolidated return.[7] Thus, the C corporation must file Form 1120 and the S corporation must file Form 1120S.

Example 1

D Inc., an S corporation, is interested in purchasing T Inc., a C corporation. T operates a hazardous waste disposal business that is quite profitable but also quite risky. D would like to structure the acquisition in such a way that it does not expose its current business to the risks associated with T's operation. D may own as little or as much of T stock that it wants since there are no rules prohibiting an S corporation from owning the stock of a C corporation.

---

[2] § 1361.

[3] § 1362(d)(2). As discussed later, however, a corporation may avoid loss of its election by applying for "inadvertent termination" relief.

[4] § 1361(b); Reg. 301.7701-5(b) includes any U.S. territory as well as states.

[5] § 1361(b)(2).

[6] Rev. Proc. 2004-48, 2004-32 I.R.B.

[7] § 1504(b)(8).

While S corporations may own stock of C corporations, the reverse is not allowed. As discussed below, S corporations generally are not allowed to have any corporate shareholders. However, an S corporation may own the stock of another corporation, and treat the wholly-owned corporation as a qualified subchapter S subsidiary (QSub).

Qualified Subchapter S Subsidiary (QSub)

A QSub is a corporation that is 100% owned by an S corporation (i.e., the parent) that elects to treat the subsidiary as a QSub.[8] The QSub is a corporation that exists as a disregarded entity for Federal income tax purposes, but is a separate corporation for most other purposes. By electing to treat the subsidiary as a QSub, the parent corporation agrees to report all of the income and deductions of the QSub along with its own tax items. If a parent S corporation acquires all of the stock of an existing corporation (C or S), it must treat the subsidiary as if it were liquidated for tax purposes when it elects QSub status for the subsidiary.[9] To elect QSub status, the parent files the election on Form 8869. If the parent elects to treat the subsidiary as a QSub, the subsidiary's income and deductions are included in the parent company's tax return (Form 1120S). If the parent does not elect QSub status, the subsidiary's income and deductions should be reported separately on the subsidiary's Form 1120.

SHAREHOLDER REQUIREMENTS

Subchapter S imposes several restrictions on S corporation shareholders. Not only is the total number of shareholders limited to 100, but certain parties are prohibited from owning stock of the corporation.

Type of Shareholder

The stock of an S corporation may be owned only by:

1. Individuals who are citizens or resident aliens of the United States,
2. Estates,
3. Certain trusts, and
4. Charitable organizations, pension trusts (not IRAs), and employee stock ownership plans.

Nonresident aliens (i.e., generally foreign citizens residing outside the United States), C corporations, other S corporations, partnerships, and most trusts are *not* allowed to hold stock in an S corporation.

Over the years, rules prohibiting trusts as shareholders have proved unduly inflexible, often intruding on sensible planning. This prohibition has been particularly troublesome in the estate and retirement planning area. For example, an individual may not want to leave the shares of his or her S corporation outright to a young child in his or her will but rather in trust for the benefit of a child. Without special rules, this obviously prudent action would be barred. Consequently, the current provisions allow some freedom in using trusts.

Eligible Trusts

The list of trusts that are eligible shareholders and a brief description of each follows below. In examining the list, note the concern for the shareholder limitation issue and how the shareholders are counted when an eligible trust holds shares.[10]

Grantor Trusts. A grantor trust is a trust that is disregarded under the trust taxation rules because of the power, control and benefits retained by the individual who established the trust (i.e., the grantor). All of the income of a grantor trust (e.g., a revocable trust that is used to avoid probate) is normally taxed to the grantor rather than the trust. If the grantor dies, the S shares normally have to be distributed to the beneficiaries within two years after the death. The grantor is treated as the shareholder for tax purposes. (See Chapter 16 for a discussion of these trusts.) If the grantor is a U.S. citizen or resident who would be eligible to hold the shares directly, the grantor trust may own shares.

---

[8] § 1361(b)(3)(B).

[9] Use Form 8869. The liquidation is nontaxable under §§ 332 and 337.

[10] § 1361(c)(2).

Beneficiary Controlled Trust or Deemed Grantor Trust. A deemed grantor trust is similar to the grantor trust, except the income of the trust is taxed to the beneficiary (rather than the grantor) because of the power that the beneficiary holds over trust property. The beneficiary is treated as the shareholder for tax purposes. As is the case with a grantor trust, the beneficiary, or *deemed grantor,* must be eligible to hold shares directly.

Qualified Subchapter S Trust (QSST). A QSST is a trust that has *only one* current income beneficiary (who must be a U.S. citizen or resident) to whom all of the income of the trust must be distributed annually and for which a proper election to be treated as a QSST has been filed in a timely manner. The trust's beneficiary (or legal guardian thereof) must file an election to include all of the trust's share of the S corporation's income, deductions and other tax items directly on the beneficiary's return as if he or she were the shareholder of the trust's stock. The beneficiary must file this election within two months and 16 days from the date the trust acquires the stock.[11] (If the trust owns shares on the date the corporation elects to become an S corporation, the beneficiary must file this election within two months and 16 days after the corporation files its S election. It is a good practice to file the two elections concurrently.) In addition to this election, there are certain other restrictions imposed on the QSST.

The trust may not distribute any of its income or property to any person other than the current income beneficiary during his or her lifetime. In addition, the trust must distribute (or be required to distribute) all of its income to this beneficiary annually. Failure to adhere to these rules properly results in the trust becoming an ineligible shareholder and thus causing loss of the S election. There have been numerous rulings allowing S corporations to continue their tax status after a trust fails to meet one of these rules. See Inadvertent Termination Relief, below.

In practice, the QSST election is often misunderstood. The result has been a multitude of private letter rulings allowing a corporation's S election to take effect, or continue in effect, after a trust has acquired the stock and the beneficiary has failed to make a timely QSST election. Accordingly, the IRS has issued an expedited relief rule for a QSST election that is no more than three years and 75 days late.[12] A trust that qualifies for this provision applies to the IRS Center where the corporation files its returns. Thus it avoids the need for a ruling request and user fee. If the QSST election is not filed within the 3 year and 75 day time-period, the corporation must apply for inadvertent termination or inadvertent invalid election relief. Relief is sought from the National Office of the IRS in the form of a letter ruling request, which must be accompanied by a user fee.

For all purposes of subchapter S, the beneficiary of the QSST is treated as the shareholder. This treatment applies to consents, allocations of income, other items, and the 100-shareholder limit.

Electing Small Business Trust (ESBT). In contrast to the QSST that has only a single beneficiary, an *ESBT* can have more than one potential current beneficiary (PCB). The trustee can have the right to accumulate or distribute income to any of the PCBs. The trustee must file a timely election for the trust to qualify. A price is paid for use of this trust since all of the income flowing from the S corporation to the trust is taxed to the trust itself (i.e., there is no deduction for distributions of the trust) and such income is taxed at the highest marginal rate (39.6% for ordinary income, plus the 3.8% net investment income tax in most cases). In addition, the ESBT must pay tax on any capital gains in the same manner as an individual taxpayer who is in the highest marginal tax bracket. This rule applies both to any capital gains passing through from the S corporation to the trust and to any gain recognized by the trust on the disposition of the S corporation stock. However, a distribution from the trust to a beneficiary is tax-free to the beneficiary and is nondeductible to the trust. In counting shareholders, each PCB is considered to be a shareholder in the S corporation. Thus each PCB must be a U.S. citizen or resident. If there are too many PCBs it could cause the number of shareholders to exceed 100, although with the family attribution rules this situation is not likely to be a frequent cause of concern. However, for administrative purposes, such as consents to the corporation's various elections, the trustee is treated as the shareholder.

---

[11] Inexplicably, this is one day longer than the grace period in which an S corporation has to file a timely S election.

[12] Rev. Proc. 2013-30, 2013-36 IRB 173.

Testamentary Trusts. A testamentary trust is one that is created by the decedent's last will and testament. A testamentary trust may only be an eligible shareholder for two years unless it also qualifies under one of the other trust rules. The estate is treated as the owner of the stock in the case of one or more testamentary trusts that are established (e.g., if three trusts are created, the estate is considered the single owner). For administrative purposes, such as consents to the corporation's various elections, the trustee is treated as the shareholder.

Charitable Organizations, Pension Trusts, and Employee Stock Ownership Plans. Charitable organizations and pension trusts can be shareholders in S corporations. However, individual retirement accounts are not allowed to hold stock in an S corporation.[13]

These organizations may find S corporation stock unappealing since they must include their share of income from the S corporation as unrelated business taxable income (UBTI). Thus these organizations would be subject to income tax on their income from the S corporation. However, an S corporation may make sufficient cash distributions to enable all shareholders to pay their income taxes on their portions of the S corporation's income. In contrast, these organizations are not subject to taxation on interest or dividend income derived from an investment in a C corporation. In addition, they are normally not taxable on gains from the disposition of stock or securities of a C corporation. However, gain from disposition of S corporation stock is UBTI to the charity. Employee Stock Ownership Plans (ESOPs) are not subject to the UBTI tax on income from an S corporation. Some ESOPs may also view investment in an S corporation unattractive since they may lose some special tax breaks to which they are entitled if they own stock in a C corporation. However, the combination of ESOP ownership and S corporation status may be quite attractive for a few corporations with broad-based participation in the ESOP.

Voting Trusts. A voting trust is a trust created primarily to hold the shares and exercise the voting power of the stock transferred to it. For a voting trust, each beneficiary is treated as a shareholder.

Number of Shareholders

As a general rule, a corporation does not qualify as an S corporation if the number of shareholders exceeds 100 at any moment during the taxable year. For purposes of counting the number of shareholders in an S corporation, members of a single family are subject to some rather broad attribution rules, which treat a family unit as a single shareholder. Specifically, the law permits six generations of descendants from common ancestors to elect to be treated as a single shareholder, but only for purposes of the shareholder count.[14] Moreover, the six generation limit applies only on the date the corporation files its S election or the date the first family member acquires stock in the corporation, whichever is later. Thereafter the number of generations is limitless. There is no requirement that members of each generation must be living. Thus it is possible to have extended generations of second, third and fourth cousins all be treated as one shareholder. A spouse (or former spouse) of any of the lineal family members is also included in this attribution. However, any of these individuals that actually holds stock at the time a corporation files an election for S status would have to consent to the election in his or her individual capacity. As a practical matter, few S corporations are troubled by this requirement.

When a permissible trust is a shareholder of the S corporation, the number of shareholders counted depends on the type of trust. As discussed above, all qualifying trusts, *except* ESBTs and voting trusts, represent one shareholder. For ESBTs and voting trusts, each beneficiary is counted as a shareholder.

When stock is held in the name of a nominee, agent, guardian, or custodian, the beneficial owner of the stock is treated as the shareholder.

---

[13] There is an extremely narrow exception for certain IRAs that held stock in banking corporations on October 22, 2004. Under a special rule, these IRAs (and no others) are permitted shareholders. See § 1361(c)(2)(A).

[14] See § 1361(c)(1) and § 1361(c)(1)(B)(ii).

Example 2

XYZ Bank and Trust, a corporation, holds legal title to stock in an S corporation. The XYZ corporation holds the stock for the benefit of R, a minor child. In this case, R, the beneficial owner, is treated as the shareholder rather than XYZ whether the trust qualifies as a QSST, an ESBT, or a deemed grantor trust. As a result, the S corporation is not denied the benefits of Subchapter S because of a corporate shareholder.

Example 3

F holds stock in an S corporation as custodian for his two minor children. For purposes of counting shareholders, F is ignored and the children are counted as one shareholder for purposes of the 100-shareholder limit.

ONE CLASS OF STOCK

In order to minimize the problems of allocating income of the S corporation among shareholders, the corporation is allowed only one class of stock outstanding. Stock that is authorized but unissued does not invalidate the election. For example, an S corporation may have authorized but unissued preferred stock. Similarly, stock rights, options, or convertible debentures may be issued without affecting the election. A corporation that has issued a second class of stock may qualify if the stock is reacquired and cancelled or held as Treasury stock.

Outstanding shares generally must provide identical distribution and liquidation rights to all shareholders. However, differences in *voting rights* are expressly authorized by the Code.[15] This exception enables control of the organization to be exercised in a manner that differs from stock ownership and income allocation.

Example 4

R organized MND, an S corporation. MND issued two classes of common stock to R: class A voting and class B nonvoting stock. The rights represented by the stock are identical except for voting rights, and thus do not invalidate the S election. Shortly after the organization of the corporation, R gives the class B nonvoting stock to her two children. Although R has shifted income and future appreciation of the stock to her children (assuming certain other requirements are satisfied), she has retained all of the voting control of the corporation.

Debt as a Second Class of Stock

In the past, the second class of stock issue has arisen where the IRS or the courts have stepped in and reclassified an S corporation's debt as stock. As discussed in Chapter 2, reclassification might occur when the corporation is thinly capitalized (e.g., the debt to equity ratio exceeds 4:1). If this were to happen to an S corporation, the result would disqualify the corporation from S status since the S corporation might be considered as having two classes

---

[15] § 1361(c)(4).

of stock. To provide S corporations and their shareholders with some certainty in this area, Congress created a safe-harbor for debt meeting certain requirements. Under these rules, an S corporation's *straight debt* will not be classified as a second class of stock if:[16]

1. The interest rate and interest payment dates are not contingent on either the corporation's profits, management's discretion, or similar factors;

2. The debt instrument is written and cannot be converted into stock; and

3. The creditor is an individual, estate, or trust, (but only if the trust is a grantor trust, QSST or ESBT) that is eligible to hold stock in an S corporation, or any person that is actively and regularly engaged in the business of lending money (e.g., a bank).

Straight debt is defined as any written unconditional promise to pay on demand, or on a specified date, a certain sum of money. Also included as straight debt are any short-term unwritten advances from a shareholder less than $10,000 in the aggregate—if treated as debt by the parties, and if expected to be repaid in a reasonable period of time.[17]

Distributions

Whether an S corporation has more than one class of stock is determined by the corporate charter, articles of incorporation, bylaws, applicable state law, and binding agreements relating to distributions and liquidation. Unintended unequal distributions will generally not cause a second class of stock, unless they are pursuant to a plan to circumvent the one class of stock rule. The corporation must also correct the situation by making a catch-up distribution or taking some other action to place all shares on an equal footing. For example, excessive compensation paid to an owner-employee may be recharacterized as a distribution by the IRS. However, regulations under § 1361 hold that this type of distribution normally will not result in a second class of stock.[18] The regulations also permit unequal distributions that occur in states that require the S corporation to withhold state taxes from distributions made to some or all of its shareholders, but only if there is a compensating distribution to shareholders who are not subject to the state withholding. Generally, the facts and circumstances of each situation will be considered. As a practical matter, there is no case or ruling under the current version of Subchapter S in which distributions have caused a corporation to lose its S status.

Election of S Corporation Status

A corporation that qualifies as a small business corporation is taxed according to the rules of Subchapter S only if the corporation elects to be an S corporation. This election exempts the business from the corporate income tax and all other Federal income taxes normally imposed on corporations except for (1) the tax on excessive passive investment income, (2) the tax on built-in gains, and (3) the investment tax credit recapture tax, which may happen when the corporation has claimed a rehabilitation credit and then disposes of the rehabilitated property. The S corporation may also be required to pay a tax on LIFO recapture income, but that tax is part of the income tax imposed on a C corporation immediately before it converts to become an S corporation. In addition, the corporation is exempt from the personal holding company tax and the accumulated earnings tax. Although the S corporation generally avoids taxation as a regular corporation, most rules governing regular corporations such as those concerning organization, redemptions, and liquidations apply. See Chapter 12 for discussion of these taxes.

MAKING THE ELECTION: MANNER AND PERIOD OF EFFECT

In order for a corporation to be subject to the rules of Subchapter S, the corporation must file an election on Form 2553 (see Appendix B). The effective date of the election, as well as the required shareholder consents, generally depend on when the election is filed. The election must be filed with the IRS center where the S corporation files its tax returns.

---

[16] § 1361(c)(5).

[17] Reg. 1.1361-1(l)(4)(ii)(B).

[18] Reg. § 1.1361-1(l)(2)(vi) Ex. 3.

Time of the Election

To be effective for the corporation's current taxable year, the election must be filed within two months and 15 days of the beginning of the corporation's taxable year.[19] Note that well-meaning shareholders or tax professionals trying to ensure a prompt election might file an election before the corporation has actually started its first taxable year. Unfortunately, an election cannot be made before the corporation is in existence and any election filed before such date would be invalid. Since the election must be filed in a particular time period—neither too early nor too late—the starting date is critical. For this purpose, the first taxable year starts on the earliest date that the corporation (1) issues shares; (2) acquires property; or (3) commences business.[20] Once the tax year begins, the election may be filed any time on or before the two months and 15 days deadline. For many years, there was no relief for taxpayers who filed a late election even if there were good reasons for the failure. However, the IRS may treat a late election as being timely filed if there is reasonable cause.[21]

Example 5

J and B decided to start a publishing corporation in 2016. The corporation issued shares on December 13, 2016 in exchange for $20,000. On January 15, 2017, the corporation opened a bank account and deposited the $20,000. On February 1, 2017, the corporation started operations. In this case, the corporation is considered to have started business on December 13, 2016 (the earliest of the dates that it issued shares, acquired property or commenced business). Consequently, the election is due on or before February 27, 2017 to be treated as timely filed. If the start date was May 1, the election is due on or before July 15. Note that in all of these examples, the third month and the start of the 15-day count begins on the same numerical day as the year began (i.e., February 13, July 1 plus 14 days yields the critical date).

If the corporation does not file a timely election or secure recognition of a late election, it will be considered a C corporation for the taxable year in question and the S election will be effective for the following tax year. Failure to make a timely election can be a crucial blunder. For instance, any losses that occurred during the C year would not flow through and any distributions could be treated as fully taxable dividends. However, since enactment of the legislation specifically enabling the acceptance of late elections, such mistakes have not been quite as costly.

Under current law, the IRS has been reasonable, if not outright lenient, in granting late elections. In 2013, the IRS authorized its Service Centers to accept S elections that are up to three years and 75 days from the intended effective date. In most cases, the corporation must specify a "reasonable cause" for the lateness of the election.[22] The election must include the consent of every person who has been a shareholder from the first day of the first year for which the election is to be effective until the day the corporation files the election with the Service Center. Each shareholder must state that he or she has not filed a tax return that is inconsistent with the corporation's S status.

If the corporation has not yet filed a tax return when it elects S status, it may file Form 2553 along with Form 1120S for the desired S year with the service center.

If the corporation has already filed Form 1120S for its first intended S year, it may file Form 2553 with the Service Center any time within three years and 75 days from the intended effective date. In this case all shareholders must state that they have filed returns that are consistent with the S election.

---

[19] §§ 1362(b)(1)(B) and (b)(2) and Reg. § 1.1362-6(a)(2)(ii).
[20] Reg. § 1.1362-6(a)(2)(ii)(c).
[21] § 1362(b)(5).
[22] Rev. Proc. 2013-30, 2013-36 IRB 173.

Example 6

This year J and B formed a calendar year corporation on May 1, 2016. Unfortunately, J and B were unaware that they needed to file the S election by July 15 (i.e., two months and 15 days after May 1) and their error was not discovered until they visited an accountant in January 2017. Under the current approach, the IRS would accept an election up to September 15, 2017, the extended due date of the return for the first year it desired S status. If the corporation has not already filed its Form 1120S for 2016, it should file its Form 2553 and 1120S simultaneously. If the corporation has already filed Form 1120S, it may file Form 2553 with the Service Center on or before July 15, 2018 (three years and 75 days after the intended effective date). If the corporation does not meet these qualifications it must apply to the IRS National Office for relief. This request must be in the form of a letter ruling request and requires payment of the user fee.

If an S corporation does not meet these criteria and still wishes to validate a late election, it must apply to the National Office of the IRS for a private letter ruling—a process that can be a very costly (e.g., the IRS fee for the ruling, currently $28,200, plus the expense of the accounting or law firm that prepares the ruling request). The IRS frequently grants favorable rulings on these requests. The fee is reduced to $2,200 if the corporation has no more than $250,000 of gross receipts. If the corporation has between $250,000 and $1,000,000 gross receipts the fee is $6,500.[23]

The IRS may accept a timely filed but defective election (e.g., second class of stock outstanding) if the reason for the defect is inadvertent. Inadvertence is a higher standard than reasonable cause. In most cases only the National Office of the IRS can approve a defective election.[24] However, if the defect is due to a late filed QSST or ESBT election, the Service Center can grant relief if the trust or beneficiary files the proper election within three years and 75 days of the date that the trust needs to qualify.

Shareholder Consent

In order for the election to be valid, the corporation must secure and file the consents of the shareholders along with the election. Consent to the election must be obtained not only from *all* shareholders holding stock (voting and nonvoting) at the time of election, but also from former shareholders who have held stock during the earlier portion of that taxable year.[25] The consent of these former shareholders is required since they will be allocated a share of the income, losses, and other items applicable to the time they held the stock. The IRS may grant an extension for filing the consent for one or more shareholders if reasonable cause can be shown.[26] If a *former* shareholder (whose signature is necessary to validate the election for the desired year) will not or does not sign the consent, the election is effective for the following taxable year. Similarly, if the corporation fails to meet any of the Subchapter S requirements during the pre-election portion of the year, the election is effective for the following taxable year.

Example 7

At the beginning of 2016, D, E, and F owned the stock of GHI Corporation, a calendar year taxpayer. On February 15, 2016, F sold all of her shares in GHI to C. On March 1, 2016 an S corporation election is desired. In order for the election to be effective for 2016, all shareholders on the date of election (C, D, and E), as well as any shareholders in the pre-election portion of the year (F), must consent. Failure to obtain F's consent would cause the election to become effective for 2017. Consent is required from both C and D even if they are family members and qualify as one shareholder for purposes of the maximum shareholder limit.

When a corporation seeks relief for filing a late S election, it must attach statements from all of the persons who have been shareholders starting with the date the corporation intended for the election to take effect. These consents are necessary, whether the corporation

---

[23] See Rev. Proc. 2015-1, 2015-1 I.R.B. 1, Appendix A for the most recent schedule of user fees.

[24] § 1362(f).

[25] §§ 1362(a)(2) and (b)(2)(B)(ii).

[26] Reg. § 1.1362-6(b)(3)(iii).

is able to obtain relief with the Service center or is required to request a letter ruling from the IRS national office.

Example 8

V and Z owned all of the stock of VZM Corporation on January 1, 2016, and intended for VZM to be an S corporation beginning on that date. In early 2017 M acquired all of V's shares in VZM. Later in 2017 VZM's CPA discovered that the corporation had not filed Form 2553. VZM files Form 2553 at the service center since it is within the three year and 75 day limit of Revenue Procedure 2013-30. V, Z, and M must attach their consents. Each of these individuals must also sign a statement that they have reported, and will continue to report, all of the items passing through from VZM as if the S election had been in effect from January 1, 2016 onwards.

Election Effective for Subsequent Years

Elections made after the first two months and 15 days of the current taxable year are effective for the following taxable year.[27] When the election becomes effective in the following taxable year, only shareholders holding stock on the date of election must consent. The consent of shareholders who acquire stock after the election is not required.

Example 9

On November 1, 2016, J Corporation filed an S election on Form 2553, including all of the shareholder consents. The election was to be effective for its next taxable year beginning on January 1, 2017. Unknowing to those handling the incorporation, one of the consenting shareholders, V, was a Canadian citizen, living in Vancouver. On December 15, 2016, the corporation discovered the problem and V agreed to sell all of his stock to one of the other shareholders. Since the corporation had a nonresident alien shareholder on the date that the election was filed, the election is not valid. The fact that the problem was corrected before the year in which the election was to be effective is irrelevant. Note, however, that if the corporation recognized the error, it could cure it by filing another Form 2553 by March 15, 2017. As an alternative, the corporation could file—at a cost—a ruling request asking the IRS to accept the inadvertently invalid election. Such requests are granted frequently.

TERMINATION OF THE ELECTION

An election to be taxed as an S corporation is effective until it is terminated. The election may be terminated when the corporation:[28]

1. Revokes the election;
2. Fails to satisfy the requirements; or
3. Receives excessive passive income.

Revocation

The S corporation election may be revoked if shareholders holding a *majority* of the shares of stock (voting and nonvoting) consent.[29] A revocation filed by the fifteenth day of the third month of the taxable year (e.g., March 15 for a calendar year corporation) normally is effective for the current taxable year.[30] In contrast, if the revocation is filed after this two months and 15-day period has elapsed, it usually becomes effective for the following taxable year.[31] In both situations, however, a date on or after the date of revocation may be specified for the termination to become effective.[32]

> **LO.2**
> Recognize the actions that terminate S status.

---

[27] § 1362(b)(3).

[28] § 1362(d).

[29] § 1362(d)(1)(B).

[30] § 1362(d)(1)(C)(i).

[31] § 1362(d)(1)(C)(ii).

[32] § 1362(d)(1)(D).

Example 10

A calendar year S corporation is owned equally by C, D, and E. On February 12, 2016, C and D consent to revoke the S corporation election. Since C and D own a majority of the outstanding shares of stock, the election is effective beginning on January 1, 2016, unless the revocation specifies February 12, 2016 or some later date.

Example 11

Same as *Example 10* above except the revocation was made on May 3, 2016. The election is effective for the following taxable year beginning January 1, 2017. If the revocation had specified, however, that the termination was to become effective May 3, 2016, the S corporation year would end on May 2, 2016.

Example 12

An S corporation has 100 shares of outstanding stock, 75 owned by J and 25 owned by B. On June 1 of this year, J sold 60 of her 75 shares to D. Since D owns a majority of the outstanding shares, he may direct the corporation to revoke the election, even if J and B are opposed to the revocation. However, the corporation must file the revocation. A statement filed by a shareholder is insufficient to revoke the election.

Failure to Meet the Eligibility Requirements

If the S corporation fails to satisfy any of the Subchapter S requirements at any time, the election is terminated on the date the disqualifying event occurs.[33] The termination can result from any violation of eligibility. Most often this results from an ineligible shareholder acquiring stock. Occasionally it happens when the corporation issues an equity instrument that can be construed as a second class of stock. In theory it is possible to exceed the shareholder limit, but the generous family attribution rules make this problem unlikely.

Excessive Passive Investment Income

When an S corporation has accumulated earnings and profits from C corporation years, it may encounter some problems. If the corporation's passive investment income does not exceed 25% of its gross receipts, it faces no special problems. However, if its passive investment income exceeds 25% of its gross receipts in any given year it may be subject to a corporate level income tax. If the situation persists for three consecutive years it becomes a C corporation on the first day of its next taxable income. The passive investment income problems are discussed in Chapter 12.

Treatment of the S Termination Year

When a corporation loses its S corporation status, the corporation is treated as an S corporation for the period ending the day before the date of termination. This often causes the corporation to have two short taxable years: one as an S corporation and one as a C corporation. As a result, the corporation must allocate income and loss for the entire year between the two years. The tax return for the short S year is due two months and 15 days after the end of the C short year, and may be extended for an additional six months.[34] For tax years beginning after 2015 the C short year return is due three months and 15 days after the end of the C short year.[35] The C return date can be extended five months.

---

[33] § 1362(d)(2).

[34] § 1362(e)(6)(B).

[35] § 6072(a).

Example 13

C, D, and E own a calendar year S corporation. On June 3 of this year, E sold her stock to a corporation. The same result would be obtained if the sale had been to a partnership or to an individual who became the 101st shareholder. The S short year includes January 1 through June 2. The C short year is June 3 through December 31. The S return is due on March 15 of the next year. The C return is due on April 15 of the next year. Both due dates may be extended to September 15.

Unless the S election termination occurs on the first day of the corporation's tax year, the termination year is split into two short periods. There are some special rules governing the allocation of income between the two short periods. The two methods that the corporation may use are the pro-rata allocation and the interim closing method.

Using the pro-rata method, each item required to be reported to the shareholders is assigned equally to each day in the entire tax year.[36] If the corporation uses the interim closing method it must separately account for activities during the S and C portions of the year.[37]

Example 14

On March 14, 2017, X Corporation terminates its S election. S uses the calendar year for tax purposes. Its income and loss items for 2017 occurred during the following periods.

	S Short Year	C Short Year	Total
Ordinary income	$80,000	$40,000	$120,000
Long-term capital gain	16,000	0	16,000
Dividend income (X holds 20% stock in payor)	0	5,000	5,000

If the corporation uses the interim closing method, it will report $80,000 of ordinary income and $16,000 of long-term capital gain to the shareholders, who will include these items on their 2017 tax returns. X would include $45,000 income, less a 70% dividends-received deduction of $3,500, on its Form 1120 for the C short year ending December 31, 2017. If the corporation pro rates all of the items, the allocation would be as follows:

	S Short Year (73/365)	C Short Year (292/365)	Total
Ordinary income	$24,000	$96,000	$120,000
Long-term capital gain	3,200	12,800	16,000
Dividend income	1,000	4,000	5,000

The corporation must use the pro-rata method unless it elects to use the interim closing, or there is a change of ownership of 50% or more of the corporation's shares within the S termination year.[38] The election is filed with the corporation's Form 1120 for the C short year. The election must be accompanied by consents of all persons who are shareholders at any time during the S short year, as well as all shareholders on the first day of the C short year.[39]

---

[36] § 1362(e)(1).

[37] § 1362(e)(3).

[38] § 1362(e)(6)(D).

[39] Reg. § 1.1362-6(a)(5).

The corporation must annualize its income and tax for the C short year. This is accomplished by grossing up the income as if it were earned ratably for a year of 365 days (366 in a leap year), and then apportioning the tax for the number of days in the C short year.

Example 15

Refer to *Example 14,* above. Assume that the corporation elects to use the interim closing method. X would report the following annualized income and tax:

Ordinary income	$ 40,000
Dividend income	5,000
Less dividends received deduction	(3,500)
Taxable income	$ 41,500
Annualization	(365/292)
Annualized taxable income	$ 51,875
Tax on $51,875	$ 7,969
Annualization	(292/365)
Annualized tax	$ 6,375

When termination is *inadvertent*, the Code authorizes the IRS to allow a corporation to continue its S status uninterrupted if the disqualifying action is corrected.[40] It is possible, for example, that if stock is transferred to an ineligible shareholder, the IRS might allow the corporation to correct the violation and continue its S status uninterrupted. Inadvertent termination relief can only be granted to a corporation that applies to the IRS National Office and pays the user fee for a letter ruling, except for QSST elections and ESBT elections discussed below.

Example 16

On the advice of his attorney, a majority shareholder transferred his S corporation shares to an ineligible trust. Neither the attorney nor the shareholder were knowledgeable about the specific rules of Subchapter S. When the shareholder discovered the transfer terminated the S corporation election, the trust transferred the stock to the previous shareholder. The IRS has ruled, under similar circumstances, that the S election was not lost since the termination of the S status was inadvertent, it occurred as the result of advice from counsel, and it was corrected as soon as the violation of S status was discovered.[41]

The same inadvertent termination rules apply to defective (not late) S corporation elections. The corporation must apply for a ruling, disclosing the defect and agreeing to treat the corporation as an S corporation. All shareholders must sign the ruling request, under penalties of perjury. Any of the Subchapter S rules may be violated and cause termination or a defective election. However, a disproportionately high number of these violations have come from the failure to make timely QSST or ESBT elections. Accordingly the IRS has authorized the Service Centers to accept these elections up to three years late, in which case the corporation may avoid the ruling request and user fee.[42]

---

[40] § 1362(f).

[41] Rev. Rul. 86-110, 1986-38 I.R.B. 4. Also, see Ltr. Ruls. 8550033 and 8608006.

[42] Rev. Proc. 2013-30, 2013-36 IRB 173.

ELECTION AFTER TERMINATION

When the election is terminated, whether voluntarily through revocation or involuntarily through failure to satisfy the Subchapter S or passive income requirements, the corporation normally may not make a new election until the fifth taxable year following the year in which the termination became effective.[43] The five-year wait is unnecessary, however, if the IRS consents to an earlier election. Consent usually is given in two instances: (1) when the corporation's ownership has changed such that more than 50% of the stock is owned by persons who did not own the stock at the time of termination, or (2) when the termination was attributable to an event that was not within the control of the corporation or its majority shareholders.[44] A corporation must apply to the IRS National Office for an early re-election. It must request a ruling and pay the user fee.

Example 17

KLZ, an S corporation, was wholly owned by G. The corporation revoked its S election effective on July 17, 2016. KLZ may not make an election until 2021 unless it obtains permission from the IRS. Permission to reelect S status prior to 2021 would ordinarily be denied unless persons other than G acquired more than 50% of the KLZ stock.

Operating the S Corporation

Once an S election is effective, a corporation officially becomes an S corporation and is subject to a special set of rules governing the measurement and reporting of its income. Under the provisions of Subchapter S, S corporations, like partnerships, are pass-through entities. While S corporations may pay taxes in certain situations (e.g., the passive investment income tax or the built-in gains tax discussed in Chapter 12), they primarily serve as conduits. Items of income, expense, gain, loss, and credit are measured at the S corporation level and then passed through to shareholders who report them on their own returns.[45] The focus of this section is on three questions:

- What items at the corporate level must be reported to the shareholder?

- How much of each item is reported to each shareholder?

- When does the shareholder report the items on his or her own tax return?

DETERMINING S CORPORATION TAXABLE INCOME

S corporations generally compute net income, gains, and losses in a manner similar to a partnership. The following discussion examines some of the more important aspects that should be considered in measuring S corporation income, particularly the differences between S corporations and partnerships.

Elections

Consistent with the partnership provisions, most special elections that must be made in determining the amount of income are made at the S corporation level and not by the shareholder.[46] Among the elections that must be made by the corporation are the corporation's overall method of accounting (e.g., cash or accrual), the inventory method (e.g., FIFO or LIFO), depreciation methods, § 179 limited expensing, the installment method (election out), and deferral of gain on involuntary conversions. The exceptions to this general approach are the same as those for partnerships and affect few taxpayers.

LO.3

Compute the taxable income or loss for an S corporation and the impact of S corporate operations on shareholders' taxable income.

---

[43] § 1362(g).

[44] Reg. § 1.1362-5(a).

[45] § 1366(a).

[46] § 1363(c).

Payments to a Shareholder-Employee

The treatment of payments to an S shareholder who works for the corporation is markedly different from that of a partner who works for the partnership. S corporation shareholders who work for the corporation are treated as *employees*. As a result, salary paid to a shareholder-employee as well as payroll taxes related to the salary are deductible by the S corporation. In contrast, a partner who works for a partnership is not considered an employee and the payment received for work for the partnership is not technically considered a salary. As discussed in Chapter 9, compensation paid to partners is referred to as a guaranteed payment. Like salaries, partnerships normally deduct guaranteed payments. However, unlike salaries, guaranteed payments are not subject to withholding or payroll taxes.[47] Instead, a partner's compensation is treated as self-employment income.

Example 18

H and W own their own company. This year the company made net income of $60,000 before consideration of any payments to H and W. Assume that H and W each receive a salary of $10,000 for total salary payments of $20,000. If the business is an S or C corporation, the salary is subject to withholding taxes and the corporation must pay FICA and unemployment taxes on it. If, however, the business is a partnership, there are no payroll taxes for owner compensation and partnership net income is $40,000 ($60,000 − $20,000), which is usually self-employment income and is subject to self-employment tax at the partner level. In addition, the salaries of $20,000 (i.e., guaranteed payments in the context of a partnership) would be subject to self-employment taxes.

For 2016 the Social Security and Medicare taxes are imposed as follows:

	Employee Portion	Employer Portion	Total
Retirement, on wage and salary income up to $118,500.....	6.2%	6.2%	12.4%
Medicare tax on all wage and salary income..............	1.45%	1.45%	2.9%
Medicare tax on wage and salary income above threshold ...	0.09%	0%	0.9%

The threshold amount is $250,000 for a married wage earner filing a joint return, $125,000 for a married wage earner filing a separate return and $200,000 for all others. Thus the combined rate of all of these taxes, including the employer and employee portions, for a single individual in 2016 is:

Wage Level	Combined Rate
$0–$118,500..	15.3%
$118,500–$200,000	2.9%
Above $200,000	3.8%

The self-employment tax applies the combined rates to the self-employment income of the same levels as the Social Security and Medicare taxes. For 2013 and later years the 0.9% surtax applies to the same levels of income for self-employment income as it does for Social Security wages. For income up to the threshold for the 0.9% surtax the taxpayer is allowed to deduct 50% of the combined Social Security and Medicare portions of the self-employment tax. The taxpayer is not allowed to deduct the 0.9% surcharge. Thus the deduction for the tax above the threshold level is approximately 38%. The deduction is an above the line deduction for AGI. It does not reduce the self-employment tax. For 2016 the comparison of the two entity classes (at this level of income) would yield the following results.

---

[47] Reg. § 1.707-1(c), Rev. Rul. 56-675, 1956-2 CB 459 and
Rev. Rul. 69-180, 1969-1 CB 256.

	Partnership	S Corporation
Net income before compensation	$60,000	$60,000
Guaranteed payment or salary.	(20,000)	(20,000)
Employer FICA tax (6.2% × $20,000)	0	(1,240)
Employer Medicare tax (1.45% × $20,000).		(290)
Federal and state unemployment tax (6.2%).	0	(868)
Flow-through income	$40,000	$37,602
Add guaranteed payment or salary	20,000	20,000
Employee FICA tax (6.2% × $20,000).	0	(1,240)
Employee Medicare tax (1.45% × $20,000)		(290)
Self-employment tax (12.4% × $60,000 × 0.9235).	(6,871)	0
Self-employment Medicare tax (2.9% × $60,000 × 0.9235)	(1,607)	
Deduction for self-employment tax	(3,435)	
Deduction for self-employment Medicare tax	(803)	
Net income after taxes.	$64,239	$57,602
Income tax, assuming 15% rate	(9,636)	(8,640)
Cash flow after tax	$37,648	$47,432

As this example demonstrates, the S corporation is preferred to the partnership if capital is to be retained in the business. This derives from the fact that the partners are subject to self-employment tax on their portions of partnership income, whether or not it is distributed. The S corporation and its shareholders, by contrast, are only subject to the FICA tax on money actually distributed to the shareholders as compensation.

Employment Taxes and Undercompensation

It is important to note that, unlike partnerships, no self-employment income passes from an S corporation to its shareholders. In the S corporation setting, the only amounts subject to employment taxes are the salaries paid. In light of this treatment, owners of S corporations are tempted to undercompensate themselves in order to avoid Social Security and other payroll taxes. To illustrate, consider the example above. In this situation, the owners took only $20,000 in salary, paying employment taxes of $3,928 ($1,240 + $290 + $868 + $1,240 + $290). This is far less than the $8,478 in self-employment tax that the owners would pay if they were partners in a partnership even though the amounts paid in both cases were identical ($20,000). The difference is due to the fact that the net income of the S corporation, $37,602, is not subject to employment taxes. However, there is another mitigating factor that reduces this difference. Each partner is allowed a deduction for AGI for one-half of the self-employment tax paid on partnership income. Indeed, it would appear that the owners could avoid all employment taxes using an S corporation by not paying themselves any salary but simply distributing the profits. As might be expected, the IRS, with the support of the courts, frowns on this technique. In situations when this occurs, that is, when shareholders are undercompensated for their services, the Service generally recharacterizes all or a part of any distributions as compensation thereby securing the applicable payroll taxes.[48]

Disguising compensation as a distribution has been a key area of concern by the IRS. Accordingly the IRS has taken on major initiatives to fight the loss of FICA taxes on income of S corporations. For new S corporations, the routine response to filing Form 2553 now contains a statement that the corporation should compensate its shareholders, and that the IRS will be enforcing this rule.[49] In addition, the Treasury Inspector General for Tax Administration has released a report decrying the tax avoidance that results from not collecting self-employment tax from S corporation shareholders.[50]

---

[48] See Rev. Rul. 74-44, 1974-1 C.B. 287, *Radtke v. U.S.*, 90-1 USTC ¶50,113 and *Spicer Accounting, Inc., v. U.S.*, 918 F.2d 90 (CA-9, 1990).

[49] IRS, CP [business filer notice] 261—Notice of Acceptance as an S Corporation.

[50] IRS, Report # 2005-30-080.

In December 2009 the United States Government Accountability Office issued a report on tax noncompliance of S corporations and their shareholders.[51] This report discussed several problem areas. One of the greatest concerns was the failure to treat payments to shareholder-employees as wage or salary payments, subject to withholding and payroll taxes. Moreover The Joint Committee on Taxation has selected employment tax of S corporation shareholders as one of the areas that needs to be revised in order to improve tax collections.[52]

There have been several cases heard by the Tax Court, district courts and appellate courts. Most of these have concerned S corporation shareholders who have been taking distributions but no salaries or wages from the corporation. The IRS imputes the appropriate withholding and FICA taxes on these distributions and assesses the corporation accordingly. No court has held for the shareholder, or even compromised the IRS's assessment. By the time these cases get to court the interest and penalties often exceed the tax liability.

Most of the cases involving undercompensation of S corporation shareholders involve compensation of officers. In general, any officer of the corporation is considered to be an employee for FICA tax purposes.[53] Only if the officer performs no more than minor services, and is not entitled to any compensation, can the officer be treated as not being an employee.[54] Thus the amount of compensation, or the amount of services, per se, is not an important factor.

Social Security Benefit Cutback

With the graying of America, the treatment of payments to S corporation owners is also becoming an increasingly important issue for Social Security purposes. An individual who retires before "normal" retirement age, must reduce his or her Social Security benefits if he or she earns income above a certain level. In 2016, the *normal retirement* age is 66 years of age. A person who is at least 62 but has not reached normal retirement age by the end of 2016 will be required to reduce his or her Social Security benefit by $1 for each $2 of earned income in excess of $15,720. After normal retirement age, an individual may receive full Social Security benefits regardless of the amount of earned income. For this reason, some owners of S corporations are tempted to take distributions from an S corporation rather than salary for services rendered. In a number of cases involving such attempts, however, the courts have upheld the Social Security Administration's bid to reclassify the distributions as wages.[55]

Employee Benefits

One of the most important differences concerning the taxation of C corporations, partnerships, and S corporations is the treatment of fringe benefits provided to the owners (e.g., health and accident insurance, group-term life insurance). The taxation of a number of these benefits depends on whether the individual is an "employee" of the business. If the individual is an employee, the employer normally is allowed to deduct the cost of the benefit and its value is never subject to income or employment taxes. On the other hand, if the individual is not an employee, the benefit is usually considered compensation deductible by the employer but is subject to income and employment taxes to the payees.

It is not always clear as to whether or not a self-employed person is considered an "employee" for fringe benefit purposes. In the case of C corporations, an owner who works for the business is considered an employee. Therefore, shareholder-employees of C corporations enjoy the best of all possible worlds: the corporation is allowed to deduct the cost of these benefits yet their value to the shareholder-employees is never subject to income or employment taxes. In contrast, a partner (much like a sole proprietor) is normally not considered an employee of the business. Consequently, several of the key fringe benefits provided by partnerships to their partners are considered compensation (i.e., guaranteed payments) that are deductible by the partnership but subject to income and self-employment taxes to the partners. Unfortunately, the treatment of these key fringe benefits by an S corporation for the most part mirrors that for partnerships rather than that for C corporations.[56]

---

[51] United States Government Accountability Office, Actions Needed to Address Noncompliance with S Corporation Tax Rules, GAO-10-195, December 2009.

[52] U.S. Congress, Joint Committee on Taxation, report JCS-02-05.

[53] § 3121(d)(1), § 3306(i).

[54] Reg. § 31.3121(d)-1(b), 31.3306(i)-1(e).

[55] *Ludeking v. Finch*, 421 F.2d 499 (CA-8, 1970).

[56] § 1372(a)(1) and (2).

In determining the treatment extended to S corporations, shareholder-employees are divided into two groups: those who own more than 2% of the stock and those who own 2% or less.[57] The treatment for the two groups is summarized below.

Shareholders Owning 2% or Less. For those S shareholders who own 2% or less, the treatment follows the C corporation rules: the benefits are deductible by the corporation and nontaxable (both income and employment) to the employee.

Shareholders Owning More than Two Percent. More-than-two-percent shareholders are treated much like partners.[58] The fringe benefits requiring employee status are considered compensation: the benefits are deductible by the corporation but are included in the shareholder's gross income.[59] Unlike a partnership where these benefits are subject to self-employment tax, the value of health insurance provided to an S corporation employee is not subject to FICA or FUTA.[60] Note also that while the more-than-two-percent shareholder is required to include the benefit in income, he or she is also entitled to treat such amount as if he or she paid for the benefit. For example, in the case of medical insurance premiums paid by the S corporation on behalf of a more-than-two-percent shareholder, the shareholder is usually eligible to deduct 100% of the premiums as a deduction for AGI.[61]

In determining whether an individual owns more-than-two-percent of an S corporation's stock, the constructive ownership rules of § 318 are applied.[62] For example, § 318 provides that an individual is deemed to own the stock of his or her spouse, children, parents or grandchildren. This rule prevents an owner (e.g., a husband) from employing a family member that does not own stock (e.g., a wife) in order to provide tax-free fringe benefits from the corporation to the family unit.

There are currently six fringe benefits which are nontaxable to owners of C corporations but which are treated as compensation to partners and more-than-two-percent shareholders. They are:

- Group-term life insurance (§ 79).

- Amounts received under accident and health (medical reimbursement) plans (§ 105).

- Premiums on employer-paid accident and health insurance (§ 106).

- Meals and lodging provided by the employer (§ 119).

- Value of transit passes [§ 132(f)].

- Parking provided by the employer (except that provided away from the business such as at a client's) [§ 132(f)(5)(E)].

The value of all of these is included in the shareholder-employee's Form W-2 as noncash compensation. Premiums on accident and health insurance are not subject to FICA tax.

Caution

This material covers only the basic income tax rules regarding health insurance plans. It does not cover the requirements of the Patient Protection Act or the Affordable Care Act. Thus all of the rules discussed in this material need to be evaluated in terms of required coverage of insurance policies, as well as the employers' rules for providing coverage to employees. Thus all readers need to be alert to the seemingly ever-changing rules regarding these requirements and penalties for failure to do so.

The remaining fringe benefits are eligible for exclusion not only by shareholder-employees of C corporations but also to partners and, therefore, more-than-two-percent shareholders of S corporations. In effect, the statutes governing these particular benefits

---

[57] § 1372(a) and (b).

[58] § 1372(a)(2).

[59] Rev. Rul. 91-26, 1991-1 C.B. 184, § 162(a) (subject to the capitalization rules of § 263), and § 61(a), respectively.

[60] Announcement 92-16, 1992-5 I.R.B. 53.

[61] §§ 162(l) and 106, respectively.

[62] § 1372(b). See Chapter 4 for discussion of § 318.

specifically explain that, for purpose of the given exclusion, partners are considered employees, thereby enabling exclusion not only for partners but also all S corporation shareholders. These include:

- Child and dependent care assistance (§ 129).

- Educational assistance plans (§ 127).

- No additional cost services [§ 132(b)].

- Qualified employee discounts [§ 132(c)].

- Working condition fringe benefits [§ 132(d)].

- *De minimis* fringes [§ 132(e)].

- Company dining room [§ 132(e)].

- On-premise athletic facilities [§ 132(h)].

- Employee achievement awards [§ 74(c)].

Subdivision of Real Estate

Under the "subdivide and conquer" rules of § 1237, *individual* taxpayers are ensured capital gain rather than ordinary income treatment when they subdivide and sell land if they meet a number of requirements. To qualify, the land must be held more than five years (unless inherited); there must be no substantial improvements to the property; and the parcel sold, or any part thereof must not have previously been held by the taxpayer primarily for resale. An S corporation (as well as a partnership) is treated in the same manner as an individual and is entitled to this special treatment.[63]

Section 291 Recapture

In most cases, an S corporation is not subject to the special rules of § 291 that require the recapture as ordinary income 20% of any straight-line depreciation claimed on residential or nonresidential real estate (see Chapter 1 for an example). However, an S corporation that was a C corporation for any of the three immediately preceding taxable years is subject to the special depreciation recapture rules of § 291(a)(1).[64]

Accounting Methods

Certain entities are prohibited from using the cash method of accounting, and consequently are required to use the accrual method. The cash method normally cannot be used by a C corporation unless its annual gross receipts average $5 million or less for the past three years, or it is a qualified personal service corporation. In contrast, an S corporation can use the cash method (unless it is required to maintain inventories to clearly reflect income).[65]

Charitable Contributions

Charitable contributions made by an S corporation are treated as if they are made directly by the shareholder. Consequently, unlike C corporations, an S corporation that uses the accrual method of accounting is not entitled to deduct accrued contributions.[66] Like an individual, contributions made by an S corporation can be deducted by the shareholders only in the tax year in which the contribution is made. Similarly, the special rule allowing C corporations to deduct the adjusted basis plus one-half of the foregone gross profit of inventory contributed to an organization for the care of the needy, the ill, or infants is not available to S corporations. C corporations and other taxpayers are permitted to take an enhanced deduction for certain food contributions, but only to the extent of 15% of the income from businesses making such contributions.[67] This rule had been temporary through 2014 but became permanent in late 2015.

---

[63] § 1237(a).

[64] See § 1363(b)(4).

[65] § 448. However, see Rev. Proc. 2001-10, which allows any taxpayer with no more than $1 million gross receipts to use the cash method. Also see Rev. Proc. 2002-28, which allows certain taxpayers with up to $10 million gross receipts to use the cash method.

[66] See § 1363, which incorporates the rules of § 702 that disallow the deduction of charitable contributions to partnerships.

[67] § 170(e)(3)(C)(ii).

Qualified Production Activities Income Deduction

The deduction for Qualified Production Activities Income (QPAI) is allowed to all tax entities. However, for the S corporation, this deduction is to be computed at the shareholder level.[68] When computing this deduction, the shareholder must aggregate qualifying income, deductions and W-2 wages of all proprietorships with those passed through from all S corporations and partnerships in which the person owns stock or other equity interests. Although this rule makes the computations rather cumbersome for the shareholder, it has an advantage over the result that would be the case if the corporation computed the deduction. The shareholder does not take this deduction into account in computing stock or debt basis. Moreover, a shareholder is allowed this deduction (subject to the passive loss limits of § 469) even if the deduction exceeds the allowable basis for the year. The shareholder uses Form 8903 to calculate and report this deduction.

Net Investment Income

Beginning in 2013, certain taxpayers became subject to the 3.8% tax on Net Investment Income. The S corporation is not subject to this tax as an entity. Instead, each shareholder must determine if he, she or it is subject to the tax. The particular S corporation items of concern are investment income passing through from the corporation to the shareholders, ordinary business income of the S corporation, gains from the sales of assets by the S corporation and gains from sales of S corporation stock by the shareholders.

Inherently, the rules are not complicated. However, the information might not always be available, especially if a minority shareholder sells some of all of his or her stock. A brief summary of Net Investment Income affecting S corporation's shareholders is:

1. If the shareholder does not materially participate in the S corporation's trade or business activities, all income flowing through from the corporation, and all gains from the sales of stock in the S corporation are parts of Net Investment Income. They will still be reported on Schedule E, Schedule B, Schedule D, and other appropriate forms.

2. If the shareholder does materially participate in the S corporation's trade or business activities, the ordinary trade or business income will not be part of Net Investment Income. However, any interest, dividends and rents flowing through from the corporation are part of Net Investment Income. Moreover, any gains from the sale of the corporation's assets are Net Investment Income if they result from the sale of the assets that produce dividends, interest or rents.

3. If the shareholder does materially participate in the S corporation's trade or business activities and then sells stock, the gain may be bifurcated. The shareholder must determine what would have been the gain from the sale of the S corporation's assets producing dividends, interest or rents, if the corporation had sold its assets and allocated the ratable portions of those gains to that shareholder.[69] The remainder of the gain from the sale of stock is not Net Investment Income.

This tax applies to shareholders whose adjusted gross income exceeds $250,000 if married filing joint returns, $125,000 for married taxpayers filing separate returns, $200,000 for other individuals. Estates and trusts can expect to have this tax apply to nearly all of their Net Investment Income, regardless of their total level of income. Shareholders use Form 8960 to report Net Investment Income and calculate the tax.

---

[68] § 199(d)(1).

[69] § 1411(c)(4)(A).

Example 19

N and I are the sole and equal shareholders in NIC Corporation, an S corporation. N materially participates in NIC's business, but I is a passive investor. Both N and I have sufficient AGI to subject them to the Net Investment Income tax. In 2016 NIC reports the following:

Item	Total	50% to Each Shareholder
Net income from business operations	$90,000	$45,000
Section 1231 gain from sale of business property	60,000	30,000
Interest income from investment in working capital.	10,000	5,000
Capital gain from sale of investment asset.	12,000	6,000

Since N materially participates in NIC's business, neither the ordinary income from the business nor the § 1231 gain are items of Net Investment Income. His NII for the year from NIC is $11,000 ($5,000 interest income + $6,000 capital gain). All of the income passing through to I is NII, since she did not materially participate in the corporation's business. Thus her NII from NIC for the year is $86,000.

REPORTING S CORPORATION INCOME

Once an S corporation identifies and measures the relevant items of income, deduction and credit, such items must be passed through to the shareholders for reporting on their own returns. The approach used is similar to that used by partnerships. Consistent with the conduit concept, the items normally retain their character when they are allocated to the shareholders. For example, charitable contributions made by the S corporation flow through and are reported as charitable contributions by the shareholders subject to all the special tax rules that apply to individuals. The amounts allocated to the shareholders are based on their percentage of stock owned during the year. Unlike partnerships, Subchapter S contains no provision for special allocations among owners. This can be a disadvantage if special allocations are desirable.

To accomplish the pass-through, the S corporation must file an annual information return, Form 1120S. Indeed, the similarity between the taxation of S corporations and partnerships becomes readily apparent when Forms 1120S and 1065 are compared. (See Exhibit 11-1 for an illustration of Form 1120S.) There are some differences in computing the net ordinary income on page one of the two tax forms, however. Unlike Form 1065, Form 1120S has a section for computing any taxes due on excessive passive investment income and Schedule D built-in gains (both are discussed in a later section of this chapter).

All income, expenses, gains, losses, and credits that may be subject to special treatment by one or more of the shareholders are reported separately on Schedule K, which is filed with Form 1120S.[70] Schedule K-1 is then prepared for the shareholders' use. (See Exhibit 11-1 for an illustration.) Again, these schedules are quite similar to the schedules applicable to partnerships and partners. There are differences, including the following:

- There are no guaranteed payments on the S corporation schedule.

- There is no self-employment income on the S corporation schedule.

- There are no reconciliations of capital accounts on the S corporation schedule.

- There is no allocation of liabilities on the S corporation schedule.

Finally, the S corporation schedule includes a section for reporting distributions. These are divided into two categories: (1) distributions from earnings of the S corporation, and (2) if it has been operated as a C corporation in previous years, distributions from earnings of the C corporation. (Distributions are discussed in a later section of this chapter.)

---

[70] § 1366(a)(1)(A).

Filing Requirements

Form 1120S, with the attached Schedule K-1s, must be filed for the S corporation on or before the 15th day of the third month following the close of its taxable year. An automatic extension of six months may be obtained. Thus a calendar year S corporation's normal due date is March 15 but may be extended until September 15. In order to obtain the extension, the corporation must file Form 7004 on or before March 15 (or two months and 15 days after the close of the corporation's fiscal year). For years beginning after 2015, partnership returns are also due on the 15th day of the third month following the close of the taxable year (e.g., March 15 for a calendar year partnership).

In addition to attaching the Schedule K-1s to Form 1120S, the S corporation is required to provide shareholders with Schedule K-1 by the due date of the return. The shareholder need not attach the K-1 to his or her Form 1040. Form 1120S and its schedules may not be the only required parts of the return. In addition to such common business forms as 4625 and 4797, S corporations, as well as other business taxpayers may now need to file Form 1125-A to disclose the details of cost of goods sold. In addition, S corporations with total receipts of $500,000 or more must attach Form 1125-E. On this form, the corporation must list all of its officers, and the compensation paid to each officer during the tax year.

Schedule M-3

If an S corporation's total assets, measured by book value, exceed $10,000,000 at the end of a taxable year it must file Form 1120S, Schedule M-3, in lieu of Schedule M-1. Any corporation may file Schedule M-3 voluntarily. Any S corporation that files Schedule M-3 must file its return with the Internal Revenue Service Center at Ogden, Utah.

Schedule M-3 provides a detailed reconciliation between financial and taxable income. If the corporation files financial statements it must reconcile to the income so reported. If it files multiple statements, it must reconcile its taxable income to its financial accounting income in the following order of priority:

1. U.S. GAAP
2. IFRS
3. Other international
4. Other regulatory
5. Other accrual method
6. Other market method
7. Cash method

The schedule requires reconciliation of approximately 50 line items between financial and tax amounts. It uses a four column format, detailing the financial amount, timing differences permanent differences and the amount reported on the tax return.

EXHIBIT 11-1   **Form 1120S**

Form **1120S**

Department of the Treasury
Internal Revenue Service

U.S. Income Tax Return for an S Corporation

▶ Do not file this form unless the corporation has filed or is attaching Form 2553 to elect to be an S corporation.
▶ Information about Form 1120S and its separate instructions is at *www.irs.gov/form1120s.*

OMB No. 1545-0123

2015

For calendar year 2015 or tax year beginning _____ , 2015, ending _____ , 20 ___

A S election effective date 1 – 1 – 2015	**TYPE** **OR** **PRINT**	Name T Company Inc.
B Business activity code number (see instructions) 448110		Number, street, and room or suite no. If a P.O. box, see instructions. 8122 South 8th Street
C Check if Sch. M-3 attached ☐		City or town, state or province, country, and ZIP or foreign postal code Norfolk, VA 23508

D Employer identification number   88 – 9138761
E Date incorporated   1 – 1 – 2015
F Total assets (see instructions) $ 322,000 | 00

G Is the corporation electing to be an S corporation beginning with this tax year? ☒ Yes ☐ No   If "Yes," attach Form 2553 if not already filed

H Check if: **(1)** ☐ Final return **(2)** ☐ Name change **(3)** ☐ Address change **(4)** ☐ Amended return **(5)** ☐ S election termination or revocation

I Enter the number of shareholders who were shareholders during any part of the tax year . . . . ▶ 1

Caution: Include **only** trade or business income and expenses on lines 1a through 21. See the instructions for more information.

Income

1a	Gross receipts or sales	**1a**	470,000	00
b	Returns and allowances	**1b**	0	00
c	Balance. Subtract line 1b from line 1a	**1c**	470,000	00
2	Cost of goods sold (attach Form 1125-A)	**2**	300,000	00
3	Gross profit. Subtract line 2 from line 1c	**3**	170,000	00
4	Net gain (loss) from Form 4797, line 17 (attach Form 4797)	**4**		
5	Other income (loss) (see instructions—attach statement)	**5**		
6	**Total income (loss).** Add lines 3 through 5 . . . . ▶	**6**	170,000	00

Deductions (see instructions for limitations)

7	Compensation of officers (see instructions—attach Form 1125-E)	**7**	24,700	00
8	Salaries and wages (less employment credits)	**8**	48,000	00
9	Repairs and maintenance	**9**	12,000	00
10	Bad debts	**10**		
11	Rents	**11**		
12	Taxes and licenses	**12**	9,000	00
13	Interest	**13**	3,300	00
14	Depreciation not claimed on Form 1125-A or elsewhere on return (attach Form 4562) . . .	**14**	15,000	00
15	Depletion **(Do not deduct oil and gas depletion.)**	**15**		
16	Advertising	**16**		
17	Pension, profit-sharing, etc., plans	**17**		
18	Employee benefit programs	**18**	1,400	00
19	Other deductions (attach statement)	**19**	6,700	00
20	**Total deductions.** Add lines 7 through 19 . . . . ▶	**20**	120,100	00
21	**Ordinary business income (loss).** Subtract line 20 from line 6	**21**	49,900	00

Tax and Payments

22a	Excess net passive income or LIFO recapture tax (see instructions) . .	**22a**			
b	Tax from Schedule D (Form 1120S)	**22b**			
c	Add lines 22a and 22b (see instructions for additional taxes) . . .		**22c**		
23a	2015 estimated tax payments and 2014 overpayment credited to 2015	**23a**			
b	Tax deposited with Form 7004	**23b**			
c	Credit for federal tax paid on fuels (attach Form 4136)	**23c**			
d	Add lines 23a through 23c		**23d**		
24	Estimated tax penalty (see instructions). Check if Form 2220 is attached . . . . . ▶ ☐		**24**		
25	**Amount owed.** If line 23d is smaller than the total of lines 22c and 24, enter amount owed . .		**25**		
26	**Overpayment.** If line 23d is larger than the total of lines 22c and 24, enter amount overpaid . .		**26**		
27	Enter amount from line 26 **Credited to 2016 estimated tax** ▶ _____ **Refunded** ▶		**27**		

Sign Here

Under penalties of perjury, I declare that I have examined this return, including accompanying schedules and statements, and to the best of my knowledge and belief, it is true, correct, and complete. Declaration of preparer (other than taxpayer) is based on all information of which preparer has any knowledge.

▶ *KL Roads*   3-1-16   ▶ President
Signature of officer   Date   Title

May the IRS discuss this return with the preparer shown below (see instructions)? ☐ Yes ☐ No

Paid Preparer Use Only

Print/Type preparer's name	Preparer's signature		Date	Check ☐ if self-employed	PTIN
Firm's name ▶				Firm's EIN ▶	
Firm's address ▶				Phone no.	

For Paperwork Reduction Act Notice, see separate instructions.   Cat. No. 11510H   Form **1120S** (2015)

EXHIBIT 11-1   **Continued**

Form 1120S (2015)   Page **2**

Schedule B	**Other Information** (see instructions)		Yes	No

1   Check accounting method: **a** ☐ Cash   **b** ☒ Accrual
         c ☐ Other (specify) ▶ ....

2   See the instructions and enter the:
     a Business activity ▶   Retail Sales   **b** Product or service ▶   Men's Clothing

3   At any time during the tax year, was any shareholder of the corporation a disregarded entity, a trust, an estate, or a nominee or similar person? If "Yes," attach Schedule B-1, Information on Certain Shareholders of an S Corporation . . | | X

4   At the end of the tax year, did the corporation:

a   Own directly 20% or more, or own, directly or indirectly, 50% or more of the total stock issued and outstanding of any foreign or domestic corporation? For rules of constructive ownership, see instructions. If "Yes," complete (i) through (v) below . . . . | | X

(i) Name of Corporation	**(ii)** Employer Identification Number (if any)	**(iii)** Country of Incorporation	**(iv)** Percentage of Stock Owned	**(v)** If Percentage in (iv) is 100%, Enter the Date (if any) a Qualified Subchapter S Subsidiary Election Was Made

b   Own directly an interest of 20% or more, or own, directly or indirectly, an interest of 50% or more in the profit, loss, or capital in any foreign or domestic partnership (including an entity treated as a partnership) or in the beneficial interest of a trust? For rules of constructive ownership, see instructions. If "Yes," complete (i) through (v) below . . . . | | X

(i) Name of Entity	**(ii)** Employer Identification Number (if any)	**(iii)** Type of Entity	**(iv)** Country of Organization	**(v)** Maximum Percentage Owned in Profit, Loss, or Capital

5 a   At the end of the tax year, did the corporation have any outstanding shares of restricted stock? . . . . | | X
     If "Yes," complete lines (i) and (ii) below.
     (i)   Total shares of restricted stock. . . . . ▶ ....
     (ii)   Total shares of non-restricted stock . . . . ▶ ....

b   At the end of the tax year, did the corporation have any outstanding stock options, warrants, or similar instruments? . | | X
     If "Yes," complete lines (i) and (ii) below.
     (i)   Total shares of stock outstanding at the end of the tax year ▶ ....
     (ii)   Total shares of stock outstanding if all instruments were executed ▶ ....

6   Has this corporation filed, or is it required to file, **Form 8918,** Material Advisor Disclosure Statement, to provide information on any reportable transaction? . . . . | | X

7   Check this box if the corporation issued publicly offered debt instruments with original issue discount . . . . ▶ ☐
     If checked, the corporation may have to file **Form 8281,** Information Return for Publicly Offered Original Issue Discount Instruments.

8   If the corporation: **(a)** was a C corporation before it elected to be an S corporation **or** the corporation acquired an asset with a basis determined by reference to the basis of the asset (or the basis of any other property) in the hands of a C corporation **and (b)** has net unrealized built-in gain in excess of the net recognized built-in gain from prior years, enter the net unrealized built-in gain reduced by net recognized built-in gain from prior years (see instructions) . . . . ▶ $ ....

9   Enter the accumulated earnings and profits of the corporation at the end of the tax year. $ ....

10   Does the corporation satisfy **both** of the following conditions?
   a   The corporation's total receipts (see instructions) for the tax year were less than $250,000 . . . .
   b   The corporation's total assets at the end of the tax year were less than $250,000   . . . . | | X
     If "Yes," the corporation is not required to complete Schedules L and M-1.

11   During the tax year, did the corporation have any non-shareholder debt that was canceled, was forgiven, or had the terms modified so as to reduce the principal amount of the debt?   . . . . | | X
     If "Yes," enter the amount of principal reduction $ ....

12   During the tax year, was a qualified subchapter S subsidiary election terminated or revoked? If "Yes," see instructions . | | X

13a   Did the corporation make any payments in 2015 that would require it to file Form(s) 1099? . . . . | X |
   b   If "Yes," did the corporation file or will it file required Forms 1099? . . . . | X |

                                     Form **1120S** (2015)

EXHIBIT 11-1   Continued

Form 1120S (2014)						Page **3**
Schedule K	**Shareholders' Pro Rata Share Items**				**Total amount**	

Income (Loss)	**1**	Ordinary business income (loss) (page 1, line 21)		**1**	49,900	00
	2	Net rental real estate income (loss) (attach Form 8825)		**2**		
	3a	Other gross rental income (loss)	**3a**			
	b	Expenses from other rental activities (attach statement)	**3b**			
	c	Other net rental income (loss). Subtract line 3b from line 3a		**3c**		
	4	Interest income		**4**		
	5	Dividends: **a** Ordinary dividends		**5a**	2,000	00
		b Qualified dividends	**5b**	2,000	00	
	6	Royalties		**6**		
	7	Net short-term capital gain (loss) (attach Schedule D (Form 1120S))		**7**		
	8a	Net long-term capital gain (loss) (attach Schedule D (Form 1120S))		**8a**	1,000	00
	b	Collectibles (28%) gain (loss)	**8b**			
	c	Unrecaptured section 1250 gain (attach statement)	**8c**			
	9	Net section 1231 gain (loss) (attach Form 4797)		**9**		
	10	Other income (loss) (see instructions) . . Type ▶		**10**		
Deductions	**11**	Section 179 deduction (attach Form 4562)		**11**	7,000	00
	12a	Charitable contributions		**12a**		
	b	Investment interest expense		**12b**		
	c	Section 59(e)(2) expenditures **(1)** Type ▶ _____ **(2)** Amount ▶		**12c(2)**		
	d	Other deductions (see instructions) . . . . Type ▶		**12d**		
Credits	**13a**	Low-income housing credit (section 42(j)(5))		**13a**		
	b	Low-income housing credit (other)		**13b**		
	c	Qualified rehabilitation expenditures (rental real estate) (attach Form 3468, if applicable)		**13c**		
	d	Other rental real estate credits (see instructions) Type ▶		**13d**		
	e	Other rental credits (see instructions) . . . Type ▶		**13e**		
	f	Biofuel producer credit (attach Form 6478)		**13f**		
	g	Other credits (see instructions) . . . . . Type ▶		**13g**	2,000	00
Foreign Transactions	**14a**	Name of country or U.S. possession ▶				
	b	Gross income from all sources		**14b**		
	c	Gross income sourced at shareholder level		**14c**		
		Foreign gross income sourced at corporate level				
	d	Passive category		**14d**		
	e	General category		**14e**		
	f	Other (attach statement)		**14f**		
		Deductions allocated and apportioned at shareholder level				
	g	Interest expense		**14g**		
	h	Other		**14h**		
		Deductions allocated and apportioned at corporate level to foreign source income				
	i	Passive category		**14i**		
	j	General category		**14j**		
	k	Other (attach statement)		**14k**		
		Other information				
	l	Total foreign taxes (check one): ▶ ☐ Paid ☐ Accrued		**14l**		
	m	Reduction in taxes available for credit (attach statement)		**14m**		
	n	Other foreign tax information (attach statement)				
Alternative Minimum Tax (AMT) Items	**15a**	Post-1986 depreciation adjustment		**15a**	4,000	00
	b	Adjusted gain or loss		**15b**		
	c	Depletion (other than oil and gas)		**15c**		
	d	Oil, gas, and geothermal properties—gross income		**15d**		
	e	Oil, gas, and geothermal properties—deductions		**15e**		
	f	Other AMT items (attach statement)		**15f**		
Items Affecting Shareholder Basis	**16a**	Tax-exempt interest income		**16a**		
	b	Other tax-exempt income		**16b**		
	c	Nondeductible expenses		**16c**		
	d	Distributions (attach statement if required) (see instructions)		**16d**	22,000	00
	e	Repayment of loans from shareholders		**16e**		

Form **1120S** (2014)

EXHIBIT 11-1 Continued

Form 1120S (2015) Page **4**

Schedule K		**Shareholders' Pro Rata Share Items** (continued)		**Total amount**
Other Information	**17a**	Investment income . . Dividends	**17a**	2,000 00
	b	Investment expenses	**17b**	
	c	Dividend distributions paid from accumulated earnings and profits	**17c**	
	d	Other items and amounts (attach statement)		
Recon-ciliation	**18**	**Income/loss reconciliation.** Combine the amounts on lines 1 through 10 in the far right column. From the result, subtract the sum of the amounts on lines 11 through 12d and 14l	**18**	45,900 00

Schedule L **Balance Sheets per Books**	Beginning of tax year		End of tax year	
Assets	**(a)**	**(b)**	**(c)**	**(d)**
1 Cash				
2a Trade notes and accounts receivable				
b Less allowance for bad debts	( )		( )	
3 Inventories				
4 U.S. government obligations				
5 Tax-exempt securities (see instructions)				
6 Other current assets (attach statement)				
7 Loans to shareholders				
8 Mortgage and real estate loans				
9 Other investments (attach statement)				
10a Buildings and other depreciable assets				
b Less accumulated depreciation	( )		( )	
11a Depletable assets				
b Less accumulated depletion	( )		( )	
12 Land (net of any amortization)				
13a Intangible assets (amortizable only)				
b Less accumulated amortization	( )		( )	
14 Other assets (attach statement)				
15 Total assets				322,000
Liabilities and Shareholders' Equity				
16 Accounts payable				
17 Mortgages, notes, bonds payable in less than 1 year				
18 Other current liabilities (attach statement)				
19 Loans from shareholders				
20 Mortgages, notes, bonds payable in 1 year or more				
21 Other liabilities (attach statement)				
22 Capital stock				
23 Additional paid-in capital				
24 Retained earnings				
25 Adjustments to shareholders' equity (attach statement)				
26 Less cost of treasury stock		( )		( )
27 Total liabilities and shareholders' equity		0		322,000

Form **1120S** (2015)

EXHIBIT 11-1	Continued

Form 1120S (2015)   Page **5**

Schedule M-1	Reconciliation of Income (Loss) per Books With Income (Loss) per Return	
	Note: The corporation may be required to file Schedule M-3 (see instructions)	

1	Net income (loss) per books	45,900	5	Income recorded on books this year not included on Schedule K, lines 1 through 10 (itemize):
2	Income included on Schedule K, lines 1, 2, 3c, 4, 5a, 6, 7, 8a, 9, and 10, not recorded on books this year (itemize) _____		a	Tax-exempt interest $ _____
3	Expenses recorded on books this year not included on Schedule K, lines 1 through 12 and 14l (itemize):		6	Deductions included on Schedule K, lines 1 through 12 and 14l, not charged against book income this year (itemize):
a	Depreciation $ _____		a	Depreciation $ _____
b	Travel and entertainment $ _____			
			7	Add lines 5 and 6	
4	Add lines 1 through 3	45,900	8	Income (loss) (Schedule K, line 18). Line 4 less line 7	45,900

Schedule M-2	Analysis of Accumulated Adjustments Account, Other Adjustments Account, and Shareholders' Undistributed Taxable Income Previously Taxed (see instructions)		

		(a) Accumulated adjustments account	(b) Other adjustments account	(c) Shareholders' undistributed taxable income previously taxed
1	Balance at beginning of tax year	0		
2	Ordinary income from page 1, line 21 . . .	49,900		
3	Other additions	3,000		
4	Loss from page 1, line 21	( )		
5	Other reductions	(7,000)	( )	
6	Combine lines 1 through 5	45,900		
7	Distributions other than dividend distributions	22,000		
8	Balance at end of tax year. Subtract line 7 from line 6	23,900		

Form **1120S** (2015)

EXHIBIT 11-1   Continued

671113

Schedule K-1 (Form 1120S)	2015		Part III	Shareholder's Share of Current Year Income, Deductions, Credits, and Other Items	

☐ Final K-1   ☐ Amended K-1   OMB No. 1545-0123

Schedule K-1
(Form 1120S)
Department of the Treasury
Internal Revenue Service

2015

For calendar year 2015, or tax
year beginning _____, 2015
ending _____, 20 _____

Shareholder's Share of Income, Deductions, Credits, etc.   ► See back of form and separate instructions.

Part I   Information About the Corporation

A Corporation's employer identification number
88 – 9138761

B Corporation's name, address, city, state, and ZIP code

T Company, Inc.
8122 South 8th Street
Norfolk, VA 23508

C IRS Center where corporation filed return
Cincinnati, OH

Part II   Information About the Shareholder

D Shareholder's identifying number
123 – 45 – 6789

E Shareholder's name, address, city, state, and ZIP code

Victor Z. Martin
1291 Maple Street
Austin, TX 78759

F Shareholder's percentage of stock
ownership for tax year . . . . _____ 100 %

For IRS Use Only

Part III   Shareholder's Share of Current Year Income, Deductions, Credits, and Other Items

1	Ordinary business income (loss) 49,900	13	Credits Rehab. 2,000
2	Net rental real estate income (loss)		
3	Other net rental income (loss)		
4	Interest income		
5a	Ordinary dividends 2,000		
5b	Qualified dividends 2,000	14	Foreign transactions
6	Royalties		
7	Net short-term capital gain (loss)		
8a	Net long-term capital gain (loss) 1,000		
8b	Collectibles (28%) gain (loss)		
8c	Unrecaptured section 1250 gain		
9	Net section 1231 gain (loss)		
10	Other income (loss)	15	Alternative minimum tax (AMT) items A 4,000
11	Section 179 deduction 7,000	16	Items affecting shareholder basis D 22,000
12	Other deductions		
		17	Other information

*

* See attached statement for additional information.

For Paperwork Reduction Act Notice, see Instructions for Form 1120S.   IRS.gov/form1120s   Cat. No. 11520D   **Schedule K-1 (Form 1120S) 2015**

EXHIBIT 11-1	**Continued**

Schedule K-1 (Form 1120S) 2015 — Page **2**

This list identifies the codes used on Schedule K-1 for all shareholders and provides summarized reporting information for shareholders who file Form 1040. For detailed reporting and filing information, see the separate Shareholder's Instructions for Schedule K-1 and the instructions for your income tax return.

1. **Ordinary business income (loss).** Determine whether the income (loss) is passive or nonpassive and enter on your return as follows:

	Report on
Passive loss	See the Shareholder's Instructions
Passive income	Schedule E, line 28, column (g)
Nonpassive loss	Schedule E, line 28, column (h)
Nonpassive income	Schedule E, line 28, column (j)

2. **Net rental real estate income (loss)**   See the Shareholder's Instructions

3. **Other net rental income (loss)**
Net income	Schedule E, line 28, column (g)
Net loss	See the Shareholder's Instructions

4. **Interest income**   Form 1040, line 8a
5a. **Ordinary dividends**   Form 1040, line 9a
5b. **Qualified dividends**   Form 1040, line 9b
6. **Royalties**   Schedule E, line 4
7. **Net short-term capital gain (loss)**   Schedule D, line 5
8a. **Net long-term capital gain (loss)**   Schedule D, line 12
8b. **Collectibles (28%) gain (loss)**   28% Rate Gain Worksheet, line 4 (Schedule D instructions)
8c. **Unrecaptured section 1250 gain**   See the Shareholder's Instructions
9. **Net section 1231 gain (loss)**   See the Shareholder's Instructions

10. **Other income (loss)**
Code
A	Other portfolio income (loss)	See the Shareholder's Instructions
B	Involuntary conversions	See the Shareholder's Instructions
C	Sec. 1256 contracts & straddles	Form 6781, line 1
D	Mining exploration costs recapture	See Pub. 535
E	Other income (loss)	See the Shareholder's Instructions

11. **Section 179 deduction**   See the Shareholder's Instructions

12. **Other deductions**
A	Cash contributions (50%)	
B	Cash contributions (30%)	
C	Noncash contributions (50%)	
D	Noncash contributions (30%)	
E	Capital gain property to a 50% organization (30%)	See the Shareholder's Instructions
F	Capital gain property (20%)	
G	Contributions (100%)	
H	Investment interest expense	Form 4952, line 1
I	Deductions—royalty income	Schedule E, line 19
J	Section 59(e)(2) expenditures	See the Shareholder's Instructions
K	Deductions—portfolio (2% floor)	Schedule A, line 23
L	Deductions—portfolio (other)	Schedule A, line 28
M	Preproductive period expenses	See the Shareholder's Instructions
N	Commercial revitalization deduction from rental real estate activities	See Form 8582 instructions
O	Reforestation expense deduction	See the Shareholder's Instructions
P	Domestic production activities information	See Form 8903 instructions
Q	Qualified production activities income	Form 8903, line 7b
R	Employer's Form W-2 wages	Form 8903, line 17
S	Other deductions	See the Shareholder's Instructions

13. **Credits**
A	Low-income housing credit (section 42(j)(5)) from pre-2008 buildings	
B	Low-income housing credit (other) from pre-2008 buildings	
C	Low-income housing credit (section 42(j)(5)) from post-2007 buildings	See the Shareholder's Instructions
D	Low-income housing credit (other) from post-2007 buildings	
E	Qualified rehabilitation expenditures (rental real estate)	
F	Other rental real estate credits	
G	Other rental credits	
H	Undistributed capital gains credit	Form 1040, line 73, box a
I	Biofuel producer credit	
J	Work opportunity credit	
K	Disabled access credit	See the Shareholder's Instructions
L	Empowerment zone employment credit	
M	Credit for increasing research activities	

Code   *Report on*

N	Credit for employer social security and Medicare taxes	
O	Backup withholding	See the Shareholder's Instructions
P	Other credits	

14. **Foreign transactions**
A	Name of country or U.S. possession	
B	Gross income from all sources	Form 1116, Part I
C	Gross income sourced at shareholder level	

Foreign gross income sourced at corporate level
D	Passive category	
E	General category	Form 1116, Part I
F	Other	

Deductions allocated and apportioned at shareholder level
G	Interest expense	Form 1116, Part I
H	Other	Form 1116, Part I

Deductions allocated and apportioned at corporate level to foreign source income
I	Passive category	
J	General category	Form 1116, Part I
K	Other	

Other information
L	Total foreign taxes paid	Form 1116, Part II
M	Total foreign taxes accrued	Form 1116, Part II
N	Reduction in taxes available for credit	Form 1116, line 12
O	Foreign trading gross receipts	Form 8873
P	Extraterritorial income exclusion	Form 8873
Q	Other foreign transactions	See the Shareholder's Instructions

15. **Alternative minimum tax (AMT) items**
A	Post-1986 depreciation adjustment	
B	Adjusted gain or loss	See the Shareholder's Instructions and the Instructions for Form 6251
C	Depletion (other than oil & gas)	
D	Oil, gas, & geothermal—gross income	
E	Oil, gas, & geothermal—deductions	
F	Other AMT items	

16. **Items affecting shareholder basis**
A	Tax-exempt interest income	Form 1040, line 8b
B	Other tax-exempt income	
C	Nondeductible expenses	See the Shareholder's Instructions
D	Distributions	
E	Repayment of loans from shareholders	

17. **Other information**
A	Investment income	Form 4952, line 4a
B	Investment expenses	Form 4952, line 5
C	Qualified rehabilitation expenditures (other than rental real estate)	See the Shareholder's Instructions
D	Basis of energy property	See the Shareholder's Instructions
E	Recapture of low-income housing credit (section 42(j)(5))	Form 8611, line 8
F	Recapture of low-income housing credit (other)	Form 8611, line 8
G	Recapture of investment credit	See Form 4255
H	Recapture of other credits	See the Shareholder's Instructions
I	Look-back interest—completed long-term contracts	See Form 8697
J	Look-back interest—income forecast method	See Form 8866
K	Dispositions of property with section 179 deductions	
L	Recapture of section 179 deduction	
M	Section 453(l)(3) information	
N	Section 453A(c) information	
O	Section 1260(b) information	
P	Interest allocable to production expenditures	See the Shareholder's Instructions
Q	CCF nonqualified withdrawals	
R	Depletion information—oil and gas	
S	Reserved	
T	Section 108(i) information	
U	Net investment income	
V	Other information	

ALLOCATIONS TO SHAREHOLDERS

All S corporation items (except distributions) are allocated among the shareholders based on their *ownership percentage* of the outstanding stock on each day of the year.[71] Thus, a shareholder owning 20% of the outstanding stock all year is deemed to have received 20% of *each item*. The allocation rate can be changed only by increasing or decreasing the percentage of stock ownership. This precludes shareholders from dividing net income or losses in any other manner. Of course, a certain amount of special allocation can be achieved through salaries and other business payments to owners. If there is no change in stock ownership during the year, each item to be allocated is multiplied by the percentage of stock owned by each shareholder. In contrast, actual distributions of assets are assigned to the shareholder who receives them.

Example 20

M owns 100 of an S corporation's 1,000 shares of common stock outstanding. Neither the number of shares outstanding nor the number owned by M has changed during the year. The S corporation items for its calendar year are allocated to M, based on her 10% ownership interest, as follows:

	Totals on Schedule K	M's 10% on Schedule K-1
Ordinary income (from Form 1120S, page 1)	$70,000	$7,000
Net capital gain	2,000	200
Charitable contributions.	4,000	400

If the ownership of stock changes during the year, there are two methods for determining the allocations for those shareholders whose interests have changed. These are (1) the *per day allocation method* and (2) the *interim closing of the books* method. Generally, the per day allocation method must be used. However, the S corporation may elect to use either method if:

1. A shareholder's ownership interest is *completely* terminated;
2. There is a disposition by one shareholder of *more than* 20% of the outstanding shares of the corporation within 30 days; or
3. The corporation issues shares to one or more new shareholders and the new shares are at least 25% of the number previously outstanding.

Per Day Allocation

This method assigns an equal amount of the S items to each day of the year.[72] When a shareholder's interest changes, the shareholder *must* report a pro rata share of each item for each day that the stock was owned. For this purpose, the seller is deemed to own the stock on the day of the sale. This computation may be expressed as follows:

Percentage of shares owned × Percentage of year stock was owned = Portion of item to be reported

---

[71] §§ 1366(a) and 1377(a).   [72] § 1377(a)(1).

Example 21

Assume the same facts as in *Example 20,* except that M sold all of her shares on August 7 to T. Because the S corporation uses the calendar year, M has held 100 shares for 219 days, or 60% of the year (219 ÷ 365). (The day of sale is considered an ownership day for the seller, M.) Thus M is allocated 6% (60% × 10%) of each corporate item while T is allocated 4% (40% × 10%). Based on the per day allocation method, M's and T's shares of the S corporation items are as follows:

	Totals on Schedule K	10% to M & T	M's Portion (10% × 219/365)	T's Portion (10% × 146/365)
Ordinary income	$70,000	$7,000	$4,200	$2,800
Net capital gain	2,000	200	120	80
Charitable contributions.	4,000	400	240	160

The per day allocation method also is applicable for a shareholder whose stock interest varies during the year; however, the computation is more complex.

Example 22

Assume the same facts as in *Example 21,* except M only sold 20 shares on August 7 to T. Thus, she owned 10% of the business the first 219 days and 8% the remaining 146 days. Based on the per day allocation method. M's and T's shares of the S corporation items are as follows:

	Totals Schedule K	1/1–8/7 (10% × 219/365)	8/8–12/31 (8% × 146/365)	M's Schedule K-1	T's Schedule K-1 (2% × 146/365)
Ordinary income	$70,000	$4,200	$2,240	$6,440	$560
Net capital gain	2,000	120	64	184	16
Charitable contributions. . .	4,000	240	128	368	32

Interim Closing of the Books

As noted above, the per day method must be used unless there is either (1) a complete termination of a shareholder's interest, (2) a disposition of more than 20% of the outstanding stock of the corporation by one shareholder within a 30-day period, or (3) issuance of shares to persons who were not previously shareholders equal to at least 25% of the number previously outstanding. In any of these situations, the corporation may elect to use the interim closing of books method instead of the per day allocation method.[73] If the corporation elects, the year is divided into two short taxable years for allocation purposes and all owners report the actual dollar amounts that were accumulated while they owned their shares. A valid election must be filed by the corporation with Form 1120S. All parties who are affected by the transaction must consent to the election by filing personal tax returns consistent with the election. This election does not require the corporation to file separate returns for each portion of the year.

---

[73] § 1377(a)(2).

Example 23

Assume the same facts as in *Example 21*, except the interim closing of books method is elected. Since M sells *all* of her shares on August 7 to T, the S corporation's year ends the day before on August 6. Corporate records show the following amounts for the first 219 days, for the last 146 days, and M's share for the first 219 days.

	First 219 Days	Last 146 Days	M's 10% on Schedule K-1	T's 10% on Schedule K-1
Ordinary income (from Form 1102S, page 1)	$15,000	$55,000	$1,500	$5,500
Net capital gain.................	1,000	1,000	100	100
Charitable contributions...........	0	4,000	0	400

The computations for M's share are the amounts for the first 219 days *multiplied* by her 10% ownership interest. T's share are the amounts for the last 146 days *multiplied* by his 10% ownership interest. The combined amounts for M and T equal the amount for M in *Example 21*.

It is also possible for an S corporation to have an ordinary loss for part of the year and ordinary income for the remaining period.

LOSSES OF THE S CORPORATION

One of the most common reasons a corporation elects Subchapter S status is because of the tax treatment for corporate losses. Recall that the C corporation's benefits are limited to those available from carrying the losses to another year to offset its own income. Refunds may be obtained to the extent *prior* year income is offset while losses carried to future years reduce the taxes due in those years. Frequently, these carryover benefits provide little or no value to the corporation. For example, many businesses report losses in the first few years so the carryback privilege is useless. In addition, many new businesses are never successful. But, even those that are successful receive no tax benefit from their losses currently—generally when the need is the greatest.

The pass-through feature of S corporations can be a significant advantage when a corporation has a net loss. Based on the flow-through concept, shareholders include their distributive shares of the S corporation's losses in their taxable income currently. Thus, the deduction for losses is transferred to the shareholder and generally results in tax savings for the current year. Even if a shareholder is unable to use the loss currently, carryover provisions may provide the shareholder with tax benefits in the near future.

Limitations

Each shareholder's deductible share of net losses may not exceed that shareholder's basis in the corporation's stock and the basis in any debt that the corporation owes to the shareholder. (Shareholder basis is discussed in more depth later in this chapter.) Any losses that exceed a shareholder's basis may be carried forward indefinitely to be used when the shareholder's basis is increased.[74] When basis is insufficient and there is more than one item that reduces basis, the flow-through of each item is determined in a pro rata manner.[75] In addition, any income items that increase basis flow through to the owner before any items that reduce basis, including distributions on stock.[76]

---

[74] § 1366(d)(2). Losses may also be subject to limitation under § 465 at-risk rules and § 469 passive activity rules.

[75] Reg. § 1.1366-2(a)(4).

[76] §§ 1366(d)(1) and 1367(a). After positive adjustments, basis is reduced by distributions and nondeductible items, before separately stated deductions and losses. See discussion below.

Example 24

G owns 200 of an S corporation's 1,000 shares of common stock outstanding and has a basis of $10,000 at the beginning of the year. Neither the number of shares outstanding nor those owned by G has changed during the year. The S corporation items for its calendar year are allocated to G, based on his 20% ownership interest, as follows:

	Totals on Schedule K	G's 20% on Schedule K-1
Ordinary loss (from Form 1120S, page 1)	$(70,000)	$(14,000)
Net capital loss	(5,000)	(1,000)
Section 1231 gain	10,000	2,000

G's share of the S corporation's losses is limited as follows:

	Basis	Loss Carryover
G's beginning basis	$10,000	
Section 1231 gain	2,000	
Limitation on losses	$12,000	
Ordinary loss*	(11,200)	$2,800
Net capital loss**	(800)	200
G's ending basis	$ 0	

* ($14,000/$15,000 × $12,000)
** ($1,000/$15,000 × $12,000)

Because G's basis is less than the $15,000 total loss, G may report ordinary loss of only $11,200 and net capital loss of $800. The remaining ordinary loss of $2,800 and net capital loss of $200 are carried forward to be used at the end of the first year that G's basis increases.

The above allocation of losses is applicable to all losses and separate deductions (e.g., investment interest and state income taxes) for owners of both the S corporation and the partnership.

Carryovers from C Corporation Years

Generally, no carryovers from a C corporation may be used during the years it is taxed as an S corporation (or vice versa). For example, a C corporation with a net operating loss may not use it to offset income in an S year. There is one exception: C corporate NOL carryforwards may be used to offset the S corporation's built-in gains (discussed in Chapter 12).[77] The S years are counted, however, when determining the expiration period of the carryover. Thus, a carryback of two years means two fiscal or calendar years regardless of whether the corporation was a C corporation or an S corporation.[78]

Determining Shareholder Basis

A shareholder's basis in his or her stock as well as any debt owed to the shareholder is critical for three principal purposes. First, upon a sale of stock, shareholders must know the basis of the stock to compute gain or loss on the sale. Second, the treatment of distributions depends on the basis of a shareholder's stock. Third, shareholders must know their stock basis as well as their debt basis in loss years since losses are deductible only to the extent of the basis in their stock and debt.

BASIS IN S CORPORATE STOCK

Conceptually, the computation of a shareholder's stock basis is similar to that for a partner's interest in a partnership. Both calculations are designed to ensure that there is neither double taxation of income nor double deduction of expenses. Consider a typical situation where two individuals form a business. Assume both parties contribute $10,000 for a 50% interest in an S corporation which immediately takes the money and invests it in land that it subsequently sells for $22,000. In this case, the S corporation has income of $2,000 ($22,000 − $20,000) and each shareholder reports his $1,000 share. Note that the shareholders report their share of the S corporation's income even if they receive no distributions from the S corporation. However, to ensure that an S corporation's income is not taxed again when it is distributed, each shareholder must keep track of his or her investment, that is, basis in the S corporation. In this case, each shareholder has an original basis equal to the amount contributed to the S corporation, $10,000. Upon the reporting of S corporation income, each shareholder adjusts basis in the S corporation interest for his or her share of income, increasing it from $10,000 to $11,000. When a shareholder actually receives the $1,000 share of the income, the distribution is treated as tax-free to the extent of basis. Each shareholder would then reduce basis by $1,000 back to the original basis of $10,000. The end result is that the shareholders have reported and received income that has been subject to only one tax. The same rationale can be applied to situations involving tax-exempt income, deductible losses and nondeductible expenses to ensure the proper result is reached.

The steps for calculating a shareholder's stock basis are shown and compared to that for a partner in Exhibit 11-2.[79] Generally, both computations begin with the owner's initial investment, increased by items of taxable and tax-exempt income then decreased by distributions, nondeductible expenditures,[80] deductible expenses and losses in that order. As may be apparent in Exhibit 11-2, the primary difference between the two calculations is that an S corporation shareholder does not include a proportionate share of corporate debt to other lenders. In addition, as illustrated in Chapter 12, the treatment of the distribution of noncash property differs from that of a partnership.

---

[77] § 1374(b)(2).

[78] §§ 1371(b) and 1362(e)(6)(A).

[79] § 1367.

[80] With respect to the order of nondeductible and deductible expenditures, there is no special rule for partnerships and in absence of sufficient basis, presumably a pro rata

portion of each type of expenditure is deducted as shown in *Example 24*. In contrast, S corporation shareholders must use the order shown unless they make a special election to reverse the order and agree to carry forward any disallowed expenses which exceed basis to reduce basis in future years. See Reg. § 1.1367-1(g).

LO.4

Determine the shareholders' basis in the S corporation stock and debt, and understand the significance for loss deductions and distributions.

	EXHIBIT 11-2	**Adjustments to Ownership Basis**

Shareholder's Basis in S Corporation Stock	*Partner's Basis in Partnership Interest*
Original Basis	**Original Basis**
Cost	Generally same as S unless received in exchange for property contributed to partnership where partner assumed or reduced liabilities. However, each partner is deemed to contribute cash equal to its share of liabilities.
Substitute for property contributed in § 351 exchange donor's basis	
Inherited basis (estate tax value from deceased shareholder) carryover (or limited) basis for stock received as gift	
Increased By	**Increased By**
Taxable income (ordinary or separately stated)	Same
Tax-exempt income	Same
Decreased (but not below zero) By	**Decreased (but not below zero) By**
Distributions of cash	Same
Distributions of property at fair market value	Partnership basis of distributed property (in most cases)
Nondeductible expenses (subject to election)*	Same
Losses (ordinary and separately stated)	Same
No Effect	**Additional Effect**
Increase in corporate liabilities	Increase partner's basis for share of liabilities
Decrease in corporate liabilities	Decrease partner's basis for share of liabilities

* Nondeductible expenses must be used to offset basis before deductible items unless the shareholder files a special election to reverse the order. Reg. § 1.1367-1(g).

BASIS IN S CORPORATION DEBT

If a shareholder's portion of the corporation's losses exceeds his or her stock basis, the shareholder must next turn to debt basis to determine whether or not any loss passing through from the corporation may be deductible. Unlike a partnership, in which a partner increases basis for his or her portion of the organization's debt to outsiders, a shareholder in an S corporation must actually loan money to the corporation in order to receive debt basis. There has been extensive litigation resulting from the IRS's disallowance of S corporation losses. Many of these cases arose because the IRS did not accept the basis claimed by a shareholder in a loss year. Although many cases involved different issues, several of them concerned shareholder guarantees of a corporation's debt to an outside lender, such as a bank. Others concerned indirect loans, in which the shareholder did not loan the money directly, but the S corporation borrowed from another entity in which the shareholder was a beneficiary, shareholder or partner. Still other controversies arose when a shareholder borrowed money and immediately loaned the same funds to the corporation. These transactions were often termed "back-to-back" loans.

In July 2014 the IRS amended Reg § 1.1366-2, principally to deal with the back to back loan controversy. The position of the regulation is that if an arrangement between a shareholder and a corporation creates valid indebtedness running directly from the corporation to the shareholder, and general tax principles give the shareholder basis in the amount loaned, there is valid debt basis.[81]

---

[81] Reg § 1.1366-2.

Example 25

Shareholder A owned all of the stock in ABC Corporation, an S corporation. A also owned stock in XYZ Corporation. In 2015 A borrowed $100,000 from XYZ and loaned $100,000 to ABC. Assuming that the loan to ABC from A is valid under state law, A has $100,000 of debt basis in ABC. However, if A were to become extremely aggressive, and borrow money from ABC and then loan it back to ABC, the IRS could disallow debt basis by treating the entire arrangement as a sham transaction.

When the IRS amended Reg § 1.1366-2 in 2014, it did not change its position that a guarantee of a corporation's borrowing from an outside lender was not a transaction that created or augmented debt or stock basis.[82] In accounting terms, the guarantee of a debt by anyone other than the actual borrower is a contingent liability, rather than an actual completed transaction. The shareholder increases basis only by paying all or a part of the obligation.

Example 26

DEF Corporation borrows $250,000 from a local bank in 2015. D, the principal shareholder of DEF, guarantees payment of the debt. In 2016 D pays $15,000 of the debt's principal on behalf of DEF. D receives no basis in 2015. In 2016 D's basis increases by $15,000.

The IRS has a long standing rule on how to create basis when a shareholder has guaranteed one or more of an S corporation's debt to an outsider. Rev. Rul. 75-144 instructs the shareholder to substitute his or her personal note to the lender, who accepts the shareholder's note as payment for all or a portion of the corporation's note.[83]

Example 27

Refer to *Example 26*. In 2016 the loan balance is $235,000, consisting of the amount DEF originally borrowed less the amount repaid in 2016. D arranges with the bank to tender his personal note in satisfaction of the balance now owed by DEF. When these steps are completed, D now has an additional $235,000 basis.

Rev. Rul. 75-144 states that subrogation is necessary to comply with its provisions. When subrogation occurs, the person who pays the loan is now the lender to the original borrower, and has all of the rights of the original creditor. However, some case law has held that subrogation is not necessary for the substitution to create basis for the shareholder.[84]

A shareholder's basis in the loan is adjusted for S corporation income and expenses *only* (1) when the actual indebtedness itself changes due to additional loans or repayment of loans, (2) when corporate net losses exceed the shareholder's basis in S stock, and (3) to restore any basis reduction due to the prior flow-through of net losses. The application of these latter two rules is somewhat tricky. As a general rule, losses first reduce the shareholder's stock basis (but not below zero). (Note that nondeductible expenses reduce basis before deductible expenses and losses unless a special election is made.) If there is insufficient stock basis to absorb the loss, the loss is deducted to the extent of the shareholder's debt basis. If there is insufficient stock and debt basis, the loss is carried over and used once there is sufficient basis to absorb the loss.

---

[82] Reg § 1.1366-2(a)(2)(ii).

[83] Rev. Rul. 75-144, 1975-1 CB 277.

[84] For example, see *Gilday*, 43 TCM 1295 (1982) and *Miller*, TC Memo 2006-125.

Example 28

An S corporation incurs a net operating loss of $30,000 in 2016. L, its sole share-holder, has a basis in the stock of $24,000 and a note due him from the corporation totals $10,000.

	Stock Basis	Debt Basis
Balance 12/31/2015	$24,000	$10,000
Loss to extent of stock basis	(24,000)	
Loss to extent of debt		(6,000)
Balance 12/31/2016	$ 0	$ 4,000

The $30,000 loss flows through to L, first to the extent of his $24,000 stock basis and the remaining $6,000 because of the $10,000 note owed to him.

If the 2016 loss had been $36,000, only $34,000 would be deductible by L, re-ducing his basis in both stock and debt to zero. The remaining $2,000 loss would be carried forward indefinitely until a positive basis adjustment occurs in stock or debt.

As the corporation reports income, the shareholder restores stock and debt basis. Debt basis is increased only for income in excess of current year distributions and deductible and nondeductible expenses and losses.[85] Thus if there are no distributions or losses during the year, the basis of the debt is increased first. However, in years where there are distributions and/or losses, the effect is to first allocate income to the stock's basis equal to the amount of any current year losses and distributions with any excess to the debt. While these rules are obviously confusing, failure to properly understand their operation may cause the share-holder to inadvertently have gain on the repayment of any corporate debt.

Example 29

Refer to *Example 28*. The S corporation has net income of $3,000 in 2017 and $8,000 in 2018. There were no losses or distributions in either of these years.

	Stock Basis	Debt Basis
Balance 12/31/2016	$ 0	$ 4,000
2017 net income	0	3,000
2018 net income	5,000	3,000
Balance 12/31/2018	$5,000	$10,000

In 2017, the excess of income over distributions and losses is $3,000 ($3,000 – $0 – $0) and, thus, the basis of the note is increased by $3,000. In 2018, the excess of income over distributions and losses is $8,000 ($8,000 – $0 – $0). Therefore the basis of the debt is increased first by $3,000 to its original $10,000 face amount ($7,000 + $3,000). The remaining income of $5,000 ($8,000 – $3,000) is used to increase the basis of the stock.

---

[85] § 1367(b)(2).

Example 30

The records of X, an S corporation, reveal the information below for 2016 and 2017. In addition, at the beginning of 2016, X's sole shareholder had a basis of $10,000 in her stock and $12,000 in a loan she had made to the corporation during 2013.

	2016	2017
Tax-exempt income.	$ 5,000	
Loss.	(30,000)	
Income		$21,000
Distribution		14,000

In 2016, the shareholder first increases the basis in her stock by the tax-exempt income of $5,000, resulting in a stock basis of $15,000. The $30,000 loss is then applied: first to the extent of her stock basis, $15,000, and then to the extent of her debt basis, $12,000. The remainder of the loss, $3,000, is carried over to 2017. These calculations are shown below:

	Stock Basis	Debt Basis
Begin 2016	$10,000	$12,000
Tax-exempt income.	5,000	
Loss $30,000.	(15,000)	(12,000)
End 2016.	$ 0	$ 0
Loss in excess of basis		3,000

In 2017, the corporation reports taxable income of $21,000 and distributes $14,000. The $21,000 income is applied in the following order:

		Stock Basis	Debt Basis
Begin 2017		$0	$ 0
Income	$21,000		
Distribution	(14,000)		7,000
Loss from 2016			(3,000)
End 2017.		$0	$4,000

The shareholder deducts $27,000 of the 2016 loss in 2016 and carries the remaining $3,000 forward. In 2017, the shareholder reports $21,000 of income and deducts the remaining $3,000 of the 2016 loss.

After a shareholder's basis in the indebtedness is reduced, repayments of the debt in excess of basis result in taxable income. If the debt is a note, bond, or other written debt instrument, the shareholder recognizes capital gain to the extent the payment exceeds basis.[86] If the debt is an *open* account, the shareholder recognizes ordinary income.[87] This ordinary income can be recharacterized as capital gain by converting the open account to a capital contribution; no gain is recognized for this conversion, even if the open account has been reduced by net losses (i.e., its basis is less than its face or market value).[88]

In accounting for repayments, the following rules must be followed:[89]

1. Only the basis of loans outstanding at the close of the year are reduced.

2. Only loans outstanding at the beginning of the year are restored.

The operation of these rules generally favors the taxpayer. Observe that the basis of any loan that is completely paid off during the year may be increased for income earned during the year but is not reduced for losses.

---

[86] § 1232 and Rev. Rul. 64-162, 1964-1 C.B. 304.

[87] Rev. Rul. 68-537, 1968-2 C.B. 372 and *Cornelius v. U.S.*, 74-1 USTC ¶9446, 33 AFTR2d 74-1331, 494 F.2d 465 (CA-5, 1974).

[88] §§ 108(e)(6) and (d)(7)(C). The holding period of the capital asset (the note) begins with the creation of the note—not the date of the unwritten loan.

[89] Reg. § 1.1367-2(d).

Example 31

J owns all of the stock of H, an S corporation. At the beginning of 2016, J had a basis in his S stock of $13,000 and a loan outstanding to the corporation of $10,000. On July 1, the corporation paid J the $10,000 it owed to him on the loan. As of July 1, the corporation's books and records revealed a loss of $15,000. The loss for the entire year was $20,000. J recognizes no gain on repayment of the loan since his basis is $10,000. Even though the losses suffered by the corporation at the date of the repayment, $15,000, and at the close of the year, $20,000, exceeded J's stock basis, there is no reduction in the basis of the loan since only the basis of a loan outstanding at the close of the year is reduced. However, J can only deduct $13,000 of the loss, the amount equal to his stock basis.

Example 32

Assume the same facts above except that the corporation repaid the loan on June 1 of the following year, 2017. In this case, J's basis in the loan at the beginning of 2017 would be $3,000 computed as follows:

	Stock Basis	Debt Basis
Begin 2016	$13,000	$10,000
Loss for 2016 $20,000	(13,000)	(7,000)
End 2016	$ 0	$ 3,000

If the corporation had no income for 2017, J would report a gain on the repayment of $7,000 ($10,000 − $3,000). On the other hand, if the corporation had income for the year of $6,000 *and* no distributions were made, the basis of the loan would be increased by the income of $6,000 to $9,000 and the gain on the repayment would be $1,000 ($10,000 − $9,000). Notice that in this latter case the basis of the loan is increased by income for the entire year even though the loan is paid off during the year. This follows from the rule that calls for loans outstanding at the first of the year to be restored.

Relationship between an S Corporation and Its Shareholders

LO.5

Recognize transactions between shareholders and their S corporations that are subject to special treatment.

The S corporation is a legal entity, distinctly separate from its owners. As a result, transactions between an S corporation and its shareholders are treated as though occurring between unrelated parties unless otherwise provided. Of course, these transactions must be conducted in an arm's-length manner, based on market values that would be used by unrelated parties.

Transactions between S Corporations and Their Shareholders

Owners may engage in *taxable transactions* with their S corporations. For example, shareholders may lend money, rent property, or sell assets to their S corporations (or vice versa). With few exceptions, owners include the interest income, rent income, or gain or loss from these transactions on their tax returns. Meanwhile, the S corporation is allowed a deduction for the interest, rent, or depreciation expense on assets purchased (if applicable).

Example 33

During the year, K received the following amounts from an S corporation in which she owns 30% of the stock outstanding:

1. $2,750 interest on a $25,000 loan made to the corporation;
2. $3,600 rental income from a storage building rented to the corporation; and
3. $6,300 for special tools sold to the corporation; the tools were acquired for personal use two years ago for $5,800.

Assume that the S corporation's net ordinary income, excluding the above items, is $40,000, and the depreciation deduction for the tools is $900. K's income is computed as follows:

	S Corporation	Shareholder K
Ordinary income (before items below)...................	$40,000	
Gain on sale of tools ($6,300 – $5,800)		$ 500
Depreciation of tools	(900)	
Interest	(2,750)	2,750
Rent	(3,600)	3,600
Ordinary income:		
Corporation	$32,750	
K ($32,750 × 30%)		9,825

There is a restriction, however, on when an S corporation may deduct expenses owed but not paid to a shareholder, regardless of the amount of stock owned. An accrual basis business (whether an S corporation or partnership) may not deduct expenses owed to a cash basis owner until the amount is paid.[90] This timing rule applies to all actual or constructive owners of any percent of the S corporation's stock.

Example 34

Assume the same facts as in *Example 33*, except that $2,000 of the $2,750 interest is accrued but not paid at the end of the current year, the S corporation is on the accrual basis, and K is on the cash basis. The corporation paid K the accrued interest of $2,000 on January 15, of the next year. Because K is a shareholder the corporation cannot deduct the $2,000 of accrued interest in the current year but must wait until it pays the amount. Consequently, the corporation will deduct the interest when it is paid in the next year. K will report the payment when she receives it.

Two special rules governing related-party transactions affect all business forms. Both are discussed in Chapter 9. *First,* realized *losses* on sales between related parties are disallowed.[91] This is not a deferral; therefore, there is no carryover of basis or holding period. However, if this property is later sold at a gain, the gain is offset by the previously disallowed losses.[92] *Second,* recognized gains on sales between related parties of *property* that will be *depreciable* to the new owner are taxed as ordinary income.[93] A related party is defined as one who owns directly or indirectly more than 50% of the business when losses are disallowed or when depreciable property is involved. (See the discussion and examples

---

[90] §§ 267(a)(2) and 267(e). This same restriction applies to a C corporation only if a cash basis shareholder owns more than 50% of its stock. § 267(b)(10).

[91] §§ 267 and 707(b)(1).

[92] § 267(d).

[93] § 1239.

in Chapter 9 regarding these transactions and the definitions of related parties.) A *third* restriction, affecting transactions between partners and their 50% owned partnerships, is *not* applicable to either S or C corporations. For these partners, recognized gains on sales of capital assets that will not be capital assets to the partnership are taxed as ordinary income.[94] In contrast, shareholders may sell capital assets to their more than 50% owned S or C corporations and the gain is capital, as long as the assets will not be depreciable property to the corporation. Note that this rule may favor the S corporation over the partnership or LLC for certain activities such as real estate development.

SELECTING A TAXABLE YEAR

LO.6

Determine the appropriate taxable year for an S corporation.

Shareholders report their shares of S corporation income, deductions, and credits in their tax years in which the corporation's year ends regardless of when distributions of assets are actually made.[95] This timing requirement makes the selection of a year-end for the owners and the business an important tax planning decision. Under current law, an S corporation normally must use the calendar year. Fiscal years are available but only if very strict conditions are met.

Currently an S corporation may have as its taxable year:

- A calendar year;

- A fiscal year if it is a natural business year;

- A fiscal year if its majority shareholders are on the same year; or

- A fiscal year under the special election of § 444.

Calendar Years

An S corporation is allowed to have a calendar year.[96] No permission is needed to adopt the calendar year. As will become evident, the severe requirements that must be met to obtain a fiscal year force the vast majority of S corporations to use the calendar year.

Natural Business Year

Section 1378 permits an S corporation to adopt a fiscal year if it "establishes a business purpose to the satisfaction of the Secretary." In this regard, the IRS has indicated that it will allow a fiscal year only in the case of a *natural business year*. An S corporation can qualify for use of a fiscal year end if it considered to have a "natural business year-end." There are two general categories of the natural business year end for S corporations: fiscal year-ends that meet a "25% gross receipts test" and fiscal year ends that meet an "annual business cycle" or "seasonal business" test. Year-ends qualifying under the gross receipts test can be adopted automatically by the S corporation. The other category requires permission of the IRS.

Automatic Adoption. A corporation that is electing S status, or a corporation that already has an S election in effect may automatically retain, adopt or change to a natural business year-end if it meets the "25 percent" test for its gross receipts of the past four years. To determine if this test is met, the corporation selects its desired year end (for example June 30) and determines its receipts for the two months ended on June 30 (May and June), and for the twelve months ending on that date in its most recent history (e.g., July through June). If the gross receipts for the final two months (e.g., May and June) exceed 25% of its gross receipts for the twelve months ending on that date (e.g., July through June), the S corporation meets the test. The S corporation must meet the test for its past three years ending on that date. A corporation that qualifies under this test may claim its fiscal year without receiving permission for the IRS, although it must file Form 1128 if it is changing its year.[97]

[94] § 707(b)(2).

[95] § 1366(a); § 706 provides a similar rule for partnerships.

[96] § 1378.

[97] See Rev. Proc. 2006-46, 2006-45 IRB 859, Sec. 5.07 and Rev. Proc. 2002-39, 2002-22 I.R.B. 1046, § 5.03(3).

Annual Business Cycle or Seasonal Business Tests. An S corporation may also qualify to apply for a natural business year-end under the annual business cycle test, or the seasonal business test. The annual business cycle test is for a corporation that has a "peak" period of receipts. The seasonal business test exists when there is a period of inactivity due to the nature of the business. Thus a retailer with peak sales during December holiday periods may qualify for the business cycle test, and a ski resort may qualify for the seasonal business test. However, the S corporation may not automatically claim a year-end based on either of these tests, but must apply to the National Office of the IRS and pay a ruling request fee.[98]

Example 35

An S corporation is organized November 1, 2016. Its net ordinary income for the first 14 months is as follows:

November 1–December 31, 2016	$ 20,000
January 1–October 31, 2017	200,000
November 1–December 31, 2017	40,000

All shareholders report on the calendar year. If the S corporation's year-end also is December 31, the owners have includible income of $20,000 in 2016 and $240,000 ($200,000 + $40,000) in 2017. If, however, the S corporation meets the natural business year requirements and receives permission for an October 31 year-end, the owners have no includible income in 2016 but have includible income of $220,000 ($20,000 + $200,000) in 2017. The $40,000 will be combined with the net income or loss for the first ten months in 2018 and reported in 2018.

Majority Ownership Year

Consistent with its concern about deferral, the IRS permits an S corporation to adopt a tax year that is identical to that of owners holding a majority of the corporation's stock.[99] For example, if an individual who operated a farm used a March 31 year-end, his wholly owned S corporation could use the same year-end since it conformed to the year of its majority owner. However, as a practical matter, this option is seldom used since most shareholders are individuals and certain trusts and they rarely use a fiscal year.

Section 444 Year

A partnership or an S corporation may elect to adopt or change its tax year to any fiscal year that does not result in a deferral period longer than three months—or, if less, the deferral period of the year currently in use.[100] This election requires the electing partnership or S corporation to make a single deposit on or before May 15 of each year computed on the deferred income at the highest tax rate imposed on individual taxpayers *plus* one percent (for 2016, 39.6% + 1% = 40.6%).[101] This deposit does *not* flow through to the shareholders. In essence, the partnership or S corporation must maintain a non-interest-bearing deposit of the income taxes that would have been deferred without this requirement. Since this option eliminates some tax benefits of income deferral and has burdensome compliance requirements, few S corporations make the election. The deposit is refunded if the S corporation's income declines in the future.

Since restrictions on C corporation year-end choices are much more lenient than those for S corporations, an election by a fiscal year C corporation to become an S corporation also may require a change in the corporate year-end. This new year is applicable to all future years, even if the Subchapter S election is cancelled and the business reverts to a C corporation.

---

[98] See Rev. Proc. 2002-39, 2002-22 I.R.B. 1046 for details.

[99] Rev. Proc. 2006-46, Sec. 6.06.

[100] § 444 and Temp. Reg. § 1.444-1T(b). Partnerships and S corporations in existence before 1987 are allowed to continue their fiscal years even if the deferral period exceeds three months (i.e., the fiscal year is "grandfathered").

[101] § 7519 and Temp. Reg § 1.7519-2T(a)(4)(ii).

Family Ownership

LO.7

Explain the unique concepts relevant to family members concerning ownership attribution, compensation, benefits and income allocation.

Many of the benefits available to family businesses from *income splitting* are dependent on which organizational form is selected. Some income splitting, however, may be achieved by employing relatives in the business regardless of the organizational form. For example, owners may hire their children to work for them. All reasonable salaries are deductible business expenses and includible salary income to the children. In addition to the tax benefits, some owners believe this provides personal advantages, including encouraging the children to take an interest in the business at an early age.

In some instances, family businesses are formed primarily for tax reasons. The most common example includes both a parent and one or more otherwise dependent children as owners. The basic tax rate structure provides considerable incentive for this type of arrangement when the child is at least 18 years of age.[102]

Rules similar to those affecting the family partnership (discussed in Chapter 10) are applicable to family S corporations.[103] Thus, if reasonable compensation is not paid for services performed or for the use of capital contributed by a family member, the IRS may reallocate S corporation income or expenses.[104] Unlike the partnership, this rule extends to all family members, including those who are *not* owners and when there is no donee/donor relationship.

Example 36

This year, Dr. F created LME Corporation, an S corporation whose business is leasing medical equipment. He gave all of the stock in LME to his son and daughter. For the year, LME has $20,000 of net rental income. If Dr. F performs services for LME and is not adequately compensated, the IRS may adjust the income of the parties to force Dr. F to include reasonable compensation in his income, and reduce LME's income accordingly. The IRS is not required to make this adjustment.

Current Distributions of Corporate Assets

LO.8

Calculate gain or loss for the S corporation and its shareholders when asset distributions are made and the S corporation has no Accumulated Earnings and Profits (AE&P).

The treatment of distributions by an S corporation borrows from some of the rules applying to distributions from partnerships and some applying to C corporations. In many cases, distributions from an S corporation, like those from a partnership, represent accumulated income that has been previously taxed to its owners. Accordingly, this income should not be taxed again when it is distributed. Consistent with this approach, most distributions by an S corporation are considered nontaxable to the extent of the shareholder's stock basis. Any distribution in excess of the shareholder's stock basis is treated as gain from the sale of the underlying stock, producing capital gain.

Problems arise if the retained earnings of an S corporation consist of any C corporation earnings and profits (i.e., AE&P as discussed in Chapter 3). As might be expected, when this occurs, clarification is required regarding how the S and C corporation rules interact. Consequently, one of the first questions that must be considered before the treatment of a distribution can be determined is whether an S corporation has AE&P. Beyond this first concern, however, still other considerations may be relevant. For example, special rules can operate if the S corporation distributes property (i.e., assets other than cash) or the distribution occurs shortly after the S corporation election terminates. Each of these issues and several others are examined below.

---

[102] Recall that many of the income-splitting advantages involving passive income are not available with children under 19 years of age.

[103] § 1366(e) and Reg. § 1.1366-3(a).

[104] Family member, as defined by the Code, is the same for the partnership and the S corporation. §§ 704(e)(3) and 1366(e).

THE E&P QUESTION

As noted above, the treatment of an S corporation distribution can depend on whether the corporation has any AE&P. Normally a corporation that has been an S corporation since its inception will not have AE&P since it never operated as a C corporation.[105] Nevertheless, AE&P could be found in the retained earnings of a lifelong S corporation if a C corporation was merged or liquidated into the S corporation. An election to treat a subsidiary corporation as a QSub is a deemed liquidation of the subsidiary, governed by Code §§ 332 and 337. Accordingly, any AE&P of the subsidiary becomes AE&P of the parent S corporation.

S CORPORATIONS WITH NO AE&P

All cash distributions by S corporations that have no AE&P are nontaxable unless they exceed the shareholder's basis in the stock.[106] It should be emphasized that the shareholder's stock basis is the critical variable in measuring the taxability of the distribution. The basis of any debt is irrelevant in this regard.

In determining whether a distribution exceeds the shareholder's stock basis, all distributions are deemed to be made on the last day of the tax year. For this purpose, the basis in the stock is increased for all positive adjustments before accounting for distributions. Like partnerships, distributions reduce the owner's basis before consideration of losses.[107] If the shareholder owns stock on the last day of the taxable year, all of the basis adjustments are made on the last day of the corporation's taxable year (or on the last day of ownership for a shareholder whose interest completely terminates). The general approach used by S corporations in accounting for distributions is illustrated below.

	Original basis (purchase, formation, inherited, gift, etc.)
+	Additional capital contributions
+	Separately stated income items (taxable and tax-exempt)
+	Nonseparately stated income items (taxable and tax-exempt)
−	Distributions
−	Nondeductible, non-capital, expenses
−	Separately and nonseparately stated deduction and loss items
=	Ending basis of stock

Example 37

D and F have been equal owners of an S corporation for five years. At the beginning of the current year, D has a basis in his stock of $40,000 while F's stock basis is $10,000. The corporation's records for the year revealed the following:

Ordinary taxable income	$50,000
Tax-exempt income	10,000
Nondeductible portion of meals and entertainment	2,000
Capital loss (not fully deductible by shareholder)	30,000

During the year, the corporation distributed $100,000, $50,000 to D and $50,000 to F. Based on these facts, the distribution to D would be nontaxable while the distribution to F would result in a capital gain of $10,000 as determined below.

---

[105] Prior to 1983, it was possible for an S corporation to generate AE&P while it was an S corporation. Starting in 1997, legislation eliminated these balances.

[106] § 1368(b).

[107] Prior to 1997, distributions of S corporations were the final item absorbed (i.e., distributions were after losses and separately stated items of deductible and nondeductible expenses).

	D's Share		F's Share	
	Taxable Income	Basis	Taxable Income	Basis
Beginning basis		$40,000		$10,000
Positive adjustments:				
Exempt income		5,000		5,000
Ordinary taxable income	$25,000	25,000	$25,000	25,000
Basis before $50,000 distribution to each		$70,000		$40,000
Nontaxable portion of distribution		(50,000)		(40,000)
Taxable portion of distribution (capital gain). . . .	0	0	10,000	0
Basis before negative adjustments		$20,000		$0
Negative adjustments:				
Nondeductible meals and entertainment		(1,000)		0
Capital loss.		(15,000)		0*
Ending basis.		$ 4,000		$ 0

* The capital loss would be allowed to F in any future year if F's basis were to increase.

In determining the treatment of the distributions, the stock basis for each shareholder is first adjusted for all positive adjustments before accounting for the distribution. In this case, the positive adjustments boost D's basis to $70,000 so that his $50,000 distribution is completely tax-free. After accounting for the distribution, D reduces his basis for his share of the nondeductible expenses and then the capital loss. The reduction to basis for the capital loss is made even though D is not able to fully deduct the loss on his own return. Any portion of the capital loss that D cannot deduct is carried over to subsequent years until it is exhausted.

The distribution to F results in a capital gain of $10,000 since his basis after positive adjustments, $40,000, is insufficient to absorb the entire $50,000 distribution. Note also that F cannot deduct any of the capital loss since losses are deductible only to the extent of the shareholder's basis. However, the capital loss carries over until such time that F has sufficient basis to enable its flow-through. Contrast the treatment of the capital loss with that of the nondeductible portion of meals and entertainment. There is no requirement that F must carry over the nondeductible expenses and reduce his basis. When it is known that distributions will exceed a shareholder's basis, the recognition of capital gain can be avoided if the shareholder increases his or her stock basis before the year ends. This may be done by (1) contributing capital to the S corporation, or (2) having debt owed this shareholder converted to capital. A loan by the shareholder to the corporation will not affect the tax free distributions, although it will allow the shareholder to deduct additional losses.

Problem Materials

DISCUSSION QUESTIONS

11-1 *Eligibility Requirements.* May the following corporations elect Subchapter S? If not, explain why.
   a. A corporation is 100% owned by another corporation.
   b. A corporation has 101 shareholders, including Mr. and Mrs. V and Mr. and Mrs. Z.
   c. A family corporation is owned by a father and his three children. Since the children are under age 18, their shares are held in a trust.
   d. A corporation has 1,000 shares of common stock outstanding and 500 shares of authorized but unissued preferred stock.
   e. A corporation has 70 unrelated shareholders and 35 shareholders who are all descendants of Mr. and Mrs. A.

11-2 *Eligibility Requirements.* Y corporation's shareholders want to elect S status. Do any of the following facts about the corporation prevent the election? Why?

   a. It has a wholly owned subsidiary.

   b. It has 99 shareholders who own their shares solely in their own name and a married couple who own the stock jointly.

   c. It has 10 shareholders, and one is the estate of a former shareholder. It is expected that the shares held by the estate will be distributed to three U.S. citizens and one Englishman who is a U.S. resident.

   d. It has 99 shareholders plus L, who owns no shares but serves as custodian for shares owned by her two minor children.

   e. What if L, in (d) above, is a nonresident alien, but the children are U.S. citizens?

   f. It has 15 owners of common stock and no owners of its authorized preferred stock.

   g. It has 10 owners of voting common stock and five owners of nonvoting common. Except for voting, all other rights of the two sets of common stock are identical.

   h. A corporation was formed many years ago by X, Y, and Z. Several generations later there are 210 shareholders, 150 of whom are descendants of X, Y, and Z.

11-3 *Eligibility Requirements and Termination.* Refer to *Problem 11-2* and assume Y corporation made its S election in 2012. Do the following facts about the corporation terminate the election? When? Why? Can the shareholders prevent the termination?

   a. Refer to (a) above. It has $5 billion in sales with various customers in the United States and $10,000 sales that it places through its subsidiary.

   b. Refer to (b) above. The married couple is divorced December 29, 2016, and each receives one-half the shares in Y that were owned jointly by them prior to that date.

   c. Refer to (c) above. The Englishman decides it is time to return home and moves to London, England, on March 3, 2016. He continues to own five shares of Y and gives up his residency in the United States.

   d. Refer to (f) above. M exchanges her 500 shares of Y common for 700 shares of Y preferred. Although the number of shares differs, the dollar value of M's holdings remains the same.

   e. The corporation elects to revoke its S election. Holders of 70% of the stock consent to the revocation. The other shareholders do not consent.

   f. On June 5, 2016 a 20% shareholder transfers her stock to a C corporation she owns.

   g. Y has $15,000 accumulated earnings and profits (AE&P) from C corporate years, and 30% of its gross receipts in 2014, 2015, and 2016 are from dividends and interest on investments.

11-4 *Stock Requirements.* A mother wishes to establish an S corporation with her two children. However, she is concerned about the one class of stock requirement. She does not want to provide her children with voting control but does wish to give them 60% of the stock. Can she achieve her wishes? Explain.

11-5 *Election.* F, M, and T are shareholders of a calendar year corporation. On February 15, 2016 they are advised they should elect Subchapter S status. All agree to the election. However, they state that they purchased a 10% ownership interest from V on January 4, 2016. V sold his interest because he said he never wanted to have any contact with F, M, or T again.

   a. Can the corporation make an S election for 2016? Explain.

   b. If the corporation files its election on or before March 15, 2016 but V does not consent, will this election be effective in any year?

11-6 *Election.* B, C, and D are shareholders, each owning 1,000 shares. On February 20, 2016 they are advised to elect S status for 2016. Can they make the election for all of 2016 under the following circumstances? Explain.

   a. B purchased 10 shares from R on January 5, 2016. R is hitchhiking across Europe and cannot be located until April 1, 2016.

   b. C sells 10% of her interest (after the election) July 7, 2016 to X. X refuses to agree to the S election and wants it terminated.

11-7 *Elections.* This year, RJ, an individual, formed ABC Corporation. ABC commenced business on April 17, 2016. The corporation issued its first shares on March 2, 2016. RJ transferred property (fair market value $100,000, adjusted basis $20,000) to the corporation on March 28, 2016 in a nontaxable § 351 exchange. ABC intends to use the calendar year for tax purposes. For the years in question ABC does not have any attribute that would disqualify it from S status.

    a.   By what date must ABC make an election to be an S corporation if the election is to be in effect for the corporation's first taxable year, assuming the corporation does not utilize any relief provisions?

    b.   Assume that ABC discovers, on February 15, 2017 that it has not made a timely S election for its year ended December 31, 2016. Could the corporation make an election to take effect for its taxable year beginning January 1, 2017?

    c.   If the corporation made an S election for its taxable year beginning January 1, 2016, would it have any exposure to the built-in gains tax?

    d.   Assume that on February 15, 2017 ABC discovered that no S election had been made. What would be needed for the corporation to make an S election to take effect for its year 2016 tax year?

    e.   Assume the same facts in (b) above except that the corporation discovered that it had not made an S election as of April 15, 2018. What would be required for the corporation to make an S election for its 2016 taxable year?

11-8 *Termination of the Election.* Compare the effects of an intentional revocation, an unintentional violation of the eligibility requirements, and a termination due to the receipt of excessive passive investment income.

11-9 *Termination of the Election.* A calendar year S corporation unexpectedly receives a government contract on April 3, 2016. The profits from the contract in 2016 will be substantial. The three equal shareholders wish to revoke the election for 2016. Can they? Explain.

11-10 *Late Election Relief.* Many corporations fail to file timely S elections. Some of these corporations seek relief at the Service Center level, whereas others apply to the National Office of the IRS. Give a brief explanation of the differences between the two venues, or state that there are no substantive differences.

    a.   Need for a statement of reasonable cause for the lateness.

    b.   Payment of a user fee.

    c.   Need for consistency of reporting by corporation and shareholders.

    d.   Three years and 75 days after intended effective date have elapsed.

11-11 *Employee-Owner.* Which of the three organizational forms—S corporation, C corporation, or partnership—treats owners who work for the business in the following manner?

    a.   The owner's compensation is a deductible business expense.

    b.   The owner's compensation is subject to FICA withholding.

    c.   The employee benefits are deductible expenses.

    d.   The employee benefits are excluded from the owner-employee's gross income.

11-12 *Schedule K-1.* Why must each shareholder of an S corporation be provided with a Schedule K-1?

11-13 *Business Income.* How is each of the following items treated by an S corporation?

    a.   Dividend income

    b.   Accrued rental expense to a shareholder

    c.   Net capital gain

    d.   Distribution of assets with a market value in excess of basis

11-14 *Family Ownership.* A taxpayer operates a retail store as an S corporation. He has a 16-year-old daughter and an 11-year-old son.

    a.   Can he employ either or both of them in the business and deduct their salaries?

    b.   Can they be shareholders in the S corporation?

    c.   Can a trust be formed to hold the shares of stock owned by a minor child?

11-15 *Family Ownership.* A mother wants to transfer a substantial portion of her ownership in an S corporation to a trust for her son and daughter. She wants to transfer value but retain voting control. She also wants to be able to exercise some control over how the assets of the trust are distributed. However, she is willing to use an independent trustee to manage the assets.

    a. Can she transfer nonvoting stock to the children and retain voting shares without creating a second class of stock?

    b. If she transfers stock to a trust, but retains the ability to remove the shares from the trust, will she disqualify the corporation from S status?

    c. How could she create a QSST for each child? What restrictions would the trusts face? Who would pay the tax on the income of the corporation allocated to the trusts' shares?

    d. What would be the advantages of using an ESBT? Who would pay the tax on the income of the corporation allocated to the trust's shares?

11-16 *Stock and Debt Basis.* What is the significance of stock basis and debt basis to a shareholder? How does a shareholder adjust basis for the activity of an S corporation for a year? How does a shareholder obtain debt basis?

PROBLEMS

11-17 *Late Election, Change Dates, and Consistency and Consents.* L Corporation intended to be an S corporation for its taxable year beginning January 1, 2015. On that date L and M were the only two shareholders, each owning 100 shares. On October 17, 2016 M sold 25 shares to N and 25 shares to O. On December 7, 2016, L sold all of his shares to P.

    L did not file a timely Form 2553. For each of the following situations describe the venue (Service Center or IRS National Office) where the corporation must apply for late S corporation election relief. State whether or not the relief request would require a user fee, and which persons would need to consent to the request, as well as the S election. State any additional actions the corporation or any of the shareholders might need to take.

    a. The corporation files the request on August 1, 2016. Neither the corporation nor any of the shareholders has yet filed a return for 2015.

    b. The corporation files the request on November 1, 2016. The corporation filed Form 1120S for 2015 on September 15, 2016. L and M filed returns for 2015, and each reported income from L Corporation.

    c. The corporation files the request on November 1, 2016. The corporation filed Form 1120S for 2015 on September 15, 2016. L had filed his returns for 2015, and reported income from L Corporation. M has not yet filed her return for 2015. The corporation files the request on November 1, 2016. The corporation filed Form 1120S for 2015 on September 15, 2016. L and M filed returns for 2015, but neither shareholder reported income from L Corporation.

    d. The corporation files the request on February 21, 2017. The corporation filed Form 1120S for 2014 on September 15, 2016. L and M filed returns for 2015, and each reported income from L Corporation. N, O and P did not report any income from L Corporation for 2015. Neither the corporation nor any of the shareholders has yet filed a return for 2016.

11-18 *Consequences of Revocation of an S Election.* In July 2017 S Inc., a calendar year corporation, revoked its S election as of August 1, 2017. The corporation's taxable income for January through December is $432,000, and the shareholders do not elect to perform an interim closing of the corporate books.

    a. What tax return(s) must S file for the year, and what are the due dates of the return(s)?

    b. Compute S's corporate taxable income for the short year for the (1) S corporation and (2) C corporation.

    c. Compute the C corporation's Federal income tax.

11-19 *Net Income from Operations.* A and B are MDs in the AB partnership. Because of limited liability considerations, their attorney has advised them to incorporate. A typical year for the MDs (who are equal partners) is as follows:

Revenues.	$400,000
Operating expenses.	190,000
Charitable contributions.	10,000
Owner compensation	200,000

  a. Calculate AB's ordinary net income if it is taxed as (1) a partnership or (2) an S corporation.

  b. Calculate the effect on A's ordinary income if AB is taxed as (1) a partnership; (2) an S corporation; or (3) a C corporation.

  c. Ignoring limited liability considerations, should the partners incorporate? If so, should they elect S status?

  d. If A and B desire partnership tax treatment, is there any business entity that would meet their needs?

11-20 *Net Income.* A calendar year S corporation has the following information for the current taxable year:

Sales	$180,000
Cost of goods sold.	(70,000)
Dividend income	5,000
Net capital loss	(4,000)
Salary to Z.	12,000
Life insurance for Z	500
Other operating expenses	40,000
Cash distributions to owners	20,000

Assume Z is single and her only other income is $30,000 salary from an unrelated employer. She is a 20% owner with a $10,000 basis in the S stock at the beginning of the year. Calculate the S corporation's net ordinary income and Z's adjusted gross income and ending basis in the S corporation stock.

11-21 *Net Losses.* A calendar year S corporation has the following information for the current taxable year:

Sales	$180,000
Cost of goods sold.	(130,000)
Net capital loss	(6,000)
Salary to Z.	18,000
Charitable contributions.	1,000
Other operating expenses	65,000
Dividend income	4,000

Assume Z is single and her only other income is $30,000 salary from an unrelated employer. She is a 40% owner with a $10,000 basis in the S stock and no corporate debt owed to her. Calculate the S corporation's net ordinary loss, Z's adjusted gross income, and the character and amount of S corporate items that flow through to her.

11-22 *Net Income/Loss and Basis.* For the current year, an S corporation reported an ordinary loss of $100,000, a net capital loss of $10,000, and a § 1231 gain of $20,000. M owns 10% of the stock and at the beginning of the year had a basis in her stock of $7,500. In addition, M loaned the corporation $5,000 during the year. She materially participates in the S corporation.
  a. Compute her deductible loss.
  b. The following year, the corporation reported ordinary income of $70,000 and made no distributions. How does this income affect M's basis in the stock and the debt?

11-23 *Allocations.* V owns 500 shares of stock of an S corporation with 2,000 shares outstanding. The calendar year S corporation's records show the following information:

Net ordinary income	$200,000
Net capital loss	(10,000)

Calculate V's share of the items if on March 15 he sells:
  a. 200 of his shares of stock;
  b. All 500 shares of his stock and the per-day allocation method is used; or
  c. All 500 shares of his stock and the interim closing of the books method is used. The records reveal that through March 15, net ordinary income was $60,000 and net capital loss was $10,000.

11-24 *Basis.* A calendar year business reports the following information as of the end of 2015 and 2016:

	2015	2016
Accounts payable to suppliers	$10,000	$11,000
Note payable to City Bank.	40,000	37,000
Note payable to H.	12,000	10,000
Cash distributions to owners		20,000
Net ordinary income	15,000	15,000

H, a 30% owner, had a basis in the business at the end of 2015 of $9,000. Calculate H's basis in his ownership interest at the end of 2016 assuming the business is:
  a. A partnership
  b. An S corporation

11-25 *Deductibility of Losses by Shareholders.* B, Inc. was incorporated and its shareholders made a valid S election for B's first taxable year. At the beginning of the current year, Shareholder Z had a basis of $14,500 in his B stock and held a $10,000 note receivable from B with a $10,000 basis. For the current year Z was allocated a $32,000 ordinary loss and a $4,000 capital loss from the corporation. B did not make any distributions to its shareholders during the current year.
  a. How much of each allocated loss may Z deduct in the current year?
  b. What happens to any losses in excess of the limits in (a) above?
  c. How much basis will Z have in his B stock and his note receivable at the end of the current year?

11-26 *Basis Adjustments—Restoration.* Refer to the facts in *Problem 11-25* above. In the next year Z is allocated $7,000 of ordinary income and $5,500 of tax-exempt income from B. B did not make any distributions to its shareholders during the year. What effect will these income allocations have on Z's basis in his B stock and note receivable?

11-27 *Losses and Basis.* J, Inc. is an S corporation that reported the following selected items as of December 31, 2016.

Ordinary loss (from Form 1120S, page 1)	$(30,000)
Long-term capital gain.	500
Tax-exempt interest income.	1,000
Notes payable to banks	30,000
(1/1/2016 balance = $20,000)	
Notes payable to LJ	5,000
(1/1/2016 balance = $0)	

The corporation is owned 60% by LJ and 40% by RS. At the beginning of the year, they had a basis in their *stock* of $12,000 and $10,000, respectively. How much income or loss will each of the shareholders report for 2016?

11-28 *Basis.* M, a 40% owner, has a basis in the S corporate stock of $15,000 and in a note receivable from the S corporation of $8,000. Compute the basis of the stock and the note and the amount of the ordinary loss and income that flow through to M in 2016 and 2017.
   a. The S corporation has a net operating loss of $45,000 in 2016.
   b. The S corporation has a net operating income of $20,000 in 2017.

11-29 *Basis.* A calendar year S corporation has the following information for the two years:

	2015	2016
Net ordinary income (or loss).	$(50,000)	$10,000
Dividend income	5,000	2,000

X, an unmarried 60% shareholder, has a basis in the stock on January 1, 2015 of $18,000 and a note receivable from the corporation for $12,000. X's only other income is salary from an unrelated business.
   a. Calculate X's basis in the stock and in the note after the above income and loss are recorded for 2015.
   b. Calculate X's basis in the stock and in the note after the above income items are recorded for 2016.
   c. Assume the corporation paid the $12,000 note on April 3, 2016. Calculate X's basis in the stock after the above income distributions are recorded for 2016, and calculate the effect on X's adjusted gross income for all 2016 items, including the payment of the note.

11-30 *Inside and Outside Basis. XYZ* is an S corporation owned equally by three shareholders. X has often disagreed with the other shareholders over business matters and now believes he should withdraw from the corporation. X's basis in his stock is $50,000. The corporation's balance sheet appears as follows:

Cash	$100,000
Accounts receivable.	50,000
Land	30,000
Equipment (net).	10,000
Accounts payable	30,000
Note payable to X	10,000
Shareholders' equity	150,000

The equipment's market value is approximately the same as its net book value, but the land is now valued at $60,000. X sells all of his stock to W for $60,000.
   How much gain must X recognize?

11-31 *Debt Basis.* T owns all of the stock of M Corporation, an S corporation. In the current year, M borrows $50,000 from a local bank T guarantees payment of the loan. State the effects of this loan on T's basis for losses, under each of the flowing scenarios.

    a. T takes no action other than guaranteeing the loan.

    b. Late in the current year T pays $10,000 of the principal on behalf of M. Early in the next year she pays an additional $15,000 of principal.

    c. T makes no cash payment on any of the principal balance of the loan. Before the end of the current year T substitutes her personal obligation for the entire $50,000 obligation. The bank accepts this note in satisfaction of the corporation's obligation.

11-32 *Debt Basis.* V owns all of the stock of R Corporation, an S corporation. V also owns all of the stock of Z Corporation. During the current year, V borrows $60,000 from Z and immediately loans $60,000 to R. The loan to R is valid under state law, and gives V rights as a creditor. Does this transaction create debt basis in R Corporation for V?

11-33 *Family Ownership.* K operates a small retail store as a proprietorship. Annual net ordinary income is expected to be $60,000 next year. The estimated value of her services to the business is $25,000. K's 14-year-old son is interested in the business. She is considering giving him a 30% ownership interest in the business. If she does this, she will be paid a salary of $25,000. K files as head of household and does not itemize deductions. Neither she nor her son has any other includible income. Ignore all payroll and self-employment taxes in the following computations.

    a. Determine next year's tax savings that will be achieved if K establishes an S corporation with her son at the beginning of the year compared with continuing the business as a proprietorship.

    b. Will K or her son have any includible income if they exchange the appreciated proprietorship assets for the 70 and 30 percent ownership interests, respectively, in the S corporation?

    c. What advice should you give K on establishing and operating the S corporation?

11-34 *Compensation Planning.* Mr. H owns and operates an accounting firm. The firm's principal business is the preparation of tax returns. Mr. H incorporated his tax practice about 10 years ago. At that time, the corporation elected to be treated as an S corporation and has operated as an S corporation ever since. This year the corporation had $100,000 of taxable income before considering the salary to be paid H. Answer the following questions.

    a. If the corporation pays H a salary of $70,000 and also make a distribution to him of $30,000, what is H's total taxable income from the corporation for the year?

    b. If the corporation pays H a salary of $30,000 and also makes a distribution to him of $70,000, what is H's total taxable income from the corporation for the year?

    c. Is H's total taxable income from the corporation in (a) and (b) the same or different?

    d. Based on the answers to the questions above, which is more preferable, (a) or (b)?

    e. Answer (a)–(d) assuming the business was operated as a partnership.

TAX RETURN PROBLEMS

11-35   Individuals Phil Smith and Kate Jones formed P&K Corporation on March 1, 1996 to provide computer consulting services. The company has been an S corporation since its formation, and the stock ownership is divided as follows: 60% to Phil and 40% to Kate. The business code and employer identification numbers are 514519 and 24-3897625, respectively. The business office is located at 3010 East Apple Street, Atlanta, Georgia 30304. Phil and Kate live nearby at 1521 South Elm Street and 3315 East Apple Street, respectively. Their Social Security numbers are 403-16-5110 for Phil and 518-72-9147 for Kate.

The calendar year, cash basis corporation's December 31, 2014 balance sheet and December 31, 2015 trial balance contain the following information:

	Balance Sheet 12/31/2014		Trial Balance 12/31/2015	
	Debit	Credit	Debit	Credit
Cash	$ 12,000		$ 22,000	
Investments (1)	14,000		14,000	
Equipment (2, 3)	150,000		190,000	
Accumulated depreciation		$ 38,000		$ 63,500
Notes payable (3, 4)		94,000		117,200
Capital stock		10,000		10,000
Accumulated adjustments account		34,000		34,000
Cash distributed to Phil			25,440	
Cash distributed to Kate			16,960	
Revenues				235,000
Dividend income (1)				1,000
Interest income (1)				400
Section 1245 gain (depreciation recapture)				3,500
Salary expense (5)			110,000	
Rent expense			12,000	
Interest expense			16,600	
Tax expense (property and payroll)			13,800	
Repair expense			5,800	
Depreciation expense			29,200	
Health insurance expense (6)			1,600	
Property insurance expense			1,500	
Office supplies expense			3,000	
Utility expense			2,200	
Charitable contributions			500	
Totals	$176,000	$176,000	$464,600	$464,600

1. The investment account consists of marketable securities of U.S. corporations and U.S. Treasury Bonds. All of the dividends are considered qualified dividends.
2. Equipment was sold May 12, 2015 for $9,800. It was purchased new on May 1 of the prior year for $10,000 and its basis when sold was $6,300.
3. New equipment was purchased March 1, 2015 with $5,000 cash and a $45,000 three-year note payable. The first note payment is March 1, 2016. (**Note:** the correct amount of tax depreciation is included in depreciation expense account in the trial balance.)
4. Notes payable are long-term except for $20,000 of the note to be paid next year.
5. Salary expense is composed of salary of $30,000 each to Phil and to Kate and $50,000 to unrelated employees.
6. Health insurance premiums paid were for the unrelated employees.

Prepare Form 1120S (including Schedules K, L, and M), and Schedule K-l for Phil. Complete all six pages, including responses to all questions. If any necessary information is missing in the problem, assume a logical answer and record it. Do not prepare Schedule K-l for Kate or other required supplemental forms at this time.

11-36 During 2015, Lisa Cutter and Jeff McMullen decided they would like to start their own gourmet hamburger business. Lisa and Jeff believed that the public would love the recipes used by Lisa's mom, Tina Woodbrook. They also thought that they had the necessary experience to enter this business, since Jeff currently owned a fast-food franchise business while Lisa had experience operating a small bakery. After doing their own market research, they established Slattery's Inc. and elected to be taxed as an S corporation. The company's address is 5432 Partridge Pl., Tulsa, Oklahoma 74105 and its employer identification number is 88-7654321.

The company started modestly. After refurbishing an old gas station that it had purchased, the company opened for business on February 25, 2015. Shortly after business began, however, business boomed. By the end of 2015, the company had established two other locations.

Slattery's has three shareholders who own stock as follows:

Shareholder	Shares
Lisa Cutter	500
Jeff McMullen	200
Tina Woodbrook	300
Total outstanding	1,000

Slattery's was formed on February 1, 2015. On that date, shareholders made contributions as follows:

- Lisa Cutter contributed $30,000 in cash and 200 shares of MND stock, a publicly held company, which had a fair market value of $20,000. Lisa had purchased the MND stock on October 3, 2002 for $8,000.
- Jeff McMullen contributed equipment worth $35,000 and with a basis of $29,000.
- Tina Woodbrook contributed $30,000 in cash.

Assume 2015 depreciation for tax purposes is $11,500, and omit the detailed computations for depreciations from Form 4562.

The company is on the accrual basis and has chosen to use the calendar year for tax purposes. Its adjusted trial balance for *financial accounting* purposes reveals the following information:

	Debit	Credit
Cash	$270,700	
Ending inventory	16,000	
Equipment	35,000	
Land	10,000	
Building	15,000	
Improvements to building	55,000	
Accumulated depreciation		$ 9,000
Notes payable		78,000
Accounts payable		40,000
Taxes payable		8,000
Salaries payable		20,000
Capital stock		115,000
Sales		400,000
Gain on sale of MND stock		18,000
Dividend from MND Corporation		2,000
Cost of goods sold	84,000	
Legal expenses	6,000	
Accounting expenses	4,000	
Miscellaneous expenses	2,100	
Premium on life insurance policy	800	
Advertising	8,600	
Utilities	8,000	
Payroll taxes	12,500	
Salary expenses	120,000	
Insurance	9,000	
Repairs	6,500	
Charitable contributions	17,600	
Depreciation per books	9,000	
Interest expense	200	

The company has provided additional information below.

The company took a physical count of inventory at the end of the year and determined that ending inventory was $16,000. Ten percent of the notes payable are due each year for the next 10 years.

The legal costs were for work done by Slattery's attorney in February for drafting the articles of incorporation and by-laws. Accounting fees were paid in May for setting up the books and the accounting system. Miscellaneous expenses included a one-time $100 fee paid in February to the State of Oklahoma to incorporate.

The MND stock was sold for $38,000 on April. Shortly before the sale, MND had declared and paid a dividend. Slattery's received $2,000 on April 1. MND was incorporated in Delaware.

Slattery's has elected not to use the limited expensing provisions of Code § 179 but has otherwise claimed the maximum depreciation with respect to all assets. Any other elections required to minimize the corporation's tax liability were made.

Lisa Cutter (Social Security No. 447-52-7943) is president of the corporation and spends 90% of her working time in the business. She received a salary of $60,000. No other officers received compensation. Social Security numbers are 306-28-6192 for Jeff and 403-34-6771 for Tina. The life insurance policy covers Lisa's life, and she has the right to name the beneficiary.

Prepare Form 1120S and other appropriate forms and schedules for Slattery's. On separate schedule(s), show all calculations used to determine all reported amounts except those for which the source is obvious or which are shown on a formal schedule to be filed with the return. If information is missing to answer a question on the return, make up an answer and circle it.

TAX RESEARCH PROBLEMS

11-37 *Expanding an S Corporation.* L Inc., an S corporation, manufactures computers. Most of its computers are sold through individually owned retail computer stores. This year it decided it wanted to expand its operations into the retail market. To this end, it has decided to acquire Micros Unlimited, which operates a chain of computer retail stores nationwide.

If L Inc. acquires all of the stock of Micro, may it operate Micro as a C corporation? May it operate Micro as a QSub? What would be some major considerations with each form of business?

11-38 *Basis and Losses.* J and K, individuals, are equal shareholders in JK, Inc., an S corporation. For the current year, the corporation anticipates a loss of approximately $200,000. Neither shareholder has any substantial stock basis. The corporation has a $200,000 loan from First National Bank. J and K have personally guaranteed the loan. They are concerned about their ability to deduct the loss in the current year. Please advise if they have debt basis due to the current arrangement. If they do not have basis, explain how they might create basis without any outlay of additional funds.

Research aids:

Raynor, 50 T.C. 762 (1968).

Rev. Rul. 75-144, 1975-l C.B. 277.

11-39 *Losses and Basis.* Q, an individual, is the sole shareholder of QR Corporation, an S corporation. In past years, Q's losses have exceeded her basis by $100,000. Now QR Corporation is insolvent and is $100,000 in debt. The lenders realize that they will have no possibility of collecting the full amount and are writing down the $100,000. After the debt reduction, QR will not be solvent. QR's tax advisors have told Q that the write-down of debt will not result in taxable income to QR due to the insolvency exception of § 108. Q understands that tax-exempt income flows through to shareholders in S corporations and increases stock basis. She asks you to find out if any income realized by QR due to the cancellation of debt will give her basis to deduct her prior suspended losses.

Research aids:

§ 108(d)(7).

Reg. § 1.1366-1(a)(2)(viii).

11-40 *Distribution Problems.* Dr. A has operated his medical practice as a sole proprietor. He has heard that there is no self-employment income passing through from an S corporation to a shareholder. He has also heard that distributions from corporations are not subject to Social Security tax. Accordingly, he intends to incorporate his medical practice. He will take no salary or other compensation for his services. Instead, he will cause the corporation to declare dividends each quarter and withdraw the profits as distributions from the corporation. He believes he will not be subject to self-employment tax or Social Security tax. Do you see any problems with this scheme?

Research aid:

Rev. Rul. 74-44, 1974-1 C.B. 287.

12

S Corporations:
Former C Corporations,
Sales and Purchases of Stock,
Comparison of Entities

Learning Objectives

Upon completion of this chapter you will be able to:

LO.1 Determine the effects on both the S corporation and the shareholder when an S corporation that has AE&P distributes cash to its shareholders.

LO.2 Calculate the special taxes on excessive passive income and on built-in gains.

LO.3 Understand how dispositions of S corporate stock differ from those of C corporate stock.

LO.4 Compare the four business organizations—proprietorships, partnerships, S corporations, and C corporations (see Exhibit 12-3).

Chapter Outline

Introduction

Chapter 11 deals with rules common to all S corporations. These rules include the all-important qualifications, as to shareholders, classes of stock and domestic corporation status. Every S corporation is also subject to the election rules. Income and loss allocation and distribution treatment are important to all S corporations. However, certain issues apply only to S corporations that are "former C" corporations.

Usually, a former C corporation is a corporation that has been in existence for one or more years as a C corporation and then elects (converts) to S corporation status. In some cases, the corporation in question might have always been an S corporation but has acquired a C corporation in a tax free reorganization, liquidation or QSub election.

In most cases, the act of becoming an S corporation does not have any immediate incidence of taxation. However, there is one important exception to this rule. If the corporation has used the LIFO inventory method, it must recognize gain in order to bring the inventory basis up to lower of FIFO cost or market (the LIFO Recapture rule). The corporation must recognize this gain on its final C corporation return.

There are other problems that can exist after conversion to S status, even though they do not trigger tax immediately. Among the most important are:

- If the corporation has any accumulated earnings and profits (AE&P) at the time of conversion, future distributions may become dividends, which the shareholders must include in gross income.

- If the corporation has any accumulated earnings and profits (AE&P) at the time of conversion, it may be limited in its passive investment income, or face some unpleasant consequences. These consequences include a corporate level tax on Excess Net Passive Investment Income, and possible termination of its election, causing it to revert to C corporation status.

- If the corporation has appreciated assets at the time of conversion, it is subject to a corporate level income tax if it recognizes gain or income from Net Recognized Built-In Gains, within five years after it becomes an S corporation.

As a percentage of all S corporations, these rules probably apply to only a small portion. However, when they do arise they can be among the most complicated and important problems in all of Subchapter S. They may have a material impact on the corporations involved and may even negate the benefits of an S election. Thus, even in an introductory text, it is important to introduce the students to these problems.

Before the Small Business Job Protection Act of 1996, there was some ambiguity as to the relevance of certain Subchapter C rules to S corporations. However, in the years that have followed, Congress and the Internal Revenue Service have created some interesting techniques for purchasing and selling S corporations. This chapter gives a brief introduction to some of these techniques, which have some unique aspects when applied to S corporations.

Finally, this chapter includes a multi-page chart that contrasts S corporations, C corporations, and partnerships. This chart includes problems such as allowable ownership, taxation of income or loss, compensation, distributions and other tax rules.

Current Distributions of Corporate Assets

LO.1

Determine the effects on both the S corporation and the shareholder when an S corporation that has AE&P distributes cash to its shareholders.

The distribution rules covered in Chapter 11 apply to corporations with no accumulated earnings and profits (AE&P). If a former C corporation has no AE&P at the time it becomes an S corporation, it is subject to all of the same rules. However, if it has AE&P when it becomes an S corporation, those accumulations are still subject to taxation as dividends when received by the shareholders. This situation leads to several complexities.

The E&P Question

As noted in Chapter 11, the treatment of an S corporation distribution can depend on whether the corporation has any AE&P. Normally a corporation that has been an S corporation since its inception will not have AE&P since it never operated as a C corporation.[1] Nevertheless, AE&P could be found in the retained earnings of a lifelong S corporation if a C corporation was merged or liquidated into the S corporation. An election to treat a subsidiary corporation as a QSub is a deemed liquidation of the subsidiary, governed by Code §§ 332 and 337. Accordingly, any AE&P of the subsidiary becomes AE&P of the parent S corporation.

An S corporation is far more likely to have AE&P if it operated as a C corporation before it elected S status. This is not at all uncommon. For example, it is estimated that due to substantial changes made by the Tax Reform Act of 1986, about 500,000 C corporations made S elections. Many of these converted C corporations are alive and operating today. There are also many other C corporations that for one reason or another have opted for S status. In these cases, AE&P is likely to exist. In any event, whether the corporation has always been an S corporation or is a converted C corporation, it is crucial to ascertain whether the corporation has AE&P. This determination often requires a long detailed study.

S Corporations with AE&P

The distribution rules for S corporations that have AE&P—regardless of the amount—are far more complex than those for S corporations without AE&P. This derives from the fact that the distributions that are out of an S corporation's earnings that were accumulated while it was a C corporation (C AE&P) are treated much differently from those out of its earnings accumulated while it was an S corporation. Distributions out of the S corporation's AE&P are treated as dividends and are fully taxable as ordinary income to the shareholder. In contrast, distributions out of the S corporation's earnings accumulated while it was an S corporation are generally nontaxable to the extent of the shareholder's stock basis. As a result, the source of the distribution is extremely important. This distinction—and a special concern about a potential abuse—requires the corporation to break down its retained earnings into several components. It is important to remember that while each of these components have its own special characteristics, all of them are simply part of the S corporation's total earnings that have been accumulated and not distributed over the years. There are four corporate level equity accounts. They are referred to as (1) the accumulated adjustments account (AAA); (2) previously taxed income (PTI); (3) AE&P; and (4) the other adjustments account (OAA). The treatment of the distributions from such accounts, as discussed below, can be summarized as follows:

Order	Source	Description	Treatment	Effect on Basis
1.	AAA	All S corps to the extent of AAA	Nontaxable unless exceeds shareholder's stock basis	Reduces stock basis to the extent thereof
2.	PTI	Distributions to shareholders who have personal pre-1983 PTI accumulations	Nontaxable unless exceeds shareholder's stock basis	Reduces stock basis to the extent thereof
3.	AE&P	S corps that have C AE&P	Ordinary dividend income	No effect
4.	OAA	All remaining distributions from S corp's tax-exempt income	Nontaxable unless exceeds shareholder's stock basis	Reduce basis to the extent thereof
5.	Paid-In Capital	All remaining distributions	Nontaxable unless exceeds shareholder's stock basis	Reduce basis to the extent thereof

Accumulated Adjustments Account

The *accumulated adjustments account* (AAA) is the initial reference point for determining the source of a distribution and therefore its treatment. All distributions are assumed to first come out of AAA to the extent thereof. While neither the name of the account nor its acronym are descriptive, this account generally represents post-1982 income of the S corporation

---

[1] Prior to 1983, it was possible for an S corporation to generate AE&P while it was an S corporation. Starting in 1997, an S corporation's C earnings and profits do not include any AE&P that was produced while it was an S corporation prior to 1983. See § 1311 of the Small Business Jobs Protection Act. (P.L. 104-88).

that has been taxed to shareholders but has not been distributed. Consequently, distributions from the account are a *nontaxable* return of the shareholder's basis in his or her stock. Distributions from the AAA that exceed the shareholder's stock basis are capital gain.[2]

The AAA is a corporate-level equity account that must be maintained if the S corporation has accumulated E&P from years when it was operated as a C corporation.[3] The AAA is the cumulative total of the S corporation's post-1982 income and gains (other than tax-exempt income) as reduced by all expenses and losses (both deductible and nondeductible other than those related to tax-exempt income) and any distributions deemed to have been made from the account. The specific formula for computing the balance in the AAA is shown in Exhibit 12-1. Note that the adjustments to the AAA are similar to those made by shareholders to their basis in their stock with some exceptions:[4]

1. Tax-exempt income increases the shareholder's stock basis but has no effect on the AAA. These items are posted to the OAA discussed below.

2. Expenses and losses related to tax-exempt income decrease the shareholder's stock basis but have no effect on the AAA. They are also posted to the OAA. (However, other nondeductible expenditures reduce the AAA as they do the shareholder's stock basis [e.g., the 50% of meal and entertainment expenses that is not deductible, fines, and penalties].)

3. The various adjustments to the AAA (other than distributions) can create either a positive or negative balance in the AAA account. In contrast, the shareholder's stock basis can never be negative.

4. The ordering rules for the AAA are somewhat different than for basis. The corporation adjusts for income, then subtracts deductions and losses (but *only* to the extent of income items) before it calculates the balance available for distributions. In a year in which the corporation has deductions and losses in excess of income items, it reduces the AAA for this excess (called the "net negative adjustment") *after* reduction for distributions.

EXHIBIT 12-1	**Accumulated Adjustments Account Computations**

Beginning Balance

Add income items:
    Taxable income
    Separately stated gains and income (not including tax-exempt income)
Less losses and deductions (not to exceed the year's income items above):
    Nondeductible losses and expenses (excluding expenses relating to tax-exempt income)
    Ordinary loss
Less distributions (to extent of beginning balance plus income less losses and deductions)
Less losses and deductions, to the extent they exceed the year's income items (the net negative adjustment)

Equals AAA end of the year

---

[2] § 1368(b).

[3] § 1368(c).

[4] § 1368(e)(1).

Example 1

In 1987, T formed ABC Inc. and operated it as a calendar year C corporation until 1994, when it elected to be treated as an S corporation. T has owned 100% of the stock since the corporation's inception. T's basis in his stock at the beginning of 2016 was $10,000. Other information related to the S corporation for 2016 is shown below.

Net ordinary income	$50,000
Charitable contribution	9,000
Tax-exempt interest income	10,000
Expenses related to tax-exempt interest income	1,000
Disallowed portion of meal expenses	2,000
Cash distributions	20,000
Beginning accumulated adjustments account	10,000

The first five items listed above flow through to T. Of these, T must include the $50,000 of ordinary taxable income on his 2016 tax return. In addition, T is allowed to report the $9,000 charitable contribution made by the corporation as an itemized deduction on his return.

T's basis and the balances in the AAA and OAA accounts at the end of the year are computed in the following manner:

	Basis	AAA	OAA
Beginning balance	$10,000	$10,000	$ 0
Positive adjustments:			
Taxable income	50,000	50,000	0
Tax-exempt income	10,000	0	$10,000
Basis before distributions	$70,000	—	—
Negative items to AAA:			
Disallowed meal expense	—	(2,000)	
Charitable contributions		(9,000)	
AAA before distribution		$49,000	
Less distribution	(20,000)	(20,000)	
Basis and AAA after distribution	$50,000	$29,000	
Negative items to basis:			
Disallowed meal expense	(2,000)		
Expenses related to tax-exempt income	(1,000)		(1,000)
Charitable contribution	(9,000)		
Final balances	$38,000	$29,000	$ 9,000

Note that for purposes of the determining the treatment of the distribution, the shareholder's stock basis is determined after the positive adjustments but before the negative adjustments. In contrast, the AAA balance available for distributions is determined after the nondeductible and deductible items (including losses) but only to the extent of the positive adjustments. Also observe that the $9,000 ($38,000 − $29,000) difference between the increase in T's basis in his stock and the corporation's AAA is attributable to the tax-exempt interest income of $10,000 less the $1,000 of expenses related to this income, neither of which affects the AAA. These items are reflected in the OAA account.

As noted above, distributions from the AAA are nontaxable to the shareholder unless they exceed the shareholder's stock basis. However, it is rare for shareholders to receive distributions from the AAA that exceed the basis in their stock. Most of the time, the aggregate basis of the shareholders will equal or exceed the AAA (e.g., see *Example 1* above). Note also that the AAA is a corporate-level account and is unaffected by either shareholder transactions or shareholder basis in the stock. Therefore, if a shareholder sells stock, new shareholders are entitled to distributions from the AAA, which will be reductions of basis. On rare occasions a distribution from the AAA will exceed a shareholder's stock basis. In such case, the excess is treated as a gain from the sale of stock.

Previously Taxed Income

The second account from which a distribution may come consists of undistributed income that has been previously taxed for S years before 1983, commonly referred to as previously taxed income (PTI).[5] As a practical matter, this account may be viewed as the AAA for years prior to 1983. The balance in this account represents taxable income that was earned by the corporation while it was an S corporation prior to 1983 and which has not been distributed to shareholders. Distributions from this account, like those from the AAA, are considered to be a nontaxable return of the shareholder's basis in his or her stock. Unlike AAA, PTI is considered a personal account and is nontransferable. Therefore buyers of a shareholder's interest do not obtain any of that shareholder's PTI.

Accumulated E&P of C Years

The third account from which a distribution may come represents earnings and profits accumulated in years when the corporation was a C corporation. Distributions from AE&P are taxable as dividend income. There is no schedule or reconciliation of AE&P on Form 1120S.

Other Adjustments Account

Schedule M-2 of Form 1120S creates a fourth classification, entitled *other adjustments account* (OAA). The OAA represents post-1982 tax-exempt income and expenses related to such income and other items that do not flow into the AAA. Thus, the OAA is used to show amounts that affect shareholder bases but not the AAA.

Schedule M-2

Schedule M-2 on page 4 of Form 1120S is a reconciliation of the beginning and ending balances in these corporate accounts: the AAA, the OAA, and shareholders' undistributed taxable income previously taxed (i.e., PTI). Interestingly, the M-2 does not reflect the ordering rules (i.e., distributions before losses and other expenses); nor does the M-2 provide for any reconciliation of AE&P.

Example 2

Same facts as in *Example 1* above. The corporation's Schedule M-2 for the year would appear as follows:

Schedule M-2	Analysis of Accumulated Adjustments Account, Other Adjustments Account, and Shareholders' Undistributed Taxable Income Previously Taxed (see instructions)		
		(a) Accumulated adjustments account	**(b)** Other adjustments account	**(c)** Shareholders' undistributed taxable income previously taxed
1	Balance at beginning of tax year	10,000		
2	Ordinary income from page 1, line 21 . . .	50,000		
3	Other additions		10,000	
4	Loss from page 1, line 21	( )		
5	Other reductions	(11,000)(| 1,000)	
6	Combine lines 1 through 5	49,000	9,000	
7	Distributions other than dividend distributions	20,000		
8	Balance at end of tax year. Subtract line 7 from line 6	29,000	9,000	

Form **1120S** (2015)

---

[5] § 1368(c).

Source of Distribution

As discussed above, the treatment of a distribution depends on its source. For this purpose, distributions are presumed to flow out of the various accounts in the following order with the treatment as described.[6]

1. *Accumulated Adjustments Account (AAA).* Distributions are first considered distributions out of the AAA and, therefore, are nontaxable to extent of the shareholder's stock basis. Any amount received out of the AAA that is in excess of the shareholder's basis is treated as a sale of the underlying stock, resulting in capital gain.

2. *Previously Taxed Income (PTI).* Distributions of PTI are nontaxable to the extent of the shareholder's stock basis with any excess treated as capital gain.

3. *Accumulated Earnings and Profits (AE&P).* Distributions of AE&P are treated as dividends income just as if distributed from a C corporation and, therefore, are fully taxable as dividend income to the shareholder.

4. *Other Adjustments Account (OAA).* Distributions out of the OAA are nontaxable to the extent of the shareholder's stock basis with any excess treated as capital gain.

5. *Remaining Distributions.* Distributions in excess of the amounts in the accounts described above (i.e., the other accounts are exhausted) are treated as returns of the shareholder's capital and are nontaxable to the extent of the shareholder's stock basis. Any excess is treated as capital gain.

Note that all of the distributions above reduce the shareholder's stock basis except amounts out of the corporation's AE&P.

Example 3

J and W have been equal owners of a calendar year S corporation for several years. It has been operated as a C and an S corporation in the past. Balances at the beginning of the year are shown below in the schedule. Operations for the year show $12,000 net ordinary income, $2,000 tax-exempt interest income, and $24,000 cash distributions. Based on the approach described above, the $24,000 cash distribution exhausts (1) all of the $18,000 AAA, (2) all of the $4,000 PTI, and (3) $2,000 ($24,000 − $18,000 − $4,000) of the AE&P. The balances at the end of the year are determined as follows:

	Corporate Accounts				Stock Basis	
	AAA	PTI	AE&P	OAA	J	W
Beginning balances	$ 6,000	$4,000	$3,000	$ 0	$10,000	$6,000
Net ordinary income	12,000				6,000	6,000
Tax-exempt interest income				2,000	1,000	1,000
Cash distributions:						
AAA	(18,000)				(9,000)	(9,000)
PTI		(4,000)			(2,000)	(2,000)
AE&P			(2,000)		0	0
Ending balances	$ 0	$ 0	$1,000	$2,000	$ 6,000	$2,000

Both J and W have $6,000 net ordinary income (from S operations) and $1,000 dividend income (from AE&P). Note that J and W recognize dividend income because tax-exempt income does not increase AAA. Also note that there is no longer any need to maintain an account for PTI once the corporation has distributed its PTI.

---

[6] § 1368(c).

Example 4

Refer to *Example 3*. Operations for the following year show net ordinary income of $9,400 and cash distributions of $16,000. The balances at the end of this year are determined as follows:

	Corporate Accounts				Stock Basis	
	AAA	AE&P	OAA		J	W
Beginning balances	$ 0	$1,000	$2,000		$6,000	$2,000
Net ordinary income	9,400				4,700	4,700
Cash distributions:						
AAA.	(9,400)				(4,700)	(4,700)
AE&P		(1,000)			0	0
OAA			(2,000)		(1,000)	(1,000)
Remaining (basis).				(3,600)	(1,800)	(1,000)
Remaining gain to W				(800)		
Ending balances.	$ 0	$ 0	$ 0		$3,200	$ 0

Both J and W have $4,700 net ordinary income and $500 dividend income (from AE&P). In addition, W has $800 capital gain since the distributions that reduce basis exceed her basis in the stock by $800. Because this S corporation no longer has AE&P, any future distributions will be nontaxable unless they exceed a shareholder's basis in the stock. Note that in this case there is no PTI component because the S corporation has no PTI.

DISTRIBUTIONS OF PROPERTY

Although most distributions consist solely of cash, an S corporation may distribute property. Rules governing property distributions of an S corporation are a unique blend of both the partnership and C corporation provisions.

Like C corporations, the amount of any property distributed by an S corporation is the fair market value of the property less any associated liabilities. Also like a C corporation, an S corporation must recognize gain—but not loss—on the distribution of property. Any gain recognized by the S corporation on the distribution passes through to be reported by the shareholders. In addition, this gain increases each shareholder's stock basis. Upon receipt of the distribution, the shareholder reduces his or her basis by the fair market value of the property received (but not below zero). Any amount in excess of the shareholder's basis is capital gain. The shareholder's basis in the property is its fair market value. The treatment of property distributions is identical to the approach described above for cash distributions.[7]

---

[7] Under current IRS instructions to Form 1120S, both property and cash reduce PTI.

Example 5

After using the following equipment for four years of its five-year MACRS life, an S corporation distributes it to H, its sole owner.

Asset	Cost	Accumulated Depreciation	Basis	Fair Market Value
Equipment	$10,000	$7,900	$2,100	$4,300

H's stock basis, after all adjustments except the equipment distribution, is $1,800.

	Includible Income	Stock Basis
H's basis, before		$1,800
S gain recognized (§ 1245: $4,300 FMV – $2,100 basis).	$2,200	2,200
Balance		$4,000
Tax-free distribution.		(4,000)
Taxable distribution	$ 300	
H's basis, after		$ 0

H must also recognize a $300 capital gain since the $4,300 FMV of the equipment exceeds his $4,000 stock basis. His basis in the equipment becomes $4,300.

ELECTIONS RELATING TO SOURCE OF DISTRIBUTIONS

While the normal rules for the sourcing of distributions usually is favored by shareholders, this is not always the case. For example, recall that an S election is terminated if an S corporation has excess passive income and AE&P for three consecutive years. In this situation and others, the corporation may want to purge itself of its AE&P to avoid losing its election. Note, however, that under the normal rules, the corporation must distribute all of its AAA before it can begin distributing its AE&P. Fortunately, the law provides possible relief and makes a special election available to the corporation to alter the source of the distribution. Section 1368(e)(3) allows the corporation to make the so-called *bypass election.* As shown in Exhibit 12-2, this election enables the corporation to bypass AAA and treat accumulated E&P as being distributed before AAA.[8] The corporation files the election by attaching an appropriate statement to a timely filed or extended return. The election applies only to the year covered by the return. Thus, if AE&P remain at the beginning of the next year, the balance will again be behind the corporation's AAA.

---

[8] Reg. § 1.1368-1(f)(2).

EXHIBIT 12-2	**Sources of Distributions**		
Distribution Order	*Normal Treatment*	*AAA and PTI Bypass Elections*	*Post-Termination Transition Period*
1	AAA	AE&P	AAA
2	PTI	AAA	CE&P
3	AE&P	PTI	AE&P
4	OAA	OAA	Unspecified return of capital

When an S corporation has PTI and needs to eliminate AE&P, the election under § 1368(e)(3) is not sufficient. The corporation must also exhaust PTI before it can start distributing AE&P. The Regulations make this possible by allowing the corporation to elect to bypass PTI when determining the treatment of its distributions.[9] If the corporation elects to bypass both AAA and PTI (as shown in Exhibit 12-2), AE&P is deemed to be the first item distributed by the S corporation.

In many cases, an S corporation identifies the need to distribute its AE&P after the close of the taxable year—normally a time when it would be too late to take action. However, the Regulations rescue the corporation in this situation with a very valuable tool: the deemed dividend election.[10] When every shareholder who receives a distribution during the year consents to this election, the corporation is treated as having made a distribution of its AE&P on the last day of its taxable year. The shareholders must first include the deemed dividend in their income and then are treated as having contributed the amount to the corporation as a contribution to capital increasing the basis in their stock. The bypass and deemed dividend elections require the consent of all "affected shareholders" (those who have received distributions or deemed distributions during the tax year).

The statutory requirement that shareholders must consent to the bypass and deemed dividend elections has become a bit of a misnomer. Originally, the regulations required that there must be a signed written consent by each shareholder included with the corporation's tax return for the year of the distribution or deemed dividend. However, this was becoming cumbersome, and ran counter to the movement to expand electronic filing. Therefore, after 2003, the corporation merely states in its return that all shareholders have consented.[11]

The bypass elections, including the deemed dividend election, may be popular options when the corporation faces excessive passive income problems, discussed below. Since this election eliminates the AE&P.

Example 6

In 2016 DJY Corporation, an S corporation has $100,000 of gross receipts. $40,000 of this total is from passive investment income sources. DJY had $35,000 of accumulated earnings and profits at the beginning of 2016. In that year DJY distributed $42,000 to its three shareholders. If DJY takes no action concerning its AE&P, it will be subject to the passive investment income tax, discussed below. Moreover, if it has had the accumulated earnings and profits and excessive passive investment income for three consecutive years, it will become a C corporation in 2017.

However, if DJY elects to treat $35,000 of the distribution as a dividend, its AE&P are exhausted at December 31. Therefore its passive investment income problems disappear. The shareholders must report their portions of the $35,000 as dividends, in addition to any income that passed trough from DJY for the year. However, with the preferred rate on dividends, saving the 35% corporate tax on passive investment income often makes this election worth the sacrifice.

---

[9] Reg. § 1.1368-1(f)(4).

[10] Reg. § 1.1368-1(f)(3).

[11] Reg. § 1.1368-1(f)(5)(iii).

On occasion, the bypass and deemed dividend elections offer some planning strategies when the corporation has no passive investment income problems. Since all S corporations are domestic corporations, dividends from these entities will be qualified dividends, subject to the long-term capital gain rate, except in the most unusual circumstances. The deemed dividend election may be useful where a shareholder is limited to loss deductions due to lack of basis, but the corporation has AE&P.

Example 7

In 2016 BBV Corporation, an S corporation has one shareholder, whose basis, before considering the year's activity, is $60,000. At the beginning of the year the corporation's AE&P were $80,000. The corporation's ordinary loss is $120,000 in 2016. The corporation made no distributions in 2016. By the time the corporation closes its books in 2017 it is too late to undertake any year-end planning strategies, such as loaning the corporation money or making a contribution to capital. However, the corporation can elect a deemed dividend, which would treat the corporation as having distributed all of its earnings and profits and a dividend on the last day of the corporation's taxable year, coupled with a simultaneous contribution to capital for the entire amount. Thus the shareholder would report $80,000 dividend income for the year, which would increase her basis to $140,000 before accounting for losses. The basis would then be sufficient to allow the shareholder to deduct all of the loss for the year.

Net Investment Income

Chapter 11 contains a brief discussion of the Net Investment Income tax of § 1411 as it relates to the pass through of income from the S corporation to the shareholders. Many S corporation distributions are not components of Net Investment Income, since they have no effect on taxable income. However, when a distribution is included in gross income, the shareholder must determine any Net Investment Income consequences.

When a distribution is not from the S corporation's earnings and profits, but exceeds the shareholder's stock basis the gain is treated as if the shareholder had sold stock. Thus if the shareholder does not materially participate in the S corporation's trade or business, the gain is Net Investment Income. If the shareholder materially participates, the gain is Net Investment Income, but only to the extent that the shareholder would have realized Net Investment Income if the corporation had sold all of its assets at fair market value on the date of the distribution. (In practice this may be a difficult amount to determine, especially if the corporation has numerous investment assets, and more so if they fluctuate in value during the year.)

A distribution from a corporation's accumulated earnings and profits is clearly within the classification as Net Investment Income. Thus the degree of participation by the shareholder is irrelevant in making this determination. The distribution can result from distribution more than the AAA balance, by election to bypass the AAA in favor of accumulated earnings and profits, or by a deemed dividend election.

Example 8

D and J are the sole and equal shareholders in DJY Corporation, an S corporation. D materially participates in DJY's business, whereas J is a passive investor. Both D and J have sufficient AGI to subject them to the Net Investment Income tax. In 2016 DJY reports the following:

Item	Total	50% to Each Shareholder
Net income from business operations	$50,000	$25,000
Distribution from AAA.	60,000	30,000
Distribution from AE&P	30,000	15,000

At the beginning of the year, D's basis was $1,000 and J's basis was $2,000. The treatment of the distributions to each shareholder is:

Item	D	J
Basis, beginning.	$ 1,000	$ 2,000
Increase for NET income	25,000	25,000
Basis before distribution.	26,000	27,000
Distribution:		
Nontaxable.	26,000	27,000
Gain	4,000	3,000
Dividend.	15,000	15,000

Since D materially participates in the corporation's business, neither the ordinary income from the business nor the gain portion of the distribution is an item of Net Investment Income. His NII for the year from DJY is $15,000, limited to the dividend from the corporation's accumulated earnings and profits. All of the income passing through to I is NII, since she did not materially participate in the corporation's business. Her NII also includes the taxable gain from the distribution, as well as the dividend. Her NII for the year is $43,000 ($25,000 + $3,000 + $15,000).

POST-TERMINATION TRANSACTIONS

Distributions

When a corporation election terminates its S election, the entity is immediately treated as a C corporation. Without special rules, this transition could be particularly severe. Recall that distributions for a C corporation are dividends to the extent of E&P. This is true even though the C corporation may have undistributed nontaxable income from S years. This could create a special hardship on a person who had been a shareholder during the corporation's final S corporation year and who had received an allocation of income from the corporation attributable to that period. In such a situation, the shareholder would not be able to withdraw money from the corporation, even to the extent necessary to pay taxes on his or her portion of the S corporation's taxable income, without the possibility of dividend treatment. To address this problem, special rules allow a shareholder to treat distributions as being from the AAA during the post-termination transition period (PTTP).

The PTTP begins the day after the S corporation's final tax year and lasts at least one year and perhaps longer.[12] During the PTTP, cash—but not property—distributions are deemed to come from AAA to the extent thereof.[13] But this is where the normal pattern of

---

[12] § 1377(b). [13] § 1371(e).

distributions ends. Any PTTP distributions in excess of AAA are *not* considered as having come from PTI or OAA but rather current or accumulated E&P. As shown in Exhibit 12-2, any distributions during the PTTP in excess of AAA would be fully taxable as dividends to the extent of the corporation's E&P. Note that this special ordering rule for distributions during the PTTP is deemed to occur unless the corporation elects not to have it apply. Also observe that a distribution during the PTTP is only treated as coming from the AAA if it is received by a person who was a shareholder on the corporation's final day as an S corporation.[14]

Losses

In some cases, a shareholder who had sustained losses prior to the termination of an S election may have lacked sufficient basis to deduct those losses. Without some relief, those losses would provide no tax benefit after the termination since the corporation is no longer an S corporation but a C corporation. However, the Code enables shareholders to secure those losses by allowing them to increase their stock basis during the PTTP.[15] Note that a loan during this period does not create basis for prior losses. Only increases in stock basis can secure losses. For example, shareholders could cancel any corporate debt owed to them and treat the cancellation as a contribution to capital with a corresponding increase in basis. Similarly, a shareholder could exchange the debt for additional stock. A shareholder could also increase the stock's basis by simply contributing additional cash or property to the capital of the corporation.

Taxes Imposed on the S Corporation

S corporations, like partnerships, normally are considered nontaxable entities. Unlike partnerships, however, S corporations may be required to pay one of the following taxes:

1. Excessive passive investment income tax
2. Tax on built-in gains
3. LIFO recapture tax

TAX ON EXCESSIVE PASSIVE INCOME

When Congress revised Subchapter S in 1982, it was concerned that C corporations with a potential accumulated earnings tax or personal holding company tax, particularly those that are mere holding companies (i.e., those whose principal assets are investment properties such as stocks, securities, and real estate projects), would attempt to escape these penalty taxes by electing to be treated as S corporations. Subchapter S can provide a refuge for these corporations since S corporations normally are exempt from both penalty taxes. To guard against this possibility, Congress enacted two provisions. First, as previously explained, when a corporation has AE&P *and* excessive passive income in three consecutive years, the corporation's S election is terminated.[16] Second, an S corporation must pay a special tax on its passive income if (1) it has AE&P at the close of its tax year, *and* (2) passive investment income exceeds 25% of its gross receipts that year.[17] Note that this tax, as well as the termination provision for excessive passive income (discussed early in this chapter), only applies to corporations that have AE&P from C corporation years at the end of the taxable year. Consequently, the tax is not imposed on corporations that have distributed all of their AE&P or that have never been C corporations, unless the corporation has acquired E&P in a tax-free reorganization, tax-free liquidation or QSub election.

The tax on excessive passive income is equal to the maximum corporate rate for the year (35% in 2015 and 2016) multiplied by *excess net passive income* (ENPI). ENPI is computed as follows:

$$\text{ENPI} = \text{Net passive income} \times \frac{\text{Passive investment income} - 25\% \text{ of gross receipts}}{\text{Passive investment income}}$$

LO.2
Calculate the special taxes on excessive passive income and on built-in gains.

---

[14] Reg. § 1.1377-2(b).

[15] § 1366(d)(3).

[16] § 1362(d)(3).

[17] § 1375(a).

In computing the tax, several rules must be observed.

1. For any taxable year, *ENPI* cannot exceed the corporation's taxable income, computed as though it were a C corporation but before reduction for the dividends-received deduction and net operating loss deduction.[18]

2. *Passive investment income* is defined the same as it is for the termination provisions of § 1362(d) discussed previously:[19] Generally gross receipts from dividends, interest (including tax-exempt interest), rents, royalties, and annuities.

3. *Net passive income* is passive investment income reduced by any allowable deductions directly connected with the production of this income. These deductions include such expenses as property taxes and depreciation related to rental property but exclude any deductions that are not directly connected with the sources of passive investment income.[20]

The amount of any tax paid reduces the amount of each item of passive investment income that flows through to shareholders. The tax is allocated proportionately based on net passive investment income.[21]

Example 9

PTC is owned equally by R and S. At the close of the year, PTC, an S corporation, reports gross receipts of $200,000 and a balance in its AE&P account of $24,000. Gross receipts include $25,000 interest and $50,000 of passive rent. Deductions directly attributable to rents were $30,000, including depreciation, maintenance, insurance, and property taxes. Using this information, PTC has excess net passive investment income of $15,000 determined as follows:

Total gross receipts:	
Gross receipts:	
Interest	$ 25,000
Rent (passive)	50,000
Total passive gross receipts	$ 75,000
Active gross receipts	125,000
Total gross receipts	$200,000
Permitted passive portion (25% × $200,000)	$ 50,000
Excess passive gross receipts ($75,000 – $50,000)	$ 25,000
Net passive income:	
Passive gross receipts	$ 75,000
Deductions connected with rent	(30,000)
Net passive income	$ 45,000
Excess net passive income:	
Excess passive gross receipts	$ 25,000
Divide by total passive gross receipts	75,000
Excess fraction ($25,000/$75,000)	⅓
Times net passive income	45,000
Excess net passive income	15,000

---

[18] § 1375(b)(1)(B) and Reg. § 1.1375-1(b)(1)(ii). [20] § 1375(b)(2).

[19] §§ 1375(b)(3) and 1362(d)(3). [21] Reg. § 1.1366-4(c).

Since the corporation has passive investment income exceeding 25% of its gross receipts ($25,000) *and* it has AE&P at the end of the taxable year, the tax on excessive passive income is imposed.

PTC's excessive passive investment income tax is $5,250 (35% × $15,000). This amount is allocated as follows:

	Interest	Rent	Total
Gross receipts	$25,000	$50,000	$75,000
Expenses	0	(30,000)	(30,000)
	$25,000	$20,000	$45,000
Tax allocation	(2,916)	(2,334)	(5,250)
	$22,084	$17,666	$39,750
To each shareholder (50%)	$11,042	$ 8,833	$19,875

TERMINATION OF S STATUS DUE TO EXCESSIVE PASSIVE INCOME

Under the passive income test, the election is terminated if the corporation has:[22]

1. Passive investment income exceeding 25% of its gross receipts for three consecutive years, and
2. C corporation accumulated earnings and profits (AE&P) at the end of each of the three consecutive years.

If both of these conditions are satisfied, the termination becomes effective at the beginning of the first year following the end of the three-year period.[23]

As reflected in the second condition above, the excessive passive income test applies only to corporations that were C corporations prior to becoming S corporations. An S corporation might also have earnings and profits if it absorbed a former C corporation in a tax free reorganization, liquidation or QSub election. In addition, the test applies to these former C corporations only if they have AE&P from C years. Accordingly, corporations that have never been C corporations as well as corporations that have distributed all AE&P cannot lose their S election because of passive investment income.

Passive investment income generally is defined as gross receipts from royalties, rents, dividends, interest (including tax-exempt interest but excluding interest on notes from sales of inventory and interest derived from a lending business), annuities, and gains on sales or exchanges of stock or securities.[24] For this purpose, rents are not considered passive income if the corporation provides significant services (e.g., room rents paid to a hotel) or if the rents are received in the ordinary course of a rental business.[25] In computing total gross receipts, costs of goods sold, returns and allowances and deductions are ignored. Before 2007, receipts from the sale or exchange of stocks and securities were included to the extent of gains (i.e., gross receipts = amount realized – adjusted basis = gain [but not loss]). In measuring the total gross receipts for a year, amounts realized from the sale or exchange of capital assets other than stocks and securities are included only to the extent of net gains (i.e., capital gains less capital losses).[26]

[22] § 1362(d)(3).
[23] § 1362(d)(3)(A)(ii).
[24] § 1362(d)(3)(D).
[25] Reg. § 1.1362-2(c)(5)(ii)(B)(2).
[26] §§ 1362(d)(3)(C) and 1222(9).

Example 10

OBJ, an S corporation, was a C corporation for several years before it elected to be taxed under Subchapter S beginning in 2014. For 2014 and 2015 the corporation had excessive passive income. In addition, at the close of 2014 and 2015, OBJ reported a balance in its AE&P that was attributable to its years as a C corporation. OBJ's income and expenses for 2016 are shown below. No distributions from its AE&P were made during the year. The corporation's passive investment income and total gross receipts, based on its reported items, are determined as follows:

	Reported	Gross Receipts	Passive Income
Sales	$200,000	$200,000	$ 0
Cost of goods sold	(150,000)	0	0
Interest income	30,000	30,000	30,000
Dividends	15,000	15,000	15,000
Rental income (passive)	40,000	40,000	40,000
Rental expenses	(28,000)	0	0
Gain on sale of stock ($20,000 − $5,000)	15,000	15,000	0
Loss on sale of stock ($10,000 − $12,000)	(2,000)	0	0
Total		$300,000	$85,000
25% of gross receipts		$ 75,000	

Because OBJ's passive investment income exceeds 25% of its gross receipts for the third consecutive year and it also has a balance of AE&P at the end of each of those years, the election is terminated beginning on January 1, 2017.

Even though a corporation may avoid having its election terminated by failing the excessive passive income test once every three years, a corporation still may be required to pay a tax on its excessive passive investment income.

TAX ON BUILT-IN GAINS

Without special rules, C corporations planning sales or distributions of appreciated property (e.g., as a dividend or in liquidation) could avoid double taxation by electing S status before making the distributions.

Example 11

R, a regular C corporation, owns land worth $50,000 (basis $10,000). If R Corporation distributes the land to its sole shareholder, D, as a dividend, the corporation recognizes a gain of $40,000 ($50,000 − $10,000) and D recognizes dividend income of $50,000. Therefore, two taxes are imposed. In contrast, compare the result that occurs if R Corporation has S status. R still recognizes a $40,000 gain. However, that gain is not taxed at the corporate level but flows through to D to be included on his tax return. In addition, D increases his basis in his stock by $40,000. On receipt of the property, D does not report any income but simply reduces the basis in his stock. As a result, there is only a *single tax* if R Corporation has S status.

To eliminate the tax-avoidance possibility of electing S status before the distribution (or a sale), Congress enacted § 1374. This section imposes a special corporate-level tax—the *built-in gains tax*—on gains recognized by an S corporation that accrued while it was a C corporation. The tax applies *only* to certain gains recognized during the five-year period following the S election. This five year period runs from the effective date of the election to the date of the gain, rather than from the date of the election to the beginning of the taxable year.

Under § 1374, it is presumed that *any* gain recognized on the sale or distribution of any property by a "converted" S corporation is subject to the built-in gains tax. However, the corporation may rebut this presumption and avoid the tax by proving either of the following: (1) the asset sold or distributed was not held on the date that the corporation elected S status; or (2) the gain had not accrued at the time of the election. As a practical matter, this approach requires every C corporation electing S status to have an independent appraisal of its assets on the date the S election becomes effective (i.e., the conversion date) in order to rebut the presumption. Note that for purposes of this tax, built-in gains are applicable to *all* assets, including inventory, unrealized receivables of a cash basis taxpayer, any gain on a long-term contract that has not been recognized (e.g., the taxpayer uses the completed contract method of accounting), and any goodwill.

As a general rule, the special tax applies only to S corporations having a *net unrealized built-in gain*. A net unrealized built-in gain is defined as the difference between the value and basis of all assets held on the conversion date. This difference represents the *maximum* amount that may be subject to the built-in gains tax.

Example 12

On November 3, 2015 T Corporation made an S election. The election was effective for calendar year 2016. On January 1, 2016 its balance sheet revealed the following assets:

	Adjusted Basis	Fair Market Value	Built-in Gain (Loss)
Equipment	$ 50,000	$ 75,000	$25,000
Land	30,000	70,000	40,000
Stock	20,000	15,000	(5,000)
	$100,000	$160,000	$60,000

T Corporation's net unrealized built-in gain is $60,000. The built-in loss on the stock effectively limits the taxpayer's future exposure to the built-in gains tax.

Only the *net recognized built-in gain* (NRBIG) is subject to tax.[27] According to the regulations, NRBIG is the lesser of:

1. The *Pre-Limitation Amount* (PLA). The PLA is the S corporation's taxable income as if its *only* recognized items for the year were its recognized built-in gains and losses. The S corporation must observe the C corporation rules in making this computation. However, in using the C rules, the corporation is not permitted to claim any dividends-received deduction or any loss carryforward.

2. The *Taxable Income Limit* (TIL). The TIL is the S corporation's taxable income computed in the same manner as a C corporation, including *all* of its recognized gross income and deductions for the taxable year. Again, the corporation may not claim the dividends-received deduction or any loss carryforward. Due to this rule, NRBIG cannot exceed the taxable income that the corporation would have had if it had been a C corporation.

---

[27] § 1374(b).

3. The *Net Unrealized Built-In Gain Limit* (NUL). In its first S corporation year, the NUL is the same as the net *unrealized* built-in gain (i.e., the maximum net built-in gain that could be recognized). In subsequent years, the NUL is the original net unrealized built-in gain reduced by all net recognized built-in gains in prior years. In this manner, the net unrealized built-in gain acts as the limiting factor on the total net recognized built-in gains that could be reported during the 5 year recognition period.

The corporation computes each of these amounts and the lowest is the NRBIG for the year. After the corporation computes this amount, it is then allowed to reduce it by any unused net operating loss carryforwards from years in which it was a C corporation. The corporation applies a flat rate of 35% to this amount, which in turn may be offset by certain credit carryforwards from prior years.

Example 13

Refer to the facts in *Example 12*. During 2016 T Corporation sold the equipment and the stock for $77,000 and $15,000, respectively. Although T recognizes a gain of $27,000 ($77,000 − $50,000) on the sale of the equipment, T's built-in gain recognized is limited to the amount accrued on the date of conversion from a C corporation to S status, $25,000. T's net recognized built-in gain that is potentially subject to tax is $20,000 (the built-in gain of $25,000 less the $5,000 built-in loss recognized.)

Example 14

Refer to the facts in *Examples 12* and *13*. Assume that during 2016, T Corporation's taxable income, including the equipment and stock sales, is $38,000. This figure is computed using the modified C corporation rules. At this point, the TIL is greater than the PLA of $20,000, so the PLA is treated as the taxable built-in gain. The corporation then computes its NUL. In its first S corporation year, the NUL is the same as the net unrealized built in gain, $60,000. As a result, the net recognized built-in-gain (NRBIG) for the year is $20,000 (the lesser of PLA of $20,000, TIL $38,000, and NUL $60,000).

If the corporation had sold the land at a gain of $40,000 instead of selling the stock, the total gain for the first S corporation year would have been $67,000 ($40,000 gain from land + $27,000 gain from equipment). However, only $60,000 of this gain would be potentially subject to the § 1374 tax because T's NUL is the maximum amount subject to the tax. Moreover, since its TIL is $38,000, the gain would be further limited to $38,000.

In subsequent years, the NUL is computed by subtracting all net recognized built-in gains to date from the original net unrealized built-in gain. In this manner, the net unrealized built-in gain may act as the limiting factor on the total net recognized built-in gains during the entire recognition period.

In determining the built-in gains tax, the net recognized built-in gain (after applying all limitations) is reduced by any NOL and capital loss carryforward from C corporate years. In addition, business tax credit carryforwards arising in a C year can be used to reduce the tax.[28] Any net recognized built-in gain not subject to tax because of the TIL is carried over to the following year and treated as if it occurred in that year. The calculation of the tax is summarized below.

---

[28] § 1374(b)(2) and (3).

	Net recognized built-in gain.	$x,xxx
−	NOL and NCL carryforward from C year	(xxx)
=	Tax base	$x,xxx
×	Top corporate tax rate	× xx%
=	Potential tax	$x,xxx
−	Business credit and AMT carryforward from C year	(xxx)
=	Tax	$x,xxx

Example 15

Refer to the facts in *Example 13*. Assume that T sold the land for $70,000 in its first S corporation year, but did not sell the equipment or stock. T recognizes a $40,000 gain, which is also the total PLA for the year. The TIL is $38,000 and the NUL is $60,000. Assume T also has a NOL carryforward of $3,000 from C corporation years. The corporation's built in gains tax is:

Least of:		
PLA	$40,000	
NUL.	$60,000	
TIL.	$38,000	$38,000
Less NOL carryforward		(3,000)
Taxable amount		$35,000
Tax rate		× 35%
Built-in gains tax		$12,250

After the S corporation calculates its built-in gains tax for the year, it needs to make some additional computations:

1. If the TIL is the least of the three net recognized built-in gain measures, the corporation will need to determine its recognized built-in gain carryforward to the next year.

2. The corporation must apportion the tax as a reduction to the income items flowing through to the shareholders, as well as the year's increment to the AAA.

3. The corporation must compute its NUL for its next taxable year.

For the corporation in *Example 14* above, the calculations are shown below.

Adjustment to next year's PLA to reflect the gain carryforward arising from the TIL for the current year.

Lesser of NUL ($60,000) or PLA ($40,000)	$40,000
Subtract TIL, if less.	(38,000)
Gain carryforward to add to next year's PLA	$ 2,000

Adjustment to next year's NUL:

NUL at beginning of current year	$60,000
Less net recognized built-in gain of current year	(38,000)
NUL for next year	$22,000

The corporation must then subtract its built-in gains tax from the income items that created the built-in gain in order to determine the pass-through of items to the shareholders. Assuming that the recognized built-in gain of $40,000 was a § 1231 gain, the corporation would reduce this gain by the tax of $12,250 and pass through $27,750 of § 1231 gain ($40,000 − $12,250) to its shareholders. Assuming that the corporation had a net ordinary loss of $2,000, to yield the TIL of $38,000, the corporation would pass the loss of $2,000 through to its shareholder's and the year's net addition to the AAA would be $25,750 computed as follows:

§ 1231 gain.	$40,000
Built-in gains tax	(12,250)
Ordinary loss.	(2,000)
Net increment to AAA.	$25,750

LIFO RECAPTURE

A corporation using the LIFO method of accounting for inventories in its last taxable year before an S election becomes effective must include in taxable income for its last C corporation year an additional amount, called the LIFO recapture amount.

The LIFO recapture amount is the excess of the inventory's value under FIFO (lower of cost or market) over its actual LIFO basis as of the end of the corporation's last C corporation taxable year.[29] The increase in tax liability is referred to as the LIFO recapture tax, although it is not a separate tax per se, and it is not imposed on the income after the corporation becomes an S corporation. This portion of the tax is payable in four equal installments, with the first installment due on the due date of the corporation's last C corporation return and the subsequent payments due on the due dates of the first three S corporation returns.[30] No interest is due if the required installments are paid on a timely basis, and there is no requirement that estimated tax payments be made with respect to any LIFO recapture tax due.[31] Finally, the inventory's basis is increased by the LIFO recapture amount. Any additional appreciation attributable to the inventory (i.e., excess of fair market value over its FIFO basis) will be subject to the built-in gains tax as the inventory is sold. However, if the corporation does not report a decrement from its initial S corporation LIFO layer during its recognition period, it will not recognize income as a built-in gain.

Example 16

H Corporation converts to S corporation status for 2016. H used the LIFO method of accounting for its inventory in 2015 and had an ending LIFO inventory basis of $90,000. At the end of 2015, the inventory's actual fair market value was $175,000 and its FIFO value was $150,000. H must add the $60,000 LIFO recapture amount (FIFO value of $150,000 − $90,000 LIFO value) to its 2015 taxable income. Assuming a 35% corporate tax rate, H Corporation's 2015 tax liability is increased by $21,000, the LIFO recapture tax. Thus, H must pay $5,250 (one-fourth) of the LIFO recapture tax on the due date of its 2015 corporate tax return and the remaining three installments of $5,250 each must be paid with H's next three tax returns. Note also that after adjusting the inventory's basis to $150,000, there is $25,000 of remaining unrealized appreciation that may be subject to the built-in gains tax as the inventory is sold. However, the future gains will be calculated by the LIFO method.

---

[29] § 1363(d)(3).

[30] § 1363(d)(2)(B).

[31] § 6655(g)(4).

ESTIMATED TAXES

S corporations are required to pay estimated taxes for (1) excessive passive investment income taxes (§ 1375), and (2) taxes on built-in gains (§ 1374). The computations of estimated taxes generally follow the rules applicable to C corporations.[32] Shareholders should include their portions of S corporation income or loss when calculating their own estimated tax payments.[33]

Disposition of Ownership Interest

Based on the entity theory, sales of stock by shareholders of an S corporation result in capital gain or loss. This, of course, is identical to how stock sales of a C corporation are treated. However, the amount of the gain or loss will differ since an S shareholder's basis is adjusted for income, losses, and distributions whereas a C shareholder's basis is not. All other stock transfers also follow the rules of an exchange or gift of a capital asset. This is a significant advantage for the S (or C) corporate shareholder when compared with the complicated and often unfavorable rules of the partnership. Shareholders who sell or otherwise dispose of their stock must report their share of the S corporation's current-year items, based either on the per-day allocation method or the interim closing-of-the-books method.

LO.3
Understand how dispositions of S corporate stock differ from those of C corporate stock.

WORTHLESS SECURITIES

S and C shareholders who hold worthless securities, including stock and debt, are subject to the same provisions with one exception. The S corporation's flow-through rules apply *before* the deduction for worthless stock or debt. The loss on worthless securities is treated as though it occurred on the last day of the *shareholder's* taxable year (not the S corporation's year) from the sale or exchange of a capital asset. Thus, it is possible for stock to become worthless before corporate activities are completed. In addition, if the S corporation's year ends *after* the stockholder's year ends, worthlessness could occur before the flow-through is available. This potential loss of deduction could be a serious disadvantage to shareholders.

The deduction for worthless stock is a capital loss unless the stock qualifies for ordinary loss treatment under § 1244.[34] Bad debts also are capital losses unless the shareholder can establish that they are business bad debts.[35] For example, the debts may have arisen as a result of a business transaction or the shareholder's employment status with the corporation. Business bad debts are ordinary losses. Nonbusiness bad debts are short-term capital losses.

Acquisitions and Dispositions of S Corporations

Chapter 5 discusses some of the tax and nontax considerations for buying and selling businesses. That chapter describes some of the tax and nontax consequences of asset and stock sales. However, that discussion was limited to C corporations. For nontax purposes, there is little, if any, difference between the two tax entities. However, the tax consequences may differ substantially.

SALE OF ASSETS OR SALE OF ENTITY

Perhaps the most important issue in the sale of a business is for both the buyer and seller to know exactly what property is changing hands. In general the buyer prefers to purchase assets, rather than the entity. One factor may be the presence of undisclosed or unknown liabilities of the entity. If the buyer purchases the assets from the entity, the entity will keep its undisclosed liabilities, which will ultimately be borne by the seller.

---

[32] See § 6655 for estimated taxes applicable to C corporations.

[33] The Code and Regulations do not expressly provide that but the language of §§ 1366 and 6654 is broad enough to require inclusion of S corporation items. See Ltr. Ruls. 8542034 and 8544011.

[34] Compare §§ 165(g) and 1367(b)(3) with § 1244(a).

[35] Compare §§ 166(a) and (d).

However, if the entity has some valuable contract or other right that cannot be assigned, the only feasible way to structure the deal may be a sale of the entity. Moreover, an asset deal may require payment of transfer taxes on real property, motor vehicles and other assets. Motor vehicles may require new licenses. The parties must examine agreements with lenders, in which a transfer of the property may trigger a "due on sale" provision. These factors may mitigate in favor of an entity deal.

However, the tax consequences generally place the buyer and the seller in adverse positions. Usually, the buyer prefers an asset purchase, whereas sellers prefer a stock sale.

Example 17

Buyco and Tarco are both S corporations. Buyco is negotiating to purchase all of Tarco's stock. The two corporations have no common ownership and are not otherwise considered to be related parties. Tarco's net asset value is $1,000,000. Tarco's aggregate asset basis is $100,000. Tarco's shareholders have an aggregate stock basis of $120,000, immediately before the deal takes place. A sale of all of Tarco's assets will result in $400,000 ordinary income and $500,000 of capital and § 1231 gain.

If Tarco sells all of its assets, the shareholders will report a mix of ordinary income and capital gain, flowing through from the corporation. In contrast, a sale of the stock would result in all of the shareholder gain being capital. Thus the shareholders might prefer the stock sale, at first impression.

However, an asset purchase would give Buyco an aggregate basis of $1,000,000 in the assets. Buyco could recover the cost through sale or depreciation of the assets. In contrast, a purchase of all of the stock would leave the asset basis of $100,000. That would leave Buyco with $900,000 of stock basis, which it could only recover by reselling the Tarco stock. Accordingly, Buyco would discount its offer price for stock substantially.

S Corporations and Asset Sales

After the sale of the assets, the S corporation remains in the hands of the prior shareholders, but no longer operates the business. The assets now held by the corporation consist primarily of the consideration received from the buyer, and perhaps assets that the buyer did not want. The shareholders now must decide to liquidate the corporation or to maintain its existence.

Liquidating a corporation or other limited liability entity will remove a shield protecting the owners. Before doing so, the owners should be aware of parties other than the government who might have claims against the corporation. They should leave sufficient assets inside the entity shell to protect the individual owners from unpleasant surprises. This is one of the areas in which advice from competent local counsel, with frank discussions with the officers and business advisors of the entity may provide a great deal of protection.

Corporate Tax Liquidation and Reorganization Rules Apply to S Corporations

The same general rules apply to both C and S corporations, although the tax may differ between the two types of corporations. Moreover, not all S corporations are subject to the same tax burdens, even with identical gains and shareholder basis. The presence or absence of built-in gains tax can have significant impact on the overall tax burdens of the corporation and its shareholders. See Chapter 5 for discussion of corporate liquidations and Chapter 7 for coverage of corporate reorganizations.

There are few special rules governing the liquidation of S corporations. In general, Subchapter S of the Internal Revenue Code provides that the rules of Subchapter C apply to S corporation, unless Subchapter S specifically modifies their applications.[36] Therefore, the S corporation recognizes all gains and loss on the distribution of property in liquidation.[37] Under the general rule of Subchapter S, gains and losses pass through to the shareholders, and adjust their stock basis at the moment of liquidation.[38]

SALE OF ENTITY: S CORPORATION

The sale of an entity means that the buyer picks up most of the tax history of the selling entity. This would include the basis of all assets, plus the elections, Accumulated Adjustments Account, accumulated earnings and profits, etc. If there is substantial appreciation in the assets of the target corporation, the purchaser would discount the offer price to reflect the loss of the benefits.

Example 18

Refer to *Example 17*. If Buyco were to purchase all of the stock of Tarco, the tax basis of the assets would be $100,000. Thus in a stock purchase, Buyco would sacrifice $900,000 in tax benefits. Buyco estimates the average period of the tax benefits to be seven years, since some would be sold immediately, and others would be depreciated over longer lives. Using a 6% discount rate, Buyco estimates that the present value of the benefits lost by purchasing the stock would be approximately $250,000 compared to the benefits of an asset purchase. Accordingly, Buyco offers $750,000 for the stock.

In the final negotiations, the parties may compromise. The selling shareholders, might reduce the price, if they can get no better offer. Alternatively, Buyco might pay a premium to recast the deal as an asset purchase. However, if the deal must be a stock transfer, there are some alternatives, discussed below. These include a § 338(h)(10) election, a § 336(e) election or a QSub sale.

Status of Target Corporation after Stock Sale

If the buyer is eligible to hold shares in an S corporation, the entity's S election continues without the necessity of any action on the buyer's part. If the buyer is not eligible to hold shares in an S corporation, the entity's S election terminates the day after the sale. Thus the entity becomes a C corporation for tax purposes.

Allocation of Income in Year of Sale

A sale of any percentage of S corporation stock does not terminate the corporation's S election, unless there is a sale to an ineligible person. However, the corporation could elect to terminate the S election immediately after the sale of stock, if the new owners instruct the officers to revoke the election.

When the sale does not terminate the S election, the parties have a choice as to allocation of the income, gains, deductions, losses and any other items that might affect a shareholder's income or basis. Under the general rule, the corporation must allocate every item throughout the entire year on a daily basis. It then allocates each item using a weighted average calculation of each day's percentage ownership.[39] If the buying and selling shareholders elect, there can be an interim closing of the books for allocation purposes, as was discussed in Chapter 11.

If the sale of the entity does cause a termination of the S election, or if the buyer causes the corporation to revoke the S election immediately, there are some other rules to follow:

If there is a sale of less than 50% of the stock during the year, the corporation must pro rate its income ratably throughout the entire tax year on a daily basis.[40] However, the corporation may elect to close the books on the date before the termination, if all of the shareholders during the pre-termination portion of the year, as well as all persons (or entities) who are shareholders on the first day as a C corporation consent to this election.[41]

---

[36] § 1371(a).
[37] § 336.
[38] §§ 1366 and 1367.
[39] § 1377(a)(1).
[40] § 1362(e)(3).
[41] § 1362(e)(3).

If more than 50% of the shares change hands during the year, the corporation must close its books as of the day before termination of the S election. The corporation cannot elect to pro rate its income.[42]

Stock Deal Treated as Asset Exchange for Federal Income Tax

The ability to treat an entity sale as an asset sale could help set a premium price for the business, and make the entity deal more attractive to prospective purchasers.

When the target business is a corporation, and the parties have decided that the entity deal is necessary or preferable, there are some techniques available. However, most of these are available only to S corporations or former subsidiaries of C corporations that file consolidated returns.

SECTION 338 ELECTIONS

A Section 338 election is only available to a corporation who purchases at least 80% of the stock of another corporation. The buying corporation must acquire at least 80% of the stock within a 12 month period, and none of the acquisitions may be from persons or other entities considered related to the corporation.[43] The acquiring corporation must make the election no later than the fifteenth day of the ninth month after the purchaser acquires the stock that puts it over the 80% threshold.[44] See Chapter 5 for a general discussion of § 338.

Variations on the Section 338 Election

Section 338 treats a newly acquired corporation as if it sold all of its assets for the fair market value of each on the acquisition date. This may be accomplished by a mere election and does not require an actual liquidation of the acquired corporation. A "new" corporation (for tax purposes only) springs into existence at the beginning of the next day. There are two variations on this election:

1. Section 338(g) treats a subsidiary corporation as if it sold all of its assets on the acquisition date, immediately *after* the stock transfer.

2. Section 338(h)(10) treats a subsidiary corporation as if it sold all of its assets on the acquisition date, immediately *before* the stock transfer.

In either case, the corporation is deemed to sell all of its assets at fair market value. The "old" corporation then terminates its existence. All of its tax attributes, including elections, tax year, basis, earnings and profits, etc. disappear. Immediately thereafter, a "new" corporation appears and buys all of the assets that the old one had sold. The purchase price is the adjusted grossed-up basis (AGUB) derived from the price paid by the purchaser for the stock. When the acquisition occurs in a single transaction, the AGUB is generally the same as the fair market value of the assets. When the acquisition is staggered, or there are still some minority shares outstanding, the computations may diverge.

Although the variances in timing between the two types of § 338 elections may not appear to be substantial, the results are substantially different.

- With the § 338(g) election, the purchaser gets no benefit for any gain recognized by the seller. To attain the step up in asset basis, the purchaser must bear the burden of a second round of taxation. Accordingly, this election is useful only in unusual situations, or in certain international transactions.

- In contrast, the gain recognized by the seller in a § 338(h)(10) deal results in a new basis to the assets immediately after the transfer, at no additional cost to the purchaser. Thus the purchaser gets the benefit of the gain recognized by the seller. When the purchaser and the target are domestic corporations, this is the most popular § 338 election.

---

[42] § 1362(e)(6)(D).

[43] § 338(h)(3).

[44] Reg. § 1.338-2(d).

Available Only to Corporation

In order to qualify for the § 338 election, both the purchaser and the target must be corporations. They may be C corporations, S corporations or one of each. For the § 338(h)(10) variation the target must be able to pass through gains and losses to the seller. Thus it is available only for S corporations, whose income passes through to shareholders, or consolidated subsidiaries, whose income is included on the seller's consolidated return for the year of the transaction.

S Corporation as Purchaser

When an S corporation acquires all (or at least 80%) of the stock of another corporation and the transaction meets all of the § 338 requirements, the S corporation can make a § 338 election with respect to the acquired corporation or may join with the seller in making an election to treat the transactions as a sale of assets under § 338(h)(10).

S Corporation as Target

Regulations under § 338 adopted in 1994 also hold that shareholders of a target S corporation can join with the purchaser in making a § 338(h)(10) election.[45] For the corporation to qualify for this election, the stock must be sold to another corporation that is eligible to make a § 338 election. The acquiring corporation may be a C corporation or an S corporation. To qualify for the § 338(h)(10) election, the purchaser must acquire all of the stock (or at least 80%) on the day (the acquisition date). The purchaser may not have acquired any stock before the acquisition date.[46]

Example 19

Refer to *Example 17,* and assume that Buyco acquired all of the stock in a single day for $1,000,000. Tarco's former shareholders would recognize capital gain of $880,000 on the sale of their stock. However, Tarco would not recognize any gain, since it was not a party to the transaction. Moreover, the § 754 election and resultant basis adjustments allowable to partnerships in such circumstances do not apply to S corporations. Thus Tarco's asset basis would remain at $100,000.

　　Now assume that Buyco made a § 338(g) election. Several complications would arise.

- On the date that Buyco acquired the stock, Tarco would have an ineligible shareholder and would be a C corporation.

- Tarco would be treated as if it sold its assets for $1,000,000 and would recognize a gain of $900,000. It is highly unlikely that Tarco would have any loss carryforwards from prior C corporation years, which might offset any or all of the gain. Thus in most situations, all of the gain would be taxable.

- Under current rates, Tarco would incur a Federal income tax liability of $306,000 ($900,000 × 0.34).

- Although Tarco's asset basis is now $1,000,000, the parties had to incur complete double tax liability to get this basis.

- The net value to Buyco would now be $694,000 ($1,000,000 − $306,000) immediately after it paid $1,000,000.

- This illustrates why the § 338(g) election is not in widespread use.

---

[45] Reg. §§ 1.1338(h)(10)-1(a), 1.338(h)(10)-1(c)(2).　　　[46] Reg. § 1.338(h)(10)-1(c)(2).

Example 20

Now assume that Tarco's selling shareholders joined with Buyco in a § 338(h)(10) election. This would preserve all of the nontax benefits of the stock sale, such as nonassignable contracts, transfer taxes, etc. However, the tax consequences would be much different from those in *Example 18*.

- At the last moment that the Tarco stock is in the hands of the selling shareholders, Tarco is treated as selling all of its assets for $1,000,000.

- Tarco remains an S corporation for this hypothetical transaction, and the gains pass through to the shareholders.

- The shareholders report $400,000 ordinary income and $500,000 of capital gain on the deemed sale of assets.

- The selling shareholders increase the aggregate stock basis from $120,000 to $1,120,000 as a result of the deemed sale.

- The selling shareholders are then deemed to sell all of their stock back to Tarco in complete liquidation of "old" Tarco for $1,000,000, the assets deemed held by Tarco after the deemed sale to Buyco.

- The next day "new" Tarco springs into existence with an aggregate asset basis of $1,000,000 and no tax history.

- Thus Buyco's $1,000,000 purchase price is reflected in the aggregate asset basis. In essence, this gives the same result as if a § 754 election were available.

When the purchaser is an S corporation, if it owns 100% of the stock, it may elect QSub status. Alternatively it may operate the newly acquired subsidiary as a C corporation.

QUALIFIED STOCK DISPOSITION: § 336(e) ELECTION

In 1986 Congress added a cryptic Subsection (e) to § 336. Section 336(e) allows a parent corporation that sells a consolidated subsidiary to treat the stock sale as an asset sale. However, this provision is only effective under regulations prescribes by the (Treasury) Secretary. For almost 27 years no such regulations appeared. Thus this rule seemed to be a dead letter.

The 2013 Regulations

After more than 26 years, the regulations appeared in May 2013.[47] Thus the rules are now in effect for qualified stock dispositions after May 15, 2013.[48] The statute describes only consolidated parent corporations as being eligible to make this election. However, the regulations allow selling shareholders of S corporation stock to elect asset sale treatment under this rule.

In substance, the rules are similar to those applicable to a § 338(h)(10) deal, except that the seller unilaterally makes the election. Thus the parties must use the residual method for allocation of the consideration, "old" target sells all of its assets at fair market value, and "new" target acquires all of the assets at adjusted-grossed up basis (AGUB).

The regulations also provide that any stock sold to a related person would not count towards the minimum 80% required disposition. In the S corporation context, that would apply to any stock purchased by a person who is already treated as a shareholder in the target corporation.[49]

There are differences between the rules under § 338(h)(10) and § 336(e). Some of the important distinctions are:

1. Section 338 requires a qualified stock "purchase" by a corporation, whereas § 336(e) requires a qualified stock "disposition" by a consolidated parent corporation or by S corporation shareholders.

---

[47] Treasury Decision 9619, 05/15/2013.

[48] Reg. § 1.336-5.

[49] Reg. § 1.336-1(b)(12).

2. Section 338(h)(10) requires a joint election by the selling shareholders and the buying corporation. With § 336(e), the seller makes a unilateral election to apply the rules.

3. For § 338(h)(10), both the buyer and the target must be corporations. In contrast, with § 336(e), the purchaser can be any entity or group. However, the target must be a corporation.

4. When an S corporation is the target in a § 338(h)(10) transaction, the purchaser must acquire at least 80% on the day of its first stock purchase, which must be the effective date of the election. The § 336(e) rules require that the qualifying disposing of 80% of the stock occur within 12 months. Whenever the sales reach the requisite 80% is the effective election date.

Example 21

Refer to the facts in *Example 17*. Assume that the buyer is an individual, or group of individuals. Thus the transaction would not qualify for § 338(h)(10), since only a corporation can make a § 338 election. However, Tarco's selling shareholders could elect to treat the sale as a § 336(e) liquidation. The sale of the requisite 80% need not occur on one day, as is the case with § 338(h)(10). However, they would need to make sure that Tarco's S election does not terminate before the sales reach the 80% threshold, since a stand alone C corporation cannot elect § 336(e) treatment.

Status of Target Corporation after § 336(e) Election

Under the fictions of § 336(e), target's existence terminates on the disposition date, with the deemed liquidation being its final act. Bright and early on the next morning a new tax entity arises. The tax status of this new entity would be a C corporation unless it is eligible to file an S election and does so. If it is eligible for S status, it should file a timely election for its year beginning on its first day of existence, or it will need to wait until the first day of its next tax year.

Sale of Qualified Subchapter S Subsidiary

Using a Qualified Subchapter S Subsidiary (QSub) to structure a stock sale may accomplish the same result as a § 338(h)(10) or § 336(e) election, in that it may treat a sock sale as an asset sale. The rationale is really quite simple. A Qualified Subchapter S Subsidiary is a domestic corporation that is 100% owned by an S corporation. The S corporation must have made an election to treat the corporation as a QSub.

A QSub is treated as a disregarded entity (DE) for Federal income tax purposes. Thus if the parent corporation sells the QSub, there must be a new tax entity created for tax purposes. This is accomplished by the following hypothetical steps:

- A sale by the parent of undivided interests in each of the assets deemed transferred to the QSub, followed by

- A contribution of all of the assets to the QSub in a § 351 exchange.[50]

None of the subsidiary's asset go anywhere, and the subsidiary receives no consideration. Thus, the subsidiary is not a direct party to the deal. However, there has been a tax fiction that the subsidiary corporation did not even exist while the QSub election was in effect. The subsidiary is no longer a QSub since it is no longer wholly owned by the parent S corporation.

Thus, there needs to be a new tax fiction that the corporation has suddenly sprung into existence, and received assets and liabilities. The Code is specific that the first hypothetical step is the sale of the assets by the parent S corporation to the purchaser.[51] Note that the Target corporation is not yet considered a party to the transaction.

---

[50] § 1361(b)(3)(C)(ii). [51] § 1361(b)(3)(C)(ii)(I).

Example 22

Assume the same facts in *Example 21,* but also assume that some of the purchasers are related to Tarco's selling shareholders, and the entire deal will fail the 80% test. Thus, to achieve the results of an asset sale but the nontax substance of a stock deal, the parties will do the following:

- The current Tarco shareholders will establish a new corporation, called Newco. Newco will make an S election to take place on the first day of the first taxable year.

- On a single day, all of the historic Tarco shareholders will exchange their Tarco stock for Newco stock.

- Newco will make an immediate QSub election for Tarco.

- The tax treatment will be a § 368(a)(1)(F) reorganization in which Newco is a continuation of Tarco. All of Tarco's assets, liabilities and tax history now belong to Newco for Federal income tax purposes.

- Newco sells all of the Tarco stock to the purchasers. However, Newco retains all of the tax characteristics of Tarco, and treats the transaction as if it sold the assets for $1,000,000.

- Newco recognizes the same gains that Tarco would recognize in an asset sale.

- Newco retains all of the tax history of Tarco, such as its Accumulated Adjustments Account, accumulated earnings and profits and elections.

- The purchasers are treated as if they acquired all of Tarco's assets and liabilities in a cost-based transaction for $1,000,000.

- The new owners are treated as if they contributed all of Tarco's assets and liabilities to a newly formed corporation. The basis in the stock is the basis of the assets deemed contributed. The basis of the assets to "new" Tarco is $1,000,000. Tarco has no tax history.

COMPARISON WITH § 338(h)(10) AND § 336(e)

In many cases, there is little difference between the QSub stock sale and the § 338(h)(10) or § 336(e) election. In either case, the purchaser acquires stock. Both of these transactions treat the deal as a sale of assets. However, there are some important distinctions.

Elective and Mandatory Treatment

The § 338(h)(10) treatment is elective, and offers a hindsight period of 8½ months after the acquisition. In contrast, the QSub rules are not elective, and must apply whenever the transaction is structured as a QSub sale. With the QSub sale there is no hindsight period in which the parties may determine the tax treatment of the transaction.

Other Factors

The QSub sale would allow the target corporation to transfer assets unwanted by the purchaser to the parent corporation in a tax-free transfer, since the parent is treated as the owner of all of the QSub's assets anyway. This makes the QSub sale a most useful technique when the purchaser wants all of the stock, but there are some assets that the seller desires to keep.

STATUS OF TARGET CORPORATION AFTER QSUB SALE

For tax purposes, the corporation is treated as a newly formed entity after the sale. Thus it will not have an S election in effect. If it is eligible, and the owners desire S corporation status, they should file the proper election. As is the case with the "new" corporation after the § 336(e) election, it is usually preferable to have the election take effect immediately.

The Code specifies that the former QSub is not eligible for an S election or QSub election for five years following its termination of QSub status.[52] However, the regulations permit a former QSub to become an S corporation or QSub of another S corporation immediately following loss of QSub status.[53] The key condition is that the newly liberated corporation must not be a C corporation for any single day.

Tax Planning

CHOICE OF ENTITY: COMPARING S CORPORATIONS, C CORPORATIONS, PARTNERSHIPS, AND LLCS

No doubt one of the most common questions asked by a taxpayer who is anticipating starting a new business or has an existing business concerns the form of organization that should be used. That decision has probably never been as confusing as it is today. For years, nontax factors, specifically the desire to limit an individual's liability, often were the key determinant in the choice of entity decision. Professional advisors, wishing to minimize the owner's personal liability, usually encouraged the owner to incorporate and secure the liability protection that the corporate entity offered. Assuming the owner took the advice, the only decision left from a tax perspective was whether the corporation would elect to be treated under the rules of Subchapter S or operate as a regular corporation subject to the rules of Subchapter C.

The limited liability company (authorized in all 50 states) has made the choice of entity decision far more difficult. This new creature, which provides limited liability yet is taxed as a partnership, has added an important new dimension to the business organization question. Business owners who seek limited liability are no longer constrained to accept the corporate form and the C or S tax treatment that accompanies it. They may now opt for partnership tax treatment provided by limited liability companies and still obtain the protection that was formerly available only with a corporation. In short, the limited liability company has for the most part made the liability factor moot. Consequently, the decision now turns on other critical factors, which for small business owners include tax considerations.

A complete comparison of these entities and the advantages and disadvantages of operating each can fill volumes and is beyond the scope of this text. Nevertheless, Exhibit 12-3 identifies some of the key transactions in the life of a business and explains how each of the various entities would be treated.

LO.4

Compare the four business organizations—proprietorships, partnerships, S corporations, and C corporations (see Exhibit 12-3).

---

[52] § 1361(b)(3)(D).　　　　[53] Reg. § 1.1361-5(c)(2).

EXHIBIT 12-3	**Comparative Analysis of Business Forms**			

Items for Comparison	Proprietorship/Proprietor	Partnership/Partner	S Corporation/Shareholder	C Corporation/Shareholder
1. What are the restrictions on the number of owners or who may be an owner?	One owner who must be an individual	None, except there must be at lease two owners	No more than 100 shareholders who must be individuals, estates, certain trusts, charities, pensions and ESOPs	None
2. Are owners liable for business debts that they have not personally guaranteed?	Yes, except if single-member LLC	Yes, for general partners but no for limited partners or partners in an LLP, LLC members	No	No
3. What are the appropriate tax forms and schedules and who files them?	Schedules C, SE, and all supporting schedules and forms	Form 1065 and Schedules K-1 are prepared by partnership; partners report on Schedules E, SE and other supporting schedules	Form 1120S and its Schedules K-1 are prepared by corporation; shareholders report on Schedule E and other supporting schedules	Form 1120 and all supporting schedules are filed for the C corporation; shareholders report dividend income on Schedule B
4. Who is the taxpayer?	Proprietor	Partners	Shareholders except tax on built-in gains, excess passive investment income, and LIFO recapture	C corporation: its shareholders are also taxed on dividend income when corporate earnings are distributed
5. Do owners have self-employment (SE) income from the business?	Yes, the net income from Schedule C	Yes, each *general* partner's share of net (SE) income plus guaranteed payments; for *limited* partners, only guaranteed payments from services	No	No
6. Must the business's taxable year be the same as that of the majority owners?	Yes	Generally, but a different year may be used if the partnership has natural business year or pays a tax on deferred income	Same as partnership	No, any period may be used except for personal service corporation
7. Are contributions of assets for an ownership interest taxable transactions?	No	No, same as proprietorship	No, *if* parties to the exchange own more than 80% of the corporation after the contribution, but otherwise, a taxable exchange with no carryover of tax attributes	Same as S corporation
8. Are distributions of cash includible income to owners?	No	No, except a distribution in excess of the partner's basis in the partnership is treated as a partial sale of the ownership interest	No, unless distribution exceeds shareholder's basis or is from accumulated E&P	Yes, if from the C corporation's earnings and profits
9. Do property distributions result in taxable income to the business or the owners?	No, basis is preserved in distributed property	No, with several exceptions	Yes, S corporation must recognize realize gain—but not loss—if a nonliquidating distribution; shareholders have dividend income if the FMV of the property exceeds AAA	Yes. Corporation recognizes gain, but not loss; shareholders have dividend income to extent of property's value or E&P
10. May an owner enter into taxable transactions (sales, loans, etc.) with the business	No	Yes, when acting in a nonpartner capacity, but subject to related-party restrictions	Yes, subject to related-party restrictions	Same as S corporation

EXHIBIT 12-3	**Continued**		

Items for Comparison	Proprietorship/Proprietor	Partnership/Partner	S Corporation/Shareholder	C Corporation/Shareholder
11. May an accrual basis business deduct accrued expenses to cash basis owners?	No, not applicable	No, deductible only when paid (except see 12 below)	Not deductible until shareholder includes in income. Applies to any shareholder	Not deductible until shareholder includes in income. Applies to >50% shareholder
12. Are accrued expenses of the business includible income to cash basis owners? If yes, when?	No, not applicable	Yes, when received, except guaranteed salary and interest on capital are includible when accrued	Yes, when received	When accrued to minority shareholders, when received by majority shareholders
13. Can owners be employees of the business and be paid salaries subject to employment taxes and withholding?	No	No	Yes	Yes
14. Are fringe benefits for owner/ employees deductible expenses?	No	Yes, but partner must include in gross income	Yes, but a more than 2% shareholder must include in gross income	Yes
15. May the business use the cash method?	Yes, depending on income and type of business unless it qualifies as a tax shelter	Yes, depending on income and type of business unless it qualifies as a tax shelter or has a C corporation as a partner	Yes, depending on income and type of business unless it qualifies as a tax shelter	No, unless gross receipts do not exceed $5 million or it qualifies under "type of business" exception
16. Is the business a conduit with the original character of the items flowing through to its owners as of the last day of the business's taxable year?	Yes	Yes	Yes	No, the business is an entity and the flow-through concept is not applicable
17. How are capital gains and losses of the business treated?	As though received by the proprietor	Flow through to each partner	Same as partnership	Net capital gain includible in corporate taxable income and taxed at regular rates; net capital losses carried back, forward five years, with no deduction against ordinary income
18. How is dividend income received by the business treated?	Includible income as though received by the proprietor (may be a subject to reduced rate)	Flows through to each partner as dividend income (may be subject to reduced rate)	Same as partnership	Includible income with a dividend-received deduction
19. How are charitable contributions treated?	An itemized deduction as though contributed by the proprietor	Flow through to each partner as an itemized deduction	Same as partnership	Deductions may not exceed 10% of taxable income before certain deductions
20. Who pays state and local income taxes on the business net income and how are they treated?	Proprietor; an itemized deduction as though paid by the proprietor	Each partner; an itemized deduction	Same as partnership, except some state and local income taxes are assessed on the S corporation	Deductible expense

EXHIBIT 12-3	Continued

Items for Comparison	Proprietorship/Proprietor	Partnership/Partner	S Corporation/Shareholder	C Corporation/Shareholder
21. How are tax credits treated?	Offsets proprietor's tax	Qualifying credits flow through to each partner subject to any limitations applicable at the partner level	Same as partnership	Computed at the corporate level and reduces corporate tax liability
22. How is net ordinary income treated?	Includible with proprietor's AGI	Flows through to each partner	Same as partnership	Included in corporate taxable income
23. How is net ordinary loss treated?	Reduction of proprietor's AGI	Flows through to each partner, potentially deductible up to that partner's basis in the partnership; any excess is carried forward	Same as partnership except that basis rules differ	Subject to carryover rules (back two years and forward 20 years or forward 20 years only) and deductible against net ordinary income
24. How are AMT adjustments and preferences treated?	Included on proprietor's return	Flow through to partners	Same as partnership	Included in corporation's AMTI; ACE adjustment required: small corporations exempt
25. Is § 291(a)(1) applicable?	No	No	Yes, if C corporation for any of three prior tax years	Yes
26. How are items allocated among the owners?	Not applicable	According to profit and loss ratio or may be specially allocated	According to stock ownership ratio; special rules for years of termination or dispositions	Not applicable
27. Is the basis of business assets adjusted when an ownership interest is sold?	Not applicable	Yes, if partnership has elected the optional adjustment to basis	No, unless § 338(h)(10) or § 336(e) election is in effect	No, unless § 338 election is in effect
28. Is basis affected by business liabilities?	Not applicable	Yes, a partner's basis includes his or her share of partnership liabilities	No, except for loans directly from shareholders	No
29. Is basis affected by business income, gains, deductions, and losses?	Not applicable	Yes, all income and gains increase basis and all expenses and losses (that flow through) decrease basis	Yes, same as partnership	No
30. What is the character of gains and losses on the sale of a business interest?	Each asset is treated as sold individually and the character of the gain or loss is dependent on that asset	Capital gain or loss except ordinary income to the extent of partner's share of unrealized receivables, depreciation recapture, or inventory. Some gain may be taxed at 25 or 28 percent.	Capital gains and losses, except losses may qualify as § 1244 ordinary losses if the corporation meets certain requirements. Some gain may be taxed at 28% (but not at 25%).	Same as S corporation, except no 28% portion. Special rules apply if stock is § 1202 stock.
31. Must a reasonable salary be allocated to family members performing services for the business?	No	Yes	Yes	No

DISCUSSION QUESTIONS

12-1 *Passive Investment Income.* An S corporation with AE&P of $5,000 is expected to receive 30% of its gross income from rents but only 18% of its net income from these rents. Will the excess passive investment income test be violated? Assume the S corporation's taxable year does not end for seven months and all income is earned equally over the year.

    a. Can any action be taken during the next seven months to ensure the test will not be violated?

    b. Could the corporation take any corrective action if it does not determine the nature of its gross receipts until after the end of its tax year?

12-2 *Property Distributions.* What effect do noncash distributions have on the S corporation and on the shareholder if the S corporation has no AE&P, and:

    a. The property's market value exceeds its basis, or

    b. The property's basis exceeds its market value?

12-3 *Distributions.* When do cash distributions result in includible income to the S shareholder?

12-4 *Post-Termination Transition Period.* What is a post-termination transition period? How is it useful?

12-5 *Taxes Imposed on S Corporations.* Which of the following taxes might apply to an S corporation?

    a. The net investment income tax

    b. The passive investment income tax

    c. The alternative minimum tax

    d. The built-in gains tax

12-6 *S Corporations with AE&P.* Which of the following may be directly affected by the presence of absence of an S corporation's accumulated earnings and profits from C corporation years?

    a. The built-in gains tax

    b. The passive investment income tax

    c. The LIFO recapture tax

    d. The treatment of distribution to shareholders

    e. The maximum number of shareholders permitted

12-7 *S Corporation without Taxable Income.* Which of the following will not be a problem if an S corporation has no taxable income for a given year?

    a. Distributions treated as dividends

    b. The built-in gains tax

    c. The tax on passive investment income

    d. Termination of an S election due to three consecutive years of excess passive investment income

    e. The LIFO recapture tax

12-8 *Post-Termination Transition Period.* Which of the following statements are true concerning the post-termination transition period?

    a. It may end one year after the corporation terminates its S election.

    b. During the post-termination transition period distributions may be tax free reductions of basis.

    c. During the post-termination transition period a shareholder may "purchase" otherwise suspended losses by making a contribution to the corporation's capital.

    d. During the post-termination transition period a shareholder may "purchase" otherwise suspended losses by making a loan to the corporation.

    e. During the post-termination transition period the corporation is not subject to the regular corporate income tax.

12-9 *Asset Sale versus Stock Sale.* Distinguish an asset sale/purchase from a stock sale/purchase with respect to the following:
   a. Gains and losses recognized by sellers
   b. Basis of assets after the deal
   c. Survival of tax history
   d. Ownership of nontax attributes, such as property and contracts

12-10 *Stock Purchase Treated as Asset Purchase.* Which of the following techniques treats a stock purchase as if it were an asset purchase from the seller's point of view?
   a. Outright purchase of the stock from the sellers
   b. Purchasing a QSub from an S corporation
   c. Outright purchase of the stock from the sellers, with a § 338(h)(10) election
   d. Outright purchase of the stock from the sellers, with a § 336(e) election

12-11 *Special Elections on Stock or Asset Sales/Purchases.* State which of the following transactions require special tax elections and who must file the elections:
   a. A straight stock sale, treated as such
   b. A straight asset sale, treated as such
   c. A stock purchase with § 338(h)(10)
   d. A stock sale with § 336(e)

12-12 *Basic Comparison.* List the tax advantages and the tax disadvantages of an S corporation when compared with:
   a. A partnership
   b. A C corporation

PROBLEMS

12-13 *Termination of Election.* T, the sole shareholder and president of T, Inc., had operated a successful automobile dealership as a regular C corporation for many years. In 2010, the corporation elected S corporation status. After T's unexpected illness in 2014, the corporation sold most of its assets and retained only a small used car operation. In 2014 and 2015, T, Inc. had paid the tax on excessive passive income and had AE&P (from its C corporation years) at the end of both years. In 2016, the corporation paid no dividends and had the following income and expenses:

Interest income	$50,000
Dividend income	5,000
Gain from prior installment sale	30,000
Used car sales	40,000
Cost of sales	20,000

Is the S election terminated, and if so, when?

12-14 *Property Distributions.* M receives the following equipment from an S corporation as a distribution of profits.

Asset	Cost	Accumulated Depreciation	Basis	Fair Market Value
Equipment	$10,000	$7,900	$2,100	$2,280

The equipment was used in the business for four years of its five-year MACRS life and will be a nonbusiness asset to M. M is a 60% owner and has a basis in the stock of $11,000 before the property distribution. Calculate the following amounts.
   a. The S corporation's recognized gain
   b. M's basis in the equipment
   c. The effect on M's basis in the stock
   d. The effect on M's adjusted gross income

12-15 *Property Distributions.* Refer to *Problem 12-14*. Calculate the same amounts if M's basis in the S corporation, before the distribution, is $1,200 instead of the $11,000.

12-16 *Property Distribution.* J purchases 20% of an S corporation's stock for $50,000 when its records show the following:

	Fair Market Value	Basis
Cash	$ 40,000	$ 40,000
Inventory	60,000	45,000
Land—investment	80,000	20,000
Other operating assets	100,000	80,000
Liabilities	(30,000)	(30,000)
Net assets	$250,000	$155,000

Six months later, all of the land is distributed in equal plats to the shareholders. What is the effect of this distribution on J?

12-17 *Computation of AAA and Basis.* J formed R Corporation in 1986. The corporation operated as a C corporation from 1986 until 2005, when it elected to be taxed as an S corporation. At the beginning of the current year, J had a basis in his stock of $100,000. The corporation's balance in the AAA at the beginning of the current year was $143,000. R's records for the current year reveal the following information:

Sales	$300,000
Cost of goods sold	(120,000)
Miscellaneous operating expenses	50,000
Salary to J	40,000
Nondeductible portion of entertainment	4,000
Tax-exempt interest income	13,000
Expenses related to tax-exempt interest income	3,000
Capital gain	7,000
Capital loss	(2,000)
Charitable contribution	5,000
Cash distribution to J	10,000

The corporation also had AE&P from C years of $4,000.

Compute J's basis in his stock and the corporation's balance in the AAA as of the end of the taxable year. Assume J is the sole shareholder.

12-18 *Treatment of Distributions: Converted C Corporation.* Assume the same facts as in *Problem 12-17* above. Explain the tax treatment to J if he receives the following distributions during the year.
a. $100,000
b. $220,000
c. $260,000

12-19 *Cash and Property Distributions—AE&P.* S, Inc. had previously been a regular C corporation, but elected to be taxed as an S corporation in 1982. It is owned equally by J and G, who have a basis in their stock of $100,000 each at the beginning of the current year. Also at the beginning of the current year, the corporation had the following balances:

Accumulated adjustments account	$90,000
Accumulated earnings and profits	30,000
Other adjustments account	0

During the current year, the corporation had ordinary income of $35,000 and distributed IM stock worth $75,000 to J and cash of $75,000 to G. The stock was purchased four years ago for $50,000.
a. What are the tax effects of the distribution on the corporation?
b. What are the consequences to each of the shareholders?

12-20 *Cash Distributions—AE&P.* A calendar year S corporation has the following balance on January 1, of the current year:

Accumulated adjustments account.	$15,000
Accumulated earnings and profits	6,000
Other adjustments account	0

This year the S corporation records show $12,000 net ordinary income, $4,000 tax-exempt income net of related expenses, and $55,000 cash distributions. Y owns 70% of the stock. Her basis in the stock on January 1, was $7,000, and she has a note receivable from the corporation of $5,000. Y is single, and her only other income is salary from an unrelated business.

a. Calculate the balances in the corporate accounts as of December 31.
b. Calculate the effect on Y's adjusted gross income for the year.
c. Calculate the basis in Y's stock and note as of December 31.

12-21 *Property Distributions—AE&P.* Assume the same facts as in *Problem 12-20* except the distribution is stock held more than one year as an investment with a market value of $55,000 and a basis of $53,000.

a. Calculate the balances in the corporate accounts as of December 31.
b. Calculate the effect on Y's adjusted gross income.
c. Calculate the basis in Y's stock and note as of December 31.

12-22 *Cash Distributions—AE&P.* D, Inc. was incorporated in 1999, and its shareholders made a valid S election for D's 2005 calendar year. At the end of the current year but before the distribution is considered, D had $19,000 of accumulated earnings and profits from 2000 through 2004, and an accumulated adjustments account of $11,000. D made only one cash distribution of $20,000 during the current year, $5,000 of which was paid to shareholder M, who owns 25% of D's stock. After all adjustments *except* any required for the distribution, M's basis in his stock was $18,000.

a. What are the tax consequences of the distribution to M, and what is M's basis in his D stock after the distribution?
b. What are the balances in D's accumulated earnings and profits account and accumulated adjustments account after the distribution?

12-23 *Cash Distribution—AE&P.* M and J have been equal owners of an S corporation for several years. It was operated as a C corporation its first two years and as an S corporation since then. This year it has $12,000 ordinary income, $2,000 tax-exempt interest income, $24,000 cash distributions, and the following balances at the end of the prior year:

Accumulated adjustments account.	$8,000
AE&P from C years	3,000

M's stock basis at the end of last year was $8,500 and J's was $13,000.

a. Calculate the balances in the corporate accounts as of December 31.
b. Calculate the effect on M's and J's adjusted gross income.
c. Calculate the basis in M's and J's stock as of December 31.

12-24 *Property Distribution—AE&P.* Refer to *Problem 12-23,* but assume the $24,000 distribution is of land that has a $23,000 basis.

12-25 *Excess Passive Investment Income.* A calendar year S corporation has AE&P of $15,000 from years when it was operated as a C corporation. Its records show the following:

Sales	$100,000
Cost of goods sold.	(55,000)
Operating expenses.	(15,000)
Dividend income	20,000
Rental income (passive).	40,000
Rental expenses.	(25,000)

The corporation is owned equally by three brothers. Determine the tax effect on the S corporation and on each brother.

12-26 *Distribution Election.* At the beginning of the current year, P Corporation, an S corporation, had $15,000 in accumulated earnings and profits and $24,000 in its Accumulated Adjustments Account. In the current year P had interest income of $45,000 and gross receipts from its active business of $55,000. P claimed deductions of $32,000 attributable to its business operations and no deductions attributable to its interest income. Assume that the sole shareholder is in the top marginal bracket for income tax purposes and is also subject to the Net Investment Income tax. P distributed $20,000 in the current year.
  a. Determine the tax consequences to the shareholder and the corporation if the corporation did not make any election regarding the distribution.
  b. How might the corporation elect to treat the distribution?
  c. Determine the tax consequences to the shareholder and the corporation if the corporation elected to bypass its AAA.
  d. What procedures would be necessary to achieve the result in (c) above?

12-27 *Distribution and Deemed Distribution Elections.* Assume the same facts in *Problem 12-26* except that the accumulated earnings and profits balance at the beginning of the current year was $45,000.
  a. Determine the tax consequences to the shareholder and the corporation if the corporation elected to bypass its AAA, but did not make a deemed dividend election.
  b. Determine the tax consequences to the shareholder and the corporation if the corporation elected to bypass its AAA, and made a deemed dividend election.
  c. What procedures would be necessary to achieve the result in (b) above?

12-28 *Tax on Built-in Gains.* A corporation, organized in 1985, was operated as a C corporation until Subchapter S was elected as of January 1, 2015, when it had total assets of $240,000 FMV and $185,000 basis. Assets held on that date ($80,000 market value and $50,000 basis) are distributed in 2016 when the market value is $90,000. Calculate the tax on built-in gains if taxable income, based on computations for a C corporation, is:
  a. $60,000
  b. $20,000

12-29 *Tax on Built-In Gains.* On February 5, 2016 L Corporation, a cash basis calendar year C corporation, elected S status effective for January 1, 2016. On January 1, L's balance sheet revealed the following assets:

	Adjusted Basis	Fair Market Value
Inventory.	$20,000	$85,000
Land	30,000	70,000
Equipment.	45,000	15,000

During the first S corporation year, L sold all of its inventory for $90,000. It also sold the equipment for $9,000 (L did not claim any more depreciation on the equipment this year, so its basis at the time of sale was $45,000). L's taxable income limitation is $100,000 for the year. Compute L Corporation's built-in gains tax.

12-30 *LIFO Recapture Tax.* T Corporation converts to S corporation status for 2016. T used the LIFO method of accounting for its inventory in 2015 and had an ending LIFO inventory basis of $540,000. The ending inventory's FIFO value was $650,000 and its fair market value was $800,000.

a.   What is T Corporation's LIFO recapture amount?

b.   Assuming its corporate tax rate is 35 percent, what is T Corporation's LIFO recapture tax?

c.   How is the LIFO recapture tax required to be paid?

12-31 *Worthless Securities.* A calendar year S corporation is bankrupt. E, a 60% owner for several years, will not receive any assets from the business. His basis in the stock as of January 1, 2016 was $70,000, and he has a note receivable of $25,000 from the corporation. Both are determined to be uncollectible July 1, 2016. The S corporation has a net ordinary loss during 2016 of $30,000; $20,000 before July 1 and $10,000 after July 1. E lent the corporation the $20,000 last year and $5,000 four months ago in an effort to protect his ownership interest in the business. Calculate E's adjusted gross income and capital loss carryovers if his adjusted gross income from other sources totals $120,000.

12-32 Purr Corporation and Tar Corporation are both S corporations. Purr is negotiating with the shareholder of Tar to purchase all of Tar's business. The assets are worth $2,500,000 and liabilities are $500,000. The aggregate basis of the assets to Tar before the deal is $800,000. Half of the gain on the sale of the assets would be § 1231 gain and the other 50% would be ordinary income. The sole shareholder of Tar has a stock basis of $900,000. Assume that the deal takes place as an asset sale for $2,000,000 plus assumption of all liabilities.

a.   What would be the amount of gain or loss recognized by the selling shareholder?

b.   What would be the character of gain or loss recognized by the selling shareholder?

c.   What assets would Purr now own, and what would be the basis?

d.   In general, what would be the tax benefit to Purr, in terms of future deductions?

12-33 Refer to *Problem 12-32.* Assume that the deal takes place as a stock sale for $2,000,000.

a.   What would be the amount of gain or loss recognized by the selling shareholder?

b.   What would be the character of gain or loss recognized by the selling shareholder?

c.   What assets would Purr now own, and what would be the basis?

d.   In general, what would be the tax benefit to Purr, in terms of future deductions?

12-34 Refer to *Problem 12-32.* Assume that the deal takes place as a stock sale for $2,000,000, and the parties decide to make a § 338(h)(10) election.

a.   Who would need to file the election, and when would it need to be filed?

b.   What would be the amount of gain or loss recognized by the selling shareholder?

c.   What would be the character of gain or loss recognized by the selling shareholder?

d.   What assets would Purr now own, and what would be the basis?

e.   In general, what would be the tax benefit to Purr, in terms of future deductions?

12-35 Refer to *Problem 12-32.* Assume that the deal takes place as a stock sale for $2,000,000, but Purr does not want to purchase the Tar stock directly. Instead Purr's shareholders, who are unrelated to Tar's shareholder, will purchase all of the stock.

a.   Can any or all of the parties make a § 338 election?

b.   If not, are there any other elections that might recast the deal as an asset sale for tax purposes?

Multijurisdictional Taxation

PART
4

13

International Taxation

Learning Objectives

Upon completion of this chapter you will be able to:

LO.1 Explain the taxation of U.S. citizens' and U.S. residents' foreign source income.

LO.2 Identify the trade-offs between the foreign tax credit, the foreign tax deduction, and, when applicable, the foreign income exclusions for individuals.

LO.3 Understand the taxation of U.S.-based corporations' foreign source income.

LO.4 Identify the various tax incentives related to the exporting of U.S. products.

LO.5 Determine the allocation of income and deductions among affiliated companies.

LO.6 Understand the tax provisions relating to foreign currency gains and losses.

LO.7 Explain the U.S. taxation of nonresident aliens.

Chapter Outline

Introduction

All industrial nations reserve the right to tax income earned within their territorial borders. This policy covers income earned by citizens, residents, nonresident aliens, and foreign businesses. In addition, the *Sixteenth Amendment* to the *Constitution of the United States* approaches taxation from a broader jurisdictional principle. It states:

> The Congress shall have the power to lay and collect taxes on income, from whatever source derived without apportionment among the several States, and without regard to any census or enumeration. (Emphasis added.)

Consequently, a U.S. citizen's or U.S. resident's worldwide income is subject to U.S. taxation. A similar jurisdictional approach has been taken by many industrial nations, including Canada, Japan, and the United Kingdom. Some governments, however, exclude income earned outside their borders from taxation. This type of exclusion applies most often to business entities rather than to individuals. For example, earnings of foreign subsidiaries are excludable income for parent corporations located in France, New Zealand, and Sweden.

With few exceptions, the United States levies taxes on income of U.S. citizens and resident aliens regardless of their place of residence and on income of U.S. corporations regardless of where their activities legally and economically occur. This policy sometimes causes the same income to be taxed at three or more levels. First, foreign-earned income is usually taxed by the host country. Second, most governments withhold taxes on dividend, interest, and royalty payments that leave their countries. Third, the gross income (income before foreign income taxes and withholding taxes are deducted) is taxable in the United States when it is constructively received by a U.S. citizen or corporation. In addition, this income may be subject to state and local income taxes in both the host country and the United States.

Taxation of U.S. Citizens

Individual U.S. citizens are taxed on their worldwide income. Since most foreign source income is also taxed in the foreign country, the Code provides three options that allow individuals to avoid, or at least decrease, the double tax burden.

1. Direct foreign income taxes may be reported as an itemized deduction.
2. Instead of a deduction, direct foreign income taxes may be claimed as a credit against U.S. income taxes.
3. Qualifying individuals may elect to exclude foreign-earned income up to certain statutory amounts.

The first option, an itemized deduction of foreign income taxes, is generally less beneficial than the foreign tax credit. Both the tax credit in option two and the exclusion in option three are subject to limitation. Those limitations applicable to tax credits are based on total foreign source income, while those applicable to exclusions are based on foreign source earned income. If the third option is elected, foreign taxes applicable to the amounts excluded cannot be claimed as a tax credit or deduction.

FOREIGN SOURCE INCOME

Earned Income

The source of earned income is determined by the place where the work is actually performed.[1] This determination is unaffected by either the location of the employer (or other contractor of services) or the method of payment. For example, salary received by a U.S. citizen for work performed in Germany is foreign source income, even if payment is made by a U.S. corporation to the employee's Indiana bank account. As might be expected, there is an exception to this rule. Treaties generally provide that salaries of U.S. government employees are not foreign source income, even though duties are performed and payments are received in another country.[2]

In addition to salaries, earned income includes professional fees, commissions, and employee benefits.[3] Companies often provide U.S. expatriates (U.S. citizens working in a foreign country) with substantial employee benefits. Common examples are extra amounts to cover higher costs of living, housing, home leaves, education for dependents, and income taxes. In some instances, these amounts exceed the employees' base salary and are substantial business costs.

Proprietors and partners have foreign-earned income to the extent that they perform services for their businesses in another country. As discussed in the partnership chapter (Chapter 9), it is helpful if these amounts are guaranteed payments rather than distributions of profits when a partnership has U.S. source income.[4] If capital is a material income-producing factor, the amount considered to be earned income is limited to 30% of the owner's share of net income.[5]

> ## Example 1
>
> A British partnership has $200,000 of net income in the current year. None of the income is from U.S. sources. J's distributive share is $40,000. He is a U.S. citizen living in London.
>
> 1. If J performs no services for the partnership, he has $40,000 unearned foreign source income.
>
> 2. If J performs services valued at $17,000, and capital is not a material income-producing factor, he has $17,000 earned foreign income and $23,000 unearned foreign income.
>
> 3. If J performs services valued at $17,000, and capital is a material income-producing factor, he has $12,000 (30% of $40,000) earned foreign income and $28,000 unearned foreign income.

The 30% limit does not apply to owners of businesses with net losses. When net losses occur, earned income is limited to an owner's share of gross profit from the business. The 30% limit also does not apply to incorporated businesses.

Unearned Income

Dividends, interest, pensions, annuities, capital gains, gambling winnings, and alimony are considered unearned income. Royalties and rents are also unearned income unless services are provided by the recipient. Unearned income usually qualifies as foreign source when it is received from a foreign resident or for property used in a foreign country and not effectively connected with U.S. sources. For example, interest is foreign source income even if the income is received in the United States when it is paid by a resident of a foreign country

LO.1

Explain the taxation of U.S. citizens' and U.S. residents' foreign source income.

---

[1] § 862(a)(3).

[2] § 911(b)(1)(B)(ii). For example, see the *North Atlantic Treaty Status of Forces Agreement* and the *Treaty of Mutual Cooperation and Security between the United States and Japan*. This is in contrast to some countries that base their sourcing rules on where services are utilized or payment is made.

[3] § 911(d)(2)(A).

[4] § 707(c); Reg. § 1.707-1(c); and *Carey v. U.S.*, 70-1 USTC ¶9455, 25 AFTR2d 70-1395, 427 F.2d 763 (Ct. Cls., 1970) compared with *Foster v. Comm.*, 64-1 USTC ¶9362, 21 AFTR2d 859, 329 F.2d 717(CA-2, 1964).

[5] § 911(d)(2)(B).

(even if that foreign resident is a U.S. citizen). In contrast, rents and royalties are foreign source income only if the property is used in a foreign country. Thus, the location of the property, not the residency of the payor, determines the source of rents and royalties.

In general, the source of income from sales of personal property (i.e., property other than real estate) is determined by the residency of the seller rather than by where title transfers. Thus, the income is U.S. source when sold by a U.S. resident and foreign source when sold by a nonresident, regardless of where title transfers.[6] There are, however, several exceptions to this rule. The source of income from the sale of:

1. Intangibles contingent on productivity, use, or disposition is generally determined by where the intangible is used, but goodwill is sourced in the country where it was generated.

2. An active affiliated foreign corporation's stock is foreign source if sold in the foreign country where the affiliate had derived more than 50% of its gross income in the previous three years.

3. Inventory is generally where title transfers.

4. Depreciable property is based on a recapture rule (i.e., the source of income, to the extent of depreciation expense, is the country where the deduction was claimed, and the source of any remaining income is determined by where title transfers).

5. Personal property other than those listed in 1 through 4 above is foreign if attributable to the seller's foreign office and is subject to a foreign income tax of at least 10 percent.

6. Personal property (other than Subpart F income, discussed later in this chapter) by a nonresident will be U.S. if attributable to a U.S. office (this rule is inapplicable if the property is inventory sold for use outside the United States and a foreign office of the seller materially participated in the sale).

These sourcing rules apply to all sales by foreign persons (other than controlled foreign corporations, discussed later in this chapter).

Very different sourcing rules apply to transportation income from an aircraft or a ship that begins or ends its trip in the United States. These earnings are divided equally between U.S. and foreign source income.[7]

In the past, some taxpayers were able to convert U.S. income to foreign source income by funneling it through a foreign corporation, especially one in a low-tax country. All dividends and interest received by U.S. shareholders from this corporation qualified as foreign source income. But the foreign source designation is limited when (1) at least 50% of the voting power or total stock value of the foreign corporation is owned by U.S. shareholders, and (2) at least 10% of the corporation's income is from U.S. sources.[8] When these two requirements are met, a pro rata amount of the dividends and interest received is U.S. source income.[9]

FOREIGN TAX CREDITS OR DEDUCTIONS

LO.2

Identify the trade-offs between the foreign tax credit, the foreign tax deduction, and, when applicable, the foreign income exclusions for individuals.

Originally, taxes paid to foreign governments were only deductible in the same manner as U.S. state and local taxes.[10] But since 1921, individuals have been able to elect to claim foreign income taxes applicable to U.S. includible income as either an itemized deduction or a credit.[11] (See discussion later in this chapter for corporations.) Elections are made annually by filing Form 1116 for the credit or Schedule A for the deduction. Foreign taxes applicable to excludable U.S. income do not qualify for either a deduction or a credit.[12]

In most instances, a tax credit provides more benefit than a deduction. However, a deduction may be more advantageous if, when compared to worldwide income, the foreign effective rate of tax is high and foreign income is small.

---

[6] § 865(a).

[7] § 863(c)(2).

[8] § 904(g).

[9] § 904(g)(1).

[10] §§ 164(a) and 275(a). Foreign income taxes include amounts paid to national and local foreign governments.

[11] §§ 164(a), 901(b), and 903. For a checklist of qualifying taxes in various countries, see Commerce Clearing House, *Standard Federal Tax Reporter*, ¶27,826.318 (after § 901).

[12] § 911(d)(6).

Foreign Tax Credit Limitations

When the foreign effective rate of tax does not exceed the U.S. effective rate, foreign taxes may be claimed as a credit without limit. However, when the foreign tax rate exceeds the U.S. rate, the foreign tax credit is limited to the U.S. effective rate.[13] That is, foreign taxes may be used to offset U.S. taxes up to but not beyond the amount of U.S. taxes attributable to foreign source income. For purposes of the foreign tax credit limitation, worldwide taxable income is computed without any deduction for personal exemptions.[14] If taxable income has already been determined, it is therefore necessary to add back the exemptions. The computation of the foreign tax credit and limitations for individuals is shown in Exhibit 13-1.

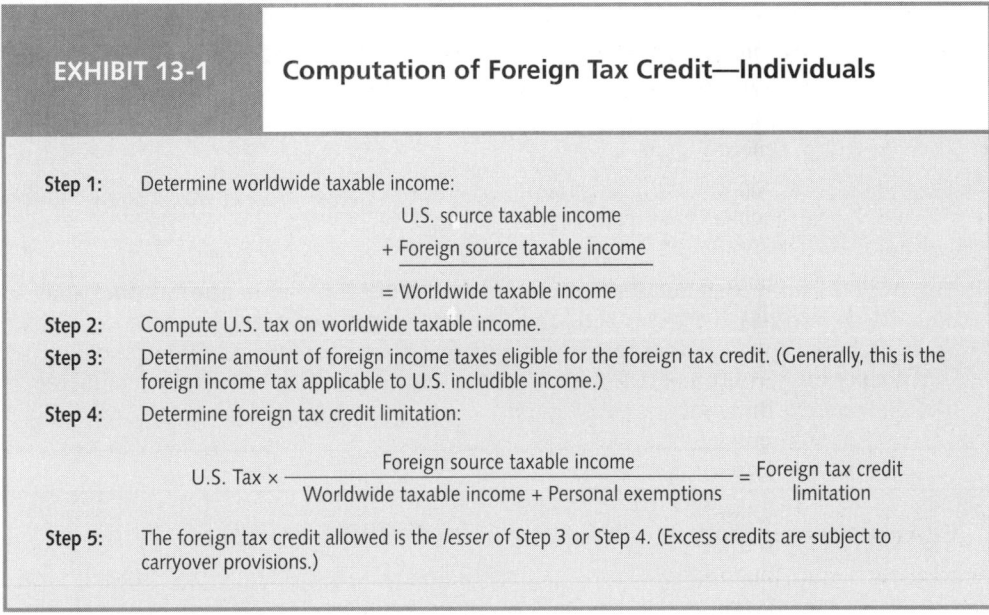

EXHIBIT 13-1	Computation of Foreign Tax Credit—Individuals

Step 1: Determine worldwide taxable income:

$$\text{U.S. source taxable income} + \text{Foreign source taxable income} = \text{Worldwide taxable income}$$

Step 2: Compute U.S. tax on worldwide taxable income.

Step 3: Determine amount of foreign income taxes eligible for the foreign tax credit. (Generally, this is the foreign income tax applicable to U.S. includible income.)

Step 4: Determine foreign tax credit limitation:

$$\text{U.S. Tax} \times \frac{\text{Foreign source taxable income}}{\text{Worldwide taxable income} + \text{Personal exemptions}} = \text{Foreign tax credit limitation}$$

Step 5: The foreign tax credit allowed is the *lesser* of Step 3 or Step 4. (Excess credits are subject to carryover provisions.)

In determining foreign source taxable income, deductions that are directly related to U.S. source income are allocated 100% to the U.S. source income. For example, investment advisory fees paid to manage a portfolio of U.S. securities would be considered a deduction that is directly related to U.S. source income. Deductions that are more general in nature and not definitely related to a specific class of gross income must be apportioned between U.S. source and foreign income. Most deductions are considered to be general in nature. If you itemize deductions, medical expenses, general sales taxes and real estate taxes on your home would fall into the general category. If you do not itemize, your standard deduction would be considered a general deduction subject to apportionment.

The calculation of the foreign tax credit limitation and the interaction of high foreign tax rates and the choice of taking foreign taxes as a credit or a deduction are demonstrated in *Examples 2* and *3* below.

Example 2

For 2016, you and your spouse have worldwide adjusted gross income of $100,000 including $20,000 of dividend income from foreign sources and $80,000 of income from U.S. sources. You paid $2,000 of withholding tax on the dividend income. You file a joint return and claim two $4,050 exemptions and itemized deductions (not including the foreign tax paid) of $13,000. None of the $13,000 of itemized deductions are directly related to a specific class of gross income.

---

[13] § 904(a).   [14] § 904(b)(1).

A comparison of the total U.S. tax assuming that you claim the $2,000 as a tax credit and the $2,000 as a tax deduction is shown below:

	Tax Credit	Tax Deduction
U.S. source taxable income	$ 80,000.00	$ 80,000.00
Foreign source taxable income	20,000.00	20,000.00
Worldwide adjusted gross income	$100,000.00	$100,000.00
Itemized deductions	(13,000.00)	(15,000.00)
Taxable income before exemptions	$ 87,000.00	$ 85,000.00
Personal exemptions	(8,100.00)	(8,100.00)
Worldwide taxable income	$ 78,900.00	$ 76,900.00
U.S. tax before the foreign tax credit	11,267.50	10,767.50
Foreign tax credit	(2,000.00)*	
U.S. tax	$ 9,267.50	$ 10,767.50

*Foreign tax credit limitation = $11,267.50 U.S. tax × $17,400/$87,000 = $2,253.50

Because the itemized deductions are not directly related to any item of income, they must be apportioned between U.S. and foreign source gross income (80% to U.S. Source income and 20% to foreign source income). Accordingly, $2,600 of the itemized deductions ($13,000 × 0.20) are allocated to the foreign source income reducing foreign source taxable income to $17,400.

Example 3

In 2016, you receive investment income of $5,000 from a foreign country which imposes a tax of $3,500 on that income. In addition to this foreign source income, you have $56,000 of taxable U.S. source income. You are single, entitled to one $4,050 exemption and have other itemized deductions of $7,000 (not including the foreign taxes of $3,500). None of $7,000 of itemized deductions are specifically related to the U.S. or foreign source income.

A comparison of the total U.S. tax assuming that you claim the $3,500 as a tax credit and the $3,500 as a tax deduction is shown below:

	Tax Credit	Tax Deduction
U.S. source income	$ 56,000.00	$ 56,000.00
Foreign source income	5,000.00	5,000.00
Worldwide adjusted gross income	$61,000.00	$61,000.00
Itemized deductions	(7,000.00)	(10,500.00)
Taxable income before exemptions	$ 54,000.00	$ 50,500.00
Personal exemptions	(4,050.00)	(4,050.00)
Worldwide taxable income	$ 49,950.00	$ 46,450.00
U.S. tax before the foreign tax credit	8,258.75	7,383.75
Foreign tax credit	(676.95)*	
U.S. tax	$ 7,581.81	$ 7,383.75

*Foreign tax credit limitation = $8,258.75 U.S. tax × $4,426.23/$54,000 = $676.95

U.S taxes are lower by $198.05 by taking the foreign taxes as a deduction rather than a credit.

Because the itemized deductions are not directly related to any item of income, they must be apportioned between U.S. and foreign source gross income (91.8033% to U.S Source income and 8.1967% to foreign source income). Accordingly, $573.77 of the itemized deductions ($7,000 × 0.081967) are allocated to the foreign source income reducing foreign source taxable income to $4,426.23.

Separate foreign tax credit computations must be made for passive income and so called general-category income which includes all other types of income. Foreign taxes paid on income in the passive "basket" may not be used to offset U.S. taxes on income in the other "basket."

Example 4

Amber is a U.S. citizen with foreign source investment income of $10,000 on which $2,500 of foreign income tax was paid. Amber also worked abroad for three months and earned a salary of $40,000 on which no foreign tax was paid due to a treaty provision between the U.S. and the foreign country.

Amber paid U.S. tax of $2,000 on the investment income and U.S. tax of $10,000 on the foreign salary. While she can use $2,000 of the foreign tax paid to offset the U.S. taxes on her investment income, the remaining $500 cannot be used to offset U.S. tax in the general category basket (her salary). Instead, it will be carried over and can be sued to offset passive category income taxes in the future.

Individuals who have only passive foreign income may elect to be exempt from the foreign tax credit limitation if their foreign taxes eligible for the foreign tax credit do not exceed $300 ($600 for a joint return).[15] The exemption is only allowed for foreign taxes for which the taxpayer received a payee statement (e.g., similar to a U.S. Form 1099). If a taxpayer makes this election, a foreign tax credit is allowed for the full amount of foreign taxes paid, and no foreign tax credit limitation applies. In *Examples 2* and *3* above, even though the taxpayers have passive foreign income, they may not elect to be exempt from the foreign tax credit limitation since the foreign taxes exceed $300 and $600 respectively.

Excess foreign tax credits may be carried to years when the reverse situation exists (i.e., years in which foreign tax credits are less than U.S. taxes on foreign source income). The carryover of credits is limited to a one-year carryback and a ten-year carryforward.[16] For example, a 2016 excess credit is carried first to 2015. Any part of the credit not used in 2015 is carried to 2017. This process continues into 2018, 2019, 2020, and through 2026. Any 2016 carryover not used before 2026 is lost. However, if a taxpayer with passive foreign income no greater than $300 ($600 if married filing jointly) elects to be exempt from the foreign tax credit for a particular year, no foreign taxes may be carried to or from that year.

FOREIGN INCOME EXCLUSIONS FOR INDIVIDUALS

The intent of legislation affecting taxation of individuals working abroad is to encourage U.S.-based multinational corporations to employ U.S. expatriates in their foreign operations. One of the expected advantages is that foreign operations managed by U.S. citizens will purchase more goods and services from the United States.

Qualifying individuals (those who meet either the bona fide resident or the physical presence test discussed later) have three special tax benefits available to them. They may elect to exclude, subject to statutory limitations, their:

1. Foreign-earned income,
2. Employer-provided foreign housing income, and
3. Employer-provided housing and meals in company foreign camps.

All three elections are made separately, but individuals may not obtain tax benefits from the same income under more than one of the exclusions. These exclusions are for income tax only, and, if self-employed, do not reduce the amount subject to the self-employment tax.

Foreign-Earned Income

The election with the most potential benefit allows qualifying taxpayers to exclude their foreign-earned income from personal services, subject to an annual limitation. The maximum exclusion is indexed for inflation and for 2016 is $101,300.[17]

---

[15] § 904(j).

[16] § 904(c) and Rev. Rul. 75-268, 1975-2 C.B. 294.

[17] §§ 911(b)(2)(A), (D), and Reg. § 1.911-1 and Rev. Proc. 2015-53.

> ### Example 5
>
> W, a U.S. citizen, meets the bona fide resident test while employed in Belgium. During 2016, she receives a salary of $65,000 and interest income from a Belgian bank of $5,000. W may elect to exclude the $65,000 earned foreign income but not the $5,000 unearned foreign income. If W received additional compensation of $40,000, she may exclude $101,300 but not the remaining $3,700 of compensation ($65,000 + $40,000 − $101,300) nor the $5,000 of interest income.

Limits are applied to each qualifying taxpayer regardless of marital status. Thus, the 2016 limit for either a husband or a wife is $101,300. If a taxpayer does not qualify for the exclusion the entire year, the exclusion is prorated on a daily basis.[18]

> ### Example 6
>
> R, a U.S. citizen, met the physical presence test while employed in Italy through October 31, 2016. R was employed in the United States the last two months of the year. Thus, she was employed in Italy 305 days and in the United States 61 days (2016 is a leap year). R's salary earned in Italy was $95,000, and her salary earned in the United States was $20,000. R's maximum exclusion is $84,417 ($101,300 × [305 ÷ 366]), which means she has $30,583 ($95,000 − $84,417 + $20,000) includible income for U.S. tax purposes.

Employer-Provided Foreign Housing Income

Many companies provide either housing or cash as a housing allowance for their expatriate employees. Employees living in employer-provided housing must include their foreign housing costs. (Note the contrast with the exclusion for certain employer-provided housing in the United States.) Individuals, however, are able to elect one of two exclusions applicable to this employee benefit. First, employer-provided housing income qualifies for the annual foreign-earned income exclusion discussed above. Alternatively, individuals may exclude a portion of their employer-provided housing income under a second election available to them. Only the excess of housing costs over a base amount may be excluded. Specifically, the second exclusion is limited to the housing cost amount, computed as follows:

1. Qualifying foreign housing expenses (limited to a maximum of 30% of the foreign earned income exclusion amount), less

2. the base housing amount, which is 16% of the foreign earned income exclusion limitation, prorated on a daily basis if the taxpayer does not qualify for the exclusion the entire year. The base housing amount for 2016 is $16,208 ($101,300 × 16%), or $44.41 per day.[19]

The maximum housing cost exclusion for 2016 is $14,182 computed as follows:

Qualifying foreign housing costs:	
2016 limit: 30% × Foreign earned income exclusion $101,300	$30,390
− Base housing amount:	
16% × Foreign earned income exclusion $101,300	(16,208)
Maximum exclusion: Housing cost amount for 2016	$14,182

As can be seen by examining the formula, the maximum exclusion is simply the product of the foreign earned income exclusion and 14% ($101,300 × [30% − 16% = 14%] = $14,182). Note that higher housing maximums are allows for certain high-cost foreign locations.[20]

Qualifying foreign housing expenses include all reasonable costs (i.e., not lavish or extravagant under the circumstances) incurred directly or as a cash allowance to house an

---

[18] § 911(b)(2)(A) and Reg. § 1.911-3(d).

[19] § 911(c)(1) and Reg. § 1.911-4.

[20] For example, in Notice 2015-33, the IRS sets the 2015 limitation on housing expenses to $108,000 in Moscow and to $114,300 in Hong Kong.

employee and also the spouse and all dependents living with the employee.[21] Examples of acceptable expenses are rent or the fair rental value of employer-owned housing, insurance, utilities, repairs, and other costs related to the housing and its furnishings, plus parking fees and local telephone charges. Acceptable expenses do not include capital expenditures, depreciation, domestic help, or expenses that can be claimed as itemized deductions, such as interest and property taxes.[22]

Example 7

C, a U.S. citizen, meets the bona fide resident test while working in Spain. During 2016, he receives a salary of $75,000, employer-provided housing costing $18,000, and other foreign employee allowances of $31,000. C's foreign-earned income totals $124,000 ($75,000 + $18,000 + $31,000). If he makes both elections, he may exclude $103,092 ($75,000 + $31,000 = $106,000 but limited to the foreign earned income exclusion of $101,300) plus $1,792 housing cost amount ($18,000 − [16% of $101,300 = $16,208]). Thus, C's includible foreign-earned income is $20,908 ($124,000 − the two exclusions of $101,300 and $1,792). Note that the $1,792 foreign housing cost exclusion is less than the maximum foreign housing cost exclusion of $14,182 for 2016.

Example 8

Mike, a U.S. citizen, works in Brazil for all of 2016. During the year, he earns $115,000 of foreign income and incurs qualified housing costs of $35,000 which exceeds the 30% maximum qualified housing expense amount of $30,390 (30% of $101,300). Accordingly, he is eligible for the maximum housing cost exclusion of $14,182 and a maximum combined exclusion of $115,482. Therefore, Mike can exclude the entire $115,000 of foreign earned income.

In most instances, the housing must be near the foreign work place, but there is one exception. If living conditions in the area are dangerous, unhealthy, or otherwise adverse, housing expenses also include money spent to maintain a separate foreign home for the spouse and dependents.[23]

The Code also provides that taxpayers who pay qualifying housing expenses and are not reimbursed by an employer may deduct the expenses for AGI. This deduction, however, may not exceed the taxpayer's includible foreign-earned income.[24] Any excess expenses may be carried forward one year and deducted to the extent there is taxable foreign-earned income in that year.[25] Regulations extend this provision for a deduction to the self-employed, to employees not receiving employer-provided housing, and to employees with only a portion of their housing costs provided by their employers.[26] According to these regulations, employees may deduct housing expenses they paid (subject to the limitations) that are not attributable to the employer.

Employer Foreign Camps

The third special exclusion is available to employees living in employer-provided camps, generally located in hardship areas. These individuals qualify as living and eating on the business premises at the convenience of their employer. As a result, all of their employer-provided meals and lodging are excludable from income.[27]

Tax Bracket

When an individual excludes income under § 911, the excluded amount is included in determining what tax bracket applies to the individual's taxable income. This generally results in a much higher tax on the included income.[28]

---

[21] § 911(c)(2)(A).

[22] Reg. § 1.911-4(b).

[23] § 911(c)(2)(B).

[24] §§ 911(c)(3)(A) and (B).

[25] § 911(c)(3)(C) and Reg. § 1.911-4(e)(2).

[26] Reg. §§ 1.911-4(d) and (e).

[27] § 119(c).

[28] § 911(f).

QUALIFYING INDIVIDUALS

Only individuals whose tax homes are in a foreign country qualify for the foreign-earned income and the housing cost exclusions.[29] In addition, these taxpayers must meet either (1) the bona fide resident or (2) the physical presence test. U.S. citizens may qualify under either test, except that income earned within a country subject to federal travel restrictions does not qualify for either exclusion.[30] U.S. residents who are citizens of another country qualify only under the physical presence test, or, if a tax treaty with their country provides, they may qualify under the bona fide resident test.

Bona Fide Resident

The bona fide resident test requires that, during an uninterrupted period that includes an entire tax year, individuals must accomplish the following:

1. Maintain bona fide resident status in one or more foreign countries.
2. Have foreign-earned income from personal services.
3. Receive the foreign income no later than the year following the service.
4. Be paid by an entity other than the U.S. government or one of its agencies or instrumentalities.

Once the bona fide resident test is met, the entire uninterrupted period of foreign residency qualifies for the exclusion provisions.

Bona fide resident status is not jeopardized if taxpayers continue to own a home in the United States or make brief business or personal trips to the United States.[31] However, there must be a clear intent to return to the foreign tax home or a new one without unreasonable delay. A bona fide foreign resident generally is expected to work outside the United States for an extended or indefinite period and establish a permanent family residence in the work area. An intention to return eventually to the United States is not relevant to the test. Residency status is denied those taxpayers who make statements to authorities in the foreign country that they are not residents, and consequently are exempted from being taxed as residents of that country.[32]

Physical Presence

Individuals unable to meet the above test may be able to qualify for foreign-earned income and employer-provided housing exclusions under the physical presence test. In addition to their tax home being in a foreign country, individuals must have been present in one or more foreign countries for at least 330 days during any 12 consecutive months.[33]

Taxpayers relying on the physical presence test may be challenged by the IRS on the basis that an assignment of less than one year is temporary.[34] At stake is the fact that a foreign residence cannot qualify as a tax home when it is temporary. Therefore, anyone expecting to work abroad for more than one year may be presumed to have established a foreign tax home.

Unlike the bona fide resident test, exclusions under the physical presence test apply only to those months that fall into one or more of the qualifying 12-month periods. Taxpayers are allowed considerable freedom in selecting the 12 months. They may be any consecutive 12 months, and two periods may overlap.

[29] §§ 911(d)(1) and (3) and Reg. § 1.911-2(c).

[30] § 911(d)(8) and Rev. Rul. 91-58, 1991-2 C.B. 340, 92-63, 1992-2 C.B. 195, and 95-63, 1995-2 C.B. 85.

[31] Reg. §§ 1.911-2(b) and (c).

[32] § 911(d)(5).

[33] § 911(d)(1)(B) and Reg. § 1.911-2(d).

[34] § 162(a)(2).

Example 9

M, a single U.S. citizen, is transferred to Vienna, Austria on March 31, 2015 by her company for an indefinite period that is expected to last more than one year. She establishes residency in Vienna, where she remains except for a two-week visit to the United States in August 2015. Unexpectedly, M's company transfers her back to the United States on May 1, 2016. She prepares her taxes on the calendar year. M does not meet the bona fide resident test because she was not a resident of Austria for an entire tax year. However, she does meet the physical presence test because she was in a foreign country more than 330 days during 12 consecutive months. In fact, she qualifies for the entire 13 months because she has two qualifying 12-month periods, even though they overlap. Her first 12-month period is April 2015 through March 2016 and her second 12-month period is May 2015 through April 2016. As a result, she may elect either or both of the foreign income exclusions for the entire 13 months.

Example 10

Refer to *Example 9,* but assume M was a resident of Vienna from March 31, 2015 until January 3, 2017 and made a total of four two-week (14 days each) trips to the United States. The trips were made in August 2015 and in January, March, and July 2016. M does not qualify under the physical presence test since she was not present in one or more foreign countries at least 330 days during any 12-month period. (For example, from April 2015 through March 2016 is 366 days (2016 is a leap year). M was in the United States for 42 days during this 12-month period. Therefore, she was physically present in a foreign country for only 324 days during this 12-month period.) However, M qualifies under the bona fide resident test because she was a resident of a foreign country during all of 2016. Since the bona fide resident test is met, M may elect the foreign income exclusions for the entire period of residency (i.e., from March 31, 2015 through January 3, 2017).

There is one exception to both the bona fide resident and the physical presence tests. If the tests are not met solely because the taxpayer was forced to leave the foreign tax home because of war, civil unrest, or other adverse condition, the minimum time requirement may be waived. Such waivers are granted by the Treasury based on information provided by the State Department.[35]

ELECTIONS TO EXCLUDE

Taxpayers have two options regarding their foreign earned income: exclusion or inclusion. Instead of excluding the income as discussed above, the taxpayer could elect to include the foreign earned income in gross income and claim a credit for the foreign taxes paid. While inclusion makes the income potentially taxable, this alternative may be more beneficial than exclusion. A greater benefit may occur if the individual's foreign earned income far exceeds the excludible amount and the foreign taxes paid exceed the U.S. tax paid on the amount excluded. It should be emphasized that an election under either exclusion provision is applicable for all future taxable years unless revoked by the taxpayer.[36] The election remains in effect but dormant if the taxpayer returns to the United States for an extended period. Although IRS permission to revoke the election is not necessary, it is advisable, because all new elections require IRS consent. If the revocation is made with permission, the IRS may grant the new election regardless of when it is made. Otherwise, a new election is not available for five years.

---

[35] § 911(d)(4), and Rev. Procs. 94-31, 1994-1 C.B. 625, 97-51, I.R.B. 1997-45, p. 9, 98-38, I.R.B. 1998-27, p. 29, 99-20 I.R.B. 1999-14, p. 7, 2000-14, I.R.B. 2000-18, p. 960, 2001-27, I.R.B. 2001-19, 2002-20, I.R.B. 2002-14, p. 732, 2003-26, I.R.B. 2003-13, and 2004-17, I.R.B. 2004-10.

[36] § 911(e) and Reg. § 1.911-7(a).

Special Rules Affecting Deductions, Credits, and Exclusions

Taxpayers electing either the annual foreign-earned income exclusion or the housing cost amount exclusion are prevented from obtaining double benefits.[37] First, this means that individuals may not elect two or more exclusions for the same income. For example, individuals may not elect to exclude employer-provided housing under both the housing cost amount and the annual exclusion provisions. In addition, the total amount excluded may not exceed foreign-earned income. Second, the Code provides that a portion of the taxpayers' deductions and credits must be allocated to the excluded foreign-earned income.

Expenses, losses and other normally deductible items that are allocated to the excluded income are not deductible. Similarly, the percentage of credits attributable to the excluded income is not allowed. These rules do not apply to items such as exemptions, alimony, charitable contributions, medical expenses, mortgage interest, real estate taxes on a personal residence or contributions to qualified retirement plans.

Allocations are made in two steps. First, all items directly related to any type of income must be allocated to that income (e.g., rental expenses are allocated to rental income). Second, those items not directly related to any type of income are allocated using the following formula: deduction × excluded foreign-earned income/total foreign-earned income. When the item to be allocated is a credit, the same formula applies except it is based on net amounts. Net means that all related deductible expenses are subtracted from both the numerator and the denominator first. Items that may be subject to the formula include moving expenses (to the foreign location and between two foreign countries), unreimbursed employee business expenses, foreign tax credits, child care credits, and the exclusion for meals and lodging provided for the convenience of employers. Generally, expenses incurred in moving back to the United States are deductible against U.S. source income and therefore are not included in the allocation formula. This is true even though employer reimbursement for these moves may qualify as compensation for past services abroad and thus as foreign source income. As noted above, the result of the allocation requirement is that a portion of the deductions and credits may not be claimed by taxpayers against their includible income. Consequently, the tax benefit of the exclusion is diminished.

Example 11

F, a U.S. citizen, lives and works in London. He is a bona fide resident of England for all of 2016. For the year, he had $202,600 of foreign earned income and he claimed the maximum exclusion of $101,300 (2016). He also had $5,000 of unreimbursed employee business expenses. Only $2,500 of the expenses are potentially deductible since 50% of his income was excluded ($5,000 × $101,300/$202,600 = $2,500).

The rules governing the payment of employment taxes require special consideration. The U.S. may have agreements with foreign countries to eliminate dual coverage and dual contributions (i.e., taxes) to Social Security systems for the same work. As a general rule, self-employed persons normally are covered by the Social Security system of the country where they reside. For a U.S. citizen the payment of self-employment taxes are generally the same whether the taxpayer is living in the U.S. or abroad. Note, however, that foreign earned income that is excluded for income tax purposes is still subject to self-employment tax.

There are a number of other tax rules that may impact a U.S. citizen who has foreign earned income. Many of these are summarized in an IRS publication, *Tax Guide for U.S. Citizens and Resident Aliens Abroad*.[38]

In addition, rules governing foreign moving expenses are more liberal than those covering moves within the United States.[39] Moving expenses are extended to include moving household goods to and from storage, and storage costs.

---

[37] § 911(d)(6).

[38] *IRS Publication 54* (available at www.irs.gov/publications/).

[39] § 217(h).

DUE DATE OF THE RETURN, EXTENSIONS

The tax law provides some relief from the basic filing requirements for taxpayers outside the U.S. For eligible taxpayers, an extension for filing income tax returns and paying the tax is automatically granted to the 15th day of the sixth month following the close of the tax year.[40] For individual taxpayers using a calendar year for reporting, the extended due date becomes June 15. In effect, an automatic two-month extension is allowed. Included among eligible taxpayers are U.S. citizens and resident aliens who on the regular due date either (1) live outside the U.S. and whose tax home is also outside of the U.S. or (2) are members of the military on duty outside the U.S. For this purpose tax home has the same meaning as that relating to the deductibility of travel expenses while away from home. For joint filers, only one of the spouses needs to qualify. To obtain the automatic two-month extension, taxpayers must attach a statement to the return explaining which of the two situations listed above qualify them for the extension.

Those who qualify for the automatic two-month extension can also request the normal six-month of extension using Form 4868 (running from the due date of the return). The form must be filed by the due date of the return, in this case June 15 for the calendar year taxpayer qualifying for the two-month extension. Note, however, that the two month extension and the six month extension start at the same time (e.g., April 15) and run concurrently. So by filing Form 4868 by June 15, the extended due date becomes October 15. In other words, the taxpayer cannot get an extension for eight months by filing Form 4868. Taxpayers who are filing for an automatic extension on or before the expiration of their two-month extension are instructed to clearly note across the top of their form their special status. While the automatic two month extension postpones the payment of the tax, interest still must be paid. Interest on any unpaid tax from the regular due date (e.g., April 15) to the date paid also must be paid.

In addition to the extensions above, taxpayers waiting to determine if they will meet the physical presence test may obtain an extension to the date they expect to meet the test. This extension is obtained using Form 2350 and normally extends the due date to 30 days beyond the date on which the taxpayer expects to qualify. Form 2350 must be filed by the due date of the return (e.g., June 15 for calendar year taxpayers who qualify for the automatic two-month extension).[41] If returns are filed prior to qualifying for the exclusions, computations must be based on the assumption that the tests will not be met. Refund claims may be filed when the tests are met.

Finally, in addition to the six month extension, taxpayers who are out of the country can request a discretionary two-month extension of time to file their returns (e.g., December 15 for calendar year taxpayers).

Taxation of U.S.-Based Corporations

When a U.S. corporation engages in international operations, new dimensions are added to the already difficult subject of taxation. As might be expected, taxing policies of each country differ in the types of taxes, rate structures, tax bases, and special provisions that are available. Some of these are modified through bilateral treaties negotiated with individual countries. In addition, the U.S. Internal Revenue Code contains numerous options for taxation of a corporation's foreign source income.

A company, for example, may find it beneficial to establish one or more separately taxed entities for its sales to foreign customers. In some instances, it has been to the company's benefit to establish a tax-haven corporation in a country that is a U.S. possession. A company may choose to generate sales through a foreign subsidiary or branch located near the customer. Although numerous factors must be considered when deciding which entity should make the sale to the foreign customer, it is essential that companies adopt a policy of systematic tax planning.

LO.3
Understand the taxation of U.S.-based corporations' foreign source income.

---

[40] Reg. § 1.6081-5(a).

[41] *IRS Publication 54* (available at www.irs.gov/publications/).

FOREIGN TAX CREDITS OR DEDUCTIONS

All direct foreign taxes actually paid (or accrued) by a U.S. corporation and all foreign taxes deemed paid (or accrued) by a U.S. corporation may be claimed as either a business deduction or a tax credit.[42] Generally, it is more advantageous to a corporation to use the foreign tax credit rather than a foreign tax deduction. Direct foreign income taxes paid include foreign withholding taxes on dividends. Foreign taxes deemed paid include those paid indirectly by the U.S. corporation on foreign source income (i.e., foreign income taxes paid by the subsidiary). In order to claim foreign taxes indirectly paid, the U.S. corporation must own at least 10% of a foreign corporation's voting stock.[43] The foreign tax credit calculations for a corporation differ from the calculations for an individual because of the foreign taxes deemed paid. The foreign source income is grossed up so that the U.S. includible income is the foreign income plus all foreign taxes deemed paid by the corporation.[44] The computation of the foreign tax credit for corporations is shown in Exhibit 13-2.

EXHIBIT 13-2	**Computation and Application of Foreign Tax Credit—Corporations**

Step 1: Determine foreign taxes actually paid by the U.S. corporation. (Generally, this is a portion of an actual distribution that is withheld by the foreign country.) This is the direct foreign tax credit.

Step 2: Determine foreign taxes deemed paid. This applies only when an actual dividend is paid by a foreign corporation to a U.S. corporation and the U.S. corporation owns at least 10% of the foreign corporation's voting stock on the date of the distribution.

$$\text{Foreign taxes deemed paid} = \frac{\text{Dividend}}{\text{Accumulated earnings profits (AEP)} \atop \text{(after 1986)}} \times {\text{Total foreign income taxes paid or} \atop \text{accrued by the foreign corporation} \atop \text{foreign corporation (after 1986)}}$$

Step 3: The foreign source dividend of the U.S. corporation is increased (grossed up) by the foreign taxes deemed paid (see *Step 2*).

Step 4: Add the grossed-up foreign dividend to U.S. source income to get worldwide taxable income.

Step 5: Determine U.S. tax on the worldwide taxable income.

Step 6: Add the results of *Step 1* (direct foreign tax credit) and *Step 2* (deemed paid foreign income tax credit) to get the total foreign tax credit before limitations. The foreign tax credit is deducted from U.S. tax in determining U.S. tax liability.

---

[42] §§ 901(b) and 903. For a checklist of qualifying taxes in various countries, see Commerce Clearing House, *Standard Federal Tax Reporter*, ¶27,826.318 (after § 901). Computations for foreign taxes deemed paid are not available to noncorporate taxpayers.

[43] § 902(a).

[44] § 78 and Reg. § 1.902-1(b)(1)(iii). The effect of the gross up is to treat the U.S. taxation of a U.S. corporation of its foreign subsidiary (if all earnings were currently distributed) somewhat similarly to the U.S. taxation of a U.S. corporation on the operations of its foreign branch.

Example 12

U.S. Parent, Inc. has taxable income in the current year from U.S. sources of $500,000. Its wholly owned Canadian subsidiary (which was acquired at the beginning of the year) has foreign source taxable income of $80,000, pays $16,000 in Canadian income taxes (20% rate), and therefore has an after-tax income of $64,000 ($80,000 – $16,000), from which a dividend of $26,000 is declared and distributed. Since the dividend is payable to a non-Canadian shareholder, it is subject to a 15% dividend-withholding tax of $3,900 ($26,000 dividend × 15% withholding rate). Parent receives $22,100 ($26,000 dividend – $3,900 withholding). Parent's direct foreign tax credit is $3,900 (Canadian withholding). The amount of foreign taxes deemed paid by Parent is $6,500 ([$26,000 dividend received ÷ $64,000 AE&P] × $16,000 total foreign taxes paid). Therefore, the total foreign tax credit is $10,400 ($3,900 + $6,500). (Assume all dollar amounts are expressed in U.S. dollars.)

Foreign source dividend	$26,000	
Foreign income taxes deemed paid	6,500	
Grossed-up foreign dividend		$ 32,500
U.S. source taxable income		500,000
Worldwide taxable income		$532,500
U.S. tax (taxable income × 34%)		$181,050
Foreign tax credit:		
Direct foreign tax credit	$ 3,900	
Foreign taxes deemed paid	6,500	
Total foreign tax credit		(10,400)
U.S. tax liability		$170,650

In *Example 12,* the foreign subsidiary was acquired in the current year, so the accumulated earnings and profits for the subsidiary was equal to the current year's earnings and profits. However, the computation of the foreign taxes deemed paid (Exhibit 13-2, Step 2) requires the use of accumulated earnings and profits.[45]

Example 13

A wholly owned foreign subsidiary has the following information (the foreign subsidiary was acquired at the beginning of 2015):

	Dividend	E&P	Foreign Income Taxes
2015	$ 0	$100,000	$20,000
2016	44,000	120,000	40,000
Total		$220,000	$60,000

The foreign income taxes deemed paid are $12,000 ([$44,000 dividend received divided by $220,000 accumulated earnings and profits] × $60,000 total foreign income taxes paid). Note that if the computation could be based on current year amounts, the taxes deemed paid would have been $14,667 ([$44,000 divided by $120,000] × $40,000).

A company with decreasing effective foreign tax rates would have the reverse of the situation illustrated in the example above. That is, a higher foreign tax credit is allowed when the effective foreign tax rate is higher for all years than it is for the current year.

Example 14

USA Corporation owns F Corporation, a foreign subsidiary that reports the following (the foreign subsidiary was acquired at the beginning of 2015):

	Tax	Dividend	Foreign Income E&P
2015	$ 0	$100,000	$40,000
2016	44,000	120,000	30,000
Total		$220,000	$70,000

The foreign income taxes deemed paid are $14,000 ([$44,000 dividend received ÷ $220,000 accumulated earnings and profits] × $70,000 total foreign income taxes paid). Note that *if* the computation were based on current year amounts, the taxes deemed paid would have been $11,000 ([$44,000 ÷ $120,000] × $30,000).

The rule governing foreign taxes deemed paid by a U.S. parent corporation extends beyond the wholly owned foreign subsidiary. In addition, if a 10% or more owned foreign corporation (first-tier) owns at least 10% of another foreign corporation (second-tier), and the second-tier corporation owns at least 10% of another foreign corporation (third-tier), a percentage of foreign taxes incurred by all of these corporations may qualify as a foreign tax credit or deduction. The indirect foreign tax credit is available for second-tier through sixth-tier corporations. However, a first-tier corporation must meet the ownership test before a second-tier corporation can qualify. Similarly, all higher tier corporations must meet the test before a sixth-tier or any other tier corporation can qualify. One further requirement is that the U.S. corporation must own indirectly at least 5% of the foreign corporation in order to claim a share of its taxes. As in the 10% requirement, the 5% ownership test must be met at the first-tier before the second-tier can qualify, and at the first- and second-tier before the third-tier can qualify and so forth to the sixth-tier. In all instances, the ownership interest must be in the form of outstanding voting stock.[46]

Example 15

X is a U.S. corporation. A, B, and C are foreign corporations. X owns 40% of A (first-tier), A owns 30% of B (second-tier), and B owns 80% of C (third-tier). The 10% test is met at all levels of ownership. In addition, X has an indirect ownership of at least 5% of each tier, determined as follows:

X owns 40% × 30% = 12% indirectly of B

X owns 12% × 80% = 9.6% indirectly of C

Thus, X may claim a portion of the foreign taxes incurred by A, B, and C. If, however, B owned 35% of C instead of 80%:

X owns 12% × 35% = 4% indirectly of C

In this situation, X may claim a portion of the foreign taxes incurred by A and B but not by C. If A only owned 8% of B, the 10% test is not met between A and B. This breaks the chain of required ownership and means that foreign taxes paid by B and C would not be deemed paid by X.

---

[46] § 902(b).

Examples 12, 13, 14, and *15* deal with a foreign subsidiary. If the foreign operation is a branch rather than a subsidiary, however, total foreign source income (or loss) and total foreign taxes for the year are included in the calculations regardless of how much income is received currently by the U.S. corporation. When there is more than one subsidiary and/or branch, foreign source income and foreign taxes from all operations in all countries are totaled and calculations are made in the same manner as illustrated in *Examples 11, 12, 13,* and *14.* This is referred to as the overall method. When income is includible from both high and low (compared to the United States) tax rate countries, this approach is particularly beneficial.

There are exceptions to the overall method. The overall method does not apply to most investment interest or dividends. Separate foreign tax credit (FTC) computations must be made for two categories of foreign source income. These foreign income categories (called baskets) are:[47]

1. Passive category income, which in general includes income that qualifies as foreign personal holding company income under Subpart F (discussed later in this chapter), but not if it (a) is subject to a foreign tax rate greater than the highest U.S. rate (e.g., 35% for corporations and 39.6% for individuals). This generally includes interest, dividends, rents, royalties, and annuities. However, it does not include export financing interest income, or rents and royalties from the active conduct of a trade or business.[48]

2. General category income, which includes all items specifically excluded from passive category income, such as highly-taxed income, export financing interest income, and rents and royalties from an active trade or business.

The object of this separate-category legislation is to segregate income (1) when the foreign tax rate is either very high (e.g., oil extraction income) or very low (e.g., dividends), or (2) when the activity can be transferred to a low tax rate country from the United States (e.g., passive income).

Foreign Tax Credit Limitations

As with individuals, the foreign tax credit for corporations is limited to the U.S. taxes attributable to foreign source income. The computation of the foreign tax credit limitation for corporations is the same as the computation for individuals shown in Exhibit 13-1, but without an adjustment for personal exemptions (since a corporation has none).

Tax planning can be very important in obtaining maximum benefits from foreign tax credits. One of the most valuable strategies involves the timing of dividends. If a year-end analysis shows an excess foreign tax credit for the year, it may be useful to have a subsidiary in a low tax rate country declare a dividend. This action gives the U.S. parent corporation access to additional cash without increasing its U.S. tax liability. Similar action is absolutely essential when excess foreign tax credits are about to expire because of the ten-year carry-forward limitation. The reverse situation is even more rewarding. That is, if U.S. taxes on foreign source income exceed foreign tax credits, a dividend declared by a subsidiary in a high tax rate country results in more cash available in the United States both from the dividend received and from a lower U.S. tax liability.

---

[47] § 904(d).   [48] Reg. § 1.904-4(b)(ii).

Example 16

Year-end analysis reveals $100,000 of grossed-up foreign source income, $20,000 of foreign taxes, and $400,000 of U.S. source income. The U.S. effective tax rate of 34% exceeds the foreign effective rate of 20% ($20,000 ÷ $100,000). If a $200,000 grossed-up dividend is made from a subsidiary with qualifying foreign taxes of $82,000, the U.S. tax liability is decreased by $14,000 ($150,000 − $136,000).

	Before Dividend	After Dividend
Foreign source income.	$100,000	$300,000
U.S. source income	400,000	400,000
Taxable income	$500,000	$700,000
U.S. tax (34% × taxable income).	$170,000	$238,000
Foreign tax credit.	(20,000)	(102,000)
U.S. tax liability	$150,000	$136,000

The limitation on foreign tax credits does not apply since the limit of $102,000 ([$300,000 ÷ $700,000] × $238,000) equals total foreign taxes of $102,000 ($20,000 + $82,000). Similar transactions involving other types of income can achieve the same results, but it generally is simpler to use the dividend approach.

Consent Dividends

In some instances, it may not be possible for a foreign subsidiary to declare a cash dividend because it does not have enough available cash or because it is politically impossible or undesirable to transfer currency out of the host country. Although seldom used in the past, a consent dividend can achieve the same effect as a cash dividend on foreign source income, foreign tax credits, and U.S. tax liabilities even though no asset is transferred.[49] The consent dividend allows a U.S. corporation to elect to be taxed currently on all or part of a foreign subsidiary's income. Generally, no withholding tax is assessed on consent dividends, since no assets leave the foreign country. An added tax planning benefit is that the decision to make a consent dividend is not required until the annual tax return is filed. This, of course, is considerably later than decisions for cash dividends, which must be declared by year-end. Because of the complexity of this strategy, however, a company is advised to obtain, when possible, a prior ruling from the tax authorities of both countries.

DIVIDENDS-RECEIVED DEDUCTION

A U.S. corporation may use the dividends-received deduction for dividends from a foreign corporation's post-1986 E&P. The U.S. corporation must own at least 10% of the foreign corporation's voting power and stock value. As might be expected, either (but not both) the dividend deduction or the FTC can be claimed.

---

[49] § 565.

Most industrial nations provide tax incentives to exporters. However, the World Trade Organization (WTO) places restrictions on the type of tax incentives they may use. The primary restriction is that WTO members may not exempt exports from direct taxes. As a result, these nations seek other alternatives. In some instances, tax incentives are given to all businesses regardless of the destination of the goods. Many nations also use the WTO restrictions to justify the depreciation of assets over a period of time considerably shorter than their expected lives. For example, allowances have been made for commercial buildings in enterprise zones to be written off in the first year in the United Kingdom. These special tax provisions for accelerated inventory and depreciation deductions meet WTO requirements since both domestic and export trade companies are treated the same and tax advantages are based on timing differences rather than on exemption from taxes.

> **LO.4**
> Identify the various tax incentives related to the exporting of U.S. products.

Several countries, including members of the European Union, rely extensively on the value added tax (VAT) for their revenues. This tax is levied on products at various stages of production. The actual value added to the product (including raw materials, labor, and profit) is determined at each stage and the tax is based on this increase in value. Since the final portion of the tax is collected at the products' destination, no VAT is charged on export sales. In contrast, a VAT is charged on all domestically sold products regardless of the country of origin. Consequently, the expected effect is that a VAT provides an incentive to export and a disincentive to import. Since a VAT is considered an indirect tax, exempting exports from it does not violate the WTO restrictions.

Without a VAT, the United States has devised other incentives. However, as discussed below, they often have not survived WTO scrutiny. The Foreign Sales Corporation (FSC), created by Congress in 1984 to encourage export activities, was found not to comply with the WTO rule prohibiting illegal subsidies, and was repealed in 2000. Congress replaced the FSC with an equally (or more) generous provision, the Extraterritorial Income Exclusion Act. The European Union requested that the WTO review the new provisions, alleging that the extraterritorial income exclusion, like the FSC, violated the WTO rules. In 2002, the WTO ruled that the extraterritorial income exclusion provisions illegally subsidized American exports, and denied an appeal by the United States. In 2004 Congress repealed the exclusion, phasing out its provisions in 2005 and 2006, with the phaseout completed in 2007. To reduce the impact of the repeal of the exclusion, Congress created a deduction for U.S. manufactured, produced, grown, or extracted property.[50] This deduction is currently 9% of the amount of qualified production activities income. The deduction does not apply to companies that engage solely in sales activities.

THE DOMESTIC INTERNATIONAL SALES CORPORATION

The Domestic International Sales Corporation (DISC) is another type of special corporation designed to yield benefits to U.S. businesses involved in exporting. Prior to 1985, extremely favorable income deferral provisions were available to DISCs, but many of these benefits have been eliminated. The form of DISC that now remains, generally called an interest-charge DISC, is available for corporations that meet certain requirements.[51] Although a limited income deferral provision still exists, interest is due to the government on the tax that would have been due if there were no deferral of income.[52] Shareholders, not the DISC itself, are responsible for any Federal income taxes assessed on DISC income.[53]

Basically, a DISC must be incorporated in the United States, maintain separate accounting records, issue only one class of stock, have a par or stated value for its outstanding stock of at least $2,500 each day of the year, derive at least 95% of its gross receipts from exports, and have at least 95% of its assets be export related.[54] The DISC is not required to be an active corporation.[55] In fact, most serve as commission DISCs, and rarely buy and sell products. Instead, they receive commissions for acting as export agents. Furthermore, DISCs commonly are wholly owned subsidiaries of U.S. corporations, exist only on paper, have no employees, and do not transact business in their own corporate names.

---

[50] § 199.

[51] § 992.

[52] § 995(f)(1).

[53] § 995(a).

[54] § 992(a)(1).

[55] Rev. Rul. 72-166, 1972-1 C.B. 220.

A DISC may be utilized to defer all of its taxable income attributable to no more than $10 million of qualified export gross receipts (QEGR).[56] As stated above, interest is due on the potential tax liability attributable to this deferred income. All DISC income attributable to QEGR in excess of $10 million is includible in the shareholders' income currently.[57]

Tax Incentives for Foreign Operations

U.S.-based multinational corporations may defer U.S. taxes on income of their foreign subsidiaries indefinitely. To accomplish this, however, funds of these subsidiaries cannot be received in the United States either directly or indirectly. Thus, if French subsidiary funds are repatriated to the U.S. parent and immediately reinvested in a Japanese subsidiary, U.S. taxes must be paid on the French income received. Alternately, if the French subsidiary transfers the funds directly to the Japanese subsidiary, the U.S. tax treatment is the same. That is, the funds are deemed to have gone first to the U.S. parent and taxed as a dividend and then reinvested in the Japanese subsidiary. This deemed dividend approach adds significantly to the cost of using funds generated within an organization for its worldwide operations.

One method used by multinationals to reduce worldwide taxes is to shift earnings to countries with favorable tax regimes including low or no taxation on income earned outside their borders. These counties (often referred to as tax havens) consciously create attractive tax advantages for multinational companies, often to the dismay of larger countries in which much of the multinationals economic activity takes place.

The MTC defines a tax haven as a jurisdiction that has no or nominal effective tax on the relevant income and: (i) has laws or practices that prevent effective exchange of information for tax purposes with other governments on taxpayers benefiting from the tax regime; (ii) has tax regime which lacks transparency; (iii) facilitates the establishment of foreign-owned entities without the need for a local substantive presence or prohibits these entities from having any commercial impact on the local economy; (iv) explicitly or implicitly excludes the jurisdiction's resident taxpayers from taking advantage of the tax regime's benefits or prohibits enterprises that benefit from the regime from operating in the jurisdiction's domestic market; or (v) has created a tax regime which is favorable for tax avoidance, based upon an overall assessment of relevant factors, including whether the jurisdiction has a significant untaxed offshore financial/other services sector relative to its overall economy.[58]

THE CONTROLLED FOREIGN CORPORATION

The objective of the Controlled Foreign Corporation (CFC) rules is to prevent corporations from being located in tax-haven countries for the sole purpose of tax avoidance. To accomplish this, the legislation provides that U.S. stockholders be taxed on CFC income when it is earned abroad, regardless of when it is received in the United States. Thus, tax deferral privileges ordinarily granted to foreign corporations are eliminated when CFC requirements are met. Placing tax-haven holding companies at the apex of an organizational structure may now result in a penalty rather than in the tax advantages previously available. Consequently, CFC requirements must be understood in order to avoid the penalties. For this reason, many U.S.-based multinationals reacted to the legislation by eliminating, reducing, or changing the activities of their tax-haven companies.

A foreign corporation may be designated a CFC and its shareholders taxed currently on its Subpart F income if it meets a control *test*. The test is met when more than 50% of its voting power or value of its outstanding stock is controlled directly or indirectly at any time during the year by U.S. stockholders who individually control at least 10% of the voting power.[59]

---

[56] §§ 993(a) and 995(b)(1)(E) and (F).

[57] § 995(b).

[58] MTC Proposed Model Statute for Combined Reporting, as approved by the Multistate Tax Commission August 17,

2006 and as amended by the Multistate Tax Commission July 29, 2011.

[59] §§ 951(b), 957(a), 958(a) and (b).

> **Example 17**
>
> If 46% of a foreign corporation's voting power (if all voting stock has equal voting rights, this is 46% of the voting stock) is owned by one U.S. shareholder and the remaining 54% is owned equally by six unrelated U.S. shareholders (9% each), it cannot be a CFC. However, if any one of the six shareholders acquires an additional percentage directly or indirectly, the foreign corporation meets the CFC control test. This change in status occurs because the 46% shareholder and the 10% shareholder together meet the 50% and 10% requirements.

U.S. shareholders who own at least 10% of the CFC's voting power are taxed currently on their shares of Subpart F income, even if it is not distributed to them.

> **Example 18**
>
> In *Example 17,* only the 46% shareholder and the 10% shareholder would be taxed on their Subpart F income currently, even if it is not distributed to them. The remaining shareholders would be taxed on their dividends from the CFC when the dividends are actually distributed.

For this reason, Subpart F income is commonly referred to as tainted income. Under prior law, this type of income had frequently been shielded from U.S. taxation through artificial arrangements with subsidiaries in tax-haven countries. Basically, there are eight types of Subpart F income:

1. Income earned from providing insurance protection for property or residents of any country other than the CFC's country.[60]
2. Income attributable to countries for which the United States does not recognize the government, has no diplomatic relations, or has designated as a country that repeatedly supports international terrorism.[61]
3. Income attributable to participation in or cooperation with an international boycott.[62]
4. Amounts equal to bribes, kickbacks, and other illegal payments to officials, employees, or agents of a foreign government.[63]
5. Passive income such as dividends, interest, rents, royalties, and gains from sale of these passive investment assets.[64]
6. Sales commissions, fees, and profits earned as a result of buying and selling goods that are neither produced nor used in the CFC's country, when one of the parties involved in the transaction is related to the CFC.[65]
7. Income for technical, managerial, engineering, architectural, scientific, skilled, industrial, commercial, or similar services performed outside the CFC's country for the benefit of a related party.[66]
8. Income derived from foreign oil and gas not extracted or consumed in the country in which the CFC is domiciled, when the CFC is a member of a related group that has at any time produced at least 1,000 barrels (or the equivalent) of oil or gas per day.[67]

The last four types of Subpart F income (numbers 5 through 8) are collectively referred to as foreign base company income (FBC income).[68]

---

[60] § 953.

[61] §§ 901(j) and 952(a)(5).

[62] §§ 952(a)(3) and 999.

[63] § 952(a)(4).

[64] §§ 954(a)(1) and (c).

[65] §§ 954(a)(2) and (d).

[66] §§ 954(a)(3) and (e).

[67] §§ 954(a)(5) and (g).

[68] §§ 952(a) and 954.

The Subpart F provisions contain several exceptions. For example, if FBC income is less than the smaller of 5% of gross income or $1 million, none of the FBC income is treated as Subpart F income. In contrast, if the sum of FBC income and gross insurance income exceeds 70% of gross income, all CFC income is Subpart F income.[69] If the foreign income cannot be repatriated to the United States because it is blocked (such as currency restrictions), it is excluded from E&P (and therefore not taxed to the U.S. shareholders) until the restrictions are removed.[70] Generally, the purpose behind these and other exceptions to Subpart F income is to avoid penalizing foreign corporations with income earned from conducting active businesses. As a result, income of a foreign corporation that is subject to a minimum effective foreign tax rate is considered not to be organized in order to reduce taxes, and is therefore not treated as Subpart F income.[71] To qualify for this exemption, the effective foreign tax rate must exceed 90% of the maximum U.S. corporate rate (e.g., 90% × 35% maximum U.S. corporate rate = 31.5%).

U.S. shareholders who own directly or indirectly at least 10% of a CFC's voting stock must include in gross income their pro rata share of Subpart F income, all previously excluded Subpart F income no longer meeting exclusion requirements (such as the removal of restrictions on blocked currency), and the increase in CFC earnings that are invested in U.S. property to the extent these earnings would be taxable dividends if distributed to the shareholders. These three types of income are taxable currently, regardless of whether any distributions are received and whether Subpart F income is directly or indirectly received by the U.S. shareholders. When dividends are distributed, however, they are not taxed again.[72] Stockholders increase their adjusted basis in CFC stock when the income is taxed in the United States and decrease their basis in the stock when these previously taxed earnings are received.[73]

Example 19

U.S. Parent owns 700 shares (70% of all stock) of Belgium Corporation. Belgium Corporation owns 100% of Liechtenstein Corporation. Belgium has no Subpart F income but all of Liechtenstein's earnings of $100,000 qualify as Subpart F income. No dividends are paid by any of the corporations. U.S. Parent's tax situation is unaffected by Belgium's earnings since Belgium did not distribute any dividends and has no Subpart F income. Parent's tax situation is affected by Liechtenstein, however, even though Liechtenstein did not distribute any dividends and is not directly owned by Parent. Parent owns 70% (70% × 100%) of Liechtenstein Corporation stock. Therefore, Liechtenstein Corporation is a CFC, and Parent will be taxed on its share of Liechtenstein Corporation's Subpart F income. Parent must recognize $70,000 dividend income (70% × 100% × $100,000) and increase its basis for Belgium's stock by $70,000.

Allocations Affecting Affiliated Companies

The differences in effective tax rates paid by companies doing business around the globe becomes particularly important when income and deductions are allocated among related companies, especially when one realizes that a substantial amount of international trade occurs between related entities. The way in which income and deductions are allocated among the members of a multinational affiliated group can have a sizable impact on the total tax liability of the group when effective tax rates differ between countries. To ensure that multinationals report their share of income from intercompany activities, most industrial nations have legislation that allows tax authorities to adjust income and deductions to reflect taxable income within their borders.

---

[69] § 954(b)(3).

[70] § 964(b).

[71] § 954(b)(4).

[72] § 951(a)(3).

[73] § 961.

ALLOCATING INCOME AMONG AFFILIATED COMPANIES

Few business decisions have greater impact on the operations of multinational organizations than those involving pricing between affiliated companies located in different countries. Tax laws throughout the world require that transactions between units of the same organization must be at arm's length. That is, prices must be based on market values, whether dealing with related or unrelated businesses. The objective of these tax laws is to ensure that all transactions are recorded as though they occurred between entities that are both legally and economically separate. The difficulty with this premise, of course, is that many multinationals do not operate in this manner. Instead, business decisions often are based on what is best for the organization as a whole. This difference in philosophy between tax authorities and multinationals creates considerable conflict worldwide.

In the United States the authority to reallocate income and deductions between affiliated companies is provided by § 482 of the Internal Revenue Code. Regulations relating to intercompany transfer pricing under § 482[74] provide several methods for setting transfer prices under different situations, as shown in Exhibit 13-3. The Regulations make it clear that the arm's-length standard is the basis for all allocations under § 482.[75]

EXHIBIT 13-3	Transfer Pricing between Members of Affiliated Groups
Type of Transaction	*Methods Available*
Interest on intercompany loans	Arm's-length interest rate
Performances of services for a related party	Arm's-length charge
Use of tangible property by a related party	Arm's-length rental charge
Intercompany transfers of tangible property	Comparable Uncontrolled Price Method (CUPM)
	Resale Price Method (RPM)
	Cost Plus Method (CPLM)
	Comparable Profits Method (CPM)
	Profit Split Method
	Another arm's-length method, if none of the five methods above can be reasonably applied
Intercompany transfers of intangible property	Comparable Uncontrolled Transaction Method (CUTM)
	Comparable Profits Method (CPM)
	Profit Split Method
	Another arm's-length method, if none of the methods above can be reasonably applied

[74] Reg. § 1.482-1 through 8.　　[75] Reg. § 1.482-1(b)(1).

The problem of intercompany transactions is complicated further by the fact that tax legislation is based on the assumption that transfer prices often are established to avoid, and possibly evade, taxation. Because of this attitude, § 482 is a preventive measure that can be used by the government but not by taxpayers. Thus, companies have the responsibility of convincing the IRS that pricing policies followed by affiliated companies are the same as those followed by unaffiliated companies. Otherwise, pricing reallocations made by the IRS must be sustained by the courts unless the taxpayer proves them to be unreasonable, arbitrary, or capricious.[76] Proving this may be nearly impossible, especially when the transactions involve unique assets or circumstances where no comparable arm's length price exists. Simply showing that the company's method is based on sound business reasons is inadequate.[77] While such evidence is relevant for disproving fraud charges, shifting income between related parties is subject to § 482 regardless of the motive. This should not, however, prevent multinationals from arranging company activities in order to minimize taxes.[78] Thus, multiple related entities may be formed as long as there is a business purpose for their existence and transactions between them are based on the arm's length standard.

No one group or organization has the authority to establish international standards for taxation. Traditionally, this regulatory authority has been exercised by each nation for transactions affecting businesses operating within its boundaries. In some instances, more than one governmental agency is delegated this authority. For example, transfer prices are of interest to both customs and income tax officials. Laws and taxing objectives differ among countries. Seldom has this been considered a serious problem by most multinationals, especially in countries other than the United States. However, tax practitioners in several countries are reporting both an increasing interest in intercompany transactions and sophistication on the part of government tax auditors. In many instances, these auditors are specialists in international matters and some are consultants with considerable business experience in the industry, occasionally even in the company under audit. These and numerous other factors are causing greater interest in the establishment of international standards for taxation.

In order to address many of the issues surrounding tax avoidance by multinational companies, the Organisation for Economic Cooperation and Development (OECD) with the blessing of the G20, embarked on a project in 2013 to develop proposals for dealing with Base Erosion and Profit Shifting (BEPS).[79] The goal of the BEPS project was to ensure that multinationals could be taxed where economic activity takes place and where value is created.

In October 2015, the BEPS Action Plan was released with recommendations relating to fifteen key areas including designing effective controlled foreign company rules (Action 3), limiting base erosion via interest deductions and other financial payments (Action 4), moving intangibles among group members (Action 8), requiring taxpayers to disclose their aggressive tax planning arrangements (Action 12) and examining transfer pricing documentation (Action 13). The OECD has also supported country-by-country reporting requiring companies to disclose the profit they make in each country along with associated measures of economic activity such as sales and employment.

As of December 2015, many countries are considering adopting changes to their international tax systems based on the recommendations in the BEPS action plan. The ultimate outcome of the project may include significant changes in the planning opportunities available to multinationals as well as a reduced appetite for aggressive tax avoidance strategies.

[76] *Eli Lilly and Co. v. U.S.*, 67-1 USTC ¶9248, 19 AFTR 712, 372 F.2d 990 (Ct. Cls., 1967).

[77] *Your Host, Inc. v. Comm.*, 74-1 USTC ¶9119, 33 AFTR2d 74-385, 489 F.2d 957 (CA-2, 1973), aff'g 58 T.C. 10 (1972).

[78] *U.S. Steel Corp. v. Comm.*, 80-1 USTC ¶9307, 45 AFTR2d 80-1081, 617 F.2d 942 (CA-2, 1980), rev'g 36 TCM 1152, T.C. Memo 1977-290.

[79] http://www.oecd.org/g20/g20-members.htm.

ALLOCATING DEDUCTIONS AMONG AFFILIATED COMPANIES

In the United States, the authority governing the allocation of deductions deemed to benefit affiliated companies is provided by Regulation § 1.861-8. The Regulations state that certain expenses are allocated according to rules specifically for those types of deductions. For example, interest expense is generally considered to be attributable to all activities and property, rather than being attributable to the specific purpose for incurring the debt.[80] Many other types of expenses are allocated to the specific class of income to which they relate.[81] These allocations are to be made to tax exempt as well as taxable income.[82] The deductions are then apportioned between U.S. source and foreign source income. Although the rules apply to all deductions, those not directly related to a specific class of income ordinarily have the most effect on foreign source income. These are primarily interest, research and development, and administrative expenses. If the multinational organization includes specially taxed corporations such as DISCs and CFCs, apportionments also require separate calculations for each type of specially taxed corporation.[83]

Allocation rules for expenses deemed not directly related to a specific class of income (e.g., interest and administrative costs) require that these expenses be combined and then allocated among the affiliated corporations, according to each one's total asset basis. Certain financial institutions are exempt from these rules, and in some instances, taxpayers will be allowed to net interest expense against related interest income.

Even though a multinational's taxable income from all sources usually remains unchanged, many are paying higher taxes as a result of numerous changes in the Regulations. This generally occurs because of the effect these changes have on the foreign tax credit limitation.[84] Recall that *Example 16* illustrated the foreign tax credit limitation as foreign source income divided by worldwide income, with the results multiplied by U.S. taxes before the credit. Thus, a shift in deductions from U.S. source income to foreign source income lowers the foreign tax credit limitation.

The issue is complicated even further if a subsequent tax audit results in a reallocation of income under § 482. This adjustment may change gross income relationships to the extent that deductions under Regulation § 1.861-8 will need to be recalculated.[85] As a result of the audit, the U.S. parent will pay more U.S. taxes because of the § 482 reallocation and also because of its effect on Regulation § 1.861-8 deductions.

RELIEF FROM DOUBLE TAXATION

Multinational organizations may be assessed income taxes on the same income by two different countries. Although this can occur in several ways, the most common double taxation situations result from adjustments made by tax authorities during an audit. In the United States, these basically fall into three categories: (1) reallocation of income or deductions under § 482, (2) reallocation of income or deductions under another Internal Revenue Code section, and (3) a reclassification of foreign source income to U.S. source income.

Worldwide interest in intercompany transactions by tax authorities causes special concern about the potential for double taxation, especially for U.S.-based multinationals. As a result, the United States has specific procedures governing § 482 audits to ensure the company has an opportunity to avoid double taxation.[86] On first encountering a situation where § 482 is applicable, the Internal Revenue agent must notify the International Examining Group. An International Examiner is assigned to the case if the issues are complex. In the event a § 482 assessment is proposed, the taxpayer must be notified in writing about the adjustment and about any international appeal procedures available for relief from double taxation.

[80] Temp. Reg. § 1.861-9T(a).
[81] Reg. § 1.861-8(b)(1).
[82] Reg. § 1.861-8(d)(2).
[83] Reg. § 1.861-8(f)(1) and (2).
[84] Reg. § 1.861-8(f)(1)(i).
[85] Reg. § 1.861-8(f)(4).
[86] Rev. Proc. 91-23, 1991-1 C.B. 534.

The parent company has several choices when notified of a § 482 adjustment. One, if there is a treaty with the foreign country involved, the parent may seek relief under the treaty's competent authority provision. Two, the parent may request an IRS administrative review of the adjustment. If this is unsuccessful, the company may then seek relief under the competent authority provision. Three, it may pursue the matter in Tax Court, the Court of Claims, or the appropriate District Court at any time. Thus, the taxpayer may turn to the courts as soon as the notice is received, after an unsuccessful administrative review, after an unsuccessful appeal through the competent authority, or during any of these procedures. Four, the parent also may decide at any time to accept the assessment and close the case.

Although no two treaties are identical, most contain a provision establishing a competent authority procedure to help protect taxpayers from double taxation. In the United States, this procedure is administered by the Foreign Operations District (formerly the Office of International Operations). The competent authority in each treaty country is responsible for pursuing an equitable solution to the double tax situation. This often includes waiving the statute of limitations when necessary. If an agreement satisfactory to the taxpayer is not reached, there are several possible outcomes. First, the competent authority may instruct the IRS to forgo the § 482 adjustments. Unless otherwise stated, however, this does not preclude the IRS from assessing the same tax under another applicable Code section. Thus, the taxpayer should ensure that the competent authority's instructions include a statement preventing such use of another Code section. Second, the IRS may allow the U.S. parent to treat the income subject to the double tax as an advance to the subsidiary. This allows the amount to be returned tax-free to the U.S. parent.[87] Nevertheless, the foreign country may choose to treat the return of funds as a dividend subject to withholding taxes. Third, some or all of the double tax may be offset by treating the amount in question as foreign source income when received in the United States. This results in a higher foreign tax credit limitation. This use of the foreign tax credit is available only to those companies that have sought relief through the competent authority.[88] Fourth, the company still has the option of requesting an IRS administrative review if it has not already done so, or to pursue the matter in U.S. courts.

Several reasons are given for not seeking assistance from the competent authority. Some taxpayers are concerned that the procedure is very time-consuming, taking from one to three years to complete after the authority becomes involved. In order to obtain competent authority help, the company must agree to the adjusted price established by the IRS. Such acceptance may affect future as well as past intercompany transactions and diminish the company's future bargaining ability with tax auditors. In addition, the competent authority acts as the company's advocate, which means the company may be required to share some of its internal documents with them. Not only are companies reluctant to share their documents with an agency of the Treasury Department in general, but there is also the fear that this information will be used to the foreign country's advantage either in audits of other intercompany transactions or in allowing this confidential information to be obtained by competitors. Treaties contain safeguards against this, but there is no guarantee. As a result of these and possibly other reasons, many U.S. companies accept the double taxation without seeking relief through the competent authority.

Competent authority procedures may not be available for double taxation that results from adjustments under Code sections other than § 482.[89] They also are not available when there is no treaty between the United States and the foreign country involved. In these situations, a request for refund may be made directly to the foreign country.[90] It is possible, however, that the request will be refused because the tax authorities believe the original amount is appropriate, because the statute of limitations prevents a review of this situation, or because of political or economic restrictions or conditions. In any event, the taxpayer still may seek IRS administrative review and a hearing by the court.

---

[87] Rev. Proc. 65-17, 1965-1 C.B. 833.

[88] Rev. Rul. 92-75, 1992-2 C.B. 197.

[89] Rev. Proc. 91-23, 1991-1 C.B. 534.

[90] Apparently, the IRS will pay interest on overpayments when the refund is of foreign taxes. Ltr. Rul. 8320004.

Foreign Currency Gains and Losses

International business is transacted in many currencies, but in most instances U.S. taxable income must be reported in dollars.[91] With some exceptions, the price of dollars is determined by supply and demand in an unregulated market. Consequently, the exchange rate from a particular currency to dollars may change.

LO.6
Understand the tax provisions relating to foreign currency gains and losses.

There are two basic methods used for translating foreign currency in determining foreign exchange gains and losses: the transaction method and the profit and loss method. The transaction method is generally used in the following situations:

1. Foreign currency transactions by taxpayers without physical locations in a foreign country; and
2. Dividend payments by foreign corporations to U.S. taxpayers.

The profit and loss method is generally used in the following situations:

1. Operations of foreign branches owned by U.S. corporations; and
2. Subpart F income of Controlled Foreign Corporations and Foreign Personal Holding Companies owned by U.S. taxpayers.

Therefore, the profit and loss method is utilized with reference to actual foreign operations when the foreign operating unit is owned by U.S. corporations/taxpayers.

Character of Gain or Loss

Whether exchange gains and losses are ordinary or capital depends on the nature of the transaction. For example, exchange gains and losses that arise in the normal course of business are ordinary.[92] However, those that result from investment or personal transactions produce capital gains or losses.[93]

Functional Currency

Generally, international transactions are recorded using the functional currency of the taxpayer.[94] Functional currency is normally the U.S. dollar, except that a qualified business unit (QBU) is to use the currency of the economic environment in which a significant part of the QBU's activities are conducted if the QBU uses that currency in keeping its books and records.[95] A QBU is any separate and clearly identified unit of a trade or business of a taxpayer that maintains separate books and records.[96]

Section 988 Transactions

Although U.S. taxpayers must generally use the U.S. dollar in recording international transactions, qualifying § 988 transactions may be denominated in another (nonfunctional) currency. Section 988 applies when the taxpayer:

1. Is the debtor or creditor of a foreign currency debt;
2. Accrues foreign currency receivables or payables for income and expense items;
3. Has foreign currency futures and forward contracts (except those qualifying under § 1256, such as hedging, which are beyond the scope of this chapter); or
4. Disposes of nonfunctional currency.[97]

Gains and losses for each of these transactions are determined in the foreign (nonfunctional) currency and then translated into U.S. dollars. The foreign currency gains and losses under § 988 are treated as ordinary gains and losses.[98]

---

[91] § 985.

[92] *Foundation Co.*, 14 T.C. 1333 (1950), acq. 1950-2 C.B. 2.

[93] Rev. Rul. 74-7, 1974 -1 C.B. 198. But, see *National-Standard Co.* 80 T.C. 551 (1983). The Tax Court allowed an ordinary loss when U.S. dollars were used to purchase Belgian francs to repay a Belgian loan originally made in francs. This decision was based on the Court's belief that no sale or exchange occurs with a mere repayment

of indebtedness. A full court review of the decision resulted in one strong dissent.

[94] § 985(a).

[95] § 985(b) and Reg. § 1.985-1(c).

[96] § 989(a).

[97] § 988(c)(1).

[98] § 988(a)(1).

Starting in 1999, an individual's foreign currency translation gains under $200 per transaction were no longer subject to U.S. taxation if they are for personal transactions (not for business or investment related expenses).[99] Small gains frequently arise when the exchange rate changes between the time that expenses are charged (e.g. using a credit card) and the time that the credit card bill is paid. This provision prevents the taxation of such small foreign currency translation gains. Foreign currency translation losses of an individual are not deductible if they are personal in nature.[100]

TRANSACTION METHOD

As stated above, exchange gains and losses for foreign currency transactions by taxpayers without a physical location in a foreign country are determined under the transaction method. Under the transaction method, the entry for the transaction is recorded at the exchange rate in effect on the date of the transaction. The exchange rate in effect on the date the collection (or payment) is made in the U.S. taxpayer's functional currency must also be determined.[101] The difference between the amount recorded on the transaction date and the actual amount received (or paid) is the exchange gain or loss due to the increase or decrease in the value of the U.S. dollar in relation to the foreign currency between the date of sale and the collection (payment) date.[102] Foreign currency exchange gains and losses are recognized when collection (or payment) is made in the U.S. taxpayer's functional currency (generally U.S. dollars), regardless of whether the accrual or cash basis of accounting is used.[103] Also, the source of foreign exchange gains and losses is generally considered to be the taxpayer's principal country of residence.

Whether the purchaser or the seller has an exchange gain or loss depends on which one bore the risk. If the transaction is conducted using the purchaser's currency, it is the seller that bears the risk and reports any exchange gain or loss.

Example 20

X Corporation (an accrual basis corporation) sold medical instruments costing $35,000 to a company located in Mexico. At the time of the sale, the exchange rate was 16 pesos to $1, and the selling price of the instruments was fixed at 880,000 pesos ($50,000). When the payment in pesos was received, the exchange rate was 17 pesos to $1, and X converted its 800,000 pesos to $47,059. Since X Corporation has no physical location in Mexico, it uses the transaction method. X's gross profit on the sale is $15,000 ($50,000 selling price on the date of the sale – $35,000 cost of medical instruments sold). X also has an ordinary (exchange) loss of $2,941 ($50,000 selling price – $47,059 actually received due to the decrease in value of the dollar in relation to pesos). The exchange loss is ordinary (rather than capital) since the transaction involved a sale of inventory.

If the transaction is conducted using the seller's currency, the risk and any resulting exchange gain or loss accrue to the buyer. Therefore, a U.S. business that negotiates all foreign purchases and sales in the U.S. dollar has no foreign currency exchange gains and losses.

Example 21

Refer to *Example 20,* but assume that both the sale and payment are denominated in U.S. dollars. The instruments are sold to the company located in Mexico for $50,000, and 30 days later payment of $50,000 is received. X Corporation has no foreign currency exchange gains and losses.

---

[99] § 988(e).

[100] § 165(c).

[101] If more than one rate is in use, the one that properly reflects income is used. See Rev. Rul. 74-222, 1974-1 C.B. 21.

[102] *Joyce-Koebel Co.*, 6 BTA 403 (1927), acq. V1-2 C.B. 4.

[103] Rev. Rul. 75-108, 1975-1 C.B. 69.

Dividend Distributions from Foreign Corporations

The transaction method is also used for actual distributions of earnings and profits to a U.S. shareholder from a foreign corporation. However, since the earnings and profits are not translated to U.S. dollars by the foreign corporation until the date the actual dividend distribution is made to the U.S. taxpayer, there is no exchange gain or loss.[104]

PROFIT AND LOSS METHOD

Foreign Branches

Foreign branches (a type of QBU) of U.S. corporations are subject to the profit and loss method for determining their exchange gains and losses. Under this method, all Federal income tax computations must be made in the foreign business's functional currency and then translated into U.S. dollars at the weighted average exchange rate for the taxable year. The U.S. corporation is taxed fully on this translated income. When distributions are made from this income, any exchange gain or loss (i.e., the difference between the exchange rate at the date of distribution and the weighted average rate used to report income) is recognized as ordinary income or loss.[105] However, translated branch losses are deductible by the U.S. taxpayer only to the extent of the U.S. taxpayer's dollar basis in the branch.

Example 22

Y Corporation's newly opened branch in France has net income of 5,500 euros. The weighted average exchange rate for the year is 0.91 euros to $1. Y received 4,000 euros from the branch on July 15, when the rate was 0.88 euros to $1. Under the profit and loss method, Y Corporation reports $6,044 (5,500 euros ÷ 0.91) ordinary income from branch operations for the year. In addition, Y reports an exchange ordinary gain of $150 ([4,000 euros ÷ 0.88 = $4,545 received] − [4,000 euros ÷ 0.91 = $4,395 taxed]).

In addition, when a branch has undistributed income attributable to more than one year, distributions must be prorated among those years for purposes of determining exchange gains and losses.

If foreign income taxes are denominated in a currency other than the taxpayer's functional currency, an election can be made to translate the foreign taxes on the date the taxes are paid rather than using the average exchange rate for the year. Once this election is made, it applies for all subsequent tax years, unless revoked with the consent of the IRS.[106]

Subpart F Income

Subpart F income of CFCs should be translated using the profit and loss method, in the same manner as income from a branch. Similarly, exchange gains and losses for these two types of income are determined when an actual distribution is made, in the same manner as they are for branches, and are generally recognized as foreign source ordinary income or loss.

BLOCKED CURRENCIES

In some instances, taxpayers are unable to convert foreign currencies into U.S. dollars because of exchange restrictions imposed by the issuing government. When this occurs, the currency is referred to as being blocked. Generally, taxpayers with income in blocked currencies may elect to defer their U.S. taxes until one of the following occurs:

1. Blockage restrictions are removed.
2. Conversion is made even though the restrictions continue.
3. The blocked currency is used for nondeductible expenditures.

---

[104] § 986(b).

[105] § 987 and Prop. Reg. §§ 1.987-1 and 1.987-2.

[106] § 986(a)(1)(D).

4. The blocked currency is disposed of in some manner, such as by gift, bequest, devise, dividend, or other distribution.

5. A taxpayer who is a resident alien terminates U.S. resident status.[107]

If one of the above occurs such that a portion, but not all, of the income deferral is removed, income is includible on a first-in, first-out basis.[108] That is, regardless of the facts, the first type of income deferred because of blockage is considered to be the first one received.

The deferral election for blocked currency generally is not available for income that is includible regardless of whether such income is distributed to the taxpayers. For example, deferral cannot be elected for includible income from a foreign personal holding company or from a foreign partnership.[109] The deferral also is not available when the taxpayer is able to use the funds in the foreign country.[110]

Expenses paid in the blocked currency are deductible only to the extent that the related income is reported.[111] Similar restrictions are placed on deductions for depreciation and on foreign tax credits.

U.S. Taxation of Aliens

LO.7

Explain the U.S. taxation of nonresident aliens.

Aliens are classified as either nonresidents or residents. Nonresident aliens are (1) individuals who are neither residents nor citizens of the United States, and (2) organizations created outside the United States.[112] The tax rate on passive-type investment income paid a nonresident alien, whether an individual or a corporation, is 30% of gross income.[113] In general, the rate is 39.6% (for individuals, estates, or trusts) and 35% (for corporate partners) on nonpassive income distributions to foreign owners of U.S. partnerships.[114] However, many treaties establish rates below these levels. Interest earned from investment funds on deposit with U.S. banks, savings and loan associations, and insurance companies are exempt from U.S. taxes.[115] In addition, there is no withholding tax for interest on portfolio investment held by nonresident aliens and foreign corporations.[116] Qualifying investments include those issued in the Eurobond market. Finally, if a nonresident alien or a foreign corporation does not engage in business in the United States at any time during the taxable year and its tax liability is fully satisfied by withholding at the source, no tax return is required.[117]

Example 23

R, a resident and citizen of Japan, receives the following income from U.S. sources in 2016: $1,000 dividend income from a U.S. corporation, $600 interest income on corporate bonds, and $300 interest income on funds deposited in a bank. The U.S.-Japanese treaty establishes a tax rate of 10% on dividends and 10% on taxable interest. These taxes must be withheld by the payors. Thus, R receives the income net of taxes as follows: $900 in dividends ($1,000 − 10% tax of $100); $540 interest ($600 − 10% tax of $60); and $300 of tax-exempt bank interest. R is not required to file a tax return. Note that, because of the treaty, the U.S. tax is the same, regardless of whether R is an individual or a foreign corporation.

---

[107] Rev. Rul. 74-351, 1974-2 C.B. 144.

[108] Rev. Rul. 57-379, 1957-2 C.B. 299.

[109] See *Elder v. Comm.*, 43-2 USTC ¶9519, 31 AFTR 627, 139 F.2d 27 (CA-2, 1943), rev'g and rem'g 47 BTA 235 and *Max Freudmann*, 10 T.C. 775 (1948), acq. 1948-2 C.B. 2.

[110] *Sanford A. Berman*, 45 TCM 1357, T.C. Memo 1983-214.

[111] Rev. Rul. 74-341, 1974-2 C.B. 128.

[112] Reg. §§ 1.871-1 and 2.

[113] §§ 871(a)(1) and 881, and Reg. § 1.871-7. In *Barba v. U.S.*, 83-1 USTC ¶9404, 52 AFTR2d 83-5272 (Ct. Cls. 1983), a nonresident alien was taxed on the full amount of his gross receipts from gambling, even though his losses far exceeded his winnings.

[114] §§ 1446 and 6401(b).

[115] § 871(i).

[116] §§ 1441(c)(9) and (10), and 871(h)(4).

[117] Reg. §§ 1.6012-1(b)(2)(i) and 1.6012-2(g)(2)(i).

Income effectively connected with a U.S. trade or business and received by a nonresident alien is subject to the regular U.S. individual or corporate tax rates on taxable income.[118] In addition, there is a 30% branch profits tax on income received by a foreign corporation from its U.S. branch.[119] This tax, however, may be overridden by tax treaty provisions.

Basically, effectively connected income is (1) income earned on assets used or held for use in a trade or business, and (2) income from activities performed within the United States by or for a trade or business. The definition, with some exceptions, includes salaries and other personal service income if material in amount (exceeds $3,000), and the U.S. net income of a trade or business.[120] Special rules apply when the income consists of capital gains.[121]

Taxable income for a nonresident business is much the same as for any similar U.S. business (i.e., effectively connected gross income less related business expenses).[122] However, taxable income for a nonresident individual is effectively connected gross income less (1) the personal exemption amount for the taxpayer (but not the standard deduction), (2) contributions to U.S. charities, (3) casualty and theft losses for property located within the United States, and (4) expenses related to the effectively connected gross income, such as travel, entertainment, moving, and state and local income tax expenses.[123] In some instances, treaty provisions extend these deductions. Nonresident aliens may receive both effectively connected income subject to the regular income tax rates and investment income subject to the 30% rate.[124]

Example 24

Refer to *Example 23*, except assume that R also earned and received $20,000 salary from a U.S. business while in the United States during June, July, and August. R, a single individual, incurred related business travel expenses of $1,700 and Kentucky state income taxes of $200. R's effectively connected taxable income is $14,100 ($20,000 − $4,000 personal exemption − $1,700 − $200). The tax is calculated on the $14,100, the same as if R were a U.S. citizen or resident. In addition, the payors must withhold the $100 on R's dividends and $60 on R's corporate investment income. Note that R's Japanese source income is not relevant to the U.S. tax calculations.

An exception covers foreign government personnel, teachers, students, and participants in certain exchange or training programs who are temporarily in the United States as nonimmigrants under the Immigration and Nationality Act. These nonresidents are taxed at the regular graduated tax rates on their includible U.S. source income.[125] They are, however, exempt from U.S. taxes on income received from foreign employers.[126]

All aliens are presumed to be nonresidents unless there is evidence to the contrary. Most foreign businesses with physical locations in the United States qualify as residents. An individual is a resident alien if he or she (1) is a lawful permanent resident under the immigration laws of the United States during any part of the calendar year, or (2) meets the substantial presence test. This test is met if the individual is present in the United States (1) at least 31 days during the calendar year, and (2) if the number of days present in the current year plus one-third of the days present in the prior year plus one-sixth of the days present in the second prior year equals at least 183 days.[127]

[118] §§ 864(c)(6) and (7), and Reg. §§ 1.864-4 and 1.882.

[119] § 884.

[120] § 864(c), and Reg. § 1.864-2.

[121] § 871(a)(2), and Reg. §§ 1.871-7(d) and 1.882-1(b)(2)(ii).

[122] § 882 and Reg. § 1.882-4(c).

[123] §§ 861(b), 863(a), and 873(b), and Reg. § 1.861-8.

[124] Reg. §§ 1.871-8 and 1.882-1.

[125] § 871(c).

[126] § 872(b)(3).

[127] § 7701(b). In addition, under certain circumstances a nonresident may elect to be treated as a resident alien.

Example 25

T, U, and V are citizens and permanent residents of Austria. They were, however, present in the United States the following number of days:

	T	U	Y
2016	25	75	150
2015	330	66	120
2014	300	42	90

T does not meet the substantial presence test in 2016 since his stay in the United States during 2016 was less than 31 days.

U also does not meet the substantial presence test in 2016. Although U was present in the United States the required minimum of 31 days during 2016, the number of days she was present in 2016 plus one-third of the number of days she was present in 2015 plus one-sixth of the number of days she was present in 2014 equals 104 days $[75 + (1/3 \times 66 = 22) + (1/6 \times 42 = 7) = 104]$, which is less than the required minimum of 183 days.

V, however, meets both portions of the substantial presence test and qualifies as a U.S. resident alien. First, he was in the United States during 2016 the required 31 days. Second, his 205 days $[150 + (1/3 \times 120 = 40) + (1/6 \times 90 = 15) = 205]$ exceeds the required minimum of 183 days.

Resident aliens are taxed in the same manner as U.S. citizens and businesses. That is, they are taxed on their worldwide income at the U.S. graduated tax rates applicable to corporations and individuals less foreign tax credits. No distinction is made between investment income and trade or business income.[128]

It is possible for aliens to qualify for nonresident status for part of the year and resident status the remainder (usually in the years of arrival and departure). In such instances, taxable income must be separated and calculated for the two classifications as though the taxpayer had been two separate taxpayers.[129] However, in a year of dual status, some restrictions are placed on an individual's tax return for income received as a resident alien. Nonresident aliens and dual status aliens may not elect to file as a head of household. In addition, married aliens must file separately in the year of dual status. Anyone who is a resident at the end of the year (or is married to such a person) may elect to be taxed as a U.S. resident for the entire year and avoid these restrictions.[130] In general, dual-status taxpayers may not claim the standard deduction.[131] In addition, personal exemptions for the resident alien's dependents and spouse cannot exceed the income received while a resident. This limitation does not, however, apply to individual residents of Canada or Mexico.[132]

Expatriation to Avoid U.S. Taxation

When an individual terminates his or her U.S. citizenship, the individual is taxed as a nonresident alien for U.S. purposes. U.S. citizens are taxed on their worldwide income while nonresident aliens are only taxed on income effectively connected with U.S. businesses and investment income from U.S. sources. However, most capital gains of nonresident aliens are not subject to U.S. tax. As a result, a U.S. citizen could escape all U.S. taxation on accrued gains on property if the person renounced his or her citizenship before selling. In addition, an expatriate could reduce or avoid any future U.S. estate or gift tax liability. To address these possible abuses, Congress has enacted several provisions.

For those who renounce their citizenship (i.e., expatriate) after June 16, 2008, the provisions of IRC § 877A apply if any of the following statements are true.

---

[128] Reg. § 1.871-1(a).

[129] Rev. Rul. 73-578, 1973-2 C.B. 39.

[130] § 6013(g) and Reg. § 1.871-1(a).

[131] § 63(c)(6)(B).

[132] Reg. § 1.873-1(b)(2)(iii).

- The taxpayer's average annual net income tax for the five years ending before the date of expatriation is more than a specified amount adjusted annually for inflation ($161,000 for 2016).[133]

- The taxpayer's net worth is $2 million or more on the date of your expatriation.

- The taxpayer fails to certify that he or she has complied with all U.S. federal tax obligations for the five years preceding the date of your expatriation.

Under the mark-to-market rule of § 877A, the expatriate is deemed to sell all of his or her property, regardless of location, on the day before he or she ceases to be taxable as a U.S. citizen or resident for their fair market value. The gains and losses are included on the expatriate's final return as a U.S. citizen. For taxable years beginning in 2016, the amount that would otherwise be includible in gross income by reason of deemed sale is reduced by $693,000 (indexed for inflation).[134] In addition, expatriates are allowed to defer payment of some or all of the tax until the property held at repatriation is actually sold. While such items as retirement benefits and deferred compensation are exempted from the mark-to-market rule, distributions are generally taxable even if distributed at a much later date.

A foreign tax credit is available for foreign taxes paid on income that is considered to be U.S. source income solely because of § 877.[135]

In order for the government to monitor individuals who might be subject to § 877, persons who terminate citizenship or long-term residency must file a statement containing identifying information, foreign residency and citizenship, and, if the individual's net worth is at least $2,000,000, information detailing the person's assets and liabilities.[136] The penalty for not providing the statement is the greater of $1,000 or 5% of the tax due as a result of § 877.

Tax Planning Considerations

Tax planning is essential for many individuals and for all businesses. However, because of the variety of available options and the interrelationships that exist among them, tax planning for those involved in international activities is even more important. The obvious difficulty is that it is impossible to accumulate and evaluate all information relevant to making decisions in an international context. Although minimizing income taxes may not be a primary goal, these taxpayers must develop an international tax strategy.

TAXATION OF U.S. CITIZENS

A U.S. citizen may elect to:

1. Report all foreign-earned income and claim the foreign taxes on that income as a credit or an itemized deduction, or

2. Exclude foreign-earned income (up to $101,300 plus the foreign housing expense allowance) and forgo claiming the foreign taxes applicable to this excluded income.

For U.S. citizens who live outside of the United States in nations with high effective tax rates, it is often better for these taxpayers to select the first option and report all foreign-earned income in order to claim the tax credit. These taxpayers will have no U.S. taxes on this income under either method, but excess foreign tax credits are larger when the exclusion is not elected. Excess credits may be carried back two years and forward five years to reduce total taxes in years when the U.S. effective rate exceeds the foreign rate. Note that if the exclusion is elected, the U.S. effective rate will be lower than it would be if it were not.

In a low tax rate country generally the exclusion should be elected. However, individuals living in such countries must remember that the decision cannot be changed annually. Once the exclusion is elected and then revoked, it is probable that the IRS will not allow its reelection for five years. Consequently, this decision must be made with consideration to future expectations as well as to the present situation.

---

[133] Rev. Proc. 2015-53.

[134] *Ibid.*

[135] § 877(b).

[136] § 6039G.

Taxpayers should determine their taxable income in the foreign country before deciding whether or not to elect the housing expense exclusion. In some countries, employer-provided housing is not taxable. Thus, electing this exclusion would have no effect on foreign tax credits. Other differences between U.S. and foreign tax bases can mean that the country appearing to have the higher effective tax rate may actually have the lower rate. Of course, the higher/lower relationship can change as the countries' tax laws and treaties are revised and as the taxpayers' taxable incomes change. These uncertainties make tax planning difficult but also show the importance of approaching it carefully.

Individuals must be aware of the tax laws of the foreign country in which they will live. One question to be resolved before the move is whether they should establish residency status in that country. As was discussed in this chapter, resident or nonresident status can affect the tax liability significantly in the United States. Similar differences also exist in many other countries.

Individuals who decide to avoid resident status may still be able to qualify for available U.S. exclusions under the physical presence test. Remember, the bona fide resident status is based on a full tax year, whereas physical presence is based on any twelve consecutive months. The shorter the expected length of time of the overseas assignment, the more important the physical presence test becomes. Taxpayers should consider the effect on this test before planning trips to the United States. Shortening the time or delaying the trip by a few days could have a significant tax impact.

A U.S. citizen moving to another country should determine if a treaty exists between that country and the United States. If there is a treaty, the taxpayer is well advised to obtain a copy and study it carefully. Treaties often grant special tax rates and treatment that are considerably more beneficial than those otherwise applicable to the taxpayer. Unfortunately, few tax advisers are aware of specific treaty provisions.

TAXATION OF U.S.-BASED CORPORATIONS

Tax planning for foreign source income requires that the most advantageous method and organizational form be selected for each type of transaction or activity. As long as the effects of taxation differ among the various corporate entities and countries, there is considerable incentive to arrange intercompany transactions with the objective of minimizing the overall tax liability of the company. The international business organization cannot afford to ignore tax consequences or make decisions and then wait until the end of the year to see how costly they were in taxes.

CONTROLLED FOREIGN CORPORATION

The intent of the CFC legislation is to penalize inactive corporations located in tax-haven countries. However, it is possible for active corporations to be subjected to these provisions unless their operations are carefully structured. Thus, a crucial tax planning strategy for all foreign corporations is to be fully aware of and alert to the CFC control test, Subpart F income computations, and all available exceptions. Particularly vulnerable to Subpart F are foreign subsidiaries that derive much of their income from providing services or from acting as selling agents for U.S. parent companies.

Strategies for avoiding CFC status can be devised to circumvent the control test. A foreign corporation cannot be a CFC unless 50% of its voting power or stock value is controlled directly or indirectly by U.S. stockholders who individually control at least 10% of the voting power. To avoid this test, a U.S. parent corporation can decontrol its wholly owned foreign subsidiary by distributing at least 50% of the subsidiary's stock as a dividend to the parent corporation's shareholders. If the parent's stock is widely held, the 10% rule will not be met. Other methods for transferring ownership of the subsidiary's stock also are available.

Decontrol of a foreign subsidiary can be accomplished by issuing preferred voting stock to unrelated non-U.S. persons to the extent that preferred shareholders own 50% of total voting stock. The U.S. parent retains 50% of the voting power by owning all of the subsidiary's common stock. Preferred stockholders must be free to exercise their voting power. If restrictions are placed on any stockholders, actual ownership will be ignored in favor of effective control.[137]

U.S. TAXATION OF ALIENS

U.S. taxation of aliens differs significantly, depending on whether an alien is classified as a resident or a nonresident. Since each alien's status is influenced by a number of factors, an individual often can arrange his or her activities in order to qualify for either classification. It is important, however, that these plans be made prior to entering the United States. Although an alien's status can be changed after arrival, this can be difficult and may cause dual-status problems in the year of change.

Special rules apply to nonresident aliens present in the United States for their foreign employer no more than 90 days during a tax year. If such an employee's U.S. earned income does not exceed $3,000, it is exempt from U.S. taxes.[138] Similarly, capital gains are exempt for nonresident aliens who are in the United States less than 183 days during a tax year. Most treaties also contain special tax benefits for temporary nonresidents. Knowledge of these rules and a little tax planning can save many aliens both tax dollars and time.

The fact that a tax year may be a fiscal rather than a calendar year allows some taxpayers even greater planning opportunities. For example, a foreign company's employee who is in the United States June through September will exceed the 90-day limit if the calendar year is used but not if a fiscal year ending July 31 is used. With the fiscal year, the alien is in the United States 61 days in each of two years. Of course, if the employee returns to the United States during the second fiscal year for more than 29 days, the limit will be exceeded in the second year.

Problem Materials

DISCUSSION QUESTIONS

13-1 *Basic Concepts.* Determine whether each of the following statements is true or false. If false, rewrite the statement so that it is true. Be prepared to explain each statement.
   a. U.S. taxation of foreign source income is based on the jurisdictional principle.
   b. A U.S. taxpayer may be a U.S. citizen living in Italy, a British citizen living in the United States, a French citizen who has never lived in the United States, or a Japanese company with no branches or subsidiaries in the United States.
   c. All industrialized nations tax their citizens on the citizens' worldwide income.
   d. A foreign-owned corporation can be a U.S. nonresident alien.
   e. A Canadian citizen living in Canada who receives dividend income from a U.S. corporation must file Form 1040 and pay U.S. taxes on the dividend income.

13-2 *Foreign Source Income.* U.S. source income, foreign source income, and foreign source earned income are taxed differently.
   a. Explain how the source is determined.
   b. List examples of foreign source earned income.
   c. Compare foreign source earned income for a U.S. citizen with effectively connected income for a nonresident alien.

---

[137] Reg. § 1.957-1(b)(2). But in July 1982 the IRS replaced its acquiescence with a nonacquiescence on the primary case in this area, *CCA, Inc.*, 64 T.C. 137 (1975), nonacq. The reason given by the Service for this change was that "the Tax Court's finding is clearly erroneous."

[138] Reg. § 1.864-2(b).

13-3 *Foreign Source Earned Income.* I and U organize the IU Computer Software Service as a U.S. partnership. Both partners are U.S. citizens. They expect net income in each of the first three years to exceed $100,000, half from the United States and half from Europe. I will live and manage the activities in the United States and U will live and manage the activities in Europe. They will divide all profits equally.

    a. Do either or both partners have foreign source income or foreign-earned income?

    b. Advise the partners how the partnership agreement can be written to maximize tax benefits from foreign source income.

13-4 *Foreign Resident Tests.* In order to qualify for certain exclusions, a U.S. citizen must meet either the bona fide resident or the physical presence tests.

    a. Define both of these tests.

    b. May a U.S. citizen qualify under either or both tests even though the citizen owns a home in the United States and expects to return to that home permanently at the end of three years?

    c. May a U.S. citizen who lives in three different countries during a two-year period qualify under either or both tests?

13-5 *Deductions for Foreign Moving Expenses.* Rules for foreign moving expenses differ from those for U.S. moves.

    a. How do they differ?

    b. Why do they differ?

13-6 *Foreign Tax Deduction versus Credit.* Is it better to deduct foreign income taxes (rather than take a credit for them) when a U.S. corporation's only foreign operation has a net taxable loss for the year?

    a. Assume the foreign business is a branch.

    b. Assume the foreign business is a corporation.

13-7 *Foreign Tax Credit—Deemed Paid.* May A Corporation claim a foreign tax credit from foreign taxes paid by D Corporation, even though A does not own any of D's stock?

    a. Assume A owns 50% of B Corporation, B Corporation owns 40% of C Corporation, and C Corporation owns 60% of D Corporation.

    b. Assume the same as (a), except that C Corporation owns 20% of D Corporation rather than 60 percent.

13-8 *Form of Organization.* AC Corporation intends to sell some of its products to several European customers. AC will establish a foreign manufacturing operation after the first three years. Start-up costs will result in losses for two years, but profits are expected in all future years. What form of organization should AC use and why?

13-9 *Code § 482.*

    a. Why is § 482 important to a U.S.-based multinational corporation?

    b. Are all transactions between the U.S. parent corporation and its subsidiaries subject to § 482?

    c. If an IRS audit results in a § 482 shift of income to the U.S. parent corporation, what is the effect on the foreign tax credit?

13-10 *Regulation § 1.861-8.*

    a. Why is Reg. § 1.861-8 important to a U.S.-based multinational corporation?

    b. If an IRS audit results in a Reg. § 1.861-8 shift of taxable income to the U.S. parent corporation, what is the effect on the foreign tax credit?

    c. What is the effect on the U.S. parent corporation and foreign subsidiary if the foreign tax authorities disallow a Reg. § 1.861-8 allocation to the foreign subsidiary?

13-11 *Foreign Currency Gains and Losses.*
   a. How are foreign currency gains and losses calculated?
   b. Are foreign currency gains and losses taxable as ordinary or capital?
   c. What effect does blocked currency have on recognition of foreign currency gains and losses?

13-12 *Resident versus Nonresident Alien Status.* Aliens subject to U.S. taxation are classified as either residents or nonresidents.
   a. How does U.S. taxation of residents differ from that of nonresidents?
   b. What is effectively connected income and how is it taxed to residents and nonresidents?
   c. How does a foreign taxpayer qualify as a resident?

PROBLEMS

13-13 *Foreign Source Income Exclusions—Partnership.* K and L form a foreign partnership to provide services to foreign clients interested in establishing businesses in the United States. They expect partnership net income, before payments to partners, to be $100,000 the first year. K and L agree that partner salaries should be $24,000 to K and $36,000 to L. Profits and losses after partners' salaries are shared equally. K will spend all of his time in the United States and L will spend all of his time in Europe. Both K and L are U.S. citizens. Calculate each partner's (1) foreign source partnership income, and (2) foreign source earned income.
   a. Assume capital is not a material income-producing factor.
   b. Assume capital is a material income-producing factor.

13-14 *Foreign Tax Credit—Individual.* T, a U.S. citizen, lives and works in the United States. In 2016, he receives a $35,000 salary from a U.S. company and $2,000 in dividends from a foreign corporation with no U.S. source income. The foreign corporation withheld $600 from the dividend and T received $1,400 cash. T is single, does not itemize deductions, and has no other taxable income and no dependents. Calculate T's U.S. Federal income tax.

13-15 *Foreign Tax Credit—Individual.* B, a U.S. citizen and resident, was single during 2016 and had the following sources of income.

Salary from a U.S. company.	$40,000
Dividends from a Mexican corporation	2,500
Interest income from a U.S. bank.	500

The gross amount of the dividend was $2,500, but the foreign corporation withheld $375 in foreign income taxes. B has $8,000 in itemized deductions for the year (excluding any foreign taxes paid). Compute B's tax liability for 2016.

13-16 *Foreign Source Income Exclusions.* Z, a U.S. citizen, works in France and meets the physical presence test. During 2016 she receives a $70,000 salary while in France for her work there, a $4,000 salary while briefly in the United States for her work here, and a $6,000 dividend while in France from stock she owns in a French company.
   a. Calculate Z's maximum exclusion.
   b. If Z receives a $25,000 bonus while in France for her work there, calculate her maximum exclusion.
   c. Calculate Z's exclusion if she receives the bonus in (b) and her employer provides housing that costs the employer $22,000.

13-17 *Foreign Income Exclusions.* J worked in Canada from August 1, 2015 through September 30, 2016. During 2016 her salary from work in Canada was $60,000 (in U.S. dollars), and her salary from work in the United States after she returned was $10,000.

   a. Calculate J's foreign earned income exclusion.

   b. Assume that a $15,000 allowance for housing is included in J's $60,000 and that the $15,000 meets the rules for qualifying foreign housing expenses. J elects to exclude foreign-earned income, but she does not make the special election to exclude employer provided foreign housing income. What is J's foreign earned income exclusion?

   c. Assume the same facts as in (b) above, except that J elects both the foreign-earned income exclusion and the exclusion for employer-provided foreign housing income. What amounts may be excluded from income? Which election(s) should J make?

13-18 *Bona Fide Resident or Physical Presence Test.* P, a U.S. citizen, moves to London, England June 1, 2016 and expects to return to the United States December 1, 2017. P is employed by a U.S.-based multinational corporation as an advisor to its British business operations during this period. Every other month, the company requires P to return to the United States for business purposes. Thus, P will be in the United States for seven days every two months, beginning with the last week in July. P's taxable year is the calendar year.

   a. Does P meet the bona fide resident test for 2016 or 2017?

   b. Does P meet the physical presence test for 2016 or 2017?

   c. What recommendations would you make to P that would enhance his situation to exclude foreign source income?

13-19 *Foreign Tax Credit—Corporations.* D, Inc. is a domestic corporation that owns 100% of F, Inc. Assume F has no Subpart F income so that the controlled foreign corporation rules do not apply. F had the following items of income and tax:

	E&P	Foreign Income Taxes
2013	$ 50,000	$12,500
2014	50,000	12,500
2015	40,000	10,000
2016	60,000	15,000
Total	$200,000	$50,000

F pays a $90,000 dividend at the end of 2016. Income taxes of $13,500 were withheld; therefore, D received $76,500. Calculate D's U.S. tax liability on this income before the foreign tax credit limitation. Assume a 34% tax rate.

13-20 *Foreign Tax Credit—Foreign Subsidiary.* The pretax income earned by a foreign corporation is $30,000. The foreign tax is 30 percent, the dividend withholding tax is 10 percent, and one-third of the after-tax foreign corporate income is remitted to stockholders. U.S. Parent Corporation income before the foreign dividend is $200,000, and it owns 100% of the foreign corporation.

   a. Calculate the U.S. taxes Parent Corporation will pay if the foreign tax is used as a tax credit.

   b. Calculate the U.S. taxes Parent Corporation will pay if the foreign tax is used as a tax credit but the foreign subsidiary pays a 20% foreign tax rate rather than the 30% one.

13-21 *Foreign Source Losses—Comparison of Business Organizations.* During the year, U.S. Parent Corporation had U.S. taxable income of $300,000, and its wholly owned foreign business organization had a taxable loss of $40,000. Calculate U.S. Parent Corporation's worldwide taxable income.

   a. Assume the business organization is a foreign branch.

   b. Assume the business organization is a foreign corporation.

13-22 *Ownership Tiers.* In each of the following independent situations, determine whether the ownership tests are met to allow V, a U.S. corporation, to claim foreign taxes paid by F Corporation, S Corporation, and T Corporation.
   a.   V owns 80% of F, F owns 20% of S, and S owns 40% of T.
   b.   V owns 80% of F, F owns 50% of S, and S owns 8% of T.
   c.   V owns 5% of F, F owns 100% of S, and S owns 80% of T.
   d.   V owns 60% of F, V and F each own 30% of S, and S owns 20% of T.

13-23 *Controlled Foreign Corporation.* AAA, Inc., a domestic corporation that manufactures automobile parts, owns 40% of NA, Inc., a Netherlands Antilles corporation. The other shareholders of NA are (1) ABC, Inc., a domestic corporation, which owns 20 percent, and (2) XYZ, Inc., a foreign corporation, which owns 40 percent. All of NA's current year income ($200,000) consists of sales commissions from buying parts from AAA, Inc. and selling them directly in Mexico. NA made no dividend distributions during the year.
   a.   Is NA a Controlled Foreign Corporation (CFC)?
   b.   How would your answer to (a) above change if ABC, Inc. were a foreign corporation?
   c.   If NA is a CFC, how much income does AAA recognize as a result of NA's activities and what is the effect on AAA's basis in NA's stock?

13-24 *Foreign Source Income—Comparison of Business Organizations.* During the year, U.S. Parent Corporation had U.S. taxable income of $300,000, and its wholly owned subsidiary organization had taxable income of $60,000. Parent Corporation received $20,000 cash from the subsidiary as a partial distribution of the subsidiary's profits for the current year. Calculate U.S. Parent Corporation's worldwide taxable income. Assume all foreign operations have no U.S. source income.
   a.   Assume the subsidiary is a foreign corporation.
   b.   Assume the subsidiary is a foreign branch.
   c.   Assume the subsidiary is a Controlled Foreign Corporation and all of its income is Subpart F income.

13-25 *Foreign Tax Credit—Comparison of Business Organizations.* U.S. Parent Corporation's taxable income before foreign source income is $100,000. Its wholly owned foreign subsidiary has foreign source taxable income of $80,000, pays a foreign tax of $12,000 (15%), and sends U.S. Parent $17,000 (one-fourth of its $68,000 after-tax income). The foreign country collects 10% withholding tax on the $17,000 and U.S. Parent receives $15,300. Calculate the U.S. Federal income taxes payable by U.S. Parent.
   a.   Assume the subsidiary is a foreign corporation.
   b.   Assume the subsidiary is a Controlled Foreign Corporation and all of its income is Subpart F income.

13-26 *Foreign Tax Credits—Tax Planning.* Assume that U.S. Corp has subsidiaries in two countries—Country A with a tax rate of 25% and Country B with a tax rate of 45%. Each subsidiary earns $10,000 of income before taxes. Subsidiary A (located in Country A) pays all of its after-tax income to the U.S. parent while Subsidiary B (located in Country B) does not pay a dividend. No withholding taxes apply to the dividend paid from Subsidiary A. Assume that the U.S. parent is subject to a 34% U.S. tax rate and has no other income.
   a.   What are the total income taxes paid in the United States, Country A and Country B?
   b.   Now assume that Subsidiary B also declares and pays a dividend equal to its after-tax income. What are the total income taxes paid in the United States, Country A and Country B?
   c.   Is this a good planning strategy?

13-27 *Foreign Currency Gains and Losses—Transaction Method.* On December 10, 2015 G, a U.S. corporation on the accrual basis, sells equipment costing $23,000 for $35,000 to a customer in the United Kingdom. Payment is to be made in British pounds, based on the December 10, 2015 exchange rate. The customer sends G 21,000 British pounds in full payment on March 10, 2016. G's wholly owned subsidiary in London has net income for 2015 of 50,000 British pounds. Its sole dividend payment was made on March 10, 2016 and the grossed-up dividend totaled 18,000 British pounds. Assume that the exchange rates were as follows:

December 10, 2015.	0.66 British pounds for $1
December 31, 2015.	0.67 British pounds for $1
Weighted average	0.65 British pounds for $1
March 10, 2016.	0.68 British pounds for $1

    a. Calculate the effect on G's 2015 taxable income.
    b. Calculate the effect on G's 2016 taxable income.

13-28 *Foreign Currency Gains and Losses—Branch.* H Corporation has a new branch operation in Canada. Branch records, stated below in Canadian dollars, reveal the following:

2015 net profits.	$13,200
Funds sent to H Corporation May 1, 2015.	9,100

Assume that the Canadian exchange rates per $1 were (1) 0.82 on May 1, 2015; (2) 0.72 on December 31, 2015; and (3) 0.78 weighted average for 2015. Calculate H Corporation's Canadian branch income in U.S. dollars for 2015 using the profit and loss method.

13-29 *Aliens.* M Corporation, an Italian business, receives the following U.S. source income: (1) $40,000 net income effectively connected with its primary business activities, (2) $2,000 dividends, less $200 U.S. tax withheld, and (3) $400 interest on funds deposited in a bank. M is exempt from the 30% branch profits tax by treaty. Calculate M's U.S. Federal income tax.
    a. M Corporation qualifies as a nonresident alien.
    b. M Corporation qualifies as a resident alien.

13-30 *Residency.* M is a Mexican citizen living and working in Mexico for a manufacturing company. The company maintains some operations in the United States. M frequently travels to the United States to supervise those operations. During 2016 M worked in the United States from January 3 through January 9 and from June 7 through June 27. In addition, he took a week's vacation in Denver during November. M also states that he was in the United States for 180 days in 2015 and 177 days in 2014. Is M's Mexican salary subject to U.S. taxation?

TAX RESEARCH PROBLEMS

13-31 U.S. Parent Corporation has two wholly owned subsidiaries. One is in West Germany and one is in Romania. The effective income tax rate in Germany is 40 percent, and repatriated earnings are subject to a 15% withholding rate. The effective income tax rate in Romania is 20 percent, and repatriated earnings are subject to a 10% withholding rate. Presently, the U.S. Parent wishes to receive all its Romanian subsidiary's income in dividends but does not want to receive any of its German income in dividends for at least five years. In order to maximize its foreign tax credits and minimize its U.S. Federal income taxes, U.S. Parent wishes to elect to be taxed on a portion of the German subsidiary's income by using a consent dividend. Since no cash is actually transferred with a consent dividend, it is not subject to the German dividend withholding tax currently. However, it increases U.S. Parent's foreign source income and foreign tax credits (see *Example 15*).

   a. How and when does U.S. Parent elect a consent dividend?

   b. How is a consent dividend recorded by the subsidiary?

   c. What is your advice to the management of U.S. Parent Corporation?

Partial list of research aids:

   § 565.

   Rev. Rul. 78-296, 1978-2 C.B. 183.

   Letter Rulings 7832023 and 8224113.

13-32 L is employed by a small town as a city manager. He is a professional and hopes some day to be the city manager of a large city. L calls you and requests a meeting. He and T, his wife, will be taking a trip in a few months and are interested in tax planning. The trip will include visits to several cities in Europe and will last six weeks. He has three weeks of paid vacation and three weeks leave of absence without pay. Since his wife is not employed, she can accompany him. In discussing the trip, you learn that L has selected the cities because they interest him professionally. He has made appointments with officials of these cities and hopes to obtain information helpful in his work as a city manager. He believes these contacts eventually will lead to increased trade between these cities and his community. In addition, he admits he and T have always wanted to visit Europe, so the trip will not be all work. He estimates he will spend approximately 20 hours each week in meetings with city officials. What is your advice to L?

   a. What constitutes a business day (activities and amount of time spent)? (Be careful, this answer requires some thinking.)

   b. How is travel time en route allocated between business and nonbusiness?

   c. How are weekends and holidays treated?

   d. Prepare a detailed list of deductible expenses, assuming L's trip does not qualify as primarily business.

   e. Prepare a detailed list of deductible expenses in addition to those in (d) if L's trip does qualify as primarily business. (Use your own knowledge to go beyond the short list you find.)

   f. Refer to (d) and (e) and explain how joint expenses are prorated between L and T assuming his trip qualifies as primarily business and hers does not. Give examples and be specific.

   g. Where are deductible expenses reported on the tax return?

14

State and Local Taxation

Learning Objectives

Upon completion of this chapter you will be able to:

LO.1 Identify the major types of taxes that states and municipalities impose on corporate taxpayers.

LO.2 Determine whether sufficient nexus exists between a corporation and a particular taxing jurisdiction in order to permit the taxing jurisdiction to impose an income tax on the corporation.

LO.3 Identify the principal modifications made to Federal taxable income to arrive at taxable income for state purposes.

LO.4 Differentiate between business and nonbusiness income.

LO.5 Determine the state to which nonbusiness income is properly allocable.

LO.6 Identify the major approaches utilized by states to apportion business income.

LO.7 Differentiate between the separate reporting, consolidated return, and combined reporting (unitary) approaches to filing state income tax returns.

LO.8 Describe the alternative approaches taken by states to taxing S corporations.

LO.9 Identify the major state issues surrounding the taxation of partnerships and LLCs.

LO.10 Identify common techniques for minimizing state taxes.

Chapter Outline

Introduction

The Federal government is not the only party that imposes taxes on business organizations. As discussed in Chapter 13, U.S. corporations conducting business abroad are frequently subject to the taxing jurisdiction of both the United States and the foreign country (or countries) in which the corporation conducts business. Similarly, even corporate taxpayers that conduct business solely within the United States are often subject to taxation at both the federal and state (and possibly local) levels.

The determination of the state tax burden of a corporate taxpayer involves a number of steps including:

1. Determining the types of taxes to which the corporation is potentially subject;
2. Determining the tax jurisdictions in which the corporation is subject to tax;
3. Determining the corporation's taxable income after taking into account various state modifications to Federal taxable income;
4. Determining what portion of the corporation's income is taxable in each state in which the corporation is subject to tax; and
5. Determining the appropriate approach to filing returns in the various states in which the corporation is subject to tax.

Different issues arise where the corporation has elected to be an S corporation for Federal income tax purposes. In addition, various planning techniques exist for minimizing a corporation's state tax liability. The determination and minimization of a corporation's state tax liability is the subject of this chapter.

Types of State and Local Taxes

LO.1

Identify the major types of taxes that states and municipalities impose on corporate taxpayers.

At the state and local level, corporations may be subjected to a variety of taxes including state and local income taxes, sales and use taxes, property taxes, and a variety of fees and taxes for the privilege of doing business in a particular jurisdiction. Each of these different types of taxes is reviewed briefly before turning our attention to an in-depth examination of what is generally the most complex of these taxes, the state corporate income tax.

STATE INCOME TAXES

The primary focus of this chapter is the state corporate income tax. At the current time, all states other than Nevada, South Dakota, Washington, and Wyoming, as well as the District of Columbia, impose an income based tax on corporations.[1] State income-based tax is imposed if a corporation possesses sufficient ties to a particular state to give rise to nexus. While state income tax rates differ significantly, most states utilize Federal taxable income as a starting point in computing state taxable income, that is, they piggyback onto the federal tax base. Individual state law may then provide for modifications to Federal taxable income to arrive at state taxable income. However, unlike the system for taxing U.S. multinationals that generally relies on complex sourcing rules and transfer prices to allocate income to specific taxing jurisdictions (that is, a separate accounting approach), multistate income taxation generally utilizes an apportionment approach at least with respect to business income.[2] Under such approach, total taxable income (after state modifications) is apportioned among the various jurisdictions in which the corporation operates based on a formula intended to reflect the way in which income is generated. In many states, the formula takes into account factors such as sales, property, and payroll.

---

[1] Texas imposes a franchise tax (also referred to as a margins tax) on corporate entities with more than $1,030,000 in total revenue on the lesser of 70% of total revenues or 100% of gross receipts after deductions for either compensation or cost of goods sold. Washington, while not imposing a tax based on net income, imposes a business and occupation tax based on gross income. These are examples of the great diversity found in the area of state and local taxation.

[2] Taxpayers occasionally employ separate accounting in their attempts to show that apportionment based on statutory formulas produces unfair results, that is, formula-based apportionment results in substantially more income being attributed to a state than the income actually earned in such state as determined utilizing separate accounting. In general, the courts have been reluctant to accept such arguments.

SALES AND USE TAXES

A sales tax is imposed on the gross receipts from the retail sale of tangible personal property and certain services. Currently, 45 states and the District of Columbia impose sales taxes.[3] Numerous local governmental bodies, such as cities, counties, and school districts, also impose sales taxes. Tax rates are stated as a percentage of the consideration received in a taxable transaction. Rates and definitions of taxable transactions vary depending on the particular state or local governmental body imposing the tax. In addition, taxing authorities generally exempt certain items, such as items purchased for resale and items used in manufacturing, from the sales tax. Exempt items vary from jurisdiction to jurisdiction.

A use tax is imposed on the use within a state or local jurisdiction of tangible personal property on which the sales tax was not paid, e.g., items purchased in another jurisdiction that imposes no sales tax or imposes tax at a rate lower than the rate in the jurisdiction in which the item is used. The tax rate normally equals that of the taxing authority's sales tax, with a credit generally being allowed for taxes actually paid to other taxing jurisdictions. It should be noted that states and other taxing authorities are generally increasing their enforcement activities with respect to use taxes in response to increases in purchases from out-of-state retailers and increased movement of assets between taxing jurisdictions.

While state and local sales taxes frequently comprise a large revenue source for state and local governments, they generally do not constitute a direct tax on corporations or other business entities making sales within a taxing jurisdiction. This is due to the fact that sales taxes are generally imposed on the ultimate consumer as opposed to the seller. The seller merely collects the tax at the time of sale, and then periodically remits the taxes to the appropriate taxing authority. It is not uncommon for a state or local government to allow the seller to retain a nominal percentage of the collected taxes to compensate it for the additional costs incurred by the seller in complying with the tax requirements. It should be noted that, while a business typically does not directly bear a sales tax, it might indirectly bear such tax to the extent that it must charge prices below what it would be able to charge in the absence of a sales tax.[4]

To help ensure that sales taxes are imposed on the ultimate consumer of a particular good, most taxing jurisdiction's sales tax statutes provide resale exemptions that exempt purchases from sales tax to the extent that the items are being purchased for resale or for incorporation into an item that will be sold. Such statutes may also provide exemptions for ancillary items such as certain packaging and tangible personal property consumed or used in the process of manufacturing property that is to be resold. It is important to note that sales and use tax statutes vary significantly from jurisdiction to jurisdiction; consequently, what may be an exempt item or transaction in one jurisdiction may be taxable in another. It is also important to note that in some cases a business entity may directly bear the burden of the sales (or use) tax to the extent that it acquires tangible personal property for its own use. For example, a business would typically be liable for sales or use tax on a purchase of office equipment or computers for its own use. This can pose a particular problem where the business acquires similar items both for its own use and for resale, for example, a computer reseller that also buys computers for use by its employees.

---

[3] Alaska, Delaware, Montana, New Hampshire, and Oregon are the states that do not currently impose a sales tax at the state level. In Alaska, local municipalities may impose a sales tax. Moreover, in Delaware, businesses may be subject to a business license tax that resembles a sales tax and are subject to a use tax on leases of personal property. As mentioned previously, the diversity of state approaches to taxation should never be underestimated.

[4] Note that a corporation may *directly* bear a sales tax where it is the ultimate consumer.

Another important type of sales tax exemption relates to casual or bulk sales of property. State statutes typically exempt sales to ultimate consumers from sales tax to the extent that the seller either engages in less than a specified number of sales transactions involving a particular type of property or sells such property in connection with a sale of substantially all of the assets of its business. Again, the specifics of these exemptions vary widely from jurisdiction to jurisdiction.

A final point to note concerning sales and use taxes is that they are often subject to a different set of nexus rules (discussed below) than those that apply for purposes of state income taxes. For example, physical presence by the corporation in the taxing state may be required to create nexus for purposes of sales and use taxes, whereas nexus may exist for purposes of income and other taxes notwithstanding the lack of physical presence.[5]

PROPERTY TAXES

Property taxes are a type of *ad valorem* tax imposed on the value of property subject to tax. A real property tax is a tax on the value of realty (land, buildings, etc.) owned by nonexempt organizations within a particular taxing jurisdiction. Rates vary with location and type of property (e.g., residential, commercial, agricultural, etc.). This type of tax normally supports local services, such as the public school system or fire department, and is levied on a recurring annual basis.

A personal property tax is levied on the value of tangible personalty located within a taxing jurisdiction. Personalty is property not classified as realty and includes items such as office furniture, machinery and equipment, inventories, and supplies. The tax normally must be paid annually, with each local jurisdiction determining its own tax rate and items subject to tax. For example, many jurisdictions exempt inventory from the imposition of the personal property tax.

While numerous jurisdictions impose a real and/or personal property tax, relatively few jurisdictions impose an intangible personal property tax. Where such tax is imposed, it is based on the value of intangible property (e.g., stocks, bonds, and accounts and notes receivable) located within a jurisdiction. As with the personal property tax, this tax is generally paid annually, with each jurisdiction setting its own tax rates and items to be taxed.

Regardless of which of the three types of taxes is being considered, it is generally imposed on the value of property located within a particular taxing jurisdiction on a given date. Such date may vary from jurisdiction to jurisdiction. To prevent tax avoidance in the case of inventory, vehicles, aircraft, and other easily movable types of property by moving it from jurisdiction to jurisdiction in such a way that it is absent from a particular taxing jurisdiction on the assessment date, taxing jurisdictions employ several anti-avoidance mechanisms. For example, the law may provide for taxation of personal property at the commercial domicile (for example, home office) of the owner if it is temporarily outside the jurisdiction. Similarly, to prevent the shifting of inventory from jurisdiction to jurisdiction or the maintenance of artificially low inventory levels on the assessment date, the statute may provide for the use of an average inventory value for the period. Conversely, to prevent multiple taxation in the case of property that is located in several taxing jurisdictions during the year (e.g., automobiles, aircraft, etc.), states may allow apportionment that results in taxation of the item based on its relative connection to the taxing jurisdiction (e.g., relative time or miles attributable to the jurisdiction).

OTHER TAXES AND FEES

State and local governments may impose a variety of other types of taxes and fees on corporations and other business organizations. Taxes and fees commonly imposed by states on corporations include franchise taxes, excise taxes, unemployment taxes, incorporation fees, license fees, and stock and/or realty transfer taxes.

---

[5] Contrast *Quill Corporation v. North Dakota*, 504 U.S. 298 (1992) with *Geoffrey, Inc. v. South Carolina Tax Comm'n.*, 437 S.E.2d 13, cert. denied, 510 U.S. 992 (1993).

Franchise Tax

A franchise tax is a tax on the privilege of doing business in a state (and, in some cases, in a locality) and, as such, is imposed on both corporations domiciled in the state and on out-of-state corporations transacting business in the state. The tax is generally imposed annually based on the value of the capital (common stock, paid-in capital, and retained earnings) employed within the particular jurisdiction. Rates vary from jurisdiction to jurisdiction and are generally stated as a percentage of capital or as a dollar amount per $1,000 of capital. Where a corporation is engaged in business in multiple states, its capital is typically apportioned among the states for purposes of computing the franchise tax. In limited cases, the corporation's home state may impose a franchise tax on the entire amount of the corporation's capital even though the corporation does business in other states. The tax is generally imposed in addition to any state corporate income tax. In a few cases, the franchise tax is imposed only if it yields a tax higher than that resulting from the imposition of the state corporate income tax or is based on net income as opposed to capital.

Excise Taxes

As in the case of the federal government, many states and municipalities impose excise taxes on a wide variety of items such as gasoline, liquor, and cigarettes, and on certain services such as motel lodging. Typically, such taxes are based on quantity (e.g., gallons) or a percentage of the sales price. Depending on the exact item in question, the tax may be imposed on the manufacturer of the item or on the consumer of the product or service. Collection and reporting responsibilities typically fall on the manufacturer (in the case of an excise tax imposed on the manufacturer) or the seller (in the case of an excise tax imposed on the consumer).

Unemployment Taxes

Most states impose an unemployment tax on employers with employees who might potentially become eligible for the particular state's unemployment benefits programs. The tax revenues are utilized to finance the cost of such programs. Such taxes are generally stated as a percentage of taxable wages up to a per employee maximum wage amount. The tax rate frequently varies from employer to employer depending on the employer's experience rate (the frequency of unemployment benefit claims by former employees). This approach provides employers with an incentive to retain employees, since there is a direct relationship between the number of employees laid off and the experience (and, in turn, tax) rate. In addition to state unemployment taxes, the federal government imposes a federal unemployment tax (FUTA) at a flat rate. A credit against such tax is allowed for all or part of state unemployment taxes.

Incorporation Fees

States typically impose a fee on domestic corporations for the privilege of incorporating within the particular state. Likewise, states frequently impose a fee on out-of-state corporations for the privilege of becoming registered to do business within the state. Such fee may constitute a fixed amount or may be based on a factor such as the par value of the corporation's authorized stock.

License Fees

Many states impose a fee for the privilege of conducting certain types of professions, trades, or businesses within their borders. Common targets of such fees are professionals such as doctors, lawyers, and accountants. Such fees are usually imposed on an annual basis, with the amount and subject occupations being determined by the particular state.

Stock/Real Estate Transfer Taxes

Some states and local governments impose a tax on transfers of stock and/or real estate. Where a stock transfer tax is imposed, it is generally based on the par or market value of the shares transferred. Certain transfers of stock are generally exempt. Where a real estate transfer tax is imposed, the consideration paid for the property generally serves as the basis for tax.

Multistate Corporate Income Taxation

As discussed earlier, most corporations are subject to state (and, in some cases, local) income taxes in one or more jurisdictions. Given such realization, the focus shifts to identifying the specific jurisdictions in which the corporation is subject to tax and the computation of its taxable income and income tax liability in each of such jurisdictions. In addition, alternative filing approaches and special rules applicable to S corporations must be considered. These topics are considered in detail in this section.

JURISDICTION TO TAX

LO.2

Determine whether sufficient nexus exists between a corporation and a particular taxing jurisdiction in order to permit the taxing jurisdiction to impose an income tax on the corporation.

Much like the Federal government is free to tax its citizens regardless of where they reside, states possess the jurisdiction to tax corporations incorporated within their borders, regardless of whether such domestic corporations actually operate within the state of incorporation.[6] A more difficult question concerns a state's ability to tax foreign corporations (i.e., corporations incorporated in other states).

The U.S. constitutional provision most frequently used to challenge a state's ability to tax is the Commerce Clause, which is found in Art. I, § 8, Cl. 3, of the Constitution of the United States. That clause provides that "[T]he Congress shall have the power … [t]o regulate Commerce with foreign Nations, and among the several States, and with the Indian Tribes." By negative implication, states are prohibited from taking any action that will contravene Congress's authority to regulate interstate commerce, including the taxation of businesses engaged in interstate commerce.

In *Complete Auto Transit v. Brady,*[7] the Supreme Court enunciated the modern four-prong Commerce Clause test that is used to determine whether a state tax is constitutional.

- First, the tax must be applied to an activity that has a substantial nexus with the state.

- Second, the tax must be fairly apportioned.

- Third, the tax must not discriminate against interstate commerce.

- Fourth, the tax must be fairly related to the services provided by the state.

Nexus

Typically, the ability of a state to tax a foreign corporation is dependent upon the existence of sufficient nexus between the corporation and the state attempting to impose the tax. Nexus refers to the degree of relationship between a state and a corporation that must be present before a state (or other taxing jurisdiction) has the right to impose a tax on the income of a foreign corporation.[8] Maintenance of an office within the state, ownership or leasing of property within the state, employment of personnel within the state, or certain other economic activities (conducted either directly or through agents or other operatives) may all potentially give rise to nexus. Generally, state law determines the degree of business activity necessary to establish nexus; however, as discussed below, the question of what specific activities give rise to nexus has been the subject of both Federal legislation and frequent judicial review.

Fair Apportionment

The second prong of *Complete Auto Transit's*[9] four-prong Commerce Clause test is that income must be fairly apportioned among the states where a multistate business is taxable. Apportionment avoids multiple taxation of the same income that would occur if each of the states where a business operated imposed tax on all of the entity's income.

At the federal level, the potential for double taxation of the same income by different jurisdictions is avoided by taxing U.S. based multinational corporations on their entire income and allowing a deduction or a credit for taxes paid to other countries. Similarly, alien corporations are taxed only on income effectively connected with the conduct of a trade or

---

[6] P.L. 86-272, Section 101(b)(1).

[7] 430 U.S. 274 (1977).

[8] As stated by Justice Frankfurter, "The simple but controlling question is whether the State has given anything (i.e., benefits and protections) for which it can ask return." [*Wisconsin v. J.C. Penney Co.* 311 U.S. 435 (1940)].

[9] *Supra*, Footnote 7.

business in the United States. Unlike the federal methodology, the states generally do not use a system of corporate income tax credits to prevent multiple taxation by differing states. Instead, they attribute portions of the tax base among the states in which the corporation does business so that each state taxes only a fair proportion of the corporation's income. A more detailed discussion of apportionment is included later in the text.

Nondiscrimination

The U.S. Supreme Court has not provided a clear-cut test for determining what constitutes discrimination prohibited under the Commerce Clause. The Court often relies on an analysis of relative tax burdens to determine if state taxes are discriminatory. Nevertheless, the Court has indicated that facially discriminatory treatment of similarly situated taxpayers is virtually per se invalid.[10] For example, in holding discriminatory a gross receipts tax on businesses selling tangible property at wholesale that exempted local manufacturers, the Court noted that a state may not tax a transaction or incident more heavily when it crosses state lines than when it occurs entirely within the state.[11]

The Court also views state tax discrimination as an interference with the businessperson's independent economic decisions regarding the location of his or her business. For example, a Louisiana use tax paid on the first use of outer continental shelf natural gas brought into the state was unconstitutional under the Commerce Clause because the tax was allowed as a credit against other Louisiana taxes and the obvious economic effect was to encourage natural gas owners to invest in mineral exploration and development within Louisiana rather than in other states.[12]

Fair Relationship

The last prong of the *Complete Auto Transit* test requires that the tax be fairly related to the services provided by the state. This prong does not require a comparison of the amount of the tax and the cost to the state of the benefits it bestowed on the taxpayer. It merely requires that the tax be reasonably related to the extent of the taxpayer's contact in the state.[13]

Public Law 86-272

Public Law 86-272, enacted by Congress in 1959 pursuant to the authority granted it by the Commerce Clause of the U.S. Constitution, prohibits a state from imposing a net income tax on a business where:

1. The business's only activity in the state is the solicitation of orders for sales (but not leases, rentals, licenses, etc.) of tangible personal property (but not real or intangible property);

2. The orders are sent outside the state for approval or rejection; and

3. If approved, the orders are filled and shipped from a point outside the state.[14]

Also protected is the solicitation of orders in the name of, or for the benefit of, a prospective customer from customers of such customer (i.e., indirect solicitation) if sales to the intermediary would be protected under the general rule stated above.

Example 1

Corporation R, domiciled in State A, sells goods to wholesalers in State B. The sales from R to the wholesalers meet the requirements of P.L. 86-272. Occasionally, R personnel solicit orders directly from retailers in State B on behalf of the wholesalers. Such activity does not cause R's sales to State B wholesalers to become taxable.

---

[10] *Oregon Waste Systems, Inc. v. Department of Environmental Quality*, 511 U.S. 93 (1994).

[11] *Armco v. Hardesty*, 467 U.S. 638 (1984).

[12] *Maryland v. Louisiana*, 451 U.S. 725 (1981).

[13] *Commonwealth Edison Co. v. Montana*, 453 U.S. 609 (1981).

[14] 15 USC 381-385. It should be noted that P.L. 86-272 does not apply to state taxes that are not based on net income.

Where in-state activities are conducted by an independent contractor, rather than by an employee, the following additional activities may be conducted without subjecting the corporation to taxation:

1. Making sales (that is, actually accepting orders); and
2. Maintaining an in-state sales office.

In order to qualify as an independent contractor for purposes of these more liberal rules, the sales representative must represent more than one principal and generally must be free from direction and control by the out-of-state seller.

P.L. 86-272 left unanswered the key question of what constitutes solicitation. The Supreme Court filled such gap by providing that solicitation of orders includes "activities that are entirely ancillary to requests for purchases—those that serve no independent business function apart from their connection to the solicitation of orders."[15] The Court went on to explain that solicitation does not include "those activities that the company would otherwise engage in but chooses to assign to its in-state sales force." Finally, the Court held that a company should not be subject to tax if its activities within a state are de minimis.

Exhibit 14-1 provides a list of activities that have generally been found sufficient to cause the taxpayer to lose the protection afforded by P.L. 86-272. Exhibit 14-2, on the other hand, provides a list of activities in which a taxpayer may generally engage without losing the protection afforded by P.L. 86-272. It is important to note that P.L. 86-272 applies only to sellers of tangible personal property; consequently, state law and relevant court decisions must be examined to determine if nexus exists in the case of service businesses or businesses involved in the sale of real or intangible property. Given differences between states and business practices in specific types of organizations, a discussion of nexus for these types of businesses is beyond the scope of this text.

EXHIBIT 14-1	Activities Not Protected under P.L. 86-272

- Approving or accepting orders
- Carrying samples for sale, exchange, or distribution in any manner for consideration or other value
- Collecting delinquent accounts
- Conducting training classes, seminars, or lectures for persons other than sales personnel
- Consigning tangible personal property to any person, including an independent contractor
- Hiring, training, or supervising personnel other than sales personnel
- Installation or supervision of installation
- Investigating creditworthiness
- Maintaining a sample or display room for more than two weeks in any one location during the taxable year
- Maintaining an office
- Making repairs or providing maintenance
- Owning, leasing, maintaining, or otherwise using any of the following facilities or property in the state: real estate; repair shop; parts department; employment office; purchasing office; warehouse; meeting place for directors, officers, or employees; stock of goods for sale; telephone answering service; or mobile stores (i.e., trucks with driver-salespersons)
- Picking up or replacing damaged or returned property
- Providing engineering services
- Repossessing property

SOURCE: "Information Concerning Practices of States under P.L. 86-272" MTC 1993, as revised to reflect the holding of the Supreme Court in *Wrigley*.

---

[15] *Wisconsin Department of Revenue v. William Wrigley, Jr., Co.*, 505 U.S. 214 (1992).

EXHIBIT 14-2	Activities Generally Protected under P.L. 86-272

- Advertising
- Carrying samples only for display or distribution without charge
- Checking customers' inventories for reorder
- Maintaining a sample or display room for two weeks or less in any one location during the taxable year*
- Owning or furnishing automobiles to salespeople
- Passing inquiries or complaints on to the home office
- Soliciting sales by an in-state resident employee, provided that the employee does not maintain a place of business in the state
- In-state recruitment, training, and evaluation of sales representatives
- Mere qualification to do business in a state
- Maintenance by an employee of a home office, provided that the use of the office is limited to solicitation and receiving orders from customers (even if the company pays the cost of maintaining the office)

* This may create nexus in a number of states.

SOURCE: "Information Concerning Practices of States under P.L. 86-272" MTC 1993, as revised to reflect the holding of the Supreme Court in *Wrigley*.

Example 2

Corporation X, which is domiciled in State T, sends employees into State L to solicit orders from customers. The employees must send the orders back to X's home office in State T for approval. If approved, the orders are shipped via common carrier from X's warehouse in State T. Under P.L. 86-272, L cannot impose an income tax on X.

Example 3

Assume the same facts as in *Example 2,* except that X maintains an office in State L. In this case, P.L. 86-272 does not protect X from taxation in State L, since maintenance of an office does not constitute a protected activity.

Example 4

Assume the same facts as in *Example 3,* except that X's salespeople in State L are properly classified as independent contractors instead of employees. In this case, State L is prevented from taxing X, since maintenance of a sales office for independent contractors is protected under P.L. 86-272.

COMPUTATION OF STATE TAXABLE INCOME

Once it has been determined that a corporation is subject to tax in a particular state, the next step in the state income tax calculation process involves computing state taxable income. This task is made considerably simpler by the fact that the majority of the states imposing a corporate income tax piggyback on Federal taxable income by specifically adopting all or

LO.3

Identify the principal modifications made to Federal taxable income to arrive at taxable income for state purposes.

part of the Internal Revenue Code or by starting with income from line 28 (taxable income before net operating loss and special deductions) or line 30 (taxable income) of Form 1120.[16] States employing the piggyback approach then specify specific adjustments to be made to such starting number to arrive at state taxable income. These adjustments, which may be either positive or negative, vary considerably from state to state; however, certain adjustments are encountered in a number of states. Several of the more commonly encountered adjustments are discussed below; however, it is always imperative that the particular state statute be consulted.

The general process for computing a multistate corporation's income tax liability in a particular state, referred to as the tax formula for multistate taxpayers, is summarized in Exhibit 14-3.

EXHIBIT 14-3	Tax Formula for Multistate Taxpayers

Federal taxable income (Form 1120, line 28 or 30)	**$ xxx,xxx**
Plus: State additions to Federal taxable income	+ xx,xxx
Minus: State subtractions from Federal taxable income	− xx,xxx
State tax base	**$ xxx,xxx**
Minus (plus): Total nonbusiness income (loss)	± xx,xxx
Total business income	**$ xxx,xxx**
Times: Apportionment percentage for state	× xx%
Business income apportioned to state	**$ xxx,xxx**
Plus (minus): Nonbusiness income (loss) allocated to state	± xx,xxx
State taxable income (Loss)	**$ xxx,xxx**
Times: State tax rate	× xx%
State income tax liability before credits	**$ xxx,xxx**
Minus: State credits	− xx,xxx
Net state income tax liability	**$ xxx,xxx**

Another factor that helps minimize differences between states is the existence of a model law known as the Uniform Division of Income for Tax Purposes Act (UDITPA). This model law written in 1957 provides standardized rules related to the taxation of multistate corporations. A number of states have adopted UDITPA in its entirety, while a number of others have either adopted UDITPA in part or modeled their laws after UDITPA. States adopting UDITPA also may become members of the Multistate Tax Compact. Such member states appoint the Multistate Tax Commission (MTC) that is charged with interpreting UDITPA through the promulgation of rules and regulations and with proposing periodic changes to UDITPA. The MTC also promotes uniformity in statutes and procedures in areas of taxation other than income taxes. The MTC substantially revised Article IV (containing the provisions of UDITPA) in July 2015.

---

[16] Moreover, even those states that do not piggyback on Federal taxable income but, rather, require that each item of income and deduction be separately stated generally employ definitions of taxable income that resemble Federal taxable income. Further, states that do piggyback on federal law typically piggyback on Federal regulations and rulings, and the outcome of the Federal tax return audit process, as well. Note, however, that this seemingly simple step can present substantial complexities depending on the way that the state statutes conform to the federal law. Some states have adopted a moving conformity system in which the computation of state taxable income begins with federal taxable income under the Internal Revenue Code (IRC) as of the *current* date. Other states have adopted a static conformity system, meaning that the computation of state taxable income begins with federal taxable income as defined in the IRC as of a *specified* date. Under a static conformity system, changes in federal law are not automatically adopted by a state. Rather the state legislature must enact legislation to change the conformity date. This allows the state flexibility in deciding whether or not to conform to the federal change. Unfortunately, it creates uncertainty in tax planning before the state legislature has enacted the conforming legislation.

Additions to Federal Taxable Income

Common additions to Federal taxable income to arrive at the state tax base include:

- Amount by which depreciation, depletion, and amortization deductions allowable for federal purposes exceed those allowable for state purposes.[17] This item may also give rise to adjustments upon the disposition of assets having differing bases for Federal and state purposes due to prior differences in allowable depreciation, depletion, or amortization deductions.

- Dividends-received deduction allowed for Federal purposes but not for state purposes (if the starting point for computing state taxable income is line 30).[18]

- Expenses deducted in computing Federal taxable income related to interest earned on U.S. obligations.

- State taxes based on net income that were deducted in computing Federal taxable income.

- Interest income on state and local bonds that is exempt for Federal income tax purposes. Some states exempt only interest earned on their own obligations in computing this adjustment.

- Net operating loss deduction for Federal income tax purposes (if the starting point for computing state taxable income is line 30).

Subtractions from Federal Taxable Income

Common subtractions from Federal taxable income to arrive at the state tax base include:

- Amount by which depreciation, depletion, and amortization deductions allowable for state purposes exceed those allowable for Federal purposes. This item may also give rise to adjustments upon the disposition of assets having differing bases for federal and state purposes due to prior differences in allowable depreciation, depletion, or amortization deductions.

- Expenses related to state or local bonds that are disallowed for Federal income tax purposes (to the extent the related interest is taxable for state purposes).

- Interest income on U.S. obligations or obligations of Federal agencies.

- Net operating loss deduction allowed for state purposes. State net operating loss deductions can differ from Federal net operating losses for a variety of reasons including differing carryover periods, required apportionment of the total Federal NOL, and state law allowing only a percentage of total losses sustained to be carried over.[19]

- Refunds of state and local taxes to the extent included in Federal taxable income.

Example 5

S Corporation is taxable only in State Z. State Z law provides for the use of Federal taxable income as the starting point in computing state taxable income. In addition, modifications are provided to reflect (1) the taxability of interest on state and local bonds of other states, (2) the nontaxability of interest on Federal obligations, (3) the mandatory use of the straight-line method of depreciation in computing state taxable

---

[17] Such differences may arise either as a result of the adoption by the state of its own cost recovery scheme or a lag in the state conforming its taxing statute to federal law. In addition, a number of states have indicated that they will not follow the Federal rules relative to bonus depreciation and increased expensing under Code Section 179.

[18] Approximately one-half of the states that impose a corporate income tax allow a deduction for dividends received comparable to that allowed for Federal purposes. A few states simply allow a full deduction for all dividends received.

[19] Similar variations between federal and state law can exist in the case of capital losses.

income, and (4) the disallowance of all state income taxes. Selected information for 20X0 is as follows:

- Federal taxable income equals $200,000.

- Excluded in computing Federal taxable income is interest on state and local bonds of $15,000. $5,000 of such interest relates to State Z bonds.

- Included in Federal taxable income is $20,000 of interest on U.S. government obligations.

- S deducted $100,000 of depreciation in computing Federal taxable income. Depreciation for 20X0 computed utilizing the straight-line method equals $60,000.

- State income taxes deducted in computing Federal taxable income totaled $15,000.

S's State Z taxable income for 20X0 is computed as follows:

Federal taxable income	$200,000
Interest on out-of-state municipal bonds	+ 10,000
Excess of Federal depreciation over state depreciation	+ 40,000
State income taxes deducted for Federal purposes	+ 15,000
Interest on U.S. government obligations	− 20,000
State Z taxable income	$245,000

BUSINESS AND NONBUSINESS INCOME

LO.4
Differentiate between business and nonbusiness income.

A critical determination in computing the taxable income of a multistate corporation involves properly distinguishing between the corporation's business income and its nonbusiness income. The reason that such distinction is important is that different sets of rules apply for dividing the two classes of income (after state modifications) among the states in which the corporation conducts business (that is, the states with which it has nexus). Business income is apportioned among the states where the corporation does business. States are constitutionally prohibited from apportioning income that does not have an operational relationship with business conducted in the state.[20] Consequently, nonbusiness income is generally allocated to a particular state. Often this is the taxpayer's state of commercial domicile or another state that has a close connection to the activity that generates the income.

A few states don't distinguish between business and nonbusiness income. In those states, all income is subject to apportionment. In the 2015 rewrite of Model Compact Article IV, the MTC moved away from referring to income as business or nonbusiness instead using the terms apportionable or non-apportionable.

Business Income

The typical presumption is that all of a corporation's income is business income.[21]

Notwithstanding the general presumption that all corporate income is business income, UDITPA defines business income as "income arising from transactions and activity in the regular course of the taxpayer's trade or business and includes income from tangible and intangible property if the acquisition, management, and disposition of the property constitute integral parts of the taxpayer's regular trade or business operations."[22]

Most states interpret the definition contained in UDITPA as incorporating two separate tests for determining whether income is business income. The tests are referred to as the transactional test and the functional test. In some states, if either test is satisfied, the income will be classified as business income. Other states require both tests to be satisfied in order for income to be classified as business income. Unfortunately, some states have not indicated whether they require one or both tests to be satisfied.

[20] *Allied Signal, Inc. v. Director, Division of Taxation,* 504 U.S. 768 (1992).

[21] According to the MTC regulations, "an item of income is nonbusiness income only if it does not meet the definitional requirements for being classified as business income."

[22] UDITPA Section 1(a).

Under the transactional test, income is considered business income if it arises from "transactions and activity in the regular course of the taxpayer's trade or business."[23] The focus is on the type of transaction giving rise to the income, and how the transaction relates to the taxpayer's regular trade or business. Under the functional test, income is considered apportionable business income if the acquisition, management, and disposition of the asset that generates the income constitute integral parts of the taxpayer's regular trade or business operations. The functional test focuses on the relationship of the asset giving rise to the taxable income, and the business itself.

Under the transactional test, the sale of a factory by a business likely would be considered unusual and extraordinary, occurring outside the normal course of business. Therefore, it would be classified as nonbusiness income. Under the functional test, however, gain or loss on the sale likely would be considered business income because the factory was acquired and used in the taxpayer's regular trade or business.

Nonbusiness Income

UDITPA defines nonbusiness income as "all income other than business income."[24] Nonbusiness income thus ordinarily consists of passive income such as dividends, interest, rents, royalties, capital gains from the sale of investment assets, and other income unrelated to the corporation's regular business operations. Care must be taken, however, in assuming that all passive income constitutes nonbusiness income. For example, income from short-term investments of working capital will generally be considered business income. Likewise, rents and royalties generated as part of the taxpayer's regular business activities are considered business income.

Example 6

X Corporation derives net nonbusiness income of $10,000 from the rental of a building located in State A. X's business income is apportioned 50% to State A and 50% to State B. State A has a corporate income tax rate of three percent, while State B's tax rate is eight percent. If the rental income constitutes business income in both States A and B, X's total state income tax liability with respect to the rental income is $550 ([$10,000 × 50% × 3%] + [$10,000 × 50% × 8%]). In contrast, if rental income constitutes nonbusiness income in both states and rents are taxable in the state in which the property is located, X's total state income tax liability with respect to the rental income is only $300 ($10,000 × 100% × 3%). Finally, if State A treats rents as nonbusiness income, while State B treats such income as business income, X's total state income tax liability with respect to the rental income equals $700 ([$10,000 × 100% × 3%] + [$10,000 × 50% × 8%]). This final situation illustrates how a multistate taxpayer may be subject to state income tax on more (or less) than 100% of its income due to inconsistencies in state laws.

ALLOCATION OF NONBUSINESS INCOME

Nonbusiness income is generally allocated to the state in which the property generating the income or loss is located, that is its business situs.[25] For example, nonbusiness rental income would typically be allocated to the state in which the property generating the income is located. If the corporation is not taxable in the state in which an income generating nonbusiness asset is located, UDITPA provides for the assignment of the income to the state in which the corporation's trade or business is directed or managed, that is, its state of commercial domicile.[26] Special rules apply in the case of certain types of income, such as rents

LO.5
Determine the state to which nonbusiness income is properly allocable.

[23] UDITPA Section 1(a).

[24] UDITPA Section 1(e).

[25] Even intangibles, such as accounts and notes receivable, may acquire a business situs if they become integral parts of a local business [*Farmer's Loan & Trust Co. v. Minnesota*, 280 U.S. 204, (1930)].

[26] UDITPA Section 1(b). It should be noted that, under this definition, a corporation's state of commercial domicile

can differ from the state in which it is incorporated, i.e., its statutory domicile [*Wheeling Steel Corp. v. Fox*, 56 S Ct. 773 (1936)]. It should also be noted that the business situs, commercial domicile, and statutory domicile approaches are not necessarily mutually exclusive; consequently, a corporation may be subject to tax in more than one jurisdiction on income from the same assets where sufficient nexus exists with each taxing jurisdiction and there are inconsistencies in state law [*Curry v. McCanless*, 307 U.S. 357 (1939)].

and royalties relating to tangible personal property and intangible assets such as patents and copyrights. UDITPA rules generally provide for allocation of receipts based on the proportionate usage of the asset within the state.[27]

Example 7

T Corporation owns investment securities that are held by a broker in State D. Dividends and interest earned on such securities constitute nonbusiness income. T is not taxable in State D. T is domiciled in State C which has adopted UDITPA; consequently, T is taxable in State C on the income earned on the investment securities even though they are physically located in State D.

APPORTIONMENT OF BUSINESS INCOME

LO.6
Identify the major approaches utilized by states to apportion business income.

Business income is typically apportioned among the states in which a corporation is taxable (i.e., the states with which it has sufficient nexus) by multiplying total business income (after state modifications) by an apportionment percentage designed to reflect the level of corporate activity within the state as a percentage of total corporate activity. Under UDITPA, a taxpayer is entitled to apportion income (as opposed to being taxable on the corporation's full income in its state of commercial domicile) if it can establish that it has income from business activity that is taxable both within and without a particular state.[28] For purposes of this rule, a taxpayer is considered taxable in a state if it may be subject to tax in such state (as a result of its having sufficient nexus with such state) even if such state does not actually impose a tax.[29]

An apportionment percentage is determined based on one or more apportionment factors. These factors are computed by taking a ratio of the amount of such factor for the state under consideration to the total amount of such factor for the company as a whole. Commonly used apportionment factors include sales, property, and payroll. Where multiple apportionment factors are utilized, they are generally averaged to arrive at the apportionment percentage. Historically, the most common apportionment formula has been a three-factor equally weighted formula. The concept is based on the theory that business profits are a function of capital employed (measured by property), labor (measured by payroll) and sales.

However, at present only nine states use an equally weighted three-factor test while 18 states utilize a three-factor formula with sales double-weighted, and 16 states utilize a one-factor sales formula. The trend over the last 15 years or so is towards increasing the weight on the sales factor.

In general, the sum of the factors is divided by no more than the number of applicable factors. If one of the factors is not present for the in-state operations of a corporation (i.e. the numerator is zero), some states allow or require that the factor be eliminated from the apportionment process. For example, for a state that has adopted an equally weighted three-factor formula, if the property factor is not present in that state, the apportionment formula may be determined by dividing the sum of the remaining two factors by two instead of three.

UDITPA contains an equitable apportionment provision allowing the state tax administrator (either upon his own volition or at the request of taxpayer) to make adjustments to the normal apportionment method in order to fairly reflect the taxpayer's business activity in the state. Among the types of adjustments allowed under this provision are:

- Separate accounting (i.e., attributing each item of income and expense to a specific location);

- The exclusion of one or more factors (for example, a factor with a zero denominator); or

- The inclusion of one or more additional factors.[30]

Finally, it is important to note that the standard formula discussed above generally applies only to manufacturers, wholesalers, retailers, and similar businesses. Special apportionment formulas are typically provided for taxpayers engaged in businesses such as banking, insurance, air transportation, trucking, and the provision of public utility services.

---

[27] UDITPA Sections 5(b) and 8(a)(1).

[28] UDITPA Section 2.

[29] UDITPA Section 3.

[30] UDITPA Section 18.

Moreover, taxpayers engaged in service businesses or other industries in which the traditional formula does not properly reflect the way income is earned should consider requesting permission to use an alternative formula.

Example 8

P Corporation derived $1,000,000 of taxable income (after state modifications) from its business activities in States Y and Z. P has no allocable income. The following table summarizes P's sales, property, and payroll in each state:

	State Y	State Z	Total
Sales	$5,000,000	$2,500,000	$7,500,000
Property	1,800,000	200,000	2,000,000
Payroll	1,000,000	250,000	1,250,000

State Y utilizes a three-factor apportionment formula in which each factor is accorded equal weight. State Z utilizes a three-factor apportionment formula which assigns double weight to sales.

P's State Y business taxable income is calculated as follows:

Computation of apportionment percentage:

Sales factor ($5,000,000/$7,500,000)	66.7%
Property factor ($1,800,000/$2,000,000)	90.0
Payroll factor ($1,000,000/$1,250,000)	80.0
Sum of apportionment factors	236.7%
	÷ 3
Apportionment percentage for State Y	78.9%

Computation of state taxable income:

Total business income (after state modifications)	$1,000,000
Times: Apportionment percentage for State Y	× 78.9%
State Y taxable income	$ 789,000

P's State Z business taxable income is calculated as follows:

Computation of apportionment percentage:

Sales factor ([$2,500,000/$7,500,000] × 2)	66.7%
Property factor ($200,000/$2,000,000)	10.0
Payroll factor ($250,000/$1,250,000)	20.0
Sum of apportionment factors	96.7%
	÷ 4
Apportionment percentage for State Z	24.2%

Computation of state taxable income:

Total business income (after state modifications)	$1,000,000
Times: Apportionment percentage for State Z	× 24.2%
State Z taxable income	$ 242,000

Note that the differing state rules regarding the weighting of sales results in P being subject to state income tax on a total of $1,031,000, notwithstanding the fact that it has only $1,000,000 of taxable income. (It should also be noted that inconsistencies in state rules may result in a corporation being subject to state income tax on less than its total taxable income.)

SALES FACTOR

The sales factor is generally computed utilizing the following formula:

$$\frac{\text{Total in-state sales (net of returns; discounts; and allowances)}}{\text{Total sales everywhere (net of returns; discounts; and allowances)}}$$

For purposes of the above factor, sales means all gross receipts derived by the taxpayer from transactions and activity in the regular course of the trade or business.[31] Accordingly, sales is generally considered to include:

- Business income from the sale of goods or the performance of services[32]

- Interest income, service charges, carrying charges, or time-price differential charges incidental to gross receipts (regardless of the place where the accounting records are maintained or the location of the contract or debt instrument)[33]

- Excise and sales taxes either passed on to the purchaser or included in the selling price[34]

- Dividends, rents, and royalties derived in the ordinary course of business[35]

- Net gain (or, in some cases, gross proceeds) from the sale or exchange of assets to the extent not excludable under various exceptions (for example, incidental or occasional sales of long-term investment assets)[36]

In determining the amount of sales includible in the numerator of the sales factor most states apply a destination rule. Under such rule, the relevant factor in determining the state in which a sales transaction (other than a sale to the Federal government) is considered to have taken place is the point of delivery, not the location at which the shipment originates. Some states apply the ultimate destination rule to dock sales (that is, sales where a purchaser utilizes its own vehicle or a common carrier to take delivery of goods at the seller's shipping dock) in the same manner in which it is applied to other sales transactions.

Example 9

Q Corporation's manufacturing plant is located in State T. Q ships goods from its manufacturing plant to customers located in States T, U, and V. Under the destination rule, sales to customers located in State T are assigned to State T, sales to customers located in State U are assigned to State U, and sales to customers located in State V are assigned to State V.

Example 10

Assume the same facts as in *Example 9,* except that certain of the customers in State U pick up the merchandise at Q's plant in State T. Income from these dock sales continues to be assigned to State U under the destination rule.[37]

---

[31] MTC Reg.IV.15.(a).(1)

[32] MTC Reg.IV.15.(a).(1)(A) and MTC Reg.IV.15(a).(1)(C)

[33] MTC Reg.IV.15.(a).(1)(A)

[34] MTC Reg.IV.15.(a)(1)(A)

[35] Particularly with respect to dividends, considerable litigation has arisen as to when dividends constitute business income. In general, such cases have held that dividends constitute business income where (1) they arise from investments of working capital or (2) they are received from an out-of-state or foreign corporation that is part of an integrated (i.e., unitary) business with the taxpayer. See, e.g., *Mobil Oil Corp. v. Commissioner of Taxes of Vt.*, 445 U.S. 425 (1980), *ASARCO, Inc. v. Idaho State Tax Com'n,* 458 U.S. 307 (1982); *F. W. Woolworth Co. v. Taxation and Revenue Department,* 458 U.S. 354 (1982). Similarly, the MTC regulations provide that dividends constitute business income if (1) the stock with respect to which the dividend was received arose out of or was acquired in the regular course of the taxpayer's trade or business or (2) the purpose of holding the stock is related to the business. MTC Reg. IV.1.(c).(4).

[36] MTC Reg. IV.18(c).

[37] Note that, in states that have not adopted the destination rule, these dock sales would be assigned to State T.

A number of states modify the ultimate destination rule in certain cases by employing a throwback rule. Under such rule, when the seller is not subject to tax in the destination state (due to the fact that it possesses insufficient nexus for such state to impose a tax, not due to the fact that the destination state does not impose an income tax) or the purchaser is the U.S. government, a sale is treated as an in-state sale of the state in which the sale originates and, thus, is included in the numerator of the sales factor for such state. In limited cases, a state may restrict the application of the throwback rules to domestic sales.

Example 11

J Corporation is domiciled in State X. In addition to making sales in State X, J makes sales in State Y; however, it is not subject to income tax in such state due to the fact that its activities in State Y are insufficient to give rise to nexus. During the current year, J has $4 million of sales in State X and $1 million of sales in State Y. All of J's property and employees are located in State X. For the current year, J has business income of $2,000,000 and no nonbusiness income. J utilizes three-factor apportionment and imposes tax at a rate of 6 percent. J's tax liability is computed as follows assuming that State X does, and does not, employ a throwback rule:

	No Throwback	Throwback
Sales factor (No throwback – [$4,000,000/$5,000,000]; throwback – [$5,000,000/$5,000,000])	80%	100%
Property factor	100%	100%
Payroll factor	100%	100%
Sum of apportionment factors	280%	300%
	÷ 3	÷ 3
Apportionment percentage for State X	93%	100%
Times: Total business income	× $2,000,000	$2,000,000
State taxable income	$1,860,000	$2,000,000
Times: State income tax rate	× 6%	× 6%
State X income tax	$ 111,600	$ 120,000

From the above table, it can be seen that the application of the throwback rule results in an $8,400 ($120,000 – $111,600) increase in J's State X tax liability.

Where sales include amounts other than gross receipts from the sale of property, for example, rents, royalties, interest, dividends, gains from the sale of property, or income from the performance of services, UDITPA provides an all-or-nothing test for determining the state to which the receipts are attributable for purposes of the numerator of the sales factor. Such rule generally attributes such receipts to the numerator of the sales factor of the state in which the greatest proportion of the income-producing activity is performed, based on costs of performance.[38] In recognition of the potential difficulties in applying the general rule and the potential for distortion inherent therein, the MTC has proposed several special rules for determining amounts includible in the numerator of the sales factor including a rule assigning receipts from the sale, lease, rental or licensing of real estate or tangible personal property to the numerator of the sales factor of the state in which the property is located or used (with an apportionment being performed if the property is present in more than one state during the year).[39] Similarly, the MTC regulations contain a rule that allocates receipts from the performance of personal services among states based on relative time where services relating to a single item of income are performed in multiple states.[40]

In recent years, a major trend is the adoption of market-based rules for sourcing services. Market-based sourcing is a destination based approach and assigns sales of services to the state in which the service is received (the jurisdiction where the consumer is located). Over twenty states have adopted market-based sourcing rules. The newly adopted revisions

[38] UDITPA Section 17.
[39] MTC Reg. IV.17.(4)(B).
[40] MTC Reg. IV.17.(4)(B)(c).

to MTC Article IV, Section 17 take this approach with a rule stating that receipts, other than receipts described in Section 16 (those from the sale of tangible personal property) are sourced to a state if the taxpayer's market for the sales is in the state. In the case of a sale of a service, the market for the sale is in the state if the service is delivered in the state.[41]

Example 12

B Corporation is domiciled in State Y. B conducts an integrated business in States X, Y, and Z. At certain times during the year, B has substantial excess funds that it invests in short-term securities. The employees who manage B's investment portfolio are headquartered in State Y. Since the management of working capital is an integral part of B's business, the interest earned on the securities constitutes apportionable business income. Moreover, for purposes of the sales factor, such interest is includible in full in the gross receipts of State Y, since the management activities are conducted in State Y.

Example 13

J Corporation, a large architectural firm, has offices in States A and B. J enters into a contract to prepare architectural drawings for a building to be constructed in State B. Portions of the drawings are prepared by employees in each of J's offices. Depending on the state, the gross receipts from the contract may be allocated between States A and B based on the time spent by employees in each office (using the cost of performance approach) or to State B only (using the market-based sourcing approach).

PROPERTY FACTOR

The property factor is generally computed utilizing the following formula:

$$\frac{\text{Average value of real and tangible personal property owned or rented and used in the state}}{\text{Average value of real and tangible personal property owned or rented and used everywhere}}$$

For purposes of the above factor, property includes:

- Land, buildings, machinery, inventory, equipment and other real and tangible property, other than coins and currency;[42]

- Proportionate share of property owned through a partnership;

- Leased property (generally valued at eight times annual rentals, net of any nonbusiness subrentals).[43]

Only property used in the production of business (apportionable) income is generally taken into account in computing the property factor. Property remains in the property factor until an identifiable event establishes its permanent withdrawal. For example, property that is idle continues to be taken into account in computing the property factor until it is sold or after the lapse of an extended period of time (normally five years). Intangibles are generally excluded.

Once the assets properly includible in the property factor have been identified, it becomes necessary to determine to which state (or states) each item of property is properly assignable. The assignment of land, machinery, equipment, fixtures, etc. to a particular state for purposes of determining the numerator of the property factor generally presents little difficulty, since these assets remain at a single location. Difficulties arise, however, in the case of assets in transit and mobile or movable property. In the former case (i.e., assets in transit between two business locations of the taxpayer), assets are generally included in the numerator of the destination state. In the latter case (e.g., trucks, construction equipment),

---

[41] MTC Article IV, Section 17(a)

[42] MTC Reg. IV.10.(a).

[43] MTC Reg.IV.11.(b)

the numerator of a state's apportionment factor is generally determined on the basis of the total time that the property was within the state during the taxable year. Under a major exception to this rule, automobiles provided to an employee are includible in the numerator of the property factor of the state to which the employee's compensation is assigned for purposes of the payroll factor or the state in which the automobile is licensed.[44] Such alternative approach serves to reduce the recordkeeping burden where an employee drives a company vehicle in multiple states.

A final issue arising in connection with the determination of the property factor involves the valuation of the assets included in the numerator and/or denominator. Leased property is generally valued at eight times annual rentals. Owned property is typically valued based on original cost, with a limited number of states allowing (or requiring) it to be valued at net book value or adjusted tax basis. Most states require that beginning and end of year cost figures be averaged to arrive at the amounts utilized in calculating the property factor. In some cases, monthly figures must be utilized if the use of beginning and end-of-year numbers results in substantial distortion. This could occur where, for example, the taxpayer makes substantial year-end asset purchases in a low-tax jurisdiction.

Example 14

Q Corporation, a calendar year taxpayer, owns property in both States Y and Z. In addition, it leases property in State Y and State Z. Both States Y and Z require computation of the property factor based on average asset values and require the inclusion of leased property based on eight times annual rentals. The states differ, however, in that State Y requires that property be valued at original cost, while State Z requires valuation based on net book value. Relevant account balances at the beginning and end of the year are as follows:

Balances at January 1	State Y	State Z	Total
Inventories.	$100,000	$150,000	$ 250,000
Buildings and machinery (cost)	400,000	200,000	600,000
Accumulated depreciation	(100,000)	(50,000)	(150,000)
Land	200,000	100,000	300,000
Total property	$600,000	$400,000	$1,000,000

Balances at December 31	State Y	State Z	Total
Inventories.	$200,000	$100,000	$ 300,000
Buildings and machinery (cost)	500,000	200,000	700,000
Accumulated depreciation	(150,000)	(100,000)	(250,000)
Land	200,000	100,000	300,000
Total property	$750,000	$300,000	$1,050,000

Total annual rental payments equal $20,000 in State Y and $5,000 in State Z.

---

[44] MTC Reg. IV.10.(d).

Q's property factors in each state are computed as follows:

State Y:

Based on Historical Cost	State Y	Total
Total property at January 1 (total property + accumulated depreciation)	$ 700,000	$1,150,000
Total property at December 31 (total property + accumulated depreciation)	900,000	1,300,000
Total	$1,600,000	$2,450,000
	÷ 2	÷ 2
Average owned property	$ 800,000	$1,225,000
Leased property (at 8 times annual rentals)	160,000	200,000
Total property for purposes of a property factor	$ 960,000	$1,425,000

$$\text{Property factor for State Y} = \frac{\$960,000}{\$1,425,000} = 67.37\%$$

State Z:

Based on Net Book Value	State Z	Total
Total property at January 1 (total property)	$400,000	$1,000,000
Total property at December 31 (total property)	300,000	1,050,000
Total	$700,000	$2,050,000
	÷ 2	÷ 2
Average owned property	$350,000	$1,025,000
Leased property (at 8 times annual rentals)	40,000	200,000
Total property for purposes of property factor	$390,000	$1,225,000

$$\text{Property factor for State Z} = \frac{\$390,000}{\$1,225,000} = 31.84\%$$

Note that the combined property factors for States Y and Z do not equal 100% (i.e., 67.37% + 31.84% = 99.21%) due to the differing state laws regarding valuation of property (that is, original cost in State Y versus net book value in State Z).

PAYROLL FACTOR

The payroll factor is generally computed utilizing the following formula:

$$\frac{\text{Total compensation paid or accrued in the state}}{\text{Total compensation paid or accrued by the corporation}}$$

For purposes of the above factor, compensation is generally considered to include wages, salaries, commissions, and similar forms of employee renumeration.[45] This typically includes fringe benefits to the extent inclludable in federal gross income.

While employees are not defined by UDITPA, states typcially define an employee for this purpose as anyone who is subject to the Federal Insurance Contributions Act rules. Accordingly, compensation paid to independent contractors is typically not included in the payroll factor.

Some states exclude the compensation of executive officers from the payroll factor. This provides an incentive for a company to locate in that state.

---

[45] UDITPA Section 1(c).

Only compensation related to the production of business (apportionable) income is taken into account in computing the payroll factor. Compensation related to the production of nonbusiness income is not taken into account. If an employee's services contribute to the production of both business and nonbusiness income, such employee's compensation must be prorated between the two classes of income in determining the payroll factor.

Once the total amount of includible compensation attributable to the production of business income has been determined, it is necessary to assign such compensation to specific states. This is generally done by treating compensation paid to an employee as attributable to the state in which the employee primarily performs services. This is generally determined based on the location of the employee's base of operations or, if the employee has no fixed base of operations, the state from which the services are directed or controlled. An exception to this latter rule exists where the employee does not actually perform services in the state from which his or her activities are controlled. In such case, the employee's compensation is attributed to his or her state of residency.[46] The net effect of these rules is generally to assign all of an employee's compensation to a single state for purposes of the numerator of the payroll factor. An allocation between states is typically not required unless an employee relocates during the year.

Example 15

E, who resides in State X, is employed by D Corporation, whose headquarters is located in State Y, as a traveling salesperson. E's territory encompasses States X, Y, and Z. D has an office in State X. All of E's compensation is attributed to State X for purposes of determining the numerator of the payroll factor.

Example 16

Assume the same facts as in *Example 15,* except that E does not have an office in any state. In such case, since E's activities are supervised from a location in State Y and E actually performs services in State Y, one hundred percent of E's compensation is attributed to State Y for purposes of determining the numerator of the payroll factor.

Example 17

Assume the same facts as in *Example 15,* except that E does not have an office and D Corporation's headquarters is located in State W. In this case, since E has no fixed base of operations and does not perform services in the state from which his activities are supervised, all of E's compensation is attributed to State X (that is, E's state of residency) for purposes of determining the numerator of the payroll factor.

Example 18

G Corporation operates in two states, A and B. Selected payroll information for the current year is as follows:

	State A	State B	Total
Salaries and wages paid to employees	$1,000,000	$1,200,000	$2,200,000
Taxable benefits.	30,000	40,000	70,000
Payments to independent contractors	400,000	0	400,000
Contributions to § 401(k) plans	60,000	70,000	130,000
Total	$1,490,000	$1,310,000	$2,800,000

---

[46] UDITPA Section 14.

The $1,000,000 paid to employees in State A includes $50,000 related to the management of nonbusiness assets. State A excludes payments to independent contractors and contributions to § 401(k) plans from the payroll factor, while State B includes § 401(k) plan contributions in the payroll factor. Both states distinguish between business and nonbusiness income in computing the payroll factor. The payroll factors for the two states are computed as follows:

$$\text{Payroll factor for State A} = \frac{\$1,490,000 - \$50,000 - \$400,000 - \$60,000}{\$2,800,000 - \$50,000 - \$400,000 - \$130,000} = 44.14\%$$

$$\text{Payroll factor for State B} = \frac{\$1,310,000}{\$2,800,000 - \$50,000 - \$400,000} = 55.74\%$$

Note that the combined payroll factors for States A and B do not equal 100% (i.e., 44.14% + 55.74% = 99.88%) due to the differing state laws regarding amounts constituting compensation.

ALTERNATIVE APPROACHES TO FILING RETURNS

LO.7

Differentiate between the separate reporting, consolidated return, and combined reporting (unitary) approaches to filing state income tax returns.

Filing requirements for multistate corporations vary considerably from state to state. Some states require each taxpayer with nexus in the state to file a separate return, while others require (or allow) related taxpayers to report income on a consolidated basis. Moreover, a number of states have adopted the so-called unitary business principle which impacts the amounts (and, in some cases, entities) included in a particular state return. The approach utilized by a particular state may affect both the nature of the return (or returns) filed in the state and the computation of includible income and the apportionment percentage. Each of the major alternative approaches to filing state returns, as well as the impact of the unitary business principle, are discussed below. Before preceding with such discussion, it is important to note that the terminology utilized to describe certain approaches to filing may vary from state to state. For example, one state may use the term consolidated to define one type of reporting while another state uses the term combined to refer to an identical method in that state. Thus, the terms used below are for illustrative purposes only.

Separate Entity Reporting

Under separate entity reporting, each corporation with sufficient nexus to a particular state is required to file its own tax return in such state. This is the case even where the corporations are included in a consolidated return for Federal purposes. Such return generally reflects that portion of the corporation's total income or loss (after state adjustments) properly allocated/apportioned to such state. In the extreme case, where a corporation operates in only a single state, a return reporting one hundred percent of its separate taxable income would be filed in such state.

Example 19

K Corporation is the 100% parent of three subsidiaries, L Corp., M Corp., and N Corp. K, L, M, and N file a consolidated return for Federal income tax purposes. K, L, and M conduct business in State A. L also conducts business in State B. N conducts business only in State B. Under separate entity reporting, K, L, and M would each be required to file a separate return in State A. In addition, L and N would be required to file separate returns in State B.

Consolidated Returns

The laws of a number of states allow or permit the filing of a single consolidated state income tax return where (1) there are two or more affiliated corporations and (2) each of the included corporations is taxable in the state. This type of filing method may also be referred to as nexus combination. The combination may be required to be made either before or after apportionment. If it is made on a pre-apportionment basis, the incomes of the entities are combined and such combined amount is apportioned to the state using a single formula that includes the factors of all the entities. In contrast, if it is made on a post-apportionment basis, each entity computes income separately and apportions the income to the state using a formula that includes only its factors. The resulting state taxable income amounts for all the entities are then combined and reported together.

Example 20

Assume the same facts as in *Example 19,* except that State A requires the filing of consolidated returns. K, L, and M would file a single income tax return in State A reporting the combined operations of the three corporations. L and N would continue to file separate returns in State B.

Combined Reporting

Combined reporting is frequently required (or permitted) where two or more separate businesses are found to comprise a unitary business (as discussed below). Under such method, the combined taxable income of all members of a unitary group of businesses is computed. Such income is then apportioned among the group members based on apportionment percentages that reflect the combined operations of the unitary group. A member of the group that has nexus with a particular state then reports its share of the total income of the unitary group apportioned to such state on either (1) a separate return or (2) a combined report reflecting the operations of all group members having nexus with the state. The key difference between combined reporting and consolidated reporting is that, under combined reporting, the income apportioned to a state may include income (or losses) of members of the unitary group that do not directly possess nexus with such state. This feature of combined reporting (and the unitary concept) has been found to be constitutional, even where the unitary group involves foreign subsidiaries of a U.S. multinational or a foreign-based multinational with both U.S. and foreign subsidiaries (worldwide combined reporting).[47]

Most states that employ worldwide combined reporting allow a taxpayer to make a so-called water's edge election under which the taxpayer may limit the apportionment of income of a unitary business to those entities which are engaged in a business within the United States.[48] States typically impose a variety of requirements on a unitary group making a water's edge election, e.g., such election may be irrevocable for a period of years. Regardless of the election, a number of states require that taxable income and apportionment factors of unitary members that are incorporated in foreign tax havens be included in the state combined return.

Example 21

Assume the same facts as in *Example 19,* except that combined reporting is utilized in State A (but not State B) and all four corporations constitute members of a unitary group. For State A filing purposes, the combined taxable income of K, L, M, and N would be computed (notwithstanding the fact that N is not subject to tax in State A on a stand-alone basis). In addition, a combined apportionment percentage would be computed taking into account the operations of the four corporations in States A and B. Total income would then be apportioned to State A based on such combined apportionment percentage. Depending on the specific laws of State A, the income apportioned to State A may be reported on a single return or split between separate returns filed by K, L, and M. L and N would continue to file separate returns in State B. Note that a portion of N's income is apportioned to State A even though N operates only in State B.

---

[47] *Container Corp. of America v. Franchise Tax Bd.,* 463 U.S. 159 (1983); *Barclays Bank PLC v. Franchise Tax Bd.,* 512 U.S. 298 (1994).

[48] See, for example, Cal. Rev. & Tax Code Section 25110.

> ## Example 22
>
> Assume the same facts as in *Example 21,* except that Corporation N is incorporated in foreign country X and operates solely in such country. If a water's edge election is made, N's activities are excluded from the computation of the group's State A taxable income and apportionment factors.

UNITARY BUSINESS PRINCIPLE

As discussed in connection with combined reporting, the general effect of the unitary business principle is to aggregate, for purposes of (1) the computation of taxable income, (2) the determination of apportionment percentages, and/or (3) the filing of returns, two or more nominally separate trades or businesses. In other words, under the unitary business principal, a taxable business is determined without regard to the business entity's legal structure. A business may generally be included in such an aggregation even if, on a separate entity basis, it conducts no business within a particular state.[49] Moreover, the unitary concept may be applied to multiple corporations, as well as separate divisions of a single enterprise.[50] Even unincorporated businesses, such as partnerships, may be treated as part of a unitary group. About half the states require or allow unitary reporting.

The seminal question in applying the unitary concept involves the determination of whether two or more nominally separate trades or businesses, in fact, constitute a single unitary business. Unfortunately, there is no uniform answer to this question; consequently, the states (and courts) have applied a variety of standards in determining whether or not two or more businesses are unitary. One commonly cited definition of a unitary business holds that two or more business operations are unitary if the operation of the portion of the business done within a state is dependent upon or contributes to the operations of the business in other states (the contribution and dependency test).[51] Such definition has been expanded to hold that a business is unitary where the following three factors are present (the three unities test):

- *Unity of ownership,* i.e., the operation of divisions within a single corporate entity or common ownership (e.g., more than 50%) of two or more corporate entities;

- *Unity of operation,* i.e., the existence of central purchasing, advertising, accounting, legal, financing, and management services; and

- *Unity of use,* i.e., the existence of a centralized executive force and general system of operation.[52]

A similar (and frequently cited) approach is found in the Supreme Court's decision in *Mobil Oil Corp. v. Commissioner of Taxes of Vermont.*[53] In such case, the court ruled that a unitary business exists where there is (1) centralized management, (2) functional integration, and (3) economies of scale.

A more restrictive (and less frequently cited) view holds that a producing, manufacturing, or mercantile company is unitary only if the basic operations are substantially interdependent, i.e., there is a substantial flow of raw materials, products, goods, and/or operational services between segments (the operational interdependency test).[54] A final approach promulgated by the MTC (the separate business test) holds that two branches or subsidiaries do not constitute a unitary business if such businesses are separate. The determination of whether two branches or subsidiaries are separate is determined based on factors such as (1) whether the business activities of the branches or subsidiaries are in the same general line, (2) the existence of vertical integration, and (3) the existence of strong centralized management.[55] The diversity of approaches taken by the courts and the MTC illustrates

---

[49] *Supra,* Footnote 47.

[50] *Edison Cal. Stores, Inc. v. McColgan,* 183 P2d 16 (Calif. 1947).

[51] *Ibid.*

[52] *Butler Bros. v. McColgan,* 315 U.S. 501 (1942).

[53] 445 U.S. 425 (1980).

[54] *Commonwealth v. ACF Indus., Inc.,* 271 A2d 273 (PA 1970).

[55] MTC Reg. IV.1.(b); *Ash Grove Cement v. Department of Revenue,* 7 OTR 6 (Ore. Tax Ct. 1977).

the difficulty of determining in practice whether two or more branches or subsidiaries constitute a unitary business and the necessity of examining all of the relevant facts and circumstances in attempting to make such determination. Finally, it should be noted that the application of the unitary business principle may operate in favor of either the revenue authority or the taxpayer depending on the particular facts and circumstances of the case at hand. This point is illustrated in greater detail in the Tax Planning section of this chapter.

Example 23

B Corp. has two wholly owned subsidiaries, C Corp. and D Corp. D, in turn, owns 100% of E Corp. B Corp. conducts no active trade or business, but performs centralized accounting, legal, and executive management functions on behalf of the other corporations. C is engaged in the manufacture and sale of Product X. D is engaged in the sale of Product Y. E manufactures Product Y. Approximately 80% of E's sales of Product Y are to D. Executives of B direct the operations of C, D, and E. Excess funds generated by one business are utilized to finance the operations of the other businesses. B, C, D, and E operate in a number of different states. The state currently under consideration employs the three unities test to determine the existence of a unitary business. Under such test, it is likely that all of the corporations would be considered to constitute a unitary business due to the existence of: (1) unity of ownership (i.e., the shareholders of B indirectly own C, D, and E as well), (2) unity of operation (i.e., B conducts centralized accounting, management, etc. for the entire group), and (3) unity of use (i.e., the executives of B direct the operations of all of the corporations).

Example 24

Assume the same facts as in *Example 23,* except that each corporation has its own executive management team. In addition, the state currently under consideration employs the contribution and dependency test. Under such test, it is clear that D and E comprise a unitary business, since D is E's major customer. It is also relatively clear that C is not part of a unitary business with D and E, since they are in different lines of business and there seem to be few links (other than the flow of excess funds) between C and the D-E group. Less clear is whether or not B is part of a unitary business with C and/or D-E.[56]

The two examples presented above illustrate the difficulties encountered in determining whether a unitary business exists in light of differing judicial definitions. They also illustrate how a group of corporations found to constitute a unitary group in one jurisdiction may be found nonunitary in another.

State Taxation of S Corporations

Most states treat S corporations in a manner consistent with the Federal tax treatment of such entities, that is, no tax is generally imposed at the corporate level and the corporation's income or loss flows through to its shareholders and is reported on their individual returns. However, some states—Connecticut, Michigan, New Hampshire, Tennessee, and Texas, as well as the District of Columbia—impose an entity-level tax on S corporations as well as certain unincorporated entities. Two states, Massachusetts and California, apply hybrid approaches in taxing S corporations—Massachusetts taxes large S corporations with gross

LO.8

Describe the alternative approaches taken by states to taxing S corporations.

---

[56] Note that if the accounting and legal services are performed under an arm's-length arrangement in a manner similar to what C, D, and E could have acquired from a third party, the likelihood that the corporations constitute a unitary business is reduced.

receipts exceeding $6 million at the corporate level, while California assesses a corporate-level tax on S corporation income but at a reduced tax rate. Even though S corporations are generally not subject to state income taxes, it should be noted that they generally continue to be subject to other state and local taxes, e.g., the corporate franchise tax, in the same manner as nonelecting corporations.

Eligibility to Elect S Status

Most states that recognize S status do not require separate filings of the equivalent of Federal Form 2553 at the state level. In contrast, a few states require separate state elections or require that a copy of Federal Form 2553 be filed with the state. In all cases, a Federal S election must be in effect in order for a state election to be valid. Moreover, a few states allow a corporation with a Federal S election in place to elect to be taxed as a C corporation for state purposes. States following Federal rules regarding election of S status also generally follow Federal rules regarding termination of S status, S termination years, post-termination transition period, reelection after termination, etc.

Taxation of S Corporations

As at the Federal level, S corporations are also generally not subject to state corporate level income taxation. Taxes imposed on S corporations at the Federal level, i.e., taxes on built-in gains and excess passive investment income, are generally imposed at the state level as well to the extent that S corporation income is allocated or apportioned to the state.

Taxation of S Corporation Shareholders

In general, resident shareholders of states that recognize the S election are taxable on their distributive shares of corporate taxable income (after state adjustments) allocated or apportioned to the state whether or not such amounts are actually distributed. Distributions received from an S corporation by resident shareholders in such states are generally nontaxable under rules similar to those employed for Federal purposes.

Where the S election is not recognized, distributions are generally taxable in the same manner as distributions by C corporations (i.e., as dividends to the extent of corporate earnings and profits). In some cases, (e.g., the District of Columbia) an exclusion or credit mechanism is provided to reduce the double taxation of distributed S corporation earnings. Undistributed earnings are generally not taxed at the shareholder level in states not recognizing S status.

Special Rules Where S Corporation Has Nonresident Shareholders

In order to help ensure collection of tax from nonresident shareholders, states employ a variety of techniques including:

- Requiring the filing of various information returns and reports identifying nonresident shareholders;

- Providing for the termination of the corporation's S election for state purposes if a nonresident shareholder fails to file and properly report his or her distributive share of S corporation income;

- Imposing a tax at the corporate level on income distributable to nonresident shareholders (either in all cases or in the event of nonfiling by a nonresident shareholder); or

- Providing for the withholding of taxes from distributions actually paid to nonresident shareholders or on the shareholders' distributive shares of corporate income (with a credit generally being allowed on the nonresident shareholders' individual returns for taxes withheld).

Example 25

D Corporation, an S corporation, is incorporated in State X. Shareholders owning 80% of D reside in State X. The shareholders owning the remaining 20% of D reside in various other states. State X imposes individual income tax at a maximum rate of 6 percent. State X law provides that an S corporation must pay tax at the highest individual rate on all income distributable to nonresident shareholders. For the current year, D has taxable income of $200,000. D must pay tax to State X of $2,400 ($200,000 × 20% × 6%). The nonresident D shareholders will not be taxed on distributions they receive from D, since the income out of which such distributions is paid has already been taxed at the corporate level.

Example 26

Assume the same facts as in *Example 25,* except that State X utilizes a withholding tax mechanism whereby taxes are withheld on distributions actually paid to nonresident shareholders. In turn, the shareholders are allowed to claim a credit on their individual returns for taxes withheld. During the year, D makes *pro rata* distributions totaling $100,000. D is required to withhold $1,200 ($100,000 × 20% × 6%). The nonresident shareholders are allowed to claim such amount as a credit on their State X individual income tax returns. (Note that such returns will reflect their distributive shares of total D taxable income, not just the amounts distributed.)

In order to increase compliance and decrease the associated burden on out-of-state shareholders, a number of states allow for the filing of composite returns. A composite return is essentially a single state individual income tax return prepared by the S corporation reporting the distributable shares of S corporation income allocable to all (or some) of the corporation's nonresident shareholders and paying the associated tax. Typically, various assumptions are made concerning filing status, exemptions, tax rates, etc. In many cases, such assumptions result in the payment of more state income tax than would be the case if the nonresident shareholders simply filed separate individual returns. Consequently, the benefit of lower compliance costs must be weighed against the cost in terms of increased state taxes in determining whether or not to file a composite return.

Basis of S Corporation Stock and Debt

As discussed in Chapter 11, a shareholder's basis in S corporation stock and debt plays a critical role in determining the ability of the shareholder to utilize passed-through losses, the taxability of S corporation distributions, and a shareholder's gain or loss on the disposition of S corporation stock. Unfortunately, approaches to the determination of basis for state purposes vary considerably. Approaches currently being employed by various states range from use of the same basis figure calculated for Federal purposes to calculation of separate state basis figures reflecting state modifications to Federal taxable income, allocation and apportionment of income, etc. In some cases, these rules can result in the omission or duplication of income. At a minimum, this lack of uniformity requires the maintenance of multiple sets of basis records in the case of a shareholder of a multistate S corporation.

State Taxation of Partnerships and LLCs

In general, states treat partnerships and limited liability companies in the same manner as they are treated for Federal purposes, that is, as nontaxable conduits. Several states do, however impose entity-level taxes on partnerships (for example, Michigan and New Hampshire) and/or LLCs (for example, Texas and New York). Partnerships and LLCs are typically required to file state returns in the states in which the entity conducts business. In addition, certain states (for example, New York and New Jersey) impose filing requirements on partnerships and LLCs with resident partners even if the partnership or LLC itself does not conduct business in the state.

LO.9

Identify the major state issues surrounding the taxation of partnerships and LLCs.

Taxation of Partners

In general, a state resident is taxable on all income from whatever source derived, including their distributive share of income from partnerships and LLCs which operate in other states. To the extent that they are also subject to tax in other states in which a partnership or LLCs operates, they are typically allowed a credit against taxes otherwise payable to their state of residency for taxes paid to such states.

A nonresident partner or LLC member is generally deemed to have nexus with those states in which the partnership owns property or conducts business. Consequently, nonresident partners and LLC members are typically taxable on their distributive shares of income to the extent allocable or apportionable to a particular state. In general, business income of a partnership or LLC is apportioned among the states in which the entity conducts business in a manner similar to a corporate taxpayer. Difficulties in performing such apportionment may occur where a partnership business is considered a portion of a unitary business conducted by one of its partners. Moreover, in limited cases, all income of a partnership or LLC may be considered nonbusiness income and allocated to the partner or member's state of residence or commercial domicile.

Depending on the state, the determination of whether entity income constitutes nonbusiness income may be made at either the entity level or the owner level. Regardless of the level at which the determination is made, partnership or LLC income classified as nonbusiness income is generally allocated to the commercial domicile or state of residence of the partner. Alternatively, in certain cases, such income may be (1) allocated to the entity's state of commercial domicile, (2) allocated to the state in which the partnership conducts the majority of its business activities, or (3) apportioned in the same fashion as business income.

Basis of Ownership Interest

Most states provide that a partner or member's basis in their ownership interest is the same for state purposes as for Federal purposes. Such approach may result in significant distortions where there are differences in Federal and state law relative to the computation of taxable income. Consequently, theoretical support exists for the maintenance of separate basis calculations for Federal and state purposes.

Disposition of Ownership Interest

As in the case of operating income, a state resident is taxable on all income from whatever source derived, including any gain derived from the sale of an interest in a partnership or LLC which operates in another state. To the extent that they are also subject to tax in other states in which a partnership or LLCs operates, they may be allowed a credit against taxes otherwise payable to their state of residency for taxes paid to such states.

In the case of a partner or member who is not a resident of the state in which the partnership or LLC operates, any gain or loss from the disposition of their ownership interest is generally treated as nonbusiness income and allocated to their state of commercial domicile or residence. Exceptions to this general rule may apply where (1) the ownership interest has acquired a business situs in another state, (2) legislation has been enacted that allocates gain or loss on sale of ownership interests in flow-through entities among states in which the partnership owns property or conducts business, or (3) the partnership or LLC interest is considered a business asset (for example, where the owner and entity are considered engaged in a unitary business).

Compliance Enhancement Measures

As in the case of S corporations, states employ a variety of mechanisms to enhance compliance by nonresident partners and LLC members. These include (1) composite returns for nonresident owners and (2) withholding from distributions to nonresident owners or on nonresident owners' distributive shares of entity income.

Tax Planning Considerations

State income taxes are a significant component of most corporations' overall tax burden. This, coupled with the opportunities afforded by differences in state tax rates and laws, has led to an increased emphasis on planning to minimize state income taxes (as well as other types of state and local taxes). A number of tax planning techniques have been developed including:

LO.10
Identify common techniques for minimizing state taxes.

- Avoiding the in-state performance of activities that create nexus with high-tax states;

- Subjecting income to apportionment by establishing nexus in low-tax states;

- Altering apportionment factors by shifting operations between states so as to minimize the overall effective state tax rate;

- Electing to file consolidated or combined returns or reports where possible when the group consists of both profit and loss members;

- Making a water's edge election where the inclusion of foreign subsidiaries subjects a disproportionate amount of income to state taxation;

- Utilizing corporations located in low tax (or no tax) states to hold passive investments; and

- Utilizing intercompany management fees and similar charges to shift income from high-tax states to low-tax states.

Each of these planning techniques will be considered in detail below. It should be noted that, while these planning techniques focus on the minimization of state income taxes, planning techniques also exist to minimize sales and use taxes and corporate franchise taxes. In the former case, for example, the structuring of a corporate acquisition as a stock sale with a § 338(h)(10) election, as opposed to an asset sale, may result in substantial sales and use tax savings. In the latter case, the use of debt, rather than equity, in the corporation's capital structure may result in significant savings of capital based franchise taxes.

AVOIDING NEXUS WITH HIGH-TAX STATES

Where a taxpayer operates in a high-tax state, it is generally advantageous to avoid taxable nexus with such state even if sales in the state will be thrown back into the taxpayer's state of commercial domicile (assuming that such state has a comparatively low tax rate). Planning in such case involves attempting to structure the taxpayer's activities in the high-tax state to fall within the protection from taxation afforded by P.L. 86-272. Possibilities include:

- Distributing free samples instead of charging a fee for sample products;

- Denying sales representatives the authority to accept or close sales; and/or

- Conducting non-sales related training seminars and other meetings out-of-state.

Example 27

T Corporation generates $1,000,000 of taxable income from the sale of Product X in States A and B. Seventy percent of T's total sales of $4,000,000 are attributable to State A, with the remaining 30% attributable to State B. T owns an office building with an original cost of $500,000 in State A. T owns no property in State B. T pays salaries of $1,000,000 to employees in State A. All of T's salespeople in State B are properly classified as independent contractors. T is domiciled in State A. State A, whose law contains a throwback provision, imposes tax at a rate of four percent, while State B imposes tax at a rate of 8 percent.

If T's activities in State B are not limited to those exempt under P.L. 86-272, its tax liability in each state is calculated as follows:

	State A	State B
Sales factor (State A – $2,800,000/$4,000,000 = 70%; State B – $1,200,000/$4,000,000 = 30%)	70%	30%
Property factor (State A – $500,000/$500,000 = 100%; State B – $0/$500,000 = 0%)	100%	0%
Payroll factor (State A – $1,000,000/$1,000,000 = 100%; State B – $0/$1,000,000 = 0%)	100%	0%
Sum of apportionment factors	270%	30%
	÷ 3	÷ 3
Apportionment percentage	90%	10%
Times: Total business income	$1,000,000	$1,000,000
State taxable income	$ 900,000	$ 100,000
Times: State income tax rate	× 4%	× 8%
State income tax	$ 36,000	$ 8,000

In contrast, if T's activities in State B are limited to those exempt under P.L. 86–272, its tax liability in each state is calculated as follows:

	State A	State B
Sales factor (State A – $4,000,000/$4,000,000 = 100%; State B – $0/$4,000,000 = 0%)	100%	0%
Property factor (State A – $500,000/$500,000 = 100%; State B – $0/$500,000 = 0%)	100%	0%
Payroll factor (State A – $1,000,000/$1,000,000 = 100%; State B – $0/$1,000,000 = 0%)	100%	0%
Sum of apportionment factors	300%	0%
	÷ 3	÷ 3
Apportionment percentage	100%	0%
Times: Total business income	$1,000,000	$1,000,000
State taxable income	$1,000,000	$ 0
Times: State income tax rate	× 4%	× 8%
State income tax	$ 40,000	$ 0

From the above, it can be seen that avoiding nexus with State B results in tax savings of $4,000 ($44,000 – $40,000). This must be compared with the cost of restructuring T's operations to avoid nexus with State B.[57]

---

[57] Note that, under the second alternative, T is taxable only in State A. A number of states do not allow a taxpayer to apportion income unless they are taxable in at least one other state.

SUBJECTING INCOME TO APPORTIONMENT

It may be advantageous to create nexus with a low (or no) tax state in order to shift income that is currently being taxed in a high-tax state into such low- (or no) tax state. This could be advantageous where, e.g., sales into a low-rate state are being thrown back into the taxpayer's state of commercial domicile that has a comparatively high tax rate. Such shifting could be accomplished by structuring the taxpayer's activities in the low tax state in a way in which they fall outside the protection afforded by P.L. 86-272. For example, the corporation could provide salespeople with tangible personal property or give them the power to approve orders (assuming that such salesmen are employees as opposed to independent contractors).

Example 28

Assume the same facts as in *Example 27,* except that the tax rate in State A is eight percent, while the tax rate in State B is four percent.

If T's activities in State B are limited to those exempt under P.L. 86-272, its tax liability in each state is calculated as follows:

	State A	State B
Sales factor (State A – $4,000,000/$4,000,000 = 100%; State B – $0/$4,000,000 = 0%)	100%	0%
Property factor (State A – $500,000/$500,000 = 100%; State B – $0/$500,000 = 0%)	100%	0%
Payroll factor (State A – $1,000,000/$1,000,000 = 100%; State B – $0/$1,000,000 = 0%)	100%	0%
Sum of apportionment factors	300%	0%
	÷ 3	÷ 3
Apportionment percentage	100%	0%
Times: Total business income	$1,000,000	$1,000,000
State taxable income	$1,000,000	$ 0
Times: State income tax rate	× 8%	× 4%
State income tax	$ 80,000	$ 0

In contrast, if T establishes sufficient nexus with State B, its tax liability in each state is calculated as follows:

	State A	State B
Sales factor (State A – $2,800,000/$4,000,000 = 70%; State B – $1,200,000/$4,000,000 = 30%)	70%	30%
Property factor (State A – $500,000/$500,000 = 100%; State B – $0/$500,000 = 0%)	100%	0%
Payroll factor (State A – $1,000,000/$1,000,000 = 100%; State B – $0/$1,000,000 = 0%)	100%	0%
Sum of apportionment factors	270%	30%
	÷ 3	÷ 3
Apportionment percentage	90%	10%
Times: Total business income	$1,000,000	$1,000,000
State taxable income	$ 900,000	$ 100,000
Times: State income tax rate	× 8%	× 4%
State income tax	$ 72,000	$ 4,000

From the above, it can be seen that creating nexus with State B results in tax savings of $4,000 ($80,000 – $76,000). This must be compared with the cost of restructuring T's operations to create nexus with State B.

ALTERING APPORTIONMENT FACTORS

A common objective of state income tax planning is to reduce the taxpayer's combined effective state income tax rate. Simple ways of accomplishing this goal are to limit the company's operations to low- (or no-) tax states or to locate profitable entities in low- (or no-) tax states. Given that these actions are often impractical in practice (or are thwarted, in the latter case, by states' application of the unitary business concept), an alternative means of accomplishing this objective is to attempt to structure the company's affairs in such a way that the apportionment factors operate to assign as much income as possible to low- (or no) tax states. Examples of possible techniques to shift income from high tax to low-tax states by altering state apportionment percentages include:

- Altering the sales factor by changing the state of destination (i.e., the state in which goods are delivered to the purchaser) from a high-tax state to a low- (or no-) tax state.[58]

- Establishing the taxpayer's distribution center in a state that does not have a throwback rule (or in a low-tax state) in order to reduce the combined sales factor below 100 percent.

- Altering the property factor by storing inventory, or establishing warehouses, manufacturing facilities, etc., in low-tax states.

- Leasing, rather than owning, property in states that do not include leased property in the property factor.[59]

- Reducing the payroll factor in high-tax states by utilizing independent contractors rather than employees in such states.[60]

- Reducing the payroll factor in high-tax states by relocating highly compensated employees to low- (or no-) tax states.

- Lowering the overall apportionment percentage by taking steps (for example, increasing operational integration) to cause two or more businesses to be treated as unitary.[61]

---

[58] Note that this may not be effective if the corporation's state of commercial domicile employs a throwback rule and the tax rate in such state is higher than the rate in the state in which the income is currently being taxed. In addition, customers may be reluctant to take delivery at an alternative location.

[59] Note that in certain cases it might be advantageous to own rather than lease property in low- (or no) tax states in order to increase the denominator of the property factor (and, thereby, decrease the property factor in high-tax states).

[60] Note that in certain cases it might be advantageous to replace independent contractors with employees in low- (or no) tax states in order to increase the denominator of the payroll factor (and, thereby, decrease the payroll factor in high-tax states).

[61] Note that in certain cases the converse also might hold true, i.e., it might be advantageous to attempt to avoid unitary classification. This would be the case where, for example, operations in a low- (or no) tax state are highly profitable or where the effect of combining the apportionment factors is to shift income from low- (or no) tax states to high-tax states.

Example 29

T Corporation generates $1,000,000 of taxable income from the sale of Product X in States A and B. 70% of T's total sales of $4,000,000 are attributable to State A, with the remaining 30% attributable to State B. T owns an office building and warehouse with an original cost of $200,000 in State A. T maintains average inventory of $300,000 in State A. T owns no property in State B. T pays salaries of $1,000,000 to employees in State A. All of T's salespeople in State B are properly classified as independent contractors. (T pays total commissions of $300,000 to such salespeople.) T's activities in State B are not protected under P.L 86-272. T is domiciled in State A. State A, whose law contains a throwback provision, imposes tax at a rate of 8 percent, while State B imposes tax at rate of four percent. Under these facts, T's state income tax liability is computed as follows:

	State A	State B
Sales factor (State A – $2,800,000/$4,000,000 = 70%; State B – $1,200,000/$4,000,000 = 30%)	70%	30%
Property factor (State A – $500,000/$500,000 = 100%; State B – $0/$500,000 = 0%)	100%	0%
Payroll factor (State A – $1,000,000/$1,000,000 = 100%; State B – $0/$1,000,000 = 0%)	100%	0%
Sum of apportionment factors	270%	30%
	÷ 3	÷ 3
Apportionment percentage	90%	10%
Times: Total business income	$1,000,000	$1,000,000
State taxable income	$ 900,000	$ 100,000
Times: State income tax rate	× 8%	× 4%
State income tax	$ 72,000	$ 4,000

In contrast, if T (1) begins warehousing its inventory in State B, (2) relocates employees earning a total of $200,000 from State A to State B, and (3) restructures its arrangements with the State B salespeople so that they become classified as employees, its tax liability in each state is calculated as follows:

	State A	State B
Sales factor (State A – $2,800,000/$4,000,000 = 70%; State B – $1,200,000/$4,000,000 = 30%)	70%	30%
Property factor (State A – $200,000/$500,000 = 40%; State B – $300,000/$500,000 = 60%)	40%	60%
Payroll factor (State A – $800,000/$1,300,000 = 62%; State B – $500,000/$1,300,000 = 38%)	62%	38%
Sum of apportionment factors	270%	128%
	÷ 3	÷ 3
Apportionment percentage	57%	43%
Times: Total business income	$1,000,000	$1,000,000
State taxable income	$ 570,000	$ 430,000
Times: State income tax rate	× 8%	× 4%
State income tax	$ 45,600	$ 17,200

From the above, it can be seen that restructuring T's operations to shift income from high-tax State A to low-tax State B results in tax savings of $13,200 ($76,000 – $62,800), i.e., a reduction in T's overall state income tax rate from 7.6% ($76,000/$1,000,000) to 6.28% ($62,800/$1,000,000). This must be compared with the nontax cost of restructuring T's operations to determine the net effect on company profitability.

Example 30

N Corporation is a wholly owned subsidiary of M Corporation. For the current year, M and N have separate taxable incomes of $2,000,000 and $3,000,000, respectively. M conducts its activities solely in State A, which imposes a 3% income tax; while N conducts its activities solely in State B, which imposes an 8% income tax. Both states employ an equally weighted three-factor apportionment formula. Sales, average property, and payroll for each of the corporations are as follows:

	M Corporation	N Corporation	Total
Sales	$6,000,000	$2,000,000	$8,000,000
Property	$3,000,000	$1,000,000	$4,000,000
Payroll.	$2,000,000	$2,000,000	$4,000,000

If M and N are treated as separate (nonunitary) entities, the combined tax liability of the two corporations is computed as follows:

State A ($2,000,000 × 3%)	$ 60,000
State B ($3,000,000 × 8%)	240,000
Total	$300,000

In contrast, if M and N comprise a unitary business, the combined tax liability of the two corporations is $233,333 ($100,000 + $133,333) computed as follows:

	State A	State B
Sales factor (State A – $6,000,000/$8,000,000 = 75%; State B – $2,000,000/$8,000,000 = 25%)	75%	25%
Property factor (State A – $3,000,000/$4,000,000 = 75%; State B – $1,000,000/$4,000,000 = 25%)	75%	25%
Payroll factor (State A – $2,000,000/$4,000,000 = 50%; State B – $2,000,000/$4,000,000 = 50%)	50%	50%
Sum of apportionment factors	200%	100%
	÷ 3	÷ 3
Apportionment percentage	67%	33%
Times: Total business income	$5,000,000	$5,000,000
State taxable income	$3,333,333	$1,666,667
Times: State income tax rate	× 3%	× 8%
State income tax	$ 100,000	$ 133,333

From the above, it can be seen that tax savings of $66,667 ($300,000 – $233,333) result from the treatment of M and N as a unitary business. Such savings result from the shifting of a portion of N's income from high-tax State B to low-tax State A through the use of a combined apportionment percentage.

ELECTING TO FILE CONSOLIDATED RETURNS

As discussed earlier, some states allow a group of affiliated corporations to elect to file a consolidated return. Filling a consolidated return may be especially advantageous where a corporate group has some members with profits and others with losses due to the fact that such amounts offset in the consolidated return. Similar results can be often be obtained by taking steps (e.g., centralizing management, integrating operational activities, etc.) to cause profit and loss corporations to be treated as members of a unitary group or by combining profitable and unprofitable activities within a single corporation.

Example 31

N Corporation is a wholly owned subsidiary of M Corporation. For the current year, M has separate taxable income of $2,000,000, while N has a separate taxable loss of $1,000,000. Both M and N conduct their activities solely in State A, which imposes a 5% income tax. State A permits the filing of consolidated returns on an elective basis. If M and N file separate returns in State A, their combined tax liability is calculated as follows:

M Corp. ($2,000,000 × 5%)	$100,000
N Corp. ([$1,000,000] × 5%)	0
Total	$100,000

On the other hand, if M and N elect to file a consolidated return, N's loss partially offsets M's taxable income, leaving income subject to tax in State A of $1,000,000 ($2,000,000 − $1,000,000) with a resulting tax liability of $50,000 ($1,000,000 × 5%).

MAKING A WATER'S EDGE ELECTION

As discussed earlier, some states allow unitary groups to elect to exclude foreign corporations from the unitary tax calculation unless they conduct domestic operations. Such election is likely to be beneficial where the foreign affiliates are extremely profitable relative to domestic corporations (e.g., due to low manufacturing costs overseas) or where their inclusion inflates in-state apportionment percentages (for example, due to the fact that foreign wage rates are substantially lower than those in the United States). Before making such election, however, any additional taxes or fees imposed by the state in which the election is being made must be considered. For example, some states impose a tax surcharge on corporations making a water's edge election.

Example 32

D Corporation, a domestic, State Z corporation, owns all of the stock of F Corporation, a foreign corporation with no United States operations. F is extremely profitable due to the fact that its overseas manufacturing costs are very low. Under the laws of State Z, D and F are considered to constitute a unitary business. If no water's edge election is made, a portion of the profits of F will be taxable in State Z (based on a combined apportionment percentage reflecting both D and F's operations). On the other hand, if a water's edge election is made, State Z will tax only the income of D.

ESTABLISHMENT OF A PASSIVE INVESTMENT COMPANY

The basic passive investment company technique involves transferring nonbusiness assets (i.e., assets whose income is subject to allocation) to a corporation located in a low- (or no-) tax state.[62] Provided that such passive investment company possesses sufficient nexus with such low- (or no) tax state (e.g., through the maintenance of an office in the state and the performance of functions that possess economic substance) and does not perform any activity establishing nexus with another state, the nonbusiness income attributable to the assets held in the passive investment company should be fully allocable to the low- (or no-) tax state. In many cases, the earnings of the investment company can then be distributed tax free to its parent due to the availability of the dividends-received deduction at the state level.[63] It is important to note that the state income tax benefits associated with the passive investment company technique generally cannot be achieved where the passive investment company is deemed to be part of a unitary business with one or more other members of the group due to the fact that the passive investment company's income would be subject to combined reporting in such case.

Example 33

Q Corporation is currently taxable only in State X that imposes an income tax at a rate of eight percent. Q has taxable income of $10,000,000, of which $1,000,000 consists of earnings on investments. Q's tax liability under its current structure is $800,000 ($10,000,000 × 8%). If Q were to transfer its investment assets to a subsidiary incorporated in Delaware, which does not tax investment income of corporations whose only in-state activity is the management of such investments, its total state income tax liability would decline to $720,000 ([$9,000,000 × 8%] in State X + $0 in Delaware). If State X allows a 100% dividends-received deduction, Q will incur no additional state income tax liability on the receipt of a distribution of the investment earnings.

---

[62] Such technique is frequently referred to as the "Delaware holding company" technique due the fact that the passive investment company is often incorporated in Delaware due to its favorable corporate laws and the fact that it does not impose state income tax on a corporation whose sole activity within the state is the maintenance and management of intangible investments and the collection and distribution of income (e.g., interest, dividends, royalties, etc.) from such investments or from tangible property physically located in another state. The continuing vitality of the Delaware holding company technique has come under attack by a number of states in recent years with varying degrees of success. Contrast *Kmart Properties, Inc. v. Taxation and Revenue Department,* New Mexico Court of Appeals, No. 21,140, where the state was successful in taxing the holding company on royalties received from an in-state subsidiary, with *The Sherwin-Williams Co. v. Commissioner of Revenue,* 2002 Mass. LEXIS 793, where the state was unsuccessful in attempting to disallow a deduction for royalties paid by an in-state corporation to a Delaware holding company.

[63] Alternatively, it may be possible to structure the group so that the parent corporation is the passive investment company, thus, eliminating the need for intercompany dividends.

INTERCOMPANY MANAGEMENT FEES AND OTHER CHARGES

Where unitary filing is not required, it may be advantageous to establish an affiliate in a low- (or no) tax state to perform services for other group members or to make loans to other group members located in high-tax states. The management fees, interest, etc. received by the payee affiliate located in the low- (or no) tax state are subject to less tax than the tax benefit received from the corresponding deduction by the payor affiliate located in a high-tax state. It should be noted that, in order for this technique to be successful, the intercompany charges must be bona fide and reflect arm's-length rates.

In addition, many states have enacted add-back statutes disallowing deductions for various expenses, interest and fees paid between related parties in certain circumstances.

Example 34

X Corporation conducts all of its operations in State A that imposes income tax at a 5% rate. State A does not require the filing of consolidated returns or combined (unitary) reporting. X establishes a subsidiary, Y Corporation, in State N that imposes no state income tax. X transfers some of its administrative employees to Y. In turn, Y bills X for administrative services at an arm's-length rate. During the current year, Y bills X $1,000,000 for administrative services and pays its employees $700,000 (the same amount that they would have been paid if they had continued to be employees of X). The effect of such arrangement is to shift $300,000 ($1,000,000 − $700,000) of taxable income from State A to State N resulting in state tax savings of $15,000 ($300,000 × 5%).

Problem Materials

DISCUSSION QUESTIONS

14-1 *Types of State Taxes.* List the different types of taxes that a state or local government may impose.

14-2 *Definition of Nexus.* What is nexus for purposes of state income taxation?

14-3 *Effect of P.L. 86-272.* What is the effect of P.L. 86-272 on corporations engaged in the interstate sale of tangible personal property?

14-4 *Factors Establishing Nexus.* List several factors that are generally sufficient to establish nexus.

14-5 *Factors Insufficient to Establish Nexus.* List several factors that may be insufficient to establish nexus.

14-6 *Computation of State Taxable Income.* What is the typical starting point in computing taxable income for state purposes? What are some of the common adjustments to such figure in arriving at state taxable income?

14-7 *Business versus Nonbusiness Income.* Briefly define business income and nonbusiness income. Why is it important to distinguish between business and nonbusiness income in computing a multistate taxpayer's income tax liability?

14-8 *Allocation of Nonbusiness Income.* What principles are generally used to determine in which state a corporation's nonbusiness income will be taxed?

14-9 *Apportionment of Business Income.* What factors generally enter into the computation of a corporation's state apportionment percentage? How is each of these factors computed?

14-10 *Sales Factor.* Does the sales factor include only gross receipts from the sale of goods or performance of services? If not, give examples of other items includible in sales.

14-11 *Sales Factor.* What is meant by double weighting sales? How does this affect the normal computation of the apportionment percentage?

14-12 *Sales Factor.* Goods are shipped from a warehouse in State X (the seller's commercial domicile) to a customer in State Y. The seller is not protected from taxation in State Y under P.L. 86-272. To what state are such sales attributed for purposes of the numerator of the sales factor?

14-13 *Sales Factor—Throwback Rule.* Same facts as in *Question 14-12,* except that the taxpayer's activities in State Y are protected under P.L 86-272. To what state are such sales attributed for purposes of the numerator of the sales factor?

14-14 *Sales Factor.* Contrast the cost of performance method of sourcing service revenue to a particular state with market-based sourcing.

14-15 *Property Factor.* Can a taxpayer generally prevent assets from being included in the property factor by leasing, rather than purchasing, them? If not, how are leased assets valued?

14-16 *Payroll Factor.* An employee performs services in several states during the taxable year. Is it generally necessary to allocate the employee's compensation among such states for purposes of the payroll factor?

14-17 *Consolidated Returns versus Combined Reporting.* Distinguish between consolidated returns and combined reports.

14-18 *Unitary Concept.* What is the significance of the unitary concept? Give two alternative approaches for identifying whether a unitary business exists; i.e., what factors are relevant in making such determination.

14-19 *Water's Edge Election.* What is the effect of a water's edge election on reporting by a unitary business?

14-20 *S Corporations.* Do most states recognize an S election for state income tax purposes? What methods do states recognizing S status utilize to ensure compliance by nonresident shareholders?

PROBLEMS

14-21 *P.L. 86-272.* Which of the following activities generally are not protected under P.L. 86-272?

    a. Soliciting orders within the state.
    b. Providing repairs pursuant to a warranty.
    c. Distributing free samples to potential customers.
    d. Providing a laptop computer to an employee.
    e. Providing an office to a sales representative who qualifies as an independent contractor.
    f. Providing a company-owned automobile to a salesperson.
    g. Giving employee-salespeople the authority to approve orders.
    h. Consigning goods to an independent vendor.
    i. Checking customers' inventories for reorder.
    j. Conducting an advertising campaign in the state.
    k. Delivering goods to customers utilizing the seller's own trucks.
    l. Qualifying to conduct business within the state.

14-22 *Modifications to Federal Taxable Income.* L Corporation is subject to tax only in State A. State A law provides for the use of Federal taxable income before net operating loss and special deductions (line 28, page 1, Form 1120) as the starting point in computing state income. State A allows a deduction for interest received on Federal obligations and disallows any deduction for state income taxes. In addition, it taxes income on municipal bonds of out-of-state issuers. Selected information for the current year is as follows:

Federal taxable income (line 28, page 1)	$500,000
Interest on U.S. Treasury bills	25,000
State income taxes	40,000
Interest on State A bonds	10,000
Interest on State B bonds	8,000

14-23 *Modifications to Federal Taxable Income.* M Corporation is subject to tax only in State B. State B law provides for the use of Federal taxable income before net operating loss and special deductions (line 28, page 1) as the starting point in computing state income. State B allows a deduction for interest received on Federal obligations and disallows any deduction for state income taxes. In addition, it taxes income on all municipal bonds. Federal depreciation differs from state depreciation due to the fact that there was a lag in State B adopting Federal depreciation methods. Selected information for the current year is as follows:

Federal taxable income (line 28, page 1)	$750,000
Interest on U.S. Treasury bills	10,000
State income taxes	50,000
Interest on State A bonds	15,000
Interest on State B bonds	5,000
Depreciation for Federal tax purposes	50,000
Depreciation for state tax purposes	60,000

14-24 *Computation of Income Taxable in Multiple States.* P Corporation conducts a multistate business that operates in States Y and Z. For the current taxable year, P generated $5,000,000 of taxable income, consisting of $4,500,000 of business income and $500,000 of nonbusiness income from investments. P manages the investments in State Y, which is also its state of commercial domicile. Both states allocate nonbusiness income and apportion business income using a three-factor formula in which sales, property, and payroll are equally weighted. Selected information for the current year is as follows:

	State Y	State Z	Total
Sales	$10,000,000	$5,000,000	$15,000,000
Property	5,000,000	3,000,000	8,000,000
Payroll	3,000,000	1,000,000	4,000,000

Determine the amount of P's taxable income that is subject to tax in each state.

14-25 *Computation of Apportionment Percentages.* Q Corporation conducts a multistate business that operates in States A and B. For the current taxable year, Q generated $3,000,000 of taxable income, consisting of $2,800,000 of business income and $200,000 of nonbusiness income from investments. P manages the investments in State A, which is also its state of commercial domicile. Both states allocate nonbusiness income and apportion business income using a three-factor formula in which sales, property (based on average historical cost), and payroll are equally weighted. Neither state takes leased property into account in computing its property factor. Selected information for the current year is as follows:

	State A	State B	Total
Sales	$8,000,000	$2,000,000	$10,000,000
Property (average cost)	$5,000,000	$1,000,000	$ 6,000,000
Average accumulated depreciation	$1,000,000	$ 500,000	$ 1,500,000
Rent expense (annual)	$ 25,000	$ 10,000	$ 35,000
Payroll	$2,000,000	$ 500,000	$ 2,500,000

Determine the current year apportionment percentages for States A and B.

14-26 *Computation of Apportionment Percentages.* Assume the same facts as *Problem 14-24,* except that State B takes property into account at average net book value. (State A continues to take property into account based on historical cost.) Determine the current year apportionment percentages for States A and B.

14-27 *Computation of Apportionment Percentages.* Assume the same facts as *Problem 14-24,* except that both states include leased assets in the property factor in accordance with UDITPA. Determine the current year apportionment percentages for States A and B.

14-28 *Computation of Apportionment Percentages.* Assume the same facts as *Problem 14-24,* except State A (but not State B) assigns a double weight to the sales factor. Determine the current year apportionment percentages for States A and B.

14-29 *Computation of Apportionment Percentages.* Shockley Products (located in State B) has $600,000 of apportionable business income from product sales in both State A and State B and has sufficient nexus to warrant income taxation in each state. The company's sales, property and payroll in each state are as follow:

	State A	State B	Total
Sales	$ 800,000	$ 1,400,000	$ 2,200,000
Property	50,000	4,000,000	4,050,000
Payroll	100,000	1,500,000	1,600,000

    a. If state A uses an equally weighted three-factor formula, how much taxable income is apportioned to A?

    b. If state A uses a three factor formula but double weights sales, how much taxable income is apportioned to A?

    c. If state A uses a single factor (sales) to apportion income, how much taxable income is apportioned *to A?*

14-30 *Sales Factor-Computation.* X Corporation, which is headquartered in State A, has sales for the current year as follows:

	Sales
Sales shipped to locations in State A	$30,000,000
Sales shipped to locations in State B	20,000,000
Sales picked up by State B purchasers at X's manufacturing facility in State A	5,000,000
Sales shipped to locations in State C	15,000,000
Sales to Federal government agencies located in numerous states	10,000,000
Total	$80,000,000

X also earns $1,000,000 of interest and dividends on investments of working capital. Such investments are managed from X's headquarters in State A. States A and B both impose a state income tax. State C does not impose a state income tax. X has sufficient activities in States A and B (but not State C) to create nexus. State A does not employ a throwback rule. Determine X's sales factor in States A and B.

14-31 *Sales Factor-Computation.* Assume the same facts as in *Problem 14-30,* except that State A law contains a throwback provision. Determine X's sales factor in States A and B.

14-32 *Property Factor-Computation.* L Corporation owns property in States X and Y, as follows:

Beginning of Year:

	State X	State Y	Total
Inventory	$ 6,000,000	$ 2,000,000	$ 8,000,000
Plant and equipment	10,000,000	15,000,000	25,000,000
Accumulated depreciation on plant and equipment	4,000,000	5,000,000	9,000,000
Land	3,000,000	2,000,000	5,000,000
Rental property (unrelated to business)	1,000,000	0	1,000,000
Accumulated depreciation on rental property	300,000	0	300,000

End of Year:

	State X	State Y	Total
Inventory	$ 2,000,000	$ 4,000,000	$ 6,000,000
Plant and equipment	11,000,000	15,000,000	26,000,000
Accumulated depreciation on plant and equipment	5,000,000	6,000,000	11,000,000
Land	3,000,000	2,000,000	5,000,000
Rental property (unrelated to business)	1,000,000	0	1,000,000
Accumulated depreciation on rental property	400,000	0	400,000

In addition, L leases property in both states. Rental expense amounts to $50,000 in State X and $20,000 in State Y. Both states value owned property at average original cost and value leased property at eight times annual rental for purposes of the property factor. Compute L's property factor in each state.

14-33 *Property Factor-Computation.* Assume the same facts as in *Problem 14-32*, except that State X does not distinguish between business and nonbusiness income. Compute L's property factor in each state.

14-34 *Payroll Factor-Computation.* T Corporation is subject to tax in States A, B, and C. T's compensation expense for the current year is summarized below:

	State A	State B	State C	Total
Compensation paid to non officers	$5,000,000*	$3,000,000	$2,000,000	$10,000,000
Officers' salaries	2,000,000	1,000,000	0	3,000,000
Total	7,000,000	4,000,000	2,000,000	13,000,000

* Includes $500,000 paid to employees engaged in the management of nonbusiness assets.

All three states include officers' salaries in compensation for purposes of the payroll factor and exclude income from nonbusiness assets from apportionable income. Compute T's payroll factor in each state.

14-35 *Payroll Factor-Computation.* Assume the same facts as in *Problem 14-34*, except that State A does not include officers' salaries in compensation for purposes of the payroll factor. Compute T's payroll factor in each state.

14-36 *Payroll Factor.* S, a district sales manager for K Corporation, earns $100,000 annually. In addition, S receives $5,000 of nontaxable fringe benefits. S spends 30% of his time in State X, 50% of his time in State Y, and 20% of his time in State Z. K's home office, from which S's activities are supervised, is located in State X. S resides in State Y. Determine how much of S's total compensation is included in the numerator of each state's payroll factor.

14-37 *Payroll Factor.* Assume the same facts as in *Problem 14-36,* except that S spends 50% of his time in State Y and 50% in State Z. Determine how much of S's total compensation is included in the numerator of each state's payroll factor.

14-38 *Franchise Tax—Computation.* P Corporation operates solely in State A that imposes a franchise tax equal to 4% of the corporation's net worth. P's balance sheet as of the close of the current year reflects assets of $5,000,000 and liabilities of $2,000,000. Determine P's State A franchise tax liability for the current year.

14-39 *Unitary Reporting.* RGS Inc., a subsidiary of RBS Inc., has taxable income of $750,000, all apportioned to state F. RBS Inc. has $1,300,000 of taxable income and does business solely in state G. Both are combined reporting states (unitary states) and use an equally weighted three-factor apportionment formula. State F has a tax rate of 10%, while state G has a tax rate of 4%.

	RGS Inc.	RBS Inc.
Sales	$ 4,000,000	$ 12,000,000
Payroll	2,000,000	5,000,000
Property	3,500,000	6,500,000

a. If RGS Inc. and RBS Inc. are not part of a unitary business group, what is their tax liability in F and G?

b. If they are members of a unitary group, what is their tax liability in each state?

Family Tax Planning

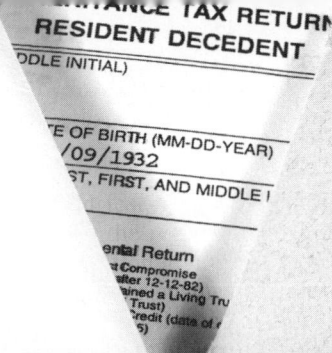

15

Estate and Gift Taxation

Learning Objectives

Upon completion of this chapter you will be able to:

LO.1 Identify the types of transfers that are subject to the Federal gift tax.

LO.2 Compute a donor's total taxable gifts for the current year, including:

- Determination of all available annual exclusions.
- Calculation of any available marital or charitable deduction.

LO.3 Explain the mechanics of the calculation of the gift tax, including the role of the unified credit.

LO.4 List the three basic steps involved in the computation of a decedent's taxable estate.

LO.5 Specify the various types of property interests that must be valued for inclusion in a decedent's gross estate.

LO.6 Describe any deductions from the gross estate.

LO.7 Explain the mechanics of the calculation of the estate tax, including the role of the unified credit.

LO.8 Discuss the purpose of the generation-skipping transfer tax.

Chapter Outline

Introduction

Since 1916 Congress has imposed taxes aimed solely at an individual's transfer of wealth: the estate tax (1916), the gift tax (1932), and the generation-skipping transfer tax (1976). As a practical matter, these taxes have produced relatively little revenue—about 1% of total revenues—and affected few individuals—also around 1 percent.[1] Despite their limited impact, the taxes have survived. However, with the inauguration of President Bush in 2001, it appeared that the estate tax itself was about to die. Under the Economic Growth and Tax Relief Reconciliation Act of 2001, the estate tax—but not the gift tax—was scheduled for repeal in 2010. As a practical matter, most believed that repeal would never happen and ultimately Congress would reach some type of compromise that would extend the estate tax in some modified form. But, the unthinkable did occur and the estate tax was repealed—but only for one year, 2010. Legislation enacted in 2010 resurrected the estate tax but only for 2011 and 2012, leaving everyone to wonder what would happen in 2013. Congress solved the mystery in the waning moments of 2012 with the enactment of the American Taxpayer Relief Act. The Act made the estate and gift tax permanent. However, the new law provided a generous exemption, $5,450,00 for 2016, that will protect all but the wealthiest of Americans.

HISTORY AND OVERVIEW

The estate tax became a permanent part of the tax system in 1916. In short, it is merely an excise tax on the transfer of the decedent's *net* wealth (fair market value of total assets less debts and expenses) that passes to his or her heirs at death. For example, if a taxpayer dies with a home worth $1,000,000 and a mortgage of $200,000, he or she is potentially taxed on the net amount of $800,000. Whether or not the taxpayer is actually taxed on such amount depends in part on a number of variables including who receives the property. For example, the law currently provides deductions for transfers to a spouse or qualifying charitable organizations.

Shortly after the enactment of the estate tax it became clear that without additional rules a taxpayer could easily avoid the estate tax simply by giving away property before he or she died. As might be expected, to prevent full scale avoidance of the estate tax Congress enacted a gift tax in 1924. A unique feature of the gift tax is the fact that unlike the income tax where the current year's tax is based on the current's year's income, the gift tax is computed on the cumulative amount of gifts made by an individual during his or her lifetime. Because of the progressive transfer tax rates, this approach makes every gift more expensive in terms of tax dollars than the last. Another important characteristic of the gift tax is the annual exclusion. To eliminate the vast administrative problems that would result if the gift tax were imposed on all gifts (e.g., birthday and Christmas presents) the gift tax is imposed only on those that exceed a certain threshold, currently $14,000 (2016) per donee per year.

Until 1976, the estate and gift tax were separate and distinct taxes. Although both taxes imposed a tax on transfers of wealth, one on lifetime transfers and one on transfers at death, they differed in several important ways. One important difference could be found in the rate structures. For many years, the gift tax rates were 25% less than estate tax rates, presumably to encourage taxpayers to transfer their assets during their lifetime rather than hoarding them until death. Another difference involved the amount of transfers exempted from tax. The gift tax had its own lifetime exemption of $30,000 while the estate tax exemption was $60,000. Any of the exemption for gifts that was not used during the taxpayer's lifetime could not be carried over and used at death but was lost. Another distinction concerned the tax computation. Transfers made during the taxpayer's lifetime (i.e., taxable gifts) did not

---

[1] Recent IRS statistics indicate the number of estate tax returns filed decreased from 108,071 in 2001 to 15,191 in 2010.

enter into the calculation of the tax on the taxpayer's transfers at death (i.e., the taxable estate). However, these distinctions came to an end with the passage of the Tax Reform Act of 1976 when the two taxes were unified. Although current practice still refers to these transfer taxes as the estate tax and the gift tax, they are really part of what is a unified transfer tax system.

The unification of the estate and gift tax eliminated the differences between the two taxes, completely integrating the two systems into the one that exists today. The new law replaced the two separate rate schedules with a single, unified transfer tax rate schedule used to compute both the estate and the gift tax. Moreover, since 1976 a decedent's taxable estate is effectively treated as an individual's final taxable gift. This is accomplished by computing the estate tax on a base that includes not only the taxable estate but also any taxable gifts made during the decedent's life. The changes in 1976 also replaced the separate exemptions with a single unified credit. The credit is unified in the sense that whatever amount is used to offset the gift tax during life is unavailable to reduce the estate tax at death. Beginning in 2011, the credit is adjusted annually for inflation. For 2016, the exemption for both the estate tax and gift tax is $5,450,000.

Another change made in 1976 was the introduction of a third Federal transfer tax on generation-skipping transfers. This tax, designed to complement the gift and estate taxes, is quite complex and highly controversial. It is discussed later in this chapter.

The Economic Recovery Tax Act of 1981 (ERTA 1981) continued the restructuring of the transfer tax system begun in 1976. The most important feature of this legislation was the unlimited marital deduction. This deduction makes gifts between spouses completely non-taxable and allows the first spouse to die to leave the family wealth to the surviving spouse at no Federal transfer tax cost. Thus, after 1981, the taxable unit for the imposition of the gift or estate tax is no longer the individual but the marital unit.

As noted above, Congress allowed the estate tax to expire for one year in 2010. Under the Tax Relief, Unemployment Insurance Reauthorization, and Job Creation Act of 2010, estates for those dying in 2010 could elect *not* to pay the estate tax, in which case the heirs had to accept the modified carryover basis rules of § 1022. Estates that did not elect and did nothing were subject to the revised rules. These rules essentially exempted taxpayers with net wealth of $5,000,000 ($10,000,000 for married couples) from the estate tax. In addition, the basis of property passing to their heirs normally was its fair market value at date of death.

Property Interests

Since the estate and gift taxes concern transfers of property, understanding the two taxes requires an appreciation of the nature of property interests and the different forms of property ownership. In the United States, each of the 50 states has its own system of *property law*—statutory rules that govern an individual's right to own and convey both real and personal property during his or her lifetime. Unfortunately, the specific property laws of each state vary considerably and therefore generalizations about property laws can be dangerous. However, the various state legal systems can be divided into two basic categories: *common law systems* and *community property systems*. The common law system, derived from English laws of property ownership, focuses on individual ownership of assets, regardless of the marital status of the individual. This system has been adopted in 41 states. The community property system is a derivation of Spanish property law and is followed in nine states: Arizona, California, Idaho, Louisiana, Nevada, New Mexico, Texas, Washington, and Wisconsin. In Alaska, individuals may opt-in to the community property system. Under either system, an individual may own property alone or jointly with another. In addition, an individual may own only a partial interest in the property such as an income interest. The different forms of co-ownership and various types of partial interests are considered below.

FORMS OF CO-OWNERSHIP

The consequences of holding property jointly with another can vary substantially, depending on the type of co-ownership. There are four forms of co-ownership: (1) tenancy in common, (2) joint tenancy, (3) tenancy by the entirety, and (4) community property ownership.

Tenancy in Common

A tenancy in common exists when two or more persons hold title to property, each owning an undivided fractional interest in the whole. The percentage of the property owned by one tenant need not be the same as the other co-tenants but can differ as the co-tenants provide. The most important feature of this type of property interest is that it is treated in virtually all respects like property that is owned outright. Thus, the interest can be sold, gifted, willed, or, when there is no will, passed to the owner's heirs according to the laws of the state. Another important characteristic of a tenancy in common is the *right of partition*. This right permits co-owners who disagree over something concerning the property to go to court to secure a division of the property among the owners. In some cases, however, a physical division is impossible (e.g., 50 acres of land where each acre's value is dependent on the whole), and consequently, the property must be sold with the proceeds split between the owners.

Joint Tenancy

Under a joint tenancy arrangement, two or more persons hold title to property, each owning the same fractional interest in the property. Joint tenancy normally implies the right of survivorship (joint tenancy with right of survivorship, or JTWROS). This means that upon the death of one joint tenant, the property automatically passes to the surviving joint tenants. Consequently, the disposition of the property is *not* controlled by the decedent's will. Like tenants in common, joint tenants have the right to sever their interest in the property. This is a particularly valuable right since the tenant may wish to disinherit the other joint tenants.

Tenancy by the Entirety

A tenancy by the entirety is a JTWROS between husband and wife. The critical difference between a tenancy by the entirety and a JTWROS is that in most states a spouse cannot sever his or her interest without the consent of the other spouse. In addition, in some states the husband has full control over the property while alive and is entitled to all the income from it.

Community Property

In a community property system, married individuals own an equal, undivided interest in all wealth acquired during the course of the marriage, regardless of which spouse made any individual contribution to the marital wealth. In addition to a half interest in such "community property," a spouse may also own property in an individual capacity as "separate property." Generally, assets acquired prior to marriage and assets received by gift or inheritance are separate property. However, in all nine community property states there exists a strong legal presumption that all property possessed during marriage is community, and that presumption can only be overcome by convincing proof of the property's separate nature.

Marital Property

Before leaving the subject of joint ownership, the concept of marital property deserves attention. Except in community property states, it is a common mistake to assume that all property acquired during marriage is jointly held. State laws vary widely on this issue. In some states, only property specifically titled as JTWROS is treated as jointly held. In these and other states, it is not unusual that property acquired during marriage belongs to the husband regardless of whose earnings were used to acquire the property. In other states, each spouse is deemed to own that which can be traced to his or her own earnings. Because of the problems with marital property, transfers of such property should be evaluated carefully to ensure that the rights of either spouse are not violated.

LIFE ESTATES, REVERSIONS, AND REMAINDERS

Persons who own property outright have virtually unlimited rights with respect to their property. They can sell it, mortgage it, or transfer it as they wish. In addition, they can divide the ownership of the property in any number of ways. In this regard, it is not uncommon for property owners to transfer ownership in property to someone temporarily. During the period of temporary ownership, the beneficiary could have the right to use, possess, and benefit from the income of the property. Assuming that the beneficiary's interest is limited to the income from the property, he or she would be treated as having an *income interest*. The time to which the beneficiary is entitled to the income from the property could be specified in any terms, such as common measures of time: days, weeks, months, or years. Alternatively, the time period could be determined by reference to the occurrence of a specific event. For example, when an individual has an income interest for life, the interest is referred to as a life estate. In this case, the person entitled to the *life estate* is called the life tenant.

The owner of property has the right to provide for one or more temporary interests, subject only to the *rule against perpetuities*. This rule requires that the property pass outright to an individual within a certain time period after the transfer. Normally, ownership of the property must vest at a date no later than 21 years after the death of persons alive at the time the interest is created.

Interestingly, a few states have recently repealed the rule. For example, trusts in Alaska, Delaware, Washington D.C., Illinois, New Jersey, South Dakota, Virginia, and Wisconsin can now be designed to last forever. Trusts in Utah and Wyoming can last for up to 1,000 years while those in Florida must end after 360 years.

After any temporary interests have been designated, the owner has the right to provide for the outright transfer of the property. If the owner specifies that the property should be returned to the owner or his or her estate, the interest following the temporary interest is referred to as a *reversionary interest*. If the property passes to someone other than the owner, the interest is called a *remainder interest*. The holder of the remainder interest is the *remainderman*.

Life estates, remainders, and reversions are property interests that can be transferred, sold, and willed (except for life estates) like other types of property. These interests can also be reached by creditors in satisfaction of their claims. However, a person can establish a trust with so-called *spendthrift* provisions, which prohibit the beneficiary from assigning or selling his or her interest (e.g., a life estate) or using the assets to satisfy creditors.

The Gift Tax

The statutory provisions regarding the Federal gift tax are contained in §§ 2501 through 2524 of the Internal Revenue Code. These rules provide the basis for the gift tax formula found in Exhibit 15-1. The various elements of this formula are discussed below.

EXHIBIT 15-1	Computation of Federal Gift Tax Liability		
Fair market value of all gifts made in the current year			$xxx,xxx
Less the sum of:			
Annual exclusions ($14,000 per donee in 2016).	$xx,xxx		
Marital deduction.	xx,xxx		
Charitable deduction	x,xxx	− xx,xxx	
Taxable gifts for current year.			$xxx,xxx
Plus: All taxable gifts made in prior years			+ xx,xxx
Taxable transfers to date			$xxx,xxx
Tentative tax on total transfers to date.			$ xx,xxx
Less the sum of:			
Gift taxes computed at current rates on prior years' taxable gifts	$ x,xxx		
Unified transfer tax credit.	x,xxx	− xx,xxx	
Gift tax due on current gifts.			$ xx,xxx

TRANSFERS SUBJECT TO TAX

LO.1

Identify the types of transfers that are subject to the Federal gift tax.

Section 2511 states that the gift tax shall apply to transfers in trust or otherwise, whether the gift is direct or indirect, real or personal, tangible or intangible. The gift tax is imposed only on transfers of property; gratuitous transfers of services are not subject to tax.[2] The types of property interests to which the gift tax applies are virtually unlimited. The tax applies to transfers of such common items as money, cars, stocks, bonds, jewelry, works of art, houses, and every other type of item normally considered property. It should be emphasized that no property is specifically excluded from the gift tax. For example, the transfer of municipal bonds is subject to the gift tax, even though the income from the bonds is tax free.

The gift tax reaches transfers of partial interests as well. One example is a transfer of property in trust where the income interest is given to someone—the income beneficiary—for his or her life, while the trust property or remainder interest is given to another person—the remainderman—upon the income beneficiary's death. In this case, the donor would be treated as having made two separate gifts, a gift of the income interest and a gift of the remainder interest.

The application of the gift tax to both direct and indirect gifts ensures that the tax reaches all transfers regardless of the method of transfer. Direct gifts encompass the common types of outright transfers (e.g., father transfers bonds to daughter, or grandmother gives cash to grandson). On the other hand, indirect gifts are represented primarily by transfers to trusts and other entities. When a transfer is made to a trust, it is considered a gift to the beneficiaries of the trust. Similarly, a transfer to a corporation or partnership is considered a gift to the shareholders or partners. However, if the donor owns an interest in a partnership or corporation, he or she is not treated as making a gift to the extent it would be a gift to himself or herself. An individual may also be treated as making a gift if he or she refuses to accept property and the property passes to another person on account of the refusal.

Most taxpayers understand that the gift tax is imposed on transfers of property motivated by affection and generosity. However, the tax may also be imposed on a transfer of property not intended as a gift within the commonly accepted definition of the word. The tax is intended to apply to any transfer of wealth by an individual that reduces his or her potential taxable estate. Therefore, § 2512 provides that any transfer of property, in return for which the transferor receives *less than adequate or full consideration* in money or money's worth, is a transfer subject to the gift tax.

Adequate Consideration

Revenue Ruling 79-384 provides an excellent example of a transfer for insufficient consideration.[3] The taxpayer in the ruling was a father, who had made an oral promise to his son to pay him $10,000 upon the son's graduation from college. The son graduated but the father refused to pay him the promised amount. The son then successfully sued the father, who was forced to transfer the $10,000. The IRS ruled that the father had received no consideration in money or money's worth for the transfer and therefore had made a taxable gift to his son.

Revenue Ruling 79-384 illustrates two important concepts. First, *donative intent* on the part of a transferor of property is *not necessary* to classify the transfer as a taxable gift.[4] Second, anything received by the transferor in exchange for the property must be subject to valuation in monetary terms if it is to be consideration within the meaning of § 2512.[5] The father did receive the satisfaction resulting from his son's graduation, and this consideration was sufficient to create an enforceable oral contract between father and son. However, because the consideration could not be objectively valued in dollar terms it was irrelevant for tax purposes.

The question of sufficiency of consideration normally arises when transfers of assets are made between family members or related parties. When properties are transferred or exchanged in a bona fide business transaction, the Regulations specify that sufficiency of consideration will be presumed because of the arm's-length negotiation between the parties.[6]

Transfers of wealth to dependent family members that represent support are not taxable gifts. The distinction between support payments and gifts is far from clear, particularly when the transferor is not legally obligated to make the payments. Section 2503(e) specifies

---

[2] Rev. Rul. 56-472, 1956-2 C.B. 21.

[3] 1979-2 C.B. 12.

[4] Reg. § 25.2511-1(g)(1).

[5] Reg. § 25.2512-8.

[6] *Ibid.*

that amounts paid on behalf of any individual for tuition to an educational organization or for medical care shall not be considered taxable gifts to such individual. However, this rule only applies if the payments are made directly to the educational institution or the health care provider.

Payments that a divorced taxpayer is legally required to make for the *support* of his or her former spouse are not taxable gifts.[7] However, Regulation § 25.2512-8 specifies that payments made prior to or after marriage in return for the recipient's relinquishment of his or her *marital property rights* are transfers for insufficient consideration and subject to the gift tax. Section 2516 provides an exception to this rule. If a transfer of property is made under the terms of a written agreement between spouses and the transfer is (1) in settlement of the spouse's marital property rights, or (2) to provide a reasonable allowance for support of any minor children of the marriage, no taxable gift will occur. For the exception to apply, divorce must occur within the three-year period beginning on the date one year before such agreement is entered into.

Retained Interest

The final criterion of a taxable transfer is that the transfer must be complete. A transfer is considered complete only if the donor has surrendered all control over the property. For this reason, when the donor alone retains the right to revoke the transfer, the transfer is incomplete and the gift tax does not apply. For example, creation of a joint bank account is not considered a completed gift since the depositor is free to withdraw the money deposited in the account. Similarly, the donor must not be able to redirect ownership of the property in the future; nonetheless, to have a completed gift it is not necessary that the donees have received the property or that the specific donees even be identified.[8]

Example 1

Donor D transfers $1 million into an irrevocable trust with an independent trustee. The trustee has the right to pay the income of the trust to beneficiaries A, B, or C *or* to accumulate the income. After 15 years, the trust will terminate and all accumulated income and principal will be divided among the surviving beneficiaries. Because D has parted with all control over the $1 million, it is a completed gift, even though neither A, B, nor C has received or is guaranteed any specified portion of the money.

VALUATION

The value of a transfer subject to the Federal gift tax is measured by the fair market value of the property transferred less the value of any consideration received by the transferor. Determining fair market value can be the most difficult aspect of computing a gift tax due. Fair market value is defined in the Regulations as "the price at which such property would change hands between a willing buyer and a willing seller, neither being under any compulsion to buy or to sell, and both having reasonable knowledge of relevant facts."[9]

The determination of an asset's fair market value must be made on the basis of all relevant facts and circumstances. The Regulations under § 2512 are quite detailed and extremely useful in that they prescribe methods for valuation of a variety of assets.

Example 2

Donor S transfers 10 shares of the publicly traded common stock of XYZ Corporation on June 8, 2016. On that date, the highest quoted selling price of the stock was $53 per share. The lowest quoted selling price was $48 per share. Regulation § 25.2512-2(b)(1) specifies that the fair market value of the XYZ stock on June 8, 2016 shall be the mean between the highest and lowest quoted selling price ([$53 + $48] ÷ 2), or $50.50 per share.

---

[7] Rev. Rul. 68-379, 1968-2 C.B. 414.

[8] Reg. § 25.2511-2(a).

[9] Reg. § 25.2512-1.

Valuation of Income and Remainder Interests

In estate planning, it is quite common for individuals to make gifts of only a partial interest of property. These arrangements usually involve transfers to a trust such as the following:

- An individual transfers property to a trust, giving away an income interest to one beneficiary and a remainder interest to another beneficiary. In this case, the taxpayer has actually made two gifts—the income interest and the remainder interest—each of which must be valued for gift tax purposes.

- An individual transfers property to a trust, retaining the income interest and giving away the remainder interest. Here there is only a single gift of the remainder interest.

- An individual transfers property to a trust, giving the income interest to a beneficiary but providing that the remainder interest reverts or returns to the individual once the income interest has expired. In this case, the taxpayer has made a single gift of the income interest.

Gifts of income and remainder interests are valued using actuarial tables. These tables take into consideration current interest rates and, if necessary, current mortality rates. In valuing the various types of transfers, the tables assume that property transferred produces income at a certain rate, regardless of the actual amount of income that is produced.

For transfers after April 30, 1989, § 7520 requires valuations using the interest rate prevailing at the time of the transfer. Specifically, the rate to be used is 120% of the applicable Federal midterm rate in effect under § 1274(d)(1) for the month in which the transfer is made.[10] These rates are published monthly. Using the appropriate rate, the values can be found in actuarial tables published by the IRS. The tables were first issued in 1989 in Notice 89-60.[11] Section 7520(c)(3) requires that the tables be revised at least once every 10 years thereafter to reflect the most recent mortality experience available. They were most recently revised in 2009 and can be found in IRS Publications 1457, 1458, or 1459.[12] These volumes reference IRS websites that provide factors for interest rates of 2.2% to 26% and annuity factors for ages 0–110. The IRS publishes the rates monthly.[13] For example, the midterm interest rate as set by Treasury for November, 2015 was 1.9 percent, making the § 7520 rate 2.0 percent.[14] Table S shows the factors for determining the value of an annuity, a life estate, or a remainder interest based on a single life. Table B shows the factors for determining the value of an annuity, a life estate or a remainder interest for a term of years Selected portions of the tables can be found in Appendix A in this book.

In examining the tables, observe that if the value of the property is split between an income interest and a remainder interest, there are two factors and the sum of those two factors equals one. In a case where the remainder factor is known but the income factor is unknown or vice versa, the income factor can be determined as follows:

Income factor = 1.000000 − Remainder factor

Example 3

In May, 20X9, H transferred $100,000 to a trust for his son, S, and his grandson, GS. According to the terms of the trust, S is to receive the income for life and upon his death, the remainder is to be paid to GS, if living, otherwise to GS's estate. S was 40 years old at the time the trust was created. H has made two gifts. The value of S's income interest is a function of three factors determined at the time of the gift: (1) S's life expectancy,

---

[10] The midterm rate is derived from the one-month average of the market yields from marketable obligations of the United States with maturities of more than three years but not more than nine years.

[11] 1989-1 C.B. 700.

[12] IRS Publication 1457, Actuarial Values, Aleph Volume (2001), Version 3A (2009); IRS Publication 1458, Actuarial Values, Beth Volume (2001), Version 3B (2009); IRS Publication 1459, Actuarial Values, Gimel Volume (2001), Version 3A (2009). The rates can be found at the following IRS website: http://www.irs.gov/Retirement-Plans/Actuarial-Tables.

[13] These rates are published monthly. For transfers after December 31, 1970 and before December 1, 1983 the interest rate used to compute the value of reversions and other interests was six percent. The factors can be found in the appropriate table contained in Reg § 20.2031-10(f). For transfers after November 30, 1983, and before May 1, 1989, the interest rate used to compute the value of reversions and other interests was 10 percent.

[14] Rev. Rul. 2015-22, 2015-44 IRB 610.

(2) the current interest rate, and (3) the value of the trust property. Assume the applicable rate for valuing the interest is five percent (120% of the May Federal mid-term rate). Using the table for valuing a remainder interest (Table S in Appendix A-1), the value of the remainder interest is $18,619 ($100,000 × 0.18619). The value of the income interest is $81,381 ($100,000 × [1 − 0.19516 = 0.81381]). Note that the sum of the remainder interest and the income interest equals the total value of the property.

Example 4

In June, 20X2, M transferred $100,000 to a trust for her daughter, D. Under the terms of the trust, D is to receive the income for 20 years at which time the trust will terminate and the property will revert to M. Assume the applicable rate for valuing the interest is 5.2% (120% of the June Federal mid-term rate). In this case, the factor for the income interest must be determined by subtracting the factor for the remainder interest from 1. Using the table for valuing a term certain remainder interest (Table B in Appendix A-2), the value of D's income interest for 20 years is $63,719 ($100,000 × 0.637185).

The valuation of a gift of a partial interest in property is subject to special rules when the donor retains an income interest. These rules are considered in Chapter 17 in conjunction with the discussion on special estate planning techniques (e.g., grantor retained income trusts, annuity trusts, and unitrusts [GRITS, GRATS, and GRUTS]).

BASIS

The basis of an asset in the hands of a donee is calculated under the rules of § 1015. Generally, the basis of property received as a gift is the basis of the asset in the hands of the donor. This carryover basis may be increased by a portion of any gift tax paid (gift tax × [value of the property − donor's basis]/amount of taxable gift). This general rule applies only if the asset is sold at a gain by the donee. If the carryover basis rule would result in a realized loss upon subsequent sale, the basis of the asset will be considered the *lesser* of the carryover basis (donor's basis) *or* the asset's fair market value at date of gift. If the asset is sold at a price greater than the fair market value at date of gift but less than its carryover basis, no gain or loss is recognized.

THE GIFT TAX EXCLUSION

When the gift tax was enacted in 1932, Congress wanted to "eliminate the necessity of keeping an account of and reporting numerous small gifts." To this end, it created an annual exclusion designed to exempt gifts under a certain threshold from the gift tax.[15] The annual exclusion was initially set at $3,000 until it was raised to $10,000 in 1981 where it remained through 2001. Starting in 2002, the exclusion has been adjusted for inflation. For 2002–2005, the exclusion was $11,000. For 2006 through 2008, the exclusion was $12,000. For 2009 through 2012 the exclusion is $13,000. For 2013 through 2016, the exclusion is $14,000.

A donor is entitled to exclude $14,000 (2016) per year per donee. However, not all gifts are eligible for the annual exclusion. Congress was concerned about the problems that could arise in determining the number of exclusions when there was only a remote possibility that a donee would receive a gift (e.g., remote and contingent beneficiaries). For this reason, to qualify for the exclusion the gift must constitute a *present* interest. Regulation § 25.2503-3(b) defines a present interest as one that gives the donee "an unrestricted right to the immediate use, possession, or enjoyment of property or the income from property." Therefore, the annual exclusion is not available for a gift that can only be enjoyed by the donee at some future date, even if the donee receives a present ownership interest in the gift.

LO.2

Compute a donor's total taxable gifts for the current year, including:

■ Determination of all available annual exclusions.

■ Calculation of any available marital or charitable deduction.

[15] § 2503(b).

> ### Example 5
>
> Donor D gifts real estate worth $20,000 to donees M and N. M is given a *life* estate (the right to the income from the property for as long as M lives) worth $8,000. N receives *the remainder interest* (complete ownership of the property upon the death of M) worth $12,000. Although both M and N have received legal property interests, D may claim only one exclusion for his gift to M. The gift to N is a gift of a future rather than a present interest. Thus D has made a taxable gift of $12,000.

Securing the tax benefit of the annual exclusion can be difficult if the gift in question is made to a minor or an incapacitated donee. In such cases, the donor may be reluctant to give an unrestricted present interest in the donated property. Strategies for making gifts to minors or incapacitated donees is included in Chapter 17.

GIFT SPLITTING

A gift made by a married individual residing in a community property state may have two donors (husband and wife) because of state property law. Property laws in the 41 non-community property states do not produce this *two donor* result. To compensate for this difference, § 2513 provides a *gift splitting* election to a married donor.

If a donor makes the proper election on his or her current gift tax return, one-half of all gifts made during the year will be considered to have been made by the donor's spouse. Both spouses must consent to gift splitting for the election to be valid. Since evidence of the spouse's consent is necessary when gift splitting is used, a gift tax return must be filed.

> ### Example 6
>
> In 2016, husband H gives $100,000 to his son and $100,000 to his daughter. His wife, W, makes a gift of $5,000 to their daughter. H and W elect gift splitting on their current gift tax returns. As a result, H reports a gift to the daughter of $52,500 ($50,000 + $2,500) and a gift to the son of $50,000, and will claim two $14,000 gift tax exclusions, resulting in total taxable gifts of $74,500 ($52,500 + $50,000 − $28,000). W will report exactly the same gifts and claim two $14,000 exclusions, resulting in the same amount of taxable gifts as her husband H, $74,500, for a total of $149,000.
>
> Without gift splitting, H would still be entitled to $28,000 of exclusions, but W could only claim an exclusion of $5,000 for her gift to the daughter. Without splitting, H and W would have total taxable gifts of $177,000 compared to $149,000 with splitting. By splitting, the couple is able to increase the exclusions by $23,000 ($14,000 for the gift to the son and $9,000 for the gift to the daughter).

GIFTS TO POLITICAL AND CHARITABLE ORGANIZATIONS

Code § 2501(a)(5) excludes gifts of money or other property to a political organization from the statutory definition of taxable transfers. If a gratuitous donation is made to a qualified charitable organization, § 2522 provides a deduction for such gift from the donor's taxable gifts for the calendar year. Thus, transfers made without sufficient consideration to qualifying political or charitable groups are not subject to the Federal gift tax.

THE GIFT TAX MARITAL DEDUCTION

Under § 2523, gifts to spouses are fully deductible by the donor. The marital deduction is permitted only if certain requirements are satisfied. A full discussion of these requirements is considered in conjunction with the discussion of the marital deduction for estate tax purposes.

The gift tax marital deduction allows an individual to make tax-free transfers of wealth to his or her spouse. This opportunity to equalize the wealth owned by husband and wife plays an essential role in family tax planning, a role that will be discussed in Chapter 17.

COMPUTATION AND FILING

LO.3

Explain the mechanics of the calculation of the gift tax, including the role of the unified credit.

Unlike the income tax, which is computed on annual taxable income, the Federal gift tax is computed on cumulative taxable gifts made during a donor's lifetime. This is done by adding taxable gifts for the current year to all taxable gifts made in prior years, calculating the gross tax on the sum of cumulative gifts, and subtracting the amount of gift tax calculated on prior years' gifts.[16] The transfer tax rate schedule currently in effect is reproduced in Exhibit 15-2. The maximum estate and gift tax rate has been gradually reduced as follows:

Year	Top Rate
2002	50%
2003	49%
2004	48%
2005	47%
2006	46%
2007–09	45%
2010–12	35%
2013–16	40%

EXHIBIT 15-2	**2016–Current Estate and Gift Tax Rates**

If Taxable Transfer Is			
Over	But Not Over	Tax Liability	Of the Amount Over
$ 0	$ 10,000	18%	$ 0
10,000	20,000	$ 1,800 + 20%	10,000
20,000	40,000	3,800 + 22%	20,000
40,000	60,000	8,200 + 24%	40,000
60,000	80,000	13,000 + 26%	60,000
80,000	100,000	18,200 + 28%	80,000
100,000	150,000	23,800 + 30%	100,000
150,000	250,000	38,800 + 32%	150,000
250,000	500,000	70,800 + 34%	250,000
500,000	750,000	155,800 + 37%	500,000
750,000	1,000,000	248,300 + 39%	750,000
Over	1,000,000	345,800 + 40%	1,000,000

Example 7

In 1995, X made his first taxable gift of $100,000 (after the exclusion). The tax (before credits) on this amount using current rates is $23,800. X made a second taxable gift of $85,000 in 2016. The tax (before credits) on the second gift is $26,200, computed as follows:

1995 taxable gift.	$100,000
2016 taxable gift.	+ 85,000
Cumulative gifts	$185,000
Tax on $185,000 ($38,800 + [32% × ($185,000 – $150,000 = $35,000)]).	$ 50,000
Less: Tax on 1995 taxable gift (computed at current rates).	– 23,800
Tax on 2016 gift before credits	$ 26,200

This cumulative system of gift taxation and the progressive rate schedule cause a higher tax on the 2016 gift, even though the 2016 gift was $15,000 ($100,000 – $85,000) *less* than the 1995 gift.

---

[16] § 2502(a). The amount of gift tax calculated on prior years' gifts is based on current gift tax rates, regardless of the rates in effect when the gifts were actually made.

Unified Credit

Both the estate and gift tax provisions have long contained exemptions to ensure that the taxes do not apply to modest transfers of wealth. As noted earlier, prior to their unification in 1976, each tax had its own separate exemption: the estate tax provided for an exemption of $60,000 while the gift tax allowed a lifetime exemption of $30,000 for otherwise taxable gifts (i.e., those not otherwise exempt by the annual exclusion). The unification in 1976 led to the creation of the unified credit. The unified credit is a lifetime credit available for offsetting the tax on all taxable transfers (i.e., the taxes imposed on taxable gifts or the taxable estate). Since 2012, the credit is adjusted annually for inflation. In 2016, the credit is $2,125,800 for both the estate tax and gift tax. This gift tax credit of $2,125,800 completely offsets the tax on $5,450,000 of taxable transfers. For example, consider a taxpayer whose first *taxable* gift is $5,450,000. The tax on the $5,450,000 taxable transfer would be $2,125,800. However, the credit of $2,125,800 would completely eliminate the tax, effectively providing an exemption from tax for transfers of up to $5,450,000.

EXHIBIT 15-3	Credit and Exemption Equivalent			
	Credit		Exemption Equivalent	
Year	*Estate Tax*	*Gift Tax*	*Estate Tax*	*Gift Tax*
1/1/77–6/30/77	$ 6,000	Same	$ 30,000	Same
7/1/77–12/31/77	30,000	Same	120,666	Same
1978	34,000	Same	134,000	Same
1979	38,000	Same	147,333	Same
1980	42,500	Same	161,563	Same
1981	47,000	Same	175,625	Same
1982	62,800	Same	225,000	Same
1983	79,300	Same	275,000	Same
1984	96,300	Same	325,000	Same
1985	121,800	Same	400,000	Same
1986	155,800	Same	500,000	Same
1987–97	192,800	Same	600,000	Same
1998	202,050	Same	625,000	Same
1999	211,300	Same	650,000	Same
2000–01	220,550	Same	675,000	Same
2002–03	345,800	Same	1,000,000	Same
2004–05	555,800	$345,800	1,500,000	$1,000,000
2006–08	780,800	345,800	2,000,000	1,000,000
2009	1,455,800	345,800	3,500,000	1,000,000
2010–11	1,730,800	345,800	5,000,000	1,000,000
2012	2,045,800	Same	5,120,000	Same
2013	2,045,800	Same	5,250,000	Same
2014	2,081,800	Same	5,340,000	Same
2015	2,117,800	Same	5,430,000	Same
2016	2,125,800	Same	5,450,000	Same

As can be seen in Exhibit 15-3, the amount of the credit has been increased over the years. In 1976, the credit was originally set so that when it was completely phased in by 1981 it would exempt from tax transfers of up to $175,625. However, by 1981, Congress and the Reagan administration viewed that amount as inadequate. Consequently, legislation was passed to gradually increase the credit so that it would reach $192,800 in 1987 where it would exempt $600,000 of transfers from tax. The credit remained at that level for more than 10 years until Congress acted again in the Taxpayer Relief Act of 1997. Beginning in

1998, the credit began to increase gradually. However, before the increase was complete, Congress changed course and moved toward ultimate repeal of the estate tax. From 2004 through 2010, the exemption amounts for the estate tax and the gift tax were no longer the same. The gift tax exemption was set at the $1,000,000 level. On the other hand, the exemption for the estate tax gradually increased to $3,500,000 in 2009. In 2010, Congress addressed the repeal of the estate tax. In so doing, it increased the exemption for the estate tax to $5,000,000 but the exemption for the gift tax for 2010 remained at $1,000,000. However, beginning in 2011, the exemptions for the estate and gift tax are united once again. For 2016, they are both $5,450,000.

The unified credit is the only credit available to offset the Federal gift tax. As noted above, the credit currently offsets the tax on $5,450,000 of taxable gifts. Thus, an individual may make substantial transfers of wealth before any tax liability is incurred. The unified credit must be used when available—a taxpayer may not decide to postpone use of the credit if he or she makes a taxable gift during the current year.[17]

Example 8

In 1995, Y made her first taxable gift of $350,000. The tax calculated on this gift was $104,800, and Y used $104,800 of her available unified credit so that the actual gift tax due was reduced to zero. In 2016, Y made her second taxable gift of $6,000,000. The tax on this gift is $404,000, computed as follows:

Taxable gift for 2016		$6,000,000
Plus: 1995 taxable gift		+ 350,000
Taxable transfers to date		$6,350,000
Tentative 2016 tax on total transfers to date (See Exhibit 15-2) ($345,800 + $2,140,000 [40%($6,350,000 – $1,000,000 = $5,350,000)])		$2,485,800
Less: Gift taxes calculated at current rates on 1995 gift		– 104,800
Tentative tax on 2016 gift		$2,381,000
Less: Remaining unified transfer tax credit:		
Total credit available for 2016	$2,125,800	
Less: Unified transfer tax credit used in 1995	– 104,800	–2,021,000
Gift tax due on 2016 gift		$ 360,000

Filing Requirements

The Federal gift tax return, Form 709, is filed annually on a calendar year basis. The due date of the return is the April 15th after the close of the taxable year. If a calendar year taxpayer obtains any extension to file his or her Federal income tax return, such extension automatically applies to any gift tax return due. If the donor dies during a taxable year for which a gift tax return is due, the gift tax return must be filed by the due date (nine months after death) plus any extensions of the donor's Federal estate tax return.[18]

THE OVERLAP BETWEEN THE GIFT AND ESTATE TAXES

A beginning student of the Federal transfer tax system might reasonably assume that an inter vivos (during life) transfer of property that is considered complete and therefore subject to the gift tax would also be considered complete for estate tax purposes, so that the transferred property would not be included in the decedent's taxable estate. This, however, is not the case. The gift tax and the estate tax are not mutually exclusive; property gifted away in

---

[17] Rev. Rul. 79-398, 1979-2 C.B. 338.   [18] § 6075(b).

earlier years can be included in the donor's taxable estate. The relationship between the two taxes is illustrated in the following diagram:

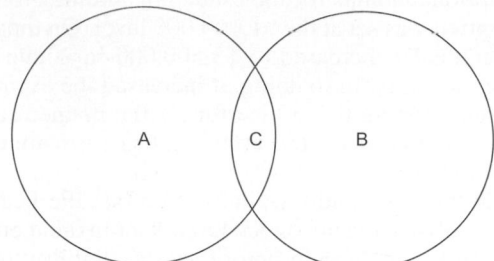

Circle A represents property transferred by the decedent during his or her lifetime and subject to the gift tax. Circle B represents the decedent's taxable estate. Overlap area C represents property already subject to a gift tax that is nevertheless included in the donor/decedent's taxable estate.

Examples of transfers that fall into the overlap area above will be presented later in the chapter. At this point, however, it is important to note that any gift tax paid on a transfer which is considered incomplete for estate tax purposes reduces the amount of estate tax payable.[19]

Transfers of Property at Death

ROLE OF A WILL

Each of the 50 states gives its citizens the right to transfer the ownership of their property at death by means of a valid will. State law provides various formal requirements for valid wills, and as a result great care must be taken that a will is drafted in strict accordance with such requirements. There are few restrictions on the right of an individual to dispose of property at death in any manner he or she chooses. The most common restriction is the right under state law of a surviving spouse to receive a specified statutory share of the deceased individual's wealth. The statutory share rules effectively prevent an individual from completely disinheriting a surviving spouse.[20]

INTESTACY

When a person dies with no will or an invalid will, the transfer of his or her wealth is determined under the intestacy laws of the deceased's state of residence. Again, the particulars of the intestacy laws of each state are different. As a general rule, property will pass in order in prescribed shares to a decedent's surviving spouse, children and lineal descendants, parents and lineal ancestors, collateral relatives, and finally, if no relatives of any degree can be located, to the state of residence itself. For example, in Indiana if the decedent is survived by his or her spouse, at least one parent and no children, ¾ of the property generally passes to the spouse and ¼ passes to the decedent's parents. If there were two children, the spouse normally would receive ½ while the children would receive ½ of the property.

PROBATE

Probate is the legal process whereby a decedent's will is established as genuine and valid, and during which creditors of the decedent may submit their claims for payment from the estate. A decedent's probate estate consists of property interests owned at death that will pass under the terms of a decedent's will (or under the laws of intestacy if no valid will exists). It is extremely important for an individual engaged in estate planning to be aware of any property interests that he or she owns but which will *not* be included in the probate estate at death. A major example of such a property interest is a joint tenancy with right of

---

[19] § 2001(b)(2).

[20] Modern statutory share laws have their origins in the English common law property concepts of the "dower" rights of a widow and the "curtesy" rights of a widower.

survivorship (JTWROS). As previously explained, upon the death of one of the joint tenants, ownership of the asset automatically shifts to the surviving joint tenant or tenants. This is true *regardless* of the provisions of the deceased joint tenant's will. Similarly, survivor benefits, such as those from a life insurance policy or an annuity, or payments from pension and profit sharing plans, usually pass directly to the beneficiary and are not controlled by the will.

It should be apparent that those individuals who have amassed any amount of wealth and who wish to control the disposition of that wealth at death should have a validly executed will. However, there are compelling reasons why *every* responsible adult should have a will. When an individual dies intestate (without a valid will), the resulting legal and administrative complications can cause unnecessary hardship and confusion for the surviving family. Finally, one of the most critical functions of a will is to name a guardian for the decedent's minor children; failure to have a will can result in years of family discord and distress.

The Taxable Estate

Code §§ 2001 through 2056A contain the statutory rules providing for the imposition of a tax on the transfer of the taxable estate of every decedent who is a citizen or resident of the United States. Sections 2101 through 2108 provide for an estate tax on the value of assets located within the United States owned by a nonresident alien decedent. Discussion of this latter tax is beyond the scope of an introductory text.

LO.4
List the three basic steps involved in the computation of a decedent's taxable estate.

Computation of a decedent's taxable estate involves three basic steps:

1. Identification and valuation of assets includible in the gross estate;
2. Identification of deductible claims against the gross estate and deductible expenses of estate administration; and
3. Identification of any deductible bequests out of the gross estate.

The formula for computing the estate tax is shown in Exhibit 15-4 below.

EXHIBIT 15-4	**Estate Tax Formula**

Gross estate (§§ 2031 through 2046)		$x,xxx,xxx
Less the sum of:		
Expenses, indebtedness, and taxes (§ 2053)	$ xx,xxx	
Losses (§ 2054)	x,xxx	
State death taxes (§ 2058)	x,xxx	
Charitable bequests (§ 2055)	xx,xxx	
Marital deduction (§ 2056)	xxx,xxx	− xxx,xxx
Taxable estate (§ 2051)		$ xxx,xxx
Plus: Taxable gifts made after December 31, 1976 [§ 2001(b)]		+ xx,xxx
Total taxable transfers		$ xxx,xxx
Tentative tax on total transfers (§ 2001)		$ xxx,xxx
Less the sum of:		
Gift taxes paid on post-1976 taxable gifts (§ 2001)	$ x,xxx	
Unified transfer tax credit (§ 2010)	xx,xxx	
Other tax credits (§§ 2012 through 2016)	x,xxx	− xx,xxx
Estate tax liability		$ xx,xxx

The Gross Estate Concept

Section 2031 broadly states that "the value of the gross estate of the decedent shall be determined by including to the extent provided for in this part the value at the time of his death of all property, real or personal, tangible or intangible, wherever situated." The Regulations under this section make it clear that property located in a foreign country is included in this definition.[21]

Sections 2033 through 2044 identify the various types of property that are includible in a decedent's gross estate. Section 2033 is the most commonly applied of these Code sections. It requires the inclusion of any property interest owned by the decedent at date of death. The property interests specified in § 2033 correspond to the legal concept of a decedent's *probate estate,* property interests that will pass to the beneficiaries under the terms of the decedent's will.[22] If the decedent dies without a valid will, these interests will be distributed to the decedent's heirs under the state intestacy laws.

All individuals are, in a sense, on the accrual method of accounting for estate tax purposes. Any legal claim to or interest in an asset that exists at death is includible in the gross estate. For example, a cash basis taxpayer who performed substantial services and was to be paid $20,000 would not report the fee as income until collected. However, if death occurred before collection, the decedent is considered to have owned a $20,000 asset, the right to the fee which would be includible in his or her gross estate.

The concept of the gross estate is much broader than the legal probate estate. Exhibit 15-5 lists the various types of property interests and assets includible in the gross estate and the statutory authority for each inclusion. These various inclusions are discussed in more detail later in the chapter.

Although the estate tax reaches virtually all types of property interests, it does not extend to property in which the decedent owned a life estate created by another. Section 2033 does not require inclusion of such property since the decedent's only legal interest in the property terminated upon death.

Example 9

Upon W's death, she transferred stock worth $300,000 in trust, giving her son, S, a life estate and the remainder to her grandson. Several years later, S died when the property was worth $900,000. However, his estate does not include the stock, since his interest terminates (i.e., was extinguished) at his death and he is not transferring the property to the grandson.

The above example illustrates why the life estate is one of the most important devices used in estate planning. Note that the son is entitled to use the property for his life, yet the property and all of the appreciation escapes taxation in his estate. In other words, the property was taxed in the first and third generations (i.e., in their estates) but not the second generation. Congress addressed this problem by enacting the generation-skipping transfer tax, discussed later in this chapter. This special tax, however, has not eliminated all of the benefits of using the life estate for family tax planning purposes.

VALUATION OF GROSS ESTATE AND BASIS

Once an asset is identified as part of the gross estate, its fair market value at date of death must be determined. Practically, valuation of assets is the most difficult and subjective problem in computing a decedent's gross estate. Many assets, such as stock in a closely held corporation, have no readily ascertainable fair market value. Fortunately, the estate tax Regulations, like their gift tax counterparts, provide detailed guidelines to the valuation of many types of assets.[23]

---

[21] Reg. § 20.2031-1(a).

[22] Reg. § 20.2031-1(a)(1).

[23] Reg. § 20.2031.

EXHIBIT 15-5	Property Included in the Gross Estate

Property	Statutory Authority
Any property interest owned by the decedent at death	Section 2033

Includes:
  Cash
  Stocks, bonds, other investment securities
  personal assets
  Personal residence
  Collectibles (antiques, etc.)
  Investment real estate
  Business interests (sole proprietorship, partnership interest)	

Certain gifts made within three years of death (limited application after 1981)	Section 2035
Assets transferred during life in which the decedent retained an income interest or control over the enjoyment of the assets or the income therefrom	Section 2036
Assets transferred during life in which the decedent retained more than a 5% reversionary interest and possession of which could only be obtained by surviving the decedent	Section 2037
Assets transferred during life if, at death, the decedent possessed the right to alter, amend, revoke, or terminate the terms of the transfer	Section 2038
Certain survivor benefits and annuities	Section 2039
Joint tenancies with right of survivorship	Section 2040
Assets over which the decedent held a general power of appointment	Section 2041

Insurance proceeds on the decedent's life if:
  1. payable to the decedent's estate; or
  2. the decedent possessed any incident of ownership in the policy at death.
	Section 2042

Assets in a QTIP trust in which the decedent had the income interest	Section 2044

ALTERNATE VALUATION DATE

Although the gross estate is normally valued as of the decedent's date of death, § 2032 allows the executor to elect an alternative valuation date of six months after death. If the election is made, the alternative valuation date must be used for every asset in the gross estate. If an asset is disposed of within six months of death, its value at the date of disposition is used. The alternate valuation date cannot be used unless it reduces both the gross estate and the estate tax liability (after all credits).

BASIS

For income tax purposes, the basis of property in the hands of a person acquiring the property from a decedent is normally the property's fair market value at date of death or on the alternate valuation date under Code § 2032.[24] Under § 1223(11), assets acquired from a decedent are presumed to have a holding period in excess of one year. In the case of community property, the adjustment to fair market value is available for the *entire property* rather than just the one-half interest that is included in the gross estate of the decedent spouse.[25]

In situations in which the Federal estate tax to be imposed on a particular estate is minimal, an executor might actually elect the alternate valuation date in order to increase the valuation of assets included in the gross estate, thus achieving maximum step-up in the basis of the assets for income tax purposes. Section 2032(c) eliminates this particular tax planning option by providing that no § 2032 election may be made unless such election will decrease the value of the gross estate *and* the amount of the Federal estate tax imposed.

SPECIAL USE VALUATION: § 2032A

The requirement that property in a decedent's gross estate be valued at fair market value can create hardship if a principal estate asset is real property used in a family business. The value of such real property as it is used in the business may be considerably less than its potential selling price on the open market. As a result, an estate might be forced to sell the real estate and terminate the family business in order to pay the Federal estate tax.

Section 2032A provides that qualifying real estate used in a closely held business may be valued based on its business usage rather than market value. The requirements for qualification under this section are formidable, but can be summarized as follows:

- *Location.* The realty must be located in the United States.

- *Qualified Heir.* The realty must pass from the decedent to a "qualified heir" (generally a family member including the taxpayer's spouse, siblings, parents, grandparents and other ancestors, or children, grandchildren and other lineal descendants).

- *Qualified Farming or Business Use.* During the eight years prior to death (or disability or the time at which he begins to receive Social Security), there were at least five years when the realty was used for farming or in business and the decedent or a member of his family materially participated in the operation of the farm or business.

- *Realty and Personal Property Value (50% Test).* The *adjusted value* of the real and personal property used in farming or business must be at least 50% of adjusted value of the gross estate. For purpose of this test and the test below, the adjusted value of the realty is the value of the property less any related debt while the adjusted value of the gross estate is the value of the gross estate less any debts related to property included in the estate.

- *Realty Value (25% Test).* The adjusted value of the real property taken by itself is at least 25% of the adjusted value of the gross estate.

If these requirements are met, the maximum reduction from highest and best use value was originally $750,000, but is now adjusted for inflation. For 2016 the amount is $1,110,000. Note also that when special valuation is elected, the basis of the realty to the heirs is the reduced value.

Example 10

F died in 2016. He owned a large farm south of a major urban center. As farming property, F's real estate was worth $4,000,000; however, developers wanting to acquire the real estate for future use as commercial and residential property had offered F $7,000,000 for the real estate. If all the qualifications of § 2032A can be met, F's real property would be valued at $5,890,000 ($7,000,000 − $1,110,000) in his gross estate, and would take an income tax basis of $5,890,000.

---

[24] § 1014(a). Decedent's dying in 2010 have a choice to not pay the estate tax in which case the basis of the property to the heirs is what is referred to as a *modified carryover basis*.

These rules are found in § 1022. These rules have limited application.

[25] § 1014(b)(6).

Recapture of Tax Savings

The estate tax savings offered by the election of qualified-use valuation is conditional upon the continued use of the qualified real property in the family farm or other business. If the heirs of the decedent dispose of the real property or discontinue its qualified use within 10 years of the decedent's death, Code § 2032A(c) requires that the heirs repay the estate tax saved by the original use of the § 2032A election.

Gross Estate Inclusions

The Federal estate tax is not a property tax levied on the value of property owned at death. Instead, it is a transfer tax levied on the value of any shift in a property interest that occurs because of a decedent's death. As a result, a decedent's gross estate may include assets not owned by a decedent at death, the transfer of which is not controlled by the terms of the decedent's will.

> **LO.5**
> Specify the various types of property interests that must be valued for inclusion in a decedent's gross estate.

INSURANCE ON THE LIFE OF THE DECEDENT

The proceeds of an insurance policy on the life of a decedent do not come into existence until the death of the insured and are paid to the beneficiaries specified in the insurance contract, not the beneficiaries named in the decedent's will. However, § 2042 provides that such proceeds shall be included in the decedent's gross estate if either of the following is true:

1. The decedent's estate is the beneficiary, or
2. The decedent, at his or her death, possessed any incident of ownership in the life insurance policy, alone or in conjunction with any other person.

The term *incident of ownership* implies any economic interest in the policy and is broadly interpreted by the IRS. The Regulations under § 2042 list the power to change the policy's beneficiary, the right to cancel or assign the policy, and the right to borrow against the policy as incidents of ownership.[26]

Example 11

In 2008, T purchased a term insurance policy on his own life. Under the terms of the policy, beneficiary B would receive $150,000 upon T's death. In 2016 T died. Immediately before T's death the policy had no value since it was term insurance. Nevertheless, the $150,000 paid to B is includible in T's gross estate.

SURVIVOR BENEFITS

Section 2039 requires that the value of an annuity or any payment receivable by a beneficiary by reason of surviving a decedent be included in the decedent's gross estate. This rule only applies to the extent that the value of the annuity or payment is attributable to contributions made by the decedent or the decedent's employer. A second condition for applicability is that the payment or annuity be payable to the decedent or that the decedent possess the right to payment at death. For example, Social Security death benefits paid to a decedent's family are not covered by § 2039 because the decedent had no right to the payments during his or her lifetime.

The value of an annuity includible under § 2039 is the replacement cost to the beneficiary of a comparable commercial annuity.[27]

---

[26] Reg. § 20.2042-1(c)(2).　　　　[27] Reg. § 20.2031-8(a).

Example 12

H purchased a self and survivor annuity contract that was to pay him $1,500 a month for his life and, upon his death, $1,000 a month to his widow, W. At the date of H's death, W would have to pay $24,000 to purchase a $1,000 a month lifetime annuity for herself. Under § 2039, the value of the annuity received by W, $24,000, is includible in H's gross estate.

JOINT INTERESTS

Nonspousal Joint Tenancies

As discussed earlier in the chapter, a joint tenancy with right of survivorship is a form of equal co-ownership of an asset that causes full ownership of the asset to vest automatically in the survivor when the first joint tenant dies. The decedent's will cannot change this result; property owned in joint tenancy is not included in a decedent's probate estate. However, some portion of the value of this property may be includible in the decedent's gross estate. Under § 2040, it is necessary to determine the proportion of the decedent's original contribution toward the acquisition of the asset. This same proportion of the value of the asset at date of death must be included in the decedent's gross estate.

Example 13

Brothers A and B decided to purchase a tract of real estate as equal joint tenants with right of survivorship. A contributed $40,000 and B contributed $10,000 toward the $50,000 purchase price. At A's death, the real estate was worth $150,000. A's gross estate must include $120,000, 80% ($40,000 ÷ [$40,000 + $10,000]) of the real estate's value. If B had died before A, only $30,000, 20% of the real estate's value, would be includible in B's gross estate.

Note in *Example 13* that in the year the real estate was acquired, A made a taxable gift to B of $15,000, the difference between half the value of the asset when purchased, $25,000, and B's $10,000 contribution. In spite of this completed gift, a portion of the property is taxed in A's gross estate under the authority of § 2040 if he dies before B.

Spousal Joint Tenancies

If a husband and wife own property as joint tenants with right of survivorship, § 2040(b) contains a rule that requires 50% of the value of the property to be included in the gross estate of the first spouse to die, regardless of the original contribution of that spouse.

Dower and Curtesy Interests

In the 41 common law states, a surviving spouse may have a legally enforceable claim against assets owned by a decedent that cannot be defeated by the terms of the decedent's will. In essence, this rule prohibit one spouse from disinheriting the other spouse. The surviving spouse in all of these states generally is guaranteed to receive the amount that he or she would have received had the decedent died intestate. For estate tax purposes, however, § 2034 states that the value of property included in the decedent's gross estate is not diminished by such a claim. In other words, the entire property is included in the decedent's estate. Of course, the martial deduction is allowed for any interest that passes to the surviving spouse so their is no effect on the taxable estate. In the nine community property states, most property owned by a married individual is community property in which both spouses have equal interests. Only one-half the value of such community property is included in a decedent's gross estate.

GENERAL POWERS OF APPOINTMENT

A *power of appointment* is a right to dispose of property that the holder of the power does not legally own. It is normally created by the will of a decedent in conjunction with a transfer of property in trust. Typically, the decedent's will provides for the transfer of property in trust, giving an individual a life estate and a power to appoint the remainder interest during his or her life or at death through a will. By so doing, the decedent transfers the ability to control the property's disposition to the holder of the power, even though the holder does not own the property. In effect, a power of appointment gives a person the right to fill in the blanks of another person's will.

A power of appointment may be *specific,* meaning that the holder of the power may only give the property to members of a specified eligible group of recipients which does *not* include the holder. Alternatively, the power may be *general,* so that the holder may appoint the property to himself or herself, or his or her creditors, estate, or creditors of that estate. The terms of the power should specify to whom ownership of the property will go if the holder deliberately or inadvertently fails to exercise the power.

A *general power of appointment* over property is tantamount to actual ownership of the property. If the holder appoints the property to another person, the exercise is treated as a taxable gift per § 2514.[28] Section 2041 provides that if a decedent holds a general power over property at his or her death, the value of the property must be included in the gross estate.

Example 14

P has the right to appoint ownership of certain real estate to any of P's children or grandchildren. He may exercise the right during life or by will. Upon P's death, his will appoints the property to his daughter, D. Because P held only a *specific power,* the value of the appointed property is not included in P's gross estate.

Example 15

M has the right to appoint ownership of certain real estate to *himself* or any of his brothers and sisters. He may exercise the right during life or by will. However, M dies without exercising the power. The terms of the power provide that if the power is not exercised the property shall go to M's uncle. Because M possessed a *general power* of appointment, the date of death value of the property must be included in M's gross estate.

Nontaxable Powers

As indicated above, a specific power of appointment over property will not result in inclusion of the property in the holder's gross estate. There are other situations where a power does not cause taxation. If the holder's power to appoint property for his or her benefit is limited to an *ascertainable standard,* it is not a general power of appointment and inclusion is not required. A power is considered limited to a standard if appointments of property may be made solely for the holder's health, education, maintenance, or support in his or her accustomed manner of living. The language used to describe the scope of the holder's power is extremely important. For example, a power is not considered limited if it permits appointments for the holder's comfort, happiness, or well-being.

---

[28] If the holder of a general power releases the power or allows it to lapse, the transfer of ownership is still considered a taxable gift made by the holder. See §§ 2514(b) and (e).

Example 16

H's will provided for the transfer of $600,000 in trust, giving his wife a life estate and a power to appoint the property to herself for her support. Upon the wife's death, nothing is included in her gross estate since she does not have a general power of appointment. The power does not cause inclusion since it is limited to an ascertainable standard.

Another nontaxable power which offers great planning flexibility is the so-called five and five power. Section 2041 generally does not require inclusion if the amount that the holder can appoint for his or her use in any one year does not exceed the greater of $5,000 or five percent of the value of the property. As long as the power is drawn within these limits, the power need not be restricted in any other manner to avoid taxation. However, in the year of the holder's death, the power is considered a general power to the extent of the greater of the two amounts and thus causes inclusion in the holder's estate to that extent.

Example 17

R created a $1,000,000 trust for his wife, giving her the income for life and the remainder to the children. R wanted to give his wife access to the corpus of the trust without causing it to be included in her estate. Therefore, he gave his wife the annual right to withdraw for her use any time during the year the greater of $5,000 or five percent of the aggregate value of the trust. As a result, assuming the value of the trust remained at $1,000,000, his wife could withdraw up to $50,000 (5% of $1,000,000) annually without having the entire corpus included in her estate. However, in the year of the wife's death, she must include $50,000 in her estate, the amount over which she might have exercised the power at death.

TRANSFERS TAKING EFFECT AT DEATH

Taxpayers who are reluctant to give away property during life but who also want to minimize the tax burden on their estate have designed a variety of inter vivos gifts with "strings attached." Such gifts are subject to a condition or restriction that enables the donor to continue to benefit from or enjoy the property until death. Such a transfer may be complete for gift tax purposes. Nevertheless, for estate tax purposes it may be classified as a transfer taking effect at death, with the result that the date of death value of the property is includible in the donor's gross estate.

Code §§ 2036, 2037, and 2038 govern transfers taking effect at death. Because these three sections were added to the Code at different times, there is a confusing amount of overlap in their coverage. The sections' requirements are very complex and difficult to apply. However, a brief description of each section can give the beginning tax student an idea of their general functions.

One important rule to remember is that all three sections can only require the inclusion in a decedent's gross estate of property that was originally owned by the decedent. A second rule is that the sections are inapplicable if the transfer of the property by the decedent was for sufficient consideration.

Transfers with a Retained Interest

Section 2036 requires that the value of any property given away by the decedent, but to which the decedent retained the right to the property's income or the right to designate who may possess or enjoy the property, shall be included in the decedent's gross estate. Section 2036 also specifies that the retention of the voting rights of shares of stock in a controlled corporation represents a retention of enjoyment.[29]

---

[29] § 2036(b)(2) defines a controlled corporation as a corporation in which the decedent controlled (directly or indirectly) at least 20% of the voting power of all classes of stock.

Example 18

In 2004, F made a completed gift of rental property to his son, S, subject to the condition that F was to receive the net rent from the property for the rest of his life. Upon F's death in the current year, the date of death value of the rental property must be included in F's gross estate since he retained a right to income (i.e., rentals), even though S is the owner of the property.

Example 19

In the current year, M transferred assets into an irrevocable trust for the sole benefit of her grandchildren. Under the terms of the trust instrument, M reserved the right to designate which of the grandchildren should receive the annual income of the trust. Because M retained the right to designate the persons who shall possess the income from the trust assets, the value of the trust assets will be included in M's gross estate upon her death.

The IRS is very aggressive in applying § 2036. For example, in a situation in which a parent gifts a family residence to a child but continues to occupy the residence rent free, the parent is considered to have retained a beneficial interest in the residence, with the result that the value of the residence will be includible in the parent's gross estate.[30]

Reversionary Interests

Section 2037 requires inclusion in a decedent's gross estate of the value of previously transferred property if two conditions are met:

1. Possession or enjoyment of the property can only be obtained by surviving the decedent,
2. The decedent owns a reversionary interest in the property, the value of which exceeds 5% of the value of the property. The value of the reversion is computed as of the moment immediately before death, based on actuarial tables.[31]

Regulation § 20.2037-1(e) gives the following example of the application of Code § 2037.

Example 20

The decedent transferred property in trust, with the income payable to his wife for life and with the remainder payable to the decedent or, if he is not living at his wife's death, to his daughter or her estate. The daughter cannot obtain possession or enjoyment of the property without surviving the decedent. Therefore, if the decedent's reversionary interest immediately before death exceeded 5% of the value of the property, the value of the property less the value of the wife's outstanding life estate is includible in the decedent's gross estate.

Note in *Example 20* that the decedent's reversionary interest was extinguished at death and did not constitute an interest in property that would be transferred under the terms of the decedent's will. However, it is the event of the decedent's death that completes the transfer of the remainder interest in the trust to the daughter or her estate.

Revocable Transfers

If, on the date of death, the decedent had the power to alter, amend, or revoke the enjoyment of any property previously given away by the decedent, § 2038 requires that the date of death value of the property be included in the decedent's gross estate. Obviously, a revocable transfer falls within § 2038. However, the scope of the section is broad enough to apply to much less obvious types of powers.

---

[30] Rev. Rul. 70-155, 1970-1 C.B. 189; and *Estate of Linderme*, 52 T.C. 305 (1966).   [31] Reg. § 20.2037-1(c)(3).

Example 21

Individual Z creates an irrevocable trust for the benefit of her children and names the trust department of a national bank as trustee. The only right retained by Z allows her to replace the trustee with a different trust department. Upon Z's death, Revenue Ruling 79-353[32] states that Code § 2038 applies and the value of the trust corpus must be included in Z's gross estate.

GIFTS IN CONTEMPLATION OF DEATH

For many years, Code § 2035 required that the date of death value of any gift made by the decedent during the three years prior to death, plus the amount of any gift tax paid on such gifts, be included in the decedent's gross estate. In 1981, Congress drastically altered this section so that it currently applies only to gifts of interests described in the sections governing transfers taking effect at death (§§ 2036, 2037, and 2038) and § 2042, relating to gifts of life insurance. In addition, § 2035 applies for determining the applicability of provisions such as § 2032A, concerning special use valuation (e.g., any property given away within three years of death is added back to the gross estate in applying the 50 and 25% tests). Notwithstanding the limited application of the general rule, § 2035(c) continues to require the inclusion in the gross estate of any gift tax paid within three years of death.

Example 22

Refer to the facts in *Example 18*. Assume that one year prior to his death, F made a gift of his retained income interest in the rental property to his granddaughter, D. Section 2035 applies to the transfer of the income interest, with the result that the date of death value of the rental property and any gift tax paid on the gift are included in F's gross estate.

TRANSFERS FOR INSUFFICIENT CONSIDERATION

A transfer for which the donor received consideration less than the value of the transferred property is vulnerable to the application of §§ 2035, 2036, 2037, or 2038 upon the donor's death. However, § 2043 does allow the estate an offset for the consideration received.[33]

Example 23

A transferred her 100 shares of stock in Famco Corporation to her daughter, D, subject to the condition that A would retain the voting rights in the shares. At date of transfer, the fair market value of the stock was $500,000, and D paid A only $300,000 cash in exchange. The transfer constituted a taxable gift of $200,000. Upon A's death, the value of the stock, $1.2 million, is includible in A's gross estate under § 2036. However, A's estate may reduce this value by $300,000, the amount of the consideration received by A.

The § 2043 consideration offset equals the value of the consideration at date of receipt. Therefore, in *Example 23* only 40% ($200,000 ÷ $500,000) of the value of the property was transferred without consideration, but 75% ([$1.2 million – $300,000] ÷ $1.2 million) of the date of death value of the property must be included in the gross estate.

---

[32] 1979-2 C.B. 325. [33] See Reg. § 20.2043-1(a).

Not all of the value of a decedent's gross estate will be available for transfer to estate beneficiaries or other individuals. Some of the value must first be used to pay off debts of the decedent and other claims against the estate. The second step in computing an individual's taxable estate is to identify the debts and claims that are deductible against the gross estate.

LO.6
Describe any deductions from the gross estate.

EXPENSES, INDEBTEDNESS, AND TAXES

The estate tax is based on the *net* wealth that is actually transferred by the decedent. Consistent with this concept, the law permits deductions for expenses associated with death as well as costs of settling the estate and other claims against the property in the estate. As might be expected, the executor cannot spend and borrow willy-nilly and expect to deduct these items. Section 2053(a) generally allows deductions for funeral and administrative expenses, mortgages on property included in the gross estate and other personal debts owed by the decedent. Under § 2053(a), these items are deductible *only* if allowed by local law and *only* to the extent they are incurred in administering property subject to claims (i.e., creditors of the decedent can seek satisfaction of their claims from these assets). This normally encompasses those expenses relating to administering the probate estate. In addition, Section 2053(b) grants deductions for expenses incurred in administering property that is included in the gross estate but which is *not* subject to the claims of the estate's creditors. For example, expenses related to a revocable trust would be deductible even though creditors cannot seek satisfaction of their claims from the trust property. These deductions are allowed because the assets of the trust are included in the gross estate [§ 2053(b)].

Funeral Expenses

Deductible funeral expenses include costs for the funeral service, clergy, mortuary, hearse, limousines, casket, cremation, pianist, singers, flowers and the like. In addition, a deduction is allowed for costs of a tombstone, monument, mausoleum crypt, or for a burial lot, either for the decedent or his family. If the decedent had acquired the burial lots prior to death, no deduction is allowed but the lots are not included in the gross estate. Deductions are also allowed for a reasonable expenditure for the future care of the lot. Transportation costs of the person bringing the body to the burial site also are deductible as funeral expenses (e.g., a corpse is flown home). Traveling expenses for beneficiaries or others to attend the decedent's funeral are not deductible (e.g., costs of flying decedent's grandchildren to the funeral are not deductible).

Administrative Expenses

Section 2053 also permits deductions for administering and settling the decedent's estate. Deductions normally include all probate costs such as those incurred in collection and preservation of probate assets (bank charges), payment of debts and distribution of property (e.g., cost of wire transfer). Common administrative expenses are fees paid to the executor or administrator of the estate, accounting and legal expenses, court costs, and appraisal fees. In addition, expenses incurred in preserving the estate, including the costs of maintaining and storing property (e.g., utility bills on the decedent's home after death) are deductible.

It should be emphasized that deductions are limited for those expenses in the administration of the estate. Those that are not "essential" to the proper settlement of the estate, but are incurred for the benefit of the heirs or others, may not be claimed as deductions. In this regard, selling expenses are deductible administrative expenses, if the assets must be sold to pay debts, expenses or taxes. Regulation § 20.2053-3(d)(2) authorizes the deduction of the expenses of selling assets of the estate only if the sale is necessary (1) to pay debts, administrative expenses or tax; (2) to preserve the estate; or (3) to effect distribution.

> ### Example 24
>
> In *Estate of David Smith,* a famous sculptor died and left over 425 pieces of his work.[34] The executors of his estate paid commissions in excess of $1,000,000 to a gallery for selling the decedent's work presumably to raise money to pay expenses of the estate. However, only $290,000 of those commissions were identified as attributable to sales needed to pay the decedent's debts, taxes, and other administration expenses. The Court held that only $290,000 of commissions were attributable to the estate's liquidity needs and denied a deduction for the remainder. Moreover, the court found no evidence that it was necessary to sell all of the works promptly. Presumably, such expenses could be claimed as selling expenses on the estate's income tax return. Note that *Smith* also stands for the proposition that assets cannot be valued in the gross estate at their value net of any expected selling expenses.

Administrative expenses incurred after death can be claimed as either a deduction on the estate tax return (Form 706) or on the estate's income tax return but not on both.[35]

The executor must be careful not to waste any deductions for administration expenses. This is a major concern when the estate owes no estate tax (e.g., due to the unlimited marital or charitable deductions or the unified credit) since the only potential benefit could be derived from deducting the expense for income tax purposes. Even if the executor properly waives the deduction for estate tax purposes, this does not ensure that an income tax benefit will be derived since the estate may have little or no income that could be reduced by the deduction. However, if the deduction exceeds income *in the year the estate terminates,* § 642(h) provides that all excess deductions pass through to the beneficiaries succeeding to the decedent's property who can then deduct them on their individual tax returns as itemized deductions. This is allowed only for the excess deductions that occur in the year of termination. If excess deductions occur in earlier years (e.g., because the estate chooses the wrong time to pay the expense) the deduction is generally lost.

Claims against the Estate

Deductions are allowed for any debts that the decedent owed at the time of death. The deduction for these items reflects the fact that the estate must pay these amounts before the property is distributed thereby reducing the amount that is transferred to the heirs by the decedent. Debts of the estate typically include unpaid mortgages or liens on property included in the gross estate, unpaid income taxes on income received by the decedent before he or she died, property taxes accrued before death as well as personal obligations of the decedent. Examples of personal liabilities are balances due on credit card accounts, utility bills, interest on mortgages accrued before death, margin accounts, and other loans outstanding at the date of death. Interest accrued after the date of death is normally not deductible on the Form 706 even if the alternate valuation date is elected.[36]

Medical expenses of the decedent are deductible as a claim against the estate. However, if such expenses are paid within one year of death, they may be claimed as income tax deduction on the final return. The expenses cannot be claimed on both returns, however.

Losses

Section 2054 allows deductions for casualty and theft losses occurring while the estate is being settled are deductible in computing the taxable estate. For example, the decedent's car may be stolen or his home destroyed by fire. The amount of the deductible loss is the value of the property reduced for any insurance proceeds received. If the alternate valuation date is elected, the property is valued at zero when determining the value of the gross estate. Therefore no loss deduction is allowed.

---

[34] 75-1 USTC ¶13,046, AFTR 2d 75-1594, 510 F.2d 479 (CA-2, 1975) aff'g 57 TC 650 (1972) cert. denied.

[35] § 642(g).

[36] Reg. § 20.2053-7.

Although casualty and theft losses are also deductible for income tax purposes, there is no double deduction allowed.[37] The loss can be deducted on either the estate tax return or the estate's income tax return, but not both. In most cases, a greater benefit could be secured by deducting the expenses on the estate tax return since such expenses may be subject to limitations for income tax purposes.

STATE DEATH TAXES

In addition to the Federal estate tax, decedents must be concerned about state death taxes. In 2015, just over 20 states imposed some type of death tax. These usually take the form of an inheritance tax, an estate tax or both. On the other hand very few states impose any type of gift tax. However, gifts made in contemplation of death (e.g., a deathbed transfer) are usually subject to the state's death tax.

State Inheritance Taxes

Several states (in 2015 Iowa, Nebraska, Pennsylvania, New Jersey, Maryland, and Kentucky) and some local jurisdictions impose an inheritance tax on the right to receive property at death. Unlike an estate tax, which is imposed on the estate according to the value of property transferred by the decedent at death, an inheritance tax is imposed on the recipient of property from an estate (although it is typically paid out of the estate). The amount of an inheritance tax payable usually is directly affected by the degree of kinship between the recipient and the decedent. The inheritance tax typically provides an exemption from the tax, which increases as the relationship between the recipient (e.g., the surviving spouse, children, grandchildren, etc.) and the decedent becomes closer. For example, under the Nebraska inheritance tax rules, transfers to a surviving spouse are exempt while transfers to the decedent's children are entitled to an exemption of $40,000. The rate of tax also differs depending on the relationship. For example, the Nebraska rate for transfers to children is 1 percent while transfers to nonrelatives is 18 percent. Observe that the small exemptions, at least in Nebraska, make even modest estates subject to state inheritance taxes even though they may be exempt from the Federal estate tax.

State Estate Taxes

These taxes are similar to the Federal estate tax and are based on the value of the property held by the decedent at the date of death. In 2015, 15 states (Washington, Oregon, Minnesota, Illinois, Tennessee, Maine, Vermont, Massachusetts, New York, New Jersey, Maryland, Rhode Island, Connecticut, Delaware, Hawaii) and the District of Columbia imposed an estate tax. Washington has the highest rate of 20 percent, followed by 11 states with a maximum rate of 16 percent. Hawaii and Delaware have the highest exemption threshold, $5,430,000 (matching the Federal exemption). New Jersey has the lowest, $675,000.

Deduction for State Death Taxes

Prior to 2005, the estate was allowed a credit for state death taxes. Beginning in 2005, however, the state death tax credit was eliminated and replaced by a deduction. Note that the deduction is for state death taxes. There is no deduction for Federal estate taxes.

Technically, § 2058 allows a deduction for the amount of any estate, inheritance, legacy, or succession taxes actually paid to any state or the District of Columbia, in respect of property included in the gross estate. The amount must be actually paid by the estate, not merely estimated or accrued. Observe that many states permit a discount for prompt payment. For example, Indiana allows a five percent discount if the tax is paid within nine months of date of death. In such case, the amount paid, not the amount assessed, is the amount of the deductible state death tax.

CHARITABLE CONTRIBUTIONS

An estate may deduct the value of any transfer of assets to a qualified charitable organization under § 2055. Qualifying organizations are specifically defined in the statute. If an individual is willing to leave his or her entire estate for public, charitable, or religious use, there will be no taxable estate.

---

[37] *Supra* Footnote 34.

For a charitable contribution to be deductible, it normally must consist of the decedent's entire interest in the underlying property. For example, if a decedent bequeaths a life interest in real estate to his son and the remainder interest in the property to charity, the value of the remainder interest is not deductible. Similarly, if the decedent bequeaths the interest in the real estate to a charity for a term of years (e.g., 20 years), and the remainder to his son, the value of the income interest is not deductible. However, this restriction does not apply if the transfer is in a specific statutory form: a *charitable lead trust,* where an income interest is given to the charity, or a *charitable remainder trust,* where a remainder interest is given to the charity.[38] A detailed description of such trusts is beyond the scope of this text, but they do allow a decedent to create both a charitable and a noncharitable interest in the same property and secure a deduction for the charitable interest. The restriction also is inapplicable to a charitable contribution of a remainder interest in a personal residence or farm and to certain contributions for conservation purposes.[39]

If an individual taxpayer is considering making bequests to charity upon his or her death, his or her tax adviser should certainly explore the possibility of having the individual make such charitable contributions during his or her life. Such inter vivos contributions would serve a dual purpose: the donated assets would be removed from the individual's potential taxable estate, and the donation would create a deduction for income tax purposes.

THE MARITAL DEDUCTION

Code § 2056 provides an unlimited deduction for the value of property passing to a surviving spouse. If a married taxpayer, no matter how wealthy, is willing to leave all his or her property to the surviving spouse, no transfer tax will be imposed on the estate.[40] Only upon the subsequent death of the spouse will the couple's wealth be subject to taxation.

In certain instances, interests transferred to the surviving spouse are not deductible—so-called *nondeductible terminable interests*. If a decedent leaves an interest in property to his or her spouse that can or will terminate at a future date *and* if after termination another person receives an interest in the property from the decedent, the value of the interest passing to the spouse is ineligible for the marital deduction.[41] Absent this rule, the interest would escape taxation entirely, since it terminates prior to or with the death of the surviving spouse and thus is not included in his or her gross estate.

Example 25

Decedent H leaves a life estate in real property to his surviving spouse, W, with the remainder after W's death left to their daughter. The interest passing to W is a terminable interest ineligible for the marital deduction. Note that without this rule barring a marital deduction, the value of the property would completely escape estate taxation since it would not be taxed in either H's estate (due to the marital deduction) or W's estate (since W's life estate terminates at her death).

The property need not pass directly to the surviving spouse to qualify for the marital deduction. Section 2056(b)(5) generally allows the deduction if the surviving spouse is entitled to annual payments of all of the income from the property for life and has a general power of appointment over the property exercisable during life or at death. In this case, the entire value of the property will be included in the estate of the surviving spouse because of his or her general power of appointment.

For many years, these two methods of leaving property to a spouse (outright or in trust with a general power of appointment to the surviving spouse) were essentially the only two techniques available if the decedent wanted to qualify the transfer for the marital deduction. This often left a married couple with a perplexing problem. Notice that in both situations, the decedent surrenders control of the property to the surviving spouse. When the surviving spouse is given a general power of appointment over the property, he or she has complete control over the ultimate disposition of the property—the same control that would have

---

[38] § 2055(e)(2).

[39] *Ibid.*

[40] No marital deduction is allowed for the value of property passing to a surviving spouse who is not a U.S. citizen unless the property is placed in a "qualified domestic trust."

[41] § 2056(b).

been obtained if he or she had received the property outright. Under either scenario, the surviving spouse is left with the choice of who will be the beneficiaries of the decedent's property. In other words, the decedent could not be assured that property that had been accumulated during marriage would reach the desired beneficiaries, typically the couple's children. For example, if the surviving spouse remarried, the decedent's property could end up being used for the benefit of the new spouse and new children, usually not the result desired by the decedent. Unfortunately, more suitable arrangements from a nontax point of view normally did not qualify for the marital deduction. Consequently, the tax law put taxpayers in an awkward position, requiring them to either give up control or face higher taxes.

In 1981, Congress addressed this problem by sanctioning the marital deduction for a life estate for the surviving spouse. Observe that without this relief provision the life estate would be considered a nondeductible terminable interest. However, as explained below, the deduction is allowed only if the property (that would normally escape tax by virtue of the life estate rules) is included in the surviving spouse's estate upon his or her death. The special rules enabling this treatment are contained in § 2056(b)(7).

Under § 2056(b)(7), a marital deduction is allowed for the value of *qualifying terminable interest property* left to a surviving spouse. Qualifying terminable interest property is property from which the entire income must be paid to the spouse at least annually. During the spouse's lifetime, no one else must be able to receive any interest in the property. Upon the spouse's death, the property may pass to anyone. If the executor elects, the entire value of the property is deductible on the decedent's estate tax return. In most cases, these requirements are met by transferring property to a trust from which the spouse receives the income for life. Such arrangements are normally referred to as QTIPs, reflecting the fact that they are created to enable the property to be considered qualifying terminable interest property.

Without further requirements, the interest described above is simply a life estate that would totally escape tax as described in *Example 25* above. However, § 2044 requires that when the surviving spouse dies, the entire value of the qualifying terminable interest property at that time must be included in the spouse's gross estate. If the surviving spouse gives away the income interest during life, § 2519 requires that the gift will consist of the entire value of the property.

Example 26

H and W, husband and wife, have been married for 10 years. They have three children, A, B, and C, ages nine, seven, and four. H wants to ensure that their children receive the couple's assets after he dies. For this reason, he does not want to leave the property outright to his spouse nor does he want to leave the property in trust to her with a general power of appointment. To this end, his will provides that upon his death, all of his assets are transferred to a trust that gives W an income interest for life and the remainder interest to A, B, and C upon W's death. Note that H has provided for W but has retained control over who ultimately receives the property. From a tax perspective, this normally would be considered a nondeductible terminable interest as described above and would not qualify for the marital deduction. However, if an election is made by the executor of H's estate, this otherwise nondeductible terminable interest becomes qualifying terminable interest property, that is, a QTIP, and qualifies for the marital deduction. When W dies, the value of the property at her death is automatically included in her gross estate. In this way, the property does not escape estate tax. Any estate tax that is attributable to inclusion of the property in the W's estate can be paid by her estate. However, if this is not suitable, the law requires that the tax will be paid from the property itself (e.g., the property could be sold to pay the estate tax and the property net of the estate tax would be passed to the children of H and W).

While the examples above provide some measure of the trade-offs that must be considered when planning with the marital deduction, these issues are just part of the story. Other factors that must be considered in order to effectively design marital bequests are discussed in Chapter 17.

LO.7

Explain the mechanics of the calculation of the estate tax, including the role of the unified credit.

Once the value of the taxable estate has been determined, the first step in computing the estate tax liability is to add the taxable estate to the amount of the decedent's *adjusted taxable gifts*. Adjusted taxable gifts are defined in Code § 2001(b) as the total amount of taxable gifts (after any available exclusion or deduction) made after December 31, 1976 *other than* gifts includible in the gross estate of the decedent.

The transfer tax rates of § 2001(c) are then applied to the sum of the taxable estate plus adjusted taxable gifts. The tentative tax calculated is then reduced by any gift taxes paid or payable at current rates for gifts made after December 31, 1976. The result is the Federal estate tax liability *before* credits.

ESTATE TAX CREDITS

There are several credits that can be used to reduce the estate tax. These are:

- Unified credit,
- Foreign death tax credit,
- Credit for taxes on prior transfers,
- Credit for pre-1977 gift taxes.

Unified Credit

The major credit available to reduce the Federal estate tax is the unified credit of Code § 2010. As seen in Exhibit 15-3, the estate and gift tax credits have varied over the years. Currently, each is $2,125,800 (2016). The mechanics of the estate tax calculation—specifically, the addition of adjusted taxable gifts ensure that the decedent's estate benefits from the credit only to the extent that it was not used to offset any gift tax during his or her lifetime. It is important to understand that the two credits combined will shelter a maximum of $5,450,000 (2016) of transfers from the imposition of any Federal transfer tax.

Portability of the Unused Unified Credit

The 2010 Tax Relief Act introduced the so-called portability rule. According to this rule, any credit that remains unused as of the death of a spouse who dies after 2010 (the "deceased spousal unused exclusion amount" or DSUE) is portable; that is, the unused amount is generally available for use by the surviving spouse as an addition to the surviving spouse's credit and can be use for taxable transfers during life or at death.[42]

Example 27

H and W are husband and wife. H died in 2011 and used $3,000,000 of his $5,000,000 exemption to eliminate his estate from tax. As a result, $2,000,000 of his exemption is unused. In 2016, W dies. W's exemption amount is $7,450,000 (her $5,450,000 + the unused amount of her last deceased husband of $2,000,000). In effect, the couple is able to exempt close to $10,450,000 million from estate taxes ($3,000,000 when H died and $7,450,000 when W died).

If a surviving spouse is predeceased by more than one spouse, the amount of unused exclusion that is available for use by such surviving spouse is limited to the amount of the unused exclusion of the last such deceased spouse.

---

[42] § 2010(c).

> ### Example 28
>
> H and W are married. H dies and his unused exclusion is $5,000,000. W remarried NH, a new husband. NH died and his unused exclusion is $2,000,000. By what amount can W increase her exemption? She can use only the unused amount of her last spouse, $2,000,000 (and not the $5,000,000 of her first spouse).

The unused exclusion amount is available to a surviving spouse only if the executor of the estate of the deceased spouse files an estate tax return on which such amount is computed and makes an election on such return that such amount may be used. The election is irrevocable. The election cannot be made unless that estate tax return is filed on a timely basis as extended. Thus, even if a decedent normally is not required to file an estate tax return, it appears that a return is now necessary simply to preserve the unused exclusion amount.

Foreign Death Tax Credit

Section 2014 allows the estate a credit for all or part of the death taxes that must be paid to a foreign country on account of property located in that country that is included in the gross estate. The amount of the credit is limited to the lesser of (1) the foreign death tax attributable to the foreign property, or (2) the Federal estate tax attributable to the foreign property.

Credit for Tax on Prior Transfers

If two family members die within a short period of time, the same property may be included in both taxable estates and be subject to two rounds of estate taxation in rapid succession. Section 2013 provides a credit to the estate of the second decedent to mitigate this excessive taxation. The credit generally is computed as a percentage of the amount of tax attributable to the inclusion of property in the estate of the first decedent. The percentage is based on the number of years between the two deaths as follows:

0–2 years..............................	100%
3–4 years..............................	80%
5–6 years..............................	60%
7–8 years..............................	40%
9–10 years............................	20%

If the second decedent outlived the first by more than 10 years, no § 2013 credit is allowed.

> ### Example 29
>
> Individual A died in March 2013. Under the terms of his will, A left $1,000,000 in assets to his younger sister, B. B died unexpectedly in May 2016 and the assets inherited from A were included in B's taxable estate. The amount of tax paid by A's estate that is attributable to the assets is calculated at $100,000. Since B died just over three years after A's death, 80% of the tax paid by A's estate is available to B's estate as a credit of $80,000 (80% × $100,000).

Gift Taxes Paid on Pre-1977 Gifts

If a taxable gift was made prior to 1977 (i.e., prior to unification) and the gifted property is included in the transferor's gross estate (e.g., under the rules of §§ 2036, 2037, or 2038), § 2012 allows a credit for any gift tax paid. The amount of the credit is limited to the lesser of the gift tax paid or the estate tax attributable to inclusion of the gifted property in the taxpayer's gross estate.

A COMPREHENSIVE EXAMPLE

The following example illustrates the complete computation of the Federal estate tax. In 1997, taxpayer M makes his first taxable gift to his son S. The fair market value of the property transferred is $200,000. The gift tax is computed as follows:

Value of gift...	$200,000
Less: Annual exclusion (1997)	− 10,000
Taxable gift	$190,000
Gift tax before credits	$ 51,600
Less: Unified credit	− 51,600
Gift tax liability for 1997	$ 0

In 1998, M makes gifts to son S and daughter D. The value of each transfer is $250,000.

Value of gifts...	$500,000
Less: Annual exclusions	− 20,000
Taxable gifts for 1998	$480,000
Plus: 1997 taxable gift...	+190,000
Taxable transfers to date	$670,000
Tentative tax on total transfers to date..................................	$218,700
Less: Tax on 1997 gift	− 51,600
Less: 1998 unified credit ($202,050 − $51,600)...........................	−150,450
1998 gift tax liability	$ 16,650

M dies in 2016, leaving a taxable estate valued at $8 million. The estate tax is computed as follows:

Taxable estate		$8,000,000
Plus: Taxable gifts made in prior years		+ 670,000
Total taxable transfers		$8,670,000
Tentative tax on total transfers ($345,800 + 40% (8,670,000 − 1,000,000 = $7,670,000))..........		$3,413,800
Less the sum of		
Gift taxes paid on post-1976 taxable gifts (on 1998 gift)*	$ 16,650	
Unified credit (2016)	2,125,800	−2,142,450
Estate tax liability.......................................		$1,271,350

* **Note:** The amount of gift taxes paid and unified credit used in prior years is recomputed under a special calculation not shown here. See § 2001(b)(2) and the instructions for Form 706 Line 7.

PAYMENT OF THE ESTATE TAX

The Federal estate tax return, Form 706, is due nine months after the date of the decedent's death, and any tax liability shown is payable with the return. However, Congress appreciates the fact that the payment of the estate tax is often unforeseen, and has provided for a variety of relief measures for the estate with a substantial tax liability and insufficient liquidity to pay the tax nine months after death.

Section 6161 authorizes the Secretary of the Treasury to extend the time of payment of the estate tax for up to 10 years past the normal due date. To obtain an extension, the executor must show reasonable cause for the delay in payment. For example, the fact that the executor of an estate requires additional time to sell a particularly illiquid asset to generate the cash with which to pay the estate tax might be accepted as reasonable cause for an extension of the payment date for the estate tax.

Section 6166 allows an estate to pay a portion of its estate tax liability in installments if a substantial portion of the estate consists of the decedent's interest in a closely held business.[43]

---

[43] § 6166(b) provides specific definition of the phrase "interest in a closely held business."

To be considered "closely-held" at least 20% of the total capital of the partnership or 20% of the total value of the corporation's voting stock must be included in the gross estate or the decedent is a partner in the partnership or a shareholder in the corporation and such partnership or corporation has 45 or fewer partners or shareholders (as increased by the 2001 legislation). An estate is eligible if more than 35% of the *adjusted gross estate* (gross estate less §§ 2053 and 2054 deductions for debts of the decedent, funeral and administrative expenses, and losses) consists of the value of such an interest. The percentage of the estate tax liability that can be deferred is based on the ratio of the value of the closely held business to the value of the adjusted gross estate.

    If a decedent owned an interest in more than one closely held business, the values of the interests can be combined to meet the 35% test *if* the decedent's interest represents 20% or more of the total value of the business.

Example 30

The taxable estate of decedent X is composed of the following:

		Value
Sole proprietorship.		$ 600,000
40% interest in closely held corporation		3,000,000
Other assets		5,000,000
Gross estate.		$8,600,000
Less sum of		
Code §§ 2053 and 2054 deductions.	$ 600,000	
Code § 2055 charitable deduction	1,000,000	–1,600,000
Taxable estate		$7,000,000

The decedent owned 100% of the value of the sole proprietorship and 40% of the value of the closely held corporation. The combined values of these interests, $3,600,000, represents 45% of the adjusted gross estate of $8,000,000 ($8,600,000 – $600,000). Therefore, the executor may elect to defer payment on 45% of the estate tax liability.

    The tax deferred under § 6166 is payable in 10 equal annual installments. The first installment is payable five years and nine months after death. The IRS does charge the estate interest on the unpaid balance for the entire 15-year period.[44] Historically the interest rate charged on the deferred tax has been substantially less than the current market rate. Legislation in 1997 cut the rate even more. Currently, the interest rate is only two-percent of the deferred tax on the so-called *two-percent portion*. The tax on the two-percent portion is limited to the tax on the sum of $1,480,000 (as adjusted for inflation in 2016) and the exemption equivalent for the year of death less the applicable unified credit. For example, the maximum two percent portion would be $592,000 in 2016 computed as follows:

Base amount	$1,480,000
Exemption equivalent (2016).	5,450,000
Two percent portion	$6,930,000
Gross tax on two percent portion ($345,800 + [40% × ($6,930,000 – $1,000,000)])	$2,717,800
Unified credit (2016)	(2,125,800)
Tax on two-percent portion.	$ 592,000

In addition, the interest rate imposed on the amount of the deferred estate tax attributable to the taxable value of the business in excess of this amount ($1,480,000 + the exemption of $5,450,000 or $6,930,000 in 2016) is reduced to 45% of the rate applicable to underpayments of estimated taxes plus the normal 3% for underpayments. No estate tax deduction is allowed for the interest paid. If the estate disposes of 50% or more of the value of the qualifying closely held interest, any outstanding amount of deferred estate tax must be paid immediately.

---

[44] See § 6601(j) for applicable interest rate.

The Generation-Skipping Transfer Tax

LO.8

Discuss the purpose of the generation-skipping transfer tax.

As part of the Tax Reform Act of 1976, Congress added a third type of transfer tax to the Internal Revenue Code. The *generation-skipping transfer tax* (GSTT) was designed to "plug a loophole" in the coverage of the gift and estate taxes. The original version of the GSTT was intimidatingly complex, and was criticized by tax practitioners from the moment of enactment.

The Tax Reform Act of 1986 retroactively repealed the 1976 version of the GSTT and replaced it with a new tax applicable to testamentary transfers occurring after the date of enactment and to inter vivos transfers made after September 25, 1985. Any tax actually paid under the 1976 GSTT is fully refundable.

A traditional generation-skipping transfer involves at least three generations of taxpayers. In its simplest form, a generation-skipping transfer occurs whenever there is a so-called *direct skip*, an outright transfer of wealth for the sole benefit of persons at least two generations younger than the transferor.[45]

Example 31

This year Grandpa made a gift to his grandchild. Although a gift tax may be imposed on Grandpa, no gift or estate tax is imposed on the intervening generation, that is, the child's father. Therefore there is a direct skip of the estate and gift tax.

A more complicated yet equally important example involves a so-called *taxable termination* as illustrated below.

Example 32

Several years ago, Mother, M, died. Her will created a trust with income to Daughter, D, for life, remainder to the grandchildren. In this case, M would pay an estate tax at the time of her death on the value of the property used to create the trust. More important, however, is the result when D dies and her interest terminates. Even though D is able to enjoy the income from the trust property for life, there is no estate tax imposed on her when she dies because her interest terminates at death. As a result, there is no estate or gift tax imposed on the second generation.

Generally, the value of property transferred in a taxable generation-skipping transaction is subject to a flat-rate tax of 40% (2016).[46] However, each transferor is allowed a lifetime exemption of $5,450,000 for 2016 for generation-skipping transfers of any type.[47] In addition, the tax is not imposed to the extent that the transfer is not subject to gift taxes (e.g., due to the annual exclusion or the exemption on transfers for medical or educational purposes). For example, small gifts from grandparents to grandchildren which fall within the annual exclusion would not be subject to the tax. Note that unlike the unified credit, any unused GSTT exemption of the transferor is not portable.

---

[45] § 2612.

[46] § 2641.

[47] § 2631.

Tax Planning Considerations

The statutory rules of Federal gift, estate, and generation-skipping taxes have been examined in this chapter. Any individual taxpayer who desires to maximize the accumulated wealth available to family members will want to minimize the burden of these three transfer taxes. Tax planning for transfer taxes would be incomplete, however, without consideration of any interrelated Federal income taxes. Many gifts are made by transfers to a trust, and the income taxation of the trust entity and its beneficiaries may have a significant impact upon the original tax minimization plan. For this reason, the Federal income taxation of trusts, estates, and beneficiaries is discussed in the next chapter (Chapter 16). The tax planning considerations for transfer taxes and any attendant income taxes are incorporated in Chapter 17, *Family Tax Planning*.

Problem Materials

DISCUSSION QUESTIONS

15-1 *Interrelation of Federal Estate and Gift Taxes.* Discuss the various reasons why the Federal gift and estate taxes can be considered as a single, unified transfer tax.

15-2 *Entity for Transfer Tax Purposes.* Why can the married couple rather than each individual spouse be considered the taxable entity for transfer tax purposes?

15-3 *What Constitutes a Gift?* Businessperson B offers X $40,000 for an asset owned by X. Although X knows the asset is worth $60,000, he is in desperate need of cash and agrees to sell. Has X made a $20,000 taxable gift to B? Explain.

15-4 *Adequate Consideration.* During the current year, K offered to pay $50,000 to his only son, S, if S would agree to live in the same town as K for the rest of K's life. K is very elderly and frail and desires to have a relative close at hand in case of emergency. Does the $50,000 payment constitute a taxable gift made by K?

15-5 *When Is a Gift Complete?* Wealthy Grandmother G wants to provide financial support for her Grandson GS. She opens a joint checking account with $20,000 of cash. At any time, G or GS may withdraw funds from this account. Has G made a completed gift to GS by opening this account? At what point is the gift complete?

15-6 *Cumulative Nature of Transfer Taxes.* The Federal income tax is computed on an annual basis. How does this contrast to the computation of the Federal gift tax?

15-7 *Purpose of Unified Transfer Tax Rates.* A decedent's taxable estate can be considered the last taxable gift the decedent makes. Why?

15-8 *Incomplete Transfers.* The Federal gift tax and estate tax are not mutually exclusive. Give examples of transfers that may be treated as taxable gifts but that do not remove the transferred assets from the donor's gross estate.

15-9 *Computation of Taxable Estate.* What are the three steps involved in computing the taxable estate of a decedent?

15-10 *Probate Estate versus Gross Estate.* How can the value of a decedent's probate estate differ from the value of his or her gross estate for tax purposes?

15-11 *Jointly Held Property.* Property held in joint tenancy with right of survivorship is often called a will substitute. In other words, if all property is held in joint tenancy, a will is unnecessary.
   a. Does joint tenancy eliminate the need for a will?
   b. Identify some of the problems that arise when property is titled in joint tenancy.

15-12 *Special Use Valuation of § 2032A.* The gross estate of decedent F consists of a very successful farming operation located 80 miles east of an expanding metropolitan area. The estate includes 2,000 acres of real estate worth $400,000 as agricultural land. However, a real estate developer is willing to pay $2 million for the property because of its potential for suburban development. Discuss the utility of § 2032A to F's estate.

15-13 *Powers of Appointment.* What are some *nontax* reasons for the creation of a power of appointment? What is the difference between a specific and a general power?

15-14 *Gifts in Contemplation of Death.* Discuss the scope of § 2035 concerning gifts made within three years of death after the enactment of ERTA 1981.

15-15 *Estate Tax Credits.* With the exception of the unified credit of § 2010, what is the basic purpose of the various estate tax credits?

15-16 *Due Date of Estate Tax Return and Payment.* Why is the tax law particularly lenient in authorizing extensions for payment of the Federal estate tax?

15-17 *Unified Transfer Tax Credit.* Section 2010 appears to allow a second $2,125,800 (2016) credit against the Federal estate tax (in addition to the credit allowed for gift tax purposes under § 2505). Is this the case?

15-18 *Generation-Skipping Transfers.* Decedent T's will created a trust, the income from which is payable to T's invalid daughter D for her life. Upon D's death, the trust assets will be paid to T's two sons (D's brothers) in equal shares. Has T made a generation-skipping transfer? Explain.

PROBLEMS

15-19 *Gift Splitting.* During 2016, Mr. and Mrs. Z made the following cash gifts to their adult children:

Mr. Z:

To son M	$30,000
To daughter N	8,000
Total	$38,000

Mrs. Z:

To son M	$ 2,000
To daughter N	12,000
To daughter O	18,000
Total	$32,000

    a. Assume Mr. and Mrs. Z do *not* elect to split their gifts per § 2513. Compute the total taxable gifts after exclusions for each.

    b. How does the amount of taxable gifts change if Mr. and Mrs. Z *elect* to split their gifts?

15-20 *Computing Gift Tax Liability.* B, a single individual, made a cash gift of $200,000 his niece C in 1996. In 2016, B gives C an additional $4,800,000 and nephew D $1,500,000. Compute B's gift tax liability for the current year.

15-21 *Computing Taxable Gifts.* C, a single individual, makes the following transfers during current year:

	Fair Market Value
Cash to sister D	$13,000
Real estate:	
Life estate to brother B	28,000
Remainder to nephew N	21,000
Cash to First Baptist Church	25,000

What is the total amount of taxable gifts C must report?

15-22 *Amount of the Gift and the Annual Exclusion.* In 2016, Mr. C decided he wanted to set up trusts for his adult daughter and his grandson. To this end, he transferred $50,000 cash to a trust. The income of the trust was payable annually to his daughter, D, for 20 years with the remainder to D's son, R. For your computations, assume 120% of the applicable Federal midterm rate is five percent.

    a. What is (are) the amount(s) of the taxable gift(s)?

    b. Same as (a) except D is to receive the income for the rest of her life (she is age 40).

15-23 *Computing Taxable Gifts.* During 2016, L, a widower, makes the following transfers:

	Fair Market Value
Tuition payment to State College for nephew N, age 32	$ 16,000
New automobile to nephew N.	9,000
Cash to a local qualified political committee.	15,000

What is the total amount of taxable gifts L must report?

15-24 *Computing Taxable Gifts.* During 2016, Z, a widow, makes the following transfers:

	Fair Market Value
Real estate located in France to son J.	$500,000
City of Philadelphia municipal bonds to daughter K.	120,000
Payment to local hospital for medical expenses of brother-in-law M	18,000

What is the total amount of taxable gifts Z must report?

15-25 *Basis of Gifted Assets.* During the current year, L received a gift of land from his grandmother. The land had a basis to the grandmother of $100,000 and a fair market value of $264,000 on the date of the gift. A gift tax of $30,000 was paid on the transfer.
  a. If L subsequently sells the land for $300,000, how much gain or loss will he recognize?
  b. What would be the amount of L's recognized gain or loss on the sale if the land had a tax basis of $325,000 (rather than $100,000) to the grandmother?

15-26 *Marital Deduction.* F died during the current year, leaving a gross estate valued at $15 million. F's will specifically provided that no amount of her wealth was to be left to her estranged husband, G. However, under applicable state law, G is legally entitled to $1 million of his deceased wife's assets. How does the payment of $1 million affect the value of:
  a. F's *gross* estate?
  b. F's *taxable* estate?

15-27 *Gross Estate Inclusions.* Q was a cash basis taxpayer who died in the current year. On the date of Q's death, he owned corporate bonds, principal amount of $50,000, with accrued interest of $3,950. On the date of death, the bonds were selling on the open market for $54,000. Six months later the market price of the bonds had dropped to $51,500; there was $3,200 of accrued interest on the bonds as of this date. Neither market price includes any payment for accrued interest.
  a. Assuming the executor of Q's estate does not elect the alternate valuation date, what amounts should be included in Q's gross estate because of his ownership of the bonds?
  b. Assuming the executor does elect the alternate valuation date, what amounts should be included in Q's gross estate?

15-28 *Interests in Trusts Included in Gross Estate.* M's mother left property in trust (Trust A), with the income payable to M for M's lifetime and the remainder to M's daughter. At M's death, Trust A was worth $6.5 million. M's grandfather created a trust (Trust B), with the income payable to M's father for his lifetime. Upon the father's death, the remainder in Trust B was payable to M or M's estate. At M's death, his 60-year-old father was still living and Trust B was worth $2.1 million. Assuming a 5.0% interest rate, what are the values of the inclusions in M's gross estate attributable to M's interests in Trust A and Trust B? (See Table S, contained in Appendix A-1.)

15-29 *Computing Gross Estate.* Upon A's death, certain assets were valued as follows:

	Fair Market Value
Probate estate...	$ 750,000
Insurance proceeds on a policy on A's life. The policy has always been owned by A's niece, the beneficiary.............................	150,000
Corpus of Trust A. A possessed the right to give the ownership of the corpus to herself or any of her family. In her will she left the corpus to cousin K............	15,000,000

Based on these facts, what is the value of A's gross estate?

15-30 *Computing Gross Estate.* Upon G's death, the following assets were valued:

	Fair Market Value
Probate estate..	$10,350,000
Life insurance proceeds on G's life payable to the estate.........................	38,000
Annuity payable to G's widow out of G's employer's pension plan..................	20,000
Corpus of revocable trust created by G for the benefit of his children 10 years prior to death. Upon G's death, the trust becomes irrevocable.............	1,000,000

What is the value of G's gross estate?

15-31 *Gifts Included in Gross Estate.* Donor D, age 66, makes a gift in trust for his grandchildren K and L. Under the terms of the trust instrument, D will receive the income from the trust for the rest of his life. Upon his death, the trust assets will be distributed equally between K and L. Upon the date of D's death, at age 77, the value of the trust assets is $2.5 million. What amount, if any, is included in D's gross estate?

15-32 *Gifts in Contemplation of Death.* In 2014, S made a taxable gift of marketable securities to his nephew and paid a gift tax of $14,250. In 2015, S gave an income interest in trust property to the same nephew and paid a gift tax of $5,000. S originally created the trust in 1990, retaining the income interest for life (the same income interest that he later gave to S) and giving the remainder to another family member. S died in 2016, when the marketable securities were worth $300,000 and the trust property was worth $972,000. Based on these facts, what amounts, if any, are included in S's gross estate?

15-33 *Gifts Included in Gross Estate.* In 1997, F transferred real estate into a trust, the income from which was payable to M during her lifetime. Upon M's death, the trust property will be distributed in equal portions among M's children. However, the trust instrument gives F the right to change the remainder beneficiaries at any time. F dies in the current year without ever having changed the original trust provisions. At date of death, the trust property is worth $3.9 million and M is 60 years old. Assuming a five percent interest rate, determine the amount, if any, to be included in F's gross estate. (See Table S, contained in Appendix A-1.)

15-34 *Gifts Included in Gross Estate.* In 1993, P transferred $500,000 of assets into an irrevocable trust for the exclusive benefit of his children. Under the terms of the trust agreement, annual income must be distributed among the children according to P's direction. When the youngest child attains the age of 25 years, the trust corpus will be distributed equally among the living children. P dies in the current year while the trust is still in existence and the corpus has a fair market value of $3,200,000. How much, if any, of the corpus must be included in P's gross estate?

15-35 *Powers of Appointment.* In 1999, donor D transferred $100,000 of assets into an irrevocable trust for the exclusive benefit of her minor grandchildren. Under the terms of the trust agreement, the grandchildren will receive the annual income from the trust, and when the youngest grandchild attains the age of 21, the trust corpus will be divided among the living grandchildren as S, D's only child, so directs. S dies in the current year while the trust is still in existence and the corpus has a fair market value of $400,000. S's valid will directs that the corpus of the trust will go entirely to grandchild Q. How much, if any, of the corpus must be included in S's gross estate?

15-36 *Including Insurance in Gross Estate.* Decedent R left a probate estate of $3,000,000. Two years prior to his death, R gave all incidents of ownership in an insurance policy on his own life to his daughter S, the policy beneficiary. Because the policy had a substantial cash surrender value, R paid a gift tax of $77,000 on the transfer. Upon death, the insurance policy paid $5,000,000 to S. What is the value of R's gross estate?

15-37 *Joint Tenancy.* In 2004, Q paid $500,000 for 100 acres of land and took title with his brother R as joint tenants with right of survivorship. R made no contribution toward the purchase price. This year Q died. At the time of his death, the land was worth $1.2 million. R became the sole owner of land upon Q's death.
   a. What are the gift tax consequences of the creation of the joint tenancy?
   b. How much of the date of death value of the land must be included in Q's gross estate?
   c. How much would be included in the gross estate of R if R, rather than Q, died in the current year?

15-38 *Computing Taxable Estate.* Decedent T left a gross estate for tax purposes of $8,000,000. T had personal debts of $60,000 and his estate incurred funeral expenses of $12,000 and legal and accounting fees of $35,000. T's will provided for $100,000 bequest to the American Cancer Society, with all other assets passing to his grandchildren. Compute T's taxable estate.

15-39 *Sections 2053 and 2054 Expenses.* Decedent D died on July 1 of the current year. D owned a sailboat valued at $85,000 as of the date of death. However, on December 1 of the current year, the boat was destroyed in a storm, and the estate was unable to collect any insurance to compensate for the loss. In December, the executor of D's estate received a $2,200 bill from the company that had stored the sailboat from January 1 through December 1 of the current year.
   a. If the executor does not elect the alternate valuation date, will the $85,000 value of the boat be included in D's gross estate? D's taxable estate?
   b. May any portion of the $2,200 storage fee be deducted on D's Federal estate tax return? On the first income tax return filed by the estate?

15-40 *Marital Deduction Assets.* J, who was employed by Gamma Inc. at the date of his death, had been an active participant in Gamma's qualified retirement plan. Under the terms of the plan, J's widow will receive an annuity of $1,500 per month for the next 20 years. The replacement value of the annuity is $145,000. In his will, J left his interest in a patent worth $50,000 to his widow; the patent will expire in eight years. To what extent will these transfers qualify for a marital deduction from J's gross estate?

15-41 *Qualified Terminable Interest Trust.* Under the will of decedent H, all his assets (fair market value of $10 million) are to be put into trust. His widow, W, age 64, will be paid all the income from the trust every quarter for the rest of her life. Upon W's death, all the assets in the trust will be distributed to the couple's children and grandchildren. During W's life, no part of the trust corpus can be distributed to anyone but W.
   a. What amount of marital deduction is available on H's estate tax return?
   b. W dies eight years after H and under the terms of H's will the trust assets are distributed. What percentage, if any, of the value of these assets must be included in W's gross estate?

15-42 *Deferring Estate Tax Payments.* Decedent X has the following taxable estate:

Sole proprietorship		$12,800,000
Ten percent interest in a closely held corporation		200,000
Other assets		1,200,000
Gross estate		$14,200,000
Less sum of:		
§§ 2053 and 2054 deductions	$800,000	
§ 2056 marital deduction	400,000	– 1,200,000
Taxable estate		$13,000,000

Assume the estate tax liability on this estate is $2,800,000.
a. How much of the liability may be deferred under § 6166?
b. If X died on November 1, 2016, when is the first installment payment of tax due?

15-43 *Computing Estate Tax Liability.* Decedent Z died in 2016 and left a taxable estate of $10 million. During his life, Z made the following unrestricted gifts and did not elect gift splitting with his wife:

	Fair Market Value
2014: Gift of 2,000 shares of Acme stock to son S	$900,000
2015: Gift of cash to daughter D	600,000
2015: Gift of cash to wife W	700,000

Compute Z's estate tax liability after utilization of the available unified credit.

15-44 *Unified Credit.* H and W are husband and wife. They own all of their property in joint tenancy with right of survivorship. This year H died. His estate included $4,000,000 (his ½ interest in all of the property). Will his unified credit be wasted?

TAX RESEARCH PROBLEMS

15-45 In 2000, JW gifted 30% of her stock in W Corporation to her favorite nephew, N. Although she retained a 50% interest in W Corporation and her husband owned the remaining 20% of the outstanding stock, JW was concerned that the family might eventually lose control of the firm. To reassure JW, the three stockholders agreed to restrict transferability of their stock by signing an agreement that any shareholder wishing to dispose of W Corporation stock must offer the stock to the corporation for a formula price based on the average net earnings per share for the three previous years. The corporation would then be obligated to purchase the stock at the formula price. At the time the buy-sell agreement was entered into, this formula resulted in a price very close to the stock's actual fair market value.

JW died in the current year at a time when the value of her W Corporation stock was substantially depreciated because of certain unfavorable local economic conditions. Several independent appraisals of the stock valued JW's 50% interest at $650,000. However, the formula under the 2000 buy-sell agreement resulted in a value of only $150,000 for the decedent's 50% interest. What is the correct value of the 50% interest in the corporation for estate tax purposes?

Research aids:

Rev. Rul. 59-60, 1959-1 C.B. 237.

Estate of Littick, 31 T.C. 181 (1958), acq. 1959-2 C.B. 5.

Code § 2703.

15-46 In 2003, Mr. and Mrs. B (residents of a common law state) created two trusts for the benefit of their children. Mr. B transferred $600,000 of his own property into trust, giving the income interest to his wife for her life, and the remainder interest to the children. Mrs. B transferred $640,000 of her own property into trust, giving the income interest to her husband for his life, and the remainder interest to the children. In the current year, Mrs. B dies. How much, if any, of the current value of the corpus of the 2003 trust created by Mrs. B will be included in her gross estate?

Research aids:

United States v. Estate of Grace, 69-1 USTC ¶12,609.

23 AFTR 2d 69-1954, 395 U.S. 316 (USSC, 1969).

16

Income Taxation of Estates and Trusts

Learning Objectives

Upon completion of this chapter you will be able to:

LO.1 Compute fiduciary accounting income and determine the required allocation of such income among the various beneficiaries of the fiduciary.

LO.2 Identify the special rules that apply to the computation of fiduciary taxable income.

LO.3 Explain the concept of income and deductions in respect of a decedent.

LO.4 Compute both the taxable and nontaxable components of a fiduciary's distributable net income.

LO.5 Describe the defining characteristics of a simple and a complex trust, including:

- The computation of the deduction for distributions to beneficiaries for both types of trusts.

- The distinction between tier one and tier two distributions from a complex trust.

LO.6 Determine the tax consequences of fiduciary distributions to the recipient beneficiaries.

Chapter Outline

Introduction

Trusts and estates are taxable entities subject to a specialized set of tax rules contained in Subchapter J of the Internal Revenue Code (§§ 641 through 692). The income taxation of trusts and estates (commonly referred to as fiduciary taxpayers) and their beneficiaries is the subject of this chapter. Grantor trusts, a type of trust not recognized as a taxable entity and therefore not subject to the rules of Subchapter J, are discussed in Chapter 17.

The Function of Estates and Trusts

ESTATES

An estate as a legal entity comes into existence upon the death of an individual. During the period of time in which the decedent's legal affairs are being settled, assets owned by the decedent are managed by an executor or administrator of the estate. Once all legal requirements have been satisfied, the estate terminates and ownership of all estate assets passes to the decedent's beneficiaries or heirs.

During its existence, the decedent's estate is a taxable entity that files a tax return and pays Federal income taxes on any income earned.[1] Normally an estate is a transitional entity that bridges the brief gap in time between the death of an individual taxpayer and the distribution of that individual's wealth to other taxpayers. However, estates as taxpayers may continue in existence for many years if the correct distribution of a decedent's wealth is in question. If the administration of a decedent's estate is unreasonably prolonged, the IRS may treat the estate as terminated for tax purposes after a reasonable amount of time for settlement of the decedent's affairs has elapsed.[2]

TRUSTS

A trust is a legal arrangement in which an individual, the *grantor*, transfers legal ownership of assets to one party, the *trustee*, and the legal right to enjoy and benefit from those assets to a second party, the *beneficiary* (or beneficiaries). Such an arrangement is usually designed for the protection of the beneficiary. Often trust beneficiaries are minor children or family members incapable of competently managing the assets themselves.

The terms of the trust, the duties of the trustee, and the rights of the various beneficiaries are specified in a legal document, the *trust instrument*. The assets put into trust are referred to as the trust *corpus*, or *principal*.

The role of the trustee is that of a fiduciary; he or she is required to act in the best interests of the trust beneficiaries rather than for his or her own interests. The position of trustee is usually filled by the professional trust department of a bank or a competent friend or family member. Professional trustees receive an annual fee to compensate them for services rendered.

The purpose of a trust is to protect and conserve trust assets for the sole benefit of the trust beneficiaries, not to operate a trade or business. A trust that becomes involved in an active, profit-making business activity runs the risk of being classified as an *association* for Federal tax purposes, with the unfavorable result that it will be taxed as a corporation rather than under the rules of Subchapter J.[3]

---

[1] § 641(a)(3).

[2] Reg. § 1.641(b)-3(a).

[3] See *Morrissey v. Comm.*, 36-1 USTC ¶9020, 16 AFTR 1274, 296 U.S. 344 (USSC, 1936), for this result.

TRUST BENEFICIARIES

An individual who desires to establish a trust has virtually unlimited discretion as to the identity of the trust beneficiaries and the nature of the interest in the trust given to each beneficiary. For example, assume grantor G creates a trust consisting of $1 million of assets. G could specify in the trust instrument that individual I is to receive all the income of the trust for I's life, and upon I's death the assets in the trust are to be distributed to individual R. In this example, both I and R are trust beneficiaries. I owns an *income interest* in the trust, while R owns a *remainder interest* (the right to the trust principal at some future date).

A grantor can give trust beneficiaries any mix of rights to trust income or principal (trust assets) that will best accomplish the goals of the trust. In the previous example, if grantor G decided that the trust income might be insufficient to provide for I, the trust document could specify that I also will receive a certain amount of trust principal every year. Alternatively, if G believed that I might not need all the trust income annually, the trust document could provide that the trustee could accumulate income to distribute to I at some later point. As may be apparent, a trust can be a very flexible arrangement for providing for the needs of specific beneficiaries.

FIDUCIARY ACCOUNTING INCOME

There is no standard accounting system that applies to fiduciaries. The accounting income of an estate or trust is determined by reference to the decedent's valid will or the trust instrument. These documents can specify how fiduciary receipts, disbursements, and other transactions affect income, principal, or both. In other words, every fiduciary may have its own unique set of rules for the computation of accounting income, and the executor or trustee must refer exclusively to this income number in carrying out his or her duties. If a will or trust instrument is silent concerning the impact of a particular transaction on accounting income, such impact must be determined by reference to controlling state law. Most states have enacted a version of the Revised Uniform Principal and Income Act, a model set of fiduciary accounting rules proposed by the Uniform Commission on State Laws.

One common difference between fiduciary accounting income and taxable income is the classification of fiduciary capital gains. Typically, capital gains represent an increase in the value of the principal of the fiduciary and normally are not available for distribution to income beneficiaries. Of course, for Federal tax purposes capital gains represent taxable income. Similarly, stock dividends are often regarded as an increase in principal rather than trust income, even though the dividend may be taxable income under the Internal Revenue Code.

Trustee fees are generally deductible for tax purposes. However, for fiduciary accounting purposes such fees may be charged *either* to trust income or to trust principal.

Depreciation may or may not have an effect on fiduciary accounting income. If local law or the trust instrument requires the fiduciary to establish a reserve for depreciation, depreciation is computed in accordance with the local law or the trust instrument and subtracted in computing trust accounting income. In effect, the fiduciary transfers cash out of income (reducing the amount that can be distributed to the income beneficiary) and sets this amount aside for future replacement of the depreciable property. Note that the amount of depreciation computed for tax purposes can be quite different than the amount of depreciation for fiduciary accounting income purposes. For this reason, tax depreciation requires special treatment as described below.

Exhibit 16-1 identifies various items of income and expense and shows how they are normally allocated between income and corpus.

LO.1

Compute fiduciary accounting income and determine the required allocation of such income among the various beneficiaries of the fiduciary.

EXHIBIT 16-1	Fiduciary Accounting Income

Typical Income Items

    Interest

    Dividends

    Royalties

    Net rental income (income less expenses) from real or personal property

    Net profits from operation of a trade or business; losses are usually charged to corpus

    All or a portion of trustee commissions

    Depreciation to the extent of any required reserve

Typical Corpus Items

    Gain or loss on the sale or exchange of trust property (capital gains)

    Casualty losses

    Stock dividends

    All or a portion of trustee commissions

Example 1

During the year, the records of a trust revealed the following information:

Receipts:	
Dividends	$10,000
Interest from municipal bonds	12,000
Long-term capital gain allocable to principal under state law	6,500
Stock dividend allocable to principal under the trust instrument	4,000
Total receipts	$32,500

Disbursements:	
Trustee fee (half allocable to trust income; half allocable to principal under the trust instrument)	$ 3,000

Based on the above, the accounting income of the trust would be $20,500, computed as follows:

Dividends	$10,000
Interest from municipal bonds	12,000
	$22,000
Less: One-half of the trustee fee ($3,000 ÷ 2)	(1,500)
Trust accounting income	$20,500

If the trustee of this particular trust was required to distribute the entire amount of trust income to a particular group of beneficiaries, the trustee would make a payment of $20,500. Note that this amount bears little relationship to the *taxable income* generated by the trust's activities.

For Federal tax purposes, fiduciaries are taxable entities.[4] Every estate that has annual gross income of $600 or more, and every trust that has either annual gross income of $600 or more *or* any taxable trust income, must file an income tax return. Furthermore, if a fiduciary has a beneficiary who is a nonresident alien, that fiduciary must file a return regardless of the amount of its gross or taxable income for the year.[5]

Form 1041, the U.S. Fiduciary Income Tax Return, must be filed by the 15th day of the fourth month following the close of the fiduciary's taxable year (see Appendix B for sample Form 1041). An estate may adopt a calendar or any fiscal taxable year. However, the taxable year of a trust must be a calendar year.[6] In the case of an estate, the first taxable year begins on the day following the date of death of the decedent.[7] In the case of a trust, the date of creation as specified in the controlling trust instrument marks the beginning of the first taxable year.

Fiduciaries generally must make quarterly estimated tax payments in the same manner as individuals. However, no estimated taxes must be paid by an estate or a grantor trust to which the residual of the grantor's estate is distributed for any taxable year ending within the two years following the decedent's death.[8] A trustee may *elect* to treat any portion of an excess estimated tax payment made by a trust as a payment of estimated tax made by a beneficiary. If the election is made, the payment is considered as having been distributed to the beneficiary on the last day of the trust's taxable year and then remitted to the government as estimated tax paid by the beneficiary on January 15th of the following year.[9]

Example 2

On April 15, 2016, Trust T made an estimated tax payment of $14,000. However, later in the year, the trustee decided to distribute all 2016 trust income to beneficiary B. Because Trust T will have no 2016 tax liability, the trustee may elect to treat the $14,000 payment as a cash distribution made to beneficiary B on December 31, 2016. Beneficiary B will report the $14,000 as part of his 2016 estimated tax payment made on January 15, 2017.

Section 641(b) provides that "the taxable income of an estate or trust shall be computed in the same manner as in the case of an individual, except as otherwise provided in this part." Thus, many of the rules governing the taxation of individuals apply to fiduciaries. Before examining the specific rules unique to fiduciary income taxation, it will be useful to look at the basic approach for computing fiduciary taxable income.

Step One: Compute fiduciary accounting income and identify any receipts and disbursements allocated to principal (under either the trust instrument or state law).

Step Two: Compute fiduciary taxable income *before* the deduction for distributions to beneficiaries authorized by Code §§ 651 and 661.

Step Three: Compute the deduction for distributions to beneficiaries. This step will require a computation of fiduciary "distributable net income" (DNI).

Step Four: Subtract the deduction for distributions to arrive at *fiduciary taxable income.*

Step One, the computation of fiduciary accounting income, was discussed earlier. Detailed discussions of Steps Two and Three constitute most of the remainder of this chapter.

---

[4] See §§ 7701(a)(6) and 641(a).

[5] § 6012(a)(3), (4), and (5).

[6] § 645. This requirement does not apply to tax-exempt and charitable trusts.

[7] See Reg. §§ 1.443-1(a)(2) and 1.461-1(b).

[8] § 6654(l).

[9] § 643(g).

Fiduciary Taxable Income

LO.2

Identify the special rules that apply to the computation of fiduciary taxable income.

Unless otherwise modified, the fiduciary computes its taxable income in a manner identical to that of an individual taxpayer. The major difference is the deduction granted for distributions made to beneficiaries, explained later in this chapter. In addition, § 642 contains a number of special provisions that must be followed in computing fiduciary taxable income and the final tax. These unique aspects of estate and trust taxation are considered below.

FIDUCIARY TAX RATES

The tax rates for estates and trusts for 2016 are shown in Exhibit 16-2. Note that the 10% rate that applies to individuals does not apply to trusts or estates. Also note that there is very little progressivity in the fiduciary rate schedule; taxable income in excess of $12,400 (2016) is taxed at the highest 39.6% rate. Net long-term capital gain and qualified dividends are taxed at a rate of 15% if the trust is in the 25, 28, or 33 percent brackets for ordinary income. A zero percent rate applies if the trust is in the 15% bracket while a 20% rate applies if the trust is in the 39.6% bracket.

EXHIBIT 16-2		Income Tax Rates for Estates and Trusts			
For Taxable Years Beginning in 2016					
If Taxable Income Is					
Over	*But Not Over*	*The Tax Is*	*+*	*% on Excess*	*Of the Amount Over*
$ 0	$ 2,550	$ 0.00		15%	$ 0
2,550	5,950	382.50	+	25%	2,550
5,950	9,050	1,232.00	+	28%	5,950
9,050	12,400	2,100.50	+	33%	9,050
12,400	—	3,206.00	+	39.6%	12,400

In determining their final tax liability, fiduciaries are subject to the alternative minimum tax provisions.[10]

Tax on Net Investment Income

The § 1411 tax of 3.8% on net investment income applies to trusts and estates as well as individuals. The special tax applies to any net investment income when the fiduciary's taxable income exceeds $12,400 (i.e., when the trust taxable income is taxed at a rate of 39.6% in 2016). Special rules must be followed in determining the amount of net investment income to be taxed to the trust and the beneficiaries.

STANDARD DEDUCTION AND PERSONAL EXEMPTION

Unlike individual taxpayers, fiduciaries are not entitled to a standard deduction.[11] However, a fiduciary, like an individual taxpayer, is entitled to a personal exemption. The amount of the exemption depends on the type of fiduciary. The personal exemption for an estate is $600. The exemption for a trust that is required by the trust instrument to distribute all trust income currently is $300. The exemption for any trust not subject to this requirement is $100.[12]

LIMITATIONS ON DEDUCTIBILITY OF FIDUCIARY EXPENSES

Because fiduciaries generally do not engage in the conduct of a business, the gross income of a fiduciary usually consists of investment income items such as dividends, interest, rents, and royalties. Fiduciary expenses are normally deductible under the authority of § 212, which provides for the deduction of ordinary and necessary expenses paid for the

---

[10] See § 59(c). A special computation is used that is beyond the scope of this text.

[11] § 63(c)(6)(D).

[12] § 642(b).

management, conservation, or maintenance of property held for the production of income. However, there are several limitations on the deduction of expenses that apply to individuals that also apply to fiduciaries.

Limitations on Deductions Related to Tax-Exempt Income

As a general rule, § 265 denies the deduction for any expenses related to tax-exempt income. In contrast, any expense that is *directly related* to taxable fiduciary income is fully deductible. For example, rent expenses are directly related to rental income and would not be subject to this limitation. Expenses that are not directly related to a particular type of income—sometimes referred to as *indirect* expenses—must be allocated proportionately between taxable and tax-exempt income.[13] For example, consider a common expenditure of trusts such as trustee commissions. These fees are viewed as relating to both taxable and tax-exempt income and, therefore, an allocation is required. Assuming 20% of the trust's income is tax-exempt, then 20% of the trustee commission would be nondeductible. On the other hand, most practitioners take the position that tax preparation fees need not be allocated to tax-exempt income since they are only related to taxable income.

The portion of an indirect expense that is not deductible can be determined using the following formula:

$$\frac{\text{Tax exempt income}}{\text{Total trust income}} \times \text{Expenses not directly related to a particular type of income} = \text{Nondeductible expenses}$$

In computing the denominator of the above formula, trust accounting income does not include capital gains unless capital gains are actually included in trust accounting income.[14] In addition, the denominator is computed using gross receipts.

Example 3

This year Trust T paid trustee fees of $7,000, $5,000 allocable to income and $2,000 allocable to corpus. Its records reveal the following additional information:

	Amounts
Rental income	$70,000
Rental expenses	(30,000)
Net rental income	$40,000
Long-term capital gains allocable to corpus	$25,000
Long-term capital losses allocable to corpus	(5,000)
Net capital gain	$20,000
Sales	$20,000
Costs of goods sold	(15,000)
Gross income	$ 5,000
Interest on State of New York bonds	$10,000

To determine the amount of commissions that are not deductible, the denominator does not include the net capital gain allocable to corpus of $20,000. However, the denominator does include the gross amounts of income received and is not reduced by expenses. Thus the denominator includes the rent of $70,000, sales of $20,000, and tax-exempt interest of $10,000 for a total of $100,000. Therefore 10% ($10,000/$100,000) of the $7,000 of trustee's commissions or $700 is not deductible, and the remaining $6,300 is deductible. Note that in computing the amount of the deductible commissions, the fact that they are allocable to income or corpus for trust accounting purposes is irrelevant.

---

[13] Reg. § 1.642(g)-2.

[14] Rev. Rul. 77-365. Other approaches may be available. For example, see *Whittemore, Jr. v. U.S.* 20 AFTR 2d 5533, 67-2 USTC ¶9670 383 F.2d 824 (CA-8, 1967).

Limitation on Double Deduction of Administrative Expenses

Section 642(g) provides a second major limitation on the deductibility of fiduciary expenses. If an administrative expense is claimed as a deduction on the estate tax return of a decedent, it may not also be claimed as a deduction on an income tax return of the decedent's estate or subsequent trust. However, Regulation § 1.642(g)-2 provides that administrative expenses that could be deducted for either estate tax or income tax purposes can be divided between the two returns in whatever portions achieve maximum tax benefit.

Limitation on Miscellaneous Itemized Deductions

Section 67(a) limits certain miscellaneous itemized deductions, including the § 212 deduction for investment expenses. Such itemized deductions are allowed only to the extent they exceed 2% of adjusted gross income. Section 67(e) provides that the deduction for expenses paid or incurred in connection with the administration of a fiduciary that would have been avoided if the property were not held by the fiduciary shall be allowable in computing the adjusted gross income of the fiduciary. In other words, fiduciary expenses such as administration fees which are incurred only because of the trust or estate form are not considered itemized deductions subject to the 2% floor. Unfortunately, whether an expense is unique to a trust or an estate is not always clear. Most of the controversy has concerned investment management and advisory expenses. However, in 2008, the Supreme Court resolved the matter, holding that investment management and advisory fees were miscellaneous itemized deductions.[15] According to the Court, if an expense of a trust or estate is commonly incurred by an individual, it is not unique to a trust. Applying this theory to fees for investment management, the Court believed that it would not be uncommon or unusual for individuals to hire an investment adviser. Therefore, it held that such expenses are miscellaneous itemized deductions. In this regard, the proposed regulations would require that trustee fees be unbundled so that the proper amounts may be allocated properly between trust or estate administration and investment advice. After the *Knight* decision, it appears that such expenses as the costs of accounting, tax return preparation, division of income or corpus among beneficiaries, will or trust contests or construction, fiduciary bond premiums and communications with beneficiaries regarding trust or estate matters would not be miscellaneous itemized deductions.

The computation of the limitation on miscellaneous itemized deductions can be quite cumbersome. Since adjusted gross income of the trust depends on the amount of the distribution deduction and the distribution deduction in turn depends on taxable income after taking into account the deduction for miscellaneous itemized deductions (taxable DNI as explained below), the calculation of allowable miscellaneous itemized deductions may require the use of simultaneous algebraic equations.

Deduction Cutback

Section 68 generally requires that the total of an individual's itemized deductions for the year be reduced by three percent of the amount of adjusted gross income in excess of an inflation adjusted threshold. This requirement is expressly inapplicable to any estate or trust.

Medical Expenses

Medical expenses paid by an estate or trust require special consideration. Medical expenses paid for the care of a *decedent* prior to his death that are paid by an estate within one year after death can be deducted either on the income tax return of the decedent (final Form 1040) or the estate tax return (Form 706), but not both. Medical expenses paid after the one-year period are deductible only as liabilities on the estate tax return (Form 706) if such return is actually filed. Medical expenses of *beneficiaries* that are paid by the trust or estate are treated as distributions of income to the beneficiaries and are not deductible per se on the fiduciary income tax return.

---

[15] *Michael J. Knight, Trustee of the William L. Rudkin Testamentary Trust,* 2008-1 USTC ¶50,132, 101 AFTR 2d 2008-544, 128 S. Ct. 782 (USSC, 2008).

CHARITABLE CONTRIBUTIONS

Section 642(c) authorizes an unlimited charitable deduction for any amount of gross income paid by a fiduciary to a qualified charitable organization. Fiduciaries are given a great deal of flexibility as to the timing of charitable contributions; if a contribution is paid after the close of one taxable year but before the close of the next taxable year, the fiduciary may elect to deduct the payment in the earlier year.[16]

If a fiduciary receives tax-exempt income that is available for charitable distribution, its deduction for any charitable contribution made normally must be reduced by that portion of the contribution attributable to tax-exempt income.[17]

Example 4

During the current year, Trust T receives $30,000 of tax-exempt interest, $25,000 of taxable interest, and $45,000 of taxable dividends. The trust makes a charitable contribution of $20,000 during the year. Because 30% of the trust's income available for distribution is nontaxable, 30% of the charitable distribution is nondeductible and the trust's deduction for charitable contributions is limited to $14,000.

DEPRECIATION, DEPLETION, AND AMORTIZATION

The total allowable amount of depreciation, depletion, and amortization that may be deducted by the fiduciary (or passed through to the beneficiaries) is determined in the normal manner. A fiduciary is entitled to bonus depreciation but not allowed to expense any portion of the cost of eligible property under § 179.

Deductions for depreciation and depletion available to a fiduciary depend upon the terms of the controlling will or trust instrument. If the controlling instrument authorizes a reserve for depreciation or depletion, any *allowable* (deductible) tax depreciation or depletion will be deductible by the fiduciary to the extent of the specified reserve. If the allowable tax depreciation or depletion exceeds the reserve, the excess deduction is allocated between the fiduciary and beneficiaries based upon the amount of fiduciary income allocable to each.[18]

Example 5

Trust R owns rental property with a basis of $300,000. The trust instrument authorizes the trustee to maintain an annual depreciation reserve of $15,000 (5% of the cost of the property). For tax purposes, however, the current year's depreciation deduction is $22,000. The trust instrument provides that one-half of annual trust income including rents will be distributed to the trust beneficiaries. For the current year, the trust is entitled to a depreciation deduction of $18,500 (5% of $300,000 + one-half the tax depreciation in excess of $15,000 [½ × $7,000 = $3,500]).

Note that if the controlling instrument is silent, depreciation and depletion deductions are simply allocated between fiduciary and beneficiaries on the basis of fiduciary income allocable to each. If a fiduciary is entitled to statutory amortization, the amortization deduction also will be apportioned among fiduciary and beneficiaries on the basis of income allocable to each.[19]

---

[16] § 642(c)(1). See Reg. § 1.642(c)-1(b) for the time and manner in which such an election is to be made.

[17] Reg. § 1.642(c)-3(b).

[18] Reg. § 1.167(h)-1; Reg. § 1.611-1(c)(4).

[19] Reg. § 1.642(f)-1.

FIDUCIARY LOSSES

Because the function of a trust generally is to conserve and protect existing wealth rather than to engage in potentially risky business activities, it is unusual for a trust to incur a net operating loss. It is not unusual, however, for an estate or trust that owns a business interest (e.g., an interest in a partnership or an S corporation) to incur this type of loss. In any case, if a net operating loss does occur, a fiduciary may carry the loss back two years and forward for 20.[20] Capital losses incurred by a fiduciary are deductible against capital gains; a maximum of $3,000 of net capital loss may be deducted against other sources of income.[21] Nondeductible net capital losses are carried forward to subsequent taxable years of the fiduciary.[22]

Fiduciaries are also subject to the limitations imposed on passive activity losses and credits by § 469.[23] Therefore, a fiduciary may only deduct current losses from passive activities against current income from passive activities. Any nondeductible loss is suspended and carried forward to subsequent taxable years. If an interest in a passive activity is distributed by a fiduciary to a beneficiary, any suspended loss of the activity is added to the tax basis of the distributed interest.[24]

Section 469(i) normally provides for a $25,000 *de minimis* offset for losses attributable to rental real estate. However, this allowance is extended only to "natural persons" and, therefore, normally does not apply to trusts or estates. This rule prevents taxpayers from circumventing the $25,000 limitation by transferring multiple properties to multiple trusts with each claiming a $25,000 allowance. However, the provision is extended to estates for losses occurring for tax years ending less than two years after the decedent's date of death.

NOLs, Capital Losses, and Excess Deductions

Unlike the net losses of a partnership or an S corporation, fiduciary losses do not flow through to beneficiaries. An exception to this rule applies for the year in which a trust or estate terminates. If the terminating fiduciary has net operating losses, capital loss carryforwards, or current year deductions in excess of current gross income, § 642(h) provides that such unused losses and excess deductions become available to the beneficiaries succeeding to the property of the fiduciary.

Example 6

D died in 2016. In 2017, the year of termination, the estate had gross income of $5,000 and legal fees of $15,000. The excess deductions of $10,000 do not create an NOL (that would carryover to the beneficiaries) since legal fees are considered a nonbusiness expense and are not deductible in computing an NOL. However, because the excess deductions occur in the year of termination, they pass through to the beneficiary who can claim the $10,000 as an itemized deduction. It should be emphasized that had this not been the year of termination, the $10,000 excess would be wasted. Due to this treatment, the fiduciary should take steps to ensure that excess deductions occur only in the year of termination. For example, a cash basis estate could postpone paying the legal fees until the final year.

Casualty losses of a fiduciary are subject to the rules pertaining to individual taxpayers. For casualty losses, the limitation of the deduction to that amount in excess of 10% of adjusted gross income applies, although the concept of adjusted gross income is normally not associated with trusts or estates.[25] In addition, § 642(g) prohibits the deduction by a fiduciary of any loss that has already been claimed as a deduction on an estate tax return.

---

[20] §§ 172(b)(1) and 642(d).

[21] § 1211(b).

[22] § 1212(b).

[23] § 469(a)(2)(A).

[24] § 469(j)(12).

[25] See Form 4684 and its instructions for this computation.

Income and Deductions in Respect of a Decedent

The death of an individual taxpayer can create a peculiar timing problem involving the reporting of income items earned or deductible expenses incurred by the taxpayer prior to death. For example, if a cash basis individual had performed all the services required to earn a $5,000 consulting fee but had not collected the fee before death, by whom shall the $5,000 of *income in respect of a decedent* (IRD) be reported? The individual taxpayer who earned the income never received payment, but the recipient of the money, the individual's estate, is not the taxpayer who earned it. Section 691(a) gives a statutory solution to this puzzling question by providing that any income of an individual not properly includible in the taxable period prior to the individual's death will be included in the gross income of the recipient of the income, typically the estate of the decedent or a beneficiary of the estate. Common IRD items include unpaid salary or commissions, retirement income (e.g., IRA), rent income, or interest accrued but unpaid at death, and the amount of a § 453 installment obligation that would have been recognized as income if payment had been received by the decedent prior to death.

Certain expenses incurred by a decedent but not properly deductible on the decedent's final return because of nonpayment are afforded similar statutory treatment. Under § 691(b), these *deductions in respect of a decedent* (DRD) are deducted by the taxpayer who is legally required to make payment. Allowable DRD items include business and income-producing expenses, interest, taxes, and depletion.

LO.3

Explain the concept of income and deductions in respect of a decedent.

ESTATE TAX TREATMENT AND THE § 691(C) DEDUCTION

Items of IRD and DRD represent assets and liabilities of the deceased taxpayer. As such, these items will be included on the decedent's estate tax return. Because IRD and DRD also have future income tax consequences, special provisions in the tax law apply to these items. First, even though the right to IRD is an asset acquired from a decedent, the basis of an IRD item does not become the item's fair market value at date of death. Instead, under § 1014(c), the basis of the item to the decedent carries over to the new owner. This special rule preserves the potential income that must be recognized when the IRD item is eventually collected. The character of IRD also is determined by reference to the decedent taxpayer.

Secondly, items of DRD that are deducted as administrative expenses on an estate tax return are *not* subject to the rule prohibiting a deduction on a subsequent income tax return.[26] Therefore, unlike administrative expenses of an estate that cannot be deducted on both the fiduciary income tax return (Form 1041) and the estate tax return (Form 706), DRD can be deducted on both.

Perhaps the most important reason for identifying items of IRD is the allowance of a special deduction for the recipient. To appreciate this deduction, consider the normal estate tax treatment given to a decedent's income. Such income is included *net* of any income tax that the decedent has paid. In contrast, items of IRD are included without reduction for the related income tax since the income tax on IRD is not a liability of the decedent but a liability of the recipient. Consequently, the amount of IRD income that is included in the gross estate is overstated and, therefore, the related estate tax is overstated. An heir who is the recipient of the income ends up with less than he would have had if the income had been taxed to the decedent and passed on to the heir net of the estate tax.

Example 7

D died on March 7, 2016. For illustration purposes, assume he was in the 40% income tax bracket and the 50% estate tax bracket. At the time of his death, D's employer owed him $10,000 of income. The following analysis shows the tax consequences that result if D had collected the $10,000 before he died as compared to those which would occur if his son, his heir, collects the $10,000 (assuming he is in the 40% tax bracket).

---

[26] § 642(g).

	D Collects before Death	Total Tax	Heir Collects after Death	Total Tax
Income	$10,000		$10,000	
Income tax to decedent	(4,000)	$4,000	0	$ 0
Aftertax income in estate	$ 6,000		$10,000	
Estate tax at 50%	3,000	3,000	5,000	5,000
Income to heir	$ 0		10,000	
Income tax to heir			$ 4,000	4,000
Total income and estate tax		$7,000		$9,000

In this case, the total income and estate tax imposed on the $10,000 if D collected the $10,000 is $7,000. In contrast, if the heir collects the $10,000 from the employer the total income and estate tax is $9,000. The $2,000 difference is attributable to the fact that the entire $10,000 is subject to estate tax in the latter case while only $6,000 ($10,000 net of the income tax of $4,000) is subject to estate tax in the first case (50% × $4,000 = $2,000).

Perhaps the best way to treat this problem is to estimate the amount of income tax that the decedent would have paid had he or she received the income and give the estate a deduction for this amount. However, because this amount would presumably be difficult to estimate, the authors of § 691 opted for an alternative that produces about the same result. Section 691(c) allows the recipient of IRD a deduction for any estate tax attributable to the income.

The deduction is a percentage of the estate tax attributable to the total *net* IRD included in an estate based on the ratio of the recognized IRD item to all IRD items. Estate tax attributable to net IRD is the excess of the actual tax over the tax computed without including the IRD in the taxable estate.

The § 691(c) deduction can be computed using the following two steps:

1. Determine the estate tax attributable to net IRD:

$$\begin{array}{l} \text{Estate tax actually incurred (including net IRD)} \\ \underline{- \ \text{Estate tax without NIRD}} \\ = \ \text{Total estate tax attributable to IRD} \end{array}$$

2. Recipient's deduction is based on the proportionate amount of IRD (not net IRD) that is received.

$$\frac{\text{IRD received}}{\text{Total IRD}} \times \text{Total estate tax attributable to IRD} = \text{Section 691(c) deduction}$$

Note that if an estate or trust is the recipient of the IRD, it is not subject to the deduction cutback for itemized deductions. In contrast, if an individual taxpayer receives the IRD, the amount is considered an itemized deduction.

Example 8

Taxpayer T's estate tax return included total IRD items valued at $145,000. DRD items totaled $20,000. If the *net* IRD of $125,000 had not been included in T's estate, the Federal estate tax liability would have decreased by $22,000. During the current year, the estate of T collected half ($72,500) of all IRD items and included this amount in estate gross income. T's estate is entitled to a § 691(c) deduction of $11,000.

The Distribution Deduction and the Taxation of Beneficiaries

The central concept of Subchapter J is that income recognized by a fiduciary will be taxed *either* to the fiduciary itself or to the beneficiaries of the fiduciary. The determination of the amount of income taxable to each depends upon the amount of annual distributions from the fiduciary to the beneficiary. Conceptually, distributions to beneficiaries represent a flow-through of trust income that will be taxed to the beneficiary. Under §§ 651 and 661, the amount of the distribution will then be available as a *deduction* to the fiduciary, reducing the taxable income the fiduciary must report. Income that flows through the fiduciary to a beneficiary retains its original character; therefore, the fiduciary acts as a *conduit*, similar to a partnership in this respect.[27]

In computing the deduction for distributions, the law generally presumes that *every distribution consists of a pro rata portion of current taxable and nontaxable income that is in fact distributable*. Sections 651 and 661 refer to this quantity as *a distributable net income* (DNI) and allow the fiduciary a deduction for amounts distributed but limit the deduction to taxable DNI. It should be emphasized that whatever amount is deductible by the fiduciary is the same amount that is taxable to the beneficiaries. This follows from the fact that the deduction merely serves to allocate taxable income from the fiduciary to the beneficiary. Distributions exceeding DNI represent accumulated income of the fiduciary that has been previously taxed, or corpus. Such amounts are neither deductible by the fiduciary nor taxable to the beneficiary.

Before further examining the computation of the deduction concept and DNI, it is important to understand that a trust or estate can make distributions of either cash or property, both of which may or may not carry out DNI (i.e., taxable and nontaxable income). However, § 663(a)(1) provides that *specific* gifts or bequests properly distributed from a fiduciary to a beneficiary under the terms of the governing instrument are distributions of principal rather than of income. Correspondingly, the fiduciary does not recognize gain or loss upon the distribution of a specific property bequest.

Example 9

During the current year, the Estate of Z recognized $30,000 of income, all of which is taxable. During the year, the executor of the estate distributed a pearl necklace to beneficiary B. The necklace had a fair market value of $6,000. If the will of decedent Z specifically provided for the distribution of the necklace to B, no estate income will be taxed to her. Alternatively, if there were no such specific bequest and B received the necklace as part of her general interest in estate assets, she will have received an income distribution.

The amount of income associated with a property distribution from a fiduciary depends upon the tax treatment of the distribution *elected* by the fiduciary. Section 643(e)(3) provides an election under which the fiduciary recognizes gain on the distribution of appreciated property as if the property had been sold at its fair market value. In this case, the amount of fiduciary income carried by the property distribution and the basis of the property in the hands of the beneficiary equals the property's fair market value. If the election is not made, the distribution of property produces no gain or loss to the fiduciary, and the amount of fiduciary income carried by the distribution is the lesser of the basis of such property in the hands of the fiduciary or the property's fair market value.[28] In the case where the election is not made, the basis of the property in the hands of the fiduciary will carry over as the basis of the property in the hands of the beneficiary.[29]

---

[27] §§ 652(b) and 662(b).

[28] § 643(e)(2).

[29] § 643(e)(1).

Example 10

During the current year, Trust T distributes property to beneficiary B. The distribution is not a specific gift of property. On the date of distribution, the property has a basis to the trust of $10,000 and a fair market value of $17,000. If the trust so elects, it will recognize a $7,000 gain on the distribution, and B will be considered to have received a $17,000 income distribution and will have a $17,000 basis in the property. If the trustee does not make the election, it will not recognize any gain upon distribution of the property. B will be considered to have received only a $10,000 income distribution and will have only a $10,000 basis in the property.

When a beneficiary is entitled to a specific gift or bequest of a sum of money (a pecuniary gift or bequest), and the fiduciary distributes property in satisfaction of such gift or bequest, any appreciation or depreciation in the property is recognized as a gain or loss to the fiduciary.[30]

Example 11

Under the terms of E's will, beneficiary M is to receive the sum of $60,000. E's executor distributes 600 shares of corporate stock to M to satisfy this pecuniary bequest. At the time of distribution, the stock has a fair market value of $100 a share and a basis to E's estate of $75 a share. Upon distribution, the estate must recognize a capital gain of $15,000 (600 shares × $25 per share appreciation). Note that because this distribution represents a specific bequest, it is not an income distribution to M and the § 643(e)(3) election is inapplicable. The basis of the stock to M will be its fair market value.

In any case in which the distribution of depreciated property by a trust or an estate to a beneficiary results in the recognition of loss, § 267 disallows any deduction of the loss by the trust.

COMPUTATION OF DISTRIBUTION DEDUCTION AND DNI

To calculate the distribution deduction available to a fiduciary and the amount of fiduciary income taxable to beneficiaries, it is first necessary to calculate the *distributable net income* (DNI) of the fiduciary. DNI represents the net income of a fiduciary available for distribution to income beneficiaries.

DNI has several important characteristics. First, it does not include taxable income that is unavailable for distribution to income beneficiaries. For example, in most states capital gains realized upon the sale of fiduciary assets are considered to represent a part of *trust principal* and are not considered *fiduciary income*. Such capital gains, while taxable, are not included in DNI. Secondly, DNI may include nontaxable income that is available for distribution to income beneficiaries.

At this point, it would appear that the amount of DNI is the same amount as fiduciary accounting income. However, there is an important difference between the two concepts. All expenses that are deductible *for tax purposes* by the fiduciary enter into the DNI calculation, even if some of these expenses are chargeable to principal and not deducted in computing fiduciary accounting income.

A beneficiary who receives a distribution from a fiduciary with both taxable and nontaxable DNI is considered to have received a proportionate share of each.[31]

---

[30] Reg. § 1.661(a)-2(f)(1).

[31] Reg. § 1.662(b)-1.

Example 12

Trust A has DNI of $80,000, $30,000 of which is nontaxable. During the year, beneficiary X receives a distribution of $16,000. This distribution consists of $10,000 of taxable DNI ($16,000 distribution × [$50,000 taxable DNI ÷ $80,000 total DNI]) and $6,000 of nontaxable DNI.

The amount of a fiduciary's *taxable* DNI represents *both* the maximum income that may be taxed to beneficiaries and the maximum deduction for distributions available to the fiduciary in computing its own taxable income.[32] Therefore, computing DNI is crucial to the correct computation of the taxable incomes of both beneficiary and fiduciary. Note that in *Example 12* Trust A is entitled to a deduction for distributions to beneficiaries of $10,000.

THE COMPUTATION OF DNI

Section 643 defines DNI as fiduciary taxable income before any deduction for distributions to beneficiaries, adjusted as follows:

LO.4

Compute both the taxable and nontaxable components of a fiduciary's distributable net income.

1. No deduction for a personal exemption is allowed.
2. No deduction against ordinary income for net capital losses is allowed.
3. Taxable income allocable to principal and not available for distribution to income beneficiaries is excluded.
4. Tax-exempt interest reduced by expenses allocable thereto is included.

Example 13

A trust that is not required to distribute all income currently has the following items of income and expense during the current year:

Tax-exempt interest	$10,000
Dividends	5,000
Rents	20,000
Long-term capital gains allocable to principal	8,000
Rent expense	6,700
Trustee fee allocable to income	3,500

The trust's taxable income before any deduction for distributions to beneficiaries is $23,700, computed as follows:

Dividends		$ 5,000
Rents		20,000
Capital gain		8,000
		$33,000
Less: Rent expense	$6,700	
Trust fee allocable to *taxable* trust income*	2,500	
Exemption	100	(9,300)
Taxable income before distribution deduction		$23,700

$$*\$3,500 \text{ fee} \times \frac{\$25,000 \text{ taxable trust income}}{\$35,000 \text{ total trust income}}$$

---

[32] §§ 651(b) and 661(c).

The trust's DNI is $24,800, computed as follows:

Trust taxable income before distribution deduction	$23,700
Add back exemption	100
	$23,800
Exclude: Nondistributable capital gain	(8,000)
Include: *Net* tax-exempt interest ($10,000 total – $1,000 allocable to trustee fee)** . . .	9,000
Distributable net income (DNI)	$24,800

$$**\$3,500 \text{ fee} \times \frac{\$10,000 \text{ tax-exempt income}}{\$35,000 \text{ total trust income}}$$

SIMPLE TRUSTS

LO.5

Describe the defining
characteristics of a simple
and a complex trust,
including:

■ The computation
of the deduction
for distributions
to beneficiaries for
both types of trusts.

■ The distinction
between tier
one and tier two
distributions from
a complex trust.

Section 651 defines a *simple trust* as one that satisfies these conditions:

1. Distributes all trust income currently.
2. Does not take a deduction for a charitable contribution for the current year.
3. Does not make any current distributions out of trust principal.

Because of the requirement that a simple trust distribute all trust income to its beneficiaries, all taxable DNI of a simple trust is taxed to the beneficiaries, based upon the relative income distributable to each.

Example 14

Trust S is required to distribute 40% of trust income to beneficiary A and 60% of trust income to B. The trust's DNI for the current year is $100,000, of which $20,000 is nontaxable. For the current year, beneficiary A must report $32,000 of trust income (40% of *taxable* DNI) and B must report $48,000 of trust income (60% of *taxable* DNI). Trust S's deduction for distributions to beneficiaries is $80,000 (i.e., taxable DNI).

In *Example 14,* the tax results would not change if the trustee had failed to make actual distributions to the beneficiaries. In the case of a simple trust, the taxability of income to beneficiaries is not dependent upon cash flow from the trust.[33]

COMPLEX TRUSTS AND ESTATES

Any trust that does not meet all three requirements of a simple trust is categorized as a *complex trust*. The categorization of a trust may vary from year to year. For example, if a trustee is required to distribute all trust income currently but also has the discretion to make distributions out of trust principal, the trust will be *simple* in any year in which principal is not distributed, but *complex* in any year in which principal is distributed.

Computing the taxable income of complex trusts and estates generally is more difficult than computing the taxable income of a simple trust. Complex trusts and estates potentially may distribute amounts of cash and property that are less than or in excess of DNI.

If distributions to beneficiaries are less than or equal to DNI, each beneficiary is required to report the amount of the distribution representing *taxable* DNI in his or her gross income. Taxable DNI remaining in the fiduciary is taxed to the fiduciary.

---

[33] § 652(a).

Example 15

In the current year, Trust C has DNI of $50,000, of which $20,000 or 40% is nontaxable. During the year, the trustee makes a $5,000 distribution to both beneficiary M and beneficiary N. M and N will each report $3,000 of income from Trust C ($5,000 distribution × [$30,000 taxable DNI ÷ $50,000 total DNI]). Trust C is allowed a $6,000 deduction for distributions to beneficiaries.[34] As a result, $24,000 of taxable DNI will be reported by (and taxed to) Trust C.

Example 16

Using the same facts as in *Example 13*, assume the trust distributes $10,000. The trust is generally entitled to a deduction for amounts distributed. However, this amount is further limited to the portion of taxable DNI contained in the distribution. In this case, the amount of the distribution deduction and the amount taxable to the beneficiaries is $6,371 computed as follows:

Distributable net income	$24,800
Net tax-exempt income ($10,000 – $1,000)	(9,000)
Taxable DNI	$15,800

$$\frac{\text{Taxable DNI}}{\text{Total DNI}} \times \text{Amount distributed} = \text{Distribution deduction}$$

$$\frac{\$15,800}{\$24,800} \times \$10,000 = \underline{\$6,371}$$

In this case, the trust did not distribute all of its DNI, $24,800, but only a portion, $10,000. Consequently, the calculation effectively treats a portion of the amount distributed as taxable (63.71% or $6,371) and a portion as nontaxable (36.29% or $3,629). Taxable income of the trust would be $17,329 as computed below.

Taxable income before distribution deduction	$23,700
Deduction for distributions	(6,371)
Trust taxable income	$17,329

When distributions to beneficiaries exceed DNI, the entire taxable portion of DNI will be reported as income by the beneficiaries. Amounts distributed in excess of DNI are nontaxable, representing either accumulated income that has been previously taxed or corpus.

Allocation of DNI

In those cases when distributions exceed DNI and there are multiple beneficiaries, DNI must be allocated among the beneficiaries. In determining the amount of DNI allocated to each beneficiary (and, therefore, the amount of taxable income and nontaxable income that is allocable to each), the distribution rules acknowledge that some beneficiaries' rights to income may be superior to those of others. For example, the trust agreement may provide that distributions of income must be made to certain beneficiaries each year while other beneficiaries receive distributions solely at the discretion of the trustee. In recognition of this possibility, the Code establishes a so-called tier system to allocate DNI.[35]

---

[34] § 661(c).   [35] §§ 662(a)(1) and (2).

Under the tier system, DNI (increased for charitable contributions) is first allocated proportionately to the distributions that are *required* to be made. These mandatory distributions are commonly referred to as *first-tier* or *tier-one* distributions. After allocating DNI to first-tier distributions, *any* DNI remaining (as reduced by first-tier distributions and charitable contributions) is allocated proportionately to *second tier* or *tier-two* distributions (i.e., discretionary distributions).

Example 17

This year Trust T reported taxable DNI of $60,000. During the year, the trust made required distributions of $40,000 to beneficiary R. In addition, the trustee made discretionary distributions of $40,000 to R and $20,000 to S. DNI would be allocated as follows:

	Total	R	S
Required distributions	$ 40,000	$40,000	0
Discretionary distributions	60,000	40,000	$20,000
Total distributions received	$100,000	$80,000	$20,000

	Total	R	S
DNI before contributions	$ 60,000		
First-tier distributions	(40,000)	$40,000	0
DNI available for charity	20,000		
Charitable distributions	(0)		
DNI for second tier	$ 20,000		
Second-tier distributions	(20,000)	13,333*	$ 6,667*
DNI received		$53,333	$ 6,667

$$*\text{DNI for second tier} \times \frac{\text{Beneficiary's second-tier distribution}}{\text{Total second-tier distribution}}$$

$20,000 × $40,000/$60,000 = $13,333 to R
$20,000 × $20,000/$60,000 = $6,667 to S

Observe that the first $40,000 of DNI must be allocated to R because this distribution was mandatory thus making it a first-tier distribution. The remaining $20,000 of DNI is allocated proportionally to the discretionary or second-tier distributions received by R and S. Note that all of the trust's DNI is allocated and taxed to the beneficiaries and none is taxed to the trust. In this case, R received $80,000 from the trust of which $53,333 is taxable while S received $20,000 of which $6,667 is taxable. The balance of each distribution represents either accumulated income or corpus. Although the trust distributed $100,000, its deduction for distributions is limited to its taxable DNI for the year, $60,000.

In determining the treatment of a beneficiary's distributions, the treatment of charitable contributions can be a bit confusing. On the one hand, a contribution is treated as an expense that reduces the trust's taxable income (i.e., it is reported on Line 13 of Form 1041 and not on a Schedule K-1). On the other hand, the charity itself is treated like a beneficiary in the sense that it absorbs taxable and nontaxable DNI just like any other beneficiary. It should be emphasized that the charity is not considered a beneficiary when computing the deduction for distributions to beneficiaries. Instead, the distribution is accounted for as an expense.[36]

Example 18

This year the F Trust reported $80,000 of dividend income. Pursuant to the trust instrument the trustee distributed $90,000 as follows: (1) a required distribution to beneficiary J of $50,000; (2) a charitable contribution of $30,000; and (3) a discretionary distribution to K of $10,000. Taxable DNI would be $50,000 ($80,000 − $30,000) all of which would be allocated to J as computed below.

DNI before contributions ($50,000 + $ 30,000)	$80,000
First-tier distribution to J	(50,000)
DNI available for charity	$30,000
Charitable distribution	(30,000)
DNI for second tier	$ 0

Note that J would report $50,000 of DNI, all of which would be taxable. In contrast, K receives no taxable DNI since there is none available after taking into account the charitable contribution. Although the trust distributed $60,000 to J and K, its distribution deduction is limited to taxable DNI of $50,000. Trust taxable income would be $0 as calculated below.

Dividends	$80,000
Contribution	(30,000)
Distribution deduction (limited to taxable DNI)	(50,000)
Trust taxable income	$ 0

CHARACTER OF BENEFICIARY'S INCOME

Not only must a beneficiary determine the amount of taxable income received from a trust or estate, but he or she must determine its character as well. As stated at the outset, estates and trusts generally serve as conduits to the extent they make distributions. Consequently, each distribution is deemed to contain a pro rata portion of each type of distributable income received by the trust or estate. For example, if a portion of a trust's income consisted of dividends, a portion of the distribution received by the beneficiary is considered dividend income.

To determine the composition of a distribution, the gross amount of each item of distributable income must be reduced by any deduction directly related to that item of income. Any other expenses may be allocated against whatever class of distributable income the fiduciary selects. However, charitable contributions are treated as consisting of a proportionate share of each type of distributable income.

LO.6
Determine the tax consequences of fiduciary distributions to the recipient beneficiaries.

---

[36] § 662(a)(2). For purposes of determining DNI available for first-tier distribution only, no charitable contribution deduction is allowed.

Example 19

This year the records of the T Trust revealed the following information, resulting in DNI of $60,000:

	Income and Expenses	DNI
Rental income	$70,000	$ 70,000
Dividends	30,000	30,000
Long-term capital gain	50,000	
Charitable contribution	10,000	(10,000)
Rent expense	23,000	(23,000)
Trustee commission allocable between income and corpus	7,000	(7,000)
DNI		$ 60,000

During the year, the trust distributed $6,000 to its only beneficiary, X. The character of the distribution is determined below.

Elements of DNI	Rents	Dividends	Total
Income	$70,000	$30,000	$100,000
Expenses:			
Rental expenses	(23,000)		(23,000)
Trustee fees		(7,000)	(7,000)
Contribution	(7,000)*	(3,000)*	(10,000)
Total DNI	$40,000	$20,000	$ 60,000
Percentage of DNI	67%	33%	100%

* $10,000 × $70,000/$100,000 = $7,000
$10,000 × $30,000/$100,000 = $3,000

Since X received 10% of the DNI ($6,000/$60,000) she is deemed to receive 10% of each item of DNI. Thus she will report rental income of $4,000 (10% × $40,000) and dividend income of $2,000 (10% × $20,000). In other words, of the $6,000 of DNI received, $4,000 or 67% is rents while $2,000 or 33% is dividends. Note how the expenses were allocated in determining the composition of DNI. The rental expenses are charged against the rental income since they are directly related. In contrast, the charitable contribution is charged proportionately against each type of distributable income. On the other hand, the trustee fees may be allocated however the trustee wishes. In this case, he elects to charge the trustee fees against the dividend income. In light of the 15% tax rate that applies to dividends, the trustee should consider allocating the fees to the rental income.

A special problem arises when the trust receives qualified dividends that are taxed at a maximum rate of 15% (5% if in the 15% tax bracket). A calculation must be made to determine the amount of qualified dividends *retained* by the trust to be taxed at the favorable rate. The amount deemed to be retained by the trust is equal to the proportion of distributable net income (DNI) retained by the trust.

Example 20

Same facts as in *Example 19*. The total DNI was $60,000 and the trust distributed 10% of the DNI ($6,000/$60,000) to the beneficiary and retained 90% ($54,000/$60,000). Thus the qualified dividends retained by the trust are $27,000 (90% × $30,000). Alternatively, the amount could be computed by using the amount of DNI allocated to the beneficiary as follows:

Qualified dividends	$30,000	$30,000
Allocation to beneficiary		
$\dfrac{\text{DNI distributed to beneficiary } \$6,000}{\text{Total DNI } \$60,000}$	× 10%	(3,000)
Allocation to trust		$27,000

Note that this method of allocating the amount of qualified dividends between the beneficiary and the trust is used solely for calculating the tax liability of the trust. The actual amount of qualified dividends to be reported on the Schedule K-1 which the beneficiary must report is not $3,000 but is $2,000 (10% × $20,000) as shown above.

REPORTING REQUIREMENTS FOR BENEFICIARIES

A beneficiary who receives a distribution from a fiduciary will receive a summary of the tax consequences of the distribution in the form of a Schedule K-1 from the executor or trustee. The K-1 will tell the beneficiary the amounts and character of the various items of income that constitute the taxable portion of the distribution.

A beneficiary also may be entitled to depreciation or depletion deductions and various tax credits because of distributions of fiduciary income. Such items are also reflected on the Schedule K-1.

If the taxable year of a beneficiary is different from that of the fiduciary, the amount of fiduciary income taxable to the beneficiary is included in the beneficiary's tax year within which the fiduciary's year ends.[37]

Example 21

Estate E is on a fiscal year ending January 31. During its fiscal year ending January 31, 2016, but prior to December 31, 2015, the estate made cash distributions to beneficiary Z, a calendar year taxpayer. Because of these distributions, Z must report income of $8,000. However, this income will be reported on Z's 2016 individual tax return.

THE SEPARATE SHARE RULE

In certain circumstances, the rules governing the taxation of beneficiaries of a complex trust can lead to an inequitable result. Assume a grantor created a single trust with two beneficiaries, A and B. The grantor intended that each beneficiary have an equal interest in trust income and principal. The trustee has considerable discretion as to the timing of distributions of income and principal. Consider a year in which beneficiary A was in exceptional need of funds and, as a result, the trustee distributed $15,000 to A as A's half of trust income for the

---

[37] §§ 652(c) and 662(c).

year *plus* $10,000 out of A's half of trust principal. Because B had no need of current funds, the trustee distributed neither income nor principal to B.

If the trust's DNI was $30,000 for the year, the normal rules of Subchapter J would dictate that A would have to report and pay tax on $25,000 of trust income. However, the clear intent of the grantor is that A only be responsible for half of trust income and no more. To reflect such intent, § 663(c) provides the following rule: if a single trust contains substantially separate and independent shares for different beneficiaries, the trust shall be treated as separate trusts for purposes of determining DNI. Therefore, using this separate share rule, beneficiary A's *separate trust* would have DNI of only $15,000, the maximum amount taxable to A in the year of distribution. This rule is inapplicable to estates.

A COMPREHENSIVE EXAMPLE

The AB Trust is a calendar year taxpayer. In the current year, the trust books show the following:

Gross rental income	$25,000
Taxable interest income	10,000
Tax-exempt interest income	15,000
Long-term capital gain	8,000
Trustee fee	6,000
Rent expenses	3,000
Contribution to charity	1,500
Distributions to:	
Beneficiary A	20,000
Beneficiary B	20,000

Under the terms of the trust instrument the capital gain and one-third of the trustee fee are allocable to principal. The trustee is required to maintain a reserve for depreciation on the rental property equal to one-tenth of annual gross rental income. (For tax purposes, assume actual tax depreciation is $1,300.) The trustee is required to make an annual distribution to beneficiary A of $12,000 and has the discretion to make additional distributions to A or beneficiary B.

Based on these facts, the computation of the income taxable to the trust and the beneficiaries is as follows. Note that this example ignores the net investment income tax.

Step One: Compute fiduciary accounting income.

Gross rental income	$25,000
Taxable interest income	10,000
Tax-exempt interest income	15,000
	$50,000
Trustee fee charged against income	(4,000)
Rent expenses	(3,000)
Depreciation (1/10 × $25,000)	(2,500)
Fiduciary accounting income	$40,500

Step Two: Compute fiduciary taxable income before the § 661 deduction for distributions to beneficiaries.

Gross rental income	$25,000
Taxable interest income	10,000
Long-term capital gain	8,000
	$43,000
Deductible trustee fee	(4,200)*
Deductible rent expense	(3,000)
Deductible depreciation allocable to fiduciary	(1,300)
Deductible charitable contribution	(1,050)*
Exemption	(100)
Taxable income before § 661 deduction	$33,350

* $35,000 ÷ $50,000 of gross fiduciary accounting income is taxable; thus, only 70% of both the $6,000 trustee fee and $1,500 charitable contribution is deductible.

Step Three: Compute DNI and the § 661 deduction for distributions to beneficiaries.

Taxable income from Step Two	$33,350
Add back:	
Exemption	100
Net tax-exempt income	12,750*
Subtract:	
Capital gain allocable to principal	(8,000)
Distributable net income (DNI)	$38,200

*$15,000 tax-exempt interest less 30% of the $6,000 trustee fee and $1,500 charitable contribution.

Step Four: Subtract the § 661 deduction for distributions to beneficiaries.

Taxable income before deduction	$33,350
Section 661 deduction for distributions	(25,450)*
Trust taxable income	$ 7,900

* Because distributions to beneficiaries exceeded DNI, the trust will deduct the entire amount of taxable DNI. $25,450 ($38,200 − $12,750).

Tax Consequences to Beneficiaries

The $40,000 cash distribution to beneficiaries exceeds the total DNI of $38,200; thus, the entire amount of DNI must be allocated to the beneficiaries.

	Total	A	B
DNI	$38,200		
Add-back charitable contribution	1,500		
DNI before charitable contribution	$39,700		
First-tier distributions	(12,000)	$12,000	—
DNI available for charity	$27,700		
Charitable distributions	(1,500)		
DNI for second tier	$26,200		
Second-tier distributions	(26,200)	7,483*	$18,717**
DNI received	(26,200)	$19,483	$18,717
Percentage of DNI received		51%	49%

$$*\text{DNI for second tier} \times \frac{\text{Beneficiary's second-tier distribution}}{\text{Total second-tier distribution}}$$

* $26,200 × $8,000/$28,000 = $7,483 to A
** $26,200 × $20,000/$28,000 = $18,717 to B

The composition of DNI is as follows:

	Rent	Taxable Interest	Tax-Exempt Interest	Total
Gross receipts	$25,000	$10,000	$15,000	$50,000
Rent expense	(3,000)			(3,000)
Depreciation	(1,300)			(1,300)
Trustee fee*		(4,200)	(1,800)	(6,000)
Charitable contribution**	(750)	(300)	(450)	(1,500)
Total	$19,950	$ 5,500	$12,750	$38,200

 * The trustee fee allocable to taxable income may be arbitrarily allocated to **any** item of taxable income. Reg. 1.652(b)-3(b).

 ** In the absence of a specific provision in the trust instrument, the charitable contribution is allocated proportionally to each class of income. Reg. § 1.642(c)-3(b)(2).

Each beneficiary should report the following:

	Rent	Taxable Interest	Tax-Exempt Interest	Total DNI Allocated
Beneficiary A (51%)	$10,175*	$2,805	$ 6,503	$19,483
Beneficiary B (49%)	9,775	2,695	6,247	18,717
Total	$19,950	$5,500	$12,750	$38,200

 * Beneficiary A's proportionate share of DNI 51% multiplied by $19,950 total rent income included in DNI equals beneficiary A's share of rent income. This same procedure is used to determine each beneficiary's share of all other items.

A completed Form 1041 for the AB Trust and Schedule K-1 for Beneficiary A are shown on the following pages.

THE SIXTY-FIVE DAY RULE

Fiduciaries may want to avoid accumulating income since such income may be taxed at very high rates. Because DNI is often not calculated until after the close of the trust's taxable year, the amount of current distributions necessary to avoid accumulation may be unknown. To alleviate this timing problem, § 663(b) provides that a trust or an estate *may elect* that any distribution made within the first 65 days of a taxable year will be considered paid to the beneficiary on the last day of the preceding taxable year.[38] This rule allows a trustee to make distributions after the close of a year to eliminate any accumulations of DNI for that year.

---

[38] See Reg. § 1.663(b)-2 for the manner and time for making such an election.

Form 1041	Department of the Treasury—Internal Revenue Service **U.S. Income Tax Return for Estates and Trusts**	**2015**	OMB No. 1545-0092

▶ Information about Form 1041 and its separate instructions is at *www.irs.gov/form1041.*

A Check all that apply:

☐ Decedent's estate
☐ Simple trust
☐ Complex trust
☐ Qualified disability trust
☐ ESBT (S portion only)
☐ Grantor type trust
☐ Bankruptcy estate-Ch. 7
☐ Bankruptcy estate-Ch. 11
☐ Pooled income fund

For calendar year 2015 or fiscal year beginning _____ , 2015, and ending _____ , 20 ___

Name of estate or trust (If a grantor type trust, see the instructions.)
AB Trust

Name and title of fiduciary

Number, street, and room or suite no. (If a P.O. box, see the instructions.)

City or town, state or province, country, and ZIP or foreign postal code

C Employer identification number

D Date entity created

E Nonexempt charitable and split-interest trusts, check applicable box(es), see instructions.
☐ Described in sec. 4947(a)(1). Check here
if not a private foundation . . . . ▶ ☐
☐ Described in sec. 4947(a)(2)

B Number of Schedules K-1 attached (see instructions) ▶

F Check applicable boxes:
☐ Initial return ☐ Final return ☐ Amended return
☐ Change in trust's name ☐ Change in fiduciary ☐ Change in fiduciary's name

☐ Net operating loss carryback
☐ Change in fiduciary's address

G Check here if the estate or filing trust made a section 645 election . . . . . . ▶ ☐ Trust TIN ▶ _____

Income

1	Interest income	1	10,000 00
2a	Total ordinary dividends	2a	
b	Qualified dividends allocable to: **(1)** Beneficiaries _____ **(2)** Estate or trust _____		
3	Business income or (loss). Attach Schedule C or C-EZ (Form 1040)	3	
4	Capital gain or (loss). Attach Schedule D (Form 1041)	4	8,000 00
5	Rents, royalties, partnerships, other estates and trusts, etc. Attach Schedule E (Form 1040) .	5	20,700 00
6	Farm income or (loss). Attach Schedule F (Form 1040)	6	
7	Ordinary gain or (loss). Attach Form 4797	7	
8	Other income. List type and amount _____	8	
9	**Total income.** Combine lines 1, 2a, and 3 through 8 . . . . ▶	9	38,700 00

Deductions

10	Interest. Check if Form 4952 is attached ▶ ☐	10	
11	Taxes	11	
12	Fiduciary fees	12	4,200 00
13	Charitable deduction (from Schedule A, line 7)	13	1,050 00
14	Attorney, accountant, and return preparer fees	14	
15a	Other deductions **not** subject to the 2% floor (attach schedule)	15a	
b	Net operating loss deduction (see instructions)	15b	
c	Allowable miscellaneous itemized deductions subject to the 2% floor	15c	
16	Add lines 10 through 15c . . . . ▶	16	5,250 00
17	Adjusted total income or (loss). Subtract line 16 from line 9 . . .	**17**	33,450 00
18	Income distribution deduction (from Schedule B, line 15). Attach Schedules K-1 (Form 1041)	18	25,450 00
19	Estate tax deduction including certain generation-skipping taxes (attach computation) . . .	19	
20	Exemption	20	100 00
21	Add lines 18 through 20 . . . . ▶	21	25,550 00

Tax and Payments

22	Taxable income. Subtract line 21 from line 17. If a loss, see instructions	22	7,900 00
23	**Total tax** (from Schedule G, line 7)	23	810 00
24	**Payments: a** 2015 estimated tax payments and amount applied from 2014 return	24a	
b	Estimated tax payments allocated to beneficiaries (from Form 1041-T)	24b	
c	Subtract line 24b from line 24a	24c	
d	Tax paid with Form 7004 (see instructions)	24d	
e	Federal income tax withheld. If any is from Form(s) 1099, check ▶ ☐	24e	
	Other payments: **f** Form 2439 _____ ; **g** Form 4136 _____ ; Total ▶	24h	
25	**Total payments.** Add lines 24c through 24e, and 24h . . . . ▶	25	
26	Estimated tax penalty (see instructions)	26	
27	**Tax due.** If line 25 is smaller than the total of lines 23 and 26, enter amount owed	27	810 00
28	**Overpayment.** If line 25 is larger than the total of lines 23 and 26, enter amount overpaid . .	28	
29	Amount of line 28 to be: **a** Credited to 2016 estimated tax ▶ _____ ; **b** Refunded ▶	29	

Sign Here

Under penalties of perjury, I declare that I have examined this return, including accompanying schedules and statements, and to the best of my knowledge and belief, it is true, correct, and complete. Declaration of preparer (other than taxpayer) is based on all information of which preparer has any knowledge.

▶ _____   _____   _____
Signature of fiduciary or officer representing fiduciary   Date   EIN of fiduciary if a financial institution

May the IRS discuss this return with the preparer shown below (see instr.)? ☐ Yes ☐ No

Paid Preparer Use Only

Print/Type preparer's name	Preparer's signature	Date	Check ☐ if self-employed	PTIN

Firm's name ▶   Firm's EIN ▶
Firm's address ▶   Phone no.

For Paperwork Reduction Act Notice, see the separate instructions.   Cat. No. 11370H   Form **1041** (2015)

Form 1041 (2015)

Page **2**

Schedule A	Charitable Deduction. Do not complete for a simple trust or a pooled income fund.			
1	Amounts paid or permanently set aside for charitable purposes from gross income (see instructions) .	1	1,500	00
2	Tax-exempt income allocable to charitable contributions (see instructions)	2	450	00
3	Subtract line 2 from line 1	3	1,050	00
4	Capital gains for the tax year allocated to corpus and paid or permanently set aside for charitable purposes	4		
5	Add lines 3 and 4	5	1,050	00
6	Section 1202 exclusion allocable to capital gains paid or permanently set aside for charitable purposes (see instructions) .	6		
7	**Charitable deduction.** Subtract line 6 from line 5. Enter here and on page 1, line 13	7	1,050	00

Schedule B	Income Distribution Deduction				
1	Adjusted total income (see instructions)		1	33,450	00
2	Adjusted tax-exempt interest		2	12,750	00
3	Total net gain from Schedule D (Form 1041), line 19, column (1) (see instructions)		3		
4	Enter amount from Schedule A, line 4 (minus any allocable section 1202 exclusion)		4		
5	Capital gains for the tax year included on Schedule A, line 1 (see instructions)		5		
6	Enter any gain from page 1, line 4, as a negative number. If page 1, line 4, is a loss, enter the loss as a positive number .		6	<8,000	00>
7	**Distributable net income.** Combine lines 1 through 6. If zero or less, enter -0-		7	38,200	00
8	If a complex trust, enter accounting income for the tax year as determined under the governing instrument and applicable local law .	8	40,500	00	
9	Income required to be distributed currently		9	12,000	00
10	Other amounts paid, credited, or otherwise required to be distributed		10	28,000	00
11	Total distributions. Add lines 9 and 10. If greater than line 8, see instructions		11	40,000	00
12	Enter the amount of tax-exempt income included on line 11		12	12,750	00
13	Tentative income distribution deduction. Subtract line 12 from line 11		13	27,250	00
14	Tentative income distribution deduction. Subtract line 2 from line 7. If zero or less, enter -0- .		14	25,450	00
15	**Income distribution deduction.** Enter the smaller of line 13 or line 14 here and on page 1, line 18		15	25,450	00

Schedule G	Tax Computation (see instructions)					
1 Tax: a	Tax on taxable income (see instructions)	1a	810	00		
b	Tax on lump-sum distributions. Attach Form 4972	1b				
c	Alternative minimum tax (from Schedule I (Form 1041), line 56)	1c				
d	**Total.** Add lines 1a through 1c . . . . ▶				1d	810	00
2a	Foreign tax credit. Attach Form 1116	2a				
b	General business credit. Attach Form 3800	2b				
c	Credit for prior year minimum tax. Attach Form 8801 . . .	2c				
d	Bond credits. Attach Form 8912	2d				
e	**Total credits.** Add lines 2a through 2d . . . . ▶				2e	0	00
3	Subtract line 2e from line 1d. If zero or less, enter -0-			3	810	00
4	Net investment income tax from Form 8960, line 21			4		
5	Recapture taxes. Check if from: ☐ Form 4255 ☐ Form 8611			5		
6	Household employment taxes. Attach Schedule H (Form 1040)			6		
7	**Total tax.** Add lines 3 through 6. Enter here and on page 1, line 23 . . . . . . ▶			7	810	00

	Other Information	Yes	No
1	Did the estate or trust receive tax-exempt income? If "Yes," attach a computation of the allocation of expenses. Enter the amount of tax-exempt interest income and exempt-interest dividends ▶ $ 15,000	X	
2	Did the estate or trust receive all or any part of the earnings (salary, wages, and other compensation) of any individual by reason of a contract assignment or similar arrangement?		X
3	At any time during calendar year 2015, did the estate or trust have an interest in or a signature or other authority over a bank, securities, or other financial account in a foreign country?		X
	See the instructions for exceptions and filing requirements for FinCEN Form 114. If "Yes," enter the name of the foreign country ▶		
4	During the tax year, did the estate or trust receive a distribution from, or was it the grantor of, or transferor to, a foreign trust? If "Yes," the estate or trust may have to file Form 3520. See instructions		X
5	Did the estate or trust receive, or pay, any qualified residence interest on seller-provided financing? If "Yes," see the instructions for required attachment		X
6	If this is an estate or a complex trust making the section 663(b) election, check here (see instructions) . . ▶ ☐		
7	To make a section 643(e)(3) election, attach Schedule D (Form 1041), and check here (see instructions) . . ▶ ☐		
8	If the decedent's estate has been open for more than 2 years, attach an explanation for the delay in closing the estate, and check here ▶ ☐		
9	Are any present or future trust beneficiaries skip persons? See instructions		X

Form **1041** (2015)

| SCHEDULE D
(Form 1041)

Department of the Treasury
Internal Revenue Service | **Capital Gains and Losses**
▶ Attach to Form 1041, Form 5227, or Form 990-T.
▶ Use Form 8949 to list your transactions for lines 1b, 2, 3, 8b, 9 and 10.
▶ Information about Schedule D and its separate instructions is at *www.irs.gov/form1041*. | OMB No. 1545-0092
2015 |

Name of estate or trust AB Trust	Employer identification number

Note: *Form 5227 filers need to complete **only** Parts I and II.*

Part I — Short-Term Capital Gains and Losses—Assets Held One Year or Less

See instructions for how to figure the amounts to enter on the lines below. This form may be easier to complete if you round off cents to whole dollars.	(d) Proceeds (sales price)	(e) Cost (or other basis)	(g) Adjustments to gain or loss from Form(s) 8949, Part I, line 2, column (g)	(h) Gain or (loss) Subtract column (e) from column (d) and combine the result with column (g)
1a Totals for all short-term transactions reported on Form 1099-B for which basis was reported to the IRS and for which you have no adjustments (see instructions). However, if you choose to report all these transactions on Form 8949, leave this line blank and go to line 1b .				
1b Totals for all transactions reported on Form(s) 8949 with **Box A** checked				
2 Totals for all transactions reported on Form(s) 8949 with **Box B** checked				
3 Totals for all transactions reported on Form(s) 8949 with **Box C** checked				

4 Short-term capital gain or (loss) from Forms 4684, 6252, 6781, and 8824	**4**	
5 Net short-term gain or (loss) from partnerships, S corporations, and other estates or trusts . . .	**5**	
6 Short-term capital loss carryover. Enter the amount, if any, from line 9 of the 2014 Capital Loss Carryover Worksheet	**6** (	)
7 **Net short-term capital gain or (loss).** Combine lines 1a through 6 in column (h). Enter here and on line 17, column (3) on the back . . . . ▶	**7**	

Part II — Long-Term Capital Gains and Losses—Assets Held More Than One Year

See instructions for how to figure the amounts to enter on the lines below. This form may be easier to complete if you round off cents to whole dollars.	(d) Proceeds (sales price)	(e) Cost (or other basis)	(g) Adjustments to gain or loss from Form(s) 8949, Part II, line 2, column (g)	(h) Gain or (loss) Subtract column (e) from column (d) and combine the result with column (g)
8a Totals for all long-term transactions reported on Form 1099-B for which basis was reported to the IRS and for which you have no adjustments (see instructions). However, if you choose to report all these transactions on Form 8949, leave this line blank and go to line 8b .				8,000
8b Totals for all transactions reported on Form(s) 8949 with **Box D** checked				
9 Totals for all transactions reported on Form(s) 8949 with **Box E** checked				
10 Totals for all transactions reported on Form(s) 8949 with **Box F** checked.				

11 Long-term capital gain or (loss) from Forms 2439, 4684, 6252, 6781, and 8824	**11**	
12 Net long-term gain or (loss) from partnerships, S corporations, and other estates or trusts . . .	**12**	
13 Capital gain distributions	**13**	
14 Gain from Form 4797, Part I	**14**	
15 Long-term capital loss carryover. Enter the amount, if any, from line 14 of the 2014 Capital Loss Carryover Worksheet	**15** (	)
16 **Net long-term capital gain or (loss).** Combine lines 8a through 15 in column (h). Enter here and on line 18a, column (3) on the back . . . . ▶	**16**	8,000

For Paperwork Reduction Act Notice, see the Instructions for Form 1041.   Cat. No. 11376V   Schedule D (Form 1041) 2015

Schedule D (Form 1041) 2015   Page **2**

Part III — Summary of Parts I and II

Caution: *Read the instructions before completing this part.*

			(1) Beneficiaries' (see instr.)	(2) Estate's or trust's	(3) Total
17	Net short-term gain or (loss)	17			
18	Net long-term gain or (loss):				
a	Total for year	18a		8,000 00	8,000 00
b	Unrecaptured section 1250 gain (see line 18 of the wrksht.)	18b			
c	28% rate gain	18c			
19	Total net gain or (loss). Combine lines 17 and 18a ►	19		8,000 00	8,000 00

Note: *If line 19, column (3), is a net gain, enter the gain on Form 1041, line 4 (or Form 990-T, Part I, line 4a). If lines 18a and 19, column (2), are net gains, go to Part V, and **do not** complete Part IV. If line 19, column (3), is a net loss, complete Part IV and the **Capital Loss Carryover Worksheet,** as necessary.*

Part IV — Capital Loss Limitation

20	Enter here and enter as a (loss) on Form 1041, line 4 (or Form 990-T, Part I, line 4c, if a trust), the **smaller** of:		
a	The loss on line 19, column (3) **or b** $3,000	20	( )

Note: *If the loss on line 19, column (3), is more than $3,000, **or** if Form 1041, page 1, line 22 (or Form 990-T, line 34), is a loss, complete the **Capital Loss Carryover Worksheet** in the instructions to figure your capital loss carryover.*

Part V — Tax Computation Using Maximum Capital Gains Rates

Form 1041 filers. Complete this part **only** if both lines 18a and 19 in column (2) are gains, or an amount is entered in Part I or Part II and there is an entry on Form 1041, line 2b(2), **and** Form 1041, line 22, is more than zero.

Caution: *Skip this part and complete the **Schedule D Tax Worksheet** in the instructions if:*

- *Either line 18b, col. (2) or line 18c, col. (2) is more than zero, or*
- *Both Form 1041, line 2b(1), and Form 4952, line 4g are more than zero.*

Form 990-T trusts. Complete this part **only** if both lines 18a and 19 are gains, or qualified dividends are included in income in Part I of Form 990-T, and Form 990-T, line 34, is more than zero. Skip this part and complete the **Schedule D Tax Worksheet** in the instructions if either line 18b, col. (2) or line 18c, col. (2) is more than zero.

21	Enter taxable income from Form 1041, line 22 (or Form 990-T, line 34)	21	7,900 00	
22	Enter the **smaller** of line 18a or 19 in column (2) but not less than zero . . LTCG	22	8,000 00	
23	Enter the estate's or trust's qualified dividends from Form 1041, line 2b(2) (or enter the qualified dividends included in income in Part I of Form 990-T)	23		
24	Add lines 22 and 23 . . LTCG	24	8,000 00	
25	If the estate or trust is filing Form 4952, enter the amount from line 4g; otherwise, enter -0- ►	25	0 00	
26	Subtract line 25 from line 24. If zero or less, enter -0- . . LTCG . .	26	8,000 00	
27	Subtract line 26 from line 21. If zero or less, enter -0-	27	0 00	
28	Enter the **smaller** of the amount on line 21 or $2,500	28	2,500 00	
29	Enter the **smaller** of the amount on line 27 or line 28	29	0 00	
30	Subtract line 29 from line 28. If zero or less, enter -0-. This amount is taxed at 0% ►	30		2,500 00
31	Enter the **smaller** of line 21 or line 26	31	7,900 00	
32	Subtract line 30 from line 26	32	5,500 00	
33	Enter the **smaller** of line 21 or $12,300	33	7,900 00	
34	Add lines 27 and 30	34	2,500 00	
35	Subtract line 34 from line 33. If zero or less, enter -0-	35	5,400 00	
36	Enter the **smaller** of line 32 or line 35	36	5,400 00	
37	Multiply line 36 by 15% ►	37		810 00
38	Enter the amount from line 31	38	7,900 00	
39	Add lines 30 and 36	39	7,900 00	
40	Subtract line 39 from line 38. If zero or less, enter -0-	40	0 00	
41	Multiply line 40 by 20% ►	41		0 00
42	Figure the tax on the amount on line 27. Use the 2015 Tax Rate Schedule for Estates and Trusts (see the Schedule G instructions in the instructions for Form 1041)	42	0 00	
43	Add lines 37, 41, and 42	43	810 00	
44	Figure the tax on the amount on line 21. Use the 2015 Tax Rate Schedule for Estates and Trusts (see the Schedule G instructions in the instructions for Form 1041)	44	1,746 00*	
45	**Tax on all taxable income.** Enter the **smaller** of line 43 or line 44 here and on Form 1041, Schedule G, line 1a (or Form 990-T, line 36) ►	45		810 00

Schedule D (Form 1041) 2015

* Using 2015 rates: $1,746($1,200 + [$7,900 − $5,950 = $1,950 × 28% = $546])

661113

☐ Final K-1	☐ Amended K-1

OMB No. 1545-0092

Schedule K-1
(Form 1041)

Department of the Treasury
Internal Revenue Service

2015

For calendar year 2015,
or tax year beginning _____, 2015,
and ending _____, 20 _____

Beneficiary's Share of Income, Deductions, Credits, etc.

► See back of form and instructions.

Part I	Information About the Estate or Trust

A Estate's or trust's employer identification number

AB Trust

B Estate's or trust's name

C Fiduciary's name, address, city, state, and ZIP code

AB Trust

D ☐ Check if Form 1041-T was filed and enter the date it was filed
_____

E ☐ Check if this is the final Form 1041 for the estate or trust

Part II	Information About the Beneficiary

F Beneficiary's identifying number

G Beneficiary's name, address, city, state, and ZIP code

Beneficiary A

H ☐ Domestic beneficiary   ☐ Foreign beneficiary

Part III	Beneficiary's Share of Current Year Income, Deductions, Credits, and Other Items

1	Interest income 2,805	**11**	Final year deductions
2a	Ordinary dividends		
2b	Qualified dividends		
3	Net short-term capital gain		
4a	Net long-term capital gain		
4b	28% rate gain	**12**	Alternative minimum tax adjustment
4c	Unrecaptured section 1250 gain		
5	Other portfolio and nonbusiness income		
6	Ordinary business income		
7	Net rental real estate income 10,175	**13**	Credits and credit recapture
8	Other rental income		
9	Directly apportioned deductions		
		14	Other information 6,503
10	Estate tax deduction		

*See attached statement for additional information.

Note. A statement must be attached showing the beneficiary's share of income and directly apportioned deductions from each business, rental real estate, and other rental activity.

For IRS Use Only

For Paperwork Reduction Act Notice, see the Instructions for Form 1041.   IRS.gov/form1041   Cat. No. 11380D   **Schedule K-1 (Form 1041) 2015**

Tax Planning Considerations

The tax planning considerations for the use of trusts are discussed in Chapter 17, *Family Tax Planning*.

Problem Materials

DISCUSSION QUESTIONS

16-1　*Trusts and Estates as Conduits.* What does it mean to describe a fiduciary as *a conduit* of income? To what extent does a fiduciary operate as a conduit?

16-2　*Purpose of Trusts.* Trusts are usually created for nonbusiness purposes. Give some examples of situations in which a trust could be useful.

16-3　*Trust as a Separate Legal Entity.* A trust cannot exist if the only trustee is also sole beneficiary. Why not?

16-4　*Trust Expenses Allocable to Principal.* For what reason might the grantor of a trust stipulate that some amount of trust expenses be paid out of trust principal rather than trust income?

16-5　*Use of Fiduciaries to Defer Income Taxation.* Although a trust must adopt a calendar year for tax purposes, an estate may adopt any fiscal year, as well as a calendar year, for reporting taxable income. Why is Congress willing to allow an estate more flexibility in the choice of taxable year?

16-6　*Trust Accounting Income versus Taxable Income.* Even though a trustee may be required to distribute all trust income currently, the trust may still have to report taxable income. Explain.

16-7　*Deductibility of Administrative Expenses.* Explain any options available to the executor of an estate with regard to the deductibility of administrative expenses incurred by the estate.

16-8　*Capital Loss Deductions.* To what extent may a fiduciary deduct any excess of capital losses over capital gains for a taxable year?

16-9　*Operating Losses of a Fiduciary.* How does the tax treatment of operating losses incurred by a fiduciary differ from the treatment of such losses by a partnership or an S corporation?

16-10　*Purpose of DNI.* Discuss the function of DNI from the point of view of the fiduciary and the point of view of beneficiaries who receive distributions from the fiduciary.

16-11　*Taxable versus Nontaxable DNI.* Why is it important to correctly identify any nontaxable component of DNI?

16-12　*Charitable Deductions.* Enumerate the differences in the charitable deduction allowable to a fiduciary and the charitable deduction allowable to an individual.

16-13　*Timing Distributions from an Estate.* Why might a beneficiary of an estate prefer *not* to receive an early distribution of property from the estate?

16-14　*Simple versus Complex Trusts.* All trusts are complex in the year of termination. Why?

16-15　*Trust Reserves for Depreciation.* Discuss the reason why a grantor of a trust would require the trustee to maintain a certain reserve for depreciation of trust assets.

16-16　*Distributions Exceeding DNI.* How are distributions in excess of distributable net income treated?

16-17　*Sixty-Five Day Rule.* Explain the sixty-five day rule and what purpose it serves.

PROBLEMS

16-18 *Computation of Fiduciary Accounting Income.* Under the terms of the trust instrument, the annual fiduciary accounting income of Trust MNO must be distributed in equal amounts to individual beneficiaries M, N, and O. The trust instrument also provides that capital gains or losses realized on the sale of trust assets are allocated to principal, and that 40% of the annual trustee fee is to be allocated to principal. For the current year, the records of the trust show the following:

Dividend income	$38,000
Tax-exempt interest income	18,900
Taxable interest income	12,400
Capital loss on sale of securities	(2,500)
Trustee fee	5,000

Based on these facts, determine the required distribution to each of the three trust beneficiaries.

16-19 *Tax Consequences of Property Distributions.* During the taxable year, beneficiary M receives 100 shares of Acme common stock from Trust T. The basis of the stock is $70 per share to the trust, and its fair market value at date of distribution is $110 per share. The trust's DNI for the year is $60,000, all of which is taxable. There were no other distributions made or required to be made by the trust.

    a. Assume the stock distribution was in satisfaction of an $11,000 pecuniary bequest to M. What is the tax result to M? To Trust T? What basis will M have in the Acme shares?

    b. Assume the distribution did not represent a specific bequest to M, and that Trust T did not make a § 643(e)(3) election. What is the tax result to M? To Trust T? What basis will M have in the Acme shares?

    c. Assume now that Trust T did make a § 643(e)(3) election with regard to the distribution of the Acme shares. What is the tax result to M? To Trust T? What basis will M have in the Acme shares?

16-20 *Trust's Depreciation Deduction.* Under the terms of the trust instrument, Trustee K is required to maintain a reserve for depreciation equal to $3,000 per year. All trust income, including rents from depreciable trust property, must be distributed currently to trust beneficiaries.

    a. Assume allowable depreciation for tax purposes is $2,000. What is the amount of the depreciation deduction available to the trust? To the trust beneficiaries?

    b. Assume allowable depreciation for tax purposes is $7,000. What is the amount of the depreciation deduction available to the trust? To the trust beneficiaries?

16-21 *Trust Losses.* Complex Trust Z has the following receipts and disbursements for the current year:

Receipts:		
Rents		$ 62,000
Proceeds from sale of securities (basis of securities = $55,000)		48,000
Dividends		12,000
Total receipts		$122,000
Disbursements:		
Rent expenses		$ 70,000
Trustee fee (100% allocable to income)		4,000
Total disbursements		$ 74,000

The trustee made no distributions to any beneficiaries during the current year. Based on these facts, compute trust taxable income for the current year.

16-22 *Deductibility of Funeral and Administrative Expenses.* Decedent L died on May 12 of the current year, and her executor elected a calendar taxable year for L's estate. Prior to December 31, L's estate paid $4,800 of funeral expenses, $19,900 of legal and accounting fees attributable to the administration of the estate, and a $6,100 executor's fee. Before consideration of any of these expenses, L's estate has taxable income of $60,000 for the period May 13 to December 31. Decedent L's taxable estate for Federal estate tax purposes is estimated at $8,600,000.

   a.   To what extent are the above expenses deductible on L's estate tax return (Form 706) or on the estate's income tax return (Form 1041) for the current year? On which return would the deductions yield the greater tax benefit?

   b.   Assume that L was married at the time of her death and that all the property included in her gross estate was left to her surviving spouse. Does this fact change your answer to (a)?

16-23 *Amount of Distribution Taxable to Beneficiary.* During the current year, Trust H has DNI of $50,000, of which $30,000 is nontaxable. The trustee made a $10,000 cash distribution to beneficiary P during the year; no other distributions were made.

   a.   How much taxable income must P report?

   b.   What deduction for distributions to beneficiaries may Trust H claim?

16-24 *Deductibility of Trust Expenses.* Trust A has the following receipts and disbursements for the current year:

Receipts:

Nontaxable interest	$ 40,000
Taxable interest	30,000
Rents	30,000
Total receipts	$100,000

Disbursements:

Charitable donation	$ 10,000
Rent expense	6,500
Total disbursements	$ 21,500

   a.   What is Trust A's deduction for charitable contributions for the current year?

   b.   How much of the trustee fee is deductible?

   c.   How much of the rent expense is deductible?

16-25 *Computation of DNI and Trust's Tax Liability.* Trust M has the following receipts disbursements for the current year:

Receipts:

Nontaxable interest	$ 4,000
Taxable interest	25,000
Rents	11,000
Long-term capital gain allocable to principal	9,000
Total receipts	$49,000

Disbursements:

Rent expense	$ 2,400
Trustee fee	1,000
Total disbursements	$ 3,400

The trustee is required to distribute all trust income to beneficiary N on a quarterly basis.

   a.   Compute Trust M's DNI for the current year.

   b.   Compute Trust M's taxable income for the current year.

   c.   Compute Trust M's tax liability for the current year.

16-26 *Taxation of Trust and Beneficiaries.* Trust B has the following receipts and disbursements for the current year:

Receipts:

Nontaxable interest	$10,000
Dividends	10,000
Rents	30,000
Long-term capital gain allocable to principal	15,000
Total receipts	$65,000

Disbursements:

Rent expense	$ 7,500
Trustee fee	5,000
Total disbursements	$12,500

During the year, the trustee distributes $20,000 to beneficiary C and $10,000 to beneficiary D. None of these distributions is subject to the throwback rule. The trust and both beneficiaries are calendar year taxpayers.
   a. Compute Trust B's DNI for the current year.
   b. Compute Trust B's taxable income for the current year.
   c. How much taxable income must each beneficiary report for the current year?

16-27 *Distributions from Complex Trusts.* Under the terms of the trust instrument, the trustee of Trust EFG is required to make an annual distribution of 50% of trust accounting income to beneficiary E. The trustee can make additional discretionary distributions out of trust income or principal to beneficiaries E, F, or G. During the current year, the trust accounting income of $85,000 equaled taxable DNI.
   a. Assume that the trustee made current distributions of $60,000 to E and $10,000 to G. How much taxable income must each beneficiary report for the current year? What is the amount of the trust's deduction for distributions to beneficiaries?
   b. Assume that the trustee made current distributions of $80,000 to E and $40,000 to G. How much taxable income must each beneficiary report for the current year? What is the amount of the trust's deduction for distributions to beneficiaries?

16-28 *First- and Second-Tier Distributions.* For the current year, Trust R has DNI of $100,000, of which $25,000 is nontaxable. The trustee is required to make an annual distribution of $60,000 to beneficiary S. Also during the year, the trustee made discretionary distributions of $40,000 to beneficiary T and $30,000 to beneficiary U. None of these distributions is subject to the throwback rules. How much taxable income must each beneficiary report?

16-29 *Distribution Exceeding DNI.* In 2014 and 2015, complex Trust C had taxable DNI of $18,000 and $28,500, respectively. No distributions were made to beneficiaries in either year and the trust paid income taxes totaling $13,041 for the two years. In 2016, trust DNI was $33,000 and the trustee distributed $100,000 to beneficiary W. Explain how such distribution is taxed.

16-30 *Income in Respect of a Decedent.* Individual K is a self-employed business consultant. In the current year, K performed services for a client and billed the client for $14,500. Unfortunately, K died on October 10 of the current year, before he received payment for his services. A check for $14,500 was received by K's executor on November 18. At the date of K's death, he owed a local attorney $1,600 for legal advice concerning a child custody suit in which K was involved. K's executor paid this bill on December 15.
   a. Assuming that K was a cash basis taxpayer, describe the tax consequences of the $14,500 receipt and the $1,600 payment by K's executor.
   b. How would your answer change if K had been an accrual basis taxpayer?

16-31 *Income in Respect of a Decedent.* Early in 2015, Z (an unmarried cash basis tax-payer) sold investment land with a basis of $50,000 for $200,000. In payment, Z received an installment note for $200,000, payable over the next ten years. Z died on December 1, 2015. As of the date of death, Z had received no principal payments on the note. Accrued interest on the note as of December 1, 2015 was $18,000, although the first interest payment was not due until early in 2016.

a. Assuming that no election is made to avoid installment sale treatment, how much of the $150,000 gain realized by Z will be included on her final income tax return? How much of the accrued interest income will be included?

b. In 2016, the estate of Z collects the first annual interest payment on the note of $19,700, and the first principal payment of $20,000. What are the income tax consequences to the estate of these collections?

c. Assume that the amount of estate tax attributable to the inclusion of the IRD represented by the installment note and the accrued interest in Z's taxable estate is $10,000, and that there are no other IRD or DRD items on the estate tax return. Compute the § 691(c) deduction available on the estate's 2016 income tax return.

TAX RETURN PROBLEM

16-32 The MKJ trust is a calendar year, cash basis taxpayer. The trust was created pursuant to the will of Murray Kyle Jacobs, who died on November 11, 2002. For 2016, the trust's book and records reflect these transactions:

Receipts:

Dividends (qualified)..		$30,000
Gross rents...		25,000
Interest:		
Bonds of the city of New York		25,000
U.S. government bonds		20,000
Capital gains:		
General Motors stock received from estate of MKJ:		
Sales price—December 2, 2016	$48,000	
Less: Basis (FMV on date of death)........................	(30,000)	18,000
Disbursements:		
Trustee commissions (50% paid out of income, 50% paid out of principal)		5,300
Legal fee		28,800
Contribution—American Cancer Society (paid out of principal)		12,000
Depreciation—rental property		2,000
Real estate tax—rental property............................		4,000
Repairs and maintenance—rental property.....................		4,200
Federal quarterly estimated tax payments......................		9,000

The legal fee was a legitimate trust expense and was incurred because of the choice of trust form. The fee was allocated by the trustee to the various income classes as follows:

Dividends	$ 0
Taxable interest..	16,000
Tax-exempt interest..	6,000
Rents..	6,800
Total legal fee	$28,800

The propriety of this allocation is *not* in question. Under the terms of the trust instrument (i.e., Mr. Jacobs' will), the $2,000 depreciation reserve equals the available tax depreciation deduction for the year. The trust instrument also specifies that all capital gains are allocable to principal and that the trustee has discretion as to the amount of trust income distributed to Brenda Jacobs, the sole individual beneficiary, and several charities specified in Mr. Jacobs' will. During 2016, the trustee distributes $24,000 of income to Brenda and $12,000 of income to the American Cancer Society.

Required: Complete Form 1041 and Schedule D for the MKJ trust. Ignore the net investment income tax. If the 2016 forms are not available, use the 2015 forms. **Note:** If the student is required to complete a Schedule K-l for Brenda Jacobs, he or she should refer to Reg. §§ 1.661(b)-1, 1.661(c)-2, and 1.661(c)-4, and the comprehensive example in this chapter in order to determine the character of any income distributed to the beneficiary.

TAX RESEARCH PROBLEM

16-33 In 2009, N transferred $600,000 of assets into an irrevocable trust for the benefit of her mother, M. The independent trustee, T, is required to distribute annually all income to M. The trust instrument also provides that any capital gains or losses realized upon the sale of trust assets are to be allocated to trust principal. In 2011, and 2013, the trustee sold trust assets and distributed an amount equal to the capital gain realized to M, in addition to the required distribution of trust income. During the current year, T sold certain trust securities and realized a net gain of $25,000. The trust also earned $10,000 of other income. During the year, $35,000 was distributed to M. Should the DNI of the trust for the current year include the $25,000 capital gain?

Family Tax Planning

17

Learning Objectives

Upon completion of this chapter you will be able to:

LO.1 Explain the concept of income shifting and the judicial constraints on this tax planning technique.

LO.2 Describe the marriage penalty and the singles penalty and identify the taxpayer situations in which either might occur.

LO.3 Identify different planning techniques that achieve tax savings by the shifting of income among family members.

LO.4 Characterize a regular corporation, an S corporation, and a partnership in terms of their viability as intrafamily income-shifting devices.

LO.5 Explain how the "kiddie tax" is computed on the unearned income of a minor child.

LO.6 Understand the role of a trust as a vehicle for intrafamily income shifting.

LO.7 Distinguish between a grantor trust and a taxable trust.

LO.8 Specify the tax advantages of inter vivos gifts as compared to testamentary transfers of wealth.

Chapter Outline

Introduction

Under the United States system of taxation, individuals are viewed as the basic unit of taxation. However, most individuals who are members of a nuclear family tend to regard the family as the economic and financial unit. For example, the individual wage earner with a spouse and three children must budget his or her income according to the needs of five people rather than one individual. Similarly, the family that includes a teenager who has received a college scholarship may perceive the scholarship as a financial benefit to all its members.

The concept of family tax planning is a product of this family-oriented economic perspective. Such planning has as its goal the minimization of taxes paid by the family unit as opposed to the separate taxes paid by individual members. Minimization of the total annual income tax bill of a family results in greater consumable income to the family unit. Minimization of transfer taxes on shifts of wealth among family members increases the total wealth that can be enjoyed by the family as a whole.

Before beginning a study of family tax planning, it is important to remember that such planning is only one aspect of the larger issue of family financial planning. Nontax considerations may often be more important to a family than the tax consequences of a course of action. For example, a family that faces the possibility of large medical expenses might be more concerned with their short-term liquidity needs than minimization of their current tax bill. A competent tax adviser must always be sensitive to the family's nontax goals and desires before he or she can design a tax plan that is truly in the family's best interests.

Family Income Shifting

A general premise in tax planning holds that, given a single amount of income, two taxpayers are always better than one. This premise results from the progressive structure of the United States income tax. As one taxpayer earns an increasing amount of income, the income is taxed at an increasing marginal rate. If the income can be diverted to a second taxpayer with less income of his or her own, the diverted amount will be taxed at a lower marginal rate. In 2016, the tax rates applicable to individuals range from 10% on the first dollar of taxable income to 39.6% on taxable income in excess of $415,050 ($466,950 for joint filers). This 25-percentage-point spread between the lowest and highest marginal rates is a powerful incentive for individuals to adopt tax plans that incorporate some type of income-shifting technique. Moreover, in light of the net investment income tax of 3.8 percent, the spread could be even greater!

A family unit composed of several individuals theoretically represents a single economic unit, which nonetheless is composed of separate taxpayers. A shift of income from one of these taxpayers to another has no effect economically. However, if the shift moves the income from a high tax bracket to a low tax bracket, the family has enjoyed a tax savings. A simple example can illustrate this basic point.

Example 1

Family F is composed of a father and his 15-year-old daughter. The father earns taxable income of $90,000 a year, an amount that represents total family income. During the summer, the daughter needs $10,000 for various personal expenses. To earn the money, she agrees to work for her father for a $10,000 salary, payment of which represents a deductible expense to him.

Based on this arrangement, the family saves $2,130 ($12,448 − [$9,948 + $370 = $10,318]) as computed below.

	Father Split	Daughter Split	Father No Split
Gross income	$80,000	$10,000	$90,000
Standard deduction	(9,300)	(6,300)	(9,300)
Exemptions	(8,100)	0	(8,100)
Taxable income	$62,600	$ 3,700	$72,600
Tax (head of household rates)	$ 9,948		$12,448
Tax (single rates)		$ 370	

Note that the father's income tax, standard deduction and exemptions are based on the fact that he would be considered a head of household and can claim an exemption for his daughter. Observe also that the fact that the daughter is a taxpayer does not prevent the father from qualifying as a head of household for filing purposes. However, because the daughter is eligible to be claimed as a dependent on her father's return she is not entitled to a personal exemption.[1]

The tax savings in the above example is attributable to two factors. First, the daughter as a taxpayer with earned income is entitled to a $6,300 (2016) standard deduction, which shelters $6,300 (2016) of the income shifted to her from any taxation at all.[2] Second, the income taxable to the daughter is subject to a 10% tax rate; if this income had been taxed on the father's return, it would have been subject to a 25% tax rate.

JUDICIAL CONSTRAINTS ON INCOME SHIFTING

The Federal courts have consistently recognized that the United States system of taxation cannot tolerate arbitrary shifting of income from one family member to another. The decisions in a number of historic cases have established clear judicial doctrine that limits the assignment of income from one taxpayer to another.[3]

The 1930 Supreme Court case of *Lucas v. Earl*[3] involved a husband and wife who entered into a contract providing that the earnings of either spouse should be considered as owned equally by each. The contract was signed in 1901, twelve years before the first Federal income tax law was written, and was legally binding upon the spouses under California law.

The taxpayers contended that because of the contract certain attorney fees earned by Mr. Earl should be taxed in equal portions to Mr. and Mrs. Earl. However, the Supreme Court agreed with the government's argument that the intent of the Federal income tax law was to tax income to the individual who earns it, an intent that cannot be avoided by anticipatory arrangements to assign the income to a different taxpayer. The decision of the Court ended with the memorable statement that the tax law must disregard arrangements "by which the fruits are attributed to a different tree from that on which they grew."[4]

LO.1

Explain the concept of income shifting and the judicial constraints on this tax planning technique.

---

[1] § 151(d)(2).

[2] § 63(c)(5).

[3] 2 USTC ¶496, 8 AFTR 10287, 281 U.S. 111 (USSC, 1930).

[4] *Ibid.* 281 U.S. 115.

The Supreme Court followed the same logic in its 1940 decision in *Helvering v. Horst*.[5] This case involved a father who owned corporate coupon bonds and who detached the negotiable interest coupons from the bonds shortly before their due date. The father then gifted the coupons to his son, who collected the interest upon maturity and reported the income on his tax return for the year.

The Court's decision focused on the fact that ownership of the corporate bonds themselves created the right to the interest payments. Because the father owned the bonds, he alone had the right to and control over the interest income. In exercising his control by gifting the interest coupons to his child, the father realized the economic benefit of the income represented by the coupons and therefore was the individual taxable on the income.

These two cases illustrate the two basic premises of the *assignment of income doctrine*. Earned income must be taxed to the individual who performs the service for which the income is paid. Investment income must be taxed to the owner of the investment capital that generated the income. All legitimate efforts to shift income from one individual to another must take into account these judicial constraints.

JOINT FILING AND THE SINGLES PENALTY

LO.2
Describe the marriage penalty and the singles penalty and identify the taxpayer situations in which either might occur.

The most obvious candidates for intrafamily income shifting are a husband and wife, one of whom has a much larger income than the other. However, since 1948 married couples have been allowed to file a joint income tax return, which reports the total income earned by the couple and taxes the income on the basis of one progressive rate schedule.[6]

Joint filing originally was intended as a benefit to married couples. Prior to 1969, the joint filing tax rates were designed to tax one-half of total marital income at the tax rates applicable to single individuals. The resultant tax was then doubled to produce the married couple's tax liability. This perfect split and the corresponding tax savings were perceived as inequitable by unmarried taxpayers, who felt they were paying an unjustifiable "singles penalty."

To illustrate, consider the situation of a single taxpayer with taxable income of $24,000. In 1965, this taxpayer owed $8,030 of income tax, with the last dollar of income taxed at a 50% marginal tax rate. A married couple with the same 1965 taxable income owed only $5,660 and faced a marginal tax rate of only 32 percent.

THE MARRIAGE PENALTY

In 1969, Congress attempted to alleviate the singles penalty by enacting a new (and lower) rate schedule for single taxpayers.[7] While this action did reduce (but not eliminate) the singles penalty, it also created a marriage penalty for certain individuals. In 2001, Congress addressed the marriage tax penalty by modifying the standard deduction and the tax rates. For 2016, the standard deduction for joint returns is exactly double that of single taxpayers. Similarly, the 10% and 15% rate brackets for joint filers are exactly twice the size of the corresponding bracket for an unmarried individual ($9,275 versus $18,550 and $37,650 versus $75,300). The brackets for the higher rates are *not* expanded to twice the corresponding single filer tax brackets. As a practical matter, these changes will eliminate the marriage tax penalty for most individuals. Nevertheless, a penalty may still result for higher income taxpayers as shown below.

[5] 40-2 USTC ¶9787, 24 AFTR 1058, 311 U.S. 112 (USSC, 1940).

[6] § 6013. Married individuals may choose to file separate returns, but they must use the rate schedule of § 1(d), which simply halves the tax brackets of the married filing jointly rate schedule of § 1(a). As a general rule, separate filing results in a greater tax than joint filing and such filing status is elected only for nontax reasons.

[7] Act. § 803(a), P.L. 91-172, Dec. 30, 1969.

Example 2

H and W are thinking about getting married and starting a family. The calculations below demonstrate what may happen if (1) H and W do not marry and H earns $150,000; (2) H and W do marry and H earns $150,000; and (3) H and W marry and both earned $150,000.

	H Single	*H & W Married*	*H & W Married*
Gross income of H....................	$150,000	$150,000	$150,000
Gross income of W	—	—	150,000
Standard deduction	(6,300)	(12,600)	(12,600)
Exemption...........................	(4,050)	(8,100)	(8,100)
Taxable income	$139,650	$129,300	$279,300
Tax	$ 32,139	$ 23,868	$ 67,582
Tax for two singles ($32,139 × 2)			(64,278)
Singles penalty ($32,139 − $23,868)........		$ 8,271	
Marriage penalty ($67,582 − $64,278)			$ 3,304

Interpretations of these results differ depending on the point of view. If H is single, he may not like the fact that his married friends who make the same income pay $8,271 less tax than he does. Obviously, he needs to find a wife! If H and W are considering getting married and W does not work, they should marry immediately since they would save $8,271 or avoid the singles penalty that H currently pays. But what happens if both individuals earn income? If each had about the same income and the amounts did not exceed about $104,993, there would be no penalty. However, if they both earn about $150,000, as seen above, getting married produces an additional tax of $3,304—some may say a small price for marital bliss. Most individuals contemplating marriage need not worry about the cost of marriage since the penalty normally occurs only at higher income levels.

Generally, a singles penalty may occur when *one* income can be taxed at married, rather than single, rates. A marriage penalty may occur when *two* incomes are combined and taxed at married, rather than single, rates. Today, two-income families have become the rule rather than the exception, and the marriage penalty has received considerable publicity. The recent changes by Congress will go a long way to putting an end to the controversy. Nevertheless there will be married couples who want to avoid the penalty. For these people who might entertain the notion of divorce, they should be wary. Because marital status is determined as of the last day of the taxable year,[8] couples have attempted to avoid the marriage penalty by obtaining a technically legal divorce shortly before year end. When a couple has immediately remarried and the only purpose of the divorce was to enable the husband and wife to file as single taxpayers, the IRS and the courts have had little trouble in concluding that the divorce was a sham transaction and therefore ineffective for tax purposes.[9]

Before leaving this topic, one last observation is worth noting. While the recent changes should eliminate most objections to the marriage tax penalty, this does not mean the system is neutral on marriage. Inequities between married and single taxpayers have not necessarily been resolved. No doubt singles who pay more taxes that their married counterparts who earn the same income will complain—much as their ancestors did in 1969. Only time will tell if Congress will once again provide relief and start the cycle once again.

INCOME SHIFTING TO CHILDREN AND OTHER FAMILY MEMBERS

Because a married couple is considered one rather than two taxpayers for Federal tax purposes, intrafamily income shifting usually involves a transfer of income from parents to children (or, less commonly, other family members) who are considered taxpayers in their own right.

---

[8] § 7703(a).

[9] Rev. Rul. 76-255, 1976-2 C.B. 40; and *Boyter v. Comm.*, 82-1 USTC ¶9117, 49 AFTR2d 451, 668 F.2d 1382 (CA-4, 1981).

The fact that children are taxpayers separate and distinct from their parents is recognized by § 73, which states "amounts received in respect of the services of a child shall be included in his gross income and not in the gross income of the parent, even though such amounts are not received by the child." The regulations elaborate by stating that the statutory rule applies even if state law entitles the parent to the earnings of a minor child.[10]

Because children typically will have little or no income of their own, a shift of family income to such children can cause the income to be taxed at a lower marginal rate. The income shifted from parent to child also represents wealth that is owned by the child rather than the parent. Thus, the future taxable estate of the parent will not include the accumulated income that is already in the hands of younger-generation family members.

Income-Shifting Techniques

LO.3

Identify different planning techniques that achieve tax savings by the shifting of income among family members.

The next section of this chapter explores a variety of techniques whereby income can be successfully shifted to family members in a lower marginal tax bracket. The circumstances of each particular family situation will dictate the specific technique to be used.

FAMILY MEMBERS AS EMPLOYEES

The first technique for intrafamily income shifting is for a low-bracket family member to become an employee of a family business. This technique does not involve the transfer of a capital interest in the business, so the family member who owns the business does not dilute his or her ownership by this technique.

In the simplest case in which the family business is a sole proprietorship, any family members who become employees must actually perform services the value of which equates to the amount of compensation received. This requirement implies that the employee is both capable and qualified for his or her job and devotes an appropriate amount of time to the performance of services.

Example 3

F owns a plumbing contracting business as a sole proprietorship. During the current year, F employs his son S as an apprentice plumber for an hourly wage of $10. The total amount paid to S for the year is $9,000.

If the father can prove to the satisfaction of the IRS that his son performed services worth $10 per hour and that the son actually worked 900 hours during the year, the father may deduct the $9,000 as wage expense on his tax return and the son will report $9,000 of compensation income on his own return.

If, on the other hand, the IRS concludes that the son was not a legitimate employee of his father's business, the transfer of $9,000 to the son would be recharacterized as a gift. As a result, the father would lose the business deduction, and no income shift from father to son would occur.

Obviously, the legitimacy of the employment relationship between father and son can only be determined by an examination of all relevant facts and circumstances. Facts to be considered would include the age of the son, his prior work experience and technical training, and his actual participation on contracted jobs requiring an apprentice plumber.

When a family member is an employee of a family business, any required payroll taxes on his or her compensation must be paid. However, compensation paid to an employer's children under the age of 18 is not subject to Federal payroll tax.[11]

FAMILY EMPLOYEES OF PARTNERSHIPS AND CORPORATIONS

If a family member wants to work as an employee of a family business operated in partnership or corporate form, the requirement that the value of his or her services equate to the amount of compensation received does not change. If the employment relationship is valid,

---

[10] Reg. § 1.73-1(a). [11] §§ 3121(b)(3)(A) and 3306(c)(5).

the partnership or corporation may deduct the compensation paid to the family member. If the family member is not performing services that justify the salary he or she is drawing from the business, the IRS may recharacterize the payment.

In the case of a partnership, the payment may be recharacterized as a constructive cash withdrawal by one or more partners followed by a constructive gift of the cash to the pseudo employee.

Example 4

Brothers X, Y, and Z are equal partners in Partnership XYZ. The partnership hires S, the sister of the partners, to act as secretary-treasurer for the business. S's salary is $20,000 per year. Assume that S has no business or clerical training and performs only minimal services for the business on a very sporadic basis. As a result, the IRS disallows a deduction to the partnership for all but $5,000 of the payment to the sister. The nondeductible $15,000 will be treated as a withdrawal by the partners that was transferred as a gift to the sister.

Constructive cash withdrawals from a partnership could have adverse tax consequences to the partners. If the withdrawal exceeds a partner's basis in his or her partnership interest, the excess constitutes capital gain to the partner.[12] Similarly, a constructive gift to a family member could result in an unexpected gift tax liability.

When the employer is a family corporation and a salary or wage paid to a nonshareholder family member is disallowed, the tax results can be extremely detrimental. Not only does the corporation lose a deduction, but the payment could be recharacterized as a constructive dividend to the family members who are shareholders, followed by a constructive gift to the family member who actually received the funds.[13] Thus, the corporate shareholders would have dividend income without any corresponding cash, and a potential gift tax liability.

The lesson to be learned from the preceding discussion should be clear. If an intrafamily income shift is to be accomplished by hiring a family member as an employee of a family business, the family member must perform as a legitimate employee. If the employment relationship has no substance, the unintended tax consequences to the family could be costly indeed.

FAMILY MEMBERS AS OWNERS OF THE FAMILY BUSINESS

A second technique for intrafamily income shifting is to make a low-bracket family taxpayer a part owner of the family business. By virtue of his or her equity or capital interest, the family member is then entitled to a portion of the income generated by the business. This is a more extreme technique in that it involves an actual transfer of a valuable asset. Moreover, the disposition of a partial ownership interest may cause dilution of the original owner's control of the business. These and other negative aspects of this technique will be discussed in greater detail later in the chapter.

The gratuitous transfer of an equity interest in a business will constitute a taxable gift to the original owner.

LO.4

Characterize a regular corporation, an S corporation, and a partnership in terms of their viability as intrafamily income-shifting devices.

Example 5

M runs a very successful business as a sole proprietorship. She wants to bring her son S into the business as an equal partner. Under the terms of a legally binding partnership agreement, she contributes her business, valued at $1 million, to the partnership. Although the son will have a 50% capital interest in the partnership, he contributes nothing. As a result, M has made a $500,000 taxable gift to S.

---

[12] § 731(a).

[13] *Duffey v. Lethert,* 63-1 USTC ¶9442, 11 AFTR2d 1317 (D.Ct. Minn., 1963).

If the transfer of the equity interest is accomplished by sale rather than gift, no initial gift tax liability will result. But in a typical family situation, the equity interest is being transferred to a family member without significant income or wealth, so that the family member lacks the funds to purchase the interest. Also, the income tax consequences of a sale could be more expensive than gift tax consequences, depending upon the facts. The prudent tax adviser should explore both possible methods of transfer when designing a particular plan.

FAMILY PARTNERSHIPS

A family partnership can be used as a vehicle for the co-ownership of a single business by a number of family members. As a partner, each family member will report his or her allocable share of partnership income (or loss) on his or her individual tax return.[14] Therefore, through use of a partnership, business income can be shifted to family members with relatively low marginal tax brackets.

If a family partnership is a service business, only a family member who performs services can receive an allocation of partnership income. In a service partnerships, the physical assets of the business (the capital of the partnership) are not a major factor of income production. Rather, it is the individual efforts and talents of the partners that produce partnership income. An attempt to allow a family member who cannot perform the appropriate services to participate in partnership income is an unwarranted assignment of earned income.

If the family partnership is one in which capital is a major income-producing factor, the mere ownership of a capital interest will entitle a family member to participate in partnership income. The determination of whether or not capital is a material income-producing factor is made by reference to the facts of each situation. However, capital is ordinarily a material income-producing factor if the operation of the business requires substantial inventories or investment in plant, machinery, or equipment.[15]

Section 704(e)(1) specifies that a family member will be recognized as a legitimate partner if he or she owns a capital interest in a partnership in which capital is a material income-producing factor. This is true even if the family member received his or her interest as a gift. However, § 704(e)(2) limits the amount of partnership income that can be shifted to such a donee partner. Under this statute, the income allocated to the partner cannot be proportionally greater than his or her interest in partnership capital.

Example 6

Grandfather F is a 50% partner in Praco Partnership. At the beginning of the current year, F gives his grandson G a 20% capital interest in Praco (leaving F with a 30% interest). For the current year Praco has taxable income of $120,000. The *maximum* amount allocable to G is $24,000 (20% × $120,000). If F wanted to increase the dollar amount of partnership income shifted to G, he must give G a greater equity interest in the partnership.

Section 704(e)(2) contains a second restriction on income allocation. A donor partner who *gifts* a capital interest must receive reasonable compensation for any services he or she renders to the partnership before any income can be allocated to the donee partner.

Example 7

Refer to the facts in *Example 6*. During the current year, F performs services for Praco worth $15,000 but for which he receives no compensation. Half of the $120,000 partnership income is still allocable to F and G with respect to their combined 50% capital interests; however, the maximum amount allocable to G decreases to $18,000 ([$60,000 − $15,000 allocated to F as compensation for services] × 40%).

---

[14] § 702(a). [15] Reg. § 1.704-1(e)(1)(iv).

Note that in the above example, Grandfather F might be willing to forgo any compensation for the services performed for Magnum in order to increase the amount of partnership income shifted to his grandson. Unfortunately, § 704(e)(2) effectively curtails this type of indirect assignment of earned income.

Family members are not able to avoid the dual limitations of § 704(e) by arranging a transfer of a capital interest to a lower-bracket family member by sale rather than by gift. Under § 704(e)(3), a capital interest in a partnership purchased by one member of a family from another is considered to be created by gift from the seller. In this context the term *family* includes an individual's spouse, ancestors, lineal descendants, and certain family trusts.

REGULAR CORPORATIONS

Family businesses are frequently owned as closely held corporations. There are a number of business reasons why the corporate form is popular. For example, shareholders in a corporation have limited liability so that creditors of the corporation cannot force the shareholders to pay the debts of the corporation out of the shareholders' personal assets. There are also tax benefits to the corporate form of business. The owners of the business can function as employees of the corporate entity. As employees, they may participate in a wide variety of tax-favored employee benefit plans, such as employer-sponsored medical reimbursement plans. If the family business were in sole proprietorship or partnership form, the owners of the business would be self-employed and ineligible to participate in such employee benefit plans.

The corporate form of business must be regarded as a mixed blessing from a tax point of view. The incorporation of a family business does result in the creation of a new taxable entity, separate and distinct from its owners. Business income has been shifted to the corporate taxpayer, and because corporate tax rates are progressive, a net tax savings to the business can be the result.[16]

> ### Example 8
>
> T, married, owns a sole proprietorship that produces $100,000 of net income before taxes. Ignoring the availability of any deductions or exemptions, T's 2016 tax on this income is $16,543 (married filing jointly rates). If T incorporates the business and draws a salary of $50,000, he will pay an individual tax of only $6,573. The corporation will also have income of $50,000 ($100,000 net income − $50,000 salary to T). The corporate tax on $50,000 is $7,500. Therefore, the *total* tax on the business income has decreased to $14,073 ($6,573 + $7,500), a savings of $2,470 ($16,543 − $14,073).

The tax savings to T's business ($2,470) achieved by incorporation is significant, particularly considering it would occur year after year. However, the potential problem created by the incorporation of T's business is that the after-tax earnings of the business are now in the corporation rather than in T's pocket. If T needs or wants more than $43,427 ($50,000 salary − $6,573 tax liability) of after-tax personal income, he may certainly have his corporation pay out some of its after-tax earnings to him as a dividend. But any dividends paid must be included in T's gross income and taxed at the individual level.

The double taxation of corporate earnings paid to shareholders as dividends can quickly offset the tax savings resulting from using a corporation as a separate entity. Therefore, shareholders in closely held corporations usually become very adept in drawing business income out of their corporations as deductible business expenses rather than nondeductible dividends.

---

[16] Because of the 5% surtax on taxable income between $100,000 and $335,000, corporations with taxable income between $335,000 and $10 million face a flat 34% tax rate rather than a progressive rate. Qualified personal service corporations pay a flat 35% of their total taxable income. § 11(b)(2).

Shareholders who are also employees will usually try to maximize the amount of compensation they receive from the corporation. Section 162(a)(1) authorizes the corporation to deduct a *reasonable* allowance for salaries or other compensation paid. If the IRS determines that the compensation paid to an owner employee is unjustifiably high and therefore *unreasonable*, the excessive compensation can be reclassified as a dividend. As a result, the corporation loses the deduction for the excessive compensation, and to a corresponding extent, business earnings are taxed twice.

Other types of deductible payments from corporations to shareholders include rents paid for corporate use of shareholder assets and interest on loans made to the corporation by shareholders. The arrangements between corporation and shareholder that give rise to such rent or interest payments will be subject to careful scrutiny by the IRS. If an arrangement lacks substance and is deemed to be a device to camouflage the payments of dividends to shareholders, the corporate deduction for the payments will be disallowed.

Because it is a taxpayer in its own right, a regular corporation cannot be effectively used to shift business income to low-bracket family members. If such family members are made shareholders in the corporation and have no other relationship to the corporate business (employee, creditor, etc.), the only way to allocate business earnings to them is by paying dividends on their stock. As previously discussed, dividend payments are usually considered prohibitively costly from a tax standpoint.

Closely held regular corporations do have tremendous utility in other areas of tax planning. However, for purposes of intrafamily income shifting, the S corporation is a highly preferable alternative to a regular corporation.

S Corporations

The complex set of statutory provisions that govern the tax treatment of S corporations is explained in Chapter 11. For family tax planning purposes, the most important characteristic of an S corporation is that the corporate income escapes taxation at the corporate level and is taxed to the corporation's shareholders. This characteristic makes an S corporation a very useful mechanism for intrafamily income shifting.

Section 1366(a) provides that the taxable income of an S corporation is allocated to the shareholders on a pro rata basis. Thus, any individual who is a shareholder will report a proportionate share of the corporate business income on his or her personal tax return for the year with or within which the S corporation's taxable year ends.

Example 9

Individual M, married, owns a sole proprietorship with an annual net income before taxes of $200,000. Ignoring the availability of any itemized deductions or exemptions, M's personal tax on this income is $42,986.50 (joint return schedule). If at the beginning of 2016 M incorporates the business, gives each of his four unmarried children 20% of the stock, and has the shareholders elect S status for the corporation, the corporate income of $200,000 will be taxed in equal $40,000 amounts to the five shareholders. Ignoring other deductions or exemptions, the 2016 tax bill on the business income will be $28,157.50 ($5,072.50 on a joint return + [4 × $5,771.50 = $23,085 on a single return]). By splitting the income, M saves $14,828 ($42,986.50 − $28,157.50).

A shareholder who is also an employee of a family-owned S corporation will not be able to divert corporate income to other shareholders by forgoing any compensation for services rendered to the corporation. Code § 1366(e) provides that if such a shareholder employee does not receive reasonable compensation from the S corporation, the IRS may reallocate corporate income to the shareholder employee so as to accurately reflect the value of his or her services.

Because shareholders of an S corporation are taxed on all the taxable income earned by the corporation, subsequent cash withdrawals of this income by shareholders are tax free.[17]

---

[17] § 1368(b).

However, the technical requirements for cash withdrawals from an S corporation are dangerously complicated. Because of the complexity of these requirements and many other tax aspects of S corporations, family tax plans involving their use should be carefully designed and monitored by the family tax adviser.

NEGATIVE ASPECTS OF OWNERSHIP TRANSFERS

A high-bracket taxpayer who desires to shift income to low-bracket family members by making such members co-owners of the taxpayer's business must reconcile himself or herself to several facts. First, the transfer of the equity interest in the business must be complete and legally binding so that the recipient of the interest has "dominion and control" over his or her new asset. A *paper* transfer by which the transferor creates only the illusion that a family member has been given an equity interest in a business will be treated as a sham transaction, ineffective for income-shifting purposes.[18]

As a general rule, the recipient of an ownership interest in a family business is free to dispose of the interest, just as he or she is free to dispose of any asset he or she owns. If the recipient is a responsible individual and supportive of the family tax planning goals, his or her legal right to assign the interest may not be a problem. But if the recipient is a spendthrift in constant need of ready cash, he or she may sell the interest to a third party, thereby completely subverting the family tax plan.

One popular technique that can prevent an unexpected and undesired disposition of an interest in a family business is a buy-sell agreement. A taxpayer can transfer an equity interest to a low-bracket family member on the condition that should the family member desire to sell the interest he or she must first offer the interest to its original owner at an independently determined market value. Such an agreement is in no way economically detrimental to the family member, yet affords a measure of protection for both the original owner and the family tax plan.

A related aspect of the requirement that the taxpayer must legally surrender the ownership of the business interest transferred is that the transfer is irrevocable. Ownership of the interest cannot be regained if future events cause the original tax plan to become undesirable. For example, an estrangement between family members could convert a highly satisfactory intrafamily income-shifting plan into a bitterly resented trap. A father who has an ill-favored son as an employee can always fire him. It is another matter entirely if the son is a 40% shareholder in the father's corporation.

A change in economic circumstances could also cause a taxpayer to regret a transfer of a business interest. Consider a situation in which a formerly high-income taxpayer suffers a severe financial downturn. A tax plan that is shifting income *away* from such a taxpayer could suddenly become an economic disaster.

PRESERVATION OF CONTROL OF THE BUSINESS

A taxpayer who is contemplating transferring an ownership interest in a business to one or more family members should also consider any resultant dilution of his or her control of the business. The taxpayer may be willing to part with an equity interest in order to shift business income to low-bracket family members, but may be very reluctant to allow such family members to participate in the management of the business.

A limited partnership can be used to bring family members into a business without allowing them a voice in management. A family member who owns a capital interest as a limited partner in a partnership may be allocated a share of business income, subject to the family partnership rules, and yet be precluded from participating in management of the business.

If the family business is in corporate form, various classes of stock with differing characteristics can be issued. For example, nonvoting stock can be given to family members without any dilution of the original owner's voting power, and hence control, over the business. If the original owner does not want to draw any dividends out of the corporate business but is willing to have dividends paid to low-bracket family members, nonvoting preferred stock can be issued to such family members.

---

[18] For example, see Reg. § 1.704-1(e)(2).

Unfortunately, this flexibility in designing a corporate capital structure that maximizes income-shifting potential while minimizing loss of control is not available to S corporations. To qualify for S status a corporation may have only one class of stock outstanding.[19] Thus, all outstanding shares of stock in an S corporation must be identical with respect to the rights they convey in the profits and assets of the corporation. However, shares of stock in S corporations may have different *voting rights* without violating the single class of stock requirement.[20]

SHIFTS OF INVESTMENT INCOME

In many ways the shifting of investment income to family members is simpler than the shifting of business income. Questions of forms of co-ownership and control are not as difficult to resolve if the income-producing asset to be transferred is in the form of an investment security rather than a business interest.

The simplest means to shift investment income from one taxpayer to another is an outright gift of the investment asset. Even gifts to minors who are under legal disabilities with regard to property ownership can be accomplished under state Uniform Gifts to Minors Acts. By using a custodian to hold the property for the benefit of a minor, the donor has shifted the investment income to the minor's tax return.[21]

Although gifting of investment property is a relatively simple technique, the donor must be aware that the transfer must be complete. The asset (and the wealth it represents) is irrevocably out of the donor's hands. If the donor attempts to retain an interest in or control over the asset, the gift may be deemed incomplete and the attempted income shift ineffectual.

If a donee receives an unrestricted right to a valuable investment asset, there is always the worry that he or she will mismanage it, or worse, assign it to a third party against the wishes of the donor. Because of these negative aspects of outright gifts, the private trust has become a very popular vehicle for the transfer of investment assets, especially when minor children are involved. A subsequent section of the chapter explores the use of trusts in family tax planning.

TAXATION OF UNEARNED INCOME OF MINOR CHILDREN

LO.5

Explain how the "kiddie tax" is computed on the unearned income of a minor child.

Tax law significantly limits the ability of parents to shift investment income to their children. Section 1(g) provides that any *net unearned income* of a minor child in excess of a $1,050 (2016) base is taxed at the marginal rate applicable to the income of the child's parents.[22] A minor child is one who by the close of the tax year has not obtained the age of 19 or is a full-time student less than the age of 24 who does not provide more than one-half of his or her support and who has at least one living parent on that date.

Net unearned income is generally defined as passive investment income such as interest and dividends, reduced by the $1,050 (2016) standard deduction available against unearned income of a dependent.[23] The amount of net unearned income for any taxable year may not exceed the child's taxable income for the year. The *source* of the unearned income is irrelevant for purposes of this so-called "kiddie tax."

Example 10

Several years ago grandchild G, age 15, received a gift of corporate bonds from her grandparents. G's 2016 interest income from the securities totaled $8,000. G had no other income or deductions for the year. G's parents claimed G as a dependent and reported taxable income of $450,000 on their joint return. G's taxable income is $6,950

---

[19] § 1361(b)(1)(D).

[20] § 1361(c)(4).

[21] Rev. Rul. 56-484, 1956-2 C.B. 23. However, income earned by the custodian account used for the support of the minor will be taxed to the person legally responsible for such support (i.e., the parent).

[22] In the case of parents who are not married, the child's tax is computed with reference to the tax rate of the custodial parent. If the parents file separate tax returns, the tax rate of the parent with the *greater* taxable income is used. § 1(g)(5).

[23] § 63(c)(5).

($8,000 gross income – $1,050 standard deduction) and her net unearned income to be taxed at her parents' rate is $5,900 ($8,000 – the $1,050 base – an $1,050 standard deduction). Thus $5,900 is taxed at her parents' rates and the balance, $1,050, is taxed at her rates, resulting in a tax liability of $2,200 computed as follows:

Tax on unearned income at parents' rates:	
($8,000 – $2,100 = $5,900 × 35%)	$2,065
Tax on remaining taxable income at child's rates:	
($1,050 × 10%)	105
Tax liability	$2,170

In this example, it is important to note that the income was interest and, therefore, subject to tax at the parents' highest tax rate. In contrast, dividend income or long-term capital gains that are shifted to a child are generally taxed at the parents' rates of 20% or 15% (or 0%) but a special computation is required. Note that this example ignores the net investment income tax of 3.8% that applies when a married couple's AGI exceeds $250,000 ($200,000 for unmarried taxpayers).

In certain cases parents may elect to include a dependent's unearned income on their return, rather than filing a separate return and making the "kiddie tax" calculation. As a general rule, this should not be done since the additional income increases the parents' adjusted gross income, which may reduce the amount of deductions that the parent may claim and have other unintended effects.

The Trust as a Tax Planning Vehicle

As discussed in Chapter 16, a private trust is a legal arrangement whereby the ownership and control of property are vested in a trustee while the beneficial interest in the property is given to one or more beneficiaries. The trustee has a fiduciary responsibility to manage the property for the sole benefit of the beneficiaries.

ADVANTAGES OF THE TRUST FORM

The use of a trust has many nontax advantages. If an individual desires to make a gift of property to a donee who is not capable of owning or managing the property, the gift can be made in trust so that a competent trustee can be selected to manage the property free from interference from the donee-beneficiary.

LO.6
Understand the role of a trust as a vehicle for intrafamily income shifting.

The trust form of property ownership is very convenient in that it allows the legal title to property to be held by a single person (the trustee) while allowing the beneficial enjoyment of the property to be shared by a number of beneficiaries. If legal ownership of the property were fragmented among the various beneficiaries, they would all have to jointly participate in management decisions regarding the property. This cumbersome and oftentimes impractical co-ownership situation is avoided when a trustee is given sole management authority over the property.

If a donor would like to give property to several donees so that the donees have sequential rather than concurrent rights in the property, the trust form for the gift is commonly the solution.

Example 11

Individual K owns a valuable tract of income-producing real estate. She would like ownership of the real estate to ultimately pass to her three minor grandchildren. She also would like to give her invalid brother an interest in the real estate so as to provide him with a future source of income. K can transfer the real estate into trust, giving her brother an income interest for a designated time period. Upon termination of the time period, ownership of the real estate will go to K's grandchildren.

TAX CONSEQUENCES OF TRANSFERS INTO TRUST

The use of the trust form can have distinct income tax advantages to a family because both the trust itself and any beneficiaries who receive income from the trust are taxpayers in their own right.

Example 12

F, a high-bracket taxpayer, transfers income-producing assets into a trust of which his four grandchildren are discretionary income beneficiaries. In the current year, the trust assets generate $100,000 of income, of which the trustee distributes $24,000 to each child. The $100,000 of investment income will be taxed to five taxpayers, the four grandchildren and the trust itself.

In determining the benefit of splitting income in *Example 12,* it is important to remember that unearned income *distributed* from a trust to a beneficiary may be subject to the kiddie tax as well as the net investment income tax. The income will be taxed at the marginal rate applicable to the beneficiary's parents, even if the parents did not create the trust. However, if the beneficiary is not subject to the kiddie tax (e.g., a grandparent), substantial savings can be obtained. Note also that any investment income accumulated in the trust that exceeds the highest tax bracket of the trust ($12,400 in 2016) would be subject to the net investment income tax of 3.8 percent.

GIFT-LEASEBACKS

A popular and controversial method for family income shifting through use of a trust involves a technique known as a gift-leaseback. Typically, a taxpayer who owns assets that he or she uses in a trade or business transfers the assets as a gift in trust for the benefit of the taxpayer's children (or other low-bracket family members). The independent trustee then leases the assets back to the taxpayer for their fair rental value. The rent paid by the taxpayer to the trust is deducted as a § 162 ordinary and necessary business expense and becomes income to the taxpayer's children because of their status as trust beneficiaries.

The IRS has refused to recognize the validity of gift-leaseback arrangements and has consistently disallowed the rent deduction to the transferor of the business assets under the theory that the entire transaction has no business purpose. However, if the trust owning the leased assets has an independent trustee and the leaseback arrangement is in written form and requires payment to the trust of a reasonable rent, the Tax Court and the Second, Third, Seventh, Eighth, and Ninth Circuits have allowed the transferor to deduct the rent paid.[24] To date, only the Fourth and Fifth Circuits have supported the government's position that gift-leaseback transactions are shams to be disregarded for tax purposes.[25]

GIFT TAX CONSIDERATIONS

The obvious income tax advantage of a family trust, such as the one described in *Example 12* above, can be offset if the original gift of property into the trust is subject to a substantial gift tax. Thus, the first step in designing a family trust is the minimization of any front-end gift tax. If the fair market value of the transferred property is less than the taxable amount sheltered by the unified credit of § 2505, no gift tax will be paid. However, the reader should bear in mind that the use of the credit against inter vivos gifts reduces the future shelter available on the donor's estate tax return.

An essential element in the minimization of any gift tax for transfers into trust is securing the $14,000 (2016) annual exclusion (§ 2503) for the amount transferred to each beneficiary-donee. This can be difficult when certain of the donees are given only a prospective or future interest in the trust property.

---

[24] See *May v. Comm.,* 76 T.C. 7(1981), *aff'd.* 84-1 USTC ¶9166, 53 AFTR2d 84-626 (CA-9. 1984).

[25] See *Mathews v. Comm.,* 75-2 USTC ¶9734, 36 AFTR2d 75-5965, 520 F.2d 323 (CA-5, 1975), cert. denied, 424 U.S. 967 (1976).

Example 13

Donor Z transfers $100,000 into trust. The independent trustee has the discretion to distribute income currently among Z's five children, or she may accumulate it for future distribution. Upon trust termination, the trust assets will be divided equally among the children. Because the five donees have only future interests in the $100,000, Z may not claim any exclusions in computing the amount of the taxable gift.[26]

SECTION 2503(c) AND CRUMMEY TRUSTS

One method of securing the exclusion for transfers into trust is to rely on the *safe harbor* rules of § 2503(c). Under this subsection a transfer into trust will not be considered a gift of a future interest if:

1. The property and income therefrom may be expended for the benefit of the donee-beneficiary before he or she reaches age 21; and

2. If any property or income is not so expended, it will pass to the donee-beneficiary at age 21 or be payable to his or her estate if he or she dies before that age.

One drawback to the "§ 2503(c) trust" is that the trust assets generally must go to the beneficiaries at age 21. Many parent-donors would prefer to postpone trust termination until their children-donees attain a more mature age. This goal can be accomplished through the use of a *Crummey trust.*[27]

A Crummey trust is one in which the beneficiaries are directly given only a future right to trust income or corpus. The term of the trust may extend well beyond the time when the beneficiaries reach age 21. However, the trust instrument contains a clause (the Crummey clause) that authorizes any beneficiary or his or her legal representative to make a current withdrawal of any current addition to the trust of up to $14,000 (2016). The withdrawal right is made noncumulative from year to year. As long as the beneficiary is given notification of this right within a reasonable period before it lapses for the year, the donor will be entitled to an exclusion for the current transfers into trust.[28] It should be noted that most donors anticipate that their donees will never exercise their withdrawal right; the Crummey clause is included in the trust instrument for the *sole purpose* of securing the $14,000 exclusion for gift tax purposes.

Grantor Trusts

LO.7
Distinguish between a grantor trust and a taxable trust.

In certain cases a taxpayer may desire to transfer property into trust but does not want to surrender complete control over the property. Alternatively, the taxpayer may want to dispose of the property (and the right to income from the property) for only a limited period of time. Prior to the enactment of the 1954 Internal Revenue Code there was no statutory guidance as to when the retention of powers over a trust by the grantor (transferor) would prevent the trust from being recognized as a separate taxable entity. Nor was there statutory guidance as to the tax status of a reversionary trust, the corpus of which reverted to the grantor after a specified length of time.

The judicial attitude toward these *grantor* trusts was reflected in the Supreme Court decision of *Helvering v. Clifford.*[29] This case involved a taxpayer who transferred securities into trust for the exclusive benefit of his wife. The trust was to last for five years, during which time the taxpayer as trustee would manage the trust corpus as well as decide how much, if any, of the trust income was to be paid to his wife. Upon trust termination, corpus was to return to the taxpayer while any accumulated income was to go to the wife.

[26] Reg. § 25.2503-3(c) Ex. 3.

[27] The amusing designation comes from the court case which established the validity of the technique—*Crummey v. Comm.,* 68-2 USTC ¶12,541, 22 AFTR2d 6023, 397 F.2d 82

(CA-9, 1968). The IRS *acquiesced* to this decision in Rev. Rul. 73-405, 1973-2 C.B. 321.

[28] Rev. Rul. 81-7, 1981-1 C.B. 27.

[29] 40-1 USTC ¶9265, 23 AFTR 1077, 309 U.S. 331 (1940).

In reaching its decision, the Court noted the lack of a precise standard or guide supplied by statute or regulations. As a result, the Court turned to a subjective evaluation of all the facts and circumstances of this particular short-term trust arrangement and held that "the short duration of the trust, the fact that the wife was the beneficiary, and the retention of control over the corpus by respondent all lead irresistibly to the conclusion that the respondent continued to be the owner."[30] As a result, the trust income was held to be taxable to the grantor rather than the trust or its beneficiary.

The authors of the 1954 Internal Revenue Code recognized that the uncertainty regarding the tax treatment of grantor trusts was undesirable and supplanted the subjective *Clifford* approach with a series of code sections (§§ 671 through 679) containing more objective rules as to the taxability of such trusts. The basic operative rule is contained in § 671. If §§ 673 through 679 specify that the grantor (or another person) shall be treated as the owner of any portion of a trust, the income, deductions, or credits attributable to that portion of the trust shall be reported on the grantor's (or other person's) tax return. If §§ 673 through 679 are inapplicable, the trust shall be treated as a separate taxable entity under the normal rules of Subchapter J (see Chapter 16).

REVERSIONARY TRUSTS

Section 673 provides that the grantor shall be treated as the owner of any portion of a trust in which he or she has a reversionary interest, if upon creation of the trust the value of the reversion exceeds 5% of the value of the assets subject to reversion.

Example 14

In the current year, grantor G transfers assets worth $500,000 into trust. Niece N, age 20, will receive the income from the trust for 15 years, after which the trust will terminate and the assets returned to G. On the date the trust is created, the reversion is properly valued at $121,000. Because the reversion is worth more than 5% of $500,000, the income will be taxed to G, even though it will be distributed to N.

Example 15

If in the previous example, N had been given the income from the trust for her life, the proper value of G's reversion would only be $13,000. Because this reversionary interest is worth only 2.6% of the value of the trust assets, the trust is not a grantor trust and the income will be taxed to N.

In the case of a trust in which a lineal descendant of the grantor (child, grandchild, etc.) is the income beneficiary, and the grantor owns a reversionary interest that takes effect only upon the death of the beneficiary prior to the age of 21, the trust *will not* be considered a grantor trust.[31]

INTEREST-FREE LOANS

Through use of a reversionary trust, a taxpayer may divert income to low-bracket family members only if he or she is willing to part with control of the trust corpus for a significant period of time. For many years the use of an interest-free demand loan between family members provided an alternative to a reversionary trust. A taxpayer could loan a sum of money to a family member on a demand basis and the money could be invested to earn income for

[30] *Ibid.*, 309 U.S. 332.   [31] § 673(b).

that family member. Because the loan was interest-free, the creditor-taxpayer had no income from the temporary shift of wealth and could call the loan (demand payment) at any time.

The IRS was understandably hostile to such loans and argued that the creditor was making a gift of the use of the money to the borrower and that the amount of the gift equaled the interest that the creditor would have charged an unrelated borrower. In 1984, Congress codified the IRS position by enacting Code § 7872, concerning below-market-rate-interest and no-interest loans. The thrust of this provision is to impute interest income to the creditor donor and correspondingly allow an interest deduction for the borrower-donee. Therefore, the creditor-donor is effectively treated as having received interest income and then gifting such income to the borrower. The deemed transfer is subject to the gift tax to the extent the interest exceeds the annual exclusion. As a result, interest-free loans are no longer an effective device for shifting income.

Example 16

On January 1 of the current year, father F loaned $175,000 to his daughter, S. The loan was interest free and F may demand repayment at any time. The current interest rate as determined by the IRS is 10% per annum. On December 31 of the current year, S is considered to have paid $17,500 of deductible interest to F, and F is considered to have received $17,500 of taxable interest income from S. On the same date, F is considered to have made a $17,500 gift to S which is eligible for the $14,000 (2016) annual gift tax exclusion.

POWER TO CONTROL BENEFICIAL ENJOYMENT

Section 674(a) contains the general rule that a grantor shall be treated as the owner of any portion of a trust of which the grantor, a nonadverse party, or both, controls the beneficial enjoyment. However, if the exercise of such control requires the approval or consent of an *adverse party*, the general rule shall not apply. An adverse party is defined in § 672(a) as any person who has a substantial beneficial interest in the trust that would be adversely affected by the exercise of the control held by the grantor.

Example 17

F transfers income-producing property into trust with City Bank as independent trustee. F's two children are named as trust beneficiaries. However, F retains the unrestricted right to designate which of the children is to receive annual distributions of trust income. This is a grantor trust with the result that all trust income is taxed to F.

Example 18

Refer to the facts in *Example 17*. Assume that the trust instrument provides that the trust income will be paid out on an annual basis in equal portions to F's two children. However, F retains the right to adjust the amount of the income distributions at any time with the consent of the older child C. Because C is an adverse party with respect to the one-half of the income to which he is entitled, only the other half of the income is considered subject to F's control. As a result, only half the trust property is deemed owned by F and only half the trust income is taxable directly to him.[32]

---

[32] Reg. § 1.672(a)-1(b).

The general rule of § 674(a) is subject to numerous exceptions contained in §§ 674(b), (c), and (d). Any tax adviser attempting to avoid the grantor trust rules should be aware of these exceptions. For example, § 674(c) provides that the power to distribute income within a class of beneficiaries will not cause the grantor trust rules to apply if the power is solely exercisable by an *independent* trustee.

> ### Example 19
>
> M transfers income-producing property into trust and names Midtown Bank as independent trustee. The trustee has the right to *sprinkle* (distribute) the annual income of the trust among M's three children in any proportion the trustee deems appropriate. Even though the power to control the enjoyment of the income is held by a nonadverse party, such party is independent of the grantor and the trust is not a grantor trust.

OTHER GRANTOR TRUSTS

Section 675 provides that the grantor shall be treated as the owner of any portion of a trust in respect of which he or she holds certain administrative or management powers.

> ### Example 20
>
> T transfers 60% of the common stock in his closely held corporation into trust with City National Bank as independent trustee. All income of the trust must be paid to T's only grandchild. However, T retains the right to vote the transferred shares. Because T has retained an administrative power specified in § 675(4), he will be taxed on the income generated by the corporate stock.

If a grantor, a nonadverse party, or both have the right to revest in the grantor the ownership of any portion of trust property, § 676 provides that such portion of the trust is considered to be owned by the grantor. Therefore, revocable trusts are grantor trusts for income tax purposes.

Under § 677, a grantor also is treated as owner of any portion of a trust the income of which *may be* distributed to the grantor or spouse without the approval of any adverse party. This rule also applies if trust income may be used to pay premiums for insurance on the life of the grantor and spouse. This provision is inapplicable if the beneficiary of the policy is a charitable organization.

> ### Example 21
>
> Individual J transfers income-producing assets into trust and designates Second National Bank as independent trustee. Under the terms of the trust instrument, the trustee may distribute trust income to either J's spouse or J's brother. In the current year the trustee distributes all trust income to J's brother. Because a nonadverse party (the trustee) could have distributed the trust income to J's spouse, this is a grantor trust and all income is taxed to J.

If trust income may be expended to discharge a legal obligation of the grantor, § 677 applies,[33] subject to two important exceptions. Section 682 creates an exception for *alimony trusts*. In certain divorce situations an individual who is required to pay alimony may fund a reversionary trust, the income from which will be paid to the grantor's former spouse in satisfaction of the alimony obligation. Under § 682, the recipient of the trust income rather than the grantor will be taxed on the income regardless of the applicability of any other of the grantor trust rules.

---

[33] Reg. § 1.677(a)-1(d).

As a second exception, § 677(b) specifies that if trust income may be distributed for the support or maintenance of a beneficiary (other than the grantor's spouse) whom the grantor is legally obligated to support, such a provision by itself will not cause the trust to be a grantor trust. However, to the extent trust income is actually distributed for such purposes, it will be taxed to the grantor.

The final type of trust that is not recognized as a separate taxable entity is described in § 678. Under this provision, a person *other than* the grantor may be treated as the owner of a portion of a trust if such person has an unrestricted right to vest trust corpus or income in himself or herself. Section 678 shall not apply to the situation in which a person, in the capacity of trustee, has the right to distribute trust income to a beneficiary whom the person is legally obligated to support. Only to the extent that trust income is actually so expended will the income be taxed to the person.

Example 22

Grantor G creates a trust with an independent corporate trustee and names his children and grandchildren as beneficiaries. The trust instrument also provides that G's sister S has the unrestricted right to withdraw up to one-third of trust corpus at anytime. S is considered the owner of one-third of the trust and will be taxed on one-third of the income, regardless of the fact that such income is not distributable to her.

GRANTOR TRUSTS AND THE TRANSFER TAX RULES

As a general rule, a transfer of assets into trust that is incomplete for income tax purposes, so that the grantor is taxed on trust income, is also incomplete for gift and estate tax purposes.

Example 23

M transfers income-producing properties into a trust but retains the right to designate which of the specified trust beneficiaries will receive a distribution of trust income. The arrangement is a grantor trust per § 674. Under the gift tax Regulations, M has not made a completed gift of the income interest in the trust, and per § 2036 the value of the trust corpus will be included in M's gross estate upon his death.

However, it should be emphasized that the general rule does not always hold.

Example 24

Grantor G transfers assets into a reversionary trust that will last only eight years. During the existence of the trust, all income must be paid to G's cousin, C. For income tax purposes, this is a grantor trust and all trust income is taxable to G. However, for gift tax purposes G has made a completed gift of the income interest to C.

Transfer Tax Planning

The first part of this chapter dealt with a variety of techniques to shift income within a family group and thereby minimize the family's income tax burden. The second part of the chapter focuses on family tax planning techniques designed to reduce any transfer tax liability on intrafamily shifts of wealth. At this point, the student should be cautioned against thinking of income tax planning and transfer tax planning as two separate areas; both types of planning should be considered as highly interrelated aspects of a single integrated family tax plan.

A second aspect of transfer tax planning of which any tax adviser should be aware is that a client's nontax estate planning goals may conflict with an optimal tax-oriented estate plan. From a client's point of view, an orderly disposition of wealth that benefits the heirs in the precise manner that the client desires may be the primary planning objective, regardless of the tax cost. A client planning for his or her own death may be most concerned with his or her own emotional and psychological needs as well as those of other family members. Minimization of the Federal estate tax levied on the estate simply may not be a central concern. A tax adviser who fails to appreciate the client's priorities and who designs an estate plan that fails to reflect the client's nontax needs is not acting in the best interest of that client.

TAX PLANNING WITH INTRAFAMILY GIFTS

LO.8

Specify the tax advantages of inter vivos gifts as compared to testamentary transfers of wealth.

Before enactment of the Tax Reform Act of 1976, the Federal transfer tax savings associated with gifting assets to family members during the donor's life rather than transferring the assets at death were obvious. The gift tax rates were only 75% of the estate tax rates, and because of the progressive nature of both rate schedules, inter vivos gifts could shift an individual's wealth out of a high marginal estate tax bracket into a lower marginal gift tax bracket.

The Tax Reform Act of 1976 integrated the gift and estate taxes by providing a single rate schedule for both taxes and by including in the estate tax base the amount of post-1976 gifts made by a decedent.[34] Thus, any inter vivos gift made by a decedent after 1976 has the effect of boosting his or her taxable estate into a higher tax bracket.

Example 25

In 2007, D made a taxable gift of $400,000, her only taxable inter vivos transfer. D dies in 2016, leaving a taxable estate of $5,450,000. The base for computing D's estate tax is $5,850,000, her taxable estate of $5,450,000 plus the $400,000 taxable gift.

Because of the integration of the gift and estate taxes, the tax benefit of inter vivos giving has been reduced but certainly not eliminated. The following advantages of making gifts have survived the integration process.

1. All appreciation in value of the transferred property that occurs after the date of gift escapes taxation in the donor's gross estate. Refer to *Example 25*. If the value of the gifted asset increased from $400,000 in 2007 to $700,000 in the current year, the $300,000 appreciation is not taxed in D's estate. It should be noted that inter vivos transfers of appreciating assets do have a negative income tax consequence. The basis of such assets to the donee will be a carryover basis from the donor, increased by the amount of any gift tax paid attributable to the difference between the value of the gift and the donor's tax basis.[35] If the donor retained the property until death, the basis of the property would be stepped up to its fair market to value at date of death.[36] Thus, a transfer of the asset during life rather than at death preserves rather than eliminates pre-death appreciation in the value of the asset that will be subject to income taxation on subsequent sale.

2. Future income generated by property that the donor has transferred will be accumulated by younger generation family members rather than in the estate of the donor.

3. The availability of the annual $14,000 (2016) exclusion allows a donor to give away a substantial amount of wealth completely tax free.

4. All other factors being equal, it is cheaper to pay a gift tax rather than an estate tax. This is true because the dollars used to pay a gift tax are never themselves subject to a Federal transfer tax. However, dollars used to pay an estate tax have been included in the taxable estate and are subject to the estate tax.

---

[34] § 2001(b).

[35] § 1015.

[36] § 1014.

For this reason, the estate tax is said to be *tax inclusive* (since the estate tax is itself taxed) while the gift tax is sometimes said to be *tax exclusive* (the gift tax itself is not taxed).

Example 26

D has $10,000,000 in assets and wants to transfer $6,000,000 to a beneficiary. Ignore the annual exclusion, the unified credit and assume a flat rate of 40%. If D dies with an estate of $10,000,000, the estate will pay a tax of $4,000,000 out of the estate's assets and $6,000,000 will be left to pass to the heirs. In contrast, if the individual had made a $6,000,000 gift before he died, he would have had to pay only a $2,400,000 tax for the privilege of transferring $6,000,000. In other words, it would cost $1,600,000 less ($4,000,000 − $2,400,000) to give $6,000,000 than to *will* such amount. In effect, if he gave $6,000,000 while he was living, he would have had $1,600,000 left to do with as he pleases. By making the gift and paying the gift tax, he is removing the gift tax amount ($2,400,000) from his estate, never to be taxed!

Example 27

W has only $1,000,000 of assets. Assume a 40% rate and ignore the unified credit and annual exclusion. If W dies and leaves the $1,000,000 to her child, W pays a tax of $400,000 and the child receives $600,000. If W had used the same $1,000,000 to make a gift and pay the tax, she could have given her child $714,286, determined as follows:

$$
\begin{aligned}
x &= \text{Amount of the gift} \\
0.40x &= \text{Gift tax} \\[6pt]
x + 0.40x &= \$1,000,000 \\
1.40x &= \$1,000,000 \\
x &= \$714,286 \\
0.40x &= \$285,714
\end{aligned}
$$

Thus if W makes a gift of $714,286, she will pay a gift tax of $285,714, exhausting the $1,000,000. Note that by giving, the child receives $714,286 rather than $600,000 or $114,286 more!

"FREEZING" THE VALUE OF ASSETS IN THE GROSS ESTATE

A long-range plan of inter vivos giving from older generation to younger generation family members is a basic component of most family tax plans. However, elderly individuals can be very reluctant about making substantial gifts of their wealth, even when they fully understand the tax advantages in doing so. Psychologically it is difficult to part with wealth that is the result of a lifetime of endeavor. Elderly individuals often fear that gifts of property might leave them without sufficient income or capital to provide for their future comfort and security. They may even worry that their children and grandchildren might "desert" them if the offspring were given the family wealth too soon.

For these and many other reasons it may be difficult for the tax adviser to persuade an older client to transfer existing wealth during his or her lifetime. However, the same client may be much more amenable to simply "freezing" the value of his or her current estate, so that future accumulations of wealth are somehow transferred to younger members of the family and therefore not subject to estate tax upon the client's death.

Gifts of Property

The simplest type of estate freeze is a gift. A gift of appreciating property is taxed at its current value for gift tax purposes and any future appreciation is forever removed from the estate tax base. Note, however, that this technique is not without problems. Taxpayers who want to maximize the amount of wealth that their heirs ultimately receive must balance the trade-offs between giving the property during their lifetime or willing the property at death.

If a taxpayer gives appreciating property during life, the gift removes any appreciation from the estate. However, the basis of the property to the donee will normally be the same as the donor's basis. In such case, the donee would be required to pay an income tax on a subsequent sale of the property. Note that this income tax would not have resulted had the property been retained till death due to the step-up in basis for inherited property. Moreover, if the taxpayer must pay gift tax on the transfer, the time value of any gift tax paid would be lost. In short, a gift of appreciating property normally saves transfer taxes at a rate up to 40% (2016) but results in an income tax of up to 15% (assuming the property is a capital asset) and loss of the time value of gift tax (net of estate tax). Conversely, retaining the property normally saves on income taxes but at the cost of an estate tax on the appreciation.

Example 28

In 2003, T purchased 300 acres of land on the far west side of Dallas for $100,000. While the land was truly in a remote area, T expected that it would one day be prime property since it is near an interstate highway. By 2016, it was clear that an increase in the value of the property was imminent. Assume the property will triple in value to $300,000 by the time T dies in 10 years. Also assume that the transfer tax rate is 40 percent, the applicable income tax rate is 15 percent, and the aftertax interest rate is 8 percent. The following is a simple comparison (ignoring present values) of what happens if (1) T gives the property now, or (2) holds it until death.

1.	*Give Property Now before It Appreciates*		Tax Cost
	Gift tax now ($100,000 × 40%)		$ 40,000
	Income tax to beneficiaries later due to carryover basis		
	Gift: ([$300,000 − $100,000 = $200,000] × 15%)		30,000
	Value of gift tax paid today lost:		
	Gift tax ($40,000 × 8% × 10 years)	$32,000	
	Estate tax ($32,000 − [40% × $32,000])	(19,200)	12,800
	Tax cost		$ 82,800

2.	*Retain Property until Death*		Tax Cost
	Estate tax later ($300,000 × 40%)		$120,000
	No income tax later		
	Bequest ($300,000 − $300,000 = $0 × 15%)		0
	Tax cost		$120,000

In this case, it would appear that giving the property away during T's life would produce a smaller overall tax cost than retaining it till death. However, this result is based on many assumptions and fails to consider many others. Nevertheless, the example illustrates some of the basic considerations that should be taken into account when doing estate planning.

Interests in Closely Held Businesses

For individuals who have a stake in a business, such as stock in a family-held C or S corporation or an interest in a partnership or LLC, the interest in the company is not only their lifeblood but in most cases represents a substantial portion of their estate. Indeed, the business often represents the bulk of the assets that they wish to leave to their heirs. Unfortunately, without proper planning, the costs associated with transferring such business (e.g., illiquidity, the estate, gift and generation-skipping transfer taxes, probate) can decimate the business, leaving the heirs with little or no inheritance. Over the years, practitioners have addressed these problems in a number of ways. Most of these plans are directed at valuation of the assets and how that value can be reduced and frozen. In this regard, it should not be forgotten that for estate and gift tax purposes, the minimum marginal tax rate is 45 percent, meaning that every $1,000 of reduced valuation produces $450 of savings!

Closely held businesses normally present valuation problems of monumental proportions. The difficulty lies in the fact that, unlike their publicly traded cousins, there is no market where closely held businesses are actively traded.

For its part, the government's primary contribution concerning the valuation problem is contained in the often cited Revenue Ruling 59-60. In this ruling, the IRS has identified a list of factors to be considered in valuing such businesses. These are:

1. Book value and financial condition of the corporation.
2. Earning capacity of the company.
3. Dividend paying capacity.
4. Whether the enterprise has goodwill or other intangible value.
5. The economic outlook in general and the condition and outlook of the specific industry in particular.
6. The nature of the business and the history of the enterprise from its inception.
7. Sales of stock and the size of the block of stock to be valued.
8. The market price of stocks of corporations engaged in the same or a similar line of business that are actively traded in a free and open market.

Unfortunately, the ruling provides little guidance regarding how these factors are to be used. The ruling simply states that the weight to be accorded each factor depends upon the facts of each case. While experts in business valuation (a niche industry in and of itself) utilize these and other widely accepted methods, there is no certainty that the value obtained is objective and unbiased. As a practical matter, the estate is left to its own devices to determine the value of the company and convince the IRS and/or judge that its method and value are correct.

Valuation: Premiums and Discounts. In establishing the value of an interest in a closely held company, additional value is generally attributed to the interest if it represents control. A so-called *control premium* is warranted since it enables the holder to extract more value from the firm through his or her ability to dominate management. For example, an individual with control can elect the entire board of directors, remove a director, control the business and affairs of the company, elect and remove all of the officers, fix their salaries, and control the declaration of dividends. The major valuation issue when control is present is determining how much value, if any should be assigned to the control element. This has often been the source of a great deal of controversy.

Example 29

The uncertainties of valuation are made abundantly clear in *Estate of Joseph E. Salsbury*.[37] In this case, the value of the company, particularly the amount of premium, was the primary issue. Salsbury died holding 51.8% of the stock of Salsbury Laboratories, a manufacturer of drug and health products for the poultry industry. At the time of his death, all of the stock of the corporation was owned by the decedent, members of his family, trusts for their benefit and a private charitable foundation. The IRS asserted an estate tax deficiency of $6,007,503 primarily attributable to the difference in values placed on the stock held by the decedent. The date of death values placed on the decedent's shares by the parties and the expert witnesses for the taxpayer and the IRS were worlds apart as shown below.

---

[37] T.C. Memo 1975-33.

Value claimed on estate tax return...	$ 372,152
Value asserted by the IRS in deficiency notice	11,655,000
Expert witness for the taxpayer	558,228
Expert witness for the IRS	8,748,152
Expert witness for the IRS	1,400,000

The sole issue of contention regarding the valuation was the amount that should be assigned to the control element held by the decedent. Note the difference in valuation even though these are valuation experts. Interestingly, the court ultimately held that the stock was worth $514,000.

Discounts. In contrast to a control premium, a *discount* may be available. Over the years, taxpayers have identified a number of reasons why a discount should be allowed.

It is well accepted that a discount may be appropriate when valuing large blocks of stock. When a taxpayer owns such a large block of stock that the price at which the stock would be traded in the market would *not* be representative of the value, a *blockage discount* may be claimed. Blockage discounts are available if the executor can show that the block of stock to be valued is so large in relation to the actual sales on the existing market that the stock could not be liquidated in a reasonable time without depressing the market.

Discounts have also been granted for the tax consequences that could result upon a disposition of the business. For example, if a taxpayer owns stock in a C corporation, the ultimate value that the owner can extract from the company can be substantially reduced because of the double taxation problems that can occur on liquidation of the corporation.

By far the most important types of discount are those available if the taxpayer's ownership represents a minority interest or where there is lack of marketability or both. In reviewing the court decisions addressing this issue, it is not uncommon to see discounts of between 25 and 50 percent and sometimes more! With proper planning, taxpayers can successfully secure these discounts to obtain literally huge savings. For this reason, understanding the justification for these discounts and the techniques used to achieve them is extremely important.

The lack of marketability discount is based on the fact that an interest in a closely held business is generally less attractive because it is illiquid—hard to convert to cash—and more difficult to sell than an interest for which there is an active trading market. This is a particularly acute problem when the majority of interests are owned by family members. Stock that if publicly traded would be worth $1,000,000 would be worth far less because it would be unlikely to find an outside buyer to purchase the stock. Adding to the discount is the fact there would be substantial costs incurred such as underwriting expenses involved if a company were to go public.

The rationale for *minority interest discounts* is founded upon the owner's limited power to influence business decisions (e.g., control day-to-day or long-range managerial decisions, affect future earnings, control efforts for growth potential, establish executive compensation or dividend policy, or compel a sale of assets or a liquidation). As a practical matter, a discount is warranted due to the fact that an unrelated party interested in purchasing an interest in a family-owned business would not pay full value for such an interest.

Example 30

D owns all of the stock of Close Corporation, which has a value of $9,000,000. If D were to die, the entire value of the stock would be included in his estate. D might be able to reduce the transfer cost substantially if he were to give one-third of the stock to his son, one-third to his daughter and die holding one-third. At first thought, it might appear that the value of the gifts would be one-third of the total or aggregate value or $3,000,000 each. However, by arguing that the each gift constitutes a minority interest, he may be able to claim a substantial discount when he makes the gifts or at death.

The IRS has not always accepted the minority discount theory, particularly when the person acquiring the interest is related. Historically, the government consistently argued that for purposes of valuing gifts and bequests of stock or partnership interests to family members, the ownership interests of the family members should be aggregated and valued as a whole.[38] Applying this approach to the example above, the IRS may take the position that no discount is allowed and the value of each gift is $3,000,000. In fact, when the IRS took this approach, using an aggregate value, it often included a control premium, and then used the increased value as the basis for assigning a value to the fraction of shares transferred.

After years of denying taxpayers minority discounts in the family setting, the IRS finally abandoned its position. In Revenue Ruling 93-12, the IRS stated that it would no longer challenge a discount solely because the transferred interest, when aggregated with interests held by family members, would be considered part of a controlling interest.[39] For example, when the taxpayer transferred all of his stock in equal gifts to each of his 11 children, the IRS ruled that the value of the gift to each is computed by considering each gift separately and not by aggregating all of the donor's holdings.[40]

Since the government's surrender in 1993, fractionalizing an owner's interest to obtain minority discounts has become virtually an indispensable part of estate planning. As explained below, corporate and partnership freezes, particularly the use of family limited partnerships, has become a staple of the estate planning industry.

Freezing the Value of the Estate: C Corporations

To freeze the transfer tax value of an interest in a C corporation, the corporation engages in a type "E" reorganization referred to as a recapitalization. The following steps are taken:

1. The owner exchanges common stock for both new voting preferred and new nonvoting common which together has a value equal to his original shares of common.

2. Pursuant to the reorganization provisions of § 368(a)(1)(E), this exchange of stock is nontaxable.

3. At the time of the exchange, the preferred stock is structured to represent the majority of the corporation's value, while the common stock has little value. The preferred stock typically carried a fixed-rate, non-cumulative dividend and preferential treatment for dividends and assets upon liquidation. Other rights and privileges may be attached.

4. The owner gives the nonvoting common stock to the heirs at little or no gift tax cost since all of the corporation's value is in the preferred stock which is held by the owner.

5. The result is that all of future appreciation of the corporation is attributable to the common stock and shifted to the donees since the preferred stock's value is locked in at time of exchange (i.e., its value is attributable to its preferred claim on assets in the event of liquidation and its yield). Also, the owner has retained income security.

Example 31

F owns all of the voting common stock of C corporation with a value of $1,500,000 (basis $100,000). Approaching retirement, F wants to transfer the ownership of the business to his daughter and do so at the least possible tax cost. In addition, he wants to maintain control of the business and retain a steady stream of income for life. To this end, he exchanged his voting common stock for nonvoting common stock worth $1,000,000 and voting preferred stock with a par value set such that it is equal to $500,000. F has a non-cumulative "put" with the corporation that enables him to sell the preferred stock back to the corporation at its par value of $500,000. The preferred stock pays a non-cumulative dividend of 15 percent. The put and the dividend enable F to claim the stock is at least worth $500,000 since at any time the stock could

---

[38] See Revenue Ruling 81-253 1981-2 C.B. 187 which held that no minority interest discount would be allowed for intrafamily transfers of stock in a corporation controlled by the family absent discord among the family members.

[39] 1993-1 C.B. 202.

[40] TAM 9449001.

be sold to the corporation for $500,000. F realizes a gain of $1,400,000 ($500,000 + $1,000,000 − $100,000) but under the reorganization provisions this gain is not recognized. F subsequently gives the common worth $1,000,000 ($1,500,000 total value − $500,000 value of preferred) to his daughter and pays no gift tax due to the unified credit which shelters the $1,000,000 taxable gift. If the value of the preferred is respected, F has (1) retained control of the corporation since he owns all of the voting stock, (2) ensured a steady stream of income for retirement since he can vote himself a dividend at any time, (3) frozen the value of his estate at $500,000, and (4) shifted all of the appreciation to his daughter who holds the common stock. As might be expected, in these situations, the Service was reluctant to accept the value placed on the preferred since it was unlikely that F would ever exercise his put nor would he ever vote himself a dividend.

While this plan can be used successfully, there are certain restrictions that limit its value as discussed below.

Freezing the Value of the Estate: Partnerships

Steps similar to that used in freezing the value of an interest in a family-held C corporation can be taken to freeze the value of an interest in a partnership (or LLC). In addition, a partnership could be used to freeze the value of appreciating property such as farms, ranches, timberland, and other unimproved or improved real estate. The partnership form provides an almost perfect vehicle to fractionalize interests in the property to create minority discounts. A partnership freeze normally involves recapitalizing an existing partnership or the formation of a new partnership. Family limited partnerships are the vehicle commonly used. The following steps are taken:

1. The owners of property (e.g., the senior members of the family such as parents or grandparents) normally transfer the property to a limited partnership in exchange for (1) a general partnership interest which represents growth interest and (2) a limited partnership interest which represents the frozen interest.

2. The exchange normally is nontaxable under § 721.

3. The transferors retain a small general partnership interest and transfer a large limited partnership interest.

Example 32

H and W transfer 1,000 acres of land worth $10,000,000 to a family limited partnership. In exchange H and W each receive one percent general partnership interests and 49% limited partnership interests. H and W then transfer the limited partnership interests to their children. Significant discounts are normally available for transfers of limited partnership interests. Normally there is a minority interest discount since limited partners have no control over the partnership (e.g., no voice in management and no right to force a liquidation) as well as a lack of marketability discount since such interests are usually illiquid.

Valuation Issues in Corporate and Partnership Freezes

The approach normally used to value the interest transferred in a corporate or partnership freeze is a residual one. The entire business is valued and then the value of the retained interest is identified. Any residual value is the value of the transferred interest. This method is show in the formula below.

$$
\begin{array}{r}
\text{FMV of business} \\
-\ \ \text{FMV of retained interest} \\
\hline
=\ \ \text{FMV of transferred interest and gift to heirs}
\end{array}
$$

For many years, planners kept the value of the transferred interest (e.g., the common stock) low by assigning valuable rights to the retained interest (e.g., the preferred stock) in order to increase the value of the retained interest. For example, in a preferred stock freeze, these included an above market-rate cumulative (and often noncumulative) dividend, conversion rights, call rights, liquidation preferences and voting rights. Even if it was clear that it was unlikely that those rights would be exercised, the courts usually took them into account in valuing the preferred stock.[41]

Congress became concerned about assigning value to these "discretionary" rights given to the owner in that such rights probably would not be exercised. To address this problem, in 1987 Congress enacted the now infamous anti-freeze rules of § 2036(c) that were so controversial that they were subsequently repealed in 1990. In their place, Congress substituted § 2701, which contains the rules currently in operation today. Section 2701 attempts to more accurately value the property that is transferred among family members when the transferor retains some interest in the business. The approach is to value certain retained discretionary rights (e.g., rights to dividends or distributions, liquidation rights, put, call, and conversion rights) at *zero* unless they meet tests that virtually guarantee their exercise. Note that if these retained rights are valued at zero, a transfer of the common stock or limited partnership interests would be treated as a gift of the full fair market value of the business.

Section 2701 generally operates only if the following conditions exist (note this is the normal pattern of a corporate or partnership freeze discussed above):

1. The taxpayer makes a transfer of an interest in a corporation or partnership.
2. The transferor controls the entity. Control is defined as ownership of at least 50% of the entity either directly or indirectly.
3. The transfer is made to a family member (i.e., spouse, lineal descendant of the transferor or spouse, or a spouse of such descendant).
4. The transferor retains an applicable retained right (distribution rights).

In general, the retained interests must provide for a periodic *qualified payment* (e.g., a dividend or distribution). If there is no provision for qualified payments, no value may be assigned to the retained interest, resulting in a gift of the full value of the business.

Qualified Payments. A qualified payment depends on the type of entity. For corporations, a qualified payment is any dividend payable at a fixed rate on a periodic basis on cumulative preferred stock. For partnerships, a qualified payment is a comparable payment at a fixed rate made with respect to any partnership interest. The value of the retained interest must be determined by calculating the present value of the future cash flows from the retained interest or more precisely discounting the qualified payment. No value is assigned to any other rights (put, call, conversion) attached to the stock or partnership interest. Note that if a very low payout rate is selected, there will be a lower annual cash payout required but there will also be a lower value placed on the preferred stock or retained partnership interest. In contrast, if there is a high payout rate, the value of the retained interest is greater, yielding a smaller gift. However, selecting a high payout rate in order to increase the value of the retained interest and reduce the value of the gifted interest has the effect of returning more value (e.g., dividends) to the taxpayer's estate. In any event, a minimum value is placed on the common stock or partnership interest that is transferred. At least 10% of the value of the business must be assigned to the gifted stock or partnership interest. This ensures that there is a gift of at least 10% of the value of the corporation.

Example 33

This year D decided to transfer her business, a C corporation, to her children. To this end, she exchanged all of her common stock in the corporation for nonvoting common and voting preferred in a transaction qualifying as a tax-free recapitalization. After the transfer, D owned 3,000 shares of $1,000 par value voting preferred stock, each share paying a cumulative annual dividend of seven percent. In addition, there are 10,000 shares of nonvoting common stock outstanding. D gave all of the common stock to her daughter. Pursuant to an appraisal, the corporation's value was

---

[41] Rev. Rul. 83-120, 1983-2 C.B. 170.

estimated to be $3,100,000. The value of the preferred stock must be determined by discounting the future dividends. Here the annual dividends are $210,000 ($1,000 par value × 7% = $70 per share × 3,000 shares). According to the regulations, the value is determined by assuming that the dividend is paid in perpetuity. Assuming the applicable federal rate is ten percent, the present value of a $210,000 annuity discounted at ten percent is $2,100,000 (1/.1 × $210,000). Thus the value of the preferred is $2,100,000 and the value of the common is $1,000,000 ($3,100,000 − $2,100,000). Consequently, D is treated as making a $1,000,000 gift. If D has not made any other taxable gifts during her lifetime, the entire transfer is tax-free. More important, if the corporation's value increases at a rate greater than the dividend rate of seven percent, all of the excess appreciation is attributable to the common and, therefore, out of her estate.

Family Limited Partnerships

Although the corporate or partnership freeze can be useful, the qualified payment requirement can be a difficult hurdle when trying to accomplish the taxpayer's goals. For this reason, some plans do not meet or do not attempt to meet the qualified payment rule. In such case, the gift is the full value of the interest. However, to minimize this problem, a family limited partnership (FLP) is often formed to create minority and marketability discounts that reduce the value of the transferred interests.

Example 34

H and W, husband and wife, together own all of the stock of a corporation worth $4,000,000. As part of a plan to transfer the stock to their children, they transfer all of the stock to a limited partnership in exchange for a one percent general partnership interest and a 99% limited partnership interest. The couple then transfers the limited partnership interest to their children, claiming minority and marketability discounts totaling 50 percent. As a result, the partnership interests transferred by each are about $1,000,000 each and totally tax free because of the unified credit.

Due to the power of the FLP, they have become extremely popular and, at the same time, frequently abused. The most flagrant situations involve transfers of publicly traded securities to FLPs and taking substantial discounts. Although the IRS retreated in their challenge of such arrangements in Revenue Ruling 93-12, it is now pursuing these with some recent successes. Only time will tell the final outcome.[42]

Sales of Property

Another technique for freezing the value of an asset in a taxpayer's estate is for the taxpayer to sell the asset to a younger generation family member.

Example 35

Grandfather G owns several acres of undeveloped real estate with a current value of $1 million. The land is located near a rapidly growing metropolitan area and its value is expected to triple over the next decade. If G sells the real estate to his granddaughter D for $1 million cash, the value of his current estate is unchanged. However, the future increase in the value of the land has been removed from G's estate and will belong to D. In addition, D's basis is at least equal to the value of the property at the time of the transfer rather than G's basis had it been gifted.

---

[42] For example, see *Estate of Charles Reichardt v. Comm.*, 114 T.C. 144 (2000).

An attractive variation of the selling technique illustrated in *Example 35* is an installment sale to the granddaughter. If D does not have $1 million of cash readily available (a most realistic assumption), G could simply accept his granddaughter's bona fide installment note as payment for the land. If the note is to be paid off over 20 years, G could use the installment sale method of reporting any taxable gain on the sale. If G had no need for cash during the term of the note, he could forgive his granddaughter's note payments and interest as they become due. Such forgiveness of indebtedness would not change the income tax consequences of the installment sale to G and would represent a gift to D eligible for the annual $14,000 (2016) exclusion.[43]

GRITs, GRATs, and GRUTs

Another freezing technique that gained popularity over the years is the so-called *GRIT*, the acronym for *grantor retained income trust*. Under this arrangement, the grantor transfers property to a trust, retains the income for a period of years, and gifts the remainder. Under the right circumstances, substantial benefits can be obtained. If the grantor survives the term, nothing is pulled back into the grantor's estate under § 2036 since the grantor did not retain an interest until death. As a result, the taxpayer has transferred the property at the cost of a gift tax on the remainder which normally represents only a fraction of the value of the entire property. In addition, all of the appreciation in the property is out of the estate. Note, however, that if the grantor does not survive the term, the property is included in the estate at its date of death value and nothing has been accomplished.

Example 36

R owns rapidly appreciating real estate. Its current value is $3,000,000. In 2016, he transferred the property to a trust, retaining the income from the property for 10 years and giving the remainder to his son. Assume the income interest is worth $2,000,000. As a result, the remainder interest is $1,000,000 and due to the unified credit there is no gift tax on the transfer. Eleven years after the transfer R died when the property was worth $9,000,000. Under prior law, nothing would be included in R's gross estate under § 2036 since he did not have an interest in the property at the time of his death. Moreover, if the property did not in reality produce any income, the $2,000,000 assigned to the retained interest is a fiction and is never subject to income or estate taxes. Thus, if R survives the transfer by more than 10 years, he was able to transfer property worth $9,000,000 and avoid all transfer tax.

Example 37

Same facts as above except R died five years after the trust was created. In such case, all of the property is included in R's gross estate at its date of death value and nothing will have been accomplished.

Historically, the value of the retained income interest in a GRIT was determined using IRS tables that often placed a higher value on the retained income interest than was justified by the actual income generated on the property. The effect of this was to deflate the value of the gift of the remainder which could be sheltered by the donor's unified credit. As might be expected, the IRS attacked this technique primarily on the grounds that the retained income interest was undervalued. Consequently, legislation was enacted to ensure that the value of the income interest was indeed real.

Under § 2702, the value of the retained income interest is *zero* and the gifted value of the remainder is the entire value of the property unless the transfer is to a *grantor retained annuity trust (GRAT)* or a grantor retained unit trust *(GRUT)*. When either of these is used, the value

---

[43] See Rev. Rul. 77-299, 1977-2 C.B. 343 for the IRS's
 negative reaction to this tax plan.

of the gift of the remainder is the value of the property less the value of the annuity or unitrust interest as shown below.

	Fair market value of property
−	Value of income interest
=	FMV of remainder and gift to heirs (no exclusion since future interest)

When the transfer is made, the grantor specifies how much income will be retained (e.g., either a fixed dollar amount [i.e., an annuity trust] or a percentage of the annual asset value [i.e., a unitrust]) as well as the period for which the annuity will last. If the grantor retains an annuity interest, the arrangement is referred to as a GRAT. If the grantor retains a unitrust interest, the arrangement is called a GRUT. Note that in either case the income interest-retained annuity effectively replaces the transferred property. One of the biggest differences between a GRIT and GRATs and GRUTs is that annual payments under GRATs and GRUTs *must be made* even if the trust assets do not generate sufficient income to make the payments. Trust principal may have to be invaded to meet the distribution requirement (however, a debt obligation may suffice).

Example 38

In 1997, R transferred land worth $1,000,000 to a GRAT. He wanted the amount of the gift of the remainder interest to be $600,000 in order to use his unified credit (exemption equivalent of $600,000 in 1997), but no more. R is 55 and he decides to use a term of 15 years to compute the required annuity. The present value of an annuity of $1 for 15 years using the IRS tables and a discount rate of 10% is $7.6061. Thus the present value of an annuity of $52,589 ($400,000/7.6061) at 10% for 15 years is $400,000. Therefore to achieve the desired result, the annuity rate is set at 5.26% and payments of $52,589 must be paid annually, even if the property does not generate sufficient income. This departs drastically from the GRIT where no payment was required if there was in fact no income. Note that if R lives the entire term, he will receive $788,835 ($52,589 × 15) which is the original $400,000 retained income interest plus the growth on the $400,000 at 10% for 15 years. Although R's estate may contain $788,835, he will have removed any appreciation from his estate. In short, if the property appreciates (or produces income at a rate exceeding the annuity rate) all of the excess appreciation or income is removed from his estate. In addition, R could remove part of this $788,835 by embarking on a gift-giving program.

CHARITABLE GIVING

Another important tool that estate planners often use to reduce a family's tax burden is the charitable transfer. Obviously, an individual can reduce or even eliminate any estate taxes by simply leaving part or all of his or her property to a qualified charity. As explained in Chapter 15, bequests to qualified charitable organizations may be deducted from the gross estate without limitation. However, from a tax planning perspective it is usually preferable for the taxpayer to make a charitable donation during life rather than at death.

While many individuals would like to make large contributions of property to a charity during their lifetime, they often delay the contribution to their deaths believing they may need the income and the property before that time. Unfortunately, these kindhearted donors, while securing the contribution deduction for estate tax purposes, lose the income tax deduction. On the other hand, some individuals may be willing to give the property and its income to a charity temporarily but ultimately want to pass the property to their heirs. Long ago charitable organizations recognized these problems and designed a solution, the so-called split interest gift.

A split-interest gift is simply a transfer of property—typically to a trust—where part of the property is given to a charity and the other part is retained by the donor. There are two common types of charitable trusts: charitable remainder trusts, and charitable lead trusts.

Charitable Remainder Trusts

With a charitable remainder trust, an individual transfers property to a trust, leaving the income from the property to a noncharitable beneficiary (e.g., a spouse or child) typically for life, and upon the beneficiary's death, the property passes to the charitable beneficiary. The beauty of a charitable remainder trust is that the donor retains the security of a steady income stream yet is entitled to an income tax deduction for the present value of the remainder interest—a deduction that would be lost had the gift been postponed until death. In order to secure the deduction for the remainder interest, a number of special requirements must be met to ensure that the charity in fact receives something once the income interest terminates.

Charitable Lead Trusts

Charities also have an answer for individuals who wish to transfer property and its income to a charity for a period of years yet want the property returned after the term has run. The solution is referred to as a charitable lead trust. In this case, the donor receives both an income and gift-tax deduction for the present value of the income interest given to the charity. However, the income tax deduction is limited to 20% of AGI, since it is for the "use of the charity" rather than "to the" charity. No carryover is allowed.

For many years, the grantor of a charitable lead trust was not charged with the income of the trust but simply got a deduction for income given to the trust that he was never taxed on! In 1969, Congress believed that this was an "unwarranted tax advantage"—a duplication of benefits—and eliminated such favorable treatment. Currently, the trust must be a grantor trust to qualify. The effect in such case is to accelerate the deduction to the current year, yet defer the income to the year it is actually received.

Using a charitable lead trust is particularly beneficial when taxpayers want to bunch all of their charitable deductions in one year. Bunching or accelerating deductions to a particular year may be advantageous in situations when taxpayers have a particularly good year with high income and need the deduction or they simply expect to be in a lower bracket in the future. As with charitable remainder trusts, a number of requirements must be met in order to secure the deduction for the income interest.

Example 39

This year J sold his business, recognizing a large amount of income. To offset some of this income, J gave $100,000 to a charitable lead trust for his alma mater, the University of Nebraska. According to the terms of the gift, the university receives the income for the next five years after which the property is returned to J. Assuming the present value of the income over the next five years is $60,000, J receives a $60,000 deduction this year. Assume that next year, the trust earns $12,000. Because J has retained a reversionary interest that reverts too quickly, the trust is a grantor trust and J is taxed on the income of $12,000.

Liquidity Planning

The Federal estate tax is literally a once-in-a-lifetime event. Because taxpayers do not have to pay the tax on a regular recurring basis, many individuals give little thought to the eventual need for cash to pay the tax.

When an individual dies leaving a large estate but little cash with which to pay death taxes and other expenses, serious problems can result. The family may be forced to sell assets at distress prices just to obtain cash. In a severe situation, a decedent's carefully designed dispositive plan may be shattered because of the failure to anticipate the liquidity needs of the estate.

One of the functions of a competent tax adviser is to foresee any liquidity problem of his or her client's potential estate and to suggest appropriate remedies. The remainder of this chapter covers some of the common solutions to the problem of a cash-poor estate.

SOURCE OF FUNDS

An excellent source of funds with which to pay an estate tax is insurance on the life of the potential decedent. For a relatively small cash outlay, a taxpayer can purchase enough insurance coverage to meet all the liquidity needs of his or her estate. It is absolutely vital that the insured individual does not possess any incidents of ownership in the policies and that his or her estate is not the beneficiary of the policies. If these two rules are observed the policy proceeds will not be included in the insured's estate and needlessly subjected to the estate tax.[44]

A second source of funds is any family business in which the decedent owned an interest. Under the terms of a binding buy-sell agreement, the business could use its cash to liquidate the decedent's interest. If the business is in corporate form, a redemption of the decedent's interest under § 303 can be a highly beneficial method of securing funds. If the fairly straightforward requirements of § 303 are met, the corporation can purchase its own stock from the decedent's estate without danger of the payment being taxed as a dividend. Because the estate's basis in the stock has been stepped up to its fair market value at date of death, the estate normally will realize little or no taxable gain on sale. The amount of the corporate distribution protected by § 303 cannot exceed the amount of death taxes and funeral and administrative expenses payable by the estate.[45]

In order for a redemption of stock to qualify under § 303, the value of the stock must exceed 35% of the value of the gross estate less § 2053 and § 2054 expenses.[46] Careful pre-death planning may be necessary to meet this requirement.

Example 40

C owns a 100% interest in F Corporation, a highly profitable business with substantial cash flow. However, the value of the F stock is only 29% of the value of C's projected estate. As C's tax adviser, you could recommend that C (1) gift away other assets to reduce the estate, or (2) transfer assets into F Corporation as a contribution to capital in order to increase the stock's value. Note, however, that any transfers within three years of death are treated as not having been made.

FLOWER BONDS

Certain issues of Treasury bonds known as *flower bonds* may be used to pay the Federal estate tax at their par value plus accrued interest.[47] Because these bonds have very low interest rates, they are obtainable on the open market at a price well below their par value. Thus, an estate can satisfy its Federal tax liability with bonds that cost much less than the amount of that liability. The bonds must be included in the decedent's estate at their par, rather than market value.[48]

PLANNING FOR DEFERRED PAYMENT OF THE ESTATE TAX

Under § 6166, an estate may be entitled to pay its Federal estate tax liability on an installment basis over a 15-year period. This provision can be a blessing for an illiquid estate. However, only estates that meet the requirements of § 6166 may use the installment method of payment. As a result, pre-death planning should be undertaken to ensure qualification.

Basically, only an amount of estate tax attributable to a decedent's interest in a closely held business may be deferred.[49] In addition, the value of the closely held business must exceed 35% of the gross estate minus Code § 2053 and § 2054 deductions. If a deferral of estate tax is desirable in a specific situation, the tax adviser should make certain that such requirements are met on a prospective basis.

---

[44] § 2042.

[45] § 303(a).

[46] § 303(b)(2)(A).

[47] § 6312 provided the authorization for such usage. However, the section was repealed with respect to bonds issued after March 3, 1971. Bonds issued before this date and still outstanding continue to be eligible for payment of the estate tax.

[48] Rev. Rul. 69-489, 1969-2 C.B. 172.

[49] § 6166(a)(2).

Conclusion

This chapter has introduced the reader to one of the most fascinating and satisfying areas of tax practice—family tax planning. Such planning involves arrangements whereby family income can be shifted to low-bracket members so as to reduce the income taxes paid by the family unit. The use of trusts also has been discussed, and grantor trusts whose income is taxed not to the trust or its beneficiaries but to the grantor have been described.

Transfer tax planning techniques for reducing the family transfer tax burden have been introduced. Such techniques include long-range programs of inter vivos giving, asset freezes, selective use of the marital deduction, and liquidity planning. The family tax planner should never lose sight of the basic premise of family tax planning: only a plan that meets the subjective nontax goals and desires of a family as well as the objective goal of tax minimization is a truly well-designed plan.

Problem Materials

DISCUSSION QUESTIONS

17-1 *Assignment of Income Doctrine.* Explain the assignment of income doctrine as it relates to earned income. How does the doctrine apply to investment income?

17-2 *Income Shifting.* Assignment of income from one taxpayer to another can result in a tax savings only in a tax system with a progressive rate structure. Discuss.

17-3 *Family Employees.* List some of the factors the IRS might consider in determining whether a particular family member is a bona fide employee of a family business.

17-4 *Shareholder/Employee.* Discuss the tax consequences if the IRS determines that a family member is receiving an amount of unreasonable compensation from a family-owned corporation if that family member is a shareholder. What if the family member is not a shareholder?

17-5 *Gift of Business Interest.* An individual who transfers an equity interest in his or her business to a family member may be accomplishing an income shift to that family member. What are some nontax risks associated with such an equity transfer?

17-6 *Buy-Sell Arrangements.* How may a buy-sell agreement be utilized when an intra-family transfer of an equity interest in a business is contemplated?

17-7 *Regular Corporation versus S Corporation.* As a general rule, a regular corporation is an inappropriate vehicle by which to shift business income to low-bracket family members. Discuss.

17-8 *Limitation on Using S Corporations.* An S corporation may have only a single class of common stock outstanding. How does this fact limit the utility of the S corporation in many family tax plans?

17-9 *Use of Grantor Trusts.* Grantor trusts are ineffective as devices for shifting income to trust beneficiaries. However, such trusts may be very useful in achieving nontax family planning goals. Explain.

17-10 *Crummey Trusts.* What is a Crummey trust and why might a grantor prefer a Crummey trust to a § 2503(c) trust?

17-11 *Reversionary Trusts and Interest-Free Loans.* Can a trust in which the grantor has the right to receive his or her property back after a specified period of time be considered a valid trust for tax purposes so that the income is taxed to the beneficiaries rather than the grantor? Can an interest-free demand loan achieve an income shift from the lender to the debtor?

17-12 *Inter Vivos Gifts.* Why are inter vivos gifts beneficial from a transfer tax planning viewpoint?

17-13 *Limitations of Inter Vivos Gifts.* For what reasons might an elderly taxpayer be reluctant to make inter vivos gifts?

17-14 *Estate Freezes.* Define an "asset freeze" as the term relates to estate planning.

17-15 *Current versus Testamentary Contributions.* Is it preferable to make a charitable contribution during a taxpayer's life or at his or her death under the terms of his or her will?

17-16 *Marital Deduction.* Discuss the tax benefits associated with the unlimited marital deduction of § 2056.

PROBLEMS

17-17 *Using Family Employees.* F runs a carpet installation and cleaning business as a sole proprietorship. In the current year, the business generates $89,000 of net income.
   a. Assume F is married, has three children (all under the age of 19), does not have any other source of taxable income, and does not itemize deductions. What is his current year tax liability?
   b. Assume F can use all three children in his business as legitimate part-time employees. He pays each child $8,000 per year, but continues to provide more than one-half of their support. Compute the family's total tax bill for the current year.

17-18 *Sole Proprietorship versus Corporation.* Single individual K owns a sole proprietorship that is K's only source of income. In the current year, the business has net income of $130,000.
   a. If K does not itemize deductions, what is her current year tax liability?
   b. If K incorporates the business on January 1 and pays herself a $40,000 salary (and no dividends), by how much will she have reduced the tax bill on her business income? (Assume the corporation will not be a personal service corporation.)

17-19 *Sole Proprietorship versus Corporation.* Mr. and Mrs. C own their own business, which they currently operate as a sole proprietorship. Annual income from the business averages $400,000. Mr. and Mrs. C are considering incorporating the business. They estimate that each of them could draw a reasonable annual salary of $75,000. In order to maintain their current standard of living, they would also have to draw an additional $50,000 cash out of the business annually in the form of dividends. Based on these facts, compute the income tax savings or cost that would result from the incorporation. In making your calculation, ignore any deductions or exemptions available on the C's joint return.

17-20 *Singles Penalty.* Single taxpayer S has current year taxable income of $35,000 (after all available deductions and exemptions). His fiancée F has a taxable income of $6,000. Assuming they both itemize deductions, and that no deductions are affected by their combined adjusted gross income, should F and S marry before or after December 31? Support your conclusion with calculations.

17-21 *Marriage Penalty.* Taxpayers H and W are married and file a joint return. Both are professionals and earn salaries of $150,000 and $120,000, respectively. Assuming H and W have no other income and do not itemize deductions, compute any *marriage penalty* they will pay.

17-22 *Unearned Income of a Minor Child.* In the current year, taxpayer M receives $12,000 of interest income and earns a salary of $2,500 from a summer job. M has no other income or deductions. M is 13 years old and is claimed as a dependent on his parents' jointly filed tax return. His parents report taxable income of $300,000. Based on these facts, compute M's income tax liability.

17-23 *Sheltering Unearned Income of a Minor Child.* Taxpayer P made a gift of investment securities to his 13-year-old dependent daughter, D, under the Uniform Gift to Minors Act. The securities generate annual interest income of $4,000. P is considering a second gift to D that would generate an additional $3,000 of investment income annually. Calculate the amount of tax savings to the family if P could employ D in his business and pay her an annual salary of $3,000, rather than making the second gift. In making your calculation, assume P is in a 40% tax bracket.

17-24 *Family Partnerships.* F owns a 70% interest in Mako Partnership, in which capital is a material income-producing factor. On January 1 of the current year, F gives his son S a 35% interest in Mako (leaving F with a 35% interest). For the current year, Mako has taxable income of $200,000.

    a. Assume F does not perform any services for Mako. What is the maximum amount of partnership income allocable to S?

    b. Assume F performs services for Mako for which he normally would receive $30,000. However, F has not charged the partnership for his services. Based on these facts, what is the maximum amount of partnership income allocable to S in the current year?

17-25 *Gift of S Corporation Stock.* Grandfather G owns all 100 shares of the outstanding stock of Sigma, Inc., a calendar year S corporation. On January 1 of the current year, G gives 10 shares of Sigma stock to each of his four minor grandchildren under the Uniform Gift to Minors Act. For the current year, Sigma reports taxable income of $70,000. To whom is this income taxed?

17-26 *Gift-Leaseback.* Taxpayer B owns land used in his sole proprietorship with a tax basis of $75,000 and a fair market value of $100,000. B gives this land to an irrevocable simple trust for the equal benefit of his three children (ages 19, 20, and 21) and leases back the land from the trust for a fair market rental of $9,000 per year.

    a. Assuming that all three children are B's dependents and have no other source of income, calculate the tax savings to the family of this gift-leaseback arrangement. In making your calculation, assume B is in a 40% tax bracket.

    b. What are the gift and estate tax consequences of this transaction to B and his family? Assume that B has made no prior taxable gifts and that he is married.

17-27 *Use of Trusts.* Grandfather Z is in the habit of giving his 20-year-old grandchild, A, $10,000 annually as a gift. Z's taxable income is consistently over $500,000 per year, and A has no income. If Z creates a valid trust with investment assets just sufficient to yield $12,000 of income a year and specifies in the trust instrument that A is to receive the trust income annually, what will be the net tax savings to the family? (For purposes of this problem, assume that A is not a full-time student and *ignore* the fact that A may be claimed as a dependent on the return of another taxpayer.)

17-28 *Reversionary Trusts.* Grantor G transfers $100,000 of assets into a trust that will last for 10 years, after which time the assets will revert to G or his estate. During the trust's existence all income must be paid to beneficiary M on a current basis. For the current year, ordinary trust income is $18,000. To whom is this income taxed?

17-29 *Reversionary Trusts.* Refer to the facts in *Problem 17-28*. Assume that under the terms of the trust agreement the trust will last for M's lifetime. Upon M's death, the trust corpus will revert to G or his estate. On the date the trust is created, M is 18 years old. For the current year, ordinary trust income is $40,000. To whom is this income taxed?

17-30 *Irrevocable Trusts.* F transfers assets into an irrevocable trust and designates First City Bank as independent trustee. F retains no control over the trust assets. The trustee may distribute income to either of F's two adult brothers or to S, F's minor son whom F is legally obligated to support. During the year, the trustee distributed all of the trust income to one of F's brothers. To whom will the income be taxed?

17-31 *Irrevocable Trusts.* M transfers assets into an irrevocable trust and appoints National Bank independent trustee. M retains no control over trust assets. Under the terms of the trust agreement, M's sister N is given the right to determine which of M's three minor children will receive trust income for the year. N herself is not a trust beneficiary. During the year, N directs that trust income be divided equally among M's three children. To whom will the income be taxed?

17-32 *Irrevocable Trusts.* Grantor B transfers assets into an irrevocable trust and designates Union State Bank independent trustee. B retains no control over trust assets. Under the terms of the trust instrument the trustee must use trust income to pay the annual insurance premium on a policy on B's life. Any remaining income must be distributed to B's grandson, GS. For the current year, trust income totals $60,000, of which $9,000 is used to pay the required insurance premium. To whom will the income be taxed?

17-33 *Grantor Trusts.* Although T is not a beneficiary of the ABC Trust, T does have the right under the terms of the trust instrument to appoint up to 10% of the trust assets to himself or any member of his family. T has never exercised this right. For the current year, the trust income of $80,000 is distributed to the income beneficiaries of the trust.

   a. To whom will the income be taxed?

   b. If T dies before exercising his right to appoint trust corpus, will the possession of the right have any estate tax consequences?

17-34 *Gift Splitting.* Every year D gives each of her nine grandchildren $20,000 in cash to be used toward their education.

   a. If D is unmarried, what is the amount of her annual taxable gift?

   b. If D is married and she and her husband elect to "gift split," what is the amount of her annual taxable gift?

17-35 *Inter Vivos Gifts.* Decedent T died in 2016 and left the following taxable estate:

	Fair Market Value
Investment real estate	$6,000,000
Cash and securities	3,500,000
Gross estate	$9,500,000
Less: § 2053 and § 2054 expenses	(500,000)
Taxable estate	$9,000,000

After payment of all death taxes, the estate will be divided equally among T's five surviving married children.

   a. If T has never made any inter vivos gifts, compute the estate's Federal estate tax liability.

   b. How much tax could have been saved if T had made cash gifts equal to the maximum annual exclusion under § 2503 to each of his children and their spouses in each of the 10 years preceding his death?

17-36 *Power of Giving.* W is thinking about the possibility of dying in the next ten years. She currently has an estate of $10,000,000. Assuming W is in the 40% transfer tax bracket, how much more could she give to her child if she made a gift to her child rather than dying with the entire $10,000,000? Ignore the annual exclusion and the unified credit.

17-37 *Liquidity Planning.* Decedent D left the following taxable estate:

	Fair Market Value
Life insurance proceeds from policy on D's life (D owned the policy at his death)	$ 8,500,000
Real estate	1,300,000
Stock in Acme Corporation (100% owned by D)	650,000
Gross estate	$10,450,000
Less: § 2053 and § 2054 expenses	(450,000)
Taxable estate	$10,000,000

   a. If D has never made any inter vivos gifts and dies in 2016, what is the estate's Federal estate tax liability (before credit for any state death tax paid)?

   b. How much tax could have been avoided if D had not been the owner of the life insurance policy?

   c. Can the Acme stock qualify for a § 303 redemption? What if the life insurance proceeds were not included in the gross estate?

TAX RESEARCH PROBLEMS

17-38 In 2006, P, a resident of St. Louis, Missouri, created an irrevocable trust for the benefit of his teenage son, S, and his brother, B. The independent trustee, T, has discretionary power to use the trust income for the "payment of tuition, books, and room and board at any institution of higher learning that S chooses to attend." After an 11-year period, the trust will terminate with any accumulated income payable to S and the trust corpus payable to B. In the current year, S received an income distribution of $7,000 from the trust, which he used to attend a state-supported school, the University of Missouri. To whom will the $7,000 of trust income be taxed?

Research aids:

Section 677 and accompanying regulations

Morrill, Jr. v. United States, 64-1 USTC ¶9463, 13 AFTR2d 1334, 228 F.Supp. 734 (D.Ct. Maine, 1964).

Braun, Jr., 48 TCM 210, T.C. Memo 1984-285.

17-39 Decedent D died on January 19, 2011. Under the terms of D's will, D's sister S, age 57, is to receive $500,000 as a specific bequest. The remainder of D's estate will be distributed to D's various grandchildren. On June 8, 2013, S decides to join a religious community and take a vow of poverty. She makes written notification to the executor of D's estate that she will not accept her bequest from her late sister, and that the $500,000 should be added to the amount to be distributed to the grandchildren. What are the transfer tax consequences of S's action?

Research aid:

Section 2518

Tax Research and Tax Practice

CHAPTER 18 Sources and Applications of Federal Tax Law

CHAPTER 19 Tax Practice and Procedure

Sources and Applications of Federal Tax Law

Learning Objectives

Upon completion of this chapter you will be able to:

LO.1 Describe the process in which Federal tax law is enacted and subsequently modified or evaluated by the judiciary.

LO.2 Understand the organization of the Internal Revenue Code.

LO.3 Identify the source of various administrative authorities.

LO.4 Understand the judicial system as it applies to tax cases.

LO.5 Identify secondary authority and distinguish it from primary authority.

LO.6 Understand the process of tax research.

Chapter Outline

Introduction

Mastery of taxation requires an understanding of how and where the rules of taxation originate. What might be called the "body of tax law" consists not only of the legislative provisions enacted by Congress, but also court decisions and administrative (Treasury Department) releases that explain and interpret the statutory provisions. In the aggregate, the statutes, court decisions, and administrative releases constitute the *legal authority* that provides the consequences given a particular set of facts. The tax treatment of any particular transaction normally must be based on some supporting authority. The tax rules contained in each of the earlier chapters all have their origin in some authoritative pronouncement. This chapter introduces the sources of tax law and explains how these and other information relating to taxes may be accessed and used in solving a particular tax question. This process of obtaining information and synthesizing it to answer a specific tax problem is referred to as tax research. The importance of *tax research* cannot be overemphasized. The vast body of tax law and its ever-changing nature place a premium on knowing how to use research materials.

Authoritative Sources of Tax Law

Sources of tax law can be classified into two broad categories: (1) the law, and (2) official interpretations of the law. The law consists primarily of the Constitution, the Acts of Congress, and tax treaties. In general, these sources are referred to as the *statutory* law. Most statutory law is written in general terms for a typical situation. Since general rules, no matter how carefully drafted, cannot be written to cover variations on the normal scheme, interpretation is usually required. The task of interpreting the statute is one of the principal duties of the Internal Revenue Service (IRS) as representative of the Secretary of the Treasury. The IRS annually produces thousands of releases that explain and clarify the law. To no one's surprise, however, taxpayers and the government do not always agree on how a particular law should be interpreted. In situations where the taxpayer or the government decides to litigate the question, the courts, as final arbiters, are given the opportunity to interpret the law. These judicial interpretations, administrative interpretations, and the statutory law are considered in detail below.

Statutory Law

The Constitution of the United States provides the Federal government with the power to tax. Disputes concerning the constitutionality of an income tax levied on taxpayers without apportionment among the states were resolved in 1913 with passage of the Sixteenth Amendment. Between 1913 and 1939, Congress enacted revenue acts that amounted to a complete rewrite of all tax law to date, including the desired changes. In 1939, due primarily to the increasing complexity of the earlier process, Congress codified all Federal tax laws into Title 26 of the *United States Code,* which was then called the *Internal Revenue Code of 1939.* Significant changes in the Federal tax laws were made during World War II and the postwar period of the late 1940s. Each change resulted in amendments to the 1939 Code. By 1954, the codification process had to be repeated in order to organize all additions to the law and to eliminate obsolete provisions. The product of this effort was the *Internal Revenue Code of 1954.* After 1954, Congress took great care to ensure that each new amendment to the 1954 Code was incorporated within its organizational structure with appropriate cross-references to any prior provisions affected by a new law. In 1986, Congress again made substantial revisions in the tax law. Consistent with this massive redesign of the 1954 Code, Congress changed the title to the *Internal Revenue Code of 1986.* Like the 1954 Code, the 1986 Code is subject to revisions introduced by a new law. Some of the many recent changes incorporated into the 1986 Code include those made by the *American Taxpayer Relief Act of 2012.*

The legislative provisions contained in the Code are by far the most important component of tax law. Although the steps necessary to enact a law are generally well known, it is important to review this process with a special emphasis on taxation. Much of the job of the tax professional is to determine how a particular rule works or how it applies. What did Congress intend when it wrote the rule? For this reason, it is critical to understand how a law is created or more specifically, the legislative process.

THE MAKING OF A TAX LAW

Who writes the tax laws? The short answer is Congress—and not the IRS. Article I, Section 7, Clause 1 of the Constitution provides that the House of Representatives of the U.S. Congress has the basic responsibility for initiating revenue bills.[1] The Ways and Means Committee of the House of Representatives must consider any tax bill before it is presented for vote by the full House of Representatives. On bills of major public interest, the Ways and Means Committee holds public hearings where interested organizations may send representatives to express their views about the bill. The first witness at such hearings is usually the Secretary of the Treasury, representing the President of the United States. In many cases, proposals for new tax legislation or changes in existing legislation come from the President as a part of his political or economic programs.

> **LO.1**
> Describe the process in which Federal tax law is enacted and subsequently modified or evaluated by the judiciary.

After the public hearings have been held, the Ways and Means Committee usually goes into closed session, where the Committee prepares the tax bill for consideration by the entire House. The members of the Committee receive invaluable assistance from their highly skilled staff, which includes economists, accountants, and lawyers. The product of this session is a proposed bill that is submitted to the entire House for debate and vote.

After a bill has been approved by the entire House, it is sent to the Senate and assigned to the Senate Finance Committee. The Senate Finance Committee may also hold hearings on the bill before its consideration by the full Senate. The Senate's bill generally differs from the House's bill. In these situations, both versions are sent to the Joint Conference Committee on Taxation, which is composed of members selected from the House Ways and Means Committee and from the Senate Finance Committee. The objective of this Joint Committee is to produce a compromise bill acceptable to both sides. On occasion, when compromise cannot be achieved by the Joint Committee or the compromise bill is unacceptable to the House or the Senate, the bill "dies." If, however, compromise is reached and the Senate and House approve the compromise bill, it is then referred to the President for his or her approval or veto. If the President vetoes the bill, the legislation is "killed" unless two-thirds of both the House and the Senate vote to override the veto. If the veto is overridden, the legislation becomes law.

When a bill is signed into law by the President it is sent to the Office of the Federal Register to be assigned a "public law number." For example, the Tax Reform Act of 1986 is designated P.L. 99-514 and is explained in the following diagram.

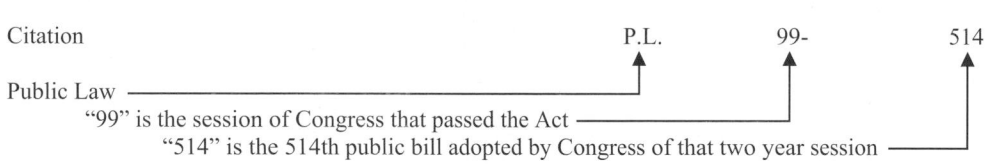

References to the various laws are often made using their public law numbers. Unfortunately, the public law number does not indicate the year in which the bill was enacted. However, the legislative session in which a public law was enacted can be determined using the following formula:

$$(\text{Session number} \times 2) - 112 = \text{Second year of session}$$

Using this formula, P.L. 99-514 was enacted during the 1985–1986 legislative session ($99 \times 2 = 198 - 112 = 86$). The Tax Relief and Health Care Act of 2006 was P.L. 109-432. Using the formula reveals that this Act was enacted during the 2005–2006 legislative session ($109 \times 2 = 218 - 112 = 106$).

---

[1] Tax bills do not originate in the Senate, except when they are attached to other bills.

COMMITTEE REPORTS

At each stage of the legislative process, various documents are generated that may be useful in assessing the intent of Congress. One of the better sources of Congressional intent is a report issued by the House Ways and Means Committee. This report contains the bill as well as a general explanation. This explanation usually provides the historical background of the proposed legislation along with the reasons for enactment. The Senate Finance Committee also issues a report similar to that of the House. Because the Senate often makes changes in the House version of the bill, the Senate's report is also an important source. Additionally, the Joint Conference Committee on Taxation issues its own report, which is sometimes helpful. Two other sources of intent are the records of the debates on the bill and publications of the initial hearings.

Committee reports and debates appear in several publications. Committee reports are officially published in pamphlet form by the U.S. Government Printing Office as the bill proceeds through Congress. The enacted bill is published in the *Internal Revenue Bulletin* and the *Internal Revenue Cumulative Bulletin*. The debates are published in the *Congressional Record*. In addition to these official government publications, several commercial publishers make this information available to subscribers.

The normal flow of a bill through the legislative process and the documents that are generated in this process are illustrated in a diagram below.

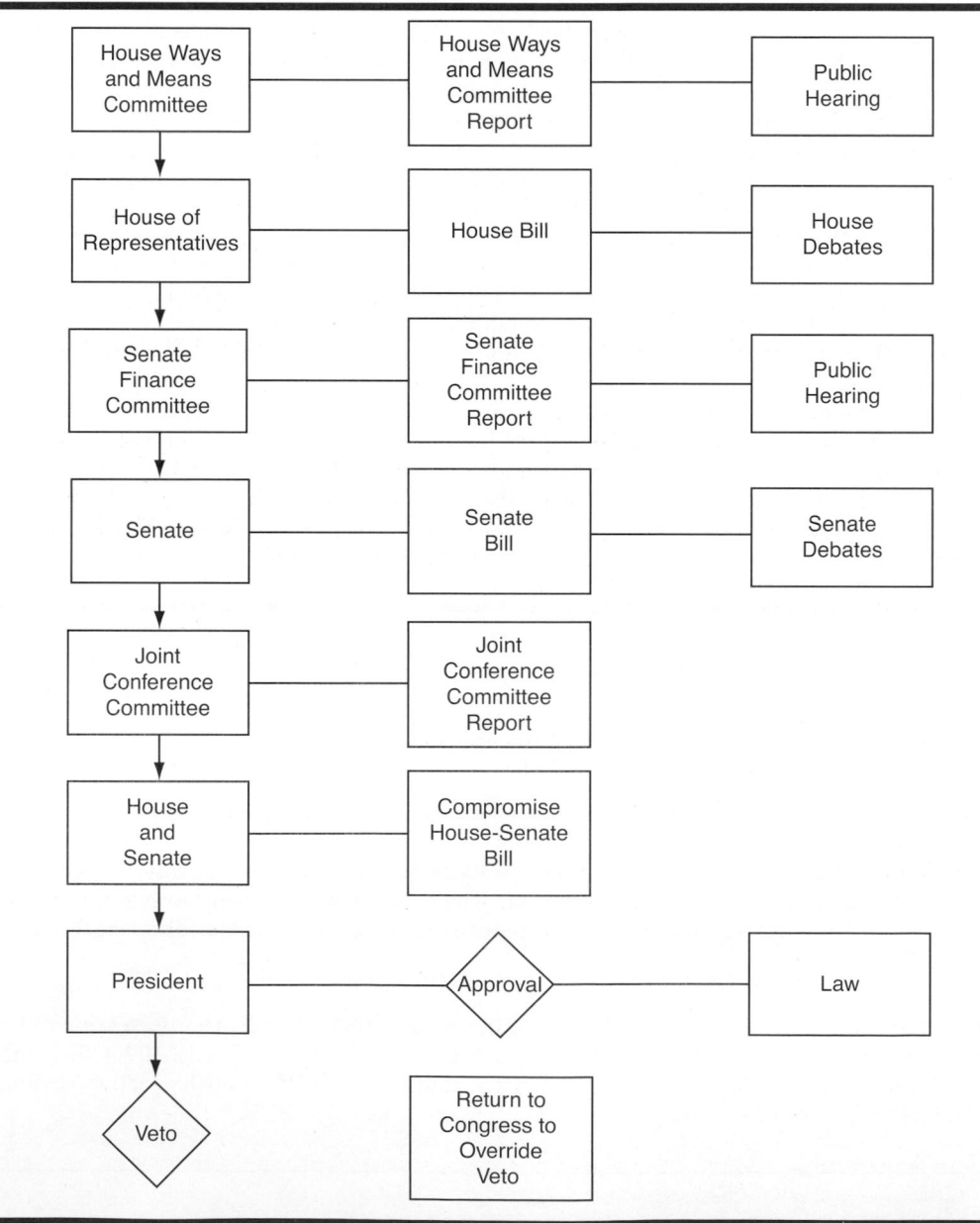

ORGANIZATION OF THE INTERNAL REVENUE CODE

Once a tax bill becomes tax law, it is incorporated into the existing structure of the U.S. federal laws known as the *United States Code*. As mentioned above, the *U.S. Code* is the collection of all laws enacted by Congress. Laws concerning the same subject matter (e.g., taxation) are consolidated in a single "title." As shown in Exhibit 18-1, there are 50 titles. Tax laws are incorporated directly into Title 26 entitled *Internal Revenue Code*.[2]

LO.2
Understand the organization of the Internal Revenue Code.

EXHIBIT 18-1	United States Code		

Title Number	Title Name	Title Number	Title Name
Title 1	General Provisions	**Title 26**	**Internal Revenue Code**
Title 2	The Congress	Title 27	Intoxicating Liquors
Title 3	The President	Title 28	Judiciary and Judicial Procedure
Title 4	Flag and Seal, Seat of Government, …	Title 29	Labor
Title 5	Government Organization and Employees	Title 30	Mineral Lands and Mining
Title 6	Domestic Security	Title 31	Money and Finance
Title 7	Agriculture	Title 32	National Guard
Title 8	Aliens and Nationality	Title 33	Navigation and Navigable Waters
Title 9	Arbitration	Title 34	Navy (repealed)
Title 10	Armed Forces	Title 35	Patents
Title 11	Bankruptcy	Title 36	Patriotic Societies and Observances
Title 12	Banks and Banking	Title 37	Pay and Allowances of the Uniformed Services
Title 13	Census	Title 38	Veterans' Benefits
Title 14	Coast Guard	Title 39	Postal Service
Title 15	Commerce and Trade	Title 40	Public Buildings, Property, and Works
Title 16	Conservation	Title 41	Public Contracts
Title 17	Copyrights	Title 42	The Public Health and Welfare
Title 18	Crimes and Criminal Procedure	Title 43	Public Lands
Title 19	Customs Duties	Title 44	Public Printing and Documents
Title 20	Education	Title 45	Railroads
Title 21	Food and Drugs	Title 46	Shipping
Title 22	Foreign Relations and Intercourse	Title 47	Telegraphs, Telephones, and Radiotelegraphs
Title 23	Highways	Title 48	Territories and Insular Possessions
Title 24	Hospitals and Asylums	Title 49	Transportation
Title 25	Indians	Title 50	War and National Defense

Title 26 (the Internal Revenue Code) is further divided as follows:

> **Title 26** of the United States Code (referred to as the Internal Revenue Code)
>> **Subtitle A**—Income Taxes
>>> **Chapter 1**—Normal Taxes and Surtaxes
>>>> **Subchapter A**—Determination of Tax Liability
>>>>> **Part I**—Tax on Individuals
>>>>>> **Sections**—1 through 5

---

[2] All future use of the term Code or Internal Revenue Code refers to the *Internal Revenue Code of 1986*, as amended.

Exhibit 18-2 reveals the contents of the various subdivisions. As a practical matter, virtually all of a tax practitioner's work is done in Subtitle A, Chapter 1, which deals with income taxes. Note that subtitles are further divided into chapters, subchapters, parts, subparts and finally the most important element: sections.

EXHIBIT 18-2	**Internal Revenue Code: Subtitles, Chapters and Subchapters**	

Subtitle	Subject	First Code Section
Subtitle A	Income taxes	§ 1
Subtitle B	Estate and gift taxes	§ 2001
Subtitle C	Employment taxes	§ 3101
Subtitle D	Miscellaneous excise taxes	§ 4001
Subtitle E	Alcohol, tobacco, and certain other excise taxes	§ 5001
Subtitle F	Procedure and administration	§ 6001
Subtitle G	The joint committee on taxation	§ 8001
Subtitle H	Financing of presidential election campaigns	§ 9001
Subtitle I	Trust fund code	§ 9501

Chapters in Subtitle A	Name	First Code Section
1	Income taxes	§ 1
2	Tax on self-employment income	§ 1401
3	Withholding of tax on nonresident aliens and foreign corporations	§ 1441
4	[Repealed]	
5	[Repealed]	§ 1491
6	Consolidated returns	§ 1501

Selected Subchapters of Chapter 1	Name	Code Sections
A	Determination of tax liability	§§ 1–59B
B	Computation of taxable income	§§ 61–291
C	Corporate distributions and adjustments	§§ 301–385
D	Deferred compensation, etc.	§§ 401–436
E	Accounting periods and methods of accounting	§§ 441–483
F	Exempt organizations	§§ 501–530
G	Corporations used to avoid income tax on shareholders	§§ 531–565
H	Banking institutions	§§ 581–597
I	Natural resources	§§ 611–638
J	Estates, trusts, beneficiaries, and decedents	§§ 641–692
K	Partners and partnerships	§§ 701–777
L	Insurance companies	§§ 801–848
M	Regulated investment companies and real estate investment trusts	§§ 851–860L
N	Tax based on income from sources within or without the United States	§§ 861–999
O	Gain or loss on disposition of property	§§ 1001–1111
P	Capital gains and losses	§§ 1201–1298
S	Tax treatment of s corporations and their shareholders	§§ 1361–1379

The most critical portions of the Internal Revenue Code are its "sections." The sections contain the laws—often referred to as provisions or rules—that a taxpayer must follow to determine taxable income and ultimately the final tax liability. For example, the starting point in determining taxable income is gross income and Code Section 61 provides the definition of gross income as follows: income. Section 61 appears below.

Section 61: Gross Income Defined

(a) *General definition. Except as otherwise provided in this subtitle (A), gross income means all income from whatever source derived, including (but not limited to) the following items:*
   (1) *Compensation for services, including fees, commissions, fringe benefits, and similar items;*
   (2) *Gross income derived from business;*
   (3) *Gains derived from dealings in property*
   (4) *Interest*
   (5) *Rents*

   .
   .
   .

   (14) *Income in respect of a decedent and*
   (15) *Income from an interest in an estate or trust.*

The ability to use the Internal Revenue Code is essential for all individuals who have any involvement with the tax laws.

When working with the tax law, it is often necessary to make reference to, or *cite*, a particular source with respect to the Code. The section of the Code is the source normally cited. A complete citation for a section of the Code would be too cumbersome. For instance, a formal citation for Section 1 of the Code would be "Subtitle A, Chapter 1, Subchapter A, Part I, Section 1." In most cases, citation of the section alone is sufficient. Sections are numbered consecutively throughout the Code so that each section number is used only once. Currently the numbers run from Section 1 through Section 9833. Not all section numbers are used, so that additional ones may be added by Congress in the future without the need for renumbering.[3]

Citation of a particular Code section in tax literature ordinarily does not require the prefix "Internal Revenue Code" because it is generally understood that, unless otherwise stated, references to section numbers concern the Internal Revenue Code of 1986 as amended. However, since most Code sections are divided into subparts, reference to a specific subpart requires more than just its section number. Section 170(a)(2)(B) serves as an example.

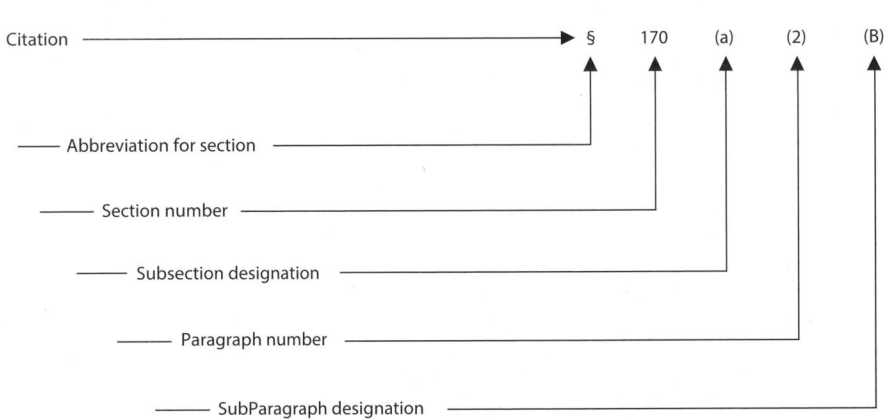

All footnote references used throughout this text are made in the form given above. In most cases, the "§" or "§§" symbols are used in place of the terms "section" or "sections," respectively.

---

[3] It is interesting to note that when it adopted the 1954 Code, Congress deliberately left section numbers unassigned to provide room for future additions. Recently, however, Congress has been forced to identify new sections by alphabetical letters following a particular section number. See, for example, Sections 280, 280A, 280B, and 280C of the 1986 Code.

Single-volume or double-volume editions of the Internal Revenue Code are published after every major change in the law. Commerce Clearing House, Inc. (CCH) and the Research Institute of America (RIA) publish these editions. Additionally, the Code is included in each of the major tax services that are discussed in a later section of this chapter.

TAX TREATIES

The laws contained in tax treaties represent the third and final component of the statutory law. Tax treaties (also referred to as tax conventions) are agreements between the United States and other countries that provide rules governing the taxation of residents of one country by another. For example, the tax treaty between the United States and France indicates how the French government taxes U.S. citizens residing in France and vice versa. Tax treaties, as law, have the same authority as those laws contained in the Code.[4] Treaty provisions may override provisions of the Internal Revenue Code under certain circumstances.[5] For this reason, persons involved with an international tax question must be aware of tax treaties and recognize that the Code may be superseded by a tax treaty. International taxation and tax treaties are considered in detail in Chapter 13.

Administrative Interpretations

LO.3

Identify the source of various administrative authorities.

After Congress has enacted a tax law, the Executive branch of the Federal government has the responsibility for enforcing it. In the process of enforcing the law, the Treasury interprets, clarifies, defines, and analyzes the Code in order to apply Congressional intention of the law to the specific facts of a taxpayer's situation. This process results in numerous administrative releases including the following:

1. Regulations
2. Revenue rulings and letter rulings
3. Revenue procedures
4. Technical advice memoranda

REGULATIONS

Regulations are the Treasury's official interpretation of the Internal Revenue Code. Code § 7805(a) authorizes the Secretary of the Treasury to "prescribe all needful rules and regulations for the enforcement of this title, including all rules and regulations as may be necessary of any alteration of law in relation to internal revenue." Section 7805(b) provides authority to the Secretary to prescribe the extent, if any, to which any ruling or regulation relating to the internal revenue laws will be applied without retroactive effect. In most cases the Secretary delegates the power to write the regulations to the Commissioner of the Internal Revenue Service. In practice, this means that the regulations are written by the technical staff of the IRS or by the office of the Chief Counsel of the IRS, an official who is also an assistant General Counsel of the Treasury Department.

Regulations are issued in the form of *Treasury Decisions* (often referred to as TDs), which are published in the Federal Register and sometimes later in the *Internal Revenue Bulletin*. The Federal Register is the official publication for regulations and legal notices issued by the executive branch of the Federal government. The Federal Register is published every business day. Before a TD is published in final form, it must be issued in proposed form, a *proposed regulation*, for a period of at least 30 days before it is scheduled to become final.

Section 7805(d) provides that any temporary regulation (discussed below) issued by the Secretary will also be issued as a proposed regulation. Any temporary regulation expires within three years after the date of issuance of such regulation.

---

[4] See Code § 7852(d)(1).   [5] § 7852(d)(2).

Upon publication, interested parties have at least 30 days to comment on proposed regulations. In theory, at the end of this comment period, the Treasury responds in any one of three ways; it may withdraw the proposed regulation, amend it, or leave it unchanged. In the latter two cases, the Treasury normally issues the regulation in its final form as a TD, published in the Federal Register. The final version of any given regulation is quite frequently significantly different from the proposed version.

Afterwards, the new regulation is included in Title 26 of the *Code of Federal Regulations*. In fact, however, proposed regulations sometimes remain in proposed form for many years. Proposed regulations do not have the force of law and are not the Treasury's official position on a particular issue.

Temporary Regulations

The National Office of the Treasury issues temporary regulations as the need arises. Often such regulations are issued in response to substantive changes in the tax law when tax practitioners, in particular, need immediate guidance in applying a new or revised statute. Such regulations usually deal with immediate filing requirements or details regarding a mandated accounting method change. Temporary regulations are effective immediately; they are not given the 30-day period for public comment provided with proposed regulations. Generally, the IRS also issues temporary regulations as proposed regulations, however. Temporary regulations expire three years after issuance and are given the same respect and precedential value as final regulations.

The primary purpose of the regulations is to explain and interpret particular Code sections. Although regulations have not been issued for all Code sections, they have been issued for the great majority. In those cases where regulations exist, they are an important authoritative source on which one can usually rely. Regulations can be classified into three groups: (1) legislative; (2) interpretive; and (3) procedural.

Legislative Regulations

Occasionally, Congress will give specific authorization to the Secretary of the Treasury to issue regulations on a particular Code section. For example, under § 1502, the Secretary is charged with prescribing the regulations for the filing of a consolidated return by an affiliated group of corporations. There are virtually no Code sections governing consolidated returns, and the regulations in effect serve in lieu of the Code. In this case and others where it occurs, the regulation has the force and effect of a law, with the result that a court reviewing the regulation usually will not substitute its judgment for that of the Treasury Department unless the Treasury has clearly abused its discretion.[6]

Interpretative Regulations

Interpretative regulations explain the meaning of a Code section and commit the Treasury and the Internal Revenue Service to a particular position relative to the Code section in question. This type of regulation is binding on the IRS but not on the courts, although it is "a body of experience and informed judgment to which courts and litigants may properly resort for guidance."[7] Interpretive regulations have considerable authority and normally are invalidated only if they are inconsistent with the Code or are unreasonable.

For many years, taxpayers and the government have disagreed over the level of deference that courts should give to regulations. In other words, how much authoritative weight should courts give to the rules that Treasury writes? The Supreme Court's recent decision in *Mayo Foundation* seems to have resolved this issue.[8]

Mayo involved a long-running controversy between the IRS and the medical community over whether medical residents are "students" and therefore exempt from employment taxes. After losing a number of cases on this issue, Treasury revoked a 50 year old regulation favorable to Mayo and the students and replaced it with one saying that anyone who works more than 40 hours a week cannot qualify for the student exemption. The primary concern of the case was the authoritative value that should be given the new regulation and whether it was valid at all. According to the *Mayo* court, all regulations should be analyzed using the standards developed in *Chevron,* a non-tax case.[9]

---

[6] *Anderson, Clayton & Co. v. U.S.*, 77-2 USTC ¶9727, 40 AFTR2d 77-6102, 562 F.2d 972 (CA-5, 1977), Cert. den. at 436 U.S. 944 (USSC, 1978).

[7] *Skidmore v. Swift and Co.*, 323 U.S. 134 (USSC, 1944).

[8] *Mayo Foundation for Medical Education and Educational Research v. U.S.*, 2011-1 USTC ¶50,143, 107 AFTR 2d 2011-341, 131 S.Ct. 704 (USSC, 2011).

[9] *Chevron USA v. Natural Resources Defense Council, Inc.*, 467 U.S. 837 (USSC, 1984).

The *Chevron* approach involves a two step inquiry. The first step asks whether Congress has directly addressed the precise question at issue. If Congress has made its intent clear, then the regulation must give effect to Congress' stated intent. If Congressional intent is not clear, the second inquiry is whether the regulation is a reasonable construction of the statute. In this case, the Court concluded that the statute that Congress had written to address the issue (the definition of a student) was unclear. so it turned to the second *Chevron* inquiry: was the regulation a reasonable interpretation of the ambiguous statute? The Court believed it was reasonable and held against the taxpayer.

The effects of *Mayo* appear to be far reaching. Most importantly, courts now must apply the two-part test of *Chevron* in evaluating regulations. Moreover, the *Mayo* court made it clear that the authority of a regulation did not depend on whether the regulation was issued at the specific direction of Congress or under the general rulemaking authority granted to the Treasury Department. Whether a regulation is legislative or interpretive now appears irrelevant. Finally, the court indicated that the history of a regulation, such as whether it represents a reversal of Treasury policy or whether it was issued because the government was losing cases, is not a consideration in determining whether the regulation is valid. According to some, the immediate effect of *Mayo* will cause challenges to regulations to ignore history and whether the regulation is legislative or interpretive and center on substance.

Procedural Regulations

Procedural regulations cover such areas as the information a taxpayer must supply to the IRS and the internal management and conduct of the IRS in certain matters. Those regulations affecting vital interests of the taxpayers are generally binding on the IRS, and those regulations stating the taxpayer's obligation to file particular forms or other types of information are given the effect of law.

Citation for Regulations

Regulations are arranged in the same sequence as the Code sections they interpret. Thus, a regulation begins with a number that designates the type of tax or administrative, definitional, or procedural matter and is followed by the applicable Code section number. For example, Treasury Regulation Section 1.614-3(f)(5) serves as an illustration of how regulations are cited throughout this text.

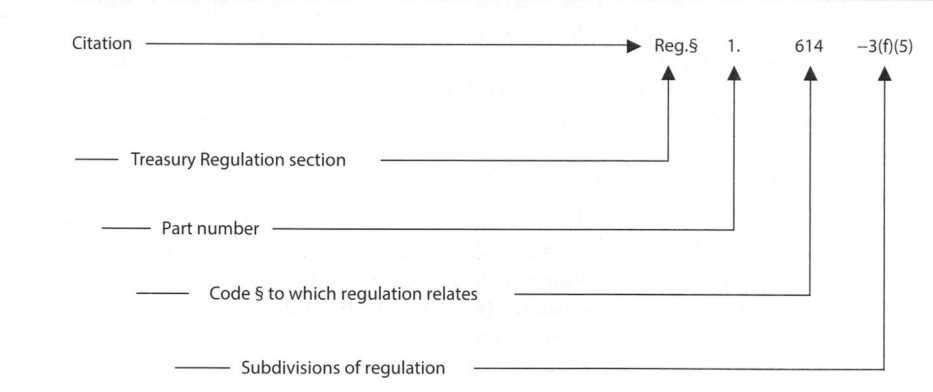

The part number of a Treasury regulation is used to identify the general area covered by the regulation as follows:

Part Number	Law Subject
1	Income Tax
20	Estate Tax
25	Gift Tax
31	Employment Tax
48–49	Excise Tax
301	Procedural Matters

The various subdivisions of a regulation are not necessarily related to a specific subdivision of the Code.

Sometimes the Treasury issues temporary regulations when it is necessary to meet a compelling need. For example, temporary regulations are often issued shortly after enactment of a major change in the tax law. These temporary regulations have the same binding effect as final regulations until they are withdrawn or replaced. Such regulations are cited as "Temp. Reg. §."

Temporary regulations should not be confused with proposed regulations. The latter have no force or effect.[10] Nevertheless, proposed regulations provide insight into how the IRS currently interprets a particular Code section. For this reason, they should not be ignored.

REVENUE RULINGS

Revenue rulings also are official interpretations of the Federal tax laws and are issued by the National Office of the IRS. Revenue rulings do not have quite the authority of regulations, however. Regulations are a direct extension of the law-making powers of Congress, whereas revenue rulings are an application of the administrative powers of the Internal Revenue Service. In contrast to rulings, regulations are usually issued only after public hearings and must be approved by the Secretary of the Treasury.

Unlike regulations, revenue rulings are limited to a given set of facts. Taxpayers may rely on revenue rulings in determining the tax consequences of their transactions; however, taxpayers must determine for themselves if the facts of their cases are substantially the same as those set forth in the revenue ruling.

Revenue rulings are published in the weekly issues of the *Internal Revenue Bulletin*. The information contained in the *Internal Revenue Bulletins* (including, among other things, revenue rulings) is accumulated and usually published semiannually in the *Cumulative Bulletin*. The *Cumulative Bulletin* reorganizes the material according to Code section. Citations for the *Internal Revenue Bulletin* and the *Cumulative Bulletin* are illustrated on the following page.

REVENUE PROCEDURES

Revenue procedures are statements reflecting the internal management practices of the IRS that affect the rights and duties of taxpayers. Occasionally they are also used to announce procedures to guide individuals in dealing with the IRS or to make public something the IRS believes should be brought to the attention of taxpayers. Revenue procedures are published in the weekly *Internal Revenue Bulletins* and bound in the *Cumulative Bulletin* along with revenue rulings issued in the same year. The citation system for revenue procedures is the same as for revenue rulings except that the prefix "Rev. Proc." is substituted for "Rev. Rul."

---

[10] Federal law (i.e., the Administrative Procedure Act) requires any federal agency, including the Internal Revenue Service, that wishes to adopt a substantive rule to publish the rule in proposed form in order to give interested persons an opportunity to comment. Proposed regulations are issued in compliance with this directive.

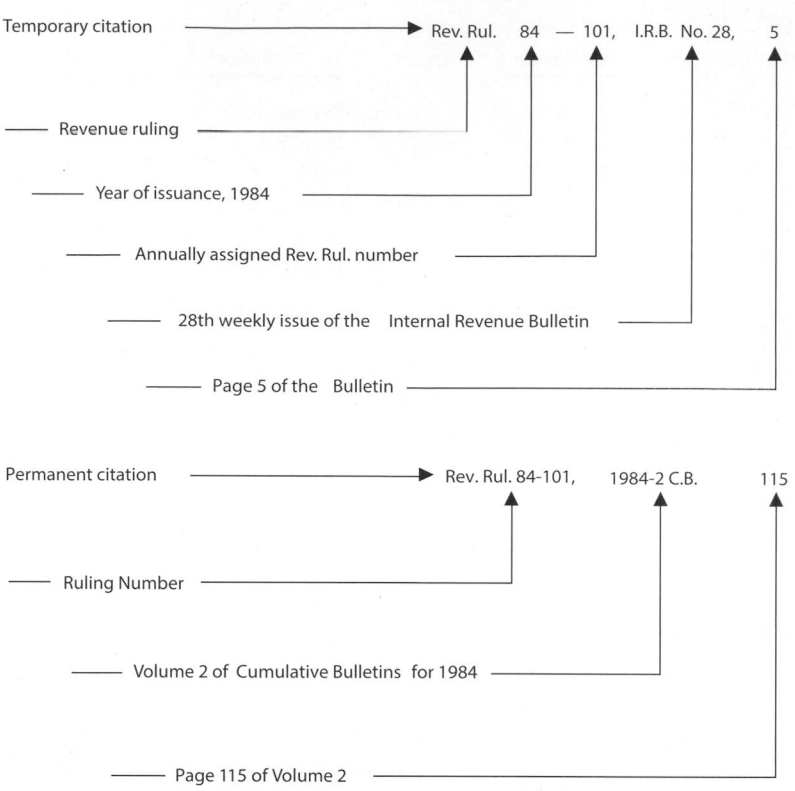

LETTER RULINGS

The term *letter ruling* actually encompasses three different types of rulings: private letter rulings, determination letters, and technical advice memoranda. These items are not published in an official government publication but are available from commercial sources.

Private Letter Ruling

Taxpayers who are in doubt about the tax consequences of a contemplated transaction can ask the National Office of the IRS for a ruling. Generally, the IRS has discretion about whether to rule or not, and it has issued guidelines describing the circumstances under which it will rule.[11]

Unlike revenue rulings, private letter rulings apply only to the particular taxpayer asking for the ruling and are thus not applicable to taxpayers in general. Section 6110(j)(3) specifically states that "unless the Secretary otherwise establishes by regulations, a written determination may not be used or cited as a precedent." Recently, however, the IRS has expanded the list of authorities constituting "substantial" authority for Section 6662 purposes to include private letter rulings. Section 6662 imposes an accuracy-related penalty equal to 20% of the underpayment unless the taxpayer can cite "substantial authority" for his or her position.

For those requesting a ruling, the IRS's response might provide insurance against surprises. As a practical matter, a favorable ruling should preclude any controversies with the IRS on an audit of that transaction, at least with respect to the matters addressed in the private letter ruling. During the process of obtaining a private letter ruling, the IRS often recommends changes in a proposed transaction to assist the taxpayer in achieving the tax result he or she wishes. Since 1976 the IRS has made individual private letter rulings publicly available after deleting names and other information that would tend to identify the taxpayer. Private letter rulings are published by both CCH and RIA.

---

[11] See Rev. Proc. 2016-1, 2016-1 I.R.B. 1, for a description of the areas in which the IRS has refused to issue advanced rulings. Note, also, that the IRS is required to charge taxpayers a fee for letter rulings, opinion letters, determination letters, and similar requests. A sense of the various fees charge can be found in Rev. Proc. 2016-1 IRB 2016-1 (Appendix A). See § 6591.

Determination Letter

A determination letter is similar to a private letter ruling, except that it is issued by the office of the local IRS district director, rather than by the National Office. Unlike private letter rulings, determination letters usually relate to completed transactions. Like private letter rulings, they are not published in any official government publication but are available commercially. In most instances, determination letters deal with issues and transactions that are not overtly controversial. Obtaining a determination letter in order to ensure that a pension plan is qualified is a typical use of a determination letter.

Technical Advice Memorandum

A technical advice memorandum ("tech advice") is typically requested by an IRS agent during an audit. The request is normally made to the National Office when the agent has a question that cannot be answered by sources in his or her local office. The technical advice memorandum only applies to the taxpayer for whose audit the technical advice was requested and cannot be relied upon by other taxpayers. Technical advice memoranda are available from private publishers but are not published by the government.

Citations for letter rulings and technical advice follow a multidigit file number system. IRS Letter Ruling 200434039 serves as an example.

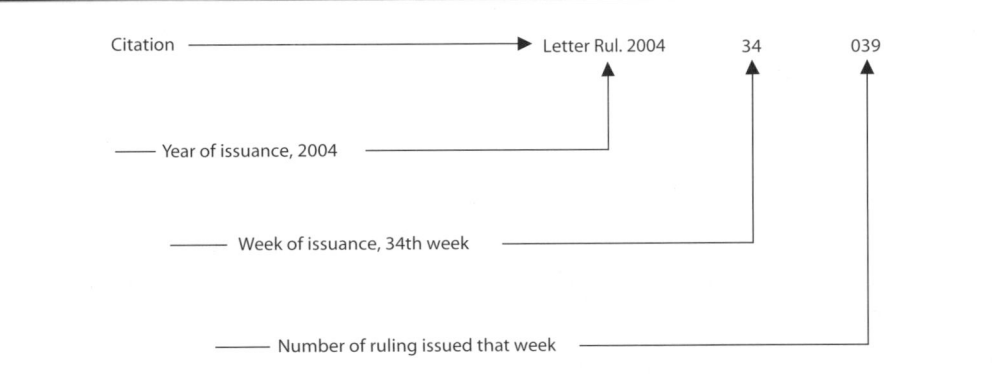

| Citation | → Letter Rul. 2004 | 34 | 039 |

- Year of issuance, 2004
- Week of issuance, 34th week
- Number of ruling issued that week

Judicial Interpretations

The Congress passes the tax law and the Executive branch of the Federal government enforces and interprets it, but under the American system of checks and balances, it is the Judiciary branch that ultimately determines whether the Executive branch's interpretation is correct. This provides yet another source of tax law—court decisions. It is therefore absolutely essential for the student of tax as well as the tax practitioner to have a grasp of the judicial system of the United States and how tax cases move through this system.

Before litigating a case in court, the taxpayer must have exhausted the administrative remedies available to him or her within the Internal Revenue Service. If the taxpayer has not exhausted his or her administrative remedies, a court will deny a hearing because the claim filed in the court is premature.

All litigation begins in what are referred to as *courts of original jurisdiction*, or *trial courts*, which "try" the case. There are three trial courts: (1) the Tax Court; (2) the U.S. District Court; and (3) the U.S. Court of Federal Claims. Note that the taxpayer may select any one (and only one) of these three courts to hear the case. If the taxpayer or government disagrees with the decision by the trial court, either party has the right to appeal to either the U.S. Court of Appeals or the U.S. Court of Appeals for the Federal Circuit, whichever is appropriate in the particular case. If a litigating party is dissatisfied with the decision by the appellate court, it may ask for review by the Supreme Court, but this is rarely granted. The judicial system is illustrated and discussed below.

LO.4

Understand the judicial system as it applies to tax cases.

TRIAL COURTS

U.S. Tax Court

The Tax Court, as its name suggests, specializes in tax matters and hears no other types of cases. The judges on the court are especially skilled in taxation. Usually, prior to being selected as a judge by the President, the individual was a practitioner or IRS official who was noted for his or her expertise. This Court is composed of 19 judges who "ride circuit" throughout the United States (i.e., they travel and hear cases in various parts of the country). Occasionally, the full Tax Court hears a case, but most cases are heard by a single judge who submits his or her opinion to the chief judge, who then decides whether the full court should review the decision.

Besides its expertise in tax matters, two other characteristics of the Tax Court should be noted. Perhaps the most important feature of the Tax Court is that the taxpayer does not pay the alleged tax deficiency before bringing his or her action before the court. The second facet of the Tax Court that bears mentioning is that a trial by jury is not available.

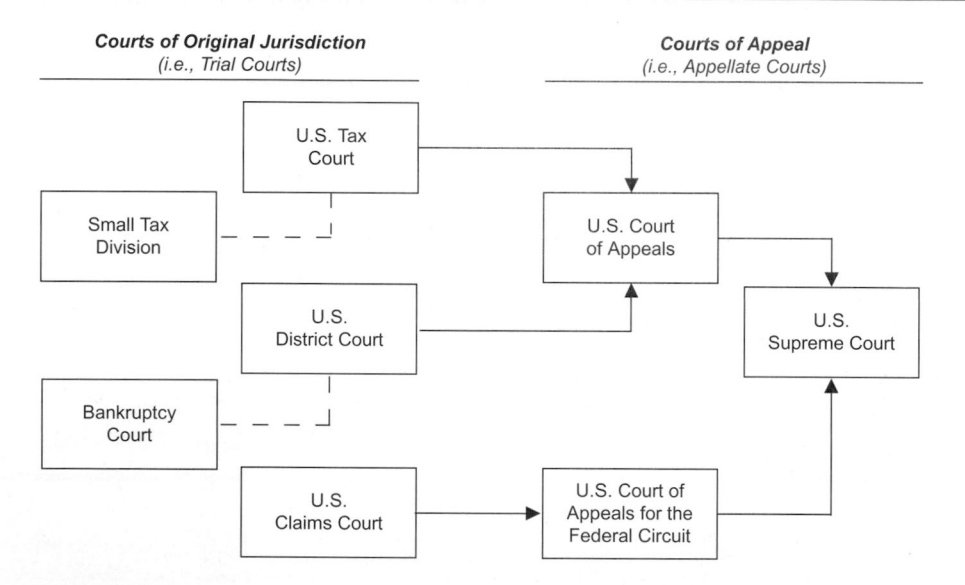

U.S. District Courts

For purposes of the Federal judicial system, the United States is divided into 11 geographic areas called circuits, which are subdivided into districts. For example, the second circuit, which is composed of Vermont, Connecticut, and New York, contains the District Court for the Southern District of New York, which covers parts of New York City. Other districts may include very large areas, such as the District Court for the State of Arizona, which covers the entire state. A taxpayer may take a case into the District Court for the district in which he or she resides, but only after the disputed tax deficiency has been paid. The taxpayer then sues the IRS for a refund of the disputed amount. The District Court is a court of general jurisdiction and hears many types of cases in addition to tax cases. This is the only court in which the taxpayer may obtain a jury trial. The jury decides matters of fact but not matters of law. However, even in issues of fact, the judge may, and occasionally does, disregard the jury's decision.

U.S. Court of Federal Claims

The United States Court of Federal Claims was established on October 1, 1982. Prior to that time it was called the "U.S. Court of Claims." The U.S. Court of Federal Claims hears cases involving certain claims against the Federal government, including tax refunds.

This Court is made up of 16 judges and usually meets in Washington, D.C. A taxpayer must pay the disputed tax deficiency before bringing an action in this court, and may not obtain a jury trial. Appeals from the U.S. Court of Federal Claims are taken to the U.S. Court of Appeals for the Federal Circuit, an appellate court created at the same time as the U.S. Court of Federal Claims.

The chart on the following page illustrates the position of the taxpayer in bringing an action in these courts.

Small Claims Cases

When the amount of a tax assessment is relatively small, the taxpayer may elect to submit the case to the division of the Tax Court hearing small claims cases, called the Small Tax Division of the Tax Court. If the amount of tax at issue is $50,000 per year or less, the taxpayer can obtain a decision with a minimum of formality, delay, and expense; but the taxpayer loses the right to appeal the decision. The Small Tax Division is administered by the chief judge of the Tax Court, who is authorized to assign small claims cases to special trial judges. These cases receive priority on the trial calendars, and relatively informal rules are followed whenever possible. The special trial judges' opinions are not published on these cases, and the decisions are not reviewed by any other court or treated as precedents in any other case.

	U.S. Tax Court	U.S. District Court	U.S. Court of Federal Claims
Jurisdiction	Nationwide	Specific district in which court is sitting	Nationwide
Subject Matter	Tax cases only	Many different types of cases, both criminal and civil	Claims against the Federal government, including tax refunds
Payment of Contested Amount	Taxpayer does not pay deficiency, but files suit against IRS Commissioner to stop collection of tax	Taxpayer pays alleged deficiency and then files suit against the U.S. government for refund	Taxpayer pays alleged deficiency and then files suit against the U.S. government for refund
Availability of Jury Trial	No	Yes	No
Appeal Taken to	U.S. Court of Appeals	U.S. Court of Appeals	U.S. Court of Appeals for the Federal Circuit
Number of Courts	1	95	1
Number of Judges per Court	19	1	16

Bankruptcy Court

Under limited circumstances, it is possible for the bankruptcy court to have jurisdiction over tax matters. The filing of a bankruptcy petition prevents creditors, including the IRS, from taking action against a taxpayer, including the filing of a proceeding before the Tax Court if a notice of deficiency is sent after the filing of a petition in bankruptcy. In such cases, a tax claim may be determined by the bankruptcy court.

APPELLATE COURTS

U.S. Courts of Appeals

Which appellate court is appropriate depends on which trial court hears the case. Taxpayer or government appeals from the District Courts and the Tax Court are taken to the U.S. Court of Appeals that has jurisdiction over the court in which the taxpayer lives. Appeals from the U.S. Court of Federal Claims are taken to the U.S. Court of Appeals for the Federal Circuit, which has the same powers and jurisdictions as any of the other Courts of Appeals except that it only hears specialized appeals. Courts of Appeals are national courts of appellate jurisdiction. With the exceptions of the Court of Appeals for the Federal Circuit and the Court of Appeals for the District of Columbia, these appellate courts are assigned various geographic areas of jurisdiction as follows:

Court of Appeals for the Federal Circuit (CA-FC)	District of Columbia Circuit (CA-DC)	First Circuit (CA-1)
U.S. Court of Federal Claims	District of Columbia	Maine
		Massachusetts
		New Hampshire
		Puerto Rico
		Rhode Island

Second Circuit (CA-2)	Third Circuit (CA-3)	Fourth Circuit (CA-4)	Fifth Circuit (CA-5)	Sixth Circuit (CA-6)
Connecticut	Delaware	Maryland	Louisiana	Kentucky
New York	New Jersey	N. Carolina	Mississippi	Michigan
Vermont	Pennsylvania	S. Carolina	Texas	Ohio
	Virgin Islands	Virginia		Tennessee
		W. Virginia		

Seventh Circuit (CA-7)	Eighth Circuit (CA-8)	Ninth Circuit (CA-9)	Tenth Circuit (CA-10)	Eleventh Circuit (CA-11)
Illinois	Arkansas	Alaska	Colorado	Alabama
Indiana	Iowa	Arizona	New Mexico	Florida
Wisconsin	Minnesota	California	Kansas	Georgia
	Missouri	Guam	Oklahoma	
	Nebraska	Hawaii	Utah	
	N. Dakota	Idaho	Wyoming	
	S. Dakota	Montana		
		Nevada		
		Oregon		
		Washington		

Taxpayers may appeal to the Courts of Appeal as a matter of right, and the Courts must hear their cases. Very often, however, the expense of such an appeal deters many from proceeding with an appeal. Appellate courts review the record of the trial court to determine whether the lower court completed its responsibility of fact finding and applied the proper law in arriving at its decision.

District Courts must follow the decision of the Appeals Court for the circuit in which they are located. For instance, the District Court in the Eastern District of Missouri must follow the decision of the Eighth Circuit Court of Appeals because Missouri is in the Eighth Circuit. If the Eighth Circuit has not rendered a decision on the particular issue involved, then the District Court may make its own decision or follow the decision in another Circuit.

The Tax Court is a national court with jurisdiction throughout the entire country. Prior to 1970, the Tax Court considered itself independent and indicated that it would not be bound by the decisions of the Circuit Court to which its decision would be appealed. In *Golsen,*[12] however, the Tax Court reversed its position. Under the *Golsen rule,* the Tax Court

---

[12] *Jack E. Golsen*, 54 T.C. 742 (1970).

now follows the decisions of the Circuit Court to which a particular case would be appealed. Even if the Tax Court disagrees with a Circuit Court's view, it will decide based upon the Circuit Court's view. On the other hand, if a similar case arises in the jurisdiction of another Circuit Court that has not yet ruled on the same issue, the Tax Court will follow its own view, despite its earlier decision following a contrary Circuit Court decision.

The U.S. Courts of Appeals generally sit in panels of three judges, although the entire court may sit in particularly important cases. They may reach a decision that affirms the lower court or that reverses the lower court. Additionally, the Appellate Court could send the case back to the lower court (remand the case) for another trial or for rehearing on another point not previously covered. It is possible for the Appellate Court to affirm the decision of the lower court on one particular issue and reverse it on another.

Generally, only one judge writes a decision for the Appeals Court, although in some cases no decision is written and an order is simply made. Such an order might hold that the lower court is sustained, or that the lower court's decision is reversed as being inconsistent with one of the Appellate Court's decisions. Sometimes other judges (besides the one assigned to write the opinion) will write additional opinions agreeing with (concurring opinion) or disagreeing with (dissenting opinion) the majority opinion. These opinions often contain valuable insights into the law controlling the case, and often set the ground for a change in the court's opinion at a later date.

U.S. Supreme Court

The Supreme Court of the United States is the highest court of the land. No one has a *right* to be heard by this Court. It only accepts cases it wishes to hear, and generally those involve issues that the Court feels are of national importance. There is no minimum dollar amount for these cases. As a practical matter, the Supreme Court generally hears very few tax cases. Consequently, taxpayers desiring a review of their trial court decision find it solely at the Court of Appeals. Technically, cases are submitted to the Supreme Court through a request process known as the *"Writ of Certiorari."* If the Supreme Court decides to hear the case, it grants the *Writ of Certiorari;* if it decides not to hear the case, it denies the *Writ of Certiorari.* It is important to note that there is another path to review by the U.S. Supreme Court—*by appeal*—as opposed to by *Writ of Certiorari.* This "review by appeal" may be available when a U.S. Court of Appeals has held that a state statute is in conflict with the laws or treaties of the United States. The "review by appeal" may also be available when the highest court in a state has decided a case on grounds that a Federal statute or treaty is invalid, or when the state court has held a state statute valid despite the claim of the losing party that the statute is in conflict with the U.S. Constitution or a Federal law. Review by the U.S. Supreme Court is still discretionary, but a *Writ of Certiorari* is not involved.

The Supreme Court, like the Courts of Appeals, does not conduct another trial. Its responsibility is to review the record and determine whether or not the trial court correctly applied the law in deciding the case. The Supreme Court also reviews the decision of the Court of Appeals to determine if the court used the correct reasoning.

In general, the Supreme Court only hears cases when one or more of the following conditions apply:

1. When a Court of Appeals has not used accepted or usual methods of judicial procedure or has sanctioned an unusual method by the trial court;

2. When a Court of Appeals has settled an important question of Federal law and the Supreme Court feels such an important question should have one more review by the most prestigious court of the nation;

3. When a decision of a Court of Appeals is in apparent conflict with a decision of the Supreme Court;

4. When two or more Courts of Appeals are in conflict on an issue; or

5. When the Supreme Court has already decided an issue but feels that the issue should be looked at again, possibly to reverse its previous decision.

CASE CITATION

Tax Court Decisions

The predecessor to the Tax Court was called the Board of Tax Appeals. It was established by Congress in 1924 in response to the absence of a suitable system for resolving disputes between taxpayers and the government. The decisions of the Board of Tax Appeals were published as the *United States Board of Tax Appeals Reports* (BTA). To the extent these decisions concern laws that are still in effect, most believe that they have the same authority of Tax Court decisions. BTA cases are cited as follows:

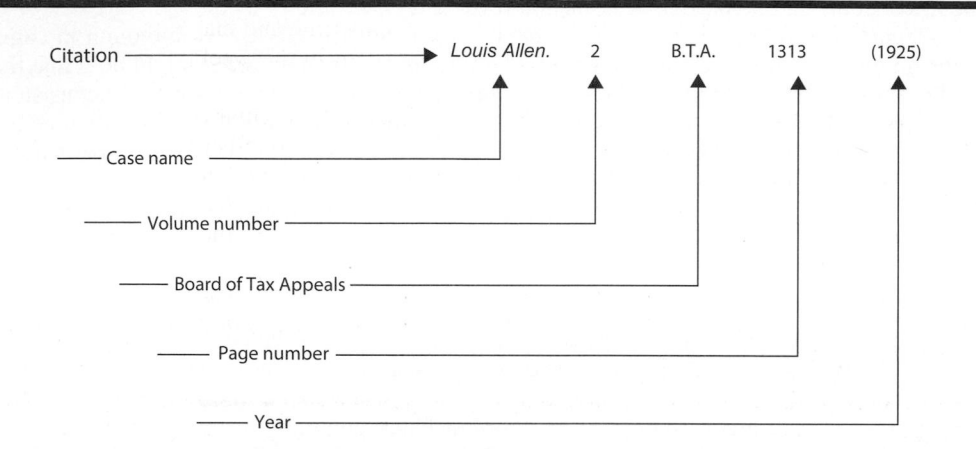

The Tax Court renders two different types of decisions with two different citation systems: regular decisions and memorandum decisions.

Tax Court *regular* decisions deal with new issues that the court has not yet resolved. In contrast, decisions that deal only with the application of already established principles of law are called *memorandum* decisions. The United States government publishes regular decisions in *United States Tax Court Reports* (T.C.). Tax Court regular decisions are cited as follows:

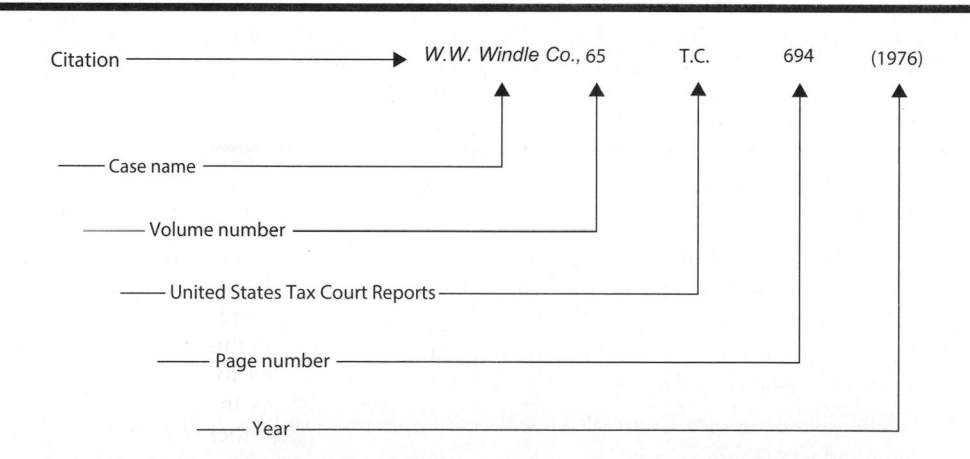

Like revenue rulings and the *Cumulative Bulletins*, there is a time lag between the date a Tax Court regular decision is issued and the date it is bound in a *U.S. Tax Court Report* volume. In this case, the citation appears as follows:

Temporary Citation

W.W. Windle Co., 65 T.C. __, No. 79 (1976).

Here the page is left out, but the citation tells the reader that this is the 79th regular decision issued by the Tax Court since Volume 64 ended. When the new volume (65th) of the Tax Court Report is issued, then the permanent citation may be substituted for the old one. Both CCH and RIA have tax services that allow the researcher to find these temporary citations.

The IRS has adopted the practice of announcing its acquiescence or nonacquiescence to the regular decisions of the Tax Court that are adverse to the position taken by the government.[13] That is, the Service announces whether it agrees with the Tax Court or not. The IRS does not follow this practice for the decisions of the other courts, or even for memorandum decisions of the Tax Court, although it occasionally announces that it will or will not follow a decision of another Federal court with a similar set of facts. The IRS may withdraw its acquiescence or nonacquiescence at any time and may do so even retroactively. Acquiescences and nonacquiescences are published in the weekly *Internal Revenue Bulletins* and the *Cumulative Bulletins*.

Although the U.S. government publishes the Tax Court's regular decisions, it does not publish memorandum decisions. However, both CCH and RIA publish them. CCH publishes the memorandum decisions under the title *Tax Court Memorandum Decisions* (TCM), while RIA publishes these decisions as *Tax Court Reporter* and *Memorandum Decisions* (T.C. Memo). In citing Tax Court memorandum decisions, some authors prefer to use both the RIA and the CCH citations for their cases.

In an effort to provide the reader the greatest latitude of research sources, this dual citation policy has been adopted for this text. The case of *Alan K. Minor* serves as an example of the dual citation of Tax Court memorandum decisions.

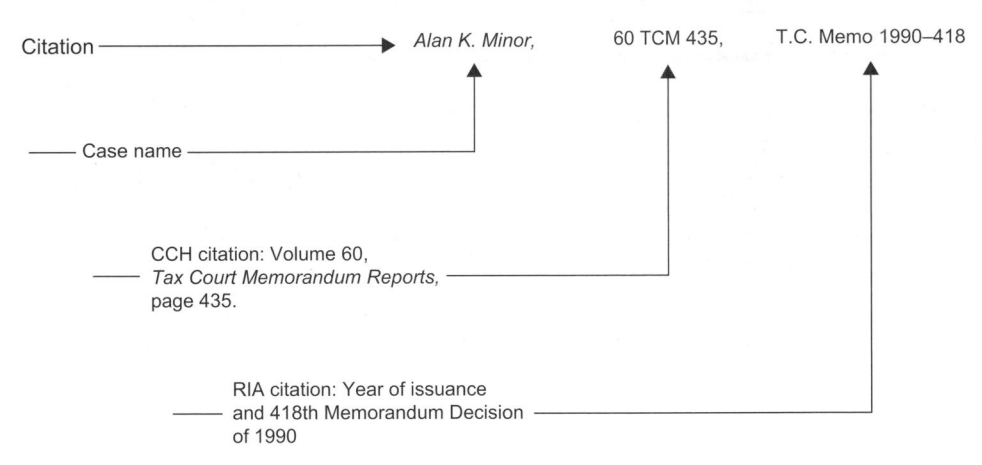

Citation ──────────────→ *Alan K. Minor,*　　60 TCM 435,　　T.C. Memo 1990–418

── Case name ──

CCH citation: Volume 60,
── *Tax Court Memorandum Reports,*
page 435.

RIA citation: Year of issuance
── and 418th Memorandum Decision
of 1990

Citations for U.S. District Court, Court of Appeals, and Court of Federal Claims

Commerce Clearing House, Research Institute of America, and West Publishing Company all publish decisions of the District Courts, Courts of Appeals, and the Court of Federal Claims. When available, all three citations of a case are provided in this text.[14] CCH publishes the decisions of these courts in its *U.S. Tax Cases* (USTC—not to be confused with the U.S. Tax Court Reports) volumes, and RIA offers these decisions in its *American Federal Tax Reports* (AFTR) series.[15] West Publishing Company reports these decisions in either

---

[13] The IRS's acquiescence is symbolized by "A" or "Acq." and its nonacquiescence by "NA" or "Nonacq."

[14] When all three publishers have not printed the case, only the citations to the cases published are provided.

[15] Until the acquisition of Prentice Hall by RIA, Prentice Hall published cases under its own name. Accordingly, researchers needing cases from before 1993 will often encounter Prentice Hall as publisher of these reporters now carried under RIA's name.

its *Federal Supplement Series* (F.Supp.—District Court decisions), or its *Federal Second Series* (F.2d—Court of Federal Claims and Courts of Appeals decisions). The citation of the U.S. District Court decision of *Cam F. Dowell, Jr. v. U.S.* is illustrated for each of the three publishing companies as follows:

CCH Citation:

Cam F. Dowell, Jr. v. U.S., 74-1 USTC ¶9243, (D.Ct. Tx., 1974).

Interpretation: This case is reported in the first volume of the *U.S. Tax Cases*, published by CCH for calendar year 1974 (74-1), located at paragraph (¶) 9243, and is a decision rendered in 1974 by a U.S. District Court located in Texas (Tx.).

RIA Citation:

Cam F. Dowell, Jr. v. U.S., 33 AFTR2d 74-739, (D.Ct. Tx., 1974).

Interpretation: Reported in the 33rd volume of the second series of the *American Federal Tax Reports* (AFTR2d), published by RIA for 1974, and located at page 739.

West Citation:

Cam F. Dowell, Jr. v. U.S., 370 F.Supp. 69 (D.Ct. Tx., 1974).

Interpretation: Located in the 370th volume of the *Federal Supplement Series* (F.Supp), published by West Publishing Company, and located at page 69.

The multiple citation of the U.S. District Court case illustrated above appears as follows:

Cam F. Dowell, Jr. v. U.S., 74-1 USTC ¶9243, 33 AFTR2d 74-739, 370 F.Supp. 69 (D.Ct. Tx., 1974).

Decisions of the Court of Federal Claims (Ct. Cls.), the Courts of Appeals (e.g., CA-1, CA-2, etc.), and the Supreme Court (USSC) are published by CCH and RIA in the same reporting source as District Court decisions (i.e., USTCs and AFTRs). Court of Federal Claims and Court of Appeals decisions are reported by West Publishing Company in its *Federal Second Series* (F.2d). Supreme Court decisions are published by West Publishing Company in its *Supreme Court Reports* (S.Ct.), and the U.S. Government Printing Office publishes Supreme Court decisions in its *Supreme Court Reports* (U.S.).

An example of the multiple citation of a Court of Appeals decision follows:

Citation:

Millar v. Comm., 78-2 USTC ¶9514, 42 AFTR2d 78-5246, 577 F.2d 212 (CA-3, 1978).

A multiple citation of a Supreme Court decision would appear as follows:

Citation:

Fausner v. Comm., 73-2 USTC ¶9515, 32 AFTR2d 73-5202, 413 U.S. 838 (USSC, 1973).

Note that in each of the citations above, the designation "Commissioner of the Internal Revenue Service" is simply abbreviated to "Comm." In some instances, the IRS or U.S. is substituted for Comm., and older cases used the Commissioner's name. For example, in *Gregory v. Helvering*, 293 U.S. 465 (USSC, 1935), Mr. Helvering was the Commissioner of the Internal Revenue Service at the time the case was brought to the Court. Also note that the citation contains a reference to the Appellate Court rendering the decision (i.e., CA-3, or USSC) and the year of issuance.

Exhibit 18-3 and Exhibit 18-4 summarize the sources of case citations from various reporter services.

EXHIBIT 18-3	**Reporters of Tax Court Decisions**		

Reporter	Abbr.	Type	Publisher
Tax Court Reports	TC	Regular	Government Printing Office
Tax Court Memorandum Decisions	TCM	Memorandum	Commerce Clearing House
Tax Court Memorandum Decisions	TC Memo	Memorandum	Research Institute of America

EXHIBIT 18-4	**Reporters of Decisions Other than Tax Court**		

Reporter	Abbr.	Courts Reported	Publisher
Supreme Court Reports	U.S.	Supreme Court	Government Printing Office
Supreme Court Reporter	S.Ct	Supreme Court	West Publishing
Federal Supplement	F.Supp	District Courts	West Publishing
Federal Reporter	F. F.2d	Cts. of Appeals and Ct. of Fed. Cls.	West Publishing
American Federal Tax Reports	AFTR AFTR2d	District Courts Ct. of Fed. Cls. Cts. of Appeals, and Supreme Ct.	Research Institute of America
United States Tax Cases	USTC	Same as AFTR and AFTR2d	Commerce Clearing House

Secondary Sources

The importance of understanding the sources discussed thus far stems from their role in the taxation process. As mentioned earlier, the statutory law and its official interpretations constitute the legal authorities that set forth the tax consequences for a particular set of facts. These legal authorities, sometimes referred to as *primary authorities*, must be distinguished from so-called *secondary sources* or *secondary authorities*. The secondary sources of tax information consist mainly of books, periodicals, articles, newsletters, and editorial judgments in tax services. When working with the tax law, it must be recognized that secondary sources are unofficial interpretations—mere opinions—that have no legal authority.

Although secondary sources should not be used as the supporting authority for a particular tax treatment (except as a supplement to primary authority or in cases where primary authority is absent), they are an indispensable aid when seeking an understanding of the tax law. Several of these secondary materials are discussed briefly below.

LO.5 Identify secondary authority and distinguish it from primary authority.

TAX SERVICES

"Tax service" is the name given to a set of organized materials that contains a vast quantity of tax-related information organized so as to make it useful and accessible to tax practitioners. In general, a tax service is a paper or electronic compilation of the following: the Code, regulations, court decisions, IRS releases, and explanations of these primary authorities by the editors. As the listing of contents suggests, a tax service is invaluable since it contains, all in one place, a wealth of tax information, including both primary and secondary sources. The major tax services are available on the Internet. Moreover, these materials are updated constantly to reflect current developments—an extremely important feature given the dynamic nature of tax law. The major tax services are:

Publisher	Name of Publications
Commerce Clearing House	Standard Federal Tax Reporter—Income Taxes
Research Institute of America	United States Tax Reporter and Federal Tax Coordinator—2nd Series
The Bureau of National Affairs, Inc.	Tax Management Portfolios—U.S. Income

The widespread use of computers has found applications in tax research. For example, *LEXIS* is a computerized data base that a user can access through his or her personal computer. The *LEXIS* data base contains almost all information available in an extensive tax library. Suppliers of tax services currently make computer-based tax libraries available to their customers. Undoubtedly computers are basic to tax research.

Commerce Clearing House, Research Institute of America, and other publishers issue daily electronic summaries of important cases and other tax developments that many practitioners and scholars find helpful in keeping current with developments in the tax field. The Bureau of National Affairs publishes the *Daily Tax Bulletin,* a comprehensive daily journal of late-breaking tax news that often reprints entire cases or regulations of particular importance. *Tax Notes,* published by Tax Analysts, is a weekly publication addressing legislative and judicial developments in the tax field. *Tax Notes* is particularly helpful in following the progress of tax legislation through the legislative process.

TAX PERIODICALS

In addition to these services, there are a number of quality publications (usually published monthly) that contain articles on a variety of important tax topics. These publications are very helpful when new tax acts are passed, because they often contain clear, concise summaries of the new law in a readable format. In addition, they serve to convey new planning opportunities and relay the latest IRS and judicial developments in many important subspecialities of the tax profession. Some of the leading periodicals include the following:

Estate Planning	Taxes—The Tax Magazine
Journal of Corporate Taxation	The International Tax Journal
Journal of Partnership Taxation	The Review of Taxation of Individuals
Journal of Real Estate Taxation	The Tax Advisor
Journal of Taxation	The Tax Executive
Tax Law Journal	The Tax Lawyer
Tax Law Review	Trusts and Estates

In addition to these publications, many law journals contain excellent articles on tax subjects.

Several indexes exist that may be used to locate a journal article. Through the use of a subject index, author index, and in some instances a Code section index, articles dealing with a particular topic may be found. Three of these indexes are:

Title	Publisher
Index to Federal Tax Articles	Warren, Gorham and Lamont
Federal Tax Articles	Commerce Clearing House
The Accountant's Index	American Institute of Certified Public Accountants

In addition, the *United States Tax Reporter*, published by RIA, contains a section entitled "Index to Tax Articles."

Having introduced the sources of tax law, the remainder of this chapter is devoted to working with the law—or more specifically, the art of tax research. Tax research may be defined as the process used to ascertain the optimal answer to a question with tax implications. Although there is no perfect technique for researching a question, the following approach normally is used:

LO.6
Understand the process of tax research.

1. Obtain all of the facts
2. Diagnose the problem from the facts
3. Locate the authorities
4. Evaluate the authorities
5. Derive the solution and possible alternative solutions
6. Communicate the answer

Each of these steps is discussed below.

OBTAINING THE FACTS

Before discussing the importance of obtaining all the facts, the distinction between closed fact research and open- or controlled-fact research should be noted. If the research relates to a problem with transactions that are complete, it is referred to as closed-fact research and normally falls within the realm of tax practice known as tax compliance. On the other hand, if the research relates to contemplated transactions, it is called controlled- or open-fact research and is an integral part of tax planning.

In researching a closed-fact problem, the first step is gathering all of the facts. Unfortunately, it is difficult to obtain all relevant facts upon first inquiry. This is true because it is essentially impossible to understand the law so thoroughly that all of the proper questions can be asked before the research task begins. After the general area of the problem is identified and research has begun, it usually becomes apparent that more facts must be obtained before an answer can be derived. Consequently, additional inquiries must be made until all facts necessary for a solution are acquired.

DIAGNOSING THE ISSUE

Once the initial set of facts is gathered, the tax issue or question must be identified. Most tax problems involve very basic questions such as these:

1. Does the taxpayer have gross income that must be recognized?
2. Is the taxpayer entitled to a deduction?
3. Is the taxpayer entitled to a credit?
4. In what period is the gross income, deduction, or credit reported?
5. What amount of gross income, deduction, or credit must be reported?

As research progresses, however, such fundamental questions can be answered only after more specific issues have been resolved.

Example 1

R's employer owns a home in which R lives. The basic question that must be asked is whether use of the home constitutes income to R. After consulting the various tax sources, it can be determined that § 61 requires virtually all benefits to be included in income unless another provision specifically grants an exclusion. In this case, § 119 allows a taxpayer to exclude the value of employer-provided housing if the housing is on the employer's premises, the lodging is furnished for the convenience of the employer, and the employee is required by the employer to accept the housing. Due to the additional research, three more specific questions must be asked:

1. Is the home on the employer's premises?
2. Is the home provided for the employer's convenience?
3. Is R required to live in the home?

As the above example suggests, diagnosing the problem requires a continuing refinement of the questions until the critical issue is identified. The refinement that occurs results from the awareness that is gained through reading and rereading the primary and secondary authorities.

Example 2

Assume the same facts as in *Example 1*. After determining that one of the issues concerns whether R's home is on the business premises, a second inquiry is made of R concerning the location of his residence. (Note that as the research progresses, additional facts must be gathered.) According to R, the house is located in a suburb, 25 miles from his employer's downtown office. However, the house is owned by the employer, and hence R suggests that he lives on the employer's premises. He also explains that he often brings work home and frequently entertains clients in his home. Having uncovered this information, the primary authorities are reexamined. Upon review, it is determined that in *Charles N. Anderson*,[16] the court indicated that an employee would be considered on the business premises if the employee performed a significant portion of his duties at the place of lodging. Again the question must be refined to ask: Do R's work and entertainment activities in the home constitute a significant portion of his duties?

LOCATING THE AUTHORITIES

Identification of the critical issue presented by any tax question begins by first locating, then reading and studying the appropriate authority. Locating the authority is ordinarily done using a tax service. With the issue stated in general terms, the subject is found in the index volume and the location is determined. At this point, the appropriate Code sections, regulations, and editorial commentary may be perused to determine their applicability to the question.

Example 3

In the case of R above, the problem stated in general terms concerns income. Using an index, the key word, *income*, could be located and a reference to information concerning the income aspects of lodging would be given.

Once information relating to the issue is identified, the authoritative materials must be read. That is, the appropriate Code sections, regulations, rulings, and cases must be examined and studied to determine how they relate to the question. As suggested above, this process normally results in refinement of the question, which in turn may require acquisition of additional facts.

---

[16] 67-1 USTC ¶9136, 19 AFTR2d 318, 371 F.2d 59 (CA-6, 1966).

EVALUATING THE AUTHORITY

After the various authorities have been identified and it has been *verified* that they are applicable, their value must be appraised. This evaluation process, as will become clear below, primarily involves appraisal of court decisions and revenue rulings.

The Code

The Internal Revenue Code is the final authority on most tax issues since it is the Federal tax law as passed by Congress. Only the courts can offset this authority by declaring part of the law unconstitutional, and this happens rarely. Most of the time, however, the Code itself is only of partial help. It is written in a style that is not always easy to understand, and it contains no examples. Accordingly, to the extent the Code can be understood as clearly applicable, no stronger authority exists, except possibly a treaty. But in most cases. the Code cannot be used to solve a tax problem without further support.

Treasury Regulations

As previously discussed, the regulations are used to expand and explain the Code. Because Congress has given its authority to make laws to the Executive branch's administrative agency—the Treasury—the regulations that are produced are a very strong source of authority, second only to the Code itself. Normally, the major issue when a regulation is under scrutiny by a Court is whether the regulation is consistent with the Code. If the regulations are inconsistent, the Court will not hesitate to invalidate them. In completing a research project, the tax professional should always discuss the Code and the applicable regulations.

Judicial Authority

The value of a court decision depends on numerous factors. On appraising a decision, the most crucial determination concerns whether the outcome is consistent with other decisions on the same issue. In other words, consideration must be given to how other decisions have evaluated the one in question. An invaluable tool in determining the validity of a case is a *citator*. A tax citator is a volume containing an alphabetical listing of virtually all tax cases. After the name of each case, there is a record of other decisions that have cited (in the text of their facts and opinions) the first case.

Example 4

Assume the same facts as in *Example 2*. Examination of the *Anderson* case in a citator reveals that it has been cited by courts in other decisions numerous times. For example, two cases in which the *Anderson* decision was discussed are *U.S. Jr. Chamber of Commerce*[17] and *Jan J. Wexler*.[18]

It is important to note that tax citators often use abbreviations for subsequent case history. For example, the abbreviations *aff'g* and *aff'd* mean "affirming" and "affirmed" and indicate that an appeals court has upheld the decision in question. Similarly, *rev'g* and *rev'd* mean "reversing" and "reversed" and indicate that a trial court's decision was overturned. Finally, *rem'g* and *rem'd* mean "remanding" and "remanded" and indicate that the case has been sent back to a lower court for reconsideration.

The validity of a particular decision may be assessed by examining how the subsequent cases viewed the cited decision. For example, subsequent cases may have agreed or disagreed with the decision in question, or distinguished the facts of the cited case from those examined in a later case.

Another important factor that must be considered in evaluating a court decision is the level of the court that issued it. Decisions issued by trial courts have less value than those issued by appellate courts. And, of course, decisions of the Supreme Court are the ultimate authority.

A court decision's value rises appreciably if the IRS agrees with its result. As discussed earlier, the IRS usually indicates whether it acquiesces or does not acquiesce to regular Tax Court decisions. The position of the Service may also be published in a revenue ruling.

[17] 64-2 USTC ¶9637, 14 AFTR2d 5223, 334 F.2d 660 (Ct. Cls., 1964).

[18] 75-1 USTC ¶9235, 35 AFTR2d 75-550, 507 F.2d 842 (CA-6, 1975).

Rulings

The significance of revenue rulings lies in the fact that they reflect current IRS policy. Since agents of the IRS are usually reluctant to vary from that policy, revenue rulings carry considerable weight.

Revenue rulings are often evaluated in court decisions. Thus, a tax service should be used to determine whether relevant rulings have been considered in any decisions. By examining the Court's view of the ruling, possible flaws may be discovered.

Private letter rulings issued to the taxpayer must be followed for that taxpayer by the IRS as long as the transaction is carried out in the manner initially approved. Variation from the facts on which the ruling was based permits the Service to revise its position. As mentioned earlier, a private letter ruling applies only to the particular taxpayer to whom it was issued. However, such a ruling should prove helpful to any other taxpayer faced with a substantially identical fact pattern.

DERIVING THE SOLUTION

Once all the relevant authorities have been evaluated, a conclusion must be drawn. Before deriving the final answer or answers, however, an important caveat is warranted: the researcher must ensure that the research reflects all current developments. The new matters section of a tax service can aid in this regard. The new matters section updates the textual discussion with any late-breaking developments. For instance, the section will contain any new cases, regulations, or pronouncements of the Internal Revenue Service that may bear on the discussion of the topic covered in the main text.

After the current validity of the research is verified, the questions that have been formulated must be answered. In some cases the answers are clear; all too often, however, they are not. In such cases, it seems that from a practical viewpoint the issue should always be resolved in the taxpayer's favor, since the probability that a particular return will be subject to audit is very low. This decision also depends on several other factors, such as a taxpayer's personal attitudes, the amount of the tax at issue, and whether the tax return contains other items that might be at risk. Prior to enactment of the Tax Equity and Fiscal Responsibility Act (TEFRA), this was often the result. Under the rules enacted by TEFRA, however, the taxpayer may be subject to a penalty. This penalty is levied if there is a substantial understatement of tax attributable to a particular treatment for which the taxpayer does not have substantial authority.[19] (No penalty is imposed if the treatment is disclosed on the return and the taxpayer has a reasonable basis for that particular treatment.) Although the criterion of substantial authority has yet to be defined, the standard probably lies somewhere between reasonable support and more likely than not. In any event, it is clear that taxpayers must be concerned with their conclusion and its supporting authority more than ever before.[20]

COMMUNICATING THE FINDINGS

The final product of the research effort is a memorandum recording the research and a letter to the interested parties. Although many formats are suitable for the memorandum, one technique typically used is structured as follows:

1. Description of the facts.
2. Statement of the issues or questions researched.
3. Report of the conclusions (brief answers to the research questions).
4. Discussion of the rationale and authorities that support the conclusions.
5. Summary of the authorities consulted in the research.

A good tax memorandum is essential. If the research findings are not communicated intelligently and effectively, the entire research effort is wasted.

---

[19] § 6662.

[20] It should be noted that the Internal Revenue Code contains penalties for improper conduct by tax return preparers as well. These penalties run the gamut from offenses such as failing to furnish a completed copy of a return to the taxpayer to penalties for negligence and fraud. These penalties are discussed in Chapter 19.

DISCUSSION QUESTIONS

18-1 *Making a New Tax Law.* Describe the Congressional process of making a tax bill into final law.

18-2 *Legislative versus Interpretative Regulations.* Explain the difference between a legislative Treasury Regulation and an interpretative Regulation.

18-3 *Proposed versus Final Regulations.* Distinguish between proposed and final Regulations. How would either type of Regulation involving Code § 704 be cited?

18-4 *Revenue Rulings and Revenue Procedures.* Distinguish between a Revenue Ruling and a Revenue Procedure. Where can either be found in printed form?

18-5 *Private versus Published Rulings.* Distinguish between a private letter ruling and a Revenue Ruling. Under what circumstances would a taxpayer prefer to rely on either of these sources?

18-6 *Technical Advice Memoranda.* What are Technical Advice Memoranda? Under what circumstances are they issued?

18-7 *Trial Courts.* Describe the trial courts that hear tax cases. What are the advantages or disadvantages of litigating a tax issue in each of these courts?

18-8 *The Appeals Process.* A taxpayer living in Indiana has exhausted her appeals within the IRS. If she chooses to litigate her case, trace the appeals process assuming she begins her effort in each of the following trial courts:
  a.   The U.S. Court of Federal Claims
  b.   The U.S. District Court
  c.   The U.S. Tax Court
  d.   The Small Tax Division of the U.S. Tax Court

18-9 *Tax Court Decisions.* Distinguish between a Regular Tax Court decision and a Memorandum decision.

18-10 *Authority of Tax Law Sources.* Assuming that you have discovered favorable support for your position taken in a controversy with an IRS agent in each of the sources listed below, indicate how you would use these authoritative sources in your discussion with the agent.
  a.   A decision of the U.S. District Court having jurisdiction over your case if litigated
  b.   Treasury Regulation
  c.   The Internal Revenue Code
  d.   A decision of the Supreme Court
  e.   A decision of the Small Claims Court
  f.   A decision of the U.S. Tax Court
  g.   A private letter ruling issued to another taxpayer
  h.   A Revenue Ruling
  i.   A tax article in a leading periodical

18-11 *Tax Services.* What materials are generally found in leading tax services? Which does your library have?

PROBLEMS

18-12 *Interpreting Citations.* Interpret each of the following citations:
  a.   Reg. § 1.721-1(a).
  b.   Rev. Rul. 60-314, 1960-2 C.B. 48.
  c.   Rev. Proc. 86-46, 1986-2 C.B. 739.
  d.   Rev. Rul. 98-36, I.R.B. No. 31, 6.
  e.   § 351.

18-13   *Citation Abbreviations.* Explain each of the abbreviations below.
   a.   B.T.A.
   b.   Acq.
   c.   D. Ct.
   d.   CA-9
   e.   F.Supp.
   f.   NA.
   g.   Ct. Cls.
   h.   USTC
   i.   AFTR
   j.   *Cert. Den.*
   k.   *aff'g* and *aff'd*
   l.   *rev'g* and *rev'd*
   m.   *rem'g* and *rem'd*

18-14   *Interpreting Citations.* Identify the publisher and interpret each of the following citations:
   a.   41 TCM 289.
   b.   93 S. Ct. 2820 (USSC, 1973).
   c.   71-1 USTC ¶9241 (CA-2, 1971).
   d.   236 F.Supp. 761 (D. Ct. Va., 1974).
   e.   T.C. Memo 1977-20.
   f.   48 T.C. 430 (1967).
   g.   6 AFTR2d 5095 (CA-2, 1960).
   h.   589 F.2d 446 (CA-9, 1979).
   i.   277 U.S. 508 (USSC, 1928).

18-15   *Citation Form.* Record the following information in its proper citation form:
   a.   Part 7, subdivision (a)(2) of the income tax Regulation under Code § 165.
   b.   The 34th Revenue Ruling issued March 2, 1987, and printed on pages 101 and 102 of the appropriate document.
   c.   The 113th letter ruling issued the last week of 1986.

18-16   *Citation Form.* Record the following information in its proper citation form:
   a.   A 1982 U.S. Tax Court case in which Roger A. Schubel sued the IRS Commissioner for a refund, published in volume 77 on pages 701 through 715 as a regular decision.
   b.   A 1974 U.S. Tax Court case in which H. N. Schilling, Jr. sued the IRS Commissioner for a refund, published by (1) Commerce Clearing House in volume 33 on pages 1097 through 1110 and (2) Prentice Hall as its 246th decision that year.
   c.   A 1966 Court of Appeals case in which Boris Nodiak sued the IRS Commissioner in the second Circuit for a refund, published by (1) Commerce Clearing House in volume 1 of that year at paragraph 9262, (2) Prentice Hall in volume 17 on pages 396 through 402, and (3) West Publishing Company in volume 356 on pages 911 through 919.

TAX RESEARCH PROBLEMS

18-17   *Using a Citator.* Use either the Commerce Clearing House or Research Institute of America Citator in your library and locate *Richard L. Kroll, Exec. v. U.S.*
   a.   Which Court of Appeals Circuit heard this case?
   b.   Was this case heard by the Supreme Court?
   c.   James B. and Doris E. Wallach are included in the listing below the citation for Kroll. In what court was the Wallach case heard?

18-18   *Using a Citator.* Using any available citator, locate the case of *Corn Products v. Comm.*, 350 U.S. 46. What effect did the decision in *Arkansas Best v. Comm.* (58 AFTR2d 86-5748, 800 F.2d 219) have on the precedential value of the *Corn Products* case?

18-19   *Locating Court Cases.* Locate the case of *Robert Autrey, Jr. v. United States*, 89-2 USTC ¶9659, and answer the following questions.
   a.   What court decided the case on appeal?
   b.   What court originally tried the case?
   c.   Was the trial court's decision upheld or reversed?

18-20 *Locating Court Cases.* Locate the case of *Fabry v. Commissioner*, 111 T.C. 305, and answer the following questions.
   a. What court tried the case?
   b. Identify the various types of precedential authority the judge used in framing his opinion.

18-21 *Locating Court Cases.* Locate the cited court cases and answer the questions below.
   a. *Stanley A. and Lorriee M. Golanty*, 72 T.C. 411 (1979). Did the taxpayers win their case?
   b. *Hamilton D. Hill*, 41 TCM 700, T.C. Memo ¶71,127 (1971). Who was the presiding judge?
   c. *Patterson (Jefferson) v. Comm.*, 72-1 USTC ¶9420, 29 AFTR2d 1181 (Ct. Cls., 1972). What was the issue being questioned in this case?

18-22 *Completing Citations.* To the extent the materials are available to you, complete the following citations:
   a. Rev. Rul. 98-60,_____ C.B. _____.
   b. *Lawrence W. McCoy*, _____ T.C. _____ (1962).
   c. *Reginald Turner*, _____ TCM _____, T.C. Memo 1954-38.
   d. *RCA Corp. v. U.S.*, _____ USTC _____ (CA-2, 1981).
   e. *RCA Corp. v. U.S.* _____ AFTR2d _____ (CA-2, 1981).
   f. *RCA Corp. v. U.S.* _____ F.2d _____ (CA-2, 1981).
   g. *Comm. v. Wilcox*, _____ S. Ct. _____ (USSC, 1946).
   h. _____, 79-1 USTC ¶9139 (USSC, 1979).
   i. _____, 34 T.C. 842 (1960).
   j. *Brian E. Knutson*, 60 TCM 540, T.C. Memo _____.
   k. *Samuel B. Levin v. Comm.*, 43 AFTR2d 79-1057 (_____).

18-23 *Examination of Tax Sources.* For each of the tax sources listed below, identify at least one of the tax issues involved. In addition, if the source has a temporary citation, provide its permanent citation (if available).
   a. *Battelstein Investment Co. v. U.S.*, 71-1 USTC ¶9227, 27 AFTR2d 71-713. 442 F.2d 87 (CA-5, 1971).
   b. *Joel Kerns*, 47 TCM, _____ T.C. Memo 1984-22.
   c. *Patterson v. U.S.*, 84-1 USTC ¶9315 (CA-6, 1984).
   d. *Webster Lair*, 95 T.C. 484 (1990).
   e. *Thompson Engineering Co., Inc.*, 80 T.C. 672 (1983).
   f. *Towne Square, Inc.*, 45 TCM 478, T.C. Memo 1983-10.
   g. Rev. Rul. 85-13, I.R.B. No. 7, 28.
   h. Rev. Proc. 85-49, I.R.B. No. 40, 26.
   i. *William F. Sutton, et al. v. Comm.*, 84 T.C. _____ No. 17.
   j. Rev. Rul. 86-103, I.R.B. No. 36, 13.
   k. *Hughes Properties, Inc.*, 86-1 USTC ¶9440, 58 AFTR2d 86-5062, _____ U.S. _____ (USSC, 1986).
   l. Rev. Rul. 98-27, I.R.B. No. 22, 4.

18-24 *Office in the Home.* T comes to you for advice regarding the deductibility of expenses for maintaining an office in his home. T is currently employed as an Executive Vice President for Zandy Corporation. He has found it impossible to complete his job responsibilities during the normal forty-hour weekly period. Although the office building in which he works is open nights and weekends, the heating and air conditioning systems are shut down at night (from 6 p.m.) and during the entire weekend. As a result, T has begun taking work home with him on a regular basis. The work is generally done in the den of T's home. Although T's employer does not require him to work at home, T is convinced that he would be fired if his work assignments were not completed on a timely basis. Given these facts, what would you advise T about taking a home-office deduction?

Partial list of research aids:

§ 280A

Proposed Reg. § 1.280A

M.G. Hill, 43 TCM 832, T.C. Memo 1982-143

18-25   *Journal Articles.* Refer to *Problem 18-24* above. Consult an index to periodicals (e.g., AICPA's *Accountants Index*; Warren, Gorham, and Lamont's *Index to Federal Tax Articles*; or CCH's *Federal Tax Articles*) and locate a journal article on the topic of tax deductions for an office in the home. Copy the article. Record the citation for the article (i.e., author's name, article title, journal name, publication date, and first and last pages of the article) at the top of your paper. Prepare a two-page summary of the article, including all relevant issues, research sources, and conclusions. Staple your two-page summary to the article. The grade for this exercise will be based on the relevance of your article to the topic, the accuracy and quality of your summary, and the quality of your written communication skills.

18-26   *Deductible Medical Expenses.* B suffers from a severe form of degenerative arthritis. Her doctor strongly recommended that she swim for at least one hour per day in order to stretch and exercise her leg and arm muscles. There are no swimming pools nearby, so B spent $15,000 to have a swimming pool installed in her back yard. This expenditure increased the fair market value of her house by $5,000. B consults you about whether she can deduct the cost of the swimming pool on her individual tax return. What do you recommend?

    Hint: You should approach this problem by using the tax service volumes of either Commerce Clearing House or Research Institute of America. Both tax services are organized according to Code Sections, so you should start with Code § 213. You will find the Code Sections on the back binding of the volumes. Research Institute of America has a very extensive index, so look under the term "medical expenses."

18-27   *Deductible Educational Expenses.* T is a CPA with a large accounting firm in Houston, Texas. He has been assigned to the international taxation group of his firm's tax department. As a result of this assignment, T enrolls in an international tax law course at the University of Houston Law School. The authorities of the University require T to enroll as a regular law student and, theoretically, if he continues to attend courses, T will graduate with a law degree. Will T be able to deduct his tuition for the international tax law course as a business expense?

    Hint: Go to either the RIA or CCH tax service and use it to find the analysis of Code § 162. When you have found the discussion of § 162, find that part of the subsection dealing with educational deductions. Read the appropriate Regulations and then note the authorities listed after the Regulations. Read over the summaries provided and then choose those you think have the most relevance to the question asked above. Read these cases and other listed authorities, and formulate a written response to the question asked in light of these cases and other authorities. Finally, for the authorities you choose, go to the RIA or CCH Citator and use it to ensure that your authorities are current.

19

Tax Practice and Procedure

Learning Objectives

Upon completion of this chapter you will be able to:

LO.1 Identify the conditions that might be likely to result in an IRS audit.

LO.2 Explain IRS audit procedures, including the procedure for proposed audit adjustments.

LO.3 Explain the procedure for appealing an adverse audit outcome.

LO.4 Understand and be able to determine the statute of limitations for assessments, collections, and refund claims.

LO.5 Determine when delinquency, accuracy-related, fraud, and information reporting penalties apply to taxpayers, and be able to compute them.

LO.6 Identify situations when interest applies to payment due to the IRS or a refund due from the IRS, and the rates applicable.

LO.7 Explain the rules for practice before the IRS.

LO.8 Identify the penalties that may apply to a tax return preparer.

LO.9 Understand the AICPA's Statements on Standards for Tax Services.

Chapter Outline

Introduction

With this chapter, the emphasis switches from issues of substantive tax law (i.e., the various rules that must be applied to determine the tax) to the procedural problems of complying with these laws. While considerations such as filing a tax return, paying the tax, and resolving disputes might seem mundane, they are a critical part of the taxation process. Indeed, if there were no provisions concerning compliance, revenues would go uncollected. The procedural aspect of taxation is the subject of this chapter.

The Compliance Process in General

The Federal tax system relies heavily on the concepts of *voluntary compliance* and *self-assessment* in order to collect tax revenues. Voluntary compliance implies that the taxpayer is responsible for reporting the appropriate tax liability to the Federal government, paying the tax, and otherwise complying with current tax laws. This is typically accomplished when the taxpayer properly reports all taxable items, deductions, and credits on a Federal tax return that is filed on or before the due date. Self-assessment is reflected in the burden imposed on the taxpayer to compute taxable income and the tax liability for that income by applying current law to the relevant facts for the tax year. The IRS generally does not determine tax liability, but instead relies on the taxpayer to compute, report, and pay the proper amount of tax.

The principles underlying the Federal tax assessment collection process differ markedly from those found in other systems of taxation. For example, contrast the Federal method with the assessment technique and *involuntary* taxpayer compliance found in a sales tax system. Under the sales tax system, a purchaser of goods pays the sales tax to the merchant that is responsible for assessing and collecting the tax at the time of the transaction. Also, compare the Federal method to that used for obtaining local property taxes. Under most property tax systems, a field employee assesses the value of the property, after which the appropriate governing body sends a tax bill to the property owner.

To maintain the integrity of the self-assessment system, Congress has charged the Secretary of the Treasury with the responsibility of administering and enforcing the Internal Revenue Code. With this responsibility, Congress also has given the Secretary the authority to prescribe the rules and Regulations necessary for enforcing the tax laws. The Secretary, in turn, has delegated this rule-making authority to the Commissioner of the Internal Revenue Service. Thus, it is the duty of the IRS to ensure compliance with the tax laws.

The mission of the IRS is to:

> Provide America's taxpayers top quality service by helping them understand and meet their tax responsibilities and by applying the tax law with integrity and fairness to all.

The IRS is organized into four operating divisions:

- *Wage & Investment.* This division includes individual taxpayers with only wage and investment income.

- *Small Business/Self-Employed.* This division includes individuals with unincorporated businesses or farms, rental or royalty income, employee business expenses, and income or losses from flow-through entities. It also includes most partnerships and S corporations, and corporations with assets under $10 million.

- *Large and Mid-Size Business.* This division includes corporations, S corporations, and partnerships with assets greater than $10 million.

- *Tax Exempt/Government Entities.* This division includes exempt organizations, employee plans, and state/local governments.

Each operating division is responsible for all activities related to that division, including all taxpayer education, filing of returns, examination of returns, and collection of tax, and is headed by its own Commissioner and Deputy Commissioner. IRS Services and Enforcement includes not only the four operating divisions, but also IRS Criminal Investigations and the Office of Professional Responsibility, which oversees tax professionals in practice before the IRS. IRS Operations Support includes the Chief Information Officer, the Human Capital Officer, the Chief Financial Officer, Mission Assurance, and general Agency-Wide Shared Services. Finally, the IRS has six specialized units: Appeals, National Taxpayer Advocate, Chief Counsel, Communications and Liaison, EEO and Diversity, and Research, Analysis and Statistics.

ADMINISTRATIVE REVIEW: THE AUDIT PROCESS

The IRS enforces the Federal tax law primarily through a systematic review of tax returns that have been filed. The review process begins when a tax return is filed. Every return is scanned for math and clerical errors as well as exclusions, deductions, and credits obviously claimed in error. This process includes matching information contained on such forms as the 1099 and the W-2 with amounts reported by the taxpayer. If any additional liability results from this review, the IRS Service Center issues an assessment for the correct amount of tax along with a brief statement explaining why the tax return was in error and a calculation of the additional amount owed. Alternatively, if a refund is owed to the taxpayer, it is issued. Typically, a taxpayer can resolve any questions concerning these adjustments by telephone or written correspondence with the IRS. This level of review is applied to *all* tax returns, as opposed to a more rigorous examination reserved only for selected tax returns.

Selection of Returns for Audit

Prior to selecting returns for audit, all returns are classified by type (e.g., individual, corporate, and partnership). Individual returns are then grouped in audit classes according to their adjusted gross incomes while corporate returns are divided into audit classes by gross assets. The selection of returns from each class is done through the use of the Discriminant Function System and through the identification of abusive tax schemes. The Discriminant Function System (DIF) is developed from data obtained in audits made in connection with the National Research Program (NRP).[1] The NRP consists of regular audits and randomly-selected audits, which, upon completion, are used to construct formulas that score returns as to their likelihood for containing significant tax error. Those returns with the highest score in each class are then scrutinized by the IRS to decide which returns it will audit, the type of audit to be performed, and how extensive the audit will be.

LO.1
Identify the conditions that might be likely to result in an IRS audit.

The factors that determine whether a return will or will not be audited have not been publicly disclosed by the IRS. Many factors may be gleaned from experience, however, including the following:

1. Exceeding "normal" ranges for itemized deductions at various income levels.
2. Previous audits that resulted in a deficiency assessment against the taxpayer.
3. Activity in sensitive areas, such as oil and gas, equipment leasing, real estate ventures, and other tax shelters.
4. Taking a deduction that may be easily abused, such as home office expenses, casualty and theft losses, and business use of automobiles.
5. Activity in a cash-transaction business where the opportunity for abuse is high and the ability to trace cash is low.
6. A discrepancy between informational returns (e.g., Form 1099 and Form 1065's Schedule K-1) and the income shown on the taxpayer's return.
7. Self-employed persons, especially those in typically high-income businesses.
8. Individuals with high gross income.
9. Information from all other sources, including but not limited to informants, financial statements, and public records.

---

[1] The NRP was instituted in 2002 in order to update the DIF formulas used in the audit selection process. The last time that the DIF formulas had been updated was 1988, using the Taxpayer Compliance Measurement Program (TCMP), which involved extensive audits of randomly selected returns. The NRP audits are expected to be much less intrusive than the TCMP audits.

Examples of these possibilities are illustrated below.

Example 1

Taxpayer A has gross income of $15,000 and claims a $10,000 deduction for interest. A may expect to be audited due to the large amount of interest deduction claimed relative to her total gross income.

Example 2

Taxpayer B's individual income tax return has been audited for each of the past five years. Each year's audit has resulted in a deficiency. B files Form 1040 for the current year in good form. B's current year return may be audited based on the record of deficiencies in prior years.

Example 3

Taxpayer C reports a net operating loss from participating as a limited partner in the XYZ Oil and Gas Partnership. C may be audited due to activity in the sensitive area of oil and gas.

Example 4

Taxpayer D files Form 1040 and claims a casualty loss deduction for the theft of $2,000 in cash. D may be audited due to the potential for abuse in deducting a casualty loss.

Example 5

Taxpayer E reports only $5,000 of gross income on Form 1040 for the entire year. E states on the return that his occupation is that of a magazine salesman. E may be audited since this is typically an occupation in which many transactions are paid for in cash.

In addition to focusing on returns selected for audit using DIF, the IRS is also focusing attention on the audit of abusive trusts where individuals attempt to conceal income and deduct personal expenses. Another area of interest is the use of offshore credit cards. While having an offshore credit card is not illegal, the funds used to pay for the credit card charges are often unreported income which has been moved to an offshore bank. These initiatives are part of the IRS's focus on high-income, high-risk tax returns.

Time Limit on Audits

In order for an assessment to be enforceable, it must be made within the statute of limitations. Accordingly, an audit generally must be performed within three years from the due date of the tax return.[2] There are circumstances and exceptions which shorten, lengthen, or suspend the period of the statute of limitations as discussed later in this chapter.

The IRS attempts to complete audits of income tax returns within 27 months or whichever comes later—the dates that they are due or are filed. The issuance of a refund check for overpayment of taxes is absolutely no indication of whether or not the IRS will audit this particular return.

Conduct of the Audit

All examinations of tax returns are conducted by the operating division that is best able to address the issues of the particular audit. Most tax returns are likely to clearly meet the criteria for a particular operating division where the taxpayer/entity best fits. The IRS is developing a set of criteria to deal with possible reassignments to other divisions where appropriate.

> **LO.2**
> Explain IRS audit procedures, including the procedure for proposed audit adjustments.

The audit is usually performed in the geographic area where the tax return was originally filed. When the taxpayer has moved to another area, when it is discovered that the records to be examined are located in another area, or when it is determined that the audit could be performed more conveniently and swiftly in another area, the audit may be moved.[3]

Auditing is conducted either in the local IRS office or in the field. Typically, only individual taxpayers are audited in the IRS office, as this imposes the burden of transporting financial data on the taxpayers most likely to have few records. In an office audit situation, the IRS usually sends an information guide instructing the taxpayer about which records are to be brought to the office. Although some individuals are audited extensively, most are required only to substantiate amounts for selected income, deductions, or credits by showing cancelled checks, receipts, or other supporting evidence. Sometimes an audit is conducted entirely through written correspondence (called a correspondence audit). If the taxpayer is requested to appear in the IRS office, he or she may go alone, or may be accompanied by an attorney, a certified public accountant, an individual enrolled to practice before the IRS, or even an unenrolled but qualified individual. If the taxpayer chooses not to appear personally, any of the individuals named above may represent the taxpayer—provided that such individual has a written power of attorney (Form 2848) executed by the taxpayer.[4] An additional form exists (Form 8821: Tax Information Authorization) that allows any person authorized by the taxpayer to receive and/or inspect that taxpayer's confidential tax return information. However, Form 8821 is *only* an authorization for disclosure of information and is not used to appoint a representative.

The field audit is conducted by revenue agents (rather than office auditors). Although the IRS's preferred audit location is the taxpayer's business, the audit may be performed in the taxpayer's home, or in the office of the taxpayer's representative. Field audits are typically conducted on businesses (e.g., large sole proprietorships, corporations, or partnerships), thus alleviating the burden of transporting to an IRS office the often voluminous records maintained by the business enterprise. A field audit of a business usually extends widely in scope, involving examination of many items and possibly several years of activity. The audit often begins with a conference between the IRS field agent and the taxpayer and the taxpayer's representative. At this time, the IRS must provide the taxpayer with an explanation of the audit process and the taxpayer's rights in the audit process.[5] The IRS may not require the taxpayer to accompany the representative unless an administrative summons is issued to the taxpayer.[6] However, the IRS may notify the taxpayer directly if it is believed that the representative is causing an unreasonable delay or hindering the IRS audit.

---

[2] § 6501 and Reg. § 301.6501.

[3] Statement of Procedural Rules, Reg. § 601.105(k).

[4] § 7521(c).

[5] § 7521(b)(1).

[6] § 7521(c).

During the initial conference, the IRS agent scrutinizes the taxpayer's records and requests explanation and substantiation of various items that he or she found to be questionable. IRS agents have the power to summon the taxpayer's records and to compel witnesses to testify.[7] Several meetings between the IRS agent conducting the audit and the taxpayer or the taxpayer's representative may take place. At such meetings, the IRS may ask for additional explanation and substantiation for items already being examined, and very possibly, the IRS may decide that it wants to expand the scope of the audit to examine additional items. The taxpayer and the IRS are allowed to make audio recordings of any interview as long as advance notice is given.[8] In addition, if at any time during the interview, the taxpayer clearly states to the IRS representative conducting the interview that he or she wishes to consult with an attorney, CPA, or any other person qualified to represent the taxpayer, then the interview shall be suspended.[9]

The IRS Restructuring and Reform Act of 1998 limited the use of "financial status" or "economic reality" audit techniques unless the IRS has a reasonable indication that there is a likelihood of unreported income.[10] Congress felt that these audit techniques, which often focused on the possibility of unreported income at the beginning of an audit, were unreasonably intrusive. In addition, the IRS must give the taxpayer reasonable advance notice when contacting third parties.[11] This does not apply to any contact authorized by the taxpayer, situations where notice might jeopardize either a person or collection of a tax, or criminal investigations.

There has been much publicity about the new burden of proof rules contained in the tax law. These new rules apply only to court proceedings, and shift the burden of proof for factual issues only to the IRS if the taxpayer introduces credible evidence regarding the facts that apply to a tax liability.[12] Unfortunately, these court burden of proof rules are likely to cause the IRS to spend additional time and be more intrusive in audits to prepare for the often remote possibility of a court action.

Proposed Audit Adjustments

In either type of audit, if the IRS does not agree with the return as filed, it may propose that adjustments be made to the tax liability. The IRS may find that the taxpayer overstated the tax liability on the return and has overpaid the actual tax bill for the period under audit. More likely, due to the Discriminant Function System, the IRS will propose that the tax liability be adjusted upward for the period audited, indicating that the taxpayer owes additional tax.[13]

The IRS findings (i.e., an overpayment, an underpayment, or no change in the tax liability for the period audited) are set out in a report called "Income Tax Examination Changes" after the audit is finished. The report explains the adjustments proposed by the IRS in terms of the dollar amounts and the issues which underlie the suggested changes. The report may be reviewed by the auditor's supervisor and subsequently by a member of the review staff of the appropriate IRS operating division. Normally, these reviewers agree with the report as is, but they may ask for more information from the taxpayers or even bring up new issues that relate to the audit.

Issues that may arise during the audit may be questions of fact, questions of law, or mixed questions of fact and law. A question of fact involves a dispute over whether something did or did not occur. For example, whether or not a business expense for office rent was actually incurred and the amount of the expense are facts that may be questioned. A question of law involves a dispute over the interpretation of a law and its application in the taxpayer's situation. For example, whether the taxpayer is permitted to deduct a particular expense under some Code provision is a question of law. A mixed question of fact and

---

[7] § 7602.

[8] § 7521(a).

[9] § 7521(b)(2).

[10] § 7602(d).

[11] § 7602(c).

[12] § 7491.

[13] § 6211.

law involves a dispute over how the law applies in a situation where the facts are ambiguous or subject to different interpretations. For instance, the IRS may question whether a company has paid its president reasonable compensation. Whether the compensation paid to the president (and principal shareholder) is to be treated as dividends or as salary may depend on the facts, such as the intentions of the parties, the amount paid, the amount of services rendered, or the value of the services. Resolution of the issue also depends on the law, which in this type of case specifies various factors that may or may not have importance in the situation, depending on how the law is interpreted. For instance, the law may be interpreted so that the value of the services rendered is of paramount importance. Alternatively, the law may be interpreted to place the highest emphasis on the amount of services rendered and little importance on the value. Clearly, the mixed questions of fact and law are the most troublesome issues raised by an audit.

A taxpayer and an IRS agent may settle any type of question by reaching an agreement on the issues raised in the audit. Questions of fact are usually the easiest to resolve as they most often deal with matters that may be traced to tangible evidence; these questions become more difficult where the subject under scrutiny is less tangible, such as the taxpayer's intent at a given time. In resolving a question of law, the IRS must follow its current policy as established by Regulations, Rulings, and other releases. The IRS may not take a position that differs from its announced policy even though the IRS has a high probability of prevailing if the issue should be tried in court. This also is true in resolving a mixed question of fact and law.

Closing the Audit

After the audit has been completed, a taxpayer who agrees with the proposed adjustments is asked to sign either the Report of Individual Income Tax Changes (issued in an office audit), the Revenue Agent's Report (issued in a field audit and generally known as the RAR Exhibit 19-1), or Form 870, Waiver of Restrictions on Assessment and Collection of Deficiency in Tax [most commonly used for situations involving partial agreements (see Exhibit 19-2)]. By signing these forms, the taxpayer waives the right to pursue the appeals process within the IRS and also waives the right to petition the Tax Court for relief. However, anyone who signs one of the above forms may pay the deficiency and, if he or she chooses, sue for a refund of the deficiency in U.S. District Court or U.S. Claims Court. This path may bypass the IRS Appeals function and procedure and take the taxpayer directly to court. The IRS encourages its personnel to try to settle issues at the audit level, and at least arrive at partial agreements to lighten the workload of the Appeals function and the Tax Court.[14] If the taxpayer and the IRS are unable to agree on one or more issues, the taxpayer may keep the case open by refusing to sign one of the above forms. By not signing and by doing nothing further, the taxpayer will receive a letter explaining the appeal process. The taxpayer must then be ready to pursue the appeal process to avoid having the proposed deficiency assessed.

The signing of a Report of Individual Income Tax Examination Changes, an RAR, or Form 870 at the audit level does *not* bar the IRS from opening new issues, requesting more information, and assessing more deficiencies (although this is somewhat unlikely), even after the taxpayer has paid the deficiency already assessed. Similarly, the taxpayer does not lose the right to use the IRS Appeals function for any *additional* issues or deficiencies raised by the IRS after an agreement has been signed. Thus, a signed agreement does nothing to bind either the IRS or the taxpayer from seeking further relief; it merely precludes the taxpayer from seeking a settlement with IRS Appeals on issues and deficiencies already in question that are covered in the agreement. The signing of Form 870 stops the running of interest on the deficiency 30 days after the form is filed.

---

[14] Rev. Rul. 266, 1953-2 C.B. 450.

EXHIBIT 19-1	**Revenue Agent's Report (RAR)**

Form **4549** (Rev. March 2005)	Department of the Treasury-Internal Revenue Service **Income Tax Examination Changes**		Page ___1___ of ___2___
Name and Address of Taxpayer		Taxpayer Identification Number	Return Form No.:
		Person with whom examination changes were discussed.	Name and Title:

1. Adjustments to Income	Period End 12/31/2007	Period End	Period End
a. Other income (Carryforward to 2007)			
b. Other deductions (Carryforward to 2007)			
c.			
d.			
e.			
f.			
g.			
h.			
i.			
j.			
k.			
l.			
m.			
n.			
o.			
p.			
2. Total Adjustments			
3. Taxable Income Per Return or as Previously Adjusted			
4. Corrected Taxable Income Tax Method Filing Status			
5. Tax			
6. Additional Taxes / Alternative Minimum Tax			
7. Corrected Tax Liability			
8. Less a. Credits b. c. d.			
9. Balance *(Line 7 less Lines 8a through 8d)*			
10. Plus Other Taxes a. b. c. d.			
11. Total Corrected Tax Liability *(Line 9 plus Lines 10a through 10d)*			
12. Total Tax Shown on Return or as Previously Adjusted			
13. Adjustments to: a. b.			
14. Deficiency-Increase in Tax or *(Overassessment-Decrease in Tax)* *(Line 11 less Line 12 adjusted by Lines 13a plus 13b)*			
15. Adjustments to Prepayment Credits - Increase *(Decrease)*			
16. Balance Due or *(Overpayment)* - *(Line 14 adjusted by Line 15)* *(Excluding interest and penalties)*			

The Internal Revenue Service has agreements with state tax agencies under which information about federal tax, including increases or decreases, is exchanged with the states. If this change affects the amount of your state income tax, you should amend your state return by filing the necessary forms.

You may be subject to backup withholding if you underreport your interest, dividend, or patronage dividend income you earned and do not pay the required tax. The IRS may order backup withholding *(withholding of a percentage of your dividend and/or interest income)* if the tax remains unpaid after it has been assessed and four notices have been issued to you over a 120-day period.

Catalog Number 23105A	www.irs.gov	Form 4549 (Rev. 3-2005)

EXHIBIT 19-1	**Continued**

Form **4549** (Rev. March 2005)	Department of the Treasury-Internal Revenue Service **Income Tax Examination Changes**		Page __2__ of __2__
Name of Taxpayer Sun City Anthem Community Association, Inc.	Taxpayer Identification Number 86-0932401		Return Form No.: 1120

17. Penalties/ Code Sections	Period End	Period End	Period End
a. Penalties, Section 6662(d) @20% of amount owed incl. interest			
b.			
c.			
d.			
e.			
f.			
g.			
h.			
i.			
j.			
k.			
l.			
m.			
18. Total Penalties			
Underreporter attributable to negligence: *(1981-1987)* *A tax addition of 50 percent of the interest due on the underpayment will accrue until it is paid or assessed.*			
Underreporter attributable to fraud: *(1981-1987)* *A tax addition of 50 percent of the interest due on the underpayment will accrue until it is paid or assessed.*			
Underreporter attributable to Tax Motivated Transactions *(TMT).* The interest will accrue and be assessed at 120% of the under-payment rate in accordance with IRC §6621(c)			
19. Summary of Taxes, Penalties and Interest:			
a. Balance due or *(Overpayment)* Taxes - *(Line 16, Page 1)*			
b. Penalties *(Line 18)* - computed to 1/31/2011			
c. Interest *(IRC § 6601)* - computed to 1/31/2011			
d. TMT Interest - computed to ___ *(on TMT underpayment)*			
e. Amount due or *(refund)* - *(sum of Lines a, b, c and d)*			

Other Information:

Examiner's Signature: Kathy Thomas	Employee ID: 09-29785	Office: 110 City Parkway, Las Vegas NV 89106	Date: 1/31/2011

Consent to Assessment and Collection- I do not wish to exercise my appeal rights with the Internal Revenue Service or to contest in the United States Tax Court the findings in this report. Therefore, I give my consent to the immediate assessment and collection of any increase in tax and penalties, and accept any decrease in tax and penalties shown above, plus additional interest as provided by law. It is understood that this report is subject to acceptance by the Area Director, Area Manager, Specialty Tax Program Chief, or Director of Field Operations.

PLEASE NOTE: *If a joint return was filed.* **BOTH** *taxpayers must sign*

Signature of Taxpayer	Date:	Signature of Taxpayer	Date:
By:		Title:	Date:

Catalog Number 23105A	www.irs.gov	Form 4549 (Rev. 3-2005)

EXHIBIT 19-2 | **Form 870**

Form **870** (Rev. March 1992)	Department of the Treasury—Internal Revenue Service **Waiver of Restrictions on Assessment and Collection of Deficiency in Tax and Acceptance of Overassessment**	Date received by Internal Revenue Service

Names and address of taxpayers *(Number, street, city or town, State, ZIP code)* | Social security or employer identification number

Increase (Decrease) in Tax and Penalties

Tax year ended	Tax	Penalties		

(For instructions, see back of form)

Consent to Assessment and Collection

I consent to the immediate assessment and collection of any deficiencies *(increase in tax and penalties)* and accept any overassessment *(decrease in tax and penalties)* shown above, plus any interest provided by law. I understand that by signing this waiver, I will not be able to contest these years in the United States Tax Court, unless additional deficiencies are determined for these years.

YOUR SIGNATURE HERE ➡		Date
SPOUSE'S SIGNATURE ➡		Date
TAXPAYER'S REPRESENTATIVE HERE ➡		Date

CORPORATE NAME ➡		
CORPORATE OFFICER(S) ➡		Title	Date
SIGN HERE ➡		Title	Date

Catalog Number 16894U | Form **870** (Rev. 3-1992)

APPEALS PROCEDURE

A taxpayer who does not agree with the outcome of an audit may choose to challenge the findings by appealing the case to a higher level of the IRS. (Contrast this with the taxpayer who pays the deficiency and signs one of the forms discussed above, then requests a refund from the IRS with the intention of bringing suit for such refund in U.S. District Court or U.S. Claims Court if the refund claim is denied. Such a taxpayer typically seeks to avoid the appellate procedure within the IRS.) The taxpayer who pursues an appeal within the IRS starts the process by refusing to sign an agreement. The IRS then sends the taxpayer a copy of the Revenue Agent's Report, a Form 870, and a so-called *30-day letter* (see Exhibit 19-3), which instructs the taxpayer to make use of the appellate procedure in the IRS. The 30-day letter typically urges the taxpayer to respond within 30 days by either agreeing to the RAR and signing either the RAR or Form 870, or requesting an appellate conference. The letter also explains that if there is no response, a "90-day letter" (discussed below) containing a statutory notice of deficiency will be issued.

LO.3

Explain the procedure for appealing an adverse audit outcome.

Written Protest

If the taxpayer wants a conference with IRS Appeals, a written protest for appeal must be filed with a request for an appellate conference. The protest is required in all cases except (1) where the deficiency is no greater than $2,500 for each tax period audited, or (2) the deficiency was assessed in an office or correspondence audit.

The protest must contain a statement that supports the taxpayer's position with regard to questions of fact as well as a statement and analysis of the law upon which the taxpayer is relying. The protest also must list the specific adjustments proposed by the audit that the taxpayer wishes to challenge.

The Appellate Conference

The IRS does not allow the taxpayer an appellate conference as a matter of right. Rather, it offers the process as a privilege for a taxpayer who wishes to dispose of a case at an administrative level (i.e., within the IRS, before reaching the trial court). The taxpayer who refuses to comply with tax laws on the basis of moral or political reasons normally is not granted an appellate conference.

The purpose of an appeals conference is to review the findings of the audit and the issues raised in hopes of arriving at a resolution of the case. The conference itself takes place in an informal manner. Usually, only the taxpayer's representative attends the conference as the taxpayer's lack of technical understanding may hinder the proceedings. As a practical matter, the taxpayer's representative often requests that the taxpayer not attend the conference. The IRS agents that performed the audit typically are not present; instead, the IRS is represented by officers of the Appeals function. Witnesses are seldom asked to testify as their sworn affidavits usually suffice.

A taxpayer should not pursue an appellate review of an IRS audit without an understanding of the risk involved. The personnel at this level usually have more experience than the agents who conducted the audit, and are likely to construct more sophisticated arguments against the taxpayer and possibly raise new issues. Also, the taxpayer must take into account the costs of professional services necessary to appeal a case. The research for and the drafting of a written protest, along with professional fees for representation at the appellate conference, may involve considerable expense. These costs should be balanced against the amount of the disputed deficiency weighted by the probability of a favorable outcome.

During the appellate conference, the taxpayer or his or her representative meets with members of the IRS Appeals function. In an effort to settle the case, the IRS may agree to resolve an issue in favor of the taxpayer in exchange for a reciprocal agreement by the taxpayer to resolve one or more other issues in favor of the IRS. This practice may occur only with issues raised at the audit level, and not with new issues that might be raised at the appellate level. The Appeals function may not raise new issues at the appellate level unless the grounds of a new issue have significant tax impact.[15]

---

[15] Statement of Procedural Rules, Reg. § 601.106(d)(1).

The Appeals function has authority to settle all cases without regard to the amount of tax involved. One of the many factors considered by Appeals is whether or not there exists a *hazard of litigation*. This term has not been clearly defined but obviously relates to the probability that the taxpayer will continue to pursue the case to the trial court level or beyond, as well as being related to the taxpayer's chances of winning there. The primary objective of Appeals is to settle cases and keep them from going to court. As a result, Appeals may offer to accept only a percentage of the deficiency proposed by the IRS. Each item might be adjusted and settled in such a manner. For example, if a question exists as to the deductibility of an item, the IRS may settle for one-half of the tax deficiency related to that item. However, this should not be construed as meaning that the Appeals function will automatically concede issues or cases involving a low tax liability.

EXHIBIT 19-3 | **Sample 30-Day Letter**

Internal Revenue Service   Department of the Treasury

Date: In Reply Refer to:

                                                                Person to Contact:

                                                                Contact Telephone Number:

                                                                Tax Year Ended and Deficiency/
                                                                  Overassessment:

Dear

  We are enclosing a report proposing adjustments to the amount of your tax for the year(s) shown above. Please read the report, decide whether you agree or disagree with us, and respond within 30 days from the date of this letter. (Our report may not reflect the results of examinations of flow-through entities [partnerships, S corporations, trusts, etc.] in which you may have an interest.)

  IF YOU AGREE, you should:

  1. Sign and date the enclosed agreement form.

  2. Return the signed agreement form to us in the enclosed envelope.

  3. Enclose payment of the tax and interest if additional tax is due, if you wish to stop the further running of interest. (The person whose name and telephone number appear above will be able to tell you how much interest is due to the date you intend to make payment. See the enclosed Publication 5 for additional payment information.)

  After we receive your signed agreement form, we will close your case and bill you for any unpaid tax or interest.

  IF YOU DO NOT AGREE and wish a conference with the Regional Office of Appeals, you MUST LET US KNOW within 30 days.

  1. If the proposed change to your tax is $2,500 OR LESS for any tax period, you may call the person whose name and telephone number appear above; he or she will arrange for your case to be forwarded to Appeals. Or, you may send us your request by checking the appropriate section at the end of this letter; an additional copy of this letter is provided for this purpose. Mail this to us in the enclosed envelope.

  2. If the proposed change to your tax is more than $2,500 but is $10,000 or less for any tax period, you must provide us with a BRIEF written statement of the disputed issues. This should be shown in the area found at the end of this letter; an additional copy of this letter is provided for this purpose. Mail this to us in the enclosed envelope.

  3. If the proposed change to your tax is MORE THAN $10,000 for any tax period, we will require a written protest. Follow the instructions in the enclosed Publication 5. Mail the protest to us in the enclosed envelope.

(over)

EXHIBIT 19-3	**Continued**

An Appeals Officer, who has not previously examined your return, will take a fresh look at your case. The Appeals Office is independent of the District Director. Most disputes considered by Appeals are resolved informally and promptly. By going to Appeals, you may avoid court costs (such as the Tax Court's $60 filing fee), clear up this matter sooner, and prevent interest from running. An Appeals Officer will telephone you and, if necessary, arrange an appointment.

Under Code section 6673, the Tax Court is authorized to award damages of up to $5,000 to the United States where a taxpayer unreasonably fails to pursue available administrative remedies. Damages could be awarded under this provision, for example, if the Court concludes that it was unreasonable for a taxpayer to bypass Appeals and then file a petition in the Tax Court. The Tax Court will make that determination based upon the facts and circumstances of each case. Generally, the Service will not ask the Court to award damages under this provision if you made a good faith effort to meet with Appeals and to settle your case before petitioning the Tax Court.

If you do not reach and agreement with Appeals or if you do not respond to this letter, we will process your case on the basis of the enclosed examination report. IF you decide to bypass Appeals and petition the Tax Court, your case will normally be assigned for settlement to an Appeals Office before the Tax Court hears the case. (References to Tax Court do not apply to excise or employment tax cases.) If YOU ARE UNSURE as to what to do or have other questions, call the person whose name and telephone number appear above. We will be glad to discuss your choices.

Sincerely yours,

Enclosures:
Copy of this letter
Examination Report
Agreement Form
Publication 5
Envelope

Statement of Disputed Issues

Check appropriate block:

☐ TAX IN DISPUTE IS $2,500 OR LESS FOR ANY TAX PERIOD (Note: You may not call us with this request if you prefer.)

   I disagree and wish a conference with an Appeals Officer.

_____   _____
Signature   Date

☐ TAX IN DISPUTE IS OVER $2,500 BUT IS $10,000 OR LESS FOR ANY TAX PERIOD

Unagreed Adjustments   Reason for Disagreement

_____   _____

_____   _____

_____   _____

                                     _____

                                     _____

(If more space is needed, attach a separate sheet.)   _____
                                     Signature   Date

Settlement with Appeals

At any stage in the appellate process, the taxpayer may be requested to sign Form 870-AD (Appellate Division), Offer of Waiver of Restrictions on Assessment and Collection of Deficiency, in order to settle the case. This form is similar to Form 870 inasmuch as it sets forth the concessions arrived at between the IRS and the taxpayer. However, the two forms differ in one important respect. As a general rule, signing Form 870 does not preclude the IRS from further audits. In contrast, acceptance of the Form 870-AD by the IRS means that the case *will not* be reopened in the absence of fraud, misrepresentation of material fact, significant error in mathematical calculation, or other administrative malfeasance. Most practitioners regard the agreement delineated on the Form 870-AD as a binding one. The issue of whether or not either party may reopen the case after the agreement is executed has not been resolved.[16]

Unlike Form 870, filing Form 870-AD does not stop the running of interest until the offer is accepted by the IRS. Also, if Form 870-AD is signed, the IRS may make a valid assessment without issuing the customary 90-day letter containing a notice of deficiency which is otherwise required.

Fast Track Mediation

The IRS has recently instituted a new mediation service available *before* the Appeals process for taxpayers under audit by the Small Business/Self-Employed Division of the IRS. Taxpayers may request Fast Track Mediation if they don't agree with any or all of the IRS findings. An Appeals Officer trained in mediation conducts discussions with the taxpayer and the IRS representative, with the goal of reaching a mutually satisfactory resolution consistent with the law. No written protest is required. The mediator has no authority to require either party to accept any resolution, and the taxpayer may withdraw from the mediation process at any time. If any issues remain unresolved, the taxpayer still has the usual appeal rights. There is also a version of Fast Track Mediation for the IRS Large and Mid-Size Business Division.

THE 90-DAY LETTER: NOTICE OF DEFICIENCY

As suggested above, the IRS is normally prohibited from assessing and collecting the tax until 90 days after the taxpayer has been notified of the tax deficiency. The required statutory notice of deficiency, commonly referred to as the 90-day letter (see Exhibit 19-4), may be issued at various times during the review process. The letter is usually sent following the rejection or denial of the taxpayer's appeal. A taxpayer who fails to settle a case with the IRS Appeals function receives the letter shortly after IRS legal counsel has reviewed the case. The 90-day letter is also sent to taxpayers who do not respond to the 30-day letter. In addition, the taxpayer may request issuance of the 90-day letter since a petition to the Tax Court cannot be filed until statutory notice of the deficiency has been received. It should be noted that issuance of the 90-day letter *suspends* the running of the statute of limitations.

Assessment

Before the tax can be collected, it must be assessed. Assessment is the act of recording the amount of tax due on the books of the government.[17] As noted above, the IRS generally cannot make an assessment of a deficiency until a 90-day letter has been mailed to the taxpayer and the 90 days of notice have elapsed. In addition, the IRS cannot assess a deficiency where the taxpayer has filed a petition with the Tax Court until the court's decision has become final.[18]

Assessments of tax shown on a return, math errors, credits taken in error, and delinquency penalties not related to a deficiency do not require the 90-day letter of statutory notice. It is required, however, for all deficiencies, penalties for fraud and negligence, and delinquency penalties related to deficiencies.

---

[16] See *W.R. Lowe*, 63-2 USTC ¶9778, 12 AFTR2d 5951, 223 F. Supp. 948 (1963); but cf. *W.A. Morse*, 59-1 USTC ¶9359, 6 AFTR2d 5353, 183 F. Supp. 847 (1959).

[17] § 6213.

[18] § 6213. Also, see § 7481 for the date that a Tax Court decision becomes final.

EXHIBIT 19-4	Sample 90-Day Letter

Internal Revenue Service   Department of the Treasury

Date:

Taxpayer Identifying Number:

Form:

Tax Year Ended and Deficiency:

Person to Contact:

Telephone Number:

NOTICE OF DEFICIENCY

We have determined that you owe additional tax or other amount, or both, as shown for the tax year(s) identified above. This letter is your NOTICE OF DEFICIENCY, as required by law. The enclosed statement shows how we figured the deficiency.

If you want to contest this determination in court before making any payment, you have 90 days from the date of this letter (150 days if addressed to your outside of the United States) to file a petition with the United States Tax Court for a redetermination of the deficiency. For a petition form, write to:

United States Tax Court
400 Second Street, NW
Washington, DC 20217

Send the completed petition form, a copy of this letter, and all relevant statements or schedules that accompanied this letter to the Tax Court at the same address. The petition must be timely filed with the court within 90 days from the above mailing date (150 days if addressed to you outside of the United Sates). However, if the petition is filed after the 90 days (or 150 day) period, it is considered timely filing if the postmark date falls within the prescribed period and the envelope containing the petition is properly addressed with the correct postage.

The time for filing a petition with the court (90 or 150 days as the case may be) is set by law and can't be extended or suspended. Thus, contacting the Service for more information or receiving other correspondence from the Service won't change the period for filing a petition with the Tax Court. The court can't consider your case if the petition is filed late.

If this letter is addressed to both a husband and wife, and both want to petition the Tax, Court, both must sign and file the petition or each must file a separate, signed petition. If more than one year is shown above, you only need to file one petition form showing the years you are contesting.

(over)

EXHIBIT 19-4	Continued

The Tax Court has a simplified procedure for small tax cases, when the dispute is for $10,000 or less for any one tax year. You can get information about this procedure as well as a petition form you can use, by writing to:

Clerk of the United States Tax Court
400 Second Street, NW
Washington, DC 20217

Do this promptly if you intend to file a petition with the Tax Court.

You may represent yourself before the Tax Court, or you may be represented by anyone admitted to practice before the court.

If you decide not to file a petition with the Tax Court, please sign and return the enclosed waiver form. This will permit us to assess the deficiency quickly and can help limit the accumulation of interest. The enclosed envelope is for your convenience.

If you decide not to sign and return the waiver, and you do not file a petition with the Tax Court within the time limit, the law requires us to assess and bill you for the deficiency after 90 days from the above mailing date of this letter (150 days if this letter is addressed to you outside the United States).

If you are a "C" corporation, Section 6621(c) of the Internal Revenue Code provides that an interest rate two percent higher than the normal rate of interest be charged on large corporate underpayments of $100,000 or more.

If you have questions about this letter, please write to the person whose name and address are shown on this letter. If you write, please attach this letter to help us identify your account. Keep the copy for your records. Also, please include your telephone number and the most convenient time to call, so we can contact you if we need additional information.

If you prefer, you may call the IRS contact person at the telephone number shown above. If this number is outside your local calling area, there will be a long distance charge to you. You may call the IRS telephone number listed in your local directory. An IRS employee there may be able to help you, but the contact person at the address shown on this letter is most familiar with your case.

Thank you for your cooperation.

Sincerely yours,

Commissioner

Enclosures:
Copy of this letter
Waiver
Envelope

BEYOND APPELLATE CONFERENCE PROCEDURES

After the appellate conference and related negotiations have been completed, an office of the Appeals function reviews the case. When a settlement was reached in the appellate conference but not approved by the reviewing officer, the taxpayer is granted a conference with the reviewing officer.[19] If the reviewer approves the appellate conference findings, he or she forwards them to the area where the case originated.

---

[19] Statement of Procedural Rules, Reg. § 601.106(f)(3).

In cases where a settlement is not reached at the appellate conference or the post-conference review, the Appeals function sends a 90-day letter to the taxpayer stating that an assessment will be made if he or she does not pay the deficiency or petition the Tax Court within 90 days. Generally, this notice marks the end of the administrative appeals process and availability of any remedies at the administrative level. Consequently, the taxpayer must either pay the deficiency and sue to recover it in District Court or the Claims Court, or he or she must file a petition for a determination of the case by the Tax Court. In the latter event, the taxpayer need not pay the deficiency before filing a claim for relief.

ADDITIONAL SETTLEMENT TECHNIQUES

As mentioned above, the taxpayer may be requested to settle the dispute during the audit by signing Form 870, or during the appellate process by signing Form 870-AD. By entering into this type of agreement, the parties avoid the statutory requirement that a notice of deficiency (i.e., a 90-day letter) be sent and that 90 days expire before an assessment is made. Other commonly used settlement methods include closing agreements, offers in compromise, and agreements to extend the statute of limitations for assessment.

Closing Agreements

A written closing agreement can be entered into by any authorized officer or employee of the IRS.[20] A closing agreement may be made at any time before the case has been heard by the Tax Court. Such agreements are considered binding in the absence of fraud, misrepresentation, or substantial error.

Offers in Compromise

It is possible, after assessment, for the taxpayer and the IRS to "compromise" or settle a tax liability for a lower amount than the tax liability (including penalties and interest) actually owed. An *offer in compromise* is *not* suitable for situations in which the taxpayer has the means to pay the entire existing tax liability in a reasonably short period of time. In fact, the IRS is *not* likely to accept an offer in compromise unless the amount offered by the taxpayer to settle his or her liability is at least equal to the net realizable value of all of the taxpayer's assets. In addition, a nonrefundable partial payment (e.g., 20% of a lump-sum offer) must be submitted with the offer in compromise. As part of the offer in compromise, the taxpayer agrees to comply with the Federal tax laws for the five-year period following acceptance of the offer. Violation of this provision, or of any other terms of the offer in compromise, will result in the entire original tax liability, plus accrued penalties and interest, becoming due. Although offers in compromise are most commonly used when there is doubt as to the collectibility of an amount owed, offers in compromise may also be used when there is doubt as to the liability assessed.[21]

Extensions of Limitation Period

An audit or an appellate review often requires more time to finish than that remaining in the limitations period. In unusual circumstances only, the IRS asks the taxpayer to agree to an extension of the limitations period.[22] This agreement must be written and it may be entered into only by an appropriate official of the IRS. The IRS, when requesting that a taxpayer consent to extend the statute of limitations, must notify the taxpayer that he or she has the right to refuse to extend the statute of limitations or to limit the extension to particular issues or to a particular period of time.[23] The taxpayer does not have to enter into the Agreement, but it is unwise to refuse to do so. Such a refusal prompts the IRS to prematurely stop negotiations and assess a deficiency against the taxpayer. This precludes further dealings with the IRS until the taxpayer files a petition with the Tax Court or pays the assessment and files a claim for a refund. An extension is executed on Form 872 or Form 872-A. The agreement

---

[20] Reg. § 301.7121-1. Also, see Rev. Proc. 68-16, 1968-1 C.B. 770.

[21] § 7122 and Reg. § 301.7122-1(a).

[22] Rev. Proc. 57-6, 1957-1 C.B. 729.

[23] § 6501(c)(4)(B).

extends the limitations period either to a specific date, or until a written notification is made by one party to the other declaring the end of the additional period. In either case, the termination of the agreement becomes effective only after the passage of an additional period of 90 days (i.e., the length of time needed for the statutory notice of deficiency) plus an extra 60 days.[24]

Example 6

Individual taxpayer A enters into an agreement with the IRS to extend the statute of limitations for 2013. The limitations period normally expires April 15, 2017, but due to unusual circumstances, A has agreed to keep the period open until June 30, 2017. The running of the period of limitation for assessment is suspended from April 15, 2017 to November 27, 2017. Ninety days for the statutory notice of assessment plus 60 extra days are added to the specified date of June 30, 2017.

Example 7

Individual taxpayer B enters into an agreement with the IRS to extend the limitations period for 2013. The limitations period normally expires on April 15, 2017, but due to unusual circumstances, B has agreed to keep the period open until one party notifies the other in writing that the extension is terminated. On July 31, 2017 B notifies the IRS in writing that the extension period is over. The running of the period of limitation for assessment is suspended from April 15, 2017 to December 28, 2017. Ninety days for the statutory notice of assessment plus 60 extra days are added to the notice date of July 31, 2017.

EXHAUSTING THE ADMINISTRATIVE REMEDIES

As mentioned above, the taxpayer may at any time during the audit and appellate process request a 90-day letter from the IRS, pay the assessed deficiency, and file a claim for refund in District Court or Claims Court. Before filing suit in either of these courts, however, the taxpayer must first exhaust his or her administrative remedies making a formal, written request for a refund from the IRS. The taxpayer's request for refund is considered by the operating division that conducted the audit. If the request is rejected, a 30-day letter is sent to the taxpayer explaining the appellate procedure. The taxpayer must follow the same appellate procedure with IRS Appeals as is followed by a taxpayer who has not yet paid a deficiency. The difference is that this taxpayer, by virtue of having already paid the deficiency, must file a suit for refund in the District Court or Claims Court, and may not go to the Tax Court for relief.

National Taxpayer Advocate

The Office of Taxpayer Advocate was designed to assist taxpayers whose problems are not resolved through normal channels, or who are suffering significant hardships.[25] The National Taxpayer Advocate reports directly to the IRS Commissioner, and is appointed by the Secretary of the Treasury, after consulting with the IRS Commissioner and the IRS Oversight Board. In addition, the law now requires that there be at least one local Taxpayer Advocate for each state, and that the local telephone numbers be published and available. As the name suggests, the Taxpayer Advocates are to act on behalf of the taxpayers. Specifically, the Taxpayer Advocate is to assist taxpayers in resolving problems with the IRS, identify areas in which taxpayers have problems in dealing with the IRS, propose changes in IRS

---

[24] § 6503(a)(1).   [25] § 7803(c).

administrative practices to ease the problems identified, and identify potential law changes which might be appropriate to reduce the identified problems.[26]

The National Taxpayer Advocate also has the power to issue a *Taxpayer Assistance Order* if a taxpayer is suffering or is about to suffer a significant hardship as a result of the manner in which the IRS is administering the tax laws.[27] The definition of a "significant hardship" includes an immediate threat of adverse action, a delay of more than 30 days in resolving taxpayer account problems, the incurring by the taxpayer of significant costs if relief is not granted, and irreparable injury or a long-term adverse impact on a taxpayer if relief is not granted. A Taxpayer Assistance Order may require that the IRS, within a specified time period, release a levy on a taxpayer's property, or cease action, take any legally allowed action, or refrain from taking action, with respect to a taxpayer in the following areas: collection, bankruptcy or receivership, discovery of liability or enforcement of title, or any other provision of the law specifically mentioned in the Taxpayer Assistance Order.[28] A Taxpayer Assistance Order may only be modified or rescinded by the National Taxpayer Advocate, the IRS Commissioner, or the IRS Deputy Commissioner, and only if a written explanation is provided to the National Taxpayer Advocate.[29] The National Taxpayer Advocate is required to submit regular reports on these matters *directly* to Congress.[30]

IRS Oversight Board

There is also an IRS Oversight Board which has the authority to oversee IRS administration, management, conduct, direction, and to supervise the execution and application of tax laws.[31] The IRS Oversight Board reviews and approves strategic and operational plans of the IRS, including making management recommendations and reviewing the IRS budget. The Board is also responsible for ensuring the proper treatment of taxpayers by IRS employees. The Board consists of nine individuals: the Treasury Secretary (or Deputy Treasury Secretary), the IRS Commissioner, an appointed Federal employee, and six appointed professionals who are not Federal employees. These six Presidentially-appointed individuals must have professional experience and expertise in at least one of a variety of areas: management of large service organizations, customer service, Federal tax laws, information technology, organizational development, needs and concerns of taxpayers, and needs and concerns of small businesses.

The Statute of Limitations

LO.4
Understand and be able to determine the statute of limitations for assessments, collections, and refund claims.

The Internal Revenue Code contains several statutes of limitation. These statutes provide that after a certain event has occurred, legal action related to the event may not be brought if a specified amount of time has passed. The statute of limitations establishes an absolute defense against any legal action brought after its expiration. In deciding the type of events that should have a limitations period and the length of that period, many factors must be considered. These factors include the significance of the event, its seriousness in nature as well as its magnitude. Also important is the availability of records, witnesses, or other evidence related to the event and the difficulty of obtaining them due to the passage of time. Other considerations involve the overall harm to the legal system that might occur if legal action is barred, including the detriment to the party that has suffered from the event as opposed to the burden imposed on the judicial system by allowing legal action to be brought on events of the more distant past. Finally, it is desirable to have events beyond a certain point of time in the past considered legally settled. This affords peace of mind to the parties involved inasmuch as the event can no longer be the cause for legal action. This too must be balanced against the harm suffered by any party in deciding whether or not to bar legal action and after what length of time.

---

[26] § 7803(c)(2)(A).

[27] § 7811(a).

[28] § 7811(b).

[29] § 7811(c).

[30] § 7811(c)(2)(B).

[31] § 7802.

ASSESSMENTS

General Rule

The general period of limitations for tax assessment is three years from the date the return is filed or the date the return is due, whichever is later.[32] Several exceptions to this rule exist, however.

Example 8

Taxpayer A files a tax return in good form on April 1, 2017 for 2016. The statute of limitations expires April 15, 2020, three years from the later of the date the return is due (April 15, 2017) or the date it was filed.

Example 9

Taxpayer E files an income tax return for 2016 in good form on April 10, 2017. On April 1, 2018, Taxpayer E files a Form 1040X to amend the 2016 tax return. The statute of limitations remains unchanged and expires on April 15, 2020, three years from the later of the date the return is due (April 15, 2017) or the date the return is actually filed.

Fraudulent Return

There is no statute of limitations barring assessment where the taxpayer has filed a false or fraudulent return with intent to evade taxes. Similarly, where the taxpayer makes a willful attempt to defeat or evade taxes other than income, estate, and gift taxes there is no limitation period for assessment.

Example 10

Taxpayer C, a waitress, files a tax return for this year, intentionally omitting $3,000 of cash she received in tips from taxable income. She hopes to evade the tax on the $3,000. No statute of limitations applies.

No Return

Where the taxpayer files no tax return, assessment may be made or a court action begun at any time.[33]

Substantial Omission of Income

If the taxpayer omits gross income from the return in an amount greater than 25% of the gross income shown on the return, the limitations period is extended to six years.[34] The limitations period also is extended to six years where a personal holding company files a return without including a schedule that itemizes income and lists major stockholders.[35]

Prompt Assessments

A request for prompt assessment of tax liability for a decedent, a decedent's estate, or a corporation in dissolution may be requested. If it is granted, the usual three-year period is shortened to 18 months from the time the request for a prompt assessment is made.[36]

---

[32] § 6501(a).

[33] § 6501(c) and Reg. § 301.6501(c)-1.

[34] § 6501(e) and Reg. § 301.6501(e)-1.

[35] § 6501(f) and Reg. § 301.6501(f)-1.

[36] Reg. § 301.6501(d)-1.

Carryback and Carryovers

If the taxpayer wishes to carry back a net operating loss or a capital loss to an earlier year, the assessment period begins with the due date of the return for the year in which the loss occurred, instead of the carryback year.[37] The period for assessment on the years that generate net operating losses and capital losses is not extended by carrying forward such items.[38]

Example 11

Corporation Y, a calendar year taxpayer, has filed an income tax return for 2016 which shows a net operating loss. The corporation carries the net operating loss back to 2014, the second tax year preceding 2016, and then, if there is still an unused loss, to 2015, the first tax year preceding 2016. The statute of limitations ends for these carryback years in three years from the later of the date that the 2016 return is due (March 15, 2017) or the date the 2016 return is actually filed. Assuming the 2016 return is filed on March 3, 2017, the statute of limitations runs out on March 15, 2020 for all three returns.

Amended Returns

Normally, an amended return does not change the length of the limitations period. However, the statute of limitations period is extended by 60 days where an amended return is filed and the normal assessment period would expire in less than 60 days from the date of filing the amended return.

Example 12

Taxpayer F files an income tax return for 2016 in good form on April 10, 2017. On April 1, 2020, Taxpayer F files a Form 1040X to amend the 2016 tax return. The statute of limitations expires 60 days after Taxpayer F files the Form 1040X, since less than 60 days remain in the original limitations period when the amended return is filed.

Suspension of Assessment Period

The running of the limitations period for assessing tax is suspended when a statutory notice of deficiency (i.e., a 90-day letter) is mailed to the taxpayer or after the taxpayer has filed a petition with the Tax Court.[39] When the statutory notice of deficiency is sent to the taxpayer, the statute of limitations stops running for the 90 days of the notice period and for 60 days thereafter. When a case is pending before the Tax Court, the statute of limitations on assessment is suspended from running until the Tax Court's decision becomes final and for 60 days thereafter. This suspension of the limitations period gives the IRS the additional time it might need to make an assessment, since it may not make an assessment during the statutory notice period or while a petition is before the Tax Court.

Example 13

Taxpayer G files an income tax return for 2015 on April 1, 2016. After an audit of this return and appeal to the IRS, a 90-day letter is sent to the taxpayer on March 1, 2019. The statute of limitations expires on July 28, 2019. The limitations period would have expired on April 15, 2019, but the 90-day letter suspends the limitations period for the 90 days following the date of the notice plus an extra 60 days.

---

[37] §§ 6501(h) and (j) and Reg. §§ 301.6501(h)-1 and 301.6501(j)-1.

[38] Reg. § 301.6501(j)-1.

[39] § 6503(a)(1).

Pass-Through Entities

The statute of limitations for an item from a pass-through entity is controlled by the date the shareholder, partner, or other beneficial owner files a return, not by the date that the pass-through entity files its return.[40] Pass-through entities include partnerships, S corporations, trusts, and estates.

Example 14

An S corporation files its 2016 return on March 15, 2017, and a shareholder of that S corporation files her 2016 individual tax return containing pass-through information from the S corporation on April 15, 2017. The statute of limitations period with regard to the pass-through item (and all other items on the return) starts on April 15, 2017, and would normally expire on April 15, 2020.

COLLECTIONS

After an assessment has been made in a proper and timely manner, the IRS must begin proceedings to collect the tax within ten years of the assessment.[41] During this time, the IRS must either levy against the taxpayer's property or initiate court proceedings to recover the tax assessed. The limitations period for tax collection may be extended by written agreement between the taxpayer and the IRS. Such an agreement may allow the taxpayer additional time needed to pay off taxes, and thus prevent a levy against the taxpayer's property. Federal tax refunds may be redirected to the states for specific legally enforceable state tax debts of that state's residents.[42] The state must first notify the taxpayer that it plans to take this action, then allow 60 days for the taxpayer to try to resolve the issue directly with the state. If a state tax debt is still due, the state then notifies the IRS, and any refunds for that person are reduced by the amount owed to the state. Finally, the Collection Appeals Program allows taxpayers to appeal IRS lien, levy, or seizure actions.

REFUND CLAIMS

The taxpayer must file a timely and valid claim in order to receive a refund for an overpayment of tax. Refunds are properly filed by individuals on Form 1040X, Individual Amended Income Tax Return, and by corporations on Form 1120X, Corporate Amended Income Tax Return.[43] Other taxpayers make refunds by filing Form 843. The rules applying to refund claims are stated below.

1. The refund claim must be filed within three years from the date on which the tax return to which it relates was filed, or within two years of the actual payment of the tax.[44]

2. If no tax return is filed, the refund claim must be filed within two years of the date the tax was paid.

3. Where a return is filed and tax is paid, the amount of the refund may not exceed the tax paid within the three-year period.

4. Where a refund is claimed after three years from the date the return is filed (or was due), but within two years of the payment of the tax, the refund amount may not exceed the amount paid during the past two years.

5. Nonfilers who receive a notice of deficiency (90-day letter) and file suit to contest it in the Tax Court during the third year after the return was due (within the normal statute of limitations) may obtain a refund of the amounts paid within the three years prior to the notice of deficiency.[45] This is an exception to the rule that a refund claim must be filed within two years of the actual payment of tax.

---

[40] § 6501(a).

[41] § 6502(a) and Reg. § 301.6502-1(a).

[42] § 6402(e).

[43] Reg. § 301.6402-3.

[44] § 6511(a) and Reg. § 301.6511(a)-1.

[45] § 6512(b)(3).

6. The statute of limitations is suspended for refunds or credits while an individual is *financially disabled*.[46] Financial disability occurs when an individual is unable to manage his or her financial affairs due to a medically determined physical or mental impairment which can be expected to result in death or which has lasted or can be expected to last at least 12 months. This suspension of the statute of limitations does not apply if the financially disabled person's spouse or another person is authorized to act on his/her behalf in financial matters.

It should be noted that estimated income tax payments and income tax withholdings on wages are deemed to be paid on the due date of the return to which they relate.

Example 15

Taxpayer A files an individual income tax return for 2016 on April 15, 2017. All of A's income tax withholding and estimated income tax payments totaling $10,000 are deemed paid April 15, 2017. On April 1, 2020, A files a refund claim for $2,000 of tax by filing Form 1040X, Amended Individual Income Tax Return. A may receive the entire $2,000 since the refund is based on a valid claim filed within three years of the date the return was filed.

Example 16

Taxpayer B files an individual income tax return for 2016 on April 15, 2017. B has paid $9,000 of her $10,000 stated tax liability in withholding and estimated tax payments by April 15, 2017. B pays the remaining $1,000 of tax due on April 15, 2019. On April 1, 2021 B claims a refund of $2,000 by filing Form 1040X, Amended Individual Income Tax Return. B may receive only $1,000, the amount she has paid during the past two years. Since three years have passed since B filed her income tax return for 2016 (on April 15, 2017), B cannot claim a refund under the three-year rule. B may claim a refund only for an amount equal to the tax paid in the past two years under the two-year rule.

Mitigation Provisions

Provisions exist to "mitigate" or reduce the effect of the statute of limitations in cases where a rigid imposition of the rule would work an unfair hardship on the IRS or the taxpayer.[47] According to these rules, where the statute of limitations has expired, adjustments may be made on a return that relates to the expired period for specified reasons. These reasons often involve cases where an item of income, deduction, or credit has been erroneously claimed in a "closed" year and the proper period for the taxpayer to claim this item is in a subsequent "open" year. Other applicable situations occur when the taxpayer has claimed an item of income, deduction, or credit that rightfully belongs to a related taxpayer.[48] In these instances, the statute of limitations is not observed so that the taxpayer is not allowed a double benefit from claiming a specific item of deduction or credit in a closed year and then again in an open year. Conversely, a taxpayer is spared the double burden of having to include an income item in both a closed year and again in an open year. In a situation where a taxpayer improperly claims an item of income, deduction, or credit that belongs to a related taxpayer, the statute of limitations is ignored so that the item may be reallocated. The purpose of the mitigations rule is to prevent the IRS or the taxpayer from maintaining *inconsistent* positions from which either would inequitably benefit, where such inconsistent positions could otherwise not be challenged due to the expiration of the limitations period.

---

[46] § 6511(h).

[47] §§ 1311 through 1314 and Reg. §§ 1.1311(a)-1 through 1.1311(c)-1.

[48] *Ibid.*

Example 17

Taxpayer H files an income tax return for 2016 that claims a deduction for the cost of repairing a building used for business. In 2017, H decides that it is more appropriate to treat the cost of the building repair as a capital expenditure and depreciate it. A depreciation deduction is taken for a portion of the cost of the repair in 2017 and subsequent years. In 2021, although the statute of limitations has expired on the 2017 return, the IRS may adjust that return and disallow the deduction for the entire cost of the repair. This prevents a double benefit for the taxpayer who has deducted the entire cost once, and now seeks to depreciate the cost over the life of the asset.

Example 18

Taxpayer J incorrectly includes in his own income the $3,500 that his minor son has earned on his summer job during 2016. The IRS audits the son in 2021 and determines that he should have filed a return reporting the $3,500 for the year 2016. The son files the 2016 return late and pays tax on the $3,500 income, plus penalty and interest. Taxpayer J may claim a refund for the tax paid (plus interest) on the $3,500 erroneously reported for 2016 even though the statute of limitations otherwise treats this year as closed. This allows the allocation of the $3,500 income away from the father to the son despite the expiration of the limitations period.

Penalties

LO.5

Determine when delinquency, accuracy-related, fraud, and information reporting penalties apply to taxpayers, and be able to compute them.

To encourage taxpayers to comply with the Federal tax laws, Congress has enacted numerous penalties. These penalties cover a variety of violations, such as failure to file and pay taxes on a timely basis, negligence in preparing the tax return, and outright fraud. The penalties are usually monetary in nature. However, where the taxpayer goes beyond these civil offenses and purposefully attempts to evade tax, criminal penalties—including jail sentences—may result. No penalty may be assessed unless the taxpayer is provided with information on the name of the penalty, the Code section of the penalty, and a computation of the penalty.[49]

Penalties are referred to by the Internal Revenue Code as "additions to the tax," "additional amounts," and "assessable penalties."[50] All such amounts are treated as additional "tax," to be assessed, collected, and paid in the same manner as regular taxes.[51] Thus, assessment procedures, restrictions on assessment, and the statute of limitations for assessment and collection apply to penalties. Some penalties are computed in the same manner as interest; nevertheless, such penalties are nondeductible since they are considered additional Federal taxes.

Civil tax penalties are categorized into four major groups:

1. Delinquency penalties
2. Accuracy-related and fraud penalties
3. Information reporting penalties
4. Protestor, promoter, and preparer penalties

Each of these penalties is discussed below.

---

[49] § 6751.

[50] See §§ 6651 through 6665, §§ 6671 through 6724.

[51] § 6665.

DELINQUENCY PENALTIES

For whatever reason, taxpayers may be inclined to postpone the inevitable; that is, the filing of a tax return and the payment of taxes. For those taxpayers who are delinquent in such duties, two penalties exist—the failure-to-file penalty and the failure-to-pay penalty. Both penalties play an integral part in the efficient operation of the Federal tax system.

Failure to File

A penalty is imposed on a taxpayer for failure to file a tax return by the due date.[52] The penalty is 5% of the net tax due for each month or part thereof that the return is late. The net tax due is the amount of tax shown on the return less any amount that is paid by the later of (1) the due date of the return, or (2) the month the penalty is assessed. The total penalty for failure to file may not exceed 25% of the net tax due.

The failure-to-file penalty does not apply in several instances. It does not apply where the taxpayer has obtained a proper extension (i.e., a timely filed extension request accompanied by 100% of the estimated tax due), and the return is filed within the extended period. Note, however, that individuals who obtain an extension and properly file their return within the extended period may still be subject to the failure-to-pay penalty discussed below. The failure-to-file penalty also is waived where the failure to file is attributable to reasonable cause (discussed below).

To encourage taxpayers who owe small amounts of tax to file a tax return, a minimum failure-to-file penalty is imposed. The minimum penalty is the lesser of (1) $135, or (2) 100% of the amount of the net tax due. The minimum penalty applies when the return is filed more than 60 days late (e.g., filed after June 14 for the calendar year taxpayer). This penalty is also waived if the failure to file is attributable to reasonable cause.

Example 19

S, a calendar year taxpayer, computed his tax for 2016 and determined that he would receive a refund of $150. He did not file his return claiming his refund until August 3, 2017. No penalty is assessed since the penalty is based on the net amount due, which was zero. Had S owed $150, the normal failure-to-file penalty would have been only $30 (5% × 4 months × $150). However, the minimum penalty of $135 would apply if S had owed $150 since the return was filed more than 60 days late (the lesser of $150 tax due or $135).

Example 20

R, a calendar year taxpayer, determined that her tax liability before prepayments for 2016 was $10,000. Estimated tax payments and withholding during the year totaled $7,000. When April 15, 2017 arrived, R had no money to pay the $3,000 in tax due so she postponed filing until August 3, 2017. The failure-to-file penalty is $600 ($3,000 × 5% × 4 months).

Failure to Pay

When a taxpayer fails to pay the tax owed at the time it is due, a penalty is imposed. The penalty normally is one-half of one percent of the net tax due for each month that the tax is unpaid. In certain situations, however, the rate of penalty is increased to one percent per month. The increased penalty applies if the IRS notifies the taxpayer of its intent to levy on the taxpayer's assets (usually the *fourth* notice sent to the taxpayer requesting payment) or gives notice and demand for payment because the collection of the tax is in jeopardy.

---

[52] § 6651(a) and Reg. § 301.6651-1(a).

The total penalty for failure to pay the tax when due may not exceed 25% of the net tax due. For example, a taxpayer that owes $1,000 on a 2016 tax return that remains unpaid until the year 2028 pays a failure to pay penalty of a maximum of $250. Note that in light of the penalty rate, 0.5% per month, 50 months—or more than four years—must pass before the maximum penalty applies. However, other penalties may also be imposed on the taxpayer when there is such a long delinquency, and in addition, interest on the amount owed is charged.

In the case of an individual, the failure-to-pay penalty does not apply if the taxpayer obtains an automatic extension and pays 90% of the total tax liability due (before any prepayments or withholding) by the original filing date. In such case, the taxpayer simply remits the balance due with the tax return. If the taxpayer fails to pay 90% of the tax by the original due date, the failure-to-pay penalty is imposed and applies on the net tax due. If the taxpayer does pay 90% of the tax by the original due date but fails to pay the balance by the extended due date, the failure-to-pay penalty applies on the net tax due.

When taxpayers fail to file a return, it is not uncommon to find that they also have not paid the tax they owe. In such case, the taxpayer is subject to both the failure-to-file and failure-to-pay penalties. However, to mitigate the harsh effect of this double penalty, the failure-to-file penalty is reduced by the failure-to-pay penalty for any month both penalties apply.[53]

Example 21

Same facts as in *Example 20* above. The failure-to-file and failure-to-pay penalties would be computed as follows:

Failure to pay (0.005 × 4 × $3,000)		$ 60
Gross failure to file (0.05 × 4 × $3,000)	$600	
Reduction for failure to pay penalty	– 60	
Failure to file		+540
Total failure to file and pay penalties		$600

In effect, a taxpayer who fails to file and pay the balance of the tax owed must pay a penalty of 5% a month (4.5% failure-to-file penalty plus 0.5% failure-to-pay penalty). If the taxpayer files a timely return *and* has an installment payment agreement in effect with the IRS, the failure to pay penalty is reduced from 0.5% per month to 0.25% per month.[54] As previously stated, each penalty independently may not exceed a maximum of 25 percent. It also should be noted that in addition to failure-to-file and failure-to-pay penalties, the taxpayer must pay interest on the amount of unpaid taxes starting on the due date of the return. In such case, the taxpayer, in all likelihood, also would be subject to the penalty for failure to pay estimated taxes—in essence, interest starting prior to the due date of the return.[55] Interest and the penalty for underpayment of taxes are discussed below. It should be noted, however, that none of these penalties are imposed if the civil fraud penalty is assessed.

Reasonable Cause

When a taxpayer shows that failure to file a tax return or to pay a tax is due to reasonable cause, no penalty is assessed. The concept of reasonable cause—as it applies to delinquency penalties—is not clearly defined by the Internal Revenue Code or the Regulations. The standard enunciated is that of "ordinary business care and prudence."[56] This obviously allows the IRS and the courts wide latitude in applying these penalties. The taxpayer carries the burden of proving reasonable cause to the IRS by showing that despite the exercise of ordinary business care and prudence, the return could not be filed or the tax paid when due.[57]

---

[53] § 6651(c)(1).

[54] § 6651(h).

[55] § 6651(d).

[56] § 6651(a) and Reg. § 301.6651-1(c).

[57] *Ibid.*

Reasonable cause includes death or serious illness of the taxpayer,[58] natural disasters or other casualties that destroy the taxpayer's records or assets, unavoidable absence of the taxpayer, and reliance on the advice of an attorney.[59] Reasonable cause does not include reliance on the advice of an accountant,[60] ignorance[61] or forgetfulness[62] of the taxpayer, or nonincapacitating illness.[63] In determining whether there is reasonable cause to abate a penalty, all the facts and circumstances for each case are considered. In addition, the IRS *must* abate any penalties or additions to tax that are a result of the taxpayer's reliance on IRS written advice, when the advice was in response to a specific written request of the taxpayer and the taxpayer provided the IRS with adequate and accurate information.[64]

FAILURE TO PAY ESTIMATED INCOME TAX

Under the "pay-as-you-go" system for collection of taxes, taxpayers are effectively required to estimate their tax for the taxable year and pay the estimated amount in installments during the year. For individuals, these payments normally are made either through the withholding system for salaries and wages or by direct payments of estimated taxes by the taxpayer. For corporate taxpayers, only the latter option is available. A penalty is imposed on any one who fails to make adequate payments of the estimated taxes. Penalties for individuals, corporations, trusts, and estates are examined below.

Individuals

The *required installment* of tax due from an individual must be paid on April 15, June 15, September 15, and January 15 of the following year. The required installment is 25% of the *required annual payment*, which is the lesser of the following:

1. 90% of the tax shown on the return before any prepayments.

2. 100% of the tax shown on the return of the individual for the preceding taxable year (110% for taxpayers whose AGI for the preceding year exceeded $150,000; $75,000 if married filing separately).[65]

3. The *annualized income installment*.[66]

For purposes of these rules, the tax on the return includes the alternative minimum tax as well as any self-employment taxes that may be due.

The effect of these rules is to allow a taxpayer to avoid penalty if quarterly installments are made of 22.5% of the current year's tax. If the 100% "safe harbor" is available to the taxpayer, the quarterly installments can be computed as 25% of last year's tax. The latter provision permits the taxpayer to base the installment on the prior year's tax even if the tax in the prior year was zero. However, it should be noted that the required installment cannot be based on the prior year's tax if the preceding year was not a taxable year of 12 months or the individual did not file a return for such year. The annualized income installment is discussed below.

If the taxpayer fails to pay the required installment—in effect 25% of the lowest of 90% of the current year's tax, 100% of the prior year's tax (110% if the prior year's AGI exceeded $150,000), or the annualized income installment—a penalty is imposed on the *amount of the underpayment*. The underpayment for any required installment is computed as follows:

> Required installment
> − Installment paid to that due date including withholding
> = Amount of the underpayment

---

[58] *Gladys Forbes Est.*, 12 TCM 176 (1953), and *Ward v. Comm.*, 58-2 USTC ¶9922 (D.Ct. Tenn., 1958).

[59] *Tennyson, Jr. v. Comm.*, 76-1 USTC ¶ 9264 (D.Ct. Ark., 1976).

[60] *Inter-American Life Ins. Co.*, 56 T.C. 497, aff'd (CA-9, 1973) 73-1 USTC ¶9127, 31 AFTR2d 73-412, 469 F.2d 697 (CA-9, 1973).

[61] *Stonegate of Blacksburg, Inc.*, 33 TCM 956, T.C. Memo 1974-213.

[62] *Christie Coal and Coke Co., Inc.*, 28 TCM 498, T.C. Memo 1978-404.

[63] *H.W. Pinkham*, 17 TCM 1071, T.C. Memo 1958-216.

[64] § 6404(f).

[65] § 6654(d)(1)(C).

[66] § 6654.

The penalty assessed on the underpayment is computed in the same manner as interest, but because it is a penalty the amount paid is not deductible. The penalty is computed as follows:

$$
\begin{array}{rl}
 & \text{Amount of underpayment for period} \\
\times & \text{Annual interest rate} \\
\times & \text{Period outstanding} \\
\hline
= & \text{Penalty on underpayment for period}
\end{array}
$$

The annual interest rate to be applied is the "average predominant prime rate quoted by commercial banks to large business" as determined by the members of the Federal Reserve System. The rate for January 1 through June 30 is the average rate charged for the six-month period running from April 1 through September 30 of the prior year.[67] Similarly, the rate from July 1 through December 31 is the average rate charged for the six-month period running from September 30 of the prior year to March 31 of the current year. The period of time for computing interest begins on the due date of the installment and runs to the earlier of the date the payment is made or the due date of the return (e.g., April 15). For this purpose, withholding is deemed to occur ratably throughout the year regardless of when it was actually made. Payments not made by the due date of the return become subject to the failure-to-pay penalty.

Example 22

During 2016, P, a single taxpayer, paid $750 of estimated tax each installment due date. His employer withheld $1,000 during the year. His tax return, filed April 15, 2017, showed a total tax before prepayments of $15,000. P's tax liability for 2015 was $8,000. P's AGI was $80,000 for 2016 and was $55,000 for 2015. Since his 2015 AGI was less than $150,000, P may take advantage of the 100% safe harbor. The required installment is $2,000 (the *lesser of* $2,000 [$8,000 × 100% × 25%] or $3,375 [$15,000 × 90% × 25%]). The underpayments and the penalty, assuming a 6% interest rate, are computed as follows:

	4/15/16	6/15/16	9/15/16	1/15/17	Total
Installment required:					
(25% × $8,000)	$ 2,000	$ 2,000	$ 2,000	$ 2,000	$8,000
Less: Amounts paid:					
Estimated tax payments . .	− 750	− 750	− 750	− 750	−3,000
Withholding (ratably)	− 250	− 250	− 250	− 250	−1,000
Underpayment amount	$ 1,000	$ 1,000	$ 1,000	$ 1,000	$4,000
Days outstanding ÷ 365	× 365/365	× 304/365	× 212/365	× 90/365	
Interest rate.	× 6%	× 6%	× 6%	× 6%	
Nondeductible penalty.	$ 60	$ 50	$ 35	$ 15	$ 160

Example 23

Same facts as *Example 22* above except P's 2015 AGI was $25,000 and his 2015 tax liability was $2,800. Since P's installment for each period exceeds $700 (25% of last year's tax of $2,800) no penalty is assessed. P may use the 100% safe harbor since his 2015 AGI was less than $150,000.

---

[67] § 6621.

Example 24

Same facts as *Example 22* above except P's 2015 AGI was $170,000. Since P's prior year AGI exceeds $150,000, the "safe harbor" based on the prior year's tax is $8,800 (110% of the $8,000 2015 tax). His required installment for each period would have to be $2,200 (25% of $8,800) in order to avoid the penalty for underestimated tax. Since P's payments were $1,000 per period ($750 estimated tax payment + $250 ratable withholding), he has *not* met the safe harbor based upon the prior year's taxes and has underpaid by $1,200 per period. The penalty will be based on the $1,200 underpayment amount for each of the four periods.

The annualized income installment is determined in two steps. First, the taxpayer must compute the total tax that would be due if income actually received through the month ending before the due date of the installment were annualized. The required installment is 22.5, 45, 67.5, and 90 percent of the annualized tax for each installment respectively.

Example 25

Assume the same as in *Example 22* above except that P's income and itemized deductions *through March* consisted of wages of $11,000, self-employment income from commissions of $1,000, and $1,916.50 of itemized deductions. P's annualized tax for the first period is computed as follows:

	Wages	$11,000
+	Self-employment income	+ 1,000
−	Self-employment tax deduction: ($1,000 × 92.35% = $923.50 × 15.3% = $141 ÷ 2)	− 71
=	Actual adjusted gross income (for one quarter of the year)	$11,929
	Annualized adjusted gross income ($11,929 × 4)	$47,716
−	Annualized itemized deductions ($1,916.50 × 4)	− 7,666
−	Exemption	− 3,650
=	Annualized taxable income	$36,400
	Tax on annualized income	$ 5,288
+	Self-employment tax ($1,000 × 92.35% = $923.50 × 15.3% = $141.29 × 4 quarters)	+ 565
	Total tax	$ 5,853

P's annualized income installment for the first period is $1,317 ($5,853 × 22.5%). Since this amount is less than the required installment based on last year's tax ($2,000 per installment from *Example 22*), P can avoid the penalty for underpayment of estimated tax by paying $1,317 per quarter.

No underpayment penalty is imposed for an individual where the balance of tax after reduction for withholding is $1,000 or less. In addition, the IRS may waive the underpayment penalty in the event of a casualty or unusual circumstances where it might be inequitable to impose the additional tax. The IRS also may waive the penalty for retired taxpayers who are age 62 or disabled where the underpayment was due to reasonable cause rather than willful neglect.

Corporations

A corporate taxpayer generally avoids penalty for failure to pay estimated taxes if 100% of the tax is paid during the year. Specifically, the corporate taxpayer must pay ¼ of this amount—25% of the tax shown on the return—on the fifteenth day of the fourth, sixth, ninth, and twelfth months of the taxable year (April 15, June 15, September 15, and December 15 assuming a calendar year taxpayer).[68] In addition, the penalty is not imposed where the *installment* for any period is:

1. At least 25% of the tax shown on the prior year's return (small corporations *only*); or
2. Equal to or exceeds 100% of the tax due for each quarter based on annualized taxable income.

No penalty is imposed on a corporate taxpayer if its tax for any year is less than $500. In addition, the exception related to the prior year (1 above) is available to so-called *large corporations* (i.e., a corporation having taxable income exceeding $1 million in any of the three preceding taxable years) for the first quarter only.

Trusts and Estates

Like individuals and corporations, trusts and estates are required to pay estimated taxes. An estate, however, need not make estimated tax payments for the first two years of its existence. The penalties for trusts and estates are computed in the same manner as individuals.

ACCURACY-RELATED PENALTIES

The 20% accuracy-related penalty applies to the portion of the tax underpayment that is attributable to negligence or disregard of the rules or regulations, substantial understatement of income tax, substantial valuation misstatement for income tax purposes, substantial overstatement of pension liabilities, or substantial estate or gift valuation understatement.[69] Only one accuracy-related penalty may be imposed on any specific underpayment of tax. The accuracy-related penalty may be imposed in conjunction with the delinquency penalties when the situation so warrants. However, it may not be imposed when a fraud penalty is assessed.[70]

Interest on the accuracy-related penalty runs from the due date of the return (including extensions) until the date the penalty is paid.[71] The accuracy-related penalty as it applies to negligence and to the substantial understatement of income tax is discussed here, as well as a new penalty for refund or credit claims for excessive amounts.

Negligence

The accuracy-related penalty may be imposed for underpayment of taxes due to negligence or disregard of the rules and regulations.[72] The penalty is 20% of the portion of the underpayment that is attributable to negligence or disregard of the rules or regulations. "Negligence" includes any failure to make a reasonable attempt to comply with the tax laws, and "disregard" includes any careless, reckless, or intentional disregard.[73]

Example 26

J filed her 2015 return on April 16, 2016. On August 16, 2019, the IRS assessed an additional $10,000 of tax attributable to her failure to report income. The accuracy-related penalty attributable to negligence is $2,000 ($10,000 × 20%). Also, interest is due on both the additional tax and the penalty.

Negligence is often found where the taxpayer fails to report income (e.g., cash receipts), or claims substantial amounts of deductions that are not substantiated (e.g., travel and entertainment) or that are not authorized by the Code. A taxpayer is automatically considered negligent for failure to report *any* type of income for which there was an information return

---

[68] § 6655.

[69] § 6662.

[70] § 6662(b).

[71] § 6601(e)(2)(B).

[72] § 6662(b)(1).

[73] § 6662(c) and Reg. § 1.6662-3(b).

(e.g., Form 1099) filed by the payer. In this case, only the portion of the underpayment of the tax related to the information return is used in computing the negligence penalty.[74]

Negligence also has been found where the taxpayer was lax in keeping books and records,[75] where the taxpayer signed erroneous returns prepared by an accountant without checking them,[76] where the taxpayer lost or failed to keep records,[77] and where the taxpayer filed incomplete tax returns.[78] Where the taxpayer had an honest misunderstanding of the facts or the law similar to what an ordinary reasonable person might have, the negligence penalty was not applied.[79] The penalty also was avoided where the taxpayer relied on an accountant's advice regarding an item of a controversial nature.[80]

Substantial Understatement of Income Tax

The accuracy-related penalty may be imposed for underpayment of taxes due to any substantial understatement of income tax.[81] This portion of the accuracy-related penalty is designed to deter taxpayers from taking unreasonable or insupportable positions on their tax returns with the hope that they will never be audited. The penalty is 20% of the portion of the underpayment that is attributable to the substantial understatement of income tax. The tax liability is considered to be substantially understated when the amount of the understatement is more than the greater of (1) 10% of the correct tax, or (2) $5,000.[82] The penalty may be totally or partially waived by the IRS when the taxpayer has substantial authority for the position taken on the return or the item is disclosed on the return *and* the taxpayer has a reasonable basis for the tax treatment of the item.[83]

Reasonable Cause

The accuracy-related penalty may be waived either totally or partially if the taxpayer can show that he or she had reasonable cause and acted in good faith with respect to the position taken on the return.[84] There has been some controversy as to whether reliance on a tax advisor qualifies as "reasonable cause." Regulations state that reasonable cause and good faith are to be determined on a case-by-case basis.[85] The regulations also state that:

> Reliance on an information return or on the advice of a professional tax advisor or an appraiser does not necessarily demonstrate reasonable cause and good faith. Similarly, reasonable cause and good faith are not necessarily indicated by reliance on facts that, unknown to the taxpayer, are incorrect.[86]

In determining whether reasonable cause and good faith exist in relying on tax advice, all facts and circumstances must be considered.[87] For example, the advice must take into account the taxpayer's purpose in entering a transaction or structuring it in a particular way. Failure of the taxpayer to disclose any relevant facts (that the taxpayer knows, or should have known) to the advisor is considered a lack of reasonable cause and good faith. In addition, the advice must not be based on any assumption that the taxpayer knows, or has reason to know, is unlikely to be true.[88]

Erroneous Refund or Credit Claims

The Small Business and Work Opportunity Tax Act of 2007 added a new penalty for refund or credit claims for an "excessive amount." The penalty is 20% of the "excessive amount," which is defined as the amount by which the claim exceeds the amount allowable under the law. This penalty may be waived if there is a reasonable basis for the excessive amount, and does not apply to claims of the earned income credit.[89]

---

[74] §§ 6662(a) and (b).

[75] *H.S. Glazer*, 40 TCM 1065, T.C. Memo 1980-337, and *H.G. Sealy*, 39 TCM 827, T.C. Memo 1980-7.

[76] *Mackay*, 11 B.T.A. 569 (1928), Acq.

[77] *Estella Collins*, 9 TCM 14 (1950), and *W.R. McKinley*, 37 TCM 1769, T.C. Memo 1978-428.

[78] *G.C. Lamb*, 32 TCM 305, T.C. Memo 1973-71.

[79] *C.B. Baker*, 40 TCM 983, T.C. Memo 1980-319; and *E.G. Harris*, 36 TCM 1426, T.C. Memo 1977-358.

[80] *R. Wolman*, 34 TCM 1143, T.C. Memo 1975-266.

[81] § 6662(b)(2).

[82] § 6662(d)(1)(A).

[83] § 6662(d)(2)(B)(ii), Reg. § 1.6662-4(d), and Rev. Proc. 96-58, 1996-2 C.B. 390.

[84] § 6664(c)(1) and Reg. § 1.6664-4.

[85] Reg. § 1.6664-4(b)(1).

[86] *Ibid.*

[87] Reg. § 1.6664-4(c)(1)(i).

[88] Reg. § 1.6664-4(c)(1)(ii).

[89] § 6676(a).

Economic Substance Doctrine

It is not surprising that some taxpayers—both individuals and businesses—go to great lengths, often concocting intricate transactions, to avoid paying taxes. Some schemes are the ingenious creation of a company's legal or accounting department, sometimes with the aid of tax professionals at big name accounting or law firms. Some are the outrageous products of charlatan promoters. Others fall somewhere in between. Interestingly, many of these plans actually adhere to the letter of the law, meeting all of the statutory and administrative requirements. Nevertheless, courts often deny taxpayers the tax benefits of these otherwise "legal" transactions" if they lack so-called *economic substance*. A transaction is said to lack economic substance if it did not result in a meaningful change to the taxpayer's economic position other than reducing federal income taxes. In short, if the transaction was solely for tax purposes, it will be disregarded. This principle is referred to as the "economic substance doctrine."

The economic substance doctrine is just one of several judicial theories that have been used to attack tax avoidance schemes. Another theory is the "business purpose doctrine." This principle says that the transaction must be motivated by business considerations and reducing taxes is not a business purpose. In other situations, where the alleged activity never took place or what took place was merely a facade, the court often asserts that the events were a "sham transaction" and disregards the outcome. Similarly, the court may disallow the tax benefits by invoking the "substance over form" principle. This well-known doctrine stands for the proposition that the tax results of an arrangement should be based on the underlying substance rather than a simple evaluation of the formal steps by which the arrangement was undertaken. Yet another weapon in the court's arsenal is the "step transaction" doctrine. This doctrine treats what are purportedly separate steps as a single transaction if the steps are integrated, interdependent, and focused toward a particular result. The purpose of each of these doctrines is to test the transactions and sort out those that are primarily or solely motivated by tax savings from those that have a substantial business purpose or economic motive.

In 2010, Congress created § 7701(o)(1) that effectively enacts into law the economic substance doctrine and its variations. Section 7701 imposes a significant penalty for transactions that fail its tests.

Under § 7701(o), a transaction has economic substance only if it (1) changes in a meaningful way (apart from federal taxes) the taxpayer's economic position and (2) the taxpayer has a substantial purpose for entering the transaction (other than federal income taxes purposes). This is a two prong test where the taxpayer must meet both tests for the transaction to be honored. The law does allow an exception for personal transactions of individuals. Individuals will be subject to the economic substance doctrine only for transactions entered in connection with a trade or business or an activity entered into for the production of income.

For transactions not meeting the two-part test, there is a penalty based on the underpayment of taxes resulting from the transaction. If the transaction is disclosed, the penalty is 20% of the underpayment. For undisclosed transactions, the penalty is doubled to 40 percent.

The impact of § 7701(o) is yet to be determined. Most commentators believe that many tax professionals will now lose a great deal of sleep wondering whether even the most common transactions have economic substance. Indeed, the provision is quite broad, and many legitimate business transactions, if tested for economic substance, could fail the statutory tests. Because of the uncertainty and because of the strict liability penalty, it does seem that taxpayers will face increased tax risk with respect to some transactions and, in some cases, will be deterred from engaging in transactions that otherwise would have been undertaken.

Uncertain Tax Positions: Financial Accounting Reporting

Part of the difficulty encountered in tax practice is uncertainty. For many transactions, the tax treatment may not be clear. In such case, companies, as might be expected, usually take positions that reduce their tax liability. For example, a company may exclude income that it may believe is tax-exempt or take a tax credit that it believes is appropriate. Similarly, a company may not file a tax return in a particular state because it believes it is not required. These positions normally have a sound legal basis and are taken in good faith. However, given the complexities and varying interpretations of the tax law, these positions may not ultimately prevail. Consequently, uncertainty exists regarding the actual benefit a company will derive from a position taken on its tax return. This has an impact not only on a company's tax return but also its financial statements.

Over time, the Financial Accounting Standards Board (FASB) became concerned about the accounting for uncertainty in income taxes and how it was reported for financial accounting purposes. In June 2006, the FASB issued FASB Interpretation (FIN) No. 48, *Accounting for Uncertainty in Income Taxes* (now contained in Accounting Standards Codification Topic 740). FIN 48 or ASC 740 was created primarily as a mechanism to provide greater transparency for uncertain tax positions and greater uniformity in the financial reporting of tax issues.

FIN 48 requires companies to identify their uncertain tax positions and determine the likelihood that they will or will not survive audit, appeals and litigation. Once that is determined, FIN 48 forces companies to disclose and create a reserve for uncertain tax positions that are more likely than not to occur. Basically, FIN 48 contains a two step-process that must be applied to all tax positions: recognition and measurement. First, a tax position is recognized for financial accounting purposes only if it is "more likely than not" (i.e., greater than 50%) that the position will be sustained upon examination by a taxing authority. Second, if the tax position is recognized, the effect is measured. Using probability techniques, measurement determines what amount of a tax position will be sustainable upon a potential examination or settlement. Finally, FIN 48 requires certain disclosures to be footnoted in the financial statements. In short, it has completely changed the way companies account for uncertainty with respect to tax positions.

Uncertain Tax Positions: Tax Reporting

It was not long after the issuance of FIN 48 that the government decided it deserved similar treatment. In 2010, the IRS created Schedule UTP that requires companies to report *on their tax returns* their uncertain tax positions. The schedule is appropriately titled Schedule UTP. Generally, a corporation that is required to file a corporate income tax return, Form 1120 (and certain others) must attach Schedule UTP if it meets the following requirements:

1. The corporation has assets that equal or exceed $10 million.
2. The corporation or a related party issued *audited* financial statements.
3. The corporation has one or more tax positions that must be reported on Schedule UTP.

Schedule UTP requires the reporting of an income tax position taken by the corporation on its tax return if it recorded a reserve for that tax position in audited financial statements or did not record a reserve because the corporation expects to litigate the position.

FRAUD PENALTIES

Civil Fraud Penalty

A penalty equal to 75% of the amount of underpayment attributable to fraud is imposed when the taxpayer is found to have been fraudulent. However, if the IRS establishes that any portion of an underpayment is attributable to fraud, then the penalty applies to the *entire* underpayment, except for any portion that the taxpayer establishes is *not* attributable to fraud.[90]

As mentioned above, when the fraud penalty is assessed, no accuracy-related penalty is assessed on the same portion of the underpayment.[91] However, if the failure to file a return is shown to be fraudulent, then the failure-to-file penalty is tripled.[92] The same reasonable cause exception that applies to the accuracy-related penalty applies to the civil fraud penalty.[93]

The IRS carries the burden to prove fraud against a taxpayer by a preponderance of the evidence.[94] Civil fraud has not been clearly defined, but requires more than negligent acts or omissions by the taxpayer. In determining the presence of fraud, all facts and circumstances of the case are considered. Fraud has been found where the taxpayer made misleading statements during the course of an examination,[95] where the taxpayer changed a book entry

---

[90] § 6663.

[91] § 6662(b).

[92] § 6651(f).

[93] § 6664(c)(1).

[94] See § 7454(a). Fraud is not presumed, and a finding of fraud by the IRS does not create a presumption that the taxpayer committed fraud. The IRS must prove taxpayer fraud in all cases where it is alleged. See *A. Windsberg*, 37 TCM 455, T.C. Memo 1978-1.

[95] *Herrald, Inc.*, 35 TCM 1129, T.C. Memo 1976-258.

to understate income,[96] where the taxpayer treated personal expenses as business expenses,[97] and where the taxpayer concealed income by having other persons report the income.[98] Fraud was not found where the taxpayer failed to report a large amount of gross income because of an error and where no intent to commit fraud existed[99] where the taxpayer with little business knowledge signed false returns prepared by his partner,[100] and where the taxpayer claimed a deduction that he or she honestly but erroneously believed to be permitted.[101] Before assessing the fraud penalty, the courts must find an "intent to defraud." This intent may be evidenced by an actual desire by the taxpayer to commit fraud or by the taxpayer's reckless disregard of the facts and circumstances.

Criminal Fraud Penalties

The law imposes not only civil penalties for fraud, but also criminal penalties.[102] A civil fraud offense must be proven by a preponderance of the evidence, and the penalty is based on the amount of tax or interest owed. In contrast, a criminal penalty must be proven beyond a reasonable doubt, and the penalty is measured by the severity of the fraud as opposed to the amount of tax underpaid. The penalties imposed for criminal fraud are the most severe imposed by the Code.

A criminal offense of fraud requires that the taxpayer *willfully* attempt to evade or defeat the tax.[103] A taxpayer may be convicted of a misdemeanor or a felony and may be subject to fines or imprisonment or both, depending on the degree of fraud. The most common offenses and highest penalties appear in Exhibit 19-5. The opinion of the IRS weighs heavily in the decision of whether to prosecute a taxpayer for criminal fraud, and if so, how much penalty to seek. The decision to prosecute is ultimately made by the Department of Justice.

A criminal penalty may be imposed for *willful* failure to pay an estimated tax, as shown in Exhibit 19-5.[104] As with other criminal offenses, the penalty is not based on the amount of tax owed, but on the severity of the offense.

EXHIBIT 19-5	Criminal Offenses and Penalties	
Offense	*Maximum Penalty*	*Source*
1. Willful attempt to evade or defeat any tax.	$100,000 fine[a] or five years imprisonment or both.	§ 7201
2. Willful failure to collect or truthfully account for and pay over any tax.	$10,000 fine or five years imprisonment or both.	§ 7202
3. Willful failure to pay a tax or an estimated tax, to make a required return, to keep required records or to supply required information.	$25,000 fine[b] or one year imprisonment or both.	§ 7203
4. Willfully furnishing an employee with a false statement regarding tax withholdings on wages.	$1,000 fine or one year imprisonment or both.	§ 7204
5. Making a declaration under penalty of perjury not believed by the maker to be true, preparing or assisting in preparation of fraudulent returns or other documents, or concealing goods or property in respect of any tax.	$100,000 fine[a] or three years imprisonment or both.	§ 7206

[a] In the case of a corporate taxpayer, no imprisonment and a $500,000 fine.
[b] In the case of a corporate taxpayer, no imprisonment and a $100,000 fine.

---

[96] *K. Haddad*, 19 TCM 599, T.C. Memo 1960-112.

[97] *Hicks Co., Inc.* 73-1 USTC ¶9109, 31 AFTR2d 73-382, 470 F.2d 87 (CA-1, 1973).

[98] *A.S. Hershenson*, 21 TCM 1204, T.C. Memo 1962-228.

[99] *U.S. v. Bank of Powers*, 39-2 USTC ¶9665, 26 AFTR 1115 (D.Ct. Ore., 1939), appeal dismissed, 23 AFTR 839, 106 F.2d 1019 (1939).

[100] *F.A. Herman*, 18 TCM 569, T.C. Memo 1959-129.

[101] *M. Bailey*, 29 TCM 272, T.C. Memo 1970-64, aff'd per curiam, 71-1 USTC ¶9359, 27 AFTR2d 71-1210, 439 F.2d 723 (CA-6, 1971), cert. den., 404 U.S. 867.

[102] § 7201, et. seq.

[103] *Ibid.*

[104] § 7203.

INFORMATION REPORTING PENALTIES

To ensure taxpayers are reporting all of the income they receive, Congress requires those who make certain payments to taxpayers to file information returns such as the well-known Forms W-2 and 1099. This information is then matched against what taxpayers actually show on their returns to determine if all income has been properly reported. Consistent with its goal to match all taxpayer returns and information returns, Congress imposes a penalty for failure to file information returns as well as a penalty for failure to provide copies of such returns to the persons to whom they relate. For many years, the penalty for failure to file information returns was quite modest, $1 per return up to $1,000, and did little to encourage taxpayers to comply. In fact, in 1979, it was estimated that fewer than 60% of the required information returns for nonemployee compensation were filed. Over the past several years, this penalty has increased significantly. The penalty is currently $50 for each failure to file correct information returns ($250,000 annual maximum),[105] $50 for each failure to furnish a correct information return to a taxpayer ($100,000 annual maximum),[106] and $50 for each failure to comply with any other information reporting requirements ($100,000 annual maximum).[107] Each of these penalties also requires that the information returns be filed with the IRS or furnished to the taxpayer on or before the required date. If the failure to file or failure to furnish a correct information return is due to the taxpayer's intentional disregard, then the penalty is $100 per failure (with no maximum penalty).[108] Information returns include such forms as those for interest (Form 1099-INT), dividends (Form 1099-DIV), wage payments (Form W-2), withholding of tax on interest and dividends, compensation for services and direct sales, rental and other business payments in excess of $600, and other items peculiar to specialized industries.[109] Criminal penalties also apply for the *willful* failure to file informational returns or the *willful* making of falsified statements regarding wage withholdings, as described in Exhibit 19-5.[110]

A penalty of $50 per partner is imposed for every month that a partnership return is not filed.[111] This penalty is assessed against the partnership itself, but the individual partners are ultimately liable for the penalty to the extent they are responsible for partnership debts.

A heavier penalty applies to taxpayers for making statements that result in reduced withholdings on wages when no reasonable basis for such statement exists.[112] The penalty imposed is $500 for each statement in civil cases. Where such a statement is *willfully* made, a criminal penalty of $1,000 (or one year imprisonment, or both) per occurrence also may be imposed.[113] The goal of this penalty is to encourage taxpayer compliance with the wage withholding system. The penalty is applied to an understatement by the taxpayer of wages upon which withholding is based, or an overstatement of the amount of itemized deductions a taxpayer is entitled to take for the purpose of claiming exemptions on withholding. Such a misstatement might be made in the taxpayer's Form W-4, Employee's Withholding Allowance Certificate, which is typically executed when an employee is hired.

OTHER PENALTIES

Frivolous Return Penalty

In recent years, high rates, complexity, and overall dissatisfaction with the system have spawned a growing number of taxpayers who resent the payment of taxes. Taxpayers who actively engage in protest activities might claim 99 dependents, attach statements to their return indicating that they will not pay because the tax is unconstitutional, or submit forms that are illegible and cannot be processed. A penalty exists for taxpayers who maintain a frivolous position on a return. A civil penalty of $5,000 may be imposed on any taxpayer who files a return with insufficient data to determine the correctness of the tax liability or a return that obviously has a substantially incorrect tax liability.[114] It must be shown that the taxpayer has the intent to assume a frivolous position or to delay or impede the administration of the income tax laws.[115] This penalty also includes "frivolous submissions," including frivolous

---

[105] § 6721(a)(1).

[106] § 6722(a).

[107] § 6723.

[108] §§ 6721(e) and 6722(c).

[109] § 6724(d).

[110] See §§ 7203 and 7204 for criminal penalties regarding informational returns.

[111] § 6698.

[112] § 6682 and Reg. § 301.6682-1.

[113] § 7205.

[114] § 6702.

[115] *Ibid.*

offers in compromise and frivolous applications for installment agreements. The IRS is also expected to issue a list of frivolous positions subject to this $5,000 penalty. Also, if the IRS sends a taxpayer a notice that a submission is considered "frivolous," the taxpayer may avoid the penalty by withdrawing the submission within 30 days. Imposition of this penalty does not preclude the levy of any other penalty that otherwise applies.

Aiding and Abetting Penalty

When a person aids or abets the preparation of a false document, a civil penalty of $1,000 may be imposed on that person for each document or return that contains an understatement of tax liability.[116] Only one penalty may be imposed on a person for each taxable event or taxable period relating to the understatement of a tax liability. Thus, if a person aids only one taxpayer in understating the tax liability in a return or a document, only one penalty may be imposed on that person for each taxable event or taxable period involved, regardless of how many understated returns or documents were prepared. More than one penalty may be imposed on a person when there is more than one taxable event involved, the understatement occurs in more than one period, or the tax liability of more than one taxpayer is understated. This penalty may be supplemented by criminal penalties for *willful* attempts to prepare or assist in preparation of fraudulent returns, as shown in Exhibit 19-5, or any other penalty except the return preparer penalty.

Unauthorized Browsing

Although this does not affect taxpayers directly, there is a civil penalty for federal employees or any other persons who knowingly or negligently, without authorization, *inspect* any tax return or return information.[117] Previously, this penalty had applied only to unauthorized *disclosure* of returns or return information, but now applies to both unauthorized inspection or disclosure. The amount of the penalty is $1,000 or actual damages, whichever is greater. There is a *good faith* exception to this penalty, and the penalty will not be applied to accidental or inadvertent inspection of returns, or to an inspection requested by the taxpayer. This law change is due to the potential ease of availability of taxpayer information in electronic format.

Criminal penalties are imposed on *willful* unauthorized inspection or disclosure of returns by federal employees, IRS contractors, and others who obtain the information as part of their government-related work.[118] The criminal penalty is $1,000 and/or one year imprisonment, plus the costs of prosecution. In addition, if a person is criminally charged with unauthorized inspection or disclosure, the IRS is required to notify the taxpayer as soon as practicable.[119]

Prohibition of Executive Branch Influence over Audits

There is a criminal penalty for certain Executive Branch influence over taxpayer audits and other tax investigations.[120] Prohibited actions include requesting that the IRS conduct or terminate an audit, but does not apply to written requests initiated by or on behalf of a taxpayer, written disclosure requests, or written requests for the purpose of implementing a change in tax policy. The penalty, if convicted of violating this provision is up to $5,000 or 5 years imprisonment, or both, plus costs of prosecution.

INTERACTION OF CIVIL PENALTIES

As mentioned previously, it is possible for certain civil penalties to be imposed on the same amount of tax underpayment as other civil penalties. However, in some situations Congress has specifically limited the multiple application of penalties. The interaction of the delinquency, accuracy-related, fraud, and several other civil penalties is shown in Exhibit 19-6.

PREPARER PENALTIES

The preparer of income tax returns is subject to several penalties regarding various acts or omissions that may occur in the preparation of a tax return or in tax practice. These penalties are discussed in greater detail in the "Tax Practice" section of this chapter.

---

[116] § 6701.

[117] § 7431.

[118] § 7213A.

[119] § 7431(e).

[120] § 7217.

Penalty	Source	Penalty Based Upon	Interaction with Other Penalties
Delinquency penalties:			Can be imposed in conjunction with other types of penalties
Failure-to-file	§ 6651(a)	Net amount of tax due (generally, the rate is 5% per month or portion of a month; maximum 25%)	Reduced by failure-to-pay penalty when failure-to-file and failure-to-pay penalties run concurrently
Failure-to-pay	§ 6651(a)	Net amount of tax due (generally, the rate is ½% per month or portion of a month; maximum 25%)	
Estimated tax penalty	§ 6654	Amount of the underpayment for the period of the underpayment (in general, 90% of the total tax is required to be paid in installments during the year; the penalty rate varies, similar to the interest rate)	
Accuracy-related penalties	§ 6662	Amount of the underpayment attributable to the particular accuracy-related penalty (generally, rate is 20%)	Only one accuracy-related penalty may be imposed on any specific underpayment of tax; can be imposed in conjunction with delinquency penalties; and cannot be imposed in same portion of underpayment on which fraud penalty is imposed
Negligence or disregard of rules or regulations			
Substantial understatement of tax			
Substantial valuation misstatement of income tax			
Substantial overstatement of pension liabilities			
Substantial estate or gift tax valuation understatement			
Civil fraud penalty	§ 6663	Amount of the underpayment attributable to fraud (generally, rate is 75%)	When fraud penalty is assessed, no accuracy-related penalties may be assessed on the same portion of the underpayment
Frivolous return penalty	§ 6702	Flat penalty of $500	Can be imposed in conjunction with any other penalties
Aiding and abetting penalty	§ 6701	Flat penalty of $1,000; $10,000 if related to the tax liability of a corporation	May be supplemented by criminal penalties for willful attempts to prepare or assist in preparation of fraudulent return(s), OR any other penalty EXCEPT the return preparer penalty

EXHIBIT 19-6 Interaction of Civil Penalties

DEPENDENTS' IDENTIFICATION NUMBERS

The IRS has long been plagued by taxpayers who claim exemptions for persons who do not exist. To deter taxpayers from making such claims, the law requires that the taxpayer who claims an exemption for a dependent *must* report the dependent's taxpayer identification number on his or her return.[121] Normally, this is the dependent's Social Security number (SSN) or, if the person is not eligible for a SSN, the individual taxpayer's identification number (ITIN) obtained from the IRS. A temporary identification number or noting "applied for" on the return are no longer accepted by the IRS. Failure to provide this number results in loss of the dependency exemption[122] and the child and dependent care credit.[123] In addition, the omission of this identification number from a return is now considered a "mathematical or clerical error,"[124] so that the IRS may simply deny the dependency exemption, child care credit, or even head of household filing status, and assess any additional tax due.

---

[121] Small Business Job Protection Act of 1996, § 1615(d)(2).

[122] § 151(e).

[123] § 21(e)(10).

[124] § 6213(g)(2)(H).

INTEREST

LO.6

Identify situations when interest applies to payment due to the IRS or a refund due from the IRS, and the rates applicable.

The Federal government generally charges a taxpayer interest whenever the assessed tax is not paid in a timely manner. Although the interest charge obviously compensates the government for use of funds legally theirs, it serves what perhaps is a more important purpose. The interest charge eliminates some of the incentive for the taxpayer either to delay payment of taxes or to avoid payment of taxes by taking aggressive positions on returns.

To provide equitable treatment between the government and taxpayers, the Code also provides for interest when there has been an overpayment of tax. Thus, taxpayers that have paid more tax than the amount owed for a given period are compensated.

Rate of Interest

Historically, the interest rate charged on underpayments has been substantially less than the market rate of interest. For example, during 1980 the tax interest rate was 12% while the average prime rate was 15.27 percent. In 1981, Congress believed that this disparity between tax and market rates of interest was leading to the increasing number and amount of delinquent accounts. For this reason, action has been taken over the years to bring tax interest rates more in line with commercial practices.[125]

The interest rate charged on both underpayments and overpayments is three percentage points *over* the Federal short-term rate.[126] The rate that applies to large corporate underpayments when the underpayment (not including any interest, penalties, or additions to tax) for the taxable period exceeds $100,000 is *five* points over the Federal short-term rate.[127] In addition, the interest rate that applies to large corporate overpayments over $10,000 is ½ point over the Federal short-term rate.[128] These rates are updated and published for each calendar quarter. The rate is based on the average market yield of short-term government obligations.

Underpayments

Interest is charged on the amount of unpaid taxes, including deficiencies and penalties, from the payment due date to the date of receipt by the IRS.[129] The due date for payment is considered to be the last date prescribed for payment of the tax *without* regard for any extension of time,[130] March 15 and April 15 for calendar year corporations and individuals, respectively.

Interest on a deficiency or other tax underpayment is computed and charged until the time of notice and demand for payment. The notice and demand for taxes to be paid is not the 90-day letter, but rather it is a formal written demand by the IRS for payment, made within 60 days after an assessment of tax.[131] If a taxpayer does not pay the amount due within 21 calendar days after the date of the notice (10 business days if the amount for which the notice and demand is made equals or exceeds $100,000), then interest is computed and charged until the actual payment is made. However, if the taxpayer pays the amount due within 21 days of the date of the notice and demand, then no interest is charged after the date of the notice.[132]

Prior to 1983, interest was not charged on the portion of an amount owed that represented interest. Since 1982, however, interest is compounded daily.[133] As a result, the extra burden of interest on interest will apply until the amount owed is paid.[134]

Form 870 and Interest

As described in an earlier section, Form 870 (Waiver of Restrictions on Assessment and Collection of Deficiency in Tax) operates as an agreement between the taxpayer and the IRS to settle a dispute over a proposed deficiency. If the taxpayer signs Form 870, interest stops accruing on the deficiency 30 days after the form is filed.[135] At any time after Form 870 is filed, the IRS may send a notice for the amount of tax deficiency plus penalties and interest.

---

[125] § 6621 and Reg. § 301.6621-1.

[126] § 6621(a)(1). For example, the interest rates in effect at the time of this writing are (1) 5% for underpayments and overpayments (4% in the case of a corporation), (2) 7% for large corporate underpayments, and (3) 2.5% for large corporate overpayments exceeding $10,000.

[127] § 6621(c).

[128] § 6621(a)(1).

[129] § 6601(a) and Reg. § 301.6601-1.

[130] § 6601(b)(1) and Reg. § 301.6601-1.

[131] §§ 6601(e)(1) and 6303 and Reg. § 301.6303-1.

[132] § 6601(e) and Reg. § 301.6601-1.

[133] § 6622.

[134] *Ibid.*

[135] § 6601(c) and Reg. § 301.6601-1.

If this notice is sent more than 30 days after Form 870 is filed, no interest accrues from the end of the 30-day period until the date of the notice.[136]

Overpayments

An overpayment of tax refunded 45 days within the later of the date the return is filed or the due date of the return does not accrue interest.[137] When an overpayment arises because of a carryback (e.g., carryback of a net operating loss, capital loss, or credit), interest begins to accrue on the later of the due date of the return in which the carryback originated or the date that the claim for the refund is filed. However, the 45-day rule still applies in this case and the interest is not paid on such overpayment if the refund is made within 45 days of the appropriate date.[138]

When an amended return (a claim for credit or refund) is filed, the IRS is not required to pay interest for the period between the time the amended return is filed and the refund is actually issued, *if* the IRS issues the refund within 45 days of the date the amended return was filed.[139] This keeps the taxpayer from benefiting from any interest accrued during the time the amended return is being processed. The taxpayer will still receive interest to the date that the amended return was filed. If the government takes more than 45 days to issue the refund, interest is paid from the later of the original due date of the return or the date the original return was filed. A similar rule allows the government, when initiating a refund or credit (e.g., from an audit adjustment), to reduce the period over which interest is paid by 45 days.[140]

When a refund is claimed on an overpayment, interest accrues from the date of the overpayment to a date not more than 30 days before the refund check is issued.[141] A taxpayer may request that the overpayment be credited to a subsequent tax period liability, instead of taking payment in a check. In such event, the interest runs from the date of the overpayment to the due date of the amount against which the credit is taken.[142]

Suspension of Interest and Penalties

For individual taxpayers who file their return on or before the return's due date (including extensions), *if* the IRS does not provide a notice specifically stating the taxpayer's liability and the basis for the liability within 36 months of the later of the due date of the return or the date the return was filed, then interest and many penalties are suspended from the 36 month date until 21 days after the notice is provided by the IRS. This suspension does not apply to failure to file and failure to pay penalties, any interest or penalty in a fraud case, any interest or penalty related to the tax liability shown on the tax return, or any criminal penalty. For example, the suspension would apply to dividend income omitted from the return, if the IRS failed to send a notice within the 36-month period, but would not apply to an audit adjustment for an incorrect tax treatment of an item on the taxpayer's tax return. It is also important to note that this suspension of interest and penalties only applies for taxpayers who file their returns by the due date (including extensions).

Tax Practice

Individuals involved in preparing tax returns, representing taxpayers in tax matters before the IRS, and providing other tax-related services must be aware of the various rules governing their conduct. Failure to follow these rules may result in penalty or loss of the right to engage in tax practice. The rules governing tax practice are contained primarily in *Treasury Circular Number 230* and various provisions of the Code. In addition, CPAs and attorneys engaged in tax practice also must follow the rules of conduct imposed by their professional organizations, the American Institute of Certified Public Accountants (AICPA) and the American Bar Association.

LO.7

Explain the rules for practice before the IRS.

---

[136] *Ibid.*

[137] §§ 6611(a) and (e), and Reg. § 301.6611-1.

[138] § 6611(f) and Reg. § 301.6611-1.

[139] § 6611(e)(2).

[140] § 6611(e)(3).

[141] § 6611(b) and Reg. § 301.6611-1.

[142] *Ibid.*

PRIVILEGED COMMUNICATION

Prior to the IRS Restructuring and Reform Act of 1998, the privilege of confidentiality for tax matters was available only under common law between attorneys and their clients. Now there is privileged (confidential) communication with respect to tax advice between a taxpayer and any *federally authorized tax practitioner* to the extent that the communication would be considered a privileged communication if it were between a taxpayer and an attorney.[143] This privilege applies only to *noncriminal* tax matters (within the scope of the practitioner's authority to practice) and does not apply to corporate tax shelters. A "federally authorized tax practitioner" is any person who is authorized under Federal law to practice before the IRS.

TAX RETURN PREPARATION

A *tax return preparer* is defined as a person who prepares for compensation, or employs a person to prepare for compensation, any return or claim for refund regarding federal taxes. This includes the preparation of a substantial portion of the return or refund claim.[144] Until recently, there were no laws or regulations that prevented any individual from becoming a tax return preparer, regardless of the individual's educational background, degree of competence, or experience. However, this all changed in 2010 when the IRS instituted sweeping changes in the rules governing tax return preparers. Before looking at these rules, it should be emphasized that *only* CPAs, attorneys, and enrolled agents are authorized to *practice* before the IRS and are therefore able to represent taxpayers beyond the initial audit.

Tax Return Preparers

After an extensive review that included significant public input, the IRS made fundamental changes in how it regulates the tax return preparation industry. In 2010, the IRS began implementing new regulations and procedures that it believes better serves taxpayers, tax administration and the tax professional industry.[145] The new requirements became effective on January 1, 2011. But, the new rules didn't last long. In 2014 in *Loving v. IRS,*[146] the court affirmed a lower court ruling that the IRS did not have the authority to enforce the tax return preparer rules. In answer, the IRS created a new voluntary program described below. Moreover, at the time of this writing, Congress is about to introduce new legislation that would override the Loving decision and give the IRS complete authority to regulate all aspects of Federal tax practice.

PTIN Requirements. One part of the IRS overhaul that still remains is a requirement concerning preparer tax identification numbers, or so-called PTINs. All tax return preparers who are compensated for preparing, or assisting in the preparation of, all or substantially all of a federal tax return after December 31, 2010 must be registered and have a PTIN. The preparer's PTIN must be disclosed on the tax return. Prior to the new rules, preparers could use either their Social Security number or their PTIN but this option no longer exists. Only the PTIN can be used.

The PTIN requirement applies to virtually anyone who prepares or assists in the preparation of a return. The rule extends to attorneys, certified public accountants, and enrolled agents who are compensated for preparing returns. Note that the IRS has indicated that students who have internships with accounting firms and who prepare returns, regardless of their simplicity, must have a PTIN. In contrast, individuals who volunteer and prepare returns as part of the IRS' VITA program (voluntary income tax assistance program) need not have PTINs.

Preparers can obtain a PTIN, using Form W-12 or an online sign-up system available through www.IRS.gov/taxpros. PTINs must be renewed annually. The cost for both a new PTIN or a renewal for 2016 is $50. All applicants must be at least 18 years old.

Competency Testing. Prior to the decision in *Loving,* individuals seeking a PTIN were required to pass a competency test covering the Form 1040 series returns. However, one ramifications of *Loving* was the elimination of the competency test requirement.

New return preparers are required to pass the competency test before they can obtain a PTIN. Attorneys, certified public accountants, and enrolled agents are exempt from the competency test requirement. Enrolled actuaries and enrolled retirement plan agents are

---

[143] § 7525.

[144] § 7701(a)(36). Reg. § 301.7701-15 defines more clearly the terms "substantial portion," and "return and claim for refund."

[145] See § 6019 and Reg. § 1.6019-2.

[146] 2014-1 USTC 50,175, 113 AFTR 2d 2014-867, 742 F.3d 1013 (CA-DC, 2014).

exempt from the competency test requirement if they only prepare returns within the limited practice areas of these groups.

Continuing Education. As originally constructed, paid preparers (other than CPAs, attorney and enrolled agents) had to meet a continuing education responsibility. The *Loving* decision ended this requirement. However, in its place the IRS created a voluntary education program.[147] The new approach referred to as the Annual Filing Season Program (AFSP) covers tax return preparers who are not attorneys, CPAs or enrolled agents. The stated purpose of the program is to recognize the efforts of non-credentialed return preparers who aspire to a higher level of professionalism. The program requires 18 hours of continuing education, including a six hour tax annual update course with a test. Upon completion, the IRS would give the individual an Annual Filing Season Program—Record of Completion. Participants who successfully complete the program will be included in a public database of return preparers found on the IRS website. The database entitled Directory of Federal Tax Return Preparers with Credentials and Select Qualifications, will contain the name, city, state, zip code, and credentials of all attorneys, CPAs, enrolled agents, enrolled retirement plan agents and enrolled actuaries with a valid PTIN, as well as all AFSP—Record of Completion holders. The IRS launched a public education campaign in 2015 encouraging taxpayers to select return preparers carefully and seek those with professional credentials or other select qualifications. One of the benefits of those participating AFSP will be somewhat greater rights to represent clients whose returns they prepare.

Tax Preparer Penalties

Various rules require certain items to be disclosed and impose an ethical standard on tax return preparers. Many penalties may be imposed by the IRS for noncompliance by preparers, in addition to the power of the IRS to obtain injunctive relief in court to stop a preparer from performing certain unauthorized acts.[148] The penalties include the following:

LO.8
Identify the penalties that may apply to a tax return preparer.

1. The greater of $5,000 per return or claim for refund or 50% of the preparer's income from the return or claim, where the preparer willfully attempts to understate the liability of the taxpayer or where the preparer understates the taxpayer's liability by reckless or intentional disregard of the rules or regulations.[149]

2. The greater of $1,000 per return or claim for refund or 50% of the preparer's income from the return or claim, where the preparer understates the liability of the taxpayer and the understatement is due to an unreasonable position, if the preparer knew (or reasonably should have known) of the position.[150] An unreasonable position generally exists when there is not substantial authority for the position. For disclosed (non tax shelter) positions, only the lesser standard of reasonable basis needs to be met in order to avoid designation as an unreasonable position.[151] If there was reasonable cause for the understatement and the preparer acted in good faith, the penalty may be waived.

3. $100 per return or claim for refund where the preparer fails to exercise due diligence with respect to determining eligibility for, or the amount of, the earned income credit. Due diligence, for these purposes, includes determination that the taxpayer is properly eligible for the credit, properly computing the amount of the credit, and questioning any information that appears to be incorrect, inconsistent, or incomplete. The preparer is also required to retain worksheets and documentation (including the identity of any person furnishing information) showing that the above due diligence requirements have been met with respect to a taxpayer.[152]

4. $500 per occurrence if the preparer endorses or otherwise negotiates a check made in respect of income taxes and issued to the taxpayer.[153]

5. $50 per occurrence if the preparer fails to furnish a copy of the return to the taxpayer, unless it is shown that such failure is due to reasonable cause and not willful neglect.[154]

6. $50 per occurrence if the preparer fails to sign a return, where the preparer is required by regulation to sign the return, unless it is shown that such failure is due to reasonable cause and not willful neglect.[155]

---

[147] Rev. Proc. 2014-42, 2014-29 IRB 192 (2014).

[148] § 7407(a).

[149] § 6694(b).

[150] § 6694(a).

[151] § 6694(a)(2)(B).

[152] § 6695(g) and I.R. Notice 97-65.

[153] § 6695(f) and Reg. § 1.6695-1(f).

[154] § 6695(a) and Reg. § 1.6695-1(a).

[155] § 6695(b) and Reg. § 1.6695-1(b).

7. $50 per occurrence if the preparer fails to furnish an identifying number where the preparer is also required to sign the return, unless it is shown that such failure is due to reasonable cause and not willful neglect.[156]

8. $50 per occurrence if the preparer fails to maintain a copy of a return, or retain a record of the return available for inspection, unless it is shown that such failure is due to reasonable cause and not willful neglect.[157]

9. $50 per occurrence where a preparer fails to make available and maintain a list of the preparer's employees during a return period, plus $50 for each failure to record a required item in the record, unless it is shown that such failure is due to reasonable cause and not willful neglect.[158]

10. $250 per occurrence where a preparer either discloses information connected to the preparation of a tax return or uses the information for anything other than the preparation of a tax return.[159]

The above penalties are intended to regulate the practices of income tax return preparers for compensation. These penalties are civil in nature. Criminal penalties include the following:

1. $10,000 or three years imprisonment, or both, for willfully making fraudulent understatements where the preparer aids or assists in the preparation of the return or document.[160]

2. $10,000 or one year imprisonment, or both, for willful disclosure of a fraudulent document by the preparer to the IRS.[161]

3. $1,000 or one year imprisonment, or both, for improper disclosure by a preparer of information used in preparation of a return.[162]

It is evident that criminal transgressions involve more severe penalties than civil infractions. In any event, all penalties indicate a desire by the Federal government and the IRS to motivate those in a position of trust (i.e., preparers) to exercise a high standard of care, and to sanction certain failures to maintain that standard.

PRACTICE BEFORE THE IRS: TREASURY CIRCULAR 230

Circular 230 prescribes the standards that an individual must satisfy to be eligible to practice before the IRS. *Practice before the IRS* does not include the preparation of a tax return, the appearance as a witness for the taxpayer, or the furnishing of information at the request of the Service. Rather, the term *practice* relates to all matters connected with a presentation to the IRS relating to a client's rights, privileges, or liabilities under the law. Such presentations include, but are not limited to, preparing and filing documents, corresponding and communicating with the IRS, giving written advice with respect to any entity, transaction, plan or arrangement, or other plan or arrangement having a potential for tax avoidance or evasion, and representing a client at conferences, hearings and meetings. In essence, satisfying the requirements of Circular 230 enables the practitioner to represent a client before the Service. As suggested above, however, individuals who merely prepare returns or give advice related to tax matters are not subject to the rules of Circular 230. As explained above, various provisions of the Code control the conduct of these persons.

Circular 230 identifies three primary categories of individuals who may practice before the IRS: attorneys, Certified Public Accountants, and enrolled agents. An enrolled agent is an individual who passes a written examination administered by the IRS, if the individual has not engaged in conduct that would justify suspension or disbarment of an attorney or CPA, or an enrolled agent.[163] An individual who is not enrolled or otherwise admitted to practice before the IRS may practice in the following circumstances:

1. An individual may represent himself or herself, his or her employer (if a full-time employee), a partnership of which he or she is a partner or full-time employee, or may represent without compensation a member of his or her immediate family.

---

[156] § 6695(c) and Reg. § 1.6695-1(c).

[157] § 6695(d) and Reg. § 1.6695-1(d).

[158] § 6695(e) and Reg. § 1.6695-1(e).

[159] § 6713.

[160] § 7206.

[161] § 7207.

[162] § 7216.

[163] 31 C.F.R. § 10.3-4. This citation refers to Title 31 of the Code of Federal Regulations, Part 10, Sections 3 and 4.

2. A corporation, trust, estate, association, or organized group may be represented by its officers or regular full-time employees.

3. Trusts, receiverships, guardianships, or estates may be represented by their trustees, receivers, guardians, administrators, executors, or their regular full-time employees.

4. Any governmental unit, agency, or authority may be represented by an officer or regular employee in the course of his or her official duties.

5. Enrollment is not required for representation outside of the United States before personnel of the IRS.

6. A person who is not under disbarment or suspension from practice before the IRS or other practice of his or her profession and who prepares or signs a return as preparer for a taxpayer may represent the taxpayer in an audit, but not in any collection actions or IRS appeals.[164]

Circular 230 also provides rules that set forth a standard of conduct for professionals who practice before the IRS. The following are duties and restrictions relating to the practice of attorneys, CPAs, or enrolled agents.

1. A practitioner must submit records or information promptly in any matter before the IRS, upon proper and lawful request by an officer or employee of the IRS, unless the practitioner believes in good faith and on reasonable grounds that the records or information are privileged.[165]

2. A practitioner who practices before the IRS must, when requested, provide information about an alleged violation of the Regulations concerning practice by any person and must also testify about such information in any proceeding, unless he or she believes in good faith and on reasonable grounds that such information is privileged.[166]

3. A practitioner must promptly advise a client of any noncompliance, error, or omission he or she knows of with respect to any return or document that the client is required to file, and of the consequences under the Code and Regulations of the noncompliance, error, or omission.[167]

4. A practitioner must exercise due diligence:
   a. In preparing, assisting in preparation, approving, and filing of documents relating to IRS matters;
   b. In determining the correctness of oral and written representation that he or she makes to the IRS; and
   c. In determining the correctness of oral and written representations that he or she makes to clients regarding matters administered by the IRS.[168]

5. No practitioner may unreasonably delay the prompt disposition of any matter before the IRS.[169]

6. No practitioner may charge a client an unconscionable fee in connection with any IRS matter.[170] A practitioner may not charge a contingent fee for preparation or advice related to an original return, but may charge a contingent fee related to an audit or a judicial matter.

7. In general, a practitioner must, at the request of a client, promptly return any and all records of the client that are necessary for the client to comply with his or her Federal tax obligations, even if there is a dispute over fees. The practitioner may retain copies of the records returned to a client. However, if applicable state law allows or permits the retention of a client's records by a practitioner in the case of a dispute over fees for services rendered, the practitioner need only return those records that must be attached to the taxpayer's return. In addition, the practitioner must provide the client with reasonable access to review and copy any additional records of the client retained by the practitioner under state law that are necessary for the client to comply with his or her Federal tax obligations.[171]

---

[164] 31 C.F.R. § 10.7.

[165] 31 C.F.R. § 10.20(a). *U.S. v. Arthur Young & Co.*, 84-1 USTC ¶9305, 53 AFTR2d 84-866, 104 S. Ct. 1495 (USSC, 1984), where the U.S. Supreme Court held that accountant-client privilege does not bar enforcement of an IRS summons for the workpapers prepared by an independent CPA during an audit of its client's finances.

[166] 31 C.F.R. § 10.20(b).

[167] 31 C.F.R. § 10.21.

[168] 31 C.F.R. § 10.22.

[169] 31 C.F.R. § 10.23.

[170] 31 C.F.R. § 10.27.

[171] 31 C.F.R. § 10.28.

8. In general, a practitioner may not represent a client before the IRS if representing that client constitutes a conflict of interest. However, if there is an apparent conflict of interest, and the practitioner believes that he or she can legally provide competent and diligent representation to each client, he or she may do so by express consent of the clients after full disclosure is made.[172]

9. No practitioner may engage in the practice of using a form of public communication or private solicitation that contains a false, fraudulent, misleading, deceptive, coercive, statement or claim.

10. No practitioner may engage in direct or indirect, uninvited written or oral solicitation of employment regarding tax matters, if the solicitation violates Federal or state law.[173]

11. A practitioner *may not sign* a return as preparer unless the practitioner has a reasonable belief that the tax treatment of each position on the return would more likely than not be sustained on its merits, or there is a reasonable basis for each position and each position on the return is adequately disclosed to the IRS. In addition, a practitioner *may not advise* a client to take a position on a return, or prepare the portion of a return on which a position is taken, unless the practitioner has a reasonable belief that the tax treatment of each position satisfies the more likely than not standard, or the position has a reasonable basis and is adequately disclosed to the IRS. "More likely than not" is defined as a greater than fifty-percent likelihood that the tax treatment will be upheld if the IRS challenges it.[174]

12. A practitioner may be censured, suspended, or disbarred from practice before the IRS if the practitioner is shown to be incompetent or disreputable, fails to comply with any practice regulations, or with intent to defraud, willfully and knowingly misleads or threatens a client or prospective client. The IRS may also impose monetary penalties on practitioners who engage in activities subject to these sanctions. In addition, a practitioner may be censured, suspended, or disbarred from practice before the IRS if the practitioner willfully, recklessly, or through gross incompetence violates the regulations for practice before the IRS.[175]

In 2005, Circular 230 was amended to include "Best practices for tax advisors" to ensure that tax advisors act fairly and with integrity.[176] The best practices include communicating clearly with the client about the form and scope of the services to be provided, establishing the relevant facts and evaluating the reasonableness of any related assumptions or client representations. The tax advisor should relate the applicable law, including court cases, to the facts and arrive at a conclusion supported by the law and facts. Finally, the client is to be advised of the conclusions reached, including whether the taxpayer may avoid accuracy-related penalties (e.g., for negligence) if the advice is followed. Tax advisors are also to take reasonable steps to ensure that their firm's procedures are in compliance with these best practices.

In addition, Section 10.35 of Circular 230 imposes stiff reporting requirements and sanctions for any practitioner who provides a "covered opinion."[177] A "covered opinion" is written advice related to any transaction that is the same or substantially similar to one that has already been identified publicly by the IRS as a tax avoidance transaction, or any plan or arrangement which has tax avoidance or evasion as a principal or significant purpose. A practitioner that provides a covered opinion must use reasonable efforts to identify and ascertain the facts of the situation, including the reasonableness of assumptions, relate the law (including court cases) to the facts, and conclusions in the covered opinion must provide the practitioner's opinion whether each significant Federal tax issue in the opinion is likely to prevail on its merits or that the practitioner is unable to reach a conclusion on the issue. Other disclosures, such as the relationship between the practitioner and the promoter of the plan or arrangement, are also required. Any practitioner who violates these provisions, whether willfully, recklessly, or through gross incompetence, may be censured, suspended, or disbarred from practice before the Internal Revenue Service.[178]

---

172 31 C.F.R. § 10.29.

173 31 C.F.R. § 10.30.

174 31 C.F.R. § 10.34.

175 31 C.F.R. §§ 10.50 through 10.52.

176 31 C.F.R. § 10.33.

177 31 C.F.R. § 10.34.

178 31 C.F.R. § 10.52.

CODES OF PROFESSIONAL CONDUCT

In addition to the rules of practice prescribed by the Code and Treasury Circular 230, CPAs and attorneys involved in tax practice must also abide by the additional rules of conduct imposed by their organizations—the American Institute of Certified Public Accountants (AICPA) and the American Bar Association. Each of these professional organizations has a code of professional ethics for its members. Failure to comply with the applicable rules may result in the member's suspension or expulsion from the organization.

Ethical codes for attorneys and CPAs have a great deal in common with the rules set forth in Circular 230 of the IRS. A professional code is written more broadly and does not necessarily cover the same material as Circular 230. Where the ethical code and Circular 230 coincide on subject matter, the professional must follow the rule that imposes the higher standard.

In 1965, the American Bar Association issued *Formal Opinion 314* regarding the ethical position of an attorney practicing before the Internal Revenue Service. This opinion states, in part, that:

> [A] lawyer who is asked to advise his client in the course of the preparation of the client's tax returns may freely urge the statement of positions most favorable to the client as long as there is a *reasonable basis* for this position.[179]

The reasonable basis standard, however, was interpreted in many ways, including merely a taxpayer's chance of being audited. In 1985, the American Bar Association, in *Formal Opinion 85-352*, introduced the *realistic possibility* standard to replace the reasonable basis standard:

> A lawyer may advise reporting a position on a tax return so long as the lawyer believes in good faith that the position is warranted in existing law or can be supported by a good faith argument for an extension, modification or reversal of existing law and there is some realistic possibility of success if the matter is litigated.[180]

AICPA Statements on Standards for Tax Services

The general rules of conduct prescribed by the AICPA concern such matters as independence, integrity and objectivity, advertising, contingent fees, and responsibilities of the accountant when undertaking an engagement—but none that relate specifically to tax practice. Acknowledging that individuals engaged in tax practice have ethical concerns beyond those covered in the general rules of conduct, the AICPA began issuing *Statements on Responsibilities in Tax Practice* in 1964, which incorporated a *reasonable support* standard similar to that in ABA *Formal Opinion 314*.

> **LO.9**
> Understand the AICPA's Statements on Standards for Tax Services.

In 1988, the AICPA issued revised Statements on Responsibilities in Tax Practice in response to changes in the tax laws and the increasing importance of tax practice to CPAs. The Statements on Responsibilities in Tax Practice were advisory in nature, intended to provide guidance as to the accountant's responsibilities in various aspects of tax practice. They were not enforceable AICPA standards. However, the Boards of Accountancy of several states added rules making the Statements enforceable for tax practice in their state. As a result, effective October 31, 2000, the AICPA Statements on Standards for Tax Services (SSTSs) superceded and replaced the Statements on Responsibilities in Tax Practice. The SSTSs are considered AICPA standards and are therefore enforceable with respect to AICPA members. Upon their last revision, effective in 2010, there are seven statements as summarized below.

1. *SSTS No. 1: Tax Return Positions.* As revised in 2010, this *Standard* explains that CPAs must observe the level of support for tax positions expected by the applicable taxing authority. However, the minimum level of support required for an undisclosed tax position recommended by a CPA is a good-faith belief that there is at least a realistic possibility of the position's being sustained administratively or judicially on its merits if challenged. This level of support applies if the taxing authority has no standards or has less rigorous standards than the realistic-possibility standard. Obviously, the CPA must adhere to the taxing authority's standards if they are higher than the

---

[179] ABA Standing Committee On Ethics And Professional Responsibility, *Formal Opinion 314* (April 27, 1965).

[180] ABA Standing Committee On Ethics And Professional Responsibility, *Formal Opinion 85-352* (July 5, 1985).

realistic-possibility standard. According to the standard, a CPA may recommend a position for which there is a reasonable basis of support if the CPA advises the client to disclose the position.[181]

2. *SSTS No. 2: Answers to Questions on the Return.* When there are questions on a return that have not been answered, the CPA should make a reasonable effort to obtain appropriate answers from the taxpayer and provide the answers to the questions on the return. The significance of the question in terms of the information's effect on taxable income or loss and tax liability may be considered in determining whether the answer to a question may be omitted. However, omission of an answer is not justified simply because the answer may prove to be disadvantageous to the taxpayer.[182]

3. *SSTS No. 3: Certain Procedural Aspects of Preparing Returns.* In preparing or signing a return, a CPA may, without verification, rely in good faith on information furnished by the taxpayer or a third party. However, the CPA cannot ignore the implications of information furnished, and should make reasonable inquiries if the information appears to be incorrect, incomplete, or inconsistent either by itself or on the basis of other facts known to the CPA. When preparing the current return, the CPA should make use of returns from prior years wherever feasible. If the tax law or regulations impose conditions with respect to the tax treatment of an item (e.g., substantiating documentation), the CPA should make appropriate inquiries to determine if the conditions are met. In addition, when preparing a return, the CPA should consider relevant information known to the CPA from the tax return of another taxpayer, but should also consider any legal limitations relating to confidentiality.[183]

4. *SSTS No. 4: Use of Estimates.* Unless it is prohibited by the Internal Revenue Code or other tax rule, a CPA may prepare returns involving the use of the taxpayers, estimates, if under the circumstances, exact data cannot be obtained in a practical manner. When estimates are used, they should be presented in such a manner as to avoid the implication of greater accuracy than that which exists. The CPA should be satisfied that estimated amounts are reasonable under the circumstances.[184]

5. *SSTS No. 5: Departure from Positions Previously Concluded in an Administrative Proceeding or Court Decision.* A CPA may recommend a tax return position that differs from the way an item was previously treated in an IRS examination, IRS appeals conference, or a court decision for that taxpayer, unless the taxpayer is bound to a specific treatment for the item in the later year (such as by a formal closing agreement). The CPA should still follow the *realistic possibility* standard in recommending tax return positions, discussed above.[185]

6. *SSTS No. 6: Knowledge of Error: Return Preparation and Administrative Proceeding.* A CPA should advise the taxpayer promptly upon learning of an error in a previously filed return, or upon learning of a taxpayer's failure to file a required return. The advice of the CPA may be oral, and should include a recommendation of the measures to be taken. The CPA is not obliged to inform the IRS and may not do so without the permission of the taxpayer, except where required by law. If the CPA is requested to prepare the current year's return and the taxpayer has not taken appropriate steps to correct an error on a prior year's return, the CPA should consider whether to withdraw from preparing the return and whether to continue a professional or employment relationship with the taxpayer.[186]

When the CPA represents a taxpayer in an administrative proceeding regarding a return with an error known to the CPA that has resulted or may result in more than an insignificant effect on the taxpayer's tax liability, the CPA should notify the taxpayer and recommend corrective measures to be taken. The recommendations may be given orally. The CPA is not obligated to inform the IRS or other taxing authority, and may not do so without the taxpayer's permission, except where required by law. However, the CPA should request permission from the taxpayer to disclose the error to the IRS. Absent such permission, the CPA should consider withdrawing from the engagement.

---

[181] American Institute of Certified Public Accountants, Statements on Standards for Tax Services (2000), SSTS No. 1.

[182] *Ibid.*, SSTS No. 2.

[183] *Ibid.*, SSTS No. 3.

[184] *Ibid.*, SSTS No. 4.

[185] *Ibid.*, SSTS No. 5

[186] *Ibid.*, SSTS No. 6.

7. *SSTS No. 7: Form and Content of Advice to Taxpayers.* In providing tax advice to a taxpayer, the CPA must use judgment to ensure that the advice reflects professional competence and appropriately serves the taxpayer's needs. There is no standard format or guidelines to be used in giving written or oral advice to a taxpayer. A CPA should assume that tax advice provided to a taxpayer will affect the manner in which items are reported on the taxpayer's tax returns and therefore should follow the *realistic possibility* and *reasonable basis* standards from Statement No. 1 or that of the applicable taxing authority. Finally, the CPA has no obligation to communicate with a taxpayer when subsequent developments affect prior advice, unless the CPA is assisting the taxpayer in implementing procedures or plan associated with the advice, or there is a specific agreement for subsequent communications.[187]

The CPA must look to the ethical standards of the accounting profession as a guideline for the level of performance and standard of care required in tax practice today. The *realistic possibility* and *reasonable basis* standards discussed in Statement No. 1 above relate to all advice provided by the CPA to the taxpayer on tax return positions. This applies not only as a general rule, but also specifically to the above Statements.

Problem Materials

DISCUSSION QUESTIONS

19-1 *Self-Assessment and Voluntary Compliance.* The Federal income tax system is based on the concepts of self-assessment and voluntary compliance. Describe how these concepts are applied in the Federal income tax system and discuss how they do or do not appear in other tax systems.

19-2 *IRS Structure.* Briefly discuss the basic differences between the IRS structure of four operating divisions and the supporting functions and shared services.

19-3 *Selection of Returns for Audit.* It is known that many factors are considered by the IRS in deciding whether or not to select a return for audit. List five or more factors and briefly discuss why each factor has importance in the return selection process.

19-4 *Return Selection and Audits.* Individual taxpayer X's income tax return has been selected for audit because the amount of mortgage interest and contributions deducted by X appear excessive in light of X's gross income. Corporate taxpayer A's income tax return has been selected for audit.
  a. Where will each audit most likely be conducted?
  b. Who will conduct each audit?

19-5 *Items Indicating Significant Tax Error.* Listed below are several items which might appear on a return. Each item may or may not suggest that a significant tax error on the return is probable. Evaluate each item as to whether it invites (or does not invite) closer scrutiny by the IRS.
  a. An individual taxpayer files Form 1040 but does not include Schedule B, Interest and Dividend Income. The taxpayer reports interest income of $425 on the Form 1040. (Form 1040 instructs the taxpayer to attach Schedule B if interest income equals or exceeds $400.)
  b. Same as (a) except the individual reports interest income of $10,000 on Form 1040.
  c. A self-employed taxpayer shows on her return gross income in the amount of $500,000 and taxable income of $50,000.
  d. A medical doctor reports gross income of $2,500 for a taxable year.
  e. A real estate broker who works out of his home deducts a home office expense, indicating that the percentage used to arrive at the deduction is based on the use of one room in the house out of seven rooms. The taxpayer also claims exemptions for eleven children.
  f. A taxpayer who works as a neighborhood ice cream salesperson reports gross income of $5,000 for the tax year.

---

[187] *Ibid.*, SSTS No. 7.

g. An individual taxpayer with gross income of $20,000, all from earnings as a factory worker, claims deductions in the amount of $7,000 for mortgage interest, $4,000 for real property taxes, and $2,000 for contributions on Schedule A, Itemized Deductions.

h. A taxpayer claims, in each respective year, a $12,000 casualty loss deduction for cash stolen in 2014, a $5,000 casualty loss deduction for a diamond necklace stolen in a burglary in 2015, and a $7,000 casualty loss deduction for bearer bonds lost in a fire in 2016.

i. A taxpayer who was audited three years ago, where the audit resulted in a tax deficiency of $200, files a return with no exceptional characteristics.

j. Same as (i) except the prior audit resulted in a tax deficiency of $50,000.

19-6 *Refund or Balance Due upon Filing.* Many taxpayers believe that receipt of a refund check after the filing of Form 1040 for a year signifies that the IRS does not intend to audit the taxpayer. Conversely, many taxpayers believe that paying a balance due (owed when the Form 1040 is filed) calls attention from the IRS to the return, making an audit more likely. Comment on the validity of these ideas and discuss why a refund or a balance due does or does not play a role in whether a return is examined.

19-7 *Types of Audits.* The IRS distinguishes between audits that are performed in the field and those that are performed in the IRS office. Describe what types of taxpayers are most likely to be involved in each kind of audit and give reasons why. Also state which type of audit is usually the most extensive and why the different types of audits may differ in scope.

19-8 *Substantiation of Items on Returns.* The IRS requires that the taxpayer show evidence during an audit of a return for various items being examined.

a. What types of supporting evidence are considered valuable for substantiating items of income or deductions?

b. What kinds of problems might arise during an audit that could prompt the IRS to disagree with the amounts of the income or the amounts of the deductions claimed on the return?

c. What types of problems might arise during an audit that would prompt the IRS to broaden the scope of the audit and call additional items into question?

19-9 *Representation/Authorization.* Describe the difference between Form 2848 (Power of Attorney) and Form 8821 (Tax Information Authorization).

19-10 *The Revenue Agent's Report.* At the end of the audit, the IRS makes proposals for adjustment (or no adjustment) of the tax liability for the return examined. The findings of the IRS in the audit, the proposals for adjustment, and the reasons for the proposed adjustments are set out by the IRS in the Revenue Agent's Report. Briefly discuss the importance of this report. State what purposes this report might fulfill from a practical standpoint in terms of the taxpayer audit and appeal process.

19-11 *Form 870.* After the audit is completed, the IRS and the taxpayer may agree on the proposed adjustments by signing Form 870. Briefly discuss the effects of signing this form and why it is important.

19-12 *30-Day Letter.* Briefly summarize what information is contained in a 30-day letter and describe the circumstances warranting its issue.

19-13 *Written Protest.* In what circumstances and in what specific conditions is a taxpayer required to file a written protest?

19-14 *Form 870 versus Form 870-AD.* Compare and contrast Form 870, which may be used after the audit, with Form 870-AD, which is used after the appeal. Specifically consider the following points:

a. Setting forth the concessions arrived at between the IRS and the taxpayer;

b. The running of interest on a proposed deficiency;

c. Further audits concerning the same tax period; and

d. The degree to which each form is considered to be a binding agreement.

19-15 *Appellate Review.* Describe what risks the taxpayer takes by pursuing an appellate review of a case. Against what possible benefits should the taxpayer balance such risks in order to decide whether to proceed further?

19-16 *Appellate Conference.* Briefly summarize what happens during an appellate conference, including which parties usually attend and why.

19-17 *Hazards of Litigation.* The term "hazards of litigation" is rather ill-defined. Try to clarify the meaning of this term and describe the role that the concept plays in the appellate review process.

19-18 *The 90-Day Letter.* Why is the 90-day letter referred to as the statutory notice of deficiency? When will this letter be sent to the taxpayer and what is its effect?

19-19 *Assessment.* The term "assessment" signifies an important event. What is this event and what is its importance?

19-20 *Settlement Authority.* During the various stages of a case, from the audit through appellate review and to the trial court, different IRS officials have the authority to settle the case. Describe what officials have authority to settle the case at the various stages.

19-21 *Additional Settlement Techniques.* The items listed below are settlement techniques used as alternatives to the signing of Form 870 or Form 870-AD. State when each of the following techniques might be used and comment on its effect.
    a. Closing agreements
    b. Offers in compromise
    c. Extensions of limitations period

19-22 *Proposed Deficiency: Alternatives.* The IRS proposes a deficiency of $10,000 for the 2016 tax return of individual T.
    a. If T agrees with the proposed deficiency, what must he do and what are the ramifications of his actions?
    b. If T disagrees with the proposed deficiency, what steps must he take to pursue the matter further within the IRS?

19-23 *National Taxpayer Advocate.* What are the duties of the National Taxpayer Advocate? When does the National Taxpayer Advocate have the power to issue a Taxpayer Assistance Order?

19-24 *IRS Oversight Board.* Briefly discuss the purpose of the IRS Oversight Board, and the benefits derived from the composition of the Board.

19-25 *Purpose of Limitations Period.* A statute that limits the amount of time in which a legal action may be brought typically seeks to strike a balance between several conflicting interests. State the nature of the conflicting interests and describe how a limitations period operates to achieve a balance.

19-26 *Limitations Periods.* The statute of limitations varies in length depending on the circumstances of the case. In each of the examples below, state the length of the limitations period and give reasons why the period is greater than (or less than) the general three-year period.
    a. The taxpayer files a tax return which omits 10% of the taxpayer's gross income. The taxpayer knows of the omission and hopes that it will not be discovered.
    b. The taxpayer has income of $1,000 and files no return for the period.
    c. Same as (b) only the taxpayer has income of $100,000.
    d. The taxpayer has income of $100,000 but reports only $75,000 as gross income on the tax return for the period.
    e. Same as (d) only the taxpayer reports $70,000 as gross income on the tax return for the period.
    f. The taxpayer is a decedent's estate, and the executor has requested that a prompt assessment of taxes be made.
    g. A corporate taxpayer files a return on March 3, 2017 that shows a net operating loss of $10,000 for 2016. The taxpayer carries the loss back and applies it to the third taxable year preceding the year of the loss.

> **h.** The taxpayer files an amended return while only 75 days remain in the three-year period from the date the original return was due (or filed, if later).
>
> **i.** Same as (h) only there are 50 days remaining in the original three-year limitation period.
>
> **j.** A 90-day letter has been mailed to the taxpayer for a certain tax year.

19-27 *Collections.* A separate statute of limitations applies to collections. When does this limitations period begin and what is its length? Discuss why the period may be extended.

19-28 *Refund Claims.* The rules that define the limitations periods for refund claims are often referred to as the "two-year or three-year" rules. Discuss why the rules are called this and briefly describe the rules.

19-29 *Mitigation Provisions.* The law provides that in certain circumstances the statute of limitations will not bar the taxpayer or the IRS from adjusting a return for a year otherwise considered closed by virtue of the limitations period. Describe in what circumstances the finality of the statute of limitations will be mitigated and why this rule serves a useful purpose.

19-30 *Failure-to-Pay Penalty.* The penalty for failure to pay is computed on a certain amount of tax. Describe this base amount and state how large this penalty can become. Include in the description the time periods for the penalty and what happens after the penalty reaches its maximum.

19-31 *Failure-to-File Penalty.* The penalty for failure to file a tax return accumulates much faster than does the penalty for failure to pay. Describe the failure-to-file penalty and give reasons why it builds so much faster than the failure-to-pay penalty.

19-32 *Delinquency Penalties.* The delinquency penalties include the failure-to-pay and the failure-to-file penalties. Briefly discuss what these two penalties have in common and the special relationship between them.

19-33 *Underpayment Penalty for Estimated Taxes.* What fundamental premises of the Federal tax system compel the need for this penalty? The rate of the penalty is indexed directly to the same provisions that fix the rate of interest used by the IRS. Briefly describe the penalty and give reasons why (or why not) the rate used to compute the penalty is appropriate.

19-34 *Accuracy-Related Penalty: Negligence.* Describe the circumstances relating to the acts or omissions of a taxpayer in which a penalty for negligence may be imposed. Briefly outline a standard for the taxpayer to follow to avoid this penalty.

19-35 *Accuracy-Related Penalty: Substantial Understatement.* The law imposes a penalty on substantial understatements of the tax liability shown on a return. Describe the rules relating to this penalty and the conditions in which it is not applied despite an understatement.

19-36 *Civil Fraud Penalty.* A penalty is imposed equal to 75% of the tax underpayment where fraud is involved. Describe the circumstances in which fraud may be found and state which party carries the burden of proof.

19-37 *Accuracy-Related and Fraud Penalties.* Contrast the accuracy-related penalty for negligence with the civil fraud penalty. Contrast the circumstances in which each one applies. Briefly state whether both penalties may be imposed concurrently and give reasons why this should or should not be allowed.

19-38 *Criminal Penalties.* Several criminal penalties apply in addition to the civil penalties in various circumstances. Contrast and compare the criminal penalty with the civil penalty, especially with regard to the standard of proof required and the manner in which the amount of the penalty is determined. Describe these criminal penalties and the acts to which they pertain. Should criminal penalties be involved every time a civil penalty applies?

19-39 *Information Reporting Penalties.* Discuss the goals of Congress in significantly increasing the information reporting penalties in recent years.

19-40 *Frivolous Return Penalty.* Describe the typical circumstances in which the frivolous return penalty is imposed. State whether or not other penalties may be imposed in addition to this penalty and give reasons why this is (or is not) a good policy.

19-41 *Aiding and Abetting Penalty.* Generally, a tax return preparer or advisor must be compensated in order to be subject to penalties. However, the aiding and abetting penalty applies whether or not the person is compensated. Discuss the goals of Congress in applying this penalty to not only compensated advisors, but also uncompensated advisors.

19-42 *Interest and Penalties.* Taxpayer B, an individual, filed for an extension, paying 90% of the tax that he believed he owed. Answer the following questions:
  a. Assuming that B's final tax liability was $10,000 and he owes $2,000 of additional tax, will he owe any interest or other penalties? Explain.
  b. Assuming that B is entitled to a refund of $1,000, is he entitled to any interest? Explain.

19-43 *Interest as an Inducement to Pay.* The Code has many penalty provisions which the IRS may invoke where a taxpayer has not paid all of the taxes owed. Discuss the purpose of interest in light of the fact that there are so many penalties available, and compare the role of interest with that of penalties.

19-44 *Interest and Accrual Dates.* Describe upon what amounts the interest is charged and when it begins and stops accruing. State how interest is compounded and whether or not the Code allows for interest to be charged on interest.

19-45 *Privileged Communication.* Compare and contrast attorney-client privilege and the privileged communication allowed for tax practitioners.

19-46 *Tax Return Preparer.* In order to become an income tax return preparer, an individual need not meet any educational or professional requirements. Describe what an individual must do to be considered an income tax return preparer. Discuss how this differs from qualification for practice before the IRS.

19-47 *Penalties for Income Tax Return Preparers.* The law imposes several penalties on the income tax return preparer for various acts and omissions. Describe five such acts or omissions and the related penalties. For each one, discuss the purpose for the rule and give reasons why (or why not) the purpose is an important one in tax practice. Generally, discuss why there are so many rules pertaining to the income tax return preparer.

19-48 *Criminal Penalties Relating to Return Preparation.* In addition to the civil penalties, the law imposes criminal penalties on certain acts relating to tax return preparation. How do these penalties differ from the civil penalties in nature? Discuss whether the criminal penalties seem fair, given their maximum limits. State why or why not.

19-49 *Tax Practitioner Guidelines.* The IRS has several guidelines pertaining to what individuals it will allow to practice before it. Describe the professional qualifications these guidelines require, and discuss why (or why not) this type of policy is beneficial. Include in the discussion what parties are benefited and how.

19-50 *Nonprofessional Tax Practitioners.* The law allows individuals other than attorneys and CPAs to practice before the IRS. What standards are set for enrolled agents admitted to practice? Discuss the importance of allowing individuals not in an organized profession to practice before the IRS.

19-51 *Other Individuals Allowed to Practice.* In various circumstances, an individual may practice before the IRS to a limited degree without being an attorney, accountant, or enrolled agent. Briefly describe four situations in which this may occur and discuss the reasons why this is (or is not) a good rule in each instance.

19-52 *"Tax Specialist" Representations.* The tax practice law and most professional ethical codes expressly prohibit a professional from making representations of special knowledge regarding tax matters. Discuss the reasons for such a rule and consider the rule in light of the lack of such a constraint on the nonprofessional tax practitioner or the income tax return preparer. Also discuss the fairness of the rule in comparison to the IRS rules that allow for the designation of personnel as revenue agents or revenue officers. Consider any unfair advantages that might be created by this scheme.

19-53 *Ethics and Statements on Standards for Tax Services.* The AICPA standards, set forth in the Statements on Standards for Tax Services, address in a general manner a set of situations typically encountered by the CPA. Focusing on one Statement, create a hypothetical example and make specific assertions about what the Statement requires, given the set of hypothetical facts. Discuss how well the Statement delineates the action to be taken in a factual situation from a practical standpoint.

19-54 *Professional Conduct.* The large amount of malpractice litigation in the accounting world relating to tax practice suggests that the professional standard of conduct in this area is still rather ill-defined. Discuss how a professional tax practitioner might ascertain a standard which, if properly followed, would provide greater security from findings of malpractice. Include in the discussion the sources to which the professional must look in order to find such a standard. Also evaluate the costs to the profession and to the public involved in the evolution of a standard.

PROBLEMS

19-55 *The Decision to Appeal.* Taxpayer Z disagrees with the findings of an audit which rest on the controversy of a single issue. The proposed IRS adjustment is a $20,000 deficiency. Z has retained counsel to take the appeal from start to finish for $6,500. Z's personal expenses to proceed with the audit, including time lost at work, amount to an estimated $1,500. Indicate whether Z should proceed with the appeal or pay the proposed deficiency (disregarding any penalties and interest) in each of the following circumstances:
   a.   The probability of winning the appeal for Z is 50 percent.
   b.   The probability of winning the appeal for Z is 40 percent.
   c.   The probability of winning the appeal for Z is 30 percent.

19-56 *Statute of Limitations.* The limitations period varies from case to case, depending on the circumstances. In each situation described below, state when the statute of limitations expires.
   a.   Calendar year taxpayer A files a 2016 individual income tax return on March 31, 2017.
   b.   Same facts as (a) except the return is for a corporation.
   c.   Taxpayer B files a 2016 return on April 1, 2017 that shows $15,000 of gross income. B actually has gross income of $16,000 but hopes to not pay tax on $1,000 by not reporting it.
   d.   Taxpayer C files a 2016 income tax return on March 1, 2017 that shows $7,500 of gross income. C actually has gross income of $10,000 but has inadvertently omitted $2,500 from the return.
   e.   Same as (d) except C reports $7,200 on the return, inadvertently omitting $2,800.
   f.   Taxpayer D has income of $25,000 for 2016 and files no returns.
   g.   Taxpayer E is an estate for an individual who died on December 31, 2016. The estate tax return is filed March 15, 2017. On April 1, 2017 the executor of Taxpayer E files a request for a prompt assessment.
   h.   Taxpayer F files a 2016 income tax return on April 10, 2017. On April 1, 2018 F files an amended return for the 2016 tax return.
   i.   Same as (h) except F files the amended return on April 1, 2020.

19-57 *Penalties.* Compute the penalties in the following situations:
  a. Taxpayer A files a 2016 income tax return on April 15, 2017 showing a tax liability of $10,000 and a balance due of $1,000. A does not pay the $1,000 until June 30, 2017.
  b. Same as (a) except A does not pay the $1,000 balance due until April 1, 2020.
  c. Taxpayer B filed no 2016 income tax return until July 31, 2017. The return shows a tax liability of $5,000 with a balance due of $100. B pays the $100 on April 15, 2017 without the return.
  d. Same as (c) except B does not pay the balance due until the return is filed.
  e. Taxpayer C files a 2016 income tax return on April 1, 2017, negligently reporting $1,000 less than C's actual tax liability.
  f. Taxpayer D files a 2016 income tax return on April 15, 2017 that fraudulently reports $500 less than D's actual tax liability.

19-58 *Interaction of Civil Penalties.* For each item below, indicate whether the penalties may be applied concurrently.
  a. Failure-to-file penalty and failure-to-pay penalty.
  b. Failure-to-file penalty and accuracy-related negligence penalty.
  c. Accuracy-related negligence penalty and accuracy-related substantial understatement of tax penalty.
  d. Accuracy-related negligence penalty and civil fraud penalty.
  e. Civil fraud penalty and frivolous return penalty.

19-59 *Estimated Taxes: Individual.* In 2016, R's gross tax liability before prepayments is $20,000. His gross tax liability in 2015 was $12,000. R's 2016 AGI is $88,000, and his 2015 AGI was $59,000.
  a. What is the lowest required estimated tax that R can make for 2016 and avoid penalty? (Ignore the annualized income installment.)
      During 2016, R (a single taxpayer) paid estimated taxes of $1,000 on each due date. In addition, R's employer withheld a total of $3,000 during the year. R filed and paid the balance of his liability on April 15, 2017. Assume the applicable interest rate charged on underpayments for 2016 is six percent.
  b. Compute R's penalty, if any, for failure to pay estimated taxes. Compute the penalty with respect to the first installment only. (Consider using the format presented in *Example 22* of this chapter.)
  c. Briefly explain the "annualized income installment" and its function.

19-60 *Estimated Taxes: Individual.* In 2016, Q's gross tax liability before prepayments is $50,000. Her gross tax liability in 2015 was $40,000. Q's 2016 AGI is $180,000, and her 2015 AGI was $162,000. What is the lowest required estimated tax that Q can make for 2016 and avoid penalty? (Ignore the annualized income installment.)

19-61 *Estimated Taxes: Corporation.* During 2015, K Corp. had taxable income of $500,000. Its taxable income for 2015 was $100,000.
  a. What is the minimum installment of estimated taxes that K must make to avoid penalty? Assume the corporation has never had taxable income greater than $500,000.
  b. Same as (a) except the corporation's taxable income in 2015 was $1.5 million.

19-62 *Interest.* The rate of interest used by the IRS has some special characteristics and applications.
  a. How frequently is the interest compounded?
  b. May the IRS charge interest on interest?
  c. How much interest may be charged on tax paid within 21 days of the date it is assessed?
  d. What happens to the accrual of interest on a tax deficiency when the taxpayer signs Form 870? Form 870-AD?
  e. When does interest begin to run on the tax overpayment if a taxpayer files a Form 1040 that requests a refund?
  f. When does interest begin to run on the tax overpayment if a taxpayer files a claim for a refund?

19-63 *Ethics.* The CPA encounters various situations that fall under ethical rules that prescribe or proscribe certain acts. Comment on the following situations and state what the CPA should do in each case.

 a. A CPA receives no compensation for preparing the income tax return of a neighbor. The neighbor requests that the CPA sign the preparer's declaration.

 b. A CPA prepares a Form 1120 for a corporation, but is unable to show a breakdown of the compensation of officers due to lack of information.

 c. A CPA assists a corporate client through an audit of a return in which it is found that an officer has received unreasonable compensation. No prospective statements are made by the IRS that specifically deal with future years. The CPA is currently assisting the client in the preparation of a current income tax return for a period when the same officer received the same compensation for the same amount of work.

 d. A CPA has knowledge of an error in the ending inventory of a prior year. The CPA is asked to prepare the return for the current year.

 e. A CPA is asked to prepare a return where the client has provided information indicating that the client pays several thousands of dollars in office rent. The CPA knows the client actually owns the office which it claims to be renting.

 f. A CPA takes a position contrary to an Income Tax Regulation (i.e., a Treasury Regulation) with reasonable support for the position.

 g. A CPA takes a position contrary to a specific section of the Internal Revenue Code with reasonable support for the position.

RESEARCH PROBLEMS

19-64 Q filed a fraudulent income tax return for 2010. In 2012, Q realized the error of his ways and filed a nonfraudulent amended income tax return for the 2010 tax year, and paid the additional taxes due. In 2016, the IRS assessed the 75% civil fraud penalty under § 6663 on Q's 2010 tax. Q asserts that the normal three-year statute of limitations expired in 2015, since he filed a nonfraudulent amended return in 2012. The position of the IRS is that there is no statute of limitations due to fraud. Which party is likely to prevail? Why?

Research aid:

 Reg. § 301.6501(a)-1(b).

19-65 On April 10, 2016, N realized that she would not be able to file her 2015 tax return by April 15, 2016. She phoned her accountant and told him that she was delayed but expected a very large refund. The accountant informed her that she would not be penalized since no tax was due. When N finished her tax return, she found that $4,000 additional tax was due. She filed her 2015 return and paid the $4,000 additional tax in July 2016. The IRS assessed failure to-file and failure-to-pay penalties. N agrees that she owes the penalty for failure to pay, but does not feel that she should be penalized for failure to file since she relied on the advice of her accountant. Should N be penalized for failure to file? Why or why not?

Research aid:

 § 6651(a).

Appendices

A

Estate and Gift Tax
Valuation Table

Appendix Outline

A-1 Table S: Single Life Factors—Various Interest Rates

Appendix A-1

Section 1

Table S
Single Life Factors Based on Life Table 2000CM
Interest at 4.4 Percent

Age	Annuity	Life Estate	Remainder	Age	Annuity	Life Estate	Remainder
0	21.4812	0.94517	0.05483	55	14.3029	0.62933	0.37067
1	21.5798	0.94951	0.05049	56	14.0285	0.61725	0.38275
2	21.5405	0.94778	0.05222	57	13.7495	0.60498	0.39502
3	21.4955	0.94580	0.05420	58	13.4666	0.59253	0.40747
4	21.4469	0.94366	0.05634	59	13.1793	0.57989	0.42011
5	21.3952	0.94139	0.05861	60	12.8873	0.56704	0.43296
6	21.3405	0.93898	0.06102	61	12.5909	0.55400	0.44600
7	21.2835	0.93647	0.06353	62	12.2910	0.54080	0.45920
8	21.2234	0.93383	0.06617	63	11.9879	0.52747	0.47253
9	21.1603	0.93105	0.06895	64	11.6816	0.51399	0.48601
10	21.0942	0.92815	0.07185	65	11.3721	0.50037	0.49963
11	21.0250	0.92510	0.07490	66	11.0563	0.48648	0.51352
12	20.9527	0.92192	0.07808	67	10.7352	0.47235	0.52765
13	20.8780	0.91863	0.08137	68	10.4101	0.45804	0.54196
14	20.8018	0.91528	0.08472	69	10.0818	0.44360	0.55640
15	20.7246	0.91188	0.08812	70	9.7511	0.42905	0.57095
16	20.6468	0.90846	0.09154	71	9.4179	0.41439	0.58561
17	20.5678	0.90498	0.09502	72	9.0829	0.39965	0.60035
18	20.4874	0.90145	0.09855	73	8.7474	0.38488	0.61512
19	20.4051	0.89783	0.10217	74	8.4129	0.37017	0.62983
20	20.3200	0.89408	0.10592	75	8.0808	0.35556	0.64444
21	20.2324	0.89023	0.10977	76	7.7521	0.34109	0.65891
22	20.1419	0.88624	0.11376	77	7.4270	0.32679	0.67321
23	20.0480	0.88211	0.11789	78	7.1061	0.31267	0.68733
24	19.9498	0.87779	0.12221	79	6.7900	0.29876	0.70124
25	19.8469	0.87326	0.12674	80	6.4795	0.28510	0.71490
26	19.7389	0.86851	0.13149	81	6.1751	0.27170	0.72830
27	19.6256	0.86353	0.13647	82	5.8772	0.25860	0.74140
28	19.5071	0.85831	0.14169	83	5.5866	0.24581	0.75419
29	19.3837	0.85288	0.14712	84	5.3036	0.23336	0.76664
30	19.2556	0.84725	0.15275	85	5.0288	0.22127	0.77873
31	19.1225	0.84139	0.15861	86	4.7626	0.20956	0.79044
32	18.9844	0.83532	0.16468	87	4.5055	0.19824	0.80176
33	18.8412	0.82901	0.17099	88	4.2573	0.18732	0.81268
34	18.6932	0.82250	0.17750	89	4.0188	0.17683	0.82317
35	18.5402	0.81577	0.18423	90	3.7900	0.16676	0.83324
36	18.3820	0.80881	0.19119	91	3.5710	0.15712	0.84288
37	18.2186	0.80162	0.19838	92	3.3619	0.14792	0.85208
38	18.0496	0.79418	0.20582	93	3.1630	0.13917	0.86083
39	17.8755	0.78652	0.21348	94	2.9739	0.13085	0.86915
40	17.6962	0.77863	0.22137	95	2.7943	0.12295	0.87705
41	17.5114	0.77050	0.22950	96	2.6249	0.11549	0.88451
42	17.3214	0.76214	0.23786	97	2.4650	0.10846	0.89154
43	17.1253	0.75352	0.24648	98	2.3142	0.10182	0.89818
44	16.9238	0.74465	0.25535	99	2.1717	0.09556	0.90444
45	16.7166	0.73553	0.26447	100	2.0391	0.08972	0.91028
46	16.5033	0.72615	0.27385	101	1.9130	0.08417	0.91583
47	16.2844	0.71651	0.28349	102	1.7964	0.07904	0.92096
48	16.0595	0.70662	0.29338	103	1.6806	0.07395	0.92605
49	15.8285	0.69645	0.30355	104	1.5740	0.06926	0.93074
50	15.5907	0.68599	0.31401	105	1.4689	0.06463	0.93537
51	15.3462	0.67523	0.32477	106	1.3375	0.05885	0.94115
52	15.0949	0.66418	0.33582	107	1.1884	0.05229	0.94771
53	14.8370	0.65283	0.34717	108	0.9478	0.04170	0.95830
54	14.5728	0.64120	0.35880	109	0.4789	0.02107	0.97893

Appendix A-1
Table S   Section 1
Single Life Factors Based on Life Table 2000CM
Interest at 4.6 Percent

Age	Annuity	Life Estate	Remainder	Age	Annuity	Life Estate	Remainder
0	20.6611	0.95041	0.04959	55	13.9887	0.64348	0.35652
1	20.7593	0.95493	0.04507	56	13.7264	0.63141	0.36859
2	20.7249	0.95335	0.04665	57	13.4595	0.61914	0.38086
3	20.6853	0.95152	0.04848	58	13.1885	0.60667	0.39333
4	20.6421	0.94954	0.05046	59	12.9130	0.59400	0.40600
5	20.5961	0.94742	0.05258	60	12.6327	0.58110	0.41890
6	20.5474	0.94518	0.05482	61	12.3478	0.56800	0.43200
7	20.4964	0.94283	0.05717	62	12.0593	0.55473	0.44527
8	20.4426	0.94036	0.05964	63	11.7673	0.54130	0.45870
9	20.3859	0.93775	0.06225	64	11.4720	0.52771	0.47229
10	20.3264	0.93501	0.06499	65	11.1733	0.51397	0.48603
11	20.2639	0.93214	0.06786	66	10.8681	0.49993	0.50007
12	20.1986	0.92913	0.07087	67	10.5574	0.48564	0.51436
13	20.1310	0.92603	0.07397	68	10.2425	0.47115	0.52885
14	20.0620	0.92285	0.07715	69	9.9241	0.45651	0.54349
15	19.9921	0.91964	0.08036	70	9.6030	0.44174	0.55826
16	19.9217	0.91640	0.08360	71	9.2792	0.42684	0.57316
17	19.8502	0.91311	0.08689	72	8.9533	0.41185	0.58815
18	19.7775	0.90976	0.09024	73	8.6265	0.39682	0.60318
19	19.7030	0.90634	0.09366	74	8.3004	0.38182	0.61818
20	19.6258	0.90279	0.09721	75	7.9763	0.36691	0.63309
21	19.5463	0.89913	0.10087	76	7.6553	0.35214	0.64786
22	19.4640	0.89535	0.10465	77	7.3375	0.33752	0.66248
23	19.3786	0.89141	0.10859	78	7.0235	0.32308	0.67692
24	19.2891	0.88730	0.11270	79	6.7139	0.30884	0.69116
25	19.1950	0.88297	0.11703	80	6.4096	0.29484	0.70516
26	19.0961	0.87842	0.12158	81	6.1109	0.28110	0.71890
27	18.9922	0.87364	0.12636	82	5.8185	0.26765	0.73235
28	18.8833	0.86863	0.13137	83	5.5330	0.25452	0.74548
29	18.7696	0.86340	0.13660	84	5.2548	0.24172	0.75828
30	18.6514	0.85797	0.14203	85	4.9844	0.22928	0.77072
31	18.5285	0.85231	0.14769	86	4.7223	0.21722	0.78278
32	18.4007	0.84643	0.15357	87	4.4689	0.20557	0.79443
33	18.2679	0.84032	0.15968	88	4.2242	0.19431	0.80569
34	18.1306	0.83401	0.16599	89	3.9889	0.18349	0.81651
35	17.9884	0.82747	0.17253	90	3.7630	0.17310	0.82690
36	17.8411	0.82069	0.17931	91	3.5467	0.16315	0.83685
37	17.6888	0.81369	0.18631	92	3.3400	0.15364	0.84636
38	17.5311	0.80643	0.19357	93	3.1433	0.14459	0.85541
39	17.3684	0.79895	0.20105	94	2.9562	0.13598	0.86402
40	17.2005	0.79122	0.20878	95	2.7784	0.12781	0.87219
41	17.0274	0.78326	0.21674	96	2.6106	0.12009	0.87991
42	16.8490	0.77506	0.22494	97	2.4522	0.11280	0.88720
43	16.6649	0.76658	0.23342	98	2.3027	0.10592	0.89408
44	16.4752	0.75786	0.24214	99	2.1614	0.09943	0.90057
45	16.2800	0.74888	0.25112	100	2.0298	0.09337	0.90663
46	16.0788	0.73962	0.26038	101	1.9047	0.08762	0.91238
47	15.8720	0.73011	0.26989	102	1.7890	0.08229	0.91771
48	15.6593	0.72033	0.27967	103	1.6740	0.07700	0.92300
49	15.4405	0.71026	0.28974	104	1.5682	0.07214	0.92786
50	15.2150	0.69989	0.30011	105	1.4638	0.06734	0.93266
51	14.9828	0.68921	0.31079	106	1.3332	0.06133	0.93867
52	14.7439	0.67822	0.32178	107	1.1851	0.05451	0.94549
53	14.4983	0.66692	0.33308	108	0.9455	0.04349	0.95651
54	14.2464	0.65533	0.34467	109	0.4780	0.02199	0.97801

Appendix A-1

Section 1

Table S

Single Life Factors Based on Life Table 2000CM

Interest at 4.8 Percent

Age	Annuity	Life Estate	Remainder	Age	Annuity	Life Estate	Remainder
0	19.8956	0.95499	0.04501	55	13.6857	0.65692	0.34308
1	19.9930	0.95966	0.04034	56	13.4349	0.64488	0.35512
2	19.9630	0.95822	0.04178	57	13.1795	0.63261	0.36739
3	19.9280	0.95654	0.04346	58	12.9198	0.62015	0.37985
4	19.8897	0.95470	0.04530	59	12.6555	0.60747	0.39253
5	19.8487	0.95274	0.04726	60	12.3863	0.59454	0.40546
6	19.8051	0.95065	0.04935	61	12.1124	0.58140	0.41860
7	19.7594	0.94845	0.05155	62	11.8347	0.56806	0.43194
8	19.7112	0.94614	0.05386	63	11.5534	0.55456	0.44544
9	19.6601	0.94369	0.05631	64	11.2686	0.54089	0.45911
10	19.6065	0.94111	0.05889	65	10.9802	0.52705	0.47295
11	19.5500	0.93840	0.06160	66	10.6852	0.51289	0.48711
12	19.4908	0.93556	0.06444	67	10.3845	0.49846	0.50154
13	19.4296	0.93262	0.06738	68	10.0793	0.48381	0.51619
14	19.3670	0.92962	0.07038	69	9.7705	0.46898	0.53102
15	19.3037	0.92658	0.07342	70	9.4587	0.45402	0.54598
16	19.2398	0.92351	0.07649	71	9.1439	0.43891	0.56109
17	19.1750	0.92040	0.07960	72	8.8267	0.42368	0.57632
18	19.1091	0.91724	0.08276	73	8.5084	0.40840	0.59160
19	19.0416	0.91400	0.08600	74	8.1904	0.39314	0.60686
20	18.9716	0.91063	0.08937	75	7.8741	0.37796	0.62204
21	18.8993	0.90717	0.09283	76	7.5605	0.36290	0.63710
22	18.8245	0.90358	0.09642	77	7.2498	0.34799	0.65201
23	18.7466	0.89984	0.10016	78	6.9425	0.33324	0.66676
24	18.6650	0.89592	0.10408	79	6.6393	0.31868	0.68132
25	18.5790	0.89179	0.10821	80	6.3409	0.30437	0.69563
26	18.4883	0.88744	0.11256	81	6.0480	0.29030	0.70970
27	18.3929	0.88286	0.11714	82	5.7608	0.27652	0.72348
28	18.2927	0.87805	0.12195	83	5.4803	0.26305	0.73695
29	18.1879	0.87302	0.12698	84	5.2067	0.24992	0.75008
30	18.0787	0.86778	0.13222	85	4.9407	0.23715	0.76285
31	17.9650	0.86232	0.13768	86	4.6825	0.22476	0.77524
32	17.8467	0.85664	0.14336	87	4.4328	0.21278	0.78722
33	17.7235	0.85073	0.14927	88	4.1916	0.20120	0.79880
34	17.5960	0.84461	0.15539	89	3.9594	0.19005	0.80995
35	17.4637	0.83826	0.16174	90	3.7364	0.17935	0.82065
36	17.3265	0.83167	0.16833	91	3.5226	0.16909	0.83091
37	17.1844	0.82485	0.17515	92	3.3183	0.15928	0.84072
38	17.0371	0.81778	0.18222	93	3.1238	0.14994	0.85006
39	16.8849	0.81048	0.18952	94	2.9387	0.14106	0.85894
40	16.7277	0.80293	0.19707	95	2.7626	0.13261	0.86739
41	16.5653	0.79513	0.20487	96	2.5965	0.12463	0.87537
42	16.3978	0.78710	0.21290	97	2.4395	0.11710	0.88290
43	16.2246	0.77878	0.22122	98	2.2913	0.10998	0.89002
44	16.0461	0.77021	0.22979	99	2.1512	0.10326	0.89674
45	15.8620	0.76138	0.23862	100	2.0207	0.09699	0.90301
46	15.6721	0.75226	0.24774	101	1.8965	0.09103	0.90897
47	15.4767	0.74288	0.25712	102	1.7816	0.08552	0.91448
48	15.2754	0.73322	0.26678	103	1.6674	0.08004	0.91996
49	15.0680	0.72326	0.27674	104	1.5624	0.07499	0.92501
50	14.8540	0.71299	0.28701	105	1.4588	0.07002	0.92998
51	14.6335	0.70241	0.29759	106	1.3290	0.06379	0.93621
52	14.4061	0.69149	0.30851	107	1.1817	0.05672	0.94328
53	14.1721	0.68026	0.31974	108	0.9433	0.04528	0.95472
54	13.9318	0.66873	0.33127	109	0.4771	0.02290	0.97710

Appendix A-1
Table S   **Section 1**
Single Life Factors Based on Life Table 2000CM
Interest at 5.0 Percent

Age	Annuity	Life Estate	Remainder	Age	Annuity	Life Estate	Remainder
0	19.1799	0.95899	0.04101	55	13.3935	0.66968	0.33032
1	19.2763	0.96382	0.03618	56	13.1536	0.65768	0.34232
2	19.2501	0.96250	0.03750	57	12.9089	0.64545	0.35455
3	19.2192	0.96096	0.03904	58	12.6600	0.63300	0.36700
4	19.1851	0.95925	0.04075	59	12.4064	0.62032	0.37968
5	19.1485	0.95742	0.04258	60	12.1477	0.60739	0.39261
6	19.1095	0.95547	0.04453	61	11.8844	0.59422	0.40578
7	19.0685	0.95342	0.04658	62	11.6170	0.58085	0.41915
8	19.0251	0.95125	0.04875	63	11.3459	0.56729	0.43271
9	18.9791	0.94895	0.05105	64	11.0711	0.55355	0.44645
10	18.9306	0.94653	0.05347	65	10.7925	0.53963	0.46037
11	18.8795	0.94397	0.05603	66	10.5073	0.52536	0.47464
12	18.8258	0.94129	0.05871	67	10.2162	0.51081	0.48919
13	18.7702	0.93851	0.06149	68	9.9204	0.49602	0.50398
14	18.7133	0.93567	0.06433	69	9.6208	0.48104	0.51896
15	18.6558	0.93279	0.06721	70	9.3180	0.46590	0.53410
16	18.5978	0.92989	0.07011	71	9.0119	0.45060	0.54940
17	18.5391	0.92695	0.07305	72	8.7032	0.43516	0.56484
18	18.4793	0.92396	0.07604	73	8.3930	0.41965	0.58035
19	18.4180	0.92090	0.07910	74	8.0829	0.40414	0.59586
20	18.3543	0.91772	0.08228	75	7.7742	0.38871	0.61129
21	18.2886	0.91443	0.08557	76	7.4677	0.37339	0.62661
22	18.2205	0.91103	0.08897	77	7.1639	0.35819	0.64181
23	18.1495	0.90748	0.09252	78	6.8631	0.34316	0.65684
24	18.0749	0.90375	0.09625	79	6.5660	0.32830	0.67170
25	17.9962	0.89981	0.10019	80	6.2736	0.31368	0.68632
26	17.9131	0.89565	0.10435	81	5.9861	0.29931	0.70069
27	17.8253	0.89127	0.10873	82	5.7042	0.28521	0.71479
28	17.7330	0.88665	0.11335	83	5.4285	0.27142	0.72858
29	17.6363	0.88181	0.11819	84	5.1594	0.25797	0.74203
30	17.5354	0.87677	0.12323	85	4.8976	0.24488	0.75512
31	17.4302	0.87151	0.12849	86	4.6433	0.23217	0.76783
32	17.3205	0.86602	0.13398	87	4.3973	0.21986	0.78014
33	17.2061	0.86030	0.13970	88	4.1594	0.20797	0.79203
34	17.0875	0.85438	0.14562	89	3.9302	0.19651	0.80349
35	16.9643	0.84822	0.15178	90	3.7101	0.18550	0.81450
36	16.8364	0.84182	0.15818	91	3.4989	0.17495	0.82505
37	16.7038	0.83519	0.16481	92	3.2969	0.16485	0.83515
38	16.5661	0.82830	0.17170	93	3.1046	0.15523	0.84477
39	16.4236	0.82118	0.17882	94	2.9213	0.14607	0.85393
40	16.2762	0.81381	0.18619	95	2.7471	0.13735	0.86265
41	16.1238	0.80619	0.19381	96	2.5825	0.12912	0.87088
42	15.9665	0.79832	0.20168	97	2.4270	0.12135	0.87865
43	15.8035	0.79018	0.20982	98	2.2800	0.11400	0.88600
44	15.6353	0.78176	0.21824	99	2.1411	0.10706	0.89294
45	15.4617	0.77308	0.22692	100	2.0116	0.10058	0.89942
46	15.2823	0.76411	0.23589	101	1.8884	0.09442	0.90558
47	15.0975	0.75487	0.24513	102	1.7743	0.08872	0.91128
48	14.9069	0.74534	0.25466	103	1.6609	0.08305	0.91695
49	14.7103	0.73551	0.26449	104	1.5566	0.07783	0.92217
50	14.5071	0.72535	0.27465	105	1.4537	0.07269	0.92731
51	14.2974	0.71487	0.28513	106	1.3247	0.06624	0.93376
52	14.0810	0.70405	0.29595	107	1.1784	0.05892	0.94108
53	13.8580	0.69290	0.30710	108	0.9410	0.04705	0.95295
54	13.6286	0.68143	0.31857	109	0.4762	0.02381	0.97619

A-2 Table B: Annuity, Income, and Remainder Interests

Appendix A-2

Section 3

Table B

Annuity, Income, and Remainder Interests for a Term Certain

	5.0%			Interest Rates		5.2%	
Years	Annuity	Income Interest	Remainder	Years	Annuity	Income Interest	Remainder
1	0.9524	.047619	.952381	1	0.9506	.045430	.950570
2	1.8594	.092971	.907029	2	1.8542	.096416	.903584
3	2.7232	.136162	.863838	3	2.7131	.141080	.858920
4	3.5460	.177298	.822702	4	3.5295	.183536	.816464
5	4.3295	.216474	.783526	5	4.3056	.223894	.776106
6	5.0757	.253785	.746215	6	5.0434	.262256	.737744
7	5.7864	.289319	.710681	7	5.7447	.298723	.701277
8	6.4632	.323161	.676839	8	6.4113	.333387	.666613
9	7.1078	.355391	.644609	9	7.0449	.366337	.633663
10	7.7217	.386087	.613913	10	7.6473	.397659	.602341
11	8.3064	.415321	.584679	11	8.2199	.427432	.572568
12	8.8633	.443163	.556837	12	8.7641	.455734	.544266
13	9.3936	.469679	.530321	13	9.2815	.482637	.517363
14	9.8986	.494932	.505068	14	9.7733	.508210	.491790
15	10.3797	.518983	.481017	15	10.2408	.532519	.467481
16	10.8378	.541888	.458112	16	10.6851	.555628	.444374
17	11.2741	.563703	.436297	17	11.1075	.577592	.422408
18	11.6896	.584479	.415521	18	11.5091	.598471	.401529
19	12.0853	.604266	.395734	19	11.8907	.618319	.381681
20	12.4622	.623111	.376889	20	12.2536	.637185	.362815
21	12.8212	.641058	.358942	21	12.5984	.655119	.344881
22	13.1630	.658150	.341850	22	12.9263	.672166	.327834
23	13.4886	.674429	.325571	23	13.2379	.688371	.311629
24	13.7986	.689932	.310068	24	13.5341	.703775	.296225
25	14.0939	.704697	.295303	25	13.8157	.718417	.281583
26	14.3752	.716759	.281241	26	14.0834	.732336	.267664
27	14.6430	.732152	.267848	27	14.3378	.745566	.254434
28	14.8981	.744906	.255094	28	14.5797	.758143	.241357
29	15.1411	.757054	.242946	29	14.8096	.770098	.229902
30	15.3725	.768623	.231377	30	15.0281	.781462	.218538
31	15.5928	.779641	.220359	31	15.2358	.792264	.207736
32	15.8027	.790134	.209666	32	15.4333	.802532	.197468
33	16.0025	.800127	.199873	33	15.6210	.812293	.187707
34	16.1929	.809645	.190355	34	15.7994	.821571	.178429
35	16.3742	.818710	.181290	35	15.9691	.830391	.169609
36	16.5469	.827343	.172657	36	16.1303	.838775	.161225
37	16.7113	.835564	.164436	37	16.2835	.846744	.153256
38	16.8679	.843395	.156605	38	16.4292	.854319	.145681
39	17.0170	.850852	.149148	39	16.5677	.861520	.138480
40	17.1591	.857954	.142046	40	16.6993	.868365	.131635
41	17.2944	.864718	.135282	41	16.6245	.874872	.125128
42	17.4232	.871160	.128840	42	16.9434	.881057	.118943
43	17.5459	.877296	.122704	43	17.0565	.886936	.113064
44	17.6628	.883139	.116861	44	17.1639	.892525	.107475
45	17.7741	.888703	.111297	45	17.2661	.897837	.102163
46	17.8801	.894003	.105997	46	17.3632	.902887	.097113
47	17.9810	.899051	.100949	47	17.4555	.907688	.092312
48	18.0772	.903858	.096142	48	17.5433	.912251	.087749
49	18.1687	.908436	.091564	49	17.6267	.916588	.083412
50	18.2559	.912796	.087204	50	17.7060	.920711	.079289
51	18.3390	.916949	.083051	51	17.7814	.924630	.075370
52	18.4181	.920904	.079096	52	17.8530	.928356	.071644
53	18.4934	.924670	.075330	53	17.9211	.931897	.068103
54	18.5651	.928257	.071743	54	17.9858	.935263	.064737
55	18.6335	.931674	.068326	55	18.0474	.938463	.061537
56	18.6985	.934927	.065073	56	18.1059	.941505	.058495
57	18.7605	.938026	.061974	57	18.1615	.944396	.055604
58	18.8195	.940977	.059023	58	18.2143	.947145	.052855
59	18.8758	.943788	.056212	59	18.2646	.949757	.050243
60	18.9293	.946464	.053536	60	18.3123	.952241	.047759

Tax Forms

B

Appendix Outline

B-1   U.S. Corporation Income Tax Return

Form **1120**	**U.S. Corporation Income Tax Return**	OMB No. 1545-0123
Department of the Treasury Internal Revenue Service	For calendar year 2015 or tax year beginning _____, 2015, ending _____, 20 ____ ▶ Information about Form 1120 and its separate instructions is at *www.irs.gov/form1120.*	**2015**

A Check if:
1a Consolidated return (attach Form 851) ☐
 b Life/nonlife consolidated return ☐
2 Personal holding co. (attach Sch. PH) ☐
3 Personal service corp. (see instructions) ☐
4 Schedule M-3 attached ☐

TYPE OR PRINT

Name

Number, street, and room or suite no. If a P.O. box, see instructions.

City or town, state, or province, country, and ZIP or foreign postal code

B Employer identification number

C Date incorporated

D Total assets (see instructions)
$

E Check if: **(1)** ☐ Initial return **(2)** ☐ Final return **(3)** ☐ Name change **(4)** ☐ Address change

Income

1a	Gross receipts or sales	1a	
b	Returns and allowances	1b	
c	Balance. Subtract line 1b from line 1a	1c	
2	Cost of goods sold (attach Form 1125-A)	2	
3	Gross profit. Subtract line 2 from line 1c	3	
4	Dividends (Schedule C, line 19)	4	
5	Interest	5	
6	Gross rents	6	
7	Gross royalties	7	
8	Capital gain net income (attach Schedule D (Form 1120))	8	
9	Net gain or (loss) from Form 4797, Part II, line 17 (attach Form 4797)	9	
10	Other income (see instructions—attach statement)	10	
11	**Total income.** Add lines 3 through 10 ▶	11	

Deductions (See instructions for limitations on deductions.)

12	Compensation of officers (see instructions—attach Form 1125-E) ▶	12	
13	Salaries and wages (less employment credits)	13	
14	Repairs and maintenance	14	
15	Bad debts	15	
16	Rents	16	
17	Taxes and licenses	17	
18	Interest	18	
19	Charitable contributions	19	
20	Depreciation from Form 4562 not claimed on Form 1125-A or elsewhere on return (attach Form 4562)	20	
21	Depletion	21	
22	Advertising	22	
23	Pension, profit-sharing, etc., plans	23	
24	Employee benefit programs	24	
25	Domestic production activities deduction (attach Form 8903)	25	
26	Other deductions (attach statement)	26	
27	**Total deductions.** Add lines 12 through 26 ▶	27	
28	Taxable income before net operating loss deduction and special deductions. Subtract line 27 from line 11.	28	
29a	Net operating loss deduction (see instructions)	29a	
b	Special deductions (Schedule C, line 20)	29b	
c	Add lines 29a and 29b	29c	

Tax, Refundable Credits, and Payments

30	**Taxable income.** Subtract line 29c from line 28 (see instructions)	30	
31	Total tax (Schedule J, Part I, line 11)	31	
32	Total payments and refundable credits (Schedule J, Part II, line 21)	32	
33	Estimated tax penalty (see instructions). Check if Form 2220 is attached ▶ ☐	33	
34	**Amount owed.** If line 32 is smaller than the total of lines 31 and 33, enter amount owed	34	
35	**Overpayment.** If line 32 is larger than the total of lines 31 and 33, enter amount overpaid	35	
36	Enter amount from line 35 you want: **Credited to 2016 estimated tax ▶** Refunded ▶	36	

Sign Here

Under penalties of perjury, I declare that I have examined this return, including accompanying schedules and statements, and to the best of my knowledge and belief, it is true, correct, and complete. Declaration of preparer (other than taxpayer) is based on all information of which preparer has any knowledge.

▶ _____   _____ ▶ _____
Signature of officer   Date   Title

May the IRS discuss this return with the preparer shown below (see instructions)? ☐ **Yes** ☐ **No**

Paid Preparer Use Only

Print/Type preparer's name	Preparer's signature	Date	Check ☐ if self-employed	PTIN
Firm's name ▶			Firm's EIN ▶	
Firm's address ▶			Phone no.	

For Paperwork Reduction Act Notice, see separate instructions.   Cat. No. 11450Q   Form **1120** (2015)

Form 1120 (2015)   Page **2**

Schedule C	Dividends and Special Deductions (see instructions)	(a) Dividends received	(b) %	(c) Special deductions (a) × (b)
1	Dividends from less-than-20%-owned domestic corporations (other than debt-financed stock)		70	
2	Dividends from 20%-or-more-owned domestic corporations (other than debt-financed stock)		80	
3	Dividends on debt-financed stock of domestic and foreign corporations		see instructions	
4	Dividends on certain preferred stock of less-than-20%-owned public utilities . . .		42	
5	Dividends on certain preferred stock of 20%-or-more-owned public utilities		48	
6	Dividends from less-than-20%-owned foreign corporations and certain FSCs . . .		70	
7	Dividends from 20%-or-more-owned foreign corporations and certain FSCs . . .		80	
8	Dividends from wholly owned foreign subsidiaries		100	
9	**Total.** Add lines 1 through 8. See instructions for limitation			
10	Dividends from domestic corporations received by a small business investment company operating under the Small Business Investment Act of 1958		100	
11	Dividends from affiliated group members		100	
12	Dividends from certain FSCs		100	
13	Dividends from foreign corporations not included on lines 3, 6, 7, 8, 11, or 12 . . .			
14	Income from controlled foreign corporations under subpart F (attach Form(s) 5471) .			
15	Foreign dividend gross-up			
16	IC-DISC and former DISC dividends not included on lines 1, 2, or 3			
17	Other dividends			
18	Deduction for dividends paid on certain preferred stock of public utilities			
19	**Total dividends.** Add lines 1 through 17. Enter here and on page 1, line 4 . . . ▶			
20	**Total special deductions.** Add lines 9, 10, 11, 12, and 18. Enter here and on page 1, line 29b . . . . ▶			

Form **1120** (2015)

Form 1120 (2015)   Page **3**

Schedule J Tax Computation and Payment (see instructions)

Part I–Tax Computation

1	Check if the corporation is a member of a controlled group (attach Schedule O (Form 1120)) ▶ ☐		
2	Income tax. Check if a qualified personal service corporation (see instructions) ▶ ☐	**2**	
3	Alternative minimum tax (attach Form 4626)	**3**	
4	Add lines 2 and 3	**4**	
5a	Foreign tax credit (attach Form 1118)	5a	
b	Credit from Form 8834 (see instructions)	5b	
c	General business credit (attach Form 3800)	5c	
d	Credit for prior year minimum tax (attach Form 8827)	5d	
e	Bond credits from Form 8912	5e	
6	**Total credits.** Add lines 5a through 5e	**6**	
7	Subtract line 6 from line 4	**7**	
8	Personal holding company tax (attach Schedule PH (Form 1120))	**8**	
9a	Recapture of investment credit (attach Form 4255)	9a	
b	Recapture of low-income housing credit (attach Form 8611)	9b	
c	Interest due under the look-back method—completed long-term contracts (attach Form 8697)	9c	
d	Interest due under the look-back method—income forecast method (attach Form 8866)	9d	
e	Alternative tax on qualifying shipping activities (attach Form 8902)	9e	
f	Other (see instructions—attach statement)	9f	
10	**Total.** Add lines 9a through 9f	**10**	
11	**Total tax.** Add lines 7, 8, and 10. Enter here and on page 1, line 31	**11**	

Part II–Payments and Refundable Credits

12	2014 overpayment credited to 2015	**12**		
13	2015 estimated tax payments	**13**		
14	2015 refund applied for on Form 4466	**14**	(	)
15	Combine lines 12, 13, and 14	**15**		
16	Tax deposited with Form 7004	**16**		
17	Withholding (see instructions)	**17**		
18	**Total payments.** Add lines 15, 16, and 17	**18**		
19	Refundable credits from:			
a	Form 2439	19a		
b	Form 4136	19b		
c	Form 8827, line 8c	19c		
d	Other (attach statement—see instructions)	19d		
20	**Total credits.** Add lines 19a through 19d	**20**		
21	**Total payments and credits.** Add lines 18 and 20. Enter here and on page 1, line 32	**21**		

Schedule K Other Information (see instructions)

		Yes	No
1	Check accounting method: **a** ☐ Cash **b** ☐ Accrual **c** ☐ Other (specify) ▶ _____		
2	See the instructions and enter the:		
a	Business activity code no. ▶ _____		
b	Business activity ▶ _____		
c	Product or service ▶ _____		
3	Is the corporation a subsidiary in an affiliated group or a parent-subsidiary controlled group?		
	If "Yes," enter name and EIN of the parent corporation ▶ _____		
4	At the end of the tax year:		
a	Did any foreign or domestic corporation, partnership (including any entity treated as a partnership), trust, or tax-exempt organization own directly 20% or more, or own, directly or indirectly, 50% or more of the total voting power of all classes of the corporation's stock entitled to vote? If "Yes," complete Part I of Schedule G (Form 1120) (attach Schedule G)		
b	Did any individual or estate own directly 20% or more, or own, directly or indirectly, 50% or more of the total voting power of all classes of the corporation's stock entitled to vote? If "Yes," complete Part II of Schedule G (Form 1120) (attach Schedule G)		

Form **1120** (2015)

Form 1120 (2015)   Page **4**

Schedule K	**Other Information** *continued* (see instructions)		Yes	No

5 At the end of the tax year, did the corporation:

a Own directly 20% or more, or own, directly or indirectly, 50% or more of the total voting power of all classes of stock entitled to vote of any foreign or domestic corporation not included on **Form 851,** Affiliations Schedule? For rules of constructive ownership, see instructions. If "Yes," complete (i) through (iv) below.

(i) Name of Corporation	**(ii)** Employer Identification Number (if any)	**(iii)** Country of Incorporation	**(iv)** Percentage Owned in Voting Stock

b Own directly an interest of 20% or more, or own, directly or indirectly, an interest of 50% or more in any foreign or domestic partnership (including an entity treated as a partnership) or in the beneficial interest of a trust? For rules of constructive ownership, see instructions. If "Yes," complete (i) through (iv) below.

(i) Name of Entity	**(ii)** Employer Identification Number (if any)	**(iii)** Country of Organization	**(iv)** Maximum Percentage Owned in Profit, Loss, or Capital

6 During this tax year, did the corporation pay dividends (other than stock dividends and distributions in exchange for stock) in excess of the corporation's current and accumulated earnings and profits? (See sections 301 and 316.) . . . .

If "Yes," file **Form 5452,** Corporate Report of Nondividend Distributions.

If this is a consolidated return, answer here for the parent corporation and on Form 851 for each subsidiary.

7 At any time during the tax year, did one foreign person own, directly or indirectly, at least 25% of **(a)** the total voting power of all classes of the corporation's stock entitled to vote or **(b)** the total value of all classes of the corporation's stock? . . . .

For rules of attribution, see section 318. If "Yes," enter:

(i) Percentage owned ▶ _____ and **(ii)** Owner's country ▶ _____

(c) The corporation may have to file **Form 5472,** Information Return of a 25% Foreign-Owned U.S. Corporation or a Foreign Corporation Engaged in a U.S. Trade or Business. Enter the number of Forms 5472 attached ▶ _____

8 Check this box if the corporation issued publicly offered debt instruments with original issue discount . . . . . . ▶ ☐

If checked, the corporation may have to file **Form 8281,** Information Return for Publicly Offered Original Issue Discount Instruments.

9 Enter the amount of tax-exempt interest received or accrued during the tax year ▶ $ _____

10 Enter the number of shareholders at the end of the tax year (if 100 or fewer) ▶ _____

11 If the corporation has an NOL for the tax year and is electing to forego the carryback period, check here . . . . . ▶ ☐

If the corporation is filing a consolidated return, the statement required by Regulations section 1.1502-21(b)(3) must be attached or the election will not be valid.

12 Enter the available NOL carryover from prior tax years (do not reduce it by any deduction on line 29a.) ▶ $ _____

13 Are the corporation's total receipts (page 1, line 1a, plus lines 4 through 10) for the tax year **and** its total assets at the end of the tax year less than $250,000? . . . .

If "Yes," the corporation is not required to complete Schedules L, M-1, and M-2. Instead, enter the total amount of cash distributions and the book value of property distributions (other than cash) made during the tax year ▶ $ _____

14 Is the corporation required to file Schedule UTP (Form 1120), Uncertain Tax Position Statement (see instructions)? . . . .

If "Yes," complete and attach Schedule UTP.

15a Did the corporation make any payments in 2015 that would require it to file Form(s) 1099? . . . .

b If "Yes," did or will the corporation file required Forms 1099? . . . .

16 During this tax year, did the corporation have an 80% or more change in ownership, including a change due to redemption of its own stock? . . . .

17 During or subsequent to this tax year, but before the filing of this return, did the corporation dispose of more than 65% (by value) of its assets in a taxable, non-taxable, or tax deferred transaction? . . . .

18 Did the corporation receive assets in a section 351 transfer in which any of the transferred assets had a fair market basis or fair market value of more than $1 million? . . . .

Form **1120** (2015)

Form 1120 (2015)   Page **5**

Schedule L	**Balance Sheets per Books**	Beginning of tax year		End of tax year	
	Assets	**(a)**	**(b)**	**(c)**	**(d)**
1	Cash				
2a	Trade notes and accounts receivable . . .				
b	Less allowance for bad debts	( )		( )	
3	Inventories				
4	U.S. government obligations				
5	Tax-exempt securities (see instructions) . .				
6	Other current assets (attach statement) . .				
7	Loans to shareholders				
8	Mortgage and real estate loans				
9	Other investments (attach statement) . . .				
10a	Buildings and other depreciable assets . .				
b	Less accumulated depreciation	( )		( )	
11a	Depletable assets				
b	Less accumulated depletion	( )		( )	
12	Land (net of any amortization)				
13a	Intangible assets (amortizable only) . . .				
b	Less accumulated amortization	( )		( )	
14	Other assets (attach statement)				
15	Total assets				
	Liabilities and Shareholders' Equity				
16	Accounts payable				
17	Mortgages, notes, bonds payable in less than 1 year				
18	Other current liabilities (attach statement) . .				
19	Loans from shareholders				
20	Mortgages, notes, bonds payable in 1 year or more				
21	Other liabilities (attach statement)				
22	Capital stock: **a** Preferred stock				
	b Common stock				
23	Additional paid-in capital				
24	Retained earnings—Appropriated (attach statement)				
25	Retained earnings—Unappropriated . . .				
26	Adjustments to shareholders' equity (attach statement)				
27	Less cost of treasury stock		( )		( )
28	Total liabilities and shareholders' equity . .				

Schedule M-1	**Reconciliation of Income (Loss) per Books With Income per Return**

Note: The corporation may be required to file Schedule M-3 (see instructions).

1	Net income (loss) per books		**7**	Income recorded on books this year not included on this return (itemize):	
2	Federal income tax per books				
3	Excess of capital losses over capital gains .			Tax-exempt interest $ _____	
4	Income subject to tax not recorded on books this year (itemize): _____			_____	
			8	Deductions on this return not charged against book income this year (itemize):	
5	Expenses recorded on books this year not deducted on this return (itemize):		**a**	Depreciation . . $ _____	
a	Depreciation . . . . $ _____		**b**	Charitable contributions $ _____	
b	Charitable contributions . $ _____			_____	
c	Travel and entertainment . $ _____				
			9	Add lines 7 and 8	
6	Add lines 1 through 5		**10**	Income (page 1, line 28)—line 6 less line 9	

Schedule M-2	**Analysis of Unappropriated Retained Earnings per Books (Line 25, Schedule L)**

1	Balance at beginning of year		**5**	Distributions: **a** Cash	
2	Net income (loss) per books			**b** Stock	
3	Other increases (itemize): _____			**c** Property . . .	
	_____		**6**	Other decreases (itemize): _____	
	_____		**7**	Add lines 5 and 6	
4	Add lines 1, 2, and 3		**8**	Balance at end of year (line 4 less line 7)	

Form **1120** (2015)

SCHEDULE PH (Form 1120) (Rev. November 2015) Department of the Treasury Internal Revenue Service	**U.S. Personal Holding Company (PHC) Tax** ▶ Attach to tax return. ▶ Information about Schedule PH (Form 1120) and its separate instructions is at *www.irs.gov/form1120.*	OMB No. 1545-0123

Name		Employer identification number

Part I   Undistributed Personal Holding Company Income (see instructions)

Additions	1	Taxable income before net operating loss deduction and special deductions. Enter amount from Form 1120, line 28	**1**	
	2	Contributions deducted in figuring line 1. Enter amount from Form 1120, line 19	**2**	
	3	Excess expenses and depreciation under section 545(b)(6). Enter amount from Part V, line 2	**3**	
	4	Total. Add lines 1 through 3	**4**	
Deductions	5	Federal and foreign income, war profits, and excess profits taxes not deducted in figuring line 1 (attach schedule)	**5**	
	6	Contributions deductible under section 545(b)(2). See instructions for limitation	**6**	
	7	Net operating loss for the preceding tax year deductible under section 545(b)(4)	**7**	
	8a	Net capital gain from Schedule D (Form 1120), line 17 . . **8a**		
	b	**Less:** Income tax on this net capital gain (see section 545(b)(5)) (attach computation) **8b**	**8c**	
	9	Deduction for dividends paid (other than dividends paid after the end of the tax year). Enter amount from Part VI, line 5	**9**	
	10	Total. Add lines 5 through 9	**10**	
	11	Subtract line 10 from line 4	**11**	
	12	Dividends paid after the end of the tax year (other than deficiency dividends defined in section 547(d)), but not more than the smaller of line 11 or 20% of Part VI, line 1 . . .	**12**	
	13	**Undistributed PHC income.** Subtract line 12 from line 11	**13**	

Note: *If the information in Part II and Part IV is not submitted with the return, the limitation period for assessment and collection of the PHC tax is any time within 6 years after the return is filed. See section 6501(f).*

Part II   Personal Holding Company Income (see instructions)

14a	Dividends	**14a**		
b	**Less:** Dividends excluded (under section 543(a)(1)(C))	**14b**	**14c**	
15a	Interest	**15a**		
b	**Less:** Amounts excluded (attach schedule)	**15b**	**15c**	
16	Royalties (other than mineral, oil, gas, or copyright royalties)		**16**	
17	Annuities		**17**	
18a	Rents	**18a**		
b	**Less:** Adjustments to rents (attach schedule)	**18b**	**18c**	
19a	Mineral, oil, and gas royalties	**19a**		
b	**Less:** Adjustments to mineral, oil, and gas royalties (attach schedule)	**19b**	**19c**	
20	Copyright royalties		**20**	
21	Produced film rents		**21**	
22	Compensation received for use of corporation property by 25% or more shareholder		**22**	
23	Amounts received under personal service contracts and from their sale		**23**	
24	Amounts includible in taxable income from estates and trusts		**24**	
25	**PHC income.** Add lines 14 through 24		**25**	

Part III   Tax on Undistributed Personal Holding Company Income (see instructions)

26	**PHC tax.** Multiply the amount on line 13 by 20%. Enter the result here and on Schedule J (Form 1120), line 8, or on the proper line of the appropriate tax return	**26**	

For Paperwork Reduction Act Notice, see the Instructions for Form 1120.   Cat. No. 11465P   Schedule PH (Form 1120) (Rev. 11-2015)

Schedule PH (Form 1120) (Rev. 11-2015)   Page **2**

Part IV Stock Ownership Requirement Under Section 542(a)(2)

Enter the names and addresses of the individuals who together owned, directly or indirectly, at any time during the last half of the tax year, more than 50% in value of the outstanding stock of the corporation.

(a) Name	(b) Address	Highest percentage of shares owned during last half of tax year	
		(c) Preferred	**(d)** Common
1		%	%
		%	%
		%	%
		%	%
		%	%
2 Add the amounts in columns (c) and (d) and enter the totals here . . . . ▶		%	%

Part V Excess of Expenses and Depreciation Over Income From Property Not Allowable Under Section 545(b)(6) (see instructions for Part I, line 3)

(a) Description of property	(b) Date acquired	(c) Cost or other basis	(d) Depreciation deduction	(e) Repairs, insurance, and other expenses (section 162) (attach schedule)	(f) Total of columns (d) and (e)	(g) Income from rent or other compensation	(h) Excess (col. (f) less col. (g))
1							

2 **Total excess of expenses and depreciation over rent or other compensation.** Add the amounts in column (h). Enter the total here and on Part I, line 3 . . . .

Note: *Attach a statement showing the names and addresses of persons from whom rent or other compensation was received for the use of, or the right to use, each property.*

Part VI Deduction for Dividends Paid Under Sections 561 and 562

1	Taxable dividends paid. Do not include dividends considered as paid in the preceding tax year under section 563 or deficiency dividends as defined in section 547	**1**	
2	Consent dividends. Attach Forms 972 and 973	**2**	
3	Taxable distributions. Add lines 1 and 2	**3**	
4	Dividend carryover from first and second preceding tax years. Attach computation	**4**	
5	**Deduction for dividends paid.** Add lines 3 and 4. Enter the total here and on Part I, line 9 . .	**5**	

Schedule PH (Form 1120) (Rev. 11-2015)

B-2   U.S. Income Tax Return for an S Corporation

Form **1120S**	**U.S. Income Tax Return for an S Corporation**	OMB No. 1545-0123
Department of the Treasury Internal Revenue Service	▶ Do not file this form unless the corporation has filed or is attaching Form 2553 to elect to be an S corporation. ▶ Information about Form 1120S and its separate instructions is at *www.irs.gov/form1120s.*	20**15**

For calendar year 2015 or tax year beginning   , 2015, ending   , 20

A S election effective date	**TYPE**	Name	**D** Employer identification number
B Business activity code number (see instructions)	**OR**	Number, street, and room or suite no. If a P.O. box, see instructions.	**E** Date incorporated
C Check if Sch. M-3 attached ☐	**PRINT**	City or town, state or province, country, and ZIP or foreign postal code	**F** Total assets (see instructions) $

G   Is the corporation electing to be an S corporation beginning with this tax year? ☐ Yes ☐ No   If "Yes," attach Form 2553 if not already filed

H   Check if: **(1)** ☐ Final return   **(2)** ☐ Name change   **(3)** ☐ Address change   **(4)** ☐ Amended return   **(5)** ☐ S election termination or revocation

I   Enter the number of shareholders who were shareholders during any part of the tax year   . . . . ▶

Caution: Include **only** trade or business income and expenses on lines 1a through 21. See the instructions for more information.

Income

1a	Gross receipts or sales	**1a**	
b	Returns and allowances	**1b**	
c	Balance. Subtract line 1b from line 1a	**1c**	
2	Cost of goods sold (attach Form 1125-A)	**2**	
3	Gross profit. Subtract line 2 from line 1c	**3**	
4	Net gain (loss) from Form 4797, line 17 (attach Form 4797)	**4**	
5	Other income (loss) (see instructions—attach statement)	**5**	
6	**Total income (loss).** Add lines 3 through 5 . . . . ▶	**6**	

Deductions (see instructions for limitations)

7	Compensation of officers (see instructions—attach Form 1125-E) . . .	**7**	
8	Salaries and wages (less employment credits)	**8**	
9	Repairs and maintenance	**9**	
10	Bad debts	**10**	
11	Rents	**11**	
12	Taxes and licenses	**12**	
13	Interest	**13**	
14	Depreciation not claimed on Form 1125-A or elsewhere on return (attach Form 4562)	**14**	
15	Depletion (**Do not deduct oil and gas depletion.**)	**15**	
16	Advertising	**16**	
17	Pension, profit-sharing, etc., plans	**17**	
18	Employee benefit programs	**18**	
19	Other deductions (attach statement)	**19**	
20	**Total deductions.** Add lines 7 through 19 . . . . ▶	**20**	
21	**Ordinary business income (loss).** Subtract line 20 from line 6	**21**	

Tax and Payments

22a	Excess net passive income or LIFO recapture tax (see instructions) . .	**22a**	
b	Tax from Schedule D (Form 1120S)	**22b**	
c	Add lines 22a and 22b (see instructions for additional taxes) . . .	**22c**	
23a	2015 estimated tax payments and 2014 overpayment credited to 2015	**23a**	
b	Tax deposited with Form 7004	**23b**	
c	Credit for federal tax paid on fuels (attach Form 4136)	**23c**	
d	Add lines 23a through 23c	**23d**	
24	Estimated tax penalty (see instructions). Check if Form 2220 is attached . . . . . . ▶ ☐	**24**	
25	**Amount owed.** If line 23d is smaller than the total of lines 22c and 24, enter amount owed . .	**25**	
26	**Overpayment.** If line 23d is larger than the total of lines 22c and 24, enter amount overpaid . .	**26**	
27	Enter amount from line 26 **Credited to 2016 estimated tax** ▶ **Refunded** ▶	**27**	

Sign Here

Under penalties of perjury, I declare that I have examined this return, including accompanying schedules and statements, and to the best of my knowledge and belief, it is true, correct, and complete. Declaration of preparer (other than taxpayer) is based on all information of which preparer has any knowledge.

▶ _____ Signature of officer   Date   ▶ _____ Title

May the IRS discuss this return with the preparer shown below (see instructions)? ☐ Yes ☐ No

Paid Preparer Use Only

Print/Type preparer's name	Preparer's signature	Date	Check ☐ if self-employed	PTIN
Firm's name ▶			Firm's EIN ▶	
Firm's address ▶			Phone no.	

For Paperwork Reduction Act Notice, see separate instructions.   Cat. No. 11510H   Form **1120S** (2015)

Form 1120S (2015)   Page **2**

Schedule B	**Other Information** (see instructions)		**Yes**	**No**

1 Check accounting method: **a** ☐ Cash   **b** ☐ Accrual

        c ☐ Other (specify) ▶ _____

2 See the instructions and enter the:

   a Business activity ▶ _____   **b** Product or service ▶ _____

3 At any time during the tax year, was any shareholder of the corporation a disregarded entity, a trust, an estate, or a nominee or similar person? If "Yes," attach Schedule B-1, Information on Certain Shareholders of an S Corporation . .

4 At the end of the tax year, did the corporation:

  a Own directly 20% or more, or own, directly or indirectly, 50% or more of the total stock issued and outstanding of any foreign or domestic corporation? For rules of constructive ownership, see instructions. If "Yes," complete (i) through (v) below . . . .

(i) Name of Corporation	**(ii)** Employer Identification Number (if any)	**(iii)** Country of Incorporation	**(iv)** Percentage of Stock Owned	**(v)** If Percentage in (iv) is 100%, Enter the Date (if any) a Qualified Subchapter S Subsidiary Election Was Made

  b Own directly an interest of 20% or more, or own, directly or indirectly, an interest of 50% or more in the profit, loss, or capital in any foreign or domestic partnership (including an entity treated as a partnership) or in the beneficial interest of a trust? For rules of constructive ownership, see instructions. If "Yes," complete (i) through (v) below . . . .

(i) Name of Entity	**(ii)** Employer Identification Number (if any)	**(iii)** Type of Entity	**(iv)** Country of Organization	**(v)** Maximum Percentage Owned in Profit, Loss, or Capital

5 a At the end of the tax year, did the corporation have any outstanding shares of restricted stock? . . . .

    If "Yes," complete lines (i) and (ii) below.

    (i)   Total shares of restricted stock . . . . ▶ _____

    (ii)   Total shares of non-restricted stock . . . . ▶ _____

  b At the end of the tax year, did the corporation have any outstanding stock options, warrants, or similar instruments? .

    If "Yes," complete lines (i) and (ii) below.

    (i)   Total shares of stock outstanding at the end of the tax year ▶ _____

    (ii)   Total shares of stock outstanding if all instruments were executed ▶ _____

6 Has this corporation filed, or is it required to file, **Form 8918**, Material Advisor Disclosure Statement, to provide information on any reportable transaction? . . . .

7 Check this box if the corporation issued publicly offered debt instruments with original issue discount . . . . ▶ ☐

    If checked, the corporation may have to file **Form 8281,** Information Return for Publicly Offered Original Issue Discount Instruments.

8 If the corporation: **(a)** was a C corporation before it elected to be an S corporation **or** the corporation acquired an asset with a basis determined by reference to the basis of the asset (or the basis of any other property) in the hands of a C corporation **and (b)** has net unrealized built-in gain in excess of the net recognized built-in gain from prior years, enter the net unrealized built-in gain reduced by net recognized built-in gain from prior years (see instructions) . . . . ▶ $ _____

9 Enter the accumulated earnings and profits of the corporation at the end of the tax year. $ _____

10 Does the corporation satisfy **both** of the following conditions?

  a The corporation's total receipts (see instructions) for the tax year were less than $250,000 . . . .

  b The corporation's total assets at the end of the tax year were less than $250,000 . . . .

    If "Yes," the corporation is not required to complete Schedules L and M-1.

11 During the tax year, did the corporation have any non-shareholder debt that was canceled, was forgiven, or had the terms modified so as to reduce the principal amount of the debt? . . . .

    If "Yes," enter the amount of principal reduction $ _____

12 During the tax year, was a qualified subchapter S subsidiary election terminated or revoked? If "Yes," see instructions .

13a Did the corporation make any payments in 2015 that would require it to file Form(s) 1099? . . . .

  b If "Yes," did the corporation file or will it file required Forms 1099? . . . .

Form **1120S** (2015)

Form 1120S (2015)   Page **3**

Schedule K		Shareholders' Pro Rata Share Items		Total amount	

Income (Loss)

1	Ordinary business income (loss) (page 1, line 21)	1		
2	Net rental real estate income (loss) (attach Form 8825)	2		
3a	Other gross rental income (loss) ... 3a			
b	Expenses from other rental activities (attach statement) ... 3b			
c	Other net rental income (loss). Subtract line 3b from line 3a	3c		
4	Interest income	4		
5	Dividends: a Ordinary dividends	5a		
	b Qualified dividends ... 5b			
6	Royalties	6		
7	Net short-term capital gain (loss) (attach Schedule D (Form 1120S))	7		
8a	Net long-term capital gain (loss) (attach Schedule D (Form 1120S))	8a		
b	Collectibles (28%) gain (loss) ... 8b			
c	Unrecaptured section 1250 gain (attach statement) ... 8c			
9	Net section 1231 gain (loss) (attach Form 4797)	9		
10	Other income (loss) (see instructions) ... Type ▶	10		

Deductions

11	Section 179 deduction (attach Form 4562)	11		
12a	Charitable contributions	12a		
b	Investment interest expense	12b		
c	Section 59(e)(2) expenditures (1) Type ▶ _____ (2) Amount ▶	12c(2)		
d	Other deductions (see instructions) ... Type ▶	12d		

Credits

13a	Low-income housing credit (section 42(j)(5))	13a		
b	Low-income housing credit (other)	13b		
c	Qualified rehabilitation expenditures (rental real estate) (attach Form 3468, if applicable)	13c		
d	Other rental real estate credits (see instructions) Type ▶	13d		
e	Other rental credits (see instructions) ... Type ▶	13e		
f	Biofuel producer credit (attach Form 6478)	13f		
g	Other credits (see instructions) ... Type ▶	13g		

Foreign Transactions

14a	Name of country or U.S. possession ▶			
b	Gross income from all sources	14b		
c	Gross income sourced at shareholder level	14c		
	Foreign gross income sourced at corporate level			
d	Passive category	14d		
e	General category	14e		
f	Other (attach statement)	14f		
	Deductions allocated and apportioned at shareholder level			
g	Interest expense	14g		
h	Other	14h		
	Deductions allocated and apportioned at corporate level to foreign source income			
i	Passive category	14i		
j	General category	14j		
k	Other (attach statement)	14k		
	Other information			
l	Total foreign taxes (check one): ▶ ☐ Paid ☐ Accrued	14l		
m	Reduction in taxes available for credit (attach statement)	14m		
n	Other foreign tax information (attach statement)			

Alternative Minimum Tax (AMT) Items

15a	Post-1986 depreciation adjustment	15a		
b	Adjusted gain or loss	15b		
c	Depletion (other than oil and gas)	15c		
d	Oil, gas, and geothermal properties—gross income	15d		
e	Oil, gas, and geothermal properties—deductions	15e		
f	Other AMT items (attach statement)	15f		

Items Affecting Shareholder Basis

16a	Tax-exempt interest income	16a		
b	Other tax-exempt income	16b		
c	Nondeductible expenses	16c		
d	Distributions (attach statement if required) (see instructions)	16d		
e	Repayment of loans from shareholders	16e		

Form **1120S** (2015)

Form 1120S (2015)   Page **4**

Schedule K	**Shareholders' Pro Rata Share Items** (continued)		Total amount	
Other Information	**17a** Investment income	**17a**		
	b Investment expenses	**17b**		
	c Dividend distributions paid from accumulated earnings and profits	**17c**		
	d Other items and amounts (attach statement)			
Recon- ciliation	**18** **Income/loss reconciliation.** Combine the amounts on lines 1 through 10 in the far right column. From the result, subtract the sum of the amounts on lines 11 through 12d and 14l	**18**		

Schedule L	**Balance Sheets per Books**	Beginning of tax year		End of tax year	
	Assets	(a)	(b)	(c)	(d)
1	Cash				
2a	Trade notes and accounts receivable . . .				
b	Less allowance for bad debts	( )		( )	
3	Inventories				
4	U.S. government obligations				
5	Tax-exempt securities (see instructions) . .				
6	Other current assets (attach statement) . . .				
7	Loans to shareholders				
8	Mortgage and real estate loans				
9	Other investments (attach statement) . . .				
10a	Buildings and other depreciable assets . . .				
b	Less accumulated depreciation	( )		( )	
11a	Depletable assets				
b	Less accumulated depletion	( )		( )	
12	Land (net of any amortization)				
13a	Intangible assets (amortizable only)				
b	Less accumulated amortization	( )		( )	
14	Other assets (attach statement)				
15	Total assets				
	Liabilities and Shareholders' Equity				
16	Accounts payable				
17	Mortgages, notes, bonds payable in less than 1 year				
18	Other current liabilities (attach statement) . .				
19	Loans from shareholders				
20	Mortgages, notes, bonds payable in 1 year or more				
21	Other liabilities (attach statement)				
22	Capital stock				
23	Additional paid-in capital				
24	Retained earnings				
25	Adjustments to shareholders' equity (attach statement)				
26	Less cost of treasury stock		( )		( )
27	Total liabilities and shareholders' equity . .				

Form **1120S** (2015)

Form 1120S (2015)   Page **5**

Schedule M-1	**Reconciliation of Income (Loss) per Books With Income (Loss) per Return**

Note: The corporation may be required to file Schedule M-3 (see instructions)

1	Net income (loss) per books		5	Income recorded on books this year not included on Schedule K, lines 1 through 10 (itemize):	
2	Income included on Schedule K, lines 1, 2, 3c, 4, 5a, 6, 7, 8a, 9, and 10, not recorded on books this year (itemize)		a	Tax-exempt interest $	
3	Expenses recorded on books this year not included on Schedule K, lines 1 through 12 and 14l (itemize):		6	Deductions included on Schedule K, lines 1 through 12 and 14l, not charged against book income this year (itemize):	
a	Depreciation $		a	Depreciation $	
b	Travel and entertainment $				
			7	Add lines 5 and 6	
4	Add lines 1 through 3		8	Income (loss) (Schedule K, line 18). Line 4 less line 7	

Schedule M-2	**Analysis of Accumulated Adjustments Account, Other Adjustments Account, and Shareholders' Undistributed Taxable Income Previously Taxed** (see instructions)

		(a) Accumulated adjustments account	**(b)** Other adjustments account	**(c)** Shareholders' undistributed taxable income previously taxed
1	Balance at beginning of tax year			
2	Ordinary income from page 1, line 21 . . .			
3	Other additions			
4	Loss from page 1, line 21	( )		
5	Other reductions	( )	( )	
6	Combine lines 1 through 5			
7	Distributions other than dividend distributions			
8	Balance at end of tax year. Subtract line 7 from line 6			

Form **1120S** (2015)

671113

| | | | Final K-1 | | Amended K-1 | OMB No. 1545-0123 |

Schedule K-1
(Form 1120S)
Department of the Treasury
Internal Revenue Service

20**15**

For calendar year 2015, or tax
year beginning _____ , 2015
ending _____ , 20 ___

Shareholder's Share of Income, Deductions, Credits, etc.   ▶ See back of form and separate instructions.

| **Part I** | **Information About the Corporation** |

A   Corporation's employer identification number

B   Corporation's name, address, city, state, and ZIP code

C   IRS Center where corporation filed return

| **Part II** | **Information About the Shareholder** |

D   Shareholder's identifying number

E   Shareholder's name, address, city, state, and ZIP code

F   Shareholder's percentage of stock
ownership for tax year   .   .   .   . _____ %

For IRS Use Only

Part III	**Shareholder's Share of Current Year Income, Deductions, Credits, and Other Items**	
1	Ordinary business income (loss)	13	Credits
2	Net rental real estate income (loss)		
3	Other net rental income (loss)		
4	Interest income		
5a	Ordinary dividends		
5b	Qualified dividends	14	Foreign transactions
6	Royalties		
7	Net short-term capital gain (loss)		
8a	Net long-term capital gain (loss)		
8b	Collectibles (28%) gain (loss)		
8c	Unrecaptured section 1250 gain		
9	Net section 1231 gain (loss)		
10	Other income (loss)	15	Alternative minimum tax (AMT) items
11	Section 179 deduction	16	Items affecting shareholder basis
12	Other deductions		
		17	Other information

* See attached statement for additional information.

For Paperwork Reduction Act Notice, see Instructions for Form 1120S.   IRS.gov/form1120s   Cat. No. 11520D   **Schedule K-1 (Form 1120S) 2015**

Schedule K-1 (Form 1120S) 2015   Page **2**

This list identifies the codes used on Schedule K-1 for all shareholders and provides summarized reporting information for shareholders who file Form 1040. For detailed reporting and filing information, see the separate Shareholder's Instructions for Schedule K-1 and the instructions for your income tax return.

1. Ordinary business income (loss). Determine whether the income (loss) is passive or nonpassive and enter on your return as follows:

	Report on
Passive loss	See the Shareholder's Instructions
Passive income	Schedule E, line 28, column (g)
Nonpassive loss	Schedule E, line 28, column (h)
Nonpassive income	Schedule E, line 28, column (j)

2. Net rental real estate income (loss)   See the Shareholder's Instructions

3. Other net rental income (loss)
Net income	Schedule E, line 28, column (g)
Net loss	See the Shareholder's Instructions

4. Interest income   Form 1040, line 8a
5a. Ordinary dividends   Form 1040, line 9a
5b. Qualified dividends   Form 1040, line 9b
6. Royalties   Schedule E, line 4
7. Net short-term capital gain (loss)   Schedule D, line 5
8a. Net long-term capital gain (loss)   Schedule D, line 12
8b. Collectibles (28%) gain (loss)   28% Rate Gain Worksheet, line 4 (Schedule D instructions)
8c. Unrecaptured section 1250 gain   See the Shareholder's Instructions
9. Net section 1231 gain (loss)   See the Shareholder's Instructions

10. Other income (loss)
Code
A	Other portfolio income (loss)	See the Shareholder's Instructions
B	Involuntary conversions	See the Shareholder's Instructions
C	Sec. 1256 contracts & straddles	Form 6781, line 1
D	Mining exploration costs recapture	See Pub. 535
E	Other income (loss)	See the Shareholder's Instructions

11. Section 179 deduction   See the Shareholder's Instructions

12. Other deductions
A	Cash contributions (50%)	
B	Cash contributions (30%)	
C	Noncash contributions (50%)	
D	Noncash contributions (30%)	See the Shareholder's Instructions
E	Capital gain property to a 50% organization (30%)	
F	Capital gain property (20%)	
G	Contributions (100%)	
H	Investment interest expense	Form 4952, line 1
I	Deductions—royalty income	Schedule E, line 19
J	Section 59(e)(2) expenditures	See the Shareholder's Instructions
K	Deductions—portfolio (2% floor)	Schedule A, line 23
L	Deductions—portfolio (other)	Schedule A, line 28
M	Preproductive period expenses	See the Shareholder's Instructions
N	Commercial revitalization deduction from rental real estate activities	See Form 8582 instructions
O	Reforestation expense deduction	See the Shareholder's Instructions
P	Domestic production activities information	See Form 8903 instructions
Q	Qualified production activities income	Form 8903, line 7b
R	Employer's Form W-2 wages	Form 8903, line 17
S	Other deductions	See the Shareholder's Instructions

13. Credits
A	Low-income housing credit (section 42(j)(5)) from pre-2008 buildings	
B	Low-income housing credit (other) from pre-2008 buildings	
C	Low-income housing credit (section 42(j)(5)) from post-2007 buildings	See the Shareholder's Instructions
D	Low-income housing credit (other) from post-2007 buildings	
E	Qualified rehabilitation expenditures (rental real estate)	
F	Other rental real estate credits	
G	Other rental credits	
H	Undistributed capital gains credit	Form 1040, line 73, box a
I	Biofuel producer credit	
J	Work opportunity credit	
K	Disabled access credit	See the Shareholder's Instructions
L	Empowerment zone employment credit	
M	Credit for increasing research activities	

	Code		*Report on*
N	Credit for employer social security and Medicare taxes		
O	Backup withholding		See the Shareholder's Instructions
P	Other credits		

14. Foreign transactions
A	Name of country or U.S. possession	
B	Gross income from all sources	Form 1116, Part I
C	Gross income sourced at shareholder level	

Foreign gross income sourced at corporate level
D	Passive category	
E	General category	Form 1116, Part I
F	Other	

Deductions allocated and apportioned at shareholder level
G	Interest expense	Form 1116, Part I
H	Other	Form 1116, Part I

Deductions allocated and apportioned at corporate level to foreign source income
I	Passive category	
J	General category	Form 1116, Part I
K	Other	

Other information
L	Total foreign taxes paid	Form 1116, Part II
M	Total foreign taxes accrued	Form 1116, Part II
N	Reduction in taxes available for credit	Form 1116, line 12
O	Foreign trading gross receipts	Form 8873
P	Extraterritorial income exclusion	Form 8873
Q	Other foreign transactions	See the Shareholder's Instructions

15. Alternative minimum tax (AMT) items
A	Post-1986 depreciation adjustment	
B	Adjusted gain or loss	See the Shareholder's Instructions and the Instructions for Form 6251
C	Depletion (other than oil & gas)	
D	Oil, gas, & geothermal—gross income	
E	Oil, gas, & geothermal—deductions	
F	Other AMT items	

16. Items affecting shareholder basis
A	Tax-exempt interest income	Form 1040, line 8b
B	Other tax-exempt income	
C	Nondeductible expenses	See the Shareholder's Instructions
D	Distributions	
E	Repayment of loans from shareholders	

17. Other information
A	Investment income	Form 4952, line 4a
B	Investment expenses	Form 4952, line 5
C	Qualified rehabilitation expenditures (other than rental real estate)	See the Shareholder's Instructions
D	Basis of energy property	See the Shareholder's Instructions
E	Recapture of low-income housing credit (section 42(j)(5))	Form 8611, line 8
F	Recapture of low-income housing credit (other)	Form 8611, line 8
G	Recapture of investment credit	See Form 4255
H	Recapture of other credits	See the Shareholder's Instructions
I	Look-back interest—completed long-term contracts	See Form 8697
J	Look-back interest—income forecast method	See Form 8866
K	Dispositions of property with section 179 deductions	
L	Recapture of section 179 deduction	
M	Section 453(l)(3) information	
N	Section 453A(c) information	
O	Section 1260(b) information	
P	Interest allocable to production expenditures	See the Shareholder's Instructions
Q	CCF nonqualified withdrawals	
R	Depletion information—oil and gas	
S	Reserved	
T	Section 108(i) information	
U	Net investment income	
V	Other information	

Form **1065**	**U.S. Return of Partnership Income**	OMB No. 1545-0123
Department of the Treasury Internal Revenue Service	For calendar year 2015, or tax year beginning _____ , 2015, ending _____ , 20 ____ . ▶ Information about Form 1065 and its separate instructions is at *www.irs.gov/form1065.*	**2015**

A Principal business activity	**Type or Print**	Name of partnership	D Employer identification number
B Principal product or service		Number, street, and room or suite no. If a P.O. box, see the instructions.	E Date business started
C Business code number		City or town, state or province, country, and ZIP or foreign postal code	F Total assets (see the instructions) $

G Check applicable boxes: **(1)** ☐ Initial return **(2)** ☐ Final return **(3)** ☐ Name change **(4)** ☐ Address change **(5)** ☐ Amended return
  (6) ☐ Technical termination - also check (1) or (2)

H Check accounting method: **(1)** ☐ Cash **(2)** ☐ Accrual **(3)** ☐ Other (specify) ▶ _____

I Number of Schedules K-1. Attach one for each person who was a partner at any time during the tax year ▶ _____

J Check if Schedules C and M-3 are attached . . . . ☐

Caution. *Include **only** trade or business income and expenses on lines 1a through 22 below. See the instructions for more information.*

Income	**1a**	Gross receipts or sales	**1a**		
	b	Returns and allowances	**1b**		
	c	Balance. Subtract line 1b from line 1a	**1c**	
	2	Cost of goods sold (attach Form 1125-A)	**2**	
	3	Gross profit. Subtract line 2 from line 1c	**3**	
	4	Ordinary income (loss) from other partnerships, estates, and trusts (attach statement) . .	**4**	
	5	Net farm profit (loss) (attach Schedule F (Form 1040))	**5**	
	6	Net gain (loss) from Form 4797, Part II, line 17 (attach Form 4797)	**6**	
	7	Other income (loss) (attach statement)	**7**	
	8	**Total income (loss).** Combine lines 3 through 7	**8**	
Deductions (see the instructions for limitations)	**9**	Salaries and wages (other than to partners) (less employment credits)	**9**	
	10	Guaranteed payments to partners	**10**	
	11	Repairs and maintenance	**11**	
	12	Bad debts	**12**	
	13	Rent	**13**	
	14	Taxes and licenses	**14**	
	15	Interest	**15**	
	16a	Depreciation (if required, attach Form 4562) .	**16a**		
	b	Less depreciation reported on Form 1125-A and elsewhere on return	**16b**	**16c**	
	17	Depletion **(Do not deduct oil and gas depletion.)**	**17**	
	18	Retirement plans, etc.	**18**	
	19	Employee benefit programs	**19**	
	20	Other deductions (attach statement)	**20**	
	21	**Total deductions.** Add the amounts shown in the far right column for lines 9 through 20 .	**21**	
	22	**Ordinary business income (loss).** Subtract line 21 from line 8	**22**	

Sign Here	Under penalties of perjury, I declare that I have examined this return, including accompanying schedules and statements, and to the best of my knowledge and belief, it is true, correct, and complete. Declaration of preparer (other than general partner or limited liability company member manager) is based on all information of which preparer has any knowledge.	May the IRS discuss this return with the preparer shown below (see instructions)? ☐ **Yes** ☐ **No**
	▶ _____ ▶ _____ Signature of general partner or limited liability company member manager Date	

Paid Preparer Use Only	Print/Type preparer's name	Preparer's signature	Date	Check ☐ if self-employed	PTIN
	Firm's name ▶			Firm's EIN ▶	
	Firm's address ▶			Phone no.	

For Paperwork Reduction Act Notice, see separate instructions.   Cat. No. 11390Z   Form **1065** (2015)

Form 1065 (2015) Page **2**

Schedule B	**Other Information**		

		Yes	No
1	What type of entity is filing this return? Check the applicable box:		

a ☐ Domestic general partnership   **b** ☐ Domestic limited partnership

c ☐ Domestic limited liability company   **d** ☐ Domestic limited liability partnership

e ☐ Foreign partnership   **f** ☐ Other ▶

2 At any time during the tax year, was any partner in the partnership a disregarded entity, a partnership (including an entity treated as a partnership), a trust, an S corporation, an estate (other than an estate of a deceased partner), or a nominee or similar person? . . . .

3 At the end of the tax year:

a Did any foreign or domestic corporation, partnership (including any entity treated as a partnership), trust, or tax-exempt organization, or any foreign government own, directly or indirectly, an interest of 50% or more in the profit, loss, or capital of the partnership? For rules of constructive ownership, see instructions. If "Yes," attach Schedule B-1, Information on Partners Owning 50% or More of the Partnership . . . .

b Did any individual or estate own, directly or indirectly, an interest of 50% or more in the profit, loss, or capital of the partnership? For rules of constructive ownership, see instructions. If "Yes," attach Schedule B-1, Information on Partners Owning 50% or More of the Partnership . . . .

4 At the end of the tax year, did the partnership:

a Own directly 20% or more, or own, directly or indirectly, 50% or more of the total voting power of all classes of stock entitled to vote of any foreign or domestic corporation? For rules of constructive ownership, see instructions. If "Yes," complete (i) through (iv) below . . . .

(i) Name of Corporation	**(ii)** Employer Identification Number (if any)	**(iii)** Country of Incorporation	**(iv)** Percentage Owned in Voting Stock

b Own directly an interest of 20% or more, or own, directly or indirectly, an interest of 50% or more in the profit, loss, or capital in any foreign or domestic partnership (including an entity treated as a partnership) or in the beneficial interest of a trust? For rules of constructive ownership, see instructions. If "Yes," complete (i) through (v) below . .

(i) Name of Entity	**(ii)** Employer Identification Number (if any)	**(iii)** Type of Entity	**(iv)** Country of Organization	**(v)** Maximum Percentage Owned in Profit, Loss, or Capital

		Yes	No
5	Did the partnership file Form 8893, Election of Partnership Level Tax Treatment, or an election statement under section 6231(a)(1)(B)(ii) for partnership-level tax treatment, that is in effect for this tax year? See Form 8893 for more details		

6 Does the partnership satisfy **all four** of the following conditions?

a The partnership's total receipts for the tax year were less than $250,000.

b The partnership's total assets at the end of the tax year were less than $1 million.

c Schedules K-1 are filed with the return and furnished to the partners on or before the due date (including extensions) for the partnership return.

d The partnership is not filing and is not required to file Schedule M-3 . . . .

If "Yes," the partnership is not required to complete Schedules L, M-1, and M-2; Item F on page 1 of Form 1065; or Item L on Schedule K-1.

7 Is this partnership a publicly traded partnership as defined in section 469(k)(2)? . . . .

8 During the tax year, did the partnership have any debt that was cancelled, was forgiven, or had the terms modified so as to reduce the principal amount of the debt? . . . .

9 Has this partnership filed, or is it required to file, Form 8918, Material Advisor Disclosure Statement, to provide information on any reportable transaction? . . . .

10 At any time during calendar year 2015, did the partnership have an interest in or a signature or other authority over a financial account in a foreign country (such as a bank account, securities account, or other financial account)? See the instructions for exceptions and filing requirements for FinCEN Form 114, Report of Foreign Bank and Financial Accounts (FBAR). If "Yes," enter the name of the foreign country. ▶

Form **1065** (2015)

Form 1065 (2015)   Page **3**

Schedule B	**Other Information** *(continued)*	Yes	No

		Yes	No
11	At any time during the tax year, did the partnership receive a distribution from, or was it the grantor of, or transferor to, a foreign trust? If "Yes," the partnership may have to file Form 3520, Annual Return To Report Transactions With Foreign Trusts and Receipt of Certain Foreign Gifts. See instructions		
12a	Is the partnership making, or had it previously made (and not revoked), a section 754 election? . . . . See instructions for details regarding a section 754 election.		
b	Did the partnership make for this tax year an optional basis adjustment under section 743(b) or 734(b)? If "Yes," attach a statement showing the computation and allocation of the basis adjustment. See instructions		
c	Is the partnership required to adjust the basis of partnership assets under section 743(b) or 734(b) because of a substantial built-in loss (as defined under section 743(d)) or substantial basis reduction (as defined under section 734(d))? If "Yes," attach a statement showing the computation and allocation of the basis adjustment. See instructions		
13	Check this box if, during the current or prior tax year, the partnership distributed any property received in a like-kind exchange or contributed such property to another entity (other than disregarded entities wholly owned by the partnership throughout the tax year) . . . . ▶ ☐		
14	At any time during the tax year, did the partnership distribute to any partner a tenancy-in-common or other undivided interest in partnership property?		
15	If the partnership is required to file Form 8858, Information Return of U.S. Persons With Respect To Foreign Disregarded Entities, enter the number of Forms 8858 attached. See instructions ▶		
16	Does the partnership have any foreign partners? If "Yes," enter the number of Forms 8805, Foreign Partner's Information Statement of Section 1446 Withholding Tax, filed for this partnership. ▶		
17	Enter the number of Forms 8865, Return of U.S. Persons With Respect to Certain Foreign Partnerships, attached to this return. ▶		
18a	Did you make any payments in 2015 that would require you to file Form(s) 1099? See instructions		
b	If "Yes," did you or will you file required Form(s) 1099?		
19	Enter the number of Form(s) 5471, Information Return of U.S. Persons With Respect To Certain Foreign Corporations, attached to this return. ▶		
20	Enter the number of partners that are foreign governments under section 892. ▶		

Designation of Tax Matters Partner (see instructions)

Enter below the general partner or member-manager designated as the tax matters partner (TMP) for the tax year of this return:

Name of designated TMP ▶ _____	Identifying number of TMP ▶ _____
If the TMP is an entity, name of TMP representative ▶ _____	Phone number of TMP ▶ _____
Address of designated TMP ▶ _____	

Form **1065** (2015)

Form 1065 (2015)   Page **4**

Schedule K — Partners' Distributive Share Items

			Total amount
Income (Loss)	**1** Ordinary business income (loss) (page 1, line 22)	**1**	
	2 Net rental real estate income (loss) (attach Form 8825)	**2**	
	3a Other gross rental income (loss) **3a**		
	b Expenses from other rental activities (attach statement) **3b**		
	c Other net rental income (loss). Subtract line 3b from line 3a	**3c**	
	4 Guaranteed payments	**4**	
	5 Interest income	**5**	
	6 Dividends: **a** Ordinary dividends	**6a**	
	b Qualified dividends **6b**		
	7 Royalties	**7**	
	8 Net short-term capital gain (loss) (attach Schedule D (Form 1065))	**8**	
	9a Net long-term capital gain (loss) (attach Schedule D (Form 1065))	**9a**	
	b Collectibles (28%) gain (loss) **9b**		
	c Unrecaptured section 1250 gain (attach statement) .. **9c**		
	10 Net section 1231 gain (loss) (attach Form 4797)	**10**	
	11 Other income (loss) (see instructions) Type ▶	**11**	
Deductions	**12** Section 179 deduction (attach Form 4562)	**12**	
	13a Contributions	**13a**	
	b Investment interest expense	**13b**	
	c Section 59(e)(2) expenditures: **(1)** Type ▶____ **(2)** Amount ▶	**13c(2)**	
	d Other deductions (see instructions) Type ▶	**13d**	
Self-Employment	**14a** Net earnings (loss) from self-employment	**14a**	
	b Gross farming or fishing income	**14b**	
	c Gross nonfarm income	**14c**	
Credits	**15a** Low-income housing credit (section 42(j)(5))	**15a**	
	b Low-income housing credit (other)	**15b**	
	c Qualified rehabilitation expenditures (rental real estate) (attach Form 3468, if applicable)	**15c**	
	d Other rental real estate credits (see instructions) Type ▶	**15d**	
	e Other rental credits (see instructions) Type ▶	**15e**	
	f Other credits (see instructions) Type ▶	**15f**	
Foreign Transactions	**16a** Name of country or U.S. possession ▶		
	b Gross income from all sources	**16b**	
	c Gross income sourced at partner level	**16c**	
	Foreign gross income sourced at partnership level		
	d Passive category ▶____ **e** General category ▶____ **f** Other ▶	**16f**	
	Deductions allocated and apportioned at partner level		
	g Interest expense ▶____ **h** Other .... ▶	**16h**	
	Deductions allocated and apportioned at partnership level to foreign source income		
	i Passive category ▶____ **j** General category ▶____ **k** Other ▶	**16k**	
	l Total foreign taxes (check one): ▶ Paid ☐ Accrued ☐ ____	**16l**	
	m Reduction in taxes available for credit (attach statement)	**16m**	
	n Other foreign tax information (attach statement)		
Alternative Minimum Tax (AMT) Items	**17a** Post-1986 depreciation adjustment	**17a**	
	b Adjusted gain or loss	**17b**	
	c Depletion (other than oil and gas)	**17c**	
	d Oil, gas, and geothermal properties—gross income	**17d**	
	e Oil, gas, and geothermal properties—deductions	**17e**	
	f Other AMT items (attach statement)	**17f**	
Other Information	**18a** Tax-exempt interest income	**18a**	
	b Other tax-exempt income	**18b**	
	c Nondeductible expenses	**18c**	
	19a Distributions of cash and marketable securities	**19a**	
	b Distributions of other property	**19b**	
	20a Investment income	**20a**	
	b Investment expenses	**20b**	
	c Other items and amounts (attach statement)		

Form **1065** (2015)

Form 1065 (2015)   Page **5**

Analysis of Net Income (Loss)

1	Net income (loss). Combine Schedule K, lines 1 through 11. From the result, subtract the sum of Schedule K, lines 12 through 13d, and 16l	**1**

2	Analysis by partner type:	**(i)** Corporate	**(ii)** Individual (active)	**(iii)** Individual (passive)	**(iv)** Partnership	**(v)** Exempt Organization	**(vi)** Nominee/Other
a	General partners						
b	Limited partners						

Schedule L   Balance Sheets per Books

	Assets	Beginning of tax year (a)	(b)	End of tax year (c)	(d)
1	Cash				
2a	Trade notes and accounts receivable . . .				
b	Less allowance for bad debts				
3	Inventories				
4	U.S. government obligations				
5	Tax-exempt securities				
6	Other current assets (attach statement) . .				
7a	Loans to partners (or persons related to partners)				
b	Mortgage and real estate loans				
8	Other investments (attach statement) . . .				
9a	Buildings and other depreciable assets . .				
b	Less accumulated depreciation				
10a	Depletable assets				
b	Less accumulated depletion				
11	Land (net of any amortization)				
12a	Intangible assets (amortizable only) . . .				
b	Less accumulated amortization				
13	Other assets (attach statement)				
14	Total assets				
	Liabilities and Capital				
15	Accounts payable				
16	Mortgages, notes, bonds payable in less than 1 year				
17	Other current liabilities (attach statement) .				
18	All nonrecourse loans				
19a	Loans from partners (or persons related to partners)				
b	Mortgages, notes, bonds payable in 1 year or more				
20	Other liabilities (attach statement)				
21	Partners' capital accounts				
22	Total liabilities and capital				

Schedule M-1   Reconciliation of Income (Loss) per Books With Income (Loss) per Return
Note. The partnership may be required to file Schedule M-3 (see instructions).

1	Net income (loss) per books		**6**	Income recorded on books this year not included on Schedule K, lines 1 through 11 (itemize):	
2	Income included on Schedule K, lines 1, 2, 3c, 5, 6a, 7, 8, 9a, 10, and 11, not recorded on books this year (itemize):		**a**	Tax-exempt interest $	
3	Guaranteed payments (other than health insurance)		**7**	Deductions included on Schedule K, lines 1 through 13d, and 16l, not charged against book income this year (itemize):	
4	Expenses recorded on books this year not included on Schedule K, lines 1 through 13d, and 16l (itemize):		**a**	Depreciation $	
a	Depreciation $		**8**	Add lines 6 and 7	
b	Travel and entertainment $		**9**	Income (loss) (Analysis of Net Income (Loss), line 1). Subtract line 8 from line 5 .	
5	Add lines 1 through 4				

Schedule M-2   Analysis of Partners' Capital Accounts

1	Balance at beginning of year . . .		**6**	Distributions: **a** Cash	
2	Capital contributed: **a** Cash . . .			**b** Property	
	b Property . .		**7**	Other decreases (itemize):	
3	Net income (loss) per books				
4	Other increases (itemize):		**8**	Add lines 6 and 7	
5	Add lines 1 through 4		**9**	Balance at end of year. Subtract line 8 from line 5	

Form **1065** (2015)

651113

☐ Final K-1   ☐ Amended K-1   OMB No. 1545-0123

Schedule K-1
(Form 1065)

20**15**

Department of the Treasury
Internal Revenue Service

For calendar year 2015, or tax

year beginning _____, 2015

ending _____, 20 _____

Partner's Share of Income, Deductions,
Credits, etc. ▶ See back of form and separate instructions.

Part I	Information About the Partnership

A Partnership's employer identification number

B Partnership's name, address, city, state, and ZIP code

C IRS Center where partnership filed return

D ☐ Check if this is a publicly traded partnership (PTP)

Part II	Information About the Partner

E Partner's identifying number

F Partner's name, address, city, state, and ZIP code

G ☐ General partner or LLC member-manager   ☐ Limited partner or other LLC member

H ☐ Domestic partner   ☐ Foreign partner

I1 What type of entity is this partner? _____

I2 If this partner is a retirement plan (IRA/SEP/Keogh/etc.), check here . . . . ☐

J Partner's share of profit, loss, and capital (see instructions):

	Beginning	Ending
Profit	%	%
Loss	%	%
Capital	%	%

K Partner's share of liabilities at year end:

Nonrecourse . . . . $ _____

Qualified nonrecourse financing . $ _____

Recourse . . . . $ _____

L Partner's capital account analysis:

Beginning capital account . . . $ _____

Capital contributed during the year $ _____

Current year increase (decrease) . $ _____

Withdrawals & distributions . . $ (_____)

Ending capital account . . . . $ _____

☐ Tax basis   ☐ GAAP   ☐ Section 704(b) book
☐ Other (explain)

M Did the partner contribute property with a built-in gain or loss?
☐ Yes   ☐ No
If "Yes," attach statement (see instructions)

Part III Partner's Share of Current Year Income,
Deductions, Credits, and Other Items

1	Ordinary business income (loss)	**15**	Credits
2	Net rental real estate income (loss)		
3	Other net rental income (loss)	**16**	Foreign transactions
4	Guaranteed payments		
5	Interest income		
6a	Ordinary dividends		
6b	Qualified dividends		
7	Royalties		
8	Net short-term capital gain (loss)		
9a	Net long-term capital gain (loss)	**17**	Alternative minimum tax (AMT) items
9b	Collectibles (28%) gain (loss)		
9c	Unrecaptured section 1250 gain		
10	Net section 1231 gain (loss)	**18**	Tax-exempt income and nondeductible expenses
11	Other income (loss)		
		19	Distributions
12	Section 179 deduction		
13	Other deductions	**20**	Other information
14	Self-employment earnings (loss)		

*See attached statement for additional information.

For IRS Use Only

For Paperwork Reduction Act Notice, see Instructions for Form 1065.   IRS.gov/form1065   Cat. No. 11394R   **Schedule K-1 (Form 1065) 2015**

Schedule K-1 (Form 1065) 2015   Page **2**

This list identifies the codes used on Schedule K-1 for all partners and provides summarized reporting information for partners who file Form 1040.
For detailed reporting and filing information, see the separate Partner's Instructions for Schedule K-1 and the instructions for your income tax return.

1. Ordinary business income (loss). Determine whether the income (loss) is passive or nonpassive and enter on your return as follows.

	Report on
Passive loss	See the Partner's Instructions
Passive income	Schedule E, line 28, column (g)
Nonpassive loss	Schedule E, line 28, column (h)
Nonpassive income	Schedule E, line 28, column (j)

2. Net rental real estate income (loss) — See the Partner's Instructions

3. Other net rental income (loss)

Net income	Schedule E, line 28, column (g)
Net loss	See the Partner's Instructions

4. Guaranteed payments — Schedule E, line 28, column (j)
5. Interest income — Form 1040, line 8a
6a. Ordinary dividends — Form 1040, line 9a
6b. Qualified dividends — Form 1040, line 9b
7. Royalties — Schedule E, line 4
8. Net short-term capital gain (loss) — Schedule D, line 5
9a. Net long-term capital gain (loss) — Schedule D, line 12
9b. Collectibles (28%) gain (loss) — 28% Rate Gain Worksheet, line 4 (Schedule D instructions)
9c. Unrecaptured section 1250 gain — See the Partner's Instructions
10. Net section 1231 gain (loss) — See the Partner's Instructions
11. Other income (loss)

Code		
A	Other portfolio income (loss)	See the Partner's Instructions
B	Involuntary conversions	See the Partner's Instructions
C	Sec. 1256 contracts & straddles	Form 6781, line 1
D	Mining exploration costs recapture	See Pub. 535
E	Cancellation of debt	Form 1040, line 21 or Form 982
F	Other income (loss)	See the Partner's Instructions

12. Section 179 deduction — See the Partner's Instructions
13. Other deductions

A	Cash contributions (50%)	
B	Cash contributions (30%)	
C	Noncash contributions (50%)	
D	Noncash contributions (30%)	See the Partner's
E	Capital gain property to a 50% organization (30%)	Instructions
F	Capital gain property (20%)	
G	Contributions (100%)	
H	Investment interest expense	Form 4952, line 1
I	Deductions—royalty income	Schedule E, line 19
J	Section 59(e)(2) expenditures	See the Partner's Instructions
K	Deductions—portfolio (2% floor)	Schedule A, line 23
L	Deductions—portfolio (other)	Schedule A, line 28
M	Amounts paid for medical insurance	Schedule A, line 1 or Form 1040, line 29
N	Educational assistance benefits	See the Partner's Instructions
O	Dependent care benefits	Form 2441, line 12
P	Preproductive period expenses	See the Partner's Instructions
Q	Commercial revitalization deduction from rental real estate activities	See Form 8582 instructions
R	Pensions and IRAs	See the Partner's Instructions
S	Reforestation expense deduction	See the Partner's Instructions
T	Domestic production activities information	See Form 8903 instructions
U	Qualified production activities income	Form 8903, line 7b
V	Employer's Form W-2 wages	Form 8903, line 17
W	Other deductions	See the Partner's Instructions

14. Self-employment earnings (loss)

Note: If you have a section 179 deduction or any partner-level deductions, see the Partner's Instructions before completing Schedule SE.

A	Net earnings (loss) from self-employment	Schedule SE, Section A or B
B	Gross farming or fishing income	See the Partner's Instructions
C	Gross non-farm income	See the Partner's Instructions

15. Credits

A	Low-income housing credit (section 42(j)(5)) from pre-2008 buildings	
B	Low-income housing credit (other) from pre-2008 buildings	
C	Low-income housing credit (section 42(j)(5)) from post-2007 buildings	See the Partner's Instructions
D	Low-income housing credit (other) from post-2007 buildings	
E	Qualified rehabilitation expenditures (rental real estate)	
F	Other rental real estate credits	
G	Other rental credits	
H	Undistributed capital gains credit	Form 1040, line 73; check box a
I	Biofuel producer credit	
J	Work opportunity credit	See the Partner's Instructions
K	Disabled access credit	

Code		*Report on*
L	Empowerment zone employment credit	
M	Credit for increasing research activities	
N	Credit for employer social security and Medicare taxes	See the Partner's Instructions
O	Backup withholding	
P	Other credits	

16. Foreign transactions

A	Name of country or U.S. possession	
B	Gross income from all sources	Form 1116, Part I
C	Gross income sourced at partner level	

Foreign gross income sourced at partnership level

D	Passive category	
E	General category	Form 1116, Part I
F	Other	

Deductions allocated and apportioned at partner level

G	Interest expense	Form 1116, Part I
H	Other	Form 1116, Part I

Deductions allocated and apportioned at partnership level to foreign source income

I	Passive category	
J	General category	Form 1116, Part I
K	Other	

Other information

L	Total foreign taxes paid	Form 1116, Part II
M	Total foreign taxes accrued	Form 1116, Part II
N	Reduction in taxes available for credit	Form 1116, line 12
O	Foreign trading gross receipts	Form 8873
P	Extraterritorial income exclusion	Form 8873
Q	Other foreign transactions	See the Partner's Instructions

17. Alternative minimum tax (AMT) items

A	Post-1986 depreciation adjustment	
B	Adjusted gain or loss	See the Partner's
C	Depletion (other than oil & gas)	Instructions and
D	Oil, gas, & geothermal—gross income	the Instructions for
E	Oil, gas, & geothermal—deductions	Form 6251
F	Other AMT items	

18. Tax-exempt income and nondeductible expenses

A	Tax-exempt interest income	Form 1040, line 8b
B	Other tax-exempt income	See the Partner's Instructions
C	Nondeductible expenses	See the Partner's Instructions

19. Distributions

A	Cash and marketable securities	
B	Distribution subject to section 737	See the Partner's Instructions
C	Other property	

20. Other information

A	Investment income	Form 4952, line 4a
B	Investment expenses	Form 4952, line 5
C	Fuel tax credit information	Form 4136
D	Qualified rehabilitation expenditures (other than rental real estate)	See the Partner's Instructions
E	Basis of energy property	See the Partner's Instructions
F	Recapture of low-income housing credit (section 42(j)(5))	Form 8611, line 8
G	Recapture of low-income housing credit (other)	Form 8611, line 8
H	Recapture of investment credit	See Form 4255
I	Recapture of other credits	See the Partner's Instructions
J	Look-back interest—completed long-term contracts	See Form 8697
K	Look-back interest—income forecast method	See Form 8866
L	Dispositions of property with section 179 deductions	
M	Recapture of section 179 deduction	
N	Interest expense for corporate partners	
O	Section 453(l)(3) information	
P	Section 453A(c) information	
Q	Section 1260(b) information	
R	Interest allocable to production expenditures	See the Partner's Instructions
S	CCF nonqualified withdrawals	
T	Depletion information—oil and gas	
U	Reserved	
V	Unrelated business taxable income	
W	Precontribution gain (loss)	
X	Section 108(i) information	
Y	Net investment income	
Z	Other information	

B-4   U.S. Income Tax Return for Estates and Trusts

Form **1041**

Department of the Treasury—Internal Revenue Service

U.S. Income Tax Return for Estates and Trusts

20**15**

OMB No. 1545-0092

▶ Information about Form 1041 and its separate instructions is at *www.irs.gov/form1041.*

A Check all that apply:

- ☐ Decedent's estate
- ☐ Simple trust
- ☐ Complex trust
- ☐ Qualified disability trust
- ☐ ESBT (S portion only)
- ☐ Grantor type trust
- ☐ Bankruptcy estate-Ch. 7
- ☐ Bankruptcy estate-Ch. 11
- ☐ Pooled income fund

For calendar year 2015 or fiscal year beginning _____ , 2015, and ending _____ , 20 ___

Name of estate or trust (If a grantor type trust, see the instructions.)

Name and title of fiduciary

Number, street, and room or suite no. (If a P.O. box, see the instructions.)

City or town, state or province, country, and ZIP or foreign postal code

C Employer identification number

D Date entity created

E Nonexempt charitable and split-interest trusts, check applicable box(es), see instructions.

☐ Described in sec. 4947(a)(1). Check here if not a private foundation . . ▶ ☐

☐ Described in sec. 4947(a)(2)

B Number of Schedules K-1 attached (see instructions) ▶ _____

F Check applicable boxes:
- ☐ Initial return
- ☐ Final return
- ☐ Amended return
- ☐ Net operating loss carryback
- ☐ Change in trust's name
- ☐ Change in fiduciary
- ☐ Change in fiduciary's name
- ☐ Change in fiduciary's address

G Check here if the estate or filing trust made a section 645 election . . . . ▶ ☐   Trust TIN ▶ _____

Income

1	Interest income	1
2a	Total ordinary dividends	2a
b	Qualified dividends allocable to: **(1)** Beneficiaries _____ **(2)** Estate or trust _____	
3	Business income or (loss). Attach Schedule C or C-EZ (Form 1040)	3
4	Capital gain or (loss). Attach Schedule D (Form 1041)	4
5	Rents, royalties, partnerships, other estates and trusts, etc. Attach Schedule E (Form 1040) .	5
6	Farm income or (loss). Attach Schedule F (Form 1040)	6
7	Ordinary gain or (loss). Attach Form 4797	7
8	Other income. List type and amount _____	8
9	**Total income.** Combine lines 1, 2a, and 3 through 8 . . . . ▶	9

Deductions

10	Interest. Check if Form 4952 is attached ▶ ☐	10
11	Taxes	11
12	Fiduciary fees	12
13	Charitable deduction (from Schedule A, line 7)	13
14	Attorney, accountant, and return preparer fees	14
15a	Other deductions **not** subject to the 2% floor (attach schedule)	15a
b	Net operating loss deduction (see instructions)	15b
c	Allowable miscellaneous itemized deductions subject to the 2% floor	15c
16	Add lines 10 through 15c . . . . ▶	16
17	Adjusted total income or (loss). Subtract line 16 from line 9 . . .	17 _____	
18	Income distribution deduction (from Schedule B, line 15). Attach Schedules K-1 (Form 1041)	18
19	Estate tax deduction including certain generation-skipping taxes (attach computation) . . .	19
20	Exemption	20
21	Add lines 18 through 20 . . . . ▶	21

Tax and Payments

22	Taxable income. Subtract line 21 from line 17. If a loss, see instructions	22
23	**Total tax** (from Schedule G, line 7)	23
24	**Payments: a** 2015 estimated tax payments and amount applied from 2014 return . . .	24a
b	Estimated tax payments allocated to beneficiaries (from Form 1041-T)	24b
c	Subtract line 24b from line 24a	24c
d	Tax paid with Form 7004 (see instructions)	24d
e	Federal income tax withheld. If any is from Form(s) 1099, check ▶ ☐	24e
	Other payments: **f** Form 2439 _____ ; **g** Form 4136 _____ ; Total ▶	24h
25	**Total payments.** Add lines 24c through 24e, and 24h . . . . ▶	25
26	Estimated tax penalty (see instructions)	26
27	**Tax due.** If line 25 is smaller than the total of lines 23 and 26, enter amount owed	27
28	**Overpayment.** If line 25 is larger than the total of lines 23 and 26, enter amount overpaid . .	28
29	Amount of line 28 to be: **a** Credited to 2016 estimated tax ▶ _____ ; **b** Refunded ▶	29

Sign Here

Under penalties of perjury, I declare that I have examined this return, including accompanying schedules and statements, and to the best of my knowledge and belief, it is true, correct, and complete. Declaration of preparer (other than taxpayer) is based on all information of which preparer has any knowledge.

▶ _____   ▶ _____

Signature of fiduciary or officer representing fiduciary   Date   EIN of fiduciary if a financial institution

May the IRS discuss this return with the preparer shown below (see instr.)? ☐ Yes ☐ No

Paid Preparer Use Only

Print/Type preparer's name	Preparer's signature	Date	Check ☐ if self-employed	PTIN
Firm's name ▶			Firm's EIN ▶	
Firm's address ▶			Phone no.	

For Paperwork Reduction Act Notice, see the separate instructions.   Cat. No. 11370H   Form **1041** (2015)

Form 1041 (2015)   Page **2**

Schedule A	**Charitable Deduction.** Do not complete for a simple trust or a pooled income fund.		
1	Amounts paid or permanently set aside for charitable purposes from gross income (see instructions)	1	
2	Tax-exempt income allocable to charitable contributions (see instructions)	2	
3	Subtract line 2 from line 1	3	
4	Capital gains for the tax year allocated to corpus and paid or permanently set aside for charitable purposes	4	
5	Add lines 3 and 4	5	
6	Section 1202 exclusion allocable to capital gains paid or permanently set aside for charitable purposes (see instructions)	6	
7	**Charitable deduction.** Subtract line 6 from line 5. Enter here and on page 1, line 13	7	

Schedule B	**Income Distribution Deduction**		
1	Adjusted total income (see instructions)	1	
2	Adjusted tax-exempt interest	2	
3	Total net gain from Schedule D (Form 1041), line 19, column (1) (see instructions)	3	
4	Enter amount from Schedule A, line 4 (minus any allocable section 1202 exclusion)	4	
5	Capital gains for the tax year included on Schedule A, line 1 (see instructions)	5	
6	Enter any gain from page 1, line 4, as a negative number. If page 1, line 4, is a loss, enter the loss as a positive number	6	
7	**Distributable net income.** Combine lines 1 through 6. If zero or less, enter -0-	7	
8	If a complex trust, enter accounting income for the tax year as determined under the governing instrument and applicable local law **8**		
9	Income required to be distributed currently	9	
10	Other amounts paid, credited, or otherwise required to be distributed	10	
11	Total distributions. Add lines 9 and 10. If greater than line 8, see instructions	11	
12	Enter the amount of tax-exempt income included on line 11	12	
13	Tentative income distribution deduction. Subtract line 12 from line 11	13	
14	Tentative income distribution deduction. Subtract line 2 from line 7. If zero or less, enter -0-	14	
15	**Income distribution deduction.** Enter the smaller of line 13 or line 14 here and on page 1, line 18	15	

Schedule G	**Tax Computation** (see instructions)			
1	**Tax: a** Tax on taxable income (see instructions)	**1a**		
	b Tax on lump-sum distributions. Attach Form 4972	**1b**		
	c Alternative minimum tax (from Schedule I (Form 1041), line 56)	**1c**		
	d Total. Add lines 1a through 1c ▶		**1d**	
2a	Foreign tax credit. Attach Form 1116	**2a**		
b	General business credit. Attach Form 3800	**2b**		
c	Credit for prior year minimum tax. Attach Form 8801	**2c**		
d	Bond credits. Attach Form 8912	**2d**		
e	**Total credits.** Add lines 2a through 2d ▶		**2e**	
3	Subtract line 2e from line 1d. If zero or less, enter -0-		**3**	
4	Net investment income tax from Form 8960, line 21		**4**	
5	Recapture taxes. Check if from: ☐ Form 4255 ☐ Form 8611		**5**	
6	Household employment taxes. Attach Schedule H (Form 1040)		**6**	
7	**Total tax.** Add lines 3 through 6. Enter here and on page 1, line 23 ▶		**7**	

	Other Information	Yes	No
1	Did the estate or trust receive tax-exempt income? If "Yes," attach a computation of the allocation of expenses. Enter the amount of tax-exempt interest income and exempt-interest dividends ▶ $ _____		
2	Did the estate or trust receive all or any part of the earnings (salary, wages, and other compensation) of any individual by reason of a contract assignment or similar arrangement?		
3	At any time during calendar year 2015, did the estate or trust have an interest in or a signature or other authority over a bank, securities, or other financial account in a foreign country?		
	See the instructions for exceptions and filing requirements for FinCEN Form 114. If "Yes," enter the name of the foreign country ▶ _____		
4	During the tax year, did the estate or trust receive a distribution from, or was it the grantor of, or transferor to, a foreign trust? If "Yes," the estate or trust may have to file Form 3520. See instructions		
5	Did the estate or trust receive, or pay, any qualified residence interest on seller-provided financing? If "Yes," see the instructions for required attachment		
6	If this is an estate or a complex trust making the section 663(b) election, check here (see instructions) ▶ ☐		
7	To make a section 643(e)(3) election, attach Schedule D (Form 1041), and check here (see instructions) ▶ ☐		
8	If the decedent's estate has been open for more than 2 years, attach an explanation for the delay in closing the estate, and check here ▶ ☐		
9	Are any present or future trust beneficiaries skip persons? See instructions		

Form **1041** (2015)

651113

□ Final K-1   □ Amended K-1   OMB No. 1545-0092

Schedule K-1
(Form 1041)
Department of the Treasury
Internal Revenue Service

20**15**

For calendar year 2015,
or tax year beginning _____ , 2015,
and ending _____ , 20 _____

Beneficiary's Share of Income, Deductions, Credits, etc.

▶ See back of form and instructions.

Part I	Information About the Estate or Trust

A Estate's or trust's employer identification number

B Estate's or trust's name

C Fiduciary's name, address, city, state, and ZIP code

D □   Check if Form 1041-T was filed and enter the date it was filed

_____

E □   Check if this is the final Form 1041 for the estate or trust

Part II	Information About the Beneficiary

F Beneficiary's identifying number

G Beneficiary's name, address, city, state, and ZIP code

H □   Domestic beneficiary   □   Foreign beneficiary

Part III	Beneficiary's Share of Current Year Income, Deductions, Credits, and Other Items

1	Interest income	**11**	Final year deductions
2a	Ordinary dividends		
2b	Qualified dividends		
3	Net short-term capital gain		
4a	Net long-term capital gain		
4b	28% rate gain	**12**	Alternative minimum tax adjustment
4c	Unrecaptured section 1250 gain		
5	Other portfolio and nonbusiness income		
6	Ordinary business income		
7	Net rental real estate income		
8	Other rental income	**13**	Credits and credit recapture
9	Directly apportioned deductions		
		14	Other information
10	Estate tax deduction		

*See attached statement for additional information.

Note. A statement must be attached showing the beneficiary's share of income and directly apportioned deductions from each business, rental real estate, and other rental activity.

For IRS Use Only

For Paperwork Reduction Act Notice, see the Instructions for Form 1041.   IRS.gov/form1041   Cat. No. 11380D   **Schedule K-1 (Form 1041) 2015**

This list identifies the codes used on Schedule K-1 for beneficiaries and provides summarized reporting information for beneficiaries who file Form 1040. For detailed reporting and filing information, see the Instructions for Schedule K-1 (Form 1041) for a Beneficiary Filing Form 1040 and the instructions for your income tax return.

Report on

1. Interest income	Form 1040, line 8a	
2a. Ordinary dividends	Form 1040, line 9a	
2b. Qualified dividends	Form 1040, line 9b	
3. Net short-term capital gain	Schedule D, line 5	
4a. Net long-term capital gain	Schedule D, line 12	
4b. 28% rate gain	28% Rate Gain Worksheet, line 4 (Schedule D Instructions)	
4c. Unrecaptured section 1250 gain	Unrecaptured Section 1250 Gain Worksheet, line 11 (Schedule D Instructions)	
5. Other portfolio and nonbusiness income	Schedule E, line 33, column (f)	
6. Ordinary business income	Schedule E, line 33, column (d) or (f)	
7. Net rental real estate income	Schedule E, line 33, column (d) or (f)	
8. Other rental income	Schedule E, line 33, column (d) or (f)	

9. Directly apportioned deductions

Code

A Depreciation	Form 8582 or Schedule E, line 33, column (c) or (e)
B Depletion	Form 8582 or Schedule E, line 33, column (c) or (e)
C Amortization	Form 8582 or Schedule E, line 33, column (c) or (e)

10. Estate tax deduction	Schedule A, line 28

11. Final year deductions

A Excess deductions	Schedule A, line 23
B Short-term capital loss carryover	Schedule D, line 5
C Long-term capital loss carryover	Schedule D, line 12; line 5 of the wksht. for Sch. D, line 18; and line 16 of the wksht. for Sch. D, line 19
D Net operating loss carryover — regular tax	Form 1040, line 21
E Net operating loss carryover — minimum tax	Form 6251, line 11

12. Alternative minimum tax (AMT) items

A Adjustment for minimum tax purposes	Form 6251, line 15
B AMT adjustment attributable to qualified dividends	
C AMT adjustment attributable to net short-term capital gain	
D AMT adjustment attributable to net long-term capital gain	
E AMT adjustment attributable to unrecaptured section 1250 gain	See the beneficiary's instructions and the Instructions for Form 6251
F AMT adjustment attributable to 28% rate gain	
G Accelerated depreciation	
H Depletion	
I Amortization	
J Exclusion items	2016 Form 8801

13. Credits and credit recapture

Code		Report on
A Credit for estimated taxes		Form 1040, line 65
B Credit for backup withholding		Form 1040, line 64
C Low-income housing credit		
D Rehabilitation credit and energy credit		
E Other qualifying investment credit		
F Work opportunity credit		
G Credit for small employer health insurance premiums		
H Biofuel producer credit		
I Credit for increasing research activities		
J Renewable electricity, refined coal, and Indian coal production credit		
K Empowerment zone employment credit		See the beneficiary's instructions
L Indian employment credit		
M Orphan drug credit		
N Credit for employer-provided child care and facilities		
O Biodiesel and renewable diesel fuels credit		
P Credit to holders of tax credit bonds		
Q Credit for employer differential wage payments		
R Recapture of credits		

14. Other information

A Tax-exempt interest	Form 1040, line 8b
B Foreign taxes	Form 1040, line 48 or Sch. A, line 8
C Qualified production activities income	Form 8903, line 7, col. (b) (also see the beneficiary's instructions)
D Form W-2 wages	Form 8903, line 17
E Net investment income	Form 4952, line 4a
F Gross farm and fishing income	Schedule E, line 42
G Foreign trading gross receipts (IRC 942(a))	See the Instructions for Form 8873
H Adjustment for section 1411 net investment income or deductions	Form 8960, line 7 (also see the beneficiary's instructions)
I Other information	See the beneficiary's instructions

Note. If you are a beneficiary who does not file a Form 1040, see instructions for the type of income tax return you are filing.

B-5   Amended Tax Return Form

Form **1120X**

(Rev. January 2011)
Department of the Treasury
Internal Revenue Service

**Amended U.S. Corporation
Income Tax Return**

OMB No. 1545-0132

For tax year ending
▶ ------------------------------
(Enter month and year.)

Please Type or Print

Name	Employer identification number
Number, street, and room or suite no. (If a P.O. box, see instructions.)	
City or town, state, and ZIP code	Telephone number (optional)

Enter name and address used on original return (If same as above, write "Same.")

Internal Revenue Service Center ▶
where original return was filed

Fill in applicable items and use Part II on the back to explain any changes

Part I   **Income and Deductions** (see instructions)

			(a) As originally reported or as previously adjusted	(b) Net change — increase or (decrease) — explain in Part II	(c) Correct amount
1	Total income	1			
2	Total deductions	2			
3	Taxable income. Subtract line 2 from line 1	3			
4	Total tax	4			

Payments and Credits (see instructions)

5a	Overpayment in prior year allowed as a credit . . .	5a			
b	Estimated tax payments	5b			
c	Refund applied for on Form 4466	5c			
d	Subtract line 5c from the sum of lines 5a and 5b . .	5d			
e	Tax deposited with Form 7004	5e			
f	Credit from Form 2439	5f			
g	Credit for federal tax on fuels and other refundable credits	5g			
6	Tax deposited or paid with (or after) the filing of the original return	6			
7	Add lines 5d through 6, column (c)	7			
8	Overpayment, if any, as shown on original return or as later adjusted	8			
9	Subtract line 8 from line 7	9			

Tax Due or Overpayment (see instructions)

10	**Tax due.** Subtract line 9 from line 4, column (c). If paying by check, make it payable to the "United States Treasury" . . . . ▶	10	
11	**Overpayment.** Subtract line 4, column (c), from line 9 . . . . ▶	11	
12	Enter the amount of line 11 you want: **Credited to 20** ____ **Estimated tax** ▶ ____ **Refunded** ▶	12	

Sign Here

Under penalties of perjury, I declare that I have filed an original return and that I have examined this amended return, including accompanying schedules and statements, and to the best of my knowledge and belief, this amended return is true, correct, and complete. Declaration of preparer (other than taxpayer) is based on all information of which preparer has any knowledge.

▶ _____ _____ ▶ _____
   Signature of officer   Date   Title

Paid Preparer Use Only

Print/Type preparer's name	Preparer's signature	Date	Check ☐ if self-employed	PTIN
Firm's name ▶			Firm's EIN ▶	
Firm's address ▶			Phone no.	

For Paperwork Reduction Act Notice, see instructions.   Cat. No. 11530Z   Form **1120X** (Rev. 1-2011)

Form 1120X (Rev. 1-2011)   Page **2**

| **Part II** | **Explanation of Changes to Items in Part I** (Enter the line number from page 1 for the items you are changing, and give the reason for each change. Show any computation in detail. Also, see **What To Attach** in the instructions.) |

If the change is due to a net operating loss carryback, a capital loss carryback, or a general business credit carryback, see **Carryback Claims** in the instructions, and check here . . . . ▶ ☐

Form **1120X** (Rev. 1-2011)

B-6   Application for Extension of Time to File Income Tax Return

Form 7004
(Rev. December 2012)
Department of the Treasury
Internal Revenue Service

Application for Automatic Extension of Time To File Certain Business Income Tax, Information, and Other Returns
► File a separate application for each return.
► Information about Form 7004 and its separate instructions is at *www.irs.gov/form7004.*

OMB No. 1545-0233

Print or Type	Name		Identifying number
	Number, street, and room or suite no. (If P.O. box, see instructions.)		
	City, town, state, and ZIP code (If a foreign address, enter city, province or state, and country (follow the country's practice for entering postal code)).		

Note. *File request for extension by the due date of the return for which the extension is granted. See instructions before completing this form.*

Part I   Automatic 5-Month Extension

1a Enter the form code for the return that this application is for (see below) . . . .

Application Is For:	Form Code	Application Is For:	Form Code
Form 1065	09	Form 1041 (estate other than a bankruptcy estate)	04
Form 8804	31	Form 1041 (trust)	05

Part II   Automatic 6-Month Extension

b Enter the form code for the return that this application is for (see below) . . . .

Application Is For:	Form Code	Application Is For:	Form Code
Form 706-GS(D)	01	Form 1120-ND (section 4951 taxes)	20
Form 706-GS(T)	02	Form 1120-PC	21
Form 1041 (bankruptcy estate only)	03	Form 1120-POL	22
Form 1041-N	06	Form 1120-REIT	23
Form 1041-QFT	07	Form 1120-RIC	24
Form 1042	08	Form 1120S	25
Form 1065-B	10	Form 1120-SF	26
Form 1066	11	Form 3520-A	27
Form 1120	12	Form 8612	28
Form 1120-C	34	Form 8613	29
Form 1120-F	15	Form 8725	30
Form 1120-FSC	16	Form 8831	32
Form 1120-H	17	Form 8876	33
Form 1120-L	18	Form 8924	35
Form 1120-ND	19	Form 8928	36

2 If the organization is a foreign corporation that does not have an office or place of business in the United States, check here . . . . ► ☐

3 If the organization is a corporation and is the common parent of a group that intends to file a consolidated return, check here . . . . ► ☐
    If checked, attach a statement, listing the name, address, and Employer Identification Number (EIN) for each member covered by this application.

Part III   All Filers Must Complete This Part

4 If the organization is a corporation or partnership that qualifies under Regulations section 1.6081-5, check here . ► ☐

5a The application is for calendar year 20___, or tax year beginning _____, 20___, and ending _____, 20___

b **Short tax year.** If this tax year is less than 12 months, check the reason: ☐ Initial return ☐ Final return
    ☐ Change in accounting period ☐ Consolidated return to be filed ☐ Other (see instructions-attach explanation)

6 Tentative total tax	**6**	
7 **Total** payments and credits (see instructions)	**7**	
8 **Balance due.** Subtract line 7 from line 6 (see instructions)	**8**	

For Privacy Act and Paperwork Reduction Act Notice, see separate Instructions.   Cat. No. 13804A   Form **7004** (Rev. 12-2012)

Form **2220**	Underpayment of Estimated Tax by Corporations	OMB No. 1545-0123
Department of the Treasury Internal Revenue Service	▶ Attach to the corporation's tax return. ▶ Information about Form 2220 and its separate instructions is at *www.irs.gov/form2220*.	20**15**

Name	Employer identification number

Note: Generally, the corporation is not required to file Form 2220 (see Part II below for exceptions) because the IRS will figure any penalty owed and bill the corporation. However, the corporation may still use Form 2220 to figure the penalty. If so, enter the amount from page 2, line 38 on the estimated tax penalty line of the corporation's income tax return, but **do not** attach Form 2220.

Part I   Required Annual Payment

1	Total tax (see instructions)		**1**
2a	Personal holding company tax (Schedule PH (Form 1120), line 26) included on line 1	**2a**	
b	Look-back interest included on line 1 under section 460(b)(2) for completed long-term contracts or section 167(g) for depreciation under the income forecast method . .	**2b**	
c	Credit for federal tax paid on fuels (see instructions)	**2c**	
d	**Total.** Add lines 2a through 2c		**2d**
3	Subtract line 2d from line 1. If the result is less than $500, **do not** complete or file this form. The corporation does not owe the penalty		**3**
4	Enter the tax shown on the corporation's 2014 income tax return (see instructions). **Caution: If the tax is zero or the tax year was for less than 12 months, skip this line and enter the amount from line 3 on line 5** . .		**4**
5	**Required annual payment.** Enter the **smaller** of line 3 or line 4. If the corporation is required to skip line 4, enter the amount from line 3		**5**

Part II   Reasons for Filing—Check the boxes below that apply. If any boxes are checked, the corporation **must** file Form 2220 even if it does not owe a penalty (see instructions).

6	☐	The corporation is using the adjusted seasonal installment method.
7	☐	The corporation is using the annualized income installment method.
8	☐	The corporation is a "large corporation" figuring its first required installment based on the prior year's tax.

Part III   Figuring the Underpayment

			(a)	(b)	(c)	(d)
9	**Installment due dates.** Enter in columns (a) through (d) the 15th day of the 4th (**Form 990-PF filers:** Use 5th month), 6th, 9th, and 12th months of the corporation's tax year	**9**				
10	**Required installments.** If the box on line 6 and/or line 7 above is checked, enter the amounts from Schedule A, line 38. If the box on line 8 (but not 6 or 7) is checked, see instructions for the amounts to enter. If none of these boxes are checked, enter 25% of line 5 above in each column	**10**				
11	Estimated tax paid or credited for each period (see instructions). For column (a) only, enter the amount from line 11 on line 15	**11**				
	Complete lines 12 through 18 of one column before going to the next column.					
12	Enter amount, if any, from line 18 of the preceding column	**12**				
13	Add lines 11 and 12	**13**				
14	Add amounts on lines 16 and 17 of the preceding column	**14**				
15	Subtract line 14 from line 13. If zero or less, enter -0-	**15**				
16	If the amount on line 15 is zero, subtract line 13 from line 14. Otherwise, enter -0-	**16**				
17	**Underpayment.** If line 15 is less than or equal to line 10, subtract line 15 from line 10. Then go to line 12 of the next column. Otherwise, go to line 18	**17**				
18	**Overpayment.** If line 10 is less than line 15, subtract line 10 from line 15. Then go to line 12 of the next column	**18**				

Go to Part IV on page 2 to figure the penalty. Do not go to Part IV if there are no entries on line 17—no penalty is owed.

For Paperwork Reduction Act Notice, see separate instructions.   Cat. No. 11746L   Form **2220** (2015)

Form 2220 (2015)   Page **2**

Part IV   Figuring the Penalty

		(a)	(b)	(c)	(d)
19	Enter the date of payment or the 15th day of the 3rd month after the close of the tax year, whichever is earlier (see instructions). *(Form 990-PF and Form 990-T filers:* Use 5th month instead of 3rd month.) **19**				
20	Number of days from due date of installment on line 9 to the date shown on line 19 . . . . **20**				
21	Number of days on line 20 after 4/15/2015 and before 7/1/2015 **21**				
22	Underpayment on line 17 × $\dfrac{\text{Number of days on line 21}}{365}$ × 3% **22**	$	$	$	$
23	Number of days on line 20 after 6/30/2015 and before 10/1/2015 **23**				
24	Underpayment on line 17 × $\dfrac{\text{Number of days on line 23}}{365}$ × 3% **24**	$	$	$	$
25	Number of days on line 20 after 9/30/2015 and before 1/1/2016 **25**				
26	Underpayment on line 17 × $\dfrac{\text{Number of days on line 25}}{365}$ × 3% **26**	$	$	$	$
27	Number of days on line 20 after 12/31/2015 and before 4/1/2016 **27**				
28	Underpayment on line 17 × $\dfrac{\text{Number of days on line 27}}{366}$ × 3% **28**	$	$	$	$
29	Number of days on line 20 after 3/31/2016 and before 7/1/2016 **29**				
30	Underpayment on line 17 × $\dfrac{\text{Number of days on line 29}}{366}$ × *% **30**	$	$	$	$
31	Number of days on line 20 after 6/30/2016 and before 10/1/2016 **31**				
32	Underpayment on line 17 × $\dfrac{\text{Number of days on line 31}}{366}$ × *% **32**	$	$	$	$
33	Number of days on line 20 after 9/30/2016 and before 1/1/2017 **33**				
34	Underpayment on line 17 × $\dfrac{\text{Number of days on line 33}}{366}$ × *% **34**	$	$	$	$
35	Number of days on line 20 after 12/31/2016 and before 2/16/2017 **35**				
36	Underpayment on line 17 × $\dfrac{\text{Number of days on line 35}}{365}$ × *% **36**	$	$	$	$
37	Add lines 22, 24, 26, 28, 30, 32, 34, and 36 . . . . **37**	$	$	$	$

38	**Penalty.** Add columns (a) through (d) of line 37. Enter the total here and on Form 1120, line 33; or the comparable line for other income tax returns . . . . **38** $

*Use the penalty interest rate for each calendar quarter, which the IRS will determine during the first month in the preceding quarter. These rates are published quarterly in an IRS News Release and in a revenue ruling in the Internal Revenue Bulletin. To obtain this information on the Internet, access the IRS website at *www.irs.gov.* You can also call 1-800-829-4933 to get interest rate information.

Form **2220** (2015)

Form 2220 (2015) Page **3**

Schedule A Adjusted Seasonal Installment Method and Annualized Income Installment Method
(see instructions)

Form 1120S filers: *For lines 1, 2, 3, and 21, below, "taxable income" refers to excess net passive income or the amount on which tax is imposed under section 1374(a), whichever applies.*

Part I **Adjusted Seasonal Installment Method (Caution:** Use this method only if the base period percentage for any 6 consecutive months is at least 70%. See instructions.)

			(a)	(b)	(c)	(d)
1	Enter taxable income for the following periods:		First 3 months	First 5 months	First 8 months	First 11 months
a	Tax year beginning in 2012	**1a**				
b	Tax year beginning in 2013	**1b**				
c	Tax year beginning in 2014	**1c**				
2	Enter taxable income for each period for the tax year beginning in 2015 (see instructions for the treatment of extraordinary items)	**2**				
3	Enter taxable income for the following periods:		First 4 months	First 6 months	First 9 months	Entire year
a	Tax year beginning in 2012	**3a**				
b	Tax year beginning in 2013	**3b**				
c	Tax year beginning in 2014	**3c**				
4	Divide the amount in each column on line 1a by the amount in column (d) on line 3a	**4**				
5	Divide the amount in each column on line 1b by the amount in column (d) on line 3b	**5**				
6	Divide the amount in each column on line 1c by the amount in column (d) on line 3c	**6**				
7	Add lines 4 through 6	**7**				
8	Divide line 7 by 3.0	**8**				
9a	Divide line 2 by line 8	**9a**				
b	Extraordinary items (see instructions)	**9b**				
c	Add lines 9a and 9b	**9c**				
10	Figure the tax on the amount on line 9c using the instructions for Form 1120, Schedule J, line 2 (or comparable line of corporation's return)	**10**				
11a	Divide the amount in columns (a) through (c) on line 3a by the amount in column (d) on line 3a	**11a**				
b	Divide the amount in columns (a) through (c) on line 3b by the amount in column (d) on line 3b	**11b**				
c	Divide the amount in columns (a) through (c) on line 3c by the amount in column (d) on line 3c	**11c**				
12	Add lines 11a through 11c	**12**				
13	Divide line 12 by 3.0	**13**				
14	Multiply the amount in columns (a) through (c) of line 10 by columns (a) through (c) of line 13. In column (d), enter the amount from line 10, column (d)	**14**				
15	Enter any alternative minimum tax for each payment period (see instructions)	**15**				
16	Enter any other taxes for each payment period (see instructions)	**16**				
17	Add lines 14 through 16	**17**				
18	For each period, enter the same type of credits as allowed on Form 2220, lines 1 and 2c (see instructions)	**18**				
19	Total tax after credits. Subtract line 18 from line 17. If zero or less, enter -0-	**19**				

Form **2220** (2015)

Form 2220 (2015)   Page **4**

Part II   Annualized Income Installment Method

			(a)	(b)	(c)	(d)
			First months	First months	First months	First months
20	Annualization periods (see instructions)	20				
21	Enter taxable income for each annualization period (see instructions for the treatment of extraordinary items) . . .	21				
22	Annualization amounts (see instructions)	22				
23a	Annualized taxable income. Multiply line 21 by line 22 . . .	23a				
b	Extraordinary items (see instructions)	23b				
c	Add lines 23a and 23b	23c				
24	Figure the tax on the amount on line 23c using the instructions for Form 1120, Schedule J, line 2 (or comparable line of corporation's return)	24				
25	Enter any alternative minimum tax for each payment period (see instructions)	25				
26	Enter any other taxes for each payment period (see instructions)	26				
27	Total tax. Add lines 24 through 26	27				
28	For each period, enter the same type of credits as allowed on Form 2220, lines 1 and 2c (see instructions)	28				
29	Total tax after credits. Subtract line 28 from line 27. If zero or less, enter -0-	29				
30	Applicable percentage	30	25%	50%	75%	100%
31	Multiply line 29 by line 30	31				

Part III   Required Installments

			1st installment	2nd installment	3rd installment	4th installment
	Note: Complete lines 32 through 38 of one column before completing the next column.					
32	If only Part I or Part II is completed, enter the amount in each column from line 19 or line 31. If both parts are completed, enter the **smaller** of the amounts in each column from line 19 or line 31 . .	32				
33	Add the amounts in all preceding columns of line 38 (see instructions)	33				
34	**Adjusted seasonal or annualized income installments.** Subtract line 33 from line 32. If zero or less, enter -0- . . .	34				
35	Enter 25% of line 5 on page 1 of Form 2220 in each column. **Note:** "Large corporations," see the instructions for line 10 for the amounts to enter	35				
36	Subtract line 38 of the preceding column from line 37 of the preceding column	36				
37	Add lines 35 and 36	37				
38	**Required installments.** Enter the **smaller** of line 34 or line 37 here and on page 1 of Form 2220, line 10 (see instructions) .	38				

Form **2220** (2015)

Form **4626**	**Alternative Minimum Tax—Corporations**	OMB No. 1545-0123
Department of the Treasury Internal Revenue Service	▶ Attach to the corporation's tax return. ▶ Information about Form 4626 and its separate instructions is at *www.irs.gov/form4626*.	20**15**

Name	Employer identification number

Note: *See the instructions to find out if the corporation is a small corporation exempt from the alternative minimum tax (AMT) under section 55(e).*

1	Taxable income or (loss) before net operating loss deduction	**1**	
2	**Adjustments and preferences:**		
a	Depreciation of post-1986 property	**2a**	
b	Amortization of certified pollution control facilities.	**2b**	
c	Amortization of mining exploration and development costs	**2c**	
d	Amortization of circulation expenditures (personal holding companies only)	**2d**	
e	Adjusted gain or loss	**2e**	
f	Long-term contracts	**2f**	
g	Merchant marine capital construction funds.	**2g**	
h	Section 833(b) deduction (Blue Cross, Blue Shield, and similar type organizations only)	**2h**	
i	Tax shelter farm activities (personal service corporations only)	**2i**	
j	Passive activities (closely held corporations and personal service corporations only)	**2j**	
k	Loss limitations	**2k**	
l	Depletion	**2l**	
m	Tax-exempt interest income from specified private activity bonds	**2m**	
n	Intangible drilling costs	**2n**	
o	Other adjustments and preferences	**2o**	
3	Pre-adjustment alternative minimum taxable income (AMTI). Combine lines 1 through 2o.	**3**	
4	**Adjusted current earnings (ACE) adjustment:**		
a	ACE from line 10 of the ACE worksheet in the instructions	**4a**	
b	Subtract line 3 from line 4a. If line 3 exceeds line 4a, enter the difference as a negative amount (see instructions)	**4b**	
c	Multiply line 4b by 75% (.75). Enter the result as a positive amount	**4c**	
d	Enter the excess, if any, of the corporation's total increases in AMTI from prior year ACE adjustments over its total reductions in AMTI from prior year ACE adjustments (see instructions). **Note:** *You **must** enter an amount on line 4d (even if line 4b is positive).*	**4d**	
e	ACE adjustment.		
	• If line 4b is zero or more, enter the amount from line 4c	**4e**	
	• If line 4b is less than zero, enter the **smaller** of line 4c or line 4d as a negative amount		
5	Combine lines 3 and 4e. If zero or less, stop here; the corporation does not owe any AMT	**5**	
6	Alternative tax net operating loss deduction (see instructions)	**6**	
7	**Alternative minimum taxable income.** Subtract line 6 from line 5. If the corporation held a residual interest in a REMIC, see instructions	**7**	
8	**Exemption phase-out** (if line 7 is $310,000 or more, skip lines 8a and 8b and enter -0- on line 8c):		
a	Subtract $150,000 from line 7 (if completing this line for a member of a controlled group, see instructions). If zero or less, enter -0-	**8a**	
b	Multiply line 8a by 25% (.25).	**8b**	
c	Exemption. Subtract line 8b from $40,000 (if completing this line for a member of a controlled group, see instructions). If zero or less, enter -0-	**8c**	
9	Subtract line 8c from line 7. If zero or less, enter -0-	**9**	
10	Multiply line 9 by 20% (.20)	**10**	
11	Alternative minimum tax foreign tax credit (AMTFTC) (see instructions)	**11**	
12	Tentative minimum tax. Subtract line 11 from line 10	**12**	
13	Regular tax liability before applying all credits except the foreign tax credit	**13**	
14	**Alternative minimum tax.** Subtract line 13 from line 12. If zero or less, enter -0-. Enter here and on Form 1120, Schedule J, line 3, or the appropriate line of the corporation's income tax return . . .	**14**	

For Paperwork Reduction Act Notice, see separate instructions.   Cat. No. 12955I   Form **4626** (2015)

B-9 Forms for Tax Credits

Form **1116**	**Foreign Tax Credit**	OMB No. 1545-0121
Department of the Treasury Internal Revenue Service (99)	(Individual, Estate, or Trust) ▶ Attach to Form 1040, 1040NR, 1041, or 990-T. ▶ Information about Form 1116 and its separate instructions is at *www.irs.gov/form1116*.	20**15** Attachment Sequence No. **19**

Name	Identifying number as shown on page 1 of your tax return

Use a separate Form 1116 for each category of income listed below. See **Categories of Income** in the instructions. Check only one box on each Form 1116. Report all amounts in U.S. dollars except where specified in Part II below.

a ☐ Passive category income   **c** ☐ Section 901(j) income   **e** ☐ Lump-sum distributions

b ☐ General category income   **d** ☐ Certain income re-sourced by treaty

f Resident of (name of country) ▶

Note: If you paid taxes to only one foreign country or U.S. possession, use column A in Part I and line A in Part II. If you paid taxes to **more than one** *foreign country or U.S. possession, use a separate column and line for each country or possession.*

Part I Taxable Income or Loss From Sources Outside the United States (for Category Checked Above)

		Foreign Country or U.S. Possession			Total (Add cols. A, B, and C.)
		A	B	C	
g	Enter the name of the foreign country or U.S. possession . . . . ▶				
1a	Gross income from sources within country shown above and of the type checked above (see instructions): _____ _____				
					1a
b	Check if line 1a is compensation for personal services as an employee, your total compensation from all sources is $250,000 or more, and you used an alternative basis to determine its source (see instructions) . . ▶ ☐				
Deductions and losses (*Caution: See instructions*):					
2	Expenses **definitely related** to the income on line 1a (attach statement)				
3	Pro rata share of other deductions **not definitely related**:				
a	Certain itemized deductions or standard deduction (see instructions)				
b	Other deductions (attach statement)				
c	Add lines 3a and 3b				
d	Gross foreign source income (see instructions) .				
e	Gross income from all sources (see instructions) .				
f	Divide line 3d by line 3e (see instructions) . . .				
g	Multiply line 3c by line 3f				
4	Pro rata share of interest expense (see instructions):				
a	Home mortgage interest (use the Worksheet for Home Mortgage Interest in the instructions) . .				
b	Other interest expense				
5	Losses from foreign sources				
6	Add lines 2, 3g, 4a, 4b, and 5				**6**
7	Subtract line 6 from line 1a. Enter the result here and on line 15, page 2 . . . . ▶				**7**

Part II Foreign Taxes Paid or Accrued (see instructions)

Country	Credit is claimed for taxes (you must check one)		Foreign taxes paid or accrued								
			In foreign currency				In U.S. dollars				
	(h) ☐ Paid (i) ☐ Accrued		Taxes withheld at source on:			(n) Other foreign taxes paid or accrued	Taxes withheld at source on:			(r) Other foreign taxes paid or accrued	(s) Total foreign taxes paid or accrued (add cols. (o) through (r))
	(j) Date paid or accrued		(k) Dividends	(l) Rents and royalties	(m) Interest		(o) Dividends	(p) Rents and royalties	(q) Interest		
A											
B											
C											
8	Add lines A through C, column (s). Enter the total here and on line 9, page 2 . . . . ▶									**8**	

For Paperwork Reduction Act Notice, see instructions.   Cat. No. 11440U   Form **1116** (2015)

Form 1116 (2015)   Page **2**

Part III Figuring the Credit

9	Enter the amount from line 8. These are your total foreign taxes paid or accrued for the category of income checked above Part I . .	**9**	
10	Carryback or carryover (attach detailed computation)	**10**	
11	Add lines 9 and 10	**11**	
12	Reduction in foreign taxes (see instructions)	**12** ( )	
13	Taxes reclassified under high tax kickout (see instructions) . .	**13**	

14	Combine lines 11, 12, and 13. This is the total amount of foreign taxes available for credit . . .	**14**
15	Enter the amount from line 7. This is your taxable income or (loss) from sources outside the United States (before adjustments) for the category of income checked above Part I (see instructions)	**15**
16	Adjustments to line 15 (see instructions)	**16**
17	Combine the amounts on lines 15 and 16. This is your net foreign source taxable income. (If the result is zero or less, you have no foreign tax credit for the category of income you checked above Part I. Skip lines 18 through 22. However, if you are filing more than one Form 1116, you must complete line 20.)	**17**
18	**Individuals:** Enter the amount from Form 1040, line 41, or Form 1040NR, line 39. **Estates and trusts:** Enter your taxable income without the deduction for your exemption	**18**
	Caution: *If you figured your tax using the lower rates on qualified dividends or capital gains, see instructions.*	
19	Divide line 17 by line 18. If line 17 is more than line 18, enter "1"	**19**
20	**Individuals:** Enter the amounts from Form 1040, lines 44 and 46. If you are a nonresident alien, enter the amounts from Form 1040NR, lines 42 and 44. **Estates and trusts:** Enter the amount from Form 1041, Schedule G, line 1a, or the total of Form 990-T, lines 36 and 37	**20**
	Caution: *If you are completing line 20 for separate category e (lump-sum distributions), see instructions.*	
21	Multiply line 20 by line 19 (maximum amount of credit)	**21**
22	Enter the **smaller** of line 14 or line 21. If this is the only Form 1116 you are filing, skip lines 23 through 27 and enter this amount on line 28. Otherwise, complete the appropriate line in Part IV (see instructions) . . . . ▶	**22**

Part IV Summary of Credits From Separate Parts III (see instructions)

23	Credit for taxes on passive category income	**23**	
24	Credit for taxes on general category income	**24**	
25	Credit for taxes on certain income re-sourced by treaty	**25**	
26	Credit for taxes on lump-sum distributions	**26**	
27	Add lines 23 through 26		**27**
28	Enter the **smaller** of line 20 or line 27		**28**
29	Reduction of credit for international boycott operations. See instructions for line 12		**29**
30	Subtract line 29 from line 28. This is your **foreign tax credit.** Enter here and on Form 1040, line 48; Form 1040NR, line 46; Form 1041, Schedule G, line 2a; or Form 990-T, line 40a . . . . . . ▶		**30**

Form **1116** (2015)

Form **3800**	**General Business Credit**	OMB No. 1545-0895

Department of the Treasury
Internal Revenue Service (99)

▶ Information about Form 3800 and its separate instructions is at *www.irs.gov/form3800*.
▶ You must attach all pages of Form 3800, pages 1, 2, and 3, to your tax return.

20**15**
Attachment
Sequence No. **22**

Name(s) shown on return

Identifying number

Part I **Current Year Credit for Credits Not Allowed Against Tentative Minimum Tax (TMT)**
(See instructions and complete Part(s) III before Parts I and II)

1	General business credit from line 2 of all Parts III with box A checked	**1**	
2	Passive activity credits from line 2 of all Parts III with box B checked **2**		
3	Enter the applicable passive activity credits allowed for 2015 (see instructions)	**3**	
4	Carryforward of general business credit to 2015. Enter the amount from line 2 of Part III with box C checked. See instructions for statement to attach	**4**	
5	Carryback of general business credit from 2016. Enter the amount from line 2 of Part III with box D checked (see instructions)	**5**	
6	Add lines 1, 3, 4, and 5	**6**	

Part II **Allowable Credit**

7	Regular tax before credits: • Individuals. Enter the sum of the amounts from Form 1040, lines 44 and 46, or the sum of the amounts from Form 1040NR, lines 42 and 44 . . . . • Corporations. Enter the amount from Form 1120, Schedule J, Part I, line 2; or the applicable line of your return . . . . • Estates and trusts. Enter the sum of the amounts from Form 1041, Schedule G, lines 1a and 1b; or the amount from the applicable line of your return	**7**	
8	Alternative minimum tax: • Individuals. Enter the amount from Form 6251, line 35 . . . . • Corporations. Enter the amount from Form 4626, line 14 . . . . • Estates and trusts. Enter the amount from Schedule I (Form 1041), line 56 . .	**8**	
9	Add lines 7 and 8	**9**	
10a	Foreign tax credit **10a**		
b	Certain allowable credits (see instructions) **10b**		
c	Add lines 10a and 10b	**10c**	
11	**Net income tax.** Subtract line 10c from line 9. If zero, skip lines 12 through 15 and enter -0- on line 16	**11**	
12	**Net regular tax.** Subtract line 10c from line 7. If zero or less, enter -0- **12**		
13	Enter 25% (.25) of the excess, if any, of line 12 over $25,000 (see instructions) **13**		
14	Tentative minimum tax: • Individuals. Enter the amount from Form 6251, line 33 . . . • Corporations. Enter the amount from Form 4626, line 12 . . . **14** • Estates and trusts. Enter the amount from Schedule I (Form 1041), line 54		
15	Enter the greater of line 13 or line 14	**15**	
16	Subtract line 15 from line 11. If zero or less, enter -0-	**16**	
17	Enter the **smaller** of line 6 or line 16	**17**	
	C corporations: See the line 17 instructions if there has been an ownership change, acquisition, or reorganization.		

For Paperwork Reduction Act Notice, see separate instructions.   Cat. No. 12392F   Form **3800** (2015)

Form 3800 (2015)   Page **2**

Part II   **Allowable Credit** *(Continued)*

Note. If you are not required to report any amounts on lines 22 or 24 below, skip lines 18 through 25 and enter -0- on line 26.

18	Multiply line 14 by 75% (.75) (see instructions)	18	
19	Enter the greater of line 13 or line 18	19	
20	Subtract line 19 from line 11. If zero or less, enter -0-	20	
21	Subtract line 17 from line 20. If zero or less, enter -0-	21	
22	Combine the amounts from line 3 of all Parts III with box A, C, or D checked	22	
23	Passive activity credit from line 3 of all Parts III with box B checked **23**		
24	Enter the applicable passive activity credit allowed for 2015 (see instructions)	24	
25	Add lines 22 and 24	25	
26	Empowerment zone and renewal community employment credit allowed. Enter the smaller of line 21 or line 25	26	
27	Subtract line 13 from line 11. If zero or less, enter -0-	27	
28	Add lines 17 and 26	28	
29	Subtract line 28 from line 27. If zero or less, enter -0-	29	
30	Enter the general business credit from line 5 of all Parts III with box A checked	30	
31	Reserved	31	
32	Passive activity credits from line 5 of all Parts III with box B checked **32**		
33	Enter the applicable passive activity credits allowed for 2015 (see instructions)	33	
34	Carryforward of business credit to 2015. Enter the amount from line 5 of Part III with box C checked and line 6 of Part III with box G checked. See instructions for statement to attach . .	34	
35	Carryback of business credit from 2016. Enter the amount from line 5 of Part III with box D checked (see instructions)	35	
36	Add lines 30, 33, 34, and 35	36	
37	Enter the **smaller** of line 29 or line 36	37	
38	**Credit allowed for the current year.** Add lines 28 and 37. Report the amount from line 38 (if smaller than the sum of Part I, line 6, and Part II, lines 25 and 36, see instructions) as indicated below or on the applicable line of your return: • Individuals. Form 1040, line 54, or Form 1040NR, line 51 • Corporations. Form 1120, Schedule J, Part I, line 5c • Estates and trusts. Form 1041, Schedule G, line 2b	38	

Form **3800** (2015)

Form 3800 (2015)   Page **3**

Name(s) shown on return	Identifying number

Part III **General Business Credits or Eligible Small Business Credits** (see instructions)

Complete a separate Part III for each box checked below. (see instructions)

A ☐ General Business Credit From a Non-Passive Activity   **E** ▨ Reserved

B ☐ General Business Credit From a Passive Activity   **F** ▨ Reserved

C ☐ General Business Credit Carryforwards   **G** ☐ Eligible Small Business Credit Carryforwards

D ☐ General Business Credit Carrybacks   **H** ▨ Reserved

I   If you are filing more than one Part III with box A or B checked, complete and attach first an additional Part III combining amounts from all Parts III with box A or B checked. Check here if this is the consolidated Part III . . . . ▶ ☐

(a) Description of credit		(b) If claiming the credit from a pass-through entity, enter the EIN	(c) Enter the appropriate amount
Note. On any line where the credit is from more than one source, a separate Part III is needed for each pass-through entity.			
1a Investment (Form 3468, Part II only) (attach Form 3468)	1a		
b Reserved	1b	▨	▨
c Increasing research activities (Form 6765)	1c		
d Low-income housing (Form 8586, Part I only)	1d		
e Disabled access (Form 8826) (see instructions for limitation)	1e		
f Renewable electricity, refined coal, and Indian coal production (Form 8835)	1f		
g Indian employment (Form 8845)	1g		
h Orphan drug (Form 8820)	1h		
i New markets (Form 8874)	1i		
j Small employer pension plan startup costs (Form 8881) (see instructions for limitation)	1j		
k Employer-provided child care facilities and services (Form 8882) (see instructions for limitation)	1k		
l Biodiesel and renewable diesel fuels (attach Form 8864)	1l		
m Low sulfur diesel fuel production (Form 8896)	1m		
n Distilled spirits (Form 8906)	1n		
o Nonconventional source fuel	1o		
p Energy efficient home (Form 8908)	1p		
q Energy efficient appliance	1q		
r Alternative motor vehicle (Form 8910)	1r		
s Alternative fuel vehicle refueling property (Form 8911)	1s		
t Reserved	1t	▨	▨
u Mine rescue team training (Form 8923)	1u		
v Agricultural chemicals security (carryforward only)	1v		
w Employer differential wage payments (Form 8932)	1w		
x Carbon dioxide sequestration (Form 8933)	1x		
y Qualified plug-in electric drive motor vehicle (Form 8936)	1y		
z Qualified plug-in electric vehicle (carryforward only)	1z		
aa New hire retention (carryforward only)	1aa		
bb General credits from an electing large partnership (Schedule K-1 (Form 1065-B))	1bb		
zz Other	1zz		
2 Add lines 1a through 1zz and enter here and on the applicable line of Part I	2	▨	
3 Enter the amount from Form 8844 here and on the applicable line of Part II .	3		
4a Investment (Form 3468, Part III) (attach Form 3468)	4a		
b Work opportunity (Form 5884)	4b		
c Biofuel producer (Form 6478)	4c		
d Low-income housing (Form 8586, Part II)	4d		
e Renewable electricity, refined coal, and Indian coal production (Form 8835)	4e		
f Employer social security and Medicare taxes paid on certain employee tips (Form 8846)	4f		
g Qualified railroad track maintenance (Form 8900)	4g		
h Small employer health insurance premiums (Form 8941)	4h		
i Reserved	4i	▨	▨
j Reserved	4j	▨	▨
z Other	4z		
5 Add lines 4a through 4z and enter here and on the applicable line of Part II .	5	▨	
6 Add lines 2, 3, and 5 and enter here and on the applicable line of Part II . .	6	▨	

Form **3800** (2015)

Form 2553
(Rev. December 2013)

Department of the Treasury
Internal Revenue Service

Election by a Small Business Corporation
(Under section 1362 of the Internal Revenue Code)

▶ See Parts II and III on page 3.
▶ You can fax this form to the IRS (see separate instructions).
▶ Information about Form 2553 and its separate instructions is at *www.irs.gov/form2553*.

OMB No. 1545-0123

Note. This election to be an S corporation can be accepted only if all the tests are met under *Who May Elect* in the instructions, all shareholders have signed the consent statement, an officer has signed below, and the exact name and address of the corporation (entity) and other required form information have been provided.

Part I   Election Information

Type or Print

Name (see instructions)

Number, street, and room or suite no. (If a P.O. box, see instructions.)

City or town, state, and ZIP code

A Employer identification number

B Date incorporated

C State of incorporation

D Check the applicable box(es) if the corporation (entity), after applying for the EIN shown in **A** above, changed its ☐ name or ☐ address

E Election is to be effective for tax year beginning (month, day, year) (see instructions) . . . . . . ▶ _____

Caution. A corporation (entity) making the election for its first tax year in existence will usually enter the beginning date of a short tax year that begins on a date other than January 1.

F Selected tax year:
(1) ☐ Calendar year
(2) ☐ Fiscal year ending (month and day) ▶ _____
(3) ☐ 52-53-week year ending with reference to the month of December
(4) ☐ 52-53-week year ending with reference to the month of ▶ _____
If box (2) or (4) is checked, complete Part II.

G If more than 100 shareholders are listed for item J (see page 2), check this box if treating members of a family as one shareholder results in no more than 100 shareholders (see test 2 under *Who May Elect* in the instructions) ▶ ☐

H Name and title of officer or legal representative who the IRS may call for more information

I Telephone number of officer or legal representative

If this S corporation election is being filed late, I declare that I had reasonable cause for not filing Form 2553 timely, and if this late election is being made by an entity eligible to elect to be treated as a corporation, I declare that I also had reasonable cause for not filing an entity classification election timely and that the representations listed in Part IV are true. See below for my explanation of the reasons the election or elections were not made on time and a description of my diligent actions to correct the mistake upon its discovery (see instructions).

Sign Here

Under penalties of perjury, I declare that I have examined this election, including accompanying documents, and, to the best of my knowledge and belief, the election contains all the relevant facts relating to the election, and such facts are true, correct, and complete.

▶ _____   _____   _____
Signature of officer   Title   Date

For Paperwork Reduction Act Notice, see separate instructions.   Cat. No. 18629R   Form **2553** (Rev. 12-2013)

Form 2553 (Rev. 12-2013)   Page **2**

Part I	**Election Information** (continued) **Note.** If you need more rows, use additional copies of page 2.					

J Name and address of each shareholder or former shareholder required to consent to the election. (see instructions)	K **Shareholder's Consent Statement** Under penalties of perjury, I declare that I consent to the election of the above-named corporation (entity) to be an S corporation under section 1362(a) and that I have examined this consent statement, including accompanying documents, and, to the best of my knowledge and belief, the election contains all the relevant facts relating to the election, and such facts are true, correct, and complete. I understand my consent is binding and may not be withdrawn after the corporation (entity) has made a valid election. If seeking relief for a late filed election, I also declare under penalties of perjury that I have reported my income on all affected returns consistent with the S corporation election for the year for which the election should have been filed (see beginning date entered on line E) and for all subsequent years.		L Stock owned or percentage of ownership (see instructions)		M Social security number or employer identification number (see instructions)	N Shareholder's tax year ends (month and day)
	Signature	Date	Number of shares or percentage of ownership	Date(s) acquired		

Form **2553** (Rev. 12-2013)

Form 2553 (Rev. 12-2013)   Page **3**

Part II   Selection of Fiscal Tax Year (see instructions)

Note. All corporations using this part must complete item O and item P, Q, or R.

O   Check the applicable box to indicate whether the corporation is:

1. ☐ A new corporation **adopting** the tax year entered in item F, Part I.
2. ☐ An existing corporation **retaining** the tax year entered in item F, Part I.
3. ☐ An existing corporation **changing** to the tax year entered in item F, Part I.

P   Complete item P if the corporation is using the automatic approval provisions of Rev. Proc. 2006-46, 2006-45 I.R.B. 859, to request **(1)** a natural business year (as defined in section 5.07 of Rev. Proc. 2006-46) or **(2)** a year that satisfies the ownership tax year test (as defined in section 5.08 of Rev. Proc. 2006-46). Check the applicable box below to indicate the representation statement the corporation is making.

1. Natural Business Year ▶ ☐ I represent that the corporation is adopting, retaining, or changing to a tax year that qualifies as its natural business year (as defined in section 5.07 of Rev. Proc. 2006-46) and has attached a statement showing separately for each month the gross receipts for the most recent 47 months (see instructions). I also represent that the corporation is not precluded by section 4.02 of Rev. Proc. 2006-46 from obtaining automatic approval of such adoption, retention, or change in tax year.

2. Ownership Tax Year ▶ ☐ I represent that shareholders (as described in section 5.08 of Rev. Proc. 2006-46) holding more than half of the shares of the stock (as of the first day of the tax year to which the request relates) of the corporation have the same tax year or are concurrently changing to the tax year that the corporation adopts, retains, or changes to per item F, Part I, and that such tax year satisfies the requirement of section 4.01(3) of Rev. Proc. 2006-46. I also represent that the corporation is not precluded by section 4.02 of Rev. Proc. 2006-46 from obtaining automatic approval of such adoption, retention, or change in tax year.

Note. If you do not use item P and the corporation wants a fiscal tax year, complete either item Q or R below. Item Q is used to request a fiscal tax year based on a business purpose and to make a back-up section 444 election. Item R is used to make a regular section 444 election.

Q   Business Purpose—To request a fiscal tax year based on a business purpose, check box Q1. See instructions for details including payment of a user fee. You may also check box Q2 and/or box Q3.

1. Check here ▶ ☐ if the fiscal year entered in item F, Part I, is requested under the prior approval provisions of Rev. Proc. 2002-39, 2002-22 I.R.B. 1046. Attach to Form 2553 a statement describing the relevant facts and circumstances and, if applicable, the gross receipts from sales and services necessary to establish a business purpose. See the instructions for details regarding the gross receipts from sales and services. If the IRS proposes to disapprove the requested fiscal year, do you want a conference with the IRS National Office?

☐ Yes   ☐ No

2. Check here ▶ ☐ to show that the corporation intends to make a back-up section 444 election in the event the corporation's business purpose request is not approved by the IRS. (See instructions for more information.)

3. Check here ▶ ☐ to show that the corporation agrees to adopt or change to a tax year ending December 31 if necessary for the IRS to accept this election for S corporation status in the event (1) the corporation's business purpose request is not approved and the corporation makes a back-up section 444 election, but is ultimately not qualified to make a section 444 election, or (2) the corporation's business purpose request is not approved and the corporation did not make a back-up section 444 election.

R   Section 444 Election—To make a section 444 election, check box R1. You may also check box R2.

1. Check here ▶ ☐ to show that the corporation will make, if qualified, a section 444 election to have the fiscal tax year shown in item F, Part I. To make the election, you must complete **Form 8716,** Election To Have a Tax Year Other Than a Required Tax Year, and either attach it to Form 2553 or file it separately.

2. Check here ▶ ☐ to show that the corporation agrees to adopt or change to a tax year ending December 31 if necessary for the IRS to accept this election for S corporation status in the event the corporation is ultimately not qualified to make a section 444 election.

Part III   Qualified Subchapter S Trust (QSST) Election Under Section 1361(d)(2)*

Income beneficiary's name and address	Social security number
Trust's name and address	Employer identification number

Date on which stock of the corporation was transferred to the trust (month, day, year) . . . . ▶

In order for the trust named above to be a QSST and thus a qualifying shareholder of the S corporation for which this Form 2553 is filed, I hereby make the election under section 1361(d)(2). Under penalties of perjury, I certify that the trust meets the definitional requirements of section 1361(d)(3) and that all other information provided in Part III is true, correct, and complete.

Signature of income beneficiary or signature and title of legal representative or other qualified person making the election	Date

*Use Part III to make the QSST election only if stock of the corporation has been transferred to the trust on or before the date on which the corporation makes its election to be an S corporation. The QSST election must be made and filed separately if stock of the corporation is transferred to the trust **after** the date on which the corporation makes the S election.

Form **2553** (Rev. 12-2013)

Form 2553 (Rev. 12-2013)   Page **4**

| **Part IV** | **Late Corporate Classification Election Representations** (see instructions) |

If a late entity classification election was intended to be effective on the same date that the S corporation election was intended to be effective, relief for a late S corporation election must also include the following representations.

1   The requesting entity is an eligible entity as defined in Regulations section 301.7701-3(a);

2   The requesting entity intended to be classified as a corporation as of the effective date of the S corporation status;

3   The requesting entity fails to qualify as a corporation solely because Form 8832, Entity Classification Election, was not timely filed under Regulations section 301.7701-3(c)(1)(i), or Form 8832 was not deemed to have been filed under Regulations section 301.7701-3(c)(1)(v)(C);

4   The requesting entity fails to qualify as an S corporation on the effective date of the S corporation status solely because the S corporation election was not timely filed pursuant to section 1362(b); **and**

5a   The requesting entity timely filed all required federal tax returns and information returns consistent with its requested classification as an S corporation for all of the years the entity intended to be an S corporation and no inconsistent tax or information returns have been filed by or with respect to the entity during any of the tax years, **or**

b   The requesting entity has not filed a federal tax or information return for the first year in which the election was intended to be effective because the due date has not passed for that year's federal tax or information return.

Form **2553** (Rev. 12-2013)

Form **8832**
(Rev. December 2013)

Department of the Treasury
Internal Revenue Service

Entity Classification Election

OMB No. 1545-1516

▶ Information about Form 8832 and its instructions is at *www.irs.gov/form8832.*

Type
or
Print

Name of eligible entity making election	Employer identification number

Number, street, and room or suite no. If a P.O. box, see instructions.

City or town, state, and ZIP code. If a foreign address, enter city, province or state, postal code and country. Follow the country's practice for entering the postal code.

▶ Check if: ☐ Address change   ☐ Late classification relief sought under Revenue Procedure 2009-41
☐ Relief for a late change of entity classification election sought under Revenue Procedure 2010-32

Part I	**Election Information**

1   **Type of election** (see instructions):

a ☐ Initial classification by a newly-formed entity. Skip lines 2a and 2b and go to line 3.
b ☐ Change in current classification. Go to line 2a.

2a Has the eligible entity previously filed an entity election that had an effective date within the last 60 months?

☐ **Yes.** Go to line 2b.
☐ **No.** Skip line 2b and go to line 3.

2b Was the eligible entity's prior election an initial classification election by a newly formed entity that was effective on the date of formation?

☐ **Yes.** Go to line 3.
☐ **No.** Stop here. You generally are not currently eligible to make the election (see instructions).

3 Does the eligible entity have more than one owner?

☐ **Yes.** You can elect to be classified as a partnership or an association taxable as a corporation. Skip line 4 and go to line 5.
☐ **No.** You can elect to be classified as an association taxable as a corporation or to be disregarded as a separate entity. Go to line 4.

4 If the eligible entity has only one owner, provide the following information:

a Name of owner ▶ _____
b Identifying number of owner ▶ _____

5 If the eligible entity is owned by one or more affiliated corporations that file a consolidated return, provide the name and employer identification number of the parent corporation:

a Name of parent corporation ▶ _____
b Employer identification number ▶ _____

For Paperwork Reduction Act Notice, see instructions.   Cat. No. 22598R   Form **8832** (Rev. 12-2013)

Form 8832 (Rev. 12-2013)   Page **2**

Part I	**Election Information** (Continued)

6   Type of entity (see instructions):

a   ☐ A domestic eligible entity electing to be classified as an association taxable as a corporation.

b   ☐ A domestic eligible entity electing to be classified as a partnership.

c   ☐ A domestic eligible entity with a single owner electing to be disregarded as a separate entity.

d   ☐ A foreign eligible entity electing to be classified as an association taxable as a corporation.

e   ☐ A foreign eligible entity electing to be classified as a partnership.

f   ☐ A foreign eligible entity with a single owner electing to be disregarded as a separate entity.

7   If the eligible entity is created or organized in a foreign jurisdiction, provide the foreign country of organization ▶

8   Election is to be effective beginning (month, day, year) (see instructions) . . . . ▶

9 Name and title of contact person whom the IRS may call for more information	**10** Contact person's telephone number

Consent Statement and Signature(s) (see instructions)

Under penalties of perjury, I (we) declare that I (we) consent to the election of the above-named entity to be classified as indicated above, and that I (we) have examined this election and consent statement, and to the best of my (our) knowledge and belief, this election and consent statement are true, correct, and complete. If I am an officer, manager, or member signing for the entity, I further declare under penalties of perjury that I am authorized to make the election on its behalf.

Signature(s)	Date	Title

Form **8832** (Rev. 12-2013)

Form 8832 (Rev. 12-2013)

Page **3**

Part II   **Late Election Relief**

11   Provide the explanation as to why the entity classification election was not filed on time (see instructions).

Under penalties of perjury, I (we) declare that I (we) have examined this election, including accompanying documents, and, to the best of my (our) knowledge and belief, the election contains all the relevant facts relating to the election, and such facts are true, correct, and complete. I (we) further declare that I (we) have personal knowledge of the facts and circumstances related to the election. I (we) further declare that the elements required for relief in Section 4.01 of Revenue Procedure 2009-41 have been satisfied.

Signature(s)	Date	Title

Form **8832** (Rev. 12-2013)

Form **4562**	**Depreciation and Amortization**	OMB No. 1545-0172
	(Including Information on Listed Property)	**2015**
Department of the Treasury Internal Revenue Service (99)	▶ Attach to your tax return. ▶ Information about Form 4562 and its separate instructions is at *www.irs.gov/form4562*.	Attachment Sequence No. **179**

Name(s) shown on return	Business or activity to which this form relates	Identifying number

Part I   Election To Expense Certain Property Under Section 179
Note: If you have any listed property, complete Part V before you complete Part I.

1	Maximum amount (see instructions)	1	
2	Total cost of section 179 property placed in service (see instructions)	2	
3	Threshold cost of section 179 property before reduction in limitation (see instructions)	3	
4	Reduction in limitation. Subtract line 3 from line 2. If zero or less, enter -0-	4	
5	Dollar limitation for tax year. Subtract line 4 from line 1. If zero or less, enter -0-. If married filing separately, see instructions	5	

6	(a) Description of property	(b) Cost (business use only)	(c) Elected cost	

7	Listed property. Enter the amount from line 29 . . . . **7**		
8	Total elected cost of section 179 property. Add amounts in column (c), lines 6 and 7	8	
9	Tentative deduction. Enter the **smaller** of line 5 or line 8	9	
10	Carryover of disallowed deduction from line 13 of your 2014 Form 4562	10	
11	Business income limitation. Enter the smaller of business income (not less than zero) or line 5 (see instructions)	11	
12	Section 179 expense deduction. Add lines 9 and 10, but do not enter more than line 11	12	
13	Carryover of disallowed deduction to 2016. Add lines 9 and 10, less line 12 ▶ **13**		

Note: Do not use Part II or Part III below for listed property. Instead, use Part V.

Part II   Special Depreciation Allowance and Other Depreciation (Do not include listed property.) (See instructions.)

14	Special depreciation allowance for qualified property (other than listed property) placed in service during the tax year (see instructions)	14	
15	Property subject to section 168(f)(1) election	15	
16	Other depreciation (including ACRS)	16	

Part III   MACRS Depreciation (Do not include listed property.) (See instructions.)

Section A

17	MACRS deductions for assets placed in service in tax years beginning before 2015	17	
18	If you are electing to group any assets placed in service during the tax year into one or more general asset accounts, check here ▶ ☐		

Section B—Assets Placed in Service During 2015 Tax Year Using the General Depreciation System

(a) Classification of property	(b) Month and year placed in service	(c) Basis for depreciation (business/investment use only—see instructions)	(d) Recovery period	(e) Convention	(f) Method	(g) Depreciation deduction
19a 3-year property						
b 5-year property						
c 7-year property						
d 10-year property						
e 15-year property						
f 20-year property						
g 25-year property			25 yrs.		S/L	
h Residential rental property			27.5 yrs.	MM	S/L	
			27.5 yrs.	MM	S/L	
i Nonresidential real property			39 yrs.	MM	S/L	
				MM	S/L	

Section C—Assets Placed in Service During 2015 Tax Year Using the Alternative Depreciation System

20a Class life					S/L	
b 12-year			12 yrs.		S/L	
c 40-year			40 yrs.	MM	S/L	

Part IV   Summary (See instructions.)

21	Listed property. Enter amount from line 28	21	
22	**Total.** Add amounts from line 12, lines 14 through 17, lines 19 and 20 in column (g), and line 21. Enter here and on the appropriate lines of your return. Partnerships and S corporations—see instructions	22	
23	For assets shown above and placed in service during the current year, enter the portion of the basis attributable to section 263A costs **23**		

For Paperwork Reduction Act Notice, see separate instructions.   Cat. No. 12906N   Form **4562** (2015)

Form 4562 (2015) Page **2**

Part V — Listed Property (Include automobiles, certain other vehicles, certain aircraft, certain computers, and property used for entertainment, recreation, or amusement.)

Note: For any vehicle for which you are using the standard mileage rate or deducting lease expense, complete **only** 24a, 24b, columns (a) through (c) of Section A, all of Section B, and Section C if applicable.

Section A—Depreciation and Other Information (Caution: See the instructions for limits for passenger automobiles.)

24a Do you have evidence to support the business/investment use claimed? ☐ Yes ☐ No   **24b** If "Yes," is the evidence written? ☐ Yes ☐ No

(a) Type of property (list vehicles first)	(b) Date placed in service	(c) Business/ investment use percentage	(d) Cost or other basis	(e) Basis for depreciation (business/investment use only)	(f) Recovery period	(g) Method/ Convention	(h) Depreciation deduction	(i) Elected section 179 cost
25 Special depreciation allowance for qualified listed property placed in service during the tax year and used more than 50% in a qualified business use (see instructions) . **25**								
26 Property used more than 50% in a qualified business use:								
		%						
		%						
		%						
27 Property used 50% or less in a qualified business use:								
		%				S/L –		
		%				S/L –		
		%				S/L –		

28 Add amounts in column (h), lines 25 through 27. Enter here and on line 21, page 1 . **28**

29 Add amounts in column (i), line 26. Enter here and on line 7, page 1 . . . . **29**

Section B—Information on Use of Vehicles

Complete this section for vehicles used by a sole proprietor, partner, or other "more than 5% owner," or related person. If you provided vehicles to your employees, first answer the questions in Section C to see if you meet an exception to completing this section for those vehicles.

	(a) Vehicle 1		(b) Vehicle 2		(c) Vehicle 3		(d) Vehicle 4		(e) Vehicle 5		(f) Vehicle 6	
30 Total business/investment miles driven during the year (**do not** include commuting miles) .												
31 Total commuting miles driven during the year												
32 Total other personal (noncommuting) miles driven												
33 Total miles driven during the year. Add lines 30 through 32												
34 Was the vehicle available for personal use during off-duty hours?	Yes	No	Yes	No	Yes	No	Yes	No	Yes	No	Yes	No
35 Was the vehicle used primarily by a more than 5% owner or related person? . .												
36 Is another vehicle available for personal use?												

Section C—Questions for Employers Who Provide Vehicles for Use by Their Employees

Answer these questions to determine if you meet an exception to completing Section B for vehicles used by employees who **are not** more than 5% owners or related persons (see instructions).

		Yes	No
37	Do you maintain a written policy statement that prohibits all personal use of vehicles, including commuting, by your employees?		
38	Do you maintain a written policy statement that prohibits personal use of vehicles, except commuting, by your employees? See the instructions for vehicles used by corporate officers, directors, or 1% or more owners . .		
39	Do you treat all use of vehicles by employees as personal use?		
40	Do you provide more than five vehicles to your employees, obtain information from your employees about the use of the vehicles, and retain the information received?		
41	Do you meet the requirements concerning qualified automobile demonstration use? (See instructions.) . . .		

Note: If your answer to 37, 38, 39, 40, or 41 is "Yes," do not complete Section B for the covered vehicles.

Part VI — Amortization

(a) Description of costs	(b) Date amortization begins	(c) Amortizable amount	(d) Code section	(e) Amortization period or percentage	(f) Amortization for this year
42 Amortization of costs that begins during your 2015 tax year (see instructions):					

43 Amortization of costs that began before your 2015 tax year **43**

44 Total. Add amounts in column (f). See the instructions for where to report **44**

Form **4562** (2015)

Form **4797**	**Sales of Business Property**	OMB No. 1545-0184
	(Also Involuntary Conversions and Recapture Amounts Under Sections 179 and 280F(b)(2))	20**15**
Department of the Treasury Internal Revenue Service	► Attach to your tax return. ► Information about Form 4797 and its separate instructions is at *www.irs.gov/form4797.*	Attachment Sequence No. **27**

Name(s) shown on return	Identifying number

1 Enter the gross proceeds from sales or exchanges reported to you for 2015 on Form(s) 1099-B or 1099-S (or substitute statement) that you are including on line 2, 10, or 20 (see instructions) . . . . | **1** |

Part I **Sales or Exchanges of Property Used in a Trade or Business and Involuntary Conversions From Other Than Casualty or Theft—Most Property Held More Than 1 Year** (see instructions)

2	**(a)** Description of property	**(b)** Date acquired (mo., day, yr.)	**(c)** Date sold (mo., day, yr.)	**(d)** Gross sales price	**(e)** Depreciation allowed or allowable since acquisition	**(f)** Cost or other basis, plus improvements and expense of sale	**(g) Gain or (loss)** Subtract (f) from the sum of (d) and (e)

3	Gain, if any, from Form 4684, line 39	**3**
4	Section 1231 gain from installment sales from Form 6252, line 26 or 37	**4**
5	Section 1231 gain or (loss) from like-kind exchanges from Form 8824	**5**
6	Gain, if any, from line 32, from other than casualty or theft.	**6**
7	Combine lines 2 through 6. Enter the gain or (loss) here and on the appropriate line as follows:	**7**

Partnerships (except electing large partnerships) and S corporations. Report the gain or (loss) following the instructions for Form 1065, Schedule K, line 10, or Form 1120S, Schedule K, line 9. Skip lines 8, 9, 11, and 12 below.

Individuals, partners, S corporation shareholders, and all others. If line 7 is zero or a loss, enter the amount from line 7 on line 11 below and skip lines 8 and 9. If line 7 is a gain and you did not have any prior year section 1231 losses, or they were recaptured in an earlier year, enter the gain from line 7 as a long-term capital gain on the Schedule D filed with your return and skip lines 8, 9, 11, and 12 below.

8	Nonrecaptured net section 1231 losses from prior years (see instructions)	**8**
9	Subtract line 8 from line 7. If zero or less, enter -0-. If line 9 is zero, enter the gain from line 7 on line 12 below. If line 9 is more than zero, enter the amount from line 8 on line 12 below and enter the gain from line 9 as a long-term capital gain on the Schedule D filed with your return (see instructions)	**9**

Part II **Ordinary Gains and Losses** (see instructions)

10 Ordinary gains and losses not included on lines 11 through 16 (include property held 1 year or less):

11	Loss, if any, from line 7	**11** ( )
12	Gain, if any, from line 7 or amount from line 8, if applicable	**12**
13	Gain, if any, from line 31	**13**
14	Net gain or (loss) from Form 4684, lines 31 and 38a	**14**
15	Ordinary gain from installment sales from Form 6252, line 25 or 36	**15**
16	Ordinary gain or (loss) from like-kind exchanges from Form 8824.	**16**
17	Combine lines 10 through 16	**17**

18 For all except individual returns, enter the amount from line 17 on the appropriate line of your return and skip lines a and b below. For individual returns, complete lines a and b below:

a If the loss on line 11 includes a loss from Form 4684, line 35, column (b)(ii), enter that part of the loss here. Enter the part of the loss from income-producing property on Schedule A (Form 1040), line 28, and the part of the loss from property used as an employee on Schedule A (Form 1040), line 23. Identify as from "Form 4797, line 18a." See instructions . . | **18a** |

b Redetermine the gain or (loss) on line 17 excluding the loss, if any, on line 18a. Enter here and on Form 1040, line 14 | **18b** |

For Paperwork Reduction Act Notice, see separate instructions.   Cat. No. 13086I   Form **4797** (2015)

Form 4797 (2015)   Page **2**

Part III Gain From Disposition of Property Under Sections 1245, 1250, 1252, 1254, and 1255 (see instructions)

	(b) Date acquired (mo., day, yr.)	**(c)** Date sold (mo., day, yr.)
19 **(a)** Description of section 1245, 1250, 1252, 1254, or 1255 property:		
A		
B		
C		
D		

	These columns relate to the properties on lines 19A through 19D. ▶		**Property A**	**Property B**	**Property C**	**Property D**
20	Gross sales price (**Note:** See line 1 before completing.)	20				
21	Cost or other basis plus expense of sale	21				
22	Depreciation (or depletion) allowed or allowable	22				
23	Adjusted basis. Subtract line 22 from line 21	23				
24	Total gain. Subtract line 23 from line 20	24				
25	**If section 1245 property:**					
a	Depreciation allowed or allowable from line 22	25a				
b	Enter the **smaller** of line 24 or 25a	25b				
26	**If section 1250 property:** If straight line depreciation was used, enter -0- on line 26g, except for a corporation subject to section 291.					
a	Additional depreciation after 1975 (see instructions)	26a				
b	Applicable percentage multiplied by the **smaller** of line 24 or line 26a (see instructions)	26b				
c	Subtract line 26a from line 24. If residential rental property **or** line 24 is not more than line 26a, skip lines 26d and 26e	26c				
d	Additional depreciation after 1969 and before 1976	26d				
e	Enter the **smaller** of line 26c or 26d	26e				
f	Section 291 amount (corporations only)	26f				
g	Add lines 26b, 26e, and 26f	26g				
27	**If section 1252 property:** Skip this section if you did not dispose of farmland or if this form is being completed for a partnership (other than an electing large partnership).					
a	Soil, water, and land clearing expenses	27a				
b	Line 27a multiplied by applicable percentage (see instructions)	27b				
c	Enter the **smaller** of line 24 or 27b	27c				
28	**If section 1254 property:**					
a	Intangible drilling and development costs, expenditures for development of mines and other natural deposits, mining exploration costs, and depletion (see instructions)	28a				
b	Enter the **smaller** of line 24 or 28a	28b				
29	**If section 1255 property:**					
a	Applicable percentage of payments excluded from income under section 126 (see instructions)	29a				
b	Enter the **smaller** of line 24 or 29a (see instructions)	29b				

Summary of Part III Gains. Complete property columns A through D through line 29b before going to line 30.

30	Total gains for all properties. Add property columns A through D, line 24	30	
31	Add property columns A through D, lines 25b, 26g, 27c, 28b, and 29b. Enter here and on line 13	31	
32	Subtract line 31 from line 30. Enter the portion from casualty or theft on Form 4684, line 33. Enter the portion from other than casualty or theft on Form 4797, line 6	32	

Part IV Recapture Amounts Under Sections 179 and 280F(b)(2) When Business Use Drops to 50% or Less (see instructions)

			(a) Section 179	**(b)** Section 280F(b)(2)
33	Section 179 expense deduction or depreciation allowable in prior years	33		
34	Recomputed depreciation (see instructions)	34		
35	Recapture amount. Subtract line 34 from line 33. See the instructions for where to report	35		

Form **4797** (2015)

Table of Cases Cited

Table of Code Sections Cited

Table of Regulations Cited

Table of Revenue Procedures and Revenue Rulings Cited

Letter Rulings

Glossary of Tax Terms

—A—

A. (*see* Acquiescence).

Accelerated Cost Recovery System (ACRS). An alternate form of depreciation enacted by the Economic Recovery Tax Act of 1981 and significantly modified by the Tax Reform Act of 1986. The modified cost recovery system applies to assets placed into service after 1986 and is referred to as MACRS. Under both systems, the cost of a qualifying asset is recovered over a set period of time. Salvage value is ignored. § 168.

Accelerated Depreciation. Various depreciation methods that produce larger depreciation deductions in the earlier years of an asset's life than straight-line depreciation. Examples: double-declining balance method (200% declining balance) and sum-of-the-years'-digits method. § 167 (*see* Depreciation).

Accounting Method. A method by which an entity's income and expenses are determined. The primary accounting methods used are the accrual method and the cash method. Other accounting methods include the installment method, the percentage-of-completion method (for construction), and various methods for valuing inventories, such as FIFO and LIFO. §§ 446 and 447 (*see also specific accounting methods*).

Accounting Period. A period of time used by a taxpayer in determining his or her income, expenses, and tax liability. An accounting period is generally a year for tax purposes, either a calendar year, a fiscal year, or a 52–53 week year. §§ 441 and 443.

Accrual Method of Accounting. The method of accounting that reflects the income earned and the expenses incurred during a given tax period. However, unearned income of an accrual basis taxpayer must generally be included in an entity's income in the year in which it is received, even if it is not actually earned by the entity until a later tax Period. § 446.

Accumulated Adjustment Account (AAA). A summary of all includible income and gains, expenses, and losses of an S Corporation for taxable years after 1982, except those that relate to excludable income, distributions, and redemptions of an S Corporation. Distributions from the AAA are not taxable to the shareholders. §§ 1368(c)(1) and (3)(1).

Accumulated Earnings Credit. A reduction in arriving at a corporation's accumulated taxable income (in computing the Accumulated Earnings Tax). Its purpose is to avoid penalizing a corporation for retaining sufficient earnings and profits to meet the reasonable needs of the business. § 535(c).

Accumulated Earnings Tax. A penalty tax on the unreasonable accumulation of earnings and profits by a corporation. It is intended to encourage the distribution of earnings and profits of a corporation to its shareholders. §§ 531–537.

Accumulated Taxable Income. The amount on which the accumulated earnings tax is imposed. §§ 531 and 535.

Accuracy-related Penalty. Any of the group of penalties that includes negligence or disregard of rules or regulations, substantial understatement of income tax, substantial valuation misstatement for income tax purposes, substantial overstatement of pension liabilities, and substantial estate or gift valuation understatement. § 6662.

Acquiescence. The public endorsement of a regular Tax Court decision by the Commissioner of the Internal Revenue Service. When the Commissioner acquiesces to a regular Tax Court decision, the IRS generally will not dispute the result in cases involving substantially similar facts (*see* Nonacquiescence).

Ad Valorem Tax. A tax based on the value of property.

Adjusted Basis. The basis (i.e., cost or other basis) of property plus capital improvements minus depreciation allowed or allowable. See § 1016 for other adjustments to basis. § 1016 (*see* Basis).

Adjusted Gross Income. A term used with reference to individual taxpayers. Adjusted gross income consists of an individual's gross income less certain deductions and business expenses. § 62.

Adjusted Ordinary Gross Income (AOGI). A term used in relation to personal holding companies. Adjusted ordinary gross income is determined by subtracting certain expenses related to rents and mineral, oil, and gas royalties, and certain interest expense from ordinary gross income § 543(b)(2).

Administrator. A person appointed by the court to administrate the estate of a deceased person. If named to perform these duties by the decedent's will, this person is called an executor (executrix).

AFTR (American Federal Tax Reports). These volumes contain the Federal tax decisions issued by the U.S. District Courts, U.S. Court of Federal Claims, U.S. Circuit Courts of Appeals, and the U.S. Supreme Court (*see* AFTR2d).

AFTR2d (American Federal Tax Reports, Second Series). The second series of the American Federal Tax Reports. These volumes contain the Federal tax decisions issued by the U.S. District Courts, U.S. Court of Federal Claims. U.S. Circuit Courts of Appeals, and the U.S. Supreme Court (*see* AFTR).

Allocation. A method of assigning nonbusiness income to the state in which the income was generated or otherwise sourced.

Alternate Valuation Date. The property contained in a decedent's gross estate must be valued at either the decedent's date of death or the alternate valuation date. The alternate valuation date is six months after the decedent's date of death, or, if the property is disposed of prior to that date. The particular property disposed of is valued as of the date of its disposition. § 2032.

Alternative Minimum Tax. A tax imposed on taxpayers only if it exceeds the "regular" tax of the taxpayer. Regular taxable income is adjusted by certain timing differences, then increased by tax preferences to arrive at alternative minimum taxable income.

Amortization. The systematic write-off (deduction) of the cost or other basis of an intangible asset over its estimated useful life. The concept is similar to depreciation (used for tangible assets) and depletion (used for natural resources) (*see* Goodwill; Intangible Asset).

Amount Realized. Any money received, plus the fair market value of any other property or services received, plus any liabilities discharged on the sale or other disposition of property. The determination of the amount realized is the first step in determining realized gain or loss. § 1001(b).

Annual Exclusion. The amount each year that a donor may exclude from Federal gift tax for each donee. Currently, the annual exclusion is $14,000 per donee. The annual exclusion does not generally apply to gifts of future interests. § 2503(b).

Annuity. A fixed amount of money payable to a person at specific intervals for either a specific period of time or for life.

Appellate Court. A court to which other court decisions are appealed. The appellate courts for Federal tax purposes include the Courts of Appeals and the Supreme Court.

Apportionment. A method of assigning business income among the states in which a corporation has established nexus using formulas based on sales, property and payroll.

Arm's-Length Transaction. A transaction entered into by unrelated parties, all acting in their own best interests. It is presumed that in an arm's length transaction the prices used are the fair market values of the properties or services being transferred in the transaction.

Articles of Incorporation. The basic instrument filed with the appropriate state agency when a business is incorporated.

Assessment of Tax. The imposition of an additional tax liability by the Internal Revenue Service (i.e., as the result of an audit).

Assignment of Income. A situation in which a taxpayer assigns income or income-producing property to another person or entity in an attempt to avoid paying taxes on that income. An assignment of income or income-producing property is generally not recognized for tax purposes, and the income is taxable to the assignor.

Association. An entity that possesses a majority of the following characteristics: associates; profit motive; continuity of life; centralized management; limited liability; free transferability of interests. Associations are taxed as corporations. § 7701(a)(3). Reg. § 301.7701-2.

At-Risk Limitation. A provision that limits a deduction for losses to the amounts "at risk." A taxpayer is generally not "at risk" in situations where nonrecourse debt is used. § 465.

Attribution. (see Constructive Ownership).

Audit. The examination of a taxpayer's return or other taxable transactions by the Internal Revenue Service in order to determine the correct tax liability. Types of audits include correspondence audits, office audits, and field audits (*see also* Correspondence Audit; Office Audit; Field Audit).

—B—

Bad Debt. An uncollectible debt. A bad debt may be classified either as a business bad debt or a nonbusiness bad debt. A business bad debt is one that has arisen in the course of the taxpayer's business (with a business purpose). Nonbusiness bad debts are treated as short-term capital losses rather than as ordinary losses. § 166.

Bargain Sale, Rental, or Purchase. A sale, rental, or purchase of property for less than its fair market value. The difference between the sale, rental, or purchase price and the property's fair market value may have its own tax consequences, such as consideration as a constructive dividend or a gift.

Bartering. The exchange of goods and services without using money.

Basis. The starting point in determining the gain or loss from the sale or other disposition of an asset, or the depreciation (or depletion or amortization) on an asset. For example, if an asset is purchased for cash, the basis of that asset is the cash paid. §§ 1012, 1014, 1015, 334, 359, 362.

Beneficiary. Someone who will benefit from an act of another, such as the beneficiary of a life insurance contract, the beneficiary of a trust (i.e., income beneficiary), or the beneficiary of an estate.

Bequest. A testamentary transfer (by will) of personal property (personalty).

Board of Tax Appeals (B.T.A.). The predecessor of the United States Tax Court, in existence from 1924 to 1942.

Bona Fide. Real; in good faith.

Bonus Depreciation. Depreciation that taxpayers can take in the year of acquisition in addition to normal depreciation and expensing for certain newly acquired property.

Boot. Cash or property that is not included in the definition of a particular type of nontaxable exchange [see §§ 351(b) and 1031(b)]. In these nontaxable exchanges, a taxpayer who receives boot must recognize gain to the extent of the boot received or the realized gain, whichever is less.

Brother-Sister Corporations. A controlled group of two or more corporations owned (in certain amounts) by five or fewer individuals, estates, or trusts. § 1563(a)(2).

Burden of Proof. The weight of evidence in a legal case or in a tax proceeding. Generally, the burden of proof is on the taxpayer in a tax case. However, the burden of proof is on the government in fraud cases. § 7454.

Business Purpose. An actual business reason for following a course of action. Tax avoidance alone is not considered to be a business purpose. In areas such as corporate formation and corporate reorganizations, business purpose is especially important.

—C—

C Corporation. A so-called regular corporation that is a separate tax-paying entity and is subject to the tax rules contained in Subchapter C of the Internal Revenue Code (as opposed to an S corporation, which is subject to the tax rules of Subchapter S of the Code).

Capital Asset. All property held by a taxpayer (e.g., house, car, clothing) except for certain assets that are specifically excluded from the definition of a capital asset, such as inventory and depreciable and real property used in a trade or business.

Capital Contribution. Cash, services, or property contributed by a partner to a partnership or by a shareholder to a corporation. Capital contributions are not income to the recipient partnership or corporation. §§ 721 and 118.

Capital Expenditure. Any amount paid for new buildings or for permanent improvements; any expenditures that add to the value or prolong the life of property or adapt the property to a new or different use. Capital expenditures should be added to the basis of the property improved. § 263.

Capital Gain. A gain from the sale or other disposition of a capital asset. § 1222.

Capital Loss. A loss from the sale or other disposition of a capital asset. § 1222.

Cash Method of Accounting. The method of accounting that reflects the income received (or constructively received) and the expenses paid during a given period. However, prepaid expenses of a cash basis taxpayer that benefit more than one year may be required to be deducted only in the periods benefited (e.g., a premium for a three-year insurance policy may have to be spread over three years).

CCH. (*see* Commerce Clearing House).

Certiorari. A *Writ of Certiorari* is the form used to appeal a lower court (U.S. Court of Appeals) decision to the Supreme Court. The Supreme Court then decides, by reviewing the *Writ of Certiorari*, whether it will accept the appeal or not. The Supreme Court generally does not accept the appeal unless a constitutional issue is involved or the lower courts are in conflict. If the Supreme Court refuses to accept the appeal, then the certiorari is denied (cert. den.).

Claim of Right Doctrine. If a taxpayer has an unrestricted claim to income, the income is included in that taxpayer's income when it is received or constructively received, even if there is a possibility that all or part of the income may have to be returned to another party.

Closely Held Corporation. A corporation whose voting stock is owned by one or a few shareholders and is operated by this person or closely knit group.

Collapsible Corporation. A corporation that liquidates before it has realized a substantial portion of its income. Shareholders treat the gain on these liquidating distributions as ordinary income (rather than dividend income or capital gains). § 341.

Combined (Unitary) Reporting. A method of multistate taxation used by about half the states in which the combined taxable income of all members of a unitary group is apportioned among the states based on apportionment percentages that reflect the combined operations of the unitary group.

Commerce Clearing House. A publisher of tax materials, including a multivolume tax service, volumes that contain the Federal courts' decisions on tax matters (USTC) and the Tax Court regular (T.C.) and memorandum (TCM) decisions.

Community Property. Property that is owned together by husband and wife, where each has an undivided one-half interest in the property due to their marital status. The nine community property states are Arizona, California, Idaho, Louisiana, Nevada, New Mexico, Texas, Washington, and Wisconsin.

Complex Trust. Any trust that does not meet the requirements of a simple trust. For example, a trust will be considered to be a complex trust if it does not distribute the trust income currently, if it takes a deduction for a charitable contribution for the current year, or if it distributes any of the trust corpus currently. § 661.

Condemnation. The taking of private property for a public use by a public authority, an exercise of the power of eminent domain. The public authority compensates the owner of the property taken in a condemnation (*see also* Involuntary Conversion).

Conduit Principle. The provisions in the tax law that allow specific tax characteristics to be passed through certain entities to the owners of the entity without losing their identity. For example, the short-term capital gains of a partnership would be passed through to the partners and retain their character as short-term capital gains on the tax returns of the partners. This principle applies in varying degrees to partnerships, S corporations, estates, and trusts.

Consent Dividend. A term used in relation to the accumulated earnings tax and the personal holding company tax. A consent dividend occurs when the shareholders consent to treat a certain amount as a taxable dividend on their tax returns even though there is no distribution of cash or property. The purpose of this is to obtain a dividends-paid deduction. § 565.

Consolidated Return. A method used to determine the tax liability of a group of affiliated corporations. The aggregate income (with certain adjustments) of a group is viewed as the income of a single enterprise. § 1501.

Consolidation. The statutory combination of two or more corporations in a *new* corporation. § 368(a)(1)(A).

Constructive Dividends. The constructive receipt of a dividend. Even though a taxable benefit was not designated as a dividend by the distributing corporation, a shareholder may be designated by the IRS as having received a dividend if the benefit has the appearance of a dividend. For example, if a shareholder uses corporate property for personal purposes rent-free, he or she will have a constructive dividend equal to the fair rental value of the corporate property.

Constructive Ownership. In certain situations, the tax law attributes the ownership of stock to persons "related" to the person or entity that actually owns the stock. The related party is said to constructively own the stock of that person. For example, under § 267(c) a father is considered to constructively own all stock actually owned by his son. §§ 267, 318, and 544(a).

Constructive Receipt. When income is available to a taxpayer, even though it is not actually received by the taxpayer, the amount is considered to be constructively received by the taxpayer and should be included in income (e.g., accrued interest on a savings account). However, if there are restrictions on the availability of the income, it is generally not considered to be constructively received until the restrictions are removed (e.g., interest on a 6-month certificate of deposit is not constructively received until the end of the 6-month period if early withdrawal would result in loss of interest or principal).

Contributions to the Capital of a Corporation. (*see* Capital Contributions).

Controlled Foreign Corporation. A foreign corporation in which more than 50% of its voting power is controlled directly or indirectly at any a time during the year by U.S. stockholders who individually control at least 10% of the voting power. U.S. shareholders are taxed on their share of the income as it is earned, rather than when it is distributed. §§ 951 through 964.

Corpus. The principal of a trust, as opposed to the income of the trust. Also called the *res* of the trust.

Correspondence Audit. An IRS audit conducted through the mail. Generally, verification or substantiation for specified items is requested by the IRS, and the taxpayer mails the requested information to the IRS (*see* Field Audit; Office Audit).

Cost Depletion. (*see* Depletion).

Court of Appeals. The U.S. Federal court system has 13 circuit Courts of Appeals, which consider cases appealed from the U.S. Court of Federal Claims, the U.S. Tax Court, and the U.S. District Courts. A *Writ of Certiorari* is used to appeal a case from a Court of Appeals to the U.S. Supreme Court (*see* Appellate Court).

Creditor. A person or entity to whom money is owed. The person or entity who owes the money is called the debtor.

—D—

Death Tax. A tax imposed on property upon the death of the owner, such as an estate tax or inheritance tax.

Debtor. A person or entity who owes money to another. The person or entity to whom the money is owed is called the creditor.

Decedent. A deceased person.

Deductions in Respect of a Decedent (DRD). Certain expenses that are incurred by a decedent but are not properly deductible on the decedent's first return because of nonpayment. Deductions in respect of a decedent are deducted by the taxpayer who is legally required to make payment. § 691(b).

Deficiency. An additional tax liability owed to the IRS by a taxpayer. A deficiency is generally proposed by the IRS through the use of a Revenue Agent's Report.

Deficit. A negative balance in retained earnings or in earnings and profits.

Dependent. A person who derives his or her primary support from another. In order for a taxpayer to claim a dependency exemption for a person, there are five tests that must be met: support test, gross income test, citizenship or residency test, relationship or member of household test, and joint return test. § 152.

Depletion. As natural resources are extracted and sold, the cost or other basis of the resource is recovered by the use of depletion. Depletion may be either cost or percentage (statutory) depletion. Cost depletion has to do with the recovery of the cost of natural resources based on the units of the resource sold. Percentage depletion uses percentages given in the Internal Revenue Code multiplied by the gross income from the interest. Subject to limitations. §§ 613 and 613A.

Depreciation. The systematic write-off of the basis of a tangible asset over the asset's estimated useful life. Depreciation is intended to reflect the wear, tear, and obsolescence of the asset (*see* Amortization; Depletion).

Depreciation Recapture. The situation in which all or part of the realized gain from the sale or other disposition of depreciable business property could be treated as ordinary income. See text for discussion of §§ 291, 1245, and 1250.

Determination Letter. A written statement regarding the tax consequences of a transaction issued by an IRS District Director in response to a written inquiry by a taxpayer that applies to a particular set of facts. Determination letters are frequently used to state whether a pension or profit-sharing plan is qualified or not, to determine the tax-exempt status of nonprofit organizations, and to clarify employee status.

Discretionary Trust. A trust in which the trustee or another party has the right to determine whether to accumulate or distribute the trust income currently, and/or which beneficiary is to receive the trust income.

Discriminant Function System (DIF). The computerized system used by the Internal Revenue Service in identifying and selecting returns for examination. This system uses secret mathematical formulas to select those returns that have a probability of tax errors.

Dissent. A disagreement with the majority opinion. The term is generally used to mean the explicit disagreement of one or more judges in a court with the majority decision on a particular case.

Distributable Net Income (DNI). The net income of a fiduciary that is available for distribution to income beneficiaries. DNI is computed by adjusting an estate's or trust's taxable income by certain modifications. § 643(a).

Distribution in Kind. A distribution of property as it is. For example, rather than selling property and distributing the proceeds to the shareholders, the property itself is distributed to the shareholders.

District Court. A trial court in which Federal tax matters can be litigated; the only trial court in which a jury trial can be obtained.

Dividend. A payment by a corporation to its shareholders authorized by the corporation's board of directors to be distributed pro rata among the outstanding shares. However, a constructive dividend does not need to be authorized by the shareholders (*see also* Constructive Dividend).

Dividends-Paid Deduction. A deduction allowed in determining the amount that is subject to the accumulated earnings tax and the personal holding company tax. §§ 561 through 565.

Dividends-Received Deduction. A deduction available to corporations on dividends received from a domestic corporation. The dividends-received deduction is generally 70% of the dividends received. If the recipient corporation owns 20% or more of the stock of the paying corporation, an 80% deduction is allowed. The dividends-received deduction is 100% of the dividends received from another member of an affiliated group, if an election is made §§ 243 through 246.

Domestic Corporation. A corporation which is created or organized in the United States or under the law of the United States or of any state. § 7701(a)(4).

Donee. The person or entity to whom a gift is made.

Donor. The person or entity who makes a gift.

Double Taxation. A situation in which income is taxed twice. For example, a regular corporation pays tax on its taxable income, and when this income is distributed to the corporation's shareholders, the shareholders are taxed on the dividend income.

—E—

Earned Income. Income from personal services. § 911(d)(2).

Earnings and Profits (E&P). The measure of a corporation's ability to pay dividends to its shareholders. Distributions made by a corporation to its shareholders are dividends to the extent of the corporation's earnings and profits. §§ 312 and 316.

Eminent Domain. (*see* Condemnation).

Employee. A person in the service of another, where the employer has the power to specify how the work is to be performed (*see* Independent Contractor).

Encumbrance. A liability.

Entity. For tax purposes, an organization that is considered to have a separate existence, such as a partnership, corporation, estate, or trust.

Escrow. Cash or other property that is held by a third party as security for an obligation.

Estate. All of the property owned by a decedent at the time of his or her death.

Estate Tax. A tax imposed on the transfer of a decedent's taxable estate. The estate, not the heirs, is liable for the estate tax. §§ 2001–2209 (*see* Inheritance Tax).

Estoppel. A bar or impediment preventing a party from asserting a fact or a claim in court that is inconsistent with a position he or she had previously taken.

Excise Tax. A tax imposed by the federal government or the states on a wide variety of items such as gasoline, alcohol and tobacco products. In contrast to sales taxes, excise taxes are typically assessed on the quantity sold rather than a dollar sales price.

Executor. A person appointed in a will to carry out the provisions in the will and to administer the estate of the decedent. (Feminine of *executor* is *executrix*.)

Exempt Organization. An organization (such as a charitable organization) that is exempt from Federal income taxes. §§ 501–528.

Exemption. A deduction allowed in computing taxable income. Personal exemptions are available for the taxpayer and his or her spouse. Dependency exemptions are available for the taxpayer's dependents. §§ 151–154 (*see* Dependent).

Expatriate (U.S.). U.S. citizen working in a foreign country.

—F—

F.2d (Federal Reporter, Second Series). Volumes in which the decisions of the U.S. Court of Federal Claims and the U.S. Courts of Appeals are published.

F. Supp. (Federal Supplement). Volumes in which the decisions of the U.S. District Courts are published.

Fair Market Value. The amount that a willing buyer would pay a willing seller in an arm's-length transaction.

Fed. (Federal Reporter). Volumes in which the decisions of the U.S. Court of Federal Claims and the U.S. Courts of Appeals are published.

FICA (Federal Insurance Contributions Act). The law dealing with Social Security taxes and benefits. §§ 3101–3126.

Fiduciary. A person or institution who holds and manages property for another, such as a guardian, trustee, executor, or administrator. § 7701(a)(6).

Field Audit. An audit conducted by the IRS at the taxpayer's place of business or at the place of business of the taxpayer's representative. Field audits are generally conducted by Revenue Agents (*see* Correspondence Audit; Office Audit).

FIFO (First-In, First-Out). A method of determining the cost of an inventory. The first inventory units acquired are considered to be the first sold. Therefore, the cost of the inventory would consist of the most recently acquired inventory.

Filing Status. The filing status of an individual taxpayer determines the tax rates that are applicable to that taxpayer. The filing statuses include Single, Head of Household, Married Filing Jointly, Married Filing Separately, and Surviving Spouse (Qualifying Widow or Widower).

Fiscal Year. A period of 12 consecutive months, other than a calendar year, used as the accounting period of a business. § 7701(a)(24).

Foreign Corporation. A corporation that is not organized under U.S. laws. Other than a domestic corporation. § 7701(a)(5).

Foreign Personal Holding Company (FPHC). A foreign corporation in which five or fewer U.S. citizens or residents owned more than 50% of the value of its outstanding stock during the taxable year and at least 50% of its gross income (or 60% if it was not an FPHC in the previous year) is foreign personal holding company income. §§ 551–558.

Foreign Sales Corporation (FSC). A corporation created or organized under the laws of a U.S. possession (other than Puerto Rico) or certain foreign countries, has no more than 25 shareholders at any time, has no outstanding preferred stock, maintains a set of records at an office outside the United States and certain records inside the United States, has at least one non-U.S. resident member of the board of directors, makes a timely FSC election, and meets foreign management and foreign economic process tests. §§ 921–927.

Foreign Source Income. Income derived from sources outside the United States. The source of earned income is determined by the place where the work is actually performed. Unearned income usually qualifies as foreign source income when it is received from a foreign resident or for property used in a foreign country and not effectively connected with U.S. sources.

Foreign Tax Credit. A credit available against taxes for foreign income taxes paid or deemed paid. A deduction may be taken for these foreign taxes as an alternative to the foreign tax credit. §§ 27 and 901–905.

Franchise Tax A tax imposed by some states and local governments on the value of capital (common stock, paid in capital and retained earnings) employed within a taxing jurisdiction.

Fraud. A willful intent to evade tax. For tax purposes, fraud is divided into civil fraud and criminal fraud. The IRS has the burden of proof of proving fraud. Civil fraud has a penalty of 75% of the underpayment [§ 6653(b)]. Criminal fraud requires a greater degree of willful intent to evade tax (§§ 7201–7207).

Freedom of Information Act. The means by which the public may obtain information held by Federal agencies.

Fringe Benefits. Benefits received by an employee in addition to his or her salary or wages, such as insurance and recreational facilities.

Functional Currency. In foreign currency translation, normally the U.S. dollar, except that a *qualified business unit* (QBU) is to use the currency of the "economic environment" in which a significant part of the QBU's activities are conducted, if the QBU uses that currency in keeping its books and records. Generally, international transactions are recorded using the *functional currency* of the taxpayer.

FUTA (Federal Unemployment Tax Act). Tax imposed on the employer on the wages of the employees. A credit is generally given for amounts contributed to state unemployment tax funds. §§ 3301–3311.

Future Interest. An interest, the possession or enjoyment of which will come into being at some point in the future. The annual exclusion for gifts applies only to gifts of present interests, as opposed to future interests.

—G—

General Partner. A partner who is jointly and severally liable for the debts of the partnership. A general partner has no limited liability (*see* Limited Partner).

Generation-Skipping Tax. Transfer tax imposed on a certain type of transfer involving a trust and at least three generations of taxpayers. The transfer generally skips a generation younger than the original transferor. The transfer therefore results in the avoidance of one generation's estate tax on the transferred property. §§ 2601–2622.

Gift. A transfer of property or money given for less than adequate consideration in money or money's worth.

Gift-Splitting. A tax provision that allows a married person who makes a gift of his or her property to elect, with the consent of his or her spouse, to treat the gift as being made one-half by each the taxpayer and his or her spouse. The effect of gift-splitting is to take advantage of the annual gift tax exclusions for both the taxpayer and his or her spouse. § 2513.

Gift Tax. A tax imposed on the donor of a gift. The tax applies to transfers in trust or otherwise, whether the gift is direct or indirect, real or personal, tangible or intangible. §§ 2501–2524.

Goodwill. An intangible that has an indefinite useful life, arising from the difference between the purchase price and the value of the assets of an acquired business. Goodwill is amortizable over a 15-year period. § 263(b).

Grantor. The person who creates a trust.

Grantor Trust. A trust in which the transferor (grantor) of the trust does not surrender complete control over the property. Generally, the income from a grantor trust is taxable to the grantor rather than to the person who receives the income. §§ 671–677.

Gross Estate. The value of all property, real or personal, tangible or intangible, owned by a decedent at the time of his or her death. §§ 2031–2046.

Gross Income. Income that is subject to Federal income tax. All income from whatever source derived, unless it is specifically excluded from income (e.g., interest on state and local bonds). § 61.

Guaranteed Payment. A payment made by a partnership to a partner for services or the use of capital, without regard to the income of the partnership. The payment generally is deductible by the partnership and taxable to the partner. § 707(c).

—H—

Half-Year Convention. When using ACRS or MACRS, personalty placed in service at any time during the year is treated as placed in service in the middle of the year, and personalty disposed of or retired at any time during the year is treated as disposed of in the middle of the year. However, if more than 40% of all personalty placed in service during the year is placed in service during the last three months of the year, the mid-quarter convention applies. § 168(d)(4)(A).

Heir. One who inherits property from a decedent.

Hobby. An activity not engaged in for profit. § 183.

Holding Period. The period of time that property is held. Holding period is used to determine whether a gain or loss is short-term or long-term. §§ 1222 and 1223.

H.R. 10 Plans. (*see* Keogh Plans).

—I—

Incident of Ownership. Any economic interest in a life insurance policy, such as the power to change the policy's beneficiary, the right to cancel or assign the policy, and the right to borrow against the policy. § 2042(2).

Income Beneficiary. The person or entity entitled to receive the income from property. Generally used in reference to trusts.

Income in Respect of a Decedent (IRD). Income that had been earned by a decedent at the time of his or her death, but is not included on the final tax return because of the decedent's method of accounting. Income in respect of a decedent is included in the decedent's gross estate and also on the tax return of the person who receives the income. § 691.

Independent Contractor. One who contracts to do a job according to his or her own methods and skills. The employer has control over the independent contractor only as to the final result of his or her work (*see* Employee).

Indirect Method. A method used by the IRS in order to determine whether a taxpayer's income is correctly reported when adequate records do not exist. Indirect methods include the Source and Applications of Funds Method and the Net Worth Method.

Information Return. A return that must be filed with the Internal Revenue Service even though no tax is imposed, such as a partnership return (Form 1065), Form W-2, and Form 1099.

Inheritance Tax. A tax imposed on the privilege of receiving property of a decedent. The tax is imposed on the heir.

Installment Method. A method of accounting under which a taxpayer spreads the recognition of his or her gain ratably over time as the payments are received. §§ 453, 453A, and 453B.

Intangible Asset. A nonphysical asset, such as goodwill, copyrights, franchises, or trademarks.

Inter Vivos Transfer. A property transfer during the life of the owner.

Intercompany Transaction. A transaction that occurs during a consolidated return year between two or more members of the same affiliated group.

Internal Revenue Service. Part of the Treasury Department, it is responsible for administering and enforcing the Federal tax laws.

Intestate. No will existing at the time of death.

Investment Tax Credit. A credit against tax that was allowed for investing in depreciable tangible personalty before 1986. The credit was equal to 10% of the qualified investment. §§ 38 and 46–48.

Investment Tax Credit Recapture. When property on which an investment credit has been taken is disposed of prior to the full time period required under the law to earn the credit, then the amount of unearned credit must be added back to the taxpayer's tax liability-this is called recapture of the investment credit. § 47.

Involuntary Conversion. The complete or partial destruction, theft, seizure, requisition, or condemnation of property. § 1033.

Itemized Deductions. Certain expenditures of a personal nature that are specifically allowed to be deductible from an individual taxpayer's adjusted gross income. Itemized deductions (e.g., medical expenses, charitable contributions, interest, taxes, and miscellaneous itemized deductions) are deductible if they exceed the taxpayer's standard deduction.

—J—

Jeopardy Assessment. If the IRS has reason to believe that the collection or assessment of a tax would be jeopardized by delay, the IRS may assess and collect the tax immediately. §§ 6861–6864.

Joint and Several Liability. The creditor has the ability to sue one or more of the parties who have a liability, or all of the liable persons together. General partners are jointly and severally liable for the debts of the partnership. Also, if a husband and wife file a joint return, they are jointly and severally liable to the IRS for the taxes due.

Joint Tenancy. Property held by two or more owners, where each has an undivided interest in the property. Joint tenancy includes the right of survivorship, which means that upon the death of an owner, his or her share passes to the surviving owner(s).

Joint Venture. A joining together of two or more persons in order to undertake a specific business project. A joint venture is not a continuing relationship like a partnership, but may be treated as a partnership for Federal income tax purposes. § 761(a).

—K—

Keogh Plans. A retirement plan available for self-employed taxpayers. § 401.

"Kiddie" Tax. Unearned income of a dependent child under age 19 is taxed at the child's parents' marginal tax rate. § 1(I).

—L—

Leaseback. A transaction in which a taxpayer sells property and then leases back the property.

Lessee. A person or entity who rents or leases property from another.

Lessor. A person or entity who rents or leases property to another.

Life Estate. A trust or legal arrangement by which a certain person (life tenant) is entitled to receive the income from designated property for his or her life.

Life Insurance. A form of insurance that will pay the beneficiary of the policy a fixed amount upon the death of the insured person.

LIFO (Last-In, First-Out). A method of determining the cost of an inventory. The last inventory units acquired are considered to be the first sold. Therefore, the cost of the inventory would consist of the earliest acquired inventory.

Like-Kind Exchange. The exchange of property held for productive use in a trade or business or for investment (but not inventory, stock, bonds, or notes) for property that is also held for productive use or for investment (i.e., realty for realty; personalty for personalty). No gain or loss is generally recognized by either party unless boot (other than qualifying property) is involved in the transaction. § 1031.

Limited Liability. The situation in which the liability of an owner of an organization for the organization's debts is limited to the owner's investment in the organization. Examples of taxpayers with limited liability are corporate shareholders and the limited partners in a limited partnership.

Limited Liability Company (LLC). A form of business entity permitted by all states in the U.S. under which the owners are treated as partners and the company is subject to the rules of partnership taxation for Federal tax purposes.

Limited Partner. A partner whose liability for partnership debts is limited to his or her investment in the partnership. A limited partner may take no active part in the management of the partnership according to the Uniform Limited Partnership Act (*see* General Partner).

Limited Partnership. A partnership with one or more general partners *and* one or more limited partners. The limited partners are liable only up to the amount of their contribution plus any personally guaranteed debt. Limited partners cannot participate in the management or control of the partnership.

Liquidation. The cessation of all or part of a corporation's operations or the corporate form of business and the distribution of the corporate assets to the shareholders. §§ 331–337.

Lump Sum Distribution. Payment at one time of an entire amount due, or the entire proceeds of a pension or profit-sharing plan, rather than installment payments.

—M—

Majority. Of legal age (*see* Minor).

Marital Deduction. Upon the transfer of property from one spouse to another, either by gift or at death, the Internal Revenue Code allows a transfer tax deduction for the amount transferred.

Market Value. (*see* Fair Market Value).

Material Participation. Occurs when a taxpayer is involved in the operations of an activity on a regular, continuous, and substantial basis. § 469(h).

Merger. The absorption of one corporation (target corporation) by another corporation (acquiring corporation). The target corporation transfers its assets to the acquiring corporation in return for stock or securities of the acquiring corporation. Then the target corporation dissolves by exchanging the acquiring corporation's stock for its own stock held by its shareholders.

Mid-Month Convention. When a taxpayer is using ACRS or MACRS, realty placed in service at any time during a month is treated as placed in service in the middle of the month, and realty disposed of or retired at any time during a month is treated as disposed of in the middle of the month. § 168(d)(4)(B).

Mid-Quarter Convention. Used for all personalty placed in service during the year if more than 40% of all personalty placed in service during the year is placed in service during the last three months of the year. § 168(d)(4)(C).

Minimum Tax. (*see* Alternative Minimum Tax).

Minor. A person who has not yet reached the age of legal majority. In most states, a minor is a person under 18 years of age.

Mortgagee. The person or entity that holds the mortgage; the lender; the creditor.

Mortgagor. The person or entity that is mortgaging the property; the debtor.

Multistate Tax Commission (MTC). An agency of state governments established to interpret UDITPA and to promote uniformity in statutes and procedures across the states.

—N—

NA. (*see* Nonacquiescence).

Negligence Penalty. A penalty imposed by the IRS on taxpayers who are negligent or intentionally disregard the rules or regulations (but are not fraudulent), in the determination of their tax liability. § 6662.

Net Investment Income Tax. Special 3.8% tax imposed by § 1411 on an individual's investment income net of related expenses. Applies only to high income individuals.

Net Operating Loss (NOL). The amount by which deductions exceed a taxpayer's gross income. § 172.

Net Worth Method. An indirect method of determining a taxpayer's income used by the IRS when adequate records do not exist. The net worth of the taxpayer is determined for the end of each year in question, and adjustments are made to the increase in net worth from year to year for nontaxable sources of income and nondeductible expenditures. This method is often used when a possibility of fraud exists.

Nexus. The degree of relationships between a state (or other taxing jurisdiction) and a business entity that must be present before a state has the right to tax the business.

Ninety-Day (90-Day) Letter. (*see* Statutory Notice of Deficiency).

Nonacquiescence. The public announcement that the Commissioner of the Internal Revenue Service disagrees with a regular Tax Court decision. When the Commissioner nonacquiesces to a regular Tax Court decision, the IRS generally will litigate cases involving similar facts (see Acquiescence).

Nonfunctional Currency. In foreign currency translation, a currency other than the functional currency of the taxpayer.

Nonresident Alien. A person who is not a resident or citizen of the United States.

—O—

Office Audit. An audit conducted by the Internal Revenue Service on IRS premises. The person conducting the audit is generally referred to as an Office Auditor (see Correspondence Audit; Field Audit).

Office Auditor. An IRS employee who conducts primarily office audits, as opposed to a Revenue Agent, who conducts primarily field audits (*see also* Revenue Agent).

Ordinary Gross Income. A term used in relation to personal holding companies. Ordinary gross income is determined by subtracting capital gains and § 1231 gains from gross income. § 1231 gains from gross income. § 543(b)(1).

—P—

Partial Liquidation. A distribution that is not essentially equivalent to a dividend, or a distribution that is attributable to the termination one of two or more businesses (that have been active businesses for at least five years). § 302(e).

Partner. (*see* General Partner; Limited Partner).

Partnership. A syndicate, group, pool, joint venture, or other unincorporated organization, through or by means of which any business, financial operation, or venture is carried on, and which is not a trust, estate, or corporation. §§ 761(a) and 7701(a)(2).

Passive Activity. Any activity that involves the conduct of any trade or business in which the taxpayer does not materially participate. Losses from passive activities generally are deductible only to the extent of passive activity income. § 469.

Passive Investment Income. A term used in relation to S corporations. Passive investment income is generally defined as gross receipts derived from royalties, rents, dividends, interest, annuities, and gains on sales or exchanges of stock or securities. § 1362(d)(3)(D).

Pecuniary Bequest. Monetary bequest (*see* Bequest).

Percentage Depletion. (*see* Depletion).

Percentage of Completion Method of Accounting. A method of accounting that may be used on certain long-term contracts in which the income is reported as the contract reaches various stages of completion.

Personal Holding Company. A corporation in which five or fewer individuals owned more than 50% of the value of its stock at any a time during the last half of the taxable year and at least 60% of the corporation's adjusted ordinary gross income consists of personal holding company income. § 542.

Personal Property. All property that is not realty; personalty. This term is also often used to mean personal use property (*see* Personal Use Property; Personalty).

Personal Use Property. Any property used for personal, rather than business, purposes. Distinguished from "personal property."

Personalty. All property that is not realty (e.g., automobiles, trucks, machinery, and equipment).

Portability. An estate tax concept. Under the portability rules, the unused unified credit of a spouse may be used by the surviving spouse if the decedent spouse files an estate tax return and makes the appropriate election.

Portfolio Income. Interest and dividends. Portfolio income, annuities, and royalties are not considered to be income from a passive activity for purposes of the passive activity loss limitations. § 469(e).

Power of Appointment. A right to dispose of property that the holder of the power does not legally own.

Preferred Stock Bailout. A scheme by which shareholders receive a nontaxable preferred stock dividend, sell this preferred stock to a third party, and report the gain as a long-term capital gain. This scheme, therefore, converts what would be ordinary dividend income to capital gain. Section 306 was created to prohibit use of this scheme.

Present Interest. An interest in which the donee has the present right to use, possess, or enjoy the donated property. The annual exclusion is available for gifts of present interests, but not for gifts of future interests (*see* Future Interest).

Previously Taxed Income (PTI). A term used to refer to the accumulated earnings and profits for the period that a Subchapter S election was in effect prior to 1983. Distributions from PTI are not taxable to the shareholders.

Private Letter Ruling. A written statement from the IRS to a taxpayer in response to a request by the taxpayer for the tax consequences of a specific set of facts. The taxpayer who receives the Private Letter Ruling is the only taxpayer that may rely on that specific ruling in case of litigation.

Property Tax. A type of *ad valorem* tax (typically imposed by local governments) on the value of certain property—typically real property and some types of personal property.

Pro Rata. Proportionately.

Probate. The court-directed administration of a decedent's estate.

Prop. Reg. (Proposed Regulation). Treasury (IRS) Regulations are generally issued first in a proposed form in order to obtain input from various sources before the regulations are changed (if necessary) and issued in final form.

—Q—

Qualified Business Unit (QBU). In foreign currency translation, any separate and clearly identified unit of trade or business of a taxpayer that maintains separate books and records. An individual may not be a QBU, but an individual's trade or business may qualify. [Reg. § 1.989(a)-1(b).] Foreign branches of U.S. corporations generally qualify as QBUs.

Qualified Residence Interest. Interest on indebtedness that is secured by the principal residence or one other residence of a taxpayer. §§ 162(h)(3) and (5)(A).

Qualified Terminable Interest Property (QTIP). Property that passes from the decedent in which the surviving spouse has a qualifying income interest for life. An election to treat the property as qualified terminable interest property has been made. § 2056(b).

—R—

RAR. (*see* Revenue Agent's Report).

Real Property. (*see* Realty).

Realized Gain or Loss. The difference between the amount realized from the sale or other disposition of an asset and the adjusted basis of the asset. § 1001.

Realty. Real estate; land, including any objects attached thereto that are not readily movable (e.g., buildings, sidewalks, trees, and fences).

Reasonable Needs of the Business. In relation to the accumulated earnings tax, a corporation may accumulate sufficient earnings and profits to meet its reasonable business needs. Examples of reasonable needs of the business include working capital needs, amounts needed for bona fide business expansion, and amounts needed for redemptions for death taxes § 537.

Recapture. The recovery of the tax benefit from a previously taken deduction or credit. The recapture of a deduction results in its inclusion in income, and the recapture of a credit results in its inclusion in tax (*see* Depreciation Recapture; Investment Credit Recapture).

Recognized Gain or Loss. The amount of the realized gain or loss that is subject to income tax. § 1001.

Redemption. The acquisition by a corporation of its own stock from a shareholder in exchange for property. § 1001.

Reg. (*see* Regulation—Treasury Department Regulation). (*see also* Regulations).

Regulations (Treasury Department Regulations). Interpretations of the Internal Revenue Code by the Internal Revenue Service.

Related Party. A person or entity that is related to another under the various code provisions for constructive ownership. §§ 267, 318, and 544(a).

Remainder Interest. Property that passes to a remainderman after the life estate or other income interest expires on the property.

Remainderman. The person entitled to the remainder interest.

Remand. The sending back of a case by an appellate court to a lower court for further action by the lower court. The abbreviation for "remanding" is "rem'g."

Reorganization. The combination, division, or restructuring of a corporation or corporations.

Research Institute of America (RIA). A publisher of tax materials, including a multivolume tax service and volumes that contain the Federal courts' decisions on tax matters (AFTR, AFTR2d).

Resident Alien. A person who is not a citizen of the United States, and who is a resident of the United States or meets the substantial presence test. § 7701(b).

Rev. Proc. (*see* Revenue Procedure).

Rev. Rul. (*see* Revenue Ruling).

Revenue Agent. An employee of the Internal Revenue Service who performs primarily field audits.

Revenue Agent's Report (RAR). The report issued by a Revenue Agent in which adjustments to a taxpayer's tax liability are proposed. (IRS Form 4549; Form 1902 is used for office audits.)

Revenue Officer. An employee of the Internal Revenue Service whose primary duty is the collection of tax. (As opposed to a Revenue Agent, who audits returns.)

Revenue Procedure (Rev. Rul.). A procedure published by the Internal Revenue Service outlining various processes and methods of handling various matters of tax practice and administration. Revenue Procedures are published first in the Internal Revenue Bulletin and then compiled annually in the Cumulative Bulletin.

Revenue Ruling (Rev. Proc.). A published interpretation by the Internal Revenue Service of the tax law as applied to specific situations. Revenue Rulings are published first in the Internal Revenue Bulletin and then compiled annually in the Cumulative Bulletin.

Reversed (Rev'd). The reverse of a lower court's decision by a higher court.

Reversing (Rev'g). The reversing of a lower court's decision by a higher court. Rev. Proc. (*see* Revenue Procedure).

Revocable Transfer. A transfer that may be revoked by the transferor. In other words, the transferor keeps the right to recover the transferred property.

Right of Survivorship. (*see* Joint Tenancy).

Royalty. Compensation for the use of property, such as natural resources or copyrighted material.

—S—

Sales and Use Taxes. Taxes imposed by state and local governments on the gross receipts from the retail sale or use of tangible personal property and certain services.

S Corporation. A corporation that qualifies as a small business corporation and elects to have §§ 1361–1379 apply. Once a Subchapter S election is made, the corporation is treated similarly to a partnership for tax purposes. An S corporation uses Form 1120S to report its income and expenses. (*see* C Corporation).

Section 179 Election. Allows taxpayers to expense immediately a limited amount of the cost of an asset in lieu of depreciating such cost.

Section 199 Domestic Production Activity Deduction. Also referred to as DPAD. Special deduction generally granted to taxpayers who engage in domestic production and manufacturing activities.

Section 751 Assets. Unrealized receivables and appreciated inventory items of a partnership. A disproportionate distribution of § 751 assets generally results in taxable income to the partners.

Section 1231 Property. Depreciable property and real estate used in a trade or business held for more than one year. Section 1231 property may also include timber, coal, domestic iron ore, livestock, and unharvested crops.

Section 1244 Stock. Stock of a small business corporation issued pursuant to § 1244. A loss on § 1244 stock is treated as an ordinary loss (rather than a capital loss) within limitations. § 1244.

Section 1245 Property. Property that is subject to depreciation recapture under § 1245.

Section 1250 Property. Property that is subject to depreciation recapture under § 1250.

Securities. Evidences of debt or of property, such as stock, bonds, and notes.

Separate Property. Property that belongs separately to only one spouse (as contrasted with community property in a community property state). In a community property state, a spouse's separate property generally includes property acquired by the spouse prior to marriage, or property acquired after marriage by gift or inheritance.

Severance Tax. At the time they are severed or removed from the earth, a tax on minerals or timber.

Sham Transaction. A transaction with no substance or bona fide business purpose that may be ignored for tax purposes.

Simple Trust. A trust that is required to distribute all of its income currently and does not pay, set aside, or use any funds for charitable purposes. § 651(a).

Small Business Corporation. There are two separate definitions of a small business corporation, one relating to S corporations and one relating to § 1244. If small business corporation status is met under § 1361(b), a corporation may elect Subchapter S. If small business corporation status is met under § 1244(c)(3), losses on § 1244 stock may be deducted as ordinary (rather than capital) losses, within limitations.

Special Use Valuation. A special method of valuing real estate for estate tax purposes. The special use valuation allows that qualifying real estate used in a closely held business may be valued based on its business usage rather than market value. § 2032A.

Specific Bequest. A bequest made by a testator in his or her will giving an heir a particular piece of property or money.

Spin-Off. A type of divisive corporate reorganization in which the original corporation transfers some of its assets to a newly formed subsidiary in exchange for all of the subsidiary's stock which it then distributes to its shareholders. The shareholders of the original corporation do not surrender any of their ownership in the original corporation for the subsidiary's stock.

Split-Off. A type of divisive corporate reorganization in which the original corporation transfers some of its assets to a newly formed subsidiary in exchange for all of the subsidiary's stock which it then distributes to some or all of its shareholders in exchange for some portion of their stock.

Split-Up. A type of divisive corporate reorganization in which the original corporation transfers some of its assets to one newly created subsidiary and the remainder of the assets to another newly created subsidiary. The original corporation then liquidates, distributing the stock of both subsidiaries in exchange for its own stock.

Standard Deduction. A deduction that is available to most individual taxpayers. The standard deduction or total itemized deductions, whichever is larger, is subtracted in computing taxable income. §§ 63(c) and (f).

Statute of Limitations. Law provisions that limit the period of time in which action may be taken after an event occurs. The limitations on the IRS for assessments and collections are included in §§ 6501–6504, and the limitations on taxpayers for credits or refunds are included in §§ 6511–6515.

Statutory Depletion. (*see* Depletion).

Stock Option. A right to purchase a specified amount of stock for a specified price at a given time or times.

Subchapter S. Sections 1361–1379 of the Internal Revenue Code (*see also* S Corporation).

Substance versus Form. The essence of a transaction as opposed to the structure or form that the transaction takes. For example, a transaction may formally meet the requirements for a specific type of tax treatment, but if what the transaction is actually accomplishing is different from the form of the transaction, the form may be ignored.

Surtax. An additional tax imposed on corporations with taxable income in excess of $100,000. The surtax is 5% of the corporation's taxable income in excess of $100,000 up to a maximum surtax of $11,750. § 11(b).

—T—

Tangible Property. Property that can be touched (e.g., machinery, automobile, desk) as opposed to intangibles, which cannot (e.g., goodwill, copyrights, patents).

Tax Avoidance. Using the tax laws to avoid paying taxes or to reduce one's tax liability (*see* Tax Evasion).

Tax Benefit Rule. The doctrine by which the amount of income that a taxpayer must include in income when the taxpayer has recovered an amount previously deducted is limited to the amount of the previous deduction that produced a tax benefit.

Tax Court (United States Tax Court). One of the three trial courts that hears cases dealing with Federal tax matters. A taxpayer need not pay his or her tax deficiency in advance if he or she decides to litigate the case in Tax Court (as opposed to the District Court or Claims Court).

Tax Credits. An amount that is deducted directly from a taxpayer's tax liability, as opposed to a deduction, which reduces taxable income.

Tax Evasion. The illegal evasion of the tax laws. § 7201 (*see* Tax Avoidance).

Tax Preference Items. Those items specifically designated in § 57 that may be subject to a special tax (*see also* Alternative Minimum Tax).

Tax Shelter. A device or scheme used by taxpayers either to reduce taxes or defer the payment of taxes.

Taxable Estate. Gross estate reduced by the expenses, indebtedness, taxes, losses, and charitable contributions of the estate, and by the marital deduction. § 2051.

Taxable Gifts. The total amount of gifts made during the calendar year, reduced by charitable gifts and the marital deduction. § 2503.

T.C. (Tax Court: United States Tax Court). This abbreviation is also used to cite the Tax Court's Regular Decisions (*see also* Tax Court; T.C. Memo).

T.C. Memo. The term used to cite the Tax Court's Memorandum Decisions (*see also* Tax Court; T.C.).

Tenancy by the Entirety. Form of ownership between a husband and wife wherein each has an undivided interest in the property, with the right of survivorship.

Tenancy in Common. A form of joint ownership wherein each owner has an undivided interest in the property, with no right of survivorship.

Testator. A person who makes or has made a will; one who dies and has left a will.

Thin Corporation. A corporation in which the amount of debt owed by the corporation is high in relationship to the amount of equity in the corporation. § 385.

Three Unities Test. A method of determining whether a business is part of a unitary group based on common ownership (unity of ownership), centralized support functions and operations (unity of operations) and a centralized executive force (unity of use).

Treasury Regulations. (*see* Regulations).

Trial Court. The first court to consider a case, as opposed to an appellate court.

Trust. A right in property that is held by one person or entity for the benefit of another. §§ 641–683.

—U—

Unearned Income. Income that is not earned or is not yet earned. The term is used to refer to both prepaid (not vet earned) income and to passive (not earned) income.

Unearned Income of a Minor Child. (*see* "Kiddie" tax).

Unified Credit. A credit available to reduce an individual's estate and gift tax. Also referred to as an exemption or applicable exclusion.

Uniform Division of Income for Tax Purposes Act (UDITPA). Provides standardized rules relating to the taxation of multistate corporations.

Uniform Gift to Minors Act. An Act that provides a way to transfer property to minors. A custodian manages the property on behalf of the minor, and the custodianship terminates when the minor achieves majority.

Unitary Business Principle. A concept employed by states in which separate legal entities may nonetheless be treated as part of the same taxable group if the businesses constitute a single unitary business. States use a number of different methods to establish whether a unitary business exists, the most common being the three unities test.

USSC (U.S. Supreme Court). This abbreviation is used to cite U.S. Supreme Court cases.

U.S. Tax Court. (*see* Tax Court).

USTC (U.S. Tax Cases). Published by Commerce Clearing House. These volumes contain all the Federal tax-related decisions of the U.S. District Courts, the U.S. Court of Federal Claims, the U.S. Courts of Appeals, and the U.S. Supreme Court.

—V—

Valuation. (*see* Fair Market Value).

Vested. Fixed or settled; having the right to absolute ownership, even if ownership will not come into being until sometime in the future.

—W—

Water's Edge Election. An election allowed by states that require or allow unitary reporting to exclude foreign corporations from the unitary group.

Modified ACRS Tables

H

Appendix Outline

Modified ACRS Accelerated Depreciation Percentages Using the Half-Year Convention for 3-, 5-, 7-, 10-, 15-, and 20-Year Property Placed in Service after December 31, 1986

Recovery Year	Property Class					
	3-Year	5-Year	7-Year	10-Year	15-Year	20-Year
1	33.33	20.00	14.29	10.00	5.00	3.750
2	44.45	32.00	24.49	18.00	9.50	7.219
3	14.81	19.20	17.49	14.40	8.55	6.677
4	7.41	11.52	12.49	11.52	7.70	6.177
5		11.52	8.93	9.22	6.93	5.713
6		5.76	8.92	7.37	6.23	5.285
7			8.93	6.55	5.90	4.888
8			4.46	6.55	5.90	4.522
9				6.56	5.91	4.462
10				6.55	5.90	4.461
11				3.28	5.91	4.462
12					5.90	4.461
13					5.91	4.462
14					5.90	4.461
15					5.91	4.462
16					2.95	4.461
17						4.462
18						4.461
19						4.462
20						4.461
21						2.231

Modified ACRS Depreciation Rates for Residential Rental Property Placed in Service after December 31, 1986

Recovery Year	Month Placed in Service					
	1	2	3	4	5	6
1	3.485	3.182	2.879	2.576	2.273	1.970
2	3.636	3.636	3.636	3.636	3.636	3.636
3	3.636	3.636	3.636	3.636	3.636	3.636
4	3.636	3.636	3.636	3.636	3.636	3.636
5	3.636	3.636	3.636	3.636	3.636	3.636
6	3.636	3.636	3.636	3.636	3.636	3.636
7	3.636	3.636	3.636	3.636	3.636	3.636
8	3.636	3.636	3.636	3.636	3.636	3.636
9	3.636	3.636	3.636	3.636	3.636	3.636
10	3.637	3.637	3.637	3.637	3.637	3.637
11	3.636	3.636	3.636	3.636	3.636	3.636
12	3.637	3.637	3.637	3.637	3.637	3.637
13	3.636	3.636	3.636	3.636	3.636	3.636
14	3.637	3.637	3.637	3.637	3.637	3.637
15	3.636	3.636	3.636	3.636	3.636	3.636
16	3.637	3.637	3.637	3.637	3.637	3.637
17	3.636	3.636	3.636	3.636	3.636	3.636
18	3.637	3.637	3.637	3.637	3.637	3.637
19	3.636	3.636	3.636	3.636	3.636	3.636
20	3.637	3.637	3.637	3.637	3.637	3.636
21	3.636	3.636	3.636	3.636	3.636	3.636
22	3.637	3.637	3.637	3.637	3.637	3.637
23	3.636	3.636	3.636	3.636	3.636	3.636
24	3.637	3.637	3.637	3.637	3.637	3.637
25	3.636	3.636	3.636	3.636	3.636	3.636
26	3.637	3.637	3.637	3.637	3.637	3.637
27	3.636	3.636	3.636	3.636	3.636	3.636
28	1.970	2.273	2.576	2.879	3.182	3.485
29	0.000	0.000	0.000	0.000	0.000	0.000

Modified ACRS Depreciation Rates for Residential Rental Property Placed in Service after December 31, 1986 (continued)

Recovery Year	Month Placed in Service					
	7	8	9	10	11	12
1	1.667	1.364	1.061	0.758	0.455	0.152
2	3.636	3.636	3.636	3.636	3.636	3.636
3	3.636	3.636	3.636	3.636	3.636	3.636
4	3.636	3.636	3.636	3.636	3.636	3.636
5	3.636	3.636	3.636	3.636	3.636	3.636
6	3.636	3.636	3.636	3.636	3.636	3.636
7	3.636	3.636	3.636	3.636	3.636	3.636
8	3.636	3.636	3.636	3.636	3.636	3.636
9	3.636	3.636	3.636	3.636	3.636	3.636
10	3.636	3.636	3.636	3.636	3.636	3.636
11	3.637	3.637	3.637	3.637	3.637	3.637
12	3.636	3.636	3.636	3.636	3.636	3.636
13	3.637	3.637	3.637	3.637	3.637	3.637
14	3.636	3.636	3.636	3.636	3.636	3.636
15	3.637	3.637	3.637	3.637	3.637	3.637
16	3.636	3.636	3.636	3.636	3.636	3.636
17	3.637	3.637	3.637	3.637	3.637	3.637
18	3.636	3.636	3.636	3.636	3.636	3.636
19	3.637	3.637	3.637	3.637	3.637	3.637
20	3.636	3.636	3.636	3.636	3.636	3.636
21	3.637	3.637	3.637	3.637	3.637	3.637
22	3.636	3.636	3.636	3.636	3.636	3.636
23	3.637	3.637	3.637	3.637	3.637	3.637
24	3.636	3.636	3.636	3.636	3.636	3.636
25	3.637	3.637	3.637	3.637	3.637	3.637
26	3.636	3.636	3.636	3.636	3.636	3.636
27	3.637	3.637	3.637	3.637	3.637	3.637
28	3.636	3.636	3.636	3.636	3.636	3.636
29	0.152	0.455	0.758	1.061	1.364	1.667

Modified ACRS Depreciation Percentages for Nonresidential Real Property Placed in Service after December 31, 1986 and before May 13, 1993

Recovery Year	Month Placed in Service					
	1	2	3	4	5	6
1	3.042	2.778	2.513	2.249	1.984	1.720
2	3.175	3.175	3.175	3.175	3.175	3.175
3	3.175	3.175	3.175	3.175	3.175	3.175
4	3.175	3.175	3.175	3.175	3.175	3.175
5	3.175	3.175	3.175	3.175	3.175	3.175
6	3.175	3.175	3.175	3.175	3.175	3.175
7	3.175	3.175	3.175	3.175	3.175	3.175
8	3.175	3.174	3.175	3.174	3.175	3.174
9	3.174	3.175	3.174	3.175	3.174	3.175
10	3.175	3.174	3.175	3.174	3.175	3.174
11	3.174	3.175	3.174	3.175	3.174	3.175
12	3.175	3.174	3.175	3.174	3.175	3.174
13	3.174	3.175	3.174	3.175	3.174	3.175
14	3.175	3.174	3.175	3.174	3.175	3.174
15	3.174	3.175	3.174	3.175	3.174	3.175
16	3.175	3.174	3.175	3.174	3.175	3.174
17	3.174	3.175	3.174	3.175	3.174	3.175
18	3.175	3.174	3.175	3.174	3.175	3.174
19	3.174	3.175	3.174	3.175	3.174	3.175
20	3.175	3.174	3.175	3.174	3.175	3.174
21	3.174	3.175	3.174	3.175	3.174	3.175
22	3.175	3.174	3.175	3.174	3.175	3.174
23	3.174	3.175	3.174	3.175	3.174	3.175
24	3.175	3.174	3.175	3.174	3.175	3.174
25	3.174	3.175	3.174	3.175	3.174	3.175
26	3.175	3.174	3.175	3.174	3.175	3.174
27	3.174	3.175	3.174	3.175	3.174	3.175
28	3.175	3.174	3.175	3.174	3.175	3.174
29	3.174	3.175	3.174	3.175	3.174	3.175
30	3.175	3.174	3.175	3.174	3.175	3.174
31	3.174	3.175	3.174	3.175	3.174	3.175
32	1.720	1.984	2.249	2.513	2.778	3.042
33	0.000	0.000	0.000	0.000	0.000	0.000

Modified ACRS Depreciation Percentages for Nonresidential Real Property Placed in Service after December 31, 1986 and before May 13, 1993 (continued)

Recovery Year	Month Placed in Service					
	7	8	9	10	11	12
1	1.455	1.190	0.926	0.661	0.397	0.132
2	3.175	3.175	3.175	3.175	3.175	3.175
3	3.175	3.175	3.175	3.175	3.175	3.175
4	3.175	3.175	3.175	3.175	3.175	3.175
5	3.175	3.175	3.175	3.175	3.175	3.175
6	3.175	3.175	3.175	3.175	3.175	3.175
7	3.175	3.175	3.175	3.175	3.175	3.175
8	3.175	3.175	3.175	3.175	3.175	3.175
9	3.174	3.175	3.175	3.175	3.174	3.175
10	3.175	3.174	3.175	3.174	3.175	3.174
11	3.174	3.175	3.174	3.175	3.174	3.175
12	3.175	3.174	3.175	3.174	3.175	3.174
13	3.174	3.175	3.174	3.175	3.174	3.175
14	3.175	3.174	3.175	3.174	3.175	3.174
15	3.174	3.175	3.174	3.175	3.174	3.175
16	3.175	3.174	3.175	3.174	3.175	3.174
17	3.174	3.175	3.174	3.175	3.174	3.175
18	3.175	3.174	3.175	3.174	3.175	3.174
19	3.174	3.175	3.174	3.175	3.174	3.175
20	3.175	3.174	3.175	3.174	3.175	3.174
21	3.174	3.175	3.174	3.175	3.174	3.175
22	3.175	3.174	3.175	3.174	3.175	3.174
23	3.174	3.175	3.174	3.175	3.174	3.175
24	3.175	3.174	3.175	3.174	3.175	3.174
25	3.174	3.175	3.174	3.175	3.174	3.175
26	3.175	3.174	3.175	3.174	3.175	3.174
27	3.174	3.175	3.174	3.175	3.174	3.175
28	3.175	3.174	3.175	3.174	3.175	3.174
29	3.174	3.175	3.174	3.175	3.174	3.175
30	3.175	3.174	3.175	3.174	3.175	3.174
31	3.174	3.175	3.174	3.175	3.174	3.175
32	3.175	3.174	3.175	3.174	3.175	3.174
33	0.132	0.397	0.661	0.926	1.190	1.455

Modified ACRS Depreciation Percentages for
Nonresidential Real Property
Placed in Service after May 12, 1993

Month Placed in Service	Recovery Year				
	1	2	...	39	40
1	2.461%	2.564%		2.564%	0.107%
2	2.247	2.564		2.564	0.321
3	2.033	2.564		2.564	0.535
4	1.819	2.564		2.564	0.749
5	1.605	2.564		2.564	0.963
6	1.391	2.564		2.564	1.177
7	1.177	2.564		2.564	1.391
8	0.963	2.564		2.564	1.605
9	0.749	2.564		2.564	1.819
10	0.535	2.564		2.564	2.033
11	0.321	2.564		2.564	2.247
12	0.107	2.564		2.564	2.461

**Modified ACRS Accelerated Depreciation
Percentages Using the Mid-Quarter Convention for
3-, 5-, 7-, 10-, 15-, and 20-Year Property Placed in
Service after December 31, 1986**

	Quarter Placed in Service			
Recovery Year	1	2	3	4
3-Year Property:				
1	58.33	41.67	25.00	8.33
2	27.78	38.89	50.00	61.11
3	12.35	14.14	16.67	20.37
4	1.54	5.30	8.33	10.19
5-Year Property:				
1	35.00	25.00	15.00	5.00
2	26.00	30.00	34.00	38.00
3	15.60	18.00	20.40	22.80
4	11.01	11.37	12.24	13.68
5	11.01	11.37	11.30	10.94
6	1.38	4.26	7.06	9.58
7-Year Property:				
1	25.00	17.85	10.71	3.57
2	21.43	23.47	25.51	27.55
3	15.31	16.76	18.22	19.68
4	10.93	11.37	13.02	14.06
5	8.75	8.87	9.30	10.04
6	8.74	8.87	8.85	8.73
7	8.75	8.87	8.86	8.73
8	1.09	3.33	5.53	7.64
10-Year Property:				
1	17.50	12.50	7.50	2.50
2	16.50	17.50	18.50	19.50
3	13.20	14.00	14.80	15.60
4	10.56	11.20	11.84	12.48
5	8.45	8.96	9.47	9.98
6	6.76	7.17	7.58	7.99
7	6.55	6.55	6.55	6.55
8	6.55	6.55	6.55	6.55
9	6.56	6.56	6.56	6.56
10	0.82	6.55	6.55	6.55
11		2.46	4.10	5.74

Modified ACRS Accelerated Depreciation Percentages Using the Mid-Quarter Convention for 3-, 5-, 7-, 10-, 15-, and 20-Year Property Placed in Service after December 31, 1986 (continued)

	Quarter Placed in Service			
Recovery Year	1	2	3	4
15-Year Property:				
1	8.75	6.25	3.75	1.25
2	9.13	9.38	9.63	9.88
3	8.21	8.44	8.66	8.89
4	7.39	7.59	7.80	8.00
5	6.65	6.83	7.02	7.20
6	5.99	6.15	6.31	6.48
7	5.90	5.91	5.90	5.90
8	5.91	5.90	5.90	5.90
9	5.90	5.91	5.91	5.90
10	5.91	5.90	5.90	5.91
11	5.90	5.91	5.91	5.90
12	5.91	5.90	5.90	5.91
13	5.90	5.91	5.91	5.90
14	5.91	5.90	5.90	5.91
15	5.90	5.91	5.91	5.90
16	0.74	2.21	3.69	5.17
20-Year Property:				
1	6.563	4.688	2.813	0.938
2	7.000	7.148	7.289	7.430
3	6.482	6.612	6.742	6.872
4	5.996	6.116	6.237	6.357
5	5.546	5.658	5.769	5.880
6	5.130	5.233	5.336	5.439
7	4.746	4.841	4.936	5.031
8	4.459	4.478	4.566	4.654
9	4.459	4.463	4.460	4.458
10	4.459	4.463	4.460	4.458
11	4.459	4.463	4.460	4.458
12	4.460	4.463	4.460	4.458
13	4.459	4.463	4.461	4.458
14	4.460	4.463	4.460	4.458
15	4.459	4.462	4.461	4.458
16	4.460	4.463	4.460	4.458
17	4.459	4.462	4.461	4.458
18	4.460	4.463	4.460	4.459
19	4.459	4.462	4.461	4.458
20	4.460	4.463	4.460	4.459
21	0.557	1.673	2.788	3.901

Alternative Depreciation System
Recovery Periods

General Rule: Recovery period is the property's class life unless:
1. There is no class life (see below), or
2. A special class life has been designated (see below).

Type of Property	Recovery Period
Personal property with no class life	12 years
Nonresidential real property with no class life	40 years
Residential rental property with no class life	40 years
Cars, light general purpose trucks, certain technological equipment, and semiconductor manufacturing equipment	5 years
Computer-based telephone central office switching equipment	9.5 years
Railroad track	10 years
Single purpose agricultural or horticultural structures	15 years
Municipal waste water treatment plants, telephone distribution plants	24 years
Low-income housing financed by tax-exempt bonds	27.5 years
Municipal sewers	50 years

**Modified ACRS and ADS Straight-Line Depreciation Percentages
Using the Half-Year Convention for 3-, 5-, 7-, 10-, 15-, and
20-Year Property Placed in Service after December 31, 1986**

Recovery Year	Property Class					
	3-Year	5-Year	7-Year	10-Year	15-Year	20-Year
1	16.67	10.00	7.14	5.00	3.33	2.50
2	33.33	20.00	14.29	10.00	6.67	5.00
3	33.33	20.00	14.29	10.00	6.67	5.00
4	16.67	20.00	14.28	10.00	6.67	5.00
5		20.00	14.29	10.00	6.67	5.00
6		10.00	14.28	10.00	6.67	5.00
7			14.29	10.00	6.67	5.00
8			7.14	10.00	6.66	5.00
9				10.00	6.67	5.00
10				10.00	6.66	5.00
11				5.00	6.67	5.00
12					6.66	5.00
13					6.67	5.00
14					6.66	5.00
15					6.67	5.00
16					3.33	5.00
17						5.00
18						5.00
19						5.00
20						5.00
21						2.50

**ADS Straight-Line Depreciation Percentages
for Real Property Using the Mid-Month
Convention for Property Placed in Service
after December 31, 1986**

Month Placed in Service	Recovery Year		
	1	2–40	41
1	2.396	2.500	0.104
2	2.188	2.500	0.312
3	1.979	2.500	0.521
4	1.771	2.500	0.729
5	1.563	2.500	0.937
6	1.354	2.500	1.146
7	1.146	2.500	1.354
8	0.938	2.500	1.562
9	0.729	2.500	1.771
10	0.521	2.500	1.979
11	0.313	2.500	2.187
12	0.104	2.500	2.396

Index

U

W

Y

Tax Formula for Corporate Taxpayers

Total income (from whatever source)	$ xxx,xxx
Less: Exclusions from gross income	− xx,xxx
Gross income	$ xxx,xxx
Less: Deductions	− xx,xxx
Taxable income	$ xxx,xxx
Applicable tax rates	× xx%
Gross tax	$ xx,xxx
Less: Tax credits and prepayments	− x,xxx
Tax due (or refund)	$ xx,xxx

Tax Formula for Individual Taxpayers

Total income (from whatever source)		$ xxx,xxx
Less: Exclusions from gross income		− xx,xxx
Gross income		$ xxx,xxx
Less: Deductions *for* adjusted gross income		− xx,xxx
Adjusted gross income		$ xxx,xxx
Less: 1. The larger of:		
a. Standard deduction	$ x,xxx	
or	or	− x,xxx
b. Total itemized deduction	$ x,xxx	
2. Number of personal and dependency exemptions × exemption amount		− x,xxx
Taxable income		$ xxx,xxx
Applicable tax rates (from tables or Schedules X, Y, or Z)		× xx%
Gross income tax		$ xx,xxx
Plus: Additional taxes (e.g., self-employment taxes and recapture of tax credits)		+ x,xxx
Less: Tax credits and prepayments		− x,xxx
Tax due (or refund)		$ xx,xxx